DOCUMENTS SUPPLEMENT TO
INTERNATIONAL HUMAN RIGHTS LAWYERING
CASES AND MATERIALS

■ ■ ■

By

Ralph G. Steinhardt
Arthur Selwyn Miller Research Professor of Law
The George Washington University Law School

Paul L. Hoffman
Schonbrun, De Simone, Seplow, Harris and Hoffman LLP

Christopher N. Camponovo
United States Department of State

AMERICAN CASEBOOK SERIES®

WEST®
A Thomson Reuters business

Mat #40769128

© 2009 Thomson Reuters
   610 Opperman Drive
   St. Paul, MN 55123
   1–800–313–9378
Printed in the United States of America

ISBN: 978–0–314–19892–1

 TEXT IS PRINTED ON 10% POST CONSUMER RECYCLED PAPER

PREFACE

This collection of human rights documents accompanies INTERNATIONAL HUMAN RIGHTS LAWYERING: CASES AND MATERIALS (West 2009), but it is also intended to be a portable, hard-copy library of primary documents for advocates in the field. Choosing which documents to exclude -- and which to include but in edited form -- has been difficult in some cases, but we were scared straight by the prospect of creating a book that either weighed too much to carry or appeared in typeface too small to read. On the other hand, we have also been guided by our belief that existing collections of human rights documents have defined the field too narrowly, excluding instruments that deal with the law of war, international labor law, the law governing treaties and consular affairs, refugee and immigration law, international criminal law, and professional ethics. Some of the most important of these instruments appear here. We also have a broad view of U.S. statutes and executive branch materials that are relevant to the contemporary human rights advocate (especialy litigators) and so have included an expansive set of domestic instruments.

The gaps that inevitably remain in this or any other collection of documents can be filled somewhat by the web-based resources that have proliferated in recent years, especially among academic institutions (like the online Human Rights Library at the University of Minnesota) and intergovernmental organizations (like the U.N. Office of the High Commissioner for Human Rights, the African Union, the Council of Europe, and the Inter-American Commission and Court of Human Rights). We encourage students and advocates to check these sites for recent developments, because human rights instruments and documents are appearing at an exponential rate, and existing instruments are sometimes revisited and amended. Of course, access to the web is not universal, and a "document" is not necessarily accurate just because it can be found on the internet, which is why a book of this type is necessary in the first place.

The authors wish to express their particular gratitude to two people at the George Washington University Law School, who have been instrumental in getting this Document Supplement across the finish line: Herb Somers, the incomparable international law librarian, and Nicole Rentz, Class of 2009 (a.k.a. "The Keeper of The Version.")

In addition to the permissions noted in the casebook (pp. xi-xix), special permissions have been granted by the athors, publishers, and organizations to reprint the following copyrighted materials herein:

Princeton University Program in Law and Public Affairs, The Princeton Principles on Universal Jurisdiction (reprinted in their entirety below);

World Bank Group, Articles of Agreement of the International Bank of Reconstruction and Development and The World Bank Inspection Panel *Operatiing Procedure.* "Permission by the World Bank for use of documents used in this publication does not imply an endorsement of the findings, interpretations and conclusions made by the authors of this casebook in relation to World Bank policies."

R.S.
P.H.
C.C.

Washington, D.C.
December 2008

TABLE OF CONTENTS

CONSTITUTION OF THE UNITED STATES

INTERNATIONAL TREATIES

REGIONAL TREATIES, RESOLUTIONS, AND DOCUMENTS

U.N. RESOLUTIONS AND OTHER U.N. MATERIALS

UNITED STATES STATUTES

UNITED STATES EXECUTIVE/LEGISLATIVE MATERIALS

TREATY COMMITTEE DOCUMENTS

INTERNATIONAL CRIMINAL TRIBUNAL DOCUMENTS

INTERNATIONAL FINANCIAL INSTITUTIONS

INTERNATIONAL CODES OF PROFESSIONAL CONDUCT

NGO DOCUMENTS

MISCELLANEOUS MATERIALS

CONSTITUTION OF THE UNITED STATES

U.S. Const. arts. I, II, III, VI, and amend. VIII

We the People of the United States, in Order to form a more perfect Union, establish Justice, insure domestic Tranquility, provide for the common defence, promote the general Welfare, and secure the Blessings of Liberty to ourselves and our Posterity, do ordain and establish this Constitution for the United States of America.

Article I

Section 1. All legislative Powers herein granted shall be vested in a Congress of the United States, which shall consist of a Senate and House of Representatives. * * *

Section 8. The Congress shall have Power To lay and collect Taxes, Duties, Imposts and Excises, to pay the Debts and provide for the common Defence and general Welfare of the United States; but all Duties, Imposts and Excises shall be uniform throughout the United States; To borrow Money on the credit of the United States; To regulate Commerce with foreign Nations, and among the several States, and with the Indian Tribes; To establish an uniform Rule of Naturalization, and uniform Laws on the subject of Bankruptcies throughout the United States; To coin Money, regulate the Value thereof, and of foreign Coin, and fix the Standard of Weights and Measures; To provide for the Punishment of counterfeiting the Securities and current Coin of the United States; To establish Post Offices and post Roads; To promote the Progress of Science and useful Arts, by securing for limited Times to Authors and Inventors the exclusive Right to their respective Writings and Discoveries; To constitute Tribunals inferior to the supreme Court; To define and punish Piracies and Felonies committed on the high Seas, and Offenses against the Law of Nations; To declare War, grant Letters of Marque and Reprisal, and make Rules concerning Captures on Land and Water; To raise and support Armies, but no Appropriation of Money to that Use shall be for a longer Term than two Years; To provide and maintain a Navy; To make Rules for the Government and Regulation of the land and naval Forces; To provide for calling forth the Militia to execute the Laws of the Union, suppress Insurrections and repel Invasions; To provide for organizing, arming, and disciplining, the Militia, and for governing such Part of them as may be employed in the Service of the United States, reserving to the States respectively, the Appointment of the Officers, and the Authority of training the Militia according to the discipline prescribed by Congress; * * * And To make all Laws which shall be necessary and proper for carrying into Execution the foregoing Powers, and all other Powers vested by this Constitution in the Government of the United States or in any Department or Officer thereof.

Section 9. * * * The Privilege of the Writ of Habeas Corpus shall not be suspended, unless when in Cases of Rebellion or Invasion the public Safety may require it. No Bill of Attainder or ex post facto Law shall be passed. No Capitation, or other direct, Tax shall be laid, unless in Proportion to the Census or Enumeration herein before directed to be taken.[1] No Tax or Duty shall be laid on Articles exported from any State. No Preference shall be given by any Regulation of Commerce or Revenue to the Ports of one State over those of another: nor shall Vessels bound to, or from, one State, be obliged to enter, clear, or pay Duties in another. No Money shall be drawn from the Treasury, but in Consequence of Appropriations made by Law, and a regular Statement and Account of the Receipts and Expenditures of all public Money shall be published from time to time. No Title of Nobility shall be granted by the United States: And no Person holding any Office of Profit or Trust under them, shall, without the Consent of the Congress, accept of any present, Emolument, Office, or Title, of any kind whatever, from any King, Prince, or foreign State.

Section 10. No State shall enter into any Treaty, Alliance, or Confederation; grant Letters of Marque and Reprisal; coin Money; emit Bills of Credit; make any Thing but gold and silver Coin a Tender in Payment of Debts; pass any Bill of Attainder, ex post facto Law, or Law impairing the Obligation of Contracts, or grant any Title of Nobility.

No State shall, without the Consent of the Congress, lay any Imposts or Duties on Imports or Exports, except what may be absolutely necessary for executing it's inspection Laws: and the net Produce

---

[1] See Sixteenth Amendment.

of all Duties and Imposts, laid by any State on Imports or Exports, shall be for the Use of the Treasury of the United States; and all such Laws shall be subject to the Revision and Control of the Congress.

No State shall, without the Consent of Congress, lay any Duty of Tonnage, keep Troops, or Ships of War in time of Peace, enter into any Agreement or Compact with another State, or with a foreign Power, or engage in War, unless actually invaded, or in such imminent Danger as will not admit of delay.

Article II

Section 1. The executive Power shall be vested in a President of the United States of America. * * *

Section 2. The President shall be Commander in Chief of the Army and Navy of the United States, and of the Militia of the several States, when called into the actual Service of the United States; he may require the Opinion, in writing, of the principal Officer in each of the executive Departments, upon any Subject relating to the Duties of their respective Offices, and he shall have Power to grant Reprieves and Pardons for Offenses against the United States, except in Cases of Impeachment.

He shall have Power, by and with the Advice and Consent of the Senate, to make Treaties, provided two thirds of the Senators present concur; and he shall nominate, and by and with the Advice and Consent of the Senate, shall appoint Ambassadors, other public Ministers and Consuls, Judges of the supreme Court, and all other Officers of the United States, whose Appointments are not herein otherwise provided for, and which shall be established by Law: but the Congress may by Law vest the Appointment of such inferior Officers, as they think proper, in the President alone, in the Courts of Law, or in the Heads of Departments. * * *

Section 3. He shall * * * shall receive Ambassadors and other public Ministers; he shall take Care that the Laws be faithfully executed, and shall Commission all the Officers of the United States. * * *

Article III

Section 1. The judicial Power of the United States, shall be vested in one supreme Court, and in such inferior Courts as the Congress may from time to time ordain and establish. * * *

Section 2. The judicial Power shall extend to all Cases, in Law and Equity, arising under this Constitution, the Laws of the United States, and Treaties made, or which shall be made, under their Authority;--to all Cases affecting Ambassadors, other public Ministers and Consuls;--to all Cases of admiralty and maritime Jurisdiction;--to Controversies to which the United States shall be a Party;--to Controversies between two or more States;--[between a State and Citizens of another State;--][2] between Citizens of different States,-- between Citizens of the same State claiming Lands under Grants of different States, [and between a State, or the Citizens thereof, and foreign States, Citizens or Subjects.][3]

In all Cases affecting Ambassadors, other public Ministers and Consuls, and those in which a State shall be Party, the supreme Court shall have original Jurisdiction. In all the other Cases before mentioned, the supreme Court shall have appellate Jurisdiction, both as to Law and Fact, with such Exceptions, and under such Regulations as the Congress shall make. * * *

Article VI

* * * This Constitution, and the Laws of the United States which shall be made in Pursuance thereof; and all Treaties made, or which shall be made, under the Authority of the United States, shall be the supreme Law of the Land; and the Judges in every State shall be bound thereby, any Thing in the Constitution or Laws of any State to the Contrary notwithstanding. * * *

Amendment VIII

Excessive bail shall not be required, nor excessive fines imposed, nor cruel and unusual punishments inflicted.

---

[2] See the Eleventh Amendment.
[3] See the Eleventh Amendment.

INTERNATIONAL TREATIES

Covenant of the League of Nations
available at http://avalon.law.yale.edu/20th_century/leagcov.asp

The High Contracting Parties
> In order to promote international co-operation and to achieve international peace and security
> by the acceptance of obligations not to resort to war,
> by the prescription of open, just and honourable relations between nations,
> by the firm establishment of the understandings of international law as the actual rule of conduct among Governments, and
> by the maintenance of justice and a scrupulous respect for all treaty obligations in the dealings of organised peoples with one another,

Agree to this Covenant of the League of Nations. * * *

Article 22

1. To those colonies and territories which as a consequence of the late war have ceased to be under the sovereignty of the States which formerly governed them and which are inhabited by peoples not yet able to stand by themselves under the strenuous conditions of the modern world, there should be applied the principle that the well-being and development of such peoples form a sacred trust of civilisation and that securities for the performance of this trust should be embodied in this Covenant.

2. The best method of giving practical effect to this principle is that the tutelage of such peoples should be entrusted to advanced nations who by reason of their resources, their experience or their geographical position can best undertake this responsibility, and who are willing to accept it, and that this tutelage should be exercised by them as Mandatories on behalf of the League.

3. The character of the mandate must differ according to the stage of the development of the people, the geographical situation of the territory, its economic conditions and other similar circumstances.

4. Certain communities formerly belonging to the Turkish Empire have reached a stage of development where their existence as independent nations can be provisionally recognized subject to the rendering of administrative advice and assistance by a Mandatory until such time as they are able to stand alone. The wishes of these communities must be a principal consideration in the selection of the Mandatory.

5. Other peoples, especially those of Central Africa, are at such a stage that the Mandatory must be responsible for the administration of the territory under conditions which will guarantee freedom of conscience and religion, subject only to the maintenance of public order and morals, the prohibition of abuses such as the slave trade, the arms traffic and the liquor traffic, and the prevention of the establishment of fortifications or military and naval bases and of military training of the natives for other than police purposes and the defence of territory, and will also secure equal opportunities for the trade and commerce of other Members of the League.

6. There are territories, such as South-West Africa and certain of the South Pacific Islands, which, owing to the sparseness of their population, or their small size, or their remoteness from the centres of civilisation, or their geographical contiguity to the territory of the Mandatory, and other circumstances, can be best administered under the laws of the Mandatory as integral portions of its territory, subject to the safeguards above mentioned in the interests of the indigenous population.

7. In every case of mandate, the Mandatory shall render to the Council an annual report in reference to the territory committed to its charge.

8. The degree of authority, control, or administration to be exercised by the Mandatory shall, if not previously agreed upon by the Members of the League, be explicitly defined in each case by the Council.

9. A permanent Commission shall be constituted to receive and examine the annual reports of the Mandatories and to advise the Council on all matters relating to the observance of the mandates.

Article 23

Subject to and in accordance with the provisions of international conventions existing or hereafter to be agreed upon, the Members of the League:

(a) will endeavour to secure and maintain fair and humane conditions of labour for men, women, and children, both in their own countries and in all countries to which their commercial and industrial relations extend, and for that purpose will establish and maintain the necessary international organisations;

(b) undertake to secure just treatment of the native inhabitants of territories under their control;

(c) will entrust the League with the general supervision over the execution of agreements with regard to the traffic in women and children, and the traffic in opium and other dangerous drugs;

(d) will entrust the League with the general supervision of the trade in arms and ammunition with the countries in which the control of this traffic is necessary in the common interest;

(e) will make provision to secure and maintain freedom of communications and of transit and equitable treatment for the commerce of all Members of the League. In this connection, the special necessities of the regions devastated during the war of 1914-1918 shall be borne in mind;

(f) will endeavour to take steps in matters of international concern for the prevention and control of disease. * * *

Article 25

The Members of the League agree to encourage and promote the establishment and co-operation of duly authorised voluntary national Red Cross organisations having as purposes the improvement of health, the prevention of disease and the mitigation of suffering throughout the world.

CHARTER OF THE UNITED NATIONS
Adopted June 26, 1945, 59 Stat. 1055, 2000 U.N.Y.B. 1451

Preamble

We the Peoples of the United Nations Determined

to save succeeding generations from the scourge of war, which twice in our lifetime has brought untold sorrow to mankind, and

to reaffirm faith in fundamental human rights, in the dignity and worth of the human person, in the equal rights of men and women and of nations large and small, and

to establish conditions under which justice and respect for the obligations arising from treaties and other sources of international law can be maintained, and

to promote social progress and better standards of life in larger freedom,

And for these Ends

to practice tolerance and live together in peace with one another as good neighbors, and

to unite our strength to maintain international peace and security, and

to ensure by the acceptance of principles and the institution of methods, that armed force shall not be used, save in the common interest, and

to employ international machinery for the promotion of the economic and social advancement of all peoples,

Have Resolved to Combine our Efforts to Accomplish these Aims

Accordingly, our respective Governments, through representatives assembled in the city of San Francisco, who have exhibited their full powers found to be in good and due form, have agreed to the present Charter of the United Nations and do hereby establish an international organization to be known as the United Nations.

Chapter I
Purposes and Principles

Article 1

The Purposes of the United Nations are:

1. To maintain international peace and security, and to that end: to take effective collective measures for the prevention and removal of threats to the peace, and for the suppression of acts of aggression or other breaches of the peace, and to bring about by peaceful means, and in conformity with the principles of justice and international law, adjustment or settlement of international disputes or situations which might lead to a breach of the peace;

2. To develop friendly relations among nations based on respect for the principle of equal rights and self-determination of peoples, and to take other appropriate measures to strengthen universal peace;

3. To achieve international cooperation in solving international problems of an economic, social, cultural, or humanitarian character, and in promoting and encouraging respect for human rights and for fundamental freedoms for all without distinction as to race, sex, language, or religion; and

4. To be a center for harmonizing the actions of nations in the attainment of these common ends.

Article 2

The Organization and its Members, in pursuit of the Purposes stated in Article 1, shall act in accordance with the following Principles.

1. The Organization is based on the principle of the sovereign equality of all its Members.

2. All Members, in order to ensure to all of them the rights and benefits resulting from membership, shall fulfill in good faith the obligations assumed by them in accordance with the present Charter.

3. All Members shall settle their international disputes by peaceful means in such a manner that international peace and security, and justice, are not endangered.

4. All Members shall refrain in their international relations from the threat or use of force against the territorial integrity or political independence of any state, or in any other manner inconsistent with the Purposes of the United Nations.

5. All Members shall give the United Nations every assistance in any action it takes in accordance with the present Charter, and shall refrain from giving assistance to any state against which the United Nations is taking preventive or enforcement action.

6. The Organization shall ensure that states which are not Members of the United Nations act in accordance with these Principles so far as may be necessary for the maintenance of international peace and security.

7. Nothing contained in the present Charter shall authorize the United Nations to intervene in matters which are essentially within the domestic jurisdiction of any state or shall require the Members to submit such matters to settlement under the present Charter; but this principle shall not prejudice the application of enforcement measures under Chapter VII. * * *

Chapter VII
Action with respect to threats to the peace, breaches of the peace, and acts of aggression

Article 39

The Security Council shall determine the existence of any threat to the peace, breach of the peace, or act of aggression and shall make recommendations, or decide what measures shall be taken in accordance with Articles 41 and 42, to maintain or restore international peace and security.

Article 40

In order to prevent an aggravation of the situation, the Security Council may, before making the recommendations or deciding upon the measures provided for in Article 39, call upon the parties concerned to comply with such provisional measures as it deems necessary or desirable. Such provisional measures shall be without prejudice to the rights, claims, or position of the parties concerned. The Security Council shall duly take account of failure to comply with such provisional measures.

Article 41

The Security Council may decide what measures not involving the use of armed force are to be employed to give effect to its decisions, and it may call upon the Members of the United Nations to apply such measures. These may include complete or partial interruption of economic relations and of rail, sea, air, postal, telegraphic, radio, and other means of communication, and the severance of diplomatic relations.

Article 42
Should the Security Council consider that measures provided for in Article 41 would be inadequate or have proved to be inadequate, it may take such action by air, sea, or land forces as may be necessary to maintain or restore international peace and security. Such action may include demonstrations, blockade, and other operations by air, sea, or land forces of Members of the United Nations. * * *

Article 49
The Members of the United Nations shall join in affording mutual assistance in carrying out the measures decided upon by the Security Council. * * *

Article 51
Nothing in the present Charter shall impair the inherent right of individual or collective self-defense if an armed attack occurs against a Member of the United Nations, until the Security Council has taken measures necessary to maintain international peace and security. Measures taken by Members in the exercise of this right of self-defense shall be immediately reported to the Security Council and shall not in any way affect the authority and responsibility of the Security Council under the present Charter to take at any time such action as it deems necessary in order to maintain or restore international peace and security. * * *

Chapter IX
International economic and social co-operation

Article 55
With a view to the creation of conditions of stability and well-being which are necessary for peaceful and friendly relations among nations based on respect for the principle of equal rights and self-determination of peoples, the United Nations shall promote:
> a. higher standards of living, full employment, and conditions of economic and social progress and development;
> b. solutions of international economic, social, health, and related problems; and international cultural and educational co-operation; and
> c. universal respect for, and observance of, human rights and fundamental freedoms for all without distinction as to race, sex, language, or religion.

Article 56
All Members pledge themselves to take joint and separate action in cooperation with the Organization for the achievement of the purposes set forth in Article 55. * * *

Article 60
Responsibility for the discharge of the functions of the Organization set forth in this Chapter shall be vested in the General Assembly and, under the authority of the General Assembly, in the Economic and Social Council, which shall have for this purpose the powers set forth in Chapter X.

Chapter X
The Economic and Social Council

Composition
Article 61
1. The Economic and Social Council shall consist of fifty-four Members of the United Nations elected by the General Assembly.

2. Subject to the provisions of paragraph 3, eighteen members of the Economic and Social Council shall be elected each year for a term of three years. A retiring member shall be eligible for immediate re-election.

3. At the first election after the increase in the membership of the Economic and Social Council from twenty-seven to fifty-four members, in addition to the members elected in place of the nine members

whose term of office expires at the end of that year, twenty-seven additional members shall be elected. Of these twenty-seven additional members, the term of office of nine members so elected shall expire at the end of one year, and of nine other members at the end of two years, in accordance with arrangements made by the General Assembly.

4. Each member of the Economic and Social Council shall have one representative.

Functions and Powers

Article 62

1. The Economic and Social Council may make or initiate studies and reports with respect to international economic, social, cultural, educational, health, and related matters and may make recommendations with respect to any such matters to the General Assembly, to the Members of the United Nations, and to the specialized agencies concerned.

2. It may make recommendations for the purpose of promoting respect for, and observance of, human rights and fundamental freedoms for all.

3. It may prepare draft conventions for submission to the General Assembly, with respect to matters falling within its competence.

4. It may call, in accordance with the rules prescribed by the United Nations, international conferences on matters falling within its competence. * * *

Article 66

1. The Economic and Social Council shall perform such functions as fall within its competence in connection with the carrying out of the recommendations of the General Assembly.

2. It may, with the approval of the General Assembly, perform services at the request of Members of the United Nations and at the request of specialized agencies.

3. It shall perform such other functions as are specified elsewhere in the present Charter or as may be assigned to it by the General Assembly. * * *

Procedure

Article 68

The Economic and Social Council shall set up commissions in economic and social fields and for the promotion of human rights, and such other commissions as may be required for the performance of its functions. * * *

Article 71

The Economic and Social Council may make suitable arrangements for consultation with non-governmental organizations which are concerned with matters within its competence. Such arrangements may be made with international organizations and, where appropriate, with national organizations after consultation with the Member of the United Nations concerned. * * *

Chapter XI
Declaration regarding non-self-governing territories

Article 73

Members of the United Nations which have or assume responsibilities for the administration of territories whose peoples have not yet attained a full measure of self-government recognize the principle that the interests of the inhabitants of these territories are paramount, and accept as a sacred trust the obligation to promote to the utmost, within the system of international peace and security established by the present Charter, the well-being of the inhabitants of these territories, and, to this end:

a. to ensure, with due respect for the culture of the peoples concerned, their political, economic, social, and educational advancement, their just treatment, and their protection against abuses;

b. to develop self-government, to take due account of the political aspirations of the peoples, and to assist them in the progressive development of their free political institutions, according to the particular circumstances of each territory and its peoples and their varying stages of advancement;

c. to further international peace and security;

d. to promote constructive measures of development, to encourage research, and to cooperate with one another and, when and where appropriate, with specialized international bodies with a view to the practical achievement of the social, economic, and scientific purposes set forth in this Article; and

e. to transmit regularly to the Secretary-General for information purposes, subject to such limitation as security and constitutional considerations may require, statistical and other information of a technical nature relating to economic, social, and educational conditions in the territories for which they are respectively responsible other than those territories to which Chapter XII and XIII apply. * * *

Chapter XII
International trusteeship system

Article 75

The United Nations shall establish under its authority an international trusteeship system for the administration and supervision of such territories as may be placed thereunder by subsequent individual agreements. These territories are hereinafter referred to as trust territories.

Article 76

The basic objectives of the trusteeship system, in accordance with the Purposes of the United Nations laid down in Article 1 of the present Charter, shall be:

a. to further international peace and security;

b. to promote the political, economic, social, and educational advancement of the inhabitants of the trust territories, and their progressive development towards self-government or independence as may be appropriate to the particular circumstances of each territory and its peoples and the freely expressed wishes of the peoples concerned, and as may be provided by the terms of each trusteeship agreement;

c. to encourage respect for human rights and for fundamental freedoms for all without distinction as to race, sex, language, or religion, and to encourage recognition of the interdependence of the peoples of the world; and

d. to ensure equal treatment in social, economic, and commercial matters for all Members of the United Nations and their nationals and also equal treatment for the latter in the administration of justice without prejudice to the attainment of the foregoing objectives and subject to the provisions of Article 80.

Article 77

1. The trusteeship system shall apply to such territories in the following categories as may be placed thereunder by means of trusteeship agreements:

a. territories now held under mandate;

b. territories which may be detached from enemy states as a result of the Second World War, and

c. territories voluntarily placed under the system by states responsible for their administration.

2. It will be a matter for subsequent agreement as to which territories in the foregoing categories will be brought under the trusteeship system and upon what terms.

Article 78

The trusteeship system shall not apply to territories which have become Members of the United Nations, relationship among which shall be based on respect for the principle of sovereign equality. * * *

Chapter XVI
Miscellaneous provisions

Article 103

In the event of a conflict between the obligations of the Members of the United Nations under the present Charter and their obligations under any other international agreement, their obligations under the present Charter shall prevail.

VIENNA CONVENTION ON THE LAW OF TREATIES (1969)

Vienna Convention on the Law of Treaties, *adopted* May 23, 1969, 1155 U.N.T.S. 331.

Article 1
Scope of the present Convention

The present Convention applies to treaties between States.

Article 2
Use of terms

1. For the purposes of the present Convention:

(a) "treaty" means an international agreement concluded between States in written form and governed by international law, whether embodied in a single instrument or in two or more related instruments and whatever its particular designation;

(b) "ratification", "acceptance", "approval" and "accession" mean in each case the international act so named whereby a State establishes on the international plane its consent to be bound by a treaty; * * *

(d) "reservation" means a unilateral statement, however phrased or named, made by a State, when signing, ratifying, accepting, approving or acceding to a treaty, whereby it purports to exclude or to modify the legal effect of certain provisions of the treaty in their application to that State; * * *

(f) "contracting State" means a State which has consented to be bound by the treaty, whether or not the treaty has entered into force;

(g) "party" means a State which has consented to be bound by the treaty and for which the treaty is in force; * * *

(i) "international organization" means an intergovernmental organization. * * *

Article 7
Full powers

1. A person is considered as representing a State for the purpose of adopting or authenticating the text of a treaty or for the purpose of expressing the consent of the State to be bound by a treaty if:

(a) he produces appropriate full powers; or

(b) it appears from the practice of the States concerned or from other circumstances that their intention was to consider that person as representing the State for such purposes and to dispense with full powers.

2. In virtue of their functions and without having to produce full powers, the following are considered as representing their State:

(a) Heads of State, Heads of Government and Ministers for Foreign Affairs, for the purpose of performing all acts relating to the conclusion of a treaty;

(b) heads of diplomatic missions, for the purpose of adopting the text of a treaty between the accrediting State and the State to which they are accredited;

(c) representatives accredited by States to an international conference or to an international organization or one of its organs, for the purpose of adopting the text of a treaty in that conference, organization or organ. * * *

Article 11
Means of expressing consent to be bound by a treaty

The consent of a State to be bound by a treaty may be expressed by signature, exchange of instruments constituting a treaty, ratification, acceptance, approval or accession, or by any other means if so agreed. * * *

Article 18
Obligation not to defeat the object and purpose
of a treaty prior to its entry into force

A State is obliged to refrain from acts which would defeat the object and purpose of a treaty when:

(a) it has signed the treaty or has exchanged instruments constituting the treaty subject to ratification, acceptance or approval, until it shall have made its intention clear not to become a party to the treaty; or

(b) it has expressed its consent to be bound by the treaty, pending the entry into force of the treaty and provided that such entry into force is not unduly delayed.

Article 19
Formulation of reservations

A State may, when signing, ratifying, accepting, approving or acceding to a treaty, formulate a reservation unless:

(a) the reservation is prohibited by the treaty;

(b) the treaty provides that only specified reservations, which do not include the reservation in question, may be made; or

(c) in cases not failing under subparagraphs (*a*) and (*b*), the reservation is incompatible with the object and purpose of the treaty.

Article 20
Acceptance of and objection to reservations

1. A reservation expressly authorized by a treaty does not require any subsequent acceptance by the other contracting States unless the treaty so provides.

2. When it appears from the limited number of the negotiating States and the object and purpose of a treaty that the application of the treaty in its entirety between all the parties is an essential condition of the consent of each one to be bound by the treaty, a reservation requires acceptance by all the parties.

3. When a treaty is a constituent instrument of an international organization and unless it otherwise provides, a reservation requires the acceptance of the competent organ of that organization.

4. In cases not falling under the preceding paragraphs and unless the treaty otherwise provides:

(a) acceptance by another contracting State of a reservation constitutes the reserving State a party to the treaty in relation to that other State if or when the treaty is in force for those States;

(b) an objection by another contracting State to a reservation does not preclude the entry into force of the treaty as between the objecting and reserving States unless a contrary intention is definitely expressed by the objecting State;

(c) an act expressing a State's consent to be bound by the treaty and containing a reservation is effective as soon as at least one other contracting State has accepted the reservation.

5. For the purposes of paragraphs 2 and 4 and unless the treaty otherwise provides, a reservation is considered to have been accepted by a State if it shall have raised no objection to the reservation by the end of a period of twelve months after it was notified of the reservation or by the date on which it expressed its consent to be bound by the treaty, whichever is later.

Article 21
Legal elects of reservations and of objections to reservations

1. A reservation established with regard to another party in accordance with articles 19, 20 and 23:

(a) modifies for the reserving State in its relations with that other party the provisions of the treaty to which the reservation relates to the extent of the reservation; and

(b) modifies those provisions to the same extent for that other party in its relations with the reserving State.

2. The reservation does not modify the provisions of the treaty for the other parties to the treaty *inter se.*

3. When a State objecting to a reservation has not opposed the entry into force of the treaty between itself and the reserving State, the provisions to which the reservation relates do not apply as between the two States to the extent of the reservation.

Article 22
Withdrawal of reservations and of objections to reservations

1. Unless the treaty otherwise provides, a reservation may be withdrawn at any time and the consent of a State which has accepted the reservation is not required for its withdrawal.

2. Unless the treaty otherwise provides, an objection to a reservation may be withdrawn at any time.

3. Unless the treaty otherwise provides, or it is otherwise agreed:

(a) the withdrawal of a reservation becomes operative in relation to another contracting State only when notice of it has been received by that State;

(b) the withdrawal of an objection to a reservation becomes operative only when notice of it has been received by the State which formulated the reservation. * * *

Article 26
"Pacta sunt servanda"

Every treaty in force is binding upon the parties to it and must be performed by them in good faith.

Article 27
Internal law and observance of treaties

A party may not invoke the provisions of its internal law as justification for its failure to perform a treaty. This rule is without prejudice to article 46. * * *

Article 28
Non-retroactivity of treaties

Unless a different intention appears from the treaty or is otherwise established, its provisions do not bind a party in relation to any act or fact which took place or any situation which ceased to exist before the date of the entry into force of the treaty with respect to that party. * * *

Article 31
General rule of interpretation

1. A treaty shall be interpreted in good faith in accordance with the ordinary meaning to be given to the terms of the treaty in their context and in the light of its object and purpose.

2. The context for the purpose of the interpretation of a treaty shall comprise, in addition to the text, including its preamble and annexes:

(a) any agreement relating to the treaty which was made between all the parties in connection with the conclusion of the treaty;

(b) any instrument which was made by one or more parties in connection with the conclusion of the treaty and accepted by the other parties as an instrument related to the treaty.

3. There shall be taken into account, together with the context:

(a) any subsequent agreement between the parties regarding the interpretation of the treaty or the application of its provisions;

(b) any subsequent practice in the application of the treaty which establishes the agreement of the parties regarding its interpretation;

(c) any relevant rules of international law applicable in the relations between the parties.

4. A special meaning shall be given to a term if it is established that the parties so intended.

Article 32
Supplementary means of interpretation

Recourse may be had to supplementary means of interpretation, including the preparatory work of the treaty and the circumstances of its conclusion, in order to confirm the meaning resulting from the application of article 31, or to determine the meaning when the interpretation according to article 31:

(a) leaves the meaning ambiguous or obscure; or

(b) leads to a result which is manifestly absurd or unreasonable.

Article 33
Interpretation of treaties authenticated in two or more languages

1. When a treaty has been authenticated in two or more languages, the text is equally authoritative in each language, unless the treaty provides or the parties agree that, in case of divergence, a particular text shall prevail.

2. A version of the treaty in a language other than one of those in which the text was authenticated shall be considered an authentic text only if the treaty so provides or the parties so agree.

3. The terms of the treaty are presumed to have the same meaning in each authentic text.

4. Except where a particular text prevails in accordance with paragraph 1, when a comparison of the authentic texts discloses a difference of meaning which the application of articles 31 and 32 does not

remove, the meaning which best reconciles the texts, having regard to the object and purpose of the treaty, shall be adopted. * * *

Article 43
Obligations imposed by international law independently of a treaty

The invalidity, termination or denunciation of a treaty, the withdrawal of a party from it, or the suspension of its operation, as a result of the application of the present Convention or of the provisions of the treaty, shall not in any way impair the duty of any State to fulfil any obligation embodied in the treaty to which it would be subject under international law independently of the treaty. * * *

Article 52
Coercion of a State by the threat or use of force

A treaty is void if its conclusion has been procured by the threat or use of force in violation of the principles of international law embodied in the Charter of the United Nations.

Article 53
Treaties conflicting with a peremptory norm of
general international law ("jus cogens")

A treaty is void if, at the time of its conclusion, it conflicts with a peremptory norm of general international law. For the purposes of the present Convention, a peremptory norm of general international law is a norm accepted and recognized by the international community of States as a whole as a norm from which no derogation is permitted and which can be modified only by a subsequent norm of general international law having the same character. * * *

Article 56
Denunciation of or withdrawal from a treaty containing no
provision regarding termination, denunciation or withdrawal

1. A treaty which contains no provision regarding its termination and which does not provide for denunciation or withdrawal is not subject to denunciation or withdrawal unless:
    (a) it is established that the parties intended to admit the possibility of denunciation or withdrawal; or
    (b) a right of denunciation or withdrawal may be implied by the nature of the treaty.
2. A party shall give not less than twelve months' notice of its intention to denounce or withdraw from a treaty under paragraph 1. * * *

Article 60
Termination or suspension of the operation of a treaty
as a consequence of its breach

1. A material breach of a bilateral treaty by one of the parties entitles the other to invoke the breach as a ground for terminating the treaty or suspending its operation in whole or in part.
2. A material breach of a multilateral treaty by one of the parties entitles:
    (a) the other parties by unanimous agreement to suspend the operation of the treaty in whole or in part or to terminate it either:
        (i) in the relations between themselves and the defaulting State; or
        (ii) as between all the parties;
    (b) a party specially affected by the breach to invoke it as a ground for suspending the operation of the treaty in whole or in part in the relations between itself and the defaulting State;
    (c) any party other than the defaulting State to invoke the breach as a ground for suspending the operation of the treaty in whole or in part with respect to itself if the treaty is of such a character that a material breach of its provisions by one party radically changes the position of every party with respect to the further performance of its obligations under the treaty.
3. A material breach of a treaty, for the purposes of this article, consists in:
    (a) a repudiation of the treaty not sanctioned by the present Convention; or
    (b) the violation of a provision essential to the accomplishment of the object or purpose of the treaty.

4. The foregoing paragraphs are without prejudice to any provision in the treaty applicable in the event of a breach.

5. Paragraphs 1 to 3 do not apply to provisions relating to the protection of the human person contained in treaties of a humanitarian character, in particular to provisions prohibiting any form of reprisals against persons protected by such treaties. * * *

Article 62
Fundamental change of circumstances

1. A fundamental change of circumstances which has occurred with regard to those existing at the time of the conclusion of a treaty, and which was not foreseen by the parties, may not be invoked as a ground for terminating or withdrawing from the treaty unless:

(a) the existence of those circumstances constituted an essential basis of the consent of the parties to be bound by the treaty; and

(b) the effect of the change is radically to transform the extent of obligations still to be performed under the treaty.

2. A fundamental change of circumstances may not be invoked as a ground for terminating or withdrawing from a treaty:

(a) if the treaty establishes a boundary; or

(b) if the fundamental change is the result of a breach by the party invoking it either of an obligation under the treaty or of any other international obligation owed to any other party to the treaty.

3. If, under the foregoing paragraphs, a party may invoke a fundamental change of circumstances as a ground for terminating or withdrawing from a treaty it may also invoke the change as a ground for suspending the operation of the treaty.

Article 63
Severance of diplomatic or consular relations

The severance of diplomatic or consular relations between parties to a treaty does not affect the legal relations established between them by the treaty except insofar as the existence of diplomatic or consular relations is indispensable for the application of the treaty.

Article 64
Emergence of a new peremptory norm of generalinternational law ("jus cogens")

If a new peremptory norm of general international law emerges, any existing treaty which is in conflict with that norm becomes void and terminates. * * *

Article 73
Cases of State succession, State responsibilityand outbreak of hostilities

The provisions of the present Convention shall not prejudge any question that may arise in regard to a treaty from a succession of States or from the international responsibility of a State or from the outbreak of hostilities between States.

Article 74
Diplomatic and consular relations and the conclusion of treaties

The severance or absence of diplomatic or consular relations between two or more States does not prevent the conclusion of treaties between those States. The conclusion of a treaty does not in itself affect the situation in regard to diplomatic or consular relations. * * *

CONSTITUTION OF THE INTERNATIONAL LABOUR ORGANIZATION (1919)

Constitution of the International Labour Organization, *signed* June 28, 1919, 15 U.N.T.S. 40

Preamble

Whereas universal and lasting peace can be established only if it is based upon social justice;

And whereas conditions of labour exist involving such injustice hardship and privation to large numbers of people as to produce unrest so great that the peace and harmony of the world are imperilled; and an improvement of those conditions is urgently required; as, for example, by the regulation of the hours of work including the establishment of a maximum working day and week, the regulation of the labour supply, the prevention of unemployment, the provision of an adequate living wage, the protection of the worker against sickness, disease and injury arising out of his employment the protection of children, young persons and women, provision for old age and injury, protection of the interests of workers when employed in countries other than their own, recognition of the principle of equal remuneration for work of equal value, recognition of the principle of freedom of association, the organization of vocational and technical education and other measures;

Whereas also the failure of any nation to adopt humane conditions of labour is an obstacle in the way of other nations which desire to improve the conditions in their own countries;

The High Contracting Parties, moved by sentiments of justice and humanity as well as by the desire to secure the permanent peace of the world, and with a view to attaining the objectives set forth in this Preamble, agree to the following Constitution of the International Labour Organization:

Chapter I: Organization

Article 1
Establishment

1. A permanent organization is hereby established for the promotion of the objects set forth in the Preamble to this Constitution and in the Declaration concerning the aims and purposes of the International Labour Organization adopted at Philadelphia on 10 May 1944 the text of which is annexed to this Constitution.
Membership
2. The Members of the International Labour Organization shall be the States which were Members of the Organization on 1 November 1945 and such other States as may become Members in pursuance of the provisions of paragraphs 3 and 4 of this article.
3. Any original member of the United Nations and any State admitted to membership of the united nations by a decision of the general assembly in accordance with the provisions of the charter may become a member of the International Labour Organization by communicating to the director-general of the international labour office its formal acceptance of the obligations of the constitution of the International Labour Organization.
4. The General Conference of the International Labour Organization may also admit Members to the Organization by a vote concurred in by two-thirds of the delegates attending the session, including two-thirds of the Government delegates present and voting. Such admission shall take effect on the communication to the Director-General of the International Labour Office by the government of the new Member of its formal acceptance of the obligations of the Constitution of the Organization.
Withdrawal
5. No Member of the International Labour Organization may withdraw from the Organization without giving notice of its intention so to do to the Director-General of the International Labour Office. Such notice shall take effect two years after the date of its reception by the Director-General, subject to the Member having at that time fulfilled all financial obligations arising out of its membership. When a Member has ratified any international labour Convention, such withdrawal shall not affect the continued validity for the period provided for in the Convention of all obligations arising thereunder or relating thereto.

Readmission

6. In the event of any State having ceased to be a Member of the Organization, its readmission to membership shall be governed by the provisions of paragraph 3 or paragraph 4 of this article as the case may be.

Article 2
Organs

The permanent organization shall consist of:

    (a) a General Conference of representatives of the Members;

    (b) a Governing Body composed as described in article 7; and

    (c) an International Labour Office controlled by the Governing Body.

Article 3
Conference Meetings and delegates

1. The meetings of the General Conference of representatives of the Members shall be held from time to time as occasion may require, and at least once in every year. It shall be composed of four representatives of each of the Members, of whom two shall be Government delegates and the two others shall be delegates representing respectively the employers and the workpeople of each of the Members.

Advisers

2. Each delegate may be accompanied by advisers, who shall not exceed two in number for each item on the agenda of the meeting. When questions specially affecting women are to be considered by the Conference, one at least of the advisers should be a woman. * * *

Nomination of non-governmental representatives

5. The Members undertake to nominate non-Government delegates and advisers chosen in agreement with the industrial organizations, if such organizations exist, which are most representative of employers or workpeople, as the case may be, in their respective countries. * * *

Article 4
Voting rights

1. Every delegate shall be entitled to vote individually on all matters which are taken into consideration by the Conference.

2. If one of the Members fails to nominate one of the non-Government delegates whom it is entitled to nominate, the other non-Government delegate shall be allowed to sit and speak at the Conference, but not to vote.

3. If in accordance with article 3 the Conference refuses admission to a delegate of one of the Members, the provisions of the present article shall apply as if that delegate had not been nominated. * * *

Article 7
Governing Body Composition

1. The Governing Body shall consist of fifty-six persons: Twenty-eight representing governments, Fourteen representing the employers, and Fourteen representing the workers.

Government representatives

2. Of the twenty-eight persons representing governments, ten shall be appointed by the Members of chief industrial importance, and eighteen shall be appointed by the Members selected for that purpose by the Government delegates to the Conference, excluding the delegates of the ten Members mentioned above.

States of chief industrial importance

3. The Governing Body shall as occasion requires determine which are the Members of the Organization of chief industrial importance and shall make rules to ensure that all questions relating to the selection of the Members of chief industrial importance are considered by an impartial committee before being decided by the Governing Body. Any appeal made by a Member from the declaration of the Governing Body as to which are the Members of chief industrial importance shall be decided by the Conference, but an appeal to the Conference shall not suspend the application of the declaration until such time as the Conference decides the appeal.

Employers' and Workers' representatives

4. The persons representing the employers and the persons representing the workers shall be elected respectively by the Employers' delegates and the Workers' delegates to the Conference.

Term of office
5. The period of office of the Governing Body shall be three years. If for any reason the Governing Body elections do not take place on the expiry of this period, the Governing Body shall remain in office until such elections are held.
Vacancies, substitutes, etc.
6. The method of filling vacancies and of appointing substitutes and other similar questions may be decided by the Governing Body subject to the approval of the Conference.
Officers
7. The Governing Body shall, from time to time, elect from its number a chairman and two vice-chairmen, of whom one shall be a person representing a government, one a person representing the employers, and one a person representing the workers.
Procedure
8. The Governing Body shall regulate its own procedure and shall fix its own times of meeting. A special meeting shall be held if a written request to that effect is made by at least sixteen of the representatives on the Governing Body.

Article 8
Director-General
1. There shall be a Director-General of the International Labour Office, who shall be appointed by the Governing Body, and, subject to the instructions of the Governing Body, shall be responsible for the efficient conduct of the International Labour Office and for such other duties as may be assigned to him.
2. The Director-General or his deputy shall attend all meetings of the Governing Body. * * *

Article 9
Staff Appointment
1. The staff of the International Labour Office shall be appointed by the Director-General under regulations approved by the Governing Body.
2. So far as is possible with due regard to the efficiency of the work of the Office, the Director-General shall select persons of different nationalities.
3. A certain number of these persons shall be women.
International character of responsibilities
4. The responsibilities of the Director-General and the staff shall be exclusively international in character. In the performance of their duties, the Director-General and the staff shall not seek or receive instructions from any government or from any other authority external to the Organization. They shall refrain from any action which might reflect on their position as international officials responsible only to the Organization.
5. Each Member of the Organization undertakes to respect the exclusively international character of the responsibilities of the Director-General and the staff and not to seek to influence them in the discharge of their responsibilities.

Article 10
Functions of the Office
1. The functions of the International Labour Office shall include the collection and distribution of information on all subjects relating to the international adjustment of conditions of industrial life and labour, and particularly the examination of subjects which it is proposed to bring before the Conference with a view to the conclusion of international Conventions, and the conduct of such special investigations as may be ordered by the Conference or by the Governing Body.
2. Subject to such directions as the Governing Body may give, the
    (a) prepare the documents on the various items of the agenda for the meetings of the Conference;
    (b) accord to governments at their request all appropriate assistance within its power in connection with the framing of laws and regulations on the basis of the decisions of the Conference and the improvement of administrative practices and systems of inspection;
    (c) carry out the duties required of it by the provisions of this Constitution in connection with the effective observance of Conventions;
    (d) edit and issue, in such languages as the Governing Body may think desirable, publications dealing with problems of industry and employment of international interest.

3. Generally, it shall have such other powers and duties as may be assigned to it by the Conference or by the Governing Body.

Article 11
Relations with governments

The government departments of any of the Members which deal with questions of industry and employment may communicate directly with the Director-General through the representative of their government on the Governing Body of the International Labour Office or, failing any such representative, through such other qualified official as the government may nominate for the purpose.

Article 12
Relations with international organizations

1. The International Labour Organization shall co-operate within the terms of this Constitution with any general international organization entrusted with the co-ordination of the activities of public international organizations having specialized responsibilities and with public international organizations having specialized responsibilities in related fields.
2. The International Labour Organization may make appropriate arrangements for the representatives of public international organizations to participate without vote in its deliberations.
3. The International Labour Organization may make suitable arrangements for such consultation as it may think desirable with recognized non-governmental international organizations, including international organizations of employers, workers, agriculturists and co-operators. * * *

Chapter II: Procedure

Article 14
Agenda for Conference

1. The agenda for all meetings of the Conference will be settled by the Governing Body, which shall consider any suggestion as to the agenda that may be made by the government of any of the Members or by any representative organization recognized for the purpose of article 3, or by any public international organization.

Preparation for Conference

2. The Governing Body shall make rules to ensure thorough technical preparation and adequate consultation of the Members primarily concerned, by means of a preparatory conference or otherwise, prior to the adoption of a Convention or Recommendation by the Conference. * * *

Article 17
Officers of Conference, procedure and committees

1. The Conference shall elect a president and three vice-presidents. One of the vice-presidents shall be a Government delegate, one an Employers' delegate and one a Workers' delegate. The Conference shall regulate its own procedure and may appoint committees to consider and report on any matter.

Voting

2. Except as otherwise expressly provided in this Constitution or by the terms of any Convention or other instrument conferring powers on the Conference or of the financial and budgetary arrangements adopted in virtue of article 13, all matters shall be decided by a simple majority of the votes cast by the delegates present.

Quorum

3. The voting is void unless the total number of votes cast is equal to half the number of the delegates attending the Conference. * * *

Article 19
Conventions and Recommendations; Decisions of the Conference

1. When the Conference has decided on the adoption of proposals with regard to an item on the agenda, it will rest with the Conference to determine whether these proposals should take the form: (a) of an international Convention, or (b) of a Recommendation to meet circumstances where the subject, or aspect of it, dealt with is not considered suitable or appropriate at that time for a Convention.

Vote required

2. In either case a majority of two-thirds of the votes cast by the delegates present shall be necessary on the final vote for the adoption of the Convention or Recommendation, as the case may be, by the Conference.

Modifications for special local conditions

3. In framing any Convention or Recommendation of general application the Conference shall have due regard to those countries in which climatic conditions, the imperfect development of industrial organization, or other special circumstances make the industrial conditions substantially different and shall suggest the modifications, if any, which it considers may be required to meet the case of such countries.

Authentic texts

4. Two copies of the Convention or Recommendation shall be authenticated by the signatures of the President of the Conference and of the Director-General. Of these copies one shall be deposited in the archives of the International Labour Office and the other with the Secretary-General of the United Nations. The Director-General will communicate a certified copy of the Convention or Recommendation to each of the Members.

Obligations of Members in respect of Conventions

5. In the case of a Convention

(a) the Convention will be communicated to all Members for ratification;

(b) each of the Members undertakes that it will, within the period of one year at most from the closing of the session of the Conference, or if it is impossible owing to exceptional circumstances to do so within the period of one year, then at the earliest practicable moment and in no case later than 18 months from the closing of the session of the Conference, bring the Convention before the authority or authorities within whose competence the matter lies, for the enactment of legislation or other action;

(c) Members shall inform the Director-General of the International Labour Office of the measures taken in accordance with this article to bring the Convention before the said competent authority or authorities, with particulars of the authority or authorities regarded as competent, and of the action taken by them;

(d) if the Member obtains the consent of the authority or authorities within whose competence the matter lies, it will communicate the formal ratification of the Convention to the Director-General and will take such action as may be necessary to make effective the provisions of such Convention;

(e) if the Member does not obtain the consent of the authority or authorities within whose competence the matter lies, no further obligation shall rest upon the Member except that it shall report to the Director-General of the International Labour Office, at appropriate intervals as requested by the Governing Body, the position of its law and practice in regard to the matters dealt with in the Convention, showing the extent to which effect has been given, or is proposed to be given, to any of the provisions of the Convention by legislation, administrative action, collective agreement or otherwise and stating the difficulties which prevent or delay the ratification of such Convention.

Obligations of Members in respect of Recommendations

6. In the case of a Recommendation-

(a) the Recommendation will be communicated to all Members for their consideration with a view to effect being given to it by national legislation or otherwise;

(b) each of the Members undertakes that it will, within a period of one year at most from the closing of the session of the Conference or if it is impossible owing to exceptional circumstances to do so within the period of one year, then at the earliest practicable moment and in no case later than 18 months after the closing of the Conference, bring the Recommendation before the authority or authorities within whose competence the matter lies for the enactment of legislation or other action;

(c) the Members shall inform the Director-General of the International Labour Office of the measures taken in accordance with this article to bring the Recommendation before the said competent authority or authorities with particulars of the authority or authorities regarded as competent, and of the action taken by them;

(d) apart from bringing the Recommendation before the said competent authority or authorities, no further obligation shall rest upon the Members, except that they shall report to the Director-General of the International Labour Office, at appropriate intervals as requested by the Governing Body, the position of the law and practice in their country in regard to the matters dealt with in the

18

Recommendation, showing the extent to which effect has been given or is proposed to be given, to the provisions of the Recommendation and such modifications of these provisions as it has been found or may be found necessary to make in adopting or applying them.

Obligations of federal States

7. In the case of a federal State, the following provisions shall apply:

(a) in respect of Conventions and Recommendations which the federal government regards as appropriate under its constitutional system for federal action, the obligations of the federal State shall be the same as those of Members which are not federal States;

(b) in respect of Conventions and Recommendations which the federal government regards as appropriate under its constitutional system in whole or in part, for action by the constituent states provinces, or cantons rather than for federal action, the federal government shall-

(i) make, in accordance with its Constitution and the Constitutions of the states, provinces or cantons concerned, effective arrangements for the reference of such Conventions and Recommendations not later than 18 months from the closing of the session of the Conference to the appropriate federal, state provincial or cantonal authorities for the enactment of legislation or other action;

(ii) arrange, subject to the concurrence of the state, provincial or cantonal governments concerned, for periodical consultations between the federal and the state, provincial or cantonal authorities with a view to promoting within the federal State co-ordinated action to give effect to the provisions of such Conventions and Recommendations;

(iii) inform the Director-General of the International Labour Office of the measures taken in accordance with this article to bring such Conventions and Recommendations before the appropriate federal state, provincial or cantonal authorities with particulars of the authorities regarded as appropriate and of the action taken by them;

(iv) in respect of each such Convention which it has not ratified report to the Director-General of the International Labour Office at appropriate intervals as requested by the Governing Body, the position of the law and practice of the federation and its constituent states, provinces or cantons in regard to the Convention, showing the extent to which effect has been given, or is proposed to be given, to any of the provisions of the Convention by legislation, administrative action, collective agreement, or otherwise;

(v) in respect of each such Recommendation, report to the Director-General of the International Labour Office, at appropriate ntervals as requested by the Governing Body, the position of the aw and practice of the federation and its constituent states provinces or cantons in regard to the Recommendation, showing the extent to which effect has been given, or is proposed to be given to the provisions of the Recommendation and such modifications of these provisions as have been found or may be found necessary in adopting or applying them.

Effect of Conventions and Recommendations on more favourable existing provisions

8. In no case shall the adoption of any Convention or Recommendation by the Conference, or the ratification of any Convention by any Member, be deemed to affect any law, award, custom or agreement which ensures more favourable conditions to the workers concerned than those provided for in the Convention or Recommendation. * * *

Article 21
Conventions not adopted by the Conference

1. If any Convention coming before the Conference for final consideration fails to secure the support of two-thirds of the votes cast by the delegates present, it shall nevertheless be within the right of any of the Members of the Organization to agree to such Convention among themselves.

2. Any Convention so agreed to shall be communicated by the governments concerned to the Director-General of the International Labour Office and to the Secretary-General of the United Nations for registration in accordance with the provisions of article 102 of the Charter of the United Nations. * * *

Article 22
Annual reports on ratified Conventions
Each of the Members agrees to make an annual report to the International Labour Office on the measures which it has taken to give effect to the provisions of Conventions to which it is a party. These reports shall be made in such form and shall contain such particulars as the Governing Body may request.

Article 23
Examination and communication of reports
1. The Director-General shall lay before the next meeting of the Conference a summary of the information and reports communicated to him by Members in pursuance of articles 19 and 22.
2. Each Member shall communicate to the representative organizations recognized for the purpose of article 3 copies of the information and reports communicated to the Director-General in pursuance of articles 19 and 22.

Article 24
Representations of non-observance of Conventions
In the event of any representation being made to the International Labour Office by an industrial association of employers or of workers that any of the Members has failed to secure in any respect the effective observance within its jurisdiction of any Convention to which it is a party, the Governing Body may communicate this representation to the government against which it is made, and may invite that government to make such statement on the subject as it may think fit.

Article 25
Publication of representation
If no statement is received within a reasonable time from the government in question, or if the statement when received is not deemed to be satisfactory by the Governing Body, the latter shall have the right to publish the representation and the statement, if any, made in reply to it.

Article 26
Complaints of non-observance
1. Any of the Members shall have the right to file a complaint with the International Labour Office if it is not satisfied that any other Member is securing the effective observance of any Convention which both have ratified in accordance with the foregoing articles.
2. The Governing Body may, if it thinks fit, before referring such a complaint to a Commission of Inquiry, as hereinafter provided for, communicate with the government in question in the manner described in article 24.
3. If the Governing Body does not think it necessary to communicate the complaint to the government in question, or if, when it has made such communication, no statement in reply has been received within a reasonable time which the Governing Body considers to be satisfactory, the Governing Body may appoint a Commission of Inquiry to consider the complaint and to report thereon.
4. The Governing Body may adopt the same procedure either of its own motion or on receipt of a complaint from a delegate to the Conference.
5. When any matter arising out of article 25 or 26 is being considered by the Governing Body, the government in question shall if not already represented thereon, be entitled to send a representative to take part in the proceedings of the Governing Body while the matter is under consideration. Adequate notice of the date on which the matter will be considered shall be given to the government in question.

Article 27
Co-operation with Commission of Inquiry
The Members agree that, in the event of the reference of a complaint to a Commission of Inquiry under article 26, they will each, whether directly concerned in the complaint or not, place at the disposal of the Commission all the information in their possession which bears upon the subject-matter of the complaint.

Article 28
Report of Commission of Inquiry

When the Commission of Inquiry has fully considered the complaint it shall prepare a report embodying its findings on all questions of fact relevant to determining the issue between the parties and containing such recommendations as it may think proper as to the steps which should be taken to meet the complaint and the time within which they should be taken.

Article 29
Action on report of Commission of Inquiry

1. The Director-General of the International Labour Office shall communicate the report of the Commission of Inquiry to the Governing Body and to each of the governments concerned in the complaint, and shall cause it to be published.

2. Each of these governments shall within three months inform the Director-General of the International Labour Office whether or not it accepts the recommendations contained in the report of the Commission; and if not, whether it proposes to refer the complaint to the International Court of Justice.

Article 30
Failure to submit Conventions or Recommendations to competent authorities

In the event of any Member failing to take the action required by paragraphs 5 (b), 6 (b) or 7 (b) (i) of article 19 with regard to a Convention or Recommendation, any other Member shall be entitled to refer the matter to the Governing Body. In the event of the Governing Body finding that there has been such a failure, it shall report the matter to the Conference.

Article 31
Decisions of International Court of Justice

The decision of the International Court of Justice in regard to a complaint or matter which has been referred to it in pursuance of article 29 shall be final.

Article 32

The International Court of Justice may affirm, vary or reverse any of the findings or recommendations of the Commission of Inquiry, if any.

Article 33
Failure to carry out recommendations of Commission of Inquiry or ICJ

In the event of any Member failing to carry out within the time specified the recommendations, if any, contained in the report of the Commission of Inquiry, or in the decision of the International Court of Justice, as the case may be, the Governing Body may recommend to the Conference such action as it may deem wise and expedient to secure compliance therewith.

Article 34
Compliance with recommendations of Commission of Inquiry or ICJ

The defaulting government may at any time inform the Governing Body that it has taken the steps necessary to comply with the recommendations of the Commission of Inquiry or with those in the decision of the International Court of Justice, as the case may be and may request it to constitute a Commission of Inquiry to verify its contention. In this case the provisions of articles 27, 28, 29, 31 and 32 shall apply, and if the report of the Commission of Inquiry or the decision of the International Court of Justice is in favour of the defaulting government, the Governing Body shall forthwith recommend the discontinuance of any action taken in pursuance of article 33.* * *

Article 37
Interpretation of Constitution and Conventions

1. Any question or dispute relating to the interpretation of this Constitution or of any subsequent Convention concluded by the Members in pursuance of the provisions of this Constitution shall be referred for decision to the International Court of Justice.

2. Notwithstanding the provisions of paragraph 1 of this article the Governing Body may make and submit to the Conference for approval rules providing for the appointment of a tribunal for the expeditious

determination of any dispute or question relating to the interpretation of a Convention which may be referred thereto by the Governing Body or in accordance with the terms of the Convention. Any applicable judgement or advisory opinion of the International Court of Justice shall be binding upon any tribunal established in virtue of this paragraph. Any award made by such a tribunal shall be circulated to the Members of the Organization and any observations which they may make thereon shall be brought before the Conference. * * *

Article 39
Legal status of Organization
The International Labour Organization shall possess full juridical personality and in particular the capacity-
> (a) to contract;
> (b) to acquire and dispose of immovable and movable property;
> (c) to institute legal proceedings.

Article 40
Privileges and immunities
1. The International Labour Organization shall enjoy in the territory of each of its Members such privileges and immunities as are necessary for the fulfilment of its purposes.
2. Delegates to the Conference, members of the Governing Body and the Director-General and officials of the Office shall likewise enjoy such privileges and immunities as are necessary for the independent exercise of their functions in connection with the Organization.
3. Such privileges and immunities shall be defined in a separate agreement to be prepared by the Organization with a view to its acceptance by the States Members.

Annex

Declaration concerning the aims and purposes of the International Labour Organisation
(DECLARATION OF PHILADELPHIA)

The General Conference of the International Labour Organization meeting in its Twenty-sixth Session in Philadelphia, hereby adopts this tenth day of May in the year nineteen hundred and forty-four the present Declaration of the aims and purposes of the International Labour Organization and of the principles which should inspire the policy of its Members.

I.
The Conference reaffirms the fundamental principles on which the Organization is based and, in particular, that-
> (a) labour is not a commodity;
> (b) freedom of expression and of association are essential to sustained progress;
> (c) poverty anywhere constitutes a danger to prosperity everywhere;
> (d) the war against want requires to be carried on with unrelenting vigor within each nation, and by continuous and concerted international effort in which the representatives of workers and employers, enjoying equal status with those of governments, join with them in free discussion and democratic decision with a view to the promotion of the common welfare.

II.
Believing that experience has fully demonstrated the truth of the statement in the Constitution of the International Labour Organization that lasting peace can be established only if it is based on social justice, the Conference affirms that-
> (a) all human beings, irrespective of race, creed or sex, have the right to pursue both their material well-being and their spiritual development in conditions of freedom and dignity, of economic security and equal opportunity;
> (b) the attainment of the conditions in which this shall be possible must constitute the central aim of national and international policy;

(c) all national and international policies and measures, in particular those of an economic and financial character, should be judged in this light and accepted only in so far as they may be held to promote and not to hinder the achievement of this fundamental objective;

(d) it is a responsibility of the International Labour Organization to examine and consider all international economic and financial policies and measures in the light of this fundamental objective;

(e) in discharging the tasks entrusted to it the International Labour Organization, having considered all relevant economic and financial factors, may include in its decisions and recommendations any provisions which it considers appropriate.

III.

The Conference recognizes the solemn obligation of the International Labour Organization to further among the nations of the world programmes which will achieve:

(a) full employment and the raising of standards of living;

(b) the employment of workers in the occupations in which they can have the satisfaction of giving the fullest measure of their skill and attainments and make their greatest contribution to the common well-being;

(c) the provision, as a means to the attainment of this end and under adequate guarantees for all concerned, of facilities for training and the transfer of labour, including migration for employment and settlement;

(d) policies in regard to wages and earnings, hours and other conditions of work calculated to ensure a just share of the fruits of progress to all, and a minimum living wage to all employed and in need of such protection;

(e) the effective recognition of the right of collective bargaining, the cooperation of management and labour in the continuous improvement of productive efficiency, and the collaboration of workers and employers in the preparation and application of social and economic measures;

(f) the extension of social security measures to provide a basic income to all in need of such protection and comprehensive medical care;

(g) adequate protection for the life and health of workers in all occupations;

(h) provision for child welfare and maternity protection;

(i) the provision of adequate nutrition, housing and facilities for recreation and culture;

(j) the assurance of equality of educational and vocational opportunity.

IV.

Confident that the fuller and broader utilization of the world's productive resources necessary for the achievement of the objectives set forth in this Declaration can be secured by effective international and national action, including measures to expand production and consumption, to avoid severe economic fluctuations to promote the economic and social advancement of the less developed regions of the world, to assure greater stability in world prices of primary products, and to promote a high and steady volume of international trade, the Conference pledges the full cooperation of the International Labour Organization with such international bodies as may be entrusted with a share of the responsibility for this great task and for the promotion of the health, education and well-being of all peoples.

V.

The conference affirms that the principles set forth in this Declaration are fully applicable to all peoples everywhere and that, while the manner of their application must be determined with due regard to the stage of social and economic development reached by each people, their progressive application to peoples who are still dependent, as well as to those who have already achieved self-government, is a matter of concern to the whole civilized world.

Amendments to the Constitution

The original text of the Constitution, established in 1919, has been modified *inter alia* by the amendment of 1922 which entered into force on 4 June 1934; the Instrument of Amendment of 1945 which entered into force on 26 September 1946; the Instrument of Amendment of 1946 which entered into force on 20 April 1948; the Instrument of Amendment of 1953 which entered into force on 20 May 1954; the Instrument of

Amendment of 1962 which entered into force on 22 May 1963; and the Instrument of Amendment of 1972 which entered into force on 1 November 1974.

SLAVERY CONVENTION (1926)

Slavery, Servitude, Forced Labour and Similar Institutions and Practices Convention of 1926 (Slavery Convention of 1926), *adopted* Sept. 25, 1926, 60 L.N.T.S. 253

Article 1

For the purpose of the present Convention, the following definitions are agreed upon:

(1) Slavery is the status or condition of a person over whom any or all of the powers attaching to the right of ownership are exercised.

(2) The slave trade includes all acts involved in the capture, acquisition or disposal of a person with intent to reduce him to slavery; all acts involved in the acquisition of a slave with a view to selling or exchanging him; all acts of disposal by sale or exchange of a slave acquired with a view to being sold or exchanged, and, in general, every act of trade or transport in slaves.

Article 2

The High Contracting Parties undertake, each in respect of the territories placed under its sovereignty, jurisdiction, protection, suzerainty or tutelage, so far as they have not already taken the necessary steps:

(a) To prevent and suppress the slave trade;

(b) To bring about, progressively and as soon as possible, the complete abolition of slavery in all its forms.

Article 3

The High Contracting Parties undertake to adopt all appropriate measures with a view to preventing and suppressing the embarkation, disembarkation and transport of slaves in their territorial waters and upon all vessels flying their respective flags. * * *

Article 4

The High Contracting Parties shall give to one another every assistance with the object of securing the abolition of slavery and the slave trade.

Article 5

The High Contracting Parties recognise that recourse to compulsory or forced labour may have grave consequences and undertake, each in respect of the territories placed under its sovereignty, jurisdiction, protection, suzerainty or tutelage, to take all necessary measures to prevent compulsory or forced labour from developing into conditions analogous to slavery.

It is agreed that:

(1) Subject to the transitional provisions laid down in paragraph (2) below, compulsory or forced labour may only be exacted for public purposes.

(2) In territories in which compulsory or forced labour for other than public purposes still survives, the High Contracting Parties shall endeavour progressively and as soon as possible to put an end to the practice. So long as such forced or compulsory labour exists, this labour shall invariably be of an exceptional character, shall always receive adequate remuneration, and shall not involve the removal of the labourers from their usual place of residence.

(3) In all cases, the responsibility for any recourse to compulsory or forced labour shall rest with the competent central authorities of the territory concerned.

Article 6

Those of the High Contracting Parties whose laws do not at present make adquate provision for the punishment of infractions of laws and regulations enacted with a view to giving effect to the purposes of the present Convention undertake to adopt the necessary measures in order that severe penalties may be imposed in respect of such infractions.

Article 7

The High Contracting Parties undertake to communicate to each other and to the Secretary-General of the League of Nations any laws and regulations which they may enact with a view to the application of the provisions of the present Convention.

Article 8

The High Contracting Parties agree that disputes arising between them relating to the interpretation or application of this Convention shall, if they cannot be settled by direct negotiation, be referred for decision to the Permanent Court of International Justice. In case either or both of the States Parties to such a dispute should not be Parties to the Protocol of December 16th, 1920, relating to the Permanent Court of International Justice, the dispute shall be referred, at the choice of the Parties and in accordance with the constitutional procedure of each State, either to the Permanent Court of International Justice or to a court of arbitration constituted in accordance with the Convention of October 18th, 1907, for the Pacific Settlement of International Disputes, or to some other court of arbitration.

Article 9

At the time of signature or of ratification or of accession, any High Contracting Party may declare that its acceptance of the present Convention does not bind some or all of the territories placed under its sovereignty, jurisdiction, protection, suzerainty or tutelage in respect of all or any provisions of the Convention; it may subsequently accede separately on behalf of any one of them or in respect of any provision to which any one of them is not a Party.

Article 10

In the event of a High Contracting Party wishing to denounce the present Convention, the denunciation shall be notified in writing to the Secretary-General of the League of Nations, who will at once communicate a certified true copy of the notification to all the other High Contracting Parties, informing them of the date on which it was received. The denunciation shall only have effect in regard to the notifying State, and one year after the notification has reached the Secretary-General of the League of Nations. Denunciation may also be made separately in respect of any territory placed under its sovereignty, jurisdiction, protection, suzerainty or tutelage.

Article 11

The present Convention, which will bear this day's date and of which the French and English texts are both authentic, will remain open for signature by the States Members of the League of Nations until April 1st, 1927. * * *

PROTOCOL AMENDING THE SLAVERY CONVENTION (1953)
Protocol amending the Slavery Convention, *adopted* Dec. 7, 1953, 182 U.N.T.S. 51.

The States Parties to the present Protocol,

Considering that under the Slavery Convention signed at Geneva on 25 September 1926 (hereinafter called "the Convention") the League of Nations was invested with certain duties and functions, and

Considering that it is expedient that these duties and functions should be continued by the United Nations,

Have agreed as follows:

Article 1

The States Parties to the present Protocol undertake that as between themselves they will, in accordance with the provisions of the Protocol, attribute full legal force and effect to and duly apply the amendments to the Convention set forth in the annex to the Protocol.

Article 2

1. The present Protocol shall be open for signature or acceptance by any of the States Parties to the Convention to which the Secretary-General has communicated for this purpose a copy of the Protocol.
2. States may become Parties to the present Protocol by:

    (a) Signature without reservation as to acceptance;
    (b) Signature with reservation as to acceptance, followed by acceptance;
    (c) Acceptance.

3. Acceptance shall be effected by the deposit of a formal instrument with the Secretary-General of the United Nations.

Article 3

1. The present Protocol shall come into force on the date on which two States shall have become Parties thereto, and shall thereafter come into force in respect of each State upon the date on which it becomes a Party to the Protocol.
2. The amendments set forth in the annex to the present Protocol shall come into force when twenty-three States shall have become Parties to the Protocol, and consequently any State becoming a Party to the Convention, after the amendments thereto have come into force, shall become a Party to the Convention as so amended.

Article 4

In accordance with paragraph I of Article 102 of the Charter of the United Nations and the regulations pursuant thereto adopted by the General Assembly, the Secretary-General of the United Nations is authorized to effect registration of the present Protocol and of the amendments made in the Convention by the Protocol on the respective dates of their entry into force and to publish the Protocol and the amended text of the Convention as soon as possible after registration.

Article 5

The present Protocol, of which the Chinese, English, French, Russian and Spanish texts are equally authentic, shall be deposited in the archives of the United Nations Secretariat. The texts of the Convention to be amended in accordance with the annex being authentic in the English and French languages only, the English and French texts of the annex shall be equally authentic, and the Chinese, Russian and Spanish texts shall be translations. The Secretary-General shall prepare certified copies of the Protocol, including the annex, for communication to States Parties to the Convention, as well as to all other States Members of the United Nations. He shall likewise prepare for communication to States including States not Members of the United Nations, upon the entry into force of the amendments as provided in article III, certified copies of the Convention as so amended.

Annex to the Protocol amending the Slavery Convention

In article 7 "the Secretary-General of the United Nations" shall be substituted for "the Secretary-General of the League of Nations".

In article 8 "the International Court of Justice" shall be substituted for the "Permanent Court of International Justice", and "the Statute of the International Court of Justice" shall be substituted for "the Protocol of December 16th, 1920, relating to the Permanent Court of International Justice".

In the first and second paragraphs of article 10 "the United Nations" shall be substituted for "the League of Nations".

The last three paragraphs of article 11 shall be deleted and the following substituted:

"The present Convention shall be open to accession by all States, including States which are not Members of the United Nations, to which the Secretary-General of the United Nations shall have communicated a certified copy of the Convention.

"Accession shall be effected by the deposit of a formal instrument with the Secretary-General of the United Nations, who shall give notice thereof to all States Parties to the Convention and to all other States contemplated in the present article, informing them of the date on which each such instrument of accession was received in deposit."

In article 12 "the United Nations" shall be substituted for "the League of Nations".

FORCED LABOUR CONVENTION (1930)

Convention Concerning Forced or Compulsory Labour (ILO No. 29), *adopted* June 28, 1930, 39 U.N.T.S. 55

Article 1

1. Each Member of the International Labour Organisation which ratifies this Convention undertakes to suppress the use of forced or compulsory labour in all its forms within the shortest possible period.
2. With a view to this complete suppression, recourse to forced or compulsory labour may be had, during the transitional period, for public purposes only and as an exceptional measure, subject to the conditions and guarantees hereinafter provided.
3. At the expiration of a period of five years after the coming into force of this Convention, and when the Governing Body of the International Labour Office prepares the report provided for in Article 31 below, the said Governing Body shall consider the possibility of the suppression of forced or compulsory labour in all its forms without a further transitional period and the desirability of placing this question on the agenda of the Conference.

Article 2

1. For the purposes of this Convention the term forced or compulsory labour shall mean all work or service which is exacted from any person under the menace of any penalty and for which the said person has not offered himself voluntarily.
2. Nevertheless, for the purposes of this Convention, the term forced or compulsory labour shall not include--

> (a) any work or service exacted in virtue of compulsory military service laws for work of a purely military character;
> (b) any work or service which forms part of the normal civic obligations of the citizens of a fully self-governing country;
> (c) any work or service exacted from any person as a consequence of a conviction in a court of law, provided that the said work or service is carried out under the supervision and control of a public authority and that the said person is not hired to or placed at the disposal of private individuals, companies or associations;
> (d) any work or service exacted in cases of emergency, that is to say, in the event of war or of a calamity or threatened calamity, such as fire, flood, famine, earthquake, violent epidemic or epizootic diseases, invasion by animal, insect or vegetable pests, and in general any circumstance that would endanger the existence or the well-being of the whole or part of the population;
> (e) minor communal services of a kind which, being performed by the members of the community in the direct interest of the said community, can therefore be considered as normal civic obligations incumbent upon the members of the community, provided that the members of the community or their direct representatives shall have the right to be consulted in regard to the need for such services.

Article 3

For the purposes of this Convention the term competent authority shall mean either an authority of the metropolitan country or the highest central authority in the territory concerned.

Article 4

1. The competent authority shall not impose or permit the imposition of forced or compulsory labour for the benefit of private individuals, companies or associations.

2. Where such forced or compulsory labour for the benefit of private individuals, companies or associations exists at the date on which a Member's ratification of this Convention is registered by the Director-General of the International Labour Office, the Member shall completely suppress such forced or compulsory labour from the date on which this Convention comes into force for that Member.

Article 5

1. No concession granted to private individuals, companies or associations shall involve any form of forced or compulsory labour for the production or the collection of products which such private individuals, companies or associations utilise or in which they trade.

2. Where concessions exist containing provisions involving such forced or compulsory labour, such provisions shall be rescinded as soon as possible, in order to comply with Article 1 of this Convention.

Article 6

Officials of the administration, even when they have the duty of encouraging the populations under their charge to engage in some form of labour, shall not put constraint upon the said populations or upon any individual members thereof to work for private individuals, companies or associations.

Article 7

1. Chiefs who do not exercise administrative functions shall not have recourse to forced or compulsory labour.

2. Chiefs who exercise administrative functions may, with the express permission of the competent authority, have recourse to forced or compulsory labour, subject to the provisions of Article 10 of this Convention.

3. Chiefs who are duly recognised and who do not receive adequate remuneration in other forms may have the enjoyment of personal services, subject to due regulation and provided that all necessary measures are taken to prevent abuses.

Article 8

1. The responsibility for every decision to have recourse to forced or compulsory labour shall rest with the highest civil authority in the territory concerned.

2. Nevertheless, that authority may delegate powers to the highest local authorities to exact forced or compulsory labour which does not involve the removal of the workers from their place of habitual residence. That authority may also delegate, for such periods and subject to such conditions as may be laid down in the regulations provided for in Article 23 of this Convention, powers to the highest local authorities to exact forced or compulsory labour which involves the removal of the workers from their place of habitual residence for the purpose of facilitating the movement of officials of the administration, when on duty, and for the transport of Government stores.

Article 9

Except as otherwise provided for in Article 10 of this Convention, any authority competent to exact forced or compulsory labour shall, before deciding to have recourse to such labour, satisfy itself--

    (a) that the work to be done or the service to be rendered is of important direct interest for the community called upon to do work or render the service;

    (b) that the work or service is of present or imminent necessity;

    (c) that it has been impossible to obtain voluntary labour for carrying out the work or rendering the service by the offer of rates of wages and conditions of labour not less favourable than those prevailing in the area concerned for similar work or service; and

    (d) that the work or service will not lay too heavy a burden upon the present population, having regard to the labour available and its capacity to undertake the work.

Article 10

1. Forced or compulsory labour exacted as a tax and forced or compulsory labour to which recourse is had for the execution of public works by chiefs who exercise administrative functions shall be progressively abolished.

2. Meanwhile, where forced or compulsory labour is exacted as a tax, and where recourse is had to forced or compulsory labour for the execution of public works by chiefs who exercise administrative functions, the authority concerned shall first satisfy itself--

> (a) that the work to be done or the service to be rendered is of important direct interest for the community called upon to do the work or render the service;
> (b) that the work or the service is of present or imminent necessity;
> (c) that the work or service will not lay too heavy a burden upon the present population, having regard to the labour available and its capacity to undertake the work;
> (d) that the work or service will not entail the removal of the workers from their place of habitual residence;
> (e) that the execution of the work or the rendering of the service will be directed in accordance with the exigencies of religion, social life and agriculture.

Article 11

1. Only adult able-bodied males who are of an apparent age of not less than 18 and not more than 45 years may be called upon for forced or compulsory labour. Except in respect of the kinds of labour provided for in Article 10 of this Convention, the following limitations and conditions shall apply:

> (a) whenever possible prior determination by a medical officer appointed by the administration that the persons concerned are not suffering from any infectious or contagious disease and that they are physically fit for the work required and for the conditions under which it is to be carried out;
> (b) exemption of school teachers and pupils and officials of the administration in general;
> (c) the maintenance in each community of the number of adult able-bodied men indispensable for family and social life;
> (d) respect for conjugal and family ties.

2. For the purposes of subparagraph (c) of the preceding paragraph, the regulations provided for in Article 23 of this Convention shall fix the proportion of the resident adult able-bodied males who may be taken at any one time for forced or compulsory labour, provided always that this proportion shall in no case exceed 25 per cent. In fixing this proportion the competent authority shall take account of the density of the population, of its social and physical development, of the seasons, and of the work which must be done by the persons concerned on their own behalf in their locality, and, generally, shall have regard to the economic and social necessities of the normal life of the community concerned.

Article 12

1. The maximum period for which any person may be taken for forced or compulsory labour of all kinds in any one period of twelve months shall not exceed sixty days, including the time spent in going to and from the place of work.

2. Every person from whom forced or compulsory labour is exacted shall be furnished with a certificate indicating the periods of such labour which he has completed.

Article 13

1. The normal working hours of any person from whom forced or compulsory labour is exacted shall be the same as those prevailing in the case of voluntary labour, and the hours worked in excess of the normal working hours shall be remunerated at the rates prevailing in the case of overtime for voluntary labour.

2. A weekly day of rest shall be granted to all persons from whom forced or compulsory labour of any kind is exacted and this day shall coincide as far as possible with the day fixed by tradition or custom in the territories or regions concerned.

Article 14

1. With the exception of the forced or compulsory labour provided for in Article 10 of this Convention, forced or compulsory labour of all kinds shall be remunerated in cash at rates not less than those prevailing

for similar kinds of work either in the district in which the labour is employed or in the district from which the labour is recruited, whichever may be the higher.

2. In the case of labour to which recourse is had by chiefs in the exercise of their administrative functions, payment of wages in accordance with the provisions of the preceding paragraph shall be introduced as soon as possible.

3. The wages shall be paid to each worker individually and not to his tribal chief or to any other authority.

4. For the purpose of payment of wages the days spent in travelling to and from the place of work shall be counted as working days.

5. Nothing in this Article shall prevent ordinary rations being given as a part of wages, such rations to be at least equivalent in value to the money payment they are taken to represent, but deductions from wages shall not be made either for the payment of taxes or for special food, clothing or accommodation supplied to a worker for the purpose of maintaining him in a fit condition to carry on his work under the special conditions of any employment, or for the supply of tools.

Article 15

1. Any laws or regulations relating to workmen's compensation for accidents or sickness arising out of the employment of the worker and any laws or regulations providing compensation for the dependants of deceased or incapacitated workers which are or shall be in force in the territory concerned shall be equally applicable to persons from whom forced or compulsory labour is exacted and to voluntary workers.

2. In any case it shall be an obligation on any authority employing any worker on forced or compulsory labour to ensure the subsistence of any such worker who, by accident or sickness arising out of his employment, is rendered wholly or partially incapable of providing for himself, and to take measures to ensure the maintenance of any persons actually dependent upon such a worker in the event of his incapacity or decease arising out of his employment.

Article 16

1. Except in cases of special necessity, persons from whom forced or compulsory labour is exacted shall not be transferred to districts where the food and climate differ so considerably from those to which they have been accustomed as to endanger their health.

2. In no case shall the transfer of such workers be permitted unless all measures relating to hygiene and accommodation which are necessary to adapt such workers to the conditions and to safeguard their health can be strictly applied.

3. When such transfer cannot be avoided, measures of gradual habituation to the new conditions of diet and of climate shall be adopted on competent medical advice.

4. In cases where such workers are required to perform regular work to which they are not accustomed, measures shall be taken to ensure their habituation to it, especially as regards progressive training, the hours of work and the provision of rest intervals, and any increase or amelioration of diet which may be necessary.

Article 17

Before permitting recourse to forced or compulsory labour for works of construction or maintenance which entail the workers remaining at the workplaces for considerable periods, the competent authority shall satisfy itself--

(1) that all necessary measures are taken to safeguard the health of the workers and to guarantee the necessary medical care, and, in particular, (a) that the workers are medically examined before commencing the work and at fixed intervals during the period of service, (b) that there is an adequate medical staff, provided with the dispensaries, infirmaries, hospitals and equipment necessary to meet all requirements, and (c) that the sanitary conditions of the workplaces, the supply of drinking water, food, fuel, and cooking utensils, and, where necessary, of housing and clothing, are satisfactory;

(2) that definite arrangements are made to ensure the subsistence of the families of the workers, in particular by facilitating the remittance, by a safe method, of part of the wages to the family, at the request or with the consent of the workers;

(3) that the journeys of the workers to and from the workplaces are made at the expense and under the responsibility of the administration, which shall facilitate such journeys by making the fullest use of all available means of transport;

(4) that, in case of illness or accident causing incapacity to work of a certain duration, the worker is repatriated at the expense of the administration;

(5) that any worker who may wish to remain as a voluntary worker at the end of his period of forced or compulsory labour is permitted to do so without, for a period of two years, losing his right to repatriation free of expense to himself.

Article 18

1. Forced or compulsory labour for the transport of persons or goods, such as the labour of porters or boatmen, shall be abolished within the shortest possible period. Meanwhile the competent authority shall promulgate regulations determining, inter alia, (a) that such labour shall only be employed for the purpose of facilitating the movement of officials of the administration, when on duty, or for the transport of Government stores, or, in cases of very urgent necessity, the transport of persons other than officials, (b) that the workers so employed shall be medically certified to be physically fit, where medical examination is possible, and that where such medical examination is not practicable the person employing such workers shall be held responsible for ensuring that they are physically fit and not suffering from any infectious or contagious disease, (c) the maximum load which these workers may carry, (d) the maximum distance from their homes to which they may be taken, (e) the maximum number of days per month or other period for which they may be taken, including the days spent in returning to their homes, and (f) the persons entitled to demand this form of forced or compulsory labour and the extent to which they are entitled to demand it.

2. In fixing the maxima referred to under (c), (d) and (e) in the foregoing paragraph, the competent authority shall have regard to all relevant factors, including the physical development of the population from which the workers are recruited, the nature of the country through which they must travel and the climatic conditions.

3. The competent authority shall further provide that the normal daily journey of such workers shall not exceed a distance corresponding to an average working day of eight hours, it being understood that account shall be taken not only of the weight to be carried and the distance to be covered, but also of the nature of the road, the season and all other relevant factors, and that, where hours of journey in excess of the normal daily journey are exacted, they shall be remunerated at rates higher than the normal rates.

Article 19

1. The competent authority shall only authorise recourse to compulsory cultivation as a method of precaution against famine or a deficiency of food supplies and always under the condition that the food or produce shall remain the property of the individuals or the community producing it.

2. Nothing in this Article shall be construed as abrogating the obligation on members of a community, where production is organised on a communal basis by virtue of law or custom and where the produce or any profit accruing from the sale thereof remain the property of the community, to perform the work demanded by the community by virtue of law or custom.

Article 20

Collective punishment laws under which a community may be punished for crimes committed by any of its members shall not contain provisions for forced or compulsory labour by the community as one of the methods of punishment.

Article 21

Forced or compulsory labour shall not be used for work underground in mines.

Article 22

The annual reports that Members which ratify this Convention agree to make to the International Labour Office, pursuant to the provisions of Article 22 of the Constitution of the International Labour Organisation, on the measures they have taken to give effect to the provisions of this Convention, shall contain as full information as possible, in respect of each territory concerned, regarding the extent to which recourse has been had to forced or compulsory labour in that territory, the purposes for which it has been employed, the sickness and death rates, hours of work, methods of payment of wages and rates of wages, and any other relevant information.

Article 23

1. To give effect to the provisions of this Convention the competent authority shall issue complete and precise regulations governing the use of forced or compulsory labour.
2. These regulations shall contain, inter alia, rules permitting any person from whom forced or compulsory labour is exacted to forward all complaints relative to the conditions of labour to the authorities and ensuring that such complaints will be examined and taken into consideration.

Article 24

Adequate measures shall in all cases be taken to ensure that the regulations governing the employment of forced or compulsory labour are strictly applied, either by extending the duties of any existing labour inspectorate which has been established for the inspection of voluntary labour to cover the inspection of forced or compulsory labour or in some other appropriate manner. Measures shall also be taken to ensure that the regulations are brought to the knowledge of persons from whom such labour is exacted.

Article 25

The illegal exaction of forced or compulsory labour shall be punishable as a penal offence, and it shall be an obligation on any Member ratifying this Convention to ensure that the penalties imposed by law are really adequate and are strictly enforced.

Article 26

1. Each Member of the International Labour Organisation which ratifies this Convention undertakes to apply it to the territories placed under its sovereignty, jurisdiction, protection, suzerainty, tutelage or authority, so far as it has the right to accept obligations affecting matters of internal jurisdiction; provided that, if such Member may desire to take advantage of the provisions of article 35 of the Constitution of the International Labour Organisation, it shall append to its ratification a declaration stating--

   (1) the territories to which it intends to apply the provisions of this Convention without modification;
   (2) the territories to which it intends to apply the provisions of this Convention with modifications, together with details of the said modifications;
   (3) the territories in respect of which it reserves its decision.

2. The aforesaid declaration shall be deemed to be an integral part of the ratification and shall have the force of ratification. It shall be open to any Member, by a subsequent declaration, to cancel in whole or in part the reservations made, in pursuance of the provisions of subparagraphs (2) and (3) of this Article, in the original declaration. * * *

Article 28

1. This Convention shall be binding only upon those Members whose ratifications have been registered with the International Labour Office.
2. It shall come into force twelve months after the date on which the ratifications of two Members of the International Labour Organisation have been registered with the Director-General.
3. Thereafter, this Convention shall come into force for any Member twelve months after the date on which the ratification has been registered.

Article 29

As soon as the ratifications of two Members of the International Labour Organisation have been registered with the International Labour Office, the Director-General of the International Labour Office shall so notify all the Members of the International Labour Organisation. He shall likewise notify them of the registration of ratifications which may be communicated subsequently by other Members of the Organisation.

Article 30

1. A Member which has ratified this Convention may denounce it after the expiration of ten years from the date on which the Convention first comes into force, by an act communicated to the Director-General of the International Labour Office for registration. Such denunciation shall not take effect until one year after the date on which it is registered with the International Labour Office.
2. Each Member which has ratified this Convention and which does not, within the year following the expiration of the period of ten years mentioned in the preceding paragraph, exercise the right of

denunciation provided for in this Article, will be bound for another period of five years and, thereafter, may denounce this Convention at the expiration of each period of five years under the terms provided for in this Article.

Article 31
At such times as it may consider necessary the Governing Body of the International Labour Office shall present to the General Conference a report on the working of this Convention and shall examine the desirability of placing on the agenda of the Conference the question of its revision in whole or in part. * * *

Article 33
The French and English texts of this Convention shall both be authentic.

CONVENTION ON THE PREVENTION AND PUNISHMENT OF THE CRIME OF GENOCIDE (1948)
Convention on the Prevention and Punishment of the Crime of Genocide, *adopted* Dec. 9, 1948, 78 U.N.T.S. 277, 102 Stat. 3045

Article I
The Contracting Parties confirm that genocide, whether committed in time of peace or in time of war, is a crime under international law which they undertake to prevent and to punish.

Article II
In the present Convention, genocide means any of the following acts committed with intent to destroy, in whole or in part, a national, ethnical, racial or religious group, as such:
(a) Killing members of the group;
(b) Causing serious bodily or mental harm to members of the group;
(c) Deliberately inflicting on the group conditions of life calculated to bring about its physical destruction in whole or in part;
(d) Imposing measures intended to prevent births within the group;
(e) Forcibly transferring children of the group to another group.

Article III
The following acts shall be punishable:
(a) Genocide;
(b) Conspiracy to commit genocide;
(c) Direct and public incitement to commit genocide;
(d) Attempt to commit genocide;
(e) Complicity in genocide.

Article IV
Persons committing genocide or any of the other acts enumerated in article III shall be punished, whether they are constitutionally responsible rulers, public officials or private individuals.

Article V
The Contracting Parties undertake to enact, in accordance with their respective Constitutions, the necessary legislation to give effect to the provisions of the present Convention, and, in particular, to provide effective penalties for persons guilty of genocide or any of the other acts enumerated in article III.

Article VI
Persons charged with genocide or any of the other acts enumerated in article III shall be tried by a competent tribunal of the State in the territory of which the act was committed, or by such international penal tribunal as may have jurisdiction with respect to those Contracting Parties which shall have accepted its jurisdiction.

Article VII

Genocide and the other acts enumerated in article III shall not be considered as political crimes for the purpose of extradition. The Contracting Parties pledge themselves in such cases to grant extradition in accordance with their laws and treaties in force.

Article VIII

Any Contracting Party may call upon the competent organs of the United Nations to take such action under the Charter of the United Nations as they consider appropriate for the prevention and suppression of acts of genocide or any of the other acts enumerated in article III.

Article IX

Disputes between the Contracting Parties relating to the interpretation, application or fulfilment of the present Convention, including those relating to the responsibility of a State for genocide or for any of the other acts enumerated in article III, shall be submitted to the International Court of Justice at the request of any of the parties to the dispute.

Article X

The present Convention, of which the Chinese, English, French, Russian and Spanish texts are equally authentic, shall bear the date of 9 December 1948.

Article XI

The present Convention shall be open until 31 December 1949 for signature on behalf of any Member of the United Nations and of any non-member State to which an invitation to sign has been addressed by the General Assembly. The present Convention shall be ratified, and the instruments of ratification shall be deposited with the Secretary-General of the United Nations. After 1 January 1950, the present Convention may be acceded to on behalf of any Member of the United Nations and of any non-member State which has received an invitation as aforesaid. Instruments of accession shall be deposited with the Secretary-General of the United Nations.

Article XII

Any Contracting Party may at any time, by notification addressed to the Secretary-General of the United Nations, extend the application of the present Convention to all or any of the territories for the conduct of whose foreign relations that Contracting Party is responsible. * * *

Article XIV

The present Convention shall remain in effect for a period of ten years as from the date of its coming into force. It shall thereafter remain in force for successive periods of five years for such Contracting Parties as have not denounced it at least six months before the expiration of the current period. Denunciation shall be effected by a written notification addressed to the Secretary-General of the United Nations. * * *

Article XVI

A request for the revision of the present Convention may be made at any time by any Contracting Party by means of a notification in writing addressed to the Secretary-General. The General Assembly shall decide upon the steps, if any, to be taken in respect of such request. * * *

GENEVA CONVENTION RELATIVE TO THE TREATMENT OF PRISONERS OF WAR (1949)

Geneva Convention Relative to the Treatment of Prisoners of War, *adopted* Aug. 12, 1949, 6 U.S.T. 3316; 75 U.N.T.S. 135

Article 1

The High Contracting Parties undertake to respect and to ensure respect for the present Convention in all circumstances.

Article 2

In addition to the provisions which shall be implemented in peace time, the present Convention shall apply to all cases of declared war or of any other armed conflict which may arise between two or more of the High Contracting Parties, even if the state of war is not recognized by one of them. The Convention shall also apply to all cases of partial or total occupation of the territory of a High Contracting Party, even if the said occupation meets with no armed resistance. Although one of the Powers in conflict may not be a party to the present Convention, the Powers who are parties thereto shall remain bound by it in their mutual relations. They shall furthermore be bound by the Convention in relation to the said Power, if the latter accepts and applies the provisions thereof.

Article 3

In the case of armed conflict not of an international character occurring in the territory of one of the High Contracting Parties, each party to the conflict shall be bound to apply, as a minimum, the following provisions:

1. Persons taking no active part in the hostilities, including members of armed forces who have laid down their arms and those placed hors de combat by sickness, wounds, detention, or any other cause, shall in all circumstances be treated humanely, without any adverse distinction founded on race, colour, religion or faith, sex, birth or wealth, or any other similar criteria.

To this end the following acts are and shall remain prohibited at any time and in any place whatsoever with respect to the above-mentioned persons:

> (a) Violence to life and person, in particular murder of all kinds, mutilation, cruel treatment and torture;
>
> (b) Taking of hostages;
>
> (c) Outrages upon personal dignity, in particular, humiliating and degrading treatment;
>
> (d) The passing of sentences and the carrying out of executions without previous judgment pronounced by a regularly constituted court affording all the judicial guarantees which are recognized as indispensable by civilized peoples.

2. The wounded and sick shall be collected and cared for.

An impartial humanitarian body, such as the International Committee of the Red Cross, may offer its services to the Parties to the conflict.

The Parties to the conflict should further endeavour to bring into force, by means of special agreements, all or part of the other provisions of the present Convention.

The application of the preceding provisions shall not affect the legal status of the Parties to the conflict.

Article 4

A. Prisoners of war, in the sense of the present Convention, are persons belonging to one of the following categories, who have fallen into the power of the enemy:

1. Members of the armed forces of a Party to the conflict as well as members of militias or volunteer corps forming part of such armed forces.

2. Members of other militias and members of other volunteer corps, including those of organized resistance movements, belonging to a Party to the conflict and operating in or outside their own territory, even if this territory is occupied, provided that such militias or volunteer corps, including such organized resistance movements, fulfil the following conditions:

> (a) That of being commanded by a person responsible for his subordinates;
>
> (b) That of having a fixed distinctive sign recognizable at a distance;
>
> (c) That of carrying arms openly;

(d) That of conducting their operations in accordance with the laws and customs of war.
3. Members of regular armed forces who profess allegiance to a government or an authority not recognized by the Detaining Power.
4. Persons who accompany the armed forces without actually being members thereof, such as civilian members of military aircraft crews, war correspondents, supply contractors, members of labour units or of services responsible for the welfare of the armed forces, provided that they have received authorization from the armed forces which they accompany, who shall provide them for that purpose with an identity card similar to the annexed model.
5. Members of crews, including masters, pilots and apprentices, of the merchant marine and the crews of civil aircraft of the Parties to the conflict, who do not benefit by more favourable treatment under any other provisions of international law.
6. Inhabitants of a non-occupied territory, who on the approach of the enemy spontaneously take up arms to resist the invading forces, without having had time to form themselves into regular armed units, provided they carry arms openly and respect the laws and customs of war.

B. The following shall likewise be treated as prisoners of war under the present Convention:
1. Persons belonging, or having belonged, to the armed forces of the occupied country, if the occupying Power considers it necessary by reason of such allegiance to intern them, even though it has originally liberated them while hostilities were going on outside the territory it occupies, in particular where such persons have made an unsuccessful attempt to rejoin the armed forces to which they belong and which are engaged in combat, or where they fail to comply with a summons made to them with a view to internment.
2. The persons belonging to one of the categories enumerated in the present Article, who have been received by neutral or non-belligerent Powers on their territory and whom these Powers are required to intern under international law, without prejudice to any more favourable treatment which these Powers may choose to give and with the exception of Articles 8, 10, 15, 30, fifth paragraph, 58-67, 92, 126 and, where diplomatic relations exist between the Parties to the conflict and the neutral or non-belligerent Power concerned, those Articles concerning the Protecting Power. Where such diplomatic relations exist, the Parties to a conflict on whom these persons depend shall be allowed to perform towards them the functions of a Protecting Power as provided in the present Convention, without prejudice to the functions which these Parties normally exercise in conformity with diplomatic and consular usage and treaties.

C. This Article shall in no way affect the status of medical personnel and chaplains as provided for in Article 33 of the present Convention.

Article 5
The present Convention shall apply to the persons referred to in Article 4 from the time they fall into the power of the enemy and until their final release and repatriation. Should any doubt arise as to whether persons, having committed a belligerent act and having fallen into the hands of the enemy, belong to any of the categories enumerated in Article 4, such persons shall enjoy the protection of the present Convention until such time as their status has been determined by a competent tribunal.

Article 6
In addition to the agreements expressly provided for in Articles 10, 23, 28, 33, 60, 65, 66, 67, 72, 73, 75, 109, 110, 118, 119, 122 and 132, the High Contracting Parties may conclude other special agreements for all matters concerning which they may deem it suitable to make separate provision. No special agreement shall adversely affect the situation of prisoners of war, as defined by the present Convention, nor restrict the rights which it confers upon them. Prisoners of war shall continue to have the benefit of such agreements as long as the Convention is applicable to them, except where express provisions to the contrary are contained in the aforesaid or in subsequent agreements, or where more favourable measures have been taken with regard to them by one or other of the Parties to the conflict.

Article 7
Prisoners of war may in no circumstances renounce in part or in entirety the rights secured to them by the present Convention, and by the special agreements referred to in the foregoing Article, if such there be.

Article 8

The present Convention shall be applied with the cooperation and under the scrutiny of the Protecting Powers whose duty it is to safeguard the interests of the Parties to the conflict. For this purpose, the Protecting Powers may appoint, apart from their diplomatic or consular staff, delegates from amongst their own nationals or the nationals of other neutral Powers. The said delegates shall be subject to the approval of the Power with which they are to carry out their duties. The Parties to the conflict shall facilitate to the greatest extent possible the task of the representatives or delegates of the Protecting Powers. The representatives or delegates of the Protecting Powers shall not in any case exceed their mission under the present Convention. They shall, in particular, take account of the imperative necessities of security of the State wherein they carry out their duties.

Article 9

The provisions of the present Convention constitute no obstacle to the humanitarian activities which the International Committee of the Red Cross or any other impartial humanitarian organization may, subject to the consent of the Parties to the conflict concerned, undertake for the protection of prisoners of war and for their relief.

Article 10

The High Contracting Parties may at any time agree to entrust to an organization which offers all guarantees of impartiality and efficacy the duties incumbent on the Protecting Powers by virtue of the present Convention. When prisoners of war do not benefit or cease to benefit, no matter for what reason, by the activities of a Protecting Power or of an organization provided for in the first paragraph above, the Detaining Power shall request a neutral State, or such an organization, to undertake the functions performed under the present Convention by a Protecting Power designated by the Parties to a conflict. If protection cannot be arranged accordingly, the Detaining Power shall request or shall accept, subject to the provisions of this Article, the offer of the services of a humanitarian organization, such as the International Committee of the Red Cross, to assume the humanitarian functions performed by Protecting Powers under the present Convention. Any neutral Power or any organization invited by the Power concerned or offering itself for these purposes, shall be required to act with a sense of responsibility towards the Party to the conflict on which persons protected by the present Convention depend, and shall be required to furnish sufficient assurances that it is in a position to undertake the appropriate functions and to discharge them impartially. No derogation from the preceding provisions shall be made by special agreements between Powers one of which is restricted, even temporarily, in its freedom to negotiate with the other Power or its allies by reason of military events, more particularly where the whole, or a substantial part, of the territory of the said Power is occupied. Whenever in the present Convention mention is made of a Protecting Power, such mention applies to substitute organizations in the sense of the present Article.

Article 11

In cases where they deem it advisable in the interest of protected persons, particularly in cases of disagreement between the Parties to the conflict as to the application or interpretation of the provisions of the present Convention, the Protecting Powers shall lend their good offices with a view to settling the disagreement. For this purpose, each of the Protecting Powers may, either at the invitation of one Party or on its own initiative, propose to the Parties to the conflict a meeting of their representatives, and in particular of the authorities responsible for prisoners of war, possibly on neutral territory suitably chosen. The Parties to the conflict shall be bound to give effect to the proposals made to them for this purpose. The Protecting Powers may, if necessary, propose for approval by the Parties to the conflict a person belonging to a neutral Power, or delegated by the International Committee of the Red Cross, who shall be invited to take part in such a meeting.

PART II
GENERAL PROTECTION OF PRISONERS OF WAR

Article 12

Prisoners of war are in the hands of the enemy Power, but not of the individuals or military units who have captured them. Irrespective of the individual responsibilities that may exist, the Detaining Power is responsible for the treatment given them. Prisoners of war may only be transferred by the Detaining Power to a Power which is a party to the Convention and after the Detaining Power has satisfied itself of the willingness and ability of such transferee Power to apply the Convention. When prisoners of war are transferred under such circumstances, responsibility for the application of the Convention rests on the Power accepting them while they are in its custody. Nevertheless if that Power fails to carry out the provisions of the Convention in any important respect, the Power by whom the prisoners of war were transferred shall, upon being notified by the Protecting Power, take effective measures to correct the situation or shall request the return of the prisoners of war. Such requests must be complied with.

Article 13
Prisoners of war must at all times be humanely treated. Any unlawful act or omission by the Detaining Power causing death or seriously endangering the health of a prisoner of war in its custody is prohibited, and will be regarded as a serious breach of the present Convention. In particular, no prisoner of war may be subjected to physical mutilation or to medical or scientific experiments of any kind which are not justified by the medical, dental or hospital treatment of the prisoner concerned and carried out in his interest. Likewise, prisoners of war must at all times be protected, particularly against acts of violence or intimidation and against insults and public curiosity. Measures of reprisal against prisoners of war are prohibited.

Article 14
Prisoners of war are entitled in all circumstances to respect for their persons and their honour. Women shall be treated with all the regard due to their sex and shall in all cases benefit by treatment as favourable as that granted to men. Prisoners of war shall retain the full civil capacity which they enjoyed at the time of their capture. The Detaining Power may not restrict the exercise, either within or without its own territory, of the rights such capacity confers except in so far as the captivity requires.

Article 15
The Power detaining prisoners of war shall be bound to provide free of charge for their maintenance and for the medical attention required by their state of health.

Article 16
Taking into consideration the provisions of the present Convention relating to rank and sex, and subject to any privileged treatment which may be accorded to them by reason of their state of health, age or professional qualifications, all prisoners of war shall be treated alike by the Detaining Power, without any adverse distinction based on race, nationality, religious belief or political opinions, or any other distinction founded on similar criteria.

PART III
CAPTIVITY

Section I
Beginning of captivity

Article 17
Every prisoner of war, when questioned on the subject, is bound to give only his surname, first names and rank, date of birth, and army, regimental, personal or serial number, or failing this, equivalent information. If he wilfully infringes this rule, he may render himself liable to a restriction of the privileges accorded to his rank or status. Each Party to a conflict is required to furnish the persons under its jurisdiction who are liable to become prisoners of war, with an identity card showing the owner's surname, first names, rank, army, regimental, personal or serial number or equivalent information, and date of birth. The identity card may, furthermore, bear the signature or the fingerprints, or both, of the owner, and may bear, as well, any other information the Party to the conflict may wish to add concerning persons belonging to its armed forces. As far as possible the card shall measure 6.5 x 10 cm. and shall be issued in duplicate. The identity card shall be shown by the prisoner of war upon demand, but may in no case be taken away from him. No physical or mental torture, nor any other form of coercion, may be inflicted on prisoners of war to secure from them information of any kind whatever. Prisoners of war who refuse to answer may not be threatened, insulted, or exposed to any unpleasant or disadvantageous treatment of any kind. Prisoners of

war who, owing to their physical or mental condition, are unable to state their identity, shall be handed over to the medical service. The identity of such prisoners shall be established by all possible means, subject to the provisions of the preceding paragraph. The questioning of prisoners of war shall be carried out in a language which they understand.

Article 18

All effects and articles of personal use, except arms, horses, military equipment and military documents shall remain in the possession of prisoners of war, likewise their metal helmets and gas masks and like articles issued for personal protection. Effects and articles used for their clothing or feeding shall likewise remain in their possession, even if such effects and articles belong to their regulation military equipment. At no time should prisoners of war be without identity documents. The Detaining Power shall supply such documents to prisoners of war who possess none. Badges of rank and nationality, decorations and articles having above all a personal or sentimental value may not be taken from prisoners of war. Sums of money carried by prisoners of war may not be taken away from them except by order of an officer, and after the amount and particulars of the owner have been recorded in a special register and an itemized receipt has been given, legibly inscribed with the name, rank and unit of the person issuing the said receipt. Sums in the currency of the Detaining Power, or which are changed into such currency at the prisoner's request, shall be placed to the credit of the prisoner's account as provided in Article 64. The Detaining Power may withdraw articles of value from prisoners of war only for reasons of security; when such articles are withdrawn, the procedure laid down for sums of money impounded shall apply. Such objects, likewise the sums taken away in any currency other than that of the Detaining Power and the conversion of which has not been asked for by the owners, shall be kept in the custody of the Detaining Power and shall be returned in their initial shape to prisoners of war at the end of their captivity.

Article 19

Prisoners of war shall be evacuated, as soon as possible after their capture, to camps situated in an area far enough from the combat zone for them to be out of danger. Only those prisoners of war who, owing to wounds or sickness, would run greater risks by being evacuated than by remaining where they are, may be temporarily kept back in a danger zone. Prisoners of war shall not be unnecessarily exposed to danger while awaiting evacuation from a fighting zone.

Article 20

The evacuation of prisoners of war shall always be effected humanely and in conditions similar to those for the forces of the Detaining Power in their changes of station. The Detaining Power shall supply prisoners of war who are being evacuated with sufficient food and potable water, and with the necessary clothing and medical attention. The Detaining Power shall take all suitable precautions to ensure their safety during evacuation, and shall establish as soon as possible a list of the prisoners of war who are evacuated. If prisoners of war must, during evacuation, pass through transit camps, their stay in such camps shall be as brief as possible.

Section II
Internment of prisoners of war

Chapter I
General observations

Article 21

The Detaining Power may subject prisoners of war to internment. It may impose on them the obligation of not leaving, beyond certain limits, the camp where they are interned, or if the said camp is fenced in, of not going outside its perimeter. Subject to the provisions of the present Convention relative to penal and disciplinary sanctions, prisoners of war may not be held in close confinement except where necessary to safeguard their health and then only during the continuation of the circumstances which make such confinement necessary. Prisoners of war may be partially or wholly released on parole or promise, in so far as is allowed by the laws of the Power on which they depend. Such measures shall be taken particularly in cases where this may contribute to the improvement of their state of health. No prisoner of war shall be compelled to accept liberty on parole or promise. Upon the outbreak of hostilities, each Party to the conflict shall notify the adverse Party of the laws and regulations allowing or forbidding its own nationals to accept liberty on parole or promise. Prisoners of war who are paroled or who have given their promise in conformity with the laws and regulations so notified, are bound on their personal honour scrupulously to fulfil, both towards the Power on which they depend and towards the Power which has captured them, the engagements of their paroles or promises. In such cases, the Power on which they depend is bound neither to require nor to accept from them any service incompatible with the parole or promise given.

Article 22
Prisoners of war may be interned only in premises located on land and affording every guarantee of hygiene and healthfulness. Except in particular cases which are justified by the interest of the prisoners themselves, they shall not be interned in penitentiaries. Prisoners of war interned in unhealthy areas, or where the climate is injurious for them, shall be removed as soon as possible to a more favourable climate. The Detaining Power shall assemble prisoners of war in camps or camp compounds according to their nationality, language and customs, provided that such prisoners shall not be separated from prisoners of war belonging to the armed forces with which they were serving at the time of their capture, except with their consent.

Article 23
No prisoner of war may at any time be sent to or detained in areas where he may be exposed to the fire of the combat zone, nor may his presence be used to render certain points or areas immune from military operations. Prisoners of war shall have shelters against air bombardment and other hazards of war, to the same extent as the local civilian population. With the exception of those engaged in the protection of their quarters against the aforesaid hazards, they may enter such shelters as soon as possible after the giving of the alarm. Any other protective measure taken in favour of the population shall also apply to them. Detaining Powers shall give the Powers concerned, through the intermediary of the Protecting Powers, all useful information regarding the geographical location of prisoner of war camps. Whenever military considerations permit, prisoner of war camps shall be indicated in the day-time by the letters PW or PG, placed so as to be clearly visible from the air. The Powers concerned may, however, agree upon any other system of marking. Only prisoner of war camps shall be marked as such.

Article 24
Transit or screening camps of a permanent kind shall be fitted out under conditions similar to those described in the present Section, and the prisoners therein shall have the same treatment as in other camps.

Chapter II
Quarters, food and clothing of prisoners of war

Article 25
Prisoners of war shall be quartered under conditions as favourable as those for the forces of the Detaining Power who are billeted in the same area. The said conditions shall make allowance for the habits and customs of the prisoners and shall in no case be prejudicial to their health. The foregoing provisions shall apply in particular to the dormitories of prisoners of war as regards both total surface and minimum cubic space, and the general installations, bedding and blankets. The premises provided for the use of prisoners of war individually or collectively, shall be entirely protected from dampness and adequately heated and lighted, in particular between dusk and lights out. All precautions must be taken against the danger of fire. In any camps in which women prisoners of war, as well as men, are accommodated, separate dormitories shall be provided for them.

Article 26
The basic daily food rations shall be sufficient in quantity, quality and variety to keep prisoners of war in good health and to prevent loss of weight or the development of nutritional deficiencies. Account shall also be taken of the habitual diet of the prisoners. The Detaining Power shall supply prisoners of war who work with such additional rations as are necessary for the labour on which they are employed. Sufficient drinking water shall be supplied to prisoners of war. The use of tobacco shall be permitted. Prisoners of war shall, as far as possible, be associated with the preparation of their meals; they may be employed for that purpose in

the kitchens. Furthermore, they shall be given the means of preparing, themselves, the additional food in their possession. Adequate premises shall be provided for messing. Collective disciplinary measures affecting food are prohibited.

Article 27

Clothing, underwear and footwear shall be supplied to prisoners of war in sufficient quantities by the Detaining Power, which shall make allowance for the climate of the region where the prisoners are detained. Uniforms of enemy armed forces captured by the Detaining Power should, if suitable for the climate, be made available to clothe prisoners of war. The regular replacement and repair of the above articles shall be assured by the Detaining Power. In addition, prisoners of war who work shall receive appropriate clothing, wherever the nature of the work demands.

Article 28

Canteens shall be installed in all camps, where prisoners of war may procure foodstuffs, soap and tobacco and ordinary articles in daily use. The tariff shall never be in excess of local market prices. The profits made by camp canteens shall be used for the benefit of the prisoners; a special fund shall be created for this purpose. The prisoners' representative shall have the right to collaborate in the management of the canteen and of this fund. When a camp is closed down, the credit balance of the special fund shall be handed to an international welfare organization, to be employed for the benefit of prisoners of war of the same nationality as those who have contributed to the fund. In case of a general repatriation, such profits shall be kept by the Detaining Power, subject to any agreement to the contrary between the Powers concerned.

Chapter III
Hygiene and medical attention

Article 29

The Detaining Power shall be bound to take all sanitary measures necessary to ensure the cleanliness and healthfulness of camps and to prevent epidemics. Prisoners of war shall have for their use, day and night, conveniences which conform to the rules of hygiene and are maintained in a constant state of cleanliness. In any camps in which women prisoners of war are accommodated, separate conveniences shall be provided for them. Also, apart from the baths and showers with which the camps shall be furnished, prisoners of war shall be provided with sufficient water and soap for their personal toilet and for washing their personal laundry; the necessary installations, facilities and time shall be granted them for that purpose.

Article 30

Every camp shall have an adequate infirmary where prisoners of war may have the attention they require, as well as appropriate diet. Isolation wards shall, if necessary, be set aside for cases of contagious or mental disease. Prisoners of war suffering from serious disease, or whose condition necessitates special treatment, a surgical operation or hospital care, must be admitted to any military or civilian medical unit where such treatment can be given, even if their repatriation is contemplated in the near future. Special facilities shall be afforded for the care to be given to the disabled, in particular to the blind, and for their rehabilitation, pending repatriation. Prisoners of war shall have the attention, preferably, of medical personnel of the Power on which they depend and, if possible, of their nationality. Prisoners of war may not be prevented from presenting themselves to the medical authorities for examination. The detaining authorities shall, upon request, issue to every prisoner who has undergone treatment, an official certificate indicating the nature of his illness or injury, and the duration and kind of treatment received. A duplicate of this certificate shall be forwarded to the Central Prisoners of War Agency. The costs of treatment, including those of any apparatus necessary for the maintenance of prisoners of war in good health, particularly dentures and other artificial appliances, and spectacles, shall be borne by the Detaining Power.

Article 31

Medical inspections of prisoners of war shall be held at least once a month. They shall include the checking and the recording of the weight of each prisoner of war. Their purpose shall be, in particular, to supervise the general state of health, nutrition and cleanliness of prisoners and to detect contagious diseases, especially tuberculosis, malaria and venereal disease. For this purpose the most efficient methods available shall be employed, e.g. periodic mass miniature radiography for the early detection of tuberculosis.

Article 32

Prisoners of war who, though not attached to the medical service of their armed forces, are physicians, surgeons, dentists, nurses or medical orderlies, may be required by the Detaining Power to exercise their medical functions in the interests of prisoners of war dependent on the same Power. In that case they shall continue to be prisoners of war, but shall receive the same treatment as corresponding medical personnel retained by the Detaining Power. They shall be exempted from any other work under Article 49.

Chapter IV
Medical personnel and chaplains retained to assist prisoners of war

Article 33

Members of the medical personnel and chaplains while retained by the Detaining Power with a view to assisting prisoners of war, shall not be considered as prisoners of war. They shall, however, receive as a minimum the benefits and protection of the present Convention, and shall also be granted all facilities necessary to provide for the medical care of, and religious ministration to, prisoners of war. They shall continue to exercise their medical and spiritual functions for the benefit of prisoners of war, preferably those belonging to the armed forces upon which they depend, within the scope of the military laws and regulations of the Detaining Power and under the control of its competent services, in accordance with their professional etiquette. They shall also benefit by the following facilities in the exercise of their medical or spiritual functions:

(a) They shall be authorized to visit periodically prisoners of war situated in working detachments or in hospitals outside the camp. For this purpose, the Detaining Power shall place at their disposal the necessary means of transport.

(b) The senior medical officer in each camp shall be responsible to the camp military authorities for everything connected with the activities of retained medical personnel. For this purpose, Parties to the conflict shall agree at the outbreak of hostilities on the subject of the corresponding ranks of the medical personnel, including that of societies mentioned in Article 26 of the Geneva Convention for the Amelioration of the Condition of the Wounded and Sick in Armed Forces in the Field of August 12, 1949. This senior medical officer, as well as chaplains, shall have the right to deal with the competent authorities of the camp on all questions relating to their duties. Such authorities shall afford them all necessary facilities for correspondence relating to these questions.

(c) Although they shall be subject to the internal discipline of the camp in which they are retained, such personnel may not be compelled to carry out any work other than that concerned with their medical or religious duties.

During hostilities, the Parties to the conflict shall agree concerning the possible relief of retained personnel and shall settle the procedure to be followed. None of the preceding provisions shall relieve the Detaining Power of its obligations with regard to prisoners of war from the medical or spiritual point of view.

Chapter V
Religious, intellectual and physical activities

Article 34

Prisoners of war shall enjoy complete latitude in the exercise of their religious duties, including attendance at the service of their faith, on condition that they comply with the disciplinary routine prescribed by the military authorities. Adequate premises shall be provided where religious services may be held. * * *

Article 37

When prisoners of war have not the assistance of a retained chaplain or of a prisoner of war minister of their faith, a minister belonging to the prisoners' or a similar denomination, or in his absence a qualified layman, if such a course is feasible from a confessional point of view, shall be appointed, at the request of the prisoners concerned, to fill this office. This appointment, subject to the approval of the Detaining Power, shall take place with the agreement of the community of prisoners concerned and, wherever necessary, with the approval of the local religious authorities of the same faith. The person thus appointed shall comply with all regulations established by the Detaining Power in the interests of discipline and military security.

Article 38

While respecting the individual preferences of every prisoner, the Detaining Power shall encourage the practice of intellectual, educational, and recreational pursuits, sports and games amongst prisoners, and shall take the measures necessary to ensure the exercise thereof by providing them with adequate premises and necessary equipment. Prisoners shall have opportunities for taking physical exercise, including sports and games, and for being out of doors. Sufficient open spaces shall be provided for this purpose in all camps.

Chapter VI
Discipline

Article 39

Every prisoner of war camp shall be put under the immediate authority of a responsible commissioned officer belonging to the regular armed forces of the Detaining Power. Such officer shall have in his possession a copy of the present Convention; he shall ensure that its provisions are known to the camp staff and the guard and shall be responsible, under the direction of his government, for its application.
Prisoners of war, with the exception of officers, must salute and show to all officers of the Detaining Power the external marks of respect provided for by the regulations applying in their own forces.
Officer prisoners of war are bound to salute only officers of a higher rank of the Detaining Power; they must, however, salute the camp commander regardless of his rank.

Article 40

The wearing of badges of rank and nationality, as well as of decorations, shall be permitted.

Article 41

In every camp the text of the present Convention and its Annexes and the contents of any special agreement provided for in Article 6, shall be posted, in the prisoners' own language, at places where all may read them. * * *

Article 42

The use of weapons against prisoners of war, especially against those who are escaping or attempting to escape, shall constitute an extreme measure, which shall always be preceded by warnings appropriate to the circumstances. * * *

Chapter VIII
Transfer of prisoners of war after their arrival in camp

Article 46

The Detaining Power, when deciding upon the transfer of prisoners of war, shall take into account the interests of the prisoners themselves, more especially so as not to increase the difficulty of their repatriation. The transfer of prisoners of war shall always be effected humanely and in conditions not less favourable than those under which the forces of the Detaining Power are transferred. Account shall always be taken of the climatic conditions to which the prisoners of war are accustomed and the conditions of transfer shall in no case be prejudicial to their health. The Detaining Power shall supply prisoners of war during transfer with sufficient food and drinking water to keep them in good health, likewise with the necessary clothing, shelter and medical attention. The Detaining Power shall take adequate precautions especially in case of transport by sea or by air, to ensure their safety during transfer, and shall draw up a complete list of all transferred prisoners before their departure.

Article 47

Sick or wounded prisoners of war shall not be transferred as long as their recovery may be endangered by the journey, unless their safety imperatively demands it. If the combat zone draws closer to a camp, the prisoners of war in the said camp shall not be transferred unless their transfer can be carried out in adequate conditions of safety, or if they are exposed to greater risks by remaining on the spot than by being transferred.

Article 48

In the event of transfer, prisoners of war shall be officially advised of their departure and of their new postal address. Such notifications shall be given in time for them to pack their luggage and inform their next of kin. They shall be allowed to take with them their personal effects, and the correspondence and parcels which have arrived for them. * * * The costs of transfers shall be borne by the Detaining Power.

Section III
Labour of prisoners of war

Article 49

The Detaining Power may utilize the labour of prisoners of war who are physically fit, taking into account their age, sex, rank and physical aptitude, and with a view particularly to maintaining them in a good state of physical and mental health. Non-commissioned officers who are prisoners of war shall only be required to do supervisory work. Those not so required may ask for other suitable work which shall, so far as possible, be found for them. If officers or persons of equivalent status ask for suitable work, it shall be found for them, so far as possible, but they may in no circumstances be compelled to work.

Article 50

Besides work connected with camp administration, installation or maintenance, prisoners of war may be compelled to do only such work as is included in the following classes:
(a) Agriculture;
(b) Industries connected with the production or the extraction of raw materials, and manufacturing industries, with the exception of metallurgical, machinery and chemical industries; public works and building operations which have no military character or purpose;
(c) Transport and handling of stores which are not military in character or purpose;
(d) Commercial business, and arts and crafts;
(e) Domestic service;
(f) Public utility services having no military character or purpose.
Should the above provisions be infringed, prisoners of war shall be allowed to exercise their right of complaint, in conformity with Article 78.

Article 51

Prisoners of war must be granted suitable working conditions, especially as regards accommodation, food, clothing and equipment; such conditions shall not be inferior to those enjoyed by nationals of the Detaining Power employed in similar work; account shall also be taken of climatic conditions. The Detaining Power, in utilizing the labour of prisoners of war, shall ensure that in areas in which prisoners are employed, the national legislation concerning the protection of labour, and, more particularly, the regulations for the safety of workers, are duly applied. Prisoners of war shall receive training and be provided with the means of protection suitable to the work they will have to do and similar to those accorded to the nationals of the Detaining Power. Subject to the provisions of Article 52, prisoners may be submitted to the normal risks run by these civilian workers. Conditions of labour shall in no case be rendered more arduous by disciplinary measures.

Article 52

Unless he be a volunteer, no prisoner of war may be employed on labour which is of an unhealthy or dangerous nature. No prisoner of war shall be assigned to labour which would be looked upon as humiliating for a member of the Detaining Power's own forces. The removal of mines or similar devices shall be considered as dangerous labour. * * *

Article 54

The working pay due to prisoners of war shall be fixed in accordance with the provisions of Article 62 of the present Convention. Prisoners of war who sustain accidents in connection with work, or who contract a disease in the course, or in consequence of their work, shall receive all the care their condition may require. The Detaining Power shall furthermore deliver to such prisoners of war a medical certificate enabling them to submit their claims to the Power on which they depend, and shall send a duplicate to the Central Prisoners of War Agency provided for in Article 123.

Article 55

The fitness of prisoners of war for work shall be periodically verified by medical examinations at least once a month. The examinations shall have particular regard to the nature of the work which prisoners of war are required to do. If any prisoner of war considers himself incapable of working, he shall be permitted to appear before the medical authorities of his camp. Physicians or surgeons may recommend that the prisoners who are, in their opinion, unfit for work, be exempted therefrom.

Article 56

The organization and administration of labour detachments shall be similar to those of prisoner of war camps. Every labour detachment shall remain under the control of and administratively part of a prisoner of war camp. The military authorities and the commander of the said camp shall be responsible, under the direction of their government, for the observance of the provisions of the present Convention in labour detachments. The camp commander shall keep an up-to-date record of the labour detachments dependent on his camp, and shall communicate it to the delegates of the Protecting Power, of the International Committee of the Red Cross, or of other agencies giving relief to prisoners of war, who may visit the camp.

Article 57

The treatment of prisoners of war who work for private persons, even if the latter are responsible for guarding and protecting them, shall not be inferior to that which is provided for by the present Convention. The Detaining Power, the military authorities and the commander of the camp to which such prisoners belong shall be entirely responsible for the maintenance, care, treatment, and payment of the working pay of such prisoners of war. Such prisoners of war shall have the right to remain in communication with the prisoners' representatives in the camps on which they depend.

Section IV
Financial resources of prisoners of war

* * *

Article 60

The Detaining Power shall grant all prisoners of war a monthly advance of pay, the amount of which shall be fixed by conversion, into the currency of the said Power, of the following amounts:

Category I: Prisoners ranking below sergeant: eight Swiss francs.

Category II: Sergeants and other non-commissioned officers, or prisoners of equivalent rank: twelve Swiss francs.

Category III: Warrant officers and commissioned officers below the rank of major or prisoners of equivalent rank: fifty Swiss francs.

Category IV: Majors, lieutenant-colonels, colonels or prisoners of equivalent rank: sixty Swiss francs.

Category V: General officers or prisoners of equivalent rank: seventy-five Swiss francs.

However, the Parties to the conflict concerned may by special agreement modify the amount of advances of pay due to prisoners of the preceding categories.

Furthermore, if the amounts indicated in the first paragraph above would be unduly high compared with the pay of the Detaining Power's armed forces or would, for any reason, seriously embarrass the Detaining Power, then, pending the conclusion of a special agreement with the Power on which the prisoners depend to vary the amounts indicated above, the Detaining Power:

(a) Shall continue to credit the accounts of the prisoners with the amounts indicated in the first paragraph above;

(b) May temporarily limit the amount made available from these advances of pay to prisoners of war for their own use, to sums which are reasonable, but which, for Category I, shall never be inferior to the amount that the Detaining Power gives to the members of its own armed forces.

The reasons for any limitations will be given without delay to the Protecting Power. * * *

Article 62

Prisoners of war shall be paid a fair working rate of pay by the detaining authorities direct. The rate shall be fixed by the said authorities, but shall at no time be less than one-fourth of one Swiss franc for a full working day. The Detaining Power shall inform prisoners of war, as well as the Power on which they depend, through the intermediary of the Protecting Power, of the rate of daily working pay that it has fixed. Working pay shall likewise be paid by the detaining authorities to prisoners of war permanently detailed to duties or to a skilled or semi-skilled occupation in connection with the administration, installation or maintenance of camps, and to the prisoners who are required to carry out spiritual or medical duties on behalf of their comrades. The working pay of the prisoners' representative, of his advisers, if any, and of his assistants, shall be paid out of the fund maintained by canteen profits. The scale of this working pay shall be fixed by the prisoners' representative and approved by the camp commander. If there is no such fund, the detaining authorities shall pay these prisoners a fair working rate of pay.

Article 63

Prisoners of war shall be permitted to receive remittances of money addressed to them individually or collectively. Every prisoner of war shall have at his disposal the credit balance of his account as provided for in the following Article, within the limits fixed by the Detaining Power, which shall make such payments as are requested. Subject to financial or monetary restrictions which the Detaining Power regards as essential, prisoners of war may also have payments made abroad. In this case payments addressed by prisoners of war to dependants shall be given priority. In any event, and subject to the consent of the Power on which they depend, prisoners may have payments made in their own country, as follows: the Detaining Power shall send to the aforesaid Power through the Protecting Power a notification giving all the necessary particulars concerning the prisoners of war, the beneficiaries of the payments, and the amount of the sums to be paid, expressed in the Detaining Power's currency. The said notification shall be signed by the prisoners and countersigned by the camp commander. The Detaining Power shall debit the prisoners' account by a corresponding amount; the sums thus debited shall be placed by it to the credit of the Power on which the prisoners depend. * * *

Article 64

The Detaining Power shall hold an account for each prisoner of war, showing at least the following:
1. The amounts due to the prisoner or received by him as advances of pay, as working pay or derived from any other source; the sums in the currency of the Detaining Power which were taken from him; the sums taken from him and converted at his request into the currency of the said Power.
2. The payments made to the prisoner in cash, or in any other similar form; the payments made on his behalf and at his request; the sums transferred under Article 63, third paragraph. * * *

Article 66

On the termination of captivity, through the release of a prisoner of war or his repatriation, the Detaining Power shall give him a statement, signed by an authorized officer of that Power, showing the credit balance then due to him. The Detaining Power shall also send through the Protecting Power to the government upon which the prisoner of war depends, lists giving all appropriate particulars of all prisoners of war whose captivity has been terminated by repatriation, release, escape, death or any other means, and showing the amount of their credit balances. Such lists shall be certified on each sheet by an authorized representative of the Detaining Power. Any of the above provisions of this Article may be varied by mutual agreement between any two Parties to the conflict. The Power on which the prisoner of war depends shall be responsible for settling with him any credit balance due to him from the Detaining Power on the termination of his captivity. * * *

Section V
Relations of prisoners of war with the exterior

Article 69

Immediately upon prisoners of war falling into its power, the Detaining Power shall inform them and the Powers on which they depend, through the Protecting Power, of the measures taken to carry out the provisions of the present Section. They shall likewise inform the parties concerned of any subsequent modifications of such measures.

Article 70

Immediately upon capture, or not more than one week after arrival at a camp, even if it is a transit camp, likewise in case of sickness or transfer to hospital or another camp, every prisoner of war shall be enabled to write direct to his family, on the one hand, and to the Central Prisoners of War Agency provided for in Article 123, on the other hand, a card similar, if possible, to the model annexed to the present Convention, informing his relatives of his capture, address and state of health. The said cards shall be forwarded as rapidly as possible and may not be delayed in any manner.

Article 71

Prisoners of war shall be allowed to send and receive letters and cards. If the Detaining Power deems it necessary to limit the number of letters and cards sent by each prisoner of war, the said number shall not be less than two letters and four cards monthly, exclusive of the capture cards provided for in Article 70, and conforming as closely as possible to the models annexed to the present Convention. Further limitations may be imposed only if the Protecting Power is satisfied that it would be in the interests of the prisoners of war concerned to do so owing to difficulties of translation caused by the Detaining Power's inability to find sufficient qualified linguists to carry out the necessary censorship. * * *

Article 72

Prisoners of war shall be allowed to receive by post or by any other means individual parcels or collective shipments containing, in particular, foodstuffs, clothing, medical supplies and articles of a religious, educational or recreational character which may meet their needs, including books, devotional articles, scientific equipment, examination papers, musical instruments, sports outfits and materials allowing prisoners of war to pursue their studies or their cultural activities. * * * The only limits which may be placed on these shipments shall be those proposed by the Protecting Power in the interest of the prisoners themselves, or by the International Committee of the Red Cross or any other organization giving assistance to the prisoners, in respect of their own shipments only, on account of exceptional strain on transport or communications. * * *

Article 76

The censoring of correspondence addressed to prisoners of war or despatched by them shall be done as quickly as possible. Mail shall be censored only by the despatching State and the receiving State, and once only by each. The examination of consignments intended for prisoners of war shall not be carried out under conditions that will expose the goods contained in them to deterioration; except in the case of written or printed matter, it shall be done in the presence of the addressee, or of a fellow-prisoner duly delegated by him. The delivery to prisoners of individual or collective consignments shall not be delayed under the pretext of difficulties of censorship. Any prohibition of correspondence ordered by Parties to the conflict, either for military or political reasons, shall be only temporary and its duration shall be as short as possible.

Section VI
Relations between Prisoners of War and the Authorities

Chapter I
Complaints of Prisoners of War respecting the conditions of Captivity

Article 78

Prisoners of war shall have the right to make known to the military authorities in whose power they are, their requests regarding the conditions of captivity to which they are subjected. They shall also have the unrestricted right to apply to the representatives of the Protecting Powers either through their prisoners' representative or, if they consider it necessary, direct, in order to draw their attention to any points on which they may have complaints to make regarding their conditions of captivity. * * *

Chapter II
Prisoner of War Representatives

Article 79

In all places where there are prisoners of war, except in those where there are officers, the prisoners shall freely elect by secret ballot, every six months, and also in case of vacancies, prisoners' representatives entrusted with representing them before the military authorities, the Protecting Powers, the International Committee of the Red Cross and any other organization which may assist them. These prisoners' representatives shall be eligible for re-election. In camps for officers and persons of equivalent status or in mixed camps, the senior officer among the prisoners of war shall be recognized as the camp prisoners' representative. In camps for officers, he shall be assisted by one or more advisers chosen by the officers; in mixed camps, his assistants shall be chosen from among the prisoners of war who are not officers and shall be elected by them. * * *

Article 80

Prisoners' representatives shall further the physical, spiritual and intellectual well-being of prisoners of war. * * * Prisoners' representatives shall not be held responsible, simply by reason of their duties, for any offences committed by prisoners of war. * * *

Chapter III
Penal and Disciplinary Sanctions

Section I
General provisions

Article 82

A prisoner of war shall be subject to the laws, regulations and orders in force in the armed forces of the Detaining Power; the Detaining Power shall be justified in taking judicial or disciplinary measures in respect of any offence committed by a prisoner of war against such laws, regulations or orders. However, no proceedings or punishments contrary to the provisions of this Chapter shall be allowed. If any law, regulation or order of the Detaining Power shall declare acts committed by a prisoner of war to be punishable, whereas the same acts would not be punishable if committed by a member of the forces of the Detaining Power, such acts shall entail disciplinary punishments only. * * *

Article 84

A prisoner of war shall be tried only by a military court, unless the existing laws of the Detaining Power expressly permit the civil courts to try a member of the armed forces of the Detaining Power in respect of the particular offence alleged to have been committed by the prisoner of war. In no circumstances whatever shall a prisoner of war be tried by a court of any kind which does not offer the essential guarantees of independence and impartiality as generally recognized, and, in particular, the procedure of which does not afford the accused the rights and means of defence provided for in Article 105.

Article 85

Prisoners of war prosecuted under the laws of the Detaining Power for acts committed prior to capture shall retain, even if convicted, the benefits of the present Convention.

Article 86

No prisoner of war may be punished more than once for the same act, or on the same charge.

Article 87

Prisoners of war may not be sentenced by the military authorities and courts of the Detaining Power to any penalties except those provided for in respect of members of the armed forces of the said Power who have committed the same acts. When fixing the penalty, the courts or authorities of the Detaining Power shall take into consideration, to the widest extent possible, the fact that the accused, not being a national of the Detaining Power, is not bound to it by any duty of allegiance, and that he is in its power as the result of circumstances independent of his own will. The said courts or authorities shall be at liberty to reduce the penalty provided for the violation of which the prisoner of war is accused, and shall therefore not be bound to apply the minimum penalty prescribed. Collective punishment for individual acts, corporal punishments, imprisonment in premises without daylight and, in general, any form of torture or cruelty, are forbidden. * * *

Article 88

Officers, non-commissioned officers and men who are prisoners of war undergoing a disciplinary or judicial punishment, shall not be subjected to more severe treatment than that applied in respect of the same punishment to members of the armed forces of the Detaining Power of equivalent rank. A woman prisoner of war shall not be awarded or sentenced to a punishment more severe, or treated whilst undergoing punishment more severely, than a woman member of the armed forces of the Detaining Power dealt with for a similar offence. In no case may a woman prisoner of war be awarded or sentenced to a punishment more severe, or treated whilst undergoing punishment more severely, than a male member of the armed forces of the Detaining Power dealt with for a similar offence. Prisoners of war who have served disciplinary or judicial sentences may not be treated differently from other prisoners of war.

Section II
Disciplinary sanctions

Article 89

The disciplinary punishments applicable to prisoners of war are the following:
1. A fine which shall not exceed 50 per cent of the advances of pay and working pay which the prisoner of war would otherwise receive under the provisions of Articles 60 and 62 during a period of not more than thirty days.
2. Discontinuance of privileges granted over and above the treatment provided for by the present Convention.
3. Fatigue duties not exceeding two hours daily.
4. Confinement.

The punishment referred to under (3) shall not be applied to officers. In no case shall disciplinary punishments be inhuman, brutal or dangerous to the health of prisoners of war.

Article 90

The duration of any single punishment shall in no case exceed thirty days. Any period of confinement awaiting the hearing of a disciplinary offence or the award of disciplinary punishment shall be deducted from an award pronounced against a prisoner of war. The maximum of thirty days provided above may not be exceeded, even if the prisoner of war is answerable for several acts at the same time when he is awarded punishment, whether such acts are related or not. The period between the pronouncing of an award of disciplinary punishment and its execution shall not exceed one month. When a prisoner of war is awarded a further disciplinary punishment, a period of at least three days shall elapse between the execution of any two of the punishments, if the duration of one of these is ten days or more.

Article 91

The escape of a prisoner of war shall be deemed to have succeeded when:
1. He has joined the armed forces of the Power on which he depends, or those of an allied Power;
2. He has left the territory under the control of the Detaining Power, or of an ally of the said Power;
3. He has joined a ship flying the flag of the Power on which he depends, or of an allied Power, in the territorial waters of the Detaining Power, the said ship not being under the control of the last-named Power.

Prisoners of war who have made good their escape in the sense of this Article and who are recaptured, shall not be liable to any punishment in respect of their previous escape.

Article 92

A prisoner of war who attempts to escape and is recaptured before having made good his escape in the sense of Article 91 shall be liable only to a disciplinary punishment in respect of this act, even if it is a repeated offence. * * *

Article 95

A prisoner of war accused of an offence against discipline shall not be kept in confinement pending the hearing unless a member of the armed forces of the Detaining Power would be so kept if he were accused of a similar offence, or if it is essential in the interests of camp order and discipline. Any period spent by a prisoner of war in confinement awaiting the disposal of an offence against discipline shall be reduced to an absolute minimum and shall not exceed fourteen days. * * *

Article 97

Prisoners of war shall not in any case be transferred to penitentiary establishments (prisons, penitentiaries, convict prisons, etc.) to undergo disciplinary punishment therein. All premises in which disciplinary punishments are undergone shall conform to the sanitary requirements set forth in Article 25. A prisoner of war undergoing punishment shall be enabled to keep himself in a state of cleanliness, in conformity with Article 29. Officers and persons of equivalent status shall not be lodged in the same quarters as non-commissioned officers or men. Women prisoners of war undergoing disciplinary punishment shall be confined in separate quarters from male prisoners of war and shall be under the immediate supervision of women.

Article 98

A prisoner of war undergoing confinement as a disciplinary punishment, shall continue to enjoy the benefits of the provisions of this Convention except in so far as these are necessarily rendered inapplicable by the mere fact that he is confined. In no case may he be deprived of the benefits of the provisions of Articles 78 and 126. A prisoner of war awarded disciplinary punishment may not be deprived of the prerogatives attached to his rank. Prisoners of war awarded disciplinary punishment shall be allowed to exercise and to stay in the open air at least two hours daily. They shall be allowed, on their request, to be present at the daily medical inspections. They shall receive the attention which their state of health requires and, if necessary, shall be removed to the camp infirmary or to a hospital. They shall have permission to read and write, likewise to send and receive letters. Parcels and remittances of money, however, may be withheld from them until the completion of the punishment; they shall meanwhile be entrusted to the prisoners' representative, who will hand over to the infirmary the perishable goods contained in such parcels.

Section III
Judicial proceedings

Article 99

No prisoner of war may be tried or sentenced for an act which is not forbidden by the law of the Detaining Power or by international law, in force at the time the said act was committed. No moral or physical coercion may be exerted on a prisoner of war in order to induce him to admit himself guilty of the act of which he is accused. No prisoner of war may be convicted without having had an opportunity to present his defence and the assistance of a qualified advocate or counsel.

Article 100

Prisoners of war and the Protecting Powers shall be informed as soon as possible of the offences which are punishable by the death sentence under the laws of the Detaining Power. Other offences shall not thereafter be made punishable by the death penalty without the concurrence of the Power upon which the prisoners of war depend. The death sentence cannot be pronounced on a prisoner of war unless the attention of the court has, in accordance with Article 87, second paragraph, been particularly called to the fact that since the accused is not a national of the Detaining Power, he is not bound to it by any duty of allegiance, and that he is in its power as the result of circumstances independent of his own will. * * *

Article 102

A prisoner of war can be validly sentenced only if the sentence has been pronounced by the same courts according to the same procedure as in the case of members of the armed forces of the Detaining Power, and if, furthermore, the provisions of the present Chapter have been observed.

Article 103

Judicial investigations relating to a prisoner of war shall be conducted as rapidly as circumstances permit and so that his trial shall take place as soon as possible. A prisoner of war shall not be confined while awaiting trial unless a member of the armed forces of the Detaining Power would be so confined if he were accused of a similar offence, or if it is essential to do so in the interests of national security. In no circumstances shall this confinement exceed three months. Any period spent by a prisoner of war in confinement awaiting trial shall be deducted from any sentence of imprisonment passed upon him and taken into account in fixing any penalty. * * *

Article 104

In any case in which the Detaining Power has decided to institute judicial proceedings against a prisoner of war, it shall notify the Protecting Power as soon as possible and at least three weeks before the opening of the trial. This period of three weeks shall run as from the day on which such notification reaches the Protecting Power at the address previously indicated by the latter to the Detaining Power. The said notification shall contain the following information:

1. Surname and first names of the prisoner of war, his rank, his army, regimental, personal or serial number, his date of birth, and his profession or trade, if any;
2. Place of internment or confinement;
3. Specification of the charge or charges on which the prisoner of war is to be arraigned, giving the legal provisions applicable;
4. Designation of the court which will try the case, likewise the date and place fixed for the opening of the trial.

The same communication shall be made by the Detaining Power to the prisoners' representative. If no evidence is submitted, at the opening of a trial, that the notification referred to above was received by the Protecting Power, by the prisoner of war and by the prisoners' representative concerned, at least three weeks before the opening of the trial, then the latter cannot take place and must be adjourned.

Article 105

The prisoner of war shall be entitled to assistance by one of his prisoner comrades, to defence by a qualified advocate or counsel of his own choice, to the calling of witnesses and, if he deems necessary, to the services of a competent interpreter. He shall be advised of these rights by the Detaining Power in due time before the trial. Failing a choice by the prisoner of war, the Protecting Power shall find him an advocate or counsel, and shall have at least one week at its disposal for the purpose. The Detaining Power shall deliver to the said Power, on request, a list of persons qualified to present the defence. Failing a choice of an advocate or counsel by the prisoner of war or the Protecting Power, the Detaining Power shall appoint a competent advocate or counsel to conduct the defence. The advocate or counsel conducting the defence on behalf of the prisoner of war shall have at his disposal a period of two weeks at least before the opening of the trial, as well as the necessary facilities to prepare the defence of the accused. He may, in particular, freely visit the accused and interview him in private. He may also confer with any witnesses for the defence, including prisoners of war. He shall have the benefit of these facilities until the term of appeal or petition has expired. Particulars of the charge or charges on which the prisoner of war is to be arraigned, as well as the documents which are generally communicated to the accused by virtue of the laws in force in the armed forces of the Detaining Power, shall be communicated to the accused prisoner of war in a language which he understands, and in good time before the opening of the trial. The same communication in the same circumstances shall be made to the advocate or counsel conducting the defence on behalf of the prisoner of war. The representatives of the Protecting Power shall be entitled to attend the trial of the case, unless, exceptionally, this is held in camera in the interest of State security. In such a case the Detaining Power shall advise the Protecting Power accordingly.

Article 106

Every prisoner of war shall have, in the same manner as the members of the armed forces of the Detaining Power, the right of appeal or petition from any sentence pronounced upon him, with a view to the quashing or revising of the sentence or the reopening of the trial. He shall be fully informed of his right to appeal or petition and of the time limit within which he may do so.

Article 107

Any judgment and sentence pronounced upon a prisoner of war shall be immediately reported to the Protecting Power in the form of a summary communication, which shall also indicate whether he has the right of appeal with a view to the quashing of the sentence or the reopening of the trial. This communication shall likewise be sent to the prisoners' representative concerned. It shall also be sent to the accused prisoner of war in a language he understands, if the sentence was not pronounced in his presence. The Detaining Power shall also immediately communicate to the Protecting Power the decision of the prisoner of war to use or to waive his right of appeal. Furthermore, if a prisoner of war is finally convicted or if a sentence pronounced on a prisoner of war in the first instance is a death sentence, the Detaining Power shall as soon as possible address to the Protecting Power a detailed communication containing:

    1. The precise wording of the finding and sentence;

    2. A summarized report of any preliminary investigation and of the trial, emphasizing in particular the elements of the prosecution and the defence;

    3. Notification, where applicable, of the establishment where the sentence will be served.

The communications provided for in the foregoing subparagraphs shall be sent to the Protecting Power at the address previously made known to the Detaining Power.

Article 108

Sentences pronounced on prisoners of war after a conviction has become duly enforceable, shall be served in the same establishments and under the same conditions as in the case of members of the armed forces of the Detaining Power. These conditions shall in all cases conform to the requirements of health and humanity. A woman prisoner of war on whom such a sentence has been pronounced shall be confined in separate quarters and shall be under the supervision of women. In any case, prisoners of war sentenced to a penalty depriving them of their liberty shall retain the benefit of the provisions of Articles 78 and 126 of the present Convention. Furthermore, they shall be entitled to receive and despatch correspondence, to receive at least one relief parcel monthly, to take regular exercise in the open air, to have the medical care required by their state of health, and the spiritual assistance they may desire. Penalties to which they may be subjected shall be in accordance with the provisions of Article 87, third paragraph.

PART IV
TERMINATION OF CAPTIVITY

Section I
Direct Repatriation and Accommodation in Neutral Countries

Article 109

Subject to the provisions of the third paragraph of this Article, Parties to the conflict are bound to send back to their own country, regardless of number or rank, seriously wounded and seriously sick prisoners of war, after having cared for them until they are fit to travel, in accordance with the first paragraph of the following Article. Throughout the duration of hostilities, Parties to the conflict shall endeavour, with the cooperation of the neutral Powers concerned, to make arrangements for the accommodation in neutral countries of the sick and wounded prisoners of war referred to in the second paragraph of the following Article. * * * No sick or injured prisoner of war who is eligible for repatriation under the first paragraph of this Article, may be repatriated against his will during hostilities.

Article 110

The following shall be repatriated direct:

    1. Incurably wounded and sick whose mental or physical fitness seems to have been gravely diminished.

    2. Wounded and sick who, according to medical opinion, are not likely to recover within one year, whose condition requires treatment and whose mental or physical fitness seems to have been gravely diminished.

    3. Wounded and sick who have recovered, but whose mental or physical fitness seems to have been gravely and permanently diminished.

The following may be accommodated in a neutral country:

1. Wounded and sick whose recovery may be expected within one year of the date of the wound or the beginning of the illness, if treatment in a neutral country might increase the prospects of a more certain and speedy recovery.

2. Prisoners of war whose mental or physical health, according to medical opinion, is seriously threatened by continued captivity, but whose accommodation in a neutral country might remove such a threat.

The conditions which prisoners of war accommodated in a neutral country must fulfil in order to permit their repatriation shall be fixed, as shall likewise their status, by agreement between the Powers concerned. In general, prisoners of war who have been accommodated in a neutral country, and who belong to the following categories, should be repatriated:

1. Those whose state of health has deteriorated so as to fulfil the conditions laid down for direct repatriation;

2. Those whose mental or physical powers remain, even after treatment, considerably impaired. * * *

Article 117

No repatriated person may be employed on active military service.

Section II
Release and Repatriation of Prisoners of War at the Close of Hostilities

Article 118

Prisoners of war shall be released and repatriated without delay after the cessation of active hostilities. * * * The costs of repatriation of prisoners of war shall in all cases be equitably apportioned between the Detaining Power and the Power on which the prisoners depend. This apportionment shall be carried out on the following basis:

(a) If the two Powers are contiguous, the Power on which the prisoners of war depend shall bear the costs of repatriation from the frontiers of the Detaining Power.

(b) If the two Powers are not contiguous, the Detaining Power shall bear the costs of transport of prisoners of war over its own territory as far as its frontier or its port of embarkation nearest to the territory of the Power on which the prisoners of war depend. The Parties concerned shall agree between themselves as to the equitable apportionment of the remaining costs of the repatriation. The conclusion of this agreement shall in no circumstances justify any delay in the repatriation of the prisoners of war. * * *

Section III
Death of Prisoners of War

Article 120

Wills of prisoners of war shall be drawn up so as to satisfy the conditions of validity required by the legislation of their country of origin, which will take steps to inform the Detaining Power of its requirements in this respect. At the request of the prisoner of war and, in all cases, after death, the will shall be transmitted without delay to the Protecting Power; a certified copy shall be sent to the Central Agency.

Death certificates in the form annexed to the present Convention, or lists certified by a responsible officer, of all persons who die as prisoners of war shall be forwarded as rapidly as possible to the Prisoner of War Information Bureau established in accordance with Article 122. The death certificates or certified lists shall show particulars of identity as set out in the third paragraph of Article 17, and also the date and place of death, the cause of death, the date and place of burial and all particulars necessary to identify the graves.

The burial or cremation of a prisoner of war shall be preceded by a medical examination of the body with a view to confirming death and enabling a report to be made and, where necessary, establishing identity.

The detaining authorities shall ensure that prisoners of war who have died in captivity are honourably buried, if possible according to the rites of the religion to which they belonged, and that their graves are respected, suitably maintained and marked so as to be found at any time. Wherever possible, deceased prisoners of war who depended on the same Power shall be interred in the same place.

Deceased prisoners of war shall be buried in individual graves unless unavoidable circumstances require the use of collective graves. Bodies may be cremated only for imperative reasons of hygiene, on account of the religion of the deceased or in accordance with his express wish to this effect. In case of cremation, the fact shall be stated and the reasons given in the death certificate of the deceased.

In order that graves may always be found, all particulars of burials and graves shall be recorded with a Graves Registration Service established by the Detaining Power. Lists of graves and particulars of the prisoners of war interred in cemeteries and elsewhere shall be transmitted to the Power on which such prisoners of war depended. Responsibility for the care of these graves and for records of any subsequent moves of the bodies shall rest on the Power controlling the territory, if a Party to the present Convention. These provisions shall also apply to the ashes, which shall be kept by the Graves Registration Service until proper disposal thereof in accordance with the wishes of the home country.

Article 121

Every death or serious injury of a prisoner of war caused or suspected to have been caused by a sentry, another prisoner of war, or any other person, as well as any death the cause of which is unknown, shall be immediately followed by an official enquiry by the Detaining Power. A communication on this subject shall be sent immediately to the Protecting Power. Statements shall be taken from witnesses, especially from those who are prisoners of war, and a report including such statements shall be forwarded to the Protecting Power. If the enquiry indicates the guilt of one or more persons, the Detaining Power shall take all measures for the prosecution of the person or persons responsible.

PART V
INFORMATION BUREAUX AND RELIEF SOCIEITIES
FOR PRISONERS OF WAR

Article 122

Upon the outbreak of a conflict and in all cases of occupation, each of the Parties to the conflict shall institute an official Information Bureau for prisoners of war who are in its power. Neutral or non-belligerent Powers who may have received within their territory persons belonging to one of the categories referred to in Article 4, shall take the same action with respect to such persons. The Power concerned shall ensure that the Prisoners of War Information Bureau is provided with the necessary accommodation, equipment and staff to ensure its efficient working. It shall be at liberty to employ prisoners of war in such a Bureau under the conditions laid down in the Section of the present Convention dealing with work by prisoners of war.

Within the shortest possible period, each of the Parties to the conflict shall give its Bureau the information referred to in the fourth, fifth and sixth paragraphs of this Article regarding any enemy person belonging to one of the categories referred to in Article 4, who has fallen into its power. Neutral or non-belligerent Powers shall take the same action with regard to persons belonging to such categories whom they have received within their territory.

The Bureau shall immediately forward such information by the most rapid means to the Powers concerned, through the intermediary of the Protecting Powers and likewise of the Central Agency provided for in Article 123.

This information shall make it possible quickly to advise the next of kin concerned. Subject to the provisions of Article 17, the information shall include, in so far as available to the Information Bureau, in respect of each prisoner of war, his surname, first names, rank, army, regimental, personal or serial number, place and full date of birth, indication of the Power on which he depends, first name of the father and maiden name of the mother, name and address of the person to be informed and the address to which correspondence for the prisoner may be sent.

The Information Bureau shall receive from the various departments concerned information regarding transfers, releases, repatriations, escapes, admissions to hospital, and deaths, and shall transmit such information in the manner described in the third paragraph above.

Likewise, information regarding the state of health of prisoners of war who are seriously ill or seriously wounded shall be supplied regularly, every week if possible. The Information Bureau shall also be responsible for replying to all enquiries sent to it concerning prisoners of war, including those who have died in captivity; it will make any enquiries necessary to obtain the information which is asked for if this is not in its possession. All written communications made by the Bureau shall be authenticated by a signature or a seal. The Information Bureau shall furthermore be charged with collecting all personal valuables, including sums in currencies other than that of the Detaining Power and documents of importance to the next of kin, left by prisoners of war who have been repatriated or released, or who have escaped or died, and shall forward the said valuables to the Powers concerned. Such articles shall be sent by the Bureau in sealed packets which shall be accompanied by statements giving clear and full particulars of the identity of the person to whom the articles belonged, and by a complete list of the contents of the parcel. Other personal effects of such prisoners of war shall be transmitted under arrangements agreed upon between the Parties to the conflict concerned.

Article 123

A Central Prisoners of War Information Agency shall be created in a neutral country. The International Committee of the Red Cross shall, if it deems necessary, propose to the Powers concerned the organization of such an Agency. The function of the Agency shall be to collect all the information it may obtain through official or private channels respecting prisoners of war, and to transmit it as rapidly as possible to the country of origin of the prisoners of war or to the Power on which they depend. It shall receive from the Parties to the conflict all facilities for effecting such transmissions. The High Contracting Parties, and in particular those whose nationals benefit by the services of the Central Agency, are requested to give the said Agency the financial aid it may require. The foregoing provisions shall in no way be interpreted as restricting the humanitarian activities of the International Committee of the Red Cross, or of the relief Societies provided for in Article 125.

Article 124

The national Information Bureaux and the Central Information Agency shall enjoy free postage for mail, likewise all the exemptions provided for in Article 74, and further, so far as possible, exemption from telegraphic charges or, at least, greatly reduced rates.

Article 125

Subject to the measures which the Detaining Powers may consider essential to ensure their security or to meet any other reasonable need, the representatives of religious organizations, relief societies, or any other organization assisting prisoners of war, shall receive from the said Powers, for themselves and their duly accredited agents, all necessary facilities for visiting the prisoners, distributing relief supplies and material, from any source, intended for religious, educational or recreative purposes, and for assisting them in organizing their leisure time within the camps. Such societies or organizations may be constituted in the territory of the Detaining Power or in any other country, or they may have an international character. The Detaining Power may limit the number of societies and organizations whose delegates are allowed to carry out their activities in its territory and under its supervision, on condition, however, that such limitation shall not hinder the effective operation of adequate relief to all prisoners of war. The special position of the International Committee of the Red Cross in this field shall be recognized and respected at all times. * * *

PART VI
EXECUTION OF THE CONVENTION

Section I
General Provisions

Article 126

Representatives or delegates of the Protecting Powers shall have permission to go to all places where prisoners of war may be, particularly to places of internment, imprisonment and labour, and shall have access to all premises occupied by prisoners of war; they shall also be allowed to go to the places of departure, passage and arrival of prisoners who are being transferred. They shall be able to interview the prisoners, and in particular the prisoners' representatives, without witnesses, either personally or through an interpreter. Representatives and delegates of the Protecting Powers shall have full liberty to select the places they wish to visit. The duration and frequency of these visits shall not be restricted. Visits may not be prohibited except for reasons of imperative military necessity, and then only as an exceptional and temporary measure. The Detaining Power and the Power on which the said prisoners of war depend may agree, if necessary, that compatriots of these prisoners of war be permitted to participate in the visits. The delegates of the International Committee of the Red Cross shall enjoy the same prerogatives. The appointment of such delegates shall be submitted to the approval of the Power detaining the prisoners of war to be visited.

Article 127

The High Contracting Parties undertake, in time of peace as in time of war, to disseminate the text of the present Convention as widely as possible in their respective countries, and, in particular, to include the study thereof in their programmes of military and, if possible, civil instruction, so that the principles thereof may become known to all their armed forces and to the entire population. Any military or other authorities, who in time of war assume responsibilities in respect of prisoners of war, must possess the text of the Convention and be specially instructed as to its provisions. * * *

Article 129

The High Contracting Parties undertake to enact any legislation necessary to provide effective penal sanctions for persons committing, or ordering to be committed, any of the grave breaches of the present Convention defined in the following Article. Each High Contracting Party shall be under the obligation to search for persons alleged to have committed, or to have ordered to be committed, such grave breaches, and shall bring such persons, regardless of their nationality, before its own courts. It may also, if it prefers, and in accordance with the provisions of its own legislation, hand such persons over for trial to another High Contracting Party concerned, provided such High Contracting Party has made out a prima facie case. Each High Contracting Party shall take measures necessary for the suppression of all acts contrary to the provisions of the present Convention other than the grave breaches defined in the following Article. In all circumstances, the accused persons shall benefit by safeguards of proper trial and defence, which shall not be less favourable than those provided by Article 105 and those following of the present Convention.

Article 130

Grave breaches to which the preceding Article relates shall be those involving any of the following acts, if committed against persons or property protected by the Convention: wilful killing, torture or inhuman treatment, including biological experiments, wilfully causing great suffering or serious injury to body or health, compelling a prisoner of war to serve in the forces of the hostile Power, or wilfully depriving a prisoner of war of the rights of fair and regular trial prescribed in this Convention.

Article 131

No High Contracting Party shall be allowed to absolve itself or any other High Contracting Party of any liability incurred by itself or by another High Contracting Party in respect of breaches referred to in the preceding Article.

Article 132

At the request of a Party to the conflict, an enquiry shall be instituted, in a manner to be decided between the interested Parties, concerning any alleged violation of the Convention. If agreement has not been reached concerning the procedure for the enquiry, the Parties should agree on the choice of an umpire who will decide upon the procedure to be followed. Once the violation has been established, the Parties to the conflict shall put an end to it and shall repress it with the least possible delay.

Section 11
Final Provisions

Article 133

The present Convention is established in English and in French. Both texts are equally authentic. The Swiss Federal Council shall arrange for official translations of the Convention to be made in the Russian and Spanish languages.

Article 134

The present Convention replaces the Convention of 27 July 1929, in relations between the High Contracting Parties. * * *

Article 137

The present Convention shall be ratified as soon as possible and the ratifications shall be deposited at Berne. A record shall be drawn up of the deposit of each instrument of ratification and certified copies of this record shall be transmitted by the Swiss Federal Council to all the Powers in whose name the Convention has been signed, or whose accession has been notified.

Article 138

The present Convention shall come into force six months after not less than two instruments of ratification have been deposited. Thereafter, it shall come into force for each High Contracting Party six months after the deposit of the instrument of ratification. * * *

Article 140

Accessions shall be notified in writing to the Swiss Federal Council, and shall take effect six months after the date on which they are received. The Swiss Federal Council shall communicate the accessions to all the Powers in whose name the Convention has been signed, or whose accession has been notified. * * *

Article 142

Each of the High Contracting Parties shall be at liberty to denounce the present Convention. The denunciation shall be notified in writing to the Swiss Federal Council, which shall transmit it to the Governments of all the High Contracting Parties. The denunciation shall take effect one year after the notification thereof has been made to the Swiss Federal Council. However, a denunciation of which notification has been made at a time when the denouncing Power is involved in a conflict shall not take effect until peace has been concluded, and until after operations connected with the release and repatriation of the persons protected by the present Convention have been terminated. The denunciation shall have effect only in respect of the denouncing Power. It shall in no way impair the obligations which the Parties to the conflict shall remain bound to fulfil by virtue of the principles of the law of nations, as they result from the usages established among civilized peoples, from the laws of humanity and the dictates of the public conscience.

Article 143

The Swiss Federal Council shall register the present Convention with the Secretariat of the United Nations. The Swiss Federal Council shall also inform the Secretariat of the United Nations of all ratifications, accessions and denunciations received by it with respect to the present Convention. * * *

GENEVA CONVENTION RELATIVE TO THE PROTECTION OF CIVILIAN PERSONS IN TIME OF WAR (1949)

Geneva Convention relative to the Protection of Civilian Persons in Time of War, *adopted* Aug. 12, 1949, 6 U.S.T. 3516; 75 U.N.T.S. 287

PART I
GENERAL PROVISIONS

Article 1

The High Contracting Parties undertake to respect and to ensure respect for the present Convention in all circumstances.

Article 2

In addition to the provisions which shall be implemented in peacetime, the present Convention shall apply to all cases of declared war or of any other armed conflict which may arise between two or more of the High Contracting Parties, even if the state of war is not recognized by one of them. The Convention shall also apply to all cases of partial or total occupation of the territory of a High Contracting Party, even if the said occupation meets with no armed resistance. Although one of the Powers in conflict may not be a party to the present Convention, the Powers who are parties thereto shall remain bound by it in their mutual relations. They shall furthermore be bound by the Convention in relation to the said Power, if the latter accepts and applies the provisions thereof.

Article 3

In the case of armed conflict not of an international character occurring in the territory of one of the High Contracting Parties, each Party to the conflict shall be bound to apply, as a minimum, the following provisions:

1. Persons taking no active part in the hostilities, including members of armed forces who have laid down their arms and those placed hors de combat by sickness, wounds, detention, or any other cause, shall in all circumstances be treated humanely, without any adverse distinction founded on race, colour, religion or faith, sex, birth or wealth, or any other similar criteria. To this end, the following acts are and shall remain prohibited at any time and in any place whatsoever with respect to the above-mentioned persons:

(a) Violence to life and person, in particular murder of all kinds, mutilation, cruel treatment and torture;
(b) Taking of hostages;
(c) Outrages upon personal dignity, in particular humiliating and degrading treatment;
(d) The passing of sentences and the carrying out of executions without previous judgment pronounced by a regularly constituted court, affording all the judicial guarantees which are recognized as indispensable by civilized peoples.

2. The wounded and sick shall be collected and cared for.

An impartial humanitarian body, such as the International Committee of the Red Cross, may offer its services to the Parties to the conflict. The Parties to the conflict should further endeavour to bring into force, by means of special agreements, all or part of the other provisions of the present Convention.

The application of the preceding provisions shall not affect the legal status of the Parties to the conflict.

Article 4

Persons protected by the Convention are those who, at a given moment and in any manner whatsoever, find themselves, in case of a conflict or occupation, in the hands of a Party to the conflict or Occupying Power of which they are not nationals. Nationals of a State which is not bound by the Convention are not protected by it. Nationals of a neutral State who find themselves in the territory of a belligerent State, and nationals of a co-belligerent State, shall not be regarded as protected persons while the State of which they are nationals has normal diplomatic representation in the State in whose hands they are. The provisions of Part II are, however, wider in application, as defined in Article 13. Persons protected by the Geneva Convention for the Amelioration of the Condition of the Wounded and Sick in Armed Forces in the Field of August 12, 1949, or by the Geneva Convention for the Amelioration of the Condition of Wounded, Sick and Shipwrecked Members of Armed Forces at Sea of August 12, 1949, or by the Geneva Convention relative to the Treatment of Prisoners of War of August 12, 1949, shall not be considered as protected persons within the meaning of the present Convention.

Article 5

Where, in the territory of a Party to the conflict, the latter is satisfied that an individual protected person is definitely suspected of or engaged in activities hostile to the security of the State, such individual person shall not be entitled to claim such rights and privileges under the present Convention as would, if exercised in the favour of such individual person, be prejudicial to the security of such State. Where in occupied territory an individual protected person is detained as a spy or saboteur, or as a person under definite suspicion of activity hostile to the security of the Occupying Power, such person shall, in those cases where absolute military security so requires, be regarded as having forfeited rights of communication under the present Convention. In each case, such persons shall nevertheless be treated with humanity, and in case of trial, shall not be deprived of the rights of fair and regular trial prescribed by the present Convention. They shall also be granted the full rights and privileges of a protected person under the present Convention at the earliest date consistent with the security of the State or Occupying Power, as the case may be.

Article 6

The present Convention shall apply from the outset of any conflict or occupation mentioned in Article 2.

In the territory of Parties to the conflict, the application of the present Convention shall cease on the general close of military operations. In the case of occupied territory, the application of the present Convention shall cease one year after the general close of military operations; however, the Occupying Power shall be bound, for the duration of the occupation, to the extent that such Power exercises the functions of government in such territory, by the provisions of the following Articles of the present Convention: 1 to 12, 27, 29 to 34, 47, 49, 51, 52, 53, 59, 61 to 77, and 143. Protected persons whose release, repatriation or re-establishment may take place after such dates shall meanwhile continue to benefit by the present Convention.

Article 7

In addition to the agreements expressly provided for in Articles 11, 14, 15, 17, 36, 108, 109, 132, 133 and 149, the High Contracting Parties may conclude other special agreements for all matters concerning which they may deem it suitable to make separate provision. No special agreement shall adversely affect the situation of protected persons, as defined by the present Convention, nor restrict the rights which it confers upon them. Protected persons shall continue to have the benefit of such agreements as long as the Convention is applicable to them, except where express provisions to the contrary are contained in the aforesaid or in subsequent agreements, or where more favourable measures have been taken with regard to them by one or other of the Parties to the conflict.

Article 8

Protected persons may in no circumstances renounce in part or in entirety the rights secured to them by the present Convention, and by the special agreements referred to in the foregoing Article, if such there be.

Article 9

The present Convention shall be applied with the cooperation and under the scrutiny of the Protecting Powers whose duty it is to safeguard the interests of the Parties to the conflict. For this purpose, the Protecting Powers may appoint, apart from their diplomatic or consular staff, delegates from amongst their own nationals or the nationals of other neutral Powers. The said delegates shall be subject to the approval of the Power with which they are to carry out their duties. The Parties to the conflict shall facilitate to the greatest extent possible the task of the representatives or delegates of the Protecting Powers. The representatives or delegates of the Protecting Powers shall not in any case exceed their mission under the present Convention. They shall, in particular, take account of the imperative necessities of security of the State wherein they carry out their duties.

Article 10

The provisions of the present Convention constitute no obstacle to the humanitarian activities which the International Committee of the Red Cross or any other impartial humanitarian organization may, subject to the consent of the Parties to the conflict concerned, undertake for the protection of civilian persons and for their relief. * * *

Article 12

In cases where they deem it advisable in the interest of protected persons, particularly in cases of disagreement between the Parties to the conflict as to the application or interpretation of the provisions of the present Convention, the Protecting Powers shall lend their good offices with a view to settling the disagreement. For this purpose, each of the Protecting Powers may, either at the invitation of one Party or on its own initiative, propose to the Parties to the conflict a meeting of their representatives, and in particular of the authorities responsible for protected persons, possibly on neutral territory suitably chosen. The Parties to the conflict shall be bound to give effect to the proposals made to them for this purpose. The Protecting Powers may, if necessary, propose for approval by the Parties to the conflict, a person belonging to a neutral Power or delegated by the International Committee of the Red Cross who shall be invited to take part in such a meeting.

PART II
GENERAL PROTECTION OF POPULATIONS AGAINST CERTAIN CONSEQUENCES OF WAR

Article 13
The provisions of Part II cover the whole of the populations of the countries in conflict, without any adverse distinction based, in particular, on race, nationality, religion or political opinion, and are intended to alleviate the sufferings caused by war.

Article 14
In time of peace, the High Contracting Parties and, after the outbreak of hostilities, the Parties thereto, may establish in their own territory and, if the need arises, in occupied areas, hospital and safety zones and localities so organized as to protect from the effects of war, wounded, sick and aged persons, children under fifteen, expectant mothers and mothers of children under seven. Upon the outbreak and during the course of hostilities, the Parties concerned may conclude agreements on mutual recognition of the zones and localities they have created. They may for this purpose implement the provisions of the Draft Agreement annexed to the present Convention, with such amendments as they may consider necessary. The Protecting Powers and the International Committee of the Red Cross are invited to lend their good offices in order to facilitate the institution and recognition of these hospital and safety zones and localities.

Article 15
Any Party to the conflict may, either directly or through a neutral State or some humanitarian organization, propose to the adverse Party to establish, in the regions where fighting is taking place, neutralized zones intended to shelter from the effects of war the following persons, without distinction:
> (a) Wounded and sick combatants or non-combatants;
> (b) Civilian persons who take no part in hostilities, and who, while they reside in the zones, perform no work of a military character.

When the Parties concerned have agreed upon the geographical position, administration, food supply and supervision of the proposed neutralized zone, a written agreement shall be concluded and signed by the representatives of the Parties to the conflict. The agreement shall fix the beginning and the duration of the neutralization of the zone.

Article 16
The wounded and sick, as well as the infirm, and expectant mothers, shall be the object of particular protection and respect. As far as military considerations allow, each Party to the conflict shall facilitate the steps taken to search for the killed and wounded, to assist the shipwrecked and other persons exposed to grave danger, and to protect them against pillage and ill-treatment.

Article 17
The Parties to the conflict shall endeavour to conclude local agreements for the removal from besieged or encircled areas, of wounded, sick, infirm, and aged persons, children and maternity cases, and for the passage of ministers of all religions, medical personnel and medical equipment on their way to such areas.

Article 18
Civilian hospitals organized to give care to the wounded and sick, the infirm and maternity cases, may in no circumstances be the object of attack, but shall at all times be respected and protected by the Parties to the conflict. States which are Parties to a conflict shall provide all civilian hospitals with certificates showing that they are civilian hospitals and that the buildings which they occupy are not used for any purpose which would deprive these hospitals of protection in accordance with Article 19. Civilian hospitals shall be marked by means of the emblem provided for in Article 38 of the Geneva Convention for the Amelioration of the Condition of the Wounded and Sick in Armed Forces in the Field of August 12, 1949, but only if so authorized by the State. The Parties to the conflict shall, in so far as military considerations permit, take the necessary steps to make the distinctive emblems indicating civilian hospitals clearly visible to the enemy land, air and naval forces in order to obviate the possibility of any hostile action. In view of the dangers to which hospitals may be exposed by being close to military objectives, it is recommended that such hospitals be situated as far as possible from such objectives.

Article 19

The protection to which civilian hospitals are entitled shall not cease unless they are used to commit, outside their humanitarian duties, acts harmful to the enemy. Protection may, however, cease only after due warning has been given, naming, in all appropriate cases, a reasonable time limit, and after such warning has remained unheeded. The fact that sick or wounded members of the armed forces are nursed in these hospitals, or the presence of small arms and ammunition taken from such combatants which have not yet been handed to the proper service, shall not be considered to be acts harmful to the enemy.

Article 20

Persons regularly and solely engaged in the operation and administration of civilian hospitals, including the personnel engaged in the search for, removal and transporting of and caring for wounded and sick civilians, the infirm and maternity cases, shall be respected and protected. In occupied territory and in zones of military operations, the above personnel shall be recognizable by means of an identity card certifying their status, bearing the photograph of the holder and embossed with the stamp of the responsible authority, and also by means of a stamped, water-resistant armlet which they shall wear on the left arm while carrying out their duties. This armlet shall be issued by the State and shall bear the emblem provided for in Article 38 of the Geneva Convention for the Amelioration of the Condition of the Wounded and Sick in Armed Forces in the Field of August 12, 1949. Other personnel who are engaged in the operation and administration of civilian hospitals shall be entitled to respect and protection and to wear the armlet, as provided in and under the conditions prescribed in this Article, while they are employed on such duties. The identity card shall state the duties on which they are employed. The management of each hospital shall at all times hold at the disposal of the competent national or occupying authorities an up-to-date list of such personnel.

Article 21

Convoys of vehicles or hospital trains on land or specially provided vessels on sea, conveying wounded and sick civilians, the infirm and maternity cases, shall be respected and protected in the same manner as the hospitals provided for in Article 18, and shall be marked, with the consent of the State, by the display of the distinctive emblem provided for in Article 38 of the Geneva Convention for the Amelioration of the Condition of the Wounded and Sick in Armed Forces in the Field of August 12, 1949.

Article 22

Aircraft exclusively employed for the removal of wounded and sick civilians, the infirm and maternity cases, or for the transport of medical personnel and equipment, shall not be attacked, but shall be respected while flying at heights, times and on routes specifically agreed upon between all the Parties to the conflict concerned. They may be marked with the distinctive emblem provided for in Article 38 of the Geneva Convention for the Amelioration of the Condition of the Wounded and Sick in Armed Forces in the Field of August 12, 1949. Unless agreed otherwise, flights over enemy or enemy-occupied territory are prohibited. Such aircraft shall obey every summons to land. In the event of a landing thus imposed, the aircraft with its occupants may continue its flight after examination, if any.

Article 23

Each High Contracting Party shall allow the free passage of all consignments of medical and hospital stores and objects necessary for religious worship intended only for civilians of another High Contracting Party, even if the latter is its adversary. It shall likewise permit the free passage of all consignments of essential foodstuffs, clothing and tonics intended for children under fifteen, expectant mothers and maternity cases. The obligation of a High Contracting Party to allow the free passage of the consignments indicated in the preceding paragraph is subject to the condition that this Party is satisfied that there are no serious reasons for fearing:

> (a) That the consignments may be diverted from their destination;
> (b) That the control may not be effective; or
> (c) That a definite advantage may accrue to the military efforts or economy of the enemy through the substitution of the above-mentioned consignments for goods which would otherwise be provided or produced by the enemy or through the release of such material, services or facilities as would otherwise be required for the production of such goods.

The Power which allows the passage of the consignments indicated in the first paragraph of this Article may make such permission conditional on the distribution to the persons benefited thereby being made under the local supervision of the Protecting Powers.

Such consignments shall be forwarded as rapidly as possible, and the Power which permits their free passage shall have the right to prescribe the technical arrangements under which such passage is allowed.

Article 24

The Parties to the conflict shall take the necessary measures to ensure that children under fifteen, who are orphaned or are separated from their families as a result of the war, are not left to their own resources, and that their maintenance, the exercise of their religion and their education are facilitated in all circumstances. Their education shall, as far as possible, be entrusted to persons of a similar cultural tradition. The Parties to the conflict shall facilitate the reception of such children in a neutral country for the duration of the conflict with the consent of the Protecting Power, if any, and under due safeguards for the observance of the principles stated in the first paragraph. They shall, furthermore, endeavour to arrange for all children under twelve to be identified by the wearing of identity discs, or by some other means.

Article 25

All persons in the territory of a Party to the conflict, or in a territory occupied by it, shall be enabled to give news of a strictly personal nature to members of their families, wherever they may be, and to receive news from them. This correspondence shall be forwarded speedily and without undue delay. * * *

Article 26

Each Party to the conflict shall facilitate enquiries made by members of families dispersed owing to the war, with the object of renewing contact with one another and of meeting, if possible. It shall encourage, in particular, the work of organizations engaged on this task provided they are acceptable to it and conform to its security regulations.

PART III
STATUS AND TREATMENT OF PROTECTED PERSONS

Section I
Provisions common to the territories of the Parties to the conflict and to occupied territories

Article 27

Protected persons are entitled, in all circumstances, to respect for their persons, their honour, their family rights, their religious convictions and practices, and their manners and customs. They shall at all times be humanely treated, and shall be protected especially against all acts of violence or threats thereof and against insults and public curiosity. Women shall be especially protected against any attack on their honour, in particular against rape, enforced prostitution, or any form of indecent assault. Without prejudice to the provisions relating to their state of health, age and sex, all protected persons shall be treated with the same consideration by the Party to the conflict in whose power they are, without any adverse distinction based, in particular, on race, religion or political opinion. However, the Parties to the conflict may take such measures of control and security in regard to protected persons as may be necessary as a result of the war.

Article 28

The presence of a protected person may not be used to render certain points or areas immune from military operations.

Article 29

The Party to the conflict in whose hands protected persons may be is responsible for the treatment accorded to them by its agents, irrespective of any individual responsibility which may be incurred.

Article 30

Protected persons shall have every facility for making application to the Protecting Powers, the International Committee of the Red Cross, the National Red Cross (Red Crescent, Red Lion and Sun) Society of the country where they may be, as well as to any organization that might assist them.

These several organizations shall be granted all facilities for that purpose by the authorities, within the bounds set by military or security considerations. Apart from the visits of the delegates of the Protecting Powers and of the International Committee of the Red Cross, provided for by Article 143, the Detaining or Occupying Powers shall facilitate as much as possible visits to protected persons by the representatives of other organizations whose object is to give spiritual aid or material relief to such persons.

Article 31
No physical or moral coercion shall be exercised against protected persons, in particular to obtain information from them or from third parties.

Article 32
The High Contracting Parties specifically agree that each of them is prohibited from taking any measure of such a character as to cause the physical suffering or extermination of protected persons in their hands. This prohibition applies not only to murder, torture, corporal punishment, mutilation and medical or scientific experiments not necessitated by the medical treatment of a protected person but also to any other measures of brutality whether applied by civilian or military agents.

Article 33
No protected person may be punished for an offence he or she has not personally committed. Collective penalties and likewise all measures of intimidation or of terrorism are prohibited.
Pillage is prohibited. Reprisals against protected persons and their property are prohibited.

Article 34
The taking of hostages is prohibited.

Section II
Aliens in the territory of a Party to the conflict

Article 35
All protected persons who may desire to leave the territory at the outset of, or during a conflict, shall be entitled to do so, unless their departure is contrary to the national interests of the State. The applications of such persons to leave shall be decided in accordance with regularly established procedures and the decision shall be taken as rapidly as possible. Those persons permitted to leave may provide themselves with the necessary funds for their journey and take with them a reasonable amount of their effects and articles of personal use. If any such person is refused permission to leave the territory, he shall be entitled to have such refusal reconsidered as soon as possible by an appropriate court or administrative board designated by the Detaining Power for that purpose. Upon request, representatives of the Protecting Power shall, unless reasons of security prevent it, or the persons concerned object, be furnished with the reasons for refusal of any request for permission to leave the territory and be given, as expeditiously as possible, the names of all persons who have been denied permission to leave.

Article 36
Departures permitted under the foregoing Article shall be carried out in satisfactory conditions as regards safety, hygiene, sanitation and food. All costs in connection therewith, from the point of exit in the territory of the Detaining Power, shall be borne by the country of destination, or, in the case of accommodation in a neutral country, by the Power whose nationals are benefited. The practical details of such movements may, if necessary, be settled by special agreements between the Powers concerned. The foregoing shall not prejudice such special agreements as may be concluded between Parties to the conflict concerning the exchange and repatriation of their nationals in enemy hands.

Article 37
Protected persons who are confined pending proceedings or serving a sentence involving loss of liberty shall during their confinement be humanely treated. As soon as they are released, they may ask to leave the territory in conformity with the foregoing Articles.

Article 38

With the exception of special measures authorized by the present Convention, in particular by Articles 27 and 41 thereof, the situation of protected persons shall continue to be regulated, in principle, by the provisions concerning aliens in time of peace. In any case, the following rights shall be granted to them:

1. They shall be enabled to receive the individual or collective relief that may be sent to them.
2. They shall, if their state of health so requires, receive medical attention and hospital treatment to the same extent as the nationals of the State concerned.
3. They shall be allowed to practise their religion and to receive spiritual assistance from ministers of their faith.
4. If they reside in an area particularly exposed to the dangers of war, they shall be authorized to move from that area to the same extent as the nationals of the State concerned.
5. Children under fifteen years, pregnant women and mothers of children under seven years shall benefit by any preferential treatment to the same extent as the nationals of the State concerned.

Article 39

Protected persons who, as a result of the war, have lost their gainful employment, shall be granted the opportunity to find paid employment. That opportunity shall, subject to security considerations and to the provisions of Article 40, be equal to that enjoyed by the nationals of the Power in whose territory they are. Where a Party to the conflict applies to a protected person methods of control which result in his being unable to support himself, and especially if such a person is prevented for reasons of security from finding paid employment on reasonable conditions, the said Party shall ensure his support and that of his dependents. Protected persons may in any case receive allowances from their country, the Protecting Power, or the relief societies referred to in Article 30.

Article 40

Protected persons may be compelled to work only to the same extent as nationals of the Party to the conflict in whose territory they are. If protected persons are of enemy nationality, they may only be compelled to do work which is normally necessary to ensure the feeding, sheltering, clothing, transport and health of human beings and which is not directly related to the conduct of military operations. * * *

Article 41

Should the Power in whose hands protected persons may be consider the measures of control mentioned in the present Convention to be inadequate, it may not have recourse to any other measure of control more severe than that of assigned residence or internment, in accordance with the provisions of Articles 42 and 43. In applying the provisions of Article 39, second paragraph, to the cases of persons required to leave their usual places of residences by virtue of a decision placing them in assigned residence elsewhere. the Detaining Power shall be guided as closely as possible by the standards of welfare set forth in Part III, Section IV of this Convention.

Article 42

The internment or placing in assigned residence of protected persons may be ordered only if the security of the Detaining Power makes it absolutely necessary. If any person, acting through the representatives of the Protecting Power, voluntarily demands internment, and if his situation renders this step necessary, he shall be interned by the Power in whose hands he may be.

Article 43

Any protected person who has been interned or placed in assigned residence shall be entitled to have such action reconsidered as soon as possible by an appropriate court or administrative board designated by the Detaining Power for that purpose. * * *

Article 44

In applying the measures of control mentioned in the present Convention, the Detaining Power shall not treat as enemy aliens exclusively on the basis of their nationality *de jure* of an enemy State, refugees who do not, in fact, enjoy the protection of any government.

Article 45

Protected persons shall not be transferred to a Power which is not a party to the Convention. This provision shall in no way constitute an obstacle to the repatriation of protected persons, or to their return to their country of residence after the cessation of hostilities. Protected persons may be transferred by the Detaining Power only to a Power which is a party to the present Convention and after the Detaining Power has satisfied itself of the willingness and ability of such transferee Power to apply the present Convention. If protected persons are transferred under such circumstances, responsibility for the application of the present Convention rests on the Power accepting them, while they are in its custody. Nevertheless, if that Power fails to carry out the provisions of the present Convention in any important respect, the Power by which the protected persons were transferred shall, upon being so notified by the Protecting Power, take effective measures to correct the situation or shall request the return of the protected persons. Such request must be complied with. In no circumstances shall a protected person be transferred to a country where he or she may have reason to fear persecution for his or her political opinions or religious beliefs. The provisions of this Article do not constitute an obstacle to the extradition, in pursuance of extradition treaties concluded before the outbreak of hostilities, of protected persons accused of offences against ordinary criminal law.

Article 46

In so far as they have not been previously withdrawn, restrictive measures taken regarding protected persons shall be cancelled as soon as possible after the close of hostilities. Restrictive measures affecting their property shall be cancelled, in accordance with the law of the Detaining Power, as soon as possible after the close of hostilities.

Section III
Occupied territories

Article 47

Protected persons who are in occupied territory shall not be deprived, in any case or in any manner whatsoever, of the benefits of the present Convention by any change introduced, as the result of the occupation of a territory, into the institutions or government of the said territory, nor by any agreement concluded between the authorities of the occupied territories and the Occupying Power, nor by any annexation by the latter of the whole or part of the occupied territory.

Article 48

Protected persons who are not nationals of the Power whose territory is occupied may avail themselves of the right to leave the territory subject to the provisions of Article 35, and decisions thereon shall be taken according to the procedure which the Occupying Power shall establish in accordance with the said Article.

Article 49

Individual or mass forcible transfers, as well as deportations of protected persons from occupied territory to the territory of the Occupying Power or to that of any other country, occupied or not, are prohibited, regardless of their motive. Nevertheless, the Occupying Power may undertake total or partial evacuation of a given area if the security of the population or imperative military reasons so demand. Such evacuations may not involve the displacement of protected persons outside the bounds of the occupied territory except when for material reasons it is impossible to avoid such displacement. Persons thus evacuated shall be transferred back to their s as soon as hostilities in the area in question have ceased. The Occupying Power undertaking such transfers or evacuations shall ensure, to the greatest practicable extent, that proper accommodation is provided to receive the protected persons, that the removals are effected in satisfactory conditions of hygiene, health, safety and nutrition, and that members of the same family are not separated. The Protecting Power shall be informed of any transfers and evacuations as soon as they have taken place. The Occupying Power shall not detain protected persons in an area particularly exposed to the dangers of war unless the security of the population or imperative military reasons so demand. The Occupying Power shall not deport or transfer parts of its own civilian population into the territory it occupies.

Article 50

The Occupying Power shall, with the cooperation of the national and local authorities, facilitate the proper working of all institutions devoted to the care and education of children. The Occupying Power shall take all necessary steps to facilitate the identification of children and the registration of their parentage. It may not, in any case, change their personal status, nor enlist them in formations or organizations subordinate to it. Should the local institutions be inadequate for the purpose, the Occupying Power shall make arrangements for the maintenance and education, if possible by persons of their own nationality, language and religion, of children who are orphaned or separated from their parents as a result of the war and who cannot be adequately cared for by a near relative or friend. A special section of the Bureau set up in accordance with Article 136 shall be responsible for taking all necessary steps to identify children whose identity is in doubt. Particulars of their parents or other near relatives should always be recorded if available. The Occupying Power shall not hinder the application of any preferential measures in regard to food, medical care and protection against the effects of war, which may have been adopted prior to the occupation in favour of children under fifteen years, expectant mothers, and mothers of children under seven years.

Article 51

The Occupying Power may not compel protected persons to serve in its armed or auxiliary forces. No pressure or propaganda which aims at securing voluntary enlistment is permitted. The Occupying Power may not compel protected persons to work unless they are over eighteen years of age, and then only on work which is necessary either for the needs of the army of occupation, or for the public utility services, or for the feeding, sheltering, clothing, transportation or health of the population of the occupied country. Protected persons may not be compelled to undertake any work which would involve them in the obligation of taking part in military operations. The Occupying Power may not compel protected persons to employ forcible means to ensure the security of the installations where they are performing compulsory labour. The work shall be carried out only in the occupied territory where the persons whose services have been requisitioned are. Every such person shall, so far as possible, be kept in his usual place of employment. Workers shall be paid a fair wage and the work shall be proportionate to their physical and intellectual capacities. The legislation in force in the occupied country concerning working conditions, and safeguards as regards, in particular, such matters as wages, hours of work, equipment, preliminary training and compensation for occupational accidents and diseases, shall be applicable to the protected persons assigned to the work referred to in this Article. In no case shall requisition of labour lead to a mobilization of workers in an organization of a military or semi-military character. * * *

Article 53

Any destruction by the Occupying Power of real or personal property belonging individually or collectively to private persons, or to the State, or to other public authorities, or to social or cooperative organizations, is prohibited, except where such destruction is rendered absolutely necessary by military operations.

Article 54

The Occupying Power may not alter the status of public officials or judges in the occupied territories, or in any way apply sanctions to or take any measures of coercion or discrimination against them, should they abstain from fulfilling their functions for reasons of conscience. This prohibition does not prejudice the application of the second paragraph of Article 51. It does not affect the right of the Occupying Power to remove public officials from their posts.

Article 55

To the fullest extent of the means available to it the Occupying Power has the duty of ensuring the food and medical supplies of the population; it should, in particular, bring in the necessary foodstuffs, medical stores and other articles if the resources of the occupied territory are inadequate. The Occupying Power may not requisition foodstuffs, articles or medical supplies available in the occupied territory, except for use by the occupation forces and administration personnel, and then only if the requirements of the civilian population have been taken into account. Subject to the provisions of other international Conventions, the Occupying Power shall make arrangements to ensure that fair value is paid for any requisitioned goods. The Protecting Power shall, at any time, be at liberty to verify the state of the food and medical supplies in occupied territories, except where temporary restrictions are made necessary by imperative military requirements.

Article 56

To the fullest extent of the means available to it, the Occupying Power has the duty of ensuring and maintaining, with the cooperation of national and local authorities, the medical and hospital establishments and services, public health and hygiene in the occupied territory, with particular reference to the adoption and application of the prophylactic and preventive measures necessary to combat the spread of contagious diseases and epidemics. Medical personnel of all categories shall be allowed to carry out their duties. * * *

Article 57

The Occupying Power may requisition civilian hospitals only temporarily and only in cases of urgent necessity for the care of military wounded and sick, and then on condition that suitable arrangements are made in due time for the care and treatment of the patients and for the needs of the civilian population for hospital accommodation. The material and stores of civilian hospitals cannot be requisitioned so long as they are necessary for the needs of the civilian population.

Article 58

The Occupying Power shall permit ministers of religion to give spiritual assistance to the members of their religious communities. The Occupying Power shall also accept consignments of books and articles required for religious needs and shall facilitate their distribution in occupied territory.

Article 59

If the whole or part of the population of an occupied territory is inadequately supplied, the Occupying Power shall agree to relief schemes on behalf of the said population, and shall facilitate them by all the means at its disposal. Such schemes, which may be undertaken either by States or by impartial humanitarian organizations such as the International Committee of the Red Cross, shall consist, in particular, of the provision of consignments of foodstuffs, medical supplies and clothing. All Contracting Parties shall permit the free passage of these consignments and shall guarantee their protection. A Power granting free passage to consignments on their way to territory occupied by an adverse Party to the conflict shall, however, have the right to search the consignments, to regulate their passage according to prescribed times and routes, and to be reasonably satisfied through the Protecting Power that these consignments are to be used for the relief of the needy population and are not to be used for the benefit of the Occupying Power.

Article 60

Relief consignments shall in no way relieve the Occupying Power of any of its responsibilities under Articles 55, 56 and 59. The Occupying Power shall in no way whatsoever divert relief consignments from the purpose for which they are intended, except in cases of urgent necessity, in the interests of the population of the occupied territory and with the consent of the Protecting Power.* * *

Article 64

The penal laws of the occupied territory shall remain in force, with the exception that they may be repealed or suspended by the Occupying Power in cases where they constitute a threat to its security or an obstacle to the application of the present Convention. Subject to the latter consideration and to the necessity for ensuring the effective administration of justice, the tribunals of the occupied territory shall continue to function in respect of all offences covered by the said laws. The Occupying Power may, however, subject the population of the occupied territory to provisions which are essential to enable the Occupying Power to fulfil its obligations under the present Convention, to maintain the orderly government of the territory, and to ensure the security of the Occupying Power, of the members and property of the occupying forces or administration, and likewise of the establishments and lines of communication used by them.

Article 65

The penal provisions enacted by the Occupying Power shall not come into force before they have been published and brought to the knowledge of the inhabitants in their own language. The effect of these penal provisions shall not be retroactive.

Article 66

In case of a breach of the penal provisions promulgated by it by virtue of the second paragraph of Article 64, the Occupying Power may hand over the accused to its properly constituted, non-political military courts, on condition that the said courts sit in the occupied country. Courts of appeal shall preferably sit in the occupied country.

Article 67

The courts shall apply only those provisions of law which were applicable prior to the offence, and which are in accordance with general principles of law, in particular the principle that the penalty shall be proportionate to the offence. They shall take into consideration the fact that the accused is not a national of the Occupying Power.

Article 68

Protected persons who commit an offence which is solely intended to harm the Occupying Power, but which does not constitute an attempt on the life or limb of members of the occupying forces or administration, nor a grave collective danger, nor seriously damage the property of the occupying forces or administration or the installations used by them, shall be liable to internment or simple imprisonment, provided the duration of such internment or imprisonment is proportionate to the offence committed. Furthermore, internment or imprisonment shall, for such offences, be the only measure adopted for depriving protected persons of liberty. The courts provided for under Article 66 of the present Convention may at their discretion convert a sentence of imprisonment to one of internment for the same period.

The penal provisions promulgated by the Occupying Power in accordance with Articles 64 and 65 may impose the death penalty on a protected person only in cases where the person is guilty of espionage, of serious acts of sabotage against the military installations of the Occupying Power or of intentional offences which have caused the death of one or more persons, provided that such offences were punishable by death under the law of the occupied territory in force before the occupation began. The death penalty may not be pronounced against a protected person unless the attention of the court has been particularly called to the fact that, since the accused is not a national of the Occupying Power, he is not bound to it by any duty of allegiance. In any case, the death penalty may not be pronounced against a protected person who was under eighteen years of age at the time of the offence.

Article 69

In all cases, the duration of the period during which a protected person accused of an offence is under arrest awaiting trial or punishment shall be deducted from any period of imprisonment awarded.

Article 70

Protected persons shall not be arrested, prosecuted or convicted by the Occupying Power for acts committed or for opinions expressed before the occupation, or during a temporary interruption thereof, with the exception of breaches of the laws and customs of war. Nationals of the Occupying Power who, before the outbreak of hostilities, have sought refuge in the territory of the occupied State, shall not be arrested, prosecuted, convicted or deported from the occupied territory, except for offences committed after the outbreak of hostilities, or for offences under common law committed before the outbreak of hostilities which, according to the law of the occupied State, would have justified extradition in time of peace.

Article 71

No sentence shall be pronounced by the competent courts of the Occupying Power except after a regular trial. Accused persons who are prosecuted by the Occupying Power shall be promptly informed, in writing, in a language which they understand, of the particulars of the charges preferred against them, and shall be brought to trial as rapidly as possible. The Protecting Power shall be informed of all proceedings instituted by the Occupying Power against protected persons in respect of charges involving the death penalty or imprisonment for two years or more; it shall be enabled, at any time, to obtain information regarding the state of such proceedings. Furthermore, the Protecting Power shall be entitled, on request, to be furnished with all particulars of these and of any other proceedings instituted by the Occupying Power against protected persons. The notification to the Protecting Power, as provided for in the second paragraph above, shall be sent immediately, and shall in any case reach the Protecting Power three weeks before the date of the first hearing. Unless, at the opening of the trial, evidence is submitted that the provisions of this Article are fully complied with, the trial shall not proceed. The notification shall include the following particulars:
    (a) Description of the accused;
    (b) Place of residence or detention;

(c) Specification of the charge or charges (with mention of the penal provisions under which it is brought);

(d) Designation of the court which will hear the case;

(e) Place and date of the first hearing.

Article 72

Accused persons shall have the right to present evidence necessary to their defence and may, in particular, call witnesses. They shall have the right to be assisted by a qualified advocate or counsel of their own choice, who shall be able to visit them freely and shall enjoy the necessary facilities for preparing the defence. Failing a choice by the accused, the Protecting Power may provide him with an advocate or counsel. When an accused person has to meet a serious charge and the Protecting Power is not functioning, the Occupying Power, subject to the consent of the accused, shall provide an advocate or counsel. Accused persons shall, unless they freely waive such assistance, be aided by an interpreter, both during preliminary investigation and during the hearing in court. They shall have the right at any time to object to the interpreter and to ask for his replacement.

Article 73

A convicted person shall have the right of appeal provided for by the laws applied by the court. He shall be fully informed of his right to appeal or petition and of the time limit within which he may do so. The penal procedure provided in the present Section shall apply, as far as it is applicable, to appeals. Where the laws applied by the Court make no provision for appeals, the convicted person shall have the right to petition against the finding and sentence to the competent authority of the Occupying Power. * * *

Article 75

In no case shall persons condemned to death be deprived of the right of petition for pardon or reprieve. No death sentence shall be carried out before the expiration of a period of at least six months from the date of receipt by the Protecting Power of the notification of the final judgment confirming such death sentence, or of an order denying pardon or reprieve. The six months period of suspension of the death sentence herein prescribed may be reduced in individual cases in circumstances of grave emergency involving an organized threat to the security of the Occupying Power or its forces, provided always that the Protecting Power is notified of such reduction and is given reasonable time and opportunity to make representations to the competent occupying authorities in respect of such death sentences.

Article 76

Protected persons accused of offences shall be detained in the occupied country, and if convicted they shall serve their sentences therein. They shall, if possible, be separated from other detainees and shall enjoy conditions of food and hygiene which will be sufficient to keep them in good health, and which will be at least equal to those obtaining in prisons in the occupied country. They shall receive the medical attention required by their state of health. They shall also have the right to receive any spiritual assistance which they may require. Women shall be confined in separate quarters and shall be under the direct supervision of women. Proper regard shall be paid to the special treatment due to minors. Protected persons who are detained shall have the right to be visited by delegates of the Protecting Power and of the International Committee of the Red Cross, in accordance with the provisions of Article 143. Such persons shall have the right to receive at least one relief parcel monthly.

Article 77

Protected persons who have been accused of offences or convicted by the courts in occupied territory shall be handed over at the close of occupation, with the relevant records, to the authorities of the liberated territory. * * *

Section IV
Regulations for the treatment of internees

Chapter I
General provisions

Article 79

The Parties to the conflict shall not intern protected persons, except in accordance with the provisions of Articles 41, 42, 43, [and] 68 * * *.

Article 80

Internees shall retain their full civil capacity and shall exercise such attendant rights as may be compatible with their status.

Article 81

Parties to the conflict who intern protected persons shall be bound to provide free of charge for their maintenance, and to grant them also the medical attention required by their state of health. No deduction from the allowances, salaries or credits due to the internees shall be made for the repayment of these costs. The Detaining Power shall provide for the support of those dependent on the internees, if such dependants are without adequate means of support or are unable to earn a living.

Article 82

The Detaining Power shall, as far as possible, accommodate the internees according to their nationality, language and customs. Internees who are nationals of the same country shall not be separated merely because they have different languages. Throughout the duration of their internment, members of the same family, and in particular parents and children, shall be lodged together in the same place of internment, except when separation of a temporary nature is necessitated for reasons of employment or health or for the purposes of enforcement of the provisions of Chapter IX of the present Section. Internees may request that their children who are left at liberty without parental care shall be interned with them. Wherever possible, interned members of the same family shall be housed in the same premises and given separate accommodation from other internees, together with facilities for leading a proper family life.

Chapter II
Places of internment

Article 83

The Detaining Power shall not set up places of internment in areas particularly exposed to the dangers of war. The Detaining Power shall give the enemy Powers, through the intermediary of the Protecting Powers, all useful information regarding the geographical location of places of internment. Whenever military considerations permit, internment camps shall be indicated by the letters IC, placed so as to be clearly visible in the daytime from the air. The Powers concerned may, however, agree upon any other system of marking. No place other than an internment camp shall be marked as such.

Article 84

Internees shall be accommodated and administered separately from prisoners of war and from persons deprived of liberty for any other reason.

Article 85

The Detaining Power is bound to take all necessary and possible measures to ensure that protected persons shall, from the outset of their internment, be accommodated in buildings or quarters which afford every possible safeguard as regards hygiene and health, and provide efficient protection against the rigours of the climate and the effects of the war. In no case shall permanent places of internment be situated in unhealthy areas or in districts the climate of which is injurious to the internees. In all cases where the district, in which a protected person is temporarily interned, is in an unhealthy area or has a climate which is harmful to his health, he shall be removed to a more suitable place of internment as rapidly as circumstances permit. The premises shall be fully protected from dampness, adequately heated and lighted, in particular between dusk and lights out. The sleeping quarters shall be sufficiently spacious and well ventilated, and the internees shall have suitable bedding and sufficient blankets, account being taken of the climate, and the age, sex, and state of health of the internees. Internees shall have for their use, day and night, sanitary conveniences which conform to the rules of hygiene and are constantly maintained in a state of cleanliness. They shall be provided with sufficient water and soap for their daily personal toilet and for washing their personal laundry; installations and facilities necessary for this purpose shall be granted to them. Showers or baths shall also be available. The necessary time shall be set aside for washing and for cleaning. Whenever it is necessary, as an exceptional and temporary measure, to accommodate women internees who are not members of a family unit in the same place of internment as men, the provision of separate sleeping quarters and sanitary conveniences for the use of such women internees shall be obligatory.

Article 86

The Detaining Power shall place at the disposal of interned persons, of whatever denomination, premises suitable for the holding of their religious services.

Article 87

Canteens shall be installed in every place of internment, except where other suitable facilities are available. Their purpose shall be to enable internees to make purchases, at prices not higher than local market prices, of foodstuffs and articles of everyday use, including soap and tobacco, such as would increase their personal well-being and comfort. Profits made by canteens shall be credited to a welfare fund to be set up for each place of internment, and administered for the benefit of the internees attached to such place of internment. The Internee Committee provided for in Article 102 shall have the right to check the management of the canteen and of the said fund. When a place of internment is closed down, the balance of the welfare fund shall be transferred to the welfare fund of a place of internment for internees of the same nationality, or, if such a place does not exist, to a central welfare fund which shall be administered for the benefit of all internees remaining in the custody of the Detaining Power. In case of a general release, the said profits shall be kept by the Detaining Power, subject to any agreement to the contrary between the Powers concerned.

Article 88

In all places of internment exposed to air raids and other hazards of war, shelters adequate in number and structure to ensure the necessary protection shall be installed. In case of alarms, the internees shall be free to enter such shelters as quickly as possible, excepting those who remain for the protection of their quarters against the aforesaid hazards. Any protective measures taken in favour of the population shall also apply to them. All due precautions must be taken in places of internment against the danger of fire.

Chapter III
Food and clothing

Article 89

Daily food rations for internees shall be sufficient in quantity, quality and variety to keep internees in a good state of health and prevent the development of nutritional deficiencies. Account shall also be taken of the customary diet of the internees. Internees shall also be given the means by which they can prepare for themselves any additional food in their possession. Sufficient drinking water shall be supplied to internees. The use of tobacco shall be permitted. Internees who work shall receive additional rations in proportion to the kind of labour which they perform. Expectant and nursing mothers and children under fifteen years of age shall be given additional food, in proportion to their physiological needs.

Article 90

When taken into custody, internees shall be given all facilities to provide themselves with the necessary clothing, footwear and change of underwear, and later on, to procure further supplies if required. Should any internees not have sufficient clothing, account being taken of the climate, and be unable to procure any, it shall be provided free of charge to them by the Detaining Power. The clothing supplied by the Detaining Power to internees and the outward markings placed on their own clothes shall not be ignominious nor expose them to ridicule. Workers shall receive suitable working outfits, including protective clothing, whenever the nature of their work so requires.

Chapter IV
Hygiene and medical attention

Article 91
Every place of internment shall have an adequate infirmary, under the direction of a qualified doctor, where internees may have the attention they require, as well as an appropriate diet. Isolation wards shall be set aside for cases of contagious or mental diseases. Maternity cases and internees suffering from serious diseases, or whose condition requires special treatment, a surgical operation or hospital care, must be admitted to any institution where adequate treatment can be given and shall receive care not inferior to that provided for the general population. Internees shall, for preference, have the attention of medical personnel of their own nationality. Internees may not be prevented from presenting themselves to the medical authorities for examination. The medical authorities of the Detaining Power shall, upon request, issue to every internee who has undergone treatment an official certificate showing the nature of his illness or injury, and the duration and nature of the treatment given. A duplicate of this certificate shall be forwarded to the Central Agency provided for in Article 140. Treatment, including the provision of any apparatus necessary for the maintenance of internees in good health, particularly dentures and other artificial appliances and spectacles, shall be free of charge to the internee. * * *

Chapter V
Religious, intellectual and physical activities

Article 93
Internees shall enjoy complete latitude in the exercise of their religious duties, including attendance at the services of their faith, on condition that they comply with the disciplinary routine prescribed by the detaining authorities. Ministers of religion who are interned shall be allowed to minister freely to the members of their community. For this purpose, the Detaining Power shall ensure their equitable allocation amongst the various places of internment in which there are internees speaking the same language and belonging to the same religion. Should such ministers be too few in number, the Detaining Power shall provide them with the necessary facilities, including means of transport, for moving from one place to another, and they shall be authorized to visit any internees who are in hospital. Ministers of religion shall be at liberty to correspond on matters concerning their ministry with the religious authorities in the country of detention and, as far as possible, with the international religious organizations of their faith. * * *

Article 94
The Detaining Power shall encourage intellectual, educational and recreational pursuits, sports and games amongst internees, whilst leaving them free to take part in them or not. It shall take all practicable measures to ensure the exercise thereof, in particular by providing suitable premises. All possible facilities shall be granted to internees to continue their studies or to take up new subjects. The education of children and young people shall be ensured; they shall be allowed to attend schools either within the place of internment or outside. Internees shall be given opportunities for physical exercise, sports and outdoor games. For this purpose, sufficient open spaces shall be set aside in all places of internment. Special playgrounds shall be reserved for children and young people.

Article 95
The Detaining Power shall not employ internees as workers, unless they so desire. Employment which, if undertaken under compulsion by a protected person not in internment, would involve a breach of Articles 40 or 51 of the present Convention, and employment on work which is of a degrading or humiliating character are in any case prohibited. After a working period of six weeks, internees shall be free to give up work at any moment, subject to eight days' notice. These provisions constitute no obstacle to the right of the Detaining Power to employ interned doctors, dentists and other medical personnel in their professional capacity on behalf of their fellow internees, or to employ internees for administrative and maintenance work in places of internment and to detail such persons for work in the kitchens or for other domestic tasks, or to require such persons to undertake duties connected with the protection of internees against aerial bombardment or other war risks. No internee may, however, be required to perform tasks for which he is, in the opinion of a medical officer, physically unsuited. The Detaining Power shall take entire responsibility for all working conditions, for medical attention, for the payment of wages, and for ensuring

that all employed internees receive compensation for occupational accidents and diseases. The standards prescribed for the said working conditions and for compensation shall be in accordance with the national laws and regulations, and with the existing practice; they shall in no case be inferior to those obtaining for work of the same nature in the same district. Wages for work done shall be determined on an equitable basis by special agreements between the internees, the Detaining Power, and, if the case arises, employers other than the Detaining Power, due regard being paid to the obligation of the Detaining Power to provide for free maintenance of internees and for the medical attention which their state of health may require. Internees permanently detailed for categories of work mentioned in the third paragraph of this Article shall be paid fair wages by the Detaining Power. The working conditions and the scale of compensation for occupational accidents and diseases to internees thus detailed shall not be inferior to those applicable to work of the same nature in the same district. * * *

Chapter VI
Personal property and financial resources

Article 97

Internees shall be permitted to retain articles of personal use. Monies, cheques, bonds, etc., and valuables in their possession may not be taken from them except in accordance with established procedure. Detailed receipts shall be given therefor. The amounts shall be paid into the account of every internee as provided for in Article 98. Such amounts may not be converted into any other currency unless legislation in force in the territory in which the owner is interned so requires or the internee gives his consent. Articles which have above all a personal or sentimental value may not be taken away. A woman internee shall not be searched except by a woman. On release or repatriation, internees shall be given all articles, monies or other valuables taken from them during internment and shall receive in currency the balance of any credit to their accounts kept in accordance with Article 98, with the exception of any articles or amounts withheld by the Detaining Power by virtue of its legislation in force. If the property of an internee is so withheld, the owner shall receive a detailed receipt. Family or identity documents in the possession of internees may not be taken away without a receipt being given. At no time shall internees be left without identity documents. If they have none, they shall be issued with special documents drawn up by the detaining authorities, which will serve as their identity papers until the end of their internment. Internees may keep on their persons a certain amount of money, in cash or in the shape of purchase coupons, to enable them to make purchases.

Article 98

All internees shall receive regular allowances, sufficient to enable them to purchase goods and articles, such as tobacco, toilet requisites, etc. Such allowances may take the form of credits or purchase coupons. Furthermore, internees may receive allowances from the Power to which they owe allegiance, the Protecting Powers, the organizations which may assist them, or their families, as well as the income on their property in accordance with the law of the Detaining Power. The amount of allowances granted by the Power to which they owe allegiance shall be the same for each category of internees (infirm, sick, pregnant women, etc.), but may not be allocated by that Power or distributed by the Detaining Power on the basis of discrimination between internees which are prohibited by Article 27 of the present Convention. The Detaining Power shall open a regular account for every internee, to which shall be credited the allowances named in the present Article, the wages earned and the remittances received, together with such sums taken from him as may be available under the legislation in force in the territory in which he is interned. Internees shall be granted all facilities consistent with the legislation in force in such territory to make remittances to their families and to other dependants. They may draw from their accounts the amounts necessary for their personal expenses, within the limits fixed by the Detaining Power. They shall at all times be afforded reasonable facilities for consulting and obtaining copies of their accounts. A statement of accounts shall be furnished to the Protecting Power on request, and shall accompany the internee in case of transfer.

Chapter VII
Administration and discipline

Article 99

Every place of internment shall be put under the authority of a responsible officer, chosen from the regular military forces or the regular civil administration of the Detaining Power. The officer in charge of the place of internment must have in his possession a copy of the present Convention in the official language, or one of the official languages, of his country and shall be responsible for its application. The staff in control of internees shall be instructed in the provisions of the present Convention and of the administrative measures adopted to ensure its application. The text of the present Convention and the texts of special agreements concluded under the said Convention shall be posted inside the place of internment, in a language which the internees understand, or shall be in the possession of the Internee Committee. Regulations, orders, notices and publications of every kind shall be communicated to the internees and posted inside the places of internment, in a language which they understand. Every order and command addressed to internees individually must likewise be given in a language which they understand.

Article 100

The disciplinary regime in places of internment shall be consistent with humanitarian principles, and shall in no circumstances include regulations imposing on internees any physical exertion dangerous to their health or involving physical or moral victimization. Identification by tattooing or imprinting signs or markings on the body is prohibited. In particular, prolonged standing and roll-calls, punishment drill, military drill and manoeuvres, or the reduction of food rations, are prohibited.

Article 101

Internees shall have the right to present to the authorities in whose power they are any petition with regard to the conditions of internment to which they are subjected. They shall also have the right to apply without restriction through the Internee Committee or, if they consider it necessary, direct to the representatives of the Protecting Power, in order to indicate to them any points on which they may have complaints to make with regard to the conditions of internment. Such petitions and complaints shall be transmitted forthwith and without alteration, and even if the latter are recognized to be unfounded, they may not occasion any punishment. Periodic reports on the situation in places of internment and as to the needs of the internees may be sent by the Internee Committees to the representatives of the Protecting Powers.

Article 102

In every place of internment, the internees shall freely elect by secret ballot every six months, the members of a Committee empowered to represent them before the Detaining and the Protecting Powers, the International Committee of the Red Cross and any other organization which may assist them. The members of the Committee shall be eligible for re-election. Internees so elected shall enter upon their duties after their election has been approved by the detaining authorities. The reasons for any refusals or dismissals shall be communicated to the Protecting Powers concerned.

Article 103

The Internee Committees shall further the physical, spiritual and intellectual well-being of the internees. In case the internees decide, in particular, to organize a system of mutual assistance amongst themselves, this organization would be within the competence of the Committees in addition to the special duties entrusted to them under other provisions of the present Convention. * * *

Chapter VIII
Relations with the exterior

Article 105

Immediately upon interning protected persons, the Detaining Power shall inform them, the Power to which they owe allegiance and their Protecting Power of the measures taken for executing the provisions of the present Chapter. The Detaining Power shall likewise inform the Parties concerned of any subsequent modifications of such measures. * * *

Article 107

Internees shall be allowed to send and receive letters and cards. If the Detaining Power deems it necessary to limit the number of letters and cards sent by each internee, the said number shall not be less than two letters and four cards monthly; these shall be drawn up so as to conform as closely as possible to the models annexed to the present Convention. If limitations must be placed on the correspondence addressed to internees, they may be ordered only by the Power to which such internees owe allegiance, possibly at the request of the Detaining Power. Such letters and cards must be conveyed with reasonable despatch; they may not be delayed or retained for disciplinary reasons. Internees who have been a long time without news, or who find it impossible to receive news from their relatives, or to give them news by the ordinary postal route, as well as those who are at a considerable distance from their s, shall be allowed to send telegrams, the charges being paid by them in the currency at their disposal. They shall likewise benefit by this provision in cases which are recognized to be urgent. As a rule, internees' mail shall be written in their own language. The Parties to the conflict may authorize correspondence in other languages.

Article 108
Internees shall be allowed to receive, by post or by any other means, individual parcels or collective shipments containing in particular foodstuffs, clothing, medical supplies, as well as books and objects of a devotional, educational or recreational character which may meet their needs. Such shipments shall in no way free the Detaining Power from the obligations imposed upon it by virtue of the present Convention. Should military necessity require the quantity of such shipments to be limited, due notice thereof shall be given to the Protecting Power and to the International Committee of the Red Cross, or to any other organization giving assistance to the internees and responsible for the forwarding of such shipments.
The conditions for the sending of individual parcels and collective shipments shall, if necessary, be the subject of special agreements between the Powers concerned, which may in no case delay the receipt by the internees of relief supplies. Parcels of clothing and foodstuffs may not include books. Medical relief supplies shall, as a rule, be sent in collective parcels. * * *

Article 112
The censoring of correspondence addressed to internees or despatched by them shall be done as quickly as possible. The examination of consignments intended for internees shall not be carried out under conditions that will expose the goods contained in them to deterioration. It shall be done in the presence of the addressee, or of a fellow-internee duly delegated by him. The delivery to internees of individual or collective consignments shall not be delayed under the pretext of difficulties of censorship. Any prohibition of correspondence ordered by the Parties to the conflict, either for military or political reasons, shall be only temporary and its duration shall be as short as possible.

Article 113
The Detaining Powers shall provide all reasonable facilities for the transmission, through the Protecting Power or the Central Agency provided for in Article 140, or as otherwise required, of wills, powers of attorney letters of authority, or any other documents intended for internees or despatched by them.
In all cases the Detaining Power shall facilitate the execution and authentication in due legal form of such documents on behalf of internees, in particular by allowing them to consult a lawyer.

Article 114
The Detaining Power shall afford internees all facilities to enable them to manage their property, provided this is not incompatible with the conditions of internment and the law which is applicable. For this purpose, the said Power may give them permission to leave the place of internment in urgent cases and if circumstances allow. * * *

Chapter IX
Penal and disciplinary sanctions

Article 117
Subject to the provisions of the present Chapter, the laws in force in the territory in which they are detained will continue to apply to internees who commit offences during internment. If general laws, regulations or orders declare acts committed by internees to be punishable, whereas the same acts are not punishable when committed by persons who are not internees, such acts shall entail disciplinary punishments only.
No internee may be punished more than once for the same act, or on the same count.

Article 118
The courts or authorities shall in passing sentence take as far as possible into account the fact that the defendant is not a national of the Detaining Power. They shall be free to reduce the penalty prescribed for

the offence with which the internee is charged and shall not be obliged, to this end, to apply the minimum sentence prescribed. Imprisonment in premises without daylight, and, in general, all forms of cruelty without exception are forbidden. Internees who have served disciplinary or judicial sentences shall not be treated differently from other internees. The duration of preventive detention undergone by an internee shall be deducted from any disciplinary or judicial penalty involving confinement to which he may be sentenced. Internee Committees shall be informed of all judicial proceedings instituted against internees whom they represent, and of their result.

Article 119
The disciplinary punishments applicable to internees shall be the following:
1. A fine which shall not exceed 50 per cent of the wages which the internee would otherwise receive under the provisions of Article 95 during a period of not more than thirty days.
2. Discontinuance of privileges granted over and above the treatment provided for by the present Convention.
3. Fatigue duties, not exceeding two hours daily, in connection with the maintenance of the place of internment.
4. Confinement.
In no case shall disciplinary penalties be inhuman, brutal or dangerous for the health of internees. Account shall be taken of the internee's age, sex and state of health.
The duration of any single punishment shall in no case exceed a maximum of thirty consecutive days, even if the internee is answerable for several breaches of discipline when his case is dealt with, whether such breaches are connected or not.

Article 120
Internees who are recaptured after having escaped or when attempting to escape shall be liable only to disciplinary punishment in respect of this act, even if it is a repeated offence. Article 118, paragraph 3, notwithstanding, internees punished as a result of escape or attempt to escape, may be subjected to special surveillance, on condition that such surveillance does not affect the state of their health, that it is exercised in a place of internment and that it does not entail the abolition of any of the safeguards granted by the present Convention. Internees who aid and abet an escape, or attempt to escape, shall be liable on this count to disciplinary punishment only.

Article 121
Escape, or attempt to escape, even if it is a repeated offence, shall not be deemed an aggravating circumstance in cases where an internee is prosecuted for offences committed during his escape.
The Parties to the conflict shall ensure that the competent authorities exercise leniency in deciding whether punishment inflicted for an offence shall be of a disciplinary or judicial nature, especially in respect of acts committed in connection with an escape, whether successful or not. * * *

Article 124
Internees shall not in any case be transferred to penitentiary establishments (prisons, penitentiaries, convict prisons, etc.) to undergo disciplinary punishment therein. The premises in which disciplinary punishments are undergone shall conform to sanitary requirements; they shall in particular be provided with adequate bedding. Internees undergoing punishment shall be enabled to keep themselves in a state of cleanliness. Women internees undergoing disciplinary punishment shall be confined in separate quarters from male internees and shall be under the immediate supervision of women. * * *

Chapter XI
Deaths

Article 129
The wills of internees shall be received for safe-keeping by the responsible authorities; and in the event of the death of an internee his will shall be transmitted without delay to a person whom he has previously designated. Deaths of internees shall be certified in every case by a doctor, and a death certificate shall be made out, showing the causes of death and the conditions under which it occurred. An official record of the death, duly registered, shall be drawn up in accordance with the procedure relating thereto in force in the

territory where the place of internment is situated, and a duly certified copy of such record shall be transmitted without delay to the Protecting Power as well as to the Central Agency referred to in Article 140.

Article 130

The detaining authorities shall ensure that internees who die while interned are honourably buried, if possible according to the rites of the religion to which they belonged, and that their graves are respected, properly maintained, and marked in such a way that they can always be recognized. Deceased internees shall be buried in individual graves unless unavoidable circumstances require the use of collective graves. Bodies may be cremated only for imperative reasons of hygiene, on account of the religion of the deceased or in accordance with his expressed wish to this effect. * * *

Article 131

Every death or serious injury of an internee, caused or suspected to have been caused by a sentry, another internee or any other person, as well as any death the cause of which is unknown, shall be immediately followed by an official enquiry by the Detaining Power. A communication on this subject shall be sent immediately to the Protecting Power. The evidence of any witnesses shall be taken, and a report including such evidence shall be prepared and forwarded to the said Protecting power. If the enquiry indicates the guilt of one or more persons, the Detaining Power shall take all necessary steps to ensure the prosecution of the person or persons responsible.

Chapter XII
Release, repatriation and accommodation in neutral countries

Article 132

Each interned person shall be released by the Detaining Power as soon as the reasons which necessitated his internment no longer exist. The Parties to the conflict shall, moreover, endeavour during the course of hostilities, to conclude agreements for the release, the repatriation, the return to places of residence or the accommodation in a neutral country of certain classes of internees, in particular children, pregnant women and mothers with infants and young children, wounded and sick, and internees who have been detained for a long time.

Article 133

Internment shall cease as soon as possible after the close of hostilities. Internees, in the territory of a Party to the conflict, against whom penal proceedings are pending for offences not exclusively subject to disciplinary penalties, may be detained until the close of such proceedings and, if circumstances require, until the completion of the penalty. The same shall apply to internees who have been previously sentenced to a punishment depriving them of liberty. By agreement between the Detaining Power and the Powers concerned, committees may be set up after the close of hostilities, or of the occupation of territories, to search for dispersed internees.

Article 134

The High Contracting Parties shall endeavour, upon the close of hostilities or occupation, to ensure the return of all internees to their last place of residence, or to facilitate their repatriation. * * *

Section V
Information Bureaux and Central Agency

Article 136

Upon the outbreak of a conflict and in all cases of occupation, each of the Parties to the conflict shall establish an official Information Bureau responsible for receiving and transmitting information in respect of the protected persons who are in its power. Each of the Parties to the conflict shall, within the shortest possible period, give its Bureau information of any measure taken by it concerning any protected persons who are kept in custody for more than two weeks, who are subjected to assigned residence or who are interned. It shall, furthermore, require its various departments concerned with such matters to provide the aforesaid Bureau promptly with information concerning all changes pertaining to these protected persons, as, for example, transfers, release, repatriations, escapes, admittances to hospitals, births and deaths.

Article 137

Each national Bureau shall immediately forward information concerning protected persons by the most rapid means to the Powers of whom the aforesaid persons are nationals, or to Powers in whose territory they resided, through the intermediary of the Protecting Powers and likewise through the Central Agency provided for in Article 140. The Bureaux shall also reply to all enquiries which may be received regarding protected persons. Information Bureaux shall transmit information concerning a protected person unless its transmission might be detrimental to the person concerned or to his or her relatives. Even in such a case, the information may not be withheld from the Central Agency which, upon being notified of the circumstances, will take the necessary precautions indicated in Article 140. All communications in writing made by any Bureau shall be authenticated by a signature or a seal.

Article 138

The information received by the national Bureau and transmitted by it shall be of such a character as to make it possible to identify the protected person exactly and to advise his next of kin quickly. The information in respect of each person shall include at least his surname, first names, place and date of birth, nationality, last residence and distinguishing characteristics, the first name of the father and the maiden name of the mother, the date, place and nature of the action taken with regard to the individual, the address at which correspondence may be sent to him and the name and address of the person to be informed. Likewise, information regarding the state of health of internees who are seriously ill or seriously wounded shall be supplied regularly and if possible every week.

Article 139

Each national Information Bureau shall, furthermore, be responsible for collecting all personal valuables left by protected persons mentioned in Article 136, in particular those who have been repatriated or released, or who have escaped or died; it shall forward the said valuables to those concerned, either direct, or, if necessary, through the Central Agency. Such articles shall be sent by the Bureau in sealed packets which shall be accompanied by statements giving clear and full identity particulars of the person to whom the articles belonged, and by a complete list of the contents of the parcel. Detailed records shall be maintained of the receipt and despatch of all such valuables.

Article 140

A Central Information Agency for protected persons, in particular for internees, shall be created in a neutral country. The International Committee of the Red Cross shall, if it deems necessary, propose to the Powers concerned the organization of such an Agency, which may be the same as that provided for in Article 123 of the Geneva Convention relative to the Treatment of Prisoners of War of August 12, 1949. The function of the Agency shall be to collect all information of the type set forth in Article 136 which it may obtain through official or private channels and to transmit it as rapidly as possible to the countries of origin or of residence of the persons concerned, except in cases where such transmissions might be detrimental to the persons whom the said information concerns, or to their relatives. It shall receive from the Parties to the conflict all reasonable facilities for effecting such transmissions. The High Contracting Parties, and in particular those whose nationals benefit by the services of the Central Agency, are requested to give the said Agency the financial aid it may require. The foregoing provisions shall in no way be interpreted as restricting the humanitarian activities of the International Committee of the Red Cross and of the relief Societies described in Article 142. * * *

PART IV
EXECUTION OF THE CONVENTION

Section I
General provisions

Article 142

Subject to the measures which the Detaining Powers may consider essential to ensure their security or to meet any other reasonable need, the representatives of religious organizations, relief societies, or any other organizations assisting the protected persons, shall receive from these Powers, for themselves or their duly accredited agents, all facilities for visiting the protected persons, for distributing relief supplies and material from any source, intended for educational, recreational or religious purposes, or for assisting them in organizing their leisure time within the places of internment. Such societies or organizations may be constituted in the territory of the Detaining Power, or in any other country, or they may have an international character. The Detaining Power may limit the number of societies and organizations whose delegates are allowed to carry out their activities in its territory and under its supervision, on condition, however, that such limitation shall not hinder the supply of effective and adequate relief to all protected persons. The special position of the International Committee of the Red Cross in this field shall be recognized and respected at all times.

Article 143

Representatives or delegates of the Protecting Powers shall have permission to go to all places where protected persons are, particularly to places of internment, detention and work. They shall have access to all premises occupied by protected persons and shall be able to interview the latter without witnesses, personally or through an interpreter. Such visits may not be prohibited except for reasons of imperative military necessity, and then only as an exceptional and temporary measure Their duration and frequency shall not be restricted. Such representatives and delegates shall have full liberty to select the places they wish to visit. The Detaining or Occupying Power, the Protecting Power and when occasion arises the Power of origin of the persons to be visited, may agree that compatriots of the internees shall be permitted to participate in the visits. The delegates of the International Committee of the Red Cross shall also enjoy the above prerogatives. The appointment of such delegates shall be submitted to the approval of the Power governing the territories where they will carry out their duties.

Article 144

The High Contracting Parties undertake, in time of peace as in time of war, to disseminate the text of the present Convention as widely as possible in their respective countries, and, in particular, to include the study thereof in their programmes of military and, if possible, civil instruction, so that the principles thereof may become known to the entire population. Any civilian, military, police or other authorities, who in time of war assume responsibilities in respect of protected persons, must possess the text of the Convention and be specially instructed as to its provisions. * * *

Article 146

The High Contracting Parties undertake to enact any legislation necessary to provide effective penal sanctions for persons committing, or ordering to be committed, any of the grave breaches of the present Convention defined in the following Article. Each High Contracting Party shall be under the obligation to search for persons alleged to have committed, or to have ordered to be committed, such grave breaches, and shall bring such persons, regardless of their nationality, before its own courts. It may also, if it prefers, and in accordance with the provisions of its own legislation, hand such persons over for trial to another High Contracting Party concerned, provided such High Contracting Party has made out a prima facie case. Each High Contracting Party shall take measures necessary for the suppression of all acts contrary to the provisions of the present Convention other than the grave breaches defined in the following Article. In all circumstances, the accused persons shall benefit by safeguards of proper trial and defence, which shall not be less favourable than those provided by Article 105 and those following of the Geneva Convention relative to the Treatment of Prisoners of War of August 12, 1949.

Article 147

Grave breaches to which the preceding Article relates shall be those involving any of the following acts, if committed against persons or property protected by the present Convention: wilful killing, torture or inhuman treatment, including biological experiments, wilfully causing great suffering or serious injury to body or health, unlawful deportation or transfer or unlawful confinement of a protected person, compelling a protected person to serve in the forces of a hostile Power, or wilfully depriving a protected person of the rights of fair and regular trial prescribed in the present Convention, taking of hostages and extensive destruction and appropriation of property, not justified by military necessity and carried out unlawfully and wantonly.

Article 148

No High Contracting Party shall be allowed to absolve itself or any other High Contracting Party of any liability incurred by itself or by another High Contracting Party in respect of breaches referred to in the preceding Article.

Article 149

At the request of a Party to the conflict, an enquiry shall be instituted, in a manner to be decided between the interested Parties, concerning any alleged violation of the Convention. If agreement has not been reached concerning the procedure for the enquiry, the Parties should agree on the choice of an umpire who will decide upon the procedure to be followed. Once the violation has been established, the Parties to the conflict shall put an end to it and shall repress it with the least possible delay.

Section II
Final provisions

Article 150

The present Convention is established in English and in French. Both texts are equally authentic.
The Swiss Federal Council shall arrange for official translations of the Convention to be made in the Russian and Spanish languages. * * *

Article 153

The present Convention shall come into force six months after not less than two instruments of ratification have been deposited. Thereafter, it shall come into force for each High Contracting Party six months after the deposit of the instrument of ratification.

Article 154

In the relations between the Powers who are bound by The Hague Conventions respecting the Laws and Customs of War on Land, whether that of 29 July, 1899, or that of 18 October, 1907, and who are parties to the present Convention, this last Convention shall be supplementary to Sections II and III of the Regulations annexed to the above-mentioned Conventions of The Hague. * * *

Article 158

Each of the High Contracting Parties shall be at liberty to denounce the present Convention.
The denunciation shall be notified in writing to the Swiss Federal Council, which shall transmit it to the Governments of all the High Contracting Parties. The denunciation shall take effect one year after the notification thereof has been made to the Swiss Federal Council. However, a denunciation of which notification has been made at a time when the denouncing Power is involved in a conflict shall not take effect until peace has been concluded, and until after operations connected with the release, repatriation and re-establishment of the persons protected by the present Convention have been terminated. The denunciation shall have effect only in respect of the denouncing Power. It shall in no way impair the obligations which the Parties to the conflict shall remain bound to fulfil by virtue of the principles of the law of nations, as they result from the usages established among civilized peoples, from the laws of humanity and the dictates of the public conscience.

Article 159

The Swiss Federal Council shall register the present Convention with the Secretariat of the United Nations. The Swiss Federal Council shall also inform the Secretariat of the United Nations of all ratifications, accessions and denunciations received by it with respect to the present Convention. * * *

PROTOCOL ADDITIONAL TO THE GENEVA CONVENTIONS OF 12 AUGUST 1949, AND RELATING TO THE PROTECTION OF VICTIMS OF INTERNATIONAL ARMED CONFLICTS (PROTOCOL I) (1977)

Protocol Additional to the Geneva Conventions of 12 August 1949, and Relating to the Protection of Victims of International Armed Conflicts (Protocol I), *adopted* June 8, 1977, 1125 U.N.T.S. 3

Part I
GENERAL PROVISIONS

Article 1. General principles and scope of application

1. The High Contracting Parties undertake to respect and to ensure respect for this Protocol in all circumstances.

2. In cases not covered by this Protocol or by other international agreements, civilians and combatants remain under the protection and authority of the principles of international law derived from established custom, from the principles of humanity and from the dictates of public conscience.

3. This Protocol, which supplements the Geneva Conventions of 12 August 1949 for the protection of war victims, shall apply in the situations referred to in Article 2 common to those Conventions.

4. The situations referred to in the preceding paragraph include armed conflicts in which peoples are fighting against colonial domination and alien occupation and against racist regimes in the exercise of their right of self-determination, as enshrined in the Charter of the United Nations and the Declaration on Principles of International Law concerning Friendly Relations and Co-operation among States in accordance with the Charter of the United Nations.

Article 2. Definitions

For the purposes of this Protocol:

(a) "First Convention", "Second Convention", "Third Convention" and "Fourth Convention" mean, respectively, the Geneva Convention for the Amelioration of the Condition of the Wounded and Sick in Armed Forces in the Field of 12 August 1949; the Geneva Convention for the Amelioration of the Condition of Wounded, Sick and Shipwrecked Members of Armed Forces at Sea of 12 August 1949; the Geneva Convention relative to the Treatment of Prisoners of War of 12 August 1949; the Geneva Convention relative to the Protection of Civilian Persons in Time of War of 12 August 1949; "the Conventions" means the four Geneva Conventions of 12 August 1949 for the protection of war victims;

(b) "Rules of international law applicable in armed conflict" means the rules applicable in armed conflict set forth in international agreements to which the Parties to the conflict are Parties and the generally recognized principles and rules of international law which are applicable to armed conflict;

(c) "Protecting Power" means a neutral or other State not a Party to the conflict which has been designated by a Party to the conflict and accepted by the adverse Party and has agreed to carry out the functions assigned to a Protecting Power under the Conventions and this Protocol;

(d) "Substitute" means an organization acting in place of a Protecting Power in accordance with Article 5.

Article 3. Beginning and end of application

Without prejudice to the provisions which are applicable at all times:

(a) The Conventions and this Protocol shall apply from the beginning of any situation referred to in Article 1 of this Protocol;

(b) The application of the Conventions and of this Protocol shall cease, in the territory of Parties to the conflict, on the general close of military operations and, in the case of occupied territories, on the termination of the occupation, except, in either circumstance, for those persons whose final release, repatriation or re-establishment takes place thereafter. These persons shall continue to benefit from the relevant provisions of the Conventions and of this Protocol until their final release, repatriation or re-establishment.

Article 4. Legal status of the Parties to the conflict

The application of the Conventions and of this Protocol, as well as the conclusion of the agreements provided for therein, shall not affect the legal status of the Parties to the conflict. Neither the occupation of a territory nor the application of the Conventions and this Protocol shall affect the legal status of the territory in question.

Article 5. Appointment of Protecting Powers and of their substitute

1. It is the duty of the Parties to a conflict from the beginning of that conflict to secure the supervision and implementation of the Conventions and of this Protocol by the application of the system of Protecting Powers, including inter alia the designation and acceptance of those Powers, in accordance with the following paragraphs. Protecting Powers shall have the duty of safeguarding the interests of the Parties to the conflict.

2. From the beginning of a situation referred to in Article 1, each Party to the conflict shall without delay designate a Protecting Power for the purpose of applying the Conventions and this Protocol and shall, likewise without delay and for the same purpose, permit the activities of a Protecting Power which has been accepted by it as such after designation by the adverse Party.

3. If a Protecting Power has not been designated or accepted from the beginning of a situation referred to in Article 1, the International Committee of the Red Cross, without prejudice to the right of any other impartial humanitarian organization to do likewise, shall offer its good offices to the Parties to the conflict with a view to the designation without delay of a Protecting Power to which the Parties to the conflict consent. For that purpose it may, inter alia , ask each Party to provide it with a list of at least five States which that Party considers acceptable to act as Protecting Power on its behalf in relation to an adverse Party, and ask each adverse Party to provide a list of at least five States which it would accept as the Protecting Power of the first Party; these lists shall be communicated to the Committee within two weeks after the receipt of the request; it shall compare them and seek the agreement of any proposed State named on both lists.

4. If, despite the foregoing, there is no Protecting Power, the Parties to the conflict shall accept without delay an offer which may be made by the International Committee of the Red Cross or by any other organization which offers all guarantees of impartiality and efficacy, after due consultations with the said Parties and taking into account the result of these consultations, to act as a substitute. The functioning of such a substitute is subject to the consent of the Parties to the conflict; every effort shall be made by the Parties to the conflict to facilitate the operations of the substitute in the performance of its tasks under the Conventions and this Protocol.

5. In accordance with Article 4, the designation and acceptance of Protecting Powers for the purpose of applying the Conventions and this Protocol shall not affect the legal status of the Parties to the conflict or of any territory, including occupied territory.

6. The maintenance of diplomatic relations between Parties to the conflict or the entrusting of the protection of a Party's interests and those of its nationals to a third State in accordance with the rules of international law relating to diplomatic relations is no obstacle to the designation of Protecting Powers for the purpose of applying the Conventions and this Protocol.

7. Any subsequent mention in this Protocol of a Protecting Power includes also a substitute.

Article 6. Qualified persons

1. The High Contracting Parties shall, also in peacetime, endeavour, with the assistance of the national Red Cross (Red Crescent, Red Lion and Sun) Societies, to train qualified personnel to facilitate the application of the Conventions and of this Protocol, and in particular the activities of the Protecting Powers.

2. The recruitment and training of such personnel are within domestic jurisdiction.

3. The International Committee of the Red Cross shall hold at the disposal of the High Contracting Parties the lists of persons so trained which the High Contracting Parties may have established and may have transmitted to it for that purpose.

4. The conditions governing the employment of such personnel outside the national territory shall, in each case, be the subject of special agreements between the Parties concerned.

Article 7. Meetings

The depositary of this Protocol shall convene a meeting of the High Contracting Parties, at the request of one or more of the said Parties and upon the approval of the majority of the said Parties, to consider general problems concerning the application of the Conventions and of the Protocol.

Part II
WOUNDED, SICK AND SHIPWRECKED

Section I. General protection

Article 8. Terminology

For the purposes of this Protocol:

(a) "Wounded" and "sick" mean persons, whether military or civilian, who, because of trauma, disease or other physical or mental disorder or disability, are in need of medical assistance or care and who refrain from any act of hostility. These terms also cover maternity cases, new-born babies and other persons who may be in need of immediate medical assistance or care, such as the infirm or expectant mothers, and who refrain from any act of hostility;

(b) "Shipwrecked" means persons, whether military or civilian, who are in peril at sea or in other waters as a result of misfortune affecting them or the vessel or aircraft carrying them and who refrain from any act of hostility. These persons, provided that they continue to refrain from any act of hostility, shall continue to be considered shipwrecked during their rescue until they acquire another status under the Conventions or this Protocol;

(c) "Medical personnel" means those persons assigned, by a Party to the conflict, exclusively to the medical purposes enumerated under subparagraph (e) or to the administration of medical units or to the operation or administration of medical transports. Such assignments may be either permanent or temporary. The term includes:

(i) Medical personnel of a Party to the conflict, whether military or civilian, including those described in the First and Second Conventions, and those assigned to civil defence organizations;

(ii) Medical personnel of national Red Cross (Red Crescent, Red Lion and Sun) Societies and other national voluntary aid societies duly recognized and authorized by a Party to the conflict;

(iii) Medical personnel of medical units or medical transports described in Article 9, paragraph 2;

(d) "Religious personnel" means military or civilian persons, such as chaplains, who are exclusively engaged in the work of their ministry and attached:

(i) To the armed forces of a Party to the conflict;

(ii) To medical units or medical transports of a Party to the conflict;

(iii) To medical units or medical transports described in Article 9, paragraph 2; or

(iv) To civil defence organizations of a Party to the conflict.

The attachment of religious personnel may be either permanent or temporary, and the relevant provisions mentioned under sub-paragraph (k) apply to them;

(e) "Medical units" means establishments and other units, whether military or civilian, organized for medical purposes, namely the search for, collection, transportation, diagnosis or treatment- including first-aid treatment-of the wounded, sick and shipwrecked, or for the prevention of disease. The term includes, for example, hospitals and other similar units, blood transfusion centres, preventive medicine centres and institutes, medical depots and the medical and pharmaceutical stores of such units. Medical units may be fixed or mobile, permanent or temporary;

(f) "Medical transportation" means the conveyance by land, water or air of the wounded, sick, shipwrecked, medical personnel, religious personnel, medical equipment or medical supplies protected by the Conventions and by this Protocol;

(g) "Medical transports" means any means of transportation. whether military or civilian, permanent or temporary, assigned exclusively to medical transportation and under the control of a competent authority of a Party to the conflict;

(h) "Medical vehicles" means any medical transports by land;

(i) "Medical ships and craft'' means any medical transports by water;

(j) "Medical aircraft" means any medical transports by air;

(k) "Permanent medical personnel'', "permanent medical units" and "permanent medical transports" mean those assigned exclusively to medical purposes for an indeterminate period. "Temporary medical personnel", "temporary medical units" and "temporary medical transports" mean those devoted exclusively to medical purposes for limited periods during the whole of such periods. Unless otherwise specified, the terms "medical personnel", "medical units" and "medical transports" cover both permanent and temporary categories;

(l) "Distinctive emblem" means the distinctive emblem of the red cross, red crescent or red lion and sun on a white ground when used for the protection of medical units and transports, or medical and religious personnel, equipment or supplies;

(m) "Distinctive signal" means any signal or message specified for the identification exclusively of medical units or transports in Chapter III of Annex I to this Protocol.

Article 9. Field of application

1. This Part, the provisions of which are intended to ameliorate the condition of the wounded, sick and shipwrecked, shall apply to all those affected by a situation referred to in Article 1, without any adverse distinction founded on race, colour, sex, language, religion or belief, political or other opinion, national or social origin, wealth, birth or other status, or on any other similar criteria.

2. The relevant provisions of Articles 27 and 32 of the First Convention shall apply to permanent medical units and transports (other than hospital ships, to which Article 25 of the Second Convention applies) and their personnel made available to a Party to the conflict for humanitarian purposes:

(a) By a neutral or other State which is not a Party to that conflict;

(b) By a recognized and authorized aid society of such a State;

(c) By an impartial international humanitarian organization.

Article 10. Protection and care

1. All the wounded, sick and shipwrecked, to whichever Party they belong, shall be respected and protected.

2. In all circumstances they shall be treated humanely and shall receive, to the fullest extent practicable and with the least possible delay, the medical care and attention required by their condition. There shall be no distinction among them founded on any grounds other than medical ones.

Article 11. Protection of persons

1. The physical or mental health and integrity of persons who are in the power of the adverse Party or who are interned, detained or otherwise deprived of liberty as a result of a situation referred to in Article 1 shall not be endangered by any unjustified act or omission. Accordingly, it is prohibited to subject the persons described in this Article to any medical procedure which is not indicated by the state of health of the person concerned and which is not consistent with generally accepted medical standards which would be applied under similar medical circumstances to persons who are nationals of the Party conducting the procedure and who are in no way deprived of liberty.

2. It is, in particular, prohibited to carry out on such persons, even with their consent:

(a) Physical mutilations;

(b) Medical or scientific experiments;

(c) Removal of tissue or organs for transplantation,

except where these acts are justified in conformity with the conditions provided for in paragraph 1.

3. Exceptions to the prohibition in paragraph 2 (c) may be made only in the case of donations of blood for transfusion or of skin for grafting, provided that they are given voluntarily and without any coercion or inducement, and then only for therapeutic purposes, under conditions consistent with generally accepted medical standards and controls designed for the benefit of both the donor and the recipient.

4. Any wilful act or omission which seriously endangers the physical or mental health or integrity of any person who is in the power of a Party other than the one on which he depends and which either violates any of the prohibitions in paragraphs 1 and 2 or fails to comply with the requirements of paragraph 3 shall be a grave breach of this Protocol.

5. The persons described in paragraph 1 have the right to refuse any surgical operation. In case of refusal, medical personnel shall endeavour to obtain a written statement to that effect, signed or acknowledged by the patient.

6. Each Party to the conflict shall keep a medical record for every donation of blood for transfusion or skin for grafting by persons referred to in paragraph 1, if that donation is made under the responsibility of that Party. In addition, each Party to the conflict shall endeavour to keep a record of all medical procedures undertaken with respect to any person who is interned, detained or otherwise deprived of liberty as a result of a situation referred to in Article 1. These records shall be available at all times for inspection by the Protecting Power.

Article 12. Protection of medical units

1. Medical units shall be respected and protected at all times and shall not be the object of attack.

2. Paragraph 1 shall apply to civilian medical units, provided that they:

    (a) Belong to one of the Parties to the conflict;

    (b) Are recognized and authorized by the competent authority of one of the Parties to the conflict; or

    (c) Are authorized in conformity with Article 9, paragraph 2, of this Protocol or Article 27 of the First Convention.

3. The Parties to the conflict are invited to notify each other of the location of their fixed medical units. The absence of such notification shall not exempt any of the Parties from the obligation to comply with the provisions of paragraph 1.

4. Under no circumstances shall medical units be used in an attempt to shield military objectives from attack. Whenever possible, the Parties to the conflict shall ensure that medical units are so sited that attacks against military objectives do not imperil their safety.

Article 13. Discontinuance of protection of civilian medical units

1. The protection to which civilian medical units are entitled shall not cease unless they are used to commit, outside their humanitarian function, acts harmful to the enemy. Protection may, however, cease only after a warning has been given setting, whenever appropriate, a reasonable time-limit, and after such warning has remained unheeded.

2. The following shall not be considered as acts harmful to the enemy;

    (a) That the personnel of the unit are equipped with light individual weapons for their own defence or for that of the wounded and sick in their charge;

    (b) That the unit is guarded by a picket or by sentries or by an escort;

    (c) That small arms and ammunition taken from the wounded and sick, and not yet handed to the proper service, are found in the units;

    (d) That members of the armed forces or other combatants are in the unit for medical reasons.

Article 14. Limitations on requisition of civilian medical units

1. The Occupying Power has the duty to ensure that the medical needs of the civilian population in occupied territory continue to be satisfied.

2. The Occupying Power shall not, therefore, requisition civilian medical units, their equipment, their matériel or the services of their personnel, so long as these resources are necessary for the provision of adequate medical services for the civilian population and for the continuing medical care of any wounded and sick already under treatment.

3. Provided that the general rule in paragraph 2 continues to be observed, the Occupying Power may requisition the said resources, subject to the following particular conditions:

    (a) That the resources are necessary for the adequate and immediate medical treatment of the wounded and sick members of the armed forces of the Occupying Power or of prisoners of war;

    (b) That the requisition continues only while such necessity exists; and

    (c) That immediate arrangements are made to ensure that the medical needs of the civilian population, as well as those of any wounded and sick under treatment who are affected by the requisition, continue to be satisfied.

Article 15. Protection of civilian medical and religious personnel

1. Civilian medical personnel shall be respected and protected.

2. If needed, all available help shall be afforded to civilian medical personnel in an area where civilian medical services are disrupted by reason of combat activity.

3. The Occupying Power shall afford civilian medical personnel in occupied territories every assistance to enable them to perform, to the best of their ability, their humanitarian functions. The Occupying Power may not require that, in the performance of those functions, such personnel shall give priority to the treatment of any person except on medical grounds. They shall not be compelled to carry out tasks which are not compatible with their humanitarian mission.

4. Civilian medical personnel shall have access to any place where their services are essential, subject to such supervisory and safety measures as the relevant Party to the conflict may deem necessary.

5. Civilian religious personnel shall be respected and protected. The provisions of the Conventions and of this Protocol concerning the protection and identification of medical personnel shall apply equally to such persons.

Article 16. General protection of medical duties

1. Under no circumstances shall any person be punished for carrying out medical activities compatible with medical ethics, regardless of the person benefiting therefrom.

2. Persons engaged in medical activities shall not be compelled to perform acts or to carry out work contrary to the rules of medical ethics or to other medical rules designed for the benefit of the wounded and sick or to the provisions of the Conventions or of this Protocol, or to refrain from performing acts or from carrying out work required by those rules and provisions.

3. No person engaged in medical activities shall be compelled to give to anyone belonging either to an adverse Party, or to his own Party except as required by the law of the latter Party, any information concerning the wounded and sick who are, or who have been, under his care, if such information would, in his opinion, prove harmful to the patients concerned or to their families. Regulations for the compulsory notification of communicable diseases shall, however, be respected.

Article 17. Role of the civilian population and of aid societies

1. The civilian population shall respect the wounded, sick and shipwrecked, even if they belong to the adverse Party, and shall commit no act of violence against them. The civilian population and aid societies, such as national Red Cross (Red Crescent, Red Lion and Sun) Societies, shall be permitted, even on their own initiative, to collect and care for the wounded, sick and shipwrecked, even in invaded or occupied areas. No one shall be harmed, prosecuted, convicted or punished for such humanitarian acts.

2. The Parties to the conflict may appeal to the civilian population and the aid societies referred to in paragraph 1 to collect and care for the wounded, sick and shipwrecked, and to search for the dead and report their location; they shall grant both protection and the necessary facilities to those who respond to this appeal. If the adverse Party gains or regains control of the area, that Party also shall afford the same protection and facilities for so long as they are needed.

Article 18. Identification

1. Each Party to the conflict shall endeavour to ensure that medical and religious personnel and medical units and transports are identifiable.

2. Each Party to the conflict shall also endeavour to adopt and to implement methods and procedures which will make it possible to recognize medical units and transports which use the distinctive emblem and distinctive signals.

3. In occupied territory and in areas where fighting is taking place or is likely to take place, civilian medical personnel and civilian religious personnel should be recognizable by the distinctive emblem and an identity card certifying their status. * * *

Article 19. Neutral and other States not Parties to the conflict

Neutral and other States not Parties to the conflict shall apply the relevant provisions of this Protocol to persons protected by this Part who may be received or interned within their territory, and to any dead of the Parties to that conflict whom they may find.

Article 20. Prohibition of reprisals

Reprisals against the persons and objects protected by this Part are prohibited.

Section II. Medical transportation

Article 21. Medical vehicles

Medical vehicles shall be respected and protected in the same way as mobile medical units under the Conventions and this Protocol.

Article 22. Hospitals ships and coastal rescue craft

1. The provisions of the Conventions relating to:

    (a) Vessels described in Articles 22, 24, 25 and 27 of the Second Convention,

    (b) Their lifeboats and small craft,

    (c) Their personnel and crews; and

    (d) The wounded, sick and shipwrecked on board,

shall also apply where these vessels carry civilian wounded, sick and shipwrecked who do not belong to any of the categories mentioned in Article 13 of the Second Convention. Such civilians shall not, however, be subject to surrender to any Party which is not their own, or to capture at sea. If they find themselves in the power of a Party to the conflict other than their own they shall be covered by the Fourth Convention and by this Protocol.

2. The protection provided by the Conventions to vessels described in Article 25 of the Second Convention shall extend to hospital ships made available for humanitarian purposes to a Party to the conflict:

    (a) By a neutral or other State which is not a Party to that conflict; or

    (b) By an impartial international humanitarian organization,

provided that, in either case, the requirements set out in that Article are complied with.

3. Small craft described in Article 27 of the Second Convention shall be protected even if the notification envisaged by that Article has not been made. The Parties to the conflict are, nevertheless, invited to inform each other of any details of such craft which will facilitate their identification and recognition. * * *

Article 24. Protection of medical aircraft

Medical aircraft shall be respected and protected, subject to the provisions of this Part.

Article 25. Medical aircraft in areas not controlled by an adverse Party

In and over land areas physically controlled by friendly forces, or in and over sea areas not physically controlled by an adverse Party, the respect and protection of medical aircraft of a Party to the conflict is not dependent on any agreement with an adverse Party. For greater safety, however, a Party to the conflict operating its medical aircraft in these areas may notify the adverse Party, as provided in Article 29, in particular when such aircraft are making flights bringing them within range of surface-to-air weapons systems of the adverse Party.

Article 26. Medical aircraft in contact or similar zones

1. In and over those parts of the contact zone which are physically controlled by friendly forces and in and over those areas the physical control of which is not clearly established, protection for medical aircraft can be fully effective only by prior agreement between the competent military authorities of the Parties to the conflict, as provided for in Article 29. Although, in the absence of such an agreement, medical aircraft operate at their own risk, they shall nevertheless be respected after they have been recognized as such.

2. "Contact zone" means any area on land where the forward elements of opposing forces are in contact with each other, especially where they are exposed to direct fire from the ground.

Article 27. Medical aircraft in areas controlled by an adverse Party

1. The medical aircraft of a Party to the conflict shall continue to be protected while flying over land or sea areas physically controlled by an adverse Patty, provided that prior agreement to such flights has been obtained from the competent authority of the adverse Party.

2. A medical aircraft which flies over an area physically controlled by an adverse Party without, or in deviation from the terms of, an agreement provided for in paragraph 1, either through navigational error or because of an emergency affecting the safety of the flight, shall make every effort to identify itself and to inform the adverse Party of the circumstances. As soon as such medical aircraft has been recognized by the adverse Party, that Party shall make all reasonable efforts to give the order to land or to alight on water,

referred to in Article 30, paragraph 1, or to take other measures to safeguard its own interests, and, in either case, to allow the aircraft time for compliance, before resorting to an attack against the aircraft.

Article 28. Restrictions on operations of medical aircraft

1. The Parties to the conflict are prohibited from using their medical aircraft to attempt to acquire any military advantage over an adverse Party. The presence of medical aircraft shall not be used in an attempt to render military objectives immune from attack.
2. Medical aircraft shall not be used to collect or transmit intelligence data and shall not carry any equipment intended for such purposes. They are prohibited from carrying any persons or cargo not included within the definition in Article 8, subparagraph (f). The carrying on board of the personal effects of the occupants or of equipment intended solely to facilitate navigation, communication or identification shall not be considered as prohibited.
3. Medical aircraft shall not carry any armament except small arms and ammunition taken from the wounded, sick and shipwrecked on board and not yet handed to the proper service, and such light individual weapons as may be necessary to enable the medical personnel on board to defend themselves and the wounded, sick and shipwrecked in their charge.
4. While carrying out the flights referred to in Articles 26 and 27, medical aircraft shall not, except by prior agreement with the adverse Party, be used to search for the wounded, sick and shipwrecked

Article 29. Notifications and agreements concerning medical aircraft

1. Notifications under Article 25, or requests for prior agreement under Articles 26, 27, 28 (paragraph 4), or 31 shall state the proposed number of medical aircraft, their flight plans and means of identification, and shall be understood to mean that every flight will be carried out in compliance with Article 28.
2. A Party which receives a notification given under Article 25 shall at once acknowledge receipt of such notification.
3. A Party which receives a request for prior agreement under Articles 26, 27, 28 (paragraph 4), or 31 shall, as rapidly as possible, notify the requesting Party:

    (a) That the request is agreed to;

    (b) That the request is denied; or

    (c) Of reasonable alternative proposals to the request. It may also propose a prohibition or restriction of other flights in the area during the time involved. If the Party which submitted the request accepts the alternative proposals, it shall notify the other Party of such acceptance.

4. The Parties shall take the necessary measures to ensure that notifications and agreements can be made rapidly.
5. The Parties shall also take the necessary measures to disseminate rapidly the substance of any such notifications and agreements to the military units concerned and shall instruct those units regarding the means of identification that will be used by the medical aircraft in question.

Article 30. Landing and inspection of medical aircraft

1. Medical aircraft flying over areas which are physically controlled by an adverse Party, or over areas the physical control of which is not clearly established, may be ordered to land or to alight on water, as appropriate, to permit inspection in accordance with the following paragraphs. Medical aircraft shall obey any such order.
2. If such an aircraft lands or alights on water, whether ordered to do so or for other reasons, it may be subjected to inspection solely to determine the matters referred to in paragraphs 3 and 4. Any such inspection shall be commenced without delay and shall be conducted expeditiously. The inspecting Party shall not require the wounded and sick to be removed from the aircraft unless their removal is essential for the inspection. That Party shall in any event ensure that the condition of the wounded and sick is not adversely affected by the inspection or by the removal.
3. If the inspection discloses that the aircraft:

    (a) Is a medical aircraft within the meaning of Article 8, subparagraph (j);

    (b) Is not in violation of the conditions prescribed in Article 28; and

    (c) Has not flown without or in breach of a prior agreement where such agreement is required;

the aircraft and those of its occupants who belong to the adverse Party or to a neutral or other State not a Party to the conflict shall be authorized to continue the flight without delay.
4. If the inspection discloses that the aircraft:

(a) Is not a medical aircraft within the meaning of Article 8, subparagraph (j);

(b) Is in violation of the conditions prescribed in Article 28; or,

(c) Has flown without or in breach of a prior agreement where such agreement is required; the aircraft may be seized. Its occupants shall be treated in conformity with the relevant provisions of the Conventions and of this Protocol. Any aircraft seized which had been assigned as a permanent medical aircraft may be used thereafter only as a medical aircraft.

Article 31. Neutral or other States not Parties to the conflict

1. Except by prior agreement, medical aircraft shall not fly over or land in the territory of a neutral or other State not a Party to the conflict. However, with such an agreement, they shall be respected throughout their flight and also for the duration of any calls in the territory. Nevertheless they shall obey any summons to land or to alight on water, as appropriate.

2. Should a medical aircraft, in the absence of an agreement or in deviation from the terms of an agreement, fly over the territory of a neutral or other State not a Party to the conflict, either through navigational error or because of an emergency affecting the safety of the flight, it shall make every effort to give notice of the flight and to identify itself. As soon as such medical aircraft is recognized, that State shall make all reasonable efforts to give the order to land or to alight on water referred to in Article 30, paragraph 1, or to take other measures to safeguard its own interests, and in either case, to allow the aircraft time for compliance, before resorting to an attack against the aircraft.

3. If a medical aircraft, either by agreement or in the circumstances mentioned in paragraph 2, lands or alights on water in the territory of a neutral or other State not Party to the conflict, whether ordered to do so or for other reasons, the aircraft shall be subject to inspection for the purposes of determining whether it is in fact a medical aircraft. The inspection shall be commenced without delay and shall be conducted expeditiously. The inspecting Party shall not require the wounded and sick of the Party operating the aircraft to be removed from it unless their removal is essential for the inspection. The inspecting Party shall in any event ensure that the condition of the wounded and sick is not adversely affected by the inspection or the removal. If the inspection discloses that the aircraft is in fact a medical aircraft, the aircraft with its occupants, other than those who must be detained in accordance with the rules of international law applicable in armed conflict, shall be allowed to resume its flight, and reasonable facilities shall be given for the continuation of the flight. If the inspection discloses that the aircraft is not a medical aircraft, it shall be seized and the occupants treated in accordance with paragraph 4.

4. The wounded, sick and shipwrecked disembarked, otherwise than temporarily, from a medical aircraft with the consent of the local authorities in the territory of a neutral or other State not a Party to the conflict shall, unless agreed otherwise between that State and the Parties to the conflict, be detained by that Sate where so required by the rules of international law applicable in armed conflict, in such a manner that they cannot again take part in the hostilities. The cost of hospital treatment and internment shall be borne by the State to which those persons belong.

5. Neutral or other States not Parties to the conflict shall apply any conditions and restrictions on the passage of medical aircraft over, or on the landing of medical aircraft in, their territory equally to all Parties to the conflict.

Section III. Missing and dead persons

Article 32. General principle

In the implementation of this Section, the activities of the High Contracting Parties, of the Parties to the conflict and of the international humanitarian organizations mentioned in the Conventions and in this Protocol shall be prompted mainly by the right of families to know the fate of their relatives.

Article 33. Missing persons

1. As soon as circumstances permit, and at the latest from the end of active hostilities, each Party to the conflict shall search for the persons who have been reported missing by an adverse Party. Such adverse Party shall transmit all relevant information concerning such persons in order to facilitate such searches.

2. In order to facilitate the gathering of information pursuant to the preceding paragraph, each Party to the conflict shall, with respect to persons who would not receive more favourable consideration under the Conventions and this Protocol:

(a) Record the information specified in Article 138 of the Fourth Convention in respect of such persons who have been detained, imprisoned or otherwise held in captivity for more than two weeks as a result of hostilities or occupation, or who have died during any period of detention;

(b) To the fullest extent possible, facilitate and, if need be, carry out the search for and the recording of information concerning such persons if they have died in other circumstances as a result of hostilities or occupation.

3. Information concerning persons reported missing pursuant to paragraph 1 and requests for such information shall be transmitted either directly or through the Protecting Power or the Central Tracing Agency of the International Committee of the Red Cross or national Red Cross (Red Crescent, Red Lion and Sun) Societies. Where the information is not transmitted through the International Committee of the Red Cross and its Central Tracing Agency, each Party to the conflict shall ensure that such information is also supplied to the Central Tracing Agency.

4. The Parties to the conflict shall endeavour to agree on arrangements for teams to search for, identify and recover the dead from battlefield areas, including arrangements, if appropriate, for such teams to be accompanied by personnel of the adverse Party while carrying out the missions in areas controlled by the adverse Party. Personnel of such teams shall be respected and protected while exclusively carrying out these duties.

Article 34. Remains of deceased

1. The remains of persons who have died for reasons related to occupation or in detention resulting from occupation or hostilities and those of persons not nationals of the country in which they have died as a result of hostilities shall be respected, and the gravesites of all such persons shall be respected, maintained and marked as provided for in Article 130 of the Fourth Convention, where their remains or gravesites would not receive more favourable consideration under the Conventions and this Protocol.

2. As soon as circumstances and the relations between the adverse Parties permit, the High Contracting Parties in whose territories graves and, as the case may be, other locations of the remains of persons who have died as a result of hostilities or during occupation or in detention are situated, shall conclude agreements in order:

(a) To facilitate access to the gravesites by relatives of the deceased and by representatives of official graves registration services and to regulate the practical arrangements for such access;

(b) To protect and maintain such gravesites permanently;

(c) To facilitate the return of the remains of the deceased and of personal effects to the country upon its request or, unless that country objects, upon the request of the next of kin.

3. In the absence of the agreements provided for in paragraph 2 (b) or (c) and if the country of such deceased is not willing to arrange at its expense for the maintenance of such gravesites, the High Contracting Party in whose territory the gravesites are situated may offer to facilitate the return of the remains of the deceased to the country. Where such an offer has not been accepted the High Contracting Party may, after the expiry of five years from the date of the offer and upon due notice to the country, adopt the arrangements laid down in its own laws relating to cemeteries and graves.

4. A High Contracting Party in whose territory the gravesites referred to in this Article are situated shall be permitted to exhume the remains only:

(a) In accordance with paragraphs 2 (c) and 3; or

(b) Where exhumation is a matter of overriding public necessity, including cases of medical and investigative necessity, in which case the High Contracting Party shall at all times respect the remains, and shall give notice to the country of its intention to exhume the remains together with details of the intended place of reinterment.

Part III
METHODS AND MEANS OF WARFARE COMBATANT AND PRISONER-OF-WAR STATUS

Section I.-Methods and means of warfare

Article 35. Basic rules

1. In any armed conflict, the right of the Parties to the conflict to choose methods or means of warfare is not unlimited.

2. It is prohibited to employ weapons, projectiles and material and methods of warfare of a nature to cause superfluous injury or unnecessary suffering.

3. It is prohibited to employ methods or means of warfare which are intended, or may be expected, to cause widespread, long-term and severe damage to the natural environment.

Article 36. New weapons

In the study, development, acquisition or adoption of a new weapon, means or method of warfare, a High Contracting Party is under an obligation to determine whether its employment would, in some or all circumstances, be prohibited by this Protocol or by any other rule of international law applicable to the High Contracting Party.

Article 37. Prohibition of perfidy

1. It is prohibited to kill, injure or capture an adversary by resort to perfidy. Acts inviting the confidence of an adversary to lead him to believe that he is entitled to, or is obliged to accord, protection under the rules of international law applicable in armed conflict, with intent to betray that confidence, shall constitute perfidy. The following acts are examples of perfidy:

    (a) The feigning of an intent to negotiate under a flag of truce or of a surrender;

    (b) The feigning of an incapacitation by wounds or sickness;

    (c) The feigning of civilian, non-combatant status; and

    (d) The feigning of protected status by the use of signs, emblems or uniforms of the United Nations or of neutral or other States not Parties to the conflict.

2. Ruses of war are not prohibited. Such ruses are acts which are intended to mislead an adversary or to induce him to act recklessly but which infringe no rule of international law applicable in armed conflict and which are not perfidious because they do not invite the confidence of an adversary with respect to protection under that law. The following are examples of such ruses: the use of camouflage, decoys, mock operations and misinformation.

Article 38. Recognized emblems

1. It is prohibited to make improper use of the distinctive emblem of the red cross, red crescent or red lion and sun or of other emblems, signs or signals provided for by the Conventions or by this Protocol. It is also prohibited to misuse deliberately in an armed conflict other internationally recognized protective emblems, signs or signals, including the flag of truce, and the protective emblem of cultural property.

2. It is prohibited to make use of the distinctive emblem of the United Nations, except as authorized by that Organization.

Article 39.B Emblems of nationality

1. It is prohibited to make use in an armed conflict of the flags or military emblems, insignia or uniforms of neutral or other States not Parties to the conflict.

2. It is prohibited to make use of the flags or military emblems, insignia or uniforms of adverse Parties while engaging in attacks or in order to shield, favour, protect or impede military operations.

3. Nothing in this Article or in Article 37, paragraph 1 (d), shall affect the existing generally recognized rules of international law applicable to espionage or to the use of flags in the conduct of armed conflict at sea.

Article 40. Quarter

It is prohibited to order that there shall be no survivors, to threaten an adversary therewith or to conduct hostilities on this basis.

Article 41. Safeguard of an enemy *hors de combat*

1. A person who is recognized or who, in the circumstances, should be recognized to be hors de combat shall not be made the object of attack.

2. A person is hors de combat if:

    (a) He is in the power of an adverse Party;

    (b) He clearly expresses an intention to surrender; or

    (c) He has been rendered unconscious or is otherwise incapacitated by wounds or sickness, and therefore is incapable of defending himself;

provided that in any of these cases he abstains from any hostile act and does not attempt to escape.

3. When persons entitled to protection as prisoners of war have fallen into the power of an adverse Party under unusual conditions of combat which prevent their evacuation as provided for in Part III, Section I, of the Third Convention, they shall be released and all feasible precautions shall be taken to ensure their safety.

Article 42. Occupants of aircraft

1. No person parachuting from an aircraft in distress shall be made the object of attack during his descent.

2. Upon reaching the ground in territory controlled by an adverse Party, a person who has parachuted from an aircraft in distress shall be given an opportunity to surrender before being made the object of attack, unless it is apparent that he is engaging in a hostile act.

3. Airborne troops are not protected by this Article.

Section II. Combatant and prisoner-of-war status

Article 43. Armed forces

1. The armed forces of a Party to a conflict consist of all organized armed forces, groups and units which are under a command responsible to that Party for the conduct of its subordinates, even if that Party is represented by a government or an authority not recognized by an adverse Party. Such armed forces shall be subject to an internal disciplinary system which, inter alia , shall enforce compliance with the rules of international law applicable in armed conflict.

2. Members of the armed forces of a Party to a conflict (other than medical personnel and chaplains covered by Article 33 of the Third Convention) are combatants, that is to say, they have the right to participate directly in hostilities.

3. Whenever a Party to a conflict incorporates a paramilitary or armed law enforcement agency into its armed forces it shall so notify the other Parties to the conflict.

Article 44. Combatants and prisoners of war

1. Any combatant, as defined in Article 43, who falls into the power of an adverse Party shall be a prisoner of war.

2. While all combatants are obliged to comply with the rules of international law applicable in armed conflict, violations of these rules shall not deprive a combatant of his right to be a combatant or, if he falls into the power of an adverse Party, of his right to be a prisoner of war, except as provided in paragraphs 3 and 4.

3. In order to promote the protection of the civilian population from the effects of hostilities, combatants are obliged to distinguish themselves from the civilian population while they are engaged in an attack or in a military operation preparatory to an attack. Recognizing, however, that there are situations in armed conflicts where, owing to the nature of the hostilities an armed combatant cannot so distinguish himself, he shall retain his status as a combatant, provided that, in such situations, he carries his arms openly:

    (a) During each military engagement, and

    (b) During such time as he is visible to the adversary while he is engaged in a military deployment preceding the launching of an attack in which he is to participate.

Acts which comply with the requirements of this paragraph shall not be considered as perfidious within the meaning of Article 37, paragraph 1 (c).

4. A combatant who falls into the power of an adverse Party while failing to meet the requirements set forth in the second sentence of paragraph 3 shall forfeit his right to be a prisoner of war, but he shall, nevertheless, be given protections equivalent in all respects to those accorded to prisoners of war by the Third Convention and by this Protocol. This protection includes protections equivalent to those accorded to prisoners of war by the Third Convention in the case where such a person is tried and punished for any offences he has committed.

5. Any combatant who falls into the power of an adverse Party while not engaged in an attack or in a military operation preparatory to an attack shall not forfeit his rights to be a combatant and a prisoner of war by virtue of his prior activities.

6. This Article is without prejudice to the right of any person to be a prisoner of war pursuant to Article 4 of the Third Convention.

7. This Article is not intended to change the generally accepted practice of States with respect to the wearing of the uniform by combatants assigned to the regular, uniformed armed units of a Party to the conflict.

8. In addition to the categories of persons mentioned in Article 13 of the First and Second Conventions, all members of the armed forces of a Party to the conflict, as defined in Article 43 of this Protocol, shall be entitled to protection under those Conventions if they are wounded or sick or, in the case of the Second Convention, shipwrecked at sea or in other waters.

Article 45. Protection of persons who have taken part in hostilities

1. A person who takes part in hostilities and falls into the power of an adverse Party shall be presumed to be a prisoner of war, and therefore shall be protected by the Third Convention, if he claims the status of prisoner of war, or if he appears to be entitled to such status, or if the Party on which he depends claims such status on his behalf by notification to the detaining Power or to the Protecting Power. Should any doubt arise as to whether any such person is entitled to the status of prisoner of war, he shall continue to have such status and, therefore, to be protected by the Third Convention and this Protocol until such time as his status has been determined by a competent tribunal.

2. If a person who has fallen into the power of an adverse Party is not held as a prisoner of war and is to be tried by that Party for an offence arising out of the hostilities, he shall have the right to assert his entitlement to prisoner-of-war status before a judicial tribunal and to have that question adjudicated. Whenever possible under the applicable procedure, this adjudication shall occur before the trial for the offence. The representatives of the Protecting Power shall be entitled to attend the proceedings in which that question is adjudicated, unless, exceptionally, the proceedings are held in camera in the interest of State security. In such a case the detaining Power shall advise the Protecting Power accordingly.

3. Any person who has taken part in hostilities, who is not entitled to prisoner-of-war status and who does not benefit from more favourable treatment in accordance with the Fourth Convention shall have the right at all times to the protection of Article 75 of this Protocol. In occupied territory, any such person, unless he is held as a spy, shall also be entitled, notwithstanding Article 5 of the Fourth Convention, to his rights of communication under that Convention.

Article 46. Spies

1. Notwithstanding any other provision of the Conventions or of this Protocol, any member of the armed forces of a Party to the conflict who falls into the power of an adverse Party while engaging in espionage shall not have the right to the status of prisoner of war and may be treated as a spy.

2. A member of the armed forces of a Party to the conflict who, on behalf of that Party and in territory controlled by an adverse Party, gathers or attempts to gather information shall not be considered as engaging in espionage if, while so acting, he is in the uniform of his armed forces.

3. A member of the armed forces of a Party to the conflict who is a resident of territory occupied by an adverse Party and who, on behalf of the Party on which he depends, gathers or attempts to gather information of military value within that territory shall not be considered as engaging in espionage unless he does so through an act of false pretences or deliberately in a clandestine manner. Moreover, such a resident shall not lose his right to the status of prisoner of war and may not be treated as a spy unless he is captured while engaging in espionage.

4. A member of the armed forces of a Party to the conflict who is not a resident of territory occupied by an adverse Party and who has engaged in espionage in that territory shall not lose his right to the status of prisoner of war and may not be treated as a spy unless he is captured before he has rejoined the armed forces to which he belongs.

Article 47. Mercenaries

1. A mercenary shall not have the right to be a combatant or a prisoner of war.

2. A mercenary is any person who:
   (a) Is specially recruited locally or abroad in order to fight in an armed conflict;
   (b) Does, in fact, take a direct part in the hostilities;
   (c) Is motivated to take part in the hostilities essentially by the desire for private gain and, in fact, is promised, by or on behalf of a Party to the conflict, material compensation substantially in excess of that promised or paid to combatants of similar ranks and functions in the armed forces of that Party;

(d) Is neither a national of a Party to the conflict nor a resident of territory controlled by a Party to the conflict;

(e) Is not a member of the armed forces of a Party to the conflict; and

(f) Has not been sent by a State which is not a Party to the conflict on official duty as a member of its armed forces.

PROTOCOL ADDITIONAL TO THE GENEVA CONVENTIONS OF 12 AUGUST 1949, AND RELATING TO THE PROTECTION OF VICTIMS OF NON-INTERNATIONAL ARMED CONFLICTS (PROTOCOL II) (1977)

Protocol Additional to the Geneva Conventions of 12 August 1949, and Relating to the Protection of Victims of Non-International Armed Conflicts (Protocol II), *adopted* June 8, 1977, 1125 U.N.T.S. 609

Part I
SCOPE OF THIS PROTOCOL

Article 1. Material field of application

1. This Protocol, which develops and supplements Article 3 common to the Geneva Conventions of 12 August 1949 without modifying its existing conditions of application, shall apply to all armed conflicts which are not covered by Article 1 of the Protocol Additional to the Geneva Conventions of 12 August 1949, and relating to the Protection of Victims of International Armed Conflicts (Protocol I) and which take place in the territory of a High Contracting Party between its armed forces and dissident armed forces or other organized armed groups which, under responsible command, exercise such control over a part of its territory as to enable them to carry out sustained and concerted military operations and to implement this Protocol.

2. This Protocol shall not apply to situations of internal disturbances and tensions, such as riots, isolated and sporadic acts of violence and other acts of a similar nature, as not being armed conflicts.

Article 2. Personal field of application

1. This Protocol shall be applied without any adverse distinction founded on race, colour, sex, language, religion or belief, political or other opinion, national or social origin, wealth, birth or other status, or on any other similar criteria (hereinafter referred to as "adverse distinction") to all persons affected by an armed conflict as defined in Article 1.

2. At the end of the armed conflict, all the persons who have been deprived of their liberty or whose liberty has been restricted for reasons related to such conflict, as well as those deprived of their liberty or whose liberty is restricted after the conflict for the same reasons, shall enjoy the protection of Articles 5 and 6 until the end of such deprivation or restriction of liberty.

Article 3. Non-intervention

1. Nothing in this Protocol shall be invoked for the purpose of affecting the sovereignty of a State or the responsibility of the government, by all legitimate means, to maintain or re-establish law and order in the State or to defend the national unity and territorial integrity of the State.

2. Nothing in this Protocol shall be invoked as a justification for intervening, directly or indirectly, for any reason whatever, in the armed conflict or in the internal or external affairs of the High Contracting Party in the territory of which that conflict occurs.

Part II
HUMANE TREATMENT

Article 4. Fundamental guarantees

1. All persons who do not take a direct part or who have ceased to take part in hostilities, whether or not their liberty has been restricted, are entitled to respect for their person, honour and convictions and

religious practices. They shall in all circumstances be treated humanely, without any adverse distinction. It is prohibited to order that there shall be no survivors.

2. Without prejudice to the generality of the foregoing, the following acts against the persons referred to in paragraph I are and shall remain prohibited at any time and in any place whatsoever:

> (a) Violence to the life, health and physical or mental well-being of persons, in particular murder as well as cruel treatment such as torture, mutilation or any form of corporal punishment;
>
> (b) Collective punishments;
>
> (c) Taking of hostages;
>
> (d) Acts of terrorism;
>
> (e) Outrages upon personal dignity, in particular humiliating and degrading treatment, rape, enforced prostitution and any form of indecent assault;
>
> (f) Slavery and the slave trade in all their forms;
>
> (g) Pillage;
>
> (h) Threats to commit any of the foregoing acts.

3. Children shall be provided with the care and aid they require, and in particular:

> (a) They shall receive an education, including religious and moral education, in keeping with the wishes of their parents, or in the absence of parents, of those responsible for their care;
>
> (b) All appropriate steps shall be taken to facilitate the reunion of families temporarily separated;
>
> (c) Children who have not attained the age of fifteen years shall neither be recruited in the armed forces or groups nor allowed to take part in hostilities;
>
> (d) The special protection provided by this Article to children who have not attained the age of fifteen years shall remain applicable to them if they take a direct part in hostilities despite the provisions of sub-paragraph (c) and are captured;
>
> (e) Measures shall be taken, if necessary, and whenever possible with the consent of their parents or persons who by law or custom are primarily responsible for their care, to remove children temporarily from the area in which hostilities are taking place to a safer area within the country and ensure that they are accompanied by persons responsible for their safety and well-being.

Article 5. Persons whose liberty has been restricted

1. In addition to the provisions of Article 4, the following provisions shall be respected as a minimum with regard to persons deprived of their liberty for reasons related to the armed conflict, whether they are interned or detained:

> (a) The wounded and the sick shall be treated in accordance with Article 7;
>
> (b) The persons referred to in this paragraph shall, to the same extent as the local civilian population, be provided with food and drinking water and be afforded safeguards as regards health and hygiene and protection against the rigours of the climate and the dangers of the armed conflict;
>
> (c) They shall be allowed to receive individual or collective relief;
>
> (d) They shall be allowed to practise their religion and, if requested and appropriate, to receive spiritual assistance from persons, such as chaplains, performing religious functions;
>
> (e) They shall, if made to work, have the benefit of working conditions and safeguards similar to those enjoyed by the local civilian population.

2. Those who are responsible for the internment or detention of the persons referred to in paragraph 1 shall also, within the limits of their capabilities, respect the following provisions relating to such persons:

> (a) Except when men and women of a family are accommodated together, women shall be held in quarters separated from those of men and shall be under the immediate supervision of women;
>
> (b) They shall be allowed to send and receive letters and cards, the number of which may be limited by the competent authority if it deems necessary;
>
> (c) Places of internment and detention shall not be located close to the combat zone. The persons referred to in paragraph 1 shall be evacuated when the places where they are interned or detained become particularly exposed to danger arising out of the armed conflict, if their evacuation can be carried out under adequate conditions of safety;
>
> (d) They shall have the benefit of medical examinations;
>
> (e) Their physical or mental health and integrity shall not be endangered by an unjustified act or omission. Accordingly, it is prohibited to subject the persons described in this Article to any medical procedure which is not indicated by the state of health of the person concerned, and which

is not consistent with the generally accepted medical standards applied to free persons under similar medical circumstances.

3. Persons who are not covered by paragraph 1 but whose liberty has been restricted in any way whatsoever for reasons related to the armed conflict shall be treated humanely in accordance with Article 4 and with paragraphs 1 (a), (c) and (d), and 2(b) of this Article.

4. If it is decided to release persons deprived of their liberty, necessary measures to ensure their safety shall be taken by those so deciding.

Article 6. Penal prosecutions

1. This Article applies to the prosecution and punishment of criminal offences related to the armed conflict.

2. No sentence shall be passed and no penalty shall be executed on a person found guilty of an offence except pursuant to a conviction pronounced by a court offering the essential guarantees of independence and impartiality. In particular:

> (a) The procedure shall provide for an accused to be informed without delay of the particulars of the offence alleged against him and shall afford the accused before and during his trial all necessary rights and means of defence;
> (b) No one shall be convicted of an offence except on the basis of individual penal responsibility;
> (c) No one shall be held guilty of any criminal offence on account of any act or omission which did not constitute a criminal offence, under the law, at the time when it was committed; nor shall a heavier penalty be imposed than that which was applicable at the time when the criminal offence was committed; if, after the commission of the offence, provision is made by law for the imposition of a lighter penalty, the offender shall benefit thereby;
> (d) Anyone charged with an offence is presumed innocent until proved guilty according to law;
> (e) Anyone charged with an offence shall have the right to be tried in his presence;
> (f) No one shall be compelled to testify against himself or to confess guilt.

3. A convicted person shall be advised on conviction of his judicial and other remedies and of the time-limits within which they may be exercised.

4. The death penalty shall not be pronounced on persons who were under the age of eighteen years at the time of the offence and shall not be carried out on pregnant women or mothers of young children.

5. At the end of hostilities, the authorities in power shall endeavour to grant the broadest possible amnesty to persons who have participated in the armed conflict, or those deprived of their liberty for reasons related to the armed conflict, whether they are interned or detained.

Part III
WOUNDED, SICK AND SHIPWRECKED

Article 7. Protection and care

1. All the wounded, sick and shipwrecked, whether or not they have taken part in the armed conflict, shall be respected and protected.

2. In all circumstances they shall be treated humanely and shall receive, to the fullest extent practicable and with the least possible delay, the medical care and attention required by their condition. There shall be no distinction among them founded on any grounds other than medical ones.

Article 8. Search

Whenever circumstances permit, and particularly after an engagement, all possible measures shall be taken, without delay, to search for and collect the wounded, sick and shipwrecked, to protect them against pillage and ill-treatment, to ensure their adequate care, and to search for the dead, prevent their being despoiled, and decently dispose of them.

Article 9. Protection of medical and religious personnel

1. Medical and religious personnel shall be respected and protected and shall be granted all available help for the performance of their duties. They shall not be compelled to carry out tasks which are not compatible with their humanitarian mission.

2. In the performance of their duties medical personnel may not be required to give priority to any person except on medical grounds.

Article 10. General protection of medical duties
1. Under no circumstances shall any person be punished for having carried out medical activities compatible with medical ethics, regardless of the person benefiting therefrom.
2. Persons engaged in medical activities shall neither be compelled to perform acts or to carry out work contrary to, nor be compelled to refrain from acts required by, the rules of medical ethics or other rules designed for the benefit of the wounded and sick, or this Protocol.
3. The professional obligations of persons engaged in medical activities regarding information which they may acquire concerning the wounded and sick under their care shall, subject to national law, be respected.
4. Subject to national law, no person engaged in medical activities may be penalized in any way for refusing or failing to give information concerning the wounded and sick who are, or who have been, under his care.

Article 11. Protection of medical units and transports
1. Medical units and transports shall be respected and protected at all times and shall not be the object of attack.
2. The protection to which medical units and transports are entitled shall not cease unless they are used to commit hostile acts, outside their humanitarian function. Protection may, however, cease only after a warning has been given setting, whenever appropriate, a reasonable time-limit, and after such warning has remained unheeded.

Article 12. The distinctive emblem
Under the direction of the competent authority concerned, the distinctive emblem of the red cross, red crescent or red lion and sun on a white ground shall be displayed by medical and religious personnel and medical units, and on medical transports. It shall be respected in all circumstances. It shall not be used improperly.

Part IV
CIVILIAN POPULATION

Article 13. Protection of the civilian population
1. The civilian population and individual civilians shall enjoy general protection against the dangers arising from military operations. To give effect to this protection, the following rules shall be observed in all circumstances.
2. The civilian population as such, as well as individual civilians, shall not be the object of attack. Acts or threats of violence the primary purpose of which is to spread terror among the civilian population are prohibited.
3. Civilians shall enjoy the protection afforded by this Part, unless and for such time as they take a direct part in hostilities.

Article 14. Protection of objects indispensable to the survival of the civilian population
Starvation of civilians as a method of combat is prohibited. It is therefore prohibited to attack, destroy, remove or render useless, for that purpose, objects indispensable to the survival of the civilian population, such as foodstuffs, agricultural areas for the production of foodstuffs, crops, livestock, drinking water installations and supplies and irrigation works.

Article 15. Protection of works and installations containing dangerous forces
Works or installations containing dangerous forces, namely dams, dykes and nuclear electrical generating stations, shall not be made the object of attack, even where these objects are military objectives, if such attack may cause the release of dangerous forces and consequent severe losses among the civilian population.

Article 16. Protection of cultural objects and of places of worship
Without prejudice to the provisions of The Hague Convention for the Protection of Cultural Property in the Event of Armed Conflict of 14 May 1954, it is prohibited to commit any acts of hostility directed against historic monuments, works of art or places of worship which constitute the cultural or spiritual heritage of peoples, and to use them in support of the military effort.

Article 17. Prohibition of forced movement of civilians

1. The displacement of the civilian population shall not be ordered for reasons related to the conflict unless the security of the civilians involved or imperative military reasons so demand. Should such displacements have to be carried out, all possible measures shall be taken in order that the civilian population may be received under satisfactory conditions of shelter, hygiene, health, safety and nutrition.

2. Civilians shall not be compelled to leave their own territory for reasons connected with the conflict.

Article 18. Relief societies and relief actions

1. Relief societies located in the territory of the High Contracting Party, such as Red Cross (Red Crescent, Red Lion and Sun) organizations, may offer their services for the performance of their traditional functions in relation to the victims of the armed conflict. The civilian population may, even on its own initiative, offer to collect and care for the wounded, sick and shipwrecked.

2. If the civilian population is suffering undue hardship owing to a lack of the supplies essential for its survival, such as foodstuffs and medical supplies, relief actions for the civilian population which are of an exclusively humanitarian and impartial nature and which are conducted without any adverse distinction shall be undertaken subject to the consent of the High Contracting Party concerned.

Part V
FINAL PROVISIONS

Article 19. Dissemination

This Protocol shall be disseminated as widely as possible. * * *

Article 23. Entry into force

1. This Protocol shall enter into force six months after two instruments of ratification or accession have been deposited.

2. For each Party to the Conventions thereafter ratifying or acceding to this Protocol, it shall enter into force six months after the deposit by such Party of its instrument of ratification or accession.

Article 24. Amendment

1. Any High Contracting Party may propose amendments to this Protocol. The text of any proposed amendment shall be communicated to the depositary which shall decide, after consultation with all the High Contracting Parties and the International Committee of the Red Cross, whether a conference should be convened to consider the proposed amendment.

2. The depositary shall invite to that conference all the High Contracting Parties as well as the Parties to the Conventions, whether or not they are signatories of this Protocol.

Article 25. Denunciation

1. In case a High Contracting Party should denounce this Protocol, the denunciation shall only take effect six months after receipt of the instrument of denunciation. If, however, on the expiry of six months, the denouncing Party is engaged in the situation referred to in Article l, the denunciation shall not take effect before the end of the armed conflict. Persons who have been deprived of liberty, or whose liberty has been restricted, for reasons related to the conflict shall nevertheless continue to benefit from the provisions of this Protocol until their final release.

2. The denunciation shall be notified in writing to the depositary, which shall transmit it to all the High Contracting Parties. * * *

Article 28. Authentic texts

The original of this Protocol, of which the Arabic, Chinese, English, French, Russian and Spanish texts are equally authentic shall be deposited with the depositary, which shall transmit certified true copies thereof to all the Parties to the Conventions.

CONVENTION RELATING TO THE STATUS OF REFUGEES (1951)

Convention Relating to the Status of Refugees, *adopted* July 28, 1951, 189 U.N.T.S. 150

Article 1
Definition of the term "refugee"

A. For the purposes of the present Convention, the term "refugee" shall apply to any person who: * * * (2) As a result of events occurring before 1 January 1951 and owing to a well-founded fear of being persecuted for reasons of race, religion, nationality, membership of a particular social group or political opinion, is outside the country of his nationality and is unable or, owing to such fear, is unwilling to avail himself of the protection of that country; or who, not having a nationality and being outside the country of his former habitual residence as a result of such events, is unable or, owing to such fear, is unwilling to return to it. In the case of a person who has more than one nationality, the term "the country of his nationality" shall mean each of the countries of which he is a national, and a person shall not be deemed to be lacking the protection of the country of his nationality if, without any valid reason based on well-founded fear, he has not availed himself of the protection of one of the countries of which he is a national. * * *

C. This Convention shall cease to apply to any person falling under the terms of section A if:

> (1) He has voluntarily re-availed himself of the protection of the country of his nationality; or
>
> (2) Having lost his nationality, he has voluntarily re-acquired it, or
>
> (3) He has acquired a new nationality, and enjoys the protection of the country of his new nationality; or
>
> (4) He has voluntarily re-established himself in the country which he left or outside which he remained owing to fear of persecution; or
>
> (5) He can no longer, because the circumstances in connexion with which he has been recognized as a refugee have ceased to exist, continue to refuse to avail himself of the protection of the country of his nationality; Provided that this paragraph shall not apply to a refugee falling under section A(1) of this article who is able to invoke compelling reasons arising out of previous persecution for refusing to avail himself of the protection of the country of nationality;
>
> (6) Being a person who has no nationality he is, because of the circumstances in connexion with which he has been recognized as a refugee have ceased to exist, able to return to the country of his former habitual residence; Provided that this paragraph shall not apply to a refugee falling under section A (1) of this article who is able to invoke compelling reasons arising out of previous persecution for refusing to return to the country of his former habitual residence. * * *

E. This Convention shall not apply to a person who is recognized by the competent authorities of the country in which he has taken residence as having the rights and obligations which are attached to the possession of the nationality of that country.

F. The provisions of this Convention shall not apply to any person with respect to whom there are serious reasons for considering that:

> (a) he has committed a crime against peace, a war crime, or a crime against humanity, as defined in the international instruments drawn up to make provision in respect of such crimes;
>
> (b) he has committed a serious non-political crime outside the country of refuge prior to his admission to that country as a refugee;
>
> (c) he has been guilty of acts contrary to the purposes and principles of the United Nations.

Article 2
General Obligations

Every refugee has duties to the country in which he finds himself, which require in particular that he conform to its laws and regulations as well as to measures taken for the maintenance of public order.

Article 3
Non-Discrimination

The Contracting States shall apply the provisions of this Convention to refugees without discrimination as to race, religion or country of origin.

Article 4
Religion

The Contracting States shall accord to refugees within their territories treatment at least as favourable as that accorded to their nationals with respect to freedom to practice their religion and freedom as regards the religious education of their children.

Article 5
Rights Granted Apart from this Convention

Nothing in this Convention shall be deemed to impair any rights and benefits granted by a Contracting State to refugees apart from this Convention. * * *

Article 9
Provisional Measures

Nothing in this Convention shall prevent a Contracting State, in time of war or other grave and exceptional circumstances, from taking provisionally measures which it considers to be essential to the national security in the case of a particular person, pending a determination by the Contracting State that that person is in fact a refugee and that the continuance of such measures is necessary in his case in the interests of national security. * * *

Article 12
Personal Status

1. The personal status of a refugee shall be governed by the law of the country of his domicile or, if he has no domicile, by the law of the country of his residence.
2. Rights previously acquired by a refugee and dependent on personal status, more particularly rights attaching to marriage, shall be respected by a Contracting State, subject to compliance, if this be necessary, with the formalities required by the law of that State, provided that the right in question is one which would have been recognized by the law of that State had he not become a refugee.

Article 13
Movable and Immovable Property

The Contracting States shall accord to a refugee treatment as favourable as possible and, in any event, not less favourable than that accorded to aliens generally in the same circumstances, as regards the acquisition of movable and immovable property and other rights pertaining thereto, and to leases and other contracts relating to movable and immovable property. * * *

Article 15
Right of Association

As regards non-political and non-profit-making associations and trade unions the Contracting States shall accord to refugees lawfully staying in their territory the most favourable treatment accorded to nationals of a foreign country, in the same circumstances.

Article 16
Access to Courts

1. A refugee shall have free access to the courts of law on the territory of all Contracting States.
2. A refugee shall enjoy in the Contracting State in which he has his habitual residence the same treatment as a national in matters pertaining to access to the Courts, including legal assistance and exemption from *cautio judicatum solvi.*
3. A refugee shall be accorded in the matters referred to in paragraph 2 in countries other than that in which he has his habitual residence the treatment granted to a national of the country of his habitual residence. * * *

Article 20
Rationing

Where a rationing system exists, which applies to the population at large and regulates the general distribution of products in short supply, refugees shall be accorded the same treatment as nationals.

Article 21
Housing

As regards housing, the Contracting States, in so far as the matter is regulated by laws or regulations or is subject to the control of public authorities, shall accord to refugees lawfully staying in their territory treatment as favourable as possible and, in any event, not less favourable than that accorded to aliens generally in the same circumstances.

Article 22
Public Housing

1. The Contracting States shall accord to refugees the same treatment as is accorded to nationals with respect to elementary education.

2. The Contracting States shall accord to refugees treatment as favourable as possible, and, in any event, not less favourable than that accorded to aliens generally in the same circumstances, with respect to education other than elementary education and, in particular, as regards access to studies, the recognition of foreign school certificates, diplomas and degrees, the remission of fees and charges and the award of scholarships. * * *

Article 26
Freedom of Movement

Each Contracting State shall accord to refugees lawfully in its territory the right to choose their place of residence to move freely within its territory, subject to any regulations applicable to aliens generally in the same circumstances. * * *

Article 31
Refugees Unlawfully in the Country of Refuge

1. The Contracting States shall not impose penalties, on account of their illegal entry or presence, on refugees who, coming directly from a territory where their life or freedom was threatened in the sense of article 1, enter or are present in their territory without authorization, provided they present themselves without delay to the authorities and show good cause for their illegal entry or presence.

2. The Contracting States shall not apply to the movements of such refugees restrictions other than those which are necessary and such restrictions shall only be applied until their status in the country is regularized or they obtain admission into another country. The Contracting States shall allow such refugees a reasonable period and all the necessary facilities to obtain admission into another country.

Article 32
Expulsion

1. The Contracting States shall not expel a refugee lawfully in their territory save on grounds of national security or public order.

2. The expulsion of such a refugee shall be only in pursuance of a decision reached in accordance with due process of law. Except where compelling reasons of national security otherwise require, the refugee shall be allowed to submit evidence to clear himself, and to appeal to and be represented for the purpose before competent authority or a person or persons specially designated by the competent authority.

3. The Contracting States shall allow such a refugee a reasonable period within which to seek legal admission into another country. The Contracting States reserve the right to apply during that period such internal measures as they may deem necessary.

Article 33
Prohibition of Expulsion or Return ("Refoulement")

1. No Contracting State shall expel or return ("refouler") a refugee in any manner whatsoever to the frontiers of territories where his life or freedom would be threatened on account of his race, religion, nationality, membership of a particular social group or political opinion.

2. The benefit of the present provision may not, however, be claimed by a refugee whom there are reasonable grounds for regarding as a danger to the security of the country in which he is, or who, having been convicted by a final judgment of a particularly serious crime, constitutes a danger to the community of that country.

Article 34
Naturalization

The Contracting States shall as far as possible facilitate the assimilation and naturalization of refugees. They shall in particular make every effort to expedite naturalization proceedings and to reduce as far as possible the charges and costs of such proceedings. * * *

Article 35
Co-operation of the National Authorities with the United Nations

1. The Contracting States undertake to co-operate with the Office of the United Nations High Commissioner for Refugees, or any other agency of the United Nations which may succeed it, in the exercise of its functions, and shall in particular facilitate its duty of supervising the application of the provisions of this Convention.
2. In order to enable the Office of the High Commissioner or any other agency of the United Nations which may succeed it, to make reports to the competent organs of the United Nations, the Contracting States undertake to provide them in the appropriate form with information and statistical data requested concerning:

    (a) The condition of refugees,

    (b) The implementation of this Convention, and;

    (c) Laws, regulations and decrees which are, or may hereafter be, in force relating to refugees. * * *

Article 38
Settlement of Disputes

Any dispute between parties to this Convention relating to its interpretation or application, which cannot be settled by other means, shall be referred to the International Court of Justice at the request of any one of the parties to the dispute. * * *

Article 40
Territorial Application Clause

1. Any State may, at the time of signature, ratification or accession, declare that this Convention shall extend to all or any of the territories for the international relations of which it is responsible. Such a declaration shall take effect when the Convention enters into force for the State concerned.
2. At any time thereafter any such extension shall be made by notification addressed to the Secretary-General of the United Nations and shall take effect as from the ninetieth day after the day of receipt by the Secretary-General of the United Nations of this notification, or as from the date of entry into force of the Convention for the State concerned, whichever is the later.
3. With respect to those territories to which this Convention is not extended at the time of signature, ratification or accession, each State concerned shall consider the possibility of taking the necessary steps in order to extend the application of this Convention to such territories, subject, where necessary for constitutional reasons, to the consent of the Governments of such territories.

Article 41
Federal Clause

In the case of a Federal or non-unitary State, the following provisions shall apply:

    (a) With respect to those articles of this Convention that come within the legislative jurisdiction of the federal legislative authority, the obligations of the Federal Government shall to this extent be the same as those of Parties which are not Federal States;

    (b) With respect to those articles of this Convention that come within the legislative jurisdiction of constituent States, provinces or cantons which are not, under the constitutional system of the federation, bound to take legislative action, the Federal Government shall bring such articles with a favourable recommendation to the notice of the appropriate authorities of states, provinces or cantons at the earliest possible moment.

    (c) A Federal State Party to this Convention shall, at the request of any other Contracting State transmitted through the Secretary-General of the United Nations, supply a statement of the law and practice of the Federation and its constituent units in regard to any particular provision of the

Convention showing the extent to which effect has been given to that provision by legislative or other action.

Article 42
Reservations

1. At the time of signature, ratification or accession, any State may make reservations to articles of the Convention other than to articles 1, 3, 4, 16(1), 33, 36-46 inclusive. * * *

PROTOCOL RELATING TO THE STATUS OF REFUGEES (1967)

Protocol Relating to the Status of Refugees, *adopted* Jan. 31, 1967, 19 U.S.T. 6223, 606 U.N.T.S. 267.

The States Parties to the Present Protocol,
Considering that the Convention relating to the Status of Refugees done at Geneva on 28 July 1951 (hereinafter referred to as the Convention) covers only those persons who have become refugees as a result of events occurring before 1 January 1951,
Considering that new refugee situations have arisen since the Convention was adopted and that the refugees concerned may therefore not fall within the scope of the Convention,
Considering that it is desirable that equal status should be enjoyed by all refugees covered by the definition in the Convention irrespective of the dateline 1 January 1951,
Have agreed as follows:

Article I
General Provision

1. The States Parties to the present Protocol undertake to apply articles 2 to 34 inclusive of the Convention to refugees as hereinafter defined.
2. For the purpose of the present Protocol, the term "refugee" shall, except as regards the application of paragraph 3 of this article, mean any person within the definition of article 1 of the Convention as if the words "As a result of events occurring before 1 January 1951 and ..." "and the words"... "a result of such events", in article 1 A (2) were omitted.
3. The present Protocol shall be applied by the States Parties hereto without any geographic limitation, save that existing declarations made by States already Parties to the Convention in accordance with article 1B(1)(a) of the Convention, shall, unless extended under article 1B(2) thereof, apply also under the present Protocol.

Article II
Co-operation of the National Authorities with the United Nations

1. The States Parties to the present Protocol undertake to co-operate with the Office of the United Nations High Commissioner for Refugees, or any other agency of the United Nations which may succeed it, in the exercise of its functions, and shall in particular facilitate its duty of supervising the application of the provisions of the present Protocol.
2. In order to enable the Office of the High Commissioner, or any other agency of the United Nations which may succeed it, to make reports to the competent organs of the United Nations, the States Parties to the present Protocol undertake to provide them with the information and statistical data requested, in the appropriate form, concerning:
> (a) The condition of refugees;
> (b) The implementation of the present Protocol;
> (c) Laws, regulations and decrees which are, or may hereafter be, in force relating to refugees.
> * * *

Article III
Information on National Legislation

The States Parties to the present Protocol shall communicate to the Secretary-General of the United Nations the laws and regulations which they may adopt to ensure the application of the present Protocol.

Article IV
Settlement of Disputes

Any dispute between States Parties to the present Protocol which relates to its interpretation or application and which cannot be settled by other means shall be referred to the International Court of Justice at the request of any one of the parties to the dispute. * * *

SUPPLEMENTARY CONVENTION ON THE ABOLITION OF SLAVERY, THE SLAVE TRADE, AND INSTITUTIONS AND PRACTICES SIMILAR TO SLAVERY (1956)

Supplementary Convention on the Abolition of Slavery, the Slave Trade, and Institutions and Practices Similar to Slavery, *adopted* Sept. 7, 1956, 226 U.N.T.S. 3

Preamble

The States Parties to the present Convention,

Considering that freedom is the birthright of every human being,

Mindful that the peoples of the United Nations reaffirmed in the Charter their faith in the dignity and worth of the human person,

Considering that the Universal Declaration of Human Rights, proclaimed by the General Assembly of the United Nations as a common standard of achievement for all peoples and all nations, states that no one shall be held in slavery or servitude and that slavery and the slave trade shall be prohibited in all their forms,

Recognizing that, since the conclusion of the Slavery Convention signed at Geneva on 25 September 1926, which was designed to secure the abolition of slavery and of the slave trade, further progress has been made towards this end,

Having regard to the Forced Labour Convention of 1930 and to subsequent action by the International Labour Organisation in regard to forced or compulsory labour,

Being aware, however, that slavery, the slave trade and institutions and practices similar to slavery have not yet been eliminated in all parts of the world,

Having decided , therefore, that the Convention of 1926, which remains operative, should now be augmented by the conclusion of a supplementary convention designed to intensify national as well as international efforts towards the abolition of slavery, the slave trade and institutions and practices similar to slavery,

Have agreed as follows:

Section I. Institutions and practices similar to slavery

Article 1

Each of the States Parties to this Convention shall take all practicable and necessary legislative and other measures to bring about progressively and as soon as possible the complete abolition or abandonment of the following institutions and practices, where they still exist and whether or not they are covered by the definition of slavery contained in article 1 of the Slavery Convention signed at Geneva on 25 September 1926:

(a) Debt bondage, that is to say, the status or condition arising from a pledge by a debtor of his personal services or of those of a person under his control as security for a debt, if the value of those services as reasonably assessed is not applied towards the liquidation of the debt or the length and nature of those services are not respectively limited and defined;

(b) Serfdom, that is to say, the condition or status of a tenant who is by law, custom or agreement bound to live and labour on land belonging to another person and to render some determinate service to such other person, whether for reward or not, and is not free to change his status;

(c) Any institution or practice whereby:

> (i) A woman, without the right to refuse, is promised or given in marriage on payment of a consideration in money or in kind to her parents, guardian, family or any other person or group; or
>
> (ii) The husband of a woman, his family, or his clan, has the right to transfer her to another person for value received or otherwise; or
>
> (iii) A woman on the death of her husband is liable to be inherited by another person;

(d) Any institution or practice whereby a child or young person under the age of 18 years, is delivered by either or both of his natural parents or by his guardian to another person, whether for reward or not, with a view to the exploitation of the child or young person or of his labour.

Article 2

With a view to bringing to an end the institutions and practices mentioned in article 1 (c) of this Convention, the States Parties undertake to prescribe, where appropriate, suitable minimum ages of marriage, to encourage the use of facilities whereby the consent of both parties to a marriage may be freely expressed in the presence of a competent civil or religious authority, and to encourage the registration of marriages.

Section II. The slave trade

Article 3

1. The act of conveying or attempting to convey slaves from one country to another by whatever means of transport, or of being accessory thereto, shall be a criminal offence under the laws of the States Parties to this Convention and persons convicted thereof shall be liable to very severe penalties.

2.   (a) The States Parties shall take all effective measures to prevent ships and aircraft authorized to fly their flags from conveying slaves and to punish persons guilty of such acts or of using national flags for that purpose.

(b) The States Parties shall take all effective measures to ensure that their ports, airfields and coasts are not used for the conveyance of slaves.

3. The States Parties to this Convention shall exchange information in order to ensure the practical co-ordination of the measures taken by them in combating the slave trade and shall inform each other of every case of the slave trade, and of every attempt to commit this criminal offence, which comes to their notice.

Article 4

Any slave who takes refuge on board any vessel of a State Party to this Convention shall ipso facto be free.

Section III. Slavery and institutions and practices similar to slavery

Article 5

In a country where the abolition or abandonment of slavery, or of the institutions or practices mentioned in article 1 of this Convention, is not yet complete, the act of mutilating, branding or otherwise marking a slave or a person of servile status in order to indicate his status, or as a punishment, or for any other reason, or of being accessory thereto, shall be a criminal offence under the laws of the States Parties to this Convention and persons convicted thereof shall be liable to punishment.

Article 6

1. The act of enslaving another person or of inducing another person to give himself or a person dependent upon him into slavery, or of attempting these acts, or being accessory thereto, or being a party to a

conspiracy to accomplish any such acts, shall be a criminal offence under the laws of the States Parties to this Convention and persons convicted thereof shall be liable to punishment.

2. Subject to the provisions of the introductory paragraph of article 1 of this Convention, the provisions of paragraph 1 of the present article shall also apply to the act of inducing another person to place himself or a person dependent upon him into the servile status resulting from any of the institutions or practices mentioned in article 1, to any attempt to perform such acts, to being accessory thereto, and to being a party to a conspiracy to accomplish any such acts.

Section IV. Definitions

Article 7

For the purposes of the present Convention:

(a) "Slavery" means, as defined in the Slavery Convention of 1926, the status or condition of a person over whom any or all of the powers attaching to the right of ownership are exercised, and "slave" means a person in such condition or status;

(b) "A person of servile status" means a person in the condition or status resulting from any of the institutions or practices mentioned in article 1 of this Convention;

(c) "Slave trade" means and includes all acts involved in the capture, acquisition or disposal of a person with intent to reduce him to slavery; all acts involved in the acquisition of a slave with a view to selling or exchanging him; all acts of disposal by sale or exchange of a person acquired with a view to being sold or exchanged; and, in general, every act of trade or transport in slaves by whatever means of conveyance.

Section V. Cooperation between States Parties and communication of information

Article 8

1. The States Parties to this Convention undertake to co-operate with each other and with the United Nations to give effect to the foregoing provisions.

2. The Parties undertake to communicate to the Secretary-General of the United Nations copies of any laws, regulations and administrative measures enacted or put into effect to implement the provisions of this Convention.

3. The Secretary-General shall communicate the information received under paragraph 2 of this article to the other Parties and to the Economic and Social Council as part of the documentation for any discussion which the Council might undertake with a view to making further recommendations for the abolition of slavery, the slave trade or the institutions and practices which are the subject of this Convention.

Section VI. Final clauses

Article 9

No reservations may be made to this Convention.

Article 10

Any dispute between States Parties to this Convention relating to its interpretation or application, which is not settled by negotiation, shall be referred to the International Court of Justice at the request of any one of the parties to the dispute, unless the parties concerned agree on another mode of settlement. * * *

Article 12

1. This Convention shall apply to all non-self-governing trust, colonial and other non-metropolitan territories for the international relations of which any State Party is responsible; the Party concerned shall, subject to the provisions of paragraph 2 of this article, at the time of signature, ratification or accession declare the non-metropolitan territory or territories to which the Convention shall apply ipso facto as a result of such signature, ratification or accession.

2. In any case in which the previous consent of a non-metropolitan territory is required by the constitutional laws or practices of the Party or of the non-metropolitan territory, the Party concerned shall endeavour to secure the needed consent of the non-metropolitan territory within the period of twelve months from the date of signature of the Convention by the metropolitan State, and when such consent has been obtained the

Party shall notify the Secretary-General. This Convention shall apply to the territory or territories named in such notification from the date of its receipt by the Secretary-General.

3. After the expiry of the twelve-month period mentioned in the preceding paragraph, the States Parties concerned shall inform the Secretary-General of the results of the consultations with those non-metropolitan territories for whose international relations they are responsible and whose consent to the application of this Convention may have been withheld.

Article 13

1. This Convention shall enter into force on the date on which two States have become Parties thereto.

2. It shall thereafter enter into force with respect to each State and territory on the date of deposit of the instrument of ratification or accession of that State or notification of application to that territory. * * *

Article 15

This Convention, of which the Chinese, English, French, Russian and Spanish texts are equally authentic, shall be deposited in the archives of the United Nations Secretariat. The Secretary-General shall prepare a certified copy thereof for communication to States Parties to this Convention, as well as to all other States Members of the United Nations and of the specialized agencies.

CONVENTION ON THE ABOLITION OF FORCED LABOUR (1957)

Abolition of Forced Labour Convention (ILO No. 105), *adopted* June 25, 1957, 320 U.N.T.S. 291

The General Conference of the International Labour Organisation,

Having been convened at Geneva by the Governing Body of the International Labour Office, and having met in its fortieth session on 5 June 1957, and

Having considered the question of forced labour, which is the fourth item on the agenda of the session, and

Having noted the provisions of the Forced Labour Convention, 1930, and

Having noted that the Slavery Convention, 1926, provides that all necessary measures shall be taken to prevent compulsory or forced labour from developing into conditions analogous to slavery and that the Supplementary Convention on the Abolition of Slavery, the Slave Trade, and Institutions and Practices Similar to Slavery, 1956, provides for the complete abolition of debt bondage and serfdom, and

Having noted that the Protection of Wages Convention, 1949, provides that wages shall be paid regularly and prohibits methods of payment which deprive the worker of a genuine possibility of terminating his employment, and

Having decided upon the adoption of further proposals with regard to the abolition of certain forms of forced or compulsory labour constituting a violation of the rights of man referred to in the Charter of the United Nations and enunciated by the Universal Declaration of Human Rights, and

Having determined that these proposals shall take the form of an international Convention,

Adopts this twenty-fifth day of June of the year one thousand nine hundred and fifty-seven the following Convention, which may be cited as the Abolition of Forced Labour Convention, 1957:

Article 1

Each Member of the International Labour Organisation which ratifies this Convention undertakes to suppress and not to make use of any form of forced or compulsory labour:

(a) As a means of political coercion or education or as a punishment for holding or expressing political views or views ideologically opposed to the established political, social or economic system;

(b) As a method of mobilising and using labour for purposes of economic development;

(c) As a means of labour discipline;

(d) As a punishment for having participated in strikes;

(e) As a means of racial, social, national or religious discrimination.

Article 2

Each Member of the International Labour Organisation which ratifies this Convention undertakes to take effective measures to secure the immediate and complete abolition of forced or compulsory labour as specified in article 1 of this Convention.

Article 3

The formal ratifications of this Convention shall be communicated to the Director-General of the International Labour Office for registration.

Article 4

1. This Convention shall be binding only upon those Members of the International Labour Organisation whose ratifications have been registered with the Director-General.

2. It shall come into force twelve months after the date on which the ratifications of two Members have been registered with the Director-General.

3. Thereafter, this Convention shall come into force for any Member twelve months after the date on which its ratification has been registered.

Article 5

1. A Member which has ratified this Convention may denounce it after the expiration of ten years from the date on which the Convention first comes into force, by an act communicated to the Director-General of the International Labour Office for registration. Such denunciation shall not take effect until one year after the date on which it is registered.

2. Each Member which has ratified this Convention and which does not, within the year following the expiration of the period of ten years mentioned in the preceding paragraph, exercise the right of denunciation provided for in this article, will be bound for another period of five years and, thereafter, may denounce this Convention at the expiration of each period of five years under the terms provided for in this article.

Article 6

1. The Director-General of the International Labour Office shall notify all Members of the International Labour Organisation of the registration of all ratifications and denunciations communicated to him by the Members of the Organisation.

2. When notifying the Members of the Organisation of the registration of the second ratification communicated to him the Director-General shall draw the attention of the Members of the Organisation to the date upon which the Convention will come into force.

Article 7

The Director-General of the International Labour Office shall communicate to the Secretary-General of the United Nations for registration in accordance with Article 102 of the Charter of the United Nations full particulars of all ratifications and acts of denunciation registered by him in accordance with the provisions of the preceding articles.

Article 8

At such times as it may consider necessary the Governing Body of the International Labour Office shall present to the General Conference a report on the working of the Convention and shall examine the desirability of placing on the agenda of the Conference the question of its revision in whole or in part.

Article 9

1. Should the Conference adopt a new Convention revising this Convention in whole or in part, then, unless the new Convention otherwise provides:

> (a) The ratification by a Member of the new revising Convention shall ipso jure involve the immediate denunciation of this Convention, notwithstanding the provisions of article 5 above, if and when the new revising Convention shall have come into force;
>
> (b) As from the date when the new revising Convention comes into force this Convention shall cease to be open to ratification by the Members.

2. This Convention shall in any case remain in force in its actual form and content for those Members which have ratified it but have not ratified the revising Convention. * * *

VIENNA CONVENTION ON CONSULAR RELATIONS (1963)

Vienna Convention on Consular Relations, *adopted* Apr. 24, 1963, 596 U.N.T.S. 261, 21 U.S.T. 77

The States Parties to the present Convention,

Recalling that consular relations have been established between peoples since ancient times, * * *

Believing that an international convention on consular relations, privileges and immunities would * * * contribute to the development of friendly relations among nations, irrespective of their differing constitutional and social systems,

Realizing that the purpose of such privileges and immunities is not to benefit individuals but to ensure the efficient performance of functions by consular posts on behalf of their respective States,

Affirming that the rules of customary international law continue to govern matters not expressly regulated by the provisions of the present Convention,

Have agreed as follows:

Article 1
Definitions

1. For the purposes of the present Convention, the following expressions shall have the meanings hereunder assigned to them:

> (a) "consular post" means any consulate-general, consulate, vice-consulate or consular agency;
>
> (b) "consular district" means the area assigned to a consular post for the exercise of consular functions;
>
> (c) "head of consular post" means the person charged with the duty of acting in that capacity;
>
> (d) "consular officer" means any person, including the head of a consular post, entrusted in that capacity with the exercise of consular functions;
>
> (e) "consular employee" means any person employed in the administrative or technical service of a consular post;
>
> (f) "member of the service staff" means any person employed in the domestic service of a consular post;
>
> (g) "members of the consular post" means consular officers, consular employees and members of the service staff;
>
> (h) "members of the consular staff" means consular officers, other than the head of a consular post, consular employees and members of the service staff;
>
> (i) "member of the private staff" means a person who is employed exclusively in the private service of a member of the consular post;
>
> (j) "consular premises" means the buildings or parts of buildings and the land ancillary thereto, irrespective of ownership, used exclusively for the purposes of the consular post;

(k) "consular archives" includes all the papers, documents, correspondence, books, films, tapes and registers of the consular post, together with the ciphers and codes, the card-indexes and any article of furniture intended for their protection or safe keeping.

2. Consular officers are of two categories, namely career consular officers and honorary consular officers. The provisions of Chapter II of the present Convention apply to consular posts headed by career consular officers, the provisions of Chapter III govern consular posts headed by honorary consular officers

3. The particular status of members of the consular posts who are nationals or permanent residents of the receiving State is governed by article 71 of the present Convention.

CHAPTER I
CONSULAR RELATIONS IN GENERAL

SECTION I. ESTABLISHMENT AND CONDUCT OF CONSULAR RELATIONS

Article 2
Establishment of consular relations

1. The establishment of consular relations between States takes place by mutual consent.
2. The consent given to the establishment of diplomatic relations between two States implies, unless otherwise stated, consent to the establishment of consular relations.
3. The severance of diplomatic relations shall not ipso facto involve the severance of consular relations.

Article 3
Exercise of consular functions

Consular functions are exercised by consular posts. They are also exercised by diplomatic missions in accordance with the provisions of the present Convention.

Article 4
Establishment of a consular post

1. A consular post may be established in the territory of the receiving State only with that State's consent.
2. The seat of the consular post, its classification and the consular district shall be established by the sending State and shall be subject to the approval of the receiving State.
3. Subsequent changes in the seat of the consular post, its classification or the consular district may be made by the sending State only with the consent of the receiving State.
4. The consent of the receiving State shall also be required if a consulate-general or a consulate desires to open a vice-consulate or a consular agency in a locality other than that in which it is itself established.
5. The prior express consent of the receiving State shall also be required for the opening of an office forming part of an existing consular post elsewhere than at the seat thereof.

Article 5
Consular functions

Consular functions consist in:

(a) protecting in the receiving State the interests of the sending State and of its nationals, both individuals and bodies corporate, within the limits permitted by international law;

(b) furthering the development of commercial, economic, cultural and scientific relations between the sending State and the receiving State and otherwise promoting friendly relations between them in accordance with the provisions of the present Convention;

(c) ascertaining by all lawful means conditions and developments in the commercial, economic, cultural and scientific life of the receiving State, reporting thereon to the Government of the sending State and giving information to persons interested;

(d) issuing passports and travel documents to nationals of the sending State, and visas or appropriate documents to persons wishing to travel to the sending State;

(e) helping and assisting nationals, both individuals and bodies corporate, of the sending State;

(f) acting as notary and civil registrar and in capacities of a similar kind, and performing certain functions of an administrative nature, provided that there is nothing contrary thereto in the laws and regulations of the receiving State;

(g) safeguarding the interests of nationals, both individuals and bodies corporate, of the sending States in cases of succession *mortis causa* in the territory of the receiving State, in accordance with the laws and regulations of the receiving State;

(h) safeguarding, within the limits imposed by the laws and regulations of the receiving State, the interests of minors and other persons lacking full capacity who are nationals of the sending State, particularly where any guardianship or trusteeship is required with respect to such persons;

(i) subject to the practices and procedures obtaining in the receiving State, representing or arranging appropriate representation for nationals of the sending State before the tribunals and other authorities of the receiving State, for the purpose of obtaining, in accordance with the laws and regulations of the receiving State, provisional measures for the preservation of the rights and interests of these nationals, where, because of absence or any other reason, such nationals are unable at the proper time to assume the defence of their rights and interests;

(j) transmitting judicial and extrajudicial documents or executing letters rogatory or commissions to take evidence for the courts of the sending State in accordance with international agreements in force or, in the absence of such international agreements, in any other manner compatible with the laws and regulations of the receiving State;

(k) exercising rights of supervision and inspection provided for in the laws and regulations of the sending State in respect of vessels having the nationality of the sending State, and of aircraft registered in that State, and in respect of their crews;

(l) extending assistance to vessels and aircraft mentioned in subparagraph (*k*) of this article, and to their crews, taking statements regarding the voyage of a vessel, examining and stamping the ship's papers, and, without prejudice to the powers of the authorities of the receiving State, conducting investigations into any incidents which occurred during the voyage, and settling disputes of any kind between the master, the officers and the seamen insofar as this may be authorized by the laws and regulations of the sending State;

(m) performing any other functions entrusted to a consular post by the sending State which are not prohibited by the laws and regulations of the receiving State or to which no objection is taken by the receiving State or which are referred to in the international agreements in force between the sending State and the receiving State. * * *

Article 11
The consular commission or notification of appointment

1. The head of a consular post shall be provided by the sending State with a document, in the form of a commission or similar instrument, made out for each appointment, certifying his capacity and showing, as a general rule, his full name, his category and class, the consular district and the seat of the consular post.

2. The sending State shall transmit the commission or similar instrument through the diplomatic or other appropriate channel to the Government of the State in whose territory the head of a consular post is to exercise his functions.

3. If the receiving State agrees, the sending State may, instead of a commission or similar instrument, send to the receiving State a notification containing the particulars required by paragraph 1 of this article.

Article 12
The exequatur

1. The head of a consular post is admitted to the exercise of his functions by an authorization from the receiving State termed an *exequatur*, whatever the form of this authorization.

2. A State which refused to grant an *exequatur* is not obliged to give to the sending State reasons for such refusal.

3. Subject to the provisions of articles 13 and 15 [excluded], the head of a consular post shall not enter upon his duties until he has received an *exequatur*. * * *

Article 19
Appointment of members of consular staff

1. Subject to the provisions of articles 20, 22 [deleted] and 23, the sending State may freely appoint the members of the consular staff.

2. The full name, category and class of all consular officers, other than the head of a consular post, shall be notified by the sending State to the receiving State in sufficient time for the receiving State, if it so wishes, to exercise its rights under paragraph 3 of article 23.

3. The sending State may, if required by its laws and regulations, request the receiving State to grant an *exequatur* to a consular officer other than the head of a consular post.

4. The receiving State may, if required by its laws and regulations, grant an *exequatur* to a consular officer other than the head of a consular post. * * *

Article 23
Persons declared "non grata"

1. The receiving State may at any time notify the sending State that a consular officer is persona non grata or that any other member of the consular staff is not acceptable. In that event, the sending State shall, as the case may be, either recall the person concerned or terminate his functions with the consular post.

2. If the sending State refuses or fails within a reasonable time to carry out its obligations under paragraph 1 of this article, the receiving State may, as the case may be, either withdraw the *exequatur* from the person concerned or cease to consider him as a member of the consular staff.

3. A person appointed as a member of a consular post may be declared unacceptable before arriving in the territory of the receiving State or, if already in the receiving State, before entering on his duties with the consular post. In any such case, the sending State shall withdraw his appointment.

4. In the cases mentioned in paragraphs 1 and 3 of this article, the receiving State is not obliged to give to the sending State reasons for its decision. * * *

SECTION II. END OF CONSULAR FUNCTIONS

Article 25
Termination of the functions of a member of a consular post

The functions of a member of a consular post shall come to an end, inter alia:

(a) on notification by the sending State to the receiving State that his functions have come to an end;

(b) on withdrawal of the *exequatur*;

(c) on notification by the receiving State to the sending State that the receiving State has ceased to consider him as a member of the consular staff.

Article 26
Departure from the territory of the receiving State

The receiving State shall, even in case of armed conflict, grant to members of the consular post and members of the private staff, other than nationals of the receiving State, and to members of their families forming part of their households irrespective of nationality, the necessary time and facilities to enable them to prepare their departure and to leave at the earliest possible moment after the termination of the functions of the members concerned. In particular, it shall, in case of need, place at their disposal the necessary means of transport for themselves and their property other than property acquired in the receiving State the export of which is prohibited at the time of departure.

Article 27
Protection of consular premises and archives and of the interests of the sending State in exceptional circumstances

1. In the event of the severance of consular relations between two States:

(a) the receiving State shall, even in case of armed conflict, respect and protect the consular premises, together with the property of the consular post and the consular archives;

(b) the sending State may entrust the custody of the consular premises, together with the property contained therein and the consular archives, to a third State acceptable to the receiving State;

(c) the sending State may entrust the protection of its interests and those of its nationals to a third State acceptable to the receiving State.

2. In the event of the temporary or permanent closure of a consular post, the provisions of subparagraph (*a*) of paragraph 1 of this article shall apply. In addition,

(a) if the sending State, although not represented in the receiving State by a diplomatic mission, has another consular post in the territory of that State, that consular post may be entrusted with the custody of the premises of the consular post which has been closed, together with the property contained therein and the consular archives, and, with the consent of the receiving State, with the exercise of consular functions in the district of that consular post; or
(b) if the sending State has no diplomatic mission and no other consular post in the receiving State, the provisions of subparagraphs (b) and (c) of paragraph 1 of this article shall apply. * * *

Article 28
Facilities for the work of the consular post
The receiving State shall accord full facilities for the performance of the functions of the consular post. * * *

Article 31
Inviolability of the consular premises
1. Consular premises shall be inviolable to the extent provided in this article.
2. The authorities of the receiving State shall not enter that part of the consular premises which is used exclusively for the purpose of the work of the consular post except with the consent of the head of the consular post or of his designee or of the head of the diplomatic mission of the sending State. The consent of the head of the consular post may, however, be assumed in case of fire or other disaster requiring prompt protective action.
3. Subject to the provisions of paragraph 2 of this article, the receiving State is under a special duty to take all appropriate steps to protect the consular premises against any intrusion or damage and to prevent any disturbance of the peace of the consular post or impairment of its dignity.
4. The consular premises, their furnishings, the property of the consular post and its means of transport shall be immune from any form of requisition for purposes of national defence or public utility. If expropriation is necessary for such purposes, all possible steps shall be taken to avoid impeding the performance of consular functions, and prompt, adequate and effective compensation shall be paid to the sending State. * * *

Article 33
Inviolability of the consular archives and documents
The consular archives and documents shall be inviolable at all times and wherever they may be. * * *

Article 35
Freedom of communication
1. The receiving State shall permit and protect freedom of communication on the part of the consular post for all official purposes. In communicating with the Government, the diplomatic missions and other consular posts, wherever situated, of the sending State, the consular post may employ all appropriate means, including diplomatic or consular couriers, diplomatic or consular bags and messages in code or cipher. However, the consular post may install and use a wireless transmitter only with the consent of the receiving State.
2. The official correspondence of the consular post shall be inviolable. Official correspondence means all correspondence relating to the consular post and its functions.
3. The consular bag shall be neither opened nor detained. Nevertheless, if the competent authorities of the receiving State have serious reason to believe that the bag contains something other than the correspondence, documents or articles referred to in paragraph 4 of this article, they may request that the bag be opened in their presence by an authorized representative of the sending State. If this request is refused by the authorities of the sending State, the bag shall be returned to its place of origin. * * *

Article 36
Communication and contact with nationals of the sending State
1. With a view to facilitating the exercise of consular functions relating to nationals of the sending State:
(a) consular officers shall be free to communicate with nationals of the sending State and to have access to them. Nationals of the sending State shall have the same freedom with respect to communication with and access to consular officers of the sending State;

113

(b) if he so requests, the competent authorities of the receiving State shall, without delay, inform the consular post of the sending State if, within its consular district, a national of that State is arrested or committed to prison or to custody pending trial or is detained in any other manner. Any communication addressed to the consular post by the person arrested, in prison, custody or detention shall be forwarded by the said authorities without delay. The said authorities shall inform the person concerned without delay of his rights under this subparagraph;

(c) consular officers shall have the right to visit a national of the sending State who is in prison, custody or detention, to converse and correspond with him and to arrange for his legal representation. They shall also have the right to visit any national of the sending State who is in prison, custody or detention in their district in pursuance of a judgement. Nevertheless, consular officers shall refrain from taking action on behalf of a national who is in prison, custody or detention if he expressly opposes such action.

2. The rights referred to in paragraph 1 of this article shall be exercised in conformity with the laws and regulations of the receiving State, subject to the proviso, however, that the said laws and regulations must enable full effect to be given to the purposes for which the rights accorded under this article are intended. * * *

Article 40
Protection of consular officers

The receiving State shall treat consular officers with due respect and shall take all appropriate steps to prevent any attack on their person, freedom or dignity.

Article 41
Personal inviolability of consular officers

1. Consular officers shall not be liable to arrest or detention pending trial, except in the case of a grave crime and pursuant to a decision by the competent judicial authority.

2. Except in the case specified in paragraph 1 of this article, consular officers shall not be committed to prison or be liable to any other form of restriction on their personal freedom save in execution of a judicial decision of final effect.

3. If criminal proceedings are instituted against a consular officer, he must appear before the competent authorities. Nevertheless, the proceedings shall be conducted with the respect due to him by reason of his official position and, except in the case specified in paragraph 1 of this article, in a manner which will hamper the exercise of consular functions as little as possible. When, in the circumstances mentioned in paragraph 1 of this article, it has become necessary to detain a consular officer, the proceedings against him shall be instituted with the minimum of delay.

Article 42
Notification of arrest, detention or prosecution

In the event of the arrest or detention, pending trial, of a member of the consular staff, or of criminal proceedings being instituted against him, the receiving State shall promptly notify the head of the consular post. Should the latter be himself the object of any such measure, the receiving State shall notify the sending State through the diplomatic channel.

Article 43
Immunity from jurisdiction

1. Consular officers and consular employees shall not be amenable to the jurisdiction of the judicial or administrative authorities of the receiving State in respect of acts performed in the exercise of consular functions.

2. The provisions of paragraph 1 of this article shall not, however, apply in respect of a civil action either:
    (a) arising out of a contract concluded by a consular officer or a consular employee in which he did not contract expressly or impliedly as an agent of the sending State; or
    (b) by a third party for damage arising from an accident in the receiving State caused by a vehicle vessel or aircraft. * * *

Article 53
Beginning and end of consular privileges and immunities

1. Every member of the consular post shall enjoy the privileges and immunities provided in the present Convention from the moment he enters the territory of the receiving State on proceeding to take up his post or, if already in its territory, from the moment when he enters on his duties with the consular post.

2. Members of the family of a member of the consular post forming part of his household and members of his private staff shall receive the privileges and immunities provided in the present Convention from the date from which he enjoys privileges and immunities in accordance with paragraph 1 of this article or from the date of their entry into the territory of the receiving State or from the date of their becoming a member of such family or private staff, whichever is the latest.

3. When the functions of a member of the consular post have come to an end, his privileges and immunities and those of a member of his family forming part of his household or a member of his private staff shall normally cease at the moment when the person concerned leaves the receiving State or on the expiry of a reasonable period in which to do so, whichever is the sooner, but shall subsist until that time, even in case of armed conflict. In the case of the persons referred to in paragraph 2 of this article, their privileges and immunities shall come to an end when they cease to belong to the household or to be in the service of a member of the consular post provided, however, that if such persons intend leaving the receiving State within a reasonable period thereafter, their privileges and immunities shall subsist until the time of their departure.

4. However, with respect to acts performed by a consular officer or a consular employee in the exercise of his functions, immunity from jurisdiction shall continue to subsist without limitation of time.

5. In the event of the death of a member of the consular post, the members of his family forming part of his household shall continue to enjoy the privileges and immunities accorded to them until they leave the receiving State or until the expiry of a reasonable period enabling them to do so, whichever is the sooner. * * *

Article 55
Respect for the laws and regulations of the receiving State

1. Without prejudice to their privileges and immunities, it is the duty of all persons enjoying such privileges and immunities to respect the laws and regulations of the receiving State. They also have a duty not to interfere in the internal affairs of the State.

2. The consular premises shall not be used in any manner incompatible with the exercise of consular functions.

3. The provisions of paragraph 2 of this article shall not exclude the possibility of offices of other institutions or agencies being installed in part of the building in which the consular premises are situated, provided that the premises assigned to them are separate from those used by the consular post. In that event, the said offices shall not, for the purposes of the present Convention, be considered to form part of the consular premises. * * *

Article 57
Special provisions concerning private gainful occupation

1. Career consular officers shall not carry on for personal profit any professional or commercial activity in the receiving State.

2. Privileges and immunities provided in this chapter shall not be accorded:

> (a) to consular employees or to members of the service staff who carry on any private gainful occupation in the receiving State;
>
> (b) to members of the family of a person referred to in subparagraph (a) of this paragraph or to members of his private staff;
>
> (c) to members of the family of a member of a consular post who themselves carry on any private gainful occupation in the receiving State. * * *

CONVENTION ON THE ELIMINATION OF ALL FORMS OF RACIAL DISCRIMINATION (1965)

Convention on the Elimination of All Forms of Racial Discrimination, *adopted* Dec. 21, 1965, S. Exec. Doc. C, 95-2 (1978); 660 U.N.T.S. 195, 212

Article 1

1. In this Convention, the term "racial discrimination" shall mean any distinction, exclusion, restriction or preference based on race, colour, descent, or national or ethnic origin which has the purpose or effect of nullifying or impairing the recognition, enjoyment or exercise, on an equal footing, of human rights and fundamental freedoms in the political, economic, social, cultural or any other field of public life.
2. This Convention shall not apply to distinctions, exclusions, restrictions or preferences made by a State Party to this Convention between citizens and non-citizens.
3. Nothing in this Convention may be interpreted as affecting in any way the legal provisions of States Parties concerning nationality, citizenship or naturalization, provided that such provisions do not discriminate against any particular nationality.
4. Special measures taken for the sole purpose of securing adequate advancement of certain racial or ethnic groups or individuals requiring such protection as may be necessary in order to ensure such groups or individuals equal enjoyment or exercise of human rights and fundamental freedoms shall not be deemed racial discrimination, provided, however, that such measures do not, as a consequence, lead to the maintenance of separate rights for different racial groups and that they shall not be continued after the objectives for which they were taken have been achieved.

Article 2

1. States Parties condemn racial discrimination and undertake to pursue by all appropriate means and without delay a policy of eliminating racial discrimination in all its forms and promoting understanding among all races, and, to this end:
    (a) Each State Party undertakes to engage in no act or practice of racial discrimination against persons, groups of persons or institutions and to en sure that all public authorities and public institutions, national and local, shall act in conformity with this obligation;
    (b) Each State Party undertakes not to sponsor, defend or support racial discrimination by any persons or organizations;
    (c) Each State Party shall take effective measures to review governmental, national and local policies, and to amend, rescind or nullify any laws and regulations which have the effect of creating or perpetuating racial discrimination wherever it exists;
    (d) Each State Party shall prohibit and bring to an end, by all appropriate means, including legislation as required by circumstances, racial discrimination by any persons, group or organization;
    (e) Each State Party undertakes to encourage, where appropriate, integrationist multiracial organizations and movements and other means of eliminating barriers between races, and to discourage anything which tends to strengthen racial division.
2. States Parties shall, when the circumstances so warrant, take, in the social, economic, cultural and other fields, special and concrete measures to ensure the adequate development and protection of certain racial groups or individuals belonging to them, for the purpose of guaranteeing them the full and equal enjoyment of human rights and fundamental freedoms. These measures shall in no case en tail as a con sequence the maintenance of unequal or separate rights for different racial groups after the objectives for which they were taken have been achieved.

Article 3

States Parties particularly condemn racial segregation and apartheid and undertake to prevent, prohibit and eradicate all practices of this nature in territories under their jurisdiction.

Article 4

States Parties condemn all propaganda and all organizations which are based on ideas or theories of superiority of one race or group of persons of one colour or ethnic origin, or which attempt to justify or promote racial hatred and discrimination in any form, and undertake to adopt immediate and positive measures designed to eradicate all incitement to, or acts of, such discrimination and, to this end, with due regard to the principles embodied in the Universal Declaration of Human Rights and the rights expressly set forth in article 5 of this Convention, inter alia:

(a) Shall declare an offence punishable by law all dissemination of ideas based on racial superiority or hatred, incitement to racial discrimination, as well as all acts of violence or incitement to such acts against any race or group of persons of another colour or ethnic origin, and also the provision of any assistance to racist activities, including the financing thereof;

(b) Shall declare illegal and prohibit organizations, and also organized and all other propaganda activities, which promote and incite racial discrimination, and shall recognize participation in such organizations or activities as an offence punishable by law;

(c) Shall not permit public authorities or public institutions, national or local, to promote or incite racial discrimination.

Article 5

In compliance with the fundamental obligations laid down in article 2 of this Convention, States Parties undertake to prohibit and to eliminate racial discrimination in all its forms and to guarantee the right of everyone, without distinction as to race, colour, or national or ethnic origin, to equality before the law, notably in the enjoyment of the following rights:

(a) The right to equal treatment before the tribunals and all other organs administering justice;

(b) The right to security of person and protection by the State against violence or bodily harm, whether inflicted by government officials or by any individual group or institution;

(c) Political rights, in particular the right to participate in elections-to vote and to stand for election-on the basis of universal and equal suffrage, to take part in the Government as well as in the conduct of public affairs at any level and to have equal access to public service;

(d) Other civil rights, in particular:

   (i) The right to freedom of movement and residence within the border of the State;
   (ii) The right to leave any country, including one's own, and to return to one's country;
   (iii) The right to nationality;
   (iv) The right to marriage and choice of spouse;
   (v) The right to own property alone as well as in association with others;
   (vi) The right to inherit;
   (vii) The right to freedom of thought, conscience and religion;
   (viii) The right to freedom of opinion and expression;
   (ix) The right to freedom of peaceful assembly and association;

(e) Economic, social and cultural rights, in particular:

   (i) The rights to work, to free choice of employment, to just and favourable conditions of work, to protection against unemployment, to equal pay for equal work, to just and favourable remuneration;
   (ii) The right to form and join trade unions;
   (iii) The right to housing;
   (iv) The right to public health, medical care, social security and social services;
   (v) The right to education and training;
   (vi) The right to equal participation in cultural activities;

(f) The right of access to any place or service intended for use by the general public, such as transport hotels, restaurants, cafes, theatres and parks.

Article 6

States Parties shall assure to everyone within their jurisdiction effective protection and remedies, through the competent national tribunals and other State institutions, against any acts of racial discrimination which violate his human rights and fundamental freedoms contrary to this Convention, as well as the right to seek from such tribunals just and adequate reparation or satisfaction for any damage suffered as a result of such discrimination.

Article 7

States Parties undertake to adopt immediate and effective measures, particularly in the fields of teaching, education, culture and information, with a view to combating prejudices which lead to racial discrimination and to promoting understanding, tolerance and friendship among nations and racial or ethnical groups, as well as to propagating the purposes and principles of the Charter of the United Nations, the Universal Declaration of Human Rights, the United Nations Declaration on the Elimination of All Forms of Racial Discrimination, and this Convention.

Article 8

1. There shall be established a Committee on the Elimination of Racial Discrimination (hereinafter referred to as the Committee) consisting of eighteen experts of high moral standing and acknowledged impartiality elected by States Parties from among their nationals, who shall serve in their personal capacity, consideration being given to equitable geographical distribution and to the representation of the different forms of civilization as well as of the principal legal systems.

2. The members of the Committee shall be elected by secret ballot from a list of persons nominated by the States Parties. Each State Party may nominate one person from among its own nationals.

3. The initial election shall be held six months after the date of the entry into force of this Convention. At least three months before the date of each election the Secretary-General of the United Nations shall address a letter to the States Parties inviting them to submit their nominations within two months. The Secretary-General shall prepare a list in alphabetical order of all persons thus nominated, indicating the States Parties which have nominated them, and shall submit it to the States Parties.

4. Elections of the members of the Committee shall be held at a meeting of States Parties convened by the Secretary-General at United Nations Headquarters. At that meeting, for which two thirds of the States Parties shall constitute a quorum, the persons elected to the Committee shall be nominees who obtain the largest number of votes and an absolute majority of the votes of the representatives of States Parties present and voting.

5.   (a) The members of the Committee shall be elected for a term of four years. However, the terms of nine of the members elected at the first election shall expire at the end of two years; immediately after the first election the names of these nine members shall be chosen by lot by the Chairman of the Committee;

(b) For the filling of casual vacancies, the State Party whose expert has ceased to function as a member of the Committee shall appoint another expert from among its nationals, subject to the approval of the Committee.

6. States Parties shall be responsible for the expenses of the members of the Committee while they are in performance of Committee duties.

Article 9

1. States Parties undertake to submit to the Secretary-General of the United Nations, for consideration by the Committee, a report on the legislative, judicial, administrative or other measures which they have adopted and which give effect to the provisions of this Convention:

(a) within one year after the entry into force of the Convention for the State concerned; and

(b) thereafter every two years and whenever the Committee so requests. The Committee may request further information from the States Parties.

2. The Committee shall report annually, through the Secretary General, to the General Assembly of the United Nations on its activities and may make suggestions and general recommendations based on the examination of the reports and information received from the States Parties. Such suggestions and general recommendations shall be reported to the General Assembly together with comments, if any, from States Parties.

Article 10

1. The Committee shall adopt its own rules of procedure.

2. The Committee shall elect its officers for a term of two years.

3. The secretariat of the Committee shall be provided by the Secretary General of the United Nations.

4. The meetings of the Committee shall normally be held at United Nations Headquarters.

Article 11

1. If a State Party considers that another State Party is not giving effect to the provisions of this Convention, it may bring the matter to the attention of the Committee. The Committee shall then transmit the communication to the State Party concerned. Within three months, the receiving State shall submit to

the Committee written explanations or statements clarifying the matter and the remedy, if any, that may have been taken by that State.

2. If the matter is not adjusted to the satisfaction of both parties, either by bilateral negotiations or by any other procedure open to them, within six months after the receipt by the receiving State of the initial communication, either State shall have the right to refer the matter again to the Committee by notifying the Committee and also the other State.

3. The Committee shall deal with a matter referred to it in accordance with paragraph 2 of this article after it has ascertained that all available domestic remedies have been invoked and exhausted in the case, in conformity with the generally recognized principles of international law. This shall not be the rule where the application of the remedies is unreasonably prolonged.

4. In any matter referred to it, the Committee may call upon the States Parties concerned to supply any other relevant information.

5. When any matter arising out of this article is being considered by the Committee, the States Parties concerned shall be entitled to send a representative to take part in the proceedings of the Committee, without voting rights, while the matter is under consideration.

Article 12

1. (a) After the Committee has obtained and collated all the information it deems necessary, the Chairman shall appoint an ad hoc Conciliation Commission (hereinafter referred to as the Commission) comprising five persons who may or may not be members of the Committee. The members of the Commission shall be appointed with the unanimous consent of the parties to the dispute, and its good offices shall be made available to the States concerned with a view to an amicable solution of the matter on the basis of respect for this Convention;
   (b) If the States parties to the dispute fail to reach agreement within three months on all or part of the composition of the Commission, the members of the Commission not agreed upon by the States parties to the dispute shall be elected by secret ballot by a two-thirds majority vote of the Committee from among its own members.

2. The members of the Commission shall serve in their personal capacity. They shall not be nationals of the States parties to the dispute or of a State not Party to this Convention.

3. The Commission shall elect its own Chairman and adopt its own rules of procedure.

4. The meetings of the Commission shall normally be held at United Nations Headquarters or at any other convenient place as determined by the Commission.

5. The secretariat provided in accordance with article 10, paragraph 3, of this Convention shall also service the Commission whenever a dispute among States Parties brings the Commission into being.

6. The States parties to the dispute shall share equally all the expenses of the members of the Commission in accordance with estimates to be provided by the Secretary-General of the United Nations.

7. The Secretary-General shall be empowered to pay the expenses of the members of the Commission, if necessary, before reimbursement by the States parties to the dispute in accordance with paragraph 6 of this article.

8. The information obtained and collated by the Committee shall be made available to the Commission, and the Commission may call upon the States concerned to supply any other relevant information.

Article 13

1. When the Commission has fully considered the matter, it shall prepare and submit to the Chairman of the Committee a report embodying its findings on all questions of fact relevant to the issue between the parties and containing such recommendations as it may think proper for the amicable solution of the dispute.

2. The Chairman of the Committee shall communicate the report of the Commission to each of the States parties to the dispute. These States shall, within three months, inform the Chairman of the Committee whether or not they accept the recommendations contained in the report of the Commission.

3. After the period provided for in paragraph 2 of this article, the Chairman of the Committee shall communicate the report of the Commission and the declarations of the States Parties concerned to the other States Parties to this Convention.

Article 14

1. A State Party may at any time declare that it recognizes the competence of the Committee to receive and consider communications from individuals or groups of individuals within its jurisdiction claiming to be

victims of a violation by that State Party of any of the rights set forth in this Convention. No communication shall be received by the Committee if it concerns a State Party which has not made such a declaration.

2. Any State Party which makes a declaration as provided for in paragraph I of this article may establish or indicate a body within its national legal order which shall be competent to receive and consider petitions from individuals and groups of individuals within its jurisdiction who claim to be victims of a violation of any of the rights set forth in this Convention and who have exhausted other available local remedies.

3. A declaration made in accordance with paragraph 1 of this article and the name of any body established or indicated in accordance with paragraph 2 of this article shall be deposited by the State Party concerned with the Secretary-General of the United Nations, who shall transmit copies thereof to the other States Parties. A declaration may be withdrawn at any time by notification to the Secretary-General, but such a withdrawal shall not affect communications pending before the Committee.

4. A register of petitions shall be kept by the body established or indicated in accordance with paragraph 2 of this article, and certified copies of the register shall be filed annually through appropriate channels with the Secretary-General on the understanding that the contents shall not be publicly disclosed.

5. In the event of failure to obtain satisfaction from the body established or indicated in accordance with paragraph 2 of this article, the petitioner shall have the right to communicate the matter to the Committee within six months.

6.   (a) The Committee shall confidentially bring any communication referred to it to the attention of the State Party alleged to be violating any provision of this Convention, but the identity of the individual or groups of individuals concerned shall not be revealed without his or their express consent. The Committee shall not receive anonymous communications;

    (b) Within three months, the receiving State shall submit to the Committee written explanations or statements clarifying the matter and the remedy, if any, that may have been taken by that State.

7.   (a) The Committee shall consider communications in the light of all information made available to it by the State Party concerned and by the petitioner. The Committee shall not consider any communication from a petitioner unless it has ascertained that the petitioner has exhausted all available domestic remedies. However, this shall not be the rule where the application of the remedies is unreasonably prolonged;

    (b) The Committee shall forward its suggestions and recommendations, if any, to the State Party concerned and to the petitioner.

8. The Committee shall include in its annual report a summary of such communications and, where appropriate, a summary of the explanations and statements of the States Parties concerned and of its own suggestions and recommendations.

9. The Committee shall be competent to exercise the functions provided for in this article only when at least ten States Parties to this Convention are bound by declarations in accordance with paragraph I of this article.

Article 15

1. Pending the achievement of the objectives of the Declaration on the Granting of Independence to Colonial Countries and Peoples, contained in General Assembly resolution 1514 (XV) of 14 December 1960, the provisions of this Convention shall in no way limit the right of petition granted to these peoples by other international instruments or by the United Nations and its specialized agencies.

2.   (a) The Committee established under article 8, paragraph 1, of this Convention shall receive copies of the petitions from, and submit expressions of opinion and recommendations on these petitions to, the bodies of the United Nations which deal with matters directly related to the principles and objectives of this Convention in their consideration of petitions from the inhabitants of Trust and Non-Self-Governing Territories and all other territories to which General Assembly resolution 1514 (XV) applies, relating to matters covered by this Convention which are before these bodies;

    (b) The Committee shall receive from the competent bodies of the United Nations copies of the reports concerning the legislative, judicial, administrative or other measures directly related to the principles and objectives of this Convention applied by the administering Powers within the Territories mentioned in subparagraph (a) of this paragraph, and shall express opinions and make recommendations to these bodies.

3. The Committee shall include in its report to the General Assembly a summary of the petitions and reports it has received from United Nations bodies, and the expressions of opinion and recommendations of the Committee relating to the said petitions and reports.

4. The Committee shall request from the Secretary-General of the United Nations all information relevant to the objectives of this Convention and available to him regarding the Territories mentioned in paragraph 2 (a) of this article.

Article 16

The provisions of this Convention concerning the settlement of disputes or complaints shall be applied without prejudice to other procedures for settling disputes or complaints in the field of discrimination laid down in the constituent instruments of, or conventions adopted by, the United Nations and its specialized agencies, and shall not prevent the States Parties from having recourse to other procedures for settling a dispute in accordance with general or special international agreements in force between them.

Article 17

1. This Convention is open for signature by any State Member of the United Nations or member of any of its specialized agencies, by any State Party to the Statute of the International Court of Justice, and by any other State which has been invited by the General Assembly of the United Nations to become a Party to this Convention.

2. This Convention is subject to ratification. Instruments of ratification shall be deposited with the Secretary-General of the United Nations.

Article 18

1. This Convention shall be open to accession by any State referred to in article 17, paragraph 1, of the Convention. 2. Accession shall be effected by the deposit of an instrument of accession with the Secretary-General of the United Nations.

Article 19

1. This Convention shall enter into force on the thirtieth day after the date of the deposit with the Secretary-General of the United Nations of the twenty-seventh instrument of ratification or instrument of accession.

2. For each State ratifying this Convention or acceding to it after the deposit of the twenty-seventh instrument of ratification or instrument of accession, the Convention shall enter into force on the thirtieth day after the date of the deposit of its own instrument of ratification or instrument of accession.

Article 20

1. The Secretary-General of the United Nations shall receive and circulate to all States which are or may become Parties to this Convention reservations made by States at the time of ratification or accession. Any State which objects to the reservation shall, within a period of ninety days from the date of the said communication, notify the Secretary-General that it does not accept it.

2. A reservation incompatible with the object and purpose of this Convention shall not be permitted, nor shall a reservation the effect of which would inhibit the operation of any of the bodies established by this Convention be allowed. A reservation shall be considered incompatible or inhibitive if at least two thirds of the States Parties to this Convention object to it.

3. Reservations may be withdrawn at any time by notification to this effect addressed to the Secretary-General. Such notification shall take effect on the date on which it is received.

Article 21

A State Party may denounce this Convention by written notification to the Secretary-General of the United Nations. Denunciation shall take effect one year after the date of receipt of the notification by the Secretary General.

Article 22

Any dispute between two or more States Parties with respect to the interpretation or application of this Convention, which is not settled by negotiation or by the procedures expressly provided for in this Convention, shall, at the request of any of the parties to the dispute, be referred to the International Court of Justice for decision, unless the disputants agree to another mode of settlement.

Article 23

1. A request for the revision of this Convention may be made at any time by any State Party by means of a notification in writing addressed to the Secretary-General of the United Nations.
2. The General Assembly of the United Nations shall decide upon the steps, if any, to be taken in respect of such a request.

Article 24

The Secretary-General of the United Nations shall inform all States referred to in article 17, paragraph 1, of this Convention of the following particulars:

    (a) Signatures, ratifications and accessions under articles 17 and 18;

    (b) The date of entry into force of this Convention under article 19;

    (c) Communications and declarations received under articles 14, 20 and 23;

    (d) Denunciations under article 21.

Article 25

1. This Convention, of which the Chinese, English, French, Russian and Spanish texts are equally authentic, shall be deposited in the archives of the United Nations.
2. The Secretary-General of the United Nations shall transmit certified copies of this Convention to all States belonging to any of the categories mentioned in article 17, paragraph 1, of the Convention.

INTERNATIONAL COVENANT ON CIVIL AND POLITICAL RIGHTS (1966)

International Covenant on Civil and Political Rights, *adopted* Dec. 16, 1966,
S. Exec. Doc. E, 95-2 (1978), 999 U.N.T.S. 171

Article 1

1. All peoples have the right of self-determination. By virtue of that right they freely determine their political status and freely pursue their economic, social and cultural development.
2. All peoples may, for their own ends, freely dispose of their natural wealth and resources without prejudice to any obligations arising out of international economic co-operation, based upon the principle of mutual benefit, and international law. In no case may a people be deprived of its own means of subsistence.
3. The States Parties to the present Covenant, including those having responsibility for the administration of Non-Self-Governing and Trust Territories, shall promote the realization of the right of self-determination, and shall respect that right, in conformity with the provisions of the Charter of the United Nations.

Article 2

1. Each State Party to the present Covenant undertakes to respect and to ensure to all individuals within its territory and subject to its jurisdiction the rights recognized in the present Covenant, without distinction of any kind, such as race, colour, sex, language, religion, political or other opinion, national or social origin, property, birth or other status.
2. Where not already provided for by existing legislative or other measures, each State Party to the present Covenant undertakes to take the necessary steps, in accordance with its constitutional processes and with the provisions of the present Covenant, to adopt such laws or other measures as may be necessary to give effect to the rights recognized in the present Covenant.
3. Each State Party to the present Covenant undertakes:

    (a) To ensure that any person whose rights or freedoms as herein recognized are violated shall have an effective remedy, notwithstanding that the violation has been committed by persons acting in an official capacity;

    (b) To ensure that any person claiming such a remedy shall have his right thereto determined by competent judicial, administrative or legislative authorities, or by any other competent authority provided for by the legal system of the State, and to develop the possibilities of judicial remedy;

(c) To ensure that the competent authorities shall enforce such remedies when granted.

Article 3
The States Parties to the present Covenant undertake to ensure the equal right of men and women to the enjoyment of all civil and political rights set forth in the present Covenant.

Article 4
1. In time of public emergency which threatens the life of the nation and the existence of which is officially proclaimed, the States Parties to the present Covenant may take measures derogating from their obligations under the present Covenant to the extent strictly required by the exigencies of the situation, provided that such measures are not inconsistent with their other obligations under international law and do not involve discrimination solely on the ground of race, colour, sex, language, religion or social origin.
2. No derogation from articles 6, 7, 8 (paragraphs I and 2), 11, 15, 16 and 18 may be made under this provision.
3. Any State Party to the present Covenant availing itself of the right of derogation shall immediately inform the other States Parties to the present Covenant, through the intermediary of the Secretary-General of the United Nations, of the provisions from which it has derogated and of the reasons by which it was actuated. A further communication shall be made, through the same intermediary, on the date on which it terminates such derogation.

Article 5
1. Nothing in the present Covenant may be interpreted as implying for any State, group or person any right to engage in any activity or perform any act aimed at the destruction of any of the rights and freedoms recognized herein or at their limitation to a greater extent than is provided for in the present Covenant.
2. There shall be no restriction upon or derogation from any of the fundamental human rights recognized or existing in any State Party to the present Covenant pursuant to law, conventions, regulations or custom on the pretext that the present Covenant does not recognize such rights or that it recognizes them to a lesser extent.

Article 6
1. Every human being has the inherent right to life. This right shall be protected by law. No one shall be arbitrarily deprived of his life.
2. In countries which have not abolished the death penalty, sentence of death may be imposed only for the most serious crimes in accordance with the law in force at the time of the commission of the crime and not contrary to the provisions of the present Covenant and to the Convention on the Prevention and Punishment of the Crime of Genocide. This penalty can only be carried out pursuant to a final judgement rendered by a competent court.
3. When deprivation of life constitutes the crime of genocide, it is understood that nothing in this article shall authorize any State Party to the present Covenant to derogate in any way from any obligation assumed under the provisions of the Convention on the Prevention and Punishment of the Crime of Genocide.
4. Anyone sentenced to death shall have the right to seek pardon or commutation of the sentence. Amnesty, pardon or commutation of the sentence of death may be granted in all cases.
5. Sentence of death shall not be imposed for crimes committed by persons below eighteen years of age and shall not be carried out on pregnant women.
6. Nothing in this article shall be invoked to delay or to prevent the abolition of capital punishment by any State Party to the present Covenant.

Article 7
No one shall be subjected to torture or to cruel, inhuman or degrading treatment or punishment. In particular, no one shall be subjected without his free consent to medical or scientific experimentation.

Article 8
1. No one shall be held in slavery; slavery and the slave-trade in all their forms shall be prohibited.
2. No one shall be held in servitude.
3.   (a) No one shall be required to perform forced or compulsory labour;

(b) Paragraph 3 (a) shall not be held to preclude, in countries where imprisonment with hard labour may be imposed as a punishment for a crime, the performance of hard labour in pursuance of a sentence to such punishment by a competent court;

(c) For the purpose of this paragraph the term "forced or compulsory labour" shall not include:

(i) Any work or service, not referred to in subparagraph (b), normally required of a person who is under detention in consequence of a lawful order of a court, or of a person during conditional release from such detention;

(ii) Any service of a military character and, in countries where conscientious objection is recognized, any national service required by law of conscientious objectors;

(iii) Any service exacted in cases of emergency or calamity threatening the life or well-being of the community;

(iv) Any work or service which forms part of normal civil obligations.

Article 9

1. Everyone has the right to liberty and security of person. No one shall be subjected to arbitrary arrest or detention. No one shall be deprived of his liberty except on such grounds and in accordance with such procedure as are established by law.

2. Anyone who is arrested shall be informed, at the time of arrest, of the reasons for his arrest and shall be promptly informed of any charges against him.

3. Anyone arrested or detained on a criminal charge shall be brought promptly before a judge or other officer authorized by law to exercise judicial power and shall be entitled to trial within a reasonable time or to release. It shall not be the general rule that persons awaiting trial shall be detained in custody, but release may be subject to guarantees to appear for trial, at any other stage of the judicial proceedings, and, should occasion arise, for execution of the judgement.

4. Anyone who is deprived of his liberty by arrest or detention shall be entitled to take proceedings before a court, in order that that court may decide without delay on the lawfulness of his detention and order his release if the detention is not lawful.

5. Anyone who has been the victim of unlawful arrest or detention shall have an enforceable right to compensation.

Article 10

1. All persons deprived of their liberty shall be treated with humanity and with respect for the inherent dignity of the human person.

2.   (a) Accused persons shall, save in exceptional circumstances, be segregated from convicted persons and shall be subject to separate treatment appropriate to their status as unconvicted persons;

(b) Accused juvenile persons shall be separated from adults and brought as speedily as possible for adjudication.

3. The penitentiary system shall comprise treatment of prisoners the essential aim of which shall be their reformation and social rehabilitation. Juvenile offenders shall be segregated from adults and be accorded treatment appropriate to their age and legal status.

Article 11

No one shall be imprisoned merely on the ground of inability to fulfil a contractual obligation.

Article 12

1. Everyone lawfully within the territory of a State shall, within that territory, have the right to liberty of movement and freedom to choose his residence.

2. Everyone shall be free to leave any country, including his own.

3. The above-mentioned rights shall not be subject to any restrictions except those which are provided by law, are necessary to protect national security, public order (ordre public), public health or morals or the rights and freedoms of others, and are consistent with the other rights recognized in the present Covenant.

4. No one shall be arbitrarily deprived of the right to enter his own country.

Article 13

An alien lawfully in the territory of a State Party to the present Covenant may be expelled therefrom only in pursuance of a decision reached in accordance with law and shall, except where compelling reasons of national security otherwise require, be allowed to submit the reasons against his expulsion and to have his case reviewed by, and be represented for the purpose before, the competent authority or a person or persons especially designated by the competent authority.

Article 14

1. All persons shall be equal before the courts and tribunals. In the determination of any criminal charge against him, or of his rights and obligations in a suit at law, everyone shall be entitled to a fair and public hearing by a competent, independent and impartial tribunal established by law. The press and the public may be excluded from all or part of a trial for reasons of morals, public order (ordre public) or national security in a democratic society, or when the interest of the private lives of the parties so requires, or to the extent strictly necessary in the opinion of the court in special circumstances where publicity would prejudice the interests of justice; but any judgement rendered in a criminal case or in a suit at law shall be made public except where the interest of juvenile persons otherwise requires or the proceedings concern matrimonial disputes or the guardianship of children.

2. Everyone charged with a criminal offence shall have the right to be presumed innocent until proved guilty according to law.

3. In the determination of any criminal charge against him, everyone shall be entitled to the following minimum guarantees, in full equality:

(a) To be informed promptly and in detail in a language which he understands of the nature and cause of the charge against him;

(b) To have adequate time and facilities for the preparation of his defence and to communicate with counsel of his own choosing;

(c) To be tried without undue delay;

(d) To be tried in his presence, and to defend himself in person or through legal assistance of his own choosing; to be informed, if he does not have legal assistance, of this right; and to have legal assistance assigned to him, in any case where the interests of justice so require, and without payment by him in any such case if he does not have sufficient means to pay for it;

(e) To examine, or have examined, the witnesses against him and to obtain the attendance and examination of witnesses on his behalf under the same conditions as witnesses against him;

(f) To have the free assistance of an interpreter if he cannot understand or speak the language used in court;

(g) Not to be compelled to testify against himself or to confess guilt.

4. In the case of juvenile persons, the procedure shall be such as will take account of their age and the desirability of promoting their rehabilitation.

5. Everyone convicted of a crime shall have the right to his conviction and sentence being reviewed by a higher tribunal according to law.

6. When a person has by a final decision been convicted of a criminal offence and when subsequently his conviction has been reversed or he has been pardoned on the ground that a new or newly discovered fact shows conclusively that there has been a miscarriage of justice, the person who has suffered punishment as a result of such conviction shall be compensated according to law, unless it is proved that the non-disclosure of the unknown fact in time is wholly or partly attributable to him.

7. No one shall be liable to be tried or punished again for an offence for which he has already been finally convicted or acquitted in accordance with the law and penal procedure of each country.

Article 15

1. No one shall be held guilty of any criminal offence on account of any act or omission which did not constitute a criminal offence, under national or international law, at the time when it was committed. Nor shall a heavier penalty be imposed than the one that was applicable at the time when the criminal offence was committed. If, subsequent to the commission of the offence, provision is made by law for the imposition of the lighter penalty, the offender shall benefit thereby.

2. Nothing in this article shall prejudice the trial and punishment of any person for any act or omission which, at the time when it was committed, was criminal according to the general principles of law recognized by the community of nations.

Article 16

Everyone shall have the right to recognition everywhere as a person before the law.

Article 17

1. No one shall be subjected to arbitrary or unlawful interference with his privacy, family, or correspondence, nor to unlawful attacks on his honour and reputation.
2. Everyone has the right to the protection of the law against such interference or attacks.

Article 18

1. Everyone shall have the right to freedom of thought, conscience and religion. This right shall include freedom to have or to adopt a religion or belief of his choice, and freedom, either individually or in community with others and in public or private, to manifest his religion or belief in worship, observance, practice and teaching.
2. No one shall be subject to coercion which would impair his freedom to have or to adopt a religion or belief of his choice.
3. Freedom to manifest one's religion or beliefs may be subject only to such limitations as are prescribed by law and are necessary to protect public safety, order, health, or morals or the fundamental rights and freedoms of others.
4. The States Parties to the present Covenant undertake to have respect for the liberty of parents and, when applicable, legal guardians to ensure the religious and moral education of their children in conformity with their own convictions.

Article 19

1. Everyone shall have the right to hold opinions without interference.
2. Everyone shall have the right to freedom of expression; this right shall include freedom to seek, receive and impart information and ideas of all kinds, regardless of frontiers, either orally, in writing or in print, in the form of art, or through any other media of his choice.
3. The exercise of the rights provided for in paragraph 2 of this article carries with it special duties and responsibilities. It may therefore be subject to certain restrictions, but these shall only be such as are provided by law and are necessary:
    (a) For respect of the rights or reputations of others;
    (b) For the protection of national security or of public order (ordre public), or of public health or morals.

Article 20

1. Any propaganda for war shall be prohibited by law.
2. Any advocacy of national, racial or religious hatred that constitutes incitement to discrimination, hostility or violence shall be prohibited by law.

Article 21

The right of peaceful assembly shall be recognized. No restrictions may be placed on the exercise of this right other than those imposed in conformity with the law and which are necessary in a democratic society in the interests of national security or public safety, public order (ordre public), the protection of public health or morals or the protection of the rights and freedoms of others.

Article 22

1. Everyone shall have the right to freedom of association with others, including the right to form and join trade unions for the protection of his interests.
2. No restrictions may be placed on the exercise of this right other than those which are prescribed by law and which are necessary in a democratic society in the interests of national security or public safety, public order (ordre public), the protection of public health or morals or the protection of the rights and freedoms of others. This article shall not prevent the imposition of lawful restrictions on members of the armed forces and of the police in their exercise of this right.
3. Nothing in this article shall authorize States Parties to the International Labour Organisation Convention of 1948 concerning Freedom of Association and Protection of the Right to Organize to take legislative

measures which would prejudice, or to apply the law in such a manner as to prejudice, the guarantees provided for in that Convention.

Article 23

1. The family is the natural and fundamental group unit of society and is entitled to protection by society and the State.
2. The right of men and women of marriageable age to marry and to found a family shall be recognized.
3. No marriage shall be entered into without the free and full consent of the intending spouses.
4. States Parties to the present Covenant shall take appropriate steps to ensure equality of rights and responsibilities of spouses as to marriage, during marriage and at its dissolution. In the case of dissolution, provision shall be made for the necessary protection of any children.

Article 24

1. Every child shall have, without any discrimination as to race, colour, sex, language, religion, national or social origin, property or birth, the right to such measures of protection as are required by his status as a minor, on the part of his family, society and the State.
2. Every child shall be registered immediately after birth and shall have a name.
3. Every child has the right to acquire a nationality.

Article 25

Every citizen shall have the right and the opportunity, without any of the distinctions mentioned in article 2 and without unreasonable restrictions:

(a) To take part in the conduct of public affairs, directly or through freely chosen representatives;
(b) To vote and to be elected at genuine periodic elections which shall be by universal and equal suffrage and shall be held by secret ballot, guaranteeing the free expression of the will of the electors;
(c) To have access, on general terms of equality, to public service in his country.

Article 26

All persons are equal before the law and are entitled without any discrimination to the equal protection of the law. In this respect, the law shall prohibit any discrimination and guarantee to all persons equal and effective protection against discrimination on any ground such as race, colour, sex, language, religion, political or other opinion, national or social origin, property, birth or other status.

Article 27

In those States in which ethnic, religious or linguistic minorities exist, persons belonging to such minorities shall not be denied the right, in community with the other members of their group, to enjoy their own culture, to profess and practise their own religion, or to use their own language.

Article 28

1. There shall be established a Human Rights Committee (hereafter referred to in the present Covenant as the Committee). It shall consist of eighteen members and shall carry out the functions hereinafter provided.
2. The Committee shall be composed of nationals of the States Parties to the present Covenant who shall be persons of high moral character and recognized competence in the field of human rights, consideration being given to the usefulness of the participation of some persons having legal experience.
3. The members of the Committee shall be elected and shall serve in their personal capacity.

Article 29

1. The members of the Committee shall be elected by secret ballot from a list of persons possessing the qualifications prescribed in article 28 and nominated for the purpose by the States Parties to the present Covenant.
2. Each State Party to the present Covenant may nominate not more than two persons. These persons shall be nationals of the nominating State.
3. A person shall be eligible for renomination.

Article 30

1. The initial election shall be held no later than six months after the date of the entry into force of the present Covenant.

2. At least four months before the date of each election to the Committee, other than an election to fill a vacancy declared in accordance with article 34, the Secretary-General of the United Nations shall address a written invitation to the States Parties to the present Covenant to submit their nominations for membership of the Committee within three months.

3. The Secretary-General of the United Nations shall prepare a list in alphabetical order of all the persons thus nominated, with an indication of the States Parties which have nominated them, and shall submit it to the States Parties to the present Covenant no later than one month before the date of each election.

4. Elections of the members of the Committee shall be held at a meeting of the States Parties to the present Covenant convened by the Secretary General of the United Nations at the Headquarters of the United Nations. At that meeting, for which two thirds of the States Parties to the present Covenant shall constitute a quorum, the persons elected to the Committee shall be those nominees who obtain the largest number of votes and an absolute majority of the votes of the representatives of States Parties present and voting.

Article 31

1. The Committee may not include more than one national of the same State.

2. In the election of the Committee, consideration shall be given to equitable geographical distribution of membership and to the representation of the different forms of civilization and of the principal legal systems.

Article 32

1. The members of the Committee shall be elected for a term of four years. They shall be eligible for re-election if renominated. However, the terms of nine of the members elected at the first election shall expire at the end of two years; immediately after the first election, the names of these nine members shall be chosen by lot by the Chairman of the meeting referred to in article 30, paragraph 4.

2. Elections at the expiry of office shall be held in accordance with the preceding articles of this part of the present Covenant.

Article 33

1. If, in the unanimous opinion of the other members, a member of the Committee has ceased to carry out his functions for any cause other than absence of a temporary character, the Chairman of the Committee shall notify the Secretary-General of the United Nations, who shall then declare the seat of that member to be vacant.

2. In the event of the death or the resignation of a member of the Committee, the Chairman shall immediately notify the Secretary-General of the United Nations, who shall declare the seat vacant from the date of death or the date on which the resignation takes effect.

Article 34

1. When a vacancy is declared in accordance with article 33 and if the term of office of the member to be replaced does not expire within six months of the declaration of the vacancy, the Secretary-General of the United Nations shall notify each of the States Parties to the present Covenant, which may within two months submit nominations in accordance with article 29 for the purpose of filling the vacancy.

2. The Secretary-General of the United Nations shall prepare a list in alphabetical order of the persons thus nominated and shall submit it to the States Parties to the present Covenant. The election to fill the vacancy shall then take place in accordance with the relevant provisions of this part of the present Covenant.

3. A member of the Committee elected to fill a vacancy declared in accordance with article 33 shall hold office for the remainder of the term of the member who vacated the seat on the Committee under the provisions of that article.

Article 35

The members of the Committee shall, with the approval of the General Assembly of the United Nations, receive emoluments from United Nations resources on such terms and conditions as the General Assembly may decide, having regard to the importance of the Committee's responsibilities.

Article 36
The Secretary-General of the United Nations shall provide the necessary staff and facilities for the effective performance of the functions of the Committee under the present Covenant.

Article 37
1. The Secretary-General of the United Nations shall convene the initial meeting of the Committee at the Headquarters of the United Nations.
2. After its initial meeting, the Committee shall meet at such times as shall be provided in its rules of procedure.
3. The Committee shall normally meet at the Headquarters of the United Nations or at the United Nations Office at Geneva.

Article 38
Every member of the Committee shall, before taking up his duties, make a solemn declaration in open committee that he will perform his functions impartially and conscientiously.

Article 39
1. The Committee shall elect its officers for a term of two years. They may be re-elected.
2. The Committee shall establish its own rules of procedure, but these rules shall provide, inter alia, that:
    (a) Twelve members shall constitute a quorum;
    (b) Decisions of the Committee shall be made by a majority vote of the members present.

Article 40
1. The States Parties to the present Covenant undertake to submit reports on the measures they have adopted which give effect to the rights recognized herein and on the progress made in the enjoyment of those rights:
    (a) Within one year of the entry into force of the present Covenant for the States Parties concerned;
    (b) Thereafter whenever the Committee so requests.
2. All reports shall be submitted to the Secretary-General of the United Nations, who shall transmit them to the Committee for consideration. Reports shall indicate the factors and difficulties, if any, affecting the implementation of the present Covenant.
3. The Secretary-General of the United Nations may, after consultation with the Committee, transmit to the specialized agencies concerned copies of such parts of the reports as may fall within their field of competence.
4. The Committee shall study the reports submitted by the States Parties to the present Covenant. It shall transmit its reports, and such general comments as it may consider appropriate, to the States Parties. The Committee may also transmit to the Economic and Social Council these comments along with the copies of the reports it has received from States Parties to the present Covenant.
5. The States Parties to the present Covenant may submit to the Committee observations on any comments that may be made in accordance with paragraph 4 of this article.

Article 41
1. A State Party to the present Covenant may at any time declare under this article that it recognizes the competence of the Committee to receive and consider communications to the effect that a State Party claims that another State Party is not fulfilling its obligations under the present Covenant. Communications under this article may be received and considered only if submitted by a State Party which has made a declaration recognizing in regard to itself the competence of the Committee. No communication shall be received by the Committee if it concerns a State Party which has not made such a declaration. Communications received under this article shall be dealt with in accordance with the following procedure:
    (a) If a State Party to the present Covenant considers that another State Party is not giving effect to the provisions of the present Covenant, it may, by written communication, bring the matter to the attention of that State Party. Within three months after the receipt of the communication the receiving State shall afford the State which sent the communication an explanation, or any other statement in writing clarifying the matter which should include, to the extent possible and

pertinent, reference to domestic procedures and remedies taken, pending, or available in the matter;

(b) If the matter is not adjusted to the satisfaction of both States Parties concerned within six months after the receipt by the receiving State of the initial communication, either State shall have the right to refer the matter to the Committee, by notice given to the Committee and to the other State;

(c) The Committee shall deal with a matter referred to it only after it has ascertained that all available domestic remedies have been invoked and exhausted in the matter, in conformity with the generally recognized principles of international law. This shall not be the rule where the application of the remedies is unreasonably prolonged;

(d) The Committee shall hold closed meetings when examining communications under this article;

(e) Subject to the provisions of subparagraph (c), the Committee shall make available its good offices to the States Parties concerned with a view to a friendly solution of the matter on the basis of respect for human rights and fundamental freedoms as recognized in the present Covenant;

(f) In any matter referred to it, the Committee may call upon the States Parties concerned, referred to in subparagraph (b), to supply any relevant information;

(g) The States Parties concerned, referred to in subparagraph (b), shall have the right to be represented when the matter is being considered in the Committee and to make submissions orally and/or in writing;

(h) The Committee shall, within twelve months after the date of receipt of notice under subparagraph (b), submit a report:

    (i) If a solution within the terms of subparagraph (e) is reached, the Committee shall confine its report to a brief statement of the facts and of the solution reached;

    (ii) If a solution within the terms of subparagraph (e) is not reached, the Committee shall confine its report to a brief statement of the facts; the written submissions and record of the oral submissions made by the States Parties concerned shall be attached to the report.

    In every matter, the report shall be communicated to the States Parties concerned.

2. The provisions of this article shall come into force when ten States Parties to the present Covenant have made declarations under paragraph I of this article. Such declarations shall be deposited by the States Parties with the Secretary-General of the United Nations, who shall transmit copies thereof to the other States Parties. A declaration may be withdrawn at any time by notification to the Secretary-General. Such a withdrawal shall not prejudice the consideration of any matter which is the subject of a communication already transmitted under this article; no further communication by any State Party shall be received after the notification of withdrawal of the declaration has been received by the Secretary-General, unless the State Party concerned has made a new declaration.

Article 42

1.   (a) If a matter referred to the Committee in accordance with article 41 is not resolved to the satisfaction of the States Parties concerned, the Committee may, with the prior consent of the States Parties concerned, appoint an ad hoc Conciliation Commission (hereinafter referred to as the Commission). The good offices of the Commission shall be made available to the States Parties concerned with a view to an amicable solution of the matter on the basis of respect for the present Covenant;

(b) The Commission shall consist of five persons acceptable to the States Parties concerned. If the States Parties concerned fail to reach agreement within three months on all or part of the composition of the Commission, the members of the Commission concerning whom no agreement has been reached shall be elected by secret ballot by a two-thirds majority vote of the Committee from among its members.

2. The members of the Commission shall serve in their personal capacity. They shall not be nationals of the States Parties concerned, or of a State not Party to the present Covenant, or of a State Party which has not made a declaration under article 41.

3. The Commission shall elect its own Chairman and adopt its own rules of procedure.

4. The meetings of the Commission shall normally be held at the Headquarters of the United Nations or at the United Nations Office at Geneva. However, they may be held at such other convenient places as the Commission may determine in consultation with the Secretary-General of the United Nations and the States Parties concerned.

5. The secretariat provided in accordance with article 36 shall also service the commissions appointed under this article.

6. The information received and collated by the Committee shall be made available to the Commission and the Commission may call upon the States Parties concerned to supply any other relevant information.

7. When the Commission has fully considered the matter, but in any event not later than twelve months after having been seized of the matter, it shall submit to the Chairman of the Committee a report for communication to the States Parties concerned:

(a) If the Commission is unable to complete its consideration of the matter within twelve months, it shall confine its report to a brief statement of the status of its consideration of the matter;

(b) If an amicable solution to the matter on tie basis of respect for human rights as recognized in the present Covenant is reached, the Commission shall confine its report to a brief statement of the facts and of the solution reached;

(c) If a solution within the terms of subparagraph (b) is not reached, the Commission's report shall embody its findings on all questions of fact relevant to the issues between the States Parties concerned, and its views on the possibilities of an amicable solution of the matter. This report shall also contain the written submissions and a record of the oral submissions made by the States Parties concerned;

(d) If the Commission's report is submitted under subparagraph (c), the States Parties concerned shall, within three months of the receipt of the report, notify the Chairman of the Committee whether or not they accept the contents of the report of the Commission.

8. The provisions of this article are without prejudice to the responsibilities of the Committee under article 41.

9. The States Parties concerned shall share equally all the expenses of the members of the Commission in accordance with estimates to be provided by the Secretary-General of the United Nations.

10. The Secretary-General of the United Nations shall be empowered to pay the expenses of the members of the Commission, if necessary, before reimbursement by the States Parties concerned, in accordance with paragraph 9 of this article.

Article 43

The members of the Committee, and of the ad hoc conciliation commissions which may be appointed under article 42, shall be entitled to the facilities, privileges and immunities of experts on mission for the United Nations as laid down in the relevant sections of the Convention on the Privileges and Immunities of the United Nations.

Article 44

The provisions for the implementation of the present Covenant shall apply without prejudice to the procedures prescribed in the field of human rights by or under the constituent instruments and the conventions of the United Nations and of the specialized agencies and shall not prevent the States Parties to the present Covenant from having recourse to other procedures for settling a dispute in accordance with general or special international agreements in force between them.

Article 45

The Committee shall submit to the General Assembly of the United Nations, through the Economic and Social Council, an annual report on its activities.

Article 46

Nothing in the present Covenant shall be interpreted as impairing the provisions of the Charter of the United Nations and of the constitutions of the specialized agencies which define the respective responsibilities of the various organs of the United Nations and of the specialized agencies in regard to the matters dealt with in the present Covenant.

Article 47

Nothing in the present Covenant shall be interpreted as impairing the inherent right of all peoples to enjoy and utilize fully and freely their natural wealth and resources.

Article 48

1. The present Covenant is open for signature by any State Member of the United Nations or member of any of its specialized agencies, by any State Party to the Statute of the International Court of Justice, and by any other State which has been invited by the General Assembly of the United Nations to become a Party to the present Covenant.

2. The present Covenant is subject to ratification. Instruments of ratification shall be deposited with the Secretary-General of the United Nations.

3. The present Covenant shall be open to accession by any State referred to in paragraph 1 of this article.

4. Accession shall be effected by the deposit of an instrument of accession with the Secretary-General of the United Nations.

5. The Secretary-General of the United Nations shall inform all States which have signed this Covenant or acceded to it of the deposit of each instrument of ratification or accession. * * *

Article 50

The provisions of the present Covenant shall extend to all parts of federal States without any limitations or exceptions.

Article 51

1. Any State Party to the present Covenant may propose an amendment and file it with the Secretary-General of the United Nations. The Secretary-General of the United Nations shall thereupon communicate any proposed amendments to the States Parties to the present Covenant with a request that they notify him whether they favour a conference of States Parties for the purpose of considering and voting upon the proposals. In the event that at least one third of the States Parties favours such a conference, the Secretary-General shall convene the conference under the auspices of the United Nations. Any amendment adopted by a majority of the States Parties present and voting at the conference shall be submitted to the General Assembly of the United Nations for approval.

2. Amendments shall come into force when they have been approved by the General Assembly of the United Nations and accepted by a two-thirds majority of the States Parties to the present Covenant in accordance with their respective constitutional processes. 3. When amendments come into force, they shall be binding on those States Parties which have accepted them, other States Parties still being bound by the provisions of the present Covenant and any earlier amendment which they have accepted.

Article 52

1. Irrespective of the notifications made under article 48, paragraph 5, the Secretary-General of the United Nations shall inform all States referred to in paragraph I of the same article of the following particulars:

(a) Signatures, ratifications and accessions under article 48;

(b) The date of the entry into force of the present Covenant under article 49 and the date of the entry into force of any amendments under article 51.

Article 53

1. The present Covenant, of which the Chinese, English, French, Russian and Spanish texts are equally authentic, shall be deposited in the archives of the United Nations. * * *

FIRST OPTIONAL PROTOCOL TO THE INTERNATIONAL COVENANT ON CIVIL AND POLITICAL RIGHTS (1966)

Optional Protocol to the International Covenant on Civil and Political Rights, *adopted* Dec. 16, 1966, 999 U.N.T.S. 302

The States Parties to the present Protocol,

Considering that in order further to achieve the purposes of the International Covenant on Civil and Political Rights (hereinafter referred to as the Covenant) and the implementation of its provisions it would be appropriate to enable the Human Rights Committee set up in * * * the Covenant (hereinafter referred to as the Committee) to receive and consider, as provided in the present Protocol, communications from individuals claiming to be victims of violations of any of the rights set forth in the Covenant.

Have agreed as follows:

Article 1
A State Party to the Covenant that becomes a Party to the present Protocol recognizes the competence of the Committee to receive and consider communications from individuals subject to its jurisdiction who claim to be victims of a violation by that State Party of any of the rights set forth in the Covenant. No communication shall be received by the Committee if it concerns a State Party to the Covenant which is not a Party to the present Protocol.

Article 2
Subject to the provisions of article 1, individuals who claim that any of their rights enumerated in the Covenant have been violated and who have exhausted all available domestic remedies may submit a written communication to the Committee for consideration.

Article 3
The Committee shall consider inadmissible any communciation under the present Protocol which is anonymous, or which it considers to be an abuse of the right of submission of such communications or to be incompatible with the provisions of the Covenant.

Article 4
1. Subject to the provisions of article 3, the Committee shall bring any communications submitted to it under the present Protocol to the attention of the State Party to the present Protocol alleged to be violating any provision of the Covenant.
2. Within six months, the receiving State shall submit to the Committee written explanations or statements clarifying the matter and the remedy, if any, that may have been taken by that State.

Article 5
1. The Committee shall consider communications received under the present Protocol in the light of all written information made available to it by the individual and by the State Party concerned.
2. The Committee shall not consider any communication from an individual unless it has ascertained that:
> (a) The same matter is not being examined under another procedure of international investigation or settlement;
> (b) The individual has exhausted all available domestic remedies. This shall not be the rule where the application of the remedies is unreasonably prolonged.
3. The Committee shall hold closed meetings when examining communications under the present Protocol.
4. The Committee shall forward its views to the State Party concerned and to the individual. * * *

Article 7
Pending the achievement of the objectives of resolution 1514(XV) adopted by the General Assembly of the United Nations on 14 December 1960 concerning the Declaration on the Granting of Independence to Colonial Countries and Peoples, the provisions of the present Protocol shall in no way limit the right of petition granted to these peoples by the Charter of the United Nations and other international conventions and instruments under the United Nations and its specialized agencies. * * *

Article 10
The provisions of the present Protocol shall extend to all parts of federal States without any limitations or exceptions.

Article 11
1. Any State Party to the present Protocol may propose an amendment and file it with the Secretary-General of the United Nations. The Secretary-General shall thereupon communicate any proposed amendments to the States Parties to the present Protocol with a request that they notify him whether they favour a conference of States Parties for the purpose of considering and voting upon the proposal. In the

event that at least one third of the States Parties favours such a conference, the Secretary-General shall convene the conference under the auspices of the United Nations. Any amendment adopted by a majority of the States Parties present and voting at the conference shall be submitted to the General Assembly of the United Nations for approval.

2. Amendments shall come into force when they have been approved by the General Assembly of the United Nations and accepted by a two-thirds majority of the States Parties to the present Protocol in accordance with their respective constitutional processes.

3. When amendments come into force, they shall be binding on those States Parties which have accepted them, other States Parties still being bound by the provisions of the present Protocol and any earlier amendment which they have accepted.

Article 12

1. Any State Party may denounce the present Protocol at any time by written notification addressed to the Secretary-General of the United Nations. Denunciation shall take effect three months after the date of receipt of the notification by the Secretary-General.

2. Denunciation shall be without prejudice to the continued application of the provisions of the present Protocol to any communication submitted under article 2 before the effective date of denunciation. * * *

Article 14

1. The present Protocol, of which the Chinese, English, French, Russian and Spanish texts are equally authentic, shall be deposited in the archives of the United Nations.

2. The Secretary-General of the United Nations shall transmit certified copies of the present Protocol to all States referred to in article 48 of the Covenant.

SECOND OPTIONAL PROTOCOL TO THE INTERNATIONAL COVENANT ON CIVIL AND POLITICAL RIGHTS, AIMING AT THE ABOLITION OF THE DEATH PENALTY (1989)

Second Optional Protocol to the International Covenant on Civil and Political Rights, aiming at the abolition of the death penalty, *adopted* Dec. 15, 1989, 1642 U.N.T.S. 414

The States Parties to the present Protocol,

Believing that abolition of the death penalty contributes to enhancement of human dignity and progressive development of human rights,

Recalling article 3 of the Universal Declaration of Human Rights, adopted on 10 December 1948, and article 6 of the International Covenant on Civil and Political Rights, adopted on 16 December 1966, * * *

Convinced that all measures of abolition of the death penalty should be considered as progress in the enjoyment of the right to life, * * *

Have agreed as follows:

Article 1

1. No one within the jurisdiction of a State Party to the present Protocol shall be executed.

2. Each State Party shall take all necessary measures to abolish the death penalty within its jurisdiction.

Article 2

1. No reservation is admissible to the present Protocol, except for a reservation made at the time of ratification or accession that provides for the application of the death penalty in time of war pursuant to a conviction for a most serious crime of a military nature committed during wartime.

2. The State Party making such a reservation shall at the time of ratification or accession communicate to the Secretary-General of the United Nations the relevant provisions of its national legislation applicable during wartime.

3. The State Party having made such a reservation shall notify the Secretary-General of the United Nations of any beginning or ending of a state of war applicable to its territory.

Article 3

The States Parties to the present Protocol shall include in the reports they submit to the Human Rights Committee, in accordance with article 40 of the Covenant, information on the measures that they have adopted to give effect to the present Protocol.

Article 4

With respect to the States Parties to the Covenant that have made a declaration under article 41, the competence of the Human Rights Committee to receive and consider communications when a State Party claims that another State Party is not fulfilling its obligations shall extend to the provisions of the present Protocol, unless the State Party concerned has made a statement to the contrary at the moment of ratification or accession.

Article 5

With respect to the States Parties to the first Optional Protocol to the International Covenant on Civil and Political Rights adopted on 16 December 1966, the competence of the Human Rights Committee to receive and consider communications from individuals subject to its jurisdiction shall extend to the provisions of the present Protocol, unless the State Party concerned has made a statement to the contrary at the moment of ratification or accession.

Article 6

1. The provisions of the present Protocol shall apply as additional provisions to the Covenant.

2. Without prejudice to the possibility of a reservation under article 2 of the present Protocol, the right guaranteed in article 1, paragraph 1, of the present Protocol shall not be subject to any derogation under article 4 of the Covenant. * * *

Article 9

The provisions of the present Protocol shall extend to all parts of federal States without any limitations or exceptions.

Article 10

The Secretary-General of the United Nations shall inform all States referred to in article 48, paragraph 1, of the Covenant of the following particulars:

    (a) Reservations, communications and notifications under article 2 of the present Protocol;

    (b) Statements made under articles 4 or 5 of the present Protocol;

    (c) Signatures, ratifications and accessions under article 7 of the present Protocol:

    (d) The date of the entry into force of the present Protocol under article 8 thereof.

Article 11

1. The present Protocol, of which the Arabic, Chinese, English, French, Russian and Spanish texts are equally authentic, shall be deposited in the archives of the United Nations.

2. The Secretary-General of the United Nations shall transmit certified copies of the present Protocol to all States referred to in article 48 of the Covenant.

INTERNATIONAL COVENANT ON ECONOMIC, SOCIAL AND CULTURAL RIGHTS (1966)

International Covenant on Economic, Social and Cultural Rights, *adopted* Dec. 16, 1966, 993 U.N.T.S. 3

Preamble

The States Parties to the present Covenant,

Considering that, in accordance with the principles proclaimed in the Charter of the United Nations, recognition of the inherent dignity and of the equal and inalienable rights of all members of the human family is the foundation of freedom, justice and peace in the world, * * *

Recognizing that, in accordance with the Universal Declaration of Human Rights, the ideal of free human beings enjoying freedom from fear and want can only be achieved if conditions are created whereby everyone may enjoy his economic, social and cultural rights, as well as his civil and political rights, * * *

Agree upon the following articles:

Article 1

1. All peoples have the right of self-determination. By virtue of that right they freely determine their political status and freely pursue their economic, social and cultural development.
2. All peoples may, for their own ends, freely dispose of their natural wealth and resources without prejudice to any obligations arising out of international economic co-operation, based upon the principle of mutual benefit, and international law. In no case may a people be deprived of its own means of subsistence.
3. The States Parties to the present Covenant, including those having responsibility for the administration of Non-Self-Governing and Trust Territories, shall promote the realization of the right of self-determination, and shall respect that right, in conformity with the provisions of the Charter of the United Nations.

Article 2

1. Each State Party to the present Covenant undertakes to take steps, individually and through international assistance and co-operation, especially economic and technical, to the maximum of its available resources, with a view to achieving progressively the full realization of the rights recognized in the present Covenant by all appropriate means, including particularly the adoption of legislative measures.
2. The States Parties to the present Covenant undertake to guarantee that the rights enunciated in the present Covenant will be exercised without discrimination of any kind as to race, colour, sex, language, religion, political or other opinion, national or social origin, property, birth or other status.
3. Developing countries, with due regard to human rights and their national economy, may determine to what extent they would guarantee the economic rights recognized in the present Covenant to non-nationals.

Article 3

The States Parties to the present Covenant undertake to ensure the equal right of men and women to the enjoyment of all economic, social and cultural rights set forth in the present Covenant.

Article 4

The States Parties to the present Covenant recognize that, in the enjoyment of those rights provided by the State in conformity with the present Covenant, the State may subject such rights only to such limitations as are determined by law only in so far as this may be compatible with the nature of these rights and solely for the purpose of promoting the general welfare in a democratic society.

Article 5

1. Nothing in the present Covenant may be interpreted as implying for any State, group or person any right to engage in any activity or to perform any act aimed at the destruction of any of the rights or freedoms recognized herein, or at their limitation to a greater extent than is provided for in the present Covenant.

2. No restriction upon or derogation from any of the fundamental human rights recognized or existing in any country in virtue of law, conventions, regulations or custom shall be admitted on the pretext that the present Covenant does not recognize such rights or that it recognizes them to a lesser extent.

Article 6

1. The States Parties to the present Covenant recognize the right to work, which includes the right of everyone to the opportunity to gain his living by work which he freely chooses or accepts, and will take appropriate steps to safeguard this right.
2. The steps to be taken by a State Party to the present Covenant to achieve the full realization of this right shall include technical and vocational guidance and training programmes, policies and techniques to achieve steady economic, social and cultural development and full and productive employment under conditions safeguarding fundamental political and economic freedoms to the individual.

Article 7

The States Parties to the present Covenant recognize the right of everyone to the enjoyment of just and favourable conditions of work which ensure, in particular:

(a) Remuneration which provides all workers, as a minimum, with:

(i) Fair wages and equal remuneration for work of equal value without distinction of any kind, in particular women being guaranteed conditions of work not inferior to those enjoyed by men, with equal pay for equal work;

(ii) A decent living for themselves and their families in accordance with the provisions of the present Covenant;

(b) Safe and healthy working conditions;

(c) Equal opportunity for everyone to be promoted in his employment to an appropriate higher level, subject to no considerations other than those of seniority and competence;

(d) Rest, leisure and reasonable limitation of working hours and periodic holidays with pay, as well as remuneration for public holidays

Article 8

1. The States Parties to the present Covenant undertake to ensure:

(a) The right of everyone to form trade unions and join the trade union of his choice, subject only to the rules of the organization concerned, for the promotion and protection of his economic and social interests. No restrictions may be placed on the exercise of this right other than those prescribed by law and which are necessary in a democratic society in the interests of national security or public order or for the protection of the rights and freedoms of others;

(b) The right of trade unions to establish national federations or confederations and the right of the latter to form or join international trade-union organizations;

(c) The right of trade unions to function freely subject to no limitations other than those prescribed by law and which are necessary in a democratic society in the interests of national security or public order or for the protection of the rights and freedoms of others;

(d) The right to strike, provided that it is exercised in conformity with the laws of the particular country.

2. This article shall not prevent the imposition of lawful restrictions on the exercise of these rights by members of the armed forces or of the police or of the administration of the State.
3. Nothing in this article shall authorize States Parties to the International Labour Organisation Convention of 1948 concerning Freedom of Association and Protection of the Right to Organize to take legislative measures which would prejudice, or apply the law in such a manner as would prejudice, the guarantees provided for in that Convention.

Article 9

The States Parties to the present Covenant recognize the right of everyone to social security, including social insurance.

Article 10

The States Parties to the present Covenant recognize that:

1. The widest possible protection and assistance should be accorded to the family, which is the natural and fundamental group unit of society, particularly for its establishment and while it is responsible for the care and education of dependent children. Marriage must be entered into with the free consent of the intending spouses.

2. Special protection should be accorded to mothers during a reasonable period before and after childbirth. During such period working mothers should be accorded paid leave or leave with adequate social security benefits.

3. Special measures of protection and assistance should be taken on behalf of all children and young persons without any discrimination for reasons of parentage or other conditions. Children and young persons should be protected from economic and social exploitation. Their employment in work harmful to their morals or health or dangerous to life or likely to hamper their normal development should be punishable by law. States should also set age limits below which the paid employment of child labour should be prohibited and punishable by law.

Article 11

1. The States Parties to the present Covenant recognize the right of everyone to an adequate standard of living for himself and his family, including adequate food, clothing and housing, and to the continuous improvement of living conditions. The States Parties will take appropriate steps to ensure the realization of this right, recognizing to this effect the essential importance of international co-operation based on free consent.

2. The States Parties to the present Covenant, recognizing the fundamental right of everyone to be free from hunger, shall take, individually and through international co-operation, the measures, including specific programmes, which are needed:

(a) To improve methods of production, conservation and distribution of food by making full use of technical and scientific knowledge, by disseminating knowledge of the principles of nutrition and by developing or reforming agrarian systems in such a way as to achieve the most efficient development and utilization of natural resources;

(b) Taking into account the problems of both food-importing and food-exporting countries, to ensure an equitable distribution of world food supplies in relation to need.

Article 12

1. The States Parties to the present Covenant recognize the right of everyone to the enjoyment of the highest attainable standard of physical and mental health.

2. The steps to be taken by the States Parties to the present Covenant to achieve the full realization of this right shall include those necessary for:

(a) The provision for the reduction of the stillbirth-rate and of infant mortality and for the healthy development of the child;

(b) The improvement of all aspects of environmental and industrial hygiene;

(c) The prevention, treatment and control of epidemic, endemic, occupational and other diseases;

(d) The creation of conditions which would assure to all medical service and medical attention in the event of sickness.

Article 13

1. The States Parties to the present Covenant recognize the right of everyone to education. They agree that education shall be directed to the full development of the human personality and the sense of its dignity, and shall strengthen the respect for human rights and fundamental freedoms. They further agree that education shall enable all persons to participate effectively in a free society, promote understanding, tolerance and friendship among all nations and all racial, ethnic or religious groups, and further the activities of the United Nations for the maintenance of peace.

2. The States Parties to the present Covenant recognize that, with a view to achieving the full realization of this right:

(a) Primary education shall be compulsory and available free to all;

(b) Secondary education in its different forms, including technical and vocational secondary education, shall be made generally available and accessible to all by every appropriate means, and in particular by the progressive introduction of free education;

(c) Higher education shall be made equally accessible to all, on the basis of capacity, by every appropriate means, and in particular by the progressive introduction of free education;
(d) Fundamental education shall be encouraged or intensified as far as possible for those persons who have not received or completed the whole period of their primary education;
(e) The development of a system of schools at all levels shall be actively pursued, an adequate fellowship system shall be established, and the material conditions of teaching staff shall be continuously improved.

3. The States Parties to the present Covenant undertake to have respect for the liberty of parents and, when applicable, legal guardians to choose for their children schools, other than those established by the public authorities, which conform to such minimum educational standards as may be laid down or approved by the State and to ensure the religious and moral education of their children in conformity with their own convictions.

4. No part of this article shall be construed so as to interfere with the liberty of individuals and bodies to establish and direct educational institutions, subject always to the observance of the principles set forth in paragraph I of this article and to the requirement that the education given in such institutions shall conform to such minimum standards as may be laid down by the State.

Article 14

Each State Party to the present Covenant which, at the time of becoming a Party, has not been able to secure in its metropolitan territory or other territories under its jurisdiction compulsory primary education, free of charge, undertakes, within two years, to work out and adopt a detailed plan of action for the progressive implementation, within a reasonable number of years, to be fixed in the plan, of the principle of compulsory education free of charge for all.

Article 15

1. The States Parties to the present Covenant recognize the right of everyone:
(a) To take part in cultural life;
(b) To enjoy the benefits of scientific progress and its applications;
(c) To benefit from the protection of the moral and material interests resulting from any scientific, literary or artistic production of which he is the author.

2. The steps to be taken by the States Parties to the present Covenant to achieve the full realization of this right shall include those necessary for the conservation, the development and the diffusion of science and culture.

3. The States Parties to the present Covenant undertake to respect the freedom indispensable for scientific research and creative activity.

4. The States Parties to the present Covenant recognize the benefits to be derived from the encouragement and development of international contacts and co-operation in the scientific and cultural fields.

Article 16

1. The States Parties to the present Covenant undertake to submit in conformity with this part of the Covenant reports on the measures which they have adopted and the progress made in achieving the observance of the rights recognized herein.

2.   (a) All reports shall be submitted to the Secretary-General of the United Nations, who shall transmit copies to the Economic and Social Council for consideration in accordance with the provisions of the present Covenant;
(b) The Secretary-General of the United Nations shall also transmit to the specialized agencies copies of the reports, or any relevant parts therefrom, from States Parties to the present Covenant which are also members of these specialized agencies in so far as these reports, or parts therefrom, relate to any matters which fall within the responsibilities of the said agencies in accordance with their constitutional instruments.

Article 17

1. The States Parties to the present Covenant shall furnish their reports in stages, in accordance with a programme to be established by the Economic and Social Council within one year of the entry into force of the present Covenant after consultation with the States Parties and the specialized agencies concerned.

2. Reports may indicate factors and difficulties affecting the degree of fulfilment of obligations under the present Covenant.

3. Where relevant information has previously been furnished to the United Nations or to any specialized agency by any State Party to the present Covenant, it will not be necessary to reproduce that information, but a precise reference to the information so furnished will suffice.

Article 18

Pursuant to its responsibilities under the Charter of the United Nations in the field of human rights and fundamental freedoms, the Economic and Social Council may make arrangements with the specialized agencies in respect of their reporting to it on the progress made in achieving the observance of the provisions of the present Covenant falling within the scope of their activities. These reports may include particulars of decisions and recommendations on such implementation adopted by their competent organs.

Article 19

The Economic and Social Council may transmit to the Commission on Human Rights for study and general recommendation or, as appropriate, for information the reports concerning human rights submitted by States in accordance with articles 16 and 17, and those concerning human rights submitted by the specialized agencies in accordance with article 18.

Article 20

The States Parties to the present Covenant and the specialized agencies concerned may submit comments to the Economic and Social Council on any general recommendation under article 19 or reference to such general recommendation in any report of the Commission on Human Rights or any documentation referred to therein.

Article 21

The Economic and Social Council may submit from time to time to the General Assembly reports with recommendations of a general nature and a summary of the information received from the States Parties to the present Covenant and the specialized agencies on the measures taken and the progress made in achieving general observance of the rights recognized in the present Covenant.

Article 22

The Economic and Social Council may bring to the attention of other organs of the United Nations, their subsidiary organs and specialized agencies concerned with furnishing technical assistance any matters arising out of the reports referred to in this part of the present Covenant which may assist such bodies in deciding, each within its field of competence, on the advisability of international measures likely to contribute to the effective progressive implementation of the present Covenant.

Article 23

The States Parties to the present Covenant agree that international action for the achievement of the rights recognized in the present Covenant includes such methods as the conclusion of conventions, the adoption of recommendations, the furnishing of technical assistance and the holding of regional meetings and technical meetings for the purpose of consultation and study organized in conjunction with the Governments concerned.

Article 24

Nothing in the present Covenant shall be interpreted as impairing the provisions of the Charter of the United Nations and of the constitutions of the specialized agencies which define the respective responsibilities of the various organs of the United Nations and of the specialized agencies in regard to the matters dealt with in the present Covenant.

Article 25

Nothing in the present Covenant shall be interpreted as impairing the inherent right of all peoples to enjoy and utilize fully and freely their natural wealth and resources.

Article 26

1. The present Covenant is open for signature by any State Member of the United Nations or member of any of its specialized agencies, by any State Party to the Statute of the International Court of Justice, and by any other State which has been invited by the General Assembly of the United Nations to become a party to the present Covenant.

2. The present Covenant is subject to ratification. Instruments of ratification shall be deposited with the Secretary-General of the United Nations. * * *

Article 27

1. The present Covenant shall enter into force three months after the date of the deposit with the Secretary-General of the United Nations of the thirty-fifth instrument of ratification or instrument of accession.

2. For each State ratifying the present Covenant or acceding to it after the deposit of the thirty-fifth instrument of ratification or instrument of accession, the present Covenant shall enter into force three months after the date of the deposit of its own instrument of ratification or instrument of accession.

Article 28

The provisions of the present Covenant shall extend to all parts of federal States without any limitations or exceptions.

Article 29

1. Any State Party to the present Covenant may propose an amendment and file it with the Secretary-General of the United Nations. The Secretary-General shall thereupon communicate any proposed amendments to the States Parties to the present Covenant with a request that they notify him whether they favour a conference of States Parties for the purpose of considering and voting upon the proposals. In the event that at least one third of the States Parties favours such a conference, the Secretary-General shall convene the conference under the auspices of the United Nations. Any amendment adopted by a majority of the States Parties present and voting at the conference shall be submitted to the General Assembly of the United Nations for approval.

2. Amendments shall come into force when they have been approved by the General Assembly of the United Nations and accepted by a two-thirds majority of the States Parties to the present Covenant in accordance with their respective constitutional processes.

3. When amendments come into force they shall be binding on those States Parties which have accepted them, other States Parties still being bound by the provisions of the present Covenant and any earlier amendment which they have accepted. * * *

Article 31

1. The present Covenant, of which the Chinese, English, French, Russian and Spanish texts are equally authentic, shall be deposited in the archives of the United Nations.

2. The Secretary-General of the United Nations shall transmit certified copies of the present Covenant to all States referred to in article 26.

CONVENTION ON THE ELIMINATION OF ALL FORMS OF DISCRIMINATION AGAINST WOMEN (1979)

Convention on the Elimination of All Forms of Discrimination against Women, *adopted* Dec. 18, 1979, 1249 U.N.T.S. 13

Article I

For the purposes of the present Convention, the term "discrimination against women" shall mean any distinction, exclusion or restriction made on the basis of sex which has the effect or purpose of impairing or nullifying the recognition, enjoyment or exercise by women, irrespective of their marital status, on a basis of equality of men and women, of human rights and fundamental freedoms in the political, economic, social, cultural, civil or any other field.

Article 2

States Parties condemn discrimination against women in all its forms, agree to pursue by all appropriate means and without delay a policy of eliminating discrimination against women and, to this end, undertake:

(a) To embody the principle of the equality of men and women in their national constitutions or other appropriate legislation if not yet incorporated therein and to ensure, through law and other appropriate means, the practical realization of this principle;

(b) To adopt appropriate legislative and other measures, including sanctions where appropriate, prohibiting all discrimination against women;

(c) To establish legal protection of the rights of women on an equal basis with men and to ensure through competent national tribunals and other public institutions the effective protection of women against any act of discrimination;

(d) To refrain from engaging in any act or practice of discrimination against women and to ensure that public authorities and institutions shall act in conformity with this obligation;

(e) To take all appropriate measures to eliminate discrimination against women by any person, organization or enterprise;

(f) To take all appropriate measures, including legislation, to modify or abolish existing laws, regulations, customs and practices which constitute discrimination against women;

(g) To repeal all national penal provisions which constitute discrimination against women.

Article 3

States Parties shall take in all fields, in particular in the political, social, economic and cultural fields, all appropriate measures, including legislation, to en sure the full development and advancement of women , for the purpose of guaranteeing them the exercise and enjoyment of human rights and fundamental freedoms on a basis of equality with men.

Article 4

1. Adoption by States Parties of temporary special measures aimed at accelerating de facto equality between men and women shall not be considered discrimination as defined in the present Convention, but shall in no way entail as a consequence the maintenance of unequal or separate standards; these measures shall be discontinued when the objectives of equality of opportunity and treatment have been achieved.
2. Adoption by States Parties of special measures, including those measures contained in the present Convention, aimed at protecting maternity shall not be considered discriminatory.

Article 5

States Parties shall take all appropriate measures:

(a) To modify the social and cultural patterns of conduct of men and women, with a view to achieving the elimination of prejudices and customary and all other practices which are based on the idea of the inferiority or the superiority of either of the sexes or on stereotyped roles for men and women;

(b) To ensure that family education includes a proper understanding of maternity as a social function and the recognition of the common responsibility of men and women in the upbringing and development of their children, it being understood that the interest of the children is the primordial consideration in all cases.

Article 6

States Parties shall take all appropriate measures, including legislation, to suppress all forms of traffic in women and exploitation of prostitution of women.

Article 7

States Parties shall take all appropriate measures to eliminate discrimination against women in the political and public life of the country and, in particular, shall ensure to women, on equal terms with men, the right:

(a) To vote in all elections and public referenda and to be eligible for election to all publicly elected bodies;

(b) To participate in the formulation of government policy and the implementation thereof and to hold public office and perform all public functions at all levels of government;

142

(c) To participate in non-governmental organizations and associations concerned with the public and political life of the country.

Article 8

States Parties shall take all appropriate measures to ensure to women, on equal terms with men and without any discrimination, the opportunity to represent their Governments at the international level and to participate in the work of international organizations.

Article 9

1. States Parties shall grant women equal rights with men to acquire, change or retain their nationality. They shall ensure in particular that neither marriage to an alien nor change of nationality by the husband during marriage shall automatically change the nationality of the wife, render her stateless or force upon her the nationality of the husband.
2. States Parties shall grant women equal rights with men with respect to the nationality of their children.

Article 10

States Parties shall take all appropriate measures to eliminate discrimination against women in order to ensure to them equal rights with men in the field of education and in particular to ensure, on a basis of equality of men and women:

(a) The same conditions for career and vocational guidance, for access to studies and for the achievement of diplomas in educational establishments of all categories in rural as well as in urban areas; this equality shall be ensured in pre-school, general, technical, professional and higher technical education, as well as in all types of vocational training;

(b) Access to the same curricula, the same examinations, teaching staff with qualifications of the same standard and school premises and equipment of the same quality;

(c) The elimination of any stereotyped concept of the roles of men and women at all levels and in all forms of education by encouraging coeducation and other types of education which will help to achieve this aim and, in particular, by the revision of textbooks and school programmes and the adaptation of teaching methods;

(d) The same opportunities to benefit from scholarships and other study grants;

(e) The same opportunities for access to programmes of continuing education, including adult and functional literacy programmes, particulary those aimed at reducing, at the earliest possible time, any gap in education existing between men and women;

(f) The reduction of female student drop-out rates and the organization of programmes for girls and women who have left school prematurely;

(g) The same Opportunities to participate actively in sports and physical education;

(h) Access to specific educational information to help to ensure the health and well-being of families, including information and advice on family planning.

Article 11

1. States Parties shall take all appropriate measures to eliminate discrimination against women in the field of employment in order to ensure, on a basis of equality of men and women, the same rights, in particular:

(a) The right to work as an inalienable right of all human beings;

(b) The right to the same employment opportunities, including the application of the same criteria for selection in matters of employment;

(c) The right to free choice of profession and employment, the right to promotion, job security and all benefits and conditions of service and the right to receive vocational training and retraining, including apprenticeships, advanced vocational training and recurrent training;

(d) The right to equal remuneration, including benefits, and to equal treatment in respect of work of equal value, as well as equality of treatment in the evaluation of the quality of work;

(e) The right to social security, particularly in cases of retirement, unemployment, sickness, invalidity and old age and other incapacity to work, as well as the right to paid leave;

(f) The right to protection of health and to safety in working conditions, including the safeguarding of the function of reproduction.

2. In order to prevent discrimination against women on the grounds of marriage or maternity and to ensure their effective right to work, States Parties shall take appropriate measures:

    (a) To prohibit, subject to the imposition of sanctions, dismissal on the grounds of pregnancy or of maternity leave and discrimination in dismissals on the basis of marital status;

    (b) To introduce maternity leave with pay or with comparable social benefits without loss of former employment, seniority or social allowances;

    (c) To encourage the provision of the necessary supporting social services to enable parents to combine family obligations with work responsibilities and participation in public life, in particular through promoting the establishment and development of a network of child-care facilities;

    (d) To provide special protection to women during pregnancy in types of work proved to be harmful to them.

3. Protective legislation relating to matters covered in this article shall be reviewed periodically in the light of scientific and technological knowledge and shall be revised, repealed or extended as necessary.

Article 12

1. States Parties shall take all appropriate measures to eliminate discrimination against women in the field of health care in order to ensure, on a basis of equality of men and women, access to health care services, including those related to family planning.

2. Notwithstanding the provisions of paragraph I of this article, States Parties shall ensure to women appropriate services in connection with pregnancy, confinement and the post-natal period, granting free services where necessary, as well as adequate nutrition during pregnancy and lactation.

Article 13

States Parties shall take all appropriate measures to eliminate discrimination against women in other areas of economic and social life in order to ensure, on a basis of equality of men and women, the same rights, in particular:

    (a) The right to family benefits;

    (b) The right to bank loans, mortgages and other forms of financial credit;

    (c) The right to participate in recreational activities, sports and all aspects of cultural life.

Article 14

1. States Parties shall take into account the particular problems faced by rural women and the significant roles which rural women play in the economic survival of their families, including their work in the non-monetized sectors of the economy, and shall take all appropriate measures to ensure the application of the provisions of the present Convention to women in rural areas.

2. States Parties shall take all appropriate measures to eliminate discrimination against women in rural areas in order to ensure, on a basis of equality of men and women, that they participate in and benefit from rural development and, in particular, shall ensure to such women the right:

    (a) To participate in the elaboration and implementation of development planning at all levels;

    (b) To have access to adequate health care facilities, including information, counselling and services in family planning;

    (c) To benefit directly from social security programmes;

    (d) To obtain all types of training and education, formal and non-formal, including that relating to functional literacy, as well as, inter alia, the benefit of all community and extension services, in order to increase their technical proficiency;

    (e) To organize self-help groups and co-operatives in order to obtain equal access to economic opportunities through employment or self employment;

    (f) To participate in all community activities;

    (g) To have access to agricultural credit and loans, marketing facilities, appropriate technology and equal treatment in land and agrarian reform as well as in land resettlement schemes;

    (h) To enjoy adequate living conditions, particularly in relation to housing, sanitation, electricity and water supply, transport and communications.

Article 15

1. States Parties shall accord to women equality with men before the law.

2. States Parties shall accord to women, in civil matters, a legal capacity identical to that of men and the same opportunities to exercise that capacity. In particular, they shall give women equal rights to conclude contracts and to administer property and shall treat them equally in all stages of procedure in courts and tribunals.

3. States Parties agree that all contracts and all other private instruments of any kind with a legal effect which is directed at restricting the legal capacity of women shall be deemed null and void.

4. States Parties shall accord to men and women the same rights with regard to the law relating to the movement of persons and the freedom to choose their residence and domicile.

Article 16

1. States Parties shall take all appropriate measures to eliminate discrimination against women in all matters relating to marriage and family relations and in particular shall ensure, on a basis of equality of men and women:

   (a) The same right to enter into marriage;

   (b) The same right freely to choose a spouse and to enter into marriage only with their free and full consent;

   (c) The same rights and responsibilities during marriage and at its dissolution;

   (d) The same rights and responsibilities as parents, irrespective of their marital status, in matters relating to their children; in all cases the interests of the children shall be paramount;

   (e) The same rights to decide freely and responsibly on the number and spacing of their children and to have access to the information, education and means to enable them to exercise these rights;

   (f) The same rights and responsibilities with regard to guardianship, wardship, trusteeship and adoption of children, or similar institutions where these concepts exist in national legislation; in all cases the interests of the children shall be paramount;

   (g) The same personal rights as husband and wife, including the right to choose a family name, a profession and an occupation;

   (h) The same rights for both spouses in respect of the ownership, acquisition, management, administration, enjoyment and disposition of property, whether free of charge or for a valuable consideration.

2. The betrothal and the marriage of a child shall have no legal effect, and all necessary action, including legislation, shall be taken to specify a minimum age for marriage and to make the registration of marriages in an official registry compulsory.

Article 17

1. For the purpose of considering the progress made in the implementation of the present Convention, there shall be established a Committee on the Elimination of Discrimination against Women (hereinafter referred to as the Committee) consisting, at the time of entry into force of the Convention, of eighteen and, after ratification of or accession to the Convention by the thirty-fifth State Party, of twenty-three experts of high moral standing and competence in the field covered by the Convention. The experts shall be elected by States Parties from among their nationals and shall serve in their personal capacity, consideration being given to equitable geographical distribution and to the representation of the different forms of civilization as well as the principal legal systems.

2. The members of the Committee shall be elected by secret ballot from a list of persons nominated by States Parties. Each State Party may nominate one person from among its own nationals.

3. The initial election shall be held six months after the date of the entry into force of the present Convention. At least three months before the date of each election the Secretary-General of the United Nations shall address a letter to the States Parties inviting them to submit their nominations within two months. The Secretary-General shall prepare a list in alphabetical order of all persons thus nominated, indicating the States Parties which have nominated them, and shall submit it to the States Parties.

4. Elections of the members of the Committee shall be held at a meeting of States Parties convened by the Secretary-General at United Nations Headquarters. At that meeting, for which two thirds of the States Parties shall constitute a quorum, the persons elected to the Committee shall be those nominees who obtain the largest number of votes and an absolute majority of the votes of the representatives of States Parties present and voting.

5. The members of the Committee shall be elected for a term of four years. However, the terms of nine of the members elected at the first election shall expire at the end of two years; immediately after the first election the names of these nine members shall be chosen by lot by the Chairman of the Committee.
6. The election of the five additional members of the Committee shall be held in accordance with the provisions of paragraphs 2, 3 and 4 of this article, following the thirty-fifth ratification or accession. The terms of two of the additional members elected on this occasion shall expire at the end of two years, the names of these two members having been chosen by lot by the Chairman of the Committee.
7. For the filling of casual vacancies, the State Party whose expert has ceased to function as a member of the Committee shall appoint another expert from among its nationals, subject to the approval of the Committee.
8. The members of the Committee shall, with the approval of the General Assembly, receive emoluments from United Nations resources on such terms and conditions as the Assembly may decide, having regard to the importance of the Committee's responsibilities.
9. The Secretary-General of the United Nations shall provide the necessary staff and facilities for the effective performance of the functions of the Committee under the present Convention.

Article 18

1. States Parties undertake to submit to the Secretary-General of the United Nations, for consideration by the Committee, a report on the legislative, judicial, administrative or other measures which they have adopted to give effect to the provisions of the present Convention and on the progress made in this respect:
    (a) Within one year after the entry into force for the State concerned;
    (b) Thereafter at least every four years and further whenever the Committee so requests.
2. Reports may indicate factors and difficulties affecting the degree of fulfilment of obligations under the present Convention.

Article 19

1. The Committee shall adopt its own rules of procedure.
2. The Committee shall elect its officers for a term of two years.

Article 20

1. The Committee shall normally meet for a period of not more than two weeks annually in order to consider the reports submitted in accordance with article 18 of the present Convention.
2. The meetings of the Committee shall normally be held at United Nations Headquarters or at any other convenient place as determined by the Committee. (amendment, status of ratification)

Article 21

1. The Committee shall, through the Economic and Social Council, report annually to the General Assembly of the United Nations on its activities and may make suggestions and general recommendations based on the examination of reports and information received from the States Parties. Such suggestions and general recommendations shall be included in the report of the Committee together with comments, if any, from States Parties.
2. The Secretary-General of the United Nations shall transmit the reports of the Committee to the Commission on the Status of Women for its information.

Article 22

The specialized agencies shall be entitled to be represented at the consideration of the implementation of such provisions of the present Convention as fall within the scope of their activities. The Committee may invite the specialized agencies to submit reports on the implementation of the Convention in areas falling within the scope of their activities.

Article 23

Nothing in the present Convention shall affect any provisions that are more conducive to the achievement of equality between men and women which may be contained:
    (a) In the legislation of a State Party; or
    (b) In any other international convention, treaty or agreement in force for that State.

Article 24

States Parties undertake to adopt all necessary measures at the national level aimed at achieving the full realization of the rights recognized in the present Convention.

Article 25

1. The present Convention shall be open for signature by all States.
2. The Secretary-General of the United Nations is designated as the depositary of the present Convention.
3. The present Convention is subject to ratification. Instruments of ratification shall be deposited with the Secretary-General of the United Nations.
4. The present Convention shall be open to accession by all States. Accession shall be effected by the deposit of an instrument of accession with the Secretary-General of the United Nations.

Article 26

1. A request for the revision of the present Convention may be made at any time by any State Party by means of a notification in writing addressed to the Secretary-General of the United Nations.
2. The General Assembly of the United Nations shall decide upon the steps, if any, to be taken in respect of such a request.

Article 27

1. The present Convention shall enter into force on the thirtieth day after the date of deposit with the Secretary-General of the United Nations of the twentieth instrument of ratification or accession.
2. For each State ratifying the present Convention or acceding to it after the deposit of the twentieth instrument of ratification or accession, the Convention shall enter into force on the thirtieth day after the date of the deposit of its own instrument of ratification or accession.

Article 28

1. The Secretary-General of the United Nations shall receive and circulate to all States the text of reservations made by States at the time of ratification or accession.
2. A reservation incompatible with the object and purpose of the present Convention shall not be permitted.
3. Reservations may be withdrawn at any time by notification to this effect addressed to the Secretary-General of the United Nations, who shall then inform all States thereof. Such notification shall take effect on the date on which it is received.

Article 29

1. Any dispute between two or more States Parties concerning the interpretation or application of the present Convention which is not settled by negotiation shall, at the request of one of them, be submitted to arbitration. If within six months from the date of the request for arbitration the parties are unable to agree on the organization of the arbitration, any one of those parties may refer the dispute to the International Court of Justice by request in conformity with the Statute of the Court.
2. Each State Party may at the time of signature or ratification of the present Convention or accession thereto declare that it does not consider itself bound by paragraph I of this article. The other States Parties shall not be bound by that paragraph with respect to any State Party which has made such a reservation.
3. Any State Party which has made a reservation in accordance with paragraph 2 of this article may at any time withdraw that reservation by notification to the Secretary-General of the United Nations.

Article 30

The present Convention, the Arabic, Chinese, English, French, Russian and Spanish texts of which are equally authentic, shall be deposited with the Secretary-General of the United Nations.

CONVENTION AGAINST TORTURE AND OTHER CRUEL, INHUMAN OR DEGRADING TREATMENT OR PUNISHMENT (1984)

Convention against Torture and Other Cruel, Inhuman or Degrading Treatment or Punishment, *adopted* Dec.10, 1984, 1465 U.N.T.S. 112

Article 1

1. For the purposes of this Convention, the term "torture" means any act by which severe pain or suffering, whether physical or mental, is intentionally inflicted on a person for such purposes as obtaining from him or a third person information or a confession, punishing him for an act he or a third person has committed or is suspected of having committed, or intimidating or coercing him or a third person, or for any reason based on discrimination of any kind, when such pain or suffering is inflicted by or at the instigation of or with the consent or acquiescence of a public official or other person acting in an official capacity. It does not include pain or suffering arising only from, inherent in or incidental to lawful sanctions.
2. This article is without prejudice to any international instrument or national legislation which does or may contain provisions of wider application.

Article 2

1. Each State Party shall take effective legislative, administrative, judicial or other measures to prevent acts of torture in any territory under its jurisdiction.
2. No exceptional circumstances whatsoever, whether a state of war or a threat of war, internal political in stability or any other public emergency, may be invoked as a justification of torture.
3. An order from a superior officer or a public authority may not be invoked as a justification of torture.

Article 3

1. No State Party shall expel, return ("refouler") or extradite a person to another State where there are substantial grounds for believing that he would be in danger of being subjected to torture.
2. For the purpose of determining whether there are such grounds, the competent authorities shall take into account all relevant considerations including, where applicable, the existence in the State concerned of a consistent pattern of gross, flagrant or mass violations of human rights.

Article 4

1. Each State Party shall ensure that all acts of torture are offences under its criminal law. The same shall apply to an attempt to commit torture and to an act by any person which constitutes complicity or participation in torture. 2. Each State Party shall make these offences punishable by appropriate penalties which take into account their grave nature.

Article 5

1. Each State Party shall take such measures as may be necessary to establish its jurisdiction over the offences referred to in article 4 in the following cases: (a) When the offences are committed in any territory under its jurisdiction or on board a ship or aircraft registered in that State; (b) When the alleged offender is a national of that State; (c) When the victim is a national of that State if that State considers it appropriate.
2. Each State Party shall likewise take such measures as may be necessary to establish its jurisdiction over such offences in cases where the alleged offender is present in any territory under its jurisdiction and it does not extradite him pursuant to article 8 to any of the States mentioned in paragraph I of this article.
3. This Convention does not exclude any criminal jurisdiction exercised in accordance with internal law.

Article 6

1. Upon being satisfied, after an examination of information available to it, that the circumstances so warrant, any State Party in whose territory a person alleged to have committed any offence referred to in article 4 is present shall take him into custody or take other legal measures to ensure his presence. The

custody and other legal measures shall be as provided in the law of that State but may be continued only for such time as is necessary to enable any criminal or extradition proceedings to be instituted.

2. Such State shall immediately make a preliminary inquiry into the facts.

3. Any person in custody pursuant to paragraph I of this article shall be assisted in communicating immediately with the nearest appropriate representative of the State of which he is a national, or, if he is a stateless person, with the representative of the State where he usually resides.

4. When a State, pursuant to this article, has taken a person into custody, it shall immediately notify the States referred to in article 5, paragraph 1, of the fact that such person is in custody and of the circumstances which warrant his detention. The State which makes the preliminary inquiry contemplated in paragraph 2 of this article shall promptly report its findings to the said States and shall indicate whether it intends to exercise jurisdiction.

Article 7

1. The State Party in the territory under whose jurisdiction a person alleged to have committed any offence referred to in article 4 is found shall in the cases contemplated in article 5, if it does not extradite him, submit the case to its competent authorities for the purpose of prosecution.

2. These authorities shall take their decision in the same manner as in the case of any ordinary offence of a serious nature under the law of that State. In the cases referred to in article 5, paragraph 2, the standards of evidence required for prosecution and conviction shall in no way be less stringent than those which apply in the cases referred to in article 5, paragraph 1.

3. Any person regarding whom proceedings are brought in connection with any of the offences referred to in article 4 shall be guaranteed fair treatment at all stages of the proceedings.

Article 8

1. The offences referred to in article 4 shall be deemed to be included as extraditable offences in any extradition treaty existing between States Parties. States Parties undertake to include such offences as extraditable offences in every extradition treaty to be concluded between them.

2. If a State Party which makes extradition conditional on the existence of a treaty receives a request for extradition from another State Party with which it has no extradition treaty, it may consider this Convention as the legal basis for extradition in respect of such offences. Extradition shall be subject to the other conditions provided by the law of the requested State.

3. States Parties which do not make extradition conditional on the existence of a treaty shall recognize such offences as extraditable offences between themselves subject to the conditions provided by the law of the requested State.

4. Such offences shall be treated, for the purpose of extradition between States Parties, as if they had been committed not only in the place in which they occurred but also in the territories of the States required to establish their jurisdiction in accordance with article 5, paragraph 1.

Article 9

1. States Parties shall afford one another the greatest measure of assistance in connection with criminal proceedings brought in respect of any of the offences referred to in article 4, including the supply of all evidence at their disposal necessary for the proceedings. * * *

Article 10

1. Each State Party shall ensure that education and information regarding the prohibition against torture are fully included in the training of law enforcement personnel, civil or military, medical personnel, public officials and other persons who may be involved in the custody, interrogation or treatment of any individual subjected to any form of arrest, detention or imprisonment.

2. Each State Party shall include this prohibition in the rules or instructions issued in regard to the duties and functions of any such person.

Article 11

Each State Party shall keep under systematic review interrogation rules, instructions, methods and practices as well as arrangements for the custody and treatment of persons subjected to any form of arrest, detention or imprisonment in any territory under its jurisdiction, with a view to preventing any cases of torture.

Article 12

Each State Party shall ensure that its competent authorities proceed to a prompt and impartial investigation, wherever there is reasonable ground to believe that an act of torture has been committed in any territory under its jurisdiction.

Article 13

Each State Party shall ensure that any individual who alleges he has been subjected to torture in any territory under its jurisdiction has the right to complain to, and to have his case promptly and impartially examined by, its competent authorities. Steps shall be taken to ensure that the complainant and witnesses are protected against all ill-treatment or intimidation as a consequence of his complaint or any evidence given.

Article 14

1. Each State Party shall ensure in its legal system that the victim of an act of torture obtains redress and has an enforceable right to fair and adequate compensation, including the means for as full rehabilitation as possible. In the event of the death of the victim as a result of an act of torture, his dependants shall be entitled to compensation.
2. Nothing in this article shall affect any right of the victim or other persons to compensation which may exist under national law.

Article 15

Each State Party shall ensure that any statement which is established to have been made as a result of torture shall not be invoked as evidence in any proceedings, except against a person accused of torture as evidence that the statement was made.

Article 16

1. Each State Party shall undertake to prevent in any territory under its jurisdiction other acts of cruel, inhuman or degrading treatment or punishment which do not amount to torture as defined in article I, when such acts are committed by or at the instigation of or with the consent or acquiescence of a public official or other person acting in an official capacity. In particular, the obligations contained in articles 10, 11, 12 and 13 shall apply with the substitution for references to torture of references to other forms of cruel, inhuman or degrading treatment or punishment.
2. The provisions of this Convention are without prejudice to the provisions of any other international instrument or national law which prohibits cruel, inhuman or degrading treatment or punishment or which relates to extradition or expulsion.

Article 17

1. There shall be established a Committee against Torture (hereinafter referred to as the Committee) which shall carry out the functions hereinafter provided. The Committee shall consist of ten experts of high moral standing and recognized competence in the field of human rights, who shall serve in their personal capacity. The experts shall be elected by the States Parties, consideration being given to equitable geographical distribution and to the usefulness of the participation of some persons having legal experience.
2. The members of the Committee shall be elected by secret ballot from a list of persons nominated by States Parties. Each State Party may nominate one person from among its own nationals. States Parties shall bear in mind the usefulness of nominating persons who are also members of the Human Rights Committee established under the International Covenant on Civil and Political Rights and who are willing to serve on the Committee against Torture.
3. Elections of the members of the Committee shall be held at biennial meetings of States Parties convened by the Secretary-General of the United Nations. At those meetings, for which two thirds of the States Parties shall constitute a quorum, the persons elected to the Committee shall be those who obtain the largest number of votes and an absolute majority of the votes of the representatives of States Parties present and voting.

4. The initial election shall be held no later than six months after the date of the entry into force of this Convention. At. least four months before the date of each election, the Secretary-General of the United Nations shall address a letter to the States Parties inviting them to submit their nominations within three months. The Secretary-General shall prepare a list in alphabetical order of all persons thus nominated, indicating the States Parties which have nominated them, and shall submit it to the States Parties.
5. The members of the Committee shall be elected for a term of four years. They shall be eligible for re-election if renominated. However, the term of five of the members elected at the first election shall expire at the end of two years; immediately after the first election the names of these five members shall be chosen by lot by the chairman of the meeting referred to in paragraph 3 of this article.
6. If a member of the Committee dies or resigns or for any other cause can no longer perform his Committee duties, the State Party which nominated him shall appoint another expert from among its nationals to serve for the remainder of his term, subject to the approval of the majority of the States Parties. The approval shall be considered given unless half or more of the States Parties respond negatively within six weeks after having been informed by the Secretary-General of the United Nations of the proposed appointment.
7. States Parties shall be responsible for the expenses of the members of the Committee while they are in performance of Committee duties.

Article 18
1. The Committee shall elect its officers for a term of two years. They may be re-elected.
2. The Committee shall establish its own rules of procedure, but these rules shall provide, *inter alia*, that:
    (a) Six members shall constitute a quorum;
    (b) Decisions of the Committee shall be made by a majority vote of the members present.
3. The Secretary-General of the United Nations shall provide the necessary staff and facilities for the effective performance of the functions of the Committee under this Convention.
4. The Secretary-General of the United Nations shall convene the initial meeting of the Committee. After its initial meeting, the Committee shall meet at such times as shall be provided in its rules of procedure.
5. The States Parties shall be responsible for expenses incurred in connection with the holding of meetings of the States Parties and of the Committee, including reimbursement to the United Nations for any expenses, such as the cost of staff and facilities, incurred by the United Nations pursuant to paragraph 3 of this article.

Article 19
1. The States Parties shall submit to the Committee, through the Secretary-General of the United Nations, reports on the measures they have taken to give effect to their undertakings under this Convention, within one year after the entry into force of the Convention for the State Party concerned. Thereafter the States Parties shall submit supplementary reports every four years on any new measures taken and such other reports as the Committee may request.
2. The Secretary-General of the United Nations shall transmit the reports to all States Parties.
3. Each report shall be considered by the Committee which may make such general comments on the report as it may consider appropriate and shall forward these to the State Party concerned. That State Party may respond with any observations it chooses to the Committee.
4. The Committee may, at its discretion, decide to include any comments made by it in accordance with paragraph 3 of this article, together with the observations thereon received from the State Party concerned, in its annual report made in accordance with article 24. If so requested by the State Party concerned, the Committee may also include a copy of the report submitted under paragraph I of this article.

Article 20
1. If the Committee receives reliable information which appears to it to contain well-founded indications that torture is being systematically practised in the territory of a State Party, the Committee shall invite that State Party to co-operate in the examination of the information and to this end to submit observations with regard to the information concerned.
2. Taking into account any observations which may have been submitted by the State Party concerned, as well as any other relevant information available to it, the Committee may, if it decides that this is warranted, designate one or more of its members to make a confidential inquiry and to report to the Committee urgently.

3. If an inquiry is made in accordance with paragraph 2 of this article, the Committee shall seek the co-operation of the State Party concerned. In agreement with that State Party, such an inquiry may include a visit to its territory.

4. After examining the findings of its member or members submitted in accordance with paragraph 2 of this article, the Commission shall transmit these findings to the State Party concerned together with any comments or suggestions which seem appropriate in view of the situation.

5. All the proceedings of the Committee referred to in paragraphs I to 4 of this article shall be confidential, and at all stages of the proceedings the co-operation of the State Party shall be sought. After such proceedings have been completed with regard to an inquiry made in accordance with paragraph 2, the Committee may, after consultations with the State Party concerned, decide to include a summary account of the results of the proceedings in its annual report made in accordance with article 24.

Article 21

1. A State Party to this Convention may at any time declare under this article that it recognizes the competence of the Committee to receive and consider communications to the effect that a State Party claims that another State Party is not fulfilling its obligations under this Convention. Such communications may be received and considered according to the procedures laid down in this article only if submitted by a State Party which has made a declaration recognizing in regard to itself the competence of the Committee. No communication shall be dealt with by the Committee under this article if it concerns a State Party which has not made such a declaration. Communications received under this article shall be dealt with in accordance with the following procedure;

 (a) If a State Party considers that another State Party is not giving effect to the provisions of this Convention, it may, by written communication, bring the matter to the attention of that State Party. Within three months after the receipt of the communication the receiving State shall afford the State which sent the communication an explanation or any other statement in writing clarifying the matter, which should include, to the extent possible and pertinent, reference to domestic procedures and remedies taken, pending or available in the matter;

 (b) If the matter is not adjusted to the satisfaction of both States Parties concerned within six months after the receipt by the receiving State of the initial communication, either State shall have the right to refer the matter to the Committee, by notice given to the Committee and to the other State;

 (c) The Committee shall deal with a matter referred to it under this article only after it has ascertained that all domestic remedies have been invoked and exhausted in the matter, in conformity with the generally recognized principles of international law. This shall not be the rule where the application of the remedies is unreasonably prolonged or is unlikely to bring effective relief to the person who is the victim of the violation of this Convention;

 (d) The Committee shall hold closed meetings when examining communications under this article;

 (e) Subject to the provisions of subparagraph (c), the Committee shall make available its good offices to the States Parties concerned with a view to a friendly solution of the matter on the basis of respect for the obligations provided for in this Convention. For this purpose, the Committee may, when appropriate, set up an ad hoc conciliation commission;

 (f) In any matter referred to it under this article, the Committee may call upon the States Parties concerned, referred to in subparagraph (b), to supply any relevant information;

 (g) The States Parties concerned, referred to in subparagraph (b), shall have the right to be represented when the matter is being considered by the Committee and to make submissions orally and/or in writing;

 (h) The Committee shall, within twelve months after the date of receipt of notice under subparagraph (b), submit a report:

  (i) If a solution within the terms of subparagraph (e) is reached, the Committee shall confine its report to a brief statement of the facts and of the solution reached;

  (ii) If a solution within the terms of subparagraph (e) is not reached, the Committee shall confine its report to a brief statement of the facts; the written submissions and record of the oral submissions made by the States Parties concerned shall be attached to the report.

In every matter, the report shall be communicated to the States Parties concerned.

2. The provisions of this article shall come into force when five States Parties to this Convention have made declarations under paragraph 1 of this article. Such declarations shall be deposited by the States Parties

with the Secretary-General of the United Nations, who shall transmit copies thereof to the other States Parties. A declaration may be withdrawn at any time by notification to the Secretary-General. Such a withdrawal shall not prejudice the consideration of any matter which is the subject of a communication already transmitted under this article; no further communication by any State Party shall be received under this article after the notification of withdrawal of the declaration has been received by the Secretary-General, unless the State Party concerned has made a new declaration.

Article 22

1. A State Party to this Convention may at any time declare under this article that it recognizes the competence of the Committee to receive and consider communications from or on behalf of individuals subject to its jurisdiction who claim to be victims of a violation by a State Party of the provisions of the Convention. No communication shall be received by the Committee if it concerns a State Party which has not made such a declaration.
2. The Committee shall consider inadmissible any communication under this article which is anonymous or which it considers to be an abuse of the right of submission of such communications or to be incompatible with the provisions of this Convention.
3. Subject to the provisions of paragraph 2, the Committee shall bring any communications submitted to it under this article to the attention of the State Party to this Convention which has made a declaration under paragraph I and is alleged to be violating any provisions of the Convention. Within six months, the receiving State shall submit to the Committee written explanations or statements clarifying the matter and the remedy, if any, that may have been taken by that State.
4. The Committee shall consider communications received under this article in the light of all information made available to it by or on behalf of the individual and by the State Party concerned.
5. The Committee shall not consider any communications from an individual under this article unless it has ascertained that:
>   (a) The same matter has not been, and is not being, examined under another procedure of international investigation or settlement;
>   (b) The individual has exhausted all available domestic remedies; this shall not be the rule where the application of the remedies is unreasonably prolonged or is unlikely to bring effective relief to the person who is the victim of the violation of this Convention.
6. The Committee shall hold closed meetings when examining communications under this article.
7. The Committee shall forward its views to the State Party concerned and to the individual.
8. The provisions of this article shall come into force when five States Parties to this Convention have made declarations under paragraph 1 of this article. Such declarations shall be deposited by the States Parties with the Secretary-General of the United Nations, who shall transmit copies thereof to the other States Parties. A declaration may be withdrawn at any time by notification to the Secretary-General. Such a withdrawal shall not prejudice the consideration of any matter which is the subject of a communication already transmitted under this article; no further communication by or on behalf of an individual shall be received under this article after the notification of withdrawal of the declaration has been received by the Secretary-General, unless the State Party has made a new declaration.

Article 23

The members of the Committee and of the ad hoc conciliation commissions which may be appointed under article 21, paragraph I (e), shall be entitled to the facilities, privileges and immunities of experts on mission for the United Nations as laid down in the relevant sections of the Convention on the Privileges and Immunities of the United Nations. * * *

Article 30

1. Any dispute between two or more States Parties concerning the interpretation or application of this Convention which cannot be settled through negotiation shall, at the request of one of them, be submitted to arbitration. If within six months from the date of the request for arbitration the Parties are unable to agree on the organization of the arbitration, any one of those Parties may refer the dispute to the International Court of Justice by request in conformity with the Statute of the Court.
2. Each State may, at the time of signature or ratification of this Convention or accession thereto, declare that it does not consider itself bound by paragraph I of this article. The other States Parties shall not be bound by paragraph I of this article with respect to any State Party having made such a reservation.

3. Any State Party having made a reservation in accordance with paragraph 2 of this article may at any time withdraw this reservation by notification to the Secretary-General of the United Nations.

Article 31

1. A State Party may denounce this Convention by written notification to the Secretary-General of the United Nations. Denunciation becomes effective one year after the date of receipt of the notification by the Secretary-General.

2. Such a denunciation shall not have the effect of releasing the State Party from its obligations under this Convention in regard to any act or omission which occurs prior to the date at which the denunciation becomes effective, nor shall denunciation prejudice in any way the continued consideration of any matter which is already under consideration by the Committee prior to the date at which the denunciation becomes effective.

3. Following the date at which the denunciation of a State Party becomes effective, the Committee shall not commence consideration of any new matter regarding that State.

* * *

CONVENTION ON THE RIGHTS OF THE CHILD (1989)

Convention on the Rights of the Child, *adopted* Nov. 20, 1989, 1577 U.N.T.S. 3

Preamble

The States Parties to the present Convention,

Considering that, in accordance with the principles proclaimed in the Charter of the United Nations, recognition of the inherent dignity and of the equal and inalienable rights of all members of the human family is the foundation of freedom, justice and peace in the world,

Bearing in mind that the peoples of the United Nations have, in the Charter, reaffirmed their faith in fundamental human rights and in the dignity and worth of the human person, and have determined to promote social progress and better standards of life in larger freedom,

Recognizing that the United Nations has, in the Universal Declaration of Human Rights and in the International Covenants on Human Rights, proclaimed and agreed that everyone is entitled to all the rights and freedoms set forth therein, without distinction of any kind, such as race, colour, sex, language, religion, political or other opinion, national or social origin, property, birth or other status,

Recalling that, in the Universal Declaration of Human Rights, the United Nations has proclaimed that childhood is entitled to special care and assistance,

Convinced that the family, as the fundamental group of society and the natural environment for the growth and well-being of all its members and particularly children, should be afforded the necessary protection and assistance so that it can fully assume its responsibilities within the community,

Recognizing that the child, for the full and harmonious development of his or her personality, should grow up in a family environment, in an atmosphere of happiness, love and understanding,

Considering that the child should be fully prepared to live an individual life in society, and brought up in the spirit of the ideals proclaimed in the Charter of the United Nations, and in particular in the spirit of peace, dignity, tolerance, freedom, equality and solidarity,

Bearing in mind that the need to extend particular care to the child has been stated in the Geneva Declaration of the Rights of the Child of 1924 and in the Declaration of the Rights of the Child adopted by the General Assembly on 20 November 1959 and recognized in the Universal Declaration of Human

Rights, in the International Covenant on Civil and Political Rights (in particular in articles 23 and 24), in the International Covenant on Economic, Social and Cultural Rights (in particular in article 10) and in the statutes and relevant instruments of specialized agencies and international organizations concerned with the welfare of children,

Bearing in mind that, as indicated in the Declaration of the Rights of the Child, "the child, by reason of his physical and mental immaturity, needs special safeguards and care, including appropriate legal protection, before as well as after birth",

Recalling the provisions of the Declaration on Social and Legal Principles relating to the Protection and Welfare of Children, with Special Reference to Foster Placement and Adoption Nationally and Internationally; the United Nations Standard Minimum Rules for the Administration of Juvenile Justice (The Beijing Rules); and the Declaration on the Protection of Women and Children in Emergency and Armed Conflict, Recognizing that, in all countries in the world, there are children living in exceptionally difficult conditions, and that such children need special consideration,

Taking due account of the importance of the traditions and cultural values of each people for the protection and harmonious development of the child, Recognizing the importance of international co-operation for improving the living conditions of children in every country, in particular in the developing countries,

Have agreed as follows:

PART I

Article 1
For the purposes of the present Convention, a child means every human being below the age of eighteen years unless under the law applicable to the child, majority is attained earlier.

Article 2
1. States Parties shall respect and ensure the rights set forth in the present Convention to each child within their jurisdiction without discrimination of any kind, irrespective of the child's or his or her parent's or legal guardian's race, colour, sex, language, religion, political or other opinion, national, ethnic or social origin, property, disability, birth or other status.
2. States Parties shall take all appropriate measures to ensure that the child is protected against all forms of discrimination or punishment on the basis of the status, activities, expressed opinions, or beliefs of the child's parents, legal guardians, or family members.

Article 3
1. In all actions concerning children, whether undertaken by public or private social welfare institutions, courts of law, administrative authorities or legislative bodies, the best interests of the child shall be a primary consideration.
2. States Parties undertake to ensure the child such protection and care as is necessary for his or her well-being, taking into account the rights and duties of his or her parents, legal guardians, or other individuals legally responsible for him or her, and, to this end, shall take all appropriate legislative and administrative measures.
3. States Parties shall ensure that the institutions, services and facilities responsible for the care or protection of children shall conform with the standards established by competent authorities, particularly in the areas of safety, health, in the number and suitability of their staff, as well as competent supervision.

Article 4
States Parties shall undertake all appropriate legislative, administrative, and other measures for the implementation of the rights recognized in the present Convention. With regard to economic, social and cultural rights, States Parties shall undertake such measures to the maximum extent of their available resources and, where needed, within the framework of international co-operation.

Article 5

States Parties shall respect the responsibilities, rights and duties of parents or, where applicable, the members of the extended family or community as provided for by local custom, legal guardians or other persons legally responsible for the child, to provide, in a manner consistent with the evolving capacities of the child, appropriate direction and guidance in the exercise by the child of the rights recognized in the present Convention.

Article 6

1. States Parties recognize that every child has the inherent right to life.
2. States Parties shall ensure to the maximum extent possible the survival and development of the child.

Article 7

1. The child shall be registered immediately after birth and shall have the right from birth to a name, the right to acquire a nationality and. as far as possible, the right to know and be cared for by his or her parents.
2. States Parties shall ensure the implementation of these rights in accordance with their national law and their obligations under the relevant international instruments in this field, in particular where the child would otherwise be stateless.

Article 8

1. States Parties undertake to respect the right of the child to preserve his or her identity, including nationality, name and family relations as recognized by law without unlawful interference.
2. Where a child is illegally deprived of some or all of the elements of his or her identity, States Parties shall provide appropriate assistance and protection, with a view to re-establishing speedily his or her identity.

Article 9

1. States Parties shall ensure that a child shall not be separated from his or her parents against their will, except when competent authorities subject to judicial review determine, in accordance with applicable law and procedures, that such separation is necessary for the best interests of the child. Such determination may be necessary in a particular case such as one involving abuse or neglect of the child by the parents, or one where the parents are living separately and a decision must be made as to the child's place of residence.
2. In any proceedings pursuant to paragraph 1 of the present article, all interested parties shall be given an opportunity to participate in the proceedings and make their views known.
3. States Parties shall respect the right of the child who is separated from one or both parents to maintain personal relations and direct contact with both parents on a regular basis, except if it is contrary to the child's best interests.
4. Where such separation results from any action initiated by a State Party, such as the detention, imprisonment, exile, deportation or death (including death arising from any cause while the person is in the custody of the State) of one or both parents or of the child, that State Party shall, upon request, provide the parents, the child or, if appropriate, another member of the family with the essential information concerning the whereabouts of the absent member(s) of the family unless the provision of the information would be detrimental to the well-being of the child. States Parties shall further ensure that the submission of such a request shall of itself entail no adverse consequences for the person(s) concerned.

Article 10

1. In accordance with the obligation of States Parties under article 9, paragraph 1, applications by a child or his or her parents to enter or leave a State Party for the purpose of family reunification shall be dealt with by States Parties in a positive, humane and expeditious manner. States Parties shall further ensure that the submission of such a request shall entail no adverse consequences for the applicants and for the members of their family.
2. A child whose parents reside in different States shall have the right to maintain on a regular basis, save in exceptional circumstances personal relations and direct contacts with both parents. Towards that end and in accordance with the obligation of States Parties under article 9, paragraph 1, States Parties shall respect the right of the child and his or her parents to leave any country, including their own, and to enter their own country. The right to leave any country shall be subject only to such restrictions as are prescribed by law and which are necessary to protect the national security, public order (ordre public), public health or morals

or the rights and freedoms of others and are consistent with the other rights recognized in the present Convention.

Article 11

1. States Parties shall take measures to combat the illicit transfer and non-return of children abroad.
2. To this end, States Parties shall promote the conclusion of bilateral or multilateral agreements or accession to existing agreements.

Article 12

1. States Parties shall assure to the child who is capable of forming his or her own views the right to express those views freely in all matters affecting the child, the views of the child being given due weight in accordance with the age and maturity of the child.
2. For this purpose, the child shall in particular be provided the opportunity to be heard in any judicial and administrative proceedings affecting the child, either directly, or through a representative or an appropriate body, in a manner consistent with the procedural rules of national law.

Article 13

1. The child shall have the right to freedom of expression; this right shall include freedom to seek, receive and impart information and ideas of all kinds, regardless of frontiers, either orally, in writing or in print, in the form of art, or through any other media of the child's choice.
2. The exercise of this right may be subject to certain restrictions, but these shall only be such as are provided by law and are necessary:
   (a) For respect of the rights or reputations of others; or
   (b) For the protection of national security or of public order (ordre public), or of public health or morals.

Article 14

1. States Parties shall respect the right of the child to freedom of thought, conscience and religion.
2. States Parties shall respect the rights and duties of the parents and, when applicable, legal guardians, to provide direction to the child in the exercise of his or her right in a manner consistent with the evolving capacities of the child.
3. Freedom to manifest one's religion or beliefs may be subject only to such limitations as are prescribed by law and are necessary to protect public safety, order, health or morals, or the fundamental rights and freedoms of others.

Article 15

1. States Parties recognize the rights of the child to freedom of association and to freedom of peaceful assembly.
2. No restrictions may be placed on the exercise of these rights other than those imposed in conformity with the law and which are necessary in a democratic society in the interests of national security or public safety, public order (ordre public), the protection of public health or morals or the protection of the rights and freedoms of others.

Article 16

1. No child shall be subjected to arbitrary or unlawful interference with his or her privacy, family, or correspondence, nor to unlawful attacks on his or her honour and reputation.
2. The child has the right to the protection of the law against such interference or attacks.

Article 17

States Parties recognize the important function performed by the mass media and shall ensure that the child has access to information and material from a diversity of national and international sources, especially those aimed at the promotion of his or her social, spiritual and moral well-being and physical and mental health.
To this end, States Parties shall:
   (a) Encourage the mass media to disseminate information and material of social and cultural benefit to the child and in accordance with the spirit of article 29;

(b) Encourage international co-operation in the production, exchange and dissemination of such information and material from a diversity of cultural, national and international sources;

(c) Encourage the production and dissemination of children's books;

(d) Encourage the mass media to have particular regard to the linguistic needs of the child who belongs to a minority group or who is indigenous;

(e) Encourage the development of appropriate guidelines for the protection of the child from information and material injurious to his or her well-being, bearing in mind the provisions of articles 13 and 18.

Article 18

1. States Parties shall use their best efforts to ensure recognition of the principle that both parents have common responsibilities for the upbringing and development of the child. Parents or, as the case may be, legal guardians, have the primary responsibility for the upbringing and development of the child. The best interests of the child will be their basic concern.

2. For the purpose of guaranteeing and promoting the rights set forth in the present Convention, States Parties shall render appropriate assistance to parents and legal guardians in the performance of their child-rearing responsibilities and shall ensure the development of institutions, facilities and services for the care of children.

3. States Parties shall take all appropriate measures to ensure that children of working parents have the right to benefit from child-care services and facilities for which they are eligible.

Article 19

1. States Parties shall take all appropriate legislative, administrative, social and educational measures to protect the child from all forms of physical or mental violence, injury or abuse, neglect or negligent treatment, maltreatment or exploitation, including sexual abuse, while in the care of parent(s), legal guardian(s) or any other person who has the care of the child.

2. Such protective measures should, as appropriate, include effective procedures for the establishment of social programmes to provide necessary support for the child and for those who have the care of the child, as well as for other forms of prevention and for identification, reporting, referral, investigation, treatment and follow-up of instances of child maltreatment described heretofore, and, as appropriate, for judicial involvement.

Article 20

1. A child temporarily or permanently deprived of his or her family environment, or in whose own best interests cannot be allowed to remain in that environment, shall be entitled to special protection and assistance provided by the State.

2. States Parties shall in accordance with their national laws ensure alternative care for such a child.

3. Such care could include, inter alia, foster placement, kafalah of Islamic law, adoption or if necessary placement in suitable institutions for the care of children. When considering solutions, due regard shall be paid to the desirability of continuity in a child's upbringing and to the child's ethnic, religious, cultural and linguistic background.

Article 21

States Parties that recognize and/or permit the system of adoption shall ensure that the best interests of the child shall be the paramount consideration and they shall:

(a) Ensure that the adoption of a child is authorized only by competent authorities who determine, in accordance with applicable law and procedures and on the basis of all pertinent and reliable information, that the adoption is permissible in view of the child's status concerning parents, relatives and legal guardians and that, if required, the persons concerned have given their informed consent to the adoption on the basis of such counselling as may be necessary;

(b) Recognize that inter-country adoption may be considered as an alternative means of child's care, if the child cannot be placed in a foster or an adoptive family or cannot in any suitable manner be cared for in the child's country of origin;

(c) Ensure that the child concerned by inter-country adoption enjoys safeguards and standards equivalent to those existing in the case of national adoption;

(d) Take all appropriate measures to ensure that, in inter-country adoption, the placement does not result in improper financial gain for those involved in it;

(e) Promote, where appropriate, the objectives of the present article by concluding bilateral or multilateral arrangements or agreements, and endeavour, within this framework, to ensure that the placement of the child in another country is carried out by competent authorities or organs.

Article 22

1. States Parties shall take appropriate measures to ensure that a child who is seeking refugee status or who is considered a refugee in accordance with applicable international or domestic law and procedures shall, whether unaccompanied or accompanied by his or her parents or by any other person, receive appropriate protection and humanitarian assistance in the enjoyment of applicable rights set forth in the present Convention and in other international human rights or humanitarian instruments to which the said States are Parties.

2. For this purpose, States Parties shall provide, as they consider appropriate, co-operation in any efforts by the United Nations and other competent intergovernmental organizations or non-governmental organizations co-operating with the United Nations to protect and assist such a child and to trace the parents or other members of the family of any refugee child in order to obtain information necessary for reunification with his or her family. In cases where no parents or other members of the family can be found, the child shall be accorded the same protection as any other child permanently or temporarily deprived of his or her family environment for any reason , as set forth in the present Convention.

Article 23

1. States Parties recognize that a mentally or physically disabled child should enjoy a full and decent life, in conditions which ensure dignity, promote self-reliance and facilitate the child's active participation in the community.

2. States Parties recognize the right of the disabled child to special care and shall encourage and ensure the extension, subject to available resources, to the eligible child and those responsible for his or her care, of assistance for which application is made and which is appropriate to the child's condition and to the circumstances of the parents or others caring for the child.

3. Recognizing the special needs of a disabled child, assistance extended in accordance with paragraph 2 of the present article shall be provided free of charge, whenever possible, taking into account the financial resources of the parents or others caring for the child, and shall be designed to ensure that the disabled child has effective access to and receives education, training, health care services, rehabilitation services, preparation for employment and recreation opportunities in a manner conducive to the child's achieving the fullest possible social integration and individual development, including his or her cultural and spiritual development

4. States Parties shall promote, in the spirit of international cooperation, the exchange of appropriate information in the field of preventive health care and of medical, psychological and functional treatment of disabled children, including dissemination of and access to information concerning methods of rehabilitation, education and vocational services, with the aim of enabling States Parties to improve their capabilities and skills and to widen their experience in these areas. In this regard, particular account shall be taken of the needs of developing countries.

Article 24

1. States Parties recognize the right of the child to the enjoyment of the highest attainable standard of health and to facilities for the treatment of illness and rehabilitation of health. States Parties shall strive to ensure that no child is deprived of his or her right of access to such health care services.

2. States Parties shall pursue full implementation of this right and, in particular, shall take appropriate measures:

(a) To diminish infant and child mortality;

(b) To ensure the provision of necessary medical assistance and health care to all children with emphasis on the development of primary health care;

(c) To combat disease and malnutrition, including within the framework of primary health care, through, inter alia, the application of readily available technology and through the provision of adequate nutritious foods and clean drinking-water, taking into consideration the dangers and risks of environmental pollution;

(d) To ensure appropriate pre-natal and post-natal health care for mothers;

(e) To ensure that all segments of society, in particular parents and children, are informed, have access to education and are supported in the use of basic knowledge of child health and nutrition, the advantages of breastfeeding, hygiene and environmental sanitation and the prevention of accidents;

(f) To develop preventive health care, guidance for parents and family planning education and services.

3. States Parties shall take all effective and appropriate measures with a view to abolishing traditional practices prejudicial to the health of children.

4. States Parties undertake to promote and encourage international co-operation with a view to achieving progressively the full realization of the right recognized in the present article. In this regard, particular account shall be taken of the needs of developing countries.

Article 25

States Parties recognize the right of a child who has been placed by the competent authorities for the purposes of care, protection or treatment of his or her physical or mental health, to a periodic review of the treatment provided to the child and all other circumstances relevant to his or her placement.

Article 26

1. States Parties shall recognize for every child the right to benefit from social security, including social insurance, and shall take the necessary measures to achieve the full realization of this right in accordance with their national law.

2. The benefits should, where appropriate, be granted, taking into account the resources and the circumstances of the child and persons having responsibility for the maintenance of the child, as well as any other consideration relevant to an application for benefits made by or on behalf of the child.

Article 27

1. States Parties recognize the right of every child to a standard of living adequate for the child's physical, mental, spiritual, moral and social development.

2. The parent(s) or others responsible for the child have the primary responsibility to secure, within their abilities and financial capacities, the conditions of living necessary for the child's development.

3. States Parties, in accordance with national conditions and within their means, shall take appropriate measures to assist parents and others responsible for the child to implement this right and shall in case of need provide material assistance and support programmes, particularly with regard to nutrition, clothing and housing.

4. States Parties shall take all appropriate measures to secure the recovery of maintenance for the child from the parents or other persons having financial responsibility for the child, both within the State Party and from abroad. In particular, where the person having financial responsibility for the child lives in a State different from that of the child, States Parties shall promote the accession to international agreements or the conclusion of such agreements, as well as the making of other appropriate arrangements.

Article 28

1. States Parties recognize the right of the child to education, and with a view to achieving this right progressively and on the basis of equal opportunity, they shall, in particular:

(a) Make primary education compulsory and available free to all;

(b) Encourage the development of different forms of secondary education, including general and vocational education, make them available and accessible to every child, and take appropriate measures such as the introduction of free education and offering financial assistance in case of need;

(c) Make higher education accessible to all on the basis of capacity by every appropriate means;

(d) Make educational and vocational information and guidance available and accessible to all children;

(e) Take measures to encourage regular attendance at schools and the reduction of drop-out rates.

2. States Parties shall take all appropriate measures to ensure that school discipline is administered in a manner consistent with the child's human dignity and in conformity with the present Convention.

3. States Parties shall promote and encourage international cooperation in matters relating to education, in particular with a view to contributing to the elimination of ignorance and illiteracy throughout the world and facilitating access to scientific and technical knowledge and modern teaching methods. In this regard, particular account shall be taken of the needs of developing countries.

Article 29

1. States Parties agree that the education of the child shall be directed to:

(a) The development of the child's personality, talents and mental and physical abilities to their fullest potential;

(b) The development of respect for human rights and fundamental freedoms, and for the principles enshrined in the Charter of the United Nations;

(c) The development of respect for the child's parents, his or her own cultural identity, language and values, for the national values of the country in which the child is living, the country from which he or she may originate, and for civilizations different from his or her own;

(d) The preparation of the child for responsible life in a free society, in the spirit of understanding, peace, tolerance, equality of sexes, and friendship among all peoples, ethnic, national and religious groups and persons of indigenous origin;

(e) The development of respect for the natural environment.

2. No part of the present article or article 28 shall be construed so as to interfere with the liberty of individuals and bodies to establish and direct educational institutions, subject always to the observance of the principle set forth in paragraph 1 of the present article and to the requirements that the education given in such institutions shall conform to such minimum standards as may be laid down by the State.

Article 30

In those States in which ethnic, religious or linguistic minorities or persons of indigenous origin exist, a child belonging to such a minority or who is indigenous shall not be denied the right, in community with other members of his or her group, to enjoy his or her own culture, to profess and practise his or her own religion, or to use his or her own language.

Article 31

1. States Parties recognize the right of the child to rest and leisure, to engage in play and recreational activities appropriate to the age of the child and to participate freely in cultural life and the arts.

2. States Parties shall respect and promote the right of the child to participate fully in cultural and artistic life and shall encourage the provision of appropriate and equal opportunities for cultural, artistic, recreational and leisure activity.

Article 32

1. States Parties recognize the right of the child to be protected from economic exploitation and from performing any work that is likely to be hazardous or to interfere with the child's education, or to be harmful to the child's health or physical, mental, spiritual, moral or social development.

2. States Parties shall take legislative, administrative, social and educational measures to ensure the implementation of the present article. To this end, and having regard to the relevant provisions of other international instruments, States Parties shall in particular:

(a) Provide for a minimum age or minimum ages for admission to employment;

(b) Provide for appropriate regulation of the hours and conditions of employment;

(c) Provide for appropriate penalties or other sanctions to ensure the effective enforcement of the present article.

Article 33

States Parties shall take all appropriate measures, including legislative, administrative, social and educational measures, to protect children from the illicit use of narcotic drugs and psychotropic substances as defined in the relevant international treaties, and to prevent the use of children in the illicit production and trafficking of such substances.

Article 34

States Parties undertake to protect the child from all forms of sexual exploitation and sexual abuse. For these purposes, States Parties shall in particular take all appropriate national, bilateral and multilateral measures to prevent:

(a) The inducement or coercion of a child to engage in any unlawful sexual activity;

(b) The exploitative use of children in prostitution or other unlawful sexual practices;

(c) The exploitative use of children in pornographic performances and materials.

Article 35

States Parties shall take all appropriate national, bilateral and multilateral measures to prevent the abduction of, the sale of or traffic in children for any purpose or in any form.

Article 36

States Parties shall protect the child against all other forms of exploitation prejudicial to any aspects of the child's welfare.

Article 37

States Parties shall ensure that:

(a) No child shall be subjected to torture or other cruel, inhuman or degrading treatment or punishment. Neither capital punishment nor life imprisonment without possibility of release shall be imposed for offences committed by persons below eighteen years of age;

(b) No child shall be deprived of his or her liberty unlawfully or arbitrarily. The arrest, detention or imprisonment of a child shall be in conformity with the law and shall be used only as a measure of last resort and for the shortest appropriate period of time;

(c) Every child deprived of liberty shall be treated with humanity and respect for the inherent dignity of the human person, and in a manner which takes into account the needs of persons of his or her age. In particular, every child deprived of liberty shall be separated from adults unless it is considered in the child's best interest not to do so and shall have the right to maintain contact with his or her family through correspondence and visits, save in exceptional circumstances;

(d) Every child deprived of his or her liberty shall have the right to prompt access to legal and other appropriate assistance, as well as the right to challenge the legality of the deprivation of his or her liberty before a court or other competent, independent and impartial authority, and to a prompt decision on any such action.

Article 38

1. States Parties undertake to respect and to ensure respect for rules of international humanitarian law applicable to them in armed conflicts which are relevant to the child.

2. States Parties shall take all feasible measures to ensure that persons who have not attained the age of fifteen years do not take a direct part in hostilities.

3. States Parties shall refrain from recruiting any person who has not attained the age of fifteen years into their armed forces. In recruiting among those persons who have attained the age of fifteen years but who have not attained the age of eighteen years, States Parties shall endeavour to give priority to those who are oldest.

4. In accordance with their obligations under international humanitarian law to protect the civilian population in armed conflicts, States Parties shall take all feasible measures to ensure protection and care of children who are affected by an armed conflict.

Article 39

States Parties shall take all appropriate measures to promote physical and psychological recovery and social reintegration of a child victim of: any form of neglect, exploitation, or abuse; torture or any other form of cruel, inhuman or degrading treatment or punishment; or armed conflicts. Such recovery and reintegration shall take place in an environment which fosters the health, self-respect and dignity of the child.

Article 40

1. States Parties recognize the right of every child alleged as, accused of, or recognized as having infringed the penal law to be treated in a manner consistent with the promotion of the child's sense of dignity and

worth, which reinforces the child's respect for the human rights and fundamental freedoms of others and which takes into account the child's age and the desirability of promoting the child's reintegration and the child's assuming a constructive role in society.

2. To this end, and having regard to the relevant provisions of international instruments, States Parties shall, in particular, ensure that:

(a) No child shall be alleged as, be accused of, or recognized as having infringed the penal law by reason of acts or omissions that were not prohibited by national or international law at the time they were committed;

(b) Every child alleged as or accused of having infringed the penal law has at least the following guarantees:

(i) To be presumed innocent until proven guilty according to law;

(ii) To be informed promptly and directly of the charges against him or her, and, if appropriate, through his or her parents or legal guardians, and to have legal or other appropriate assistance in the preparation and presentation of his or her defence;

(iii) To have the matter determined without delay by a competent, independent and impartial authority or judicial body in a fair hearing according to law, in the presence of legal or other appropriate assistance and, unless it is considered not to be in the best interest of the child, in particular, taking into account his or her age or situation, his or her parents or legal guardians;

(iv) Not to be compelled to give testimony or to confess guilt; to examine or have examined adverse witnesses and to obtain the participation and examination of witnesses on his or her behalf under conditions of equality;

(v) If considered to have infringed the penal law, to have this decision and any measures imposed in consequence thereof reviewed by a higher competent, independent and impartial authority or judicial body according to law;

(vi) To have the free assistance of an interpreter if the child cannot understand or speak the language used;

(vii) To have his or her privacy fully respected at all stages of the proceedings.

3. States Parties shall seek to promote the establishment of laws, procedures, authorities and institutions specifically applicable to children alleged as, accused of, or recognized as having infringed the penal law, and, in particular:

(a) The establishment of a minimum age below which children shall be presumed not to have the capacity to infringe the penal law;

(b) Whenever appropriate and desirable, measures for dealing with such children without resorting to judicial proceedings, providing that human rights and legal safeguards are fully respected. 4. A variety of dispositions, such as care, guidance and supervision orders; counselling; probation; foster care; education and vocational training programmes and other alternatives to institutional care shall be available to ensure that children are dealt with in a manner appropriate to their well-being and proportionate both to their circumstances and the offence.

Article 41

Nothing in the present Convention shall affect any provisions which are more conducive to the realization of the rights of the child and which may be contained in:

(a) The law of a State party; or

(b) International law in force for that State.

PART II

Article 42

States Parties undertake to make the principles and provisions of the Convention widely known, by appropriate and active means, to adults and children alike.

Article 43

1. For the purpose of examining the progress made by States Parties in achieving the realization of the obligations undertaken in the present Convention, there shall be established a Committee on the Rights of the Child, which shall carry out the functions hereinafter provided.

2. The Committee shall consist of eighteen experts of high moral standing and recognized competence in the field covered by this Convention. The members of the Committee shall be elected by States Parties from among their nationals and shall serve in their personal capacity, consideration being given to equitable geographical distribution, as well as to the principal legal systems.

3. The members of the Committee shall be elected by secret ballot from a list of persons nominated by States Parties. Each State Party may nominate one person from among its own nationals.

4. The initial election to the Committee shall be held no later than six months after the date of the entry into force of the present Convention and thereafter every second year. At least four months before the date of each election, the Secretary-General of the United Nations shall address a letter to States Parties inviting them to submit their nominations within two months. The Secretary-General shall subsequently prepare a list in alphabetical order of all persons thus nominated, indicating States Parties which have nominated them, and shall submit it to the States Parties to the present Convention.

5. The elections shall be held at meetings of States Parties convened by the Secretary-General at United Nations Headquarters. At those meetings, for which two thirds of States Parties shall constitute a quorum, the persons elected to the Committee shall be those who obtain the largest number of votes and an absolute majority of the votes of the representatives of States Parties present and voting.

6. The members of the Committee shall be elected for a term of four years. They shall be eligible for re-election if renominated. The term of five of the members elected at the first election shall expire at the end of two years; immediately after the first election, the names of these five members shall be chosen by lot by the Chairman of the meeting.

7. If a member of the Committee dies or resigns or declares that for any other cause he or she can no longer perform the duties of the Committee, the State Party which nominated the member shall appoint another expert from among its nationals to serve for the remainder of the term, subject to the approval of the Committee.

8. The Committee shall establish its own rules of procedure.

9. The Committee shall elect its officers for a period of two years.

10. The meetings of the Committee shall normally be held at United Nations Headquarters or at any other convenient place as determined by the Committee. The Committee shall normally meet annually. The duration of the meetings of the Committee shall be determined, and reviewed, if necessary, by a meeting of the States Parties to the present Convention, subject to the approval of the General Assembly.

11. The Secretary-General of the United Nations shall provide the necessary staff and facilities for the effective performance of the functions of the Committee under the present Convention.

12. With the approval of the General Assembly, the members of the Committee established under the present Convention shall receive emoluments from United Nations resources on such terms and conditions as the Assembly may decide.

Article 44

1. States Parties undertake to submit to the Committee, through the Secretary-General of the United Nations, reports on the measures they have adopted which give effect to the rights recognized herein and on the progress made on the enjoyment of those rights

    (a) Within two years of the entry into force of the Convention for the State Party concerned;

    (b) Thereafter every five years.

2. Reports made under the present article shall indicate factors and difficulties, if any, affecting the degree of fulfilment of the obligations under the present Convention. Reports shall also contain sufficient information to provide the Committee with a comprehensive understanding of the implementation of the Convention in the country concerned.

3. A State Party which has submitted a comprehensive initial report to the Committee need not, in its subsequent reports submitted in accordance with paragraph 1 (b) of the present article, repeat basic information previously provided.

4. The Committee may request from States Parties further information relevant to the implementation of the Convention.

5. The Committee shall submit to the General Assembly, through the Economic and Social Council, every two years, reports on its activities.

6. States Parties shall make their reports widely available to the public in their own countries.

Article 45

In order to foster the effective implementation of the Convention and to encourage international co-operation in the field covered by the Convention:

(a) The specialized agencies, the United Nations Children's Fund, and other United Nations organs shall be entitled to be represented at the consideration of the implementation of such provisions of the present Convention as fall within the scope of their mandate. The Committee may invite the specialized agencies, the United Nations Children's Fund and other competent bodies as it may consider appropriate to provide expert advice on the implementation of the Convention in areas falling within the scope of their respective mandates. The Committee may invite the specialized agencies, the United Nations Children's Fund, and other United Nations organs to submit reports on the implementation of the Convention in areas falling within the scope of their activities;

(b) The Committee shall transmit, as it may consider appropriate, to the specialized agencies, the United Nations Children's Fund and other competent bodies, any reports from States Parties that contain a request, or indicate a need, for technical advice or assistance, along with the Committee's observations and suggestions, if any, on these requests or indications;

(c) The Committee may recommend to the General Assembly to request the Secretary-General to undertake on its behalf studies on specific issues relating to the rights of the child;

(d) The Committee may make suggestions and general recommendations based on information received pursuant to articles 44 and 45 of the present Convention. Such suggestions and general recommendations shall be transmitted to any State Party concerned and reported to the General Assembly, together with comments, if any, from States Parties.

PART III

Article 46

The present Convention shall be open for signature by all States.

Article 47

The present Convention is subject to ratification. Instruments of ratification shall be deposited with the Secretary-General of the United Nations. * * *

Article 50

1. Any State Party may propose an amendment and file it with the Secretary-General of the United Nations. The Secretary-General shall thereupon communicate the proposed amendment to States Parties, with a request that they indicate whether they favour a conference of States Parties for the purpose of considering and voting upon the proposals. In the event that, within four months from the date of such communication, at least one third of the States Parties favour such a conference, the Secretary-General shall convene the conference under the auspices of the United Nations. Any amendment adopted by a majority of States Parties present and voting at the conference shall be submitted to the General Assembly for approval.

2. An amendment adopted in accordance with paragraph 1 of the present article shall enter into force when it has been approved by the General Assembly of the United Nations and accepted by a two-thirds majority of States Parties.

3. When an amendment enters into force, it shall be binding on those States Parties which have accepted it, other States Parties still being bound by the provisions of the present Convention and any earlier amendments which they have accepted.

Article 51

1. The Secretary-General of the United Nations shall receive and circulate to all States the text of reservations made by States at the time of ratification or accession.

2. A reservation incompatible with the object and purpose of the present Convention shall not be permitted.

3. Reservations may be withdrawn at any time by notification to that effect addressed to the Secretary-General of the United Nations, who shall then inform all States. Such notification shall take effect on the date on which it is received by the Secretary-General

Article 52

A State Party may denounce the present Convention by written notification to the Secretary-General of the United Nations. Denunciation becomes effective one year after the date of receipt of the notification by the Secretary-General. * * *

Article 54

The original of the present Convention, of which the Arabic, Chinese, English, French, Russian and Spanish texts are equally authentic, shall be deposited with the Secretary-General of the United Nations. In witness thereof the undersigned plenipotentiaries, being duly authorized thereto by their respective Governments, have signed the present Convention.

OPTIONAL PROTOCOL TO THE CONVENTION ON THE RIGHTS OF THE CHILD ON THE INVOLVEMENT OF CHILDREN IN ARMED CONFLICT (2000)

Optional Protocol to the Convention on the Rights of the Child on the Involvement of Children in Armed Conflict, *adopted* May 25, 2000, S. Treaty Doc. No. 106-37, 2173 U.N.T.S. 236

The States Parties to the present Protocol,

Encouraged by the overwhelming support for the Convention on the Rights of the Child, demonstrating the widespread commitment that exists to strive for the promotion and protection of the rights of the child,

Reaffirming that the rights of children require special protection, and calling for continuous improvement of the situation of children without distinction, as well as for their development and education in conditions of peace and security,

Disturbed by the harmful and widespread impact of armed conflict on children and the long-term consequences it has for durable peace, security and development,

Condemning the targeting of children in situations of armed conflict and direct attacks on objects protected under international law, including places that generally have a significant presence of children, such as schools and hospitals,

Noting the adoption of the Rome Statute of the International Criminal Court, in particular, the inclusion therein as a war crime, of conscripting or enlisting children under the age of 15 years or using them to participate actively in hostilities in both international and non-international armed conflict,

Considering therefore that to strengthen further the implementation of rights recognized in the Convention on the Rights of the Child there is a need to increase the protection of children from involvement in armed conflict, * * *

Convinced that an optional protocol to the Convention that raises the age of possible recruitment of persons into armed forces and their participation in hostilities will contribute effectively to the implementation of the principle that the best interests of the child are to be a primary consideration in all actions concerning children, * * *

Welcoming the unanimous adoption, in June 1999, of International Labour Organization Convention No. 182 on the Prohibition and Immediate Action for the Elimination of the Worst Forms of Child Labour, which prohibits, inter alia, forced or compulsory recruitment of children for use in armed conflict,

Condemning with the gravest concern the recruitment, training and use within and across national borders of children in hostilities by armed groups distinct from the armed forces of a State, and recognizing the responsibility of those who recruit, train and use children in this regard,

Recalling the obligation of each party to an armed conflict to abide by the provisions of international humanitarian law, * * *

Recognizing the special needs of those children who are particularly vulnerable to recruitment or use in hostilities contrary to the present Protocol owing to their economic or social status or gender,

Mindful of the necessity of taking into consideration the economic, social and political root causes of the involvement of children in armed conflict, * * *

Have agreed as follows:

Article 1
States Parties shall take all feasible measures to ensure that members of their armed forces who have not attained the age of 18 years do not take a direct part in hostilities.

Article 2
States Parties shall ensure that persons who have not attained the age of 18 years are not compulsorily recruited into their armed forces.

Article 3
1. States Parties shall raise the minimum age for the voluntary recruitment of persons into their national armed forces from that set out in article 38, paragraph 3, of the Convention on the Rights of the Child, taking account of the principles contained in that article and recognizing that under the Convention persons under the age of 18 years are entitled to special protection.
2. Each State Party shall deposit a binding declaration upon ratification of or accession to the present Protocol that sets forth the minimum age at which it will permit voluntary recruitment into its national armed forces and a description of the safeguards it has adopted to ensure that such recruitment is not forced or coerced.
3. States Parties that permit voluntary recruitment into their national armed forces under the age of 18 years shall maintain safeguards to ensure, as a minimum, that:
    (a) Such recruitment is genuinely voluntary;
    (b) Such recruitment is carried out with the informed consent of the person's parents or legal guardians;
    (c) Such persons are fully informed of the duties involved in such military service;
    (d) Such persons provide reliable proof of age prior to acceptance into national military service.
4. Each State Party may strengthen its declaration at any time by notification to that effect addressed to the Secretary-General of the United Nations, who shall inform all States Parties. Such notification shall take effect on the date on which it is received by the Secretary-General.
5. The requirement to raise the age in paragraph 1 of the present article does not apply to schools operated by or under the control of the armed forces of the States Parties, in keeping with articles 28 and 29 of the Convention on the Rights of the Child.

Article 4
1. Armed groups that are distinct from the armed forces of a State should not, under any circumstances, recruit or use in hostilities persons under the age of 18 years.
2. States Parties shall take all feasible measures to prevent such recruitment and use, including the adoption of legal measures necessary to prohibit and criminalize such practices.
3. The application of the present article shall not affect the legal status of any party to an armed conflict.

Article 5

Nothing in the present Protocol shall be construed as precluding provisions in the law of a State Party or in international instruments and international humanitarian law that are more conducive to the realization of the rights of the child.

Article 6

1. Each State Party shall take all necessary legal, administrative and other measures to ensure the effective implementation and enforcement of the provisions of the present Protocol within its jurisdiction.
2. States Parties undertake to make the principles and provisions of the present Protocol widely known and promoted by appropriate means, to adults and children alike.
3. States Parties shall take all feasible measures to ensure that persons within their jurisdiction recruited or used in hostilities contrary to the present Protocol are demobilized or otherwise released from service. States Parties shall, when necessary, accord to such persons all appropriate assistance for their physical and psychological recovery and their social reintegration.

Article 7

1. States Parties shall cooperate in the implementation of the present Protocol, including in the prevention of any activity contrary thereto and in the rehabilitation and social reintegration of persons who are victims of acts contrary thereto, including through technical cooperation and financial assistance. Such assistance and cooperation will be undertaken in consultation with the States Parties concerned and the relevant international organizations.
2. States Parties in a position to do so shall provide such assistance through existing multilateral, bilateral or other programmes or, inter alia, through a voluntary fund established in accordance with the rules of the General Assembly.

Article 8

1. Each State Party shall, within two years following the entry into force of the present Protocol for that State Party, submit a report to the Committee on the Rights of the Child providing comprehensive information on the measures it has taken to implement the provisions of the Protocol, including the measures taken to implement the provisions on participation and recruitment.
2. Following the submission of the comprehensive report, each State Party shall include in the reports it submits to the Committee on the Rights of the Child, in accordance with article 44 of the Convention, any further information with respect to the implementation of the Protocol. Other States Parties to the Protocol shall submit a report every five years.
3. The Committee on the Rights of the Child may request from States Parties further information relevant to the implementation of the present Protocol.

Article 9

1. The present Protocol is open for signature by any State that is a party to the Convention or has signed it.
2. The present Protocol is subject to ratification and is open to accession by any State. Instruments of ratification or accession shall be deposited with the Secretary-General of the United Nations.
3. The Secretary-General, in his capacity as depositary of the Convention and the Protocol, shall inform all States Parties to the Convention and all States that have signed the Convention of each instrument of declaration pursuant to article 3.

Article 10

1. The present Protocol shall enter into force three months after the deposit of the tenth instrument of ratification or accession.
2. For each State ratifying the present Protocol or acceding to it after its entry into force, the Protocol shall enter into force one month after the date of the deposit of its own instrument of ratification or accession.

Article 11

1. Any State Party may denounce the present Protocol at any time by written notification to the Secretary-General of the United Nations, who shall thereafter inform the other States Parties to the Convention and all States that have signed the Convention. The denunciation shall take effect one year after the date of receipt of the notification by the Secretary-General. If, however, on the expiry of that year the denouncing

State Party is engaged in armed conflict, the denunciation shall not take effect before the end of the armed conflict.

2. Such a denunciation shall not have the effect of releasing the State Party from its obligations under the present Protocol in regard to any act that occurs prior to the date on which the denunciation becomes effective. Nor shall such a denunciation prejudice in any way the continued consideration of any matter that is already under consideration by the Committee on the Rights of the Child prior to the date on which the denunciation becomes effective.

Article 12

1. Any State Party may propose an amendment and file it with the Secretary-General of the United Nations. The Secretary-General shall thereupon communicate the proposed amendment to States Parties with a request that they indicate whether they favour a conference of States Parties for the purpose of considering and voting upon the proposals. In the event that, within four months from the date of such communication, at least one third of the States Parties favour such a conference, the Secretary-General shall convene the conference under the auspices of the United Nations. Any amendment adopted by a majority of States Parties present and voting at the conference shall be submitted to the General Assembly of the United Nations for approval.

2. An amendment adopted in accordance with paragraph 1 of the present article shall enter into force when it has been approved by the General Assembly and accepted by a two-thirds majority of States Parties.

3. When an amendment enters into force, it shall be binding on those States Parties that have accepted it, other States Parties still being bound by the provisions of the present Protocol and any earlier amendments they have accepted.

Article 13

1. The present Protocol, of which the Arabic, Chinese, English, French, Russian and Spanish texts are equally authentic, shall be deposited in the archives of the United Nations.

2. The Secretary-General of the United Nations shall transmit certified copies of the present Protocol to all States Parties to the Convention and all States that have signed the Convention.

OPTIONAL PROTOCOL TO THE CONVENTION ON THE RIGHTS OF THE CHILD ON THE SALE OF CHILDREN, CHILD PROSTITUTION AND CHILD PORNOGRAPHY (2000)

Optional Protocol to the Convention on the Rights of the Child on the Sale of Children, Child Prostitution and Child Pornography, *adopted* May 25, 2000, S. Treaty Doc. No. 106-37, 2171 U.N.T.S. 247

The States Parties to the present Protocol,

Considering that, in order further to achieve the purposes of the Convention on the Rights of the Child and the implementation of its provisions, especially articles 1, 11, 21, 32, 33, 34, 35 and 36, it would be appropriate to extend the measures that States Parties should undertake in order to guarantee the protection of the child from the sale of children, child prostitution and child pornography,

Considering also that the Convention on the Rights of the Child recognizes the right of the child to be protected from economic exploitation and from performing any work that is likely to be hazardous or to interfere with the child's education, or to be harmful to the child's health or physical, mental, spiritual, moral or social development,

Gravely concerned at the significant and increasing international traffic in children for the purpose of the sale of children, child prostitution and child pornography,

Deeply concerned at the widespread and continuing practice of sex tourism, to which children are especially vulnerable, as it directly promotes the sale of children, child prostitution and child pornography,

Recognizing that a number of particularly vulnerable groups, including girl children, are at greater risk of sexual exploitation and that girl children are disproportionately represented among the sexually exploited,

Concerned about the growing availability of child pornography on the Internet and other evolving technologies, and recalling the International Conference on Combating Child Pornography on the Internet, held in Vienna in 1999, in particular its conclusion calling for the worldwide criminalization of the production, distribution, exportation, transmission, importation, intentional possession and advertising of child pornography, and stressing the importance of closer cooperation and partnership between Governments and the Internet industry,

Believing that the elimination of the sale of children, child prostitution and child pornography will be facilitated by adopting a holistic approach, addressing the contributing factors, including underdevelopment, poverty, economic disparities, inequitable socio-economic structure, dysfunctioning families, lack of education, urban-rural migration, gender discrimination, irresponsible adult sexual behaviour, harmful traditional practices, armed conflicts and trafficking in children,

Believing also that efforts to raise public awareness are needed to reduce consumer demand for the sale of children, child prostitution and child pornography, and believing further in the importance of strengthening global partnership among all actors and of improving law enforcement at the national level,

Noting the provisions of international legal instruments relevant to the protection of children, including the Hague Convention on Protection of Children and Cooperation in Respect of Intercountry Adoption, the Hague Convention on the Civil Aspects of International Child Abduction, the Hague Convention on Jurisdiction, Applicable Law, Recognition, Enforcement and Cooperation in Respect of Parental Responsibility and Measures for the Protection of Children, and International Labour Organization Convention No. 182 on the Prohibition and Immediate Action for the Elimination of the Worst Forms of Child Labour,

Encouraged by the overwhelming support for the Convention on the Rights of the Child, demonstrating the widespread commitment that exists for the promotion and protection of the rights of the child,

Recognizing the importance of the implementation of the provisions of the Programme of Action for the Prevention of the Sale of Children, Child Prostitution and Child Pornography and the Declaration and Agenda for Action adopted at the World Congress against Commercial Sexual Exploitation of Children, held in Stockholm from 27 to 31 August 1996, and the other relevant decisions and recommendations of pertinent international bodies,

Taking due account of the importance of the traditions and cultural values of each people for the protection and harmonious development of the child, Have agreed as follows:

Article 1
States Parties shall prohibit the sale of children, child prostitution and child pornography as provided for by the present Protocol.

Article 2
For the purposes of the present Protocol:
> (a) Sale of children means any act or transaction whereby a child is transferred by any person or group of persons to another for remuneration or any other consideration;
> (b) Child prostitution means the use of a child in sexual activities for remuneration or any other form of consideration;
> (c) Child pornography means any representation, by whatever means, of a child engaged in real or simulated explicit sexual activities or any representation of the sexual parts of a child for primarily sexual purposes.

Article 3

1. Each State Party shall ensure that, as a minimum, the following acts and activities are fully covered under its criminal or penal law, whether such offences are committed domestically or transnationally or on an individual or organized basis:

(a) In the context of sale of children as defined in article 2:

(i) Offering, delivering or accepting, by whatever means, a child for the purpose of:

a. Sexual exploitation of the child;

b. Transfer of organs of the child for profit;

c. Engagement of the child in forced labour;

(ii) Improperly inducing consent, as an intermediary, for the adoption of a child in violation of applicable international legal instruments on adoption;

(b) Offering, obtaining, procuring or providing a child for child prostitution, as defined in article 2;

(c) Producing, distributing, disseminating, importing, exporting, offering, selling or possessing for the above purposes child pornography as defined in article 2.

2. Subject to the provisions of the national law of a State Party, the same shall apply to an attempt to commit any of the said acts and to complicity or participation in any of the said acts.

3. Each State Party shall make such offences punishable by appropriate penalties that take into account their grave nature.

4. Subject to the provisions of its national law, each State Party shall take measures, where appropriate, to establish the liability of legal persons for offences established in paragraph 1 of the present article. Subject to the legal principles of the State Party, such liability of legal persons may be criminal, civil or administrative.

5. States Parties shall take all appropriate legal and administrative measures to ensure that all persons involved in the adoption of a child act in conformity with applicable international legal instruments.

Article 4

1. Each State Party shall take such measures as may be necessary to establish its jurisdiction over the offences referred to in article 3, paragraph 1, when the offences are commited in its territory or on board a ship or aircraft registered in that State.

2. Each State Party may take such measures as may be necessary to establish its jurisdiction over the offences referred to in article 3, paragraph 1, in the following cases:

(a) When the alleged offender is a national of that State or a person who has his habitual residence in its territory;

(b) When the victim is a national of that State.

3. Each State Party shall also take such measures as may be necessary to establish its jurisdiction over the aforementioned offences when the alleged offender is present in its territory and it does not extradite him or her to another State Party on the ground that the offence has been committed by one of its nationals.

4. The present Protocol does not exclude any criminal jurisdiction exercised in accordance with internal law.

Article 5

1. The offences referred to in article 3, paragraph 1, shall be deemed to be included as extraditable offences in any extradition treaty existing between States Parties and shall be included as extraditable offences in every extradition treaty subsequently concluded between them, in accordance with the conditions set forth in such treaties.

2. If a State Party that makes extradition conditional on the existence of a treaty receives a request for extradition from another State Party with which it has no extradition treaty, it may consider the present Protocol to be a legal basis for extradition in respect of such offences. Extradition shall be subject to the conditions provided by the law of the requested State.

3. States Parties that do not make extradition conditional on the existence of a treaty shall recognize such offences as extraditable offences between themselves subject to the conditions provided by the law of the requested State.

4. Such offences shall be treated, for the purpose of extradition between States Parties, as if they had been committed not only in the place in which they occurred but also in the territories of the States required to establish their jurisdiction in accordance with article 4.

5. If an extradition request is made with respect to an offence described in article 3, paragraph 1, and the requested State Party does not or will not extradite on the basis of the nationality of the offender, that State shall take suitable measures to submit the case to its competent authorities for the purpose of prosecution.

Article 6

1. States Parties shall afford one another the greatest measure of assistance in connection with investigations or criminal or extradition proceedings brought in respect of the offences set forth in article 3, paragraph 1, including assistance in obtaining evidence at their disposal necessary for the proceedings.
2. States Parties shall carry out their obligations under paragraph 1 of the present article in conformity with any treaties or other arrangements on mutual legal assistance that may exist between them. In the absence of such treaties or arrangements, States Parties shall afford one another assistance in accordance with their domestic law.

Article 7

States Parties shall, subject to the provisions of their national law:
(a) Take measures to provide for the seizure and confiscation, as appropriate, of:
(i) Goods, such as materials, assets and other instrumentalities used to commit or facilitate offences under the present protocol;
(ii) Proceeds derived from such offences;
(b) Execute requests from another State Party for seizure or confiscation of goods or proceeds referred to in subparagraph (a);
(c) Take measures aimed at closing, on a temporary or definitive basis, premises used to commit such offences.

Article 8

1. States Parties shall adopt appropriate measures to protect the rights and interests of child victims of the practices prohibited under the present Protocol at all stages of the criminal justice process, in particular by:
(a) Recognizing the vulnerability of child victims and adapting procedures to recognize their special needs, including their special needs as witnesses;
(b) Informing child victims of their rights, their role and the scope, timing and progress of the proceedings and of the disposition of their cases;
(c) Allowing the views, needs and concerns of child victims to be presented and considered in proceedings where their personal interests are affected, in a manner consistent with the procedural rules of national law;
(d) Providing appropriate support services to child victims throughout the legal process;
(e) Protecting, as appropriate, the privacy and identity of child victims and taking measures in accordance with national law to avoid the inappropriate dissemination of information that could lead to the identification of child victims;
(f) Providing, in appropriate cases, for the safety of child victims, as well as that of their families and witnesses on their behalf, from intimidation and retaliation;
(g) Avoiding unnecessary delay in the disposition of cases and the execution of orders or decrees granting compensation to child victims.
2. States Parties shall ensure that uncertainty as to the actual age of the victim shall not prevent the initiation of criminal investigations, including investigations aimed at establishing the age of the victim.
3. States Parties shall ensure that, in the treatment by the criminal justice system of children who are victims of the offences described in the present Protocol, the best interest of the child shall be a primary consideration.
4. States Parties shall take measures to ensure appropriate training, in particular legal and psychological training, for the persons who work with victims of the offences prohibited under the present Protocol.
5. States Parties shall, in appropriate cases, adopt measures in order to protect the safety and integrity of those persons and/or organizations involved in the prevention and/or protection and rehabilitation of victims of such offences.
6. Nothing in the present article shall be construed to be prejudicial to or inconsistent with the rights of the accused to a fair and impartial trial.

Article 9

1. States Parties shall adopt or strengthen, implement and disseminate laws, administrative measures, social policies and programmes to prevent the offences referred to in the present Protocol. Particular attention shall be given to protect children who are especially vulnerable to such practices.

2. States Parties shall promote awareness in the public at large, including children, through information by all appropriate means, education and training, about the preventive measures and harmful effects of the offences referred to in the present Protocol. In fulfilling their obligations under this article, States Parties shall encourage the participation of the community and, in particular, children and child victims, in such information and education and training programmes, including at the international level.

3. States Parties shall take all feasible measures with the aim of ensuring all appropriate assistance to victims of such offences, including their full social reintegration and their full physical and psychological recovery.

4. States Parties shall ensure that all child victims of the offences described in the present Protocol have access to adequate procedures to seek, without discrimination, compensation for damages from those legally responsible.

5. States Parties shall take appropriate measures aimed at effectively prohibiting the production and dissemination of material advertising the offences described in the present Protocol.

Article 10

1. States Parties shall take all necessary steps to strengthen international cooperation by multilateral, regional and bilateral arrangements for the prevention, detection, investigation, prosecution and punishment of those responsible for acts involving the sale of children, child prostitution, child pornography and child sex tourism. States Parties shall also promote international cooperation and coordination between their authorities, national and international non-governmental organizations and international organizations.

2. States Parties shall promote international cooperation to assist child victims in their physical and psychological recovery, social reintegration and repatriation.

3. States Parties shall promote the strengthening of international cooperation in order to address the root causes, such as poverty and underdevelopment, contributing to the vulnerability of children to the sale of children, child prostitution, child pornography and child sex tourism.

4. States Parties in a position to do so shall provide financial, technical or other assistance through existing multilateral, regional, bilateral or other programmes.

Article 11

Nothing in the present Protocol shall affect any provisions that are more conducive to the realization of the rights of the child and that may be contained in:

(a) The law of a State Party;

(b) International law in force for that State.

Article 12

1. Each State Party shall, within two years following the entry into force of the present Protocol for that State Party, submit a report to the Committee on the Rights of the Child providing comprehensive information on the measures it has taken to implement the provisions of the Protocol.

2. Following the submission of the comprehensive report, each State Party shall include in the reports they submit to the Committee on the Rights of the Child, in accordance with article 44 of the Convention, any further information with respect to the implementation of the present Protocol. Other States Parties to the Protocol shall submit a report every five years.

3. The Committee on the Rights of the Child may request from States Parties further information relevant to the implementation of the present Protocol.

Article 13

1. The present Protocol is open for signature by any State that is a party to the Convention or has signed it.

2. The present Protocol is subject to ratification and is open to accession by any State that is a party to the Convention or has signed it. Instruments of ratification or accession shall be deposited with the Secretary-General of the United Nations.

Article 14

1. The present Protocol shall enter into force three months after the deposit of the tenth instrument of ratification or accession.

2. For each State ratifying the present Protocol or acceding to it after its entry into force, the Protocol shall enter into force one month after the date of the deposit of its own instrument of ratification or accession.

Article 15

1. Any State Party may denounce the present Protocol at any time by written notification to the Secretary-General of the United Nations, who shall thereafter inform the other States Parties to the Convention and all States that have signed the Convention. The denunciation shall take effect one year after the date of receipt of the notification by the Secretary-General.

2. Such a denunciation shall not have the effect of releasing the State Party from its obligations under the present Protocol in regard to any offence that occurs prior to the date on which the denunciation becomes effective. Nor shall such a denunciation prejudice in any way the continued consideration of any matter that is already under consideration by the Committee on the Rights of the Child prior to the date on which the denunciation becomes effective.

Article 16

1. Any State Party may propose an amendment and file it with the Secretary-General of the United Nations. The Secretary-General shall thereupon communicate the proposed amendment to States Parties with a request that they indicate whether they favour a conference of States Parties for the purpose of considering and voting upon the proposals. In the event that, within four months from the date of such communication, at least one third of the States Parties favour such a conference, the Secretary-General shall convene the conference under the auspices of the United Nations. Any amendment adopted by a majority of States Parties present and voting at the conference shall be submitted to the General Assembly of the United Nations for approval.

2. An amendment adopted in accordance with paragraph 1 of the present article shall enter into force when it has been approved by the General Assembly and accepted by a two-thirds majority of States Parties.

3. When an amendment enters into force, it shall be binding on those States Parties that have accepted it, other States Parties still being bound by the provisions of the present Protocol and any earlier amendments they have accepted.

Article 17

1. The present Protocol, of which the Arabic, Chinese, English, French, Russian and Spanish texts are equally authentic, shall be deposited in the archives of the United Nations.

2. The Secretary-General of the United Nations shall transmit certified copies of the present Protocol to all States Parties to the Convention and all States that have signed the Convention.

INTERNATIONAL CONVENTION ON THE PROTECTION OF THE RIGHTS OF ALL MIGRANT WORKERS AND MEMBERS OF THEIR FAMILIES (1990)

International Convention on the Protection of the Rights of All Migrant Workers and Members of their Families, *adopted* Dec. 18, 1990, 2220 U.N.T.S. 93

Preamble

The States Parties to the present Convention,

Taking into account the principles embodied in the basic instruments of the United Nations concerning human rights, in particular the Universal Declaration of Human Rights, the International Covenant on Economic, Social and Cultural Rights, the International Covenant on Civil and Political Rights, the International Convention on the Elimination of All Forms of Racial Discrimination, the Convention on the

Elimination of All Forms of Discrimination against Women and the Convention on the Rights of the Child,
* * *

Recalling that one of the objectives of the International Labour Organisation, as stated in its Constitution, is the protection of the interests of workers when employed in countries other than their own, and bearing in mind the expertise and experience of that organization in matters related to migrant workers and members of their families, * * *

Recognizing also the progress made by certain States on a regional or bilateral basis towards the protection of the rights of migrant workers and members of their families, as well as the importance and usefulness of bilateral and multilateral agreements in this field,

Realizing the importance and extent of the migration phenomenon, which involves millions of people and affects a large number of States in the international community,

Aware of the impact of the flows of migrant workers on States and people concerned, and desiring to establish norms which may contribute to the harmonization of the attitudes of States through the acceptance of basic principles concerning the treatment of migrant workers and members of their families,

Considering the situation of vulnerability in which migrant workers and members of their families frequently-find themselves owing, among other things, to their absence from their State of origin and to the difficulties they may encounter arising from their presence in the State of employment,

Convinced that the rights of migrant workers and members of their families have not been sufficiently recognized everywhere and therefore require appropriate international protection,

Taking into account the fact that migration is often the cause of serious problems for the members of the families of migrant workers as well as for the workers themselves, in particular because of the scattering of the family,

Bearing in mind that the human problems involved in migration are even more serious in the case of irregular migration and convinced therefore that appropriate action should be encouraged in order to prevent and eliminate clandestine movements and trafficking in migrant workers, while at the same time assuring the protection of their fundamental human rights,

Considering that workers who are non-documented or in an irregular situation are frequently employed under less favourable conditions of work than other workers and that certain employers find this an inducement to seek such labour in order to reap the benefits of unfair competition,

Considering also that recourse to the employment of migrant workers who are in an irregular situation will be discouraged if the fundamental human rights of all migrant workers are more widely recognized and, moreover, that granting certain additional rights to migrant workers and members of their families in a regular situation will encourage all migrants and employers to respect and comply with the laws and procedures established by the States concerned,

Convinced, therefore, of the need to bring about the international protection of the rights of all migrant workers and members of their families, reaffirming and establishing basic norms in a comprehensive convention which could be applied universally,

Have agreed as follows:

Part I: Scope and Definitions

Article 1
1. The present Convention is applicable, except as otherwise provided hereafter, to all migrant workers and members of their families without distinction of any kind such as sex, race, colour, language, religion or

175

conviction, political or other opinion, national, ethnic or social origin, nationality, age, economic position, property, marital status, birth or other status.

2. The present Convention shall apply during the entire migration process of migrant workers and members of their families, which comprises preparation for migration, departure, transit and the entire period of stay and remunerated activity in the State of employment as well as return to the State of origin or the State of habitual residence.

Article 2

For the purposes of the present Convention:

1. The term "migrant worker" refers to a person who is to be engaged, is engaged or has been engaged in a remunerated activity in a State of which he or she is not a national.

2.   (a) The term "frontier worker" refers to a migrant worker who retains his or her habitual residence in a neighbouring State to which he or she normally returns every day or at least once a week;

(b) The term "seasonal worker" refers to a migrant worker whose work by its character is dependent on seasonal conditions and is performed only during part of the year;

(c) The term "seafarer", which includes a fisherman, refers to a migrant worker employed on board a vessel registered in a State of which he or she is not a national;

(d) The term "worker on an offshore installation" refers to a migrant worker employed on an offshore installation that is under the jurisdiction of a State of which he or she is not a national;

(e) The term "itinerant worker'' refers to a migrant worker who, having his or her habitual residence in one State, has to travel to another State or States for short periods, owing to the nature of his or her occupation;

(f) The term "project-tied worker" refers to a migrant worker admitted to a State of employment for a defined period to work solely on a specific project being carried out in that State by his or her employer;

(g) The term "specified-employment worker" refers to a migrant worker:

(i) Who has been sent by his or her employer for a restricted and defined period of time to a State of employment to undertake a specific assignment or duty; or

(ii) Who engages for a restricted and defined period of time in work that requires professional, commercial, technical or other highly specialized skill; or

(iii) Who, upon the request of his or her employer in the State of employment, engages for a restricted and defined period of time in work whose nature is transitory or brief; and who is required to depart from the State of employment either at the expiration of his or her authorized period of stay, or earlier if he or she no longer undertakes that specific assignment or duty or engages in that work;

(h) The term "self-employed worker" refers to a migrant worker who is engaged in a remunerated activity otherwise than under a contract of employment and who earns his or her living through this activity normally working alone or together with members of his or her family, and to any other migrant worker recognized as self-employed by applicable legislation of the State of employment or bilateral or multilateral agreements.

Article 3

The present Convention shall not apply to:

(a) Persons sent or employed by international organizations and agencies or persons sent or employed by a State outside its territory to perform official functions, whose admission and status are regulated by general international law or by specific international agreements or conventions;

(b) Persons sent or employed by a State or on its behalf outside its territory who participate in development programmes and other co-operation programmes, whose admission and status are regulated by agreement with the State of employment and who, in accordance with that agreement, are not considered migrant workers;

(c) Persons taking up residence in a State different from their State of origin as investors;

(d) Refugees and stateless persons, unless such application is provided for in the relevant national legislation of, or international instruments in force for, the State Party concerned;

(e) Students and trainees;

(f) Seafarers and workers on an offshore installation who have not been admitted to take up residence and engage in a remunerated activity in the State of employment.

Article 4

For the purposes of the present Convention the term "members of the family" refers to persons married to migrant workers or having with them a relationship that, according to applicable law, produces effects equivalent to marriage, as well as their dependent children and other dependent persons who are recognized as members of the family by applicable legislation or applicable bilateral or multilateral agreements between the States concerned.

Article 5

For the purposes of the present Convention, migrant workers and members of their families:
(a) Are considered as documented or in a regular situation if they are authorized to enter, to stay and to engage in a remunerated activity in the State of employment pursuant to the law of that State and to international agreements to which that State is a party;
(b) Are considered as non-documented or in an irregular situation if they do not comply with the conditions provided for in subparagraph (a) of the present article.

Article 6

For the purposes of the present Convention:
(a) The term "State of origin" means the State of which the person concerned is a national;
(b) The term "State of employment" means a State where the migrant worker is to be engaged, is engaged or has been engaged in a remunerated activity, as the case may be;
(c) The term "State of transit,' means any State through which the person concerned passes on any journey to the State of employment or from the State of employment to the State of origin or the State of habitual residence.

Part II: Non-discrimination with Respect to Rights

Article 7

States Parties undertake, in accordance with the international instruments concerning human rights, to respect and to ensure to all migrant workers and members of their families within their territory or subject to their jurisdiction the rights provided for in the present Convention without distinction of any kind such as to sex, race, colour, language, religion or conviction, political or other opinion, national, ethnic or social origin, nationality, age, economic position, property, marital status, birth or other status.

Part III: Human Rights of All Migrant Workers and Members of their Families

Article 8

1. Migrant workers and members of their families shall be free to leave any State, including their State of origin. This right shall not be subject to any restrictions except those that are provided by law, are necessary to protect national security, public order (ordre public), public health or morals or the rights and freedoms of others and are consistent with the other rights recognized in the present part of the Convention.
2. Migrant workers and members of their families shall have the right at any time to enter and remain in their State of origin.

Article 9

The right to life of migrant workers and members of their families shall be protected by law.

Article 10

No migrant worker or member of his or her family shall be subjected to torture or to cruel, inhuman or degrading treatment or punishment.

Article 11

1. No migrant worker or member of his or her family shall be held in slavery or servitude.

2. No migrant worker or member of his or her family shall be required to perform forced or compulsory labour.

3. Paragraph 2 of the present article shall not be held to preclude, in States where imprisonment with hard labour may be imposed as a punishment for a crime, the performance of hard labour in pursuance of a sentence to such punishment by a competent court.

4. For the purpose of the present article the term "forced or compulsory labour" shall not include:

(a) Any work or service not referred to in paragraph 3 of the present article normally required of a person who is under detention in consequence of a lawful order of a court or of a person during conditional release from such detention;

(b) Any service exacted in cases of emergency or clamity threatening the life or well-being of the community;

(c) Any work or service that forms part of normal civil obligations so far as it is imposed also on citizens of the State concerned.

Article 12

1. Migrant workers and members of their families shall have the right to freedom of thought, conscience and religion. This right shall include freedom to have or to adopt a religion or belief of their choice and freedom either individually or in community with others and in public or private to manifest their religion or belief in worship, observance, practice and teaching.

2. Migrant workers and members of their families shall not be subject to coercion that would impair their freedom to have or to adopt a religion or belief of their choice.

3. Freedom to manifest one's religion or belief may be subject only to such limitations as are prescribed by law and are necessary to protect public safety, order, health or morals or the fundamental rights and freedoms of others.

4. States Parties to the present Convention undertake to have respect for the liberty of parents, at least one of whom is a migrant worker, and, when applicable, legal guardians to ensure the religious and moral education of their children in conformity with their own convictions.

Article 13

1. Migrant workers and members of their families shall have the right to hold opinions without interference.

2. Migrant workers and members of their families shall have the right to freedom of expression; this right shall include freedom to seek, receive and impart information and ideas of all kinds, regardless of frontiers, either orally, in writing or in print, in the form of art or through any other media of their choice.

3. The exercise of the right provided for in paragraph 2 of the present article carries with it special duties and responsibilities. It may therefore be subject to certain restrictions, but these shall only be such as are provided by law and are necessary:

(a) For respect of the rights or reputation of others;

(b) For the protection of the national security of the States concerned or of public order (ordre public) or of public health or morals;

(c) For the purpose of preventing any propaganda for war;

(d) For the purpose of preventing any advocacy of national, racial or religious hatred that constitutes incitement to discrimination, hostility or violence.

Article 14

No migrant worker or member of his or her family shall be subjected to arbitrary or unlawful interference with his or her privacy, family, , correspondence or other communications, or to unlawful attacks on his or her honour and reputation. Each migrant worker and member of his or her family shall have the right to the protection of the law against such interference or attacks.

Article 15

No migrant worker or member of his or her family shall be arbitrarily deprived of property, whether owned individually or in association with others. Where, under the legislation in force in the State of employment, the assets of a migrant worker or a member of his or her family are expropriated in whole or in part, the person concerned shall have the right to fair and adequate compensation.

Article 16

1. Migrant workers and members of their families shall have the right to liberty and security of person.

2. Migrant workers and members of their families shall be entitled to effective protection by the State against violence, physical injury, threats and intimidation, whether by public officials or by private individuals, groups or institutions.

3. Any verification by law enforcement officials of the identity of migrant workers or members of their families shall be carried out in accordance with procedure established by law.

4. Migrant workers and members of their families shall not be subjected individually or collectively to arbitrary arrest or detention; they shall not be deprived o their liberty except on such grounds and in accordance with such procedures as are established by law.

5. Migrant workers and members of their families who are arrested shall be informed at the time of arrest as far as possible in a language they understand of the reasons for their arrest and they shall be promptly informed in a language they understand of any charges against them.

6. Migrant workers and members of their families who are arrested or detained on a criminal charge shall be brought promptly before a judge or other officer authorized by law to exercise judicial power and shall be entitled to trial within a reasonable time or to release. It shall not be the general rule that while awaiting trial they shall be detained in custody, but release may be subject to guarantees to appear for trial, at any other stage of the judicial proceedings and, should the occasion arise, for the execution of the judgement.

7. When a migrant worker or a member of his or her family is arrested or committed to prison or custody pending trial or is detained in any other manner:

> (a) The consular or diplomatic authorities of his or her State of origin or of a State representing the interests of that State shall, if he or she so requests, be informed without delay of his or her arrest or detention and of the reasons therefor;

> (b) The person concerned shall have the right to communicate with the said authorities. Any communication by the person concerned to the said authorities shall be forwarded without delay, and he or she shall also have the right to receive communications sent by the said authorities without delay;

> (c) The person concerned shall be informed without delay of this right and of rights deriving from relevant treaties, if any, applicable between the States concerned, to correspond and to meet with representatives of the said authorities and to make arrangements with them for his or her legal representation.

8. Migrant workers and members of their families who are deprived of their liberty by arrest or detention shall be entitled to take proceedings before a court, in order that that court may decide without delay on the lawfulness of their detention and order their release if the detention is not lawful. When they attend such proceedings, they shall have the assistance, if necessary without cost to them, of an interpreter, if they cannot understand or speak the language used.

9. Migrant workers and members of their families who have been victims of unlawful arrest or detention shall have an enforceable right to compensation.

Article 17

1. Migrant workers and members of their families who are deprived of their liberty shall be treated with humanity and with respect for the inherent dignity of the human person and for their cultural identity.

2. Accused migrant workers and members of their families shall, save in exceptional circumstances, be separated from convicted persons and shall be subject to separate treatment appropriate to their status as unconvicted persons. Accused juvenile persons shall be separated from adults and brought as speedily as possible for adjudication.

3. Any migrant worker or member of his or her family who is detained in a State of transit or in a State of employment for violation of provisions relating to migration shall be held, in so far as practicable, separately from convicted persons or persons detained pending trial.

4. During any period of imprisonment in pursuance of a sentence imposed by a court of law, the essential aim of the treatment of a migrant worker or a member of his or her family shall be his or her reformation and social rehabilitation. Juvenile offenders shall be separated from adults and be accorded treatment appropriate to their age and legal status.

5. During detention or imprisonment, migrant workers and members of their families shall enjoy the same rights as nationals to visits by members of their families.

6. Whenever a migrant worker is deprived of his or her liberty, the competent authorities of the State concerned shall pay attention to the problems that may be posed for members of his or her family, in particular for spouses and minor children.

7. Migrant workers and members of their families who are subjected to any form of detention or imprisonment in accordance with the law in force in the State of employment or in the State of transit shall enjoy the same rights as nationals of those States who are in the same situation.

8. If a migrant worker or a member of his or her family is detained for the purpose of verifying any infraction of provisions related to migration, he or she shall not bear any costs arising therefrom.

Article 18

1. Migrant workers and members of their families shall have the right to equality with nationals of the State concerned before the courts and tribunals. In the determination of any criminal charge against them or of their rights and obligations in a suit of law, they shall be entitled to a fair and public hearing by a competent, independent and impartial tribunal established by law.

2. Migrant workers and members of their families who are charged with a criminal offence shall have the right to be presumed innocent until proven guilty according to law.

3. In the determination of any criminal charge against them, migrant workers and members of their families shall be entitled to the following minimum guarantees:

(a) To be informed promptly and in detail in a language they understand of the nature and cause of the charge against them;

(b) To have adequate time and facilities for the preparation of their defence and to communicate with counsel of their own choosing;

(c) To be tried without undue delay;

(d) To be tried in their presence and to defend themselves in person or through legal assistance of their own choosing; to be informed, if they do not have legal assistance, of this right; and to have legal assistance assigned to them, in any case where the interests of justice so require and without payment by them in any such case if they do not have sufficient means to pay;

(e) To examine or have examined the witnesses against them and to obtain the attendance and examination of witnesses on their behalf under the same conditions as witnesses against them;

(f) To have the free assistance of an interpreter if they cannot understand or speak the language used in court;

(g) Not to be compelled to testify against themselves or to confess guilt.

4. In the case of juvenile persons, the procedure shall be such as will take account of their age and the desirability of promoting their rehabilitation.

5. Migrant workers and members of their families convicted of a crime shall have the right to their conviction and sentence being reviewed by a higher tribunal according to law.

6. When a migrant worker or a member of his or her family has, by a final decision, been convicted of a criminal offence and when subsequently his or her conviction has been reversed or he or she has been pardoned on the ground that a new or newly discovered fact shows conclusively that there has been a miscarriage of justice, the person who has suffered punishment as a result of such conviction shall be compensated according to law, unless it is proved that the non-disclosure of the unknown fact in time is wholly or partly attributable to that person.

7. No migrant worker or member of his or her family shall be liable to be tried or punished again for an offence for which he or she has already been finally convicted or acquitted in accordance with the law and penal procedure of the State concerned.

Article 19

1. No migrant worker or member of his or her family shall be held guilty of any criminal offence on account of any act or omission that did not constitute a criminal offence under national or international law at the time when the criminal offence was committed, nor shall a heavier penalty be imposed than the one that was applicable at the time when it was committed. If, subsequent to the commission of the offence, provision is made by law for the imposition of a lighter penalty, he or she shall benefit thereby.

2. Humanitarian considerations related to the status of a migrant worker, in particular with respect to his or her right of residence or work, should be taken into account in imposing a sentence for a criminal offence committed by a migrant worker or a member of his or her family.

Article 20

1. No migrant worker or member of his or her family shall be imprisoned merely on the ground of failure to fulfil a contractual obligation.

2. No migrant worker or member of his or her family shall be deprived of his or her authorization of residence or work permit or expelled merely on the ground of failure to fulfil an obligation arising out of a work contract unless fulfilment of that obligation constitutes a condition for such authorization or permit.

Article 21

It shall be unlawful for anyone, other than a public official duly authorized by law, to confiscate, destroy or attempt to destroy identity documents, documents authorizing entry to or stay, residence or establishment in the national territory or work permits. No authorized confiscation of such documents shall take place without delivery of a detailed receipt. In no case shall it be permitted to destroy the passport or equivalent document of a migrant worker or a member of his or her family.

Article 22

1. Migrant workers and members of their families shall not be subject to measures of collective expulsion. Each case of expulsion shall be examined and decided individually.

2. Migrant workers and members of their families may be expelled from the territory of a State Party only in pursuance of a decision taken by the competent authority in accordance with law.

3. The decision shall be communicated to them in a language they understand. Upon their request where not otherwise mandatory, the decision shall be communicated to them in writing and, save in exceptional circumstances on account of national security, the reasons for the decision likewise stated. The persons concerned shall be informed of these rights before or at the latest at the time the decision is rendered.

4. Except where a final decision is pronounced by a judicial authority, the person concerned shall have the right to submit the reason he or she should not be expelled and to have his or her case reviewed by the competent authority, unless compelling reasons of national security require otherwise. Pending such review, the person concerned shall have the right to seek a stay of the decision of expulsion.

5. If a decision of expulsion that has already been executed is subsequently annulled, the person concerned shall have the right to seek compensation according to law and the earlier decision shall not be used to prevent him or her from re-entering the State concerned.

6. In case of expulsion, the person concerned shall have a reasonable opportunity before or after departure to settle any claims for wages and other entitlements due to him or her and any pending liabilities.

7. Without prejudice to the execution of a decision of expulsion, a migrant worker or a member of his or her family who is subject to such a decision may seek entry into a State other than his or her State of origin.

8. In case of expulsion of a migrant worker or a member of his or her family the costs of expulsion shall not be borne by him or her. The person concerned may be required to pay his or her own travel costs.

9. Expulsion from the State of employment shall not in itself prejudice any rights of a migrant worker or a member of his or her family acquired in accordance with the law of that State, including the right to receive wages and other entitlements due to him or her.

Article 23

Migrant workers and members of their families shall have the right to have recourse to the protection and assistance of the consular or diplomatic authorities of their State of origin or of a State representing the interests of that State whenever the rights recognized in the present Convention are impaired. In particular, in case of expulsion, the person concerned shall be informed of this right without delay and the authorities of the expelling State shall facilitate the exercise of such right.

Article 24

Every migrant worker and every member of his or her family shall have the right to recognition everywhere as a person before the law.

Article 25

1. Migrant workers shall enjoy treatment not less favourable than that which applies to nationals of the State of employment in respect of remuneration and:

(a) Other conditions of work, that is to say, overtime, hours of work, weekly rest, holidays with pay, safety, health, termination of the employment relationship and any other conditions of work which, according to national law and practice, are covered by these terms;

(b) Other terms of employment, that is to say, minimum age of employment, restriction on work and any other matters which, according to national law and practice, are considered a term of employment.

2. It shall not be lawful to derogate in private contracts of employment from the principle of equality of treatment referred to in paragraph 1 of the present article.

3. States Parties shall take all appropriate measures to ensure that migrant workers are not deprived of any rights derived from this principle by reason of any irregularity in their stay or employment. In particular, employers shall not be relieved of any legal or contractual obligations, nor shall their obligations be limited in any manner by reason of such irregularity.

Article 26

1. States Parties recognize the right of migrant workers and members of their families:

(a) To take part in meetings and activities of trade unions and of any other associations established in accordance with law, with a view to protecting their economic, social, cultural and other interests, subject only to the rules of the organization concerned;

(b) To join freely any trade union and any such association as aforesaid, subject only to the rules of the organization concerned;

(c) To seek the aid and assistance of any trade union and of any such association as aforesaid.

2. No restrictions may be placed on the exercise of these rights other than those that are prescribed by law and which are necessary in a democratic society in the interests of national security, public order (ordre public) or the protection of the rights and freedoms of others.

Article 27

1. With respect to social security, migrant workers and members of their families shall enjoy in the State of employment the same treatment granted to nationals in so far as they fulfil the requirements provided for by the applicable legislation of that State and the applicable bilateral and multilateral treaties. The competent authorities of the State of origin and the State of employment can at any time establish the necessary arrangements to determine the modalities of application of this norm.

2. Where the applicable legislation does not allow migrant workers and members of their families a benefit, the States concerned shall examine the possibility of reimbursing interested persons the amount of contributions made by them with respect to that benefit on the basis of the treatment granted to nationals who are in similar circumstances.

Article 28

Migrant workers and members of their families shall have the right to receive any medical care that is urgently required for the preservation of their life or the avoidance of irreparable harm to their health on the basis of equality of treatment with nationals of the State concerned. Such emergency medical care shall not be refused them by reason of any irregularity with regard to stay or employment.

Article 29

Each child of a migrant worker shall have the right to a name, to registration of birth and to a nationality.

Article 30

Each child of a migrant worker shall have the basic right of access to education on the basis of equality of treatment with nationals of the State concerned. Access to public pre-school educational institutions or schools shall not be refused or limited by reason of the irregular situation with respect to stay or employment of either parent or by reason of the irregularity of the child's stay in the State of employment.

Article 31

1. States Parties shall ensure respect for the cultural identity of migrant workers and members of their families and shall not prevent them from maintaining their cultural links with their State of origin. 2. States Parties may take appropriate measures to assist and encourage efforts in this respect.

Article 32

Upon the termination of their stay in the State of employment, migrant workers and members of their families shall have the right to transfer their earnings and savings and, in accordance with the applicable legislation of the States concerned, their personal effects and belongings.

Article 33

1. Migrant workers and members of their families shall have the right to be informed by the State of origin, the State of employment or the State of transit as the case may be concerning:

(a) Their rights arising out of the present Convention;

(b) The conditions of their admission, their rights and obligations under the law and practice of the State concerned and such other matters as will enable them to comply with administrative or other formalities in that State. 2. States Parties shall take all measures they deem appropriate to disseminate the said information or to ensure that it is provided by employers, trade unions or other appropriate bodies or institutions. As appropriate, they shall co-operate with other States concerned.

3. Such adequate information shall be provided upon request to migrant workers and members of their families, free of charge, and, as far as possible, in a language they are able to understand.

Article 34

Nothing in the present part of the Convention shall have the effect of relieving migrant workers and the members of their families from either the obligation to comply with the laws and regulations of any State of transit and the State of employment or the obligation to respect the cultural identity of the inhabitants of such States.

Article 35

Nothing in the present part of the Convention shall be interpreted as implying the regularization of the situation of migrant workers or members of their families who are non-documented or in an irregular situation or any right to such regularization of their situation, nor shall it prejudice the measures intended to ensure sound and equitable-conditions for international migration as provided in part VI of the present Convention.

Part IV: Other Rights of Migrant Workers and Members of their Families who are Documented or in a Regular Situation

Article 36

Migrant workers and members of their families who are documented or in a regular situation in the State of employment shall enjoy the rights set forth in the present part of the Convention in addition to those set forth in part III.

Article 37

Before their departure, or at the latest at the time of their admission to the State of employment, migrant workers and members of their families shall have the right to be fully informed by the State of origin or the State of employment, as appropriate, of all conditions applicable to their admission and particularly those concerning their stay and the remunerated activities in which they may engage as well as of the requirements they must satisfy in the State of employment and the authority to which they must address themselves for any modification of those conditions.

Article 38

1. States of employment shall make every effort to authorize migrant workers and members of the families to be temporarily absent without effect upon their authorization to stay or to work, as the case may be. In doing so, States of employment shall take into account the special needs and obligations of migrant workers and members of their families, in particular in their States of origin.

2. Migrant workers and members of their families shall have the right to be fully informed of the terms on which such temporary absences are authorized.

Article 39

1. Migrant workers and members of their families shall have the right to liberty of movement in the territory of the State of employment and freedom to choose their residence there.

2. The rights mentioned in paragraph 1 of the present article shall not be subject to any restrictions except those that are provided by law, are necessary to protect national security, public order (ordre public), public health or morals, or the rights and freedoms of others and are consistent with the other rights recognized in the present Convention.

Article 40

1. Migrant workers and members of their families shall have the right to form associations and trade unions in the State of employment for the promotion and protection of their economic, social, cultural and other interests.

2. No restrictions may be placed on the exercise of this right other than those that are prescribed by law and are necessary in a democratic society in the interests of national security, public order (ordre public) or the protection of the rights and freedoms of others.

Article 41

1. Migrant workers and members of their families shall have the right to participate in public affairs of their State of origin and to vote and to be elected at elections of that State, in accordance with its legislation.

2. The States concerned shall, as appropriate and in accordance with their legislation, facilitate the exercise of these rights.

Article 42

1. States Parties shall consider the establishment of procedures or institutions through which account may be taken, both in States of origin and in States of employment, of special needs, aspirations and obligations of migrant workers and members of their families and shall envisage, as appropriate, the possibility for migrant workers and members of their families to have their freely chosen representatives in those institutions.

2. States of employment shall facilitate, in accordance with their national legislation, the consultation or participation of migrant workers and members of their families in decisions concerning the life and administration of local communities.

3. Migrant workers may enjoy political rights in the State of employment if that State, in the exercise of its sovereignty, grants them such rights.

Article 43

1. Migrant workers shall enjoy equality of treatment with nationals of the State of employment in relation to:

> (a) Access to educational institutions and services subject to the admission requirements and other regulations of the institutions and services concerned;
> (b) Access to vocational guidance and placement services;
> (c) Access to vocational training and retraining facilities and institutions;
> (d) Access to housing, including social housing schemes, and protection against exploitation in respect of rents;
> (e) Access to social and health services, provided that the requirements for participation in the respective schemes are met;
> (f) Access to co-operatives and self-managed enterprises, which shall not imply a change of their migration status and shall be subject to the rules and regulations of the bodies concerned;
> (g) Access to and participation in cultural life.

2. States Parties shall promote conditions to ensure effective equality of treatment to enable migrant workers to enjoy the rights mentioned in paragraph 1 of the present article whenever the terms of their stay, as authorized by the State of employment, meet the appropriate requirements.

3. States of employment shall not prevent an employer of migrant workers from establishing housing or social or cultural facilities for them. Subject to article 70 of the present Convention, a State of employment may make the establishment of such facilities subject to the requirements generally applied in that State concerning their installation.

Article 44

1. States Parties, recognizing that the family is the natural and fundamental group unit of society and is entitled to protection by society and the State, shall take appropriate measures to ensure the protection of the unity of the families of migrant workers.

2. States Parties shall take measures that they deem appropriate and that fall within their competence to facilitate the reunification of migrant workers with their spouses or persons who have with the migrant worker a relationship that, according to applicable law, produces effects equivalent to marriage, as well as with their minor dependent unmarried children.

3. States of employment, on humanitarian grounds, shall favourably consider granting equal treatment, as set forth in paragraph 2 of the present article, to other family members of migrant workers.

Article 45

1. Members of the families of migrant workers shall, in the State of employment, enjoy equality of treatment with nationals of that State in relation to:

   (a) Access to educational institutions and services, subject to the admission requirements and other regulations of the institutions and services concerned;

   (b) Access to vocational guidance and training institutions and services, provided that requirements for participation are met;

   (c) Access to social and health services, provided that requirements for participation in the respective schemes are met;

   (d) Access to and participation in cultural life.

2. States of employment shall pursue a policy, where appropriate in collaboration with the States of origin, aimed at facilitating the integration of children of migrant workers in the local school system, particularly in respect of teaching them the local language.

3. States of employment shall endeavour to facilitate for the children of migrant workers the teaching of their mother tongue and culture and, in this regard, States of origin shall collaborate whenever appropriate.

4. States of employment may provide special schemes of education in the mother tongue of children of migrant workers, if necessary in collaboration with the States of origin.

Article 46

Migrant workers and members of their families shall, subject to the applicable legislation of the States concerned, as well as relevant international agreements and the obligations of the States concerned arising out of their participation in customs unions, enjoy exemption from import and export duties and taxes in respect of their personal and household effects as well as the equipment necessary to engage in the remunerated activity for which they were admitted to the State of employment:

   (a) Upon departure from the State of origin or State of habitual residence;

   (b) Upon initial admission to the State of employment;

   (c) Upon final departure from the State of employment;

   (d) Upon final return to the State of origin or State of habitual residence.

Article 47

1. Migrant workers shall have the right to transfer their earnings and savings, in particular those funds necessary for the support of their families, from the State of employment to their State of origin or any other State. Such transfers shall be made in conformity with procedures established by applicable legislation of the State concerned and in conformity with applicable international agreements.

2. States concerned shall take appropriate measures to facilitate such transfers.

Article 48

1. Without prejudice to applicable double taxation agreements, migrant workers and members of their families shall, in the matter of earnings in the State of employment:

   (a) Not be liable to taxes, duties or charges of any description higher or more onerous than those imposed on nationals in similar circumstances;

   (b) Be entitled to deductions or exemptions from taxes of any description and to any tax allowances applicable to nationals in similar circumstances, including tax allowances for dependent members of their families. 2. States Parties shall endeavour to adopt appropriate measures to avoid double taxation of the earnings and savings of migrant workers and members of their families.

Article 49

1. Where separate authorizations to reside and to engage in employment are required by national legislation, the States of employment shall issue to migrant workers authorization of residence for at least the same period of time as their authorization to engage in remunerated activity.

2. Migrant workers who in the State of employment are allowed freely to choose their remunerated activity shall neither be regarded as in an irregular situation nor shall they lose their authorization of residence by the mere fact of the termination of their remunerated activity prior to the expiration of their work permits or similar authorizations.

3. In order to allow migrant workers referred to in paragraph 2 of the present article sufficient time to find alternative remunerated activities, the authorization of residence shall not be withdrawn at least for a period corresponding to that during which they may be entitled to unemployment benefits.

Article 50

1. In the case of death of a migrant worker or dissolution of marriage, the State of employment shall favourably consider granting family members of that migrant worker residing in that State on the basis of family reunion an authorization to stay; the State of employment shall take into account the length of time they have already resided in that State.

2. Members of the family to whom such authorization is not granted shall be allowed before departure a reasonable period of time in order to enable them to settle their affairs in the State of employment.

3. The provisions of paragraphs I and 2 of the present article may not be interpreted as adversely affecting any right to stay and work otherwise granted to such family members by the legislation of the State of employment or by bilateral and multilateral treaties applicable to that State.

Article 51

Migrant workers who in the State of employment are not permitted freely to choose their remunerated activity shall neither be regarded as in an irregular situation nor shall they lose their authorization of residence by the mere fact of the termination of their remunerated activity prior to the expiration of their work permit, except where the authorization of residence is expressly dependent upon the specific remunerated activity for which they were admitted. Such migrant workers shall have the right to seek alternative employment, participation in public work schemes and retraining during the remaining period of their authorization to work, subject to such conditions and limitations as are specified in the authorization to work.

Article 52

1. Migrant workers in the State of employment shall have the right freely to choose their remunerated activity, subject to the following restrictions or conditions.

2. For any migrant worker a State of employment may:

(a) Restrict access to limited categories of employment, functions, services or activities where this is necessary in the interests of this State and provided for by national legislation;

(b) Restrict free choice of remunerated activity in accordance with its legislation concerning recognition of occupational qualifications acquired outside its territory. However, States Parties concerned shall endeavour to provide for recognition of such qualifications.

3. For migrant workers whose permission to work is limited in time, a State of employment may also:

(a) Make the right freely to choose their remunerated activities subject to the condition that the migrant worker has resided lawfully in its territory for the purpose of remunerated activity for a period of time prescribed in its national legislation that should not exceed two years;

(b) Limit access by a migrant worker to remunerated activities in pursuance of a policy of granting priority to its nationals or to persons who are assimilated to them for these purposes by virtue of legislation or bilateral or multilateral agreements. Any such limitation shall cease to apply to a migrant worker who has resided lawfully in its territory for the purpose of remunerated activity for a period of time prescribed in its national legislation that should not exceed five years.

4. States of employment shall prescribe the conditions under which a migrant worker who has been admitted to take up employment may be authorized to engage in work on his or her own account. Account shall be taken of the period during which the worker has already been lawfully in the State of employment.

Article 53

1. Members of a migrant worker's family who have themselves an authorization of residence or admission that is without limit of time or is automatically renewable shall be permitted freely to choose their remunerated activity under the same conditions as are applicable to the said migrant worker in accordance with article 52 of the present Convention.

2. With respect to members of a migrant worker's family who are not permitted freely to choose their remunerated activity, States Parties shall consider favourably granting them priority in obtaining permission to engage in a remunerated activity over other workers who seek admission to the State of employment, subject to applicable bilateral and multilateral agreements.

Article 54

1. Without prejudice to the terms of their authorization of residence or their permission to work and the rights provided for in articles 25 and 27 of the present Convention, migrant workers shall enjoy equality of treatment with nationals of the State of employment in respect of:

    (a) Protection against dismissal;

    (b) Unemployment benefits;

    (c) Access to public work schemes intended to combat unemployment;

    (d) Access to alternative employment in the event of loss of work or termination of other remunerated activity, subject to article 52 of the present Convention.

2. If a migrant worker claims that the terms of his or her work contract have been violated by his or her employer, he or she shall have the right to address his or her case to the competent authorities of the State of employment, on terms provided for in article 18, paragraph 1, of the present Convention.

Article 55

Migrant workers who have been granted permission to engage in a remunerated activity, subject to the conditions attached to such permission, shall be entitled to equality of treatment with nationals of the State of employment in the exercise of that remunerated activity.

Article 56

1. Migrant workers and members of their families referred to in the present part of the Convention may not be expelled from a State of employment, except for reasons defined in the national legislation of that State, and subject to the safeguards established in part III.

2. Expulsion shall not be resorted to for the purpose of depriving a migrant worker or a member of his or her family of the rights arising out of the authorization of residence and the work permit.

3. In considering whether to expel a migrant worker or a member of his or her family, account should be taken of humanitarian considerations and of the length of time that the person concerned has already resided in the State of employment.

Part V: Provisions Applicable to Particular Categories of Migrant Workers and Members of their Families

Article 57

The particular categories of migrant workers and members of their families specified in the present part of the Convention who are documented or in a regular situation shall enjoy the rights set forth in part m and, except as modified below, the rights set forth in part IV.

Article 58

1. Frontier workers, as defined in article 2, paragraph 2 (a), of the present Convention, shall be entitled to the rights provided for in part IV that can be applied to them by reason of their presence and work in the territory of the State of employment, taking into account that they do not have their habitual residence in that State.

2. States of employment shall consider favourably granting frontier workers the right freely to choose their remunerated activity after a specified period of time. The granting of that right shall not affect their status as frontier workers.

Article 59

1. Seasonal workers, as defined in article 2, paragraph 2 (b), of the present Convention, shall be entitled to the rights provided for in part IV that can be applied to them by reason of their presence and work in the territory of the State of employment and that are compatible with their status in that State as seasonal workers, taking into account the fact that they are present in that State for only part of the year.

2. The State of employment shall, subject to paragraph 1 of the present article, consider granting seasonal workers who have been employed in its territory for a significant period of time the possibility of taking up other remunerated activities and giving them priority over other workers who seek admission to that State, subject to applicable bilateral and multilateral agreements.

Article 60

Itinerant workers, as defined in article 2, paragraph 2 (A), of the present Convention, shall be entitled to the rights provided for in part IV that can be granted to them by reason of their presence and work in the territory of the State of employment and that are compatible with their status as itinerant workers in that State.

Article 61

1. Project-tied workers, as defined in article 2, paragraph 2 (of the present Convention, and members of their families shall be entitled to the rights provided for in part IV except the provisions of article 43, paragraphs I (b) and (c), article 43, paragraph I (d), as it pertains to social housing schemes, article 45, paragraph I (b), and articles 52 to 55.

2. If a project-tied worker claims that the terms of his or her work contract have been violated by his or her employer, he or she shall have the right to address his or her case to the competent authorities of the State which has jurisdiction over that employer, on terms provided for in article 18, paragraph 1, of the present Convention.

3. Subject to bilateral or multilateral agreements in force for them, the States Parties concerned shall endeavour to enable project-tied workers to remain adequately protected by the social security systems of their States of origin or habitual residence during their engagement in the project. States Parties concerned shall take appropriate measures with the aim of avoiding any denial of rights or duplication of payments in this respect.

4. Without prejudice to the provisions of article 47 of the present Convention and to relevant bilateral or multilateral agreements, States Parties concerned shall permit payment of the earnings of project-tied workers in their State of origin or habitual residence.

Article 62

1. Specified-employment workers as defined in article 2, paragraph 2 (g), of the present Convention, shall be entitled to the rights provided for in part IV, except the provisions of article 43, paragraphs I (b) and (c), article 43, paragraph I (d), as it pertains to social housing schemes, article 52, and article 54, paragraph 1 (d).

2. Members of the families of specified-employment workers shall be entitled to the rights relating to family members of migrant workers provided for in part IV of the present Convention, except the provisions of article 53.

Article 63

1. Self-employed workers, as defined in article 2, paragraph 2 (h), of the pre sent Convention , shall be entitled to the rights provided for in part IV with the exception of those rights which are exclusively applicable to workers having a contract of employment.

2. Without prejudice to articles 52 and 79 of the present Convention, the termination of the economic activity of the self-employed workers shall not in itself imply the withdrawal of the authorization for them or for the members of their families to stay or to engage in a remunerated activity in the State of employment except where the authorization of residence is expressly dependent upon the specific remunerated activity for which they were admitted.

Part VI: Promotion of sound, equitable, humane and lawful conditions in connection with international migration of workers and members of their families

Article 64

1. Without prejudice to article 79 of the present Convention, the States Parties concerned shall as appropriate consult and co-operate with a view to promoting sound, equitable and humane conditions in connection with international migration of workers and members of their families.
2. In this respect, due regard shall be paid not only to labour needs and resources, but also to the social, economic, cultural and other needs of migrant workers and members of their families involved, as well as to the consequences of such migration for the communities concerned.

Article 65

1. States Parties shall maintain appropriate services to deal with questions concerning international migration of workers and members of their families. Their functions shall include, inter alia :
   (a) The formulation and implementation of policies regarding such migration;
   (b) An exchange of information. consultation and co-operation with the competent authorities of other States Parties involved in such migration;
   (c) The provision of appropriate information, particularly to employers, workers and their organizations on policies, laws and regulations relating to migration and employment, on agreements concluded with other States concerning migration and on other relevant matters;
   (d) The provision of information and appropriate assistance to migrant workers and members of their families regarding requisite authorizations and formalities and arrangements for departure, travel, arrival, stay, remunerated activities, exit and return, as well as on conditions of work and life in the State of employment and on customs, currency, tax and other relevant laws and regulations.
2. States Parties shall facilitate as appropriate the provision of adequate consular and other services that are necessary to meet the social, cultural and other needs of migrant workers and members of their families.

Article 66

1. Subject to paragraph 2 of the present article, the right to undertake operations with a view to the recruitment of workers for employment in another State shall be restricted to:
   (a) Public services or bodies of the State in which such operations take place;
   (b) Public services or bodies of the State of employment on the basis of agreement between the States concerned;
   (c) A body established by virtue of a bilateral or multilateral agreement.
2. Subject to any authorization, approval and supervision by the public authorities of the States Parties concerned as may be established pursuant to the legislation and practice of those States, agencies, prospective employers or persons acting on their behalf may also be permitted to undertake the said operations.

Article 67

1. States Parties concerned shall co-operate as appropriate in the adoption of measures regarding the orderly return of migrant workers and members of their families to the State of origin when they decide to return or their authorization of residence or employment expires or when they are in the State of employment in an irregular situation.
2. Concerning migrant workers and members of their families in a regular situation, States Parties concerned shall co-operate as appropriate, on terms agreed upon by those States, with a view to promoting adequate economic conditions for their resettlement and to facilitating their durable social and cultural reintegration in the State of origin.

Article 68

1. States Parties, including States of transit, shall collaborate with a view to preventing and eliminating illegal or clandestine movements and employment of migrant workers in an irregular situation. The measures to be taken to this end within the jurisdiction of each State concerned shall include:

(a) Appropriate measures against the dissemination of misleading information relating to emigration and immigration;

(b) Measures to detect and eradicate illegal or clandestine movements of migrant workers and members of their families and to impose effective sanctions on persons, groups or entities which organize, operate or assist in organizing or operating such movements;

(c) Measures to impose effective sanctions on persons, groups or entities which use violence, threats or intimidation against migrant workers or members of their families in an irregular situation.

2. States of employment shall take all adequate and effective measures to eliminate employment in their territory of migrant workers in an irregular situation, including, whenever appropriate, sanctions on employers of such workers. The rights of migrant workers vis-à-vis their employer arising from employment shall not be impaired by these measures.

Article 69

1. States Parties shall, when there are migrant workers and members of their families within their territory in an irregular situation, take appropriate measures to ensure that such a situation does not persist.

2. Whenever States Parties concerned consider the possibility of regularizing the situation of such persons in accordance with applicable national legislation and bilateral or multilateral agreements, appropriate account shall be taken of the circumstances of their entry, the duration of their stay in the States of employment and other relevant considerations, in particular those relating to their family situation.

Article 70

States Parties shall take measures not less favourable than those applied to nationals to ensure that working and living conditions of migrant workers and members of their families in a regular situation are in keeping with the standards of fitness, safety, health and principles of human dignity.

Article 71

1. States Parties shall facilitate, whenever necessary, the repatriation to the State of origin of the bodies of deceased migrant workers or members of their families.

2. As regards compensation matters relating to the death of a migrant worker or a member of his or her family, States Parties shall, as appropriate, provide assistance to the persons concerned with a view to the prompt settlement of such matters. Settlement of these matters shall be carried out on the basis of applicable national law in accordance with the provisions of the present Convention and any relevant bilateral or multilateral agreements.

Part VII: Application of the Convention

Article 72

1. (a) For the purpose of reviewing the application of the present Convention, there shall be established a Committee on the Protection of the Rights of All Migrant Workers and Members of Their Families (hereinafter referred to as "the Committee");

(b) The Committee shall consist, at the time of entry into force of the present Convention, of ten and, after the entry into force of the Convention for the forty-first State Party, of fourteen experts of high moral standing, impartiality and recognized competence in the field covered by the Convention.

2. (a) Members of the Committee shall be elected by secret ballot by the States Parties from a list of persons nominated by the States Parties, due consideration being given to equitable geographical distribution, including both States of origin and States of employment, and to the representation of the principal legal systems. Each State Party may nominate one person from among its own nationals;

(b) Members shall be elected and shall serve in their personal capacity.

3. The initial election shall be held no later than six months after the date of the entry into force of the present Convention and subsequent elections every second year. At least four months before the date of each election, the Secretary-General of the United Nations shall address a letter to all States Parties inviting them to submit their nominations within two months. The Secretary-General shall prepare a list in alphabetical order of all persons thus nominated, indicating the States Parties that have nominated them,

and shall submit it to the States Parties not later than one month before the date of the corresponding election, together with the curricula vitae of the persons thus nominated.

4. Elections of members of the Committee shall be held at a meeting of States Parties convened by the Secretary-General at United Nations Headquarters. At that meeting, for which two thirds of the States Parties shall constitute a quorum, the persons elected to the Committee shall be those nominees who obtain the largest number of votes and an absolute majority of the votes of the States Parties present and voting.

5.　　　(a) The members of the Committee shall serve for a term of four years. However, the terms of five of the members elected in the first election shall expire at the end of two years; immediately after the first election, the names of these five members shall be chosen by lot by the Chairman of the meeting of States Parties;

(b) The election of the four additional members of the Committee shall be held in accordance with the provisions of paragraphs 2, 3 and 4 of the present article, following the entry into force of the Convention for the forty-first State Party. The term of two of the additional members elected on this occasion shall expire at the end of two years; the names of these members shall be chosen by lot by the Chairman of the meeting of States Parties;

(c) The members of the Committee shall be eligible for re-election if renominated.

6. If a member of the Committee dies or resigns or declares that for any other cause he or she can no longer perform the duties of the Committee, the State Party that nominated the expert shall appoint another expert from among its own nationals for the remaining part of the term. The new appointment is subject to the approval of the Committee.

7. The Secretary-General of the United Nations shall provide the necessary staff and facilities for the effective performance of the functions of the Committee.

8. The members of the Committee shall receive emoluments from United Nations resources on such terms and conditions as the General Assembly may decide.

9. The members of the Committee shall be entitled to the facilities, privileges and immunities of experts on mission for the United Nations as laid down in the relevant sections of the Convention on the Privileges and Immunities of the United Nations.

Article 73

1. States Parties undertake to submit to the Secretary-General of the United Nations for consideration by the Committee a report on the legislative, judicial, administrative and other measures they have taken to give effect to the provisions of the present Convention:

(a) Within one year after the entry into force of the Convention for the State Party concerned;

(b) Thereafter every five years and whenever the Committee so requests.

2. Reports prepared under the present article shall also indicate factors and difficulties, if any, affecting the implementation of the Convention and shall include information on the characteristics of migration flows in which the State Party concerned is involved.

3. The Committee shall decide any further guidelines applicable to the content of the reports.

4. States Parties shall make their reports widely available to the public in their own countries.

Article 74

1. The Committee shall examine the reports submitted by each State Party and shall transmit such comments as it may consider appropriate to the State Party concerned. This State Party may submit to the Committee observations on any comment made by the Committee in accordance with the present article. The Committee may request supplementary information from States Parties when considering these reports.

2. The Secretary-General of the United Nations shall, in due time before the opening of each regular session of the Committee, transmit to the Director-General of the International Labour Office copies of the reports submitted by States Parties concerned and information relevant to the consideration of these reports, in order to enable the Office to assist the Committee with the expertise the Office may provide regarding those matters dealt with by the present Convention that fall within the sphere of competence of the International Labour Organisation. The Committee shall consider in its deliberations such comments and materials as the Office may provide.

3. The Secretary-General of the United Nations may also, after consultation with the Committee, transmit to other specialized agencies as well as to intergovernmental organizations, copies of such parts of these reports as may fall within their competence.

4. The Committee may invite the specialized agencies and organs of the United Nations, as well as intergovernmental organizations and other concerned bodies to submit, for consideration by the Committee, written information on such matters dealt with in the present Convention as fall within the scope of their activities.

5. The International Labour Office shall be invited by the Committee to appoint representatives to participate, in a consultative capacity, in the meetings of the Committee.

6. The Committee may invite representatives of other specialized agencies and organs of the United Nations, as well as of intergovernmental organizations, to be present and to be heard in its meetings whenever matters falling within their field of competence are considered.

7. The Committee shall present an annual report to the General Assembly of the United Nations on the implementation of the present Convention, containing its own considerations and recommendations, based, in particular, on the examination of the reports and any observations presented by States Parties.

8. The Secretary-General of the United Nations shall transmit the annual reports of the Committee to the States Parties to the present Convention, the Economic and Social Council, the Commission on Human Rights of the United Nations, the Director-General of the International Labour Office and other relevant organizations.

Article 75

1. The Committee shall adopt its own rules of procedure.
2. The Committee shall elect its officers for a term of two years.
3. The Committee shall normally meet annually.
4. The meetings of the Committee shall normally be held at United Nations Headquarters.

Article 76

1. A State Party to the present Convention may at any time declare under this article that it recognizes the competence of the Committee to receive and consider communications to the effect that a State Party claims that another State Party is not fulfilling its obligations under the present Convention. Communications under this article may be received and considered only if submitted by a State Party that has made a declaration recognizing in regard to itself the competence of the Committee. No communication shall be received by the Committee if it concerns a State Party which has not made such a declaration. Communications received under this article shall be dealt with in accordance with the following procedure:

(a) If a State Party to the present Convention considers that another State Party is not fulfilling its obligations under the present Convention, it may, by written communication, bring the matter to the attention of that State Party. The State Party may also inform the Committee of the matter. Within three months after the receipt of the communication the receiving State shall afford the State that sent the communication an explanation, or any other statement in writing clarifying the matter which should include, to the extent possible and pertinent, reference to domestic procedures and remedies taken, pending or available in the matter;

(b) If the matter is not adjusted to the satisfaction of both States Parties concerned within six months after the receipt by the receiving State of the initial communication, either State shall have the right to refer the matter to the Committee, by notice given to the Committee and to the other State;

(c) The Committee shall deal with a matter referred to it only after it has ascertained that all available domestic remedies have been invoked and exhausted in the matter, in conformity with the generally recognized principles of international law. This shall not be the rule where, in the view of the Committee, the application of the remedies is unreasonably prolonged;

(d) Subject to the provisions of subparagraph (c) of the present paragraph, the Committee shall make available its good offices to the States Parties concerned with a view to a friendly solution of the matter on the basis of the respect for the obligations set forth in the present Convention;

(e) The Committee shall hold closed meetings when examining communications under the present article;

(f) In any matter referred to it in accordance with subparagraph (b) of the present paragraph, the Committee may call upon the States Parties concerned, referred to in subparagraph (b), to supply any relevant information;

(g) The States Parties concerned, referred to in subparagraph (b) of the present paragraph, shall have the right to be represented when the matter is being considered by the Committee and to make submissions orally and/or in writing;

(h) The Committee shall, within twelve months after the date of receipt of notice under subparagraph (b) of the present paragraph, submit a report, as follows:

(i) If a solution within the terms of subparagraph (d) of the present paragraph is reached, the Committee shall confine its report to a brief statement of the facts and of the solution reached;

(ii) If a solution within the terms of subparagraph (d) is not reached, the Committee shall, in its report, set forth the relevant facts concerning the issue between the States Parties concerned. The written submissions and record of the oral submissions made by the States Parties concerned shall be attached to the report. The Committee may also communicate only to the States Parties concerned any views that it may consider relevant to the issue between them.

In every matter, the report shall be communicated to the States Parties concerned.

2. The provisions of the present article shall come into force when ten States Parties to the present Convention have made a declaration under paragraph 1 of the present article. Such declarations shall be deposited by the States Parties with the Secretary-General of the United Nations, who shall transmit copies thereof to the other States Parties. A declaration may be withdrawn at any time by notification to the Secretary-General. Such a withdrawal shall not prejudice the consideration of any matter that is the subject of a communication already transmitted under the present article; no further communication by any State Party shall be received under the present article after the notification of withdrawal of the declaration has been received by the Secretary-General, unless the State Party concerned has made a new declaration.

Article 77

1. A State Party to the present Convention may at any time declare under the present article that it recognizes the competence of the Committee to receive and consider communications from or on behalf of individuals subject to its jurisdiction who claim that their individual rights as established by the present Convention have been violated by that State Party. No communication shall be received by the Committee if it concerns a State Party that has not made such a declaration.

2. The Committee shall consider inadmissible any communication under the present article which is anonymous or which it considers to be an abuse of the right of submission of such communications or to be incompatible with the provisions of the present Convention.

3. The Committee shall not consider any communication from an individual under the present article unless it has ascertained that:

(a) The same matter has not been, and is not being, examined under another procedure of international investigation or settlement;

(b) The individual has exhausted all available domestic remedies; this shall not be the rule where, in the view of the Committee, the application of the remedies is unreasonably prolonged or is unlikely to bring effective relief to that individual.

4. Subject to the provisions of paragraph 2 of the present article, the Committee shall bring any communications submitted to it under this article to the attention of the State Party to the present Convention that has made a declaration under paragraph 1 and is alleged to be violating any provisions of the Convention. Within six months, the receiving State shall submit to the Committee written explanations or statements clarifying the matter and the remedy, if any, that may have been taken by that State.

5. The Committee shall consider communications received under the present article in the light of all information made available to it by or on behalf of the individual and by the State Party concerned.

6. The Committee shall hold closed meetings when examining communications under the present article.

7. The Committee shall forward its views to the State Party concerned and to the individual.

8. The provisions of the present article shall come into force when ten States Parties to the present Convention have made declarations under paragraph 1 of the present article. Such declarations shall be deposited by the States Parties with the Secretary-General of the United Nations, who shall transmit copies thereof to the other States Parties. A declaration may be withdrawn at any time by notification to the Secretary-General. Such a withdrawal shall not prejudice the consideration of any matter that is the subject of a communication already transmitted under the present article; no further communication by or on behalf

of an individual shall be received under the present article after the notification of withdrawal of the declaration has been received by the Secretary-General, unless the State Party has made a new declaration.

Article 78

The provisions of article 76 of the present Convention shall be applied without prejudice to any procedures for settling disputes or complaints in the field covered by the present Convention laid down in the constituent instruments of, or in conventions adopted by, the United Nations and the specialized agencies and shall not prevent the States Parties from having recourse to any procedures for settling a dispute in accordance with international agreements in force between them.

Part VIII: General provisions

Article 79

Nothing in the present Convention shall affect the right of each State Party to establish the criteria governing admission of migrant workers and members of their families. Concerning other matters related to their legal situation and treatment as migrant workers and members of their families, States Parties shall be subject to the limitations set forth in the present Convention.

Article 80

Nothing in the present Convention shall be interpreted as impairing the provisions of the Charter of the United Nations and of the constitutions of the specialized agencies which define the respective responsibilities of the various organs of the United Nations and of the specialized agencies in regard to the matters dealt with in the present Convention.

Article 81

1. Nothing in the present Convention shall affect more favourable rights or freedoms granted to migrant workers and members of their families by virtue of:
> (a) The law or practice of a State Party; or
> (b) Any bilateral or multilateral treaty in force for the State Party concerned.
2. Nothing in the present Convention may be interpreted as implying for any State, group or person any right to engage in any activity or perform any act that would impair any of the rights and freedoms as set forth in the present Convention.

Article 82

The rights of migrant workers and members of their families provided for in the present Convention may not be renounced. It shall not be permissible to exert any form of pressure upon migrant workers and members of their families with a view to their relinquishing or foregoing any of the said rights. It shall not be possible to derogate by contract from rights recognized in the present Convention. States Parties shall take appropriate measures to ensure that these principles are respected.

Article 83

Each State Party to the present Convention undertakes:
> (a) To ensure that any person whose rights or freedoms as herein recognized are violated shall have an effective remedy, notwithstanding that the violation has been committed by persons acting in an official capacity;
> (b) To ensure that any persons seeking such a remedy shall have his or her claim reviewed and decided by competent judicial, administrative or legislative authorities, or by any other competent authority provided for by the legal system of the State, and to develop the possibilities of judicial remedy;
> (c) To ensure that the competent authorities shall enforce such remedies when granted.

Article 84

Each State Party undertakes to adopt the legislative and other measures that are necessary to implement the provisions of the present Convention.

Part IX: Final provisions

* * *

Article 87

1. The present Convention shall enter into force on the first day of the month following a period of three months after the date of the deposit of the twentieth instrument of ratification or accession.

2. For each State ratifying or acceding to the present Convention after its entry into force, the Convention shall enter into force on the first day of the month following a period of three months after the date of the deposit of its own instrument of ratification or accession.

Article 88

A State ratifying or acceding to the present Convention may not exclude the application of any Part of it, or, without prejudice to article 3, exclude any particular category of migrant workers from its application.

Article 89

1. Any State Party may denounce the present Convention, not earlier than five years after the Convention has entered into force for the State concerned, by means of a notification in writing addressed to the Secretary-General of the United Nations.

2. Such denunciation shall become effective on the first day of the month following the expiration of a period of twelve months after the date of the receipt of the notification by the Secretary-General of the United Nations.

3. Such a denunciation shall not have the effect of releasing the State Party from its obligations under the present Convention in regard to any act or omission which occurs prior to the date at which the denunciation becomes effective, nor shall denunciation prejudice in any way the continued consideration of any matter which is already under consideration by the Committee prior to the date at which the denunciation becomes effective.

4. Following the date at which the denunciation of a State Party becomes effective, the Committee shall not commence consideration of any new matter regarding that State.

Article 90

1. After five years from the entry into force of the Convention a request for the revision of the Convention may be made at any time by any State Party by means of a notification in writing addressed to the Secretary-General of the United Nations. The Secretary-General shall thereupon communicate any proposed amendments to the States Parties with a request that they notify him whether they favour a conference of States Parties for the purpose of considering and voting upon the proposals. In the event that within four months from the date of such communication at least one third of the States Parties favours such a conference, the Secretary-General shall convene the conference under the auspices of the United Nations. Any amendment adopted by a majority of the States Parties present and voting shall be submitted to the General Assembly for approval.

2. Amendments shall come into force when they have been approved by the General Assembly of the United Nations and accepted by a two-thirds majority of the States Parties in accordance with their respective constitutional processes.

3. When amendments come into force, they shall be binding on those States Parties that have accepted them, other States Parties still being bound by the provisions of the present Convention and any earlier amendment that they have accepted.

Article 91

1. The Secretary-General of the United Nations shall receive and circulate to all States the text of reservations made by States at the time of signature, ratification or accession.

2. A reservation incompatible with the object and purpose of the present Convention shall not be permitted.

3. Reservations may be withdrawn at any time by notification to this effect addressed to the Secretary-General of the United Nations, who shall then inform all States thereof. Such notification shall take effect on the date on which it is received.

Article 92

1. Any dispute between two or more States Parties concerning the interpretation or application of the present Convention that is not settled by negotiation shall, at the request of one of them, be submitted to

arbitration. If within six months from the date of the request for arbitration the Parties are unable to agree on the organization of the arbitration, any one of those Parties may refer the dispute to the International Court of Justice by request in conformity with the Statute of the Court.

2. Each State Party may at the time of signature or ratification of the present Convention or accession thereto declare that it does not consider itself bound by paragraph 1 of the present article. The other States Parties shall not be bound by that paragraph with respect to any State Party that has made such a declaration.

3. Any State Party that has made a declaration in accordance with paragraph 2 of the present article may at any time withdraw that declaration by notification to the Secretary-General of the United Nations.

Article 93

1. The present Convention, of which the Arabic, Chinese, English, French, Russian and Spanish texts are equally authentic, shall be deposited with the Secretary-General of the United Nations.

2. The Secretary-General of the United Nations shall transmit certified copies of the present Convention to all States.

CONVENTION FOR THE PROTECTION OF ALL PERSONS FROM ENFORCED DISAPPEARANCE
(not in force as of November 2008)

Convention for the Protection of All Persons from Enforced Disappearance, G.A. Res. 61/177, Annex, U.N. GAOR, 61st Sess., 82d Plen. Mtg., U.N. Doc. A/RES/61/177 (Dec. 20, 2006), *available at* http://treaties.un.org/doc/Publication/CTC/Ch_IV_16.pdf

Preamble

The States Parties to this Convention,

Considering the obligation of States under the Charter of the United Nations to promote universal respect for, and observance of, human rights and fundamental freedoms,

Having regard to the Universal Declaration of Human Rights,

Recalling the International Covenant on Economic, Social and Cultural Rights, the International Covenant on Civil and Political Rights and the other relevant international instruments in the fields of human rights, humanitarian law and international criminal law,

Also *recalling* the Declaration on the Protection of All Persons from Enforced Disappearance adopted by the General Assembly of the United Nations in its resolution 47/133 of 18 December 1992 ,

Aware of the extreme seriousness of enforced disappearance, which constitutes a crime and, in certain circumstances defined in international law, a crime against humanity,

Determined to prevent enforced disappearances and to combat impunity for the crime of enforced disappearance,

Considering the right of any person not to be subjected to enforced disappearance, the right of victims to justice and to reparation,

Affirming the right of any victim to know the truth about the circumstances of an enforced disappearance and the fate of the disappeared person, and the right to freedom to seek, receive and impart information to this end,

Have agreed on the following articles:

Part I

Article 1

1. No one shall be subjected to enforced disappearance.
2. No exceptional circumstances whatsoever, whether a state of war or a threat of war, internal political instability or any other public emergency, may be invoked as a justification for enforced disappearance.

Article 2

For the purposes of this Convention, "enforced disappearance" is considered to be the arrest, detention, abduction or any other form of deprivation of liberty by agents of the State or by persons or groups of persons acting with the authorization, support or acquiescence of the State, followed by a refusal to acknowledge the deprivation of liberty or by concealment of the fate or whereabouts of the disappeared person, which place such a person outside the protection of the law.

Article 3

Each State Party shall take appropriate measures to investigate acts defined in article 2 committed by persons or groups of persons acting without the authorization, support or acquiescence of the State and to bring those responsible to justice.

Article 4

Each State Party shall take the necessary measures to ensure that enforced disappearance constitutes an offence under its criminal law.

Article 5

The widespread or systematic practice of enforced disappearance constitutes a crime against humanity as defined in applicable international law and shall attract the consequences provided for under such applicable international law.

Article 6

1. Each State Party shall take the necessary measures to hold criminally responsible at least:
   (a) Any person who commits, orders, solicits or induces the commission of, attempts to commit, is an accomplice to or participates in an enforced disappearance;
   (b) A superior who:
      (i) Knew, or consciously disregarded information which clearly indicated, that subordinates under his or her effective authority and control were committing or about to commit a crime of enforced disappearance;
      (ii) Exercised effective responsibility for and control over activities which were concerned with the crime of enforced disappearance; and
      (iii) Failed to take all necessary and reasonable measures within his or her power to prevent or repress the commission of an enforced disappearance or to submit the matter to the competent authorities for investigation and prosecution;
   (c) Subparagraph (b) above is without prejudice to the higher standards of responsibility applicable under relevant international law to a military commander or to a person effectively acting as a military commander.
2. No order or instruction from any public authority, civilian, military or other, may be invoked to justify an offence of enforced disappearance.

Article 7

1. Each State Party shall make the offence of enforced disappearance punishable by appropriate penalties which take into account its extreme seriousness.
2. Each State Party may establish:
   (a) Mitigating circumstances, in particular for persons who, having been implicated in the commission of an enforced disappearance, effectively contribute to bringing the disappeared

person forward alive or make it possible to clarify cases of enforced disappearance or to identify the perpetrators of an enforced disappearance;

(b) Without prejudice to other criminal procedures, aggravating circumstances, in particular in the event of the death of the disappeared person or the commission of an enforced disappearance in respect of pregnant women, minors, persons with disabilities or other particularly vulnerable persons.

Article 8

Without prejudice to article 5,

1. A State Party which applies a statute of limitations in respect of enforced disappearance shall take the necessary measures to ensure that the term of limitation for criminal proceedings:

(a) Is of long duration and is proportionate to the extreme seriousness of this offence;

(b) Commences from the moment when the offence of enforced disappearance ceases, taking into account its continuous nature.

2. Each State Party shall guarantee the right of victims of enforced disappearance to an effective remedy during the term of limitation.

Article 9

1. Each State Party shall take the necessary measures to establish its competence to exercise jurisdiction over the offence of enforced disappearance:

(a) When the offence is committed in any territory under its jurisdiction or on board a ship or aircraft registered in that State;

(b) When the alleged offender is one of its nationals;

(c) When the disappeared person is one of its nationals and the State Party considers it appropriate.

2. Each State Party shall likewise take such measures as may be necessary to establish its competence to exercise jurisdiction over the offence of enforced disappearance when the alleged offender is present in any territory under its jurisdiction, unless it extradites or surrenders him or her to another State in accordance with its international obligations or surrenders him or her to an international criminal tribunal whose jurisdiction it has recognized.

3. This Convention does not exclude any additional criminal jurisdiction exercised in accordance with national law.

Article 10

1. Upon being satisfied, after an examination of the information available to it, that the circumstances so warrant, any State Party in whose territory a person suspected of having committed an offence of enforced disappearance is present shall take him or her into custody or take such other legal measures as are necessary to ensure his or her presence. The custody and other legal measures shall be as provided for in the law of that State Party but may be maintained only for such time as is necessary to ensure the person's presence at criminal, surrender or extradition proceedings.

2. A State Party which has taken the measures referred to in paragraph 1 of this article shall immediately carry out a preliminary inquiry or investigations to establish the facts. It shall notify the States Parties referred to in article 9, paragraph 1, of the measures it has taken in pursuance of paragraph 1 of this article, including detention and the circumstances warranting detention, and of the findings of its preliminary inquiry or its investigations, indicating whether it intends to exercise its jurisdiction.

3. Any person in custody pursuant to paragraph 1 of this article may communicate immediately with the nearest appropriate representative of the State of which he or she is a national, or, if he or she is a stateless person, with the representative of the State where he or she usually resides.

Article 11

1. The State Party in the territory under whose jurisdiction a person alleged to have committed an offence of enforced disappearance is found shall, if it does not extradite that person or surrender him or her to another State in accordance with its international obligations or surrender him or her to an international criminal tribunal whose jurisdiction it has recognized, submit the case to its competent authorities for the purpose of prosecution.

2. These authorities shall take their decision in the same manner as in the case of any ordinary offence of a serious nature under the law of that State Party. In the cases referred to in article 9, paragraph 2, the

standards of evidence required for prosecution and conviction shall in no way be less stringent than those which apply in the cases referred to in article 9, paragraph 1.

3. Any person against whom proceedings are brought in connection with an offence of enforced disappearance shall be guaranteed fair treatment at all stages of the proceedings. Any person tried for an offence of enforced disappearance shall benefit from a fair trial before a competent, independent and impartial court or tribunal established by law.

Article 12

1. Each State Party shall ensure that any individual who alleges that a person has been subjected to enforced disappearance has the right to report the facts to the competent authorities, which shall examine the allegation promptly and impartially and, where necessary, undertake without delay a thorough and impartial investigation. Appropriate steps shall be taken, where necessary, to ensure that the complainant, witnesses, relatives of the disappeared person and their defence counsel, as well as persons participating in the investigation, are protected against all ill-treatment or intimidation as a consequence of the complaint or any evidence given.

2. Where there are reasonable grounds for believing that a person has been subjected to enforced disappearance, the authorities referred to in paragraph 1 of this article shall undertake an investigation, even if there has been no formal complaint.

3. Each State Party shall ensure that the authorities referred to in paragraph 1 of this article:

(a) Have the necessary powers and resources to conduct the investigation effectively, including access to the documentation and other information relevant to their investigation;

(b) Have access, if necessary with the prior authorization of a judicial authority, which shall rule promptly on the matter, to any place of detention or any other place where there are reasonable grounds to believe that the disappeared person may be present.

4. Each State Party shall take the necessary measures to prevent and sanction acts that hinder the conduct of an investigation. It shall ensure in particular that persons suspected of having committed an offence of enforced disappearance are not in a position to influence the progress of an investigation by means of pressure or acts of intimidation or reprisal aimed at the complainant, witnesses, relatives of the disappeared person or their defence counsel, or at persons participating in the investigation.

Article 13

1. For the purposes of extradition between States Parties, the offence of enforced disappearance shall not be regarded as a political offence or as an offence connected with a political offence or as an offence inspired by political motives. Accordingly, a request for extradition based on such an offence may not be refused on these grounds alone.

2. The offence of enforced disappearance shall be deemed to be included as an extraditable offence in any extradition treaty existing between States Parties before the entry into force of this Convention.

3. States Parties undertake to include the offence of enforced disappearance as an extraditable offence in any extradition treaty subsequently to be concluded between them.

4. If a State Party which makes extradition conditional on the existence of a treaty receives a request for extradition from another State Party with which it has no extradition treaty, it may consider this Convention as the necessary legal basis for extradition in respect of the offence of enforced disappearance.

5. States Parties which do not make extradition conditional on the existence of a treaty shall recognize the offence of enforced disappearance as an extraditable offence between themselves.

6. Extradition shall, in all cases, be subject to the conditions provided for by the law of the requested State Party or by applicable extradition treaties, including, in particular, conditions relating to the minimum penalty requirement for extradition and the grounds upon which the requested State Party may refuse extradition or make it subject to certain conditions.

7. Nothing in this Convention shall be interpreted as imposing an obligation to extradite if the requested State Party has substantial grounds for believing that the request has been made for the purpose of prosecuting or punishing a person on account of that person's sex, race, religion, nationality, ethnic origin, political opinions or membership of a particular social group, or that compliance with the request would cause harm to that person for any one of these reasons.

Article 14

1. States Parties shall afford one another the greatest measure of mutual legal assistance in connection with criminal proceedings brought in respect of an offence of enforced disappearance, including the supply of all evidence at their disposal that is necessary for the proceedings.

2. Such mutual legal assistance shall be subject to the conditions provided for by the domestic law of the requested State Party or by applicable treaties on mutual legal assistance, including, in particular, the conditions in relation to the grounds upon which the requested State Party may refuse to grant mutual legal assistance or may make it subject to conditions.

Article 15

States Parties shall cooperate with each other and shall afford one another the greatest measure of mutual assistance with a view to assisting victims of enforced disappearance, and in searching for, locating and releasing disappeared persons and, in the event of death, in exhuming and identifying them and returning their remains.

Article 16

1. No State Party shall expel, return ("refouler"), surrender or extradite a person to another State where there are substantial grounds for believing that he or she would be in danger of being subjected to enforced disappearance.

2. For the purpose of determining whether there are such grounds, the competent authorities shall take into account all relevant considerations, including, where applicable, the existence in the State concerned of a consistent pattern of gross, flagrant or mass violations of human rights or of serious violations of international humanitarian law.

Article 17

1. No one shall be held in secret detention.

2. Without prejudice to other international obligations of the State Party with regard to the deprivation of liberty, each State Party shall, in its legislation:

    (a) Establish the conditions under which orders of deprivation of liberty may be given;

    (b) Indicate those authorities authorized to order the deprivation of liberty;

    (c) Guarantee that any person deprived of liberty shall be held solely in officially recognized and supervised places of deprivation of liberty;

    (d) Guarantee that any person deprived of liberty shall be authorized to communicate with and be visited by his or her family, counsel or any other person of his or her choice, subject only to the conditions established by law, or, if he or she is a foreigner, to communicate with his or her consular authorities, in accordance with applicable international law;

    (e) Guarantee access by the competent and legally authorized authorities and institutions to the places where persons are deprived of liberty, if necessary with prior authorization from a judicial authority;

    (f) Guarantee that any person deprived of liberty or, in the case of a suspected enforced disappearance, since the person deprived of liberty is not able to exercise this right, any persons with a legitimate interest, such as relatives of the person deprived of liberty, their representatives or their counsel, shall, in all circumstances, be entitled to take proceedings before a court, in order that the court may decide without delay on the lawfulness of the deprivation of liberty and order the person's release if such deprivation of liberty is not lawful.

3. Each State Party shall assure the compilation and maintenance of one or more up-to-date official registers and/or records of persons deprived of liberty, which shall be made promptly available, upon request, to any judicial or other competent authority or institution authorized for that purpose by the law of the State Party concerned or any relevant international legal instrument to which the State concerned is a party. The information contained therein shall include, as a minimum:

    (a) The identity of the person deprived of liberty;

    (b) The date, time and place where the person was deprived of liberty and the identity of the authority that deprived the person of liberty;

    (c) The authority that ordered the deprivation of liberty and the grounds for the deprivation of liberty;

    (d) The authority responsible for supervising the deprivation of liberty;

(e) The place of deprivation of liberty, the date and time of admission to the place of deprivation of liberty and the authority responsible for the place of deprivation of liberty;

(f) Elements relating to the state of health of the person deprived of liberty;

(g) In the event of death during the deprivation of liberty, the circumstances and cause of death and the destination of the remains;

(h) The date and time of release or transfer to another place of detention, the destination and the authority responsible for the transfer.

Article 18

1. Subject to articles 19 and 20, each State Party shall guarantee to any person with a legitimate interest in this information, such as relatives of the person deprived of liberty, their representatives or their counsel, access to at least the following information:

(a) The authority that ordered the deprivation of liberty;

(b) The date, time and place where the person was deprived of liberty and admitted to the place of deprivation of liberty;

(c) The authority responsible for supervising the deprivation of liberty;

(d) The whereabouts of the person deprived of liberty, including, in the event of a transfer to another place of deprivation of liberty, the destination and the authority responsible for the transfer;

(e) The date, time and place of release;

(f) Elements relating to the state of health of the person deprived of liberty;

(g) In the event of death during the deprivation of liberty, the circumstances and cause of death and the destination of the remains.

2. Appropriate measures shall be taken, where necessary, to protect the persons referred to in paragraph 1 of this article, as well as persons participating in the investigation, from any ill-treatment, intimidation or sanction as a result of the search for information concerning a person deprived of liberty.

Article 19

1. Personal information, including medical and genetic data, which is collected and/or transmitted within the framework of the search for a disappeared person shall not be used or made available for purposes other than the search for the disappeared person. This is without prejudice to the use of such information in criminal proceedings relating to an offence of enforced disappearance or the exercise of the right to obtain reparation.

2. The collection, processing, use and storage of personal information, including medical and genetic data, shall not infringe or have the effect of infringing the human rights, fundamental freedoms or human dignity of an individual.

Article 20

1. Only where a person is under the protection of the law and the deprivation of liberty is subject to judicial control may the right to information referred to in article 18 be restricted, on an exceptional basis, where strictly necessary and where provided for by law, and if the transmission of the information would adversely affect the privacy or safety of the person, hinder a criminal investigation, or for other equivalent reasons in accordance with the law, and in conformity with applicable international law and with the objectives of this Convention. In no case shall there be restrictions on the right to information referred to in article 18 that could constitute conduct defined in article 2 or be in violation of article 17, paragraph 1.

2. Without prejudice to consideration of the lawfulness of the deprivation of a person's liberty, States Parties shall guarantee to the persons referred to in article 18, paragraph 1, the right to a prompt and effective judicial remedy as a means of obtaining without delay the information referred to in article 18, paragraph 1. This right to a remedy may not be suspended or restricted in any circumstances.

Article 21

Each State Party shall take the necessary measures to ensure that persons deprived of liberty are released in a manner permitting reliable verification that they have actually been released. Each State Party shall also take the necessary measures to assure the physical integrity of such persons and their ability to exercise fully their rights at the time of release, without prejudice to any obligations to which such persons may be subject under national law.

Article 22

Without prejudice to article 6, each State Party shall take the necessary measures to prevent and impose sanctions for the following conduct:

(a) Delaying or obstructing the remedies referred to in article 17, paragraph 2 (f), and article 20, paragraph 2;

(b) Failure to record the deprivation of liberty of any person, or the recording of any information which the official responsible for the official register knew or should have known to be inaccurate;

(c) Refusal to provide information on the deprivation of liberty of a person, or the provision of inaccurate information, even though the legal requirements for providing such information have been met.

Article 23

1. Each State Party shall ensure that the training of law enforcement personnel, civil or military, medical personnel, public officials and other persons who may be involved in the custody or treatment of any person deprived of liberty includes the necessary education and information regarding the relevant provisions of this Convention, in order to:

(a) Prevent the involvement of such officials in enforced disappearances;

(b) Emphasize the importance of prevention and investigations in relation to enforced disappearances;

(c) Ensure that the urgent need to resolve cases of enforced disappearance is recognized.

2. Each State Party shall ensure that orders or instructions prescribing, authorizing or encouraging enforced disappearance are prohibited. Each State Party shall guarantee that a person who refuses to obey such an order will not be punished.

3. Each State Party shall take the necessary measures to ensure that the persons referred to in paragraph 1 of this article who have reason to believe that an enforced disappearance has occurred or is planned report the matter to their superiors and, where necessary, to the appropriate authorities or bodies vested with powers of review or remedy.

Article 24

1. For the purposes of this Convention, "victim" means the disappeared person and any individual who has suffered harm as the direct result of an enforced disappearance.

2. Each victim has the right to know the truth regarding the circumstances of the enforced disappearance, the progress and results of the investigation and the fate of the disappeared person. Each State Party shall take appropriate measures in this regard.

3. Each State Party shall take all appropriate measures to search for, locate and release disappeared persons and, in the event of death, to locate, respect and return their remains.

4. Each State Party shall ensure in its legal system that the victims of enforced disappearance have the right to obtain reparation and prompt, fair and adequate compensation.

5. The right to obtain reparation referred to in paragraph 4 of this article covers material and moral damages and, where appropriate, other forms of reparation such as:

(a) Restitution;

(b) Rehabilitation;

(c) Satisfaction, including restoration of dignity and reputation;

(d) Guarantees of non-repetition.

6. Without prejudice to the obligation to continue the investigation until the fate of the disappeared person has been clarified, each State Party shall take the appropriate steps with regard to the legal situation of disappeared persons whose fate has not been clarified and that of their relatives, in fields such as social welfare, financial matters, family law and property rights.

7. Each State Party shall guarantee the right to form and participate freely in organizations and associations concerned with attempting to establish the circumstances of enforced disappearances and the fate of disappeared persons, and to assist victims of enforced disappearance.

Article 25

1. Each State Party shall take the necessary measures to prevent and punish under its criminal law:

(a) The wrongful removal of children who are subjected to enforced disappearance, children whose father, mother or legal guardian is subjected to enforced disappearance or children born during the captivity of a mother subjected to enforced disappearance;

(b) The falsification, concealment or destruction of documents attesting to the true identity of the children referred to in subparagraph (a) above.

2. Each State Party shall take the necessary measures to search for and identify the children referred to in paragraph 1 (a) of this article and to return them to their families of origin, in accordance with legal procedures and applicable international agreements.

3. States Parties shall assist one another in searching for, identifying and locating the children referred to in paragraph 1 (a) of this article.

4. Given the need to protect the best interests of the children referred to in paragraph 1 (a) of this article and their right to preserve, or to have re-established, their identity, including their nationality, name and family relations as recognized by law, States Parties which recognize a system of adoption or other form of placement of children shall have legal procedures in place to review the adoption or placement procedure, and, where appropriate, to annul any adoption or placement of children that originated in an enforced disappearance.

5. In all cases, and in particular in all matters relating to this article, the best interests of the child shall be a primary consideration, and a child who is capable of forming his or her own views shall have the right to express those views freely, the views of the child being given due weight in accordance with the age and maturity of the child.

Part II

Article 26

1. A Committee on Enforced Disappearances (hereinafter referred to as "the Committee") shall be established to carry out the functions provided for under this Convention. The Committee shall consist of ten experts of high moral character and recognized competence in the field of human rights, who shall serve in their personal capacity and be independent and impartial. The members of the Committee shall be elected by the States Parties according to equitable geographical distribution. Due account shall be taken of the usefulness of the participation in the work of the Committee of persons having relevant legal experience and of balanced gender representation.

2. The members of the Committee shall be elected by secret ballot from a list of persons nominated by States Parties from among their nationals, at biennial meetings of the States Parties convened by the Secretary-General of the United Nations for this purpose. At those meetings, for which two thirds of the States Parties shall constitute a quorum, the persons elected to the Committee shall be those who obtain the largest number of votes and an absolute majority of the votes of the representatives of States Parties present and voting.

3. The initial election shall be held no later than six months after the date of entry into force of this Convention. Four months before the date of each election, the Secretary-General of the United Nations shall address a letter to the States Parties inviting them to submit nominations within three months. The Secretary-General shall prepare a list in alphabetical order of all persons thus nominated, indicating the State Party which nominated each candidate, and shall submit this list to all States Parties.

4. The members of the Committee shall be elected for a term of four years. They shall be eligible for re-election once. However, the term of five of the members elected at the first election shall expire at the end of two years; immediately after the first election, the names of these five members shall be chosen by lot by the chairman of the meeting referred to in paragraph 2 of this article.

5. If a member of the Committee dies or resigns or for any other reason can no longer perform his or her Committee duties, the State Party which nominated him or her shall, in accordance with the criteria set out in paragraph 1 of this article, appoint another candidate from among its nationals to serve out his or her term, subject to the approval of the majority of the States Parties. Such approval shall be considered to have been obtained unless half or more of the States Parties respond negatively within six weeks of having been informed by the Secretary-General of the United Nations of the proposed appointment.

6. The Committee shall establish its own rules of procedure.

7. The Secretary-General of the United Nations shall provide the Committee with the necessary means, staff and facilities for the effective performance of its functions. The Secretary-General of the United Nations shall convene the initial meeting of the Committee.

8. The members of the Committee shall be entitled to the facilities, privileges and immunities of experts on mission for the United Nations, as laid down in the relevant sections of the Convention on the Privileges and Immunities of the United Nations.

9. Each State Party shall cooperate with the Committee and assist its members in the fulfilment of their mandate, to the extent of the Committee's functions that the State Party has accepted.

Article 27

A Conference of the States Parties will take place at the earliest four years and at the latest six years following the entry into force of this Convention to evaluate the functioning of the Committee and to decide, in accordance with the procedure described in article 44, paragraph 2, whether it is appropriate to transfer to another body - without excluding any possibility - the monitoring of this Convention, in accordance with the functions defined in articles 28 to 36.

Article 28

1. In the framework of the competencies granted by this Convention, the Committee shall cooperate with all relevant organs, offices and specialized agencies and funds of the United Nations, with the treaty bodies instituted by international instruments, with the special procedures of the United Nations and with the relevant regional intergovernmental organizations or bodies, as well as with all relevant State institutions, agencies or offices working towards the protection of all persons against enforced disappearances.

2. As it discharges its mandate, the Committee shall consult other treaty bodies instituted by relevant international human rights instruments, in particular the Human Rights Committee instituted by the International Covenant on Civil and Political Rights, with a view to ensuring the consistency of their respective observations and recommendations.

Article 29

1. Each State Party shall submit to the Committee, through the Secretary-General of the United Nations, a report on the measures taken to give effect to its obligations under this Convention, within two years after the entry into force of this Convention for the State Party concerned.

2. The Secretary-General of the United Nations shall make this report available to all States Parties.

3. Each report shall be considered by the Committee, which shall issue such comments, observations or recommendations as it may deem appropriate. The comments, observations or recommendations shall be communicated to the State Party concerned, which may respond to them, on its own initiative or at the request of the Committee.

4. The Committee may also request States Parties to provide additional information on the implementation of this Convention.

Article 30

1. A request that a disappeared person should be sought and found may be submitted to the Committee, as a matter of urgency, by relatives of the disappeared person or their legal representatives, their counsel or any person authorized by them, as well as by any other person having a legitimate interest.

2. If the Committee considers that a request for urgent action submitted in pursuance of paragraph 1 of this article:

> (a) Is not manifestly unfounded;
> (b) Does not constitute an abuse of the right of submission of such requests;
> (c) Has already been duly presented to the competent bodies of the State Party concerned, such as those authorized to undertake investigations, where such a possibility exists;
> (d) Is not incompatible with the provisions of this Convention; and
> (e) The same matter is not being examined under another procedure of international investigation or settlement of the same nature;

it shall request the State Party concerned to provide it with information on the situation of the persons sought, within a time limit set by the Committee.

3. In the light of the information provided by the State Party concerned in accordance with paragraph 2 of this article, the Committee may transmit recommendations to the State Party, including a request that the State Party should take all the necessary measures, including interim measures, to locate and protect the person concerned in accordance with this Convention and to inform the Committee, within a specified period of time, of measures taken, taking into account the urgency of the situation. The Committee shall

inform the person submitting the urgent action request of its recommendations and of the information provided to it by the State as it becomes available.

4. The Committee shall continue its efforts to work with the State Party concerned for as long as the fate of the person sought remains unresolved. The person presenting the request shall be kept informed.

Article 31

1. A State Party may at the time of ratification of this Convention or at any time afterwards declare that it recognizes the competence of the Committee to receive and consider communications from or on behalf of individuals subject to its jurisdiction claiming to be victims of a violation by this State Party of provisions of this Convention. The Committee shall not admit any communication concerning a State Party which has not made such a declaration.

2. The Committee shall consider a communication inadmissible where:

    (a) The communication is anonymous;

    (b) The communication constitutes an abuse of the right of submission of such communications or is incompatible with the provisions of this Convention;

    (c) The same matter is being examined under another procedure of international investigation or settlement of the same nature; or where

    (d) All effective available domestic remedies have not been exhausted. This rule shall not apply where the application of the remedies is unreasonably prolonged.

3. If the Committee considers that the communication meets the requirements set out in paragraph 2 of this article, it shall transmit the communication to the State Party concerned, requesting it to provide observations and comments within a time limit set by the Committee.

4. At any time after the receipt of a communication and before a determination on the merits has been reached, the Committee may transmit to the State Party concerned for its urgent consideration a request that the State Party will take such interim measures as may be necessary to avoid possible irreparable damage to the victims of the alleged violation. Where the Committee exercises its discretion, this does not imply a determination on admissibility or on the merits of the communication.

5. The Committee shall hold closed meetings when examining communications under the present article. It shall inform the author of a communication of the responses provided by the State Party concerned. When the Committee decides to finalize the procedure, it shall communicate its views to the State Party and to the author of the communication.

Article 32

A State Party to this Convention may at any time declare that it recognizes the competence of the Committee to receive and consider communications in which a State Party claims that another State Party is not fulfilling its obligations under this Convention. The Committee shall not receive communications concerning a State Party which has not made such a declaration, nor communications from a State Party which has not made such a declaration.

Article 33

1. If the Committee receives reliable information indicating that a State Party is seriously violating the provisions of this Convention, it may, after consultation with the State Party concerned, request one or more of its members to undertake a visit and report back to it without delay.

2. The Committee shall notify the State Party concerned, in writing, of its intention to organize a visit, indicating the composition of the delegation and the purpose of the visit. The State Party shall answer the Committee within a reasonable time.

3. Upon a substantiated request by the State Party, the Committee may decide to postpone or cancel its visit.

4. If the State Party agrees to the visit, the Committee and the State Party concerned shall work together to define the modalities of the visit and the State Party shall provide the Committee with all the facilities needed for the successful completion of the visit.

5. Following its visit, the Committee shall communicate to the State Party concerned its observations and recommendations.

Article 34

If the Committee receives information which appears to it to contain well-founded indications that enforced disappearance is being practised on a widespread or systematic basis in the territory under the jurisdiction of a State Party, it may, after seeking from the State Party concerned all relevant information on the situation, urgently bring the matter to the attention of the General Assembly of the United Nations, through the Secretary-General of the United Nations.

Article 35

1. The Committee shall have competence solely in respect of enforced disappearances which commenced after the entry into force of this Convention.

2. If a State becomes a party to this Convention after its entry into force, the obligations of that State vis-à-vis the Committee shall relate only to enforced disappearances which commenced after the entry into force of this Convention for the State concerned.

Article 36

1. The Committee shall submit an annual report on its activities under this Convention to the States Parties and to the General Assembly of the United Nations.

2. Before an observation on a State Party is published in the annual report, the State Party concerned shall be informed in advance and shall be given reasonable time to answer. This State Party may request the publication of its comments or observations in the report.

Part III

Article 37

Nothing in this Convention shall affect any provisions which are more conducive to the protection of all persons from enforced disappearance and which may be contained in:

    (a) The law of a State Party;

    (b) International law in force for that State.

Article 38

1. This Convention is open for signature by all Member States of the United Nations.

2. This Convention is subject to ratification by all Member States of the United Nations. Instruments of ratification shall be deposited with the Secretary-General of the United Nations.

3. This Convention is open to accession by all Member States of the United Nations. Accession shall be effected by the deposit of an instrument of accession with the Secretary-General. * * *

Article 40

The Secretary-General of the United Nations shall notify all States Members of the United Nations and all States which have signed or acceded to this Convention of the following:

    (a) Signatures, ratifications and accessions under article 38;

    (b) The date of entry into force of this Convention under article 39.

Article 41

The provisions of this Convention shall apply to all parts of federal States without any limitations or exceptions.

Article 42

1. Any dispute between two or more States Parties concerning the interpretation or application of this Convention which cannot be settled through negotiation or by the procedures expressly provided for in this Convention shall, at the request of one of them, be submitted to arbitration. If within six months from the date of the request for arbitration the Parties are unable to agree on the organization of the arbitration, any one of those Parties may refer the dispute to the International Court of Justice by request in conformity with the Statute of the Court.

2. A State may, at the time of signature or ratification of this Convention or accession thereto, declare that it does not consider itself bound by paragraph 1 of this article. The other States Parties shall not be bound by paragraph 1 of this article with respect to any State Party having made such a declaration.

3. Any State Party having made a declaration in accordance with the provisions of paragraph 2 of this article may at any time withdraw this declaration by notification to the Secretary-General of the United Nations.

Article 43
This Convention is without prejudice to the provisions of international humanitarian law, including the obligations of the High Contracting Parties to the four Geneva Conventions of 12 August 1949 and the two Additional Protocols thereto of 8 June 1977, or to the opportunity available to any State Party to authorize the International Committee of the Red Cross to visit places of detention in situations not covered by international humanitarian law.

Article 44
1. Any State Party to this Convention may propose an amendment and file it with the Secretary-General of the United Nations. The Secretary-General shall thereupon communicate the proposed amendment to the States Parties to this Convention with a request that they indicate whether they favour a conference of States Parties for the purpose of considering and voting upon the proposal. In the event that within four months from the date of such communication at least one third of the States Parties favour such a conference, the Secretary-General shall convene the conference under the auspices of the United Nations.
2. Any amendment adopted by a majority of two thirds of the States Parties present and voting at the conference shall be submitted by the Secretary-General of the United Nations to all the States Parties for acceptance.
3. An amendment adopted in accordance with paragraph 1 of this article shall enter into force when two thirds of the States Parties to this Convention have accepted it in accordance with their respective constitutional processes.
4. When amendments enter into force, they shall be binding on those States Parties which have accepted them, other States Parties still being bound by the provisions of this Convention and any earlier amendment which they have accepted.

Article 45
1. This Convention, of which the Arabic, Chinese, English, French, Russian and Spanish texts are equally authentic, shall be deposited with the Secretary-General of the United Nations.
2. The Secretary-General of the United Nations shall transmit certified copies of this Convention to all States referred to in article 38.

INTERNATIONAL CONVENTION ON THE RIGHTS OF PERSONS WITH DISABILITIES (2008)

International Convention on the Protection and Promotion of the Rights and Dignity of Persons with Disabilities, G.A. Res. 61/106, Annex I, U.N. GAOR, 61st Sess., Supp. No. 49, U.N. Doc. A/RES/61/106 (Dec. 13, 2008), *available at* http://treaties.un.org/doc/Publication/CTC/Ch_IV_15.pdf

Preamble
The States Parties to the present Convention,
(a) *Recalling* the principles proclaimed in the Charter of the United Nations which recognize the inherent dignity and worth and the equal and inalienable rights of all members of the human family as the foundation of freedom, justice and peace in the world,
(b) *Recognizing* that the United Nations, in the Universal Declaration of Human Rights and in the International Covenants on Human Rights, has proclaimed and agreed that everyone is entitled to all the rights and freedoms set forth therein, without distinction of any kind,
(c) *Reaffirming* the universality, indivisibility, interdependence and interrelatedness of all human rights and fundamental freedoms and the need for persons with disabilities to be guaranteed their full enjoyment without discrimination,
(d) *Recalling* the International Covenant on Economic Social and Cultural Rights, the International Covenant on Civil and Political Rights, the International Convention on the Elimination of All Forms of

Racial Discrimination, the Convention on the Elimination of All Forms of Discrimination against Women, the Convention against Torture and Other Cruel, Inhuman or Degrading Treatment or Punishment, the Convention on the Rights of the Child, and the International Convention on the Protection of the Rights of All Migrant Workers and Members of Their Families,

(e) *Recognizing* that disability is an evolving concept and that disability results from the interaction between persons with impairments and attitudinal and environmental barriers that hinders their full and effective participation in society on an equal basis with others,

(f) *Recognizing* the importance of the principles and policy guidelines contained in the World Programme of Action concerning Disabled Persons and in the Standard Rules on the Equalization of Opportunities for Persons with Disabilities in influencing the promotion, formulation and evaluation of the policies, plans, programmes and actions at the national, regional and international levels to further equalize opportunities for persons with disabilities,

(g) *Emphasizing* the importance of mainstreaming disability issues as an integral part of relevant strategies of sustainable development,

(h) *Recognizing* also that discrimination against any person on the basis of disability is a violation of the inherent dignity and worth of the human person,

(i) *Recognizing* further the diversity of persons with disabilities,

(j) *Recognizing* the need to promote and protect the human rights of all persons with disabilities, including those who require more intensive support,

(k) *Concerned* that, despite these various instruments and undertakings, persons with disabilities continue to face barriers in their participation as equal members of society and violations of their human rights in all parts of the world,

(l) *Recognizing* the importance of international cooperation for improving the living conditions of persons with disabilities in every country, particularly in developing countries,

(m) *Recognizing* the valued existing and potential contributions made by persons with disabilities to the overall well-being and diversity of their communities, and that the promotion of the full enjoyment by persons with disabilities of their human rights and fundamental freedoms and of full participation by persons with disabilities will result in their enhanced sense of belonging and in significant advances in the human, social and economic development of society and the eradication of poverty,

(n) *Recognizing* the importance for persons with disabilities of their individual autonomy and independence, including the freedom to make their own choices,

(o) *Considering* that persons with disabilities should have the opportunity to be actively involved in decision-making processes about policies and programmes, including those directly concerning them,

(p) *Concerned* about the difficult conditions faced by persons with disabilities who are subject to multiple or aggravated forms of discrimination on the basis of race, colour, sex, language, religion, political or other opinion, national, ethnic, indigenous or social origin, property, birth, age or other status,

(q) *Recognizing* that women and girls with disabilities are often at greater risk, both within and outside the of violence, injury or abuse, neglect or negligent treatment, maltreatment or exploitation,

(r) *Recognizing* that children with disabilities should have full enjoyment of all human rights and fundamental freedoms on an equal basis with other children, and recalling obligations to that end undertaken by States Parties to the Convention on the Rights of the Child,

(s) *Emphasizing* the need to incorporate a gender perspective in all efforts to promote the full enjoyment of human rights and fundamental freedoms by persons with disabilities,

(t) *Highlighting* the fact that the majority of persons with disabilities live in conditions of poverty, and in this regard recognizing the critical need to address the negative impact of poverty on persons with disabilities,

(u) *Bearing in mind* that conditions of peace and security based on full respect for the purposes and principles contained in the Charter of the United Nations and observance of applicable human rights instruments are indispensable for the full protection of persons with disabilities, in particular during armed conflicts and foreign occupation,

(v) *Recognizing* the importance of accessibility to the physical, social, economic and cultural environment, to health and education and to information and communication, in enabling persons with disabilities to fully enjoy all human rights and fundamental freedoms,

(w) *Realizing* that the individual, having duties to other individuals and to the community to which he or she belongs, is under a responsibility to strive for the promotion and observance of the rights recognized in the International Bill of Human Rights,

(x) *Convinced* that the family is the natural and fundamental group unit of society and is entitled to protection by society and the State, and that persons with disabilities and their family members should receive the necessary protection and assistance to enable families to contribute towards the full and equal enjoyment of the rights of persons with disabilities,

(y) *Convinced* that a comprehensive and integral international convention to promote and protect the rights and dignity of persons with disabilities will make a significant contribution to redressing the profound social disadvantage of persons with disabilities and promote their participation in the civil, political, economic, social and cultural spheres with equal opportunities, in both developing and developed countries,

Have agreed as follows:

Article 1
Purpose

The purpose of the present Convention is to promote, protect and ensure the full and equal enjoyment of all human rights and fundamental freedoms by all persons with disabilities, and to promote respect for their inherent dignity. Persons with disabilities include those who have long-term physical, mental, intellectual or sensory impairments which in interaction with various barriers may hinder their full and effective participation in society on an equal basis with others.

Article 2
Definitions

For the purposes of the present Convention:

"Communication" includes languages, display of text, Braille, tactile communication, large print, accessible multimedia as well as written, audio, plain-language, human-reader and augmentative and alternative modes, means and formats of communication, including accessible information and communication technology;

"Language" includes spoken and signed languages and other forms of non-spoken languages;

"Discrimination on the basis of disability" means any distinction, exclusion or restriction on the basis of disability which has the purpose or effect of impairing or nullifying the recognition, enjoyment or exercise, on an equal basis with others, of all human rights and fundamental freedoms in the political, economic, social, cultural, civil or any other field. It includes all forms of discrimination, including denial of reasonable accommodation;

"Reasonable accommodation" means necessary and appropriate modification and adjustments not imposing a disproportionate or undue burden, where needed in a particular case, to ensure to persons with disabilities the enjoyment or exercise on an equal basis with others of all human rights and fundamental freedoms;

"Universal design" means the design of products, environments, programmes and services to be usable by all people, to the greatest extent possible, without the need for adaptation or specialized design. "Universal design" shall not exclude assistive devices for particular groups of persons with disabilities where this is needed.

Article 3
General principles

The principles of the present Convention shall be:

(a) Respect for inherent dignity, individual autonomy including the freedom to make one's own choices, and independence of persons;

(b) Non-discrimination;

(c) Full and effective participation and inclusion in society;

(d) Respect for difference and acceptance of persons with disabilities as part of human diversity and humanity;

(e) Equality of opportunity;

(f) Accessibility;

(g) Equality between men and women;

(h) Respect for the evolving capacities of children with disabilities and respect for the right of children with disabilities to preserve their identities.

Article 4
General obligations

1. States Parties undertake to ensure and promote the full realization of all human rights and fundamental freedoms for all persons with disabilities without discrimination of any kind on the basis of disability. To this end, States Parties undertake:

(a) To adopt all appropriate legislative, administrative and other measures for the implementation of the rights recognized in the present Convention;

(b) To take all appropriate measures, including legislation, to modify or abolish existing laws, regulations, customs and practices that constitute discrimination against persons with disabilities;

(c) To take into account the protection and promotion of the human rights of persons with disabilities in all policies and programmes;

(d) To refrain from engaging in any act or practice that is inconsistent with the present Convention and to ensure that public authorities and institutions act in conformity with the present Convention;

(e) To take all appropriate measures to eliminate discrimination on the basis of disability by any person, organization or private enterprise;

(f) To undertake or promote research and development of universally designed goods, services, equipment and facilities, as defined in article 2 of the present Convention, which should require the minimum possible adaptation and the least cost to meet the specific needs of a person with disabilities, to promote their availability and use, and to promote universal design in the development of standards and guidelines;

(g) To undertake or promote research and development of, and to promote the availability and use of new technologies, including information and communications technologies, mobility aids, devices and assistive technologies, suitable for persons with disabilities, giving priority to technologies at an affordable cost;

(h) To provide accessible information to persons with disabilities about mobility aids, devices and assistive technologies, including new technologies, as well as other forms of assistance, support services and facilities;

(i) To promote the training of professionals and staff working with persons with disabilities in the rights recognized in this Convention so as to better provide the assistance and services guaranteed by those rights.

2. With regard to economic, social and cultural rights, each State Party undertakes to take measures to the maximum of its available resources and, where needed, within the framework of international cooperation, with a view to achieving progressively the full realization of these rights, without prejudice to those obligations contained in the present Convention that are immediately applicable according to international law.

3. In the development and implementation of legislation and policies to implement the present Convention, and in other decision-making processes concerning issues relating to persons with disabilities, States Parties shall closely consult with and actively involve persons with disabilities, including children with disabilities, through their representative organizations.

4. Nothing in the present Convention shall affect any provisions which are more conducive to the realization of the rights of persons with disabilities and which may be contained in the law of a State Party or international law in force for that State. There shall be no restriction upon or derogation from any of the human rights and fundamental freedoms recognized or existing in any State Party to the present Convention pursuant to law, conventions, regulation or custom on the pretext that the present Convention does not recognize such rights or freedoms or that it recognizes them to a lesser extent.

5. The provisions of the present Convention shall extend to all parts of federal states without any limitations or exceptions.

Article 5
Equality and non-discrimination

1. States Parties recognize that all persons are equal before and under the law and are entitled without any discrimination to the equal protection and equal benefit of the law.

2. States Parties shall prohibit all discrimination on the basis of disability and guarantee to persons with disabilities equal and effective legal protection against discrimination on all grounds.

3. In order to promote equality and eliminate discrimination, States Parties shall take all appropriate steps to ensure that reasonable accommodation is provided.

4. Specific measures which are necessary to accelerate or achieve de facto equality of persons with disabilities shall not be considered discrimination under the terms of the present Convention.

Article 6
Women with disabilities

1. States Parties recognize that women and girls with disabilities are subject to multiple discrimination, and in this regard shall take measures to ensure the full and equal enjoyment by them of all human rights and fundamental freedoms.

2. States Parties shall take all appropriate measures to ensure the full development, advancement and empowerment of women, for the purpose of guaranteeing them the exercise and enjoyment of the human rights and fundamental freedoms set out in the present Convention.

Article 7
Children with disabilities

1. States Parties shall take all necessary measures to ensure the full enjoyment by children with disabilities of all human rights and fundamental freedoms on an equal basis with other children.

2. In all actions concerning children with disabilities, the best interests of the child shall be a primary consideration.

3. States Parties shall ensure that children with disabilities have the right to express their views freely on all matters affecting them, their views being given due weight in accordance with their age and maturity, on an equal basis with other children, and to be provided with disability and age-appropriate assistance to realize that right.

Article 8
Awareness-raising

1. States Parties undertake to adopt immediate, effective and appropriate measures:
> (a) To raise awareness throughout society, including at the family level, regarding persons with disabilities, and to foster respect for the rights and dignity of persons with disabilities;
> (b) To combat stereotypes, prejudices and harmful practices relating to persons with disabilities, including those based on sex and age, in all areas of life;
> (c) To promote awareness of the capabilities and contributions of persons with disabilities.

2. Measures to this end include:
> (a) Initiating and maintaining effective public awareness campaigns designed:
>> (i) To nurture receptiveness to the rights of persons with disabilities;
>> (ii) To promote positive perceptions and greater social awareness towards persons with disabilities;
>> (iii) To promote recognition of the skills, merits and abilities of persons with disabilities, and of their contributions to the workplace and the labour market;
> (b) Fostering at all levels of the education system, including in all children from an early age, an attitude of respect for the rights of persons with disabilities;
> (c) Encouraging all organs of the media to portray persons with disabilities in a manner consistent with the purpose of the present Convention;
> (d) Promoting awareness-training programmes regarding persons with disabilities and the rights of persons with disabilities.

Article 9
Accessibility

1. To enable persons with disabilities to live independently and participate fully in all aspects of life, States Parties shall take appropriate measures to ensure to persons with disabilities access, on an equal basis with others, to the physical environment, to transportation, to information and communications, including information and communications technologies and systems, and to other facilities and services open or provided to the public, both in urban and in rural areas. These measures, which shall include the identification and elimination of obstacles and barriers to accessibility, shall apply to, inter alia:

(a) Buildings, roads, transportation and other indoor and outdoor facilities, including schools, housing, medical facilities and workplaces;

(b) Information, communications and other services, including electronic services and emergency services.

2. States Parties shall also take appropriate measures to:

(a) Develop, promulgate and monitor the implementation of minimum standards and guidelines for the accessibility of facilities and services open or provided to the public;

(b) Ensure that private entities that offer facilities and services which are open or provided to the public take into account all aspects of accessibility for persons with disabilities;

(c) Provide training for stakeholders on accessibility issues facing persons with disabilities;

(d) Provide in buildings and other facilities open to the public signage in Braille and in easy to read and understand forms;

(e) Provide forms of live assistance and intermediaries, including guides, readers and professional sign language interpreters, to facilitate accessibility to buildings and other facilities open to the public;

(f) Promote other appropriate forms of assistance and support to persons with disabilities to ensure their access to information;

(g) Promote access for persons with disabilities to new information and communications technologies and systems, including the Internet;

(h) Promote the design, development, production and distribution of accessible information and communications technologies and systems at an early stage, so that these technologies and systems become accessible at minimum cost.

Article 10
Right to life

States Parties reaffirm that every human being has the inherent right to life and shall take all necessary measures to ensure its effective enjoyment by persons with disabilities on an equal basis with others.

Article 11
Situations of risk and humanitarian emergencies

States Parties shall take, in accordance with their obligations under international law, including international humanitarian law and international human rights law, all necessary measures to ensure the protection and safety of persons with disabilities in situations of risk, including situations of armed conflict, humanitarian emergencies and the occurrence of natural disasters.

Article 12
Equal recognition before the law

1. States Parties reaffirm that persons with disabilities have the right to recognition everywhere as persons before the law.

2. States Parties shall recognize that persons with disabilities enjoy legal capacity on an equal basis with others in all aspects of life.

3. States Parties shall take appropriate measures to provide access by persons with disabilities to the support they may require in exercising their legal capacity.

4. States Parties shall ensure that all measures that relate to the exercise of legal capacity provide for appropriate and effective safeguards to prevent abuse in accordance with international human rights law. Such safeguards shall ensure that measures relating to the exercise of legal capacity respect the rights, will and preferences of the person, are free of conflict of interest and undue influence, are proportional and tailored to the person's circumstances, apply for the shortest time possible and are subject to regular review by a competent, independent and impartial authority or judicial body. The safeguards shall be proportional to the degree to which such measures affect the person's rights and interests.

5. Subject to the provisions of this article, States Parties shall take all appropriate and effective measures to ensure the equal right of persons with disabilities to own or inherit property, to control their own financial affairs and to have equal access to bank loans, mortgages and other forms of financial credit, and shall ensure that persons with disabilities are not arbitrarily deprived of their property.

Article 13
Access to justice

1. States Parties shall ensure effective access to justice for persons with disabilities on an equal basis with others, including through the provision of procedural and age-appropriate accommodations, in order to facilitate their effective role as direct and indirect participants, including as witnesses, in all legal proceedings, including at investigative and other preliminary stages.

2. In order to help to ensure effective access to justice for persons with disabilities, States Parties shall promote appropriate training for those working in the field of administration of justice, including police and prison staff.

Article 14
Liberty and security of the person

1. States Parties shall ensure that persons with disabilities, on an equal basis with others:

   (a) Enjoy the right to liberty and security of person;

   (b) Are not deprived of their liberty unlawfully or arbitrarily, and that any deprivation of liberty is in conformity with the law, and that the existence of a disability shall in no case justify a deprivation of liberty.

2. States Parties shall ensure that if persons with disabilities are deprived of their liberty through any process, they are, on an equal basis with others, entitled to guarantees in accordance with international human rights law and shall be treated in compliance with the objectives and principles of this Convention, including by provision of reasonable accommodation.

Article 15
Freedom from torture or cruel, inhuman or degrading treatment or punishment

1. No one shall be subjected to torture or to cruel, inhuman or degrading treatment or punishment. In particular, no one shall be subjected without his or her free consent to medical or scientific experimentation.

2. States Parties shall take all effective legislative, administrative, judicial or other measures to prevent persons with disabilities, on an equal basis with others, from being subjected to torture or cruel, inhuman or degrading treatment or punishment.

Article 16
Freedom from exploitation, violence and abuse

1. States Parties shall take all appropriate legislative, administrative, social, educational and other measures to protect persons with disabilities, both within and outside the home, from all forms of exploitation, violence and abuse, including their gender-based aspects.

2. States Parties shall also take all appropriate measures to prevent all forms of exploitation, violence and abuse by ensuring, inter alia, appropriate forms of gender- and age-sensitive assistance and support for persons with disabilities and their families and caregivers, including through the provision of information and education on how to avoid, recognize and report instances of exploitation, violence and abuse. States Parties shall ensure that protection services are age-, gender- and disability-sensitive.

3. In order to prevent the occurrence of all forms of exploitation, violence and abuse, States Parties shall ensure that all facilities and programmes designed to serve persons with disabilities are effectively monitored by independent authorities.

4. States Parties shall take all appropriate measures to promote the physical, cognitive and psychological recovery, rehabilitation and social reintegration of persons with disabilities who become victims of any form of exploitation, violence or abuse, including through the provision of protection services. Such recovery and reintegration shall take place in an environment that fosters the health, welfare, self-respect, dignity and autonomy of the person and takes into account gender- and age-specific needs.

5. States Parties shall put in place effective legislation and policies, including women- and child-focused legislation and policies, to ensure that instances of exploitation, violence and abuse against persons with disabilities are identified, investigated and, where appropriate, prosecuted.

Article 17
Protecting the integrity of the person

Every person with disabilities has a right to respect for his or her physical and mental integrity on an equal basis with others.

Article 18
Liberty of movement and nationality

1. States Parties shall recognize the rights of persons with disabilities to liberty of movement, to freedom to choose their residence and to a nationality, on an equal basis with others, including by ensuring that persons with disabilities:

(a) Have the right to acquire and change a nationality and are not deprived of their nationality arbitrarily or on the basis of disability;

(b) Are not deprived, on the basis of disability, of their ability to obtain, possess and utilize documentation of their nationality or other documentation of identification, or to utilize relevant processes such as immigration proceedings, that may be needed to facilitate exercise of the right to liberty of movement;

(c) Are free to leave any country, including their own;

(d) Are not deprived, arbitrarily or on the basis of disability, of the right to enter their own country.

2. Children with disabilities shall be registered immediately after birth and shall have the right from birth to a name, the right to acquire a nationality and, as far as possible, the right to know and be cared for by their parents.

Article 19
Living independently and being included in the community

States Parties to this Convention recognize the equal right of all persons with disabilities to live in the community, with choices equal to others, and shall take effective and appropriate measures to facilitate full enjoyment by persons with disabilities of this right and their full inclusion and participation in the community, including by ensuring that:

(a) Persons with disabilities have the opportunity to choose their place of residence and where and with whom they live on an equal basis with others and are not obliged to live in a particular living arrangement;

(b) Persons with disabilities have access to a range of in-, residential and other community support services, including personal assistance necessary to support living and inclusion in the community, and to prevent isolation or segregation from the community;

(c) Community services and facilities for the general population are available on an equal basis to persons with disabilities and are responsive to their needs.

Article 20
Personal mobility

States Parties shall take effective measures to ensure personal mobility with the greatest possible independence for persons with disabilities, including by:

(a) Facilitating the personal mobility of persons with disabilities in the manner and at the time of their choice, and at affordable cost;

(b) Facilitating access by persons with disabilities to quality mobility aids, devices, assistive technologies and forms of live assistance and intermediaries, including by making them available at affordable cost;

(c) Providing training in mobility skills to persons with disabilities and to specialist staff working with persons with disabilities;

(d) Encouraging entities that produce mobility aids, devices and assistive technologies to take into account all aspects of mobility for persons with disabilities.

Article 21
Freedom of expression and opinion, and access to information

States Parties shall take all appropriate measures to ensure that persons with disabilities can exercise the right to freedom of expression and opinion, including the freedom to seek, receive and impart information and ideas on an equal basis with others and through all forms of communication of their choice, as defined in article 2 of the present Convention, including by:

(a) Providing information intended for the general public to persons with disabilities in accessible formats and technologies appropriate to different kinds of disabilities in a timely manner and without additional cost;

(b) Accepting and facilitating the use of sign languages, Braille, augmentative and alternative communication, and all other accessible means, modes and formats of communication of their choice by persons with disabilities in official interactions;

(c) Urging private entities that provide services to the general public, including through the Internet, to provide information and services in accessible and usable formats for persons with disabilities;

(d) Encouraging the mass media, including providers of information through the Internet, to make their services accessible to persons with disabilities;

(e) Recognizing and promoting the use of sign languages.

Article 22
Respect for privacy

1. No person with disabilities, regardless of place of residence or living arrangements, shall be subjected to arbitrary or unlawful interference with his or her privacy, family, or correspondence or other types of communication or to unlawful attacks on his or her honour and reputation. Persons with disabilities have the right to the protection of the law against such interference or attacks.

2. States Parties shall protect the privacy of personal, health and rehabilitation information of persons with disabilities on an equal basis with others.

Article 23
Respect for and the family

1. States Parties shall take effective and appropriate measures to eliminate discrimination against persons with disabilities in all matters relating to marriage, family, parenthood and relationships, on an equal basis with others, so as to ensure that:

(a) The right of all persons with disabilities who are of marriageable age to marry and to found a family on the basis of free and full consent of the intending spouses is recognized;

(b) The rights of persons with disabilities to decide freely and responsibly on the number and spacing of their children and to have access to age-appropriate information, reproductive and family planning education are recognized, and the means necessary to enable them to exercise these rights are provided;

(c) Persons with disabilities, including children, retain their fertility on an equal basis with others.

2. States Parties shall ensure the rights and responsibilities of persons with disabilities, with regard to guardianship, wardship, trusteeship, adoption of children or similar institutions, where these concepts exist in national legislation; in all cases the best interests of the child shall be paramount. States Parties shall render appropriate assistance to persons with disabilities in the performance of their child-rearing responsibilities.

3. States Parties shall ensure that children with disabilities have equal rights with respect to family life. With a view to realizing these rights, and to prevent concealment, abandonment, neglect and segregation of children with disabilities, States Parties shall undertake to provide early and comprehensive information, services and support to children with disabilities and their families.

4. States Parties shall ensure that a child shall not be separated from his or her parents against their will, except when competent authorities subject to judicial review determine, in accordance with applicable law and procedures, that such separation is necessary for the best interests of the child. In no case shall a child be separated from parents on the basis of a disability of either the child or one or both of the parents.

5. States Parties shall, where the immediate family is unable to care for a child with disabilities, undertake every effort to provide alternative care within the wider family, and failing that, within the community in a family setting.

Article 24
Education

1. States Parties recognize the right of persons with disabilities to education. With a view to realizing this right without discrimination and on the basis of equal opportunity, States Parties shall ensure an inclusive education system at all levels and life long learning directed to:

    (a) The full development of human potential and sense of dignity and self-worth, and the strengthening of respect for human rights, fundamental freedoms and human diversity;

    (b) The development by persons with disabilities of their personality, talents and creativity, as well as their mental and physical abilities, to their fullest potential;

    (c) Enabling persons with disabilities to participate effectively in a free society.

2. In realizing this right, States Parties shall ensure that:

    (a) Persons with disabilities are not excluded from the general education system on the basis of disability, and that children with disabilities are not excluded from free and compulsory primary education, or from secondary education, on the basis of disability;

    (b) Persons with disabilities can access an inclusive, quality and free primary education and secondary education on an equal basis with others in the communities in which they live;

    (c) Reasonable accommodation of the individual's requirements is provided;

    (d) Persons with disabilities receive the support required, within the general education system, to facilitate their effective education;

    (e) Effective individualized support measures are provided in environments that maximize academic and social development, consistent with the goal of full inclusion.

3. States Parties shall enable persons with disabilities to learn life and social development skills to facilitate their full and equal participation in education and as members of the community. To this end, States Parties shall take appropriate measures, including:

    (a) Facilitating the learning of Braille, alternative script, augmentative and alternative modes, means and formats of communication and orientation and mobility skills, and facilitating peer support and mentoring;

    (b) Facilitating the learning of sign language and the promotion of the linguistic identity of the deaf community;

    (c) Ensuring that the education of persons, and in particular children, who are blind, deaf or deafblind, is delivered in the most appropriate languages and modes and means of communication for the individual, and in environments which maximize academic and social development.

4. In order to help ensure the realization of this right, States Parties shall take appropriate measures to employ teachers, including teachers with disabilities, who are qualified in sign language and/or Braille, and to train professionals and staff who work at all levels of education. Such training shall incorporate disability awareness and the use of appropriate augmentative and alternative modes, means and formats of communication, educational techniques and materials to support persons with disabilities.

5. States Parties shall ensure that persons with disabilities are able to access general tertiary education, vocational training, adult education and lifelong learning without discrimination and on an equal basis with others. To this end, States Parties shall ensure that reasonable accommodation is provided to persons with disabilities.

Article 25
Health

States Parties recognize that persons with disabilities have the right to the enjoyment of the highest attainable standard of health without discrimination on the basis of disability. States Parties shall take all appropriate measures to ensure access for persons with disabilities to health services that are gender-sensitive, including health-related rehabilitation. In particular, States Parties shall:

    (a) Provide persons with disabilities with the same range, quality and standard of free or affordable health care and programmes as provided to other persons, including in the area of sexual and reproductive health and population-based public health programmes;

    (b) Provide those health services needed by persons with disabilities specifically because of their disabilities, including early identification and intervention as appropriate, and services designed to minimize and prevent further disabilities, including among children and older persons;

    (c) Provide these health services as close as possible to people's own communities, including in rural areas;

(d) Require health professionals to provide care of the same quality to persons with disabilities as to others, including on the basis of free and informed consent by, inter alia, raising awareness of the human rights, dignity, autonomy and needs of persons with disabilities through training and the promulgation of ethical standards for public and private health care;

(e) Prohibit discrimination against persons with disabilities in the provision of health insurance, and life insurance where such insurance is permitted by national law, which shall be provided in a fair and reasonable manner;

(f) Prevent discriminatory denial of health care or health services or food and fluids on the basis of disability.

Article 26
Habilitation and rehabilitation

1. States Parties shall take effective and appropriate measures, including through peer support, to enable persons with disabilities to attain and maintain maximum independence, full physical, mental, social and vocational ability, and full inclusion and participation in all aspects of life. To that end, States Parties shall organize, strengthen and extend comprehensive habilitation and rehabilitation services and programmes, particularly in the areas of health, employment, education and social services, in such a way that these services and programmes:

(a) Begin at the earliest possible stage, and are based on the multidisciplinary assessment of individual needs and strengths;

(b) Support participation and inclusion in the community and all aspects of society, are voluntary, and are available to persons with disabilities as close as possible to their own communities, including in rural areas.

2. States Parties shall promote the development of initial and continuing training for professionals and staff working in habilitation and rehabilitation services.

3. States Parties shall promote the availability, knowledge and use of assistive devices and technologies, designed for persons with disabilities, as they relate to habilitation and rehabilitation.

Article 27
Work and employment

1. States Parties recognize the right of persons with disabilities to work, on an equal basis with others; this includes the right to the opportunity to gain a living by work freely chosen or accepted in a labour market and work environment that is open, inclusive and accessible to persons with disabilities. States Parties shall safeguard and promote the realization of the right to work, including for those who acquire a disability during the course of employment, by taking appropriate steps, including through legislation, to, inter alia:

(a) Prohibit discrimination on the basis of disability with regard to all matters concerning all forms of employment, including conditions of recruitment, hiring and employment, continuance of employment, career advancement and safe and healthy working conditions;

(b) Protect the rights of persons with disabilities, on an equal basis with others, to just and favourable conditions of work, including equal opportunities and equal remuneration for work of equal value, safe and healthy working conditions, including protection from harassment, and the redress of grievances;

(c) Ensure that persons with disabilities are able to exercise their labour and trade union rights on an equal basis with others;

(d) Enable persons with disabilities to have effective access to general technical and vocational guidance programmes, placement services and vocational and continuing training;

(e) Promote employment opportunities and career advancement for persons with disabilities in the labour market, as well as assistance in finding, obtaining, maintaining and returning to employment;

(f) Promote opportunities for self-employment, entrepreneurship, the development of cooperatives and starting one's own business;

(g) Employ persons with disabilities in the public sector;

(h) Promote the employment of persons with disabilities in the private sector through appropriate policies and measures, which may include affirmative action programmes, incentives and other measures;

(i) Ensure that reasonable accommodation is provided to persons with disabilities in the workplace;

(j) Promote the acquisition by persons with disabilities of work experience in the open labour market;

(k) Promote vocational and professional rehabilitation, job retention and return-to-work programmes for persons with disabilities.

2. States Parties shall ensure that persons with disabilities are not held in slavery or in servitude, and are protected, on an equal basis with others, from forced or compulsory labour.

Article 28
Adequate standard of living and social protection

1. States Parties recognize the right of persons with disabilities to an adequate standard of living for themselves and their families, including adequate food, clothing and housing, and to the continuous improvement of living conditions, and shall take appropriate steps to safeguard and promote the realization of this right without discrimination on the basis of disability.

2. States Parties recognize the right of persons with disabilities to social protection and to the enjoyment of that right without discrimination on the basis of disability, and shall take appropriate steps to safeguard and promote the realization of this right, including measures:

(a) To ensure equal access by persons with disabilities to clean water services, and to ensure access to appropriate and affordable services, devices and other assistance for disability-related needs;

(b) To ensure access by persons with disabilities, in particular women and girls with disabilities and older persons with disabilities, to social protection programmes and poverty reduction programmes;

(c) To ensure access by persons with disabilities and their families living in situations of poverty to assistance from the State with disability-related expenses, including adequate training, counselling, financial assistance and respite care;

(d) To ensure access by persons with disabilities to public housing programmes;

(e) To ensure equal access by persons with disabilities to retirement benefits and programmes.

Article 29
Participation in political and public life

States Parties shall guarantee to persons with disabilities political rights and the opportunity to enjoy them on an equal basis with others, and shall undertake to:

(a) Ensure that persons with disabilities can effectively and fully participate in political and public life on an equal basis with others, directly or through freely chosen representatives, including the right and opportunity for persons with disabilities to vote and be elected, inter alia, by:

(i) Ensuring that voting procedures, facilities and materials are appropriate, accessible and easy to understand and use;

(ii) Protecting the right of persons with disabilities to vote by secret ballot in elections and public referendums without intimidation, and to stand for elections, to effectively hold office and perform all public functions at all levels of government, facilitating the use of assistive and new technologies where appropriate;

(iii) Guaranteeing the free expression of the will of persons with disabilities as electors and to this end, where necessary, at their request, allowing assistance in voting by a person of their own choice;

(b) Promote actively an environment in which persons with disabilities can effectively and fully participate in the conduct of public affairs, without discrimination and on an equal basis with others, and encourage their participation in public affairs, including:

(i) Participation in non-governmental organizations and associations concerned with the public and political life of the country, and in the activities and administration of political parties;

(ii) Forming and joining organizations of persons with disabilities to represent persons with disabilities at international, national, regional and local levels.

Article 30
Participation in cultural life, recreation, leisure and sport

1. States Parties recognize the right of persons with disabilities to take part on an equal basis with others in cultural life, and shall take all appropriate measures to ensure that persons with disabilities:

(a) Enjoy access to cultural materials in accessible formats;

(b) Enjoy access to television programmes, films, theatre and other cultural activities, in accessible formats;

(c) Enjoy access to places for cultural performances or services, such as theatres, museums, cinemas, libraries and tourism services, and, as far as possible, enjoy access to monuments and sites of national cultural importance.

2. States Parties shall take appropriate measures to enable persons with disabilities to have the opportunity to develop and utilize their creative, artistic and intellectual potential, not only for their own benefit, but also for the enrichment of society.

3. States Parties shall take all appropriate steps, in accordance with international law, to ensure that laws protecting intellectual property rights do not constitute an unreasonable or discriminatory barrier to access by persons with disabilities to cultural materials.

4. Persons with disabilities shall be entitled, on an equal basis with others, to recognition and support of their specific cultural and linguistic identity, including sign languages and deaf culture.

5. With a view to enabling persons with disabilities to participate on an equal basis with others in recreational, leisure and sporting activities, States Parties shall take appropriate measures:

(a) To encourage and promote the participation, to the fullest extent possible, of persons with disabilities in mainstream sporting activities at all levels;

(b) To ensure that persons with disabilities have an opportunity to organize, develop and participate in disability-specific sporting and recreational activities and, to this end, encourage the provision, on an equal basis with others, of appropriate instruction, training and resources;

(c) To ensure that persons with disabilities have access to sporting, recreational and tourism venues;

(d) To ensure that children with disabilities have equal access with other children to participation in play, recreation and leisure and sporting activities, including those activities in the school system;

(e) To ensure that persons with disabilities have access to services from those involved in the organization of recreational, tourism, leisure and sporting activities.

Article 31
Statistics and data collection

1. States Parties undertake to collect appropriate information, including statistical and research data, to enable them to formulate and implement policies to give effect to the present Convention. The process of collecting and maintaining this information shall:

(a) Comply with legally established safeguards, including legislation on data protection, to ensure confidentiality and respect for the privacy of persons with disabilities;

(b) Comply with internationally accepted norms to protect human rights and fundamental freedoms and ethical principles in the collection and use of statistics.

2. The information collected in accordance with this article shall be disaggregated, as appropriate, and used to help assess the implementation of States Parties' obligations under the present Convention and to identify and address the barriers faced by persons with disabilities in exercising their rights.

3. States Parties shall assume responsibility for the dissemination of these statistics and ensure their accessibility to persons with disabilities and others.

Article 32
International cooperation

1. States Parties recognize the importance of international cooperation and its promotion, in support of national efforts for the realization of the purpose and objectives of the present Convention, and will undertake appropriate and effective measures in this regard, between and among States and, as appropriate, in partnership with relevant international and regional organizations and civil society, in particular organizations of persons with disabilities. Such measures could include, inter alia:

(a) Ensuring that international cooperation, including international development programmes, is inclusive of and accessible to persons with disabilities;

(b) Facilitating and supporting capacity-building, including through the exchange and sharing of information, experiences, training programmes and best practices;

(c) Facilitating cooperation in research and access to scientific and technical knowledge;

(d) Providing, as appropriate, technical and economic assistance, including by facilitating access to and sharing of accessible and assistive technologies, and through the transfer of technologies.

2. The provisions of this article are without prejudice to the obligations of each State Party to fulfil its obligations under the present Convention.

Article 33
National implementation and monitoring

1. States Parties, in accordance with their system of organization, shall designate one or more focal points within government for matters relating to the implementation of the present Convention, and shall give due consideration to the establishment or designation of a coordination mechanism within government to facilitate related action in different sectors and at different levels.

2. States Parties shall, in accordance with their legal and administrative systems, maintain, strengthen, designate or establish within the State Party, a framework, including one or more independent mechanisms, as appropriate, to promote, protect and monitor implementation of the present Convention. When designating or establishing such a mechanism, States Parties shall take into account the principles relating to the status and functioning of national institutions for protection and promotion of human rights.

3. Civil society, in particular persons with disabilities and their representative organizations, shall be involved and participate fully in the monitoring process.

Article 34
Committee on the Rights of Persons with Disabilities

1. There shall be established a Committee on the Rights of Persons with Disabilities (hereafter referred to as "the Committee"), which shall carry out the functions hereinafter provided.

2. The Committee shall consist, at the time of entry into force of the present Convention, of twelve experts. After an additional sixty ratifications or accessions to the Convention, the membership of the Committee shall increase by six members, attaining a maximum number of eighteen members.

3. The members of the Committee shall serve in their personal capacity and shall be of high moral standing and recognized competence and experience in the field covered by the present Convention. When nominating their candidates, States Parties are invited to give due consideration to the provision set out in article 4.3 of the present Convention.

4. The members of the Committee shall be elected by States Parties, consideration being given to equitable geographical distribution, representation of the different forms of civilization and of the principal legal systems, balanced gender representation and participation of experts with disabilities.

5. The members of the Committee shall be elected by secret ballot from a list of persons nominated by the States Parties from among their nationals at meetings of the Conference of States Parties. At those meetings, for which two thirds of States Parties shall constitute a quorum, the persons elected to the Committee shall be those who obtain the largest number of votes and an absolute majority of the votes of the representatives of States Parties present and voting.

6. The initial election shall be held no later than six months after the date of entry into force of the present Convention. At least four months before the date of each election, the Secretary-General of the United Nations shall address a letter to the States Parties inviting them to submit the nominations within two months. The Secretary-General shall subsequently prepare a list in alphabetical order of all persons thus nominated, indicating the State Parties which have nominated them, and shall submit it to the States Parties to the present Convention.

7. The members of the Committee shall be elected for a term of four years. They shall be eligible for re-election once. However, the term of six of the members elected at the first election shall expire at the end of two years; immediately after the first election, the names of these six members shall be chosen by lot by the chairperson of the meeting referred to in paragraph 5 of this article.

8. The election of the six additional members of the Committee shall be held on the occasion of regular elections, in accordance with the relevant provisions of this article.

9. If a member of the Committee dies or resigns or declares that for any other cause she or he can no longer perform her or his duties, the State Party which nominated the member shall appoint another expert possessing the qualifications and meeting the requirements set out in the relevant provisions of this article, to serve for the remainder of the term.

10. The Committee shall establish its own rules of procedure.

11. The Secretary-General of the United Nations shall provide the necessary staff and facilities for the effective performance of the functions of the Committee under the present Convention, and shall convene its initial meeting.

12. With the approval of the General Assembly, the members of the Committee established under the present Convention shall receive emoluments from United Nations resources on such terms and conditions as the Assembly may decide, having regard to the importance of the Committee's responsibilities.

13. The members of the Committee shall be entitled to the facilities, privileges and immunities of experts on mission for the United Nations as laid down in the relevant sections of the Convention on the Privileges and Immunities of the United Nations.

Article 35
Reports by States Parties

1. Each State Party shall submit to the Committee, through the Secretary-General of the United Nations, a comprehensive report on measures taken to give effect to its obligations under the present Convention and on the progress made in that regard, within two years after the entry into force of the present Convention for the State Party concerned.

2. Thereafter, States Parties shall submit subsequent reports at least every four years and further whenever the Committee so requests.

3. The Committee shall decide any guidelines applicable to the content of the reports.

4. A State Party which has submitted a comprehensive initial report to the Committee need not, in its subsequent reports, repeat information previously provided. When preparing reports to the Committee, States Parties are invited to consider doing so in an open and transparent process and to give due consideration to the provision set out in article 4.3 of the present Convention.

5. Reports may indicate factors and difficulties affecting the degree of fulfilment of obligations under the present Convention.

Article 36
Consideration of reports

1. Each report shall be considered by the Committee, which shall make such suggestions and general recommendations on the report as it may consider appropriate and shall forward these to the State Party concerned. The State Party may respond with any information it chooses to the Committee. The Committee may request further information from States Parties relevant to the implementation of the present Convention.

2. If a State Party is significantly overdue in the submission of a report, the Committee may notify the State Party concerned of the need to examine the implementation of the present Convention in that State Party, on the basis of reliable information available to the Committee, if the relevant report is not submitted within three months following the notification. The Committee shall invite the State Party concerned to participate in such examination. Should the State Party respond by submitting the relevant report, the provisions of paragraph 1 of this article will apply.

3. The Secretary-General of the United Nations shall make available the reports to all States Parties.

4. States Parties shall make their reports widely available to the public in their own countries and facilitate access to the suggestions and general recommendations relating to these reports.

5. The Committee shall transmit, as it may consider appropriate, to the specialized agencies, funds and programmes of the United Nations, and other competent bodies, reports from States Parties in order to address a request or indication of a need for technical advice or assistance contained therein, along with the Committee's observations and recommendations, if any, on these requests or indications.

Article 37
Cooperation between States Parties and the Committee

1. Each State Party shall cooperate with the Committee and assist its members in the fulfilment of their mandate.

2. In its relationship with States Parties, the Committee shall give due consideration to ways and means of enhancing national capacities for the implementation of the present Convention, including through international cooperation.

Article 38
Relationship of the Committee with other bodies
In order to foster the effective implementation of the present Convention and to encourage international cooperation in the field covered by the present Convention:

(a) The specialized agencies and other United Nations organs shall be entitled to be represented at the consideration of the implementation of such provisions of the present Convention as fall within the scope of their mandate. The Committee may invite the specialized agencies and other competent bodies as it may consider appropriate to provide expert advice on the implementation of the Convention in areas falling within the scope of their respective mandates. The Committee may invite specialized agencies and other United Nations organs to submit reports on the implementation of the Convention in areas falling within the scope of their activities;

(b) The Committee, as it discharges its mandate, shall consult, as appropriate, other relevant bodies instituted by international human rights treaties, with a view to ensuring the consistency of their respective reporting guidelines, suggestions and general recommendations, and avoiding duplication and overlap in the performance of their functions.

Article 39
Report of the Committee
The Committee shall report every two years to the General Assembly and to the Economic and Social Council on its activities, and may make suggestions and general recommendations based on the examination of reports and information received from the States Parties. Such suggestions and general recommendations shall be included in the report of the Committee together with comments, if any, from States Parties.

Article 40
Conference of States Parties
1. The States Parties shall meet regularly in a Conference of States Parties in order to consider any matter with regard to the implementation of the present Convention.
2. No later than six months after the entry into force of the present Convention, the Conference of the States Parties shall be convened by the Secretary-General of the United Nations. The subsequent meetings shall be convened by the Secretary-General of the United Nations biennially or upon the decision of the Conference of States Parties. * * *

Article 43
Consent to be bound
The present Convention shall be subject to ratification by signatory States and to formal confirmation by signatory regional integration organizations. It shall be open for accession by any State or regional integration organization which has not signed the Convention.

Article 44
Regional integration organizations
1. "Regional integration organization" shall mean an organization constituted by sovereign States of a given region, to which its member States have transferred competence in respect of matters governed by this Convention. Such organizations shall declare, in their instruments of formal confirmation or accession, the extent of their competence with respect to matters governed by this Convention. Subsequently, they shall inform the depositary of any substantial modification in the extent of their competence.
2. References to "States Parties" in the present Convention shall apply to such organizations within the limits of their competence.
3. For the purposes of article 45, paragraph 1, and article 47, paragraphs 2 and 3, any instrument deposited by a regional integration organization shall not be counted.
4. Regional integration organizations, in matters within their competence, may exercise their right to vote in the Conference of States Parties, with a number of votes equal to the number of their member States that

are Parties to this Convention. Such an organization shall not exercise its right to vote if any of its member States exercises its right, and vice versa. * * *

Article 46
Reservations
1. Reservations incompatible with the object and purpose of the present Convention shall not be permitted.
2. Reservations may be withdrawn at any time.

Article 47
Amendments
1. Any State Party may propose an amendment to the present Convention and submit it to the Secretary-General of the United Nations. The Secretary-General shall communicate any proposed amendments to States Parties, with a request to be notified whether they favour a conference of States Parties for the purpose of considering and deciding upon the proposals. In the event that, within four months from the date of such communication, at least one third of the States Parties favour such a conference, the Secretary-General shall convene the conference under the auspices of the United Nations. Any amendment adopted by a majority of two thirds of the States Parties present and voting shall be submitted by the Secretary-General to the General Assembly for approval and thereafter to all States Parties for acceptance.
2. An amendment adopted and approved in accordance with paragraph 1 of this article shall enter into force on the thirtieth day after the number of instruments of acceptance deposited reaches two thirds of the number of States Parties at the date of adoption of the amendment. Thereafter, the amendment shall enter into force for any State Party on the thirtieth day following the deposit of its own instrument of acceptance. An amendment shall be binding only on those States Parties which have accepted it.
3. If so decided by the Conference of States Parties by consensus, an amendment adopted and approved in accordance with paragraph 1 of this article which relates exclusively to articles 34, 38, 39 and 40 shall enter into force for all States Parties on the thirtieth day after the number of instruments of acceptance deposited reaches two thirds of the number of States Parties at the date of adoption of the amendment.

Article 48
Denunciation
A State Party may denounce the present Convention by written notification to the Secretary-General of the United Nations. The denunciation shall become effective one year after the date of receipt of the notification by the Secretary-General.

Article 49
Accessible format
The text of the present Convention shall be made available in accessible formats. * * *

REGIONAL TREATIES, RESOLUTIONS AND DOCUMENTS

AFRICA

AFRICAN (BANJUL) CHARTER ON HUMAN AND PEOPLES' RIGHTS
African Charter on Human and Peoples' Rights, *adopted* June 27, 1981, 1520 U.N.T.S. 217, 245.

Preamble
The African States members of the Organization of African Unity, parties to the present convention entitled "African Charter on Human and Peoples' Rights", * * *

Considering the Charter of the Organization of African Unity, which stipulates that "freedom, equality, justice and dignity are essential objectives for the achievement of the legitimate aspirations of the African peoples";

Reaffirming the pledge they solemnly made in Article 2 of the said Charter to eradicate all forms of colonialism from Africa, to coordinate and intensify their cooperation and efforts to achieve a better life for the peoples of Africa and to promote international cooperation having due regard to the Charter of the United Nations. and the Universal Declaration of Human Rights;

Taking into consideration the virtues of their historical tradition and the values of African civilization which should inspire and characterize their reflection on the concept of human and peoples' rights;

Recognizing on the one hand, that fundamental human rights stem from the attributes of human beings which justifies their national and international protection and on the other hand that the reality and respect of peoples rights should necessarily guarantee human rights;

Considering that the enjoyment of rights and freedoms also implies the performance of duties on the part of everyone; Convinced that it is henceforth essential to pay a particular attention to the right to development and that civil and political rights cannot be dissociated from economic, social and cultural rights in their conception as well as universality and that the satisfaction of economic, social and cultural rights ia a guarantee for the enjoyment of civil and political rights;

Conscious of their duty to achieve the total liberation of Africa, the peoples of which are still struggling for their dignity and genuine independence, and undertaking to eliminate colonialism, neo-colonialism, apartheid, zionism and to dismantle aggressive foreign military bases and all forms of discrimination, particularly those based on race, ethnic group, color, sex. language, religion or political opinions;

Reaffirming their adherence to the principles of human and peoples' rights and freedoms contained in the declarations, conventions and other instrument adopted by the Organization of African Unity, the Movement of Non-Aligned Countries and the United Nations;

Firmly convinced of their duty to promote and protect human and people' rights and freedoms taking into account the importance traditionally attached to these rights and freedoms in Africa;

Have agreed as follows:

Part I: Rights and Duties

Chapter I: Human and Peoples' Rights

Article 1
The Member States of the Organization of African Unity parties to the present Charter shall recognize the rights, duties and freedoms enshrined in this Chapter and shall undertake to adopt legislative or other measures to give effect to them.

Article 2
Every individual shall be entitled to the enjoyment of the rights and freedoms recognized and guaranteed in the present Charter without distinction of any kind such as race, ethnic group, color, sex, language, religion, political or any other opinion, national and social origin, fortune, birth or other status.

Article 3
1. Every individual shall be equal before the law.
2. Every individual shall be entitled to equal protection of the law.

Article 4

Human beings are inviolable. Every human being shall be entitled to respect for his life and the integrity of his person. No one may be arbitrarily deprived of this right.

Article 5

Every individual shall have the right to the respect of the dignity inherent in a human being and to the recognition of his legal status. All forms of exploitation and degradation of man particularly slavery, slave trade, torture, cruel, inhuman or degrading punishment and treatment shall be prohibited.

Article 6

Every individual shall have the right to liberty and to the security of his person. No one may be deprived of his freedom except for reasons and conditions previously laid down by law. In particular, no one may be arbitrarily arrested or detained.

Article 7

1. Every individual shall have the right to have his cause heard. This comprises: (a) the right to an appeal to competent national organs against acts of violating his fundamental rights as recognized and guaranteed by conventions, laws, regulations and customs in force; (b) the right to be presumed innocent until proved guilty by a competent court or tribunal; (c) the right to defense, including the right to be defended by counsel of his choice; (d) the right to be tried within a reasonable time by an impartial court or tribunal.
2. No one may be condemned for an act or omission which did not constitute a legally punishable offence at the time it was committed. No penalty may be inflicted for an offence for which no provision was made at the time it was committed. Punishment is personal and can be imposed only on the offender.

Article 8

Freedom of conscience, the profession and free practice of religion shall be guaranteed. No one may, subject to law and order, be submitted to measures restricting the exercise of these freedoms.

Article 9

1. Every individual shall have the right to receive information.
2. Every individual shall have the right to express and disseminate his opinions within the law.

Article 10

1. Every individual shall have the right to free association provided that he abides by the law.
2. Subject to the obligation of solidarity provided for in 29 no one may be compelled to join an association.

Article 11

Every individual shall have the right to assemble freely with others. The exercise of this right shall be subject only to necessary restrictions provided for by law in particular those enacted in the interest of national security, the safety, health, ethics and rights and freedoms of others.

Article 12

1. Every individual shall have the right to freedom of movement and residence within the borders of a State provided he abides by the law.
2. Every individual shall have the right to leave any country including his own, and to return to his country. This right may only be subject to restrictions, provided for by law for the protection of national security, law and order, public health or morality.
3. Every individual shall have the right, when persecuted, to seek and obtain asylum in other countries in accordance with laws of those countries and international conventions.
4. A non-national legally admitted in a territory of a State Party to the present Charter, may only be expelled from it by virtue of a decision taken in accordance with the law.
5. The mass expulsion of non-nationals shall be prohibited. Mass expulsion shall be that which is aimed at national, racial, ethnic or religious groups.

Article 13

1. Every citizen shall have the right to participate freely in the government of his country, either directly or through freely chosen representatives in accordance with the provisions of the law.
2. Every citizen shall have the right of equal access to the public service of his country.
3. Every individual shall have the right of access to public property and services in strict equality of all persons before the law.

Article 14

The right to property shall be guaranteed. It may only be encroached upon in the interest of public need or in the general interest of the community and in accordance with the provisions of appropriate laws.

Article 15

Every individual shall have the right to work under equitable and satisfactory conditions, and shall receive equal pay for equal work.

Article 16

1. Every individual shall have the right to enjoy the best attainable state of physical and mental health.
2. States parties to the present Charter shall take the necessary measures to protect the health of their people and to ensure that they receive medical attention when they are sick.

Article 17

1. Every individual shall have the right to education.
2. Every individual may freely, take part in the cultural life of his community.
3. The promotion and protection of morals and traditional values recognized by the community shall be the duty of the State.

Article 18

1. The family shall be the natural unit and basis of society. It shall be protected by the State which shall take care of its physical health and moral.
2. The State shall have the duty to assist the family which is the custodian or morals and traditional values recognized by the community.
3. The State shall ensure the elimination of every discrimination against women and also ensure the protection of the rights of the woman and the child as stipulated in international declarations and conventions.
4. The aged and the disabled shall also have the right to special measures of protection in keeping with their physical or moral needs.

Article 19

All peoples shall be equal; they shall enjoy the same respect and shall have the same rights. Nothing shall justify the domination of a people by another.

Article 20

1. All peoples shall have the right to existence. They shall have the unquestionable and inalienable right to self- determination. They shall freely determine their political status and shall pursue their economic and social development according to the policy they have freely chosen.
2. Colonized or oppressed peoples shall have the right to free themselves from the bonds of domination by resorting to any means recognized by the international community.
3. All peoples shall have the right to the assistance of the States parties to the present Charter in their liberation struggle against foreign domination, be it political, economic or cultural.

Article 21

1. All peoples shall freely dispose of their wealth and natural resources. This right shall be exercised in the exclusive interest of the people. In no case shall a people be deprived of it.
2. In case of spoliation the dispossessed people shall have the right to the lawful recovery of its property as well as to an adequate compensation.
3. The free disposal of wealth and natural resources shall be exercised without prejudice to the obligation of

promoting international economic cooperation based on mutual respect, equitable exchange and the principles of international law.

4. States parties to the present Charter shall individually and collectively exercise the right to free disposal of their wealth and natural resources with a view to strengthening African unity and solidarity.

5. States parties to the present Charter shall undertake to eliminate all forms of foreign economic exploitation particularly that practiced by international monopolies so as to enable their peoples to fully benefit from the advantages derived from their national resources.

Article 22

1. All peoples shall have the right to their economic, social and cultural development with due regard to their freedom and identity and in the equal enjoyment of the common heritage of mankind.

2. States shall have the duty, individually or collectively, to ensure the exercise of the right to development.

Article 23

1. All peoples shall have the right to national and international peace and security. The principles of solidarity and friendly relations implicitly affirmed by the Charter of the United Nations and reaffirmed by that of the Organization of African Unity shall govern relations between States.

2. For the purpose of strengthening peace, solidarity and friendly relations, States parties to the present Charter shall ensure that: (a) any individual enjoying the right of asylum under 12 of the present Charter shall not engage in subversive activities against his country of origin or any other State party to the present Charter; (b) their territories shall not be used as bases for subversive or terrorist activities against the people of any other State party to the present Charter.

Article 24

All peoples shall have the right to a general satisfactory environment favorable to their development.

Article 25

States parties to the present Charter shall have the duty to promote and ensure through teaching, education and publication, the respect of the rights and freedoms contained in the present Charter and to see to it that these freedoms and rights as well as corresponding obligations and duties are understood.

Article 26

States parties to the present Charter shall have the duty to guarantee the independence of the Courts and shall allow the establishment and improvement of appropriate national institutions entrusted with the promotion and protection of the rights and freedoms guaranteed by the present Charter.

Chapter II: Duties

Article 27

1. Every individual shall have duties towards his family and society, the State and other legally recognized communities and the international community.

2. The rights and freedoms of each individual shall be exercised with due regard to the rights of others, collective security, morality and common interest.

Article 28

Every individual shall have the duty to respect and consider his fellow beings without discrimination, and to maintain relations aimed at promoting, safeguarding and reinforcing mutual respect and tolerance.

Article 29

The individual shall also have the duty:

1. To preserve the harmonious development of the family and to work for the cohesion and respect of the family; to respect his parents at all times, to maintain them in case of need;

2. To serve his national community by placing his physical and intellectual abilities at its service;

3. Not to compromise the security of the State whose national or resident he is;

4. To preserve and strengthen social and national solidarity, particularly when the latter is threatened;

5. To preserve and strengthen the national independence and the territorial integrity of his country and to

contribute to its defense in accordance with the law;

6. To work to the best of his abilities and competence, and to pay taxes imposed by law in the interest of the society;

7. To preserve and strengthen positive African cultural values in his relations with other members of the society, in the spirit of tolerance, dialogue and consultation and, in general, to contribute to the promotion of the moral well being of society;

8. To contribute to the best of his abilities, at all times and at all levels, to the promotion and achievement of African unity.

Part II: Measures of Safeguard

Chapter I: Establishment and Organization of the African Commission on Human and Peoples' Rights

Article 30
An African Commission on Human and Peoples' Rights, hereinafter called "the Commission", shall be established within the Organization of African Unity to promote human and peoples' rights and ensure their protection in Africa.

Article 31
1. The Commission shall consist of eleven members chosen from amongst African personalities of the highest reputation, known for their high morality, integrity, impartiality and competence in matters of human and peoples' rights; particular consideration being given to persons having legal experience.
2. The members of the Commission shall serve in their personal capacity.

Article 32
The Commission shall not include more than one national of the same state.

Article 33
The members of the Commission shall be elected by secret ballot by the Assembly of Heads of State and Government, from a list of persons nominated by the States parties to the present Charter.

Article 34
Each State party to the present Charter may not nominate more than two candidates. The candidates must have the nationality of one of the States party to the present Charter. When two candidates are nominated by a State, one of them may not be a national of that State.

Article 35
1. The Secretary General of the Organization of African Unity shall invite States parties to the present Charter at least four months before the elections to nominate candidates;
2. The Secretary General of the Organization of African Unity shall make an alphabetical list of the persons thus nominated and communicate it to the Heads of State and Government at least one month before the elections.

Article 36
The members of the Commission shall be elected for a six year period and shall be eligible for re-election. However, the term of office of four of the members elected at the first election shall terminate after two years and the term of office of three others, at the end of four years.

Article 37
Immediately after the first election, the Chairman of the Assembly of Heads of State and Government of the Organization of African Unity shall draw lots to decide the names of those members referred to in Article 36.

Article 38

After their election, the members of the Commission shall make a solemn declaration to discharge their duties impartially and faithfully.

Article 39

1. In case of death or resignation of a member of the Commission the Chairman of the Commission shall immediately inform the Secretary General of the Organization of African Unity, who shall declare the seat vacant from the date of death or from the date on which the resignation takes effect.
2. If, in the unanimous opinion of other members of the Commission, a member has stopped discharging his duties for any reason other than a temporary absence, the Chairman of the Commission shall inform the Secretary General of the Organization of African Unity, who shall then declare the seat vacant.
3. In each of the cases anticipated above, the Assembly of Heads of State and Government shall replace the member whose seat became vacant for the remaining period of his term unless the period is less than six months.

Article 40

Every member of the Commission shall be in office until the date his successor assumes office.

Article 41

The Secretary General of the Organization of African Unity shall appoint the Secretary of the Commission. He shall also provide the staff and services necessary for the effective discharge of the duties of the Commission. The Organization of African Unity shall bear the costs of the staff and services.

Article 42

1. The Commission shall elect its Chairman and Vice Chairman for a two-year period. They shall be eligible for re-election.
2. The Commission shall lay down its rules of procedure.
3. Seven members shall form the quorum.
4. In case of an equality of votes, the Chairman shall have a casting vote.
5. The Secretary General may attend the meetings of the Commission. He shall not participate in deliberations nor shall he be entitled to vote. The Chairman of the Commission may, however, invite him to speak.

Article 43

In discharging their duties, members of the Commission shall enjoy diplomatic privileges and immunities provided for in the General Convention on the Privileges and Immunities of the Organization of African Unity.

Article 44

Provision shall be made for the emoluments and allowances of the members of the Commission in the Regular Budget of the Organization of African Unity.

Chapter II -- Mandate of the Commission

Article 45

The functions of the Commission shall be:
1. To promote Human and Peoples' Rights and in particular:
   (a) To collect documents, undertake studies and researches on African problems in the field of human and peoples' rights, organize seminars, symposia and conferences, disseminate information, encourage national and local institutions concerned with human and peoples' rights, and should the case arise, give its views or make recommendations to Governments.
   (b) To formulate and lay down, principles and rules aimed at solving legal problems relating to human and peoples' rights and fundamental freedoms upon which African Governments may base their legislations.

(c)   Co-operate with other African and international institutions concerned with the promotion and protection of human and peoples' rights.

2. Ensure the protection of human and peoples' rights under conditions laid down by the present Charter.

3. Interpret all the provisions of the present Charter at the request of a State party, an institution of the OAU or an African Organization recognized by the OAU.

4. Perform any other tasks which may be entrusted to it by the Assembly of Heads of State and Government.

Chapter III -- Procedure of the Commission

Article 46

The Commission may resort to any appropriate method of investigation; it may hear from the Secretary General of the Organization of African Unity or any other person capable of enlightening it.

Communication from States

Article 47

If a State party to the present Charter has good reasons to believe that another State party to this Charter has violated the provisions of the Charter, it may draw, by written communication, the attention of that State to the matter. This communication shall also be addressed to the Secretary General of the OAU and to the Chairman of the Commission. Within three months of the receipt of the communication, the State to which the communication is addressed shall give the enquiring State, written explanation or statement elucidating the matter. This should include as much as possible relevant information relating to the laws and rules of procedure applied and applicable, and the redress already given or course of action available.

Article 48

If within three months from the date on which the original communication is received by the State to which it is addressed, the issue is not settled to the satisfaction of the two States involved through bilateral negotiation or by any other peaceful procedure, either State shall have the right to submit the matter to the Commission through the Chairman and shall notify the other States involved.

Article 49

Notwithstanding the provisions of 47, if a State party to the present Charter considers that another State party has violated the provisions of the Charter, it may refer the matter directly to the Commission by addressing a communication to the Chairman, to the Secretary General of the Organization of African Unity and the State concerned.

Article 50

The Commission can only deal with a matter submitted to it after making sure that all local remedies, if they exist, have been exhausted, unless it is obvious to the Commission that the procedure of achieving these remedies would be unduly prolonged.

Article 51

1. The Commission may ask the States concerned to provide it with all relevant information.

2. When the Commission is considering the matter, States concerned may be represented before it and submit written or oral representation.

Article 52

After having obtained from the States concerned and from other sources all the information it deems necessary and after having tried all appropriate means to reach an amicable solution based on the respect of Human and Peoples' Rights, the Commission shall prepare, within a reasonable period of time from the notification referred to in 48, a report stating the facts and its findings. This report shall be sent to the States concerned and communicated to the Assembly of Heads of State and Government.

Article 53
While transmitting its report, the Commission may make to the Assembly of Heads of State and Government such recommendations as it deems useful.

Article 54
The Commission shall submit to each ordinary Session of the Assembly of Heads of State and Government a report on its activities.

Other Communications

Article 55
1. Before each Session, the Secretary of the Commission shall make a list of the communications other than those of States parties to the present Charter and transmit them to the members of the Commission, who shall indicate which communications should be considered by the Commission.
2. A communication shall be considered by the Commission if a simple majority of its members so decide.

Article 56
Communications relating to human and peoples' rights referred to in 55 received by the Commission, shall be considered if they:
1. Indicate their authors even if the latter request anonymity,
2. Are compatible with the Charter of the Organization of African Unity or with the present Charter,
3. Are not written in disparaging or insulting language directed against the State concerned and its institutions or to the Organization of African Unity,
4. Are not based exclusively on news discriminated through the mass media,
5. Are sent after exhausting local remedies, if any, unless it is obvious that this procedure is unduly prolonged,
6. Are submitted within a reasonable period from the time local remedies are exhausted or from the date the Commission is seized of the matter, and
7. Do not deal with cases which have been settled by these States involved in accordance with the principles of the Charter of the United Nations, or the Charter of the Organization of African Unity or the provisions of the present Charter.

Article 57
Prior to any substantive consideration, all communications shall be brought to the knowledge of the State concerned by the Chairman of the Commission.

Article 58
1. When it appears after deliberations of the Commission that one or more communications apparently relate to special cases which reveal the existence of a series of serious or massive violations of human and peoples' rights, the Commission shall draw the attention of the Assembly of Heads of State and Government to these special cases.
2. The Assembly of Heads of State and Government may then request the Commission to undertake an in depth study of these cases and make a factual report, accompanied by its findings and recommendations.
3. A case of emergency duly noticed by the Commission shall be submitted by the latter to the Chairman of the Assembly of Heads of State and Government who may request an in-depth study.

Article 59
1. All measures taken within the provisions of the present Charter shall remain confidential until such a time as the Assembly of Heads of State and Government shall otherwise decide.
2. However, the report shall be published by the Chairman of the Commission upon the decision of the Assembly of Heads of State and Government.
3. The report on the activities of the Commission shall be published by its Chairman after it has been considered by the Assembly of Heads of State and Government.

Chapter IV -- Applicable Principles

Article 60

The Commission shall draw inspiration from international law on human and peoples' rights, particularly from the provisions of various African instruments on human and peoples' rights, the Charter of the United Nations, the Charter of the Organization of African Unity, the Universal Declaration of Human Rights, other instruments adopted by the United Nations and by African countries in the field of human and peoples' rights as well as from the provisions of various instruments adopted within the Specialized Agencies of the United Nations of which the parties to the present Charter are members.

Article 61

The Commission shall also take into consideration, as subsidiary measures to determine the principles of law, other general or special international conventions, laying down rules expressly recognized by member states of the Organization of African Unity, African practices consistent with international norms on human and people's rights, customs generally accepted as law, general principles of law recognized by African states as well as legal precedents and doctrine.

Article 62

Each state party shall undertake to submit every two years, from the date the present Charter comes into force, a report on the legislative or other measures taken with a view to giving effect to the rights and freedoms recognized and guaranteed by the present Charter.

Article 63

1. The present Charter shall be open to signature, ratification or adherence of the member states of the Organization of African Unity.
2. The instruments of ratification or adherence to the present Charter shall be deposited with the Secretary General of the Organization of African Unity.
3. The present Charter shall come into force three months after the reception by the Secretary General of the instruments of ratification or adherence of a simple majority of the member states of the Organization of African Unity.

Part III: General Provisions

Article 64

1. After the coming into force of the present Charter, members of the Commission shall be elected in accordance with the relevant Articles of the present Charter.
2. The Secretary General of the Organization of African Unity shall convene the first meeting of the Commission at the Headquarters of the Organization within three months of the constitution of the Commission. Thereafter, the Commission shall be convened by its Chairman whenever necessary but at least once a year.

Article 65

For each of the States that will ratify or adhere to the present Charter after its coming into force, the Charter shall take effect three months after the date of the deposit by that State of its instrument of ratification or adherence.

Article 66

Special protocols or agreements may, if necessary, supplement the provisions of the present Charter.

Article 67

The Secretary General of the Organization of African Unity shall inform member states of the Organization of the deposit of each instrument of ratification or adherence.

Article 68

The present Charter may be amended if a State party makes a written request to that effect to the Secretary General of the Organization of African Unity. The Assembly of Heads of State and Government may only consider the draft amendment after all the States parties have been duly informed of it and the Commission has given its opinion on it at the request of the sponsoring State. The amendment shall be approved by a simple majority of the States parties. It shall come into force for each State which has accepted it in accordance with its constitutional procedure three months after the Secretary General has received notice of the acceptance.

AFRICAN COMMISSION ON HUMAN AND PEOPLES' RIGHTS INFORMATION SHEET NO. 2: GUIDELINES ON THE SUBMISSION OF COMMUNICATIONS

African Comm'n on Human and Peoples' Rights Information Sheet No. 2, *Guidelines on the Submission of Communications, available at* http://www.achpr.org/english/_info/guidelines_communications_en.html

Introduction

Most people who suffer human rights abuses sometimes do not know that their rights have been violated, and even if they know, they do not know where or who to turn to for help even within their own countries. It is very important for NGOs and governments to educate people about their human rights and inform them of the local and international remedies available to them when their rights are violated. International intervention is always chosen as a last resort when the local justice delivery system has failed to reinstate the victim in his or her rights.

One of the main functions of the Commission is to attend to communications submitted by individuals, NGOs and States Parties to the African Charter, alleging violations of human rights by these states.

Any person, group of persons of State party alleging a violation, should first of all ascertain whether the State committing the violating has ratified the Charter, and in the case of a State, it must have ratified the Charter before submitting a complaint against another State party to the Charter.

By submitting a communication to the African commission on human and Peoples Rights, victims of human rights abuses who for one reason or another could not obtain justice in their countries after exhausting all the available legal remedies, may obtain help.

Under article 46 of the Charter, the Commission has the power to use any appropriate method of investigation into allegations of human rights abuses. Where the Commission finds that violations have occurred, it makes recommendations to the State(s) concerned; to ensure that the occurrences are investigated, that the victim(s) is compensated (if necessary) and that measures are taken to prevent the recurrence of the violations.

The Commission's recommendations are submitted to the Assembly of Heads of State and Government of the OAU for adoption. The decision of the Assembly is final.

The Rights and Freedoms protected in the Charter
Understanding the rights and freedoms guaranteed in the Charter is particularly important for the submission of a communication because for any communication to be considered by the Commission, it must in one way or another demonstrate that the State has violated one or some of the rights in the charter. The complainant need not mention the specific article of the Charter alleged to have been violated, but the facts of the communication should be such that the Commission can deduce therefrom the violations alleged.

Two main categories of rights are covered in the Charter.

(1) **Individual Rights**
These are the rights and freedoms one enjoys as an individual and not because one belongs to a particular community or social grouping or any other association.

These individual rights are divided into civil and political rights on one hand and economic, social and cultural rights on the other.

(a) Civil and Political Rights
- the right not to be discriminated against **(article 2)**
- equality before the law (article 3)
- the right to inherent dignity and freedom from exploitation, slavery and slave trade; freedom from torture, cruel, inhuman or degrading punishment and treatment **(article 5)**
- the right to personal liberty and security of the person **(article 6)**
- the right to a fair trial **(article 7)**
- freedom of conscience, worship and religion **(article 8)**
- the right to receive information and freedom of expression **(article 9)**
- freedom of association **(article 10)**
- freedom of assembly **(article 11)**
- freedom of movement, including the right to leave and enter one's country and the right to seek and obtain asylum when persecuted **(article 12)**
- the right to participate in the government of one's country and the right of equal access to public service **(article 13)**

(b) Economic, Social and Cultural Rights
- The right to own property **(article 14)**
- the right to work under equitable and satisfactory conditions and receive equal pay for equal work **(article 15)**
- the right to physical and mental health **(article 16)**
- the right to education and the freedom to take part in cultural activities in one's community **(article 17)**
- the family right to protection and assistance from the state, the right to special measures of protection for the aged and disable and the freedom from discrimination of women and children **(article18)**

(2) Peoples' Rights
Although the terms 'peoples rights' have not been defined in the Charter, these rights generally refer to the rights of a community (be it ethnic or national) to determine how they should be governed, how their economies and cultures should develop; they include other rights such as the right to national and international peace and security, the right to a clean and satisfactory environment. This category of rights is also called group or solidarity rights.

Who can submit a communication to the commission?
Anybody, either on his or her own behalf or on behalf of someone else, can submit a communication to the commission denouncing a violation of human rights. Ordinary citizens, a group of individuals, NGOs, and states Parties to the Charter can all put in claims. The complainant or author of the communication need not be related to the victim of the abuse in any way, but the victim must be mentioned.

Complaining on behalf of someone else, for example, a prisoner who can't submit a communication himself or who does not want the authorities to know that he is petitioning is very helpful.

Legal Representation
Since the preparation, submission and processing of a communication is a relatively straightforward procedure, a complainant or author can act on his or her own without the need for professional assistance. However, it is always useful to seek the help of a lawyer. A lawyer would understand the technical aspects better and would therefore be able to advise, recommend, help to interpret the rights alleged to have been violated, draw up additional arguments, and set out the case in an efficient manner that will demonstrate to the Commission that one or more rights have been violated.

The complainant or his/her legal representative (if any), need not travel to the Commission's session to present or defend a case. The case can be started and concluded only through correspondence with the Secretariat of the Commission. However, should the complainant opt to be present at any session of the Commission, the Commission will grant him or her audience.

It should be noted that the Commission does not offer legal assistance to complainants. Persons in need of such assistance may approach one of the various legal assistance groups which exist in most countries or the National Bar Association.

Conditions for submitting a communication.

Article 56 of the African charter outlines seven conditions that must be met before a communication can be considered by the Commission. These are as follows:

- the communication must include the author's name even if the author wants to remain anonymous;
- the communication must be compatible with the Charter of the OAU and with the present Charter.
- the communication must not be written in insulting language directed against the state or the OAU;
- the communication must not be based exclusively on news from the media;
- the complainant must have exhausted all available domestic legal remedies;
- the communication must be submitted within a reasonable time from the date of exhaustion of domestic remedies;
- the communication must not deal with a matter which has already been settled by some other international human rights body.

How Many Violations per communication

From the wordings of article 58(1), of the Charter, it would seem that the Commission can only consider a communication when the latter reveals a series of serious and massive violation of human and peoples' rights, and only after the Assembly of Heads of state and Government has requested it to do so. However, the practice of the Commission has been to consider every communication even if it refers to only a single violation of the Charter. The rationale behind this practice is that a single violation still violates the dignity of the victim and is an affront to international human rights norms.

What a communication should include in order to be valid

All communication must be in writing, and addressed to the Secretary or chairman of the African commission on Human and Peoples' Rights. There is no form or special format that must be followed, but a communication should contain all the relevant information. If the communication is submitted by an individual or group of individuals, it should include the name(s) of the complainant or complainants, their nationalities, occupation or profession, addresses and signatures. If the communication emanates from an NGO, it should include the address of the institution and the names and signatures of its legal representatives.

If the communication is from a State Party, the names and signature of the State representative, together with the national seal would be required.

Each communication should described the violation of human and/or peoples' rights that took place, indicate the date, time (if possible), and place where it occurred. It should also identify the State concerned. The communication should also include the victim's names (even if the latter wants to remain anonymous, in which case, this should be stated), and if possible, the names of any authority familiar with the facts of the case.

It should also provide information indicating that all domestic legal remedies have been exhausted. If all remedies were not exhausted,the communication should indicate the reasons it was not possible to do so.

The complaint should also indicate whether the communication has been or is being considered before any other international human rights body, for instance, the UN human Rights committee.

As a general rule, the communication should state only the facts and not be written in vulgar or insulting language. The complaints should be drafted in a clear, simple and straightforward manner, free from unnecessary rhetoric. Any complainant failing to meet these requirements will be notified and where necessary, asked to furnish the commission with further information.

Emergency Communications

Every communication should indicate if the victim's life, personal integrity or health is in imminent danger. In such emergency situations, the Commission has the powers under **Rule 111** of its Rules of Procedure adopt provisional measures, thereby urging the State concerned not to take any action that will cause irreparable damage to the victim until the case has been heard by the Commission. The Commission can also adopt other urgent measures as it sees fit.

Standard format for the Submission of Communications

As mentioned earlier, there is no hard and fast rule or format for the submission of communications to the commission, but the following simplified guidelines will make it much easier for would-be complainants to submit their communications.

The guidelines are in two categories: (inter-State communications) and other (or individual communications)

(A) Guidelines on how to submit communication under article 48 and 49 (Communications from States)

1. **Complaining State(s)** (should state amongst other things, its name, official language, and year in which it ratified the Charter).
2. State party accused of the violation (state the year the State ratified the African Charter, its official language).
3. Facts constituting the violation (Please explain in as much a factual detail as possible what happened, specifying place, time and dates of the violation, if possible).
4. Exhaustion of local remedies (indicate measures that have been taken to resolve the matter amicable why this measure failed, or why it wasn't used at all. Also indicate measures taken to exhaust local remedies. Please attach all relevant documents).
5. Domestic legal remedies not yet pursued (please give reasons why this has not been done).
6. Other International avenues (state whether the case has also been referred to any other international settlement body either at the UN or within the OAU system).
7. Complaints submitted to the Secretary General of the OAU and to the accused State. These complaint letters should be accompanied by any response from these two sources.

(B) Guidelines on how to submit a communication pursuant to article 5 of the Charter (other communications)

1. **Complainant (s)** (please indicate whether you are acting on your behalf or on behalf of someone else. Also indicate in your communication whether you are an NGO and whether you wish to remain anonymous).

Name ....
Age ....
Nationality ....
Occupation and/or Profession ....
Address ....
Telephone/Fax no ....

2. **Government accused of the Violation** (please make sure it is a State Party to the African charter).
3. **Facts constituting alleged violation** (Explain in as much a factual detail as possible what happened, specifying place, time and dates of the violation).
4. **Urgency of the case** (Is it a case which could result in loss of life/lives or serious bodily harm if not addressed immediately? State the nature of the case and why you think it deserves immediate action from the Commission).

5. **Provisions of the Charter alleged to have been violated** (if you are unsure of the specific articles, please do not mention any).

6. **Names and titles of government authorities** who committed the violation. (if it is a government institution please give the name of the institution as well as that of the head).

7. **Witness to the violation** (include addresses and if possible telephone numbers of witnesses).

8. **Documentary proofs of the violation** (attach for example, letters, legal documents, photos, autopsies, tape recordings etc., to show proof of the violation).

9. **Domestic legal remedies pursued** (Also indicate for example, the courts you've been to, attach copies of court judgments, writs of habeas corpus etc.

10. **Other International Avenue** (Please state whether the case has already been decided or is being heard by some other international human rights body; specify this body and indicate the stage at which the case has reached).

PROTOCOL TO THE AFRICAN CHARTER ON HUMAN AND PEOPLES` RIGHTS ON THE ESTABLISHMENT OF AN AFRICAN COURT ON HUMAN AND PEOPLES` RIGHTS

Protocol to the African Charter on Human and Peoples' Rights on the Establishment of the African Court on Human and Peoples' Rights, *adopted* June 9, 1998, O.A.U. Doc. OAU/LEG/EXP/AFCHPR/PROT (III), *available at* http://www.africa-union.org/root/AU/Documents/Treaties/Text/africancourt-humanrights.pdf

The Member States of the Organization of African Unity hereinafter referred to as the OAU, States Parties to the African Charter on Human and Peoples` Rights.

Considering that the Charter of the Organization of African Unity recognizes that freedom, equality, justice, peace and dignity are essential objectives for the achievement of the legitimate aspirations of the African Peoples;

Noting that the African Charter on Human and Peoples` Rights reaffirms adherence to the principles of Human and Peoples` Rights, freedoms and duties contained in the declarations, conventions and other instruments adopted by the Organization of African Unity, and other international organizations;

Recognizing that the twofold objective of the African Commission on Human and Peoples` Rights is to ensure on the one hand promotion and on the other protection of Human and Peoples` Rights, freedom and duties;

Recognizing further, the efforts of the African Charter on Human and Peoples` Rights in the promotion and protection of Human and Peoples` Rights since its inception in 1987;

Recalling resolution AHGéRes.230 (XXX) adopted by the Assembly of Heads of State and Government in June 1994 in Tunis, Tunisia, requesting the Secretary-General to convene a Government experts` meeting to ponder, in conjunction with the African Commission, over the means to enhance the efficiency of the African commission and to consider in particular the establishment of an African Court on Human and Peoples' Rights; * * *

Firmly convinced that the attainment of the objectives of the African Charter on Human and Peoples` Rights requires the establishment of an African Court on Human and Peoples` Rights to complement and reinforce the functions of the African Commission on Human and Peoples` Rights.

Have agreed as follows:

Article 1
Establishment of the Court

There shall be established within the Organization of African Unity an African Court Human and Peoples` Rights hereinafter referred to as "the Court", the organization, jurisdiction and functioning of which shall be governed by the present Protocol.

Article 2
Relationship between the Court and the Commission

The Court shall, bearing in mind the provisions of this Protocol, complement the protective mandate of the African Commission on Human and Peoples` Rights hereinafter referred to as "the Commission", conferred upon it by the African Charter on Human and Peoples` Rights, hereinafter referred to as "the Charter".

Article 3
Jurisdiction

1. The jurisdiction of the Court shall extend to all cases and disputes submitted to it concerning the interpretation and application of the Charter, this Protocol and any other relevant Human Rights instrument ratified by the States concerned.
2. In the event of a dispute as to whether the Court has jurisdiction, the Court shall decide.

Article 4
Advisory Opinions

1. At the request of a Member State of the OAU, the OAU, any of its organs, or any African organization recognized by the OAU, the Court may provide an opinion on any legal matter relating to the Charter or any other relevant human rights instruments, provided that the subject matter of the opinion is not related to a matter being examined by the Commission.
2. The Court shall give reasons for its advisory opinions provided that every judge shall be entitled to deliver a separate of dissenting decision.

Article 5
Access to the Court

1. The following are entitled to submit cases to the Court:
   a) The Commission
   b) The State Party which had lodged a complaint to the Commission
   c) The State Party against which the complaint has been lodged at the Commission
   d) The State Party whose citizen is a victim of human rights violation
   e) African Intergovernmental Organizations
2. When a State Party has an interest in a case, it may submit a request to the Court to be permitted to join.
3. The Court may entitle relevant Non Governmental organizations (NGOs) with observer status before the Commission, and individuals to institute cases directly before it, in accordance with article 34 (6) of this Protocol.

Article 6
Admissibility of Cases

1. The Court, when deciding on the admissibility of a case instituted under article 5 (3) of this Protocol, may request the opinion of the Commission which shall give it as soon as possible.
2. The Court shall rule on the admissibility of cases taking into account the provisions of article 56 of the Charter.
3. The Court may consider cases or transfer them to the Commission.

Article 7
Sources of Law

238

The Court shall apply the provision of the Charter and any other relevant human rights instruments ratified by the States concerned.

Article 8
Consdieration of Cases

The Rules of Procedure of the Court shall lay down the detailed conditions under which the Court shall consider cases brought before it, bearing in mind the complementarity between the Commission and the Court.

Article 9
Amicable Settlement

The Court may try to reach an amicable settlement in a case pending before it in accordance with the provisions of the Charter.

Article 10
Hearings and Representation

1. The Court shall conduct its proceedings in public. The Court may, however, conduct proceedings in camera as may be provided for in the Rules of Procedure.
2. Any party to a case shall be entitled to be represented by a legal representative of the party's choice. Free legal representation may be provided where the interests of justice so require.
3. Any person, witness or representative of the parties, who appears before the Court, shall enjoy protection and all facilities, in accordance with international law, necessary for the discharging of their functions, tasks and duties in relation to the Court.

Article 11
Composition

1. The Court shall consist of eleven judges, nationals of Member States of the OAU, elected in an individual capacity from among jurists of high moral character and of recognized practical, judicial or academic competence and experience in the field of human and peoples` rights.
2. No two judges shall be nationals of the same State.

Article 12
Nominations

1. States Parties to the Protocol may each propose up to three candidates, at least two of whom shall be nationals of that State.
2. Due consideration shall be given to adequate gender representation in nomination process.

Article 13
List of Candidates

1. Upon entry into force of this Protocol, the Secretary-general of the OAU shall request each State Party to the Protocol to present, within ninety (90) days of such a request, its nominees for the office of judge of the Court.
2. The Secretary-General of the OAU shall prepare a list in alphabetical order of the candidates nominated and transmit it to the Member States of the OAU at least thirty days prior to the next session of the Assembly of Heads of State and Government of the OAU hereinafter referred to as "the Assembly".

Article 14
Elections

1. The judges of the Court shall be elected by secret ballot by the Assembly from the list referred to in Article 13 (2) of the present Protocol.
2. The Assembly shall ensure that in the Court as a whole there is representation of the main regions of Africa and of their principal legal traditions.
3. In the election of the judges, the Assembly shall ensure that there is adequate gender representation.

Article 15

Term of Office

1. The judges of the Court shall be elected for a period of six years and may be re-elected only once. The terms of four judges elected at the first election shall expire at the end of two years, and the terms of four more judges shall expire at the end of four years.

2. The judges whose terms are to expire at the end of the initial periods of two and four years shall be chosen by lot to be drawn by the Secretary-General of the OAU immediately after the first election has been completed.

3. A judge elected to replace a judge whose term of office has not expired shall hold office for the remainder of the predecessor's term.

4. All judges except the President shall perform their functions on a part-time basis. However, the Assembly may change this arrangement as it deems appropriate.

Article 16
Oath of office

After their election, the judges of the Court shall make a solemn declaration to discharge their duties impartially and faithfully.

Article 17
Independence

1. The independence of the judges shall be fully ensured in accordance with international law.

2. No judge may hear any case in which the same judge has previously taken part as agent, counsel or advocate for one of the parties or as a member of a national or international court or a commission of enquiry or in any other capacity. Any doubt on this point shall be settled by decision of the Court.

3. The judges of the Court shall enjoy, from the moment of their election and throughout their term of office, the immunities extended to diplomatic agents in accordance with international law.

4. At no time shall the judges of the Court be held liable for any decision or opinion issued in the exercise of their functions.

Article 18
Incompatibility

The position of judge of the court is incompatible with any activity that might interfere with the independence or impartiality of such a judge or the demands of the office as determined in the Rules of Procedure of the Court.

Article 19
Cessation of Office

1. A judge shall not be suspended or removed from office unless, by the unanimous decision of the other judges of the Court, the judge concerned has been found to be no longer fulfilling the required conditions to be a judge of the Court.

2. Such a decision of the Court shall become final unless it is set aside by the Assembly at its next session.

Article 20
Vacancies

1. In case of death or resignation of a judge of the Court, the President of the Court shall immediately inform the Secretary General of the Organization of African Unity, who shall declare the seat vacant from the date of death or from the date on which the resignation takes effect.

2. The Assembly shall replace the judge whose office became vacant unless the remaining period of the term is less than one hundred and eighty (180) days.

3. The same procedure and considerations as set out in Articles 12, 13 and 14 shall be followed for the filling of vacancies.

Article 21
Presidency of the Court

1. The Court shall elect its President and one Vice-President for a period of two years. They may be re-elected only once.

2. The President shall perform judicial functions on a full-time basis and shall reside at the seat of the

Court.

3. The functions of the President and the Vice-President shall be set out in the Rules of Procedure of the Court.

Article 22
Exclusion

If the judge is a national of any State which is a party to a case submitted to the Court, that judge shall not hear the case.

Article 23
Quorum

The Court shall examine cases brought before it, if it has a quorum of at least seven judges.

Article 24
Registry of the Court

1. The Court shall appoint its own Registrar and other staff of the registry from among nationals of Member States of the OAU according to the Rules of Procedure.

2. The office and residence of the Registrar shall be at the place where the Court has its seat.

Article 25
Seat of the Court

1. The Court shall have its seat at the place determined by the Assembly from among States parties to this Protocol. However, it may convene in the territory of any Member State of the OAU when the majority of the Court considers it desirable, and with the prior consent of the State concerned.

2. The seat of the Court may be changed by the Assembly after due consultation with the Court.

Article 26
Evidence

1. The Court shall hear submissions by all parties and if deemed necessary, hold an enquiry. The States concerned shall assist by providing relevant facilities for the efficient handling of the case.

2. The Court may receive written and oral evidence including expert testimony and shall make its decision on the basis of such evidence.

Article 27
Findings

1. If the Court finds that there has been violation of a human or peoples' rights, it shall make appropriate orders to remedy the violation, including the payment of fair compensation or reparation.

2. In cases of extreme gravity and urgency, and when necessary to avoid irreparable harm to persons, the Court shall adopt such provisional measures as it deems necessary.

Article 28
Judgment

1. The Court shall render its judgment within ninety (90) days of having completed its deliberations.

2. The judgment of the Court decided by majority shall be final and not subject to appeal.

3. Without prejudice to sub-article 2 above, the Court may review its decision in the light of new evidence under conditions to be set out in the Rules of Procedure.

4. The Court may interpret its own decision.

5. The judgment of the Court shall be read in open court, due notice having been given to the parties.

6. Reasons shall be given for the judgment of the Court.

7. If the judgment of the court does not represent, in whole or in part, the unanimous decision of the judges, any judge shall be entitled to deliver a separate or dissenting opinion.

Article 29
Notification of Judgment

1. The parties to the case shall be notified of the judgment of the Court and it shall be transmitted to the Member States of the OAU and the Commission.

2. The Council of Ministers shall also be notified of the judgment and shall monitor its execution on behalf of the Assembly.

Article 30
Execution of Judgment

The States Parties to the present Protocol undertake to comply with the judgment in any case to which they are parties within the time stipulated by the Court and to guarantee its execution.

Article 31
Report

The Court shall submit to each regular session of the Assembly, a report on its work during the previous year. The report shall specify, in particular, the cases in which a State has not complied with the Court's judgment.

Article 32
Budget

Expenses of the Court, emoluments and allowances for judges and the budget of its registry, shall be determined and borne by the OAU, in accordance with criteria laid down by the OAU in consultation with the Court.

Article 33
Rules of Procedure

The Court shall draw up its Rules and determine its own procedures. The Court shall consult the Commission as appropriate.

Article 34
Ratification

1. This Protocol shall be open for signature and ratification or accession by any State Party to the Charter.
2. The instrument of ratification or accession to the present Protocol shall be deposited with the Secretary-General of the OAU.
3. The Protocol shall come into force thirty days after fifteen instruments of ratification or accession have been deposited.
4. For any State Party ratifying or acceding subsequently, the present Protocol shall come into force in respect of that State on the date of the deposit of its instrument of ratification or accession.
5. The Secretary-General of the OAU shall inform all Member States of the entry into force of the present Protocol.
6. At the time of the ratification of this Protocol or any time thereafter, the State shall make a declaration accepting the competence of the Court to receive cases under article 5 (3) of this Protocol. The Court shall not receive any petition under article 5 (3) involving a State Party which has not made such a declaration.
7. Declarations made under sub-article (6) above shall be deposited with the Secretary-General, who shall transmit copies thereof to the State parties.

Article 35
Amendments

1. The present Protocol may be amended if a State Party to the Protocol makes a written request to that effect to the Secretary-General of the OAU. The Assembly may adopt, by simple majority, the draft amendment after all the State Parties to the present Protocol have been duly informed of it and the Court has given its opinion on the amendment.
2. The Court shall also be entitled to propose such amendments to the present Protocol as it may deem necessary, through the Secretary-General of the OAU.
3. The amendment shall come into force for each State Party which has accepted it thirty days after the Secretary-General of the OAU has received notice of the acceptance.

CONSTITUTIVE ACT OF THE AFRICAN UNION

Constitutive Act of the African Union, *adopted* July 11, 2000, 2158 U.N.T.S. 3

We, the Heads of State and Government of the Member States of the Organization of the African Unity (OAU): * * *

Inspired by the noble ideals which guided the founding fathers of our Continental Organization and generations of Pan Africanists in their determination to promote unity, solidarity, cohesion and cooperation among the peoples of Africa and African States;

Considering the principles and objectives stated in the Charter of the Organization of African Unity and the Treaty establishing the African Economic Community;

Recalling the heroic struggles waged by out peoples and our countries for political independence, human dignity and economic emancipation;

Considering that since its inception, the Organization of African Unity has played a determining and invaluable role in the liberation of the continent, the affirmation of a common identity and the process of attainment of the unity of our continent and has provided a unique framework for our collective action in Africa and in our relations with the rest of the world;

Determined to take up the multifaceted challenges that confront our continent and peoples in the light of the social, economic and political changes taking place in the world;

Convinced of the need to accelerate the process of implementing the Treaty establishing the African Economic Community in order to promote the socio-economic development of Africa and to face more effectively the challenges posed by globalization;

Guided by our common vision of a united and strong Africa and by the need to build a partnership between governments and all segments of civil society, in particular women, youth and the private sector, in order to strengthen solidarity and cohesion among our peoples;

Conscious of the fact that the scourge of conflicts in Africa constitutes a major impediment to the socio-economic development of the continent and of the need to promote peace, security and stability as a prerequisite for the implementation of our development and integration agenda;

Determined to promote and protect human and people's rights, consolidate democratic institutions and culture, and to ensure good governance and the rule of law;

Further determined to take all necessary measures to strengthen our common institutions and provide them with the necessary powers and resources to enable them discharge their respective mandates effectively;

Recalling the Declaration which we adopted at the Fourth Extraordinary Session of our Assembly in Sirte, the Great Socialist People's Libyan Arab Jamahiriya, on 9.9.99, in which we decided to establish an African Union, in conformity with the ultimate objectives of the Charter of our Continental Organization and the Treaty establishing the African Economic Community;

Have agreed as follows:

Article 1
Definitions

In this Constitutive Act:

"Act" means the present Constitutive Act;

"AEC" means the African Economic Community;
"Assembly" means the Assembly of Heads of State and Government of the Union;
"Charter" means the Charter of the OAU;
"Commission" means the Secretariat of the Union;
"Committee" means a Specialized Technical Committee of the Union;
"Council" means the Economic, Social and Cultural Council of the Union;
"Court" means the Court of Justice of the Union;
"Executive Council" means the Executive Council of Ministers of the Union;
"Member State" means a Member State of the Union;
"OAU" means the Organization of African Unity;
"Parliament" means the Pan African Parliament of the Union;
"Union" means the African Union established by the present Constitutive Act.

Article 2
Establishment
The African Union is hereby established in accordance with the provisions of this Act.

Article 3
Objectives
The objectives of the Union shall be to:
(a) achieve greater unity and solidarity between the African countries and the peoples of Africa;
(b) defend the sovereignty, territorial integrity and independence of its Member States;
(c) accelerate the political and socio-economic integration of the continent;
(d) promote and defend African common positions on issues of interest to the continent and its peoples;
(e) encourage international cooperation, taking due account of the Charter of the United Nations and the Universal Declaration of Human Rights;
(f) promote peace, security, and stability on the continent;
(g) promote democratic principles and institutions, popular participation and good governance;
(h) Promote and protect human and people's rights in accordance with the African Charter on Human and People's Rights and other relevant human rights instruments;
(i) establish the necessary conditions which enable the continent to play its rightful role in the global economy and in international negotiations;
(j) promote sustainable development at the economic, social and cultural levels as well as the integration of African economies;
(k) promote co-operation in all fields of human activity to raise the living standards of African peoples;
(l) coordinate and harmonize the policies between the existing and future Regional Economic Communities for the gradual attainment of the objectives of the Union;
(m) advance the development of the continent by promoting research in all fields, in particular in science and technology;
(n) work with relevant international partners in the eradication of preventable diseases and the promotion of good health on the continent.

Article 4
Principles
The Union shall function in accordance with the following principles:
(a) sovereign equality and interdependence among Member States of the Union;
(b) respect of borders existing on achievement of independence;
(c) participation of the African peoples in the activities of the Union;
(d) establishment of a common defense policy for the African Continent;
(e) peaceful resolution of conflicts among Member States of the Union through such appropriate means as may be decided upon by the Assembly;
(f) prohibition of the use of force or threat to use force among Member States of the Union;
(g) non-interference by any Member State in the internal affairs of another;
(h) the right of the Union to intervene in a Member State pursuant to a decision of the Assembly in respect of grave circumstances, namely: war crimes, genocide and crimes against humanity;
(i) peaceful co-existence of Member States and their right to live in peace and security;

(j) the right of Member States to request intervention from the Union in order to restore peace and security;

(k) promotion of self-reliance within the framework of the Union;

(l) promotion of gender equality;

(m) respect for democratic principles, human rights, the rule of law and good governance;

(n) promotion of social justice to ensure balanced economic development;

(o) respect for the sanctity of human life, condemnation and rejection of impunity and political assassination, acts of terrorism and subversive activities;

(p) condemnation and rejection of unconstitutional changes of governments.

Article 5
Organs of the Union

1. The organs of the Union shall be:
    (a) The Assembly of the Union;
    (b) The Executive Council;
    (c) The Pan African Parliament;
    (d) The Court of Justice;
    (e) The Commission;
    (f) The Permanent Representatives Committee;
    (g) The Specialized Technical Committees;
    (h) The Economic, Social and Cultural Council;
    (i) The Financial Institutions;
2. Other organs that the Assembly may decide to establish.

Article 6
The Assembly

1. The Assembly shall be composed of Heads of State and Government or their duly accredited representatives.

2. The Assembly shall be the supreme organ of the Union.

3. The Assembly shall meet at least once a year in ordinary session. At the request of any Member State and on approval by a two-thirds majority of the Member States, the Assembly shall meet in extraordinary session.

4. The Office of the Chairman of the Assembly shall be held for a period of one year by a Head State or Government elected after consultations among the Member States.

Article 7
Decisions of the Assembly

1. The Assembly shall take its decisions by consensus or, failing which, by a two- thirds majority of the Member States of the Union. However, procedural matters, including the question of whether a matter is one of procedure or not, shall be decided by a simple majority.

2. Two-thirds of the total membership of the Union shall forma quorum at any meeting of the Assembly.

Article 8
Rules of Procedure of the Assembly

The Assembly shall adopt its own Rules of Procedure.

Article 9
Powers and Functions of the Assembly

1. The functions of the Assembly shall be to:
    (a) determine the common policies of the Union;
    (b) receive, consider and take decisions on reports and recommendations from the other organs of the Union;
    (c) consider requests for Membership of the Union;
    (d) establish any organ of the Union;
    (e) monitor the implementation of policies and decisions of the Union as well as ensure compliance by all Member States;
    (f) adopt the budget of the Union;

(g) give directives to the Executive Council on the management of conflicts, war and other emergency situations and the restoration of peace;

(h) appoint and terminate the appointment of the judges of the Court of Justice;

(i) appoint the Chairman of the Commission and his or her deputy or deputies and Commissioners of the Commission and determine their functions and terms of office.

2. The Assembly may delegate any of its powers and functions to any organ of the Union.

Article 10
The Executive Council

1. The Executive Council shall be composed of Ministers of Foreign Affairs or such other Ministers or Authorities as are designated by the Governments of Member States.

2. The Executive Council shall meet at least twice a year in ordinary session. It shall also meet in an extraordinary session at the request of any Member State and upon approval by two-thirds of all Member States.

Article 11
Decisions of the Executive Council

1. The Executive Council shall take its decisions by consensus or, failing which, by a two-thirds majority of the Member States. However, procedural matters, including the question of whether a matter is one of procedure or not, shall be decided by a simple majority.

2. Two-thirds of the total membership of the Union shall form a quorum at any meeting of the Executive Council.

Article 12
Rules of Procedure of the Executive Council

The Executive Council shall adopt its own Rules of Procedure.

Article 13
Functions of the Executive Council

1. The Executive Council shall coordinate and take decisions on policies in areas of common interest to the Member States, including the following:

(a) foreign trade;

(b) energy, industry and mineral resources;

(c) food, agricultural and animal resources, livestock production and forestry;

(d) water resources and irrigation;

(e) environmental protection, humanitarian action and disaster response and relief;

(f) transport and communications;

(g) insurance;

(h) education, culture, health and human resources development;

(i) science and technology

(j) nationality, residency and immigration matters;

(k) social security, including the formulation of mother and child care policies, as well as policies relating to the disabled and the handicapped;

(l) establishment of a system of African awards, medals and prizes.

2. The Executive Council shall be responsible to the Assembly. It shall consider issues referred to it and monitor the implementation of policies formulated by the Assembly.

3. The Executive Council may delegate any of its powers and functions mentioned in paragraph 1 of this Article to the Specialized Technical Committees established under Article 14 of this Act.

Article 14
The Specialized Technical Committees Establishment and Composition

1. There is hereby established the following Specialized Technical Committees, which shall be responsible to the Executive Council:

(a) The Committee on Rural Economy and Agricultural Matters;

(b) The Committee on Monetary and Financial Affairs;

(c) The Committee on Trade, Customs and Immigration Matters;

(d) The Committee on Industry, Science and Technology, Energy, Natural Resources and Environment;

(e) The Committee on Transport, Communications and Tourism;

(f) The Committee on Health, Labour and Social Affairs; and

(g) The Committee on Education, Culture and Human Resources.

2. The Assembly shall, whenever it deems appropriate, restructure the existing Committees or establish other Committees.

3. The Specialized Technical Committees shall be composed of Ministers or senior officials responsible for sectors falling within their respective areas of competence.

Article 15
Functions of the Specialized Technical Committees

Each Committee shall within its field of competence:

(a) prepare projects and programmes of the Union and submit it to the Executive Council;

(b) ensure the supervision, follow-up and the evaluation of the implementation of decisions taken by the organs of the Union;

(c) ensure the coordination and harmonization of projects and programmes of the Union;

(d) submit to the Executive Council either on its own initiative or at the request of the Executive Council, reports and recommendations on the implementation of the provisions of this Act; and

(e) carry out any other functions assigned to it for the purpose of ensuring the implementation of the provisions of this Act.

Article 16
Meetings

Subject to any directives given by the Executive Council, each Committee shall meet as often as necessary and shall prepare its Rules of Procedure and submit them to the Executive Council for approval.

Article 17
The Pan African Parliament

1. In order to ensure the full participation of African peoples in the development and economic integration of the continent, a Pan African Parliament shall be established.

2. The composition, powers, functions and organization of the Pan African Parliament shall be defined in a protocol relating thereto.

Article 18
The Court of Justice

1. A Court of Justice of the Union shall be established;

2. The statute, composition and functions of the Court of Justice shall be defined in a protocol relating thereto.

Article 19
The Financial Institutions

The Union shall have the following financial institutions whose rules and regulations shall be defined in protocols relating thereto:

(a) The Africa Central Bank

(b) The African Monetary Fund;

(c) The African Investment Bank.

Article 20
The Commission

1. There shall be established a Commission of the Union, which shall be the Secretariat of the Union.

2. The commission shall be composed of the Chairman, his or her deputy or deputies and the Commissioners. They shall be assisted by the necessary staff for the smooth functioning of the Commission.

3. The structure, functions and regulations of the Commission shall be determined by the Assembly.

Article 21
The Permanent Representatives Committee

1. There shall be established a Permanent Representatives Committee. IT shall be composed of Permanent Representatives to the Union and other Plenipotentiaries of Member States.
2. The Permanent Representatives Committee shall be charged with the responsibility of preparing the work of the Executive Council and acting on the Executive Council's instructions. It may set up such sub-committees or working groups as it may deem necessary.

Article 22
The Economic, Social and Cultural Council

1. The Economic, Social and Cultural Council shall be an advisory organ composed of different social and professional groups of the Member States of the Union.
2. The functions, powers, composition and organization of the Economic, Social and Cultural Council shall be determined by the Assembly.

Article 23
Imposition of Sanctions

1. The Assembly shall determine the appropriate sanctions to be imposed on any Member State that defaults in the payment of its contributions to the budget of the Union in the following manner: denial of the right to speak at meetings, to vote, to present candidates for any position or post within the Union or to benefit from any activity or commitments, therefrom;
2. Furthermore, any Member State that fails to comply with the decisions and policies of the Union may be subjected to other sanctions, such as the denial of transport and communications links with other Member States, and other measures of a political and economic nature to be determined by the Assembly.

Article 24
The Headquarters of the Union

1. The Headquarters of the Union shall be in Addis Ababa in the Federal Democratic Republic of Ethiopia.
2. There may be established such other offices of the Union as the Assembly may, on the recommendation of the Executive Council, determine.

Article 25
Working languages

The working languages of the Union and all its institutions shall be, if possible, African languages, Arabic, English, French and Portuguese.

Article 26
Interpretation

The Court shall be seized with matters of interpretation arising from the application or implementation of this Act. Pending its establishment, such matters shall be submitted to the Assembly of the Union, which shall decide by two-thirds majority.

Article 27
Signature, Ratification and Accession

1. This Act shall be open to Signature, ratification and accession by the Member States of the OAU in accordance with their respective constitutional procedures.
2. The instruments of ratification shall be deposited with the Secretary General of the OAU.
3. Any Member State if the OAU acceding to this Act after its entry into force shall deposit the instrument of accession with the Chairman of the Commission.

Article 28
Entry into Force

This Act shall enter into force thirty (30) days after the deposit of the instruments of ratification by two-thirds of the Member States of the OAU.

Article 29
Admission to Membership

1. Any African State may, at any time after the entry into force of this Act, notify the Chairman of the Commission of its intention to accede to this Act and to be admitted as a member of the Union.
2. The Chairman of the Commission shall, upon receipt of such notification, transmit copies thereof to all Member States. Admission shall be decided by a simple majority of the Member States. The decision of each Member State shall be transmitted to the Chairman of the Commission who shall, upon receipt of the required number of votes, communicate the decision to the State concerned.

Article 30
Suspension

Governments which shall come to power through unconstitutional means shall not be allowed to participate in the activities of the Union.

Article 31
Cessation of Membership

1. Any State which desires to renounce its membership shall forward a written notification to the Chairman of the Commission, who shall inform Member States thereof. At the end of one year from the date of such notification, if not withdrawn, the Act shall cease to apply with respect to the renouncing State, which shall thereby cease to belong to the Union.
2. During the period of one year referred to in paragraph 1 of this Article, any Member State wishing to withdraw from the Union shall comply with the provisions of this Act shall be bound to discharge its obligations under this Act up to the date of its withdrawal.

Article 32
Amendment and Revision

1. Any Member State may submit proposals for the amendment or revision of this Act;
2. Proposals for amendment or revision shall be submitted to the Chairman of the Commission who shall transmit same to Member States within thirty (30) days of receipt thereof;
3. The Assembly, upon the advice of the Executive Council, shall examine these proposals within a period of one year following notification of Member States, in accordance with the provisions of paragraph 2 of this Article;
4. Amendments or revisions shall be adopted by the Assembly by consensus or, failing which, by a two-thirds majority and submitted for ratification by all Member States in accordance with their respective constitutional procedures. They shall enter into force thirty (30) days after the deposit of the instruments of ratification with the Chairman of the Commission by a two-thirds majority of the Member States.

Article 33
Transitional Arrangements and Final Provisions

1. This Act shall replace the Charter of the Organization of African Unity. However, the Charter shall remain operative for a transitional period of one year or such further period as may be determined by the Assembly, following the entry into force of the Act, for the purpose of enabling the OAU / AEC to undertake the necessary measures regarding the devolution of its assets and liabilities to the Union and all matters relating thereto.
2. The provisions of this Act shall take precedence over and supercede any inconsistent or contrary provisions of the Treaty establishing the African Economic Community.
3. Upon the entry into force of this Act, all necessary measures shall be undertaken to implement its provisions and to ensure the establishment of the organs provided for under the Act in accordance with any directives or decisions which may be adopted in this regard by the Parties thereto within the transitional period stipulated above.
4. Pending the establishment of the Commission, the OAU General Secretariat shall be the interim Secretariat of the Union.

5. This Act, drawn up in four (4) original texts in the Arabic, English, French and Portuguese languages, all four (4) being equally authentic, shall be deposited with the Secretary General of the OAU and, after its entry into force, with the Chairman of the Commission who shall transmit a certified true copy of the Act to the Government of each signatory State. The Secretary General of the OAU and the Chairman of the Commission shall notify all signatory States of the dates of the deposit of the instruments of ratification or accession and shall upon entry into force of this Act register the same with the Secretariat of the United Nations.

AFRICAN COURT ON HUMAN AND PEOPLES' RIGHTS INTERIM RULES OF COURT

African Court on Human and Peoples' Rights Interim Rules of Court,
http://www.chr.up.ac.za/hr_docs/documents/courtrules.pdf

PREAMBLE

The Court,

In accordance with the African Charter on Human and Peoples' Rights of 27 June 1981 and the Protocol thereof on the Establishment of an African Court on Human and Peoples' Rights dated 10 June 1998,

And in pursuance of article 33 of the Protocol,

Adopts the following Rules of Court which shall be known as the "Interim Rules of Court".

Rule 1
Definitions

For the purposes of these Rules, unless the context otherwise indicates:
a. "Assembly" means the Assembly of Heads of State and Government of the African Union;
b. "Charter" means the African Charter on Human and Peoples' Rights;
c. "Commission" means the African Commission on Human and Peoples' Rights;
d. "Constitutive Act" means the Constitutive Act of the African Union;
e. "Court" means the African Court on Human and Peoples' Rights;
f. "Executive Council" means the Executive Council of the African Union;
g. "Judge" means a Member of the Court;
h. "Member State" means a Member State of the African Union;
i. "President" means the President of the Court;
j. "Protocol" means the Protocol to the African Charter on Human and Peoples' Rights on the Establishment of an African Court on Human and Peoples' Rights;
k. "Registrar" means the Registrar of the Court;
l. "Registry" means Registry of the Court;
m. "Rules" mean the present Rules;
n. "State Party" means a State Party to the Protocol to the African Charter on Human and Peoples' Rights on the Establishment of an African Court on Human and Peoples' Rights;
o. "Vice President" means the Vice President of the Court.

PART I - THE COURT

CHAPTER I - MEMBERS OF THE COURT

Rule 2
Term of Office

1. The newly elected Judges will assume duty on the first day of the first ordinary session following their election. Before assuming duty, the elected Judges shall take an oath of office or make a declaration in accordance with Rule 4 of these Rules.

2. Notwithstanding the foregoing sub-rule, outgoing Members of the Court shall remain in office until such time as they are replaced; after they are replaced, they shall continue to sit until the completion of all stages of any case in which the Court has met for an oral hearing prior to the date of replacement.

Rule 3
Precedence

1. The Members of the Court, in the exercise of their functions, are of equal status, irrespective of age, date of election or length of service.

2. Members of the Court shall, except as provided in sub-rule 4 and 5 of this Rule, take precedence according to the date on which their terms of office respectively began pursuant to Rule 2 of these Rules.

3. Members of the Court who assume duty on the same date shall take precedence, in relation to one another, according to seniority of age.

4. A Member of the Court who is re-elected to a new term of office which is continuous with his/her previous term shall retain his/her precedence.

5. The President and the Vice-President of the Court, while holding these offices, shall take precedence before all other Members of the Court.

6. The Member of the Court who is, in accordance with the foregoing subrules, next in precedence after the President and the Vice-President, is in these Rules designated as "the Senior Member of the Court". Whenever that Member is unable to act, the Member of the Court who is next after him in precedence and able to act shall be considered the Senior Member of the Court.

Rule 4
Oath of Office or Solemn Declaration

1. Pursuant to article 16 of the Protocol, each Member of the Court shall make the following oath or solemn declaration: "I …….. (full names of Judge) do swear or solemnly declare that I will perform my duties and exercise my powers as a Member of the Court honourably, faithfully, impartially and conscientiously, and that I will preserve the confidentiality of its deliberations even after my term of office has expired".

2. This oath/declaration shall be taken/made in a public sitting as soon as possible after his/her election, and if necessary, a special public sitting shall be held for this purpose.

3. A Member of the Court who is re-elected shall take/make a new oath/declaration only if his/her new term is not continuous with his/her previous one.

Rule 5
Incompatibility

1. In accordance with the terms of article 18 of the Protocol, during their term in office, no Members of the Court shall participate in any other activity of a nature that will compromise the independence and impartiality of such a Judge or the demands of the office.

2. In particular, the Members of the Court may not hold political, diplomatic or administrative positions or function as government legal advisers at the national level.

3. Each Member of the Court shall declare any other activities to the Court.

Rule 6
Resignation

1. In the event of the resignation of a Member of the Court, the notice of resignation shall be tendered to the President of the Court, who shall notify the Chairperson of the African Union Commission of the same. Upon the latter notification, the seat shall be considered vacant.

2. Where the Member of the Court who decides to resign is the President, he/she shall announce his/her decision to the Vice President who shall notify the Chairperson of the African Union Commission and the resignation shall take effect in accordance with the terms of sub-rule 1 of the present Rule.

Rule 7
Suspension or Removal

251

1. Where the application of article 19(1) of the Protocol is under consideration, the President or, if the circumstances so require, the Vice-President, shall inform the Member of the Court concerned accordingly, in a written statement which shall include the grounds thereof and any relevant evidence. He/she shall, subsequently, at a private session of the Court specially convened for the purpose, be afforded an opportunity of making a statement, of furnishing any information or explanations he/she wishes to give, and of supplying answers, orally or in writing, to any questions put to him/her. At a further private session, at which the Member of the Court concerned shall not be present, the matter shall be considered; each Member of the Court shall state his/her opinion and, if requested, a vote shall be taken.

2. Any decision to suspend or remove a Member of the Court shall be communicated to the Chairperson of the African Union Commission.

Rule 8
Inability to Sit, Exemption and Withdrawal

1. Any Member of the Court who is unable to attend a sitting of the Court shall notify the President as early as possible.

2. In accordance with article 22 of the Protocol, any Member of the Court who is a national of a State that is party to a case shall abstain from hearing that case.

3. A Member of the Court shall also abstain from hearing cases in which the State by virtue of which he/she was elected is a party.

4. No Member of the Court shall take part in the consideration of any case if:

> a) he/she has previously acted, in relation to the case, as agent, counsel or advocate for one of the parties, or as a member of a national or international court or a commission of inquiry or in any other capacity;
> b) he/she has a personal interest in the case, including a spousal, parental or other close family, personal or professional relationship, or a subordinate relationship with any of the parties;
> c) he/she has expressed opinions publicly, through the communications media, in writing, through his or her public actions or otherwise, that may, objectively adversely affect his or her impartiality;
> d) for any other reason, his/her independence or impartiality may, legitimately, be called into doubt;

5. If a Member intends to withdraw for any of the aforesaid reasons he/she shall, accordingly, notify the President of the Court, who shall exempt such Judge from participation in the hearing of the matter.

6. In the event of any doubt as to the existence of any of the grounds for withdrawal listed in this Rule, the Member concerned shall make his/her disclosures to the Court, and deliberations and voting on the matter shall be carried out in his/her absence.

CHAPTER II – THE OFFICE OF THE PRESIDENT AND VICE-PRESIDENT

Rule 9
Term of Office

1. The President and Vice President shall be elected for a priod of two (2) years and may be re-elected only once. However, none of them may continue to hold office should they cease to be a Member of the Court.

2. The term of office of the President and Vice President shall begin to run on the commencement date of the terms of office of the Members of the Court elected in a biennial election, pursuant to Rule 2 of these Rules.

3. The elections of the President and Vice-President shall be held on the above mentioned date or shortly thereafter. The outgoing President or Vice-President, if still a Member of the Court, shall continue to exercise the functions of his/her office until the election has taken place.

4. If for any reason, the President or the Vice President ceases to be a Member of the Court before the expiry of his/her term of office, the Court shall elect a successor for the remainder of the term.

Rule 10
Elections

1. If on the date of the election to the Presidency, the outgoing President is still a Member of the Court, he/she shall conduct the election. If he/she has ceased to be a Member of the Court, is unable to act, or is himself/herself a candidate, the election shall be conducted by the Member of the Court exercising the functions of the Presidency pursuant to Rule 12, sub-rule 1 of these Rules.

2. The vote shall be taken by secret ballot after the Member of the Court acting as President indicates the number of votes required to be elected.

3. The Member of the Court obtaining the votes of the absolute majority of all the Judges of the Court shall be declared elected.

4. If no Member of the Court obtains the absolute majority required during the first ballot, the Judge having obtained the least number of votes shall withdraw. If during the second ballot no candidate receives the majority required, a third round shall take place between the two candidates having obtained the greatest number of votes. An additional round or additional rounds shall take place until one candidate has achieved the required majority. In the event of a tied vote, preference shall be given to the Judge having precedence under the terms of Rule 3 of these Rules.

5. The Member of the Court who is elected President shall take office immediately.

6. The incoming President shall conduct the election of the Vice President, either at the same or at the following sitting. The provisions of sub-rule 2 to 5 above shall also apply to this election.

Rule 11
Functions

1. The functions of the President are to:
> a) represent the Court;
> b) preside at the sittings of the Court;
> c) direct the work and supervise the administration of the Court;
> d) promote the activities of the Court;
> e) present a detailed Annual Report to the Court on the Court's activities and on his/her own activities as President over the year;
> f) pursuant to article 31 of the Protocol, prepare and present an Annual Report to the Assembly;
> g) carry out any other duties assigned to him/her by the Protocol or the present Rules, or entrusted to him/her by the Court.

2. The Vice-President shall assist the President in performing his/her functions. He/she shall replace him/her in the event of inability to act or of a vacancy in the presidency, or at the request of the President.

Rule 12
Exercise of Functions

1. In the event of the office of the President becoming vacant or the President being unable to act, his/her functions shall be performed by the Vice-President and, in default, by the Senior Member of the Court.

2. When the President is precluded from hearing a case under the terms of article 22 of the Protocol and Rule 8 hereof, he/she shall continue to act as President for all purposes save in respect of the said case; the same shall apply to the Vice President.

3. The President shall take the necessary measures to ensure the continuous exercise of the functions of the presidency at the Seat of the Court. In the event of his/her absence, he/she may, so far as is compatible with the Protocol and the present Rules, arrange for these functions to be exercised by the Vice President or in default, by the Senior Member of the Court.

4. If the President decides to resign the Presidency, he/she shall communicate his decision in writing to the Court through the Vice President, or, failing that, through the Senior Member of the Court. If the Vice President decides to resign from his office, he/she shall communicate his/her decision to the President.

Rule 13
Adequate gender representation, main legal traditions and main regions of Africa

In electing to office or making appointments governed by this Chapter and Part II of these Rules, the Members of the Court shall pursue, to the greatest extent possible, a policy aimed at securing a balanced representation of gender, the principal legal traditions and the main regions of Africa.

CHAPTER III – INTERNAL FUNCTIONING OF THE COURT

Rule 14
Ordinary Sessions

1. The Court shall hold four ordinary sessions per annum, each of which shall last about fifteen days.

2. The sessions of the Court shall be convened on the dates set by the Court during its previous session. Under exceptional circumstances, the President may, in consultation with the other Members of the Court, change the dates of a session.

3. The invitation letter shall indicate the dates, agenda, duration and venue of the session as well as any other relevant information. The letter shall be sent to the Members of the Court at least thirty (30) calendar days before the session is held.

Rule 15
Extraordinary Sessions

1. Extraordinary sessions may also be convened by the President on his own initiative or at the request of a majority of the Members of the Court.

2. The invitation letter shall indicate the dates, agenda, duration and venue of the sessions as well as any other relevant information. The letter shall be sent to the Members of the Court at least fifteen (15) calendar days before the session is held.

Rule 16
Venue of Meeting

The sessions shall normally take place at the Seat of the Court. However, the Court may, pursuant to article 25 (1) of the Protocol, decide to sit in the territory of any other Member State of the African Union.

Rule 17
Quorum

1. The quorum of seven (7) Judges stipulated under article 23 of the Protocol shall apply to all sittings of the Court.

2. If at the commencement of a sitting, the quorum is not met, the President shall adjourn it.

3. If during a sitting, the quorum ceases to exist, the President shall adjourn the sitting.

Rule 18
Official and Working languages

1. The official languages of the Court shall be the official languages of the African Union.

2. The working languages of the Court shall be the working languages of the African Union. However, the Court may, whenever the need arises, select one or more of these languages as its working languages.

3. Notwithstanding the provisions of sub-rules 1 and 2 of this Rule, the Court may permit any person appearing before it to use a language of his or her choice, if it is shown that he or she does not have sufficient knowledge of any of the official languages of the Court.

4. The terms and conditions for obtaining interpreters for implementation of sub-rule 3 of this Rule shall be determined by the Court.

Rule 19
Internal Judicial Practice and Practice Directions

Subject to the provisions of the Protocol and these Rules, the judicial practice and procedure followed by the Court shall be governed by relevant resolutions or practice directions of the Court.

PART II: THE REGISTRY

Rule 20
Composition and Organisation of the Registry

1. The Registry shall comprise the Registrar, the Deputy Registrar, and such other staff as the Court may require for the effective exercise of its functions.

2. The Court shall prescribe the organisation of the Registry.

3. Instructions for the Registry shall be drawn up by the Court.

4. The staff of the Registry shall be subject to Staff Rules and Regulations drawn up by the Court.

Rule 21
Appointment and Term of Office of the Registrar

1. The Court shall appoint its Registrar.

2. Candidates for the position of Registrar shall be of the highest moral standing and shall possess the necessary legal, administrative and linguistic knowledge and experience for the discharge of the functions linked to the post.

3. The Registrar shall be appointed for a term of five years. He/she may be re-appointed.

4. The process of recruiting the Registrar shall be conducted in accordance with the procedure established by the Court and consistent with the norms of the African Union.

5. The applications shall include all relevant information concerning the applicant, and in particular, information as to age, nationality, sex, current occupation, academic qualifications as well as the knowledge and experience required in sub-rule 2 above.

Rule 22
Appointment and Term of Office of the Deputy Registrar

1. The Court shall appoint a Deputy Registrar.

2. The provisions of Rule 21 of these Rules shall apply to the appointment and term of office of the Deputy Registrar.

Rule 23
Oath/Solemn Declaration

1. Upon assumption of office, the Registrar shall take the following oath/make the following declaration before the Court: "I ... (full names of Registrar) swear/solemnly declare that I will discharge the duties incumbent upon me as Registrar of the African Court on Human and Peoples' Rights with all loyalty, discretion and good conscience; that I will preserve the confidentiality of the information to which I have access in the exercise, or due to the exercise of my functions, and that I will faithfully observe all the provisions of the Protocol and of the Rules of the Court."

2. Upon assumption of office, the Deputy Registrar shall take a similar oath or make a similar declaration before the Court.

3. These oaths/declarations shall be recorded in the minutes of the Court.

Rule 24
Appointment of the Other Staff of the Registry

1. Other staff members of the Registry shall be appointed by the Court under such terms and conditions as it shall determine in accordance with the norms of the African Union. Appointments to such other positions as the Court shall determine may, however, be made by the Registrar with the approval of the President.

2. Upon assumption of duty, every staff member shall take the following oath/make the following declaration before the President, in the presence of the Registrar: "I .... (full names of official) swear/solemnly declare that I will discharge the duties incumbent upon me as an official of the Registry of the African Court on Human and Peoples' Rights with all loyalty, discretion and good conscience; that I will preserve the confidentiality of the information to which I have access in the exercise or due to the exercise of my functions, and that I will faithfully observe all the provisions of the Protocol and of the Rules of the Court."

Rule 25
Functions of the Registrar

1. The Registrar shall assist the Court in the exercise of its judicial function and shall be in charge of the general administration of the Court's Registry. He or she shall be responsible for the supervision and coordination of all the operations and activities of the Registry.

2. In the discharge of his/her duties, the Registrar shall:

    a) keep, in such form as may be prescribed by the Court, a General List of all cases, entered and numbered in the order in which the documents instituting proceedings or requesting an advisory opinion are received in the Registry;

    b) be the regular channel of communication to and from the Court, and in particular effect all communications, notifications and transmission of documents required by the Protocol or by these Rules and ensure that the date of dispatch and receipt thereof are readily verifiable;

    c) transmit to the parties copies of all pleadings and documents annexed thereto upon receipt thereof in the Registry;

d) be present, in person or by his/her duly qualified representative, at the sittings of the Court, and be responsible for the preparation of minutes of such sittings;

e) sign the minutes referred to in subparagraph (d) above;

f) inspect documentation submitted to the Court to establish authenticity thereof;

g) have custody of the seal, the official stamp and all the records and archives of the Court;

h) make arrangements for such provision or verification of translations and interpretations into the Court's official languages as the Court may require;

i) be responsible for the printing and publication of the Court's judgments, advisory opinions and orders, the pleadings and statements, and minutes of public sittings in each case, and of such other documents as the Court may direct to be published;

j) communicate to the government of the country in which the Court is sitting, and any other governments which may be concerned, the necessaryinformation as to the persons from time to time entitled, under the Protocol and any relevant agreements, to privileges, immunities, or facilities;

k) transmit documents to the Members of the Court, States party to the Protocol and to the Chairperson of the African Union Commission as well as other organs of the African Union where required;

l) deal with enquiries concerning the Court and its work;

m) prepare the draft budget of the Court;

n) be responsible for the sound management of all accounts and financial administration in accordance with the applicable financial rules of the African Union and the financial regulations of the Court;

o) assist in maintaining relations between the Court and the departments of the African Union Commission as well as those of the other organs of the African Union;

p) ensure that information concerning the Court and its activities is made accessible to governments, the highest national courts of justice, professional associations, learned societies, faculties and schools of law, and public information media;

3. The Court may entrust additional duties to the Registrar.

4. In the exercise of his/her functions, the Registrar shall work under the direction and supervision of the President and be answerable to the Court.

PART III: JURISDICTION

Rule 26
Jurisdiction

1. Pursuant to the Protocol, the Court shall have jurisdiction:

a) to deal with all cases and all disputes submitted to it concerning interpretation and application of the Charter, the Protocol and any other relevant human rights instrument ratified by the States concerned;

b) to render an advisory opinion on any legal matter relating to the Charter or any other relevant human rights instruments, provided that the subject of the opinion is not related to a matter being examined by the Commission;

c) to promote amicable settlement in cases pending before it in accordance with the provisions of the Charter;

d) to interpret a judgment rendered by itself; and

e) to review its own judgment in light of new evidence in conformity with Rule 67 of these Rules.

2. In the event of a dispute as to whether the Court has jurisdiction, the Court shall decide.

PART IV: CONTENTIOUS PROCEDURE

CHAPTER I: GENERAL PROVISIONS

Rule 27
Phases of Proceedings

1. The procedure before the Court shall consist of written, and if necessary, oral proceedings.

2. The written procedure shall consist of the communication to the Court, the parties, as well as the Commission, as appropriate, of applications, statements of the case, defences and observations and of replies if any, as well as all papers and documents in support, or of certified copies thereof.
3. The oral proceedings shall consist of a hearing by the Court of representatives of parties, witnesses, experts, or such other persons as the Court may decide to hear.

Rule 28
Representation
Every party to a case shall be entitled to be represented or to be assisted by legal counsel and/or by any other person of the party's choice.

Rule 29
Relations between the Court and the Commission
1. In a case brought before the Court by the Commission under article 5(1)(a) of the Protocol, the Commission shall, together with its report, also transmit to the Court all such documents that are pertinent to the proceedings. The Court may, if need be, hear one or several members of the Commission.
2. Where pursuant to article 6 (1) of the Protocol, the Court decides to solicit the opinion of the Commission on the admissibility of a case, it shall transmit to the Commission a copy of the pertinent sections of the case file indicating the time limit within which it wishes to receive the opinion.
3. Where the Court decides to transfer a case to the Commission pursuant to article 6 (3) of the Protocol, it shall transmit to the Commission a copy of the entire pleadings so far filed in the matter.
4. In accordance with article 33 of the Protocol, the Court shall consult the Commission, as appropriate, on all procedural issues relating to the relationship between the two institutions.

Rule 30
Legal Costs
Unless otherwise decided by the Court, each party shall bear its own costs.

Rule 31
Legal Assistance
Pursuant to article 10 (2) of the Protocol, the Court may, in the interest of justice and within the limits of the financial resources available, decide to provide free legal representation and/or legal assistance to any party.

Rule 32
Cooperation of the States
1. The States Parties to a case have the obligation to cooperate so as to ensure that all notices, communications or summonses addressed to persons residing in their territory or falling under their jurisdiction are duly executed.
2. The same rule shall apply to any proceeding that the Court decides to conduct or order in the territory of a State Party to a case.
3. When the performance of any of the measures referred to in the preceding paragraphs requires the cooperation of any other State, the President shall request the government concerned to provide the requisite assistance.

CHAPTER II: WRITTEN PROCEEDINGS

Rule 33
Access to the Court
1. Pursuant to the provisions of articles 5 and 34 (6) of the Protocol, the following are entitled to submit cases to the Court:
    a. The Commission;
    b. The State Party which has lodged an application to the Commission;
    c. The State Party against which an application has been lodged at the Commission;

d. The State Party whose citizen is a victim of a human rights violation;

e. An African Intergovernmental Organization;

f. An individual or a Non-Governmental Organization which has observer status before the Commission provided the requirements of article 34(6) of the Protocol are met.

2. In accordance with article 5(2) of the Protocol, a State Party which has an interest in a case may submit a request to the Court to be permitted to join in accordance with the procedure established in Rule 53 of these Rules.

Rule 34
Commencement of Proceedings

1. The Applicant shall file in the Court Registry, one (1) copy of the application containing a summary of the facts of the case and of the evidence intended to be adduced. The said application shall be signed by the Applicant or by his/her representative. The Registrar shall acknowledge receipt of the application.

2. Any application addressed to the Court shall give clear particulars of the Applicant and of the party or parties against whom such application has been brought. The application shall also contain the names and addresses of the persons designated as the Applicant's representatives.

3. The application shall be written in one of the official languages of the Court, and the original forwarded to the Court Registry.

4. The application shall specify the alleged violation, evidence of exhaustion of local remedies or of the inordinate delay of such local remedies as well as the orders or the injunctions sought. All applications filed by individuals and Non-Governmental Organizations shall meet the other admissibility conditions as set out in article 56 of the Charter and Rule 40 of these Rules.

5. Any Applicant who on his/her own behalf or on behalf of the victim wishes to be granted reparation pursuant to article 27(1) of the Protocol shall include the request for the reparation in the application in accordance with sub-rule 4 above. The amount of the reparation and the evidence relating thereto may be submitted subsequently within the time limit set by the Court.

6. The Registrar shall effect service of the application on the other party by registered post together with a request to acknowledge receipt.

Rule 35
Transmission of Applications

1. Upon the receipt of an application filed in accordance with article 5(1) and (3) of the Protocol, the Registrar shall transmit a copy thereof together with any annexes, to the President and other Members of the Court.

2. Unless otherwise decided by the Court, the Registrar shall forward copies of the application where applicable to the:

a) State Party against which the application has been filed, in accordance with Rule 34 (6) of these Rules;

b) State Party whose citizen is a victim of the alleged violation;

c) State Party against which an application has been filed at the Commission;

d) Commission;

e) Individual or legal entity or the Non-Governmental Organization that has filed an application at the Commission by virtue of article 55 of the Charter.

3. The Registrar shall also inform the Chairperson of the African Union Commission and through him/her, the Executive Council of the African Union, and all the other States Parties to the Protocol, of the filing of the application;

4. In forwarding applications as stipulated in sub-rules 2 and 3 of this Rule, the Registrar shall invite:

a) the Respondent State Party to indicate, within thirty (30) days of receipt of the application, the names and addresses of its representatives;

b) any other State Party that may wish to intervene in the proceedings under article 5(2) of the Protocol, to inform the Registrar accordingly, within the time stipulated in Rule 53;

c) if applicable, the Commission to forward to the Registrar, within thirty (30) days the names and addresses of its representatives;

d) if applicable, the individual or legal entity or the Non-Governmental Organization that has filed an application at the Commission under article 55 of the Charter, to set out, within thirty (30) days, if he/she/it wishes to participate in the proceedings before the Court and in the affirmative, the names and addresses of his/her/its representatives.

Rule 36
Registration and Transmission of Pleadings
1. All pleadings received by the Registrar shall be registered and a copy thereof transmitted to the other party.
2. The Registrar shall acknowledge receipt of all such pleadings.

Rule 37
Time Limit for Reply
The State Party against which an application has been filed shall respond thereto within sixty (60) days provided that the Court may, if the need arises, grant an extension of time.

Rule 38
Dismissal of Application without Merit
Whenever the Court finds that there is no merit in an application, it shall dismiss such application giving reasons for its decision, and may not have to summon the parties to the hearing, provided its decision and the reasons thereof are communicated to all the parties.

Rule 39
Preliminary Examination of the Competence of the Court and of Admissibility of Applications
1. The Court shall conduct preliminary examination of its jurisdiction and the admissibility of the application in accordance with articles 50 and 56 of the Charter, and Rule 40 of these Rules.
2. Pursuant to sub-rule 1 of this Rule, the Court may request the parties to submit any factual information, documents or other material considered by the Court to be relevant.

Rule 40
Conditions for Admissibility of Applications
Pursuant to the provisions of article 56 of the Charter to which article 6(2) of the Protocol refers, applications to the Court shall comply with the following conditions:
> 1. disclose the identity of the Applicant notwithstanding the latter's request for anonymity;
> 2. comply with the Constitutive Act of the Union and the Charter ;
> 3. not contain any disparaging or insulting language;
> 4. not be based exclusively on news disseminated through the mass media;
> 5. be filed after exhausting local remedies, if any, unless it is obvious that this procedure is unduly prolonged;
> 6. be filed within a reasonable time from the date local remedies were exhausted or from the date set by the Court as being the commencement of the time limit within which it shall be seized with the matter; and
> 7. not raise any mater or issues previously settled by the parties in accordance with the principles of the Charter of the United Nations, the Constitutive Act of the African Union, the provisions of the Charter or of any legal instrument of the African Union.

Rule 41
Filing of Documents
The Court may, before the commencement of or during the course of the proceedings, call upon the parties to file any pertinent document or to provide any relevant explanation. The Court shall formally note any refusal to comply.

CHAPTER III: ORAL PROCEEDINGS

Rule 42
Fixing of the Date of Hearing
When the case is ready for hearing, the President shall, after consulting the parties or the representatives of the Commission, if applicable, fix the date of the hearing. The Registrar shall notify them accordingly.

Rule 43
Public Hearings

1. Cases shall be heard in open court.

2. However, the Court may, of its own accord or at the request of a party, hold its hearings *in camera* if, in its opinion, it is in the interest of public morality, safety or public order to do so.

3. Whenever the Court orders that any proceedings shall not be conducted in public, the Court shall give one or more of the reasons specified in sub-rule 2 of this Rule as the basis of its decision. The parties or their legal representatives shall be permitted to be present and heard *in camera*.

Rule 44
Conduct of Hearings

The Presiding Judge shall conduct the hearing. He/she shall prescribe the order in which the representatives of the parties and where applicable, the representatives of the Commission, are to be heard.

Rule 45
Measures for Taking Evidence

1. The Court may, of its own accord, or at the request of a party, or the representatives of the Commission, where applicable, obtain any evidence which in its opinion may provide clarification of the facts of a case. The Court may, *inter alia*, decide to hear as a witness or expert or in any other capacity any person whose evidence, assertions or statements it deems likely to assist it in carrying out its task.

2. The Court may ask any person or institution of its choice to obtain information, express an opinion or submit a report to it on any specific point.

3. The Court may, at any time during the proceedings, assign one or more of its Members to conduct an enquiry, carry out a visit to the scene or take evidence in any other manner.

Rule 46
Witnesses, Experts and Other Persons

1. The Registrar shall issue summons to any witness, expert or other person the Court decides to hear.

2. After verification of his/her identity and before giving evidence, every witness shall take the following oath or make the following solemn declaration:

> "I swear/solemnly declare upon my honour and conscience that I will tell the truth, the whole truth and nothing but the truth."

The oath or solemn declaration shall be recorded.

3. After verification of his/her identity and before carrying out his/her task, every expert shall take the following oath or make the following solemn declaration:

> "I swear/solemnly declare that I will discharge my functions as expert on my honour and conscience."

The oath or solemn declaration shall be recorded.

4. The oath or declaration referred to in sub-rules 2 and 3 of this Rule shall be taken or made before the Court.

5. The Court shall rule on any challenge arising from an objection to a witness or expert.

Rule 47
Questions Put During Hearings

1. The Presiding Judge, or any Judge, may put questions to the representatives of the parties, and if applicable, the representative of the Commission, the witnesses, experts, and other persons appearing before the Court.

2. The witnesses, experts and other persons who appear before the Court may be examined by the representatives of the parties, and if applicable by the representatives of the Commission. The persons referred to in this paragraph may be subjected to cross-examination, followed by a reexamination.

Rule 48
Verbatim Record of Hearings

1. The Registrar shall be responsible for making a verbatim record of each hearing. The verbatim record shall include the:

a) composition of the Court at the hearing;

b) list of the persons appearing before the Court;

c) text of statements made, questions put and answers given;

d) text of any decision delivered by the Court during the hearing.

2. The representatives of the parties, and the representatives of the Commission, if applicable, shall receive the verbatim record of their arguments, statements or evidence, in order that they may, under the responsibility of the Registrar, make corrections, provided that such corrections do not affect the substance of what was said. The Registrar shall fix the time-limits granted for this purpose.

3. Once corrected, the verbatim record shall be signed by the President and the Registrar; and shall then constitute a true reflection of the proceedings.

Rule 49
Recording of Hearings

The proceedings of the hearing shall be recorded and such recordings shall be conserved in the archives of the Court.

Rule 50
New Evidence

No party may file additional evidence after the closure of pleadings except by leave of Court.

CHAPTER IV: SPECIFIC PROCEDURES

Rule 51
Interim Measures

1. Pursuant to article 27(2) of the Protocol, the Court may, at the request of a party, the Commission or on its own accord, prescribe to the parties any interim measure which it deems necessary to adopt in the interest of the parties or of justice.

2. In case of extreme urgency, the President may convene an extraordinary session of the Court to decide on measures to be taken. He/she may, in this regard, and by all reliable means, enlist the views of the Members not present.

3. The Court shall duly notify the parties to the case, the Commission, the Assembly, the Executive Council and the African Union Commission of the aforesaid interim measures.

4. In the Annual Report submitted by the Court to the Assembly pursuant to article 31 of the Protocol, the Court shall disclose the interim measures it ordered during the period under review. In the event of non-compliance with these measures by the State concerned, the Court shall make all such recommendations as it deems appropriate.

5. The Court may invite the parties to provide it with information on any issue relating to implementation of the interim measures adopted by it.

Rule 52
Preliminary Objections

1. Any party served with the application may raise preliminary objections to any part or parts thereof.

2. Preliminary objections shall be raised at the latest before the date fixed by the Court for the filing of the first set of pleadings to be submitted by the party who intends to raise the objections.

3. The submission of preliminary objections shall not cause the proceedings on the substantive case to be suspended unless the Court so decides. In any case, the Court shall rule on the objections or incorporate its ruling in its decision on the substantive case.

4. Every preliminary objection shall set out the facts and the law on which the objection is based as well as the submissions and a list of the documents in support, if any; it shall also specify any evidence which the party intends to produce. Certified copies of all supporting documents shall be attached.

5. Where a party raises a preliminary objection, the Court shall invite the other party to submit, its written observations in reply before ruling on the preliminary objection, the Court may decide to invite the parties to submit further observations in writing.

6. Before deciding on the preliminary objection, the Court may, on the request of a party, or of its own accord, decide to hold a hearing if it deems it necessary.

7. The Court shall give reasons for its ruling on the preliminary objection.

Rule 53
Intervention

1. An application for leave to intervene, in accordance with article 5 (2) of the Protocol shall be filed as soon as possible, and, in any case, before the closure of the written proceedings.
2. The application shall state the names of the Applicant's representatives. It shall specify the case to which it relates, and shall set out:

      a) the legal interest which, in the view of the State applying to intervene, has been affected;

      b) the precise object of the intervention; and

      c) the basis of the jurisdiction which, in the view of the State applying to intervene, exists between it and the parties to the case.

3. The application shall be accompanied by a list of the supporting documents attached thereto and shall be duly reasoned.
4. Certified copies of the application for leave to intervene shall be communicated forthwith to the parties to the case, who shall be entitled to submit their written observations within a time-limit to be fixed by the Court, or by the President if the Court is not in session. The Registrar shall also transmit copies of the application to any other concerned entity mentioned in Rule 35 of these Rules.
5. If the Court rules that the application is admissible, it shall fix a time limit within which the intervening State shall submit its written observations. Such observations shall be forwarded by the Registrar to the parties to the case, who shall be entitled to file written observations in reply within the timeframe fixed by the Court.
6. The intervening State shall be entitled, in the course of the oral proceedings, if any, to present its submissions in respect of the subject of the intervention.

Rule 54
Joinder of Cases and Pleadings

The Court may at any stage of the pleadings either on its own volition or in response to an application by any of the parties, order the joinder of interrelated cases and pleadings where it deems it appropriate, both in fact and in law.

Rule 55
Judgments in Default

1. Whenever a party does not appear before the Court, or fails to defend its case, the Court may, on the application of the other party, pass judgement in default after it has satisfied itself that the defaulting party has been duly served with the application and all other documents pertinent to the proceedings.
2. Before acceding to the application of the party before it, the Court shall satisfy itself that it has jurisdiction in the case, and that the application is admissible and well founded in fact and in law.

Rule 56
Out-of-Court Settlement

1. Parties to a case may settle their dispute amicably at any time before the Court gives its judgment.
2. Any settlement between the parties shall be reported to the Court, which shall render judgment limited to a brief statement on the facts and the solution adopted.
3. However, the Court may, having regard to its discretion under the Protocol, decide to proceed with a case notwithstanding the notice of such amicable settlement.

Rule 57
Amicable Settlement Under the Auspices of the Court

1. Pursuant to article 9 of the Protocol, the Court may promote amicable settlement of cases pending before it. To that end, it may contact the parties and take appropriate measures to facilitate amicable settlement of the dispute, based on respect for human and peoples' rights as recognized by the Charter.
2. Any negotiations entered into with a view to reaching an amicable settlement shall be confidential and without prejudice to the parties' observations in the proceedings before the Court. No written or oral communication and no offer of concession made as part of such negotiations shall be mentioned or referred to in the proceedings before the Court.

3. In the event of an amicable settlement of a case, the Court shall render a judgment, which shall be limited to a brief statement of the facts and of the solution adopted.

4 However, pursuant to its discretion under the Protocol, the Court may decide to proceed with the hearing of the application notwithstanding the notice of amicable settlement.

Rule 58
Discontinuance

Where an Applicant notifies the Registrar of its intention not to proceed with the case, the Court shall take due note thereof, and shall strike the application off the Court's cause list. If at the date of receipt by the Registry of the notice of the intention not to proceed with the case, the Respondent State has already taken measures to proceed with the case, its consent shall be required.

CHAPTER V: JUDGMENTS OF THE COURT

Rule 59
Decision of the Court

1. Upon the conclusion of the hearing of a case, the Court shall close the proceedings for its deliberations and judgment.

2. The decision of the Court shall be rendered by the Court within ninety (90) days from the date of completion of the deliberations.

Rule 60
Court's Deliberations

1. The deliberations of the Court shall be held *in camera* and shall remain confidential.

2. Only Judges who were Members of the Panel that heard the case shall participate in the deliberations of the Court.

3. The decision of the Court shall be made by a majority of the Members of the Panel present.

4. In the event of a tied vote, the Presiding Judge shall have a casting vote.

5. Any Member of the Court who heard the case may deliver a separate or dissenting opinion.

Rule 61
Judgment

1. In accordance with article 28(6) of the Protocol, every judgment of the Court shall state the reasons on which it is based.

2. The judgment shall indicate the names of Judges who have taken part in the deliberations.

3. The judgment shall be signed by all the Judges and certified by the Presiding Judge and the Registrar. It shall be read in open Court, due notice having been given to the parties.

4. Subject to article 28(3) of the Protocol, the judgment of the Court shall be final.

5. The judgment of the Court shall be binding on the parties.

Rule 62
Contents of Judgments

A judgment shall contain:

    a) the date on which it was delivered;
    b) the names of the parties;
    c) the names of the representatives of the parties;
    d) a summary of the proceedings;
    e) the submissions of the parties, and as may be required, those of the Commission's representatives;
    f) a statement of the facts of the case;
    g) the legal grounds;
    h) the operative provisions of the judgment;
    i) the decision, if any, on costs;
    j) the number of Judges constituting the majority;
    k) a statement as to the authentic text of the judgment.

Rule 63
Judgment on Reparation

The Court shall rule on the request for the reparation, submitted in accordance with Rule 34 (5) of these Rules, by the same decision establishing the violation of a human and peoples' right or, if the circumstances so require, by a separate decision.

Rule 64
Notification of Judgment

1. In accordance with article 29 of the Protocol, the Court shall duly notify the parties to the case, the Commission, the Assembly, the African Union Commission and any person or institution concerned of the judgment by certified true copies thereof.
2. The Executive Council shall also be notified of the judgment and shall monitor its execution on behalf of the Assembly.
3. The original copy of the judgment, duly signed and sealed, shall be conserved in the archives of the Court.

Rule 65
Publication of Judgments

Final judgments of the Court shall be published in accordance with Rule 25(2)(i), under the authority of the Registrar.

Rule 66
Application for Interpretation of a Judgment

1. Pursuant to article 28(4) of the Protocol, any party may, for the purpose of executing a judgment, apply to the Court for interpretation of the judgment within twelve months from the date the judgment was delivered unless the Court, in the interest of justice, decides otherwise.
2. The application shall be filed in the Registry. It shall state clearly the point or points in the operative provisions of the judgment on which interpretation is required.
3. Upon the instruction of the Court, the Registrar shall transmit the application for interpretation to any other parties concerned and shall invite them to submit their written comments, if any, within the time limit established by the President. The President shall also fix the date for the hearing of the application, in the event the Court decides to hold one. The Court's decision shall take the form of a judgment.
4. When considering an application for interpretation, the Court shall be composed of the same Judges who delivered judgment on the substantive case. However, where it is not possible for any Judge to participate in the proceedings, such Judge shall, if necessary, be replaced.
5. An application for interpretation shall not stay the execution of the judgment unless the Court decides otherwise.

Rule 67
Request for Review of a Judgment

1. Pursuant to article 28(3) of the Protocol, a party may apply to the Court to review its judgment in the event of the discovery of evidence, which was not within the knowledge of the party at the time the judgment was delivered. Such application shall be filed within six (6) months after that party acquired knowledge of the evidence so discovered.
2. The application shall specify the judgment in respect of which revision is requested, contain the information necessary to show that the conditions laid down in sub-rule 1 of this Rule have been met, and shall be accompanied by a copy of all relevant supporting documents. The application as well as the supporting documents shall be filed in the Registry.
3. Upon the instructions of the Court, the Registrar shall transmit a copy of the application to any other party/parties concerned and shall invite them to submit written observations, if any, within the time limit set by the President. The President shall also fix the date of the hearing should the Court decide to hold one. The Court shall rule on the admissibility of such application and its decision shall take the form of a judgment.

4. If the application is declared admissible, the Court shall, after consultation with the parties, determine the time limit for all future proceedings on the substance of the application it may deem necessary.

5. An application for review shall not stay the execution of a judgment unless the Court decides otherwise.

PART V: ADVISORY PROCEDURE

Rule 68
Request for Advisory Opinion

1. Requests for advisory opinions pursuant to article 4 of the Protocol may be filed with the Court by a Member State, by the African Union, by any organ of the African Union or by an African Organization recognized by the African Union. The request shall be on legal matters and shall state with precision the specific questions on which the opinion of the Court is being sought.

2. Any request for advisory opinion shall specify the provisions of the Charter or of any other international human rights instrument in respect of which the advisory opinion is being sought, the circumstances giving rise to the request as well as the names and addresses of the representatives of the entities making the request.

3. The subject matter of the request for advisory opinion shall not relate to an application pending before the Commission.

Rule 69
Transmission of Request for Advisory Opinion

Subsequent to the receipt of a request for advisory opinion, the Registrar shall transmit copies thereof to Member States, the Commission and to any other interested entity.

Rule 70
Written Submissions

1. The Court shall establish the time limit for the filing of written submissions by States Parties and by any other interested entity.

2. Any other States Parties may submit written submissions on any of the issues raised in the request. Any other interested entity may be authorized by the Court to do the same.

Rule 71
Oral Proceedings

After consideration of the written submissions, the Court shall decide whether or not there should be oral proceedings, and if so, shall fix a date for such hearing.

Rule 72
Application of Provisions Relating to Contentious Procedure

The Court shall apply, *mutatis mutandis* the provisions of Part IV of these Rules to the extent that it deems them to be appropriate and acceptable.

Rule 73
Advisory Opinion

1. The delivery of an advisory opinion shall take place in open Court. However, where the circumstances so require, the Court may decide otherwise.

2. Pursuant to article 4(2) of the Protocol, the Court's advisory opinion shall be accompanied by reasons, and any Judge who has participated in the hearing of an advisory request shall be entitled to deliver a separate or dissenting opinion.

PART VI: MISCELLANEOUS

Rule 74
Amendments

1. These Rules may be amended only by the Court.
2. A proposal to amend any Rule of the Court shall be submitted in writing to the President who shall, accordingly, direct the Registrar to notify all Judges.
3. The proposed amendment shall contain the Rule to be amended and its proposed replacement, if any.
4. Members of the Court shall be notified of the date and venue of the meeting at which the proposed amendment shall be discussed, ninety (90) days prior to the date of the said meeting.
5. No amendment of a Rule shall be passed unless it is supported by not less than seven Judges of the Court. * * *

Rule 76
Entry into Force and Authentic Text

These Rules, the texts of which in the working languages of the Court are equally authentic, shall enter into force on 20 June 2008.

THE AMERICAS

AMERICAN DECLARATION OF THE RIGHTS AND DUTIES OF MAN

American Declaration on the Rights and Duties of Man, O.A.S. Res. XXX (May 2, 1948), *reprinted in* Basic Documents Pertaining to Human Rights in the Inter-American System, O.A.S. Doc. OAS/Ser.L/V/I.4 rev.12 (2007), *available at* http://www.cidh.org/Basicos/English/Basic2.American%20Declaration.htm

Whereas:

The American peoples have acknowledged the dignity of the individual, and their national constitutions recognize that juridical and political institutions, which regulate life in human society, have as their principal aim the protection of the essential rights of man and the creation of circumstances that will permit him to achieve spiritual and material progress and attain happiness;

The American States have on repeated occasions recognized that the essential rights of man are not derived from the fact that he is a national of a certain state, but are based upon attributes of his human personality;

The international protection of the rights of man should be the principal guide of an evolving American law;

The affirmation of essential human rights by the American States together with the guarantees given by the internal regimes of the states establish the initial system of protection considered by the American States as being suited to the present social and juridical conditions, not without a recognition on their part that they should increasingly strengthen that system in the international field as conditions become more favorable,

Preamble

All men are born free and equal, in dignity and in rights, and, being endowed by nature with reason and conscience, they should conduct themselves as brothers one to another.

The fulfillment of duty by each individual is a prerequisite to the rights of all. Rights and duties are interrelated in every social and political activity of man. While rights exalt individual liberty, duties express the dignity of that liberty.

Duties of a juridical nature presuppose others of a moral nature which support them in principle and constitute their basis.

Inasmuch as spiritual development is the supreme end of human existence and the highest expression thereof, it is the duty of man to serve that end with all his strength and resources.

Since culture is the highest social and historical expression of that spiritual development, it is the duty of man to preserve, practice and foster culture by every means within his power.

And, since moral conduct constitutes the noblest flowering of culture, it is the duty of every man always to hold it in high respect.

CHAPTER ONE
Rights

Article I
Right to life, liberty and personal security
Every human being has the right to life, liberty and the security of his person.

Article II
Right to equality before law
All persons are equal before the law and have the rights and duties established in this Declaration, without distinction as to race, sex, language, creed or any other factor.

Article III
Right to religious freedom and worship
Every person has the right freely to profess a religious faith, and to manifest and practice it both in public and in private.

Article IV
Right to freedom of investigation, opinion, expression and dissemination
Every person has the right to freedom of investigation, of opinion, and of the expression and dissemination of ideas, by any medium whatsoever.

Article V
Right to protection of honor, personal reputation, and private and family life
Every person has the right to the protection of the law against abusive attacks upon his honor, his reputation, and his private and family life.

Article VI
Right to a family and to protection thereof
Every person has the right to establish a family, the basic element of society, and to receive protection therefor.

Article VII
Right to protection for mothers and children
All women, during pregnancy and the nursing period, and all children have the right to special protection, care and aid.

Article VIII
Right to residence and movement
Every person has the right to fix his residence within the territory of the state of which he is a national, to move about freely within such territory, and not to leave it except by his own will.

Article IX

Right to inviolability of the home

Every person has the right to the inviolability of his home.

Article X
Right to the inviolability and transmission of correspondence

Every person has the right to the inviolability and transmission of his correspondence.

Article XI
Right to the preservation of health and to well-being

Every person has the right to the preservation of his health through sanitary and social measures relating to food, clothing, housing and medical care, to the extent permitted by public and community resources.

Article XII
Right to education

Every person has the right to an education, which should be based on the principles of liberty, morality and human solidarity. Likewise every person has the right to an education that will prepare him to attain a decent life, to raise his standard of living, and to be a useful member of society. The right to an education includes the right to equality of opportunity in every case, in accordance with natural talents, merit and the desire to utilize the resources that the state or the community is in a position to provide. Every person has the right to receive, free, at least a primary education.

Article XIII
Right to the benefits of culture

Every person has the right to take part in the cultural life of the community, to enjoy the arts, and to participate in the benefits that result from intellectual progress, especially scientific discoveries. He likewise has the right to the protection of his moral and material interests as regards his inventions or any literary, scientific or artistic works of which he is the author.

Article XIV
Right to work and to fair remuneration

Every person has the right to work, under proper conditions, and to follow his vocation freely, insofar as existing conditions of employment permit. Every person who works has the right to receive such remuneration as will, in proportion to his capacity and skill, assure him a standard of living suitable for himself and for his family.

Article XV
Right to leisure time and to the use thereof

Every person has the right to leisure time, to wholesome recreation, and to the opportunity for advantageous use of his free time to his spiritual, cultural and physical benefit.

Article XVI
Right to social security

Every person has the right to social security which will protect him from the consequences of unemployment, old age, and any disabilities arising from causes beyond his control that make it physically or mentally impossible for him to earn a living.

Article XVII
Right to recognition of juridical personality and civil rights

Every person has the right to be recognized everywhere as a person having rights and obligations, and to enjoy the basic civil rights.

Article XVIII
Right to a fair trial

Every person may resort to the courts to ensure respect for his legal rights. There should likewise be available to him a simple, brief procedure whereby the courts will protect him from acts of authority that, to his prejudice, violate any fundamental constitutional rights.

Article XIX
Right to nationality

Every person has the right to the nationality to which he is entitled by law and to change it, if he so wishes, for the nationality of any other country that is willing to grant it to him.

Article XX
Right to vote and to participate in government

Every person having legal capacity is entitled to participate in the government of his country, directly or through his representatives, and to take part in popular elections, which shall be by secret ballot, and shall be honest, periodic and free.

Article XXI
Right of assembly

Every person has the right to assemble peaceably with others in a formal public meeting or an informal gathering, in connection with matters of common interest of any nature.

Article XXII
Right of association

Every person has the right to associate with others to promote, exercise and protect his legitimate interests of a political, economic, religious, social, cultural, professional, labor union or other nature.

Article XXIII
Right to property

Every person has a right to own such private property as meets the essential needs of decent living and helps to maintain the dignity of the individual and of the home.

Article XXIV
Right of petition

Every person has the right to submit respectful petitions to any competent authority, for reasons of either general or private interest, and the right to obtain a prompt decision thereon.

Article XXV
Right of protection from arbitrary arrest

No person may be deprived of his liberty except in the cases and according to the procedures established by pre-existing law. No person may be deprived of liberty for nonfulfillment of obligations of a purely civil character. Every individual who has been deprived of his liberty has the right to have the legality of his detention ascertained without delay by a court, and the right to be tried without undue delay or, otherwise, to be released. He also has the right to humane treatment during the time he is in custody.

Article XXVI
Right to due process of law

Every accused person is presumed to be innocent until proved guilty. Every person accused of an offense has the right to be given an impartial and public hearing, and to be tried by courts previously established in accordance with pre-existing laws, and not to receive cruel, infamous or unusual punishment.

Article XXVII
Right of asylum

Every person has the right, in case of pursuit not resulting from ordinary crimes, to seek and receive asylum in foreign territory, in accordance with the laws of each country and with international agreements.

Article XXVIII

Scope of the rights of man

The rights of man are limited by the rights of others, by the security of all, and by the just demands of the general welfare and the advancement of democracy.

CHAPTER TWO
Duties

Article XXIX
Duties to society

It is the duty of the individual so to conduct himself in relation to others that each and every one may fully form and develop his personality.

Article XXX
Duties toward children and parents

It is the duty of every person to aid, support, educate and protect his minor children, and it is the duty of children to honor their parents always and to aid, support and protect them when they need it.

Article XXXI
Duty to receive instruction

It is the duty of every person to acquire at least an elementary education.

Article XXXII
Duty to vote

It is the duty of every person to vote in the popular elections of the country of which he is a national, when he is legally capable of doing so.

Article XXXIII
Duty to obey the law

It is the duty of every person to obey the law and other legitimate commands of the authorities of his country and those of the country in which he may be.

Article XXXIV
Duty to serve the community and the nation

It is the duty of every able-bodied person to render whatever civil and military service his country may require for its defense and preservation, and, in case of public disaster, to render such services as may be in his power. It is likewise his duty to hold any public office to which he may be elected by popular vote in the state of which he is a national.

Article XXXV
Duties with respect to social security and welfare

It is the duty of every person to cooperate with the state and the community with respect to social security and welfare, in accordance with his ability and with existing circumstances.

Article XXXVI
Duty to pay taxes

It is the duty of every person to pay the taxes established by law for the support of public services.

Article XXXVII
Duty to work

It is the duty of every person to work, as far as his capacity and possibilities permit, in order to obtain the means of livelihood or to benefit his community.

Article XXXVIII

Duty to refrain from political activities in a foreign country

It is the duty of every person to refrain from taking part in political activities that, according to law, are reserved exclusively to the citizens of the state in which he is an alien.

AMERICAN CONVENTION ON HUMAN RIGHTS
"PACT OF SAN JOSE"

American Convention on Human Rights, *adopted* Nov. 21, 1969, O.A.S. T.S. No. 36, 1144 U.N.T.S. 143

Preamble

The American states signatory to the present Convention,

Reaffirming their intention to consolidate in this hemisphere, within the framework of democratic institutions, a system of personal liberty and social justice based on respect for the essential rights of man;

Recognizing that the essential rights of man are not derived from one's being a national of a certain state, but are based upon attributes of the human personality, and that they therefore justify international protection in the form of a convention reinforcing or complementing the protection provided by the domestic law of the American states;

Considering that these principles have been set forth in the Charter of the Organization of American States, in the American Declaration of the Rights and Duties of Man, and in the Universal Declaration of Human Rights, and that they have been reaffirmed and refined in other international instruments, worldwide as well as regional in scope;

Reiterating that, in accordance with the Universal Declaration of Human Rights, the ideal of free men enjoying freedom from fear and want can be achieved only if conditions are created whereby everyone may enjoy his economic, social, and cultural rights, as well as his civil and political rights; and

Considering that the Third Special Inter-American Conference (Buenos Aires, 1967) approved the incorporation into the Charter of the Organization itself of broader standards with respect to economic, social, and educational rights and resolved that an inter-American convention on human rights should determine the structure, competence, and procedure of the organs responsible for these matters,

Have agreed upon the following:

PART I - STATE OBLIGATIONS AND RIGHTS PROTECTED

CHAPTER I - GENERAL OBLIGATIONS

Article 1
Obligation to Respect Rights

1. The States Parties to this Convention undertake to respect the rights and freedoms recognized herein and to ensure to all persons subject to their jurisdiction the free and full exercise of those rights and freedoms, without any discrimination for reasons of race, color, sex, language, religion, political or other opinion, national or social origin, economic status, birth, or any other social condition.

2. For the purposes of this Convention, "person" means every human being.

Article 2
Domestic Legal Effects

Where the exercise of any of the rights or freedoms referred to in Article 1 is not already ensured by legislative or other provisions, the States Parties undertake to adopt, in accordance with their constitutional processes and the provisions of this Convention, such legislative or other measures as may be necessary to give effect to those rights or freedoms.

CHAPTER II - CIVIL AND POLITICAL RIGHTS

Article 3
Right to Juridical Personality

Every person has the right to recognition as a person before the law.

Article 4
Right to Life

1. Every person has the right to have his life respected. This right shall be protected by law and, in general, from the moment of conception. No one shall be arbitrarily deprived of his life.
2. In countries that have not abolished the death penalty, it may be imposed only for the most serious crimes and pursuant to a final judgment rendered by a competent court and in accordance with a law establishing such punishment, enacted prior to the commission of the crime. The application of such punishment shall not be extended to crimes to which it does not presently apply.
3. The death penalty shall not be reestablished in states that have abolished it.
4. In no case shall capital punishment be inflicted for political offenses or related common crimes.
5. Capital punishment shall not be imposed upon persons who, at the time the crime was committed, were under 18 years of age or over 70 years of age; nor shall it be applied to pregnant women.
6. Every person condemned to death shall have the right to apply for amnesty, pardon, or commutation of sentence, which may be granted in all cases. Capital punishment shall not be imposed while such a petition is pending decision by the competent authority.

Article 5
Right to Humane Treatment

1. Every person has the right to have his physical, mental, and moral integrity respected.
2. No one shall be subjected to torture or to cruel, inhuman, or degrading punishment or treatment. All persons deprived of their liberty shall be treated with respect for the inherent dignity of the human person.
3. Punishment shall not be extended to any person other than the criminal.
4. Accused persons shall, save in exceptional circumstances, be segregated from convicted persons, and shall be subject to separate treatment appropriate to their status as unconvicted persons.
5. Minors while subject to criminal proceedings shall be separated from adults and brought before specialized tribunals, as speedily as possible, so that they may be treated in accordance with their status as minors.
6. Punishments consisting of deprivation of liberty shall have as an essential aim the reform and social readaptation of the prisoners.

Article 6
Freedom from Slavery

1. No one shall be subject to slavery or to involuntary servitude, which are prohibited in all their forms, as are the slave trade and traffic in women.
2. No one shall be required to perform forced or compulsory labor. This provision shall not be interpreted to mean that, in those countries in which the penalty established for certain crimes is deprivation of liberty at forced labor, the carrying out of such a sentence imposed by a competent court is prohibited. Forced labor shall not adversely affect the dignity or the physical or intellectual capacity of the prisoner.
3. For the purposes of this article, the following do not constitute forced or compulsory labor:
   a. work or service normally required of a person imprisoned in execution of a sentence or formal decision passed by the competent judicial authority. Such work or service shall be carried out under the supervision and control of public authorities, and any persons performing such work or service shall not be placed at the disposal of any private party, company, or juridical person;

b. military service and, in countries in which conscientious objectors are recognized, national service that the law may provide for in lieu of military service;

c. service exacted in time of danger or calamity that threatens the existence or the well-being of the community; or

d. work or service that forms part of normal civic obligations.

Article 7
Right to Personal Liberty

1. Every person has the right to personal liberty and security.

2. No one shall be deprived of his physical liberty except for the reasons and under the conditions established beforehand by the constitution of the State Party concerned or by a law established pursuant thereto.

3. No one shall be subject to arbitrary arrest or imprisonment.

4. Anyone who is detained shall be informed of the reasons for his detention and shall be promptly notified of the charge or charges against him.

5. Any person detained shall be brought promptly before a judge or other officer authorized by law to exercise judicial power and shall be entitled to trial within a reasonable time or to be released without prejudice to the continuation of the proceedings. His release may be subject to guarantees to assure his appearance for trial.

6. Anyone who is deprived of his liberty shall be entitled to recourse to a competent court, in order that the court may decide without delay on the lawfulness of his arrest or detention and order his release if the arrest or detention is unlawful. In States Parties whose laws provide that anyone who believes himself to be threatened with deprivation of his liberty is entitled to recourse to a competent court in order that it may decide on the lawfulness of such threat, this remedy may not be restricted or abolished. The interested party or another person in his behalf is entitled to seek these remedies.

7. No one shall be detained for debt. This principle shall not limit the orders of a competent judicial authority issued for nonfulfillment of duties of support.

Article 8
Right to a Fair Trial

1. Every person has the right to a hearing, with due guarantees and within a reasonable time, by a competent, independent, and impartial tribunal, previously established by law, in the substantiation of any accusation of a criminal nature made against him or for the determination of his rights and obligations of a civil, labor, fiscal, or any other nature.

2. Every person accused of a criminal offense has the right to be presumed innocent so long as his guilt has not been proven according to law. During the proceedings, every person is entitled, with full equality, to the following minimum guarantees:

a. the right of the accused to be assisted without charge by a translator or interpreter, if he does not understand or does not speak the language of the tribunal or court;

b. prior notification in detail to the accused of the charges against him;

c. adequate time and means for the preparation of his defense;

d. the right of the accused to defend himself personally or to be assisted by legal counsel of his own choosing, and to communicate freely and privately with his counsel;

e. the inalienable right to be assisted by counsel provided by the state, paid or not as the domestic law provides, if the accused does not defend himself personally or engage his own counsel within the time period established by law;

f. the right of the defense to examine witnesses present in the court and to obtain the appearance, as witnesses, of experts or other persons who may throw light on the facts;

g. the right not to be compelled to be a witness against himself or to plead guilty; and

h. the right to appeal the judgment to a higher court.

3. A confession of guilt by the accused shall be valid only if it is made without coercion of any kind.

4. An accused person acquitted by a nonappealable judgment shall not be subjected to a new trial for the same cause.

5. Criminal proceedings shall be public, except insofar as may be necessary to protect the interests of justice.

Article 9
Freedom from *Ex Post Facto* Laws

No one shall be convicted of any act or omission that did not constitute a criminal offense, under the applicable law, at the time it was committed. A heavier penalty shall not be imposed than the one that was applicable at the time the criminal offense was committed. If subsequent to the commission of the offense the law provides for the imposition of a lighter punishment, the guilty person shall benefit therefrom.

Article 10
Right to Compensation

Every person has the right to be compensated in accordance with the law in the event he has been sentenced by a final judgment through a miscarriage of justice.

Article 11
Right to Privacy

1. Everyone has the right to have his honor respected and his dignity recognized.
2. No one may be the object of arbitrary or abusive interference with his private life, his family, his home, or his correspondence, or of unlawful attacks on his honor or reputation.
3. Everyone has the right to the protection of the law against such interference or attacks.

Article 12
Freedom of Conscience and Religion

1. Everyone has the right to freedom of conscience and of religion. This right includes freedom to maintain or to change one's religion or beliefs, and freedom to profess or disseminate one's religion or beliefs, either individually or together with others, in public or in private.
2. No one shall be subject to restrictions that might impair his freedom to maintain or to change his religion or beliefs.
3. Freedom to manifest one's religion and beliefs may be subject only to the limitations prescribed by law that are necessary to protect public safety, order, health, or morals, or the rights or freedoms of others.
4. Parents or guardians, as the case may be, have the right to provide for the religious and moral education of their children or wards that is in accord with their own convictions.

Article 13
Freedom of Thought and Expression

1. Everyone has the right to freedom of thought and expression. This right includes freedom to seek, receive, and impart information and ideas of all kinds, regardless of frontiers, either orally, in writing, in print, in the form of art, or through any other medium of one's choice.
2. The exercise of the right provided for in the foregoing paragraph shall not be subject to prior censorship but shall be subject to subsequent imposition of liability, which shall be expressly established by law to the extent necessary to ensure:
    a. respect for the rights or reputations of others; or
    b. the protection of national security, public order, or public health or morals.
3. The right of expression may not be restricted by indirect methods or means, such as the abuse of government or private controls over newsprint, radio broadcasting frequencies, or equipment used in the dissemination of information, or by any other means tending to impede the communication and circulation of ideas and opinions.
4. Notwithstanding the provisions of paragraph 2 above, public entertainments may be subject by law to prior censorship for the sole purpose of regulating access to them for the moral protection of childhood and adolescence.
5. Any propaganda for war and any advocacy of national, racial, or religious hatred that constitute incitements to lawless violence or to any other similar action against any person or group of persons on any grounds including those of race, color, religion, language, or national origin shall be considered as offenses punishable by law.

Article 14

Right of Reply

1. Anyone injured by inaccurate or offensive statements or ideas disseminated to the public in general by a legally regulated medium of communication has the right to reply or to make a correction using the same communications outlet, under such conditions as the law may establish.
2. The correction or reply shall not in any case remit other legal liabilities that may have been incurred.
3. For the effective protection of honor and reputation, every publisher, and every newspaper, motion picture, radio, and television company, shall have a person responsible who is not protected by immunities or special privileges.

Article 15
Right of Assembly

The right of peaceful assembly, without arms, is recognized. No restrictions may be placed on the exercise of this right other than those imposed in conformity with the law and necessary in a democratic society in the interest of national security, public safety or public order, or to protect public health or morals or the rights or freedom of others.

Article 16
Freedom of Association

1. Everyone has the right to associate freely for ideological, religious, political, economic, labor, social, cultural, sports, or other purposes.
2. The exercise of this right shall be subject only to such restrictions established by law as may be necessary in a democratic society, in the interest of national security, public safety or public order, or to protect public health or morals or the rights and freedoms of others.
3. The provisions of this article do not bar the imposition of legal restrictions, including even deprivation of the exercise of the right of association, on members of the armed forces and the police.

Article 17
Rights of the Family

1. The family is the natural and fundamental group unit of society and is entitled to protection by society and the state.
2. The right of men and women of marriageable age to marry and to raise a family shall be recognized, if they meet the conditions required by domestic laws, insofar as such conditions do not affect the principle of nondiscrimination established in this Convention.
3. No marriage shall be entered into without the free and full consent of the intending spouses.
4. The States Parties shall take appropriate steps to ensure the equality of rights and the adequate balancing of responsibilities of the spouses as to marriage, during marriage, and in the event of its dissolution. In case of dissolution, provision shall be made for the necessary protection of any children solely on the basis of their own best interests.
5. The law shall recognize equal rights for children born out of wedlock and those born in wedlock.

Article 18
Right to a Name

Every person has the right to a given name and to the surnames of his parents or that of one of them. The law shall regulate the manner in which this right shall be ensured for all, by the use of assumed names if necessary.

Article 19
Rights of the Child

Every minor child has the right to the measures of protection required by his condition as a minor on the part of his family, society, and the state.

Article 20
Right to Nationality

1. Every person has the right to a nationality.
2. Every person has the right to the nationality of the state in whose territory he was born if he does not have the right to any other nationality.

3. No one shall be arbitrarily deprived of his nationality or of the right to change it.

Article 21
Right to Property

1. Everyone has the right to the use and enjoyment of his property. The law may subordinate such use and enjoyment to the interest of society.
2. No one shall be deprived of his property except upon payment of just compensation, for reasons of public utility or social interest, and in the cases and according to the forms established by law.
3. Usury and any other form of exploitation of man by man shall be prohibited by law.

Article 22
Freedom of Movement and Residence

1. Every person lawfully in the territory of a State Party has the right to move about in it, and to reside in it subject to the provisions of the law.
2. Every person has the right lo leave any country freely, including his own.
3. The exercise of the foregoing rights may be restricted only pursuant to a law to the extent necessary in a democratic society to prevent crime or to protect national security, public safety, public order, public morals, public health, or the rights or freedoms of others.
4. The exercise of the rights recognized in paragraph 1 may also be restricted by law in designated zones for reasons of public interest.
5. No one can be expelled from the territory of the state of which he is a national or be deprived of the right to enter it.
6. An alien lawfully in the territory of a State Party to this Convention may be expelled from it only pursuant to a decision reached in accordance with law.
7. Every person has the right to seek and be granted asylum in a foreign territory, in accordance with the legislation of the state and international conventions, in the event he is being pursued for political offenses or related common crimes.
8. In no case may an alien be deported or returned to a country, regardless of whether or not it is his country of origin, if in that country his right to life or personal freedom is in danger of being violated because of his race, nationality, religion, social status, or political opinions.
9. The collective expulsion of aliens is prohibited.

Article 23
Right to Participate in Government

1. Every citizen shall enjoy the following rights and opportunities:
> a. to take part in the conduct of public affairs, directly or through freely chosen representatives;
> b. to vote and to be elected in genuine periodic elections, which shall be by universal and equal suffrage and by secret ballot that guarantees the free expression of the will of the voters; and
> c. to have access, under general conditions of equality, to the public service of his country.
2. The law may regulate the exercise of the rights and opportunities referred to in the preceding paragraph only on the basis of age, nationality, residence, language, education, civil and mental capacity, or sentencing by a competent court in criminal proceedings.

Article 24
Right to Equal Protection

All persons are equal before the law. Consequently, they are entitled, without discrimination, to equal protection of the law.

Article 25
Right to Judicial Protection

1. Everyone has the right to simple and prompt recourse, or any other effective recourse, to a competent court or tribunal for protection against acts that violate his fundamental rights recognized by the constitution or laws of the state concerned or by this Convention, even though such violation may have been committed by persons acting in the course of their official duties.
2. The States Parties undertake:

a. to ensure that any person claiming such remedy shall have his rights determined by the competent authority provided for by the legal system of the state;

b. to develop the possibilities of judicial remedy; and

c. to ensure that the competent authorities shall enforce such remedies when granted.

CHAPTER III - ECONOMIC, SOCIAL, AND CULTURAL RIGHTS

Article 26
Progressive Development

The States Parties undertake to adopt measures, both internally and through international cooperation, especially those of an economic and technical nature, with a view to achieving progressively, by legislation or other appropriate means, the full realization of the rights implicit in the economic, social, educational, scientific, and cultural standards set forth in the Charter of the Organization of American States as amended by the Protocol of Buenos Aires.

CHAPTER IV - SUSPENSION OF GUARANTEES, INTERPRETATION, AND APPLICATION

Article 27
Suspension of Guarantees

1. In time of war, public danger, or other emergency that threatens the independence or security of a State Party, it may take measures derogating from its obligations under the present Convention to the extent and for the period of time strictly required by the exigencies of the situation, provided that such measures are not inconsistent with its other obligations under international law and do not involve discrimination on the ground of race, color, sex, language, religion, or social origin.

2. The foregoing provision does not authorize any suspension of the following articles: Article 3 (Right to Juridical Personality), Article 4 (Right to Life), Article 5 (Right to Humane Treatment), Article 6 (Freedom from Slavery), Article 9 (Freedom from *Ex Post Facto* Laws), Article 12 (Freedom of Conscience and Religion), Article 17 (Rights of the Family), Article 18 (Right to a Name), Article 19 (Rights of the Child), Article 20 (Right to Nationality), and Article 23 (Right to Participate in Government), or of the judicial guarantees essential for the protection of such rights.

3. Any State Party availing itself of the right of suspension shall immediately inform the other States Parties, through the Secretary General of the Organization of American States, of the provisions the application of which it has suspended, the reasons that gave rise to the suspension, and the date set for the termination of such suspension.

Article 28
Federal Clause

1. Where a State Party is constituted as a federal state, the national government of such State Party shall implement all the provisions of the Convention over whose subject matter it exercises legislative and judicial jurisdiction.

2. With respect to the provisions over whose subject matter the constituent units of the federal state have jurisdiction, the national government shall immediately take suitable measures, in accordance with its constitution and its laws, to the end that the competent authorities of the constituent units may adopt appropriate provisions for the fulfillment of this Convention.

3. Whenever two or more States Parties agree to form a federation or other type of association, they shall take care that the resulting federal or other compact contains the provisions necessary for continuing and rendering effective the standards of this Convention in the new state that is organized.

Article 29
Restrictions Regarding Interpretation

No provision of this Convention shall be interpreted as:

        a. permitting any State Party, group, or person to suppress the enjoyment or exercise of the rights and freedoms recognized in this Convention or to restrict them to a greater extent than is provided for herein;

        b. restricting the enjoyment or exercise of any right or freedom recognized by virtue of the laws of any State Party or by virtue of another convention to which one of the said states is a party;

        c. precluding other rights or guarantees that are inherent in the human personality or derived from representative democracy as a form of government; or

        d. excluding or limiting the effect that the American Declaration of the Rights and Duties of Man and other international acts of the same nature may have.

Article 30
Scope of Restrictions

The restrictions that, pursuant to this Convention, may be placed on the enjoyment or exercise of the rights or freedoms recognized herein may not be applied except in accordance with laws enacted for reasons of general interest and in accordance with the purpose for which such restrictions have been established.

Article 31
Recognition of Other Rights

Other rights and freedoms recognized in accordance with the procedures established in Articles 76 and 77 may be included in the system of protection of this Convention.

CHAPTER V - PERSONAL RESPONSIBILITIES

Article 32
Relationship between Duties and Rights

1. Every person has responsibilities to his family, his community, and mankind.
2. The rights of each person are limited by the rights of others, by the security of all, and by the just demands of the general welfare, in a democratic society.

PART II - MEANS OF PROTECTION

CHAPTER VI - COMPETENT ORGANS

Article 33

The following organs shall have competence with respect to matters relating to the fulfillment of the commitments made by the States Parties to this Convention:

        a. the Inter-American Commission on Human Rights, referred to as "The Commission;" and

        b. the Inter-American Court of Human Rights, referred to as "The Court."

CHAPTER VII - INTER-AMERICAN COMMISSION ON HUMAN RIGHTS

Section 1. Organization

Article 34

The Inter-American Commission on Human Rights shall be composed of seven members, who shall be persons of high moral character and recognized competence in the field of human rights.

Article 35

The Commission shall represent all the member countries of the Organization of American States.

Article 36

1. The members of the Commission shall be elected in a personal capacity by the General Assembly of the Organization from a list of candidates proposed by the governments of the member states.
2. Each of those governments may propose up to three candidates, who may be nationals of the states proposing them or of any other member state of the Organization of American States. When a slate of three

is proposed, at least one of the candidates shall be a national of a state other than the one proposing the slate.

Article 37

1. The members of the Commission shall be elected for a term of four years and may be reelected only once, but the terms of three of the members chosen in the first election shall expire at the end of two years. Immediately following that election the General Assembly shall determine the names of those three members by lot.

2. No two nationals of the same state may be members of the Commission.

Article 38

Vacancies that may occur on the Commission for reasons other than the normal expiration of a term shall be filled by the Permanent Council of the Organization in accordance with the provisions of the Statute of the Commission.

Article 39

The Commission shall prepare its Statute, which it shall submit to the General Assembly for approval. It shall establish its own Regulations.

Article 40

Secretariat services for the Commission shall be furnished by the appropriate specialized unit of the General Secretariat of the Organization. This unit shall be provided with the resources required to accomplish the tasks assigned to it by the Commission.

Section 2. Functions

Article 41

The main function of the Commission shall be to promote respect for and defense of human rights. In the exercise of its mandate, it shall have the following functions and powers:

a. to develop an awareness of human rights among the peoples of America;

b. to make recommendations to the governments of the member states, when it considers such action advisable, for the adoption of progressive measures in favor of human rights within the framework of their domestic law and constitutional provisions as well as appropriate measures to further the observance of those rights;

c. to prepare such studies or reports as it considers advisable in the performance of its duties;

d. to request the governments of the member states to supply it with information on the measures adopted by them in matters of human rights;

e. to respond, through the General Secretariat of the Organization of American States, to inquiries made by the member states on matters related to human rights and, within the limits of its possibilities, to provide those states with the advisory services they request;

f. to take action on petitions and other communications pursuant to its authority under the provisions of Articles 44 through 51 of this Convention; and

g. to submit an annual report to the General Assembly of the Organization of American States.

Article 42

The States Parties shall transmit to the Commission a copy of each of the reports and studies that they submit annually to the Executive Committees of the Inter-American Economic and Social Council and the Inter-American Council for Education, Science, and Culture, in their respective fields, so that the Commission may watch over the promotion of the rights implicit in the economic, social, educational, scientific, and cultural standards set forth in the Charter of the Organization of American States as amended by the Protocol of Buenos Aires.

Article 43

The States Parties undertake to provide the Commission with such information as it may request of them as to the manner in which their domestic law ensures the effective application of any provisions of this Convention.

Section 3. Competence

Article 44

Any person or group of persons, or any nongovernmental entity legally recognized in one or more member states of the Organization, may lodge petitions with the Commission containing denunciations or complaints of violation of this Convention by a State Party.

Article 45

1. Any State Party may, when it deposits its instrument of ratification of or adherence to this Convention, or at any later time, declare that it recognizes the competence of the Commission to receive and examine communications in which a State Party alleges that another State Party has committed a violation of a human right set forth in this Convention.
2. Communications presented by virtue of this article may be admitted and examined only if they are presented by a State Party that has made a declaration recognizing the aforementioned competence of the Commission. The Commission shall not admit any communication against a State Party that has not made such a declaration.
3. A declaration concerning recognition of competence may be made to be valid for an indefinite time, for a specified period, or for a specific case.
4. Declarations shall be deposited with the General Secretariat of the Organization of American States, which shall transmit copies thereof to the member states of that Organization.

Article 46

1. Admission by the Commission of a petition or communication lodged in accordance with Articles 44 or 45 shall be subject to the following requirements:
    a. that the remedies under domestic law have been pursued and exhausted in accordance with generally recognized principles of international law;
    b. that the petition or communication is lodged within a period of six months from the date on which the party alleging violation of his rights was notified of the final judgment;
    c. that the subject of the petition or communication is not pending in another international proceeding for settlement; and
    d. that, in the case of Article 44, the petition contains the name, nationality, profession, domicile, and signature of the person or persons or of the legal representative of the entity lodging the petition.
2. The provisions of paragraphs 1.a and 1.b of this article shall not be applicable when:
    a. the domestic legislation of the state concerned does not afford due process of law for the protection of the right or rights that have allegedly been violated;
    b. the party alleging violation of his rights has been denied access to the remedies under domestic law or has been prevented from exhausting them; or
    c. there has been unwarranted delay in rendering a final judgment under the aforementioned remedies.

Article 47

The Commission shall consider inadmissible any petition or communication submitted under Articles 44 or 45 if:
    a. any of the requirements indicated in Article 46 has not been met;
    b. the petition or communication does not state facts that tend to establish a violation of the rights guaranteed by this Convention;
    c. the statements of the petitioner or of the state indicate that the petition or communication is manifestly groundless or obviously out of order; or
    d. the petition or communication is substantially the same as one previously studied by the Commission or by another international organization.

Section 4. Procedure

Article 48

1. When the Commission receives a petition or communication alleging violation of any of the rights protected by this Convention, it shall proceed as follows:

a. If it considers the petition or communication admissible, it shall request information from the government of the state indicated as being responsible for the alleged violations and shall furnish that government a transcript of the pertinent portions of the petition or communication. This information shall be submitted within a reasonable period to be determined by the Commission in accordance with the circumstances of each case.

b. After the information has been received, or after the period established has elapsed and the information has not been received, the Commission shall ascertain whether the grounds for the petition or communication still exist. If they do not, the Commission shall order the record to be closed.

c. The Commission may also declare the petition or communication inadmissible or out of order on the basis of information or evidence subsequently received.

d. If the record has not been closed, the Commission shall, with the knowledge of the parties, examine the matter set forth in the petition or communication in order to verify the facts. If necessary and advisable, the Commission shall carry out an investigation, for the effective conduct of which it shall request, and the states concerned shall furnish to it, all necessary facilities.

e. The Commission may request the states concerned to furnish any pertinent information and, if so requested, shall hear oral statements or receive written statements from the parties concerned.

f. The Commission shall place itself at the disposal of the parties concerned with a view to reaching a friendly settlement of the matter on the basis of respect for the human rights recognized in this Convention.

2. However, in serious and urgent cases, only the presentation of a petition or communication that fulfills all the formal requirements of admissibility shall be necessary in order for the Commission to conduct an investigation with the prior consent of the state in whose territory a violation has allegedly been committed.

Article 49

If a friendly settlement has been reached in accordance with paragraph 1.f of Article 48, the Commission shall draw up a report, which shall be transmitted to the petitioner and to the States Parties to this Convention, and shall then be communicated to the Secretary General of the Organization of American States for publication. This report shall contain a brief statement of the facts and of the solution reached. If any party in the case so requests, the fullest possible information shall be provided to it.

Article 50

1. If a settlement is not reached, the Commission shall, within the time limit established by its Statute, draw up a report setting forth the facts and stating its conclusions. If the report, in whole or in part, does not represent the unanimous agreement of the members of the Commission, any member may attach to it a separate opinion. The written and oral statements made by the parties in accordance with paragraph 1.e of Article 48 shall also be attached to the report.

2. The report shall be transmitted to the states concerned, which shall not be at liberty to publish it.

3. In transmitting the report, the Commission may make such proposals and recommendations as it sees fit.

Article 51

1. If, within a period of three months from the date of the transmittal of the report of the Commission to the states concerned, the matter has not either been settled or submitted by the Commission or by the state concerned to the Court and its jurisdiction accepted, the Commission may, by the vote of an absolute majority of its members, set forth its opinion and conclusions concerning the question submitted for its consideration.

2. Where appropriate, the Commission shall make pertinent recommendations and shall prescribe a period within which the state is to take the measures that are incumbent upon it to remedy the situation examined.

3. When the prescribed period has expired, the Commission shall decide by the vote of an absolute majority of its members whether the state has taken adequate measures and whether to publish its report.

CHAPTER VIII - INTER-AMERICAN COURT OF HUMAN RIGHTS

Section 1. Organization

Article 52

1. The Court shall consist of seven judges, nationals of the member states of the Organization, elected in an individual capacity from among jurists of the highest moral authority and of recognized competence in the field of human rights, who possess the qualifications required for the exercise of the highest judicial functions in conformity with the law of the state of which they are nationals or of the state that proposes them as candidates.
2. No two judges may be nationals of the same state.

Article 53

1. The judges of the Court shall be elected by secret ballot by an absolute majority vote of the States Parties to the Convention, in the General Assembly of the Organization, from a panel of candidates proposed by those states.
2. Each of the States Parties may propose up to three candidates, nationals of the state that proposes them or of any other member state of the Organization of American States. When a slate of three is proposed, at least one of the candidates shall be a national of a state other than the one proposing the slate.

Article 54

1. The judges of the Court shall be elected for a term of six years and may be reelected only once. The term of three of the judges chosen in the first election shall expire at the end of three years. Immediately after the election, the names of the three judges shall be determined by lot in the General Assembly.
2. A judge elected to replace a judge whose term has not expired shall complete the term of the latter.
3. The judges shall continue in office until the expiration of their term. However, they shall continue to serve with regard to cases that they have begun to hear and that are still pending, for which purposes they shall not be replaced by the newly elected judges.

Article 55

1. If a judge is a national of any of the States Parties to a case submitted to the Court, he shall retain his right to hear that case.
2. If one of the judges called upon to hear a case should be a national of one of the States Parties to the case, any other State Party in the case may appoint a person of its choice to serve on the Court as an *ad hoc* judge.
3. If among the judges called upon to hear a case none is a national of any of the States Parties to the case, each of the latter may appoint an *ad hoc* judge.
4. An *ad hoc* judge shall possess the qualifications indicated in Article 52.
5. If several States Parties to the Convention should have the same interest in a case, they shall be considered as a single party for purposes of the above provisions. In case of doubt, the Court shall decide.

Article 56

Five judges shall constitute a quorum for the transaction of business by the Court.

Article 57

The Commission shall appear in all cases before the Court.

Article 58

1. The Court shall have its seat at the place determined by the States Parties to the Convention in the General Assembly of the Organization; however, it may convene in the territory of any member state of the Organization of American States when a majority of the Court considers it desirable, and with the prior consent of the state concerned. The seat of the Court may be changed by the States Parties to the Convention in the General Assembly by a two-thirds vote.
2. The Court shall appoint its own Secretary.
3. The Secretary shall have his office at the place where the Court has its seat and shall attend the meetings that the Court may hold away from its seat.

Article 59

The Court shall establish its Secretariat, which shall function under the direction of the Secretary of the Court, in accordance with the administrative standards of the General Secretariat of the Organization in all respects not incompatible with the independence of the Court. The staff of the Court's Secretariat shall be appointed by the Secretary General of the Organization, in consultation with the Secretary of the Court.

Article 60

The Court shall draw up its Statute which it shall submit to the General Assembly for approval. It shall adopt its own Rules of Procedure.

Section 2. Jurisdiction and Functions

Article 61

1. Only the States Parties and the Commission shall have the right to submit a case to the Court.
2. In order for the Court to hear a case, it is necessary that the procedures set forth in Articles 48 and 50 shall have been completed.

Article 62

1. A State Party may, upon depositing its instrument of ratification or adherence to this Convention, or at any subsequent time, declare that it recognizes as binding, *ipso facto,* and not requiring special agreement, the jurisdiction of the Court on all matters relating to the interpretation or application of this Convention.
2. Such declaration may be made unconditionally, on the condition of reciprocity, for a specified period, or for specific cases. It shall be presented to the Secretary General of the Organization, who shall transmit copies thereof to the other member states of the Organization and to the Secretary of the Court.
3. The jurisdiction of the Court shall comprise all cases concerning the interpretation and application of the provisions of this Convention that are submitted to it, provided that the States Parties to the case recognize or have recognized such jurisdiction, whether by special declaration pursuant to the preceding paragraphs, or by a special agreement.

Article 63

1. If the Court finds that there has been a violation of a right or freedom protected by this Convention, the Court shall rule that the injured party be ensured the enjoyment of his right or freedom that was violated. It shall also rule, if appropriate, that the consequences of the measure or situation that constituted the breach of such right or freedom be remedied and that fair compensation be paid to the injured party.
2. In cases of extreme gravity and urgency, and when necessary to avoid irreparable damage to persons, the Court shall adopt such provisional measures as it deems pertinent in matters it has under consideration. With respect to a case not yet submitted to the Court, it may act at the request of the Commission.

Article 64

1. The member states of the Organization may consult the Court regarding the interpretation of this Convention or of other treaties concerning the protection of human rights in the American states. Within their spheres of competence, the organs listed in Chapter X of the Charter of the Organization of American States, as amended by the Protocol of Buenos Aires, may in like manner consult the Court.
2. The Court, at the request of a member state of the Organization, may provide that state with opinions regarding the compatibility of any of its domestic laws with the aforesaid international instruments.

Article 65

To each regular session of the General Assembly of the Organization of American States the Court shall submit, for the Assembly's consideration, a report on its work during the previous year. It shall specify, in particular, the cases in which a state has not complied with its judgments, making any pertinent recommendations.

Section 3. Procedure

Article 66

1. Reasons shall be given for the judgment of the Court.

2. If the judgment does not represent in whole or in part the unanimous opinion of the judges, any judge shall be entitled to have his dissenting or separate opinion attached to the judgment.

Article 67

The judgment of the Court shall be final and not subject to appeal. In case of disagreement as to the meaning or scope of the judgment, the Court shall interpret it at the request of any of the parties, provided the request is made within ninety days from the date of notification of the judgment.

Article 68

1. The States Parties to the Convention undertake to comply with the judgment of the Court in any case to which they are parties.
2. That part of a judgment that stipulates compensatory damages may be executed in the country concerned in accordance with domestic procedure governing the execution of judgments against the state.

Article 69

The parties to the case shall be notified of the judgment of the Court and it shall be transmitted to the States Parties to the Convention.

CHAPTER IX - COMMON PROVISIONS

Article 70

1. The judges of the Court and the members of the Commission shall enjoy, from the moment of their election and throughout their term of office, the immunities extended to diplomatic agents in accordance with international law. During the exercise of their official function they shall, in addition, enjoy the diplomatic privileges necessary for the performance of their duties.
2. At no time shall the judges of the Court or the members of the Commission be held liable for any decisions or opinions issued in the exercise of their functions.

Article 71

The position of judge of the Court or member of the Commission is incompatible with any other activity that might affect the independence or impartiality of such judge or member, as determined in the respective statutes.

Article 72

The judges of the Court and the members of the Commission shall receive emoluments and travel allowances in the form and under the conditions set forth in their statutes, with due regard for the importance and independence of their office. Such emoluments and travel allowances shall be determined in the budget of the Organization of American States, which shall also include the expenses of the Court and its Secretariat. To this end, the Court shall draw up its own budget and submit it for approval to the General Assembly through the General Secretariat. The latter may not introduce any changes in it.

Article 73

The General Assembly may, only at the request of the Commission or the Court, as the case may be, determine sanctions to be applied against members of the Commission or judges of the Court when there are justifiable grounds for such action as set forth in the respective statutes. A vote of a two-thirds majority of the member states of the Organization shall be required for a decision in the case of members of the Commission and, in the case of judges of the Court, a two-thirds majority vote of the States Parties to the Convention shall also be required.

PART III - GENERAL AND TRANSITORY PROVISIONS

CHAPTER X - SIGNATURE, RATIFICATION, RESERVATIONS, AMENDMENTS, PROTOCOLS, AND DENUNCIATION

Article 74

1. This Convention shall be open for signature and ratification by or adherence of any member state of the Organization of American States.

2. Ratification of or adherence to this Convention shall be made by the deposit of an instrument of ratification or adherence with the General Secretariat of the Organization of American States. As soon as eleven states have deposited their instruments of ratification or adherence, the Convention shall enter into force. With respect to any state that ratifies or adheres thereafter, the Convention shall enter into force on the date of the deposit of its instrument of ratification or adherence.

3. The Secretary General shall inform all member states of the Organization of the entry into force of the Convention.

Article 75

This Convention shall be subject to reservations only in conformity with the provisions of the Vienna Convention on the Law of Treaties signed on May 23, 1969.

Article 76

1. Proposals to amend this Convention may be submitted to the General Assembly for the action it deems appropriate by any State Party directly, and by the Commission or the Court through the Secretary General.

2. Amendments shall enter into force for the States ratifying them on the date when two thirds of the States Parties to this Convention have deposited their respective instruments of ratification. With respect to the other States Parties, the amendments shall enter into force on the dates on which they deposit their respective instruments of ratification.

Article 77

1. In accordance with Article 31, any State Party and the Commission may submit proposed protocols to this Convention for consideration by the States Parties at the General Assembly with a view to gradually including other rights and freedoms within its system of protection.

2. Each protocol shall determine the manner of its entry into force and shall be applied only among the States Parties to it.

Article 78

1. The States Parties may denounce this Convention at the expiration of a five-year period from the date of its entry into force and by means of notice given one year in advance. Notice of the denunciation shall be addressed to the Secretary General of the Organization, who shall inform the other States Parties.

2. Such a denunciation shall not have the effect of releasing the State Party concerned from the obligations contained in this Convention with respect to any act that may constitute a violation of those obligations and that has been taken by that state prior to the effective date of denunciation.

CHAPTER XI - TRANSITORY PROVISIONS

Section 1. Inter-American Commission on Human Rights

Article 79

Upon the entry into force of this Convention, the Secretary General shall, in writing, request each member state of the Organization to present, within ninety days, its candidates for membership on the Inter-American Commission on Human Rights. The Secretary General shall prepare a list in alphabetical order of the candidates presented, and transmit it to the member states of the Organization at least thirty days prior to the next session of the General Assembly.

Article 80

The members of the Commission shall be elected by secret ballot of the General Assembly from the list of candidates referred to in Article 79. The candidates who obtain the largest number of votes and an absolute majority of the votes of the representatives of the member states shall be declared elected. Should it become necessary to have several ballots in order to elect all the members of the Commission, the candidates who receive the smallest number of votes shall be eliminated successively, in the manner determined by the General Assembly.

Section 2. Inter-American Court of Human Rights

Article 81

Upon the entry into force of this Convention, the Secretary General shall, in writing, request each State Party to present, within ninety days, its candidates for membership on the Inter-American Court of Human Rights. The Secretary General shall prepare a list in alphabetical order of the candidates presented and transmit it to the States Parties at least thirty days prior to the next session of the General Assembly.

Article 82

The judges of the Court shall be elected from the list of candidates referred to in Article 81, by secret ballot of the States Parties to the Convention in the General Assembly. The candidates who obtain the largest number of votes and an absolute majority of the votes of the representatives of the States Parties shall be declared elected. Should it become necessary to have several ballots in order to elect all the judges of the Court, the candidates who receive the smallest number of votes shall be eliminated successively, in the manner determined by the States Parties.

ADDITIONAL PROTOCOL TO THE AMERICAN CONVENTION ON HUMAN RIGHTS IN THE AREA OF ECONOMIC, SOCIAL, AND CULTURAL RIGHTS ("PROTOCOL OF SAN SALVADOR")

O.A.S. Treaty Series No. 69 (1988), *entered into force* November 16, 1999, OEA/Ser.L.V/II.82 doc.6 rev.1 at 67 (1992)

Preamble

The States Parties to the American Convention on Human Rights * * *

Reaffirming their intention to consolidate in this hemisphere, within the framework of democratic institutions, a system of personal liberty and social justice based on respect for the essential rights of man;

Recognizing that the essential rights of man are not derived from one's being a national of a certain State, but are based upon attributes of the human person, for which reason they merit international protection in the form of a convention reinforcing or complementing the protection provided by the domestic law of the American States;

Considering the close relationship that exists between economic, social and cultural rights, and civil and political rights, in that the different categories of rights constitute an indivisible whole based on the recognition of the dignity of the human person, for which reason both require permanent protection and promotion if they are to be fully realized, and the violation of some rights in favor of the realization of others can never be justified;

Recognizing the benefits that stem from the promotion and development of cooperation among States and international relations;

Recalling that, in accordance with the Universal Declaration of Human Rights and the American Convention on Human Rights, the ideal of free human beings enjoying freedom from fear and want can only be achieved if conditions are created whereby everyone may enjoy his economic, social and cultural rights as well as his civil and political rights;

Bearing in mind that, although fundamental economic, social and cultural rights have been recognized in earlier international instruments of both world and regional scope, it is essential that those rights be reaffirmed, developed, perfected and protected in order to consolidate in America, on the basis of full respect for the rights of the individual, the democratic representative form of government as well as the right of its peoples to development, self-determination, and the free disposal of their wealth and natural resources; and

Considering that the American Convention on Human Rights provides that draft additional protocols to that Convention may be submitted for consideration to the States Parties, meeting together on the occasion of the General Assembly of the Organization of American States, for the purpose of gradually incorporating other rights and freedoms into the protective system thereof,

Have agreed upon the following Additional Protocol to the American Convention on Human Rights * * *:

Article 1
Obligation to Adopt Measures

The States Parties to this Additional Protocol to the American Convention on Human Rights undertake to adopt the necessary measures, both domestically and through international cooperation, especially economic and technical, to the extent allowed by their available resources, and taking into account their degree of development, for the purpose of achieving progressively and pursuant to their internal legislations, the full observance of the rights recognized in this Protocol.

Article 2
Obligation to Enact Domestic Legislation

If the exercise of the rights set forth in this Protocol is not already guaranteed by legislative or other provisions, the States Parties undertake to adopt, in accordance with their constitutional processes and the provisions of this Protocol, such legislative or other measures as may be necessary for making those rights a reality.

Article 3
Obligation of nondiscrimination

The State Parties to this Protocol undertake to guarantee the exercise of the rights set forth herein without discrimination of any kind for reasons related to race, color, sex, language, religion, political or other opinions, national or social origin, economic status, birth or any other social condition.

Article 4
Inadmissibility of Restrictions

A right which is recognized or in effect in a State by virtue of its internal legislation or international conventions may not be restricted or curtailed on the pretext that this Protocol does not recognize the right or recognizes it to a lesser degree.

Article 5
Scope of Restrictions and Limitations

The State Parties may establish restrictions and limitations on the enjoyment and exercise of the rights established herein by means of laws promulgated for the purpose of preserving the general welfare in a democratic society only to the extent that they are not incompatible with the purpose and reason underlying those rights.

Article 6
Right to Work

1. Everyone has the right to work, which includes the opportunity to secure the means for living a dignified and decent existence by performing a freely elected or accepted lawful activity.
2. The State Parties undertake to adopt measures that will make the right to work fully effective, especially with regard to the achievement of full employment, vocational guidance, and the development of technical and vocational training projects, in particular those directed to the disabled. The States Parties also undertake to implement and strengthen programs that help to ensure suitable family care, so that women may enjoy a real opportunity to exercise the right to work.

Article 7
Just, Equitable, and Satisfactory Conditions of Work

The States Parties to this Protocol recognize that the right to work to which the foregoing article refers presupposes that everyone shall enjoy that right under just, equitable, and satisfactory conditions, which the States Parties undertake to guarantee in their internal legislation, particularly with respect to:

a. Remuneration which guarantees, as a minimum, to all workers dignified and decent living conditions for them and their families and fair and equal wages for equal work, without distinction;

b. The right of every worker to follow his vocation and to devote himself to the activity that best fulfills his expectations and to change employment in accordance with the pertinent national regulations;

c. The right of every worker to promotion or upward mobility in his employment, for which purpose account shall be taken of his qualifications, competence, integrity and seniority; d. Stability of employment, subject to the nature of each industry and occupation and the causes for just separation. In cases of unjustified dismissal, the worker shall have the right to indemnity or to reinstatement on the job or any other benefits provided by domestic legislation;

d. Safety and hygiene at work;

e. The prohibition of night work or unhealthy or dangerous working conditions and, in general, of all work which jeopardizes health, safety, or morals, for persons under 18 years of age. As regards minors under the age of 16, the work day shall be subordinated to the provisions regarding compulsory education and in no case shall work constitute an impediment to school attendance or a limitation on benefiting from education received;

f. A reasonable limitation of working hours, both daily and weekly. The days shall be shorter in the case of dangerous or unhealthy work or of night work;

g. Rest, leisure and paid vacations as well as remuneration for national holidays.

Article 8
Trade Union Rights

1. The States Parties shall ensure:

a. The right of workers to organize trade unions and to join the union of their choice for the purpose of protecting and promoting their interests. As an extension of that right, the States Parties shall permit trade unions to establish national federations or confederations, or to affiliate with those that already exist, as well as to form international trade union organizations and to affiliate with that of their choice. The States Parties shall also permit trade unions, federations and confederations to function freely;

b. The right to strike.

2. The exercise of the rights set forth above may be subject only to restrictions established by law, provided that such restrictions are characteristic of a democratic society and necessary for safeguarding public order or for protecting public health or morals or the rights and freedoms of others. Members of the armed forces and the police and of other essential public services shall be subject to limitations and restrictions established by law.

3. No one may be compelled to belong to a trade union.

Article 9
Right to Social Security

1. Everyone shall have the right to social security protecting him from the consequences of old age and of disability which prevents him, physically or mentally, from securing the means for a dignified and decent existence. In the event of the death of a beneficiary, social security benefits shall be applied to his dependents.

2. In the case of persons who are employed, the right to social security shall cover at least medical care and an allowance or retirement benefit in the case of work accidents or occupational disease and, in the case of women, paid maternity leave before and after childbirth.

Article 10
Right to Health

1. Everyone shall have the right to health, understood to mean the enjoyment of the highest level of physical, mental and social well-being.

2. In order to ensure the exercise of the right to health, the States Parties agree to recognize health as a public good and, particularly, to adopt the following measures to ensure that right:

    a. Primary health care, that is, essential health care made available to all individuals and families in the community;

    b. Extension of the benefits of health services to all individuals subject to the State's jurisdiction;

    c. Universal immunization against the principal infectious diseases;

    d. Prevention and treatment of endemic, occupational and other diseases;

    e. Education of the population on the prevention and treatment of health problems, and

    f. Satisfaction of the health needs of the highest risk groups and of those whose poverty makes them the most vulnerable.

Article 11
Right to a Healthy Environment

1. Everyone shall have the right to live in a healthy environment and to have access to basic public services.
2. The States Parties shall promote the protection, preservation, and improvement of the environment.

Article 12
Right to Food

1. Everyone has the right to adequate nutrition which guarantees the possibility of enjoying the highest level of physical, emotional and intellectual development.
2. In order to promote the exercise of this right and eradicate malnutrition, the States Parties undertake to improve methods of production, supply and distribution of food, and to this end, agree to promote greater international cooperation in support of the relevant national policies.

Article 13
Right to Education

1. Everyone has the right to education.
2. The States Parties to this Protocol agree that education should be directed towards the full development of the human personality and human dignity and should strengthen respect for human rights, ideological pluralism, fundamental freedoms, justice and peace. They further agree that education ought to enable everyone to participate effectively in a democratic and pluralistic society and achieve a decent existence and should foster understanding, tolerance and friendship among all nations and all racial, ethnic or religious groups and promote activities for the maintenance of peace.
3. The States Parties to this Protocol recognize that in order to achieve the full exercise of the right to education:

    a. Primary education should be compulsory and accessible to all without cost;

    b. Secondary education in its different forms, including technical and vocational secondary education, should be made generally available and accessible to all by every appropriate means, and in particular, by the progressive introduction of free education;

    c. Higher education should be made equally accessible to all, on the basis of individual capacity, by every appropriate means, and in particular, by the progressive introduction of free education;

    d. Basic education should be encouraged or intensified as far as possible for those persons who have not received or completed the whole cycle of primary instruction;

    e. Programs of special education should be established for the handicapped, so as to provide special instruction and training to persons with physical disabilities or mental deficiencies.

4. In conformity with the domestic legislation of the States Parties, parents should have the right to select the type of education to be given to their children, provided that it conforms to the principles set forth above.
5. Nothing in this Protocol shall be interpreted as a restriction of the freedom of individuals and entities to establish and direct educational institutions in accordance with the domestic legislation of the States Parties.

Article 14
Right to the Benefits of Culture

1. The States Parties to this Protocol recognize the right of everyone:

    a. To take part in the cultural and artistic life of the community;

b. To enjoy the benefits of scientific and technological progress;

c. To benefit from the protection of moral and material interests deriving from any scientific, literary or artistic production of which he is the author.

2. The steps to be taken by the States Parties to this Protocol to ensure the full exercise of this right shall include those necessary for the conservation, development and dissemination of science, culture and art.

3. The States Parties to this Protocol undertake to respect the freedom indispensable for scientific research and creative activity.

4. The States Parties to this Protocol recognize the benefits to be derived from the encouragement and development of international cooperation and relations in the fields of science, arts and culture, and accordingly agree to foster greater international cooperation in these fields.

Article 15
Right to the Formation and the Protection of Families

1. The family is the natural and fundamental element of society and ought to be protected by the State, which should see to the improvement of its spiritual and material conditions.

2. Everyone has the right to form a family, which shall be exercised in accordance with the provisions of the pertinent domestic legislation.

3. The States Parties hereby undertake to accord adequate protection to the family unit and in particular:

a. To provide special care and assistance to mothers during a reasonable period before and after childbirth;

b. To guarantee adequate nutrition for children at the nursing stage and during school attendance years;

c. To adopt special measures for the protection of adolescents in order to ensure the full development of their physical, intellectual and moral capacities;

d. To undertake special programs of family training so as to help create a stable and positive environment in which children will receive and develop the values of understanding, solidarity, respect and responsibility.

Article 16
Rights of Children

Every child, whatever his parentage, has the right to the protection that his status as a minor requires from his family, society and the State. Every child has the right to grow under the protection and responsibility of his parents; save in exceptional, judicially-recognized circumstances, a child of young age ought not to be separated from his mother. Every child has the right to free and compulsory education, at least in the elementary phase, and to continue his training at higher levels of the educational system.

Article 17
Protection of the Elderly

Everyone has the right to special protection in old age. With this in view the States Parties agree to take progressively the necessary steps to make this right a reality and, particularly, to:

a. Provide suitable facilities, as well as food and specialized medical care, for elderly individuals who lack them and are unable to provide them for themselves;

b. Undertake work programs specifically designed to give the elderly the opportunity to engage in a productive activity suited to their abilities and consistent with their vocations or desires;

c. Foster the establishment of social organizations aimed at improving the quality of life for the elderly.

Article 18
Protection of the Handicapped

Everyone affected by a diminution of his physical or mental capacities is entitled to receive special attention designed to help him achieve the greatest possible development of his personality. The States Parties agree to adopt such measures as may be necessary for this purpose and, especially, to:

a. Undertake programs specifically aimed at providing the handicapped with the resources and environment needed for attaining this goal, including work programs consistent with their possibilities and freely accepted by them or their legal representatives, as the case may be;

b. Provide special training to the families of the handicapped in order to help them solve the problems of coexistence and convert them into active agents in the physical, mental and emotional development of the latter;

c. Include the consideration of solutions to specific requirements arising from needs of this group as a priority component of their urban development plans;

d. Encourage the establishment of social groups in which the handicapped can be helped to enjoy a fuller life.

Article 19
Means of Protection

1. Pursuant to the provisions of this article and the corresponding rules to be formulated for this purpose by the General Assembly of the Organization of American States, the States Parties to this Protocol undertake to submit periodic reports on the progressive measures they have taken to ensure due respect for the rights set forth in this Protocol. 2. All reports shall be submitted to the Secretary General of the OAS, who shall transmit them to the Inter-American Economic and Social Council and the Inter-American Council for Education, Science and Culture so that they may examine them in accordance with the provisions of this article. The Secretary General shall send a copy of such reports to the Inter-American Commission on Human Rights.

2. The Secretary General of the Organization of American States shall also transmit to the specialized organizations of the inter-American system of which the States Parties to the present Protocol are members, copies or pertinent portions of the reports submitted, insofar as they relate to matters within the purview of those organizations, as established by their constituent instruments.

3. The specialized organizations of the inter-American system may submit reports to the Inter-American Economic and Social Council and the Inter-American Council for Education, Science and Culture relative to compliance with the provisions of the present Protocol in their fields of activity.

4. The annual reports submitted to the General Assembly by the Inter-American Economic and Social Council and the Inter-American Council for Education, Science and Culture shall contain a summary of the information received from the States Parties to the present Protocol and the specialized organizations concerning the progressive measures adopted in order to ensure respect for the rights acknowledged in the Protocol itself and the general recommendations they consider to be appropriate in this respect.

5. Any instance in which the rights established in paragraph a) of Article 8 and in Article 13 are violated by action directly attributable to a State Party to this Protocol may give rise, through participation of the Inter-American Commission on Human Rights and, when applicable, of the Inter-American Court of Human Rights, to application of the system of individual petitions governed by Article 44 through 51 and 61 through 69 of the American Convention on Human Rights.

6. Without prejudice to the provisions of the preceding paragraph, the Inter-American Commission on Human Rights may formulate such observations and recommendations as it deems pertinent concerning the status of the economic, social and cultural rights established in the present Protocol in all or some of the States Parties, which it may include in its Annual Report to the General Assembly or in a special report, whichever it considers more appropriate.

7. The Councils and the Inter-American Commission on Human Rights, in discharging the functions conferred upon them in this article, shall take into account the progressive nature of the observance of the rights subject to protection by this Protocol. Article 20 Reservations

The States Parties may, at the time of approval, signature, ratification or accession, make reservations to one or more specific provisions of this Protocol, provided that such reservations are not incompatible with the object and purpose of the Protocol.

Article 21
Signature, Ratification or Accession. Entry into Effect

1. This Protocol shall remain open to signature and ratification or accession by any State Party to the American Convention on Human Rights.

2. Ratification of or accession to this Protocol shall be effected by depositing an instrument of ratification or accession with the General Secretariat of the Organization of American States.

3. The Protocol shall enter into effect when eleven States have deposited their respective instruments of ratification or accession.

4. The Secretary General shall notify all the member states of the Organization of American States of the entry of the Protocol into effect.

Article 22
Inclusion of other Rights and Expansion of those Recognized

1. Any State Party and the Inter-American Commission on Human Rights may submit for the consideration of the States Parties meeting on the occasion of the General Assembly proposed amendments to include the recognition of other rights or freedoms or to extend or expand rights or freedoms recognized in this Protocol.

2. Such amendments shall enter into effect for the States that ratify them on the date of deposit of the instrument of ratification corresponding to the number representing two thirds of the States Parties to this Protocol. For all other States Parties they shall enter into effect on the date on which they deposit their respective instrument of ratification.

PROTOCOL TO THE AMERICAN CONVENTION ON HUMAN RIGHTS TO ABOLISH THE DEATH PENALTY

O.A.S. Treaty Series No. 73 (1990), *adopted* June 8, 1990,
OEA/Ser.L.V/II.82 doc.6 rev.1 at 80 (1992)

PREAMBLE

The States Parties to this Protocol, *Considering*:

That Article 4 of the American Convention on Human Rights recognizes the right to life and restricts the application of the death penalty; That everyone has the inalienable right to respect for his life, a right that cannot be suspended for any reason; That the tendency among the American States is to be in favor of abolition of the death penalty; That application of the death penalty has irrevocable consequences, forecloses the correction of judicial error, and precludes any possibility of changing or rehabilitating those convicted; That the abolition of the death penalty helps to ensure more effective protection of the right to life; That an international agreement must be arrived at that will entail a progressive development of the American Convention on Human Rights, and That States Parties to the American Convention on Human Rights have expressed their intention to adopt an international agreement with a view to consolidating the practice of not applying the death penalty in the Americas,

Have agreed to sign the following Protocol to the American Convention on Human Rights to Abolish the Death Penalty:

Article 1

The States Parties to this Protocol shall not apply the death penalty in their territory to any person subject to their jurisdiction.

Article 2

1. No reservations may be made to this Protocol. However, at the time of ratification or accession, the States Parties to this instrument may declare that they reserve the right to apply the death penalty in wartime in accordance with international law, for extremely serious crimes of a military nature.

2. The State Party making this reservation shall, upon ratification or accession, inform the Secretary General of the Organization of American States of the pertinent provisions of its national legislation applicable in wartime, as referred to in the preceding paragraph.

3. Said State Party shall notify the Secretary General of the Organization of American States of the beginning or end of any state of war in effect in its territory.

Article 3

1. This Protocol shall be open for signature and ratification or accession by any State Party to the American Convention on Human Rights.

2. Ratification of this Protocol or accession thereto shall be made through the deposit of an instrument of ratification or accession with the General Secretariat of the Organization of American States.

Article 4

This Protocol shall enter into force among the States that ratify or accede to it when they deposit their respective instruments of ratification or accession with the General Secretariat of the Organization of American States.

STATUTE OF THE INTER-AMERICAN COMMISSION ON HUMAN RIGHTS

O.A.S. Res. 447 (IX-0/79), O.A.S. Off. Rec. OEA/Ser.P/IX.0.2/80, Vol. 1 at 88, Annual Report of the Inter-American Commission on Human Rights, OEA/Ser.L/V/11.50 doc.13 rev. 1 at 10 (1980)

I. NATURE AND PURPOSES

Article 1

1. The Inter-American Commission on Human Rights is an organ of the Organization of the American States, created to promote the observance and defense of human rights and to serve as consultative organ of the Organization in this matter.

2. For the purposes of the present Statute, human rights are understood to be:

> a. The rights set forth in the American Convention on Human Rights, in relation to the States Parties thereto;
>
> b. The rights set forth in the American Declaration of the Rights and Duties of Man, in relation to the other member states.

II. MEMBERSHIP AND STRUCTURE

Article 2

1. The Inter-American Commission on Human Rights shall be composed of seven members, who shall be persons of high moral character and recognized competence in the field of human rights.

2. The Commission shall represent all the member states of the Organization.

Article 3

1. The members of the Commission shall be elected in a personal capacity by the General Assembly of the Organization from a list of candidates proposed by the governments of the member states.

2. Each government may propose up to three candidates, who may be nationals of the state proposing them or of any other member state of the Organization. When a slate of three is proposed, at least one of the candidates shall be a national of a state other then the proposing state.

Article 4

1. At least six months prior to completion of the terms of office for which the members of the Commission were elected, the Secretary General shall request, in writing, each member state of the Organization to present its candidates within 90 days.

2. The Secretary General shall prepare a list in alphabetical order of the candidates nominated, and shall transmit it to the member states of the Organization at least thirty days prior to the next General Assembly.

Article 5

The members of the Commission shall be elected by secret ballot of the General Assembly from the list of candidates referred to in Article 3(2). The candidates who obtain the largest number of votes and an absolute majority of the votes of the member states shall be declared elected. Should it become necessary to hold several ballots to elect all the members of the Commission, the candidates who receive the smallest number of votes shall be eliminated successively, in the manner determined by the General Assembly.

Article 6

The members of the Commission shall be elected for a term of four years and may be reelected only once. Their terms of office shall begin on January 1 of the year following the year in which they are elected.

Article 7

No two nationals of the same state may be members of the Commission.

Article 8

1. Membership on the Inter-American Commission on Human Rights is incompatible with engaging in other functions that might affect the independence or impartiality of the member or the dignity or prestige of his post on the Commission.
2. The Commission shall consider any case that may arise regarding incompatibility in accordance with the provisions of the first paragraph of this Article, and in accordance with the procedures provided by its Regulations. If the Commission decides, by an affirmative vote of a least five of its members, that a case of incompatibility exists, it will submit the case, with its background, to the General Assembly for decision.
3. A declaration of incompatibility by the General Assembly shall be adopted by a majority of two thirds of the member states of the Organization and shall occasion the immediate removal of the member of the Commission from his post, but it shall not invalidate any action in which he may have participated.

Article 9

The duties of the members of the Commission are:
1. Except when justifiably prevented, to attend the regular and special meetings the Commission holds at its permanent headquarters or in any other place to which it may have decided to move temporarily.
2. To serve, except when justifiably prevented, on the special committees which the Commission may form to conduct on-site observations, or to perform any other duties within their ambit.
3. To maintain absolute secrecy about all matters which the Commission deems confidential.
4. To conduct themselves in their public and private life as befits the high moral authority of the office and the importance of the mission entrusted to the Commission.

Article 10

1. If a member commits a serious violation of any of the duties referred to in Article 9, the Commission, on the affirmative vote of five of its members, shall submit the case to the General Assembly of the Organization, which shall decide whether he should be removed from office.
2. The Commission shall hear the member in question before taking its decision.

Article 11

1. When a vacancy occurs for reasons other than the normal completion of a member's term of office, the Chairman of the Commission shall immediately notify the Secretary General of the Organization, who shall in turn inform the member states of the Organization.
2. In order to fill vacancies, each government may propose a candidate within a period of 30 days from the date of receipt of the Secretary General's communication that a vacancy has occurred.
3. The Secretary General shall prepare an alphabetical list of the candidates and shall transmit it to the Permanent Council of the Organization, which shall fill the vacancy.
4. When the term of office is due to expire within six months following the date on which a vacancy occurs, the vacancy shall not be filled.

Article 12

1. In those member states of the Organization that are Parties to the American Convention on Human Rights, the members of the Commission shall enjoy, from the time of their election and throughout their term of office, such immunities as are granted to diplomatic agents under international law. While in office, they shall also enjoy the diplomatic privileges required for the performance of their duties.

2. In those member states of the Organization that are not Parties to the American Convention on Human Rights, the members of the Commission shall enjoy the privileges and immunities pertaining to their posts that are required for them to perform their duties with independence.

3. The system of privileges and immunities of the members of the Commission may be regulated or supplemented by multilateral or bilateral agreements between the Organization and the member states.

Article 13

The members of the Commission shall receive travel allowances and per diem and fees, as appropriate, for their participation in the meetings of the Commission or in other functions which the Commission, in accordance with its Regulations, entrusts to them, individually or collectively. Such travel and per diem allowances and fees shall be included in the budget of the Organization, and their amounts and conditions shall be determined by the General Assembly.

Article 14

1. The Commission shall have a Chairman, a First Vice-Chairman and a Second Vice-Chairman, who shall be elected by an absolute majority of its members for a period of one year; they may be re-elected only once in each four-year period.

2. The Chairman and the two Vice-Chairmen shall be the officers of the Commission, and their functions shall be set forth in the Regulations.

Article 15

The Chairman of the Commission may go to the Commission's headquarters and remain there for such time as may be necessary for the performance of his duties.

III. HEADQUARTERS AND MEETINGS

Article 16

1. The headquarters of the Commission shall be in Washington, D.C.

2. The Commission may move to and meet in the territory of any American State when it so decides by an absolute majority of votes, and with the consent, or at the invitation of the government concerned.

3. The Commission shall meet in regular and special sessions, in conformity with the provisions of the Regulations.

Article 17

1. An absolute majority of the members of the Commission shall constitute a quorum.

2. In regard to those States that are Parties to the Convention, decisions shall be taken by an absolute majority vote of the members of the Commission in those cases established by the American Convention on Human Rights and the present Statute. In other cases, an absolute majority of the members present shall be required.

3. In regard to those States that are not Parties to the Convention, decisions shall be taken by an absolute majority vote of the members of the Commission, except in matters of procedure, in which case, the decisions shall be taken by simple majority.

IV. FUNCTIONS AND POWERS

Article 18

The Commission shall have the following powers with respect to the member states of the Organization of American States:

   a. to develop an awareness of human rights among the peoples of the Americas;

   b. to make recommendations to the governments of the states on the adoption of progressive measures in favor of human rights in the framework of their legislation, constitutional provisions and international commitments, as well as appropriate measures to further observance of those rights;

   c. to prepare such studies or reports as it considers advisable for the performance of its duties;

   d. to request that the governments of the states provide it with reports on measures they adopt in matters of human rights;

e. to respond to inquiries made by any member state through the General Secretariat of the Organization on matters related to human rights in the state and, within its possibilities, to provide those states with the advisory services they request;

f. to submit an annual report to the General Assembly of the Organization, in which due account shall be taken of the legal regime applicable to those States Parties to the American Convention on Human Rights and of that system applicable to those that are not Parties;

g. to conduct on-site observations in a state, with the consent or at the invitation of the government in question; and

h. to submit the program-budget of the Commission to the Secretary General, so that he may present it to the General Assembly.

Article 19

With respect to the States Parties to the American Convention on Human Rights, the Commission shall discharge its duties in conformity with the powers granted under the Convention and in the present Statute, and shall have the following powers in addition to those designated in Article 18:

a. to act on petitions and other communications, pursuant to the provisions of Articles 44 to 51 of the Convention;

b. to appear before the Inter-American Court of Human Rights in cases provided for in the Convention;

c. to request the Inter-American Court of Human Rights to take such provisional measures as it considers appropriate in serious and urgent cases which have not yet been submitted to it for consideration, whenever this becomes necessary to prevent irreparable injury to persons;

d. to consult the Court on the interpretation of the American Convention on Human Rights or of other treaties concerning the protection of human rights in the American states;

e. to submit additional draft protocols to the American Convention on Human Rights to the General Assembly, in order to progressively include other rights and freedoms under the system of protection of the Convention, and

f. to submit to the General Assembly, through the Secretary General, proposed amendments to the American Convention on Human Rights, for such action as the General Assembly deems appropriate.

Article 20

In relation to those member states of the Organization that are not parties to the American Convention on Human Rights, the Commission shall have the following powers, in addition to those designated in Article 18:

a. to pay particular attention to the observance of the human rights referred to in Articles I, II, III, IV, XVIII, XXV, and XXVI of the American Declaration of the Rights and Duties of Man;

b. to examine communications submitted to it and any other available information, to address the government of any member state not a Party to the Convention for information deemed pertinent by this Commission, and to make recommendations to it, when it finds this appropriate, in order to bring about more effective observance of fundamental human rights; and,

c. to verify, as a prior condition to the exercise of the powers granted under subparagraph b. above, whether the domestic legal procedures and remedies of each member state not a Party to the Convention have been duly applied and exhausted.

V. SECRETARIAT

Article 21

1. The Secretariat services of the Commission shall be provided by a specialized administrative unit under the direction of an Executive Secretary. This unit shall be provided with the resources and staff required to accomplish the tasks the Commission may assign to it.

2. The Executive Secretary, who shall be a person of high moral character and recognized competence in the field of human rights, shall be responsible for the work of the Secretariat and shall assist the Commission in the performance of its duties in accordance with the Regulations.

3. The Executive Secretary shall be appointed by the Secretary General of the Organization, in consultation with the Commission. Furthermore, for the Secretary General to be able to remove the Executive Secretary, he shall consult with the Commission and inform its members of the reasons for his decision.

VI. STATUTE AND REGULATIONS

Article 22
1. The present Statute may be amended by the General Assembly.
2. The Commission shall prepare and adopt its own Regulations, in accordance with the present Statute.

Article 23
1. In accordance with the provisions of Articles 44 to 51 of the American Convention on Human Rights, the Regulations of the Commission shall determine the procedure to be followed in cases of petitions or communications alleging violation of any of the rights guaranteed by the Convention, and imputing such violation to any State Party to the Convention.
2. If the friendly settlement referred to in Articles 44-51 of the Convention is not reached, the Commission shall draft, within 180 days, the report required by Article 50 of the Convention.

Article 24
1. The Regulations shall establish the procedure to be followed in cases of communications containing accusations or complaints of violations of human rights imputable to States that are not Parties to the American Convention on Human Rights.
2. The Regulations shall contain, for this purpose, the pertinent rules established in the Statute of the Commission approved by the Council of the Organization in resolutions adopted on May 25 and June 8, 1960, with the modifications and amendments introduced by Resolution XXII of the Second Special Inter-American Conference, and by the Council of the Organization at its meeting held on April 24, 1968, taking into account resolutions CP/RES. 253 (343/78), "Transition from the present Inter-American Commission on Human Rights to the Commission provided for in the American Convention on Human Rights," adopted by the Permanent Council of the Organization on September 20, 1979.

VII. TRANSITORY PROVISIONS

* * *

Article 26
1. The present Statute shall enter into effect 30 days after its approval by the General Assembly.
2. The Secretary General shall order immediate publication of the Statute, and shall give it the widest possible distribution.

STATUTE OF THE INTER-AMERICAN COURT OF HUMAN RIGHTS
O.A.S. Res. 448 (IX-0/79), O.A.S. Off. Rec. OEA/Ser.P/IX.0.2/80, Vol. 1 at 98

CHAPTER I
GENERAL PROVISIONS

Article 1. Nature and Legal Organization
The Inter-American Court of Human Rights is an autonomous judicial institution whose purpose is the application and interpretation of the American Convention on Human Rights. The Court exercises its functions in accordance with the provisions of the aforementioned Convention and the present Statute.

Article 2. Jurisdiction

The Court shall exercise adjudicatory and advisory jurisdiction:
1. Its adjudicatory jurisdiction shall be governed by the provisions of Articles 61, 62 and 63 of the Convention, and
2. Its advisory jurisdiction shall be governed by the provisions of Article 64 of the Convention.

Article 3. Seat

1. The seat of the Court shall be San Jose, Costa Rica; however, the Court may convene in any member state of the Organization of American States (OAS) when a majority of the Court considers it desirable, and with the prior consent of the State concerned.
2. The seat of the Court may be changed by a vote of two-thirds of the States Parties to the Convention, in the OAS General Assembly.

CHAPTER II
COMPOSITION OF THE COURT

Article 4. Composition

1. The Court shall consist of seven judges, nationals of the member states of the OAS, elected in an individual capacity from among jurists of the highest moral authority and of recognized competence in the field of human rights, who possess the qualifications required for the exercise of the highest judicial functions under the law of the State of which they are nationals or of the State that proposes them as candidates.
2. No two judges may be nationals of the same State.

Article 5. Judicial Terms

1. The judges of the Court shall be elected for a term of six years and may be reelected only once. A judge elected to replace a judge whose term has not expired shall complete that term.
2. The terms of office of the judges shall run from January 1 of the year following that of their election to December 31 of the year in which their terms expire.
3. The judges shall serve until the end of their terms. Nevertheless, they shall continue to hear the cases they have begun to hear and that are still pending, and shall not be replaced by the newly elected judges in the handling of those cases.

Article 6. Election of the Judges - Date

1. Election of judges shall take place, insofar as possible, during the session of the OAS General Assembly immediately prior to the expiration of the term of the outgoing judges.
2. Vacancies on the Court caused by death, permanent disability, resignation or dismissal of judges shall, insofar as possible, be filled at the next session of the OAS General Assembly. However, an election shall not be necessary when a vacancy occurs within six months of the expiration of a term.
3. If necessary in order to preserve a quorum of the Court, the States Parties to the Convention, at a meeting of the OAS Permanent Council, and at the request of the President of the Court, shall appoint one or more interim judges who shall serve until such time as they are replaced by elected judges.

Article 7. Candidates

1. Judges shall be elected by the States Parties to the Convention, at the OAS General Assembly, from a list of candidates nominated by those States.
2. Each State Party may nominate up to three candidates, nationals of the state that proposes them or of any other member state of the OAS.
3. When a slate of three is proposed, at least one of the candidates must be a national of a state other than the nominating state.

Article 8. Election - Preliminary Procedures

1. Six months prior to expiration of the terms to which the judges of the Court were elected, the Secretary General of the OAS shall address a written request to each State Party to the Convention that it nominate its candidates within the next ninety days.

2. The Secretary General of the OAS shall draw up an alphabetical list of the candidates nominated, and shall forward it to the States Parties, if possible, at least thirty days before the next session of the OAS General Assembly.
3. In the case of vacancies on the Court, as well as in cases of the death or permanent disability of a candidate, the aforementioned time periods shall be shortened to a period that the Secretary General of the OAS deems reasonable.

Article 9. Voting
1. The judges shall be elected by secret ballot and by an absolute majority of the States Parties to the Convention, from among the candidates referred to in Article 7 of the present Statute.
2. The candidates who obtain the largest number of votes and an absolute majority shall be declared elected. Should several ballots be necessary, those candidates who receive the smallest number of votes shall be eliminated successively, in the manner determined by the States Parties.

Article 10. *Ad Hoc* Judges
1. If a judge is a national of any of the States Parties to a case submitted to the Court, he shall retain his right to hear that case.
2. If one of the judges called upon to hear a case is a national of one of the States Parties to the case, any other State Party to the case may appoint a person to serve on the Court as an *ad hoc* judge.
3. If among the judges called upon to hear a case, none is a national of the States Parties to the case, each of the latter may appoint an *ad hoc* judge. Should several States have the same interest in the case, they shall be regarded as a single party for purposes of the above provisions. In case of doubt, the Court shall decide.
4. The right of any State to appoint an *ad hoc* judge shall be considered relinquished if the State should fail to do so within thirty days following the written request from the President of the Court.
5. The provisions of Articles 4, 11, 15, 16, 18, 19 and 20 of the present Statute shall apply to *ad hoc* judges.

Article 11. Oath
1. Upon assuming office, each judge shall take the following oath or make the following solemn declaration: " swear"- or " solemnly declare"- "hat I shall exercise my functions as a judge honorably, independently and impartially and that I shall keep secret all deliberations."
2. The oath shall be administered by the President of the Court and, if possible, in the presence of the other judges.

CHAPTER III
STRUCTURE OF THE COURT

Article 12. Presidency
1. The Court shall elect from among its members a President and Vice-President who shall serve for a period of two years; they may be reelected.
2. The President shall direct the work of the Court, represent it, regulate the disposition of matters brought before the Court, and preside over its sessions.
3. The Vice-President shall take the place of the President in the latter's temporary absence, or if the office of the President becomes vacant. In the latter case, the Court shall elect a new Vice-President to serve out the term of the previous Vice-President.
4. In the absence of the President and the Vice-President, their duties shall be assumed by other judges, following the order of precedence established in Article 13 of the present Statute.

Article 13. Precedence
1. Elected judges shall take precedence after the President and Vice-President according to their seniority in office.
2. Judges having the same seniority in office shall take precedence according to age.
3. Ad hoc and interim judges shall take precedence after the elected judges, according to age. However, if an *ad hoc* or interim judge has previously served as an elected judge, he shall have precedence over any other ad hoc or interim judge.

Article 14. Secretariat

1. The Secretariat of the Court shall function under the immediate authority of the Secretary, in accordance with the administrative standards of the OAS General Secretariat, in all matters that are not incompatible with the independence of the Court.

2. The Secretary shall be appointed by the Court. He shall be a full-time employee serving in a position of trust to the Court, shall have his office at the seat of the Court and shall attend any meetings that the Court holds away from its seat.

3. There shall be an Assistant Secretary who shall assist the Secretary in his duties and shall replace him in his temporary absence.

4. The Staff of the Secretariat shall be appointed by the Secretary General of the OAS, in consultation with the Secretary of the Court.

CHAPTER IV
RIGHTS, DUTIES AND RESPONSIBILITIES

Article 15. Privileges and Immunities

1. The judges of the Court shall enjoy, from the moment of their election and throughout their term of office, the immunities extended to diplomatic agents under international law. During the exercise of their functions, they shall, in addition, enjoy the diplomatic privileges necessary for the performance of their duties.

2. At no time shall the judges of the Court be held liable for any decisions or opinions issued in the exercise of their functions.

3. The Court itself and its staff shall enjoy the privileges and immunities provided for in the Agreement on Privileges and Immunities of the Organization of American States, of May 15, 1949, *mutatis mutandis*, taking into account the importance and independence of the Court.

4. The provision of paragraphs 1, 2 and 3 of this article shall apply to the States Parties to the Convention. They shall also apply to such other member states of the OAS as expressly accept them, either in general or for specific cases.

5. The system of privileges and immunities of the judges of the Court and of its staff may be regulated or supplemented by multilateral or bilateral agreements between the Court, the OAS and its member states.

Article 16. Service

1. The judges shall remain at the disposal of the Court, and shall travel to the seat of the Court or to the place where the Court is holding its sessions as often and for as long a time as may be necessary, as established in the Regulations.

2. The President shall render his service on a permanent basis.

Article 17. Emoluments

1. The emoluments of the President and the judges of the Court shall be set in accordance with the obligations and incompatibilities imposed on them by Articles 16 and 18, and bearing in mind the importance and independence of their functions.

2. The *ad hoc* judges shall receive the emoluments established by Regulations, within the limits of the Court's budget.

3. The judges shall also receive *per diem* and travel allowances, when appropriate.

Article 18. Incompatibilities

1. The position of judge of the Inter-American Court of Human Rights is incompatible with the following positions and activities:

> a. Members or high-ranking officials of the executive branch of government, except for those who hold positions that do not place them under the direct control of the executive branch and those of diplomatic agents who are not Chiefs of Missions to the OAS or to any of its member states;
> b. Officials of international organizations;
> c. Any others that might prevent the judges from discharging their duties, or that might affect their independence or impartiality, or the dignity and prestige of the office.

2. In case of doubt as to incompatibility, the Court shall decide. If the incompatibility is not resolved, the provisions of Article 73 of the Convention and Article 20(2) of the present Statute shall apply.

3. Incompatibilities may lead only to dismissal of the judge and the imposition of applicable liabilities, but shall not invalidate the acts and decisions in which the judge in question participated.

Article 19. Disqualification

1. Judges may not take part in matters in which, in the opinion of the Court, they or members of their family have a direct interest or in which they have previously taken part as agents, counsel or advocates, or as members of a national or international court or an investigatory committee, or in any other capacity.

2. If a judge is disqualified from hearing a case or for some other appropriate reason considers that he should not take part in a specific matter, he shall advise the President of his disqualification. Should the latter disagree, the Court shall decide.

3. If the President considers that a judge has cause for disqualification or for some other pertinent reason should not take part in a given matter, he shall advise him to that effect. Should the judge in question disagree, the Court shall decide.

4. When one or more judges are disqualified pursuant to this article, the President may request the States Parties to the Convention, in a meeting of the OAS Permanent Council, to appoint interim judges to replace them.

Article 20. Disciplinary Regime

1. In the performance of their duties and at all other times, the judges and staff of the Court shall conduct themselves in a manner that is in keeping with the office of those who perform an international judicial function. They shall be answerable to the Court for their conduct, as well as for any violation, act of negligence or omission committed in the exercise of their functions.

2. The OAS General Assembly shall have disciplinary authority over the judges, but may exercise that authority only at the request of the Court itself, composed for this purpose of the remaining judges. The Court shall inform the General Assembly of the reasons for its request.

3. Disciplinary authority over the Secretary shall lie with the Court, and over the rest of the staff, with the Secretary, who shall exercise that authority with the approval of the President.

4. The Court shall issue disciplinary rules, subject to the administrative regulations of the OAS General Secretariat insofar as they may be applicable in accordance with Article 59 of the Convention.

Article 21. Resignation - Incapacity

1. Any resignation from the Court shall be submitted in writing to the President of the Court. The resignation shall not become effective until the Court has accepted it.

2. The Court shall decide whether a judge is incapable of performing his functions.

3. The President of the Court shall notify the Secretary General of the OAS of the acceptance of a resignation or a determination of incapacity, for appropriate action.

CHAPTER V
THE WORKINGS OF THE COURT

Article 22. Sessions

1. The Court shall hold regular and special sessions.

2. Regular sessions shall be held as determined by the Regulations of the Court.

3. Special sessions shall be convoked by the President or at the request of a majority of the judges.

Article 23. Quorum

1. The quorum for deliberations by the Court shall be five judges.

2. Decisions of the Court shall be taken by a majority vote of the judges present.

3. In the event of a tie, the President shall cast the deciding vote.

Article 24. Hearings, Deliberations, Decisions

1. The hearings shall be public, unless the Court, in exceptional circumstances, decides otherwise.

2. The Court shall deliberate in private. Its deliberations shall remain secret, unless the Court decides otherwise.

3. The decisions, judgments and opinions of the Court shall be delivered in public session, and the parties shall be given written notification thereof. In addition, the decisions, judgments and opinions shall be

published, along with judges' individual votes and opinions and with such other data or background information that the Court may deem appropriate.

Article 25. Rules and Regulations

1. The Court shall draw up its Rules of Procedure.
2. The Rules of Procedure may delegate to the President or to Committees of the Court authority to carry out certain parts of the legal proceedings, with the exception of issuing final rulings or advisory opinions. Rulings or decisions issued by the President or the Committees of the Court that are not purely procedural in nature may be appealed before the full Court.
3. The Court shall also draw up its own Regulations.

Article 26. Budget, Financial System

1. The Court shall draw up its own budget and shall submit it for approval to the General Assembly of the OAS, through the General Secretariat. The latter may not introduce any changes in it.
2. The Court shall administer its own budget.

CHAPTER VI
RELATIONS WITH GOVERNMENTS AND ORGANIZATIONS

Article 27. Relations with the Host Country, Governments
and Organizations

1. The relations of the Court with the host country shall be governed through a headquarters agreement. The seat of the Court shall be international in nature.
2. The relations of the Court with governments, with the OAS and its organs, agencies and entities and with other international governmental organizations involved in promoting and defending human rights shall be governed through special agreements.

Article 28. Relations with the Inter-American Commission
on Human Rights

The Inter-American Commission on Human Rights shall appear as a party before the Court in all cases within the adjudicatory jurisdiction of the Court, pursuant to Article 2(1) of the present Statute. * * *

Article 30. Report to the OAS General Assembly

The Court shall submit a report on its work of the previous year to each regular session of the OAS General Assembly. It shall indicate those cases in which a State has failed to comply with the Court's ruling. It may also submit to the OAS General Assembly proposals or recommendations on ways to improve the inter-American system of human rights, insofar as they concern the work of the Court.

CHAPTER VII
FINAL PROVISIONS

Article 31. Amendments to the Statute

The present Statute may be amended by the OAS General Assembly, at the initiative of any member state or of the Court itself.

Article 32. Entry into Force

The present Statute shall enter into force on January 1, 1980.

INTER-AMERICAN CONVENTION TO PREVENT AND PUNISH TORTURE

O.A.S. Treaty Series No. 67, *entered into force* Feb. 28, 1987
OEA/Ser.L.V/II.82 doc.6 rev.1 at 83 (1992)

The American States signatory to the present Convention,

Aware of the provision of the American Convention on Human Rights that no one shall be subjected to torture or to cruel, inhuman, or degrading punishment or treatment;

Reaffirming that all acts of torture or any other cruel, inhuman, or degrading treatment or punishment constitute an offense against human dignity and a denial of the principles set forth in the Charter of the Organization of American States and in the Charter of the United Nations and are violations of the fundamental human rights and freedoms proclaimed in the American Declaration of the Rights and Duties of Man and the Universal Declaration of Human Rights;

Noting that, in order for the pertinent rules contained in the aforementioned global and regional instruments to take effect, it is necessary to draft an Inter-American Convention that prevents and punishes torture;

Reaffirming their purpose of consolidating in this hemisphere the conditions that make for recognition of and respect for the inherent dignity of man, and ensure the full exercise of his fundamental rights and freedoms,

Have agreed upon the following:

Article 1
The State Parties undertake to prevent and punish torture in accordance with the terms of this Convention.

Article 2
For the purposes of this Convention, torture shall be understood to be any act intentionally performed whereby physical or mental pain or suffering is inflicted on a person for purposes of criminal investigation, as a means of intimidation, as personal punishment, as a preventive measure, as a penalty, or for any other purpose. Torture shall also be understood to be the use of methods upon a person intended to obliterate the personality of the victim or to diminish his physical or mental capacities, even if they do not cause physical pain or mental anguish. The concept of torture shall not include physical or mental pain or suffering that is inherent in or solely the consequence of lawful measures, provided that they do not include the performance of the acts or use of the methods referred to in this article.

Article 3
The following shall be held guilty of the crime of torture:
    a. A public servant or employee who acting in that capacity orders, instigates or induces the use of torture, or who directly commits it or who, being able to prevent it, fails to do so.
    b. A person who at the instigation of a public servant or employee mentioned in subparagraph (a) orders, instigates or induces the use of torture, directly commits it or is an accomplice thereto.

Article 4
The fact of having acted under orders of a superior shall not provide exemption from the corresponding criminal liability.

Article 5
The existence of circumstances such as a state of war, threat of war, state of siege or of emergency, domestic disturbance or strife, suspension of constitutional guarantees, domestic political instability, or other public emergencies or disasters shall not be invoked or admitted as justification for the crime of torture. Neither the dangerous character of the detainee or prisoner, nor the lack of security of the prison establishment or penitentiary shall justify torture.

Article 6

In accordance with the terms of Article 1, the States Parties shall take effective measures to prevent and punish torture within their jurisdiction. The States Parties shall ensure that all acts of torture and attempts to commit torture are offenses under their criminal law and shall make such acts punishable by severe penalties that take into account their serious nature. The States Parties likewise shall take effective measures to prevent and punish other cruel, inhuman, or degrading treatment or punishment within their jurisdiction.

Article 7
The States Parties shall take measures so that, in the training of police officers and other public officials responsible for the custody of persons temporarily or definitively deprived of their freedom, special emphasis shall be put on the prohibition of the use of torture in interrogation, detention, or arrest. The States Parties likewise shall take similar measures to prevent other cruel, inhuman, or degrading treatment or punishment.

Article 8
The States Parties shall guarantee that any person making an accusation of having been subjected to torture within their jurisdiction shall have the right to an impartial examination of his case. Likewise, if there is an accusation or well-grounded reason to believe that an act of torture has been committed within their jurisdiction, the States Parties shall guarantee that their respective authorities will proceed properly and immediately to conduct an investigation into the case and to initiate, whenever appropriate, the corresponding criminal process. After all the domestic legal procedures of the respective State and the corresponding appeals have been exhausted, the case may be submitted to the international fora whose competence has been recognized by that State.

Article 9
The States Parties undertake to incorporate into their national laws regulations guaranteeing suitable compensation for victims of torture. None of the provisions of this article shall affect the right to receive compensation that the victim or other persons may have by virtue of existing national legislation.

Article 10
No statement that is verified as having been obtained through torture shall be admissible as evidence in a legal proceeding, except in a legal action taken against a person or persons accused of having elicited it through acts of torture, and only as evidence that the accused obtained such statement by such means.

Article 11
The States Parties shall take the necessary steps to extradite anyone accused of having committed the crime of torture or sentenced for commission of that crime, in accordance with their respective national laws on extradition and their international commitments on this matter.

Article 12
Every State Party shall take the necessary measures to establish its jurisdiction over the crime described in this Convention in the following cases:
     a. When torture has been committed within its jurisdiction;
     b. When the alleged criminal is a national of that State; or
     c. When the victim is a national of that State and it so deems appropriate.
Every State Party shall also take the necessary measures to establish its jurisdiction over the crime described in this Convention when the alleged criminal is within the area under its jurisdiction and it is not appropriate to extradite him in accordance with Article 11. This Convention does not exclude criminal jurisdiction exercised in accordance with domestic law.

Article 13
The crime referred to in Article 2 shall be deemed to be included among the extraditable crimes in every extradition treaty entered into between States Parties. The States Parties undertake to include the crime of torture as an extraditable offence in every extradition treaty to be concluded between them. Every State Party that makes extradition conditional on the existence of a treaty may, if it receives a request for extradition from another State Party with which it has no extradition treaty, consider this Convention as the

legal basis for extradition in respect of the crime of torture. Extradition shall be subject to the other conditions that may be required by the law of the requested State. States Parties which do not make extradition conditional on the existence of a treaty shall recognize such crimes as extraditable offences between themselves, subject to the conditions required by the law of the requested State. Extradition shall not be granted nor shall the person sought be returned when there are grounds to believe that his life is in danger, that he will be subjected to torture or to cruel, inhuman or degrading treatment, or that he will be tried by special or ad hoc courts in the requesting State.

Article 14
When a State Party does not grant the extradition, the case shall be submitted to its competent authorities as if the crime had been committed within its jurisdiction, for the purposes of investigation, and when appropriate, for criminal action, in accordance with its national law. Any decision adopted by these authorities shall be communicated to the State that has requested the extradition.

Article 15
No provision of this Convention may be interpreted as limiting the right of asylum, when appropriate, nor as altering the obligations of the States Parties in the matter of extradition.

Article 16
This Convention shall not limit the provisions of the American Convention on Human Rights, other conventions on the subject, or the Statutes of the Inter-American Commission on Human Rights, with respect to the crime of torture.

Article 17
The States Parties undertake to inform the Inter-American Commission on Human Rights of any legislative, judicial, administrative, or other measures they adopt in application of this Convention. In keeping with its duties and responsibilities, the Inter-American Commission on Human Rights will endeavor in its annual report to analyze the existing situation in the member states of the Organization of American States in regard to the prevention and elimination of torture.

Article 18
This Convention is open to signature by the member states of the Organization of American States. * * *

Article 21
The States Parties may, at the time of approval, signature, ratification, or accession, make reservations to this Convention, provided that such reservations are not incompatible with the object and purpose of the Convention and concern one or more specific provisions.

Article 22
This Convention shall enter into force on the thirtieth day following the date on which the second instrument of ratification is deposited. For each State ratifying or acceding to the Convention after the second instrument of ratification has been deposited, the Convention shall enter into force on the thirtieth day following the date on which that State deposits its instrument of ratification or accession.

Article 23
This Convention shall remain in force indefinitely, but may be denounced by any State Party. The instrument of denunciation shall be deposited with the General Secretariat of the Organization of American States. After one year from the date of deposit of the instrument of denunciation, this Convention shall cease to be in effect for the denouncing State but shall remain in force for the remaining States Parties.

Article 24
The original instrument of this Convention, the English, French, Portuguese, and Spanish texts of which are equally authentic, shall be deposited with the General Secretariat of the Organization of American States, which shall send a certified copy to the Secretariat of the United Nations for registration and publication, in accordance with the provisions of Article 102 of the United Nations Charter. The General Secretariat of the Organization of American States shall notify the member states of the Organization and the States that have

acceded to the Convention of signatures and of deposits of instruments of ratification, accession, and denunciation, as well as reservations, if any.

_____

INTER-AMERICAN CONVENTION ON THE PREVENTION, PUNISHMENT AND ERADICATION OF VIOLENCE AGAINST WOMEN ("CONVENTION OF BELEM DO PARA")

Inter-American Convention on the Prevention, Punishment and Eradication of Violence against Women, *adopted* June 9, 1994, O.A.S. T.S. No. A-61, *reprinted in* Basic Documents Pertaining to Human Rights in the Inter-American System, O.A.S. Doc. OAS/Ser.L/V/I.4 rev.12 (2007), *available at* http://www.cidh.org/Basicos/English/basic13.Conv%20of%20Belem%20Do%20Para.htm

The States Parties to this Convention,

Recognizing that full respect for human rights has been enshrined in the American Declaration of the Rights and Duties of Man and the Universal Declaration of Human Rights, and reaffirmed in other international and regional instruments;

Affirming that violence against women constitutes a violation of their human rights and fundamental freedoms, and impairs or nullifies the observance, enjoyment and exercise of such rights and freedoms;

Concerned that violence against women is an offense against human dignity and a manifestation of the historically unequal power relations between women and men;

Recalling the Declaration on the Elimination of Violence against Women, adopted by the Twenty-fifth Assembly of Delegates of the Inter-American Commission of Women, and affirming that violence against women pervades every sector of society regardless of class, race or ethnic group, income, culture, level of education, age or religion and strikes at its very foundations:

Convinced that the elimination of violence against women is essential for their individual and social development and their full and equal participation in all walks of life; and

Convinced that the adoption of a convention on the prevention, punishment and eradication of all forms of violence against women within the framework of the Organization of American States is a positive contribution to protecting the rights of women and eliminating violence against them,

Have agreed to the following:

CHAPTER I
DEFINITION AND SCOPE OF APPLICATION

Article 1
For the purposes of this Convention, violence against women shall be understood as any act or conduct, based on gender, which causes death or physical, sexual or psychological harm or suffering to women, whether in the public or the private sphere.

Article 2

Violence against women shall be understood to include physical, sexual and psychological violence:

a. that occurs within the family or domestic unit or within any other interpersonal relationship, whether or not the perpetrator shares or has shared the same residence with the woman, including, among others, rape, battery and sexual abuse;

b. that occurs in the community and is perpetrated by any person, including, among others, rape, sexual abuse, torture, trafficking in persons, forced prostitution, kidnapping and sexual harassment in the workplace, as well as in educational institutions, health facilities or any other place; and

c. that is perpetrated or condoned by the state or its agents regardless of where it occurs.

CHAPTER II
RIGHTS PROTECTED

Article 3

Every woman has the right to be free from violence in both the public and private spheres.

Article 4

Every woman has the right to the recognition, enjoyment, exercise and protection of all human rights and freedoms embodied in regional and international human rights instruments. These rights include, among others:

a. The right to have her life respected;

b. The right to have her physical, mental and moral integrity respected;

c. The right to personal liberty and security;

d. The right not to be subjected to torture;

e. The rights to have the inherent dignity of her person respected and her family protected;

f. The right to equal protection before the law and of the law;

g. The right to simple and prompt recourse to a competent court for protection against acts that violate her rights;

h. The right to associate freely;

i. The right of freedom to profess her religion and beliefs within the law; and

j. The right to have equal access to the public service of her country and to take part in the conduct of public affairs, including decision-making.

Article 5

Every woman is entitled to the free and full exercise of her civil, political, economic, social and cultural rights, and may rely on the full protection of those rights as embodied in regional and international instruments on human rights. The States Parties recognize that violence against women prevents and nullifies the exercise of these rights.

Article 6

The right of every woman to be free from violence includes, among others:

a. The right of women to be free from all forms of discrimination; and

b. The right of women to be valued and educated free of stereotyped patterns of behavior and social and cultural practices based on concepts of inferiority or subordination.

CHAPTER III
DUTIES OF THE STATES

Article 7

The States Parties condemn all forms of violence against women and agree to pursue, by all appropriate means and without delay, policies to prevent, punish and eradicate such violence and undertake to:

a. refrain from engaging in any act or practice of violence against women and to ensure that their authorities, officials, personnel, agents, and institutions act in conformity with this obligation;

b. apply due diligence to prevent, investigate and impose penalties for violence against women;

c. include in their domestic legislation penal, civil, administrative and any other type of provisions that may be needed to prevent, punish and eradicate violence against women and to adopt appropriate administrative measures where necessary;

d. adopt legal measures to require the perpetrator to refrain from harassing, intimidating or threatening the woman or using any method that harms or endangers her life or integrity, or damages her property;

e. take all appropriate measures, including legislative measures, to amend or repeal existing laws and regulations or to modify legal or customary practices which sustain the persistence and tolerance of violence against women;

f. establish fair and effective legal procedures for women who have been subjected to violence which include, among others, protective measures, a timely hearing and effective access to such procedures;

g. establish the necessary legal and administrative mechanisms to ensure that women subjected to violence have effective access to restitution, reparations or other just and effective remedies; and

h. adopt such legislative or other measures as may be necessary to give effect to this Convention.

Article 8

The States Parties agree to undertake progressively specific measures, including programs:

a. to promote awareness and observance of the right of women to be free from violence, and the right of women to have their human rights respected and protected;

b. to modify social and cultural patterns of conduct of men and women, including the development of formal and informal educational programs appropriate to every level of the educational process, to counteract prejudices, customs and all other practices which are based on the idea of the inferiority or superiority of either of the sexes or on the stereotyped roles for men and women which legitimize or exacerbate violence against women;

c. to promote the education and training of all those involved in the administration of justice, police and other law enforcement officers as well as other personnel responsible for implementing policies for the prevention, punishment and eradication of violence against women;

d. to provide appropriate specialized services for women who have been subjected to violence, through public and private sector agencies, including shelters, counseling services for all family members where appropriate, and care and custody of the affected children;

e. to promote and support governmental and private sector education designed to raise the awareness of the public with respect to the problems of and remedies for violence against women;

f. to provide women who are subjected to violence access to effective readjustment and training programs to enable them to fully participate in public, private and social life;

g. to encourage the communications media to develop appropriate media guidelines in order to contribute to the eradication of violence against women in all its forms, and to enhance respect for the dignity of women;

h. to ensure research and the gathering of statistics and other relevant information relating to the causes, consequences and frequency of violence against women, in order to assess the effectiveness of measures to prevent, punish and eradicate violence against women and to formulate and implement the necessary changes; and

i. to foster international cooperation for the exchange of ideas and experiences and the execution of programs aimed at protecting women who are subjected to violence.

Article 9

With respect to the adoption of the measures in this Chapter, the States Parties shall take special account of the vulnerability of women to violence by reason of, among others, their race or ethnic background or their status as migrants, refugees or displaced persons. Similar consideration shall be given to women subjected to violence while pregnant or who are disabled, of minor age, elderly, socioeconomically disadvantaged, affected by armed conflict or deprived of their freedom.

CHAPTER IV
INTER-AMERICAN MECHANISMS OF PROTECTION

Article 10

In order to protect the rights of every woman to be free from violence, the States Parties shall include in their national reports to the Inter-American Commission of Women information on measures adopted to prevent and prohibit violence against women, and to assist women affected by violence, as well as on any difficulties they observe in applying those measures, and the factors that contribute to violence against women.

Article 11

The States Parties to this Convention and the Inter-American Commission of Women may request of the Inter-American Court of Human Rights advisory opinions on the interpretation of this Convention.

Article 12

Any person or group of persons, or any nongovernmental entity legally recognized in one or more member states of the Organization, may lodge petitions with the Inter-American Commission on Human Rights containing denunciations or complaints of violations of Article 7 of this Convention by a State Party, and the Commission shall consider such claims in accordance with the norms and procedures established by the American Convention on Human Rights and the Statutes and Regulations of the Inter-American Commission on Human Rights for lodging and considering petitions.

CHAPTER V
GENERAL PROVISIONS

Article 13

No part of this Convention shall be understood to restrict or limit the domestic law of any State Party that affords equal or greater protection and guarantees of the rights of women and appropriate safeguards to prevent and eradicate violence against women.

Article 14

No part of this Convention shall be understood to restrict or limit the American Convention on Human Rights or any other international convention on the subject that provides for equal or greater protection in this area.

Article 15

This Convention is open to signature by all the member states of the Organization of American States.

Article 16

This Convention is subject to ratification. The instruments of ratification shall be deposited with the General Secretariat of the Organization of American States.

Article 17

This Convention is open to accession by any other state. Instruments of accession shall be deposited with the General Secretariat of the Organization of American States.

Article 18

Any State may, at the time of approval, signature, ratification, or accession, make reservations to this Convention provided that such reservations are:

> a. not incompatible with the object and purpose of the Convention, and
> b. not of a general nature and relate to one or more specific provisions.

Article 19

Any State Party may submit to the General Assembly, through the Inter-American Commission of Women, proposals for the amendment of this Convention. Amendments shall enter into force for the states ratifying them on the date when two-thirds of the States Parties to this Convention have deposited their respective instruments of ratification. With respect to the other States Parties, the amendments shall enter into force on the dates on which they deposit their respective instruments of ratification.

Article 20

If a State Party has two or more territorial units in which the matters dealt with in this Convention are governed by different systems of law, it may, at the time of signature, ratification or accession, declare that this Convention shall extend to all its territorial units or to only one or more of them.

Such a declaration may be amended at any time by subsequent declarations, which shall expressly specify the territorial unit or units to which this Convention applies. Such subsequent declarations shall be transmitted to the General Secretariat of the Organization of American States, and shall enter into force thirty days after the date of their receipt.

Article 21

This Convention shall enter into force on the thirtieth day after the date of deposit of the second instrument of ratification. For each State that ratifies or accedes to the Convention after the second instrument of ratification is deposited, it shall enter into force thirty days after the date on which that State deposited its instrument of ratification or accession.

Article 22

The Secretary General shall inform all member states of the Organization of American States of the entry into force of this Convention.

Article 23

The Secretary General of the Organization of American States shall present an annual report to the member states of the Organization on the status of this Convention, including the signatures, deposits of instruments of ratification and accession, and declarations, and any reservations that may have been presented by the States Parties, accompanied by a report thereon if needed.

Article 24

This Convention shall remain in force indefinitely, but any of the States Parties may denounce it by depositing an instrument to that effect with the General Secretariat of the Organization of American States. One year after the date of deposit of the instrument of denunciation, this Convention shall cease to be in effect for the denouncing State but shall remain in force for the remaining States Parties.

Article 25

The original instrument of this Convention, the English, French, Portuguese and Spanish texts of which are equally authentic, shall be deposited with the General Secretariat of the Organization of American States, which shall send a certified copy to the Secretariat of the United Nations for registration and publication in accordance with the provisions of Article 102 of the United Nations Charter.

INTER-AMERICAN CONVENTION ON FORCED DISAPPEARANCE OF PERSONS

Inter-American Convention on Forced Disappearance of Persons, *adopted* June 9, 1994, O.A.S. T.S. No. A-60, *reprinted in* Basic Documents Pertaining to Human Rights in the Inter-American System, O.A.S. Doc. OAS/Ser.L/V/I.4 rev.12 (2007), *available at* http://www.cidh.org/Basicos/English/Basic11.Disappearance.htm

Preamble

The Member States of the Organization of American States signatory to the present Convention,

Disturbed by the persistence of the forced disappearance of persons;

310

Reaffirming that the true meaning of American solidarity and good neighborliness can be none other than that of consolidating in this Hemisphere, in the framework of democratic institutions, a system of individual freedom and social justice based on respect for essential human rights;

Considering that the forced disappearance of persons in an affront to the conscience of the Hemisphere and a grave and abominable offense against the inherent dignity of the human being, and one that contradicts the principles and purposes enshrined in the Charter of the Organization of American States;

Considering that the forced disappearance of persons of persons violates numerous non-derogable and essential human rights enshrined in the American Convention on Human Rights, in the American Declaration of the Rights and Duties of Man, and in the Universal Declaration of Human Rights;

Recalling that the international protection of human rights is in the form of a convention reinforcing or complementing the protection provided by domestic law and is based upon the attributes of the human personality;

Reaffirming that the systematic practice of the forced disappearance of persons constitutes a crime against humanity;

Hoping that this Convention may help to prevent, punish, and eliminate the forced disappearance of persons in the Hemisphere and make a decisive contribution to the protection of human rights and the rule of law,

Resolve to adopt the following Inter-American Convention on Forced Disappearance of Persons:

Article I

The States Parties to this Convention undertake:

> a. Not to practice, permit, or tolerate the forced disappearance of persons, even in states of emergency or suspension of individual guarantees;
> b. To punish within their jurisdictions, those persons who commit or attempt to commit the crime of forced disappearance of persons and their accomplices and accessories;
> c. To cooperate with one another in helping to prevent, punish, and eliminate the forced disappearance of persons;
> d. To take legislative, administrative, judicial, and any other measures necessary to comply with the commitments undertaken in this Convention.

Article II

For the purposes of this Convention, forced disappearance is considered to be the act of depriving a person or persons of his or their freedom, in whatever way, perpetrated by agents of the state or by persons or groups of persons acting with the authorization, support, or acquiescence of the state, followed by an absence of information or a refusal to acknowledge that deprivation of freedom or to give information on the whereabouts of that person, thereby impeding his or her recourse to the applicable legal remedies and procedural guarantees.

Article III

The States Parties undertake to adopt, in accordance with their constitutional procedures, the legislative measures that may be needed to define the forced disappearance of persons as an offense and to impose an appropriate punishment commensurate with its extreme gravity. This offense shall be deemed continuous or permanent as long as the fate or whereabouts of the victim has not been determined. The States Parties may establish mitigating circumstances for persons who have participated in acts constituting forced disappearance when they help to cause the victim to reappear alive or provide information that sheds light on the forced disappearance of a person.

Article IV

The acts constituting the forced disappearance of persons shall be considered offenses in every State Party. Consequently, each State Party shall take measures to establish its jurisdiction over such cases in the following instances:

  a. When the forced disappearance of persons or any act constituting such offense was committed within its jurisdiction;

  b. When the accused is a national of that state;

  c .When the victim is a national of that state and that state sees fit to do so.

Every State Party shall, moreover, take the necessary measures to establish its jurisdiction over the crime described in this Convention when the alleged criminal is within its territory and it does not proceed to extradite him. This Convention does not authorize any State Party to undertake, in the territory of another State Party, the exercise of jurisdiction or the performance of functions that are placed within the exclusive purview of the authorities of that other Party by its domestic law.

Article V

The forced disappearance of persons shall not be considered a political offense for purposes of extradition. The forced disappearance of persons shall be deemed to be included among the extraditable offenses in every extradition treaty entered into between States Parties. The States Parties undertake to include the offense of forced disappearance as one which is extraditable in every extradition treaty to be concluded between them in the future. Every State Party that makes extradition conditional on the existence of a treaty and receives a request for extradition from another State Party with which it has no extradition treaty may consider this Convention as the necessary legal basis for extradition with respect to the offense of forced disappearance. States Parties which do not make extradition conditional on the existence of a treaty shall recognize such offense as extraditable, subject to the conditions imposed by the law of the requested state. Extradition shall be subject to the provisions set forth in the constitution and other laws of the request state.

Article VI

When a State Party does not grant the extradition, the case shall be submitted to its competent authorities as if the offense had been committed within its jurisdiction, for the purposes of investigation and when appropriate, for criminal action, in accordance with its national law. Any decision adopted by these authorities shall be communicated to the state that has requested the extradition.

Article VII

Criminal prosecution for the forced disappearance of persons and the penalty judicially imposed on its perpetrator shall not be subject to statutes of limitations. However, if there should be a norm of a fundamental character preventing application of the stipulation contained in the previous paragraph, the period of limitation shall be equal to that which applies to the gravest crime in the domestic laws of the corresponding State Party.

Article VIII

The defense of due obedience to superior orders or instructions that stipulate, authorize, or encourage forced disappearance shall not be admitted. All persons who receive such orders have the right and duty not to obey them. The States Parties shall ensure that the training of public law-enforcement personnel or officials includes the necessary education on the offense of forced disappearance of persons.

Article IX

Persons alleged to be responsible for the acts constituting the offense of forced disappearance of persons may be tried only in the competent jurisdictions of ordinary law in each state, to the exclusion of all other special jurisdictions, particularly military jurisdictions. The acts constituting forced disappearance shall not be deemed to have been committed in the course of military duties. Privileges, immunities, or special dispensations shall not be admitted in such trials, without prejudice to the provisions set forth in the Vienna Convention on Diplomatic Relations.

Article X

In no case may exceptional circumstances such as a state of war, the threat of war, internal political instability, or any other public emergency be invoked to justify the forced disappearance of persons. In such cases, the right to expeditious and effective judicial procedures and recourse shall be retained as a means of determining the whereabouts or state of health of a person who has been deprived of freedom, or of identifying the official who ordered or carried out such deprivation of freedom. In pursuing such procedures or recourse, and in keeping with applicable domestic law, the competent judicial authorities shall have free and immediate access to all detention centers and to each of their units, and to all places where there is reason to believe the disappeared person might be found including places that are subject to military jurisdiction.

Article XI

Every person deprived of liberty shall be held in an officially recognized place of detention and be brought before a competent judicial authority without delay, in accordance with applicable domestic law. The States Parties shall establish and maintain official up-to-date registries of their detainees and, in accordance with their domestic law, shall make them available to relatives, judges, attorneys, any other person having a legitimate interest, and other authorities.

Article XII

The States Parties shall give each other mutual assistance in the search for, identification, location, and return of minors who have been removed to another state or detained therein as a consequence of the forced disappearance of their parents or guardians.

Article XIII

For the purposes of this Convention, the processing of petitions or communications presented to the Inter-American Commission on Human Rights alleging the forced disappearance of persons shall be subject to the procedures established in the American Convention on Human Rights and to the Statue and Regulations of the Inter-American Commission on Human Rights and to the Statute and Rules of Procedure of the Inter-American Court of Human Rights, including the provisions on precautionary measures.

Article XIV

Without prejudice to the provisions of the preceding article, when the Inter-American Commission on Human Rights receives a petition or communication regarding an alleged forced disappearance, its Executive Secretariat shall urgently and confidentially address the respective government, and shall request that government to provide as soon as possible information as to the whereabouts of the allegedly disappeared person together with any other information it considers pertinent, and such request shall be without prejudice as to the admissibility of the petition.

Article XV

None of the provisions of this Convention shall be interpreted as limiting other bilateral or multilateral treaties or other agreements signed by the Parties. This Convention shall not apply to the international armed conflicts governed by the 1949 Geneva Conventions and their Protocols, concerning protection of wounded, sick, and shipwrecked members of the armed forces; and prisoners of war and civilians in time of war.

Article XVI

This Convention is open for signature by the member states of the Organization of American States.

Article XVII

This Convention is subject to ratification. The instruments of ratification shall be deposited with the General Secretariat of the Organization of American States.

Article XVIII

This Convention shall be open to accession by any other state. The instruments of accession shall be deposited with the General Secretariat of the Organization of American States.

Article XIX

The states may express reservations with respect to this Convention when adopting, signing, ratifying or acceding to it, unless such reservations are incompatible with the object and purpose of the Convention and as long as they refer to one or more specific provisions.

Article XX

This Convention shall enter into force for the ratifying states on the thirtieth day from the date of deposit of the second instrument of ratification. For each state ratifying or acceding to the Convention after the second instrument of ratification has been deposited, the Convention shall enter into force on the thirtieth day from the date on which that state deposited its instrument of ratification or accession.

Article XXI

This Convention shall remain in force indefinitely, buy may be denounced by any State Party. The instrument of denunciation shall be deposited with the General Secretariat of the Organization of American States. The Convention shall cease to be in effect for the denouncing state and shall remain in force for the other States Parties one year from the date of deposit of the instrument of denunciation.

Article XXII

The original instrument of this Convention, the Spanish, English, Portuguese, and French texts of which are equally authentic, shall be deposited with the General Secretariat of the Organization of American States, which shall forward certified copies thereof to the United Nations Secretariat, for registration and publication, in accordance with Article 102 of the Charter of the United Nations. The General Secretariat of the Organization of American States shall notify member states of the Organization and states acceding to the Convention of the signatures and deposit of instruments of ratification, accession or denunciation, as well as of any reservations that may be expressed.

INTER-AMERICAN DEMOCRATIC CHARTER

Inter-American Democratic Charter, *adopted* Sept. 11, 2001, O.A.S. Doc. AG/doc.8 (XXVIII-E/01), *reprinted in* Basic Documents Pertaining to Human Rights in the Inter-American System, O.A.S. Doc. OAS/Ser.L/V/I.4 rev.12 (2007), *available at* http://www.cidh.org/Basicos/English/Basic23.IA%20Domocratic%20Charter.htm

THE GENERAL ASSEMBLY,

Considering that the Charter of the Organization of American States recognizes that representative democracy is indispensable for the stability, peace, and development of the region, and that one of the purposes of the OAS is to promote and consolidate representative democracy, with due respect for the principle of nonintervention;

Recognizing the contributions of the OAS and other regional and sub-regional mechanisms to the promotion and consolidation of democracy in the Americas;

Recalling that the Heads of State and Government of the Americas, gathered at the Third Summit of the Americas, held from April 20 to 22, 2001 in Quebec City, adopted a democracy clause which establishes that any unconstitutional alteration or interruption of the democratic order in a state of the Hemisphere constitutes an insurmountable obstacle to the participation of that state's government in the Summits of the Americas process;

Bearing in mind that existing democratic provisions in regional and subregional mechanisms express the same objectives as the democracy clause adopted by the Heads of State and Government in Quebec City;

Reaffirming that the participatory nature of democracy in our countries in different aspects of public life contributes to the consolidation of democratic values and to freedom and solidarity in the Hemisphere;

Considering that solidarity among and cooperation between American states require the political organization of those states based on the effective exercise of representative democracy, and that economic growth and social development based on justice and equity, and democracy are interdependent and mutually reinforcing;

Reaffirming that the fight against poverty, and especially the elimination of extreme poverty, is essential to the promotion and consolidation of democracy and constitutes a common and shared responsibility of the American states;

Bearing in mind that the American Declaration on the Rights and Duties of Man and the American Convention on Human Rights contain the values and principles of liberty, equality, and social justice that are intrinsic to democracy;

Reaffirming that the promotion and protection of human rights is a basic prerequisite for the existence of a democratic society, and recognizing the importance of the continuous development and strengthening of the inter-American human rights system for the consolidation of democracy;

Considering that education is an effective way to promote citizens' awareness concerning their own countries and thereby achieve meaningful participation in the decision-making process, and reaffirming the importance of human resource development for a sound democratic system;

Recognizing that a safe environment is essential to the integral development of the human being, which contributes to democracy and political stability;

Bearing in mind that the Protocol of San Salvador on Economic, Social, and Cultural Rights emphasizes the great importance of the reaffirmation, development, improvement, and protection of those rights in order to consolidate the system of representative democratic government;

Recognizing that the right of workers to associate themselves freely for the defense and promotion of their interests is fundamental to the fulfillment of democratic ideals;

Taking into account that, in the Santiago Commitment to Democracy and the Renewal of the Inter-American System, the ministers of foreign affairs expressed their determination to adopt a series of effective, timely, and expeditious procedures to ensure the promotion and defense of representative democracy, with due respect for the principle of nonintervention; and that resolution AG/RES. 1080 (XXI-O/91) therefore established a mechanism for collective action in the case of a sudden or irregular interruption of the democratic political institutional process or of the legitimate exercise of power by the democratically-elected government in any of the Organization's member states, thereby fulfilling a long-standing aspiration of the Hemisphere to be able to respond rapidly and collectively in defense of democracy; * * *

Recognizing that all the rights and obligations of member states under the OAS Charter represent the foundation on which democratic principles in the Hemisphere are built; and

Bearing in mind the progressive development of international law and the advisability of clarifying the provisions set forth in the OAS Charter and related basic instruments on the preservation and defense of democratic institutions, according to established practice,

Resolves: To adopt the following:

INTER-AMERICAN DEMOCRATIC CHARTER

I
Democracy and the Inter-American System

Article 1

The peoples of the Americas have a right to democracy and their governments have an obligation to promote and defend it. Democracy is essential for the social, political, and economic development of the peoples of the Americas.

Article 2
The effective exercise of representative democracy is the basis for the rule of law and of the constitutional regimes of the member states of the Organization of American States. Representative democracy is strengthened and deepened by permanent, ethical, and responsible participation of the citizenry within a legal framework conforming to the respective constitutional order.

Article 3
Essential elements of representative democracy include, *inter alia*, respect for human rights and fundamental freedoms, access to and the exercise of power in accordance with the rule of law, the holding of periodic, free, and fair elections based on secret balloting and universal suffrage as an expression of the sovereignty of the people, the pluralistic system of political parties and organizations, and the separation of powers and independence of the branches of government.

Article 4
Transparency in government activities, probity, responsible public administration on the part of governments, respect for social rights, and freedom of expression and of the press are essential components of the exercise of democracy. The constitutional subordination of all state institutions to the legally constituted civilian authority and respect for the rule of law on the part of all institutions and sectors of society are equally essential to democracy.

Article 5
The strengthening of political parties and other political organizations is a priority for democracy. Special attention will be paid to the problems associated with the high cost of election campaigns and the establishment of a balanced and transparent system for their financing.

Article 6
It is the right and responsibility of all citizens to participate in decisions relating to their own development. This is also a necessary condition for the full and effective exercise of democracy. Promoting and fostering diverse forms of participation strengthens democracy.

II
Democracy and Human Rights

Article 7
Democracy is indispensable for the effective exercise of fundamental freedoms and human rights in their universality, indivisibility and interdependence, embodied in the respective constitutions of states and in inter-American and international human rights instruments.

Article 8
Any person or group of persons who consider that their human rights have been violated may present claims or petitions to the inter-American system for the promotion and protection of human rights in accordance with its established procedures. Member states reaffirm their intention to strengthen the inter-American system for the protection of human rights for the consolidation of democracy in the Hemisphere.

Article 9
The elimination of all forms of discrimination, especially gender, ethnic and race discrimination, as well as diverse forms of intolerance, the promotion and protection of human rights of indigenous peoples and migrants, and respect for ethnic, cultural and religious diversity in the Americas contribute to strengthening democracy and citizen participation.

Article 10

The promotion and strengthening of democracy requires the full and effective exercise of workers' rights and the application of core labor standards, as recognized in the International Labour Organization (ILO) Declaration on Fundamental Principles and Rights at Work, and its Follow-up, adopted in 1998, as well as other related fundamental ILO conventions. Democracy is strengthened by improving standards in the workplace and enhancing the quality of life for workers in the Hemisphere.

III
Democracy, Integral Development, and Combating Poverty

Article 11
Democracy and social and economic development are interdependent and are mutually reinforcing.

Article 12
Poverty, illiteracy, and low levels of human development are factors that adversely affect the consolidation of democracy. The OAS member states are committed to adopting and implementing all those actions required to generate productive employment, reduce poverty, and eradicate extreme poverty, taking into account the different economic realities and conditions of the countries of the Hemisphere. This shared commitment regarding the problems associated with development and poverty also underscores the importance of maintaining macroeconomic equilibria and the obligation to strengthen social cohesion and democracy.

Article 13
The promotion and observance of economic, social, and cultural rights are inherently linked to integral development, equitable economic growth, and to the consolidation of democracy in the states of the Hemisphere.

Article 14
Member states agree to review periodically the actions adopted and carried out by the Organization to promote dialogue, cooperation for integral development, and the fight against poverty in the Hemisphere, and to take the appropriate measures to further these objectives.

Article 15
The exercise of democracy promotes the preservation and good stewardship of the environment. It is essential that the states of the Hemisphere implement policies and strategies to protect the environment, including application of various treaties and conventions, to achieve sustainable development for the benefit of future generations.

Article 16
Education is key to strengthening democratic institutions, promoting the development of human potential, and alleviating poverty and fostering greater understanding among our peoples. To achieve these ends, it is essential that a quality education be available to all, including girls and women, rural inhabitants, and minorities.

IV
Strengthening and Preservation of Democratic Institutions

Article 17
When the government of a member state considers that its democratic political institutional process or its legitimate exercise of power is at risk, it may request assistance from the Secretary General or the Permanent Council for the strengthening and preservation of its democratic system.

Article 18
When situations arise in a member state that may affect the development of its democratic political institutional process or the legitimate exercise of power, the Secretary General or the Permanent Council may, with prior consent of the government concerned, arrange for visits or other actions in order to analyze the situation. The Secretary General will submit a report to the Permanent Council, which will undertake a

collective assessment of the situation and, where necessary, may adopt decisions for the preservation of the democratic system and its strengthening.

Article 19

Based on the principles of the Charter of the OAS and subject to its norms, and in accordance with the democracy clause contained in the Declaration of Quebec City, an unconstitutional interruption of the democratic order or an unconstitutional alteration of the constitutional regime that seriously impairs the democratic order in a member state, constitutes, while it persists, an insurmountable obstacle to its government's participation in sessions of the General Assembly, the Meeting of Consultation, the Councils of the Organization, the specialized conferences, the commissions, working groups, and other bodies of the Organization.

Article 20

In the event of an unconstitutional alteration of the constitutional regime that seriously impairs the democratic order in a member state, any member state or the Secretary General may request the immediate convocation of the Permanent Council to undertake a collective assessment of the situation and to take such decisions as it deems appropriate. The Permanent Council, depending on the situation, may undertake the necessary diplomatic initiatives, including good offices, to foster the restoration of democracy. If such diplomatic initiatives prove unsuccessful, or if the urgency of the situation so warrants, the Permanent Council shall immediately convene a special session of the General Assembly. The General Assembly will adopt the decisions it deems appropriate, including the undertaking of diplomatic initiatives, in accordance with the Charter of the Organization, international law, and the provisions of this Democratic Charter. The necessary diplomatic initiatives, including good offices, to foster the restoration of democracy, will continue during the process.

Article 21

When the special session of the General Assembly determines that there has been an unconstitutional interruption of the democratic order of a member state, and that diplomatic initiatives have failed, the special session shall take the decision to suspend said member state from the exercise of its right to participate in the OAS by an affirmative vote of two thirds of the member states in accordance with the Charter of the OAS. The suspension shall take effect immediately. The suspended member state shall continue to fulfill its obligations to the Organization, in particular its human rights obligations. Notwithstanding the suspension of the member state, the Organization will maintain diplomatic initiatives to restore democracy in that state.

Article 22

Once the situation that led to suspension has been resolved, any member state or the Secretary General may propose to the General Assembly that suspension be lifted. This decision shall require the vote of two thirds of the member states in accordance with the OAS Charter.

V
Democracy and Electoral Observation Missions

Article 23

Member states are responsible for organizing, conducting, and ensuring free and fair electoral processes. Member states, in the exercise of their sovereignty, may request that the Organization of American States provide advisory services or assistance for strengthening and developing their electoral institutions and processes, including sending preliminary missions for that purpose.

Article 24

The electoral observation missions shall be carried out at the request of the member state concerned. To that end, the government of that state and the Secretary General shall enter into an agreement establishing the scope and coverage of the electoral observation mission in question. The member state shall guarantee conditions of security, free access to information, and full cooperation with the electoral observation mission. Electoral observation missions shall be carried out in accordance with the principles and norms of the OAS. The Organization shall ensure that these missions are effective and independent and shall provide them with the necessary resources for that purpose. They shall be conducted in an objective, impartial, and transparent manner and with the appropriate technical expertise. Electoral observation missions shall present a report on their activities in a timely manner to the Permanent Council, through the General Secretariat.

Article 25

The electoral observation missions shall advise the Permanent Council, through the General Secretariat, if the necessary conditions for free and fair elections do not exist. The Organization may, with the consent of the state concerned, send special missions with a view to creating or improving said conditions.

VI
Promotion of a Democratic Culture

Article 26

The OAS will continue to carry out programs and activities designed to promote democratic principles and practices and strengthen a democratic culture in the Hemisphere, bearing in mind that democracy is a way of life based on liberty and enhancement of economic, social, and cultural conditions for the peoples of the Americas. The OAS will consult and cooperate on an ongoing basis with member states and take into account the contributions of civil society organizations working in those fields.

Article 27

The objectives of the programs and activities will be to promote good governance, sound administration, democratic values, and the strengthening of political institutions and civil society organizations. Special attention shall be given to the development of programs and activities for the education of children and youth as a means of ensuring the continuance of democratic values, including liberty and social justice.

Article 28

States shall promote the full and equal participation of women in the political structures of their countries as a fundamental element in the promotion and exercise of a democratic culture.

DRAFT AMERICAN DECLARATION ON THE RIGHTS OF INDIGENOUS PEOPLES

Draft American Declaration on the Rights of Indigenous Peoples, consolidated text, O.A.S. Doc. GT/DADIN/doc.171/04 rev. 4 (May 30, 2003), *available at* http://www.oas.org/consejo/CAJP/Indigenous%20documents.asp

PREAMBLE

The Member States of the Organization of American States (hereinafter "the States"),

Recognizing that the rights of indigenous peoples constitute a fundamental and historically significance issue for the present and future of the Americas;

Recognizing, moreover, the importance for humankind of preserving the indigenous cultures of the Americas;

1. *Indigenous peoples and national strengthening*
    Recognizing that indigenous peoples are foundational societies that form an integral part of the Americas and that their values and cultures are inextricably linked to the identity both of the countries they live in and of the region as a whole.
    Aware that the indigenous peoples of the Americas play a special role in strengthening the institutions of the State and in achieving national unity based on democratic principles.

Recalling that some of the democratic institutions and concepts embodied in the constitutions of the American States have their origins in institutions of the indigenous peoples, and that many of their present participatory systems for decision-making and for authority contribute to the improvement of the democracies in the Americas.

Mindful of the cultural wealth and diversity of the indigenous peoples of the Americas, the variety of national situations, and the varying degrees of indigenous presence in the States.

Recalling the need to develop and strengthen national legal frameworks and policies to respect the cultural diversity of our societies.

2. *The eradication of poverty*

Recognizing that eradicating poverty is a common and shared responsibility of the States, and concerned about the severe impoverishment and vulnerability of the indigenous peoples in various regions of the Hemisphere.

Reiterating that the Charter of the Organization of American States establishes as one of its essential purposes eradicating extreme poverty, indicating that constitutes an obstacle to the full democratic development of the peoples of the Hemisphere.

Mindful of the importance the Inter-American Democratic Charter accords to the relationship among democracy, integral development, and fighting poverty.

Recalling the commitments assumed by the Heads of State and Government at the Third Summit of the Americas with respect to the indigenous peoples regarding the need to adopt special measures so that said peoples can attain their full potential, and the importance of their inclusion to strengthen our democracies and economies.

Reaffirming the right of indigenous peoples to develop in accordance with their own traditions, needs, and interests.

3. *Indigenous culture and ecology*

Recognizing the respect the indigenous peoples of the Americas have for the environment and ecology.

Recognizing, moreover, the value of the cultures, knowledge, and practices of the indigenous peoples for maintaining sustainable development and for living in harmony with nature.

4. *Lands, territories, and resources*

Recognizing the special relationship that the indigenous peoples maintain with their lands, territories, and resources.

Recognizing, that for the indigenous peoples their traditional collective forms of ownership and use of lands, territories, resources, waters, and coastal zones are a necessary conditions for their survival, social organization, development, spirituality, and individual and collective well-being.

5. *Harmonious relations, respect, and non-discrimination*

Considering the importance of eliminating the various forms of *de facto* and *de jure* discrimination that still affect indigenous peoples.

Mindful of the responsibility of the States to combat racial and ethnic discrimination, xenophobia, and other related forms of intolerance.

6. *Human rights instruments and other legal advances*

Reiterating the universality, indivisibility, and interdependence of the human rights and fundamental freedoms recognized by the international community.

Noting the progress made at international level in recognizing the rights of indigenous peoples, and, in particular, the Convention concerning Indigenous and Tribal Peoples in Independent Countries (Convention No. 169) of the International Labor Organization.

Recalling the importance that the Inter-American Democratic Charter assigns to the promotion and protection of the human rights of indigenous peoples, and to respect for ethnic and cultural diversity in the Americas.

Considering the national constitutional, legislative, and jurisprudential progress made in the Americas to guarantee, promote, and protect the rights and institutions of indigenous peoples, as well as the political will of the States to continue moving forward in recognizing the rights of indigenous peoples in the Americas.

Section One: Scope of Application

Article I

1. This Declaration applies to the indigenous peoples of the Americas and their members, who within the national States descend from a native culture that predates European colonization and who conserve their fundamental distinctive features, such as their language, normative systems, usages and customs, artistic expressions, beliefs, and social, economic, cultural, and political institutions.
2. Self-identification as indigenous peoples will be a fundamental criterion for determining to whom this Declaration applies. The States shall ensure respect for self-identification as indigenous, individually and collectively, in keeping with the institutions of each indigenous people.

Article II

The States recognize the multiethnic and multicultural character of their societies.

Article III.

Within the States, the right to self-determination of the indigenous peoples is recognized, pursuant to which they can define their forms of organization and promote their economic, social, and cultural development.

Article IV

Nothing in this Declaration shall be construed so as to authorize or foster any action aimed at breaking up or diminishing, fully or in part, the territorial integrity, sovereignty, and political independence of the States, or other principles contained in the Charter of the Organization of American States.

Section Two: Human Rights

Article V
Full effect and observance of human rights

Indigenous peoples and persons have the right to the full and effective enjoyment of the human rights and fundamental freedoms recognized in the Charter of the OAS, the American Declaration of the Rights and Duties of Man, and, where applicable, the American Convention on Human Rights, and other international human rights instruments. Nothing in this Declaration may be interpreted so as to limit, restrict, or deny in any way those rights, or so as to authorize any action that is not in keeping with the principles of international law, including international human rights law.

Article VI
Collective rights

1. Indigenous peoples have collective rights that are indispensable for their continued existence, well-being, and development as peoples, and for the enjoyment of the individual rights of their members.
2. In this regard, the States recognize, *inter alia*, the right of the indigenous peoples to their collective action; to their social, political, and economic organization; to their own cultures; to profess and practice their spiritual beliefs, and to use their languages.

Article VII
Gender equality

All the rights and freedoms recognized in the present Declaration are guaranteed equally to indigenous women and men. The States condemn violence based on gender or age, which impedes and diminishes the exercise of those rights.

Article VIII
Right to belong to an indigenous people

Indigenous persons and communities have the right to belong to a given indigenous people, in accordance with the traditions and customs of that people.

Article IX
Juridical personality

Indigenous peoples and communities have the right to recognition of their juridical personality by the States. The States shall adopt the necessary measures to ensure that said juridical personality respects the indigenous forms of organization and allows for the full exercise of the rights recognized in this Declaration.

Article X
Rejection of assimilation

1. Indigenous peoples have the right to maintain, express, and freely develop their cultural identity in all respects, free from any external attempt at assimilation.
2. The States shall not adopt any policy to assimilate the indigenous peoples or to destroy their cultures.
3. Indigenous peoples have the right to not be subjected to any form of genocide or attempts to exterminate them.

Article XI
Special guarantees against racism, racial discrimination, xenophobia, and related forms of intolerance

1. Indigenous peoples have the right to protection from racism, racial discrimination, xenophobia, and related forms of intolerance. In this regard, the States shall adopt special measures, when necessary, for the full enjoyment of internationally and nationally recognized human rights, and shall adopt all necessary measures so that indigenous women, men, and children can enjoy their civil, political, economic, social, cultural, and spiritual rights.
2. Indigenous peoples have the right to participate in the determination of those special guarantees.

Section Three: Cultural identity

Article XII
Right to cultural identity

1. Indigenous peoples have the right to their cultural integrity and to their historical and ancestral heritage, which are important for their collective continuity, and for their identity and that of their members and their States.
2. Indigenous peoples have the right to restitution of the property that is part of that heritage of which they have been dispossessed, or, when restitution is not possible, to fair and equitable compensation.
3. The States shall guarantee respect for and non-discrimination against the indigenous ways of life, world views, usages and customs, traditions, forms of social organization, institutions, practices, beliefs, values, dress, and languages.

Article XIII
Logical conceptions and language

1. Indigenous peoples have the right to use, develop, revitalize, and transmit to future generations their own histories, languages, oral traditions, philosophies, systems of writing, and literature; and to designate and retain their own names for their communities, members, and places. The States shall adopt adequate measures to protect the exercise of this right, in consultation with the peoples concerned.
2. The States shall take measures to promote the broadcast of radio and television programming by the mass media in indigenous languages in regions with a large indigenous presence. The States shall also support the creation of indigenous radio stations and other means of communication.
3. The States shall take effective measures so that the members of the indigenous peoples can understand administrative, judicial, and political rules and procedures, and be understood in such proceedings. The States shall make the necessary efforts for the indigenous languages to be established as official languages in the areas where indigenous languages predominate.

Article XIV
Education

1. The States shall include in their national educational systems content that reflects the intercultural, multiethnic, and multilingual nature of their societies. The indigenous peoples have the right to bilingual intercultural education that incorporates their own world view, history, knowledge, values, spiritual practices, and ways of life.

2. Indigenous peoples have the right to:

      a) define and implement their own educational programs, institutions, and facilities;

      b) prepare and apply their own plans, programs, curricula, and teaching materials; and,

      c) educate, train, and accredit their teachers and administrators.

The States shall take the necessary measures to ensure that the indigenous education systems guarantee equal educational opportunity and teachers for the general population and complementarity with the national educational systems.

3. The States shall guarantee that the indigenous educational systems have the same level of quality, efficiency, accessibility, and in every other respect as those provided for the general population. In addition, the States shall facilitate access for indigenous children who live outside of their communities to learning in their own languages and cultures.

4. The States shall take measures to guarantee for the members of the indigenous peoples education of equal quality as for the general population at all levels. The States shall adopt effective measures to provide adequate resources for these purposes.

Article XV
Indigenous spirituality and freedom of conscience

1. Indigenous peoples and their members have the right to freedom of expression, conscience, spirituality, and religion or belief, and to express them both in public and in private, individually or collectively.

2. The States shall take the necessary measures to prohibit efforts to convert or impose beliefs on the indigenous peoples or their members without their free and informed consent.

3. The States shall adopt the necessary measures, in consultation with the indigenous peoples, to preserve, respect, and protect their sacred sites and objects, including their burial grounds, human remains, and relics.

4. The States and their institutions shall guarantee that society as a whole respect the integrity of indigenous symbols, practices, sacred ceremonies, expressions, and spiritual protocols.

Article XVI
Family relations and ties

1. The indigenous family shall be respected and protected by society and the State. The State shall recognize the various indigenous forms of family, particularly the extended family, matrimonial union, filiation, family name, and all other rights of the indigenous family. These indigenous forms of family organization shall be respected by public and private persons, including cooperation and development agencies. In all cases, the criteria of gender and generational equity shall be recognized and respected.

2. In determining the best interest of the child in matters related to the adoption of indigenous children, severance of the ties, and other similar circumstances, the courts and other relevant institutions shall take into account the customary law and shall consider the points of view, rights, and interests of the respective people, including the positions of individuals, the family, and the community. The indigenous institutions shall have primary jurisdiction for determining the custody of indigenous children.

Article XVII
Health

1. Indigenous peoples have the right to the exercise and legal recognition of their traditional indigenous medicine, pharmacopoeia, health practices and promotion, including those aimed at prevention and rehabilitation, as well as the right to use, maintain, develop, and administer their own health services; all in accordance with internationally recognized standards.

2. Indigenous peoples have the right to the use and protection of the plants, animals, and minerals for medicinal use in their ancestral lands and territories, as necessary for the practice of indigenous medicine.

3. The States shall take measures to prevent indigenous peoples from being subject to programs of biological or medical experimentation without their free and informed consent.

4. Indigenous peoples have the right to use, without any discrimination whatsoever, all the health and medical care institutions and services accessible to the general population. The States shall promote an intercultural approach in the medical and health services provided to indigenous persons, including the formation of indigenous technical and professional health care personnel.

5. The States shall provide the necessary means for the indigenous peoples to improve the health conditions in their communities insofar as they fall short of the standards accepted for the general population.

Article XVIII
Right to environmental protection

1. Indigenous peoples have the right to live in harmony with nature and to a healthy and safe environment, which are essential conditions for enjoyment of the right to life, to their spirituality, and to collective well-being.

2. Indigenous peoples have the right to conserve, restore, make use of, and protect their environment, and to the sustainable management of their lands, territories, and resources.

3. Indigenous peoples have the right to be informed and consulted with respect to measures that may affect their environment, as well as to participate in actions and decisions that may affect it.

4. Indigenous peoples have the right to participate fully in the formulation, planning, organization, and implementation of government programs and policies to conserve and exploit their lands, territories, and resources.

5. Indigenous peoples have the right to assistance from their States for the purpose of protecting the environment, and from international organizations, in keeping with the procedures established in the national legislations, and without discrimination.

6. The States shall prohibit, punish, and prevent, in conjunction with the indigenous authorities, the introduction, abandonment, or deposit of radioactive materials or waste, or toxic substances or waste, in violation of legal provisions in force; as well as the production, introduction, transit, possession, or use of chemical, biological, or nuclear weapons on indigenous lands and territories.

7. When the State declares an indigenous territory to be a protected area or subject to wildlife reserve conditions and in the case of lands and territories claimed by indigenous peoples, the conservation areas shall not be subject to any natural resources development without the informed participation of the peoples concerned.

Section IV: Organizational and Political Rights

Article XIX
Rights of association, assembly, and freedom of expression and thought

1. Indigenous peoples and their members have rights of association, assembly, organization, and expression, without interference and in accordance with their values, usages, customs, ancestral traditions, beliefs, and spirituality.

2. Indigenous peoples have the right to assembly and to make use of their sacred and ceremonial areas.

3. Indigenous peoples have the right to maintain full contact, bonds, and common activities with their members who inhabit the territory of neighboring States.

4. The States shall adopt measures aimed at facilitating the exercise of the rights recognized in this article, mindful of the rights of third persons.

Article XX
Right to self-government

1. Indigenous peoples, in the exercise of the right to self-determination within the States, have the right to autonomy or self-government with respect to, *inter alia*, culture, language, spirituality, education, information, means of communication, health, housing, employment, social well-being, maintenance of community security, family relations, economic activities, administration of land and resources, environment and entry of non-members; and to determine the ways and means of financing these autonomous functions.

2. Indigenous peoples have the right to participate without discrimination in decision-making at all levels, in relation to matters that may directly affect their rights, lives, and destiny. They may do so either directly or through their representatives elected by them in accordance with their own procedures. They also have

the right to maintain and develop their own indigenous decision-making institutions; and to equal opportunity for gaining access to and participating in all national institutions and fora.

Article XXI
Indigenous law and jurisdiction

1. Indigenous law shall be recognized as part of the legal system and of the States' framework for social and economic development.

2. Indigenous peoples have the right to maintain and strengthen their legal systems for addressing internal matters in their communities, and to apply them in accordance with their own rules and procedures, including matters related to the resolution of conflicts within and between indigenous peoples, and to the preservation of peace and harmony.

3. The matters referring to indigenous persons or to their interests in the jurisdiction of each State shall be conducted so as to provide for the right of the indigenous to full representation with dignity and equality before the law, and, if necessary, the use of interpreters.

4. The States shall take measures to reinforce the judicial capacity of the indigenous peoples, to establish their jurisdiction, and to coordinate it with all other national jurisdictions, as appropriate. In addition, the States shall take measures to ensure that the judiciary is knowledgeable of and applies indigenous law and custom, and to ensure that it is taught in the law schools.

Article XXII
Contributions of the indigenous legal and organizational systems

1. The States shall facilitate the inclusion, within their national organizational structures, as appropriate, of the traditional institutions and practices of the indigenous peoples, in consultation with and with the consent of said peoples.

2. The relevant institutions of each State that serve the indigenous peoples, as well as their respective public policies, shall be designed in consultation with and with the participation of the peoples concerned to reinforce and promote the identity, culture, traditions, organization, and values of those peoples.

Article XXIII
Treaties, agreements, and constructive arrangements

Indigenous peoples have the right to the recognition, observance, and application of the treaties, conventions, and other arrangements that the States or their successors may have concluded, in keeping with their spirit and intent, and to have the same be respected and observed by the States.

Section Five: Social, Economic, and Property Rights

Article XXIV
Traditional forms of property and cultural survival. Right to land, territory, and resources

1. Indigenous peoples have the right to the recognition of their property rights and ownership rights with respect to the lands and territories that they historically occupy, as well as the use of the lands to which they have traditionally had access for carrying out their traditional activities and for sustenance, respecting the principles of the legal system of each State. These rights also include the waters, coastal seas, flora, fauna, and all other resources of that habitat, as well as their environment, preserving these for themselves and future generations.

2. Indigenous peoples have the right to legal recognition of the various and particular modalities and forms of property, possession, and ownership of their lands and territories, in accordance with the principles of the legal system of each State. The States shall establish the special regimes appropriate for such recognition, and for their effective demarcation or titling.

3. The rights of the indigenous peoples to their lands and territories they occupy or use historically are permanent, exclusive, inalienable, imprescriptible, and indefeasible.

4. The titles may only be modified by mutual agreement between the State and the respective indigenous peoples, with full knowledge and understanding by their members with respect to the nature and attributes of that property and of the proposed modification. The agreement by the indigenous people concerned shall be given following its practices, usages and customs.

5. Indigenous peoples have the right to attribute ownership within the community in accordance with the values, usages, and customs of each peoples.

6. The States shall take adequate measures to avert, prevent, and punish any intrusion or use of such lands, territories, or resources by persons from outside to claim for themselves the property, possession, or right to use the same.

7. In case the property rights over the minerals or resources of the subsoil belong to the State, or it has rights over other resources existing in the lands and territories of the indigenous peoples, the States shall establish or maintain procedures for the participation of the peoples concerned for determining whether the interests of those peoples would be prejudiced and to what extent, before undertaking or authorizing any program involving prospecting, planning, or exploitation of the resources existing on their lands and territories. The peoples concerned shall participate in the benefits of such activities, and receive fair compensation for any harm they might suffer as a result of such activities.

8. The States shall provide, within their legal systems, a legal framework and effective legal remedies to protect the rights of the indigenous peoples referred to in this article.

Article XXV
On transfers and relocations

1. The States may not transfer or relocate indigenous peoples without their free, genuine, public, and informed consent, unless there are causes involving a national emergency or other exceptional circumstance of public interest that makes it necessary; and, in all cases, with the immediate replacement by adequate lands of equal or better quality and legal status, guaranteeing the right to return if the causes that gave rise to the displacement cease to exist.

2. Compensation shall be paid to the indigenous peoples and to their members who are transferred or relocated for any loss or harm they may have suffered as a result of their displacement.

Article XXVI
Indigenous peoples in voluntary isolation

1. Indigenous peoples in voluntary isolation have the right to remain in that condition and to live freely and in accordance with their ancestral traditions.

2. The States shall adopt adequate measures to protect the territories, environment, and cultures of the indigenous peoples in voluntary isolation, as well as the personal integrity of their members. These measures shall include those necessary to prevent intrusion into their territories.

Article XXVII
Labor rights

1. Indigenous peoples and persons enjoy the rights and guarantees recognized in labor legislation and have the right to special measures to correct, repair, and prevent the discrimination to which they are subjected. The States shall adopt immediate and effective measures to guarantee that indigenous children are protected from all forms of labor exploitation.

2. In case they are not protected effectively by the legislation applicable to workers in general, the States shall take the special and immediate measures that may be necessary in order to:

    a) protect workers and employees who are members of indigenous peoples in relation to contracting, and to obtain fair and equal conditions of employment, in both formal and informal labor arrangements;

    b) establish and improve the labor inspection service and the enforcement of rules in the regions, companies, or salaried labor activities in which indigenous workers or employees participate;

    c) guarantee that indigenous workers:

        i. enjoy equal opportunities and treatment in all employment conditions, in promotions and raises; and other conditions stipulated in international law;

        ii. enjoy the right to association, the right to engage freely in trade union activities, and the right to enter into collective bargaining agreements with employers or workers' organizations, directly or through their traditional authorities;

        iii. are not submitted to racial, sexual, or any other type of harassment;

iv. are not subject to coercive hiring systems, including debt servitude or any other type of servitude, whether they arise from law, custom, or an individual or collective arrangement, which in each case shall be deemed absolutely null and void;

v. are not subject to work that endangers their health and personal safety; and

vi. receive special protection when they provide their services as seasonal, occasional, or migrant workers, as well as when they are contracted by labor contractors such that they receive the benefits of the national legislation and practices, which shall be in accordance with the international human rights standards established for this category of workers; and

vii. ensure that the employers of indigenous workers are fully aware of the rights of indigenous workers according to the national legislation and international standards, and of the remedies and actions available to them to protect those rights.

Article XXVIII
Protection of Cultural Patrimony and Intellectual Property

1. Indigenous peoples have the right to the recognition of the property, control, development, and protection of their cultural patrimony through special regimes that recognizes the communal nature of said property. Such regimes shall be established with their informed consent and participation.

2. Indigenous peoples also have the right to the legal protection of that property through patents, commercial trademarks, copyright, and other general procedures of intellectual property.

3. The patrimony of indigenous peoples includes, *inter alia*, the knowledge, ancestral designs and procedures, artistic, spiritual, technological, scientific, and biogenetic expressions, as well as the knowledge and developments of their own related to the utility and qualities of medicinal plants.

Article XXIX
Right to development

1. Indigenous peoples have the right to determine and implement autonomously the values, options, objectives, priorities, and strategies for their development. This right includes participation in determining and developing health and housing programs, and other economic and social programs that affect them, and, when possible, in administering these programs through their own institutions. The indigenous peoples have the right, without any discrimination whatsoever, to obtain adequate means for their own development, including those from international cooperation, and to contribute in their own ways to national development.

2. The States shall take the necessary measures to ensure that the decisions referring to any plan, program, or project subject to directly affecting the rights or living conditions of the indigenous peoples are made in consultation with those peoples so that their preferences may be recognized, and so that no provision whatsoever is included that impact them directly. Such consultations shall be carried out in good faith and in a manner appropriate to the circumstances, for the purpose of reaching an agreement or securing consent to the measures proposed.

3. Indigenous peoples have the right to fair and equitable compensation for any damage caused to them by the implementation of such plans, programs, or projects, despite the precautions established in this article; and for measures to be adopted to mitigate adverse ecological, economic, social, cultural, or spiritual impacts.

Article XXX
Protection in the event of armed conflicts

In the event of armed conflicts, the States shall take special measures, with the agreement of the indigenous peoples concerned, to protect the human rights, institutions, lands, territories, and resources of the indigenous peoples.

Section Six: General provisions

Article XXXI

The States shall guarantee the full enjoyment of the fundamental civil, political, economic, social, and cultural rights and spirituality of the indigenous peoples, and shall adopt the legislative and other necessary measures to enforce the rights recognized in this Declaration.

327

Article XXXII

The nature and scope of the measures that shall be taken to implement this Declaration shall be determined with flexibility, taking into account the particular conditions of each country, and in genuine and informed consultation with the indigenous peoples concerned.

Article XXXIII

Any interpretation and application of the present Declaration shall respect the fundamental human rights, the democracy, and the constitutional principles of each State.

Article XXXIV

Nothing in this Declaration may be interpreted as to diminish or eliminate rights in force or that may be recognized in the future.

Article XXXV

The rights recognized in this Declaration constitute the minimum standard for the survival, dignity, and well-being of the indigenous peoples of the Americas.

EUROPE

CONVENTION FOR THE PROTECTION OF HUMAN RIGHTS AND FUNDAMENTAL FREEDOMS AS AMENDED BY PROTOCOL NO. 11

Convention for the Protection of Human Rights and Fundamental Freedoms, *adopted* Nov. 4, 1950, 213 U.N.T.S. 221
as amended by
Protocol No. 11 to the Convention for the Protection of Human Rights and Fundamental Freedoms of 4 November 1950, restructuring the control machinery established thereby, *adopted* May 11, 1994, 2061 U.N.T.S. 7.

The governments signatory hereto, being members of the Council of Europe,

Considering the Universal Declaration of Human Rights proclaimed by the General Assembly of the United Nations on 10th December 1948;

Considering that this Declaration aims at securing the universal and effective recognition and observance of the Rights therein declared;

Considering that the aim of the Council of Europe is the achievement of greater unity between its members and that one of the methods by which that aim is to be pursued is the maintenance and further realisation of human rights and fundamental freedoms;

Reaffirming their profound belief in those fundamental freedoms which are the foundation of justice and peace in the world and are best maintained on the one hand by an effective political democracy and on the other by a common understanding and observance of the human rights upon which they depend;

Being resolved, as the governments of European countries which are like minded and have a common heritage of political traditions, ideals, freedom and the rule of law, to take the first steps for the collective enforcement of certain of the rights stated in the Universal Declaration,

Have agreed as follows:

Article 1 – Obligation to respect human rights

The High Contracting Parties shall secure to everyone within their jurisdiction the rights and freedoms defined in Section I of this Convention.

Section I – Rights and freedoms

Article 2 – Right to life

1 Everyone's right to life shall be protected by law. No one shall be deprived of his life intentionally save in the execution of a sentence of a court following his conviction of a crime for which this penalty is provided by law.

2 Deprivation of life shall not be regarded as inflicted in contravention of this article when it results from the use of force which is no more than absolutely necessary:

    a. in defence of any person from unlawful violence;

    b. in order to effect a lawful arrest or to prevent the escape of a person lawfully detained;

    c. in action lawfully taken for the purpose of quelling a riot or insurrection.

Article 3 – Prohibition of torture

No one shall be subjected to torture or to inhuman or degrading treatment or punishment.

Article 4 – Prohibition of slavery and forced labour

1. No one shall be held in slavery or servitude.

2. No one shall be required to perform forced or compulsory labour.

3. For the purpose of this article the term "forced or compulsory labour" shall not include:

    a. any work required to be done in the ordinary course of detention imposed according to the provisions of Article 5 of this Convention or during conditional release from such detention;

    b. any service of a military character or, in case of conscientious objectors in countries where they are recognised, service exacted instead of compulsory military service;

    c. any service exacted in case of an emergency or calamity threatening the life or well being of the community;

    d. any work or service which forms part of normal civic obligations.

Article 5 – Right to liberty and security

1. Everyone has the right to liberty and security of person. No one shall be deprived of his liberty save in the following cases and in accordance with a procedure prescribed by law:

    a. the lawful detention of a person after conviction by a competent court;

    b. the lawful arrest or detention of a person for non compliance with the lawful order of a court or in order to secure the fulfilment of any obligation prescribed by law;

    c. the lawful arrest or detention of a person effected for the purpose of bringing him before the competent legal authority on reasonable suspicion of having committed an offence or when it is reasonably considered necessary to prevent his committing an offence or fleeing after having done so;

    d. the detention of a minor by lawful order for the purpose of educational supervision or his lawful detention for the purpose of bringing him before the competent legal authority;

    e. the lawful detention of persons for the prevention of the spreading of infectious diseases, of persons of unsound mind, alcoholics or drug addicts or vagrants;

    f. the lawful arrest or detention of a person to prevent his effecting an unauthorised entry into the country or of a person against whom action is being taken with a view to deportation or extradition.

2. Everyone who is arrested shall be informed promptly, in a language which he understands, of the reasons for his arrest and of any charge against him.

3. Everyone arrested or detained in accordance with the provisions of paragraph 1.c of this article shall be brought promptly before a judge or other officer authorised by law to exercise judicial power and shall be entitled to trial within a reasonable time or to release pending trial. Release may be conditioned by guarantees to appear for trial.

4. Everyone who is deprived of his liberty by arrest or detention shall be entitled to take proceedings by which the lawfulness of his detention shall be decided speedily by a court and his release ordered if the

detention is not lawful.

5. Everyone who has been the victim of arrest or detention in contravention of the provisions of this article shall have an enforceable right to compensation.

Article 6 – Right to a fair trial

1. In the determination of his civil rights and obligations or of any criminal charge against him, everyone is entitled to a fair and public hearing within a reasonable time by an independent and impartial tribunal established by law. Judgment shall be pronounced publicly but the press and public may be excluded from all or part of the trial in the interests of morals, public order or national security in a democratic society, where the interests of juveniles or the protection of the private life of the parties so require, or to the extent strictly necessary in the opinion of the court in special circumstances where publicity would prejudice the interests of justice.

2. Everyone charged with a criminal offence shall be presumed innocent until proved guilty according to law.

3. Everyone charged with a criminal offence has the following minimum rights:

> a. to be informed promptly, in a language which he understands and in detail, of the nature and cause of the accusation against him;
> b. to have adequate time and facilities for the preparation of his defence;
> c. to defend himself in person or through legal assistance of his own choosing or, if he has not sufficient means to pay for legal assistance, to be given it free when the interests of justice so require;
> d. to examine or have examined witnesses against him and to obtain the attendance and examination of witnesses on his behalf under the same conditions as witnesses against him;
> e. to have the free assistance of an interpreter if he cannot understand or speak the language used in court.

Article 7 – No punishment without law

1. No one shall be held guilty of any criminal offence on account of any act or omission which did not constitute a criminal offence under national or international law at the time when it was committed. Nor shall a heavier penalty be imposed than the one that was applicable at the time the criminal offence was committed.

2. This article shall not prejudice the trial and punishment of any person for any act or omission which, at the time when it was committed, was criminal according to the general principles of law recognised by civilised nations.

Article 8 – Right to respect for private and family life

1. Everyone has the right to respect for his private and family life, his home and his correspondence.

2. There shall be no interference by a public authority with the exercise of this right except such as is in accordance with the law and is necessary in a democratic society in the interests of national security, public safety or the economic well being of the country, for the prevention of disorder or crime, for the protection of health or morals, or for the protection of the rights and freedoms of others.

Article 9 – Freedom of thought, conscience and religion

1. Everyone has the right to freedom of thought, conscience and religion; this right includes freedom to change his religion or belief and freedom, either alone or in community with others and in public or private, to manifest his religion or belief, in worship, teaching, practice and observance.

2. Freedom to manifest one's religion or beliefs shall be subject only to such limitations as are prescribed by law and are necessary in a democratic society in the interests of public safety, for the protection of public order, health or morals, or for the protection of the rights and freedoms of others.

Article 10 – Freedom of expression

1. Everyone has the right to freedom of expression. This right shall include freedom to hold opinions and to receive and impart information and ideas without interference by public authority and regardless of frontiers. This article shall not prevent States from requiring the licensing of broadcasting, television or cinema enterprises.

2. The exercise of these freedoms, since it carries with it duties and responsibilities, may be subject to such

formalities, conditions, restrictions or penalties as are prescribed by law and are necessary in a democratic society, in the interests of national security, territorial integrity or public safety, for the prevention of disorder or crime, for the protection of health or morals, for the protection of the reputation or rights of others, for preventing the disclosure of information received in confidence, or for maintaining the authority and impartiality of the judiciary.

Article 11 – Freedom of assembly and association

1. Everyone has the right to freedom of peaceful assembly and to freedom of association with others, including the right to form and to join trade unions for the protection of his interests.
2. No restrictions shall be placed on the exercise of these rights other than such as are prescribed by law and are necessary in a democratic society in the interests of national security or public safety, for the prevention of disorder or crime, for the protection of health or morals or for the protection of the rights and freedoms of others. This article shall not prevent the imposition of lawful restrictions on the exercise of these rights by members of the armed forces, of the police or of the administration of the State.

Article 12 – Right to marry

Men and women of marriageable age have the right to marry and to found a family, according to the national laws governing the exercise of this right.

Article 13 – Right to an effective remedy

Everyone whose rights and freedoms as set forth in this Convention are violated shall have an effective remedy before a national authority notwithstanding that the violation has been committed by persons acting in an official capacity.

Article 14 – Prohibition of discrimination

The enjoyment of the rights and freedoms set forth in this Convention shall be secured without discrimination on any ground such as sex, race, colour, language, religion, political or other opinion, national or social origin, association with a national minority, property, birth or other status.

Article 15 – Derogation in time of emergency

1. In time of war or other public emergency threatening the life of the nation any High Contracting Party may take measures derogating from its obligations under this Convention to the extent strictly required by the exigencies of the situation, provided that such measures are not inconsistent with its other obligations under international law.
2. No derogation from Article 2, except in respect of deaths resulting from lawful acts of war, or from Articles 3, 4 (paragraph 1) and 7 shall be made under this provision.
3. Any High Contracting Party availing itself of this right of derogation shall keep the Secretary General of the Council of Europe fully informed of the measures which it has taken and the reasons therefor. It shall also inform the Secretary General of the Council of Europe when such measures have ceased to operate and the provisions of the Convention are again being fully executed.

Article 16 – Restrictions on political activity of aliens

Nothing in Articles 10, 11 and 14 shall be regarded as preventing the High Contracting Parties from imposing restrictions on the political activity of aliens.

Article 17 – Prohibition of abuse of rights

Nothing in this Convention may be interpreted as implying for any State, group or person any right to engage in any activity or perform any act aimed at the destruction of any of the rights and freedoms set forth herein or at their limitation to a greater extent than is provided for in the Convention.

Article 18 – Limitation on use of restrictions on rights

The restrictions permitted under this Convention to the said rights and freedoms shall not be applied for any purpose other than those for which they have been prescribed.

Section II – European Court of Human Rights

331

Article 19 – Establishment of the Court
To ensure the observance of the engagements undertaken by the High Contracting Parties in the Convention and the Protocols thereto, there shall be set up a European Court of Human Rights, hereinafter referred to as "the Court". It shall function on a permanent basis.

Article 20 – Number of judges
The Court shall consist of a number of judges equal to that of the High Contracting Parties.

Article 21 – Criteria for office
1. The judges shall be of high moral character and must either possess the qualifications required for appointment to high judicial office or be jurisconsults of recognised competence.
2. The judges shall sit on the Court in their individual capacity.
3. During their term of office the judges shall not engage in any activity which is incompatible with their independence, impartiality or with the demands of a full-time office; all questions arising from the application of this paragraph shall be decided by the Court.

Article 22 – Election of judges
1. The judges shall be elected by the Parliamentary Assembly with respect to each High Contracting Party by a majority of votes cast from a list of three candidates nominated by the High Contracting Party.
2. The same procedure shall be followed to complete the Court in the event of the accession of new High Contracting Parties and in filling casual vacancies.

Article 23 – Terms of office
1. The judges shall be elected for a period of six years. They may be re-elected. However, the terms of office of one-half of the judges elected at the first election shall expire at the end of three years.
2. The judges whose terms of office are to expire at the end of the initial period of three years shall be chosen by lot by the Secretary General of the Council of Europe immediately after their election.
3. In order to ensure that, as far as possible, the terms of office of one-half of the judges are renewed every three years, the Parliamentary Assembly may decide, before proceeding to any subsequent election, that the term or terms of office of one or more judges to be elected shall be for a period other than six years but not more than nine and not less than three years.
4. In cases where more than one term of office is involved and where the Parliamentary Assembly applies the preceding paragraph, the allocation of the terms of office shall be effected by a drawing of lots by the Secretary General of the Council of Europe immediately after the election.
5. A judge elected to replace a judge whose term of office has not expired shall hold office for the remainder of his predecessor's term.
6. The terms of office of judges shall expire when they reach the age of 70.
7. The judges shall hold office until replaced. They shall, however, continue to deal with such cases as they already have under consideration.

Article 24 – Dismissal
No judge may be dismissed from his office unless the other judges decide by a majority of two-thirds that he has ceased to fulfil the required conditions.

Article 25 – Registry and legal secretaries
The Court shall have a registry, the functions and organisation of which shall be laid down in the rules of the Court. The Court shall be assisted by legal secretaries.

Article 26 – Plenary Court
The plenary Court shall
a. elect its President and one or two Vice-Presidents for a period of three years; they may be re elected;
b. set up Chambers, constituted for a fixed period of time;
c. elect the Presidents of the Chambers of the Court; they may be re-elected;
d. adopt the rules of the Court, and
e. elect the Registrar and one or more Deputy Registrars.

Article 27 – Committees, Chambers and Grand Chamber

1. To consider cases brought before it, the Court shall sit in committees of three judges, in Chambers of seven judges and in a Grand Chamber of seventeen judges. The Court's Chambers shall set up committees for a fixed period of time.

2. There shall sit as an ex officio member of the Chamber and the Grand Chamber the judge elected in respect of the State Party concerned or, if there is none or if he is unable to sit, a person of its choice who shall sit in the capacity of judge.

3. The Grand Chamber shall also include the President of the Court, the Vice-Presidents, the Presidents of the Chambers and other judges chosen in accordance with the rules of the Court. When a case is referred to the Grand Chamber under Article 43, no judge from the Chamber which rendered the judgment shall sit in the Grand Chamber, with the exception of the President of the Chamber and the judge who sat in respect of the State Party concerned.

Article 28 – Declarations of inadmissibility by committees

A committee may, by a unanimous vote, declare inadmissible or strike out of its list of cases an application submitted under Article 34 where such a decision can be taken without further examination. The decision shall be final.

Article 29 – Decisions by Chambers on admissibility and merits

1. If no decision is taken under Article 28, a Chamber shall decide on the admissibility and merits of individual applications submitted under Article 34.

2. A Chamber shall decide on the admissibility and merits of inter-State applications submitted under Article 33.

3. The decision on admissibility shall be taken separately unless the Court, in exceptional cases, decides otherwise.

Article 30 – Relinquishment of jurisdiction to the Grand Chamber

Where a case pending before a Chamber raises a serious question affecting the interpretation of the Convention or the protocols thereto, or where the resolution of a question before the Chamber might have a result inconsistent with a judgment previously delivered by the Court, the Chamber may, at any time before it has rendered its judgment, relinquish jurisdiction in favour of the Grand Chamber, unless one of the parties to the case objects.

Article 31 – Powers of the Grand Chamber

The Grand Chamber shall

a. determine applications submitted either under Article 33 or Article 34 when a Chamber has relinquished jurisdiction under Article 30 or when the case has been referred to it under Article 43; and

b. consider requests for advisory opinions submitted under Article 47.

Article 32 – Jurisdiction of the Court

1. The jurisdiction of the Court shall extend to all matters concerning the interpretation and application of the Convention and the protocols thereto which are referred to it as provided in Articles 33, 34 and 47.

2. In the event of dispute as to whether the Court has jurisdiction, the Court shall decide.

Article 33 – Inter-State cases

Any High Contracting Party may refer to the Court any alleged breach of the provisions of the Convention and the protocols thereto by another High Contracting Party.

Article 34 – Individual applications

The Court may receive applications from any person, non-governmental organisation or group of individuals claiming to be the victim of a violation by one of the High Contracting Parties of the rights set forth in the Convention or the protocols thereto. The High Contracting Parties undertake not to hinder in any way the effective exercise of this right.

Article 35 – Admissibility criteria

1. The Court may only deal with the matter after all domestic remedies have been exhausted, according to the generally recognised rules of international law, and within a period of six months from the date on which the final decision was taken.

2. The Court shall not deal with any application submitted under Article 34 that
> a. is anonymous; or
> b. is substantially the same as a matter that has already been examined by the Court or has already been submitted to another procedure of international investigation or settlement and contains no relevant new information.

3. The Court shall declare inadmissible any individual application submitted under Article 34 which it considers incompatible with the provisions of the Convention or the protocols thereto, manifestly ill founded, or an abuse of the right of application.

4. The Court shall reject any application which it considers inadmissible under this Article. It may do so at any stage of the proceedings.

Article 36 – Third party intervention

1. In all cases before a Chamber or the Grand Chamber, a High Contracting Party one of whose nationals is an applicant shall have the right to submit written comments and to take part in hearings.

2. The President of the Court may, in the interest of the proper administration of justice, invite any High Contracting Party which is not a party to the proceedings or any person concerned who is not the applicant to submit written comments or take part in hearings.

Article 37 – Striking out applications

1. The Court may at any stage of the proceedings decide to strike an application out of its list of cases where the circumstances lead to the conclusion that
> a. the applicant does not intend to pursue his application; or
> b. the matter has been resolved; or
> c. for any other reason established by the Court, it is no longer justified to continue the examination of the application.

However, the Court shall continue the examination of the application if respect for human rights as defined in the Convention and the protocols thereto so requires.

2. The Court may decide to restore an application to its list of cases if it considers that the circumstances justify such a course.

Article 38 – Examination of the case and friendly settlement proceedings

1. If the Court declares the application admissible, it shall
> a. pursue the examination of the case, together with the representatives of the parties, and if need be, undertake an investigation, for the effective conduct of which the States concerned shall furnish all necessary facilities;
> b. place itself at the disposal of the parties concerned with a view to securing a friendly settlement of the matter on the basis of respect for human rights as defined in the Convention and the protocols thereto.

2. Proceedings conducted under paragraph 1.b shall be confidential.

Article 39 – Finding of a friendly settlement

If a friendly settlement is effected, the Court shall strike the case out of its list by means of a decision which shall be confined to a brief statement of the facts and of the solution reached.

Article 40 – Public hearings and access to documents

1. Hearings shall be in public unless the Court in exceptional circumstances decides otherwise.

2. Documents deposited with the Registrar shall be accessible to the public unless the President of the Court decides otherwise.

Article 41 – Just satisfaction

If the Court finds that there has been a violation of the Convention or the protocols thereto, and if the internal law of the High Contracting Party concerned allows only partial reparation to be made, the Court shall, if necessary, afford just satisfaction to the injured party.

Article 42 – Judgments of Chambers
Judgments of Chambers shall become final in accordance with the provisions of Article 44, paragraph 2.

Article 43 – Referral to the Grand Chamber
1. Within a period of three months from the date of the judgment of the Chamber, any party to the case may, in exceptional cases, request that the case be referred to the Grand Chamber.
2. A panel of five judges of the Grand Chamber shall accept the request if the case raises a serious question affecting the interpretation or application of the Convention or the protocols thereto, or a serious issue of general importance.
3. If the panel accepts the request, the Grand Chamber shall decide the case by means of a judgment.

Article 44 – Final judgments
1. The judgment of the Grand Chamber shall be final.
2. The judgment of a Chamber shall become final
   a. when the parties declare that they will not request that the case be referred to the Grand Chamber; or
   b. three months after the date of the judgment, if reference of the case to the Grand Chamber has not been requested; or
   c. when the panel of the Grand Chamber rejects the request to refer under Article 43.
3. The final judgment shall be published.

Article 45 – Reasons for judgments and decisions
1. Reasons shall be given for judgments as well as for decisions declaring applications admissible or inadmissible.
2. If a judgment does not represent, in whole or in part, the unanimous opinion of the judges, any judge shall be entitled to deliver a separate opinion.

Article 46 – Binding force and execution of judgments
1. The High Contracting Parties undertake to abide by the final judgment of the Court in any case to which they are parties.
2. The final judgment of the Court shall be transmitted to the Committee of Ministers, which shall supervise its execution.

Article 47 – Advisory opinions
1. The Court may, at the request of the Committee of Ministers, give advisory opinions on legal questions concerning the interpretation of the Convention and the protocols thereto.
2. Such opinions shall not deal with any question relating to the content or scope of the rights or freedoms defined in Section I of the Convention and the protocols thereto, or with any other question which the Court or the Committee of Ministers might have to consider in consequence of any such proceedings as could be instituted in accordance with the Convention.
3. Decisions of the Committee of Ministers to request an advisory opinion of the Court shall require a majority vote of the representatives entitled to sit on the Committee.

Article 48 – Advisory jurisdiction of the Court
The Court shall decide whether a request for an advisory opinion submitted by the Committee of Ministers is within its competence as defined in Article 47.

Article 49 – Reasons for advisory opinions
1. Reasons shall be given for advisory opinions of the Court.
2. If the advisory opinion does not represent, in whole or in part, the unanimous opinion of the judges, any judge shall be entitled to deliver a separate opinion.
3. Advisory opinions of the Court shall be communicated to the Committee of Ministers.

Article 50 – Expenditure on the Court
The expenditure on the Court shall be borne by the Council of Europe.

Article 51 – Privileges and immunities of judges
The judges shall be entitled, during the exercise of their functions, to the privileges and immunities provided for in Article 40 of the Statute of the Council of Europe and in the agreements made thereunder.

Section III – Miscellaneous provisions

Article 52 – Inquiries by the Secretary General
On receipt of a request from the Secretary General of the Council of Europe any High Contracting Party shall furnish an explanation of the manner in which its internal law ensures the effective implementation of any of the provisions of the Convention.

Article 53 – Safeguard for existing human rights
Nothing in this Convention shall be construed as limiting or derogating from any of the human rights and fundamental freedoms which may be ensured under the laws of any High Contracting Party or under any other agreement to which it is a Party.

Article 54 – Powers of the Committee of Ministers
Nothing in this Convention shall prejudice the powers conferred on the Committee of Ministers by the Statute of the Council of Europe.

Article 55 – Exclusion of other means of dispute settlement
The High Contracting Parties agree that, except by special agreement, they will not avail themselves of treaties, conventions or declarations in force between them for the purpose of submitting, by way of petition, a dispute arising out of the interpretation or application of this Convention to a means of settlement other than those provided for in this Convention.

Article 56 – Territorial application
1. Any State may at the time of its ratification or at any time thereafter declare by notification addressed to the Secretary General of the Council of Europe that the present Convention shall, subject to paragraph 4 of this Article, extend to all or any of the territories for whose international relations it is responsible.
2. The Convention shall extend to the territory or territories named in the notification as from the thirtieth day after the receipt of this notification by the Secretary General of the Council of Europe.
3. The provisions of this Convention shall be applied in such territories with due regard, however, to local requirements.
4. Any State which has made a declaration in accordance with paragraph 1 of this article may at any time thereafter declare on behalf of one or more of the territories to which the declaration relates that it accepts the competence of the Court to receive applications from individuals, non-governmental organisations or groups of individuals as provided by Article 34 of the Convention.

Article 57 – Reservations
1. Any State may, when signing this Convention or when depositing its instrument of ratification, make a reservation in respect of any particular provision of the Convention to the extent that any law then in force in its territory is not in conformity with the provision. Reservations of a general character shall not be permitted under this article.
2. Any reservation made under this article shall contain a brief statement of the law concerned.

Article 58 – Denunciation
1. A High Contracting Party may denounce the present Convention only after the expiry of five years from the date on which it became a party to it and after six months' notice contained in a notification addressed to the Secretary General of the Council of Europe, who shall inform the other High Contracting Parties.
2. Such a denunciation shall not have the effect of releasing the High Contracting Party concerned from its obligations under this Convention in respect of any act which, being capable of constituting a violation of

such obligations, may have been performed by it before the date at which the denunciation became effective.

3. Any High Contracting Party which shall cease to be a member of the Council of Europe shall cease to be a Party to this Convention under the same conditions.

4. The Convention may be denounced in accordance with the provisions of the preceding paragraphs in respect of any territory to which it has been declared to extend under the terms of Article 56.

Article 59 – Signature and ratification

1. This Convention shall be open to the signature of the members of the Council of Europe. It shall be ratified. Ratifications shall be deposited with the Secretary General of the Council of Europe.

2. The present Convention shall come into force after the deposit of ten instruments of ratification.

3. As regards any signatory ratifying subsequently, the Convention shall come into force at the date of the deposit of its instrument of ratification.

4. The Secretary General of the Council of Europe shall notify all the members of the Council of Europe of the entry into force of the Convention, the names of the High Contracting Parties who have ratified it, and the deposit of all instruments of ratification which may be effected subsequently.

PROTOCOL NO. 14 TO THE CONVENTION FOR THE PROTECTION OF HUMAN RIGHTS AND FUNDAMENTAL FREEDOMS, AMENDING THE CONTROL SYSTEM OF THE CONVENTION

Protocol No. 14 to the Convention for the Protection of Human Rights and Fundamental Freedoms, amending the control system of the Convention, *adopted* May 13, 2004, C.E.T.S. No. 194, *available at* http://conventions.coe.int/Treaty/EN/Treaties/Html/194.htm

Preamble

The member States of the Council of Europe, signatories to this Protocol to the Convention for the Protection of Human Rights and Fundamental Freedoms, signed at Rome on 4 November 1950 (hereinafter referred to as "the Convention"), * * *

Considering the urgent need to amend certain provisions of the Convention in order to maintain and improve the efficiency of the control system for the long term, mainly in the light of the continuing increase in the workload of the European Court of Human Rights and the Committee of Ministers of the Council of Europe;

Considering, in particular, the need to ensure that the Court can continue to play its pre-eminent role in protecting human rights in Europe,

Have agreed as follows:

Article 1

Paragraph 2 of Article 22 of the Convention shall be deleted.

Article 2

Article 23 of the Convention shall be amended to read as follows:

"Article 23 – Terms of office and dismissal

1. The judges shall be elected for a period of nine years. They may not be re-elected.

2. The terms of office of judges shall expire when they reach the age of 70.

3. The judges shall hold office until replaced. They shall, however, continue to deal with such cases as they already have under consideration.

4. No judge may be dismissed from office unless the other judges decide by a majority of two thirds that that judge has ceased to fulfil the required conditions."

Article 3

Article 24 of the Convention shall be deleted.

Article 4

Article 25 of the Convention shall become Article 24 and its text shall be amended to read as follows:
"Article 24 – Registry and rapporteurs
1. The Court shall have a registry, the functions and organisation of which shall be laid down in the rules of the Court.
2. When sitting in a single-judge formation, the Court shall be assisted by rapporteurs who shall function under the authority of the President of the Court. They shall form part of the Court's registry."

Article 5

Article 26 of the Convention shall become Article 25 ("Plenary Court") and its text shall be amended as follows:
1. At the end of paragraph d, the comma shall be replaced by a semi-colon and the word "and" shall be deleted.
2. At the end of paragraph e, the full stop shall be replaced by a semi-colon.
3. A new paragraph f shall be added which shall read as follows:
"f. make any request under Article 26, paragraph 2."

Article 6

Article 27 of the Convention shall become Article 26 and its text shall be amended to read as follows:
"Article 26 – Single-judge formation, committees, Chambers and Grand Chamber
1. To consider cases brought before it, the Court shall sit in a single-judge formation, in committees of three judges, in Chambers of seven judges and in a Grand Chamber of seventeen judges. The Court's Chambers shall set up committees for a fixed period of time.
2. At the request of the plenary Court, the Committee of Ministers may, by a unanimous decision and for a fixed period, reduce to five the number of judges of the Chambers.
3. When sitting as a single judge, a judge shall not examine any application against the High Contracting Party in respect of which that judge has been elected.
4. There shall sit as an ex officio member of the Chamber and the Grand Chamber the judge elected in respect of the High Contracting Party concerned. If there is none or if that judge is unable to sit, a person chosen by the President of the Court from a list submitted in advance by that Party shall sit in the capacity of judge.
5. The Grand Chamber shall also include the President of the Court, the Vice-Presidents, the Presidents of the Chambers and other judges chosen in accordance with the rules of the Court. When a case is referred to the Grand Chamber under Article 43, no judge from the Chamber which rendered the judgment shall sit in the Grand Chamber, with the exception of the President of the Chamber and the judge who sat in respect of the High Contracting Party concerned."

Article 7

After the new Article 26, a new Article 27 shall be inserted into the Convention, which shall read as follows:
"Article 27 – Competence of single judges
1. A single judge may declare inadmissible or strike out of the Court's list of cases an application submitted under Article 34, where such a decision can be taken without further examination.
2. The decision shall be final.
3. If the single judge does not declare an application inadmissible or strike it out, that judge shall forward it to a committee or to a Chamber for further examination."

Article 8

Article 28 of the Convention shall be amended to read as follows:
"Article 28 – Competence of committees
1. In respect of an application submitted under Article 34, a committee may, by a unanimous vote,

a. declare it inadmissible or strike it out of its list of cases, where such decision can be taken without further examination; or

b. declare it admissible and render at the same time a judgment on the merits, if the underlying question in the case, concerning the interpretation or the application of the Convention or the Protocols thereto, is already the subject of well-established case-law of the Court.

2. Decisions and judgments under paragraph 1 shall be final.

3. If the judge elected in respect of the High Contracting Party concerned is not a member of the committee, the committee may at any stage of the proceedings invite that judge to take the place of one of the members of the committee, having regard to all relevant factors, including whether that Party has contested the application of the procedure under paragraph 1.b."

Article 9

Article 29 of the Convention shall be amended as follows:

1. Paragraph 1 shall be amended to read as follows: "If no decision is taken under Article 27 or 28, or no judgment rendered under Article 28, a Chamber shall decide on the admissibility and merits of individual applications submitted under Article 34. The decision on admissibility may be taken separately."

2. At the end of paragraph 2 a new sentence shall be added which shall read as follows: "The decision on admissibility shall be taken separately unless the Court, in exceptional cases, decides otherwise."

3. Paragraph 3 shall be deleted.

Article 10

Article 31 of the Convention shall be amended as follows:

1. At the end of paragraph a, the word "and" shall be deleted.

2. Paragraph b shall become paragraph c and a new paragraph b shall be inserted and shall read as follows:
   "b. decide on issues referred to the Court by the Committee of Ministers in accordance with Article 46, paragraph 4; and".

Article 11

Article 32 of the Convention shall be amended as follows:

At the end of paragraph 1, a comma and the number 46 shall be inserted after the number 34.

Article 12

Paragraph 3 of Article 35 of the Convention shall be amended to read as follows:
   "3. The Court shall declare inadmissible any individual application submitted under Article 34 if it considers that :
      a. the application is incompatible with the provisions of the Convention or the Protocols thereto, manifestly ill-founded, or an abuse of the right of individual application; or
      b. the applicant has not suffered a significant disadvantage, unless respect for human rights as defined in the Convention and the Protocols thereto requires an examination of the application on the merits and provided that no case may be rejected on this ground which has not been duly considered by a domestic tribunal."

Article 13

A new paragraph 3 shall be added at the end of Article 36 of the Convention, which shall read as follows:
   "3. In all cases before a Chamber or the Grand Chamber, the Council of Europe Commissioner for Human Rights may submit written comments and take part in hearings."

Article 14

Article 38 of the Convention shall be amended to read as follows:
   "Article 38 – Examination of the case
   The Court shall examine the case together with the representatives of the parties and, if need be, undertake an investigation, for the effective conduct of which the High Contracting Parties concerned shall furnish all necessary facilities."

Article 15

Article 39 of the Convention shall be amended to read as follows:
    "Article 39 – Friendly settlements
    1. At any stage of the proceedings, the Court may place itself at the disposal of the parties concerned with a view to securing a friendly settlement of the matter on the basis of respect for human rights as defined in the Convention and the Protocols thereto.
    2. Proceedings conducted under paragraph 1 shall be confidential.
    3. If a friendly settlement is effected, the Court shall strike the case out of its list by means of a decision which shall be confined to a brief statement of the facts and of the solution reached.
    4. This decision shall be transmitted to the Committee of Ministers, which shall supervise the execution of the terms of the friendly settlement as set out in the decision."

Article 16

Article 46 of the Convention shall be amended to read as follows:
    "Article 46 – Binding force and execution of judgments
    1. The High Contracting Parties undertake to abide by the final judgment of the Court in any case to which they are parties.
    2. The final judgment of the Court shall be transmitted to the Committee of Ministers, which shall supervise its execution.
    3. If the Committee of Ministers considers that the supervision of the execution of a final judgment is hindered by a problem of interpretation of the judgment, it may refer the matter to the Court for a ruling on the question of interpretation. A referral decision shall require a majority vote of two thirds of the representatives entitled to sit on the Committee.
    4. If the Committee of Ministers considers that a High Contracting Party refuses to abide by a final judgment in a case to which it is a party, it may, after serving formal notice on that Party and by decision adopted by a majority vote of two thirds of the representatives entitled to sit on the Committee, refer to the Court the question whether that Party has failed to fulfil its obligation under paragraph 1.
    5. If the Court finds a violation of paragraph 1, it shall refer the case to the Committee of Ministers for consideration of the measures to be taken. If the Court finds no violation of paragraph 1, it shall refer the case to the Committee of Ministers, which shall close its examination of the case."

Article 17

Article 59 of the Convention shall be amended as follows:
1. A new paragraph 2 shall be inserted which shall read as follows:
    "2. The European Union may accede to this Convention."
2. Paragraphs 2, 3 and 4 shall become paragraphs 3, 4 and 5 respectively.

Final and transitional provisions

Article 18

1. This Protocol shall be open for signature by member States of the Council of Europe signatories to the Convention, which may express their consent to be bound by
    a. signature without reservation as to ratification, acceptance or approval; or
    b. signature subject to ratification, acceptance or approval, followed by ratification, acceptance or approval.
2. The instruments of ratification, acceptance or approval shall be deposited with the Secretary General of the Council of Europe.

Article 19

This Protocol shall enter into force on the first day of the month following the expiration of a period of three months after the date on which all Parties to the Convention have expressed their consent to be bound by the Protocol, in accordance with the provisions of Article 18.

Article 20

1. From the date of the entry into force of this Protocol, its provisions shall apply to all applications pending before the Court as well as to all judgments whose execution is under supervision by the

Committee of Ministers.

2. The new admissibility criterion inserted by Article 12 of this Protocol in Article 35, paragraph 3.b of the Convention, shall not apply to applications declared admissible before the entry into force of the Protocol. In the two years following the entry into force of this Protocol, the new admissibility criterion may only be applied by Chambers and the Grand Chamber of the Court.

Article 21

The term of office of judges serving their first term of office on the date of entry into force of this Protocol shall be extended ipso jure so as to amount to a total period of nine years. The other judges shall complete their term of office, which shall be extended ipso jure by two years.

Article 22

The Secretary General of the Council of Europe shall notify the member States of the Council of Europe of:
    a. any signature;
    b. the deposit of any instrument of ratification, acceptance or approval;
    c. the date of entry into force of this Protocol in accordance with Article 19; and
    d. any other act, notification or communication relating to this Protocol.

EUROPEAN SOCIAL CHARTER
European Treaties Series No. 35 (October 18, 1961)

Preamble

The governments signatory hereto, being members of the Council of Europe,

Considering that the aim of the Council of Europe is the achievement of greater unity between its members for the purpose of safeguarding and realising the ideals and principles which are their common heritage and of facilitating their economic and social progress, in particular by the maintenance and further realisation of human rights and fundamental freedoms;

Considering that in the Convention for the Protection of Human Rights and Fundamental Freedoms signed at Rome on 4th November 1950, and the Protocol thereto signed at Paris on 20th March 1952, the member States of the Council of Europe agreed to secure to their populations the civil and political rights and freedoms therein specified;

Considering that the enjoyment of social rights should be secured without discrimination on grounds of race, colour, sex, religion, political opinion, national extraction or social origin;

Being resolved to make every effort in common to improve the standard of living and to promote the social well-being of both their urban and rural populations by means of appropriate institutions and action,

Have agreed as follows:

Part I

The Contracting Parties accept as the aim of their policy, to be pursued by all appropriate means, both national and international in character, the attainment of conditions in which the following rights and principles may be effectively realised:
1. Everyone shall have the opportunity to earn his living in an occupation freely entered upon.
2. All workers have the right to just conditions of work.
3. All workers have the right to safe and healthy working conditions.
4. All workers have the right to a fair remuneration sufficient for a decent standard of living for themselves and their families.

5. All workers and employers have the right to freedom of association in national or international organisations for the protection of their economic and social interests.
6. All workers and employers have the right to bargain collectively.
7. Children and young persons have the right to a special protection against the physical and moral hazards to which they are exposed.
8. Employed women, in case of maternity, and other employed women as appropriate, have the right to a special protection in their work.
9. Everyone has the right to appropriate facilities for vocational guidance with a view to helping him choose an occupation suited to his personal aptitude and interests.
10. Everyone has the right to appropriate facilities for vocational training.
11. Everyone has the right to benefit from any measures enabling him to enjoy the highest possible standard of health attainable.
12. All workers and their dependents have the right to social security.
13. Anyone without adequate resources has the right to social and medical assistance.
14. Everyone has the right to benefit from social welfare services.
15. Disabled persons have the right to vocational training, rehabilitation and resettlement, whatever the origin and nature of their disability.
16. The family as a fundamental unit of society has the right to appropriate social, legal and economic protection to ensure its full development.
17. Mothers and children, irrespective of marital status and family relations, have the right to appropriate social and economic protection.
18. The nationals of any one of the Contracting Parties have the right to engage in any gainful occupation in the territory of any one of the others on a footing of equality with the nationals of the latter, subject to restrictions based on cogent economic or social reasons.
19. Migrant workers who are nationals of a Contracting Party and their families have the right to protection and assistance in the territory of any other Contracting Party.

Part II

The Contracting Parties undertake, as provided for in Part III, to consider themselves bound by the obligations laid down in the following articles and paragraphs.

Article 1 – The right to work
With a view to ensuring the effective exercise of the right to work, the Contracting Parties undertake:
1. to accept as one of their primary aims and responsibilities the achievement and maintenance of as high and stable a level of employment as possible, with a view to the attainment of full employment;
2. to protect effectively the right of the worker to earn his living in an occupation freely entered upon;
3. to establish or maintain free employment services for all workers;
4. to provide or promote appropriate vocational guidance, training and rehabilitation.

Article 2 – The right to just conditions of work
With a view to ensuring the effective exercise of the right to just conditions of work, the Contracting Parties undertake:
1. to provide for reasonable daily and weekly working hours, the working week to be progressively reduced to the extent that the increase of productivity and other relevant factors permit;
2. to provide for public holidays with pay;
3. to provide for a minimum of two weeks annual holiday with pay;
4. to provide for additional paid holidays or reduced working hours for workers engaged in dangerous or unhealthy occupations as prescribed;
5. to ensure a weekly rest period which shall, as far as possible, coincide with the day recognised by tradition or custom in the country or region concerned as a day of rest.

Article 3 – The right to safe and healthy working conditions

342

With a view to ensuring the effective exercise of the right to safe and healthy working conditions, the Contracting Parties undertake:

1. to issue safety and health regulations;
2. to provide for the enforcement of such regulations by measures of supervision;
3. to consult, as appropriate, employers' and workers' organisations on measures intended to improve industrial safety and health.

Article 4 – The right to a fair remuneration

With a view to ensuring the effective exercise of the right to a fair remuneration, the Contracting Parties undertake:

1. to recognise the right of workers to a remuneration such as will give them and their families a decent standard of living;
2. to recognise the right of workers to an increased rate of remuneration for overtime work, subject to exceptions in particular cases;
3. to recognise the right of men and women workers to equal pay for work of equal value;
4. to recognise the right of all workers to a reasonable period of notice for termination of employment;
5. to permit deductions from wages only under conditions and to the extent prescribed by national laws or regulations or fixed by collective agreements or arbitration awards.
   The exercise of these rights shall be achieved by freely concluded collective agreements, by statutory wage-fixing machinery, or by other means appropriate to national conditions.

Article 5 – The right to organise

With a view to ensuring or promoting the freedom of workers and employers to form local, national or international organisations for the protection of their economic and social interests and to join those organisations, the Contracting Parties undertake that national law shall not be such as to impair, nor shall it be so applied as to impair, this freedom. The extent to which the guarantees provided for in this article shall apply to the police shall be determined by national laws or regulations. The principle governing the application to the members of the armed forces of these guarantees and the extent to which they shall apply to persons in this category shall equally be determined by national laws or regulations.

Article 6 – The right to bargain collectively

With a view to ensuring the effective exercise of the right to bargain collectively, the Contracting Parties undertake:

1. to promote joint consultation between workers and employers;
2. to promote, where necessary and appropriate, machinery for voluntary negotiations between employers or employers' organisations and workers' organisations, with a view to the regulation of terms and conditions of employment by means of collective agreements;
3. to promote the establishment and use of appropriate machinery for conciliation and voluntary arbitration for the settlement of labour disputes;
   and recognise:
4. the right of workers and employers to collective action in cases of conflicts of interest, including the right to strike, subject to obligations that might arise out of collective agreements previously entered into.

Article 7 – The right of children and young persons to protection

With a view to ensuring the effective exercise of the right of children and young persons to protection, the Contracting Parties undertake:

1. to provide that the minimum age of admission to employment shall be 15 years, subject to exceptions for children employed in prescribed light work without harm to their health, morals or education;
2. to provide that a higher minimum age of admission to employment shall be fixed with respect to prescribed occupations regarded as dangerous or unhealthy;
3. to provide that persons who are still subject to compulsory education shall not be employed in such work as would deprive them of the full benefit of their education;

4. to provide that the working hours of persons under 16 years of age shall be limited in accordance with the needs of their development, and particularly with their need for vocational training;

5. to recognise the right of young workers and apprentices to a fair wage or other appropriate allowances;

6. to provide that the time spent by young persons in vocational training during the normal working hours with the consent of the employer shall be treated as forming part of the working day;

7. to provide that employed persons of under 18 years of age shall be entitled to not less than three weeks' annual holiday with pay;

8. to provide that persons under 18 years of age shall not be employed in night work with the exception of certain occupations provided for by national laws or regulations;

9. to provide that persons under 18 years of age employed in occupations prescribed by national laws or regulations shall be subject to regular medical control;

10. to ensure special protection against physical and moral dangers to which children and young persons are exposed, and particularly against those resulting directly or indirectly from their work.

Article 8 – The right of employed women to protection

With a view to ensuring the effective exercise of the right of employed women to protection, the Contracting Parties undertake:

1. to provide either by paid leave, by adequate social security benefits or by benefits from public funds for women to take leave before and after childbirth up to a total of at least 12 weeks;

2. to consider it as unlawful for an employer to give a woman notice of dismissal during her absence on maternity leave or to give her notice of dismissal at such a time that the notice would expire during such absence;

3. to provide that mothers who are nursing their infants shall be entitled to sufficient time off for this purpose;

4.
   a. to regulate the employment of women workers on night work in industrial employment;
   b. to prohibit the employment of women workers in underground mining, and, as appropriate, on all other work which is unsuitable for them by reason of its dangerous, unhealthy, or arduous nature.

Article 9 – The right to vocational guidance

With a view to ensuring the effective exercise of the right to vocational guidance, the Contracting Parties undertake to provide or promote, as necessary, a service which will assist all persons, including the handicapped, to solve problems related to occupational choice and progress, with due regard to the individual's characteristics and their relation to occupational opportunity: this assistance should be available free of charge, both to young persons, including school children, and to adults.

Article 10 – The right to vocational training

With a view to ensuring the effective exercise of the right to vocational training, the Contracting Parties undertake:

1. to provide or promote, as necessary, the technical and vocational training of all persons, including the handicapped, in consultation with employers' and workers' organisations, and to grant facilities for access to higher technical and university education, based solely on individual aptitude;

2. to provide or promote a system of apprenticeship and other systematic arrangements for training young boys and girls in their various employments;

3. to provide or promote, as necessary:
   a. adequate and readily available training facilities for adult workers;
   b. special facilities for the re-training of adult workers needed as a result of technological development or new trends in employment;

4. to encourage the full utilisation of the facilities provided by appropriate measures such as:
   a. reducing or abolishing any fees or charges;
   b. granting financial assistance in appropriate cases;
   c. including in the normal working hours time spent on supplementary training taken by the worker, at the request of his employer, during employment;

d.   ensuring, through adequate supervision, in consultation with the employers' and workers' organisations, the efficiency of apprenticeship and other training arrangements for young workers, and the adequate protection of young workers generally.

Article 11 – The right to protection of health

With a view to ensuring the effective exercise of the right to protection of health, the Contracting Parties undertake, either directly or in co-operation with public or private organisations, to take appropriate measures designed *inter alia:*

1. to remove as far as possible the causes of ill-health;
2. to provide advisory and educational facilities for the promotion of health and the encouragement of individual responsibility in matters of health;
3. to prevent as far as possible epidemic, endemic and other diseases.

Article 12 – The right to social security

With a view to ensuring the effective exercise of the right to social security, the Contracting Parties undertake:

1. to establish or maintain a system of social security;
2. to maintain the social security system at a satisfactory level at least equal to that required for ratification of International Labour Convention No. 102 Concerning Minimum Standards of Social Security;
3. to endeavour to raise progressively the system of social security to a higher level;
4. to take steps, by the conclusion of appropriate bilateral and multilateral agreements, or by other means, and subject to the conditions laid down in such agreements, in order to ensure:
   a.   equal treatment with their own nationals of the nationals of other Contracting Parties in respect of social security rights, including the retention of benefits arising out of social security legislation, whatever movements the persons protected may undertake between the territories of the Contracting Parties;
   b.   the granting, maintenance and resumption of social security rights by such means as the accumulation of insurance or employment periods completed under the legislation of each of the Contracting Parties.

Article 13 – The right to social and medical assistance

With a view to ensuring the effective exercise of the right to social and medical assistance, the Contracting Parties undertake:

1. to ensure that any person who is without adequate resources and who is unable to secure such resources either by his own efforts or from other sources, in particular by benefits under a social security scheme, be granted adequate assistance, and, in case of sickness, the care necessitated by his condition;
2. to ensure that persons receiving such assistance shall not, for that reason, suffer from a diminution of their political or social rights;
3. to provide that everyone may receive by appropriate public or private services such advice and personal help as may be required to prevent, to remove, or to alleviate personal or family want;
4. to apply the provisions referred to in paragraphs 1, 2 and 3 of this article on an equal footing with their nationals to nationals of other Contracting Parties lawfully within their territories, in accordance with their obligations under the European Convention on Social and Medical Assistance, signed at Paris on 11th December 1953.

Article 14 – The right to benefit from social welfare services

With a view to ensuring the effective exercise of the right to benefit from social welfare services, the Contracting Parties undertake:

1. to promote or provide services which, by using methods of social work, would contribute to the welfare and development of both individuals and groups in the community, and to their adjustment to the social environment;
2. to encourage the participation of individuals and voluntary or other organisations in the establishment and maintenance of such services.

Article 15 – The right of physically or mentally disabled persons to vocational training, rehabilitation and social resettlement

With a view to ensuring the effective exercise of the right of the physically or mentally disabled to vocational training, rehabilitation and resettlement, the Contracting Parties undertake:

1. to take adequate measures for the provision of training facilities, including, where necessary, specialised institutions, public or private;
2. to take adequate measures for the placing of disabled persons in employment, such as specialised placing services, facilities for sheltered employment and measures to encourage employers to admit disabled persons to employment.

Article 16 – The right of the family to social, legal and economic protection

With a view to ensuring the necessary conditions for the full development of the family, which is a fundamental unit of society, the Contracting Parties undertake to promote the economic, legal and social protection of family life by such means as social and family benefits, fiscal arrangements, provision of family housing, benefits for the newly married, and other appropriate means.

Article 17 – The right of mothers and children to social and economic protection

With a view to ensuring the effective exercise of the right of mothers and children to social and economic protection, the Contracting Parties will take all appropriate and necessary measures to that end, including the establishment or maintenance of appropriate institutions or services.

Article 18 – The right to engage in a gainful occupation in the territory of other Contracting Parties

With a view to ensuring the effective exercise of the right to engage in a gainful occupation in the territory of any other Contracting Party, the Contracting Parties undertake:

1. to apply existing regulations in a spirit of liberality;
2. to simplify existing formalities and to reduce or abolish chancery dues and other charges payable by foreign workers or their employers;
3. to liberalise, individually or collectively, regulations governing the employment of foreign workers;
   and recognise:
4. the right of their nationals to leave the country to engage in a gainful occupation in the territories of the other Contracting Parties.

Article 19 – The right of migrant workers and their families to protection and assistance

With a view to ensuring the effective exercise of the right of migrant workers and their families to protection and assistance in the territory of any other Contracting Party, the Contracting Parties undertake:

1. to maintain or to satisfy themselves that there are maintained adequate and free services to assist such workers, particularly in obtaining accurate information, and to take all appropriate steps, so far as national laws and regulations permit, against misleading propaganda relating to emigration and immigration;
2. to adopt appropriate measures within their own jurisdiction to facilitate the departure, journey and reception of such workers and their families, and to provide, within their own jurisdiction, appropriate services for health, medical attention and good hygienic conditions during the journey;
3. to promote co-operation, as appropriate, between social services, public and private, in emigration and immigration countries;
4. to secure for such workers lawfully within their territories, insofar as such matters are regulated by law or regulations or are subject to the control of administrative authorities, treatment not less favourable than that of their own nationals in respect of the following matters:
   a. remuneration and other employment and working conditions;
   b. membership of trade unions and enjoyment of the benefits of collective bargaining;
   c. accommodation;
5. to secure for such workers lawfully within their territories treatment not less favourable than that of their own nationals with regard to employment taxes, dues or contributions payable in respect of employed persons;

6. to facilitate as far as possible the reunion of the family of a foreign worker permitted to establish himself in the territory;
7. to secure for such workers lawfully within their territories treatment not less favourable than that of their own nationals in respect of legal proceedings relating to matters referred to in this article;
8. to secure that such workers lawfully residing within their territories are not expelled unless they endanger national security or offend against public interest or morality;
9. to permit, within legal limits, the transfer of such parts of the earnings and savings of such workers as they may desire;
10. to extend the protection and assistance provided for in this article to self-employed migrants insofar as such measures apply.

Part III

Article 20 – Undertakings

1. Each of the Contracting Parties undertakes:
   a. to consider Part I of this Charter as a declaration of the aims which it will pursue by all appropriate means, as stated in the introductory paragraph of that part;
   b. to consider itself bound by at least five of the following articles of Part II of this Charter: Articles 1, 5, 6, 12, 13, 16 and 19;
   c. in addition to the articles selected by it in accordance with the preceding sub-paragraph, to consider itself bound by such a number of articles or numbered paragraphs of Part II of the Charter as it may select, provided that the total number of articles or numbered paragraphs by which it is bound is not less than 10 articles or 45 numbered paragraphs.
2. The articles or paragraphs selected in accordance with sub-paragraphs b and c of paragraph 1 of this article shall be notified to the Secretary General of the Council of Europe at the time when the instrument of ratification or approval of the Contracting Party concerned is deposited.
3. Any Contracting Party may, at a later date, declare by notification to the Secretary General that it considers itself bound by any articles or any numbered paragraphs of Part II of the Charter which it has not already accepted under the terms of paragraph 1 of this article. Such undertakings subsequently given shall be deemed to be an integral part of the ratification or approval, and shall have the same effect as from the thirtieth day after the date of the notification.
4. The Secretary General shall communicate to all the signatory governments and to the Director General of the International Labour Office any notification which he shall have received pursuant to this part of the Charter.
5. Each Contracting Party shall maintain a system of labour inspection appropriate to national conditions.

Part IV

Article 21 – Reports concerning accepted provisions
The Contracting Parties shall send to the Secretary General of the Council of Europe a report at two-yearly intervals, in a form to be determined by the Committee of Ministers, concerning the application of such provisions of Part II of the Charter as they have accepted.

Article 22 – Reports concerning provisions which are not accepted
The Contracting Parties shall send to the Secretary General, at appropriate intervals as requested by the Committee of Ministers, reports relating to the provisions of Part II of the Charter which they did not accept at the time of their ratification or approval or in a subsequent notification. The Committee of Ministers shall determine from time to time in respect of which provisions such reports shall be requested and the form of the reports to be provided.

Article 23 – Communication of copies
1. Each Contracting Party shall communicate copies of its reports referred to in Articles 21 and 22 to such of its national organisations as are members of the international organisations of employers and trade unions to be invited under Article 27, paragraph 2, to be represented at meetings of the Sub-committee of the Governmental Social Committee.

2. The Contracting Parties shall forward to the Secretary General any comments on the said reports received from these national organisations, if so requested by them.

Article 24 – Examination of the reports

The reports sent to the Secretary General in accordance with Articles 21 and 22 shall be examined by a Committee of Experts, who shall have also before them any comments forwarded to the Secretary General in accordance with paragraph 2 of Article 23.

Article 25 – Committee of Experts

1. The Committee of Experts shall consist of not more than seven members appointed by the Committee of Ministers from a list of independent experts of the highest integrity and of recognised competence in international social questions, nominated by the Contracting Parties.
2. The members of the committee shall be appointed for a period of six years. They may be reappointed. However, of the members first appointed, the terms of office of two members shall expire at the end of four years.
3. The members whose terms of office are to expire at the end of the initial period of four years shall be chosen by lot by the Committee of Ministers immediately after the first appointment has been made.
4. A member of the Committee of Experts appointed to replace a member whose term of office has not expired shall hold office for the remainder of his predecessor's term.

Article 26 – Participation of the International Labour Organisation

The International Labour Organisation shall be invited to nominate a representative to participate in a consultative capacity in the deliberations of the Committee of Experts.

Article 27 – Sub-committee of the Governmental Social Committee

1. The reports of the Contracting Parties and the conclusions of the Committee of Experts shall be submitted for examination to a sub-committee of the Governmental Social Committee of the Council of Europe.
2. The sub-committee shall be composed of one representative of each of the Contracting Parties. It shall invite no more than two international organisations of employers and no more than two international trade union organisations as it may designate to be represented as observers in a consultative capacity at its meetings. Moreover, it may consult no more than two representatives of international non-governmental organisations having consultative status with the Council of Europe, in respect of questions with which the organisations are particularly qualified to deal, such as social welfare, and the economic and social protection of the family.
3. The sub-committee shall present to the Committee of Ministers a report containing its conclusions and append the report of the Committee of Experts.

Article 28 – Consultative Assembly

The Secretary General of the Council of Europe shall transmit to the Consultative Assembly the conclusions of the Committee of Experts. The Consultative Assembly shall communicate its views on these conclusions to the Committee of Ministers.

Article 29 – Committee of Ministers

By a majority of two-thirds of the members entitled to sit on the Committee, the Committee of Ministers may, on the basis of the report of the sub-committee, and after consultation with the Consultative Assembly, make to each Contracting Party any necessary recommendations.

Part V

Article 30 – Derogations in time of war or public emergency

1. In time of war or other public emergency threatening the life of the nation any Contracting Party may take measures derogating from its obligations under this Charter to the extent strictly required by the exigencies of the situation, provided that such measures are not inconsistent with its other obligations under international law.

2. Any Contracting Party which has availed itself of this right of derogation shall, within a reasonable lapse of time, keep the Secretary General of the Council of Europe fully informed of the measures taken and of the reasons therefor. It shall likewise inform the Secretary General when such measures have ceased to operate and the provisions of the Charter which it has accepted are again being fully executed.

3. The Secretary General shall in turn inform other Contracting Parties and the Director General of the International Labour Office of all communications received in accordance with paragraph 2 of this article.

Article 31 – Restrictions

1. The rights and principles set forth in Part I when effectively realised, and their effective exercise as provided for in Part II, shall not be subject to any restrictions or limitations not specified in those parts, except such as are prescribed by law and are necessary in a democratic society for the protection of the rights and freedoms of others or for the protection of public interest, national security, public health, or morals.

2. The restrictions permitted under this Charter to the rights and obligations set forth herein shall not be applied for any purpose other than that for which they have been prescribed.

Article 32 – Relations between the Charter and domestic law or international agreements

The provisions of this Charter shall not prejudice the provisions of domestic law or of any bilateral or multilateral treaties, conventions or agreements which are already in force, or may come into force, under which more favourable treatment would be accorded to the persons protected.

Article 33 – Implementation by collective agreements

1. In member States where the provisions of paragraphs 1, 2, 3, 4 and 5 of Article 2, paragraphs 4, 6 and 7 of Article 7 and paragraphs 1, 2, 3 and 4 of Article 10 of Part II of this Charter are matters normally left to agreements between employers or employers' organisations and workers' organisations, or are normally carried out otherwise than by law, the undertakings of those paragraphs may be given and compliance with them shall be treated as effective if their provisions are applied through such agreements or other means to the great majority of the workers concerned.

2. In member States where these provisions are normally the subject of legislation, the undertakings concerned may likewise be given, and compliance with them shall be regarded as effective if the provisions are applied by law to the great majority of the workers concerned.

Article 34 – Territorial application

1. This Charter shall apply to the metropolitan territory of each Contracting Party. Each signatory government may, at the time of signature or of the deposit of its instrument of ratification or approval, specify, by declaration addressed to the Secretary General of the Council of Europe, the territory which shall be considered to be its metropolitan territory for this purpose.

2. Any Contracting Party may, at the time of ratification or approval of this Charter or at any time thereafter, declare by notification addressed to the Secretary General of the Council of Europe, that the Charter shall extend in whole or in part to a non-metropolitan territory or territories specified in the said declaration for whose international relations it is responsible or for which it assumes international responsibility. It shall specify in the declaration the articles or paragraphs of Part II of the Charter which it accepts as binding in respect of the territories named in the declaration.

3. The Charter shall extend to the territory or territories named in the aforesaid declaration as from the thirtieth day after the date on which the Secretary General shall have received notification of such declaration.

4. Any Contracting Party may declare at a later date, by notification addressed to the Secretary General of the Council of Europe, that, in respect of one or more of the territories to which the Charter has been extended in accordance with paragraph 2 of this article, it accepts as binding any articles or any numbered paragraphs which it has not already accepted in respect of that territory or territories. Such undertakings subsequently given shall be deemed to be an integral part of the

original declaration in respect of the territory concerned, and shall have the same effect as from the thirtieth day after the date of the notification.

5. The Secretary General shall communicate to the other signatory governments and to the Director General of the International Labour Office any notification transmitted to him in accordance with this article.

Article 35 – Signature, ratification and entry into force

1. This Charter shall be open for signature by the members of the Council of Europe. It shall be ratified or approved. Instruments of ratification or approval shall be deposited with the Secretary General of the Council of Europe.
2. This Charter shall come into force as from the thirtieth day after the date of deposit of the fifth instrument of ratification or approval.
3. In respect of any signatory government ratifying subsequently, the Charter shall come into force as from the thirtieth day after the date of deposit of its instrument of ratification or approval.
4. The Secretary General shall notify all the members of the Council of Europe and the Director General of the International Labour Office of the entry into force of the Charter, the names of the Contracting Parties which have ratified or approved it and the subsequent deposit of any instruments of ratification or approval.

Article 36 – Amendments

Any member of the Council of Europe may propose amendments to this Charter in a communication addressed to the Secretary General of the Council of Europe. The Secretary General shall transmit to the other members of the Council of Europe any amendments so proposed, which shall then be considered by the Committee of Ministers and submitted to the Consultative Assembly for opinion. Any amendments approved by the Committee of Ministers shall enter into force as from the thirtieth day after all the Contracting Parties have informed the Secretary General of their acceptance. The Secretary General shall notify all the members of the Council of Europe and the Director General of the International Labour Office of the entry into force of such amendments.

Article 37 – Denunciation

1. Any Contracting Party may denounce this Charter only at the end of a period of five years from the date on which the Charter entered into force for it, or at the end of any successive period of two years, and, in each case, after giving six months notice to the Secretary General of the Council of Europe who shall inform the other Parties and the Director General of the International Labour Office accordingly. Such denunciation shall not affect the validity of the Charter in respect of the other Contracting Parties provided that at all times there are not less than five such Contracting Parties.
2. Any Contracting Party may, in accordance with the provisions set out in the preceding paragraph, denounce any article or paragraph of Part II of the Charter accepted by it provided that the number of articles or paragraphs by which this Contracting Party is bound shall never be less than 10 in the former case and 45 in the latter and that this number of articles or paragraphs shall continue to include the articles selected by the Contracting Party among those to which special reference is made in Article 20, paragraph 1, sub-paragraph b.
3. Any Contracting Party may denounce the present Charter or any of the articles or paragraphs of Part II of the Charter, under the conditions specified in paragraph 1 of this article in respect of any territory to which the said Charter is applicable by virtue of a declaration made in accordance with paragraph 2 of Article 34.

Article 38 – Appendix

The appendix to this Charter shall form an integral part of it.

Done at Turin, this 18th day of October 1961, in English and French, both texts being equally authoritative, in a single copy which shall be deposited within the archives of the Council of Europe. The Secretary General shall transmit certified copies to each of the Signatories.

Appendix to the Social Charter
Scope of the Social Charter in terms of persons protected

1. Without prejudice to Article 12, paragraph 4, and Article 13, paragraph 4, the persons covered by Articles 1 to 17 include foreigners only insofar as they are nationals of other Contracting Parties lawfully resident or working regularly within the territory of the Contracting Party concerned, subject to the understanding that these articles are to be interpreted in the light of the provisions of Articles 18 and 19.

   This interpretation would not prejudice the extension of similar facilities to other persons by any of the Contracting Parties.

2. Each Contracting Party will grant to refugees as defined in the Convention relating to the Status of Refugees, signed at Geneva on 28th July 1951, and lawfully staying in its territory, treatment as favourable as possible, and in any case not less favourable than under the obligations accepted by the Contracting Party under the said Convention and under any other existing international instruments applicable to those refugees.

Part I, paragraph 18, and Part II, Article 18, paragraph 1

It is understood that these provisions are not concerned with the question of entry into the territories of the Contracting Parties and do not prejudice the provisions of the European Convention on Establishment, signed at Paris on 13th December 1955.

Part II

Article 1, paragraph 2

This provision shall not be interpreted as prohibiting or authorising any union security clause or practice.

Article 4, paragraph 4

This provision shall be so understood as not to prohibit immediate dismissal for any serious offence.

Article 4, paragraph 5

It is understood that a Contracting Party may give the undertaking required in this paragraph if the great majority of workers are not permitted to suffer deductions from wages either by law or through collective agreements or arbitration awards, the exceptions being those persons not so covered.

Article 6, paragraph 4

It is understood that each Contracting Party may, insofar as it is concerned, regulate the exercise of the right to strike by law, provided that any further restriction that this might place on the right can be justified under the terms of Article 31.

Article 7, paragraph 8

It is understood that a Contracting Party may give the undertaking required in this paragraph if it fulfils the spirit of the undertaking by providing by law that the great majority of persons under 18 years of age shall not be employed in night work.

Article 12, paragraph 4

The words "and subject to the conditions laid down in such agreements" in the introduction to this paragraph are taken to imply *inter alia* that with regard to benefits which are available independently of any insurance contribution a Contracting Party may require the completion of a prescribed period of residence before granting such benefits to nationals of other Contracting Parties.

Article 13, paragraph 4

Governments not Parties to the European Convention on Social and Medical Assistance may ratify the Social Charter in respect of this paragraph provided that they grant to nationals of other Contracting Parties a treatment which is in conformity with the provisions of the said Convention.

Article 19, paragraph 6

For the purpose of this provision, the term "family of a foreign worker" is understood to mean at least his wife and dependent children under the age of 21 years.

Part III

It is understood that the Charter contains legal obligations of an international character, the application of which is submitted solely to the supervision provided for in Part IV thereof.

Article 20, paragraph 1

It is understood that the "numbered paragraphs" may include articles consisting of only one paragraph.

Part V
Article 30

The term "in time of war or other public emergency" shall be so understood as to cover also the threat of war.

EUROPEAN CONVENTION FOR THE PREVENTION OF TORTURE AND INHUMAN OR DEGRADING TREATMENT OR PUNISHMENT
European Treaty Series No. 126

The member States of the Council of Europe, signatory hereto,

Having regard to the provisions of the Convention for the Protection of Human Rights and Fundamental Freedoms,

Recalling that, under Article 3 of the same Convention, "no one shall be subjected to torture or to inhuman or degrading treatment or punishment";

Noting that the machinery provided for in that Convention operates in relation to persons who allege that they are victims of violations of Article 3;

Convinced that the protection of persons deprived of their liberty against torture and inhuman or degrading treatment or punishment could be strengthened by non-judicial means of a preventive character based on visits,

Have agreed as follows:

Chapter I
Article 1

There shall be established a European Committee for the Prevention of Torture and Inhuman or Degrading Treatment or Punishment (hereinafter referred to as "the Committee"). The Committee shall, by means of visits, examine the treatment of persons deprived of their liberty with a view to strengthening, if necessary, the protection of such persons from torture and from inhuman or degrading treatment or punishment.

Article 2

Each Party shall permit visits, in accordance with this Convention, to any place within its jurisdiction where persons are deprived of their liberty by a public authority.

Article 3

In the application of this Convention, the Committee and the competent national authorities of the Party concerned shall co-operate with each other.

<h2 style="text-align:center">Chapter II</h2>
<h3 style="text-align:center">Article 4</h3>

1. The Committee shall consist of a number of members equal to that of the Parties.

2. The members of the Committee shall be chosen from among persons of high moral character, known for their competence in the field of human rights or having professional experience in the areas covered by this Convention.

3. No two members of the Committee may be nationals of the same State.

4. The members shall serve in their individual capacity, shall be independent and impartial, and shall be available to serve the Committee effectively.

<h3 style="text-align:center">Article 5</h3>

1. The members of the Committee shall be elected by the Committee of Ministers of the Council of Europe by an absolute majority of votes, from a list of names drawn up by the Bureau of the Consultative Assembly of the Council of Europe; each national delegation of the Parties in the Consultative Assembly shall put forward three candidates, of whom two at least shall be its nationals. Where a member is to be elected to the Committee in respect of a non-member State of the Council of Europe, the Bureau of the Consultative Assembly shall invite the Parliament of that State to put forward three candidates, of whom two at least shall be its nationals. The election by the Committee of Ministers shall take place after consultation with the Party concerned.

2. The same procedure shall be followed in filling casual vacancies.

3. The members of the Committee shall be elected for a period of four years. They may be re-elected twice. However, among the members elected at the first election, the terms of three members shall expire at the end of two years. The members whose terms are to expire at the end of the initial period of two years shall be chosen by lot by the Secretary General of the Council of Europe immediately after the first election has been completed.

4. In order to ensure that, as far as possible, one half of the membership of the Committee shall be renewed every two years, the Committee of Ministers may decide, before proceeding to any subsequent election, that the term or terms of office of one or more members to be elected shall be for a period other than four years but not more than six and not less than two years.

5. In cases where more than one term of office is involved and the Committee of Ministers applies the preceding paragraph, the allocation of the terms of office shall be effected by the drawing of lots by the Secretary General, immediately after the election.

<h3 style="text-align:center">Article 6</h3>

1. The Committee shall meet *in camera*. A quorum shall be equal to the majority of its members. The decisions of the Committee shall be taken by a majority of the members present, subject to the provisions of Article 10, paragraph 2.

2. The Committee shall draw up its own rules of procedure.

3. The Secretariat of the Committee shall be provided by the Secretary General of the Council of Europe.

<h2 style="text-align:center">Chapter III</h2>
<h3 style="text-align:center">Article 7</h3>

1. The Committee shall organise visits to places referred to in Article 2. Apart from periodic visits, the Committee may organise such other visits as appear to it to be required in the circumstances.

2. As a general rule, the visits shall be carried out by at least two members of the Committee. The Committee may, if it considers it necessary, be assisted by experts and interpreters.

<h3 style="text-align:center">Article 8</h3>

1. The Committee shall notify the Government of the Party concerned of its intention to carry out a visit. After such notification, it may at any time visit any place referred to in Article 2.

2. A Party shall provide the Committee with the following facilities to carry out its task:

    a. access to its territory and the right to travel without restriction;

    b. full information on the places where persons deprived of their liberty are being held;

c. unlimited access to any place where persons are deprived of their liberty, including the right to move inside such places without restriction;

d. other information available to the Party which is necessary for the Committee to carry out its task. In seeking such information, the Committee shall have regard to applicable rules of national law and professional ethics.

3. The Committee may interview in private persons deprived of their liberty.

4. The Committee may communicate freely with any person whom it believes can supply relevant information.

5. If necessary, the Committee may immediately communicate observations to the competent authorities of the Party concerned.

Article 9

1. In exceptional circumstances, the competent authorities of the Party concerned may make representations to the Committee against a visit at the time or to the particular place proposed by the Committee. Such representations may only be made on grounds of national defence, public safety, serious disorder in places where persons are deprived of their liberty, the medical condition of a person or that an urgent interrogation relating to a serious crime is in progress.

2. Following such representations, the Committee and the Party shall immediately enter into consultations in order to clarify the situation and seek agreement on arrangements to enable the Committee to exercise its functions expeditiously. Such arrangements may include the transfer to another place of any person whom the Committee proposed to visit. Until the visit takes place, the Party shall provide information to the Committee about any person concerned.

Article 10

1. After each visit, the Committee shall draw up a report on the facts found during the visit, taking account of any observations which may have been submitted by the Party concerned. It shall transmit to the latter its report containing any recommendations it considers necessary. The Committee may consult with the Party with a view to suggesting, if necessary, improvements in the protection of persons deprived of their liberty.

2. If the Party fails to co-operate or refuses to improve the situation in the light of the Committee's recommendations, the Committee may decide, after the Party has had an opportunity to make known its views, by a majority of two-thirds of its members to make a public statement on the matter.

Article 11

1. The information gathered by the Committee in relation to a visit, its report and its consultations with the Party concerned shall be confidential.

2. The Committee shall publish its report, together with any comments of the Party concerned, whenever requested to do so by that Party.

3. However, no personal data shall be published without the express consent of the person concerned.

Article 12

Subject to the rules of confidentiality in Article 11, the Committee shall every year submit to the Committee of Ministers a general report on its activities which shall be transmitted to the Consultative Assembly and to any non-member State of the Council of Europe which is a party to the Convention, and made public.

Article 13

The members of the Committee, experts and other persons assisting the Committee are required, during and after their terms of office, to maintain the confidentiality of the facts or information of which they have become aware during the discharge of their functions.

Article 14

1. The names of persons assisting the Committee shall be specified in the notification under Article 8, paragraph 1.

2. Experts shall act on the instructions and under the authority of the Committee. They shall have particular knowledge and experience in the areas covered by this Convention and shall be bound by the same duties of independence, impartiality and availability as the members of the Committee.

3. A Party may exceptionally declare that an expert or other person assisting the Committee may not be allowed to take part in a visit to a place within its jurisdiction.

Chapter IV

Article 15

Each Party shall inform the Committee of the name and address of the authority competent to receive notifications to its Government, and of any liaison officer it may appoint.

Article 16

The Committee, its members and experts referred to in Article 7, paragraph 2 shall enjoy the privileges and immunities set out in the annex to this Convention.

Article 17

1. This Convention shall not prejudice the provisions of domestic law or any international agreement which provide greater protection for persons deprived of their liberty.

2. Nothing in this Convention shall be construed as limiting or derogating from the competence of the organs of the European Convention on Human Rights or from the obligations assumed by the Parties under that Convention.

3. The Committee shall not visit places which representatives or delegates of Protecting Powers or the International Committee of the Red Cross effectively visit on a regular basis by virtue of the Geneva Conventions of 12 August 1949 and the Additional Protocols of 8 June 1977 thereto.

Chapter V

Article 18

1. This Convention shall be open for signature by the member States of the Council of Europe. It is subject to ratification, acceptance or approval. Instruments of ratification, acceptance or approval shall be deposited with the Secretary General of the Council of Europe.

2. The Committee of Ministers of the Council of Europe may invite any non-member State of the Council of Europe to accede to the Convention.

Article 19

1. This Convention shall enter into force on the first day of the month following the expiration of a period of three months after the date on which seven member States of the Council of Europe have expressed their consent to be bound by the Convention in accordance with the provisions of Article 18.

2. In respect of any State which subsequently expresses its consent to be bound by it, the Convention shall enter into force on the first day of the month following the expiration of a period of three months after the date of the deposit of the instrument of ratification, acceptance, approval or accession.

Article 20

1. Any State may at the time of signature or when depositing its instrument of ratification, acceptance, approval or accession, specify the territory or territories to which this Convention shall apply.

2. Any State may at any later date, by a declaration addressed to the Secretary General of the Council of Europe, extend the application of this Convention to any other territory specified in the declaration. In respect of such territory the Convention shall enter into force on the first day of the month following the expiration of a period of three months after the date of receipt of such declaration by the Secretary General.

3. Any declaration made under the two preceding paragraphs may, in respect of any territory specified in such declaration, be withdrawn by a notification addressed to the Secretary General. The withdrawal shall become effective on the first day of the month following the expiration of a period of three months after the date of receipt of such notification by the Secretary General.

Article 21

No reservation may be made in respect of the provisions of this Convention.

Article 22

1. Any Party may, at any time, denounce this Convention by means of a notification addressed to the Secretary General of the Council of Europe.
2. Such denunciation shall become effective on the first day of the month following the expiration of a period of twelve months after the date of receipt of the notification by the Secretary General.

Article 23

The Secretary General of the Council of Europe shall notify the member States and any non-member State of the Council of Europe party to the Convention of:

    a. any signature;

    b. the deposit of any instrument of ratification, acceptance, approval or accession;

    c. any date of entry into force of this Convention in accordance with Articles 19 and 20;

    d. any other act, notification or communication relating to this Convention, except for action taken in pursuance of Articles 8 and 10.

In witness whereof, the undersigned, being duly authorised thereto, have signed this Convention.

Annex
Privileges and immunities
(Article 16)

1. For the purpose of this annex, references to members of the Committee shall be deemed to include references to experts mentioned in Article 7, paragraph 2.
2. The members of the Committee shall, while exercising their functions and during journeys made in the exercise of their functions, enjoy the following privileges and immunities:

    a. immunity from personal arrest or detention and from seizure of their personal baggage and, in respect of words spoken or written and all acts done by them in their official capacity, immunity from legal process of every kind;

    b. exemption from any restrictions on their freedom of movement on exit from and return to their country of residence, and entry into and exit from the country in which they exercise their functions, and from alien registration in the country which they are visiting or through which they are passing in the exercise of their functions.

3. In the course of journeys undertaken in the exercise of their functions, the members of the Committee shall, in the matter of customs and exchange control, be accorded:

    a. by their own Government, the same facilities as those accorded to senior officials travelling abroad on temporary official duty;

    b. by the Governments of other Parties, the same facilities as those accorded to representatives of foreign Governments on temporary official duty.

4.   Documents and papers of the Committee, in so far as they relate to the business of the Committee, shall be inviolable.
The official correspondence and other official communications of the Committee may not be held up or subjected to censorship.
5. In order to secure for the members of the Committee complete freedom of speech and complete independence in the discharge of their duties, the immunity from legal process in respect of words spoken or written and all acts done by them in discharging their duties shall continue to be accorded, notwithstanding that the persons concerned are no longer engaged in the discharge of such duties.
6. Privileges and immunities are accorded to the members of the Committee, not for the personal benefit of the individuals themselves but in order to safeguard the independent exercise of their functions. The Committee alone shall be competent to waive the immunity of its members; it has not only the right, but is under a duty, to waive the immunity of one of its members in any case where, in its opinion, the immunity would impede the course of justice, and where it can be waived without prejudice to the purpose for which the immunity is accorded.

EUROPEAN SOCIAL CHARTER (REVISED)
European Treaty Series No. 163 (1996)

Preamble

The governments signatory hereto, being members of the Council of Europe,

Considering that the aim of the Council of Europe is the achievement of greater unity between its members for the purpose of safeguarding and realising the ideals and principles which are their common heritage and of facilitating their economic and social progress, in particular by the maintenance and further realisation of human rights and fundamental freedoms;

Considering that in the Convention for the Protection of Human Rights and Fundamental Freedoms signed at Rome on 4 November 1950, and the Protocols thereto, the member States of the Council of Europe agreed to secure to their populations the civil and political rights and freedoms therein specified;

Considering that in the European Social Charter opened for signature in Turin on 18 October 1961 and the Protocols thereto, the member States of the Council of Europe agreed to secure to their populations the social rights specified therein in order to improve their standard of living and their social well-being;

Recalling that the Ministerial Conference on Human Rights held in Rome on 5 November 1990 stressed the need, on the one hand, to preserve the indivisible nature of all human rights, be they civil, political, economic, social or cultural and, on the other hand, to give the European Social Charter fresh impetus;

Resolved * * * to update and adapt the substantive contents of the Charter in order to take account in particular of the fundamental social changes which have occurred since the text was adopted;

Recognising the advantage of embodying in a Revised Charter, designed progressively to take the place of the European Social Charter, the rights guaranteed by the Charter as amended, the rights guaranteed by the Additional Protocol of 1988 and to add new rights,

Have agreed as follows:

Part I

The Parties accept as the aim of their policy, to be pursued by all appropriate means both national and international in character, the attainment of conditions in which the following rights and principles may be effectively realised:

1. Everyone shall have the opportunity to earn his living in an occupation freely entered upon.
2. All workers have the right to just conditions of work.
3. All workers have the right to safe and healthy working conditions.
4. All workers have the right to a fair remuneration sufficient for a decent standard of living for themselves and their families.
5. All workers and employers have the right to freedom of association in national or international organisations for the protection of their economic and social interests.
6. All workers and employers have the right to bargain collectively.
7. Children and young persons have the right to a special protection against the physical and moral hazards to which they are exposed.
8. Employed women, in case of maternity, have the right to a special protection.
9. Everyone has the right to appropriate facilities for vocational guidance with a view to helping him choose an occupation suited to his personal aptitude and interests.
10. Everyone has the right to appropriate facilities for vocational training.
11. Everyone has the right to benefit from any measures enabling him to enjoy the highest possible standard of health attainable.
12. All workers and their dependents have the right to social security.
13. Anyone without adequate resources has the right to social and medical assistance.
14. Everyone has the right to benefit from social welfare services.

15. Disabled persons have the right to independence, social integration and participation in the life of the community.
16. The family as a fundamental unit of society has the right to appropriate social, legal and economic protection to ensure its full development.
17. Children and young persons have the right to appropriate social, legal and economic protection.
18. The nationals of any one of the Parties have the right to engage in any gainful occupation in the territory of any one of the others on a footing of equality with the nationals of the latter, subject to restrictions based on cogent economic or social reasons.
19. Migrant workers who are nationals of a Party and their families have the right to protection and assistance in the territory of any other Party.
20. All workers have the right to equal opportunities and equal treatment in matters of employment and occupation without discrimination on the grounds of sex.
21. Workers have the right to be informed and to be consulted within the undertaking.
22. Workers have the right to take part in the determination and improvement of the working conditions and working environment in the undertaking.
23. Every elderly person has the right to social protection.
24. All workers have the right to protection in cases of termination of employment.
25. All workers have the right to protection of their claims in the event of the insolvency of their employer.
26. All workers have the right to dignity at work.
27. All persons with family responsibilities and who are engaged or wish to engage in employment have a right to do so without being subject to discrimination and as far as possible without conflict between their employment and family responsibilities.
28. Workers' representatives in undertakings have the right to protection against acts prejudicial to them and should be afforded appropriate facilities to carry out their functions.
29. All workers have the right to be informed and consulted in collective redundancy procedures.
30. Everyone has the right to protection against poverty and social exclusion.
31. Everyone has the right to housing.

Part II

The Parties undertake, as provided for in Part III, to consider themselves bound by the obligations laid down in the following articles and paragraphs.

Article 1 – The right to work

With a view to ensuring the effective exercise of the right to work, the Parties undertake:
1. to accept as one of their primary aims and responsibilities the achievement and maintenance of as high and stable a level of employment as possible, with a view to the attainment of full employment;
2. to protect effectively the right of the worker to earn his living in an occupation freely entered upon;
3. to establish or maintain free employment services for all workers;
4. to provide or promote appropriate vocational guidance, training and rehabilitation.

Article 2 – The right to just conditions of work

With a view to ensuring the effective exercise of the right to just conditions of work, the Parties undertake:
1. to provide for reasonable daily and weekly working hours, the working week to be progressively reduced to the extent that the increase of productivity and other relevant factors permit;
2. to provide for public holidays with pay;
3. to provide for a minimum of four weeks' annual holiday with pay;
4. to eliminate risks in inherently dangerous or unhealthy occupations, and where it has not yet been possible to eliminate or reduce sufficiently these risks, to provide for either a reduction of working hours or additional paid holidays for workers engaged in such occupations;
5. to ensure a weekly rest period which shall, as far as possible, coincide with the day recognised by tradition or custom in the country or region concerned as a day of rest;

6. to ensure that workers are informed in written form, as soon as possible, and in any event not later than two months after the date of commencing their employment, of the essential aspects of the contract or employment relationship;

7. to ensure that workers performing night work benefit from measures which take account of the special nature of the work.

Article 3 – The right to safe and healthy working conditions

With a view to ensuring the effective exercise of the right to safe and healthy working conditions, the Parties undertake, in consultation with employers' and workers' organisations:

1. to formulate, implement and periodically review a coherent national policy on occupational safety, occupational health and the working environment. The primary aim of this policy shall be to improve occupational safety and health and to prevent accidents and injury to health arising out of, linked with or occurring in the course of work, particularly by minimising the causes of hazards inherent in the working environment;

2. to issue safety and health regulations;

3. to provide for the enforcement of such regulations by measures of supervision;

4. to promote the progressive development of occupational health services for all workers with essentially preventive and advisory functions.

Article 4 – The right to a fair remuneration

With a view to ensuring the effective exercise of the right to a fair remuneration, the Parties undertake:

1. to recognise the right of workers to a remuneration such as will give them and their families a decent standard of living;

2. to recognise the right of workers to an increased rate of remuneration for overtime work, subject to exceptions in particular cases;

3. to recognise the right of men and women workers to equal pay for work of equal value;

4. to recognise the right of all workers to a reasonable period of notice for termination of employment;

5. to permit deductions from wages only under conditions and to the extent prescribed by national laws or regulations or fixed by collective agreements or arbitration awards.
   The exercise of these rights shall be achieved by freely concluded collective agreements, by statutory wage-fixing machinery, or by other means appropriate to national conditions.

Article 5 – The right to organise

With a view to ensuring or promoting the freedom of workers and employers to form local, national or international organisations for the protection of their economic and social interests and to join those organisations, the Parties undertake that national law shall not be such as to impair, nor shall it be so applied as to impair, this freedom. The extent to which the guarantees provided for in this article shall apply to the police shall be determined by national laws or regulations. The principle governing the application to the members of the armed forces of these guarantees and the extent to which they shall apply to persons in this category shall equally be determined by national laws or regulations.

Article 6 – The right to bargain collectively

With a view to ensuring the effective exercise of the right to bargain collectively, the Parties undertake:

1. to promote joint consultation between workers and employers;

2. to promote, where necessary and appropriate, machinery for voluntary negotiations between employers or employers' organisations and workers' organisations, with a view to the regulation of terms and conditions of employment by means of collective agreements;

3. to promote the establishment and use of appropriate machinery for conciliation and voluntary arbitration for the settlement of labour disputes;
   and recognise:

4. the right of workers and employers to collective action in cases of conflicts of interest, including the right to strike, subject to obligations that might arise out of collective agreements previously entered into.

Article 7 – The right of children and young persons to protection

With a view to ensuring the effective exercise of the right of children and young persons to protection, the Parties undertake:

1. to provide that the minimum age of admission to employment shall be 15 years, subject to exceptions for children employed in prescribed light work without harm to their health, morals or education;

2. to provide that the minimum age of admission to employment shall be 18 years with respect to prescribed occupations regarded as dangerous or unhealthy;

3. to provide that persons who are still subject to compulsory education shall not be employed in such work as would deprive them of the full benefit of their education;

4. to provide that the working hours of persons under 18 years of age shall be limited in accordance with the needs of their development, and particularly with their need for vocational training;

5. to recognise the right of young workers and apprentices to a fair wage or other appropriate allowances;

6. to provide that the time spent by young persons in vocational training during the normal working hours with the consent of the employer shall be treated as forming part of the working day;

7. to provide that employed persons of under 18 years of age shall be entitled to a minimum of four weeks' annual holiday with pay;

8. to provide that persons under 18 years of age shall not be employed in night work with the exception of certain occupations provided for by national laws or regulations;

9. to provide that persons under 18 years of age employed in occupations prescribed by national laws or regulations shall be subject to regular medical control;

10. to ensure special protection against physical and moral dangers to which children and young persons are exposed, and particularly against those resulting directly or indirectly from their work.

Article 8 – The right of employed women to protection of maternity

With a view to ensuring the effective exercise of the right of employed women to the protection of maternity, the Parties undertake:

1. to provide either by paid leave, by adequate social security benefits or by benefits from public funds for employed women to take leave before and after childbirth up to a total of at least fourteen weeks;

2. to consider it as unlawful for an employer to give a woman notice of dismissal during the period from the time she notifies her employer that she is pregnant until the end of her maternity leave, or to give her notice of dismissal at such a time that the notice would expire during such a period;

3. to provide that mothers who are nursing their infants shall be entitled to sufficient time off for this purpose;

4. to regulate the employment in night work of pregnant women, women who have recently given birth and women nursing their infants;

5. to prohibit the employment of pregnant women, women who have recently given birth or who are nursing their infants in underground mining and all other work which is unsuitable by reason of its dangerous, unhealthy or arduous nature and to take appropriate measures to protect the employment rights of these women.

Article 9 – The right to vocational guidance

With a view to ensuring the effective exercise of the right to vocational guidance, the Parties undertake to provide or promote, as necessary, a service which will assist all persons, including the handicapped, to solve problems related to occupational choice and progress, with due regard to the individual's characteristics and their relation to occupational opportunity: this assistance should be available free of charge, both to young persons, including schoolchildren, and to adults.

Article 10 – The right to vocational training

With a view to ensuring the effective exercise of the right to vocational training, the Parties undertake:

1. to provide or promote, as necessary, the technical and vocational training of all persons, including the handicapped, in consultation with employers' and workers' organisations, and to grant facilities for access to higher technical and university education, based solely on individual aptitude;

2. to provide or promote a system of apprenticeship and other systematic arrangements for training young boys and girls in their various employments;
3. to provide or promote, as necessary:
   a. adequate and readily available training facilities for adult workers;
   b. special facilities for the retraining of adult workers needed as a result of technological development or new trends in employment;
4. to provide or promote, as necessary, special measures for the retraining and reintegration of the long-term unemployed;
5. to encourage the full utilisation of the facilities provided by appropriate measures such as:
   a. reducing or abolishing any fees or charges;
   b. granting financial assistance in appropriate cases;
   c. including in the normal working hours time spent on supplementary training taken by the worker, at the request of his employer, during employment;
   d. ensuring, through adequate supervision, in consultation with the employers' and workers' organisations, the efficiency of apprenticeship and other training arrangements for young workers, and the adequate protection of young workers generally.

Article 11 – The right to protection of health

With a view to ensuring the effective exercise of the right to protection of health, the Parties undertake, either directly or in cooperation with public or private organisations, to take appropriate measures designed *inter alia:*
1. to remove as far as possible the causes of ill-health;
2. to provide advisory and educational facilities for the promotion of health and the encouragement of individual responsibility in matters of health;
3. to prevent as far as possible epidemic, endemic and other diseases, as well as accidents.

Article 12 – The right to social security

With a view to ensuring the effective exercise of the right to social security, the Parties undertake:
1. to establish or maintain a system of social security;
2. to maintain the social security system at a satisfactory level at least equal to that necessary for the ratification of the European Code of Social Security;
3. to endeavour to raise progressively the system of social security to a higher level;
4. to take steps, by the conclusion of appropriate bilateral and multilateral agreements or by other means, and subject to the conditions laid down in such agreements, in order to ensure:
   a. equal treatment with their own nationals of the nationals of other Parties in respect of social security rights, including the retention of benefits arising out of social security legislation, whatever movements the persons protected may undertake between the territories of the Parties;
   b. the granting, maintenance and resumption of social security rights by such means as the accumulation of insurance or employment periods completed under the legislation of each of the Parties.

Article 13 – The right to social and medical assistance

With a view to ensuring the effective exercise of the right to social and medical assistance, the Parties undertake:
1. to ensure that any person who is without adequate resources and who is unable to secure such resources either by his own efforts or from other sources, in particular by benefits under a social security scheme, be granted adequate assistance, and, in case of sickness, the care necessitated by his condition;
2. to ensure that persons receiving such assistance shall not, for that reason, suffer from a diminution of their political or social rights;
3. to provide that everyone may receive by appropriate public or private services such advice and personal help as may be required to prevent, to remove, or to alleviate personal or family want;
4. to apply the provisions referred to in paragraphs 1, 2 and 3 of this article on an equal footing with their nationals to nationals of other Parties lawfully within their territories, in accordance with

their obligations under the European Convention on Social and Medical Assistance, signed at
Paris on 11 December 1953.

Article 14 – The right to benefit from social welfare services

With a view to ensuring the effective exercise of the right to benefit from social welfare services, the
Parties undertake:

1. to promote or provide services which, by using methods of social work, would contribute to the
   welfare and development of both individuals and groups in the community, and to their adjustment
   to the social environment;
2. to encourage the participation of individuals and voluntary or other organisations in the
   establishment and maintenance of such services.

Article 15 – The right of persons with disabilities to independence, social integration and participation in the life of the community

With a view to ensuring to persons with disabilities, irrespective of age and the nature and origin of their
disabilities, the effective exercise of the right to independence, social integration and participation in the
life of the community, the Parties undertake, in particular:

1. to take the necessary measures to provide persons with disabilities with guidance, education and
   vocational training in the framework of general schemes wherever possible or, where this is not
   possible, through specialised bodies, public or private;
2. to promote their access to employment through all measures tending to encourage employers to
   hire and keep in employment persons with disabilities in the ordinary working environment and to
   adjust the working conditions to the needs of the disabled or, where this is not possible by reason
   of the disability, by arranging for or creating sheltered employment according to the level of
   disability. In certain cases, such measures may require recourse to specialised placement and
   support services;
3. to promote their full social integration and participation in the life of the community in particular
   through measures, including technical aids, aiming to overcome barriers to communication and
   mobility and enabling access to transport, housing, cultural activities and leisure.

Article 16 – The right of the family to social, legal and economic protection

With a view to ensuring the necessary conditions for the full development of the family, which is a
fundamental unit of society, the Parties undertake to promote the economic, legal and social protection of
family life by such means as social and family benefits, fiscal arrangements, provision of family housing,
benefits for the newly married and other appropriate means.

Article 17 – The right of children and young persons to social, legal and economic protection

With a view to ensuring the effective exercise of the right of children and young persons to grow up in an
environment which encourages the full development of their personality and of their physical and mental
capacities, the Parties undertake, either directly or in co-operation with public and private organisations, to
take all appropriate and necessary measures designed:

1.
    a. to ensure that children and young persons, taking account of the rights and duties of their
       parents, have the care, the assistance, the education and the training they need, in
       particular by providing for the establishment or maintenance of institutions and services
       sufficient and adequate for this purpose;
    b. to protect children and young persons against negligence, violence or exploitation;
    c. to provide protection and special aid from the state for children and young persons
       temporarily or definitively deprived of their family's support;
2. to provide to children and young persons a free primary and secondary education as well as to
   encourage regular attendance at schools.

Article 18 – The right to engage in a gainful occupation in the territory of other Parties

With a view to ensuring the effective exercise of the right to engage in a gainful occupation in the territory of any other Party, the Parties undertake:

1. to apply existing regulations in a spirit of liberality;
2. to simplify existing formalities and to reduce or abolish chancery dues and other charges payable by foreign workers or their employers;
3. to liberalise, individually or collectively, regulations governing the employment of foreign workers;

    and recognise:

4. the right of their nationals to leave the country to engage in a gainful occupation in the territories of the other Parties.

Article 19 – The right of migrant workers and their families to protection and assistance

With a view to ensuring the effective exercise of the right of migrant workers and their families to protection and assistance in the territory of any other Party, the Parties undertake:

1. to maintain or to satisfy themselves that there are maintained adequate and free services to assist such workers, particularly in obtaining accurate information, and to take all appropriate steps, so far as national laws and regulations permit, against misleading propaganda relating to emigration and immigration;
2. to adopt appropriate measures within their own jurisdiction to facilitate the departure, journey and reception of such workers and their families, and to provide, within their own jurisdiction, appropriate services for health, medical attention and good hygienic conditions during the journey;
3. to promote co-operation, as appropriate, between social services, public and private, in emigration and immigration countries;
4. to secure for such workers lawfully within their territories, insofar as such matters are regulated by law or regulations or are subject to the control of administrative authorities, treatment not less favourable than that of their own nationals in respect of the following matters:
    a. remuneration and other employment and working conditions;
    b. membership of trade unions and enjoyment of the benefits of collective bargaining;
    c. accommodation;
5. to secure for such workers lawfully within their territories treatment not less favourable than that of their own nationals with regard to employment taxes, dues or contributions payable in respect of employed persons;
6. to facilitate as far as possible the reunion of the family of a foreign worker permitted to establish himself in the territory;
7. to secure for such workers lawfully within their territories treatment not less favourable than that of their own nationals in respect of legal proceedings relating to matters referred to in this article;
8. to secure that such workers lawfully residing within their territories are not expelled unless they endanger national security or offend against public interest or morality;
9. to permit, within legal limits, the transfer of such parts of the earnings and savings of such workers as they may desire;
10. to extend the protection and assistance provided for in this article to self-employed migrants insofar as such measures apply;
11. to promote and facilitate the teaching of the national language of the receiving state or, if there are several, one of these languages, to migrant workers and members of their families;
12. to promote and facilitate, as far as practicable, the teaching of the migrant worker's mother tongue to the children of the migrant worker.

Article 20 – The right to equal opportunities and equal treatment in matters of employment and occupation without discrimination on the grounds of sex

With a view to ensuring the effective exercise of the right to equal opportunities and equal treatment in matters of employment and occupation without discrimination on the grounds of sex, the Parties undertake to recognise that right and to take appropriate measures to ensure or promote its application in the following fields:

a. access to employment, protection against dismissal and occupational reintegration;
b. vocational guidance, training, retraining and rehabilitation;

c. terms of employment and working conditions, including remuneration;
d. career development, including promotion.

Article 21 – The right to information and consultation

With a view to ensuring the effective exercise of the right of workers to be informed and consulted within the undertaking, the Parties undertake to adopt or encourage measures enabling workers or their representatives, in accordance with national legislation and practice:

a to be informed regularly or at the appropriate time and in a comprehensible way about the economic and financial situation of the undertaking employing them, on the understanding that the disclosure of certain information which could be prejudicial to the undertaking may be refused or subject to confidentiality; and
b to be consulted in good time on proposed decisions which could substantially affect the interests of workers, particularly on those decisions which could have an important impact on the employment situation in the undertaking.

Article 22 – The right to take part in the determination and improvement of the working conditions and working environment

With a view to ensuring the effective exercise of the right of workers to take part in the determination and improvement of the working conditions and working environment in the undertaking, the Parties undertake to adopt or encourage measures enabling workers or their representatives, in accordance with national legislation and practice, to contribute:

a. to the determination and the improvement of the working conditions, work organisation and working environment;
b. to the protection of health and safety within the undertaking;
c. to the organisation of social and socio-cultural services and facilities within the undertaking;
d. to the supervision of the observance of regulations on these matters.

Article 23 – The right of elderly persons to social protection

With a view to ensuring the effective exercise of the right of elderly persons to social protection, the Parties undertake to adopt or encourage, either directly or in co-operation with public or private organisations, appropriate measures designed in particular:

- to enable elderly persons to remain full members of society for as long as possible, by means of:
  a. adequate resources enabling them to lead a decent life and play an active part in public, social and cultural life;
  b. provision of information about services and facilities available for elderly persons and their opportunities to make use of them;
- to enable elderly persons to choose their life-style freely and to lead independent lives in their familiar surroundings for as long as they wish and are able, by means of:
  a. provision of housing suited to their needs and their state of health or of adequate support for adapting their housing;
  b. the health care and the services necessitated by their state;
- to guarantee elderly persons living in institutions appropriate support, while respecting their privacy, and participation in decisions concerning living conditions in the institution.

Article 24 – The right to protection in cases of termination of employment

With a view to ensuring the effective exercise of the right of workers to protection in cases of termination of employment, the Parties undertake to recognise:

a. the right of all workers not to have their employment terminated without valid reasons for such termination connected with their capacity or conduct or based on the operational requirements of the undertaking, establishment or service;
b. the right of workers whose employment is terminated without a valid reason to adequate compensation or other appropriate relief.

To this end the Parties undertake to ensure that a worker who considers that his employment has been terminated without a valid reason shall have the right to appeal to an impartial body.

Article 25 – The right of workers to the protection of their claims in the event of the insolvency of their employer

With a view to ensuring the effective exercise of the right of workers to the protection of their claims in the event of the insolvency of their employer, the Parties undertake to provide that workers' claims arising from contracts of employment or employment relationships be guaranteed by a guarantee institution or by any other effective form of protection.

Article 26 – The right to dignity at work

With a view to ensuring the effective exercise of the right of all workers to protection of their dignity at work, the Parties undertake, in consultation with employers' and workers' organisations:

1. to promote awareness, information and prevention of sexual harassment in the workplace or in relation to work and to take all appropriate measures to protect workers from such conduct;
2. to promote awareness, information and prevention of recurrent reprehensible or distinctly negative and offensive actions directed against individual workers in the workplace or in relation to work and to take all appropriate measures to protect workers from such conduct.

Article 27 – The right of workers with family responsibilities to equal opportunities and equal treatment

With a view to ensuring the exercise of the right to equality of opportunity and treatment for men and women workers with family responsibilities and between such workers and other workers, the Parties undertake:

1. to take appropriate measures:
    a. to enable workers with family responsibilities to enter and remain in employment, as well as to reenter employment after an absence due to those responsibilities, including measures in the field of vocational guidance and training;
    b. to take account of their needs in terms of conditions of employment and social security;
    c. to develop or promote services, public or private, in particular child daycare services and other childcare arrangements;
2. to provide a possibility for either parent to obtain, during a period after maternity leave, parental leave to take care of a child, the duration and conditions of which should be determined by national legislation, collective agreements or practice;
3. to ensure that family responsibilities shall not, as such, constitute a valid reason for termination of employment.

Article 28 – The right of workers' representatives to protection in the undertaking and facilities to be accorded to them

With a view to ensuring the effective exercise of the right of workers' representatives to carry out their functions, the Parties undertake to ensure that in the undertaking:

a. they enjoy effective protection against acts prejudicial to them, including dismissal, based on their status or activities as workers' representatives within the undertaking;
b. they are afforded such facilities as may be appropriate in order to enable them to carry out their functions promptly and efficiently, account being taken of the industrial relations system of the country and the needs, size and capabilities of the undertaking concerned.

Article 29 – The right to information and consultation in collective redundancy procedures

With a view to ensuring the effective exercise of the right of workers to be informed and consulted in situations of collective redundancies, the Parties undertake to ensure that employers shall inform and consult workers' representatives, in good time prior to such collective redundancies, on ways and means of avoiding collective redundancies or limiting their occurrence and mitigating their consequences, for example by recourse to accompanying social measures aimed, in particular, at aid for the redeployment or retraining of the workers concerned.

Article 30 – The right to protection against poverty and social exclusion

With a view to ensuring the effective exercise of the right to protection against poverty and social exclusion, the Parties undertake:

a. to take measures within the framework of an overall and co-ordinated approach to promote the effective access of persons who live or risk living in a situation of social exclusion or poverty, as well as their families, to, in particular, employment, housing, training, education, culture and social and medical assistance;

b. to review these measures with a view to their adaptation if necessary.

Article 31 – The right to housing

With a view to ensuring the effective exercise of the right to housing, the Parties undertake to take measures designed:

1. to promote access to housing of an adequate standard;
2. to prevent and reduce homelessness with a view to its gradual elimination;
3. to make the price of housing accessible to those without adequate resources.

Part III

Article A – Undertakings

1. Subject to the provisions of Article B below, each of the Parties undertakes:
   a. to consider Part I of this Charter as a declaration of the aims which it will pursue by all appropriate means, as stated in the introductory paragraph of that part;
   b. to consider itself bound by at least six of the following nine articles of Part II of this Charter: Articles 1, 5, 6, 7, 12, 13, 16, 19 and 20;
   c. to consider itself bound by an additional number of articles or numbered paragraphs of Part II of the Charter which it may select, provided that the total number of articles or numbered paragraphs by which it is bound is not less than sixteen articles or sixty-three numbered paragraphs.
2. The articles or paragraphs selected in accordance with sub-paragraphs b and c of paragraph 1 of this article shall be notified to the Secretary General of the Council of Europe at the time when the instrument of ratification, acceptance or approval is deposited.
3. Any Party may, at a later date, declare by notification addressed to the Secretary General that it considers itself bound by any articles or any numbered paragraphs of Part II of the Charter which it has not already accepted under the terms of paragraph 1 of this article. Such undertakings subsequently given shall be deemed to be an integral part of the ratification, acceptance or approval and shall have the same effect as from the first day of the month following the expiration of a period of one month after the date of the notification.
4. Each Party shall maintain a system of labour inspection appropriate to national conditions.

Article B – Links with the European Social Charter and the 1988 Additional Protocol

1. No Contracting Party to the European Social Charter or Party to the Additional Protocol of 5 May 1988 may ratify, accept or approve this Charter without considering itself bound by at least the provisions corresponding to the provisions of the European Social Charter and, where appropriate, of the Additional Protocol, to which it was bound.
2. Acceptance of the obligations of any provision of this Charter shall, from the date of entry into force of those obligations for the Party concerned, result in the corresponding provision of the European Social Charter and, where appropriate, of its Additional Protocol of 1988 ceasing to apply to the Party concerned in the event of that Party being bound by the first of those instruments or by both instruments.

Part IV

Article C – Supervision of the implementation of the undertakings contained in this Charter

The implementation of the legal obligations contained in this Charter shall be submitted to the same supervision as the European Social Charter.

Article D – Collective complaints

1. The provisions of the Additional Protocol to the European Social Charter providing for a system of collective complaints shall apply to the undertakings given in this Charter for the States which have ratified the said Protocol.

2. Any State which is not bound by the Additional Protocol to the European Social Charter providing for a system of collective complaints may when depositing its instrument of ratification, acceptance or approval of this Charter or at any time thereafter, declare by notification addressed to the Secretary General of the Council of Europe, that it accepts the supervision of its obligations under this Charter following the procedure provided for in the said Protocol.

Part V

Article E – Non-discrimination

The enjoyment of the rights set forth in this Charter shall be secured without discrimination on any ground such as race, colour, sex, language, religion, political or other opinion, national extraction or social origin, health, association with a national minority, birth or other status.

Article F – Derogations in time of war or public emergency

1. In time of war or other public emergency threatening the life of the nation any Party may take measures derogating from its obligations under this Charter to the extent strictly required by the exigencies of the situation, provided that such measures are not inconsistent with its other obligations under international law.
2. Any Party which has availed itself of this right of derogation shall, within a reasonable lapse of time, keep the Secretary General of the Council of Europe fully informed of the measures taken and of the reasons therefor. It shall likewise inform the Secretary General when such measures have ceased to operate and the provisions of the Charter which it has accepted are again being fully executed.

Article G – Restrictions

1. The rights and principles set forth in Part I when effectively realised, and their effective exercise as provided for in Part II, shall not be subject to any restrictions or limitations not specified in those parts, except such as are prescribed by law and are necessary in a democratic society for the protection of the rights and freedoms of others or for the protection of public interest, national security, public health, or morals.
2. The restrictions permitted under this Charter to the rights and obligations set forth herein shall not be applied for any purpose other than that for which they have been prescribed.

Article H – Relations between the Charter and domestic law or international agreements

The provisions of this Charter shall not prejudice the provisions of domestic law or of any bilateral or multilateral treaties, conventions or agreements which are already in force, or may come into force, under which more favourable treatment would be accorded to the persons protected.

Article I – Implementation of the undertakings given

1. Without prejudice to the methods of implementation foreseen in these articles the relevant provisions of Articles 1 to 31 of Part II of this Charter shall be implemented by:
   a. laws or regulations;
   b. agreements between employers or employers' organisations and workers' organisations;
   c. a combination of those two methods;
   d. other appropriate means.
2. Compliance with the undertakings deriving from the provisions of paragraphs 1, 2, 3, 4, 5 and 7 of Article 2, paragraphs 4, 6 and 7 of Article 7, paragraphs 1, 2, 3 and 5 of Article 10 and Articles 21 and 22 of Part II of this Charter shall be regarded as effective if the provisions are applied, in accordance with paragraph 1 of this article, to the great majority of the workers concerned.

Article J – Amendments

1. Any amendment to Parts I and II of this Charter with the purpose of extending the rights guaranteed in this Charter as well as any amendment to Parts III to VI, proposed by a Party or by the Governmental Committee, shall be communicated to the Secretary General of the Council of Europe and forwarded by the Secretary General to the Parties to this Charter.

2. Any amendment proposed in accordance with the provisions of the preceding paragraph shall be examined by the Governmental Committee which shall submit the text adopted to the Committee of Ministers for approval after consultation with the Parliamentary Assembly. After its approval by the Committee of Ministers this text shall be forwarded to the Parties for acceptance.

3. Any amendment to Part I and to Part II of this Charter shall enter into force, in respect of those Parties which have accepted it, on the first day of the month following the expiration of a period of one month after the date on which three Parties have informed the Secretary General that they have accepted it.

    In respect of any Party which subsequently accepts it, the amendment shall enter into force on the first day of the month following the expiration of a period of one month after the date on which that Party has informed the Secretary General of its acceptance.

4. Any amendment to Parts III to VI of this Charter shall enter into force on the first day of the month following the expiration of a period of one month after the date on which all Parties have informed the Secretary General that they have accepted it.

Part VI

Article K – Signature, ratification and entry into force

1. This Charter shall be open for signature by the member States of the Council of Europe. It shall be subject to ratification, acceptance or approval. Instruments of ratification, acceptance or approval shall be deposited with the Secretary General of the Council of Europe.

2. This Charter shall enter into force on the first day of the month following the expiration of a period of one month after the date on which three member States of the Council of Europe have expressed their consent to be bound by this Charter in accordance with the preceding paragraph.

3. In respect of any member State which subsequently expresses its consent to be bound by this Charter, it shall enter into force on the first day of the month following the expiration of a period of one month after the date of the deposit of the instrument of ratification, acceptance or approval.

Article L – Territorial application

1. This Charter shall apply to the metropolitan territory of each Party. Each signatory may, at the time of signature or of the deposit of its instrument of ratification, acceptance or approval, specify, by declaration addressed to the Secretary General of the Council of Europe, the territory which shall be considered to be its metropolitan territory for this purpose.

2. Any signatory may, at the time of signature or of the deposit of its instrument of ratification, acceptance or approval, or at any time thereafter, declare by notification addressed to the Secretary General of the Council of Europe, that the Charter shall extend in whole or in part to a non-metropolitan territory or territories specified in the said declaration for whose international relations it is responsible or for which it assumes international responsibility. It shall specify in the declaration the articles or paragraphs of Part II of the Charter which it accepts as binding in respect of the territories named in the declaration.

3. The Charter shall extend its application to the territory or territories named in the aforesaid declaration as from the first day of the month following the expiration of a period of one month after the date of receipt of the notification of such declaration by the Secretary General.

4. Any Party may declare at a later date by notification addressed to the Secretary General of the Council of Europe that, in respect of one or more of the territories to which the Charter has been applied in accordance with paragraph 2 of this article, it accepts as binding any articles or any numbered paragraphs which it has not already accepted in respect of that territory or territories. Such undertakings subsequently given shall be deemed to be an integral part of the original declaration in respect of the territory concerned, and shall have the same effect as from the first day of the month following the expiration of a period of one month after the date of receipt of such notification by the Secretary General.

Article M – Denunciation

1. Any Party may denounce this Charter only at the end of a period of five years from the date on which the Charter entered into force for it, or at the end of any subsequent period of two years, and

in either case after giving six months' notice to the Secretary General of the Council of Europe who shall inform the other Parties accordingly.

2. Any Party may, in accordance with the provisions set out in the preceding paragraph, denounce any article or paragraph of Part II of the Charter accepted by it provided that the number of articles or paragraphs by which this Party is bound shall never be less than sixteen in the former case and sixty-three in the latter and that this number of articles or paragraphs shall continue to include the articles selected by the Party among those to which special reference is made in Article A, paragraph 1, sub-paragraph b.

3. Any Party may denounce the present Charter or any of the articles or paragraphs of Part II of the Charter under the conditions specified in paragraph 1 of this article in respect of any territory to which the said Charter is applicable, by virtue of a declaration made in accordance with paragraph 2 of Article L.

Article N – Appendix

The appendix to this Charter shall form an integral part of it.

Article O – Notifications

The Secretary General of the Council of Europe shall notify the member States of the Council and the Director General of the International Labour Office of:

a. any signature;
b. the deposit of any instrument of ratification, acceptance or approval;
c. any date of entry into force of this Charter in accordance with Article K;
d. any declaration made in application of Articles A, paragraphs 2 and 3, D, paragraphs 1 and 2, F, paragraph 2, L, paragraphs 1, 2, 3 and 4;
e. any amendment in accordance with Article J;
f. any denunciation in accordance with Article M;
g. any other act, notification or communication relating to this Charter.

In witness whereof, the undersigned, being duly authorised thereto, have signed this revised Charter.

Done at Strasbourg, this 3rd day of May 1996, in English and French, both texts being equally authentic, in a single copy which shall be deposited in the archives of the Council of Europe. The Secretary General of the Council of Europe shall transmit certified copies to each member State of the Council of Europe and to the Director General of the International Labour Office.

Appendix to the European Social Charter (Revised)

Scope of the Revised European Social Charter in terms of persons protected

1. Without prejudice to Article 12, paragraph 4, and Article 13, paragraph 4, the persons covered by Articles 1 to 17 and 20 to 31 include foreigners only in so far as they are nationals of other Parties lawfully resident or working regularly within the territory of the Party concerned, subject to the understanding that these articles are to be interpreted in the light of the provisions of Articles 18 and 19.

   This interpretation would not prejudice the extension of similar facilities to other persons by any of the Parties.

2. Each Party will grant to refugees as defined in the Convention relating to the Status of Refugees, signed in Geneva on 28 July 1951 and in the Protocol of 31 January 1967, and lawfully staying in its territory, treatment as favourable as possible, and in any case not less favourable than under the obligations accepted by the Party under the said convention and under any other existing international instruments applicable to those refugees.

3. Each Party will grant to stateless persons as defined in the Convention on the Status of Stateless Persons done in New York on 28 September 1954 and lawfully staying in its territory, treatment as favourable as possible and in any case not less favourable than under the obligations accepted by the Party under the said instrument and under any other existing international instruments applicable to those stateless persons.

Part I, paragraph 18, and Part II, Article 18, paragraph 1

It is understood that these provisions are not concerned with the question of entry into the territories of the Parties and do not prejudice the provisions of the European Convention on Establishment, signed in Paris on 13 December 1955.

Part II

Article 1, paragraph 2
This provision shall not be interpreted as prohibiting or authorising any union security clause or practice.

Article 2, paragraph 6
Parties may provide that this provision shall not apply:
- a. to workers having a contract or employment relationship with a total duration not exceeding one month and/or with a working week not exceeding eight hours;
- b. where the contract or employment relationship is of a casual and/or specific nature, provided, in these cases, that its non-application is justified by objective considerations.

Article 3, paragraph 4
It is understood that for the purposes of this provision the functions, organisation and conditions of operation of these services shall be determined by national laws or regulations, collective agreements or other means appropriate to national conditions.

Article 4, paragraph 4
This provision shall be so understood as not to prohibit immediate dismissal for any serious offence.

Article 4, paragraph 5
It is understood that a Party may give the undertaking required in this paragraph if the great majority of workers are not permitted to suffer deductions from wages either by law or through collective agreements or arbitration awards, the exceptions being those persons not so covered.

Article 6, paragraph 4
It is understood that each Party may, insofar as it is concerned, regulate the exercise of the right to strike by law, provided that any further restriction that this might place on the right can be justified under the terms of Article G.

Article 7, paragraph 2
This provision does not prevent Parties from providing in their legislation that young persons not having reached the minimum age laid down may perform work in so far as it is absolutely necessary for their vocational training where such work is carried out in accordance with conditions prescribed by the competent authority and measures are taken to protect the health and safety of these young persons.

Article 7, paragraph 8
It is understood that a Party may give the undertaking required in this paragraph if it fulfils the spirit of the undertaking by providing by law that the great majority of persons under eighteen years of age shall not be employed in night work.

Article 8, paragraph 2
This provision shall not be interpreted as laying down an absolute prohibition. Exceptions could be made, for instance, in the following cases:
- a. if an employed woman has been guilty of misconduct which justifies breaking off the employment relationship;
- b. if the undertaking concerned ceases to operate;
- c. if the period prescribed in the employment contract has expired.

Article 12, paragraph 4

The words "and subject to the conditions laid down in such agreements" in the introduction to this paragraph are taken to imply *inter alia* that with regard to benefits which are available independently of any insurance contribution, a Party may require the completion of a prescribed period of residence before granting such benefits to nationals of other Parties.

Article 13, paragraph 4

Governments not Parties to the European Convention on Social and Medical Assistance may ratify the Charter in respect of this paragraph provided that they grant to nationals of other Parties a treatment which is in conformity with the provisions of the said convention.

Article 16

It is understood that the protection afforded in this provision covers single-parent families.

Article 17

It is understood that this provision covers all persons below the age of 18 years, unless under the law applicable to the child majority is attained earlier, without prejudice to the other specific provisions provided by the Charter, particularly Article 7. This does not imply an obligation to provide compulsory education up to the above-mentioned age.

Article 19, paragraph 6

For the purpose of applying this provision, the term "family of a foreign worker" is understood to mean at least the worker's spouse and unmarried children, as long as the latter are considered to be minors by the receiving State and are dependent on the migrant worker.

Article 20

1. It is understood that social security matters, as well as other provisions relating to unemployment benefit, old age benefit and survivor's benefit, may be excluded from the scope of this article.
2. Provisions concerning the protection of women, particularly as regards pregnancy, confinement and the post-natal period, shall not be deemed to be discrimination as referred to in this article.
3. This article shall not prevent the adoption of specific measures aimed at removing *de facto* inequalities.
4. Occupational activities which, by reason of their nature or the context in which they are carried out, can be entrusted only to persons of a particular sex may be excluded from the scope of this article or some of its provisions. This provision is not to be interpreted as requiring the Parties to embody in laws or regulations a list of occupations which, by reason of their nature or the context in which they are carried out, may be reserved to persons of a particular sex.

Articles 21 and 22

1. For the purpose of the application of these articles, the term "workers' representatives" means persons who are recognised as such under national legislation or practice.
2. The terms "national legislation and practice" embrace as the case may be, in addition to laws and regulations, collective agreements, other agreements between employers and workers' representatives, customs as well as relevant case law.
3. For the purpose of the application of these articles, the term "undertaking" is understood as referring to a set of tangible and intangible components, with or without legal personality, formed to produce goods or provide services for financial gain and with power to determine its own market policy.
4. It is understood that religious communities and their institutions may be excluded from the application of these articles, even if these institutions are "undertakings" within the meaning of paragraph 3. Establishments pursuing activities which are inspired by certain ideals or guided by certain moral concepts, ideals and concepts which are protected by national legislation, may be excluded from the application of these articles to such an extent as is necessary to protect the orientation of the undertaking.
5. It is understood that where in a state the rights set out in these articles are exercised in the various establishments of the undertaking, the Party concerned is to be considered as fulfilling the obligations deriving from these provisions.

371

6. The Parties may exclude from the field of application of these articles, those undertakings employing less than a certain number of workers, to be determined by national legislation or practice.

Article 22

1. This provision affects neither the powers and obligations of states as regards the adoption of health and safety regulations for workplaces, nor the powers and responsibilities of the bodies in charge of monitoring their application.
2. The terms "social and socio-cultural services and facilities" are understood as referring to the social and/or cultural facilities for workers provided by some undertakings such as welfare assistance, sports fields, rooms for nursing mothers, libraries, children's holiday camps, etc.

Article 23, paragraph 1

For the purpose of the application of this paragraph, the term "for as long as possible" refers to the elderly person's physical, psychological and intellectual capacities.

Article 24

1. It is understood that for the purposes of this article the terms "termination of employment" and "terminated" mean termination of employment at the initiative of the employer.
2. It is understood that this article covers all workers but that a Party may exclude from some or all of its protection the following categories of employed persons:
   a. workers engaged under a contract of employment for a specified period of time or a specified task;
   b. workers undergoing a period of probation or a qualifying period of employment, provided that this is determined in advance and is of a reasonable duration;
   c. workers engaged on a casual basis for a short period.
3. For the purpose of this article the following, in particular, shall not constitute valid reasons for termination of employment:
   a. trade union membership or participation in union activities outside working hours, or, with the consent of the employer, within working hours;
   b. seeking office as, acting or having acted in the capacity of a workers' representative;
   c. the filing of a complaint or the participation in proceedings against an employer involving alleged violation of laws or regulations or recourse to competent administrative authorities;
   d. race, colour, sex, marital status, family responsibilities, pregnancy, religion, political opinion, national extraction or social origin;
   e. maternity or parental leave;
   f. temporary absence from work due to illness or injury.
4. It is understood that compensation or other appropriate relief in case of termination of employment without valid reasons shall be determined by national laws or regulations, collective agreements or other means appropriate to national conditions.

Article 25

1. It is understood that the competent national authority may, by way of exemption and after consulting organisations of employers and workers, exclude certain categories of workers from the protection provided in this provision by reason of the special nature of their employment relationship.
2. It is understood that the definition of the term "insolvency" must be determined by national law and practice.
3. The workers' claims covered by this provision shall include at least:
   a. the workers' claims for wages relating to a prescribed period, which shall not be less than three months under a privilege system and eight weeks under a guarantee system, prior to the insolvency or to the termination of employment;
   b. the workers' claims for holiday pay due as a result of work performed during the year in which the insolvency or the termination of employment occurred;

c. the workers' claims for amounts due in respect of other types of paid absence relating to a prescribed period, which shall not be less than three months under a privilege system and eight weeks under a guarantee system, prior to the insolvency or the termination of the employment.

4. National laws or regulations may limit the protection of workers' claims to a prescribed amount, which shall be of a socially acceptable level.

Article 26

It is understood that this article does not require that legislation be enacted by the Parties. It is understood that paragraph 2 does not cover sexual harassment.

Article 27

It is understood that this article applies to men and women workers with family responsibilities in relation to their dependent children as well as in relation to other members of their immediate family who clearly need their care or support where such responsibilities restrict their possibilities of preparing for, entering, participating in or advancing in economic activity. The terms "dependent children" and "other members of their immediate family who clearly need their care and support" mean persons defined as such by the national legislation of the Party concerned.

Articles 28 and 29

For the purpose of the application of this article, the term "workers' representatives" means persons who are recognised as such under national legislation or practice.

Part III

It is understood that the Charter contains legal obligations of an international character, the application of which is submitted solely to the supervision provided for in Part IV thereof.

Article A, paragraph 1

It is understood that the numbered paragraphs may include articles consisting of only one paragraph.

Article B, paragraph 2

For the purpose of paragraph 2 of Article B, the provisions of the revised Charter correspond to the provisions of the Charter with the same article or paragraph number with the exception of:

a. Article 3, paragraph 2, of the revised Charter which corresponds to Article 3, paragraphs 1 and 3, of the Charter;
b. Article 3, paragraph 3, of the revised Charter which corresponds to Article 3, paragraphs 2 and 3, of the Charter;
c. Article 10, paragraph 5, of the revised Charter which corresponds to Article 10, paragraph 4, of the Charter;
d. Article 17, paragraph 1, of the revised Charter which corresponds to Article 17 of the Charter.

Part V

Article E

A differential treatment based on an objective and reasonable justification shall not be deemed discriminatory.

Article F

The terms "in time of war or other public emergency" shall be so understood as to cover also the threat of war.

Article I

It is understood that workers excluded in accordance with the appendix to Articles 21 and 22 are not taken into account in establishing the number of workers concerned.

Article J

The term "amendment" shall be extended so as to cover also the addition of new articles to the Charter

---

FRAMEWORK CONVENTION FOR THE PROTECTION OF NATIONAL MINORITIES

European Treaty Series No. 157

Available at http://conventions.coe.int/Treaty/EN/Treaties/Html/157.htm

The member States of the Council of Europe and the other States, signatories to the present framework Convention,

Considering that the aim of the Council of Europe is to achieve greater unity between its members for the purpose of safeguarding and realising the ideals and principles which are their common heritage;

Considering that one of the methods by which that aim is to be pursued is the maintenance and further realisation of human rights and fundamental freedoms;

Wishing to follow-up the Declaration of the Heads of State and Government of the member States of the Council of Europe adopted in Vienna on 9 October 1993;

Being resolved to protect within their respective territories the existence of national minorities;

Considering that the upheavals of European history have shown that the protection of national minorities is essential to stability, democratic security and peace in this continent;

Considering that a pluralist and genuinely democratic society should not only respect the ethnic, cultural, linguistic and religious identity of each person belonging to a national minority, but also create appropriate conditions enabling them to express, preserve and develop this identity;

Considering that the creation of a climate of tolerance and dialogue is necessary to enable cultural diversity to be a source and a factor, not of division, but of enrichment for each society;

Considering that the realisation of a tolerant and prosperous Europe does not depend solely on co-operation between States but also requires transfrontier co-operation between local and regional authorities without prejudice to the constitution and territorial integrity of each State;

Having regard to the Convention for the Protection of Human Rights and Fundamental Freedoms and the Protocols thereto;

Having regard to the commitments concerning the protection of national minorities in United Nations conventions and declarations and in the documents of the Conference on Security and Co-operation in Europe, particularly the Copenhagen Document of 29 June 1990;

Being resolved to define the principles to be respected and the obligations which flow from them, in order to ensure, in the member States and such other States as may become Parties to the present instrument, the effective protection of national minorities and of the rights and freedoms of persons belonging to those minorities, within the rule of law, respecting the territorial integrity and national sovereignty of states;

Being determined to implement the principles set out in this framework Convention through national legislation and appropriate governmental policies,

Have agreed as follows:

Section I

Article 1

The protection of national minorities and of the rights and freedoms of persons belonging to those minorities forms an integral part of the international protection of human rights, and as such falls within the scope of international co-operation.

Article 2

The provisions of this framework Convention shall be applied in good faith, in a spirit of understanding and tolerance and in conformity with the principles of good neighbourliness, friendly relations and co-operation between States.

Article 3

Every person belonging to a national minority shall have the right freely to choose to be treated or not to be treated as such and no disadvantage shall result from this choice or from the exercise of the rights which are connected to that choice. Persons belonging to national minorities may exercise the rights and enjoy the freedoms flowing from the principles enshrined in the present framework Convention individually as well as in community with others.

Section II

Article 4

The Parties undertake to guarantee to persons belonging to national minorities the right of equality before the law and of equal protection of the law. In this respect, any discrimination based on belonging to a national minority shall be prohibited. The Parties undertake to adopt, where necessary, adequate measures in order to promote, in all areas of economic, social, political and cultural life, full and effective equality between persons belonging to a national minority and those belonging to the majority. In this respect, they shall take due account of the specific conditions of the persons belonging to national minorities. The measures adopted in accordance with [the second sentence of this article] shall not be considered to be an act of discrimination.

Article 5

The Parties undertake to promote the conditions necessary for persons belonging to national minorities to maintain and develop their culture, and to preserve the essential elements of their identity, namely their religion, language, traditions and cultural heritage. Without prejudice to measures taken in pursuance of their general integration policy, the Parties shall refrain from policies or practices aimed at assimilation of persons belonging to national minorities against their will and shall protect these persons from any action aimed at such assimilation.

Article 6

The Parties shall encourage a spirit of tolerance and intercultural dialogue and take effective measures to promote mutual respect and understanding and co-operation among all persons living on their territory, irrespective of those persons' ethnic, cultural, linguistic or religious identity, in particular in the fields of education, culture and the media. The Parties undertake to take appropriate measures to protect persons who may be subject to threats or acts of discrimination, hostility or violence as a result of their ethnic, cultural, linguistic or religious identity.

Article 7

The Parties shall ensure respect for the right of every person belonging to a national minority to freedom of peaceful assembly, freedom of association, freedom of expression, and freedom of thought, conscience and religion.

Article 8

The Parties undertake to recognise that every person belonging to a national minority has the right to manifest his or her religion or belief and to establish religious institutions, organisations and associations.

Article 9

The Parties undertake to recognise that the right to freedom of expression of every person belonging to a national minority includes freedom to hold opinions and to receive and impart information and ideas in the minority language, without interference by public authorities and regardless of frontiers. The Parties shall ensure, within the framework of their legal systems, that persons belonging to a national minority are not discriminated against in their access to the media. [This provision] shall not prevent Parties from requiring the licensing, without discrimination and based on objective criteria, of sound radio and television broadcasting, or cinema enterprises. The Parties shall not hinder the creation and the use of printed media by persons belonging to national minorities. In the legal framework of sound radio and television broadcasting, they shall ensure, as far as possible, and taking into account the provisions of [the first sentence of this article], that persons belonging to national minorities are granted the possibility of creating and using their own media. In the framework of their legal systems, the Parties shall adopt adequate measures in order to facilitate access to the media for persons belonging to national minorities and in order to promote tolerance and permit cultural pluralism.

Article 10

The Parties undertake to recognise that every person belonging to a national minority has the right to use freely and without interference his or her minority language, in private and in public, orally and in writing. In areas inhabited by persons belonging to national minorities traditionally or in substantial numbers, if those persons so request and where such a request corresponds to a real need, the Parties shall endeavour to ensure, as far as possible, the conditions which would make it possible to use the minority language in relations between those persons and the administrative authorities. The Parties undertake to guarantee the right of every person belonging to a national minority to be informed promptly, in a language which he or she understands, of the reasons for his or her arrest, and of the nature and cause of any accusation against him or her, and to defend himself or herself in this language, if necessary with the free assistance of an interpreter.

Article 11

The Parties undertake to recognise that every person belonging to a national minority has the right to use his or her surname (patronym) and first names in the minority language and the right to official recognition of them, according to modalities provided for in their legal system. The Parties undertake to recognise that every person belonging to a national minority has the right to display in his or her minority language signs, inscriptions and other information of a private nature visible to the public. In areas traditionally inhabited by substantial numbers of persons belonging to a national minority, the Parties shall endeavour, in the framework of their legal system, including, where appropriate, agreements with other States, and taking into account their specific conditions, to display traditional local names, street names and other topographical indications intended for the public also in the minority language when there is a sufficient demand for such indications.

Article 12

The Parties shall, where appropriate, take measures in the fields of education and research to foster knowledge of the culture, history, language and religion of their national minorities and of the majority. In this context the Parties shall *inter alia* provide adequate opportunities for teacher training and access to textbooks, and facilitate contacts among students and teachers of different communities. The Parties undertake to promote equal opportunities for access to education at all levels for persons belonging to national minorities.

Article 13

Within the framework of their education systems, the Parties shall recognise that persons belonging to a national minority have the right to set up and to manage their own private educational and training establishments. The exercise of this right shall not entail any financial obligation for the Parties.

Article 14

The Parties undertake to recognise that every person belonging to a national minority has the right to learn his or her minority language. In areas inhabited by persons belonging to national minorities traditionally or in substantial numbers, if there is sufficient demand, the Parties shall endeavour to ensure, as far as possible and within the framework of their education systems, that persons belonging to those minorities have adequate opportunities for being taught the minority language or for receiving instruction in this language. * * * [T]his article shall be implemented without prejudice to the learning of the official language or the teaching in this language.

Article 15

The Parties shall create the conditions necessary for the effective participation of persons belonging to national minorities in cultural, social and economic life and in public affairs, in particular those affecting them.

Article 16

The Parties shall refrain from measures which alter the proportions of the population in areas inhabited by persons belonging to national minorities and are aimed at restricting the rights and freedoms flowing from the principles enshrined in the present framework Convention.

Article 17

The Parties undertake not to interfere with the right of persons belonging to national minorities to establish and maintain free and peaceful contacts across frontiers with persons lawfully staying in other States, in particular those with whom they share an ethnic, cultural, linguistic or religious identity, or a common cultural heritage. The Parties undertake not to interfere with the right of persons belonging to national minorities to participate in the activities of non-governmental organisations, both at the national and international levels.

Article 18

The Parties shall endeavour to conclude, where necessary, bilateral and multilateral agreements with other States, in particular neighbouring States, in order to ensure the protection of persons belonging to the national minorities concerned. Where relevant, the Parties shall take measures to encourage transfrontier co-operation.

Article 19

The Parties undertake to respect and implement the principles enshrined in the present framework Convention making, where necessary, only those limitations, restrictions or derogations which are provided for in international legal instruments, in particular the Convention for the Protection of Human Rights and Fundamental Freedoms, in so far as they are relevant to the rights and freedoms flowing from the said principles.

Section III

Article 20

In the exercise of the rights and freedoms flowing from the principles enshrined in the present framework Convention, any person belonging to a national minority shall respect the national legislation and the rights of others, in particular those of persons belonging to the majority or to other national minorities.

Article 21

Nothing in the present framework Convention shall be interpreted as implying any right to engage in any activity or perform any act contrary to the fundamental principles of international law and in particular of the sovereign equality, territorial integrity and political independence of States.

Article 22

Nothing in the present framework Convention shall be construed as limiting or derogating from any of the human rights and fundamental freedoms which may be ensured under the laws of any Contracting Party or under any other agreement to which it is a Party.

Article 23

The rights and freedoms flowing from the principles enshrined in the present framework Convention, in so far as they are the subject of a corresponding provision in the Convention for the Protection of Human Rights and Fundamental Freedoms or in the Protocols thereto, shall be understood so as to conform to the latter provisions.

Section IV

Article 24

The Committee of Ministers of the Council of Europe shall monitor the implementation of this framework Convention by the Contracting Parties. The Parties which are not members of the Council of Europe shall participate in the implementation mechanism, according to modalities to be determined.

Article 25

Within a period of one year following the entry into force of this framework Convention in respect of a Contracting Party, the latter shall transmit to the Secretary General of the Council of Europe full information on the legislative and other measures taken to give effect to the principles set out in this framework Convention. Thereafter, each Party shall transmit to the Secretary General on a periodical basis and whenever the Committee of Ministers so requests any further information of relevance to the implementation of this framework Convention. The Secretary General shall forward to the Committee of Ministers the information transmitted under the terms of this article.

Article 26

In evaluating the adequacy of the measures taken by the Parties to give effect to the principles set out in this framework Convention the Committee of Ministers shall be assisted by an advisory committee, the members of which shall have recognised expertise in the field of the protection of national minorities. The composition of this advisory committee and its procedure shall be determined by the Committee of Ministers within a period of one year following the entry into force of this framework Convention.

Section V

Article 27

This framework Convention shall be open for signature by the member States of the Council of Europe. Up until the date when the Convention enters into force, it shall also be open for signature by any other State so invited by the Committee of Ministers. It is subject to ratification, acceptance or approval. Instruments of ratification, acceptance or approval shall be deposited with the Secretary General of the Council of Europe.

Article 28

This framework Convention shall enter into force on the first day of the month following the expiration of a period of three months after the date on which twelve member States of the Council of Europe have expressed their consent to be bound by the Convention in accordance with the provisions of Article 27. In respect of any member State which subsequently expresses its consent to be bound by it, the framework Convention shall enter into force on the first day of the month following the expiration of a period of three months after the date of the deposit of the instrument of ratification, acceptance or approval.

Article 29

After the entry into force of this framework Convention and after consulting the Contracting States, the Committee of Ministers of the Council of Europe may invite to accede to the Convention, by a decision taken by the majority provided for in Article 20.d of the Statute of the Council of Europe, any non-member State of the Council of Europe which, invited to sign in accordance with the provisions of Article 27, has not yet done so, and any other non-member State. In respect of any acceding State, the framework Convention shall enter into force on the first day of the month following the expiration of a period of three months after the date of the deposit of the instrument of accession with the Secretary General of the Council of Europe.

378

Article 30

Any State may at the time of signature or when depositing its instrument of ratification, acceptance, approval or accession, specify the territory or territories for whose international relations it is responsible to which this framework Convention shall apply. Any State may at any later date, by a declaration addressed to the Secretary General of the Council of Europe, extend the application of this framework Convention to any other territory specified in the declaration. In respect of such territory the framework Convention shall enter into force on the first day of the month following the expiration of a period of three months after the date of receipt of such declaration by the Secretary General. Any declaration made under the two preceding [sentences] may, in respect of any territory specified in such declaration, be withdrawn by a notification addressed to the Secretary General. The withdrawal shall become effective on the first day of the month following the expiration of a period of three months after the date of receipt of such notification by the Secretary General.

Article 31

Any Party may at any time denounce this framework Convention by means of a notification addressed to the Secretary General of the Council of Europe. Such denunciation shall become effective on the first day of the month following the expiration of a period of six months after the date of receipt of the notification by the Secretary General.

Article 32

The Secretary General of the Council of Europe shall notify the member States of the Council, other signatory States and any State which has acceded to this framework Convention, of: any signature; the deposit of any instrument of ratification, acceptance, approval or accession; any date of entry into force of this framework Convention in accordance with Articles 28, 29 and 30; any other act, notification or communication relating to this framework Convention.

Done at Strasbourg, this 1st day of February 1995, in English and French, both texts being equally authentic, in a single copy which shall be deposited in the archives of the Council of Europe. The Secretary General of the Council of Europe shall transmit certified copies to each member State of the Council of Europe and to any State invited to sign or accede to this framework Convention.

THE ARAB WORLD

ARAB CHARTER ON HUMAN RIGHTS

entered into force March 15, 2008, *available at* www.umn.edu/humanrts/instree/loas2005.html

Based on the faith of the Arab nation in the dignity of the human person whom God has exalted ever since the beginning of creation and in the fact that the Arab homeland is the cradle of religions and civilizations whose lofty human values affirm the human right to a decent life based on freedom, justice and equality,

In furtherance of the eternal principles of fraternity, equality and tolerance among human beings consecrated by the noble Islamic religion and the other divinely-revealed religions,

Being proud of the humanitarian values and principles that the Arab nation has established throughout its long history, which have played a major role in spreading knowledge between East and West, so making the region a point of reference for the whole world and a destination for seekers of knowledge and wisdom,

Believing in the unity of the Arab nation, which struggles for its freedom and defends the right of nations to self-determination, to the preservation of their wealth and to development; believing in the sovereignty of the law and its contribution to the protection of universal and interrelated human rights and convinced that the human person's enjoyment of freedom, justice and equality of opportunity is a fundamental measure of the value of any society,

Rejecting all forms of racism and Zionism, which constitute a violation of human rights and a threat to international peace and security, recognizing the close link that exists between human rights and international peace and security, reaffirming the principles of the Charter of the United Nations, the Universal Declaration of Human Rights and the provisions of the International Covenant on Civil and Political Rights and the International Covenant on Economic, Social and Cultural Rights, and having regard to the Cairo Declaration on Human Rights in Islam,

The States parties to the Charter have agreed as follows:

Article 1
The present Charter seeks, within the context of the national identity of the Arab States and their sense of belonging to a common civilization, to achieve the following aims:
1. To place human rights at the centre of the key national concerns of Arab States, making them lofty and fundamental ideals that shape the will of the individual in Arab States and enable him to improve his life in accordance with noble human values.
2. To teach the human person in the Arab States pride in his identity, loyalty to his country, attachment to his land, history and common interests and to instill in him a culture of human brotherhood, tolerance and openness towards others, in accordance with universal principles and values and with those proclaimed in international human rights instruments.
3. To prepare the new generations in Arab States for a free and responsible life in a civil society that is characterized by solidarity, founded on a balance between awareness of rights and respect for obligations, and governed by the values of equality, tolerance and moderation.
4. To entrench the principle that all human rights are universal, indivisible, interdependent and interrelated.

Article 2
1. All peoples have the right of self-determination and to control over their natural wealth and resources, and the right to freely choose their political system and to freely pursue their economic, social and cultural development.
2. All peoples have the right to national sovereignty and territorial integrity.
3. All forms of racism, Zionism and foreign occupation and domination constitute an impediment to human dignity and a major barrier to the exercise of the fundamental rights of peoples; all such practices must be condemned and efforts must be deployed for their elimination.
4. All peoples have the right to resist foreign occupation.

Article 3
1. Each State party to the present Charter undertakes to ensure to all individuals subject to its jurisdiction the right to enjoy the rights and freedoms set forth herein, without distinction on grounds of race, colour, sex, language, religious belief, opinion, thought, national or social origin, wealth, birth or physical or mental disability.
2. The States parties to the present Charter shall take the requisite measures to guarantee effective equality in the enjoyment of all the rights and freedoms enshrined in the present Charter in order to ensure protection against all forms of discrimination based on any of the grounds mentioned in the preceding paragraph.
3. Men and women are equal in respect of human dignity, rights and obligations within the framework of the positive discrimination established in favour of women by the Islamic Shariah, other divine laws and by applicable laws and legal instruments. Accordingly, each State party pledges to take all the requisite measures to guarantee equal opportunities and effective equality between men and women in the enjoyment of all the rights set out in this Charter.

Article 4
1. In exceptional situations of emergency which threaten the life of the nation and the existence of which is officially proclaimed, the States parties to the present Charter may take measures derogating from their obligations under the present Charter, to the extent strictly required by the exigencies of the situation, provided that such measures are not inconsistent with their other obligations under international law and do not involve discrimination solely on the grounds of race, colour, sex, language, religion or social origin.

2. In exceptional situations of emergency, no derogation shall be made from the following articles: article 5, article 8, article 9, article 10, article 13, article 14, paragraph 6, article 15, article 18, article 19, article 20, article 22, article 27, article 28, article 29 and article 30. In addition, the judicial guarantees required for the protection of the aforementioned rights may not be suspended.

3. Any State party to the present Charter availing itself of the right of derogation shall immediately inform the other States parties, through the intermediary of the Secretary-General of the League of Arab States, of the provisions from which it has derogated and of the reasons by which it was actuated. A further communication shall be made, through the same intermediary, on the date on which it terminates such derogation.

Article 5

1. Every human being has the inherent right to life.
2. This right shall be protected by law. No one shall be arbitrarily deprived of his life.

Article 6

Sentence of death may be imposed only for the most serious crimes in accordance with the laws in force at the time of commission of the crime and pursuant to a final judgment rendered by a competent court. Anyone sentenced to death shall have the right to seek pardon or commutation of the sentence.

Article 7

1. Sentence of death shall not be imposed on persons under 18 years of age, unless otherwise stipulated in the laws in force at the time of the commission of the crime.
2. The death penalty shall not be inflicted on a pregnant woman prior to her delivery or on a nursing mother within two years from the date of her delivery; in all cases, the best interests of the infant shall be the primary consideration.

Article 8

1. No one shall be subjected to physical or psychological torture or to cruel, degrading, humiliating or inhuman treatment.
2. Each State party shall protect every individual subject to its jurisdiction from such practices and shall take effective measures to prevent them. The commission of, or participation in, such acts shall be regarded as crimes that are punishable by law and not subject to any statute of limitations. Each State party shall guarantee in its legal system redress for any victim of torture and the right to rehabilitation and compensation.

Article 9

No one shall be subjected to medical or scientific experimentation or to the use of his organs without his free consent and full awareness of the consequences and provided that ethical, humanitarian and professional rules are followed and medical procedures are observed to ensure his personal safety pursuant to the relevant domestic laws in force in each State party. Trafficking in human organs is prohibited in all circumstances.

Article 10

1. All forms of slavery and trafficking in human beings are prohibited and are punishable by law. No one shall be held in slavery and servitude under any circumstances.
2. Forced labor, trafficking in human beings for the purposes of prostitution or sexual exploitation, the exploitation of the prostitution of others or any other form of exploitation or the exploitation of children in armed conflict are prohibited.

Article 11

All persons are equal before the law and have the right to enjoy its protection without discrimination.

Article 12

All persons are equal before the courts and tribunals. The States parties shall guarantee the independence of the judiciary and protect magistrates against any interference, pressure or threats. They shall also guarantee every person subject to their jurisdiction the right to seek a legal remedy before courts of all levels.

Article 13

1. Everyone has the right to a fair trial that affords adequate guarantees before a competent, independent and impartial court that has been constituted by law to hear any criminal charge against him or to decide on his rights or his obligations. Each State party shall guarantee to those without the requisite financial resources legal aid to enable them to defend their rights.

2. Trials shall be public, except in exceptional cases that may be warranted by the interests of justice in a society that respects human freedoms and rights.

Article 14

1. Everyone has the right to liberty and security of person. No one shall be subjected to arbitrary arrest, search or detention without a legal warrant.

2. No one shall be deprived of-his liberty except on such grounds and in such circumstances as are determined by law and in accordance with such procedure as is established thereby.

3. Anyone who is arrested shall be informed, at the time of arrest, in a language that he understands, of the reasons for his arrest and shall be promptly informed of any charges against him. He shall be entitled to contact his family members.

4. Anyone who is deprived of his liberty by arrest or detention shall have the right to request a medical examination and must be informed of that right.

5. Anyone arrested or detained on a criminal charge shall be brought promptly before a judge or other officer authorized by law to exercise judicial power and shall be entitled to trial within a reasonable time or to release. His release may be subject to guarantees to appear for trial. Pre-trial detention shall in no case be the general rule.

6. Anyone who is deprived of his liberty by arrest or detention shall be entitled to petition a competent court in order that it may decide without delay on the lawfulness of his arrest or detention and order his release if the arrest or detention is unlawful.

7. Anyone who has been the victim of arbitrary or unlawful arrest or detention shall be entitled to compensation.

Article 15

No crime and no penalty can be established without a prior provision of the law. In all circumstances, the law most favorable to the defendant shall be applied.

Article 16

Everyone charged with a criminal offence shall be presumed innocent until proved guilty by a final judgment rendered according to law and, in the course of the investigation and trial, he shall enjoy the following minimum guarantees:

1. The right to be informed promptly, in detail and in a language which he understands, of the charges against him.

2. The right to have adequate time and facilities for the preparation of his defense and to be allowed to communicate with his family.

3. The right to be tried in his presence before an ordinary court and to defend himself in person or through a lawyer of his own choosing with whom he can communicate freely and confidentially.

4. The right to the free assistance of a lawyer who will defend him if he cannot defend himself or if the interests of justice so require, and the right to the free assistance of an interpreter if he cannot understand or does not speak the language used in court.

5. The right to examine or have his lawyer examine the prosecution witnesses and to on defense according to the conditions applied to the prosecution witnesses.

6. The right not to be compelled to testify against himself or to confess guilt.

7. The right, if convicted of the crime, to file an appeal in accordance with the law before a higher tribunal.

8. The right to respect for his security of person and his privacy in all circumstances.

Article 17

Each State party shall ensure in particular to any child at risk or any delinquent charged with an offence the right to a special legal system for minors in all stages of investigation, trial and enforcement of sentence, as well as to special treatment that takes account of his age, protects his dignity, facilitates his rehabilitation and reintegration and enables him to play a constructive role in society.

Article 18
No one who is shown by a court to be unable to pay a debt arising from a contractual obligation shall be imprisoned.

Article 19
1. No one may be tried twice for the same offence. Anyone against whom such proceedings are brought shall have the right to challenge their legality and to demand his release.
2. Anyone whose innocence is established by a final judgment shall be entitled to compensation for the damage suffered.

Article 20
1. All persons deprived of their liberty shall be treated with humanity and with respect for the inherent dignity of the human person.
2. Persons in pre-trial detention shall be separated from convicted persons and shall be treated in a manner consistent with their status as unconvicted persons.
3. The aim of the penitentiary system shall be to reform prisoners and effect their social rehabilitation.

Article 21
1. No one shall be subjected to arbitrary or unlawful interference with regard to his privacy, family, home or correspondence, nor to unlawful attacks on his honour or his reputation.
2. Everyone has the right to the protection of the law against such interference or attacks.

Article 22
Everyone shall have the right to recognition as a person before the law.

Article 23
Each State party to the present Charter undertakes to ensure that any person whose rights or freedoms as herein recognized are violated shall have an effective remedy, notwithstanding that the violation has been committed by persons acting in an official capacity.

Article 24
Every citizen has the right:
1. To freely pursue a political activity.
2. To take part in the conduct of public affairs, directly or through freely chosen representatives.
3. To stand for election or choose his representatives in free and impartial elections, in conditions of equality among all citizens that guarantee the free expression of his will.
4. To the opportunity to gain access, on an equal footing with others, to public office in his country in accordance with the principle of equality of opportunity.
5. To freely form and join associations with others.
6. To freedom of association and peaceful assembly.
7. No restrictions may be placed on the exercise of these rights other than those which are prescribed by law and which are necessary in a democratic society in the interests of national security or public safety, public health or morals or the protection of the rights and freedoms of others.

Article 25
Persons belonging to minorities shall not be denied the right to enjoy their own culture, to use their own language and to practice their own religion. The exercise of these rights shall be governed by law.

Article 26

1. Everyone lawfully within the territory of a State party shall, within that territory, have the right to freedom of movement and to freely choose his residence in any part of that territory in conformity with the laws in force.

2. No State party may expel a person who does not hold its nationality but is lawfully in its territory, other than in pursuance of a decision reached in accordance with law and after that person has been allowed to submit a petition to the competent authority, unless compelling reasons of national security preclude it. Collective expulsion is prohibited under all circumstances.

Article 27

1. No one may be arbitrarily or unlawfully prevented from leaving any country, including his own, nor prohibited from residing, or compelled to reside, in any part of that country.

2. No one may be exiled from his country or prohibited from returning thereto.

Article 28

Everyone has the right to seek political asylum in another country in order to escape persecution. This right may not be invoked by persons facing prosecution for an offence under ordinary law. Political refugees may not be extradited.

Article 29

1. Everyone has the right to nationality. No one shall be arbitrarily or unlawfully deprived of his nationality.

2. States parties shall take such measures as they deem appropriate, in accordance with their domestic laws on nationality, to allow a child to acquire the mother's nationality, having due regard, in all cases, to the best interests of the child.

3. Non one shall be denied the right to acquire another nationality, having due regard for the domestic legal procedures in his country.

Article 30

1. Everyone has the right to freedom of thought, conscience and religion and no restrictions may be imposed on the exercise of such freedoms except as provided for by law.

2. The freedom to manifest one's religion or beliefs or to perform religious observances, either alone or in community with others, shall be subject only to such limitations as are prescribed by law and are necessary in a tolerant society that respects human rights and freedoms for the protection of public safety, public order, public health or morals or the fundamental rights and freedoms of others.

3. Parents or guardians have the freedom to provide for the religious and moral education of their children.

Article 31

Everyone has a guaranteed right to own private property, and shall not under any circumstances be arbitrarily or unlawfully divested of all or any part of his property.

Article 32

1. The present Charter guarantees the right to information and to freedom of opinion and expression, as well as the right to seek, receive and impart information and ideas through any medium, regardless of geographical boundaries.

2. Such rights and freedoms shall be exercised in conformity with the fundamental values of society and shall be subject only to such limitations as are required to ensure respect for the rights or reputation of others or the protection of national security, public order and public health or morals.

Article 33

1. The family is the natural and fundamental group unit of society; it is based on marriage between a man and a woman. Men and women of marrying age have the right to marry and to found a family according to the rules and conditions of marriage. No marriage can take place without the full and free consent of both parties. The laws in force regulate the rights and duties of the man and woman as to marriage, during marriage and at its dissolution.

2. The State and society shall ensure the protection of the family, the strengthening of family ties, the protection of its members and the prohibition of all forms of violence or abuse in the relations among its

members, and particularly against women and children. They shall also ensure the necessary protection and care for mothers, children, older persons and persons with special needs and shall provide adolescents and young persons with the best opportunities for physical and mental development.

3. The States parties shall take all necessary legislative, administrative and judicial measures to guarantee the protection, survival, development and well-being of the child in an atmosphere of freedom and dignity and shall ensure, in all cases, that the child's best interests are the basic criterion for all measures taken in his regard, whether the child is at risk of delinquency or is a juvenile offender.

4. The States parties shall take all the necessary measures to guarantee, particularly to young persons, the right to pursue a sporting activity.

Article 34

1. The right to work is a natural right of every citizen. The State shall endeavor to provide, to the extent possible, a job for the largest number of those willing to work, while ensuring production, the freedom to choose one's work and equality of opportunity without discrimination of any kind on grounds of race, colour, sex, religion, language, political opinion, membership in a union, national origin, social origin, disability or any other situation.

2. Every worker has the right to the enjoyment of just and favourable conditions of work which ensure appropriate remuneration to meet his essential needs and those of his family and regulate working hours, rest and holidays with pay, as well as the rules for the preservation of occupational health and safety and the protection of women, children and disabled persons in the place of work.

3. The States parties recognize the right of the child to be protected from economic exploitation and from being forced to perform any work that is likely to be hazardous or to interfere with the child's education or to be harmful to the child's health or physical, mental, spiritual, moral or social development. To this end, and having regard to the relevant provisions of other international instruments, States parties shall in particular:

    (a) Define a minimum age for admission to employment;

    (b) Establish appropriate regulation of working hours and conditions;

    (c) Establish appropriate penalties or other sanctions to ensure the effective endorsement of these provisions.

4. There shall be no discrimination between men and women in their enjoyment of the right to effectively benefit from training, employment and job protection and the right to receive equal remuneration for equal work.

5. Each State party shall ensure to workers who migrate to its territory the requisite protection in accordance with the laws in force.

Article 35

1. Every individual has the right to freely form trade unions or to join trade unions and to freely pursue trade union activity for the protection of his interests.

2. No restrictions shall be placed on the exercise of these rights and freedoms except such as are prescribed by the laws in force and that are necessary for the maintenance of national security, public safety or order or for the protection of public health or morals or the rights and freedoms of others.

3. Every State party to the present Charter guarantees the right to strike within the limits laid down by the laws in force.

Article 36

The States parties shall ensure the right of every citizen to social security, including social insurance.

Article 37

The right to development is a fundamental human right and all States are required to establish the development policies and to take the measures needed to guarantee this right. They have a duty to give effect to the values of solidarity and cooperation among them and at the international level with a view to eradicating poverty and achieving economic, social, cultural and political development. By virtue of this right, every citizen has the right to participate in the realization of development and to enjoy the benefits and fruits thereof.

Article 38

Every person has the right to an adequate standard of living for himself and his family, which ensures their well-being and a decent life, including food, clothing, housing, services and the right to a healthy environment. The States parties shall take the necessary measures commensurate with their resources to guarantee these rights.

Article 39

1. The States parties recognize the right of every member of society to the enjoyment of the highest attainable standard of physical and mental health and the right of the citizen to free basic health-care services and to have access to medical facilities without discrimination of any kind.
2. The measures taken by States parties shall include the following:
   (a) Development of basic health-care services and the guaranteeing of free and easy access to the centres that provide these services, regardless of geographical location or economic status.
   (b) efforts to control disease by means of prevention and cure in order to reduce the morality rate.
   (c) promotion of health awareness and health education.
   (d) suppression of traditional practices which are harmful to the health of the individual.
   (e) provision of the basic nutrition and safe drinking water for all.
   (f) Combating environmental pollution and providing proper sanitation systems;
   (g) Combating drugs, psychotropic substances, smoking and substances that are damaging to health.

Article 40

1. The States parties undertake to ensure to persons with mental or physical disabilities a decent life that guarantees their dignity, and to enhance their self-reliance and facilitate their active participation in society.
2. The States parties shall provide social services free of charge for all persons with disabilities, shall provide the material support needed by those persons, their families or the families caring for them, and shall also do whatever is needed to avoid placing those persons in institutions. They shall in all cases take account of the best interests of the disabled person.
3. The States parties shall take all necessary measures to curtail the incidence of disabilities by all possible means, including preventive health programmes, awareness raising and education.
4. The States parties shall provide full educational services suited to persons with disabilities, taking into account the importance of integrating these persons in the educational system and the importance of vocational training and apprenticeship and the creation of suitable job opportunities in the public or private sectors.
5. The States parties shall provide all health services appropriate for persons with disabilities, including the rehabilitation of these persons with a view to integrating them into society.
6. The States parties shall enable persons with disabilities to make use of all public and private services.

Article 41

1. The eradication of illiteracy is a binding obligation upon the State and everyone has the right to education.
2. The States parties shall guarantee their citizens free education at least throughout the primary and basic levels. All forms and levels of primary education shall be compulsory and accessible to all without discrimination of any kind.
3. The States parties shall take appropriate measures in all domains to ensure partnership between men and women with a view to achieving national development goals.
4. The States parties shall guarantee to provide education directed to the full development of the human person and to strengthening respect for human rights and fundamental freedoms.
5. The States parties shall endeavour to incorporate the principles of human rights and fundamental freedoms into formal and informal education curricula and educational and training programmes.
6. The States parties shall guarantee the establishment of the mechanisms necessary to provide ongoing education for every citizen and shall develop national plans for adult education.

Article 42

1. Every person has the right to take part in cultural life and to enjoy the benefits of scientific progress and its application.

2. The States parties undertake to respect the freedom of scientific research and creative activity and to ensure the protection of moral and material interests resulting form scientific, literary and artistic production.

3. The state parties shall work together and enhance cooperation among them at all levels, with the full participation of intellectuals and inventors and their organizations, in order to develop and implement recreational, cultural, artistic and scientific programmes.

Article 43

Nothing in this Charter may be construed or interpreted as impairing the rights and freedoms protected by the domestic laws of the States parties or those set force in the international and regional human rights instruments which the states parties have adopted or ratified, including the rights of women, the rights of the child and the rights of persons belonging to minorities.

Article 44

The states parties undertake to adopt, in conformity with their constitutional procedures and with the provisions of the present Charter, whatever legislative or non-legislative measures that may be necessary to give effect to the rihts set forth herein.

Article 45

1. Pursuant to this Charter, an "Arab Human Rights Committee", hereinafter refered to as "the Committee" shall be established. This Committee shall consist of seven members who shall be elected by secret ballot by the states parties to this Charter.

2. The Committee shall consist of nationals of the states parties to the present Charter, who must be highly experienced and competent in the Committee's field of work. The members of the Committee shall serve in their personal capacity and shall be fully independent and impartial.

3. The Committee shall include among its members not more than one national of a State party; such member may be re-elected only once. Due regard shall be given to the rotation principle.

4. The members of the Committee shall be elected for a four-year term, although the mandate of three of the members elected during the first election shall be for two years and shall be renewed by lot.

5. Six months prior to the date of the election, the Secretary-General of the League of Arab States shall invite the States parties to submit their nominations within the following three months. He shall transmit the list of candidates to the States parties two months prior to the date the election. The candidates who obtain the largest number of votes cast shall be elected to membership of the Committee. If, because two or more candidates have an equal number of votes, the number of candidates with the largest number of votes exceeds the number required, a second ballot will be held between the persons with equal numbers of votes. If the votes are again equal, the member or members shall be selected by lottery. The first election for membership of the Committee shall be held at least six months after the Charter enters into force.

6. The Secretary-General shall invite the States parties to a meeting at the headquarters the League of Arab States in order to elect the member of the Committee. The presence of the majority of the States parties shall constitute a quorum. If there is no quorum, the secretary-General shall call another meeting at which at least two thirds of the States parties must be present. If there is still no quorum, the Secretary-General shall call a third meeting, which will be held regardless of the number of States parties present.

7. The Secretary-General shall convene the first meeting of the Committee, during the course of which the Committee shall elect its Chairman from among its members, for a two-year n which may be renewed only once and for an identical period. The Committee shall establish its own rules of procedure and methods of work and shall determine how often it shall et. The Committee shall hold its meetings at the headquarters of the League of Arab States. ~ay also meet in any other State party to the present Charter at that party's invitation.

Article 46

1. The Secretary-General shall declare a seat vacant after being notified by the Chairman of a member's:
   (a) Death;
   (b) Resignation; or
   (c) If, in the unanimous, opinion of the other members, a member of the Committee has ceased to perform his functions without offering an acceptable justification or for any reason other than a temporary absence.

2. If a member's seat is declared vacant pursuant to the provisions of paragraph 1 and the term of office of the member to be replaced does not expire within six months from the date on which the vacancy was declared, the Secretary-General of the League of Arab States shall refer the matter to the States parties to the present Charter, which may, within two months, submit nominations, pursuant to article 45, in order to fill the vacant seat.

3. The Secretary-General of the League of Arab States shall draw up an alphabetical list of all the duly nominated candidates, which he shall transmit to the States parties to the present Charter. The elections to fill the vacant seat shall be held in accordance with the relevant provisions.

4. Any member of the Committee elected to fill a seat declared vacant in accordance with the provisions of paragraph 1 shall remain a member of the Committee until the expiry of the remainder of the term of the member whose seat was declared vacant pursuant to the provisions of that paragraph.

5. The Secretary-General of the League of Arab States shall make provision within the budget of the League of Arab States for all the necessary financial and human resources and facilities that the Committee needs to discharge its functions effectively. The Committee's experts shall be afforded the same treatment with respect to remuneration and reimbursement of expenses as experts of the secretariat of the League of Arab States.

Article 47

The States parties undertake to ensure that members of the Committee shall enjoy the immunities necessary for their protection against any form of harassment or moral or material pressure or prosecution on account of the positions they take or statements they make while carrying out their functions as members of the Committee.

Article 48

1.. The States parties undertake to submit reports to the Secretary-General of the League of Arab States on the measures they have taken to give effect to the rights and freedoms recognized in this Charter and on the progress made towards the enjoyment thereof. The Secretary-General shall transmit these reports to the Committee for its consideration.

2. Each State party shall submit an initial report to the Committee within one year from the date on which the Charter enters into force and a periodic report every three years thereafter. The Committee may request the States parties to supply it with additional information relating to the implementation of the Charter.

3. The Committee shall consider the reports submitted by the States parties under paragraph 2 of this article in the presence of the representative of the State party whose report is being considered.

4. The Committee shall discuss the report, comment thereon and make the necessary recommendations in accordance with the aims of the Charter.

5. The Committee shall submit an annual report containing its comments and recommendations to the Council of the League, through the intermediary of the Secretary-General.

6. The Committee's reports, concluding observations and recommendations shall be public documents which the Committee shall disseminate widely.

Article 49

1. The Secretary-General of the League of Arab States shall submit the present Charter, once it has been approved by the Council of the League, to the States members for signature, ratification or accession.

2. The present Charter shall enter into effect two months from the date on which the seventh instrument of ratification is deposited with the secretariat of the League of Arab States.

3. After its entry into force, the present Charter shall become effective for each State two months after the State in question has deposited its instrument of ratification or accession with the secretariat.

4. The Secretary-General shall notify the States members of the deposit of each instrument of ratification or accession.

Article 50

Any State party may submit written proposals, though the Secretary-General, for the amendment of the present Charter. After these amendments have been circulated among the States members, the Secretary-General shall invite the States parties to consider the proposed amendments before submitting them to the Council of the League for adoption.

Article 51
The amendments shall take effect, with regard to the States parties that have approved them, once they have been approved by two thirds of the States parties.

Article 52
Any State party may propose additional optional protocols to the present Charter and they shall be adopted in accordance with the procedures used for the adoption of amendments to the Charter.

Article 53
1. Any State party, when signing this Charter, depositing the instruments of ratification or acceding hereto, may make a reservation to any article of the Charter, provided that such reservation does not conflict with the aims and fundamental purposes of the Charter.
2. Any State party that has made a reservation pursuant to paragraph 1 of this article may withdraw it at any time by addressing a notification to the Secretary-General of the League of Arab States.

U.N. RESOLUTIONS AND OTHER U.N. MATERIALS

UNIVERSAL DECLARATION OF HUMAN RIGHTS
Universal Declaration of Human Rights, G.A. Res. 217A (III), U.N. Doc. A/810 at 71 (Dec. 10, 1948)

Preamble

Whereas recognition of the inherent dignity and of the equal and inalienable rights of all members of the human family is the foundation of freedom, justice and peace in the world,

Whereas disregard and contempt for human rights have resulted in barbarous acts which have outraged the conscience of mankind, and the advent of a world in which human beings shall enjoy freedom of speech and belief and freedom from fear and want has been proclaimed as the highest aspiration of the common people,

Whereas it is essential, if man is not to be compelled to have recourse, as a last resort, to rebellion against tyranny and oppression, that human rights should be protected by the rule of law,

Whereas it is essential to promote the development of friendly relations between nations,

Whereas the peoples of the United Nations have in the Charter reaffirmed their faith in fundamental human rights, in the dignity and worth of the human person and in the equal rights of men and women and have determined to promote social progress and better standards of life in larger freedom,

Whereas Member States have pledged themselves to achieve, in cooperation with the United Nations, the promotion of universal respect for and observance of human rights and fundamental freedoms,

Whereas a common understanding of these rights and freedoms is of the greatest importance for the full realization of this pledge,

Now, therefore,

The General Assembly,

Proclaims this Universal Declaration of Human Rights as a common standard of achievement for all peoples and all nations, to the end that every individual and every organ of society, keeping this Declaration constantly in mind, shall strive by teaching and education to promote respect for these rights and freedoms and by progressive measures, national and international, to secure their universal and effective recognition and observance, both among the peoples of Member States themselves and among the peoples of territories under their jurisdiction.

Article 1
All human beings are born free and equal in dignity and rights. They are endowed with reason and conscience and should act towards one another in a spirit of brotherhood.

Article 2
Everyone is entitled to all the rights and freedoms set forth in this Declaration, without distinction of any kind, such as race, colour, sex, language, religion, political or other opinion, national or social origin, property, birth or other status. Furthermore, no distinction shall be made on the basis of the political, jurisdictional or international status of the country or territory to which a person belongs, whether it be independent, trust, non-self-governing or under any other limitation of sovereignty.

Article 3
Everyone has the right to life, liberty and security of person.

Article 4
No one shall be held in slavery or servitude; slavery and the slave trade shall be prohibited in all their forms.

Article 5
No one shall be subjected to torture or to cruel, inhuman or degrading treatment or punishment.

Article 6
Everyone has the right to recognition everywhere as a person before the law.

Article 7
All are equal before the law and are entitled without any discrimination to equal protection of the law. All are entitled to equal protection against any discrimination in violation of this Declaration and against any incitement to such discrimination.

Article 8
Everyone has the right to an effective remedy by the competent national tribunals for acts violating the fundamental rights granted him by the constitution or by law.

Article 9
No one shall be subjected to arbitrary arrest, detention or exile.

Article 10
Everyone is entitled in full equality to a fair and public hearing by an independent and impartial tribunal, in the determination of his rights and obligations and of any criminal charge against him.

Article 11
1. Everyone charged with a penal offence has the right to be presumed innocent until proved guilty according to law in a public trial at which he has had all the guarantees necessary for his defence.

2. No one shall be held guilty of any penal offence on account of any act or omission which did not constitute a penal offence, under national or international law, at the time when it was committed. Nor shall a heavier penalty be imposed than the one that was applicable at the time the penal offence was committed.

Article 12
No one shall be subjected to arbitrary interference with his privacy, family, home or correspondence, nor to attacks upon his honour and reputation. Everyone has the right to the protection of the law against such interference or attacks.

Article 13
1. Everyone has the right to freedom of movement and residence within the borders of each State.
2. Everyone has the right to leave any country, including his own, and to return to his country.

Article 14
1. Everyone has the right to seek and to enjoy in other countries asylum from persecution.
2. This right may not be invoked in the case of prosecutions genuinely arising from non-political crimes or from acts contrary to the purposes and principles of the United Nations.

Article 15
1. Everyone has the right to a nationality.
2. No one shall be arbitrarily deprived of his nationality nor denied the right to change his nationality.

Article 16
1. Men and women of full age, without any limitation due to race, nationality or religion, have the right to marry and to found a family. They are entitled to equal rights as to marriage, during marriage and at its dissolution.
2. Marriage shall be entered into only with the free and full consent of the intending spouses.
3. The family is the natural and fundamental group unit of society and is entitled to protection by society and the State.

Article 17
1. Everyone has the right to own property alone as well as in association with others.
2. No one shall be arbitrarily deprived of his property.

Article 18
Everyone has the right to freedom of thought, conscience and religion; this right includes freedom to change his religion or belief, and freedom, either alone or in community with others and in public or private, to manifest his religion or belief in teaching, practice, worship and observance.

Article 19
Everyone has the right to freedom of opinion and expression; this right includes freedom to hold opinions without interference and to seek, receive and impart information and ideas through any media and regardless of frontiers.

Article 20
1. Everyone has the right to freedom of peaceful assembly and association.
2. No one may be compelled to belong to an association.

Article 21
1. Everyone has the right to take part in the government of his country, directly or through freely chosen representatives.
2. Everyone has the right to equal access to public service in his country.

3. The will of the people shall be the basis of the authority of government; this will shall be expressed in periodic and genuine elections which shall be by universal and equal suffrage and shall be held by secret vote or by equivalent free voting procedures.

Article 22

Everyone, as a member of society, has the right to social security and is entitled to realization, through national effort and international co-operation and in accordance with the organization and resources of each State, of the economic, social and cultural rights indispensable for his dignity and the free development of his personality.

Article 23

1. Everyone has the right to work, to free choice of employment, to just and favourable conditions of work and to protection against unemployment.
2. Everyone, without any discrimination, has the right to equal pay for equal work.
3. Everyone who works has the right to just and favourable remuneration ensuring for himself and his family an existence worthy of human dignity, and supplemented, if necessary, by other means of social protection.
4. Everyone has the right to form and to join trade unions for the protection of his interests.

Article 24

Everyone has the right to rest and leisure, including reasonable limitation of working hours and periodic holidays with pay.

Article 25

1. Everyone has the right to a standard of living adequate for the health and well-being of himself and of his family, including food, clothing, housing and medical care and necessary social services, and the right to security in the event of unemployment, sickness, disability, widowhood, old age or other lack of livelihood in circumstances beyond his control.
2. Motherhood and childhood are entitled to special care and assistance. All children, whether born in or out of wedlock, shall enjoy the same social protection.

Article 26

1. Everyone has the right to education. Education shall be free, at least in the elementary and fundamental stages. Elementary education shall be compulsory. Technical and professional education shall be made generally available and higher education shall be equally accessible to all on the basis of merit.
2. Education shall be directed to the full development of the human personality and to the strengthening of respect for human rights and fundamental freedoms. It shall promote understanding, tolerance and friendship among all nations, racial or religious groups, and shall further the activities of the United Nations for the maintenance of peace.
3. Parents have a prior right to choose the kind of education that shall be given to their children.

Article 27

1. Everyone has the right freely to participate in the cultural life of the community, to enjoy the arts and to share in scientific advancement and its benefits.
2. Everyone has the right to the protection of the moral and material interests resulting from any scientific, literary or artistic production of which he is the author.

Article 28

Everyone is entitled to a social and international order in which the rights and freedoms set forth in this Declaration can be fully realized.

Article 29

1. Everyone has duties to the community in which alone the free and full development of his personality is possible.
2. In the exercise of his rights and freedoms, everyone shall be subject only to such limitations as are determined by law solely for the purpose of securing due recognition and respect for the rights and

freedoms of others and of meeting the just requirements of morality, public order and the general welfare in a democratic society.

3. These rights and freedoms may in no case be exercised contrary to the purposes and principles of the United Nations.

Article 30

Nothing in this Declaration may be interpreted as implying for any State, group or person any right to engage in any activity or to perform any act aimed at the destruction of any of the rights and freedoms set forth herein.

STANDARD MINIMUM RULES FOR THE TREATMENT OF PRISONERS

Standard Minimum Rules for the Treatment of Prisoners, Report of the First U.N. Congress on the Prevention of Crime and the Treatment of Offenders, U.N. Doc. A/CONF.6/1, Annex IA (Aug. 30, 1955), *approved by* U.N. Econ. & Soc. Council Res. 663C (XXIV), U.N. ESCOR, 24th Sess., Supp. No. 1 at 11, U.N. Doc. E/3048 (July 31, 1957), *amended by* U.N. Econ. & Soc. Council Res. 2076 (LXII), U.N. ESCOR, 62d Sess., Supp. No. 1 at 35, U.N. Doc. E/5988 (May 13, 1977), *available at* http://www.unhchr.ch/html/menu3/b/h_comp34.htm

Preliminary Observations

1. The following rules are not intended to describe in detail a model system of penal institutions. They seek only, on the basis of the general consensus of contemporary thought and the essential elements of the most adequate systems of today, to set out what is generally accepted as being good principle and practice in the treatment of prisoners and the management of institutions.

2. In view of the great variety of legal, social, economic and geographical conditions of the world, it is evident that not all of the rules are capable of application in all places and at all times. They should, however, serve to stimulate a constant endeavour to overcome practical difficulties in the way of their application, in the knowledge that they represent, as a whole, the minimum conditions which are accepted as suitable by the United Nations.

3. On the other hand, the rules cover a field in which thought is constantly developing. They are not intended to preclude experiment and practices, provided these are in harmony with the principles and seek to further the purposes which derive from the text of the rules as a whole. It will always be justifiable for the central prison administration to authorize departures from the rules in this spirit.

4. (1) Part I of the rules covers the general management of institutions, and is applicable to all categories of prisoners, criminal or civil, untried or convicted, including prisoners subject to "security measures" or corrective measures ordered by the judge.

(2) Part II contains rules applicable only to the special categories dealt with in each section. Nevertheless, the rules under section A, applicable to prisoners under sentence, shall be equally applicable to categories of prisoners dealt with in sections B, C and D, provided they do not conflict with the rules governing those categories and are for their benefit.

5. (1) The rules do not seek to regulate the management of institutions set aside for young persons such as Borstal institutions or correctional schools, but in general part I would be equally applicable in such institutions.

(2) The category of young prisoners should include at least all young persons who come within the jurisdiction of juvenile courts. As a rule, such young persons should not be sentenced to imprisonment.

PART I
RULES OF GENERAL APPLICATION

Basic principle

6. (1) The following rules shall be applied impartially. There shall be no discrimination on grounds of race, colour, sex, language, religion, political or other opinion, national or social origin, property, birth or other status.

(2) On the other hand, it is necessary to respect the religious beliefs and moral precepts of the group to which a prisoner belongs.

Register

7. (1) In every place where persons are imprisoned there shall be kept a bound registration book with numbered pages in which shall be entered in respect of each prisoner received:

      (a) Information concerning his identity;

      (b) The reasons for his commitment and the authority therefor;

      (c) The day and hour of his admission and release.

(2) No person shall be received in an institution without a valid commitment order of which the details shall have been previously entered in the register. Separation of categories

8. The different categories of prisoners shall be kept in separate institutions or parts of institutions taking account of their sex, age, criminal record, the legal reason for their detention and the necessities of their treatment. Thus,

      (a) Men and women shall so far as possible be detained in separate institutions; in an institution which receives both men and women the whole of the premises allocated to women shall be entirely separate;

      (b) Untried prisoners shall be kept separate from convicted prisoners;

      (c) Persons imprisoned for debt and other civil prisoners shall be kept separate from persons imprisoned by reason of a criminal offence;

      (d) Young prisoners shall be kept separate from adults. Accommodation

9. (1) Where sleeping accommodation is in individual cells or rooms, each prisoner shall occupy by night a cell or room by himself. If for special reasons, such as temporary overcrowding, it becomes necessary for the central prison administration to make an exception to this rule, it is not desirable to have two prisoners in a cell or room.

(2) Where dormitories are used, they shall be occupied by prisoners carefully selected as being suitable to associate with one another in those conditions. There shall be regular supervision by night, in keeping with the nature of the institution.

10. All accommodation provided for the use of prisoners and in particular all sleeping accommodation shall meet all requirements of health, due regard being paid to climatic conditions and particularly to cubic content of air, minimum floor space, lighting, heating and ventilation.

11. In all places where prisoners are required to live or work,

      (a) The windows shall be large enough to enable the prisoners to read or work by natural light, and shall be so constructed that they can allow the entrance of fresh air whether or not there is artificial ventilation;

      (b) Artificial light shall be provided sufficient for the prisoners to read or work without injury to eyesight.

12. The sanitary installations shall be adequate to enable every prisoner to comply with the needs of nature when necessary and in a clean and decent manner.

13. Adequate bathing and shower installations shall be provided so that every prisoner may be enabled and required to have a bath or shower, at a temperature suitable to the climate, as frequently as necessary for general hygiene according to season and geographical region, but at least once a week in a temperate climate.

14. All pans of an institution regularly used by prisoners shall be properly maintained and kept scrupulously clean at all times.

Personal hygiene

15. Prisoners shall be required to keep their persons clean, and to this end they shall be provided with water and with such toilet articles as are necessary for health and cleanliness.

16. In order that prisoners may maintain a good appearance compatible with their self-respect, facilities shall be provided for the proper care of the hair and beard, and men shall be enabled to shave regularly.

Clothing and bedding

17. (1) Every prisoner who is not allowed to wear his own clothing shall be provided with an outfit of clothing suitable for the climate and adequate to keep him in good health. Such clothing shall in no manner be degrading or humiliating.

(2) All clothing shall be clean and kept in proper condition. Underclothing shall be changed and washed as often as necessary for the maintenance of hygiene.

(3) In exceptional circumstances, whenever a prisoner is removed outside the institution for an authorized purpose, he shall be allowed to wear his own clothing or other inconspicuous clothing.

18. If prisoners are allowed to wear their own clothing, arrangements shall be made on their admission to the institution to ensure that it shall be clean and fit for use.

19. Every prisoner shall, in accordance with local or national standards, be provided with a separate bed, and with separate and sufficient bedding which shall be clean when issued, kept in good order and changed often enough to ensure its cleanliness.

Food

20. (1) Every prisoner shall be provided by the administration at the usual hours with food of nutritional value adequate for health and strength, of wholesome quality and well prepared and served.

(2) Drinking water shall be available to every prisoner whenever he needs it.

Exercise and sport

21. (1) Every prisoner who is not employed in outdoor work shall have at least one hour of suitable exercise in the open air daily if the weather permits.

(2) Young prisoners, and others of suitable age and physique, shall receive physical and recreational training during the period of exercise. To this end space, installations and equipment should be provided.

Medical services

22. (1) At every institution there shall be available the services of at least one qualified medical officer who should have some knowledge of psychiatry. The medical services should be organized in close relationship to the general health administration of the community or nation. They shall include a psychiatric service for the diagnosis and, in proper cases, the treatment of states of mental abnormality.

(2) Sick prisoners who require specialist treatment shall be transferred to specialized institutions or to civil hospitals. Where hospital facilities are provided in an institution, their equipment, furnishings and pharmaceutical supplies shall be proper for the medical care and treatment of sick prisoners, and there shall be a staff of suitable trained officers.

(3) The services of a qualified dental officer shall be available to every prisoner.

23. (1) In women's institutions there shall be special accommodation for all necessary pre-natal and post-natal care and treatment. Arrangements shall be made wherever practicable for children to be torn in a hospital outside the institution. If a child is born in prison, this fact shall not be mentioned in the birth certificate.

(2) Where nursing infants are allowed to remain in the institution with their mothers, provision shall be made for a nursery staffed by qualified persons, where the infants shall be placed when they are not in the care of their mothers.

24. The medical officer shall see and examine every prisoner as soon as possible after his admission and thereafter as necessary, with a view particularly to the discovery of physical or mental illness and the taking of all necessary measures; the segregation of prisoners suspected of infectious or contagious conditions; the noting of physical or mental defects which might hamper rehabilitation, and the determination of the physical capacity of every prisoner for work.

25. (1) The medical officer shall have the care of the physical and mental health of the prisoners and should daily see all sick prisoners, all who complain of illness, and any prisoner to whom his attention is specially directed.

(2) The medical officer shall report to the director whenever he considers that a prisoner's physical or mental health has been or will be injuriously affected by continued imprisonment or by any condition of imprisonment.

26. (1) The medical officer shall regularly inspect and advise the director upon:

      (a) The quantity, quality, preparation and service of food;

      (b) The hygiene and cleanliness of the institution and the prisoners;

      (c) The sanitation, heating, lighting and ventilation of the institution;

      (d) The suitability and cleanliness of the prisoners' clothing and bedding;

      (e) The observance of the rules concerning physical education and sports, in cases where there is no technical personnel in charge of these activities.

(2) The director shall take into consideration the reports and advice that the medical officer submits according to rules 25 (2) and 26 and, in case he concurs with the recommendations made, shall take immediate steps to give effect to those recommendations; if they are not within his competence or if he does not concur with them, he shall immediately submit his own report and the advice of the medical officer to higher authority.

Discipline and punishment

27. Discipline and order shall be maintained with firmness, but with no more restriction than is necessary for safe custody and well-ordered community life.

28. (1) No prisoner shall be employed, in the service of the institution, in any disciplinary capacity.

(2) This rule shall not, however, impede the proper functioning of systems based on self-government, under which specified social, educational or sports activities or responsibilities are entrusted, under supervision, to prisoners who are formed into groups for the purposes of treatment.

29. The following shall always be determined by the law or by the regulation of the competent administrative authority:

      (a) Conduct constituting a disciplinary offence;

      (b) The types and duration of punishment which may be inflicted;

      (c) The authority competent to impose such punishment.

30. (1) No prisoner shall be punished except in accordance with the terms of such law or regulation, and never twice for the same offence.

(2) No prisoner shall be punished unless he has been informed of the offence alleged against him and given a proper opportunity of presenting his defence. The competent authority shall conduct a thorough examination of the case.

(3) Where necessary and practicable the prisoner shall be allowed to make his defence through an interpreter.

31. Corporal punishment, punishment by placing in a dark cell, and all cruel, inhuman or degrading punishments shall be completely prohibited as punishments for disciplinary offences.

32. (1) Punishment by close confinement or reduction of diet shall never be inflicted unless the medical officer has examined the prisoner and certified in writing that he is fit to sustain it.

(2) The same shall apply to any other punishment that may be prejudicial to the physical or mental health of a prisoner. In no case may such punishment be contrary to or depart from the principle stated in rule 31.

(3) The medical officer shall visit daily prisoners undergoing such punishments and shall advise the director if he considers the termination or alteration of the punishment necessary on grounds of physical or mental health.

Instruments of restraint

33. Instruments of restraint, such as handcuffs, chains, irons and strait-jacket, shall never be applied as a punishment. Furthermore, chains or irons shall not be used as restraints. Other instruments of restraint shall not be used except in the following circumstances:

      (a) As a precaution against escape during a transfer, provided that they shall be removed when the prisoner appears before a judicial or administrative authority;

      (b) On medical grounds by direction of the medical officer; (c) By order of the director, if other methods of control fail, in order to prevent a prisoner from injuring himself or others or from damaging property; in such instances the director shall at once consult the medical officer and report to the higher administrative authority.

34. The patterns and manner of use of instruments of restraint shall be decided by the central prison administration. Such instruments must not be applied for any longer time than is strictly necessary.

Information to and complaints by prisoners

35. (1) Every prisoner on admission shall be provided with written information about the regulations governing the treatment of prisoners of his category, the disciplinary requirements of the institution, the authorized methods of seeking information and making complaints, and all such other matters as are necessary to enable him to understand both his rights and his obligations and to adapt himself to the life of the institution.

(2) If a prisoner is illiterate, the aforesaid information shall be conveyed to him orally.

36. (1) Every prisoner shall have the opportunity each week day of making requests or complaints to the director of the institution or the officer authorized to represent him.

(2) It shall be possible to make requests or complaints to the inspector of prisons during his inspection. The prisoner shall have the opportunity to talk to the inspector or to any other inspecting officer without the director or other members of the staff being present.

(3) Every prisoner shall be allowed to make a request or complaint, without censorship as to substance but in proper form, to the central prison administration, the judicial authority or other proper authorities through approved channels.

(4) Unless it is evidently frivolous or groundless, every request or complaint shall be promptly dealt with and replied to without undue delay.

Contact with the outside world

37. Prisoners shall be allowed under necessary supervision to communicate with their family and reputable friends at regular intervals, both by correspondence and by receiving visits.

38. (1) Prisoners who are foreign nationals shall be allowed reasonable facilities to communicate with the diplomatic and consular representatives of the State to which they belong. (2) Prisoners who are nationals of States without diplomatic or consular representation in the country and refugees or stateless persons shall be allowed similar facilities to communicate with the diplomatic representative of the State which takes charge of their interests or any national or international authority whose task it is to protect such persons.

39. Prisoners shall be kept informed regularly of the more important items of news by the reading of newspapers, periodicals or special institutional publications, by hearing wireless transmissions, by lectures or by any similar means as authorized or controlled by the administration.

Books

40. Every institution shall have a library for the use of all categories of prisoners, adequately stocked with both recreational and instructional books, and prisoners shall be encouraged to make full use of it.

Religion

41. (1) If the institution contains a sufficient number of prisoners of the same religion, a qualified representative of that religion shall be appointed or approved. If the number of prisoners justifies it and conditions permit, the arrangement should be on a full-time basis.

(2) A qualified representative appointed or approved under paragraph (1) shall be allowed to hold regular services and to pay pastoral visits in private to prisoners of his religion at proper times.

(3) Access to a qualified representative of any religion shall not be refused to any prisoner. On the other hand, if any prisoner should object to a visit of any religious representative, his attitude shall be fully respected.

42. So far as practicable, every prisoner shall be allowed to satisfy the needs of his religious life by attending the services provided in the institution and having in his possession the books of religious observance and instruction of his denomination.

Retention of prisoners' property

43. (1) All money, valuables, clothing and other effects belonging to a prisoner which under the regulations of the institution he is not allowed to retain shall on his admission to the institution be placed in safe custody. An inventory thereof shall be signed by the prisoner. Steps shall be taken to keep them in good condition. (2) On the release of the prisoner all such articles and money shall be returned to him except in so far as he has been authorized to spend money or send any such property out of the institution, or it has been found necessary on hygienic grounds to destroy any article of clothing. The prisoner shall sign a receipt for the articles and money returned to him.

(3) Any money or effects received for a prisoner from outside shall be treated in the same way.

(4) If a prisoner brings in any drugs or medicine, the medical officer shall decide what use shall be made of them.

Notification of death, illness, transfer, etc.

44. (1) Upon the death or serious illness of, or serious injury to a prisoner, or his removal to an institution for the treatment of mental affections, the director shall at once inform the spouse, if the prisoner is married, or the nearest relative and shall in any event inform any other person previously designated by the prisoner.

(2) A prisoner shall be informed at once of the death or serious illness of any near relative. In case of the critical illness of a near relative, the prisoner should be authorized, whenever circumstances allow, to go to his bedside either under escort or alone.

(3) Every prisoner shall have the right to inform at once his family of his imprisonment or his transfer to another institution.

Removal of prisoners

45. (1) When the prisoners are being removed to or from an institution, they shall be exposed to public view as little as possible, and proper safeguards shall be adopted to protect them from insult, curiosity and publicity in any form.

(2) The transport of prisoners in conveyances with inadequate ventilation or light, or in any way which would subject them to unnecessary physical hardship, shall be prohibited.

(3) The transport of prisoners shall be carried out at the expense of the administration and equal conditions shall obtain for all of them.

Institutional personnel

46. (1) The prison administration, shall provide for the careful selection of every grade of the personnel, since it is on their integrity, humanity, professional capacity and personal suitability for the work that the proper administration of the institutions depends.

(2) The prison administration shall constantly seek to awaken and maintain in the minds both of the personnel and of the public the conviction that this work is a social service of great importance, and to this end all appropriate means of informing the public should be used.

(3) To secure the foregoing ends, personnel shall be appointed on a full-time basis as professional prison officers and have civil service status with security of tenure subject only to good conduct, efficiency and physical fitness. Salaries shall be adequate to attract and retain suitable men and women; employment benefits and conditions of service shall be favourable in view of the exacting nature of the work.

47. (1) The personnel shall possess an adequate standard of education and intelligence.

(2) Before entering on duty, the personnel shall be given a course of training in their general and specific duties and be required to pass theoretical and practical tests.

(3) After entering on duty and during their career, the personnel shall maintain and improve their knowledge and professional capacity by attending courses of in-service training to be organized at suitable intervals.

48. All members of the personnel shall at all times so conduct themselves and perform their duties as to influence the prisoners for good by their example and to command their respect.

49. (1) So far as possible, the personnel shall include a sufficient number of specialists such as psychiatrists, psychologists, social workers, teachers and trade instructors.

(2) The services of social workers, teachers and trade instructors shall be secured on a permanent basis, without thereby excluding part-time or voluntary workers.

50. (1) The director of an institution should be adequately qualified for his task by character, administrative ability, suitable training and experience.

(2) He shall devote his entire time to his official duties and shall not be appointed on a part-time basis.

(3) He shall reside on the premises of the institution or in its immediate vicinity. (4) When two or more institutions are under the authority of one director, he shall visit each of them at frequent intervals. A responsible resident official shall be in charge of each of these institutions.

51. (1) The director, his deputy, and the majority of the other personnel of the institution shall be able to speak the language of the greatest number of prisoners, or a language understood by the greatest number of them.

(2) Whenever necessary, the services of an interpreter shall be used.

52. (1) In institutions which are large enough to require the services of one or more full-time medical officers, at least one of them shall reside on the premises of the institution or in its immediate vicinity.

(2) In other institutions the medical officer shall visit daily and shall reside near enough to be able to attend without delay in cases of urgency.

53. (1) In an institution for both men and women, the part of the institution set aside for women shall be under the authority of a responsible woman officer who shall have the custody of the keys of all that part of the institution.

(2) No male member of the staff shall enter the part of the institution set aside for women unless accompanied by a woman officer.

(3) Women prisoners shall be attended and supervised only by women officers. This does not, however, preclude male members of the staff, particularly doctors and teachers, from carrying out their professional duties in institutions or parts of institutions set aside for women.

54. (1) Officers of the institutions shall not, in their relations with the prisoners, use force except in self-defence or in cases of attempted escape, or active or passive physical resistance to an order based on law or regulations. Officers who have recourse to force must use no more than is strictly necessary and must report the incident immediately to the director of the institution.

(2) Prison officers shall be given special physical training to enable them to restrain aggressive prisoners.

(3) Except in special circumstances, staff performing duties which bring them into direct contact with prisoners should not be armed. Furthermore, staff should in no circumstances be provided with arms unless they have been trained in their use.

Inspection

55. There shall be a regular inspection of penal institutions and services by qualified and experienced inspectors appointed by a competent authority. Their task shall be in particular to ensure that these institutions are administered in accordance with existing laws and regulations and with a view to bringing about the objectives of penal and correctional services.

PART II
RULES APPLICABLE TO SPECIAL CATEGORIES

A. PRISONERS UNDER SENTENCE

Guiding principles

56. The guiding principles hereafter are intended to show the spirit in which penal institutions should be administered and the purposes at which they should aim, in accordance with the declaration made under Preliminary Observation I of the present text.

57. Imprisonment and other measures which result in cutting off an offender from the outside world are afflictive by the very fact of taking from the person the right of self-determination by depriving him of his liberty. Therefore the prison system shall not, except as incidental to justifiable segregation or the maintenance of discipline, aggravate the suffering inherent in such a situation.

58. The purpose and justification of a sentence of imprisonment or a similar measure deprivative of liberty is ultimately to protect society against crime. This end can only be achieved if the period of imprisonment is used to ensure, so far as possible, that upon his return to society the offender is not only willing but able to lead a law-abiding and self-supporting life.

59. To this end, the institution should utilize all the remedial, educational, moral, spiritual and other forces and forms of assistance which are appropriate and available, and should seek to apply them according to the individual treatment needs of the prisoners.

60. (1) The regime of the institution should seek to minimize any differences between prison life and life at liberty which tend to lessen the responsibility of the prisoners or the respect due to their dignity as human beings.

(2) Before the completion of the sentence, it is desirable that the necessary steps be taken to ensure for the prisoner a gradual return to life in society. This aim may be achieved, depending on the case, by a pre-release regime organized in the same institution or in another appropriate institution, or by release on trial under some kind of supervision which must not be entrusted to the police but should be combined with effective social aid. 61. The treatment of prisoners should emphasize not their exclusion from the community, but their continuing part in it. Community agencies should, therefore, be enlisted wherever possible to assist the staff of the institution in the task of social rehabilitation of the prisoners. There should be in connection with every institution social workers charged with the duty of maintaining and improving all desirable relations of a prisoner with his family and with valuable social agencies. Steps should be taken to safeguard, to the maximum extent compatible with the law and the sentence, the rights relating to civil interests, social security rights and other social benefits of prisoners.

62. The medical services of the institution shall seek to detect and shall treat any physical or mental illnesses or defects which may hamper a prisoner's rehabilitation. All necessary medical, surgical and psychiatric services shall be provided to that end.

63. (1) The fulfilment of these principles requires individualization of treatment and for this purpose a flexible system of classifying prisoners in groups; it is therefore desirable that such groups should be distributed in separate institutions suitable for the treatment of each group.

(2) These institutions need not provide the same degree of security for every group. It is desirable to provide varying degrees of security according to the needs of different groups. Open institutions, by the very fact that they provide no physical security against escape but rely on the self-discipline of the inmates, provide the conditions most favourable to rehabilitation for carefully selected prisoners.

(3) It is desirable that the number of prisoners in closed institutions should not be so large that the individualization of treatment is hindered. In some countries it is considered that the population of such institutions should not exceed five hundred. In open institutions the population should be as small as possible.

(4) On the other hand, it is undesirable to maintain prisons which are so small that proper facilities cannot be provided.

64. The duty of society does not end with a prisoner's release. There should, therefore, be governmental or private agencies capable of lending the released prisoner efficient after-care directed towards the lessening of prejudice against him and towards his social rehabilitation.

Treatment

65. The treatment of persons sentenced to imprisonment or a similar measure shall have as its purpose, so far as the length of the sentence permits, to establish in them the will to lead law-abiding and self-supporting lives after their release and to fit them to do so. The treatment shall be such as will encourage their self-respect and develop their sense of responsibility.

66. (1) To these ends, all appropriate means shall be used, including religious care in the countries where this is possible, education, vocational guidance and training, social casework, employment counselling, physical development and strengthening of moral character, in accordance with the individual needs of each prisoner, taking account of his social and criminal history, his physical and mental capacities and aptitudes, his personal temperament, the length of his sentence and his prospects after release.

(2) For every prisoner with a sentence of suitable length, the director shall receive, as soon as possible after his admission, full reports on all the matters referred to in the foregoing paragraph. Such reports shall always include a report by a medical officer, wherever possible qualified in psychiatry, on the physical and mental condition of the prisoner.

(3) The reports and other relevant documents shall be placed in an individual file. This file shall be kept up to date and classified in such a way that it can be consulted by the responsible personnel whenever the need arises.

Classification and individualization

67. The purposes of classification shall be:

> (a) To separate from others those prisoners who, by reason of their criminal records or bad characters, are likely to exercise a bad influence;
> (b) To divide the prisoners into classes in order to facilitate their treatment with a view to their social rehabilitation.

68. So far as possible separate institutions or separate sections of an institution shall be used for the treatment of the different classes of prisoners.

69. As soon as possible after admission and after a study of the personality of each prisoner with a sentence of suitable length, a programme of treatment shall be prepared for him in the light of the knowledge obtained about his individual needs, his capacities and dispositions.

Privileges

70. Systems of privileges appropriate for the different classes of prisoners and the different methods of treatment shall be established at every institution, in order to encourage good conduct, develop a sense of responsibility and secure the interest and co-operation of the prisoners in their treatment.

Work

71. (1) Prison labour must not be of an afflictive nature.

(2) All prisoners under sentence shall be required to work, subject to their physical and mental fitness as determined by the medical officer.

(3) Sufficient work of a useful nature shall be provided to keep prisoners actively employed for a normal working day.

(4) So far as possible the work provided shall be such as will maintain or increase the prisoners, ability to earn an honest living after release.

(5) Vocational training in useful trades shall be provided for prisoners able to profit thereby and especially for young prisoners.

(6) Within the limits compatible with proper vocational selection and with the requirements of institutional administration and discipline, the prisoners shall be able to choose the type of work they wish to perform.

72. (1) The organization and methods of work in the institutions shall resemble as closely as possible those of similar work outside institutions, so as to prepare prisoners for the conditions of normal occupational life.

(2) The interests of the prisoners and of their vocational training, however, must not be subordinated to the purpose of making a financial profit from an industry in the institution.

73. (1) Preferably institutional industries and farms should be operated directly by the administration and not by private contractors.

(2) Where prisoners are employed in work not controlled by the administration, they shall always be under the supervision of the institution's personnel. Unless the work is for other departments of the government

the full normal wages for such work shall be paid to the administration by the persons to whom the labour is supplied, account being taken of the output of the prisoners.

74. (1) The precautions laid down to protect the safety and health of free workmen shall be equally observed in institutions.

(2) Provision shall be made to indemnify prisoners against industrial injury, including occupational disease, on terms not less favourable than those extended by law to free workmen.

75. (1) The maximum daily and weekly working hours of the prisoners shall be fixed by law or by administrative regulation, taking into account local rules or custom in regard to the employment of free workmen.

(2) The hours so fixed shall leave one rest day a week and sufficient time for education and other activities required as part of the treatment and rehabilitation of the prisoners.

76. (1) There shall be a system of equitable remuneration of the work of prisoners.

(2) Under the system prisoners shall be allowed to spend at least a part of their earnings on approved articles for their own use and to send a part of their earnings to their family.

(3) The system should also provide that a part of the earnings should be set aside by the administration so as to constitute a savings fund to be handed over to the prisoner on his release.

Education and recreation

77. (1) Provision shall be made for the further education of all prisoners capable of profiting thereby, including religious instruction in the countries where this is possible. The education of illiterates and young prisoners shall be compulsory and special attention shall be paid to it by the administration.

(2) So far as practicable, the education of prisoners shall be integrated with the educational system of the country so that after their release they may continue their education without difficulty. 78. Recreational and cultural activities shall be provided in all institutions for the benefit of the mental and physical health of prisoners.

Social relations and after-care

79. Special attention shall be paid to the maintenance and improvement of such relations between a prisoner and his family as are desirable in the best interests of both.

80. From the beginning of a prisoner's sentence consideration shall be given to his future after release and he shall be encouraged and assisted to maintain or establish such relations with persons or agencies outside the institution as may promote the best interests of his family and his own social rehabilitation.

81. (1) Services and agencies, governmental or otherwise, which assist released prisoners to re-establish themselves in society shall ensure, so far as is possible and necessary, that released prisoners be provided with appropriate documents and identification papers, have suitable homes and work to go to, are suitably and adequately clothed having regard to the climate and season, and have sufficient means to reach their destination and maintain themselves in the period immediately following their release.

(2) The approved representatives of such agencies shall have all necessary access to the institution and to prisoners and shall be taken into consultation as to the future of a prisoner from the beginning of his sentence.

(3) It is desirable that the activities of such agencies shall be centralized or co-ordinated as far as possible in order to secure the best use of their efforts.

B. INSANE AND MENTALLY ABNORMAL PRISONERS

82. (1) Persons who are found to be insane shall not be detained in prisons and arrangements shall be made to remove them to mental institutions as soon as possible.

(2) Prisoners who suffer from other mental diseases or abnormalities shall be observed and treated in specialized institutions under medical management.

(3) During their stay in a prison, such prisoners shall be placed under the special supervision of a medical officer.

(4) The medical or psychiatric service of the penal institutions shall provide for the psychiatric treatment of all other prisoners who are in need of such treatment.

83. It is desirable that steps should be taken, by arrangement with the appropriate agencies, to ensure if necessary the continuation of psychiatric treatment after release and the provision of social-psychiatric after-care.

401

C. PRISONERS UNDER ARREST OR AWAITING TRIAL

84. (1) Persons arrested or imprisoned by reason of a criminal charge against them, who are detained either in police custody or in prison custody (jail) but have not yet been tried and sentenced, will be referred to as "untried prisoners,' hereinafter in these rules.

(2) Unconvicted prisoners are presumed to be innocent and shall be treated as such.

(3) Without prejudice to legal rules for the protection of individual liberty or prescribing the procedure to be observed in respect of untried prisoners, these prisoners shall benefit by a special regime which is described in the following rules in its essential requirements only.

85. (1) Untried prisoners shall be kept separate from convicted prisoners.

(2) Young untried prisoners shall be kept separate from adults and shall in principle be detained in separate institutions.

86. Untried prisoners shall sleep singly in separate rooms, with the reservation of different local custom in respect of the climate.

87. Within the limits compatible with the good order of the institution, untried prisoners may, if they so desire, have their food procured at their own expense from the outside, either through the administration or through their family or friends. Otherwise, the administration shall provide their food.

88. (1) An untried prisoner shall be allowed to wear his own clothing if it is clean and suitable.

(2) If he wears prison dress, it shall be different from that supplied to convicted prisoners.

89. An untried prisoner shall always be offered opportunity to work, but shall not be required to work. If he chooses to work, he shall be paid for it.

90. An untried prisoner shall be allowed to procure at his own expense or at the expense of a third party such books, newspapers, writing materials and other means of occupation as are compatible with the interests of the administration of justice and the security and good order of the institution.

91. An untried prisoner shall be allowed to be visited and treated by his own doctor or dentist if there is reasonable ground for his application and he is able to pay any expenses incurred.

92. An untried prisoner shall be allowed to inform immediately his family of his detention and shall be given all reasonable facilities for communicating with his family and friends, and for receiving visits from them, subject only to restrictions and supervision as are necessary in the interests of the administration of justice and of the security and good order of the institution.

93. For the purposes of his defence, an untried prisoner shall be allowed to apply for free legal aid where such aid is available, and to receive visits from his legal adviser with a view to his defence and to prepare and hand to him confidential instructions. For these purposes, he shall if he so desires be supplied with writing material. Interviews between the prisoner and his legal adviser may be within sight but not within the hearing of a police or institution official.

D. CIVIL PRISONERS

94. In countries where the law perm its imprisonment for debt, or by order of a court under any other non-criminal process, persons so imprisoned shall not be subjected to any greater restriction or severity than is necessary to ensure safe custody and good order. Their treatment shall be not less favourable than that of untried prisoners, with the reservation, however, that they may possibly be required to work.

E. PERSONS ARRESTED OR DETAINED WITHOUT CHARGE

95. Without prejudice to the provisions of article 9 of the International Covenant on Civil and Political Rights, persons arrested or imprisoned without charge shall be accorded the same protection as that accorded under part I and part II, section C. Relevant provisions of part II, section A, shall likewise be applicable where their application may be conducive to the benefit of this special group of persons in custody, provided that no measures shall be taken implying that re-education or rehabilitation is in any way appropriate to persons not convicted of any criminal offence.

U.N. ECONOMIC AND SOCIAL COUNCIL RESOLUTION 1296 ARRANGEMENTS FOR CONSULTATION WITH NON-GOVERNMENTAL ORGANIZATIONS

U.N. Econ. & Soc. Council Res. 1296 (XLIV), U.N. Doc. E/RES/1296(XLIV) (May 23, 1968)

The Economic and Social Council,

Having regard to Article 71 of the Charter of the United Nations,

Recognizing that arrangements for consultation with non-governmental organizations provide an important means of furthering the purposes and principles of the United Nations.

Considering that consultations between the Council and its subsidiary organs and the non-governmental organizations should be developed to the fullest practicable extent,

Approves the following arrangements, which supersede those set out in its resolution 288 B (X) of 27 February 1950:

ARRANGEMENTS FOR CONSULTATION WITH NON-GOVERNMENTAL ORGANIZATIONS

Part I
PRINCIPLES TO BE APPLIED IN THE ESTABLISHMENT OF CONSULTATIVE RELATIONS

The following principles shall be applied in establishing consultative relations with non-governmental organizations

1. The organization shall be concerned with matters falling within the competence of the Economic and Social Council with respect to international economic, social, cultural, educational, health, scientific, technological and related matters and to questions of human rights.
2. The aims and purposes of the organization shall be in conformity with the spirit, purposes and principles of the Charter of the United Nations.
3. The organization shall undertake to support the work of the United Nations and to promote knowledge of its principles and activities, in accordance with its own aims and purposes and the nature and scope of its competence and activities.
4. The organization shall be of representative character and of recognized international standing; it shall represent a substantial proportion, and express the views of major sections, of the population or of the organized persons within the particular field of its competence, covering, where possible, a substantial number of countries in different regions of the world. Where there exist a number of organizations with similar objectives, interests and basic views in a given field, they shall, for the purposes of consultation with the Council, form a joint committee or other body authorized to carry on such consultation for the group as a whole. It is understood that when a minority opinion develops on a particular point within such a committee, it shall be presented along with the opinion of the majority.
5. The organization shall have an established headquarters, with an executive officer. It shall have a democratically adopted constitution, a copy of which shall be deposited with the Secretary-General of the United Nations, and which shall provide for the determination of policy by a conference, congress or other representative body, and for an executive organ responsible to the policy-making body.
6. The organization shall have authority to speak for its members through its authorized representatives. Evidence of this authority shall be presented, if requested.

7. Subject to paragraph 9 below, the organization shall be international in its structure, with members who exercise voting rights in relation to the policies or action of the international organization. Any international organization which is not established by intergovernmental agreement shall be considered as a non-governmental organization for the purpose of these arrangements, including organizations which accept members designated by governmental authorities, provided that such membership does not interfere with the free expression of views of the organization.

8. The basic resources of the international organization shall be derived in the main part from contributions of the national affiliates or other components or from individual members. Where voluntary contributions have been received, their amounts and donors shall be faithfully revealed to the Council Committee on Non-Governmental Organizations. Where, however, the above criterion is not fulfilled and an organization is financed from other sources, it must explain to the satisfaction of the Committee its reasons for not meeting the requirements laid down in this paragraph. Any financial contribution or other support, direct or indirect, from a Government to the international organization shall be openly declared to the Committee through the Secretary-General and fully recorded in the financial and other records of the organization and shall be devoted to purposes in accordance with the aims of the United Nations.

9. National organizations shall normally present their views through international non-governmental organizations to which they belong. It would not, save in exceptional cases, be appropriate to admit national organizations which are affiliated to an international non-governmental organization covering the same subjects on an international basis. National organizations, however, may be admitted after consultation with the Member State concerned in order to help achieve a balanced and effective representation of non-governmental organizations reflecting major interests of all regions and areas of the world or where they have special experience upon which the Council may wish to draw.

10. Consultative arrangements shall not normally be made with an international organization which is a member of a committee or group composed of international organizations with which consultative arrangements have been made.

11. In considering the establishment of consultative relations with a non-governmental organization, the Council will take into account whether the field of activity of the organization is wholly or mainly within the field of a specialized agency, and whether or not it could be admitted when it has, or may have, a consultative arrangement with a specialized agency.

Part II
PRINCIPLES GOVERNING THE NATURE OF THE CONSULTATIVE ARRANGEMENTS

12. A clear distinction is drawn in the Charter of the United Nations between participation without vote in the deliberations of the Council and the arrangements for consultation. Under Articles 69 and 70, participation is provided for only in the case of States not members of the Council, and of specialized agencies. Article 71, applying to non-governmental organizations, provides for suitable arrangements for consultation. This distinction, deliberately made in the Charter, is fundamental and the arrangements for consultation should not be such as to accord to non-governmental organizations the same rights of participation as are accorded to States not members of the Council and to the specialized agencies brought into relationship with the United Nations.

13. The arrangements should not be such as to overburden the Council or transform it from a body for co-ordination of policy and action, as contemplated in the Charter, into a general forum for discussion.

14. Decisions on arrangements for consultation should be guided by the principle that consultative arrangements are to be made, on the one hand, for the purpose of enabling the Council or one of its bodies to secure expert information or advice from organizations having special competence in the subjects for which consultative arrangements are made, and, on the other hand, to enable organizations which represent important elements of public opinion in a large number of countries to express their views. Therefore, the arrangements for consultation made with each organization should involve only the subjects for which that organization has a special competence or in which it has a special interest. The organizations given consultative status should be limited to those whose international activities in fields set out in paragraph 1 above qualify them to make a significant contribution to the work of the Council and should, in sum, as far as possible reflect in a balanced way the major viewpoints or interests in these fields in all areas and regions of the world.

Part III

ESTABLISHMENT OF CONSULTATIVE RELATIONSHIPS

15. In establishing consultative relationships with each organization, regard shall be had to the nature and scope of its activities and to the assistance it may be expected to give to the Council or its subsidiary bodies in carrying out the functions set out in Chapters IX and X of the Charter of the United Nations.

16. In establishing consultative relations with organizations, the Council will distinguish between:

(a) Organizations which are concerned with most of the activities of the Council and can demonstrate to the satisfaction of the Council that they have marked and sustained contributions to make to the achievement of the objectives of the United Nations in the fields set out in paragraph 1 above, and are closely involved with the economic and social life of the peoples of the areas they represent and whose membership, which should be considerable, is broadly representative of major segments of population in a large number of countries (to be known as organizations in general consultative status, category I);

(b) Organizations which have a special competence in, and are concerned specifically with, only a few the fields of activity covered by the Council, which are known internationally within the fields for which they have or seek consultative status (to be known as organizations in special consultative status, category II).

17. Organizations accorded consultative status in category II because of their interest in the field of human rights should have a general international concern with this matter, not restricted to the interests of a particular group of persons, a single nationality of the situation in a single State or restricted group States. Special consideration shall be given to the applications of organizations in this field whose aims place stress on combating colonialism, apartheid, racial intolerance and other gross violations of human rights and fundamental freedoms.

18. Major organizations one of whose primary purposes is to promote the aims, objectives and purposes of the United Nations and a furtherance of the understanding of its work may be accorded consultative status in category II.

19. Other organizations which do not have general or special consultative status but which the Council, or the Secretary-General of the United Nations, in consultation with the Council or its Committee on Non-Governmental Organizations, considers can make occasional and useful contributions to the work of the Council or its subsidiary bodies or other United Nations bodies within their competence shall be included in a list (to be known as the Roster). This list may also include organizations in consultative status or similar relationship with a specialized agency or a United Nations body. These organizations shall be available for consultation at the request of the Council or its subsidiary bodies. The fact that an organization is on the Roster shall not in itself be regarded as a qualification for general or special consultative should an organization seek such status.

Part IV
CONSULTATION WITH THE COUNCIL

Provisional agenda

20. The provisional agenda of the Council shall be communicated to organizations in categories I and II and to those on the Roster.

21. Organizations in category I may propose to the Council Committee on Non-Governmental Organizations that the Committee request the Secretary-General to place items of special interest to the organizations on the provisional agenda of the Council.

22. Organizations in categories I and II may designate authorized representatives to sit as observers at public meetings of the Council and its subsidiary bodies. Those on the Roster may have representatives present at such meetings concerned with matters within their field of competence.

Written statements

23. Written statements relevant to the work of the Council may be submitted by organizations in categories I and II on subjects in which these organizations have special competence. Such statements shall be circulated by the Secretary-General of the United Nations to the members of the Council, except those statements which have become obsolete, for example, those dealing with matters already disposed of and those which had already been circulated in some other form.

24. The following conditions shall be observed regarding the submission and circulation of such statements:

(a) The written statement shall be submitted in one of the official languages.

(b) It shall be submitted in sufficient time for appropriate Consultation to take place between the Secretary-General and the organization before circulation.

(c) The organization shall give due consideration to any comments which the Secretary-General may make in the course of such consultation before transmitting the statement in final form.

(d) A written statement submitted by an organization in category I will be circulated in full if it does not exceed 2,000 words. Where a statement is in excess of 2,000 words, the organizations shall submit a summary which will be circulated or shall supply sufficient copies of the full text in the working languages for distribution. A statement will also be circulated in full, however, upon a specific request of the Council or its Committee on Non-Governmental Organizations.

(e) A written statement submitted by an organization in category II or on the Roster will be circulated in full if it does not exceed 500 words. Where a statement is in excess of 500 words, the organization shall submit a summary which will be circulated; such statements will be circulated in full, however, upon a specific request of the Council or its Committee on Non-Governmental Organizations.

(f) The Secretary-General in consultation with the President of the Council, or the Council or its Committee on Non-Governmental Organizations, may invite organizations on the Roster to submit written statements. The provisions of sub-paragraphs (a), (b), (c) and (e) above shall apply to such statements.

(g) A written statement or summary, as the case may be, will be circulated by the Secretary-General in the working languages, and, upon the request of a member of the Council, in any of the official languages.

Hearings

25.　　(a) The Council Committee on Non-Governmental Organizations shall make recommendations to the Council as to which organizations in category I should be heard by the Council or by its sessional committees and on which items they should be heard. Such organizations shall be entitled to make one statement to the Council or the appropriate sessional committee, subject to the approval of the Council or of the sessional committee concerned. In the absence of a subsidiary body, of the Council with jurisdiction in a major field of interest to the Council and to an organization in category II, the Committee may recommend that an organization in category II be heard by the Council on the subject in its field of interest.

(b) Whenever the Council discusses the substance of an item proposed by a non-governmental organization in category I and included in the agenda of the Council, such an organization shall be entitled to present orally to the Council or a sessional committee of the Council, as appropriate, an introductory statement of an expository nature. Such an organization may be invited by the President of the Council or the Chairman of the committee, with the consent of the relevant body, to make, in the course of the discussion of the item before the Council or before the committee, an additional statement for purposes of clarification.

Part V
CONSULTATION WITH COMMISSIONS AND OTHER SUBSIDIARY ORGANS OF THE COUNCIL

26. The provisional agenda of sessions of commissions and other subsidiary organs of the Council shall be communicated to organizations in categories I and II and those on the Roster.

27. Organizations in category I may propose items for the provisional .agenda of commissions, subject to the following conditions:

(a) An organization which intends to propose such an item shall inform the Secretary-General of the United Nations at least sixty-three days before the commencement of the session and before formally proposing an item shall give due consideration to any comments the Secretary-General may make.

(b) The proposal shall be formally submitted with the relevant basic documentation not later than forty-nine days before the commencement of the session, The item shall be included in the agenda of the commission if it is adopted by a two-thirds majority of those present and voting.

Attendance at meetings

28. Organizations in categories I and II may designate authorized representatives to sit as observers at public meetings of the commissions and other subsidiary organs of the Council. Organizations on the Roster may have representatives present at such meetings which are concerned with matters within their field of competence.

Written statements

29. Written statements relevant to the work of the commissions or other subsidiary organs may be submitted by organizations in categories I and II on subjects for which these organizations have a special competence. Such statements shall be circulated by the Secretary-General to members of the commission or other subsidiary organs, except those statements which have become obsolete, for example those dealing with matters already disposed of and those which have already been circulated in some other form to members of the commission or other subsidiary organs.

30. The following conditions shall be observed regarding the submission and circulation of such written statements:

(a) The written statement shall be submitted in one of the official languages.

(b) It shall be submitted in sufficient time for appropriate consultation to take place between the Secretary-General and the organization before circulation,

(c) the organization shall give due consideration to any comments which the Secretary-General may make in the course of such consultation before transmitting the statement in final form.

(d) A written statement submitted by an organization in category I will be circulated in full if it does not exceed 2,000 words. Where a statement is in excess of 2,000 words, the organization shall submit a summary, which will be circulated, or shall supply sufficient copies of the full text in the working languages for distribution. A statement will also be circulated in full, however, upon the specific request of the commission or other subsidiary organs.

(e) A written statement submitted by an organization in category II will be circulated in full if it does not exceed 1,500 words. Where a statement is in excess of 1,500 words, the organization shall submit a summary which will be circulated, or shall supply sufficient copies of the full text in the working languages for distribution. A statement will also be circulated in full, however, upon the specific request of the commission or other subsidiary organs.

(f) The Secretary-General, consultation with the Chairman of the relevant commission or other subsidiary organ, or the commission of other subsidiary organ itself, may invite organizations on the Roster to submit written statements. The provisions in sub-paragraphs (a), (b), (c) and (e) above shall apply to such statements.

(g) A written statement or summary, as the case may be, will be circulated by the Secretary-General in the working languages and, upon the request of a member of the commission or other subsidiary organ, in any of the official languages.

Hearings

31.　　(a) The commission or other subsidiary organs may consult with organizations in categories I and II either directly or through a committee or committees established for the purpose. In all cases, such consultations may be arranged on the request of the organization.

(b) On the recommendation of the Secretary-General and at the request of the commission or other subsidiary organs, organizations on the Roster may also be heard by the commission or other subsidiary organs.

Special studies

32. Subject to the relevant rules of procedure on financial implications, a commission may recommend that an organization which has special competence in a particular field should undertake specific studies or investigations or prepare specific papers for the commission. The limitations of paragraph 30 (d) and (e) above shall not apply in this case.

Part VI
CONSULTATIONS WITH AD HOC COMMITTEES OF THE COUNCIL

33. The arrangements for consultation between ad hoc committees of the Council authorized to meet between sessions of the Council and organizations in categories I and II and on the Roster shall follow those approved for commissions of the Council, unless the Council or the committee decides otherwise.

Part VII

CONSULTATION WITH INTERNATIONAL CONFERENCES CALLED BY THE COUNCIL

34. The Council may invite non-governmental organizations in categories I and II and on the Roster to take part in conferences called by the Council under Article 62, paragraph 4, of the Charter of the United Nations. The organizations shall be entitled to the same rights and privileges and shall undertake the same responsibilities as at sessions of the Council itself, unless the Council decides otherwise.

Part VIII
SUSPENSION AND WITHDRAWAL OF CONSULTATIVE STATUS

35. Organizations granted consultative status by the Council and those on the Roster shall conform at all times to the principles governing the establishment and nature of their consultative relations with the Council. In periodically reviewing the activities of the non-governmental organizations on the basis of reports submitted under paragraph 40 (b) below and other relevant information, the Council Committee on Non-Governmental Organizations shall determine the extent to which the organizations have complied with the principles governing consultative status and have contributed to the work of the Council, and may recommend to the Council suspension or exclusion from consultative status of organizations which have not met the requirements for consultative status as set forth in the present resolution.

36. The consultative status of non-governmental organizations with the Economic and Social Council and the listing of those on the Roster shall be suspended up to three years or withdrawn in the following cases:

> (a) If there exists substantiated evidence of secret governmental financial influence to induce an organization to undertake acts contrary to the purposes and principles of the Charter of the United Nations;
>
> (b) If the organization clearly abuses its consultative status by systematically engaging in unsubstantiated or politically motivated acts against States Members of the United Nations contrary to and incompatible with the principles of the Charter;
>
> (c) If, within the preceding three years, an organization had not made any positive or effective contribution to the work of the Council or its commissions or other subsidiary organs.

37. The consultative status of organizations on the categories I and II and the listing of those on the Roster will be suspended or withdrawn by the decision of the Economic and Social Council on the recommendation of its Committee on Non-Governmental Organizations.

38. An organization whose consultative status or whose listing on the Roster is withdrawn may be entitled to reapply for consultative status or for inclusion on the Roster not sooner than three years after the effective date of such withdrawal.

Part IX
COUNCIL COMMITTEE ON NON-GOVERNMENTAL ORGANIZATIONS

39. The members of the Council Committee on Non-Governmental Organizations shall be elected at the first session of the Council each year, on the basis of equitable geographic representation, in accordance with Council resolution 1099 (XL) of 4 March 1966 and rule 82 of the rules of procedure of the Council. The Committee shall elect its Chairman and other officers as necessary. A member shall serve until the next election unless it ceases to be a member of the Council.

40. The functions of the Committee shall include the following:

> (a) The Committee shall hold a session before the first session of the Council each year to consider applications for consultative status in categories I and II and for listing on the Roster made by non-governmental organizations and request for changes in status, and to make recommendations thereon to the Council. Organizations shall give due consideration to any comments on technical matters which the Secretary-General of the United Nations may make in receiving such applications for the Committee. The Committee shall consider at each such session applications received by the Secretary-General not later than June 1 of the preceding year, on which sufficient data have been distributed to the members of the Committee not later than six weeks before the applications are considered by the Committee at the earliest at its first session in the second year following the session at which the substance of the previous application or request was considered, unless at the time of such consideration it was decided otherwise.

(b) Organizations in consultative status in categories I and II shall submit to the Council Committee on Non-Governmental Organizations through the Secretary-General every fourth year a brief report of their activities, specifically as regards the support they have given to the work of the United Nations, Based on findings of the Committee's examination of the report and other relevant information, the Committee may recommend to the Council any reclassification in status of the organization concerned as it deems appropriate. However, under exceptional circumstances, the Committee may ask for such a report from an individual organization in category I or II or on the Roster, between the regular reporting dates.

(c) The Committee may consult, in connexion with sessions of the Council or at such other times as it may decide, with organizations in categories I and II on matters within their competence, other than items on the agenda of the Council or the Committee or the organization requests consultation. The Committee shall report to the Council on such consultations.

(d) The Committee may consult, in connexion with any particular session of the Council, with organizations in categories I and II on matters within the competence of the organizations concerning specific items on the provisional agenda of the Council on which the Council of the Committee or the organization requests consultation, and shall make recommendation as to which organizations, subject to the provisions of paragraph 25 (a) above, should be heard by the Council or the appropriate committee and regarding which subjects should be heard, The Committee shall report to the Council on such consultations.

(e) The Committee shall consider matters concerning non-governmental organizations which may be referred to it by the Council or by commissions.

(f) The Committee shall consult with the Secretary-General, as appropriate, on matters affecting the consultative arrangements under Article 71 of the Charter, and arising therefrom.

41. The Committee, in considering a request from a non-governmental organization in category I that an item be placed on the agenda of the Council, shall take into account, among other things:

(a) The adequacy of the documentation submitted by the organization;

(b) The extent to which it is considered that the item lends itself to early and constructive action by the Council;

(c) The possibility that the item might be more appropriately dealt with elsewhere than in the Council.

42. Any decision by the Council Committee on Non-Governmental Organizations not to grant a request submitted by a non-governmental organization in category I that an item be placed on the provisional agenda of the Council shall be considered as final unless the Council decides otherwise.

Part X
CONSULTATION WITH THE SECRETARIAT

43. The Secretariat should be so organized as to enable it to carry out the duties assigned to it concerning the consultative arrangements as set forth in the present resolution.

44. All organizations in consultative relationship shall be able to consult with officers of the appropriate sections of the Secretariat on matters in which there is a mutual interest or a mutual concern. Such consultation shall be upon the request of the non-governmental organization or upon the request of the Secretary-General of the United Nations.

45. The Secretary-General may request organizations in categories I and II and those on the Roster to carry out specific studies or prepare specific papers, subject to the relevant financial regulations.

46. The Secretary-General shall be authorized, within the means at his disposal, to offer to non-governmental organizations in consultative relationship facilities which include:

(a) Prompt and efficient distribution of such documents of the Council and its subsidiary bodies as shall in the judgement of the Secretary-General be appropriate;

(b) Access to the press documentation services provided by the United Nations;

(c) Arrangement of informal discussions on matters of special interest to groups or organizations;

(d) Use of the libraries of the United Nations;

(e) Provision of accommodation for conferences or smaller meetings of consultative organizations on the work of the Economic and Social Council;

(f) Appropriate seating arrangements and facilities for obtaining documents during public meetings of the General Assembly dealing with matters in the economic and social fields.

CODE OF CONDUCT FOR LAW ENFORCEMENT OFFICIALS

Adopted by General Assembly resolution 34/169 of 17 December 1979

Article 1

Law enforcement officials shall at all times fulfil the duty imposed upon them by law, by serving the community and by protecting all persons against illegal acts, consistent with the high degree of responsibility required by their profession.

Commentary:

(a) The term "law enforcement officials", includes all officers of the law, whether appointed or elected, who exercise police powers, especially the powers of arrest or detention.

(b) In countries where police powers are exercised by military authorities, whether uniformed or not, or by State security forces, the definition of law enforcement officials shall be regarded as including officers of such services.

(c) Service to the community is intended to include particularly the rendition of services of assistance to those members of the community who by reason of personal, economic, social or other emergencies are in need of immediate aid.

(d) This provision is intended to cover not only all violent, predatory and harmful acts, but extends to the full range of prohibitions under penal statutes. It extends to conduct by persons not capable of incurring criminal liability.

Article 2

In the performance of their duty, law enforcement officials shall respect and protect human dignity and maintain and uphold the human rights of all persons.

Commentary:

(a) The human rights in question are identified and protected by national and international law. Among the relevant international instruments are the Universal Declaration of Human Rights, the International Covenant on Civil and Political Rights, the Declaration on the Protection of All Persons from Being Subjected to Torture and Other Cruel, Inhuman or Degrading Treatment or Punishment, the United Nations Declaration on the Elimination of All Forms of Racial Discrimination, the International Convention on the Elimination of All Forms of Racial Discrimination, the International Convention on the Suppression and Punishment of the Crime of Apartheid, the Convention on the Prevention and Punishment of the Crime of Genocide, the Standard Minimum Rules for the Treatment of Prisoners and the Vienna Convention on Consular Relations.

(b) National commentaries to this provision should indicate regional or national provisions identifying and protecting these rights.

Article 3

Law enforcement officials may use force only when strictly necessary and to the extent required for the performance of their duty.

Commentary:

(a) This provision emphasizes that the use of force by law enforcement officials should be exceptional; while it implies that law enforcement officials may be authorized to use force as is reasonably necessary under the circumstances for the prevention of crime or in effecting or assisting in the lawful arrest of offenders or suspected offenders, no force going beyond that may be used.

(b) National law ordinarily restricts the use of force by law enforcement officials in accordance with a principle of proportionality. It is to be understood that such national principles of proportionality are to be respected in the interpretation of this provision. In no case should this provision be interpreted to authorize the use of force which is disproportionate to the legitimate objective to be achieved.

(c) The use of firearms is considered an extreme measure. Every effort should be made to exclude the use of firearms, especially against children. In general, firearms should not be used except when a suspected offender offers armed resistance or otherwise jeopardizes the lives of others and less extreme measures are not sufficient to restrain or apprehend the suspected offender. In every instance in which a firearm is discharged, a report should be made promptly to the competent authorities.

Article 4

Matters of a confidential nature in the possession of law enforcement officials shall be kept confidential , unless the performance of duty or the needs of justice strictly require otherwise.

Commentary:

By the nature of their duties, law enforcement officials obtain information which may relate to private lives or be potentially harmful to the interests, and especially the reputation, of others. Great care should be exercised in safeguarding and using such information, which should be disclosed only in the performance of duty or to serve the needs of justice. Any disclosure of such information for other purposes is wholly improper.

Article 5

No law enforcement official may inflict, instigate or tolerate any act of torture or other cruel, inhuman or degrading treatment or punishment, nor may any law enforcement official invoke superior orders or exceptional circumstances such as a state of war or a threat of war, a threat to national security, internal political instability or any other public emergency as a justification of torture or other cruel, inhuman or degrading treatment or punishment .

Commentary:

(a) This prohibition derives from the Declaration on the Protection of All Persons from Being Subjected to Torture and Other Cruel, Inhuman or Degrading Treatment or Punishment, adopted by the General Assembly, according to which: "[Such an act is] an offence to human dignity and shall be condemned as a denial of the purposes of the Charter of the United Nations and as a violation of the human rights and fundamental freedoms proclaimed in the Universal Declaration of Human Rights [and other international human rights instruments]."
(b) The Declaration defines torture as follows:
". . . torture means any act by which severe pain or suffering, whether physical or mental, is intentionally inflicted by or at the instigation of a public official on a person for such purposes as obtaining from him or a third person information or confession, punishing him for an act he has committed or is suspected of having committed, or intimidating him or other persons. It does not include pain or suffering arising only from, inherent in or incidental to, lawful sanctions to the extent consistent with the Standard Minimum Rules for the Treatment of Prisoners."
(c) The term "cruel, inhuman or degrading treatment or punishment" has not been defined by the General Assembly but should be interpreted so as to extend the widest possible protection against abuses, whether physical or mental.

Article 6

Law enforcement officials shall ensure the full protection of the health of persons in their custody and, in particular, shall take immediate action to secure medical attention whenever required.

Commentary:

(a) "Medical attention", which refers to services rendered by any medical personnel, including certified medical practitioners and paramedics, shall be secured when needed or requested.
(b) While the medical personnel are likely to be attached to the law enforcement operation, law enforcement officials must take into account the judgement of such personnel when they recommend providing the person in custody with appropriate treatment through, or in consultation with, medical personnel from outside the law enforcement operation.
(c) It is understood that law enforcement officials shall also secure medical attention for victims of violations of law or of accidents occurring in the course of violations of law.

Law enforcement officials shall not commit any act of corruption. They shall also rigorously oppose and combat all such acts.

Commentary:

(a) Any act of corruption, in the same way as any other abuse of authority, is incompatible with the profession of law enforcement officials. The law must be enforced fully with respect to any law enforcement official who commits an act of corruption, as Governments cannot expect to enforce the law among their citizens if they cannot, or will not, enforce the law against their own agents and within their agencies.

(b) While the definition of corruption must be subject to national law, it should be understood to encompass the commission or omission of an act in the performance of or in connection with one's duties, in response to gifts, promises or incentives demanded or accepted, or the wrongful receipt of these once the act has been committed or omitted.

(c) The expression "act of corruption" referred to above should be understood to encompass attempted corruption.

Article 8

Law enforcement officials shall respect the law and the present Code. They shall also, to the best of their capability, prevent and rigorously oppose any violations of them.

Law enforcement officials who have reason to believe that a violation of the present Code has occurred or is about to occur shall report the matter to their superior authorities and, where necessary, to other appropriate authorities or organs vested with reviewing or remedial power.

Commentary:

(a) This Code shall be observed whenever it has been incorporated into national legislation or practice. If legislation or practice contains stricter provisions than those of the present Code, those stricter provisions shall be observed.

(b) The article seeks to preserve the balance between the need for internal discipline of the agency on which public safety is largely dependent, on the one hand, and the need for dealing with violations of basic human rights, on the other. Law enforcement officials shall report violations within the chain of command and take other lawful action outside the chain of command only when no other remedies are available or effective. It is understood that law enforcement officials shall not suffer administrative or other penalties because they have reported that a violation of this Code has occurred or is about to occur.

(c) The term "appropriate authorities or organs vested with reviewing or remedial power" refers to any authority or organ existing under national law, whether internal to the law enforcement agency or independent thereof, with statutory, customary or other power to review grievances and complaints arising out of violations within the purview of this Code.

(d) In some countries, the mass media may be regarded as performing complaint review functions similar to those described in subparagraph (c) above. Law enforcement officials may, therefore, be justified if, as a last resort and in accordance with the laws and customs of their own countries and with the provisions of article 4 of the present Code, they bring violations to the attention of public opinion through the mass media.

(e) Law enforcement officials who comply with the provisions of this Code deserve the respect, the full support and the co-operation of the community and of the law enforcement agency in which they serve, as well as the law enforcement profession.

BASIC PRINCIPLES ON THE USE OF FORCE AND FIREARMS BY LAW ENFORCEMENT OFFICIALS

U.N. Basic Principles on the Use of Force and Firearms by Law Enforcement Officials, Report of the Eighth U.N. Congress on the Prevention of Crime and the Treatment Offenders, U.N. Doc.

Whereas the work of law enforcement officials is a social service of great importance and there is, therefore, a need to maintain and, whenever necessary, to improve the working conditions and status of these officials,

Whereas a threat to the life and safety of law enforcement officials must be seen as a threat to the stability of society as a whole,

Whereas law enforcement officials have a vital role in the protection of the right to life, liberty and security of the person, as guaranteed in the Universal Declaration of Human Rights and reaffirmed in the International Covenant on Civil and Political Rights,

Whereas the Standard Minimum Rules for the Treatment of Prisoners provide for the circumstances in which prison officials may use force in the course of their duties,

Whereas article 3 of the Code of Conduct for Law Enforcement Officials provides that law enforcement officials may use force only when strictly necessary and to the extent required for the performance of their duty,

Whereas the preparatory meeting for the Seventh United Nations Congress on the Prevention of Crime and the Treatment of Offenders, held at Varenna, Italy, agreed on elements to be considered in the course of further work on restraints on the use of force and firearms by law enforcement officials,

Whereas the Seventh Congress, in its resolution 14, inter alia, emphasizes that the use of force and firearms by law enforcement officials should be commensurate with due respect for human rights,

Whereas the Economic and Social Council, in its resolution 1986/10, section IX, of 21 May 1986, invited Member States to pay particular attention in the implementation of the Code to the use of force and firearms by law enforcement officials, and the General Assembly, in its resolution 41/149 of 4 December 1986, inter alia, welcomed this recommendation made by the Council,

Whereas it is appropriate that, with due regard to their personal safety, consideration be given to the role of law enforcement officials in relation to the administration of justice, to the protection of the right to life, liberty and security of the person, to their responsibility to maintain public safety and social peace and to the importance of their qualifications, training and conduct,

The basic principles set forth below, which have been formulated to assist Member States in their task of ensuring and promoting the proper role of law enforcement officials, should be taken into account and respected by Governments within the framework of their national legislation and practice, and be brought to the attention of law enforcement officials as well as other persons, such as judges, prosecutors, lawyers, members of the executive branch and the legislature, and the public.

General provisions

1. Governments and law enforcement agencies shall adopt and implement rules and regulations on the use of force and firearms against persons by law enforcement officials. In developing such rules and regulations, Governments and law enforcement agencies shall keep the ethical issues associated with the use of force and firearms constantly under review.

2. Governments and law enforcement agencies should develop a range of means as broad as possible and equip law enforcement officials with various types of weapons and ammunition that would allow for a differentiated use of force and firearms. These should include the development of non-lethal incapacitating weapons for use in appropriate situations, with a view to increasingly restraining the application of means capable of causing death or injury to persons. For the same purpose, it should also be possible for law enforcement officials to be equipped with self-defensive equipment such as shields, helmets, bullet-proof vests and bullet-proof means of transportation, in order to decrease the need to use weapons of any kind.

3. The development and deployment of non-lethal incapacitating weapons should be carefully evaluated in order to minimize the risk of endangering uninvolved persons, and the use of such weapons should be carefully controlled.

4. Law enforcement officials, in carrying out their duty, shall, as far as possible, apply non-violent means before resorting to the use of force and firearms. They may use force and firearms only if other means remain ineffective or without any promise of achieving the intended result.

5. Whenever the lawful use of force and firearms is unavoidable, law enforcement officials shall:

> (a) Exercise restraint in such use and act in proportion to the seriousness of the offence and the legitimate objective to be achieved;
>
> (b) Minimize damage and injury, and respect and preserve human life;
>
> (c) Ensure that assistance and medical aid are rendered to any injured or affected persons at the earliest possible moment;
>
> (d) Ensure that relatives or close friends of the injured or affected person are notified at the earliest possible moment.

6. Where injury or death is caused by the use of force and firearms by law enforcement officials, they shall report the incident promptly to their superiors, in accordance with principle 22.

7. Governments shall ensure that arbitrary or abusive use of force and firearms by law enforcement officials is punished as a criminal offence under their law.

8. Exceptional circumstances such as internal political instability or any other public emergency may not be invoked to justify any departure from these basic principles.

Special provisions

9. Law enforcement officials shall not use firearms against persons except in self-defence or defence of others against the imminent threat of death or serious injury, to prevent the perpetration of a particularly serious crime involving grave threat to life, to arrest a person presenting such a danger and resisting their authority, or to prevent his or her escape, and only when less extreme means are insufficient to achieve these objectives. In any event, intentional lethal use of firearms may only be made when strictly unavoidable in order to protect life.

10. In the circumstances provided for under principle 9, law enforcement officials shall identify themselves as such and give a clear warning of their intent to use firearms, with sufficient time for the warning to be observed, unless to do so would unduly place the law enforcement officials at risk or would create a risk of death or serious harm to other persons, or would be clearly inappropriate or pointless in the circumstances of the incident.

11. Rules and regulations on the use of firearms by law enforcement officials should include guidelines that:

> (a) Specify the circumstances under which law enforcement officials are authorized to carry firearms and prescribe the types of firearms and ammunition permitted;
>
> (b) Ensure that firearms are used only in appropriate circumstances and in a manner likely to decrease the risk of unnecessary harm;
>
> (c) Prohibit the use of those firearms and ammunition that cause unwarranted injury or present an unwarranted risk;
>
> (d) Regulate the control, storage and issuing of firearms, including procedures for ensuring that law enforcement officials are accountable for the firearms and ammunition issued to them;
>
> (e) Provide for warnings to be given, if appropriate, when firearms are to be discharged;
>
> (f) Provide for a system of reporting whenever law enforcement officials use firearms in the performance of their duty.

Policing unlawful assemblies

12. As everyone is allowed to participate in lawful and peaceful assemblies, in accordance with the principles embodied in the Universal Declaration of Human Rights and the International Covenant on Civil and Political Rights, Governments and law enforcement agencies and officials shall recognize that force and firearms may be used only in accordance with principles 13 and 14.

13. In the dispersal of assemblies that are unlawful but non-violent, law enforcement officials shall avoid the use of force or, where that is not practicable, shall restrict such force to the minimum extent necessary.

14. In the dispersal of violent assemblies, law enforcement officials may use firearms only when less dangerous means are not practicable and only to the minimum extent necessary. Law enforcement officials shall not use firearms in such cases, except under the conditions stipulated in principle 9.

Policing persons in custody or detention

15. Law enforcement officials, in their relations with persons in custody or detention, shall not use force, except when strictly necessary for the maintenance of security and order within the institution, or when personal safety is threatened.

16. Law enforcement officials, in their relations with persons in custody or detention, shall not use firearms, except in self-defence or in the defence of others against the immediate threat of death or serious injury, or when strictly necessary to prevent the escape of a person in custody or detention presenting the danger referred to in principle 9.

17. The preceding principles are without prejudice to the rights, duties and responsibilities of prison officials, as set out in the Standard Minimum Rules for the Treatment of Prisoners, particularly rules 33, 34 and 54.

Qualifications, training and counselling

18. Governments and law enforcement agencies shall ensure that all law enforcement officials are selected by proper screening procedures, have appropriate moral, psychological and physical qualities for the effective exercise of their functions and receive continuous and thorough professional training. Their continued fitness to perform these functions should be subject to periodic review.

19. Governments and law enforcement agencies shall ensure that all law enforcement officials are provided with training and are tested in accordance with appropriate proficiency standards in the use of force. Those law enforcement officials who are required to carry firearms should be authorized to do so only upon completion of special training in their use.

20. In the training of law enforcement officials, Governments and law enforcement agencies shall give special attention to issues of police ethics and human rights, especially in the investigative process, to alternatives to the use of force and firearms, including the peaceful settlement of conflicts, the understanding of crowd behaviour, and the methods of persuasion, negotiation and mediation, as well as to technical means, with a view to limiting the use of force and firearms. Law enforcement agencies should review their training programmes and operational procedures in the light of particular incidents.

21. Governments and law enforcement agencies shall make stress counselling available to law enforcement officials who are involved in situations where force and firearms are used.

Reporting and review procedures

22. Governments and law enforcement agencies shall establish effective reporting and review procedures for all incidents referred to in principles 6 and 11 (f). For incidents reported pursuant to these principles, Governments and law enforcement agencies shall ensure that an effective review process is available and that independent administrative or prosecutorial authorities are in a position to exercise jurisdiction in appropriate circumstances. In cases of death and serious injury or other grave consequences, a detailed report shall be sent promptly to the competent authorities responsible for administrative review and judicial control.

23. Persons affected by the use of force and firearms or their legal representatives shall have access to an independent process, including a judicial process. In the event of the death of such persons, this provision shall apply to their dependants accordingly.

24. Governments and law enforcement agencies shall ensure that superior officers are held responsible if they know, or should have known, that law enforcement officials under their command are resorting, or have resorted, to the unlawful use of force and firearms, and they did not take all measures in their power to prevent, suppress or report such use.

25. Governments and law enforcement agencies shall ensure that no criminal or disciplinary sanction is imposed on law enforcement officials who, in compliance with the Code of Conduct for Law Enforcement Officials and these basic principles, refuse to carry out an order to use force and firearms, or who report such use by other officials.

26. Obedience to superior orders shall be no defence if law enforcement officials knew that an order to use force and firearms resulting in the death or serious injury of a person was manifestly unlawful and had a

reasonable opportunity to refuse to follow it. In any case, responsibility also rests on the superiors who gave the unlawful orders.

DECLARATION ON THE PROTECTION OF ALL PERSONS FROM ENFORCED DISAPPEARANCE

Declaration on the Protection of all Persons from Enforced Disappearances, G.A. Res. 47/133, U.N. GAOR, 47th Sess., Supp. No. 49, U.N. Doc. A/RES/47/133 (Dec. 18, 1992)

The General Assembly,

Considering that, in accordance with the principles proclaimed in the Charter of the United Nations and other international instruments, recognition of the inherent dignity and of the equal and inalienable rights of all members of the human family is the foundation of freedom, justice and peace in the world,

Bearing in mind the obligation of States under the Charter, in particular Article 55, to promote universal respect for, and observance of, human rights and fundamental freedoms,

Deeply concerned that in many countries, often in a persistent manner, enforced disappearances occur, in the sense that persons are arrested, detained or abducted against their will or otherwise deprived of their liberty by officials of different branches or levels of Government, or by organized groups or private individuals acting on behalf of, or with the support, direct or indirect, consent or acquiescence of the Government, followed by a refusal to disclose the fate or whereabouts of the persons concerned or a refusal to acknowledge the deprivation of their liberty, which places such persons outside the protection of the law,

Considering that enforced disappearance undermines the deepest values of any society committed to respect for the rule of law, human rights and fundamental freedoms, and that the systematic practice of such acts is of the nature of a crime against humanity,

Recalling its resolution 33/173 of 20 December 1978, in which it expressed concern about the reports from various parts of the world relating to enforced or involuntary disappearances, as well as about the anguish and sorrow caused by those disappearances, and called upon Governments to hold law enforcement and security forces legally responsible for excesses which might lead to enforced or involuntary disappearances of persons,

Recalling also the protection afforded to victims of armed conflicts by the Geneva Conventions of 12 August 1949 and the Additional Protocols thereto, of 1977,

Having regard in particular to the relevant articles of the Universal Declaration of Human Rights and the International Covenant on Civil and Political Rights, which protect the right to life, the right to liberty and security of the person, the right not to be subjected to torture and the right to recognition as a person before the law,

Having regard also to the Convention against Torture and Other Cruel, Inhuman or Degrading Treatment or Punishment, which provides that States parties shall take effective measures to prevent and punish acts of torture,

Bearing in mind the Code of Conduct for Law Enforcement Officials, the Basic Principles on the Use of Force and Firearms by Law Enforcement officials, the Declaration of Basic Principles of Justice for Victims of Crime and Abuse of Power and the Standard Minimum Rules for the Treatment of Prisoners,

Affirming that, in order to prevent enforced disappearances, it is necessary to ensure strict compliance with the Body of Principles for the Protection of All Persons under any form of Detention or Imprisonment

416

contained in the annex to its resolution 43/173 of 9 December 1988, and with the Principles on the Effective Prevention and Investigation of Extra-legal, Arbitrary and Summary Executions, set forth in the annex to Economic and Social Council resolution 1989/65 of 24 May 1989 and endorsed by the General Assembly in its resolution 44/162 of 15 December 1989,

Bearing in mind that, while the acts which comprise enforced disappearance constitute a violation of the prohibition found in the aforementioned international instruments, it is none the less important to devise an instrument which characterizes all acts of enforced disappearance of persons as very serious offences and sets forth standards designed to punish and prevent their commission,

1. Proclaims the present Declaration on the Protection of all Persons from Enforced Disappearance, as a body of principles for all States;
2. Urges that all efforts be made so that the Declaration becomes generally known and respected;

Article 1

1. Any act of enforced disappearance is an offence to human dignity. It is condemned as a denial of the purposes of the Charter of the United Nations and as a grave and flagrant violation of the human rights and fundamental freedoms proclaimed in the Universal Declaration of Human Rights and reaffirmed and developed in international instruments in this field.
2. Any act of enforced disappearance places the persons subjected thereto outside the protection of the law and inflicts severe suffering on them and their families. It constitutes a violation of the rules of international law guaranteeing, inter alia, the right to recognition as a person before the law, the right to liberty and security of the person and the right not to be subjected to torture and other cruel, inhuman or degrading treatment or punishment. It also violates or constitutes a grave threat to the right to life.

Article 2

1. No State shall practise, permit or tolerate enforced disappearances.
2. States shall act at the national and regional levels and in cooperation with the United Nations to contribute by all means to the prevention and eradication of enforced disappearance.

Article 3

Each State shall take effective legislative, administrative, judicial or other measures to prevent and terminate acts of enforced disappearance in any territory under its jurisdiction.

Article 4

1. All acts of enforced disappearance shall be offences under criminal law punishable by appropriate penalties which shall take into account their extreme seriousness.
2. Mitigating circumstances may be established in national legislation for persons who, having participated in enforced disappearances, are instrumental in bringing the victims forward alive or in providing voluntarily information which would contribute to clarifying cases of enforced disappearance.

Article 5

In addition to such criminal penalties as are applicable, enforced disappearances render their perpetrators and the State or State authorities which organize, acquiesce in or tolerate such disappearances liable under civil law, without prejudice to the international responsibility of the State concerned in accordance with the principles of international law.

Article 6

1. No order or instruction of any public authority, civilian, military or other, may be invoked to justify an enforced disappearance. Any person receiving such an order or instruction shall have the right and duty not to obey it.
2. Each State shall ensure that orders or instructions directing, authorizing or encouraging any enforced disappearance are prohibited.
3. Training of law enforcement officials shall emphasize the provisions in paragraphs 1 and 2 of the present article.

Article 7

No circumstances whatsoever, whether a threat of war, a state of war, internal political instability or any other public emergency, may be invoked to justify enforced disappearances.

Article 8

1. No State shall expel, return (refouler) or extradite a person to another State where there are substantial grounds to believe that he would be in danger of enforced disappearance.
2. For the purpose of determining whether there are such grounds, the competent authorities shall take into account all relevant considerations including, where applicable, the existence in the State concerned of a consistent pattern of gross, flagrant or mass violations of human rights.

Article 9

1. The right to a prompt and effective judicial remedy as a means of determining the whereabouts or state of health of persons deprived of their liberty and/or identifying the authority ordering or carrying out the deprivation of liberty is required to prevent enforced disappearances under all circumstances, including those referred to in article 7 above.
2. In such proceedings, competent national authorities shall have access to all places where persons deprived of their liberty are being held and to each part of those places, as well as to any place in which there are grounds to believe that such persons may be found.
3. Any other competent authority entitled under the law of the State or by any international legal instrument to which the State is a party may also have access to such places.

Article 10

1. Any person deprived of liberty shall be held in an officially recognized place of detention and, in conformity with national law. be brought before a judicial authority promptly after detention.
2. Accurate information on the detention of such persons and their place or places of detention, including transfers. shall be made promptly available to their family members, their counsel or to any other persons having a legitimate interest in the information unless a wish to the contrary has been manifested by the persons concerned.
3. An official up-to-date register of all persons deprived of their liberty shall be maintained in every place of detention. Additionally, each State shall take steps to maintain similar centralized registers. The information contained in these registers shall be made available to the persons mentioned in the preceding paragraph, to any judicial or other competent and independent national authority and to any other competent authority entitled under the law of the State concerned or any international legal instrument to which a State concerned is a party, seeking to trace the whereabouts of a detained person.

Article 11

All persons deprived of liberty must be released in a manner permitting reliable verification that they have actually been released and, further, have been released in conditions in which their physical integrity and ability fully to exercise their rights are assured.

Article 12

1. Each State shall establish rules under its national law indicating those officials authorized to order deprivation of liberty, establishing the conditions under which such orders may be given, and stipulating penalties for officials who, without legal justification, refuse to provide information on any detention.
2. Each State shall likewise ensure strict supervision, including a clear chain of command, of all law enforcement officials responsible for apprehensions, arrests, detentions, custody, transfers and imprisonment, and of other officials authorized by law to use force and firearms.

Article 13

1. Each State shall ensure that any person having knowledge or a legitimate interest who alleges that a person has been subjected to enforced disappearance has the right to complain to a competent and independent State authority and to have that complaint promptly, thoroughly and impartially investigated by that authority. Whenever there are reasonable grounds to believe that an enforced disappearance has

been committed, the State shall promptly refer the matter to that authority for such an investigation, even if there has been no formal complaint. No measure shall be taken to curtail or impede the investigation.

2. Each State shall ensure that the competent authority shall have the necessary powers and resources to conduct the investigation effectively, including powers to compel attendance of witnesses and production of relevant documents and to make immediate on-site visits.

3. Steps shall be taken to ensure that all involved in the investigation, including the complainant, counsel, witnesses and those conducting the investigation, are protected against ill-treatment, intimidation or reprisal.

4. The findings of such an investigation shall be made available upon request to all persons concerned, unless doing so would jeopardize an ongoing criminal investigation.

5. Steps shall be taken to ensure that any ill-treatment, intimidation or reprisal or any other form of interference on the occasion of the lodging of a complaint or during the investigation procedure is appropriately punished.

6. An investigation, in accordance with the procedures described above, should be able to be conducted for as long as the fate of the victim of enforced disappearance remains unclarified.

Article 14

Any person alleged to have perpetrated an act of enforced disappearance in a particular State shall, when the facts disclosed by an official investigation so warrant, be brought before the competent civil authorities of that State for the purpose of prosecution and trial unless he has been extradited to another State wishing to exercise jurisdiction in accordance with the relevant international agreements in force. All States should take any lawful and appropriate action available to them to bring to justice all persons presumed responsible for an act of enforced disappearance, who are found to be within their jurisdiction or under their control.

Article 15

The fact that there are grounds to believe that a person has participated in acts of an extremely serious nature such as those referred to in article 4, paragraph 1, above, regardless of the motives, shall be taken into account when the competent authorities of the State decide whether or not to grant asylum.

Article 16

1. Persons alleged to have committed any of the acts referred to in article 4, paragraph 1, above, shall be suspended from any official duties during the investigation referred to in article 13 above.

2. They shall be tried only by the competent ordinary courts in each State, and not by any other special tribunal, in particular military courts.

3. No privileges, immunities or special exemptions shall be admitted in such trials, without prejudice to the provisions contained in the Vienna Convention on Diplomatic Relations.

4. The persons presumed responsible for such acts shall be guaranteed fair treatment in accordance with the relevant provisions of the Universal Declaration of Human Rights and other relevant international agreements in force at all stages of the investigation and eventual prosecution and trial.

Article 17

1. Acts constituting enforced disappearance shall be considered a continuing offence as long as the perpetrators continue to conceal the fate and the whereabouts of persons who have disappeared and these facts remain unclarified.

2. When the remedies provided for in article 2 of the International Covenant on Civil and Political Rights are no longer effective, the statute of limitations relating to acts of enforced disappearance shall be suspended until these remedies are re-established.

3. Statutes of limitations, where they exist, relating to acts of enforced disappearance shall be substantial and commensurate with the extreme seriousness of the offence.

Article 18

1. Persons who have or are alleged to have committed offences referred to in article 4, paragraph 1, above, shall not benefit from any special amnesty law or similar measures that might have the effect of exempting them from any criminal proceedings or sanction.

2. In the exercise of the right of pardon, the extreme seriousness of acts of enforced disappearance shall be taken into account.

Article 19

The victims of acts of enforced disappearance and their family shall obtain redress and shall have the right to adequate compensation, including the means for as complete a rehabilitation as possible. In the event of the death of the victim as a result of an act of enforced disappearance, their dependants shall also be entitled to compensation.

Article 20

1. States shall prevent and suppress the abduction of children of parents subjected to enforced disappearance and of children born during their mother's enforced disappearance, and shall devote their efforts to the search for and identification of such children and to the restitution of the children to their families of origin.
2. Considering the need to protect the best interests of children referred to in the preceding paragraph, there shall be an opportunity, in States which recognize a system of adoption, for a review of the adoption of such children and, in particular, for annulment of any adoption which originated in enforced disappearance. Such adoption should, however, continue to be in force if consent is given, at the time of the review, by the child's closest relatives.
3. The abduction of children of parents subjected to enforced disappearance or of children born during their mother's enforced disappearance, and the act of altering or suppressing documents attesting to their true identity, shall constitute an extremely serious offence, which shall be punished as such.
4. For these purposes, States shall, where appropriate, conclude bilateral and multilateral agreements.

Article 21

The provisions of the pre sent Declaration are without prejudice to the provisions enunciated in the Universal Declaration of Human Rights or in any other international instrument, and shall not be construed as restricting or derogating from any of those provisions.

DECLARATION ON THE ELIMINATION OF VIOLENCE AGAINST WOMEN

Declaration on the Elimination of Violence against Women, G.A. Res. 48/104, U.N. GAOR, 48th Sess., Supp. No. 49, U.N. Doc. A/RES/48/104 (Dec. 20, 1993)

The General Assembly,

Recognizing the urgent need for the universal application to women of the rights and principles with regard to equality, security, liberty, integrity and dignity of all human beings,

Noting that those rights and principles are enshrined in international instruments, including the Universal Declaration of Human Rights, the International Covenant on Civil and Political Rights, the International Covenant on Economic, Social and Cultural Rights, the Convention on the Elimination of All Forms of Discrimination against Women and the Convention against Torture and Other Cruel, Inhuman or Degrading Treatment or Punishment,

Recognizing that effective implementation of the Convention on the Elimination of All Forms of Discrimination against Women would contribute to the elimination of violence against women and that the Declaration on the Elimination of Violence against Women, set forth in the present resolution, will strengthen and complement that process,

Concerned that violence against women is an obstacle to the achievement of equality, development and peace, as recognized in the Nairobi Forward-looking Strategies for the Advancement of Women, in which a set of measures to combat violence against women was recommended, and to the full implementation of the Convention on the Elimination of All Forms of Discrimination against Women,

Affirming that violence against women constitutes a violation of the rights and fundamental freedoms of women and impairs or nullifies their enjoyment of those rights and freedoms, and concerned about the long-standing failure to protect and promote those rights and freedoms in the case of violence against women,

Recognizing that violence against women is a manifestation of historically unequal power relations between men and women, which have led to domination over and discrimination against women by men and to the prevention of the full advancement of women, and that violence against women is one of the crucial social mechanisms by which women are forced into a subordinate position compared with men,

Concerned that some groups of women, such as women belonging to minority groups, indigenous women, refugee women, migrant women, women living in rural or remote communities, destitute women, women in institutions or in detention, female children, women with disabilities, elderly women and women in situations of armed conflict, are especially vulnerable to violence,

Recalling the conclusion in paragraph 23 of the annex to Economic and Social Council resolution 1990/15 of 24 May 1990 that the recognition that violence against women in the family and society was pervasive and cut across lines of income, class and culture had to be matched by urgent and effective steps to eliminate its incidence,

Recalling also Economic and Social Council resolution 1991/18 of 30 May 1991, in which the Council recommended the development of a framework for an international instrument that would address explicitly the issue of violence against women,

Welcoming the role that women's movements are playing in drawing increasing attention to the nature, severity and magnitude of the problem of violence against women,

Alarmed that opportunities for women to achieve legal, social, political and economic equality in society are limited, inter alia, by continuing and endemic violence,

Convinced that in the light of the above there is a need for a clear and comprehensive definition of violence against women, a clear statement of the rights to be applied to ensure the elimination of violence against women in all its forms, a commitment by States in respect of their responsibilities, and a commitment by the international community at large to the elimination of violence against women,

Solemnly proclaims the following Declaration on the Elimination of Violence against Women and urges that every effort be made so that it becomes generally known and respected:

Article 1
For the purposes of this Declaration, the term "violence against women" means any act of gender-based violence that results in, or is likely to result in, physical, sexual or psychological harm or suffering to women, including threats of such acts, coercion or arbitrary deprivation of liberty, whether occurring in public or in private life.

Article 2
Violence against women shall be understood to encompass, but not be limited to, the following:
(a) Physical, sexual and psychological violence occurring in the family, including battering, sexual abuse of female children in the household, dowry-related violence, marital rape, female genital mutilation and other traditional practices harmful to women, non-spousal violence and violence related to exploitation;

421

(b) Physical, sexual and psychological violence occurring within the general community, including rape, sexual abuse, sexual harassment and intimidation at work, in educational institutions and elsewhere, trafficking in women and forced prostitution;

(c) Physical, sexual and psychological violence perpetrated or condoned by the State, wherever it occurs.

Article 3

Women are entitled to the equal enjoyment and protection of all human rights and fundamental freedoms in the political, economic, social, cultural, civil or any other field. These rights include, inter alia:

(a) The right to life;

(b) The right to equality;

(c) The right to liberty and security of person;

(d) The right to equal protection under the law;

(e) The right to be free from all forms of discrimination;

(f) The right to the highest standard attainable of physical and mental health;

(g) The right to just and favourable conditions of work;

(h) The right not to be subjected to torture, or other cruel, inhuman or degrading treatment or punishment.

Article 4

States should condemn violence against women and should not invoke any custom, tradition or religious consideration to avoid their obligations with respect to its elimination. States should pursue by all appropriate means and without delay a policy of eliminating violence against women and, to this end, should:

(a) Consider, where they have not yet done so, ratifying or acceding to the Convention on the Elimination of All Forms of Discrimination against Women or withdrawing reservations to that Convention;

(b) Refrain from engaging in violence against women;

(c) Exercise due diligence to prevent, investigate and, in accordance with national legislation, punish acts of violence against women, whether those acts are perpetrated by the State or by private persons;

(d) Develop penal, civil, labour and administrative sanctions in domestic legislation to punish and redress the wrongs caused to women who are subjected to violence; women who are subjected to violence should be provided with access to the mechanisms of justice and, as provided for by national legislation, to just and effective remedies for the harm that they have suffered; States should also inform women of their rights in seeking redress through such mechanisms;

(e) Consider the possibility of developing national plans of action to promote the protection of women against any form of violence, or to include provisions for that purpose in plans already existing, taking into account, as appropriate, such cooperation as can be provided by non-governmental organizations, particularly those concerned with the issue of violence against women;

(f) Develop, in a comprehensive way, preventive approaches and all those measures of a legal, political, administrative and cultural nature that promote the protection of women against any form of violence, and ensure that the re-victimization of women does not occur because of laws insensitive to gender considerations, enforcement practices or other interventions;

(g) Work to ensure, to the maximum extent feasible in the light of their available resources and, where needed, within the framework of international cooperation, that women subjected to violence and, where appropriate, their children have specialized assistance, such as rehabilitation, assistance in child care and maintenance, treatment, counselling, and health and social services, facilities and programmes, as well as support structures, and should take all other appropriate measures to promote their safety and physical and psychological rehabilitation;

(h) Include in government budgets adequate resources for their activities related to the elimination of violence against women;

(i) Take measures to ensure that law enforcement officers and public officials responsible for implementing policies to prevent, investigate and punish violence against women receive training to sensitize them to the needs of women;

(j) Adopt all appropriate measures, especially in the field of education, to modify the social and cultural patterns of conduct of men and women and to eliminate prejudices, customary practices and all other practices based on the idea of the inferiority or superiority of either of the sexes and on stereotyped roles for men and women;

(k) Promote research, collect data and compile statistics, especially concerning domestic violence, relating to the prevalence of different forms of violence against women and encourage research on the causes, nature, seriousness and consequences of violence against women and on the effectiveness of measures implemented to prevent and redress violence against women; those statistics and findings of the research will be made public;

(l) Adopt measures directed towards the elimination of violence against women who are especially vulnerable to violence;

(m) Include, in submitting reports as required under relevant human rights instruments of the United Nations, information pertaining to violence against women and measures taken to implement the present Declaration;

(n) Encourage the development of appropriate guidelines to assist in the implementation of the principles set forth in the present Declaration;

(o) Recognize the important role of the women's movement and non-governmental organizations world wide in raising awareness and alleviating the problem of violence against women;

(p) Facilitate and enhance the work of the women's movement and non-governmental organizations and cooperate with them at local, national and regional levels;

(q) Encourage intergovernmental regional organizations of which they are members to include the elimination of violence against women in their programmes, as appropriate.

Article 5

The organs and specialized agencies of the United Nations system should, within their respective fields of competence, contribute to the recognition and realization of the rights and the principles set forth in the present Declaration and, to this end, should, inter alia:

(a) Foster international and regional cooperation with a view to defining regional strategies for combating violence, exchanging experiences and financing programmes relating to the elimination of violence against women;

(b) Promote meetings and seminars with the aim of creating and raising awareness among all persons of the issue of the elimination of violence against women;

(c) Foster coordination and exchange within the United Nations system between human rights treaty bodies to address the issue of violence against women effectively;

(d) Include in analyses prepared by organizations and bodies of the United Nations system of social trends and problems, such as the periodic reports on the world social situation, examination of trends in violence against women;

(e) Encourage coordination between organizations and bodies of the United Nations system to incorporate the issue of violence against women into ongoing programmes, especially with reference to groups of women particularly vulnerable to violence;

(f) Promote the formulation of guidelines or manuals relating to violence against women, taking into account the measures referred to in the present Declaration;

(g) Consider the issue of the elimination of violence against women, as appropriate, in fulfilling their mandates with respect to the implementation of human rights instruments;

(h) Cooperate with non-governmental organizations in addressing the issue of violence against women.

Article 6

Nothing in the present Declaration shall affect any provision that is more conducive to the elimination of violence against women that may be contained in the legislation of a State or in any international convention, treaty or other instrument in force in a State.

PRINCIPLES RELATING TO THE STATUS OF NATIONAL INSTITUTIONS (The Paris Principles)

Principles Relating to the Status of National Institutions, G.A. Res. 48/134, Annex, U.N. GAOR, 48th Sess., Supp. No. 49, U.N. Doc. A/RES/48/134 (Dec. 20, 1993)

Competence and responsibilities

1. A national institution shall be vested with competence to promote and protect human rights.

2. A national institution shall be given as broad a mandate as possible, which shall be clearly set forth in a constitutional or legislative text, specifying its composition and its sphere of competence.

3. A national institution shall, inter alia, have the following responsibilities:

(a) To submit to the Government, Parliament and any other competent body, on an advisory basis either at the request of the authorities concerned or through the exercise of its power to hear a matter without higher referral, opinions, recommendations, proposals and reports on any matters concerning the promotion and protection of human rights; the national institution may decide to publicize them; these opinions, recommendations, proposals and reports, as well as any prerogative of the national institution, shall relate to the following areas:

(i) Any legislative or administrative provisions, as well as provisions relating to judicial organizations, intended to preserve and extend the protection of human rights; in that connection, the national institution shall examine the legislation and administrative provisions in force, as well as bills and proposals, and shall make such recommendations as it deems appropriate in order to ensure that these provisions conform to the fundamental principles of human rights; it shall, if necessary, recommend the adoption of new legislation, the amendment of legislation in force and the adoption or amendment of administrative measures;

(ii) Any situation of violation of human rights which it decides to take up;

(iii) The preparation of reports on the national situation with regard to human rights in general, and on more specific matters;

(iv) Drawing the attention of the Government to situations in any part of the country where human rights are violated and making proposals to it for initiatives to put an end to such situations and, where necessary, expressing an opinion on the positions and reactions of the Government;

(b) To promote and ensure the harmonization of national legislation, regulations and practices with the international human rights instruments to which the State is a party, and their effective implementation;

(c) To encourage ratification of the above-mentioned instruments or accession to those instruments, and to ensure their implementation;

(d) To contribute to the reports which States are required to submit to United Nations bodies and committees, and to regional institutions, pursuant to their treaty obligations and, where necessary, to express an opinion on the subject, with due respect for their independence;

(e) To cooperate with the United Nations and any other orgnization in the United Nations system, the regional institutions and the national institutions of other countries that are competent in the areas of the protection and promotion of human rights;

(f) To assist in the formulation of programmes for the teaching of, and research into, human rights and to take part in their execution in schools, universities and professional circles;

(g) To publicize human rights and efforts to combat all forms of discrimination, in particular racial discrimination, by increasing public awareness, especially through information and education and by making use of all press organs.

Composition and guarantees of independence and pluralism

1. The composition of the national institution and the appointment of its members, whether by means of an election or otherwise, shall be established in accordance with a procedure which affords all necessary guarantees to ensure the pluralist representation of the social forces (of civilian society) involved in the protection and promotion of human rights, particularly by powers which will enable effective cooperation to be established with, or through the presence of, representatives of:

(a) Non-governmental organizations responsible for human rights and efforts to combat racial discrimination, trade unions, concerned social and professional organizations, for example, associations of lawyers, doctors, journalists and eminent scientists;

(b) Trends in philosophical or religious thought;

(c) Universities and qualified experts;

(d) Parliament;

(e) Government departments (if these are included, their representatives should participate in the deliberations only in an advisory capacity).

2. The national institution shall have an infrastructure which is suited to the smooth conduct of its activities, in particular adequate funding. The purpose of this funding should be to enable it to have its own staff and premises, in order to be independent of the Government and not be subject to financial control which might affect its independence.

3. In order to ensure a stable mandate for the members of the national institution, without which there can be no real independence, their appointment shall be effected by an official act which shall establish the specific duration of the mandate. This mandate may be renewable, provided that the pluralism of the institution's membership is ensured.

Methods of operation

Within the framework of its operation, the national institution shall:

(a) Freely consider any questions falling within its competence, whether they are submitted by the Government or taken up by it without referral to a higher authority, on the proposal of its members or of any petitioner,

(b) Hear any person and obtain any information and any documents necessary for assessing situations falling within its competence;

(c) Address public opinion directly or through any press organ, particularly in order to publicize its opinions and recommendations;

(d) Meet on a regular basis and whenever necessary in the presence of all its members after they have been duly concerned;

(e) Establish working groups from among its members as necessary, and set up local or regional sections to assist it in discharging its functions;

(f) Maintain consultation with the other bodies, whether jurisdictional or otherwise, responsible for the promotion and protection of human rights (in particular, ombudsmen, mediators and similar institutions);

(g) In view of the fundamental role played by the non-governmental organizations in expanding the work of the national institutions, develop relations with the non-governmental organizations devoted to promoting and protecting human rights, to economic and social development, to combating racism, to protecting particularly vulnerable groups (especially children, migrant workers, refugees, physically and mentally disabled persons) or to specialized areas.

Additional principles concerning the status of commissions with quasi-jurisdictional competence

A national institution may be authorized to hear and consider complaints and petitions concerning individual situations. Cases may be brought before it by individuals, their representatives, third parties, non-governmental organizations, associations of trade unions or any other representative organizations. In such circumstances, and without prejudice to the principles stated above concerning the other powers of the commissions, the functions entrusted to them may be based on the following principles:

(a) Seeking an amicable settlement through conciliation or, within the limits prescribed by the law, through binding decisions or, where necessary, on the basis of confidentiality;

(b) Informing the party who filed the petition of his rights, in particular the remedies available to him, and promoting his access to them;

(c) Hearing any complaints or petitions or transmitting them to any other competent authority within the limits prescribed by the law;

(d) Making recommendations to the competent authorities, especially by proposing amendments or reforms of the laws, regulations and administrative practices, especially if they have created the difficulties encountered by the persons filing the petitions in order to assert their rights.

U.N. ECONOMIC AND SOCIAL COUNCIL RESOLUTION 1996/31 CONSULTATIVE RELATIONSHIP BETWEEN THE UNITED NATIONS AND NON-GOVERNMENTAL ORGANIZATIONS

U.N. Econ. & Soc. Council Res.1996/31, U.N. Doc. E/1996/96 (July 25, 1996)

The Economic and Social Council,

Recalling Article 71 of the Charter of the United Nations,

Recalling also its resolution 1993/80 of 30 July 1993, in which it requested a general review of arrangements for consultation with non-governmental organizations, with a view to updating, if necessary, Council resolution 1296 (XLIV) of 23 May 1968, as well as introducing coherence in the rules governing the participation of non-governmental organizations in international conferences convened by the United Nations, and also an examination of ways and means of improving practical arrangements for the work of the Committee on Non-Governmental Organizations and the Non-Governmental Organizations Section of the Secretariat,

Recalling further its decision 1995/304 of 26 July 1995,

Confirming the need to take into account the full diversity of the non-governmental organizations at the national, regional and international levels,

Acknowledging the breadth of non-governmental organizations' expertise and the capacity of non-governmental organizations to support the work of the United Nations,

Taking into account the changes in the non-governmental sector, including the emergence of a large number of national and regional organizations,

Calling upon the governing bodies of the relevant organizations, bodies and specialized agencies of the United Nations system to examine the principles and practices relating to their consultations with non-governmental organizations and to take action, as appropriate, to promote coherence in the light of the provisions of the present resolution,

Approves the following update of the arrangements set out in its resolution 1296 (XLIV) of 23 May 1968:

ARRANGEMENTS FOR CONSULTATION WITH NON-GOVERNMENTAL ORGANIZATIONS

Part I
PRINCIPLES TO BE APPLIED IN THE ESTABLISHMENT OF CONSULTATIVE RELATIONS

The following principles shall be applied in establishing consultative relations with non-governmental organizations:

1. The organization shall be concerned with matters falling within the competence of the Economic and Social Council and its subsidiary bodies.
2. The aims and purposes of the organization shall be in conformity with the spirit, purposes and principles of the Charter of the United Nations.
3. The organization shall undertake to support the work of the United Nations and to promote knowledge of its principles and activities, in accordance with its own aims and purposes and the nature and scope of its competence and activities.
4. Except where expressly stated otherwise, the term "organization" shall refer to non-governmental organizations at the national, subregional, regional or international levels.

5. Consultative relationships may be established with international, regional, subregional and national organizations, in conformity with the Charter of the United Nations and the principles and criteria established under the present resolution. The Committee, in considering applications for consultative status, should ensure, to the extent possible, participation of non-governmental organizations from all regions, and particularly from developing countries, in order to help achieve a just, balanced, effective and genuine involvement of non-governmental organizations from all regions and areas of the world. The Committee shall also pay particular attention to non-governmental organizations that have special expertise or experience upon which the Council may wish to draw.

6. Greater participation of non-governmental organizations from developing countries in international conferences convened by the United Nations should be encouraged.

7. Greater involvement of non-governmental organizations from countries with economies in transition should be encouraged.

8. Regional, subregional and national organizations, including those affiliated to an international organization already in status, may be admitted provided that they can demonstrate that their programme of work is of direct relevance to the aims and purposes of the United Nations and, in the case of national organizations, after consultation with the Member State concerned. The views expressed by the Member State, if any, shall be communicated to the non-governmental organization concerned, which shall have the opportunity to respond to those views through the Committee on Non-Governmental Organizations.

9. The organization shall be of recognized standing within the particular field of its competence or of a representative character. Where there exist a number of organizations with similar objectives, interests and basic views in a given field, they may, for the purposes of consultation with the Council, form a joint committee or other body authorized to carry on such consultation for the group as a whole.

10. The organization shall have an established headquarters, with an executive officer. It shall have a democratically adopted constitution, a copy of which shall be deposited with the Secretary-General of the United Nations, and which shall provide for the determination of policy by a conference, congress or other representative body, and for an executive organ responsible to the policy-making body.

11. The organization shall have authority to speak for its members through its authorized representatives. Evidence of this authority shall be presented, if requested.

12. The organization shall have a representative structure and possess appropriate mechanisms of accountability to its members, who shall exercise effective control over its policies and actions through the exercise of voting rights or other appropriate democratic and transparent decision-making processes. Any such organization that is not established by a governmental entity or intergovernmental agreement shall be considered a non-governmental organization for the purpose of these arrangements, including organizations that accept members designated by governmental authorities, provided that such membership does not interfere with the free expression of views of the organization.

13. The basic resources of the organization shall be derived in the main part from contributions of the national affiliates or other components or from individual members. Where voluntary contributions have been received, their amounts and donors shall be faithfully revealed to the Council Committee on Non-Governmental Organizations. Where, however, the above criterion is not fulfilled and an organization is financed from other sources, it must explain to the satisfaction of the Committee its reasons for not meeting the requirements laid down in this paragraph. Any financial contribution or other support, direct or indirect, from a Government to the organization shall be openly declared to the Committee through the Secretary-General and fully recorded in the financial and other records of the organization and shall be devoted to purposes in accordance with the aims of the United Nations.

14. In considering the establishment of consultative relations with a non-governmental organization, the Council will take into account whether the field of activity of the organization is wholly or mainly within the field of a specialized agency, and whether or not it could be admitted when it has, or may have, a consultative arrangement with a specialized agency.

15. The granting, suspension and withdrawal of consultative status, as well as the interpretation of norms and decisions relating to this matter, are the prerogative of Member States exercised through the Economic and Social Council and its Committee on Non-Governmental Organizations. A non-governmental organization applying for general or special consultative status or a listing on the Roster shall have the opportunity to respond to any objections being raised in the Committee before the Committee takes its decision.

16. The provisions of the present resolution shall apply to the United Nations regional commissions and their subsidiary bodies mutatis mutandis.

17. In recognizing the evolving relationship between the United Nations and non-governmental organizations, the Economic and Social Council, in consultation with the Committee on Non-Governmental Organizations, will consider reviewing the consultative arrangements as and when necessary to facilitate, in the most effective manner possible, the contributions of non-governmental organizations to the work of the United Nations.

Part II
PRINCIPLES GOVERNING THE NATURE OF THE CONSULTATIVE ARRANGEMENTS

18. A clear distinction is drawn in the Charter of the United Nations between participation without vote in the deliberations of the Council and the arrangements for consultation. Under Articles 69 and 70, participation is provided for only in the case of States not members of the Council, and of specialized agencies. Article 71, applying to non-governmental organizations, provides for suitable arrangements for consultation. This distinction, deliberately made in the Charter, is fundamental and the arrangements for consultation should not be such as to accord to non-governmental organizations the same rights of participation as are accorded to States not members of the Council and to the specialized agencies brought into relationship with the United Nations.
19. The arrangements should not be such as to overburden the Council or transform it from a body for coordination of policy and action, as contemplated in the Charter, into a general forum for discussion.
20. Decisions on arrangements for consultation should be guided by the principle that consultative arrangements are to be made, on the one hand, for the purpose of enabling the Council or one of its bodies to secure expert information or advice from organizations having special competence in the subjects for which consultative arrangements are made, and, on the other hand, to enable international, regional, subregional and national organizations that represent important elements of public opinion to express their views. Therefore, the arrangements for consultation made with each organization should relate to the subjects for which that organization has a special competence or in which it has a special interest. The organizations given consultative status should be limited to those whose activities in fields set out in paragraph 1 above qualify them to make a significant contribution to the work of the Council and should, in sum, as far as possible reflect in a balanced way the major viewpoints or interests in these fields in all areas and regions of the world.

Part III
ESTABLISHMENT OF CONSULTATIVE RELATIONSHIPS

21. In establishing consultative relationships with each organization, regard shall be had to the nature and scope of its activities and to the assistance it may be expected to give to the Council or its subsidiary bodies in carrying out the functions set out in Chapters IX and X of the Charter of the United Nations.
22. Organizations that are concerned with most of the activities of the Council and its subsidiary bodies and can demonstrate to the satisfaction of the Council that they have substantive and sustained contributions to make to the achievement of the objectives of the United Nations in fields set out in paragraph 1 above, and are closely involved with the economic and social life of the peoples of the areas they represent and whose membership, which should be considerable, is broadly representative of major segments of society in a large number of countries in different regions of the world shall be known as organizations in general consultative status.
23. Organizations that have a special competence in, and are concerned specifically with, only a few of the fields of activity covered by the Council and its subsidiary bodies, and that are known within the fields for which they have or seek consultative status shall be known as organizations in special consultative status.
24. Other organizations that do not have general or special consultative status but that the Council, or the Secretary-General of the United Nations in consultation with the Council or its Committee on Non-Governmental Organizations, considers can make occasional and useful contributions to the work of the Council or its subsidiary bodies or other United Nations bodies within their competence shall be included in a list (to be known as the Roster). This list may also include organizations in consultative status or a similar relationship with a specialized agency or a United Nations body. These organizations shall be available for consultation at the request of the Council or its subsidiary bodies. The fact that an organization is on the Roster shall not in itself be regarded as a qualification for general or special consultative status should an organization seek such status.

25. Organizations to be accorded special consultative status because of their interest in the field of human rights should pursue the goals of promotion and protection of human rights in accordance with the spirit of the Charter of the United Nations, the Universal Declaration of Human Rights and the Vienna Declaration and Programme of Action.

26. Major organizations one of whose primary purposes is to promote the aims, objectives and purposes of the United Nations and a furtherance of the understanding of its work may be accorded consultative status.

Part IV

CONSULTATION WITH THE COUNCIL

Provisional agenda

27. The provisional agenda of the Council shall be communicated to organizations in general consultative status and special consultative status and to those on the Roster.

28. Organizations in general consultative status may propose to the Council Committee on Non-Governmental Organizations that the Committee request the Secretary-General to place items of special interest to the organizations in the provisional agenda of the Council.

Attendance at meetings

29. Organizations in general consultative status and special consultative status may designate authorized representatives to sit as observers at public meetings of the Council and its subsidiary bodies. Those on the Roster may have representatives present at such meetings concerned with matters within their field of competence. These attendance arrangements may be supplemented to include other modalities of participation.

Written statements

30. Written statements relevant to the work of the Council may be submitted by organizations in general consultative status and special consultative status on subjects in which these organizations have a special competence. Such statements shall be circulated by the Secretary-General of the United Nations to the members of the Council, except those statements that have become obsolete, for example, those dealing with matters already disposed of and those that had already been circulated in some other form.

31. The following conditions shall be observed regarding the submission and circulation of such statements:

(a) The written statement shall be submitted in one of the official languages;

(b) It shall be submitted in sufficient time for appropriate consultation to take place between the Secretary-General and the organization before circulation;

(c) The organization shall give due consideration to any comments that the Secretary-General may make in the course of such consultation before transmitting the statement in final form;

(d) A written statement submitted by an organization in general consultative status will be circulated in full if it does not exceed 2,000 words. Where a statement is in excess of 2,000 words, the organizations shall submit a summary which will be circulated or shall supply sufficient copies of the full text in the working languages for distribution. A statement will also be circulated in full, however, upon a specific request of the Council or its Committee on Non-Governmental Organizations;

(e) A written statement submitted by an organization in special consultative status or on the Roster will be circulated in full if it does not exceed 500 words. Where a statement is in excess of 500 words, the organization shall submit a summary which will be circulated; such statements will be circulated in full, however, upon a specific request of the Council or its Committee on Non-Governmental Organizations;

(f) The Secretary-General, in consultation with the President of the Council, or the Council or its Committee on Non-Governmental Organizations, may invite organizations on the Roster to submit written statements. The provisions of subparagraphs (a), (b), (c) and (e) above shall apply to such statements;

(g) A written statement or summary, as the case may be, will be circulated by the Secretary-General in the working languages, and, upon the request of a member of the Council, in any of the official languages.

Oral presentations during meetings

32.   (a) The Council Committee on Non-Governmental Organizations shall make recommendations to the Council as to which organizations in general consultative status should make an oral presentation to the Council and on which items they should be heard. Such organizations shall be entitled to make one statement to the Council, subject to the approval of the Council. In the absence of a subsidiary body of the Council with jurisdiction in a major field of interest to the Council and to organizations in special consultative status, the Committee may recommend that organizations in special consultative status be heard by the Council on the subject in its field of interest;

(b) Whenever the Council discusses the substance of an item proposed by a non-governmental organization in general consultative status and included in the agenda of the Council, such an organization shall be entitled to present orally to the Council, as appropriate, an introductory statement of an expository nature. Such an organization may be invited by the President of the Council, with the consent of the relevant body, to make, in the course of the discussion of the item before the Council, an additional statement for purposes of clarification.

Part V

CONSULTATION WITH COMMISSIONS AND OTHER SUBSIDIARY ORGANS OF THE COUNCIL

Provisional agenda

33. The provisional agenda of sessions of commissions and other subsidiary organs of the Council shall be communicated to organizations in general consultative status and special consultative status and those on the Roster.

34. Organizations in general consultative status may propose items for the provisional agenda of commissions, subject to the following conditions:

(a) An organization that intends to propose such an item shall inform the Secretary-General of the United Nations at least 63 days before the commencement of the session and before formally proposing an item shall give due consideration to any comments the Secretary- General may make;

(b) The proposal shall be formally submitted with the relevant basic documentation not later than 49 days before the commencement of the session. The item shall be included in the agenda of the commission if it is adopted by a two-thirds majority of those present and voting.

Attendance at meetings

35. Organizations in general consultative status and special consultative status may designate authorized representatives to sit as observers at public meetings of the commissions and other subsidiary organs of the Council. Organizations on the Roster may have representatives present at such meetings that are concerned with matters within their field of competence. These attendance arrangements may be supplemented to include other modalities of participation.

Written statements

36. Written statements relevant to the work of the commissions or other subsidiary organs may be submitted by organizations in general consultative status and special consultative status on subjects for which these organizations have a special competence. Such statements shall be circulated by the Secretary-General to members of the commission or other subsidiary organs, except those statements that have become obsolete, for example, those dealing with matters already disposed of and those that have already been circulated in some other form to members of the commission or other subsidiary organs.

37. The following conditions shall be observed regarding the submission and circulation of such written statements:

(a) The written statement shall be submitted in one of the official languages;

(b) It shall be submitted in sufficient time for appropriate consultation to take place between the Secretary-General and the organization before circulation;

(c) The organization shall give due consideration to any comments that the Secretary-General may make in the course of such consultation before transmitting the statement in final form;

(d) A written statement submitted by an organization in general consultative status will be circulated in full if it does not exceed 2,000 words. Where a statement is in excess of 2,000 words, the organization shall submit a summary, which will be circulated, or shall supply sufficient copies of the full text in the working languages for distribution. A statement will also be circulated in full, however, upon the specific request of the commission or other subsidiary organs;

(e) A written statement submitted by an organization in special consultative status will be circulated in full if it does not exceed 1,500 words. Where a statement is in excess of 1,500 words, the organization shall submit a summary, which will be circulated, or shall supply sufficient copies of the full text in the working languages for distribution. A statement will also be circulated in full, however, upon the specific request of the commission or other subsidiary organs;

(f) The Secretary-General, in consultation with the chairman of the relevant commission or other subsidiary organ, or the commission or other subsidiary organ itself, may invite organizations on the Roster to submit written statements. The provisions in subparagraphs (a), (b), (c) and (e) above shall apply to such statements;

(g) A written statement or summary, as the case may be, will be circulated by the Secretary-General in the working languages and, upon the request of a member of the commission or other subsidiary organ, in any of the official languages.

Oral presentations during meetings

38.   (a) The commission or other subsidiary organs may consult with organizations in general consultative status and special consultative status either directly or through a committee or committees established for the purpose. In all cases, such consultations may be arranged upon the request of the organization;

(b) On the recommendation of the Secretary-General and at the request of the commission or other subsidiary organs, organizations on the Roster may also be heard by the commission or other subsidiary organs.

Special studies

39. Subject to the relevant rules of procedure on financial implications, a commission or other subsidiary organ may recommend that an organization that has special competence in a particular field should undertake specific studies or investigations or prepare specific papers for the commission. The limitations of paragraphs 37 (d) and (e) above shall not apply in this case.

Part VI
CONSULTATIONS WITH AD HOC COMMITTEES OF THE COUNCIL

40. The arrangements for consultation between ad hoc committees of the Council authorized to meet between sessions of the Council and organizations in general consultative status and special consultative status and on the Roster shall follow those approved for commissions of the Council, unless the Council or the committee decides otherwise.

Part VII
PARTICIPATION OF NON-GOVERNMENTAL ORGANIZATIONS IN INTERNATIONAL CONFERENCES CONVENED BY THE UNITED NATIONS AND THEIR PREPARATORY PROCESS

41. Where non-governmental organizations have been invited to participate in an international conference convened by the United Nations, their accreditation is the prerogative of Member States, exercised through the respective preparatory committee. Such accreditation should be preceded by an appropriate process to determine their eligibility.

42. Non-governmental organizations in general consultative status, special consultative status and on the Roster, that express their wish to attend the relevant international conferences convened by the United Nations and the meetings of the preparatory bodies of the said conferences shall as a rule be accredited for participation. Other non-governmental organizations wishing to be accredited may apply to the secretariat of the conference for this purpose in accordance with the following requirements.

43. The secretariat of the conference shall be responsible for the receipt and preliminary evaluation of requests from non-governmental organizations for accreditation to the conference and its preparatory process. In the discharge of its functions, the secretariat of the conference shall work in close cooperation and coordination with the Non-Governmental Organizations Section of the Secretariat, and shall be guided by the relevant provisions of Council resolution 1296 (XLIV) as updated.

44. All such applications must be accompanied by information on the competence of the organization and the relevance of its activities to the work of the conference and its preparatory committee, with an indication of the particular areas of the conference agenda and preparations to which such competence and relevance pertain, and should include, inter alia, the following information:

      (a) The purpose of the organization;

      (b) Information as to the programmes and activities of the organization in areas relevant to the conference and its preparatory process and the country or countries in which they are carried out. Non-governmental organizations seeking accreditation shall be asked to confirm their interest in the goals and objectives of the conference;

      (c) Confirmation of the activities of the organization at the national, regional or international level;

      (d) Copies of the annual or other reports of the organization with financial statements, and a list of financial sources and contributions, including governmental contributions;

      (e) A list of members of the governing body of the organization and their countries of nationality;

      (f) A description of the membership of the organization, indicating the total number of members, the names of organizations that are members and their geographical distribution;

      (g) A copy of the constitution and/or by-laws of the organization.

45. In the evaluation of the relevance of applications of non-governmental organizations for accreditation to the conference and its preparatory process, it is agreed that a determination shall be made based on their background and involvement in the subject areas of the conference.

46. The secretariat shall publish and disseminate to Member States on a periodic basis the updated list of applications received. Member States may submit comments on any of the applications on the list 14 days from receipt of the above-mentioned list by Member States. The comments of Member States shall be communicated to the non-governmental organization concerned, which shall have the opportunity to respond.

47. In cases where the secretariat believes, on the basis of the information provided in accordance with the present resolution, that the organization has established its competence and the relevance of its activities to the work of the preparatory committee, it shall recommend to the preparatory committee that the organization be accredited. In cases where the secretariat does not recommend the granting of accreditation, it shall make available to the preparatory committee its reasons for not doing so. The secretariat should ensure that its recommendations are available to members of the preparatory committee at least one week prior to the start of each session. The secretariat must notify such applicants of the reasons for non-recommendation and provide an opportunity to respond to objections and furnish additional information as may be required.

48. The preparatory committee shall decide on all recommendations for accreditation within 24 hours after the recommendations of the secretariat have been taken up by the preparatory committee in plenary meeting. In the event of a decision not being taken within this period, interim accreditation shall be accorded until such time as a decision is taken.

49. A non-governmental organization that has been granted accreditation to attend a session of the preparatory committee, including related preparatory meetings of regional commissions, may attend all its future sessions, as well as the conference itself.

50. In recognition of the intergovernmental nature of the conference and its preparatory process, active participation of non-governmental organizations therein, while welcome, does not entail a negotiating role.

51. The non-governmental organizations accredited to the international conference may be given, in accordance with established United Nations practice and at the discretion of the chairperson and the consent of the body concerned, an opportunity to briefly address the preparatory committee and the conference in plenary meetings and their subsidiary bodies.

52. Non-governmental organizations accredited to the conference may make written presentations during the preparatory process in the official languages of the United Nations as they deem appropriate. Those written presentations shall not be issued as official documents except in accordance with United Nations rules of procedure.

53. Non-governmental organizations without consultative status that participate in international conferences and wish to obtain consultative status later on should apply through the normal procedures established under Council resolution 1296 (XLIV) as updated. Recognizing the importance of the participation of non-governmental organizations that attend a conference in the follow-up process, the Committee on Non-Governmental Organizations, in considering their application, shall draw upon the documents already submitted by that organization for accreditation to the conference and any additional information submitted

by the non-governmental organization supporting its interest, relevance and capacity to contribute to the implementation phase. The Committee shall review such applications as expeditiously as possible so as to allow participation of the respective organization in the implementation phase of the conference. In the interim, the Economic and Social Council shall decide on the participation of non-governmental organizations accredited to an international conference in the work of the relevant functional commission on the follow-up to and implementation of that conference.

54. The suspension and withdrawal of the accreditation of non-governmental organizations to United Nations international conferences at all stages shall be guided by the relevant provisions of the present resolution.

Part VIII
SUSPENSION AND WITHDRAWAL OF CONSULTATIVE STATUS

55. Organizations granted consultative status by the Council and those on the Roster shall conform at all times to the principles governing the establishment and nature of their consultative relations with the Council. In periodically reviewing the activities of non-governmental organizations on the basis of the reports submitted under paragraph 61 (c) below and other relevant information, the Council Committee on Non-Governmental Organizations shall determine the extent to which the organizations have complied with the principles governing consultative status and have contributed to the work of the Council, and may recommend to the Council suspension of or exclusion from consultative status of organizations that have not met the requirements for consultative status as set forth in the present resolution.

56. In cases where the Committee on Non-Governmental Organizations has decided to recommend that the general or special consultative status of a non-governmental organization or its listing on the Roster be suspended or withdrawn, the non-governmental organization concerned shall be given written reasons for that decision and shall have an opportunity to present its response for appropriate consideration by the Committee as expeditiously as possible.

57. The consultative status of non-governmental organizations with the Economic and Social Council and the listing of those on the Roster shall be suspended up to three years or withdrawn in the following cases:

(a) If an organization, either directly or through its affiliates or representatives acting on its behalf, clearly abuses its status by engaging in a pattern of acts contrary to the purposes and principles of the Charter of the United Nations including unsubstantiated or politically motivated acts against Member States of the United Nations incompatible with those purposes and principles;

(b) If there exists substantiated evidence of influence from proceeds resulting from internationally recognized criminal activities such as the illicit drugs trade, money-laundering or the illegal arms trade;

(c) If, within the preceding three years, an organization did not make any positive or effective contribution to the work of the United Nations and, in particular, of the Council or its commissions or other subsidiary organs.

58. The consultative status of organizations in general consultative status and special consultative status and the listing of those on the Roster shall be suspended or withdrawn by the decision of the Economic and Social Council on the recommendation of its Committee on Non-Governmental Organizations.

59. An organization whose consultative status or whose listing on the Roster is withdrawn may be entitled to reapply for consultative status or for inclusion on the Roster not sooner than three years after the effective date of such withdrawal.

Part IX
COUNCIL COMMITTEE ON NON-GOVERNMENTAL ORGANIZATIONS

60. The members of the Committee on Non-Governmental Organizations shall be elected by the Council on the basis of equitable geographical representation, in accordance with the relevant Council resolutions and decisions and rules of procedure of the Council. The Committee shall elect its Chairman and other officers as necessary.

61. The functions of the Committee shall include the following:

(a) The Committee shall be responsible for regular monitoring of the evolving relationship between non-governmental organizations and the United Nations. With a view to fulfilling this responsibility, the Committee shall hold, before each of its sessions, and at other times as necessary, consultations with organizations in consultative status to discuss questions of interest to the Committee or to the organizations relating to the relationship between the non-governmental organizations and the United Nations. A report on such consultations shall be transmitted to the Council for appropriate action;

(b) The Committee shall hold its regular session before the substantive session of the Council each year and preferably before the sessions of functional commissions of the Council to consider applications for general consultative status and special consultative status and for listing on the Roster made by non-governmental organizations and requests for changes in status, and to make recommendations thereon to the Council. Upon approval by the Council, the Committee may hold other meetings as required to fulfil its mandated responsibilities. Organizations shall give due consideration to any comments on technical matters that the Secretary-General of the United Nations may make in receiving such applications for the Committee. The Committee shall consider at each such session applications received by the Secretary-General not later than 1 June of the preceding year, on which sufficient data have been distributed to the members of the Committee not later than six weeks before the applications are to be considered. Transitional arrangements, if possible, may be made during the current year only. Reapplication by an organization for status, or a request for a change in status, shall be considered by the Committee at the earliest at its first session in the second year following the session at which the substance of the previous application or request was considered, unless at the time of such consideration it was decided otherwise;

(c) Organizations in general consultative status and special consultative status shall submit to the Council Committee on Non-Governmental Organizations through the Secretary-General every fourth year a brief report of their activities, specifically as regards the support they have given to the work of the United Nations. Based on findings of the Committee's examination of the report and other relevant information, the Committee may recommend to the Council any reclassification in status of the organization concerned as it deems appropriate. However, under exceptional circumstances, the Committee may ask for such a report from an individual organization in general consultative status or special consultative status or on the Roster, between the regular reporting dates;

(d) The Committee may consult, in connection with sessions of the Council or at such other times as it may decide, with organizations in general consultative status and special consultative status on matters within their competence, other than items in the agenda of the Council, on which the Council or the Committee or the organization requests consultation. The Committee shall report to the Council on such consultations;

(e) The Committee may consult, in connection with any particular session of the Council, with organizations in general consultative status and special consultative status on matters within the competence of the organizations concerning specific items already in the provisional agenda of the Council on which the Council or the Committee or the organization requests consultation, and shall make recommendations as to which organizations, subject to the provisions of paragraph 32 (a) above, should be heard by the Council or the appropriate committee and regarding which subjects should be heard. The Committee shall report to the Council on such consultations;

(f) The Committee shall consider matters concerning non-governmental organizations that may be referred to it by the Council or by commissions;

(g) The Committee shall consult with the Secretary-General, as appropriate, on matters affecting the consultative arrangements under Article 71 of the Charter, and arising therefrom;

(h) An organization that applies for consultative status should attest that it has been in existence for at least two years as at the date of receipt of the application by the Secretariat. Evidence of such existence shall be furnished to the Secretariat.

62. The Committee, in considering a request from a non-governmental organization in general consultative status that an item be placed in the agenda of the Council, shall take into account, among other things:

(a) The adequacy of the documentation submitted by the organization;

(b) The extent to which it is considered that the item lends itself to early and constructive action by the Council;

(c) The possibility that the item might be more appropriately dealt with elsewhere than in the Council.

63. Any decision by the Council Committee on Non-Governmental Organizations not to grant a request submitted by a non-governmental organization in general consultative status that an item be placed in the provisional agenda of the Council shall be considered final unless the Council decides otherwise.

Part X
CONSULTATION WITH THE SECRETARIAT

64. The Secretariat should be so organized as to enable it to carry out the duties assigned to it concerning the consultative arrangements and the accreditation of non-governmental organizations to United Nations international conferences as set forth in the present resolution.

65. All organizations in consultative relationship shall be able to consult with officers of the appropriate sections of the Secretariat on matters in which there is a mutual interest or a mutual concern. Such consultation shall be upon the request of the non-governmental organization or upon the request of the Secretary-General of the United Nations.

66. The Secretary-General may request organizations in general consultative status and special consultative status and those on the Roster to carry out specific studies or prepare specific papers, subject to the relevant financial regulations.

67. The Secretary-General shall be authorized, within the means at his disposal, to offer to non-governmental organizations in consultative relationship facilities that include:

    (a) Prompt and efficient distribution of such documents of the Council and its subsidiary bodies as shall in the judgement of the Secretary-General be appropriate;

    (b) Access to the press documentation services provided by the United Nations;

    (c) Arrangement of informal discussions on matters of special interest to groups or organizations;

    (d) Use of the libraries of the United Nations;

    (e) Provision of accommodation for conferences or smaller meetings of consultative organizations on the work of the Economic and Social Council;

    (f) Appropriate seating arrangements and facilities for obtaining documents during public meetings of the General Assembly dealing with matters in the economic, social and related fields.

Part XI
SECRETARIAT SUPPORT

68. Adequate Secretariat support shall be required for fulfilment of the mandate defined for the Committee on Non-Governmental Organizations with respect to carrying out the wider range of activities in which the enhanced involvement of non-governmental organizations is envisaged. The Secretary-General is requested to provide the necessary resources for this purpose and to take steps for improving the coordination within the Secretariat of units dealing with non-governmental organizations.

69. The Secretary-General is requested to make every effort to enhance and streamline as appropriate Secretariat support arrangements, and to improve practical arrangements on such matters as greater use of modern information and communication technology, establishment of an integrated database of non-governmental organizations, wide and timely dissemination of information on meetings, distribution of documentation, provision of access and transparent, simple and streamlined procedures for the attendance of non-governmental organizations in United Nations meetings, and to facilitate their broad-based participation.

70. The Secretary-General is requested to make the present resolution widely known, through proper channels, to facilitate the involvement of non-governmental organizations from all regions and areas of the world.

SET OF PRINCIPLES FOR THE PROTECTION AND PROMOTION OF HUMAN RIGHTS THROUGH ACTION TO COMBAT IMPUNITY

U.N. Comm'n on Human Rights, Sub-Comm'n on Prevention of Discrimination and Protection of Minorities, *The Administration of Justice and Human Rights of Detainees, Question of the Impunity of Perpetrators of Human Rights Violations (Civil and Political)*, Annex II, U.N. Doc. E/CN.4/SUB.2/1997/20/REV.1 (Oct. 2, 1997) (*prepared by* Louis Joinet)

PREAMBLE

The General Assembly,

Recalling the Preamble of the Universal Declaration of Human Rights, which states that disregard and contempt for human rights have resulted in barbarous acts which have outraged the conscience of mankind,

Aware that there is always a risk that such acts may reoccur,

Reaffirming the commitment made by the Member States under Article 56 of the Charter of the United Nations to take joint and separate action, giving full importance to developing effective international cooperation for the achievement of the purposes set forth in Article 55 of the Charter concerning universal respect for, and observance of, human rights and fundamental freedoms for all,

Considering that the duty of every State under international law to respect and to secure respect for human rights requires that effective measures should be taken to combat impunity,

Aware that there can be no just and lasting reconciliation unless the need for justice is effectively satisfied,

Equally aware that forgiveness, which may be an important factor of reconciliation, implies, insofar as it is a private act, that the victim or the victim's beneficiaries know the perpetrator of the violations and that the latter has recognized the deeds and shown repentance,

Recalling the recommendation contained in paragraph 91 of Part II of the Vienna Declaration and Programme of Action, wherein the World Conference on Human Rights (June 1993) expressed its concern about the impunity of perpetrators of human rights violations and encouraged the efforts of the Commission on Human Rights and the Sub-Commission on Prevention of Discrimination and Protection of Minorities to examine all aspects of the issue,

Convinced, therefore, that national and international measures must be taken for that purpose with a view to securing jointly, in the interests of the victims of human rights violations, observance of the right to know and, by implication, the right to the truth, the right to justice and the right to reparation, without which there can be no effective remedy against the pernicious effects of impunity,

Decides, pursuant to the Vienna Declaration and Programme of Action, solemnly to proclaim the following principles for the guidance of States engaged in combating impunity.

DEFINITIONS

A. "Impunity" means the impossibility, *de jure* or de facto, of bringing the perpetrators of human rights violations to account - whether in criminal, civil, administrative or disciplinary proceedings - since they are not subject to any inquiry that might lead to their being accused, arrested, tried and, if found guilty, sentenced to appropriate penalties, and to making reparations to their victims.

B. Serious crimes under international law. This term, as used in these principles, covers war crimes, crimes against humanity, including genocide, and grave breaches of international humanitarian law.

C. Restoration of or transition to democracy and/or peace. This expression, as used in these principles, refers to situations leading, within the framework of a national movement towards democracy or peace negotiations aimed at ending an armed conflict, to an agreement, in whatever form, by which the actors or parties concerned agree to take measures against impunity and the recurrence of human rights violations.

I. THE RIGHT TO KNOW

A. General principles

PRINCIPLE 1. THE INALIENABLE RIGHT TO THE TRUTH
Every people has the inalienable right to know the truth about past events and about the circumstances and reasons which led, through systematic, gross violations of human rights, to the perpetration of heinous crimes. Full and effective exercise of the right to the truth is essential to avoid any recurrence of violations in the future.

PRINCIPLE 2. THE DUTY TO REMEMBER
A people's knowledge of the history of its oppression is part of its heritage and, as such, must be preserved by appropriate measures in fulfilment of the State's duty to remember. Such measures shall be aimed at preserving the collective memory from extinction and, in particular, at guarding against the development of revisionist and negationist arguments.

PRINCIPLE 3. THE VICTIMS' RIGHT TO KNOW
Irrespective of any legal proceedings, victims, their families and relatives have the imprescriptible right to know the truth about the circumstances in which violations took place and, in the event of death or disappearance, the victim's fate.

PRINCIPLE 4. GUARANTEES TO GIVE EFFECT TO THE RIGHT TO KNOW
States must take appropriate action to give effect to the right to know. If judicial institutions are wanting in that respect, priority should initially be given to establishing extrajudicial commissions of inquiry and to ensuring the preservation of, and access to, the archives concerned.

B. Extrajudicial Commissions of Inquiry

PRINCIPLE 5. ROLE OF THE EXTRAJUDICIAL COMMISSIONS OF INQUIRY
Extrajudicial commissions of inquiry shall have the task of establishing the facts so that the truth may be ascertained, and of preventing the disappearance of evidence.

In order to restore the dignity of victims, families and human rights advocates, these investigations shall be conducted with the object of securing recognition of such parts of the truth as were formerly constantly denied.

PRINCIPLE 6. GUARANTEES OF INDEPENDENCE AND IMPARTIALITY
In order to found their legitimacy upon incontestable guarantees of independence and impartiality, the terms of reference of the commissions, even when they are international in character, must respect the following principles:

(a) Commissions shall be established by law. If the process of the restoration of or transition to democracy and/or peace has begun, commissions may be established by an act of general application or treaty clause concluding a process of national dialogue or a peace accord;

(b) They shall be constituted in accordance with criteria making clear to the public the competence in the field of human rights and the impartiality of their members and on conditions ensuring their independence, in particular by the irremovability of their members for the duration of their terms of office;

(c) Their members shall enjoy whatever privileges and immunities are necessary for their safety, including in the period following their mission, especially in respect of any defamation proceedings or other civil or criminal action brought against them on the grounds of facts or opinions contained in the report.

PRINCIPLE 7. DEFINITION OF THE COMMISSIONS' TERMS OF REFERENCE
To avoid conflicts of jurisdiction, the commissions' terms of reference must be clearly defined. They shall incorporate at least the following stipulations and limitations:

(a) The commissions are not intended to act as substitutes for the civil, administrative or criminal courts, which shall alone have jurisdiction to establish individual criminal or other responsibility, with a view as appropriate to passing judgement and imposing a sentence;

(b) The conditions subject to which they may seek the assistance of law enforcement authorities, if required, including for the purpose, subject to the terms of principle 9 (a), of calling for testimonies, or inspect any places concerned in their investigations, or call for the delivery of relevant documents;

(c) If the commissions have reason to believe that the life, health or safety of a person concerned by their inquiry is threatened or that there is a risk of losing an element of proof, they may seek court action, under an emergency procedure, to end such threat or risk;

(d) Their investigations shall relate to all persons cited in allegations of human rights violations, whether they ordered them or actually committed them, acting as perpetrators or accomplices, and whether they are public officials or members of quasi-governmental or private armed groups with any kind of link to the State, or of non-governmental armed movements having the status of belligerents. Their investigations may also extend to crimes allegedly committed by any other organized, armed, non-governmental group;

(e) The Commissions shall have jurisdiction to consider all forms of human rights violations. Their investigations shall focus as a matter of priority on those violations which constitute serious crimes under international law, and shall pay particular attention to violations of the basic rights of women. They shall endeavour:

(i) To analyse and describe the State mechanisms of the violating system, and to identify the victims and the administrations, agencies and private entities implicated by retracing their roles;
(ii) To safeguard evidence for later use in the administration of justice.

PRINCIPLE 8. GUARANTEES FOR PERSONS IMPLICATED

Any persons implicated when the facts are established shall be entitled, especially if the commission is permitted under its terms of reference to divulge their names, to the following guarantees based on the adversarial principle:

(a) The commission must try to corroborate any information gathered by other sources;

(b) The person implicated shall, after being heard or having at least been convened to a hearing, have the opportunity to make a statement setting out his or her version of the facts or, within the time prescribed by the instrument establishing the commission, to submit a document equivalent to a right of reply for inclusion in the file. The rules of evidence provided for in principle 16 (c) shall apply.

PRINCIPLE 9. GUARANTEES FOR VICTIMS AND WITNESSES TESTIFYING ON THEIR BEHALF

Steps shall be taken to ensure the security and protection of victims and witnesses testifying on their behalf:

(a) They may be called upon to testify before the commission only on a strictly voluntary basis;

(b) If anonymity is deemed necessary in their interests, it may be allowed only on three conditions, namely:

(i) That it is an exceptional measure, except in the case of victims of aggression or sexual assault;
(ii) That the chairman and one member of the commission are entitled to verify that the request for anonymity is warranted and to ascertain, in confidence, the identity of the witness, so as to be able to give assurances to the other members of the Commission;
(iii) That the report will normally refer to the gist of the testimony if it is accepted by the commission;

(c) As far as possible, social workers and mental health-care practitioners shall be authorized to assist victims, preferably in their own language, both during and after their testimony, especially in cases of aggression or sexual assault;

(d) All expenses incurred by those giving testimony shall be borne by the State.

PRINCIPLE 10. OPERATION OF THE COMMISSIONS

The commissions shall be provided with:

(a) Transparent funding to ensure that their independence is never in doubt;

(b) Sufficient material and human resources to ensure that their credibility is never in doubt.

PRINCIPLE 11. ADVISORY FUNCTIONS OF THE COMMISSIONS

The commissions' terms of reference shall include provisions calling for them to make recommendations on action to combat impunity in their final report.

These recommendations shall contain proposals aimed:

On the basis of the facts and responsibilities established, at encouraging the perpetrators of violations to admit their guilt;

At inviting the Government to accede to any relevant international instruments it has not yet ratified;

At setting out legislative or other measures to put this set of principles into effect and to prevent any recurrence of violations. These measures shall primarily concern the army, police and judicial system and the strengthening of democratic institutions, and, where applicable, reparation for violations of the fundamental rights of women and prevention of their recurrence.

PRINCIPLE 12. PUBLICIZING THE COMMISSIONS' REPORTS

For security reasons or in order to avoid pressure on witnesses and commission members, the commissions' terms of reference may stipulate that the inquiry shall be kept confidential. The final report, on the other hand, shall be made public in full and shall be disseminated as widely as possible.

C. Preservation of and access to archives bearing witness to violations

PRINCIPLE 13. MEASURES FOR THE PRESERVATION OF ARCHIVES

The right to know implies that archives should be preserved. Technical measures and penalties shall be applied to prevent any removal, destruction, concealment or falsification of archives, especially for the purpose of ensuring the impunity of perpetrators of human rights violations.

PRINCIPLE 14. MEASURES FOR FACILITATING ACCESS TO ARCHIVES

Access to archives shall be facilitated in order to enable victims and persons related to claim their rights.

Access should also be facilitated, as necessary, for persons implicated, who request it for their defence.

When access is requested in the interest of historical research, authorization formalities shall normally be intended only to monitor access and may not be used for purposes of censorship.

PRINCIPLE 15. COOPERATION BETWEEN ARCHIVE DEPARTMENTS AND THE COURTS AND EXTRAJUDICIAL COMMISSIONS OF INQUIRY

The courts and extrajudicial commissions of inquiry, as well as the investigators reporting to them, must have free access to archives. Considerations of national security may not be invoked to prevent access. By virtue of their sovereign power of discretion, however, the courts and extrajudicial commissions of inquiry may decide, in exceptional circumstances, not to make certain information public if such publication might jeopardize the preservation or restoration of the rule of law.

PRINCIPLE 16. SPECIFIC MEASURES RELATING TO ARCHIVES CONTAINING NAMES

(a) For the purposes of this principle, archives containing names shall be understood to be those archives containing information that make it possible, in any way whatsoever, directly or indirectly, to identify the individuals to whom they relate, regardless of whether such archives are on paper or in computer files.

(b) All persons shall be entitled to know whether their name appears in the archives and, if it does, by virtue of their right of access, to challenge the validity of the information concerning them by exercising a right of reply. The document containing their own version shall be attached to the document challenged.

(c) Except where it relates to top officials and established staff of those services, information relating to individuals which appears in intelligence service archives shall not by itself constitute incriminating evidence, unless it is corroborated by several other reliable sources.

PRINCIPLE 17. SPECIFIC MEASURES RELATED TO THE RESTORATION OF OR TRANSITION TO DEMOCRACY AND/OR PEACE

(a) Measures shall be taken to place each archive centre under the responsibility of a specifically designated person. If that person was already in charge of the archive centre, he or she must be explicitly reappointed by special decision, subject to the modalities and guarantees provided in principle 41;

(b) Priority shall initially be given to inventorying stored archives and to ascertaining the reliability of existing inventories. Special attention shall be given to archives relating to places of detention, in particular when the existence of such places was not officially recognized;

(c) The inventory shall be extended to relevant archives held by third countries, who shall be expected to cooperate with a view to communicating or restituting archives for the purpose of establishing the truth.

II. RIGHT TO JUSTICE

A. General principles

PRINCIPLE 18. DUTIES OF STATES WITH REGARD TO THE ADMINISTRATION OF JUSTICE

Impunity arises from a failure by States to meet their obligations to investigate violations, to take appropriate measures in respect of the perpetrators, particularly in the area of justice, by ensuring that they are prosecuted, tried and duly punished, to provide victims with effective remedies and reparation for the injuries suffered, and to take steps to prevent any recurrence of such violations.

Although the decision to prosecute lies primarily within the competence of the State, supplementary procedural rules should be introduced to enable victims to institute proceedings, on either an individual or a collective basis, where the authorities fail to do so, particularly as civil plaintiffs. This option should be extended to non-governmental organizations with recognized long-standing activities on behalf of the victims concerned.

B. Distribution of jurisdiction between national, foreign and international courts

PRINCIPLE 19. JURISDICTION OF INTERNATIONAL CRIMINAL COURTS

It shall remain the rule that national courts normally have jurisdiction. An international criminal court may have concurrent jurisdiction where national courts cannot yet offer satisfactory guarantees of independence and impartiality, or are physically unable to function.

In such an event, the international criminal court may at any point in the proceedings require the national court to relinquish a case to it.

PRINCIPLE 20. JURISDICTION OF FOREIGN COURTS

The jurisdiction of foreign courts may be exercised by virtue either of a universal jurisdiction clause contained in a treaty in force or of a provision of domestic law establishing a rule of extraterritorial jurisdiction for serious crimes under international law.

PRINCIPLE 21. MEASURES FOR STRENGTHENING THE EFFECTIVENESS OF TREATY CLAUSES CONCERNING UNIVERSAL JURISDICTION

(a) An appropriate clause concerning universal jurisdiction should be included in all relevant international human rights instruments.

(b) In ratifying such instruments, States shall undertake, by the effect of that clause, to seek out and prosecute persons against whom there are specific, consistent accusations of violations of human rights principles laid down in those instruments, with a view to bringing them to trial or extraditing them. They are consequently bound to take legislative or other measures under domestic law to ensure the implementation of the clause on universal jurisdiction.

PRINCIPLE 22. MEASURES FOR DETERMINING EXTRATERRITORIAL JURISDICTION IN DOMESTIC LAW

In the absence of ratification making it possible to apply a universal jurisdiction clause to the country where a violation was committed, States may take practical measures in their domestic legislation to establish extraterritorial jurisdiction over serious crimes under international law committed outside their territory, which by their nature fall within the scope not only of domestic criminal law but also of an international punitive system which disregards the concept of frontiers.

C. Restrictions on rules of law justified by action to combat impunity

PRINCIPLE 23. NATURE OF RESTRICTIVE MEASURES

Safeguards must be introduced against any abuse for purposes of impunity of rules pertaining to prescription, amnesty, right to asylum, refusal to extradite, absence of <u>in absentia</u> procedure, due obedience, repentance, the jurisdiction of military courts and the irremovability of judges.

PRINCIPLE 24: RESTRICTIONS ON PRESCRIPTION

Prescription - of prosecution or penalty - in criminal cases shall not run for such period as no effective remedy is available.

Prescription shall not apply to serious crimes under international law, which are by their nature imprescriptible.

When it does apply, prescription shall not be effective against civil or administrative actions brought by victims seeking reparation for their injuries.

PRINCIPLE 25. RESTRICTIONS AND OTHER MEASURES RELATING TO AMNESTY

Even when intended to establish conditions conducive to a peace agreement or to foster national reconciliation, amnesty and other measures of clemency shall be kept within the following bounds:

(a) The perpetrators of serious crimes under international law may not benefit from such measures until such time as the State has met the obligations referred to in principle 18;

(b) They shall be without effect with respect to the victims' right to reparation, as referred to in principles 33 to 36;

(c) Insofar as it may be interpreted as an admission of guilt, amnesty cannot be imposed on individuals prosecuted or sentenced for acts connected with the peaceful exercise of their right to freedom of opinion and expression. When they have merely exercised this legitimate right, as guaranteed by articles 18 to 20 of the Universal Declaration of Human Rights and 18, 19, 21 and 22 of the International Covenant on Civil and Political Rights, the law shall consider any judicial or other decision concerning them to be null and void; their detention shall be ended unconditionally and without delay;

(d) Any individual convicted of offences other than those referred to in paragraph (c) of this principle who comes within the scope of an amnesty is entitled to refuse it and request a retrial, if he or she has been tried without benefit of the right to a fair hearing guaranteed by articles 10 and 11 of the Universal Declaration of Human Rights and articles 9, 14 and 15 of the International Covenant on Civil and Political Rights, or if he or she has been subjected to inhuman or degrading interrogation, especially under torture.

PRINCIPLE 26. RESTRICTIONS ON THE RIGHT OF ASYLUM

Under article 1, paragraph 2, of the Declaration on Territorial Asylum, adopted by the General Assembly on 14 December 1967, and article 1 F of the Convention relating to the Status of Refugees of 28 July 1951, States may not extend such protective status, including diplomatic asylum, to persons with respect to whom there are serious reasons to believe that they have committed a serious crime under international law.

PRINCIPLE 27. RESTRICTIONS ON EXTRADITION

Persons who have committed serious crimes under international law may not, in order to avoid extradition, avail themselves of the favourable provisions generally relating to political offences or of the principle of non-extradition of nationals. Extradition should always be denied, however, especially by abolitionist countries, if the individual concerned risks the death penalty in the requesting country.

PRINCIPLE 28. RESTRICTIONS ON THE EXCLUSION OF IN ABSENTIA PROCEDURE

In order to avoid establishing a guarantee of impunity, non-recognition of in absentia procedure by a legal system should be limited to the judgement stage, so that the necessary investigations, including the hearing of witnesses and victims, may be carried out and charges may be preferred, followed by wanted notices and arrest warrants, if necessary international, executed according to the procedures laid down in the Constitution of the International Criminal Police Organization (ICPO - Interpol).

PRINCIPLE 29. RESTRICTIONS ON JUSTIFICATIONS RELATED TO DUE OBEDIENCE

(a) The fact that the perpetrator of violations acted on the orders of his Government or of a superior does not exempt him from criminal or other responsibility but may be regarded as grounds for reducing the sentence, if applicable.

(b) The fact that violations have been committed by a subordinate does not exempt that subordinate's superiors from criminal or other responsibility if they knew or had at the time reason to believe that the subordinate was committing or about to commit such a crime and they did not take all action within their power to prevent or punish the crime. The official status of the perpetrator of a crime under international law - even if acting as head of State or government - does not exempt him or her from criminal responsibility and is not grounds for a reduction of sentence.

PRINCIPLE 30. RESTRICTIONS ON THE EFFECTS OF LEGISLATION ON REPENTANCE RELATED TO THE RESTORATION OF OR TRANSITION TO DEMOCRACY AND/OR PEACE

The fact that, once the period of persecution is over, a perpetrator discloses the violations that he or others have committed in order to benefit from the favourable provisions of legislation on repentance cannot exempt him or her from criminal or other responsibility. The disclosure may only provide grounds for a reduction of sentence in order to encourage revelation of the truth.

When disclosures were made during the period of persecution, the reduction of sentence may be extended to absolute discharge on grounds of the risks the person ran at the time. In that case, principle 26 notwithstanding, the person making the disclosure may be granted asylum - not refugee status - in order to facilitate revelation of the truth.

PRINCIPLE 31. RESTRICTIONS ON THE JURISDICTION OF MILITARY COURTS

In order to avoid military courts, in those countries where they have not yet been abolished, helping to perpetuate impunity owing to a lack of independence resulting from the chain of command to which all or some of their members are subject, their jurisdiction must be restricted solely to specifically military offences committed by military personnel, to the exclusion of human rights violations, which shall come under the jurisdiction of the ordinary domestic courts or, where appropriate, in the case of serious crimes under international law, that of an international criminal court.

PRINCIPLE 32. RESTRICTIONS ON THE PRINCIPLE OF THE IRREMOVABILITY OF JUDGES

The principle of irremovability, as the basic guarantee of the independence of judges, must be observed in respect of judges who have been appointed in conformity with the rule of law. Conversely, judges unlawfully appointed or who derive their judicial power from an act of allegiance may be relieved of their functions by law in accordance with the principle of parallelism. They may ask to be afforded the guarantees laid down in principles 41 and 42, in particular with a view to seeking reinstatement, where applicable.

III. RIGHT TO REPARATION

A. General principles

PRINCIPLE 33. RIGHTS AND DUTIES ARISING OUT OF THE OBLIGATION TO MAKE REPARATION

Any human rights violation gives rise to a right to reparation on the part of the victim or his or her beneficiaries, implying a duty on the part of the State to make reparation and the possibility for the victim to seek redress from the perpetrator.

PRINCIPLE 34. REPARATION PROCEDURES

All victims shall have access to a readily available, prompt and effective remedy in the form of criminal, civil, administrative or disciplinary proceedings subject to the restrictions on prescription set out in principle 24. In exercising this right, they shall be afforded protection against intimidation and reprisals.

Exercise of the right to reparation includes access to the applicable international procedures.

PRINCIPLE 35. PUBLICIZING REPARATION PROCEDURES

Ad hoc procedures enabling victims to exercise their right to reparation should be given the widest possible publicity by private as well as public communication media. Such dissemination should take place both within and outside the country, including through consular services, particularly in countries to which large numbers of victims have been forced into exile.

PRINCIPLE 36. SCOPE OF THE RIGHT TO REPARATION

The right to reparation shall cover all injuries suffered by the victim; it shall include individual measures concerning the right to restitution, compensation and rehabilitation, and general measures of satisfaction as provided by the set of basic principles and rules concerning the right to reparation (see paragraph 41 above).

In the case of forced disappearances, when the fate of the disappeared person has become known, that person's family has the imprescriptible right to be informed thereof and, in the event of decease, the person's body must be returned to the family as soon as it has been identified, whether the perpetrators have been identified, prosecuted or tried or not.

B. Guarantees of non-recurrence of violations

PRINCIPLE 37. AREAS AFFECTED BY GUARANTEES OF NON-RECURRENCE

The State shall take appropriate measures to ensure that the victims do not again have to endure violations which harm their dignity. Priority consideration shall be given to:

(a) Measures to disband parastatal armed groups;

(b) Measures repealing emergency provisions, legislative or otherwise, which are conducive to violations;

(c) Administrative or other measures against State officials implicated in gross human rights violations.

PRINCIPLE 38. DISBANDMENT OF UNOFFICIAL ARMED GROUPS DIRECTLY OR INDIRECTLY LINKED TO THE STATE AND OF PRIVATE GROUPS BENEFITING FROM THE A STATE'S PASSIVITY

In order to ensure the effective disbandment of such groups, especially in the event of attempts to ensure the restoration of or transition to democracy and/or peace, measures shall be taken as a matter of priority to:

(a) Retrace organizational structures, by firstly identifying agents and showing their position, if any, in the administration, particularly in the army or police forces, and by secondly determining the covert links which they maintained with their active or passive masters, belonging particularly to intelligence and security services or, in the event, to pressure groups. The information thus acquired shall be made public;

(b) Thoroughly investigate intelligence and security services with a view to redirecting their activities;

(c) Secure the cooperation of third countries which might have contributed to the creation and development of such groups, particularly through financial or logistical support;

(d) Draw up a reconversion plan to ensure that members of such groups are not tempted to join the ranks of organized crime.

PRINCIPLE 39. REPEAL OF EMERGENCY LEGISLATION AND ABOLITION OF EMERGENCY COURTS

Emergency legislation and courts of any kind must be repealed or abolished insofar as they infringe the fundamental rights and freedoms guaranteed in the Universal Declaration of Human Rights and the International Covenant on Civil and Political Rights.

Habeas corpus, whatever name it may be known by, must be considered a fundamental right of the individual and as such a non-derogable right.

PRINCIPLE 40. ADMINISTRATIVE AND OTHER MEASURES RELATING TO STATE OFFICIALS IMPLICATED IN GROSS HUMAN RIGHTS VIOLATIONS

Such measures should be of a preventive, not punitive character; they may therefore be taken by administrative decision, provided that appropriate implementation procedures are provided for by law. When a process has begun to ensure the restoration of or transition to democracy and/or peace, such measures may be taken under an act of general application or a treaty clause, with the intention of avoiding any administrative obstacle or challenge to the process.

These measures are invariably quite distinct from the punitive and judicial measures provided for in principles 18 et seq., which are to be applied by the courts to persons prosecuted and tried for human rights violations.

PRINCIPLE 41. IMPLEMENTATION OF ADMINISTRATIVE MEASURES

When a peace process has begun, the implementation of administrative measures should be preceded by a survey of positions of responsibility with influential decision-making powers and therefore an obligation of loyalty to the process. In that survey, priority consideration should be given to positions of responsibility in the army, the police and the judiciary.

In assessing the situation of serving officials, consideration will be given to:

(a) Their human rights records, particularly during the period of repression;

(b) Non-involvement in corruption;

(c) Professional competence;

(d) Willingness to promote the peace and/or democratization process, particularly with regard to the observance of constitutional guarantees and human rights.

Decisions shall be taken by the head of Government or, under his responsibility, by the minister under whom the official works, after the official concerned has been informed of the complaints against him and has been given a due hearing or summons for this purpose.

The official may appeal to the appropriate administrative court.

However, in view of the special circumstances inherent in any transition process, the appeal may be heard in that case by an ad hoc commission with exclusive jurisdiction, provided that it meets the criteria of independence, impartiality and procedure laid down in principles 6 (a) and (b), 7 (a), 8 and 10.

PRINCIPLE 42. NATURE OF MEASURES THAT CAN BE TAKEN AGAINST STATE OFFICIALS

Except where the official has been confirmed in his or her appointment, the official concerned may be:

(a) Suspended from certain duties;

(b) Suspended altogether pending his or her confirmation or appointment to another post;

(c) Transferred;

(d) Demoted;

(e) Given early retirement;

(f) Dismissed.

In relation to the irremovability of judges, the decision shall be taken in the light of the relevant guarantees set out in principle 32.

DECLARATION ON FUNDAMENTAL PRINCIPLES AND RIGHTS AT WORK (1998)

Declaration on Fundamental Principles and Rights at Work, *adopted* June 19, 1998, 37 I.L.M. 1233

Whereas the ILO was founded in the conviction that social justice is essential to universal and lasting peace;

Whereas economic growth is essential but not sufficient to ensure equity, social progress and the eradication of poverty, confirming the need for the ILO to promote strong social policies, justice and democratic institutions;

Whereas the ILO should, now more than ever, draw upon all its standard-setting, technical cooperation and research resources in all its areas of competence, in particular employment, vocational training and working conditions, to ensure that, in the context of a global strategy for economic and social development, economic and social policies are mutually reinforcing components in order to create broad-based sustainable development;

Whereas the ILO should give special attention to the problems of persons with special social needs, particularly the unemployed and migrant workers, and mobilize and encourage international, regional and national efforts aimed at resolving their problems, and promote effective policies aimed at job creation;

Whereas, in seeking to maintain the link between social progress and economic growth, the guarantee of fundamental principles and rights at work is of particular significance in that it enables the persons concerned, to claim freely and on the basis of equality of opportunity, their fair share of the wealth which they have helped to generate, and to achieve fully their human potential;

Whereas the ILO is the constitutionally mandated international organization and the competent body to set and deal with international labour standards, and enjoys universal support and acknowledgement in promoting Fundamental Rights at Work as the expression of its constitutional principles;

Whereas it is urgent, in a situation of growing economic interdependence, to reaffirm the immutable nature of the fundamental principles and rights embodied in the Constitution of the Organization and to promote their universal application;

The International Labour Conference

1. Recalls:
> (a) that in freely joining the ILO, all Members have endorsed the principles and rights set out in its Constitution and in the Declaration of Philadelphia, and have undertaken to work towards attaining the overall objectives of the Organization to the best of their resources and fully in line with their specific circumstances;
> (b) that these principles and rights have been expressed and developed in the form of specific rights and obligations in Conventions recognized as fundamental both inside and outside the Organization.

2. Declares that all Members, even if they have not ratified the Conventions in question, have an obligation arising from the very fact of membership in the Organization to respect, to promote and to realize, in good faith and in accordance with the Constitution, the principles concerning the fundamental rights which are the subject of those Conventions, namely:
> (a) freedom of association and the effective recognition of the right to collective bargaining;
> (b) the elimination of all forms of forced or compulsory labour;
> (c) the effective abolition of child labour; and
> (d) the elimination of discrimination in respect of employment and occupation.

3. Recognizes the obligation on the Organization to assist its Members, in response to their established and expressed needs, in order to attain these objectives by making full use of its constitutional, operational and budgetary resources, including, by the mobilization of external resources and support, as well as by encouraging other international organizations with which the ILO has established relations, pursuant to article 12 of its Constitution, to support these efforts:
> (a) by offering technical cooperation and advisory services to promote the ratification and implementation of the fundamental Conventions;
> (b) by assisting those Members not yet in a position to ratify some or all of these Conventions in their efforts to respect, to promote and to realize the principles concerning fundamental rights which are the subject of these Conventions; and
> (c) by helping the Members in their efforts to create a climate for economic and social development.

4. Decides that, to give full effect to this Declaration, a promotional follow-up, which is meaningful and effective, shall be implemented in accordance with the measures specified in the annex hereto, which shall be considered as an integral part of this Declaration.

5. Stresses that labour standards should not be used for protectionist trade purposes, and that nothing in this Declaration and its follow-up shall be invoked or otherwise used for such purposes; in addition, the

comparative advantage of any country should in no way be called into question by this Declaration and its follow-up.

THE SECRETARY GENERAL'S GLOBAL COMPACT
TEN PRINCIPLES
U.N. Global Compact, Ten Principles,
http://www.unglobalcompact.org/AboutTheGC/TheTenPrinciples/index.html

Human Rights
> Principle 1: Businesses should support and respect the protection of internationally proclaimed human rights; and
> Principle 2: make sure that they are not complicit in human rights abuses.

Labour Standards
> Principle 3: Businesses should uphold the freedom of association and the effective recognition of the right to collective bargaining;
> Principle 4: the elimination of all forms of forced and compulsory labour;
> Principle 5: the effective abolition of child labour; and
> Principle 6: the elimination of discrimination in respect of employment and occupation.

Environment
> Principle 7: Businesses should support a precautionary approach to environmental challenges;
> Principle 8: undertake initiatives to promote greater environmental responsibility; and
> Principle 9: encourage the development and diffusion of environmentally friendly technologies.

Anti-Corruption
> Principle 10: Businesses should work against corruption in all its forms, including extortion and bribery.

RESOLUTION ESTABLISHING THE UNITED NATIONS HUMAN RIGHTS COUNCIL
G.A. Res. 60/251, UN DOC A/RES/60/251 (3 April 2006)

The General Assembly,

Reaffirming the purposes and principles contained in the Charter of the United Nations, including developing friendly relations among nations based on respect for the principle of equal rights and self-determination of peoples, and achieving international cooperation in solving international problems of an economic, social, cultural or humanitarian character and in promoting and encouraging respect for human rights and fundamental freedoms for all,

Reaffirming also the Universal Declaration of Human Rights1 and the Vienna Declaration and Programme of Action,2 and recalling the International Covenant on Civil and Political Rights,3 the International Covenant on Economic, Social and Cultural Rights3 and other human rights instruments,

Reaffirming further that all human rights are universal, indivisible, interrelated, interdependent and mutually reinforcing, and that all human rights must be treated in a fair and equal manner, on the same footing and with the same emphasis,

Reaffirming that, while the significance of national and regional particularities and various historical, cultural and religious backgrounds must be borne in mind, all States, regardless of their political, economic and cultural systems, have the duty to promote and protect all human rights and fundamental freedoms,

Emphasizing the responsibilities of all States, in conformity with the Charter, to respect human rights and fundamental freedoms for all, without distinction of any kind as to race, colour, sex, language or religion, political or other opinion, national or social origin, property, birth or other status,

Acknowledging that peace and security, development and human rights are the pillars of the United Nations system and the foundations for collective security and well-being, and recognizing that development, peace and security and human rights are interlinked and mutually reinforcing,

Affirming the need for all States to continue international efforts to enhance dialogue and broaden understanding among civilizations, cultures and religions, and emphasizing that States, regional organizations, non-governmental organizations, religious bodies and the media have an important role to play in promoting tolerance, respect for and freedom of religion and belief,

Recognizing the work undertaken by the Commission on Human Rights and the need to preserve and build on its achievements and to redress its shortcomings,

Recognizing also the importance of ensuring universality, objectivity and non-selectivity in the consideration of human rights issues, and the elimination of double standards and politicization,

Recognizing further that the promotion and protection of human rights should be based on the principles of cooperation and genuine dialogue and aimed at strengthening the capacity of Member States to comply with their human rights obligations for the benefit of all human beings,

Acknowledging that non-governmental organizations play an important role at the national, regional and international levels, in the promotion and protection of human rights,

Reaffirming the commitment to strengthen the United Nations human rights machinery, with the aim of ensuring effective enjoyment by all of all human rights, civil, political, economic, social and cultural rights, including the right to development, and to that end, the resolve to create a Human Rights Council,

1. *Decides* to establish the Human Rights Council, based in Geneva, in replacement of the Commission on Human Rights, as a subsidiary organ of the General Assembly; the Assembly shall review the status of the Council within five years;
2. *Decides* that the Council shall be responsible for promoting universal respect for the protection of all human rights and fundamental freedoms for all, without distinction of any kind and in a fair and equal manner;
3. *Decides* also that the Council should address situations of violations of human rights, including gross and systematic violations, and make recommendations thereon. It should also promote the effective coordination and the mainstreaming of human rights within the United Nations system;
4. *Decides* further that the work of the Council shall be guided by the principles of universality, impartiality, objectivity and non-selectivity, constructive international dialogue and cooperation, with a view to enhancing the promotion and protection of all human rights, civil, political, economic, social and cultural rights, including the right to development;
5. *Decides* that the Council shall, inter alia:
> (a) Promote human rights education and learning as well as advisory services, technical assistance and capacity-building, to be provided in consultation with and with the consent of Member States concerned;
> (b) Serve as a forum for dialogue on thematic issues on all human rights;
> (c) Make recommendations to the General Assembly for the further development of international law in the field of human rights;
> (d) Promote the full implementation of human rights obligations undertaken by States and follow-up to the goals and commitments related to the promotion and protection of human rights emanating from United Nations conferences and summits;
> (e) Undertake a universal periodic review, based on objective and reliable information, of the fulfilment by each State of its human rights obligations and commitments in a manner which ensures universality of coverage and equal treatment with respect to all States; the review shall be

a cooperative mechanism, based on an interactive dialogue, with the full involvement of the country concerned and with consideration given to its capacity-building needs; such a mechanism shall complement and not duplicate the work of treaty bodies; the Council shall develop the modalities and necessary time allocation for the universal periodic review mechanism within one year after the holding of its first session;

(f) Contribute, through dialogue and cooperation, towards the prevention of human rights violations and respond promptly to human rights emergencies;

(g) Assume the role and responsibilities of the Commission on Human Rights relating to the work of the Office of the United Nations High Commissioner for Human Rights, as decided by the General Assembly in its resolution 48/141 of 20 December 1993;

(h) Work in close cooperation in the field of human rights with Governments, regional organizations, national human rights institutions and civil society;

(i) Make recommendations with regard to the promotion and protection of human rights;

(j) Submit an annual report to the General Assembly;

6. *Decides* also that the Council shall assume, review and, where necessary, improve and rationalize all mandates, mechanisms, functions and responsibilities of the Commission on Human Rights in order to maintain a system of special procedures, expert advice and a complaint procedure; the Council shall complete this review within one year after the holding of its first session;

7. *Decides* further that the Council shall consist of forty-seven Member States, which shall be elected directly and individually by secret ballot by the majority of the members of the General Assembly; the membership shall be based on equitable geographical distribution, and seats shall be distributed as follows among regional groups: Group of African States, thirteen; Group of Asian States, thirteen; Group of Eastern European States, six; Group of Latin American and Caribbean States, eight; and Group of Western European and other States, seven; the members of the Council shall serve for a period of three years and shall not be eligible for immediate re-election after two consecutive terms;

8. *Decides* that the membership in the Council shall be open to all States Members of the United Nations; when electing members of the Council, Member States shall take into account the contribution of candidates to the promotion and protection of human rights and their voluntary pledges and commitments made thereto; the General Assembly, by a two-thirds majority of the members present and voting, may suspend the rights of membership in the Council of a member of the Council that commits gross and systematic violations of human rights;

9. *Decides* also that members elected to the Council shall uphold the highest standards in the promotion and protection of human rights, shall fully cooperate with the Council and be reviewed under the universal periodic review mechanism during their term of membership;

10. *Decides* further that the Council shall meet regularly throughout the year and schedule no fewer than three sessions per year, including a main session, for a total duration of no less than ten weeks, and shall be able to hold special sessions, when needed, at the request of a member of the Council with the support of one third of the membership of the Council;

11. *Decides* that the Council shall apply the rules of procedure established for committees of the General Assembly, as applicable, unless subsequently otherwise decided by the Assembly or the Council, and also decides that the participation of and consultation with observers, including States that are not members of the Council, the specialized agencies, other intergovernmental organizations and national human rights institutions, as well as non-governmental organizations, shall be based on arrangements, including Economic and Social Council resolution 1996/31 of 25 July 1996 and practices observed by the Commission on Human Rights, while ensuring the most effective contribution of these entities;

12. *Decides* also that the methods of work of the Council shall be transparent, fair and impartial and shall enable genuine dialogue, be results-oriented, allow for subsequent follow-up discussions to recommendations and their implementation and also allow for substantive interaction with special procedures and mechanisms;

13. *Recommends* that the Economic and Social Council request the Commission on Human Rights to conclude its work at its sixty-second session, and that it abolish the Commission on 16 June 2006;

14. *Decides* to elect the new members of the Council; the terms of membership shall be staggered, and such decision shall be taken for the first election by the drawing of lots, taking into consideration equitable geographical distribution;

15. *Decides* also that elections of the first members of the Council shall take place on 9 May 2006, and that the first meeting of the Council shall be convened on 19 June 2006;

16. *Decides* further that the Council shall review its work and functioning five years after its establishment and report to the General Assembly.

U.N. DRAFT DECLARATION ON THE RIGHTS OF INDIGENOUS PEOPLES

U.N. Draft Declaration on the Rights of Indigenous Peoples, G.A. Res. 61/295, Annex, U.N. GAOR, 61st Sess., U.N. Doc. A/RES/61/295 (Sept. 13, 2007)

The General Assembly,

Guided by the purposes and principles of the Charter of the United Nations, and good faith in the fulfilment of the obligations assumed by States in accordance with the Charter,

Affirming that indigenous peoples are equal to all other peoples, while recognizing the right of all peoples to be different, to consider themselves different, and to be respected as such,

Affirming also that all peoples contribute to the diversity and richness of civilizations and cultures, which constitute the common heritage of humankind,

Affirming further that all doctrines, policies and practices based on or advocating superiority of peoples or individuals on the basis of national origin or racial, religious, ethnic or cultural differences are racist, scientifically false, legally invalid, morally condemnable and socially unjust,

Reaffirming that indigenous peoples, in the exercise of their rights, should be free from discrimination of any kind,

Concerned that indigenous peoples have suffered from historic injustices as a result of, inter alia, their colonization and dispossession of their lands, territories and resources, thus preventing them from exercising, in particular, their right to development in accordance with their own needs and interests,

Recognizing the urgent need to respect and promote the inherent rights of indigenous peoples which derive from their political, economic and social structures and from their cultures, spiritual traditions, histories and philosophies, especially their rights to their lands, territories and resources,

Recognizing also the urgent need to respect and promote the rights of indigenous peoples affirmed in treaties, agreements and other constructive arrangements with States,

Welcoming the fact that indigenous peoples are organizing themselves for political, economic, social and cultural enhancement and in order to bring to an end all forms of discrimination and oppression wherever they occur,

Convinced that control by indigenous peoples over developments affecting them and their lands, territories and resources will enable them to maintain and strengthen their institutions, cultures and traditions, and to promote their development in accordance with their aspirations and needs,

Recognizing that respect for indigenous knowledge, cultures and traditional practices contributes to sustainable and equitable development and proper management of the environment,

Emphasizing the contribution of the demilitarization of the lands and territories of indigenous peoples to peace, economic and social progress and development, understanding and friendly relations among nations and peoples of the world,

Recognizing in particular the right of indigenous families and communities to retain shared responsibility for the upbringing, training, education and well-being of their children, consistent with the rights of the child,

Considering that the rights affirmed in treaties, agreements and other constructive arrangements between States and indigenous peoples are, in some situations, matters of international concern, interest, responsibility and character,

Considering also that treaties, agreements and other constructive arrangements, and the relationship they represent, are the basis for a strengthened partnership between indigenous peoples and States,

Acknowledging that the Charter of the United Nations, the International Covenant on Economic, Social and Cultural Rights and the International Covenant on Civil and Political Rights,2 as well as the Vienna Declaration and Programme of Action, affirm the fundamental importance of the right to self-determination of all peoples, by virtue of which they freely determine their political status and freely pursue their economic, social and cultural development,

Bearing in mind that nothing in this Declaration may be used to deny any peoples their right to self-determination, exercised in conformity with international law,

Convinced that the recognition of the rights of indigenous peoples in this Declaration will enhance harmonious and cooperative relations between the State and indigenous peoples, based on principles of justice, democracy, respect for human rights, non-discrimination and good faith,

Encouraging States to comply with and effectively implement all their obligations as they apply to indigenous peoples under international instruments, in particular those related to human rights, in consultation and cooperation with the peoples concerned,

Emphasizing that the United Nations has an important and continuing role to play in promoting and protecting the rights of indigenous peoples,

Believing that this Declaration is a further important step forward for the recognition, promotion and protection of the rights and freedoms of indigenous peoples and in the development of relevant activities of the United Nations system in this field,

Recognizing and reaffirming that indigenous individuals are entitled without discrimination to all human rights recognized in international law, and that indigenous peoples possess collective rights which are indispensable for their existence, well-being and integral development as peoples,

Recognizing that the situation of indigenous peoples varies from region to region and from country to country and that the significance of national and regional particularities and various historical and cultural backgrounds should be taken into consideration,

Solemnly proclaims the following United Nations Declaration on the Rights of Indigenous Peoples as a standard of achievement to be pursued in a spirit of partnership and mutual respect:

Article 1
Indigenous peoples have the right to the full enjoyment, as a collective or as individuals, of all human rights and fundamental freedoms as recognized in the Charter of the United Nations, the Universal Declaration of Human Rights and international human rights law.

Article 2
Indigenous peoples and individuals are free and equal to all other peoples and individuals and have the right to be free from any kind of discrimination, in the exercise of their rights, in particular that based on their indigenous origin or identity.

Article 3

Indigenous peoples have the right to self-determination. By virtue of that right they freely determine their political status and freely pursue their economic, social and cultural development.

Article 4

Indigenous peoples, in exercising their right to self-determination, have the right to autonomy or self-government in matters relating to their internal and local affairs, as well as ways and means for financing their autonomous functions.

Article 5

Indigenous peoples have the right to maintain and strengthen their distinct political, legal, economic, social and cultural institutions, while retaining their right to participate fully, if they so choose, in the political, economic, social and cultural life of the State.

Article 6

Every indigenous individual has the right to a nationality.

Article 7

1. Indigenous individuals have the rights to life, physical and mental integrity, liberty and security of person.
2. Indigenous peoples have the collective right to live in freedom, peace and security as distinct peoples and shall not be subjected to any act of genocide or any other act of violence, including forcibly removing children of the group to another group.

Article 8

1. Indigenous peoples and individuals have the right not to be subjected to forced assimilation or destruction of their culture.
2. States shall provide effective mechanisms for prevention of, and redress for:
    (a) Any action which has the aim or effect of depriving them of their integrity as distinct peoples, or of their cultural values or ethnic identities;
    (b) Any action which has the aim or effect of dispossessing them of their lands, territories or resources;
    (c) Any form of forced population transfer which has the aim or effect of violating or undermining any of their rights;
    (d) Any form of forced assimilation or integration;
    (e) Any form of propaganda designed to promote or incite racial or ethnic discrimination directed against them.

Article 9

Indigenous peoples and individuals have the right to belong to an indigenous community or nation, in accordance with the traditions and customs of the community or nation concerned. No discrimination of any kind may arise from the exercise of such a right.

Article 10

Indigenous peoples shall not be forcibly removed from their lands or territories. No relocation shall take place without the free, prior and informed consent of the indigenous peoples concerned and after agreement on just and fair compensation and, where possible, with the option of return.

Article 11

1. Indigenous peoples have the right to practise and revitalize their cultural traditions and customs. This includes the right to maintain, protect and develop the past, present and future manifestations of their cultures, such as archaeological and historical sites, artefacts, designs, ceremonies, technologies and visual and performing arts and literature.
2. States shall provide redress through effective mechanisms, which may include restitution, developed in conjunction with indigenous peoples, with respect to their cultural, intellectual, religious and spiritual

property taken without their free, prior and informed consent or in violation of their laws, traditions and customs.

Article 12

1. Indigenous peoples have the right to manifest, practise, develop and teach their spiritual and religious traditions, customs and ceremonies; the right to maintain, protect, and have access in privacy to their religious and cultural sites; the right to the use and control of their ceremonial objects; and the right to the repatriation of their human remains.

2. States shall seek to enable the access and/or repatriation of ceremonial objects and human remains in their possession through fair, transparent and effective mechanisms developed in conjunction with indigenous peoples concerned.

Article 13

1. Indigenous peoples have the right to revitalize, use, develop and transmit to future generations their histories, languages, oral traditions, philosophies, writing systems and literatures, and to designate and retain their own names for communities, places and persons.

2. States shall take effective measures to ensure that this right is protected and also to ensure that indigenous peoples can understand and be understood in political, legal and administrative proceedings, where necessary through the provision of interpretation or by other appropriate means.

Article 14

1. Indigenous peoples have the right to establish and control their educational systems and institutions providing education in their own languages, in a manner appropriate to their cultural methods of teaching and learning.

2. Indigenous individuals, particularly children, have the right to all levels and forms of education of the State without discrimination.

3. States shall, in conjunction with indigenous peoples, take effective measures, in order for indigenous individuals, particularly children, including those living outside their communities, to have access, when possible, to an education in their own culture and provided in their own language.

Article 15

1. Indigenous peoples have the right to the dignity and diversity of their cultures, traditions, histories and aspirations which shall be appropriately reflected in education and public information.

2. States shall take effective measures, in consultation and cooperation with the indigenous peoples concerned, to combat prejudice and eliminate discrimination and to promote tolerance, understanding and good relations among indigenous peoples and all other segments of society.

Article 16

1. Indigenous peoples have the right to establish their own media in their own languages and to have access to all forms of non-indigenous media without discrimination.

2. States shall take effective measures to ensure that State-owned media duly reflect indigenous cultural diversity. States, without prejudice to ensuring full freedom of expression, should encourage privately owned media to adequately reflect indigenous cultural diversity.

Article 17

1. Indigenous individuals and peoples have the right to enjoy fully all rights established under applicable international and domestic labour law.

2. States shall in consultation and cooperation with indigenous peoples take specific measures to protect indigenous children from economic exploitation and from performing any work that is likely to be hazardous or to interfere with the child's education, or to be harmful to the child's health or physical, mental, spiritual, moral or social development, taking into account their special vulnerability and the importance of education for their empowerment.

3. Indigenous individuals have the right not to be subjected to any discriminatory conditions of labour and, *inter alia*, employment or salary.

Article 18

Indigenous peoples have the right to participate in decision-making in matters which would affect their rights, through representatives chosen by themselves in accordance with their own procedures, as well as to maintain and develop their own indigenous decision-making institutions.

Article 19

States shall consult and cooperate in good faith with the indigenous peoples concerned through their own representative institutions in order to obtain their free, prior and informed consent before adopting and implementing legislative or administrative measures that may affect them.

Article 20

1. Indigenous peoples have the right to maintain and develop their political, economic and social systems or institutions, to be secure in the enjoyment of their own means of subsistence and development, and to engage freely in all their traditional and other economic activities.
2. Indigenous peoples deprived of their means of subsistence and development are entitled to just and fair redress.

Article 21

1. Indigenous peoples have the right, without discrimination, to the improvement of their economic and social conditions, including, inter alia, in the areas of education, employment, vocational training and retraining, housing, sanitation, health and social security.
2. States shall take effective measures and, where appropriate, special measures to ensure continuing improvement of their economic and social conditions. Particular attention shall be paid to the rights and special needs of indigenous elders, women, youth, children and persons with disabilities.

Article 22

1. Particular attention shall be paid to the rights and special needs of indigenous elders, women, youth, children and persons with disabilities in the implementation of this Declaration.
2. States shall take measures, in conjunction with indigenous peoples, to ensure that indigenous women and children enjoy the full protection and guarantees against all forms of violence and discrimination.

Article 23

Indigenous peoples have the right to determine and develop priorities and strategies for exercising their right to development. In particular, indigenous peoples have the right to be actively involved in developing and determining health, housing and other economic and social programmes affecting them and, as far as possible, to administer such programmes through their own institutions.

Article 24

1. Indigenous peoples have the right to their traditional medicines and to maintain their health practices, including the conservation of their vital medicinal plants, animals and minerals. Indigenous individuals also have the right to access, without any discrimination, to all social and health services.
2. Indigenous individuals have an equal right to the enjoyment of the highest attainable standard of physical and mental health. States shall take the necessary steps with a view to achieving progressively the full realization of this right.

Article 25

Indigenous peoples have the right to maintain and strengthen their distinctive spiritual relationship with their traditionally owned or otherwise occupied and used lands, territories, waters and coastal seas and other resources and to uphold their responsibilities to future generations in this regard.

Article 26

1. Indigenous peoples have the right to the lands, territories and resources which they have traditionally owned, occupied or otherwise used or acquired.
2. Indigenous peoples have the right to own, use, develop and control the lands, territories and resources that they possess by reason of traditional ownership or other traditional occupation or use, as well as those which they have otherwise acquired.
3. States shall give legal recognition and protection to these lands, territories and resources. Such

recognition shall be conducted with due respect to the customs, traditions and land tenure systems of the indigenous peoples concerned.

Article 27
States shall establish and implement, in conjunction with indigenous peoples concerned, a fair, independent, impartial, open and transparent process, giving due recognition to indigenous peoples' laws, traditions, customs and land tenure systems, to recognize and adjudicate the rights of indigenous peoples pertaining to their lands, territories and resources, including those which were traditionally owned or otherwise occupied or used. Indigenous peoples shall have the right to participate in this process.

Article 28
1. Indigenous peoples have the right to redress, by means that can include restitution or, when this is not possible, just, fair and equitable compensation, for the lands, territories and resources which they have traditionally owned or otherwise occupied or used, and which have been confiscated, taken, occupied, used or damaged without their free, prior and informed consent.
2. Unless otherwise freely agreed upon by the peoples concerned, compensation shall take the form of lands, territories and resources equal in quality, size and legal status or of monetary compensation or other appropriate redress.

Article 29
1. Indigenous peoples have the right to the conservation and protection of the environment and the productive capacity of their lands or territories and resources. States shall establish and implement assistance programmes for indigenous peoples for such conservation and protection, without discrimination.
2. States shall take effective measures to ensure that no storage or disposal of hazardous materials shall take place in the lands or territories of indigenous peoples without their free, prior and informed consent.
3. States shall also take effective measures to ensure, as needed, that programmes for monitoring, maintaining and restoring the health of indigenous peoples, as developed and implemented by the peoples affected by such materials, are duly implemented.

Article 30
1. Military activities shall not take place in the lands or territories of indigenous peoples, unless justified by a relevant public interest or otherwise freely agreed with or requested by the indigenous peoples concerned.
2. States shall undertake effective consultations with the indigenous peoples concerned, through appropriate procedures and in particular through their representative institutions, prior to using their lands or territories for military activities.

Article 31
1. Indigenous peoples have the right to maintain, control, protect and develop their cultural heritage, traditional knowledge and traditional cultural expressions, as well as the manifestations of their sciences, technologies and cultures, including human and genetic resources, seeds, medicines, knowledge of the properties of fauna and flora, oral traditions, literatures, designs, sports and traditional games and visual and performing arts. They also have the right to maintain, control, protect and develop their intellectual property over such cultural heritage, traditional knowledge, and traditional cultural expressions.
2. In conjunction with indigenous peoples, States shall take effective measures to recognize and protect the exercise of these rights.

Article 32
1. Indigenous peoples have the right to determine and develop priorities and strategies for the development or use of their lands or territories and other resources.
2. States shall consult and cooperate in good faith with the indigenous peoples concerned through their own representative institutions in order to obtain their free and informed consent prior to the approval of any project affecting their lands or territories and other resources, particularly in connection with the development, utilization or exploitation of mineral, water or other resources.
3. States shall provide effective mechanisms for just and fair redress for any such activities, and appropriate measures shall be taken to mitigate adverse environmental, economic, social, cultural or spiritual impact.

Article 33

1. Indigenous peoples have the right to determine their own identity or membership in accordance with their customs and traditions. This does not impair the right of indigenous individuals to obtain citizenship of the States in which they live.

2. Indigenous peoples have the right to determine the structures and to select the membership of their institutions in accordance with their own procedures.

Article 34

Indigenous peoples have the right to promote, develop and maintain their institutional structures and their distinctive customs, spirituality, traditions, procedures, practices and, in the cases where they exist, juridical systems or customs, in accordance with international human rights standards.

Article 35

Indigenous peoples have the right to determine the responsibilities of individuals to their communities.

Article 36

1. Indigenous peoples, in particular those divided by international borders, have the right to maintain and develop contacts, relations and cooperation, including activities for spiritual, cultural, political, economic and social purposes, with their own members as well as other peoples across borders.

2. States, in consultation and cooperation with indigenous peoples, shall take effective measures to facilitate the exercise and ensure the implementation of this right.

Article 37

1. Indigenous peoples have the right to the recognition, observance and enforcement of treaties, agreements and other constructive arrangements concluded with States or their successors and to have States honour and respect such treaties, agreements and other constructive arrangements.

2. Nothing in this Declaration may be interpreted as diminishing or eliminating the rights of indigenous peoples contained in treaties, agreements and other constructive arrangements.

Article 38

States in consultation and cooperation with indigenous peoples, shall take the appropriate measures, including legislative measures, to achieve the ends of this Declaration.

Article 39

Indigenous peoples have the right to have access to financial and technical assistance from States and through international cooperation, for the enjoyment of the rights contained in this Declaration.

Article 40

Indigenous peoples have the right to access to and prompt decision through just and fair procedures for the resolution of conflicts and disputes with States or other parties, as well as to effective remedies for all infringements of their individual and collective rights. Such a decision shall give due consideration to the customs, traditions, rules and legal systems of the indigenous peoples concerned and international human rights.

Article 41

The organs and specialized agencies of the United Nations system and other intergovernmental organizations shall contribute to the full realization of the provisions of this Declaration through the mobilization, inter alia, of financial cooperation and technical assistance. Ways and means of ensuring participation of indigenous peoples on issues affecting them shall be established.

Article 42

The United Nations, its bodies, including the Permanent Forum on Indigenous Issues, and specialized agencies, including at the country level, and States shall promote respect for and full application of the provisions of this Declaration and follow up the effectiveness of this Declaration.

Article 43

The rights recognized herein constitute the minimum standards for the survival, dignity and well-being of the indigenous peoples of the world.

Article 44

All the rights and freedoms recognized herein are equally guaranteed to male and female indigenous individuals.

Article 45

Nothing in this Declaration may be construed as diminishing or extinguishing the rights indigenous peoples have now or may acquire in the future.

Article 46

1. Nothing in this Declaration may be interpreted as implying for any State, people, group or person any right to engage in any activity or to perform any act contrary to the Charter of the United Nations or construed as authorizing or encouraging any action which would dismember or impair, totally or in part, the territorial integrity or political unity of sovereign and independent States.
2. In the exercise of the rights enunciated in the present Declaration, human rights and fundamental freedoms of all shall be respected. The exercise of the rights set forth in this Declaration shall be subject only to such limitations as are determined by law and in accordance with international human rights obligations. Any such limitations shall be non-discriminatory and strictly necessary solely for the purpose of securing due recognition and respect for the rights and freedoms of others and for meeting the just and most compelling requirements of a democratic society.
3. The provisions set forth in this Declaration shall be interpreted in accordance with the principles of justice, democracy, respect for human rights, equality, non-discrimination, good governance and good faith.

SELECT RESOLUTIONS RELATING TO THE WAR IN IRAQ

U.N. SECURITY RESOLUTION 780
S.C. Res. 780, U.N. Doc S/RES/780 (Oct. 6, 1992)

The Security Council,

Reaffirming its resolutions 713 (1991) of 25 September 1991 and all subsequent relevant resolutions,

Recalling paragraph 10 of its resolution 764 (1992) of 13 July 1992, in which it reaffirmed that all parties are bound to comply with the obligations under international humanitarian law and in particular the Geneva Conventions of 12 August 1949, and that persons who commit or order the commission of grave breaches of the Conventions are individually responsible in respect of such breaches,

Recalling also its resolution 771 (1992) of 13 August 1992, in which, inter alia, it demanded that all parties and others concerned in the former Yugoslavia, and all military forces in Bosnia and Herzegovina, immediately cease and desist from all breaches of international humanitarian law,

Expressing once again its grave alarm at continuing reports of widespread violations of international humanitarian law occurring within the territory of the former Yugoslavia and especially in Bosnia and Herzegovina, including reports of mass killings and the continuance of the practice of "ethnic cleansing",

1. *Reaffirms* its call, in paragraph 5 of resolution 771 (1992), upon States and, as appropriate, international humanitarian organizations to collate substantiated information in their possession or submitted to them relating to the violations of humanitarian law, including grave breaches of the Geneva Conventions being

committed in the territory of the former Yugoslavia, and requests States, relevant United Nations bodies, and relevant organizations to make this information available within thirty days of the adoption of the present resolution and as appropriate thereafter, and to provide other appropriate assistance to the Commission of Experts referred to in paragraph 2 below;

2. *Request* the Secretary-General to establish, as a matter of urgency, an impartial Commission of Experts to examine and analyse the information submitted pursuant to resolution 771 (1992) and the present resolution, together with such further information as the Commission of Experts may obtain through its own investigations or efforts, of other persons or bodies pursuant to resolution 771 (1992), with a view to providing the Secretary-General with its conclusions on the evidence of grave breaches of the Geneva Conventions and other violations of international humanitarian law committed in the territory of the former Yugoslavia;

3. *Also requests* the Secretary-General to report to the Council on the establishment of the Commission of Experts;

4. *Further request* the Secretary-General to report to the Council on the conclusions of the Commission of Experts and to take account of these conclusions in any recommendatins for further appropriate steps called for by resolution 771 (1992);

5. *Decides* to remain actively seized of the matter.

U.N. SECURITY COUNCIL RESOLUTION 929
S.C. Res. 929, U.N. Doc. S/RES/929 (June 22, 1994)

The Security Council,

Reaffirming all its previous resolutions on the situation in Rwanda, in particular its resolutions 912 (1994) of 21 April 1994, 918 (1994) of 17 May 1994 and 925 (1994) of 8 June 1994, which set out the mandate and force level of the United Nations Assistance Mission for Rwanda (UNAMIR),

Determined to contribute to the resumption of the process of political settlement under the Arusha Peace Agreement and encouraging the Secretary-General and his Special Representative for Rwanda to continue and redouble their efforts at the national, regional and international levels to promote these objectives,

Stressing the importance of the cooperation of all parties for the fulfilment of the objectives of the United Nations in Rwanda, Having considered the letter of the Secretary-General of 19 June 1994 (S/1994/728),

Taking into account the time needed to gather the necessary resources for the effective deployment of UNAMIR, as expanded in resolutions 918 (1994) and 925 (1994),

Noting the offer by Member States to cooperate with the Secretary-General towards the fulfilment of the objectives of the United Nations in Rwanda (S/1994/734), and stressing the strictly humanitarian character of this operation which shall be conducted in an impartial and neutral fashion, and shall not constitute an interposition force between the parties,

Welcoming the cooperation between the United Nations, the Organization of African Unity (OAU) and neighbouring States to bring peace to Rwanda,

Deeply concerned by the continuation of systematic and widespread killings of the civilian population in Rwanda,

Recognizing that the current situation in Rwanda constitutes a unique case which demands an urgent response by the international community,

Determining that the magnitude of the humanitarian crisis in Rwanda constitutes a threat to peace and security in the region,

1. *Welcomes* the Secretary-General's letter dated 19 June 1994 (S/1994/728) and agrees that a multinational operation may be set up for humanitarian purposes in Rwanda until UNAMIR is brought up to the necessary strength;

2. *Welcomes* also the offer by Member States (S/1994/734) to cooperate with the Secretary-General in order to achieve the objectives of the United Nations in Rwanda through the establishment of a temporary operation under national command and control aimed at contributing, in an impartial way, to the security and protection of displaced persons, refugees and civilians at risk in Rwanda, on the understanding that the costs of implementing the offer will be borne by the Member States concerned;

3. *Acting* under Chapter VII of the Charter of the United Nations, *authorizes* the Member States cooperating with the Secretary-General to conduct the operation referred to in paragraph 2 above using all necessary means to achieve the humanitarian objectives set out in subparagraphs 4 (a) and (b) of resolution 925 (1994);

4. *Decides* that the mission of Member States cooperating with the Secretary-General will be limited to a period of two months following the adoption of the present resolution, unless the Secretary-General determines at an earlier date that the expanded UNAMIR is able to carry out its mandate;

5. *Commends* the offers already made by Member States of troops for the expanded UNAMIR;

6. *Calls upon* all Member States to respond urgently to the Secretary-General's request for resources, including logistical support, in order to enable expanded UNAMIR to fulfil its mandate effectively as soon as possible and *requests* the Secretary-General to identify and coordinate the supply of the essential equipment required by troops committed to the expanded UNAMIR;

7. *Welcomes*, in this respect, the offers already made by Member States of equipment for troop contributors to UNAMIR and *calls on* other Members to offer such support, including the possibility of comprehensive provision of equipment to specific troop contributors, to speed UNAMIR's expanded force deployment;

8. *Requests* Member States cooperating with the Secretary-General to coordinate closely with UNAMIR and *also requests* the Secretary-General to set up appropriate mechanisms to this end;

9. *Demands* that all parties to the conflict and others concerned immediately bring to an end all killings of civilian populations in areas under their control and allow Member States cooperating with the Secretary-General to implement fully the mission set forth in paragraph 3 above;

10. *Requests* the States concerned and the Secretary-General, as appropriate, to report to the Council on a regular basis, the first such report to be made no later than fifteen days after the adoption of this resolution, on the implementation of this operation and the progress made towards the fulfilment of the objectives referred to in paragraphs 2 and 3 above;

11. *Also requests* the Secretary-General to report on the progress made towards completing the deployment of the expanded UNAMIR within the framework of the report due no later than 9 August 1994 under paragraph 17 of resolution 925 (1994), as well as on progress towards the resumption of the process of political settlement under the Arusha Peace Agreement;

12. *Decides* to remain actively seized of the matter.

U.N. SECURITY RESOLUTION 1483
S.C. Res. 1483, U.N. Doc. S/RES/1483 (May 22, 2003)

The Security Council,

Recalling all its previous relevant resolutions,

Reaffirming the sovereignty and territorial integrity of Iraq,

Reaffirming also the importance of the disarmament of Iraqi weapons of mass destruction and of eventual confirmation of the disarmament of Iraq,

Stressing the right of the Iraqi people freely to determine their own political future and control their own natural resources, welcoming the commitment of all parties concerned to support the creation of an environment in which they may do so as soon as possible, and expressing resolve that the day when Iraqis govern themselves must come quickly,

Encouraging efforts by the people of Iraq to form a representative government based on the rule of law that affords equal rights and justice to all Iraqi citizens without regard to ethnicity, religion, or gender, and, in this connection, recalls resolution 1325 (2000) of 31 October 2000,

Welcoming the first steps of the Iraqi people in this regard, and noting in this connection the 15 April 2003 Nasiriyah statement and the 28 April 2003 Baghdad statement,

Resolved that the United Nations should play a vital role in humanitarian relief, the reconstruction of Iraq, and the restoration and establishment of national and local institutions for representative governance,

Noting the statement of 12 April 2003 by the Ministers of Finance and Central Bank Governors of the Group of Seven Industrialized Nations in which the members recognized the need for a multilateral effort to help rebuild and develop Iraq and for the need for assistance from the International Monetary Fund and the World Bank in these efforts,

Welcoming also the resumption of humanitarian assistance and the continuing efforts of the Secretary-General and the specialized agencies to provide food and medicine to the people of Iraq,

Welcoming the appointment by the Secretary-General of his Special Adviser on Iraq,

Affirming the need for accountability for crimes and atrocities committed by the previous Iraqi regime,

Stressing the need for respect for the archaeological, historical, cultural, and religious heritage of Iraq, and for the continued protection of archaeological, historical, cultural, and religious sites, museums, libraries, and monuments,

Noting the letter of 8 May 2003 from the Permanent Representatives of the United States of America and the United Kingdom of Great Britain and Northern Ireland to the President of the Security Council (S/2003/538) and recognizing the specific authorities, responsibilities, and obligations under applicable international law of these states as occupying powers under unified command (the "Authority"),

Noting further that other States that are not occupying powers are working now or in the future may work under the Authority,

Welcoming further the willingness of Member States to contribute to stability and security in Iraq by contributing personnel, equipment, and other resources under the Authority,

Concerned that many Kuwaitis and Third-State Nationals still are not accounted for since 2 August 1990,

Determining that the situation in Iraq, although improved, continues to constitute a threat to international peace and security,

Acting under Chapter VII of the Charter of the United Nations,

1. *Appeals* to Member States and concerned organizations to assist the people of Iraq in their efforts to reform their institutions and rebuild their country, and to contribute to conditions of stability and security in Iraq in accordance with this resolution;
2. *Calls* upon all Member States in a position to do so to respond immediately to the humanitarian appeals of the United Nations and other international organizations for Iraq and to help meet the humanitarian and other needs of the Iraqi people by providing food, medical supplies, and resources necessary for reconstruction and rehabilitation of Iraq's economic infrastructure;
3. *Appeals* to Member States to deny safe haven to those members of the previous Iraqi regime who are alleged to be responsible for crimes and atrocities and to support actions to bring them to justice;

4. *Calls upon* the Authority, consistent with the Charter of the United Nations and other relevant international law, to promote the welfare of the Iraqi people through the effective administration of the territory, including in particular working towards the restoration of conditions of security and stability and the creation of conditions in which the Iraqi people can freely determine their own political future;

5. *Calls upon* all concerned to comply fully with their obligations under international law including in particular the Geneva Conventions of 1949 and the Hague Regulations of 1907;

6. *Calls upon* the Authority and relevant organizations and individuals to continue efforts to locate, identify, and repatriate all Kuwaiti and Third-State Nationals or the remains of those present in Iraq on or after 2 August 1990, as well as the Kuwaiti archives, that the previous Iraqi regime failed to undertake, and, in this regard, *directs* the High-Level Coordinator, in consultation with the International Committee of the Red Cross and the Tripartite Commission and with the appropriate support of the people of Iraq and in coordination with the Authority, to take steps to fulfil his mandate with respect to the fate of Kuwaiti and Third-State National missing persons and property;

7. *Decides* that all Member States shall take appropriate steps to facilitate the safe return to Iraqi institutions, of Iraqi cultural property and other items of archaeological, historical, cultural, rare scientific, and religious importance illegally removed from the Iraq National Museum, the National Library, and other locations in Iraq since the adoption of resolution 661 (1990) of 2 August 1990, including by establishing a prohibition on trade in or transfer of such items and items with respect to which reasonable suspicion exists that they have been illegally removed, and calls upon the United Nations Educational, Scientific, and Cultural Organization, Interpol, and other international organizations, as appropriate, to assist in the implementation of this paragraph;

8. *Requests* the Secretary-General to appoint a Special Representative for Iraq whose independent responsibilities shall involve reporting regularly to the Council on his activities under this resolution, coordinating activities of the United Nations in post-conflict processes in Iraq, coordinating among United Nations and international agencies engaged in humanitarian assistance and reconstruction activities in Iraq, and, in coordination with the Authority, assisting the people of Iraq through:

(a) coordinating humanitarian and reconstruction assistance by United Nations agencies and between United Nations agencies and non-governmental organizations;

(b) promoting the safe, orderly, and voluntary return of refugees and displaced persons;

(c) working intensively with the Authority, the people of Iraq, and others concerned to advance efforts to restore and establish national and local institutions for representative governance, including by working together to facilitate a process leading to an internationally recognized, representative government of Iraq;

(d) facilitating the reconstruction of key infrastructure, in cooperation with other international organizations;

(e) promoting economic reconstruction and the conditions for sustainable development, including through coordination with national and regional organizations, as appropriate, civil society, donors and the international financial institutions;

(f) encouraging international efforts to contribute to basic civilian administration functions;

(g) promoting the protection of human rights;

(h) encouraging international efforts to rebuild the capacity of the Iraqi civilian police force; and

(i) encouraging international efforts to promote legal and judicial reform;

9. *Supports* the formation, by the people of Iraq with the help of the Authority and working with the Special Representative, of an Iraqi interim administration as a transitional administration run by Iraqis, until an internationally recognized, representative government is established by the people of Iraq and assumes the responsibilities of the Authority;

10. *Decides* that, with the exception of prohibitions related to the sale or supply to Iraq of arms and related materiel other than those arms and related materiel required by the Authority to serve the purposes of this and other related resolutions, all prohibitions related to trade with Iraq and the provision of financial or economic resources to Iraq established by resolution 661 (1990) and subsequent relevant resolutions, including resolution 778 (1992) of 2 October 1992, shall no longer apply;

11. *Reaffirms* that Iraq must meet its disarmament obligations, *encourages* the United Kingdom of Great Britain and Northern Ireland and the United States of America to keep the Council informed of their activities in this regard, and *underlines* the intention of the Council to revisit the mandates of the United Nations Monitoring and Verification Commission and the International Atomic Energy Agency as set forth

in resolutions 687 (1991) of 3 April 1991, 1284 (1999) of 17 December 1999, and 1441 (2002) of 8 November 2002;

12. *Notes* the establishment of a Development Fund for Iraq to be held by the Central Bank of Iraq and to be audited by independent public accountants approved by the International Advisory and Monitoring Board of the Development Fund for Iraq and looks forward to the early meeting of that International Advisory and Monitoring Board, whose members shall include duly qualified representatives of the Secretary-General, of the Managing Director of the International Monetary Fund, of the Director-General of the Arab Fund for Social and Economic Development, and of the President of the World Bank;

13. *Notes further* that the funds in the Development Fund for Iraq shall be disbursed at the direction of the Authority, in consultation with the Iraqi interim administration, for the purposes set out in paragraph 14 below;

14. *Underlines* that the Development Fund for Iraq shall be used in a transparent manner to meet the humanitarian needs of the Iraqi people, for the economic reconstruction and repair of Iraq's infrastructure, for the continued disarmament of Iraq, and for the costs of Iraqi civilian administration, and for other purposes benefiting the people of Iraq;

15. *Calls upon* the international financial institutions to assist the people of Iraq in the reconstruction and development of their economy and to facilitate assistance by the broader donor community, and welcomes the readiness of creditors, including those of the Paris Club, to seek a solution to Iraq's sovereign debt problems;

16. *Requests also* that the Secretary-General, in coordination with the Authority, continue the exercise of his responsibilities under Security Council resolution 1472 (2003) of 28 March 2003 and 1476 (2003) of 24 April 2003, for a period of six months following the adoption of this resolution, and terminate within this time period, in the most cost effective manner, the ongoing operations of the "Oil-for-Food" Programme (the "Programme"), both at headquarters level and in the field, transferring responsibility for the administration of any remaining activity under the Programme to the Authority, including by taking the following necessary measures:

(a) to facilitate as soon as possible the shipment and authenticated delivery of priority civilian goods as identified by the Secretary-General and representatives designated by him, in coordination with the Authority and the Iraqi interim administration, under approved and funded contracts previously concluded by the previous Government of Iraq, for the humanitarian relief of the people of Iraq, including, as necessary, negotiating adjustments in the terms or conditions of these contracts and respective letters of credit as set forth in paragraph 4 (d) of resolution 1472 (2003);

(b) to review, in light of changed circumstances, in coordination with the Authority and the Iraqi interim administration, the relative utility of each approved and funded contract with a view to determining whether such contracts contain items required to meet the needs of the people of Iraq both now and during reconstruction, and to postpone action on those contracts determined to be of questionable utility and the respective letters of credit until an internationally recognized, representative government of Iraq is in a position to make its own determination as to whether such contracts shall be fulfilled;

(c) to provide the Security Council within 21 days following the adoption of this resolution, for the Security Council's review and consideration, an estimated operating budget based on funds already set aside in the account established pursuant to paragraph 8 (d) of resolution 986 (1995) of 14 April 1995, identifying:

(i) all known and projected costs to the United Nations required to ensure the continued functioning of the activities associated with implementation of the present resolution, including operating and administrative expenses associated with the relevant United Nations agencies and programmes responsible for the implementation of the Programme both at Headquarters and in the field;

(ii) all known and projected costs associated with termination of the Programme;

(iii) all known and projected costs associated with restoring Government of Iraq funds that were provided by Member States to the Secretary-General as requested in paragraph 1 of resolution 778 (1992) of 2 October 1992; and

(iv) all known and projected costs associated with the Special Representative and the qualified representative of the Secretary-General identified to serve on the International

Advisory and Monitoring Board, for the six month time period defined above, following which these costs shall be borne by the United Nations;

(d) to consolidate into a single fund the accounts established pursuant to paragraphs 8 (a) and 8 (b) of resolution 986 (1995);

(e) to fulfil all remaining obligations related to the termination of the Programme, including negotiating, in the most cost effective manner, any necessary settlement payments, which shall be made from the escrow accounts established pursuant to paragraphs 8 (a) and 8 (b) of resolution 986 (1995), with those parties that previously have entered into contractual obligations with the Secretary-General under the Programme, and to determine, in coordination with the Authority and the Iraqi interim administration, the future status of contracts undertaken by the United Nations and related United Nations agencies under the accounts established pursuant to paragraphs 8 (b) and 8 (d) of resolution 986 (1995);

(f) to provide the Security Council, 30 days prior to the termination of the Programme, with a comprehensive strategy developed in close coordination with the Authority and the Iraqi interim administration that would lead to the delivery of all relevant documentation and the transfer of all operational responsibility of the Programme to the Authority;

17. *Requests further* that the Secretary-General transfer as soon as possible to the Development Fund for Iraq 1 billion United States dollars from unencumbered funds in the accounts established pursuant to paragraphs 8 (a) and 8 (b) of resolution 986 (1995), restore Government of Iraq funds that were provided by Member States to the Secretary-General as requested in paragraph 1 of resolution 778 (1992), and *decides* that, after deducting all relevant United Nations expenses associated with the shipment of authorized contracts and costs to the Programme outlined in paragraph 16 (c) above, including residual obligations, all surplus funds in the escrow accounts established pursuant to paragraphs 8 (a), 8 (b), 8 (d), and 8 (f) of resolution 986 (1995) shall be transferred at the earliest possible time to the Development Fund for Iraq;

18. *Decides* to terminate effective on the adoption of this resolution the functions related to the observation and monitoring activities undertaken by the Secretary-General under the Programme, including the monitoring of the export of petroleum and petroleum products from Iraq;

19. *Decides* to terminate the Committee established pursuant to paragraph 6 of resolution 661 (1990) at the conclusion of the six months period called for in paragraph 16 above and *further decides* that the Committee shall identify individuals and entities referred to in paragraph 23 below;

20. *Decides* that all export sales of petroleum, petroleum products, and natural gas from Iraq following the date of the adoption of this resolution shall be made consistent with prevailing international market best practices, to be audited by independent public accountants reporting to the International Advisory and Monitoring Board referred to in paragraph 12 above in order to ensure transparency, and *decides further* that, except as provided in paragraph 21 below, all proceeds from such sales shall be deposited into the Development Fund for Iraq, until such time as an internationally recognized, representative government of Iraq is properly constituted;

21. *Decides further* that 5 percent of the proceeds referred to in paragraph 20 above shall be deposited into the Compensation Fund established in accordance with resolution 687 (1991) of 3 April 1991 and subsequent relevant resolutions and that, unless an internationally recognized, representative government of Iraq and the Governing Council of the United Nations Compensation Commission, in the exercise of its authority over methods of ensuring that payments are made into the Compensation Fund, decide otherwise, this requirement shall be binding on a properly constituted, internationally recognized, representative government of Iraq and any successor thereto;

22. *Noting* the relevance of the establishment of an internationally recognized, representative government of Iraq and the desirability of prompt completion of the restructuring of Iraq's debt as referred to in paragraph 15 above, further *decides* that, until December 31, 2007, unless the Council decides otherwise, petroleum, petroleum products, and natural gas originating in Iraq shall be immune, until title passes to the initial purchaser, from legal proceedings against them and not be subject to any form of attachment, garnishment, or execution, and that all States shall take any steps that may be necessary under their respective domestic legal systems to assure this protection, and that proceeds and obligations arising from sales thereof, as well as the Development Fund for Iraq, shall enjoy privileges and immunities equivalent to those enjoyed by the United Nations except that the above-mentioned privileges and immunities will not apply with respect to any legal proceeding in which recourse to such proceeds or obligations is necessary to

satisfy liability for damages assessed in connection with an ecological accident, including an oil spill, that occurs after the date of adoption of this resolution;

23. *Decides* that all Member States in which there are:

(a) funds or other financial assets or economic resources of the previous Government of Iraq or its state bodies, corporations, or agencies, located outside Iraq as of the date of this resolution, or

(b) funds or other financial assets or economic resources that have been removed from Iraq, or acquired, by Saddam Hussein or other senior officials of the former Iraqi regime and their immediate family members, including entities owned or controlled, directly or indirectly, by them or by persons acting on their behalf or at their direction,

shall freeze without delay those funds or other financial assets or economic resources and, unless these funds or other financial assets or economic resources are themselves the subject of a prior judicial, administrative, or arbitral lien or judgement, immediately shall cause their transfer to the Development Fund for Iraq, it being understood that, unless otherwise addressed, claims made by private individuals or non-government entities on those transferred funds or other financial assets may be presented to the internationally recognized, representative government of Iraq; and *decides further* that all such funds or other financial assets or economic resources shall enjoy the same privileges, immunities, and protections as provided under paragraph 22;

24. *Requests* the Secretary-General to report to the Council at regular intervals on the work of the Special Representative with respect to the implementation of this resolution and on the work of the International Advisory and Monitoring Board and *encourages* the United Kingdom of Great Britain and Northern Ireland and the United States of America to inform the Council at regular intervals of their efforts under this resolution;

25. *Decides* to review the implementation of this resolution within twelve months of adoption and to consider further steps that might be necessary;

26. *Calls upon* Member States and international and regional organizations to contribute to the implementation of this resolution;

27. *Decides* to remain seized of this matter.

UNITED STATES STATUTES

ALIEN TORT CLAIMS ACT
Alien Tort Claims Act, 28 U.S.C. § 1350 (2006)

TITLE 28--JUDICIARY AND JUDICIAL PROCEDURE
PART IV--JURISDICTION AND VENUE
CHAPTER 85--DISTRICT COURTS; JURISDICTION

Sec. 1350. Alien's action for tort
The district courts shall have original jurisdiction of any civil action by an alien for a tort only, committed in violation of the law of nations or a treaty of the United States.

TORTURE VICTIM PROTECION ACT
Torture Victim Protection Act of 1991, Pub. L. No. 102-256, 106 Stat. 73

SECTION 1. SHORT TITLE.
This Act may be cited as the 'Torture Victim Protection Act of 1991'.

SEC. 2. ESTABLISHMENT OF CIVIL ACTION.

(a) Liability.--An individual who, under actual or apparent authority, or color of law, of any foreign nation—

> (1) subjects an individual to torture shall, in a civil action, be liable for damages to that individual; or

> (2) subjects an individual to extrajudicial killing shall, in a civil action, be liable for damages to the individual's legal representative, or to any person who may be a claimant in an action for wrongful death.

(b) Exhaustion of Remedies.--A court shall decline to hear a claim under this section if the claimant has not exhausted adequate and available remedies in the place in which the conduct giving rise to the claim occurred.

(c) Statute of Limitations.--No action shall be maintained under this section unless it is commenced within 10 years after the cause of action arose.

SEC. 3. DEFINITIONS.

(a) Extrajudicial Killing.--For the purposes of this Act, the term 'extrajudicial killing' means a deliberated killing not authorized by a previous judgment pronounced by a regularly constituted court affording all the judicial guarantees which are recognized as indispensable by civilized peoples. Such term, however, does not include any such killing that, under international law, is lawfully carried out under the authority of a foreign nation.

(b) Torture.--For the purposes of this Act—

> (1) the term 'torture' means any act, directed against an individual in the offender's custody or physical control, by which severe pain or suffering (other than pain or suffering arising only from or inherent in, or incidental to, lawful sanctions), whether physical or mental, is intentionally inflicted on that individual   for such purposes as obtaining from that individual or a third person information or a confession, punishing that individual for an act that individual or a third person has committed or is suspected of having committed, intimidating or coercing that individual or a third person, or for any reason based on discrimination of any kind; and

> (2) mental pain or suffering refers to prolonged mental harm caused by or resulting from—

>> (A) the intentional infliction or threatened infliction of severe physical pain or suffering;

>> (B) the administration or application, or threatened administration or application, of mind altering substances or other procedures calculated to disrupt profoundly the senses or the personality;

>> (C) the threat of imminent death; or

>> (D) the threat that another individual will imminently be subjected to death, severe physical pain or suffering, or the administration or application of mind altering substances or other procedures calculated to disrupt profoundly the senses or personality.

FOREIGN SOVEREIGN IMMUNITIES ACT

Foreign Sovereign Immunities Act, 28 U.S.C. §§ 1602-1611 (2006)

TITLE 28--JUDICIARY AND JUDICIAL PROCEDURE
PART IV--JURISDICTION AND VENUE
CHAPTER 97--JURISDICTIONAL IMMUNITIES OF FOREIGN STATES

Sec. 1602. Findings and declaration of purpose

The Congress finds that the determination by United States courts of the claims of foreign states to immunity from the jurisdiction of such courts would serve the interests of justice and would protect the rights of both foreign states and litigants in United States courts. Under international law, states are not immune from the jurisdiction of foreign courts insofar as their commercial activities are concerned, and their commercial property may be levied upon for the satisfaction of judgments rendered against them in connection with their commercial activities. Claims of foreign states to immunity should henceforth be decided by courts of the United States and of the States in conformity with the principles set forth in this chapter.

Sec. 1603. Definitions

For purposes of this chapter--

(a) A "foreign state", except as used in section 1608 of this title, includes a political subdivision of a foreign state or an agency or instrumentality of a foreign state as defined in subsection (b).

(b) An "agency or instrumentality of a foreign state" means any entity--

(1) which is a separate legal person, corporate or otherwise, and

(2) which is an organ of a foreign state or political subdivision thereof, or a majority of whose shares or other ownership interest is owned by a foreign state or political subdivision thereof, and

(3) which is neither a citizen of a State of the United States as defined in section 1332(c) and (e) of this title, nor created under the laws of any third country.

(c) The "United States" includes all territory and waters, continental or insular, subject to the jurisdiction of the United States.

(d) A "commercial activity" means either a regular course of commercial conduct or a particular commercial transaction or act. The commercial character of an activity shall be determined by reference to the nature of the course of conduct or particular transaction or act, rather than by reference to its purpose.

(e) A "commercial activity carried on in the United States by a foreign state" means commercial activity carried on by such state and having substantial contact with the United States.

Sec. 1604. Immunity of a foreign state from jurisdiction

Subject to existing international agreements to which the United States is a party at the time of enactment of this Act a foreign state shall be immune from the jurisdiction of the courts of the United States and of the States except as provided in sections 1605 to 1607 of this chapter.

Sec. 1605. General exceptions to the jurisdictional immunity of a foreign state

(a) A foreign state shall not be immune from the jurisdiction of courts of the United States or of the States in any case--

(1) in which the foreign state has waived its immunity either explicitly or by implication, notwithstanding any withdrawal of the waiver which the foreign state may purport to effect except in accordance with the terms of the waiver;

(2) in which the action is based upon a commercial activity carried on in the United States by the foreign state; or upon an act performed in the United States in connection with a commercial activity of the foreign state elsewhere; or upon an act outside the territory of the United States in connection with a commercial activity of the foreign state elsewhere and that act causes a direct effect in the United States;

(3) in which rights in property taken in violation of international law are in issue and that property or any property exchanged for such property is present in the United States in connection with a commercial activity carried on in the United States by the foreign state; or that property or any property exchanged for such property is owned or operated by an agency or instrumentality of the foreign state and that agency or instrumentality is engaged in a commercial activity in the United States;

(4) in which rights in property in the United States acquired by succession or gift or rights in immovable property situated in the United States are in issue;

(5) not otherwise encompassed in paragraph (2) above, in which money damages are sought against a foreign state for personal injury or death, or damage to or loss of property, occurring in the United States and caused by the tortious act or omission of that foreign state or of any official or employee of that foreign state while acting within the scope of his office or employment; except this paragraph shall not apply to--

(A) any claim based upon the exercise or performance or the failure to exercise or perform a discretionary function regardless of whether the discretion be abused, or

(B) any claim arising out of malicious prosecution, abuse of process, libel, slander, misrepresentation, deceit, or interference with contract rights; or

(6) in which the action is brought, either to enforce an agreement made by the foreign state with or for the benefit of a private party to submit to arbitration all or any differences which have arisen or which may arise between the parties with respect to a defined legal relationship, whether contractual or not, concerning a subject matter capable of settlement by arbitration under the laws of the United States, or to confirm an award made pursuant to such an agreement to arbitrate, if (A) the arbitration takes place or is intended to take place in the United States, (B) the agreement or award is or may be governed by a treaty or other international agreement in force for the United States calling for the recognition and enforcement of arbitral awards, (C) the underlying claim, save for the agreement to arbitrate, could have been brought in a United States court under this section or section 1607, or (D) paragraph (1) of this subsection is otherwise applicable.

(7) Repealed. Pub.L. 110-181, Div. A, § 1083(b)(1)(A)(iii), Jan. 28, 2008, 122 Stat. 341

(b) A foreign state shall not be immune from the jurisdiction of the courts of the United States in any case in which a suit in admiralty is brought to enforce a maritime lien against a vessel or cargo of the foreign state, which maritime lien is based upon a commercial activity of the foreign state: Provided, That--

(1) notice of the suit is given by delivery of a copy of the summons and of the complaint to the person, or his agent, having possession of the vessel or cargo against which the maritime lien is asserted; and if the vessel or cargo is arrested pursuant to process obtained on behalf of the party bringing the suit, the service of process of arrest shall be deemed to constitute valid delivery of such notice, but the party bringing the suit shall be liable for any damages sustained by the foreign state as a result of the arrest if the party bringing the suit had actual or constructive knowledge that the vessel or cargo of a foreign state was involved; and

(2) notice to the foreign state of the commencement of suit as provided in section 1608 of this title is initiated within ten days either of the delivery of notice as provided in paragraph (1) of this subsection or, in the case of a party who was unaware that the vessel or cargo of a foreign state was involved, of the date such party determined the existence of the foreign state's interest.

(c) Whenever notice is delivered under subsection (b)(1), the suit to enforce a maritime lien shall thereafter proceed and shall be heard and determined according to the principles of law and rules of practice of suits in rem whenever it appears that, had the vessel been privately owned and possessed, a suit in rem might have been maintained. A decree against the foreign state may include costs of the suit and, if the decree is for a money judgment, interest as ordered by the court, except that the court may not award judgment against the foreign state in an amount greater than the value of the vessel or cargo upon which the maritime lien arose. Such value shall be determined as of the time notice is served under subsection (b)(1). Decrees shall be subject to appeal and revision as provided in other cases of admiralty and maritime jurisdiction. Nothing shall preclude the plaintiff in any proper case from seeking relief in personam in the same action brought to enforce a maritime lien as provided in this section.

(d) A foreign state shall not be immune from the jurisdiction of the courts of the United States in any action brought to foreclose a preferred mortgage, as defined in section 31301 of title 46. Such action shall be brought, heard, and determined in accordance with the provisions of chapter 313 of title 46 and in accordance with the principles of law and rules of practice of suits in rem, whenever it appears that had the vessel been privately owned and possessed a suit in rem might have been maintained.

(e), (f) Repealed. Pub.L. 110-181, Div. A, Title X, § 1083(b)(1)(B), Jan. 28, 2008, 122 Stat. 341 [see Section 1605A, *infra*.]

(g) Limitation on discovery.--

(1) In general.—

(A) Subject to paragraph (2), if an action is filed that would otherwise be barred by section 1604, but for section 1605A, the court, upon request of the Attorney General, shall stay any request, demand, or order for discovery on the United States that the Attorney General certifies would significantly interfere with a criminal investigation or prosecution, or a national security operation, related to the incident that gave rise to the cause of action, until such time as the Attorney General advises the court that such request, demand, or order will no longer so interfere.

(B) A stay under this paragraph shall be in effect during the 12-month period beginning on the date on which the court issues the order to stay discovery. The court shall renew the order to stay discovery for additional 12-month periods upon motion by the United States if the Attorney General certifies that discovery would significantly interfere with a criminal investigation or prosecution, or a national security operation, related to the incident that gave rise to the cause of action.

(2) Sunset.—

(A) Subject to subparagraph (B), no stay shall be granted or continued in effect under paragraph (1) after the date that is 10 years after the date on which the incident that gave rise to the cause of action occurred.

(B) After the period referred to in subparagraph (A), the court, upon request of the Attorney General, may stay any request, demand, or order for discovery on the United States that the court finds a substantial likelihood would--

(i) create a serious threat of death or serious bodily injury to any person;

(ii) adversely affect the ability of the United States to work in cooperation with foreign and international law enforcement agencies in investigating violations of United States law; or

(iii) obstruct the criminal case related to the incident that gave rise to the cause of action or undermine the potential for a conviction in such case.

(3) Evaluation of evidence.--The court's evaluation of any request for a stay under this subsection filed by the Attorney General shall be conducted ex parte and in camera.

(4) Bar on motions to dismiss.--A stay of discovery under this subsection shall constitute a bar to the granting of a motion to dismiss under rules 12(b)(6) and 56 of the Federal Rules of Civil Procedure.

(5) Construction.--Nothing in this subsection shall prevent the United States from seeking protective orders or asserting privileges ordinarily available to the United States.

Sec. 1605A. Terrorism exception to the jurisdictional immunity of a foreign state

(a) In general.--

(1) No immunity.--A foreign state shall not be immune from the jurisdiction of courts of the United States or of the States in any case not otherwise covered by this chapter in which money damages are sought against a foreign state for personal injury or death that was caused by an act of torture, extrajudicial killing, aircraft sabotage, hostage taking, or the provision of material support or resources for such an act if such act or provision of material support or resources is engaged in by an official, employee, or agent of such foreign state while acting within the scope of his or her office, employment, or agency.

(2) Claim heard.--The court shall hear a claim under this section if--

(A)(i)(I) the foreign state was designated as a state sponsor of terrorism at the time the act described in paragraph (1) occurred, or was so designated as a result of such act, and, subject to subclause (II), either remains so designated when the claim is filed under this section or was so designated within the 6-month period before the claim is filed under this section; or

(II) in the case of an action that is refiled under this section by reason of section 1083(c)(2)(A) of the National Defense Authorization Act for Fiscal Year 2008 or is filed under this section by reason of section 1083(c)(3) of that Act, the foreign state was designated as a state sponsor of terrorism when the original action or the related action under section 1605(a)(7) (as in effect before the enactment of this section) or section 589 of the Foreign Operations, Export Financing, and Related Programs Appropriations Act, 1997 (as contained in section 101(c) of division A of Public Law 104-208) was filed;

(ii) the claimant or the victim was, at the time the act described in paragraph (1) occurred--

(I) a national of the United States;

(II) a member of the armed forces; or

(III) otherwise an employee of the Government of the United States, or of an individual performing a contract awarded by the United

States Government, acting within the scope of the employee's employment; and

(iii) in a case in which the act occurred in the foreign state against which the claim has been brought, the claimant has afforded the foreign state a reasonable opportunity to arbitrate the claim in accordance with the accepted international rules of arbitration; or

(B) the act described in paragraph (1) is related to Case Number 1:00CV03110 (EGS) in the United States District Court for the District of Columbia.

(b) Limitations.--An action may be brought or maintained under this section if the action is commenced, or a related action was commenced under section 1605(a)(7) (before the date of the enactment of this section) or section 589 of the Foreign Operations, Export Financing, and Related Programs Appropriations Act, 1997 (as contained in section 101(c) of division A of Public Law 104-208) not later than the latter of--

(1) 10 years after April 24, 1996; or

(2) 10 years after the date on which the cause of action arose.

(c) Private right of action.--A foreign state that is or was a state sponsor of terrorism as described in subsection (a)(2)(A)(i), and any official, employee, or agent of that foreign state while acting within the scope of his or her office, employment, or agency, shall be liable to--

(1) a national of the United States,

(2) a member of the armed forces,

(3) an employee of the Government of the United States, or of an individual performing a contract awarded by the United States Government, acting within the scope of the employee's employment, or

(4) the legal representative of a person described in paragraph (1), (2), or (3),

for personal injury or death caused by acts described in subsection (a) (1) of that foreign state, or of an official, employee, or agent of that foreign state, for which the courts of the United States may maintain jurisdiction under this section for money damages. In any such action, damages may include economic damages, solatium, pain and suffering, and punitive damages. In any such action, a foreign state shall be vicariously liable for the acts of its officials, employees, or agents.

(d) Additional damages.--After an action has been brought under subsection (c), actions may also be brought for reasonably foreseeable property loss, whether insured or uninsured, third party liability, and loss claims under life and property insurance policies, by reason of the same acts on which the action under subsection (c) is based.

(e) Special masters.--

(1) In general.--The courts of the United States may appoint special masters to hear damage claims brought under this section.

(2) Transfer of funds.--The Attorney General shall transfer, from funds available for the program under section 1404C of the Victims of Crime Act of 1984 (42 U.S.C. 10603c), to the Administrator of the United States district court in which any case is pending which has been brought or maintained under this section such funds as may be required to cover the costs of special masters appointed under paragraph (1). Any amount paid in compensation to any such special master shall constitute an item of court costs.

(f) Appeal.--In an action brought under this section, appeals from orders not conclusively ending the litigation may only be taken pursuant to section 1292(b) of this title.

(g) Property disposition.--

(1) In general.--In every action filed in a United States district court in which jurisdiction is alleged under this section, the filing of a notice of pending action pursuant to this section, to which is attached a copy of the complaint filed in the action, shall have the effect of establishing a lien of lis pendens upon any real property or tangible personal property that is--

(A) subject to attachment in aid of execution, or execution, under section 1610;

(B) located within that judicial district; and

(C) titled in the name of any defendant, or titled in the name of any entity controlled by any defendant if such notice contains a statement listing such controlled entity.

468

(2) Notice.--A notice of pending action pursuant to this section shall be filed by the clerk of the district court in the same manner as any pending action and shall be indexed by listing as defendants all named defendants and all entities listed as controlled by any defendant.

(3) Enforceability.--Liens established by reason of this subsection shall be enforceable as provided in chapter 111 of this title.

(h) Definitions.--For purposes of this section--

(1) the term "aircraft sabotage" has the meaning given that term in Article 1 of the Convention for the Suppression of Unlawful Acts Against the Safety of Civil Aviation;

(2) the term "hostage taking" has the meaning given that term in Article 1 of the International Convention Against the Taking of Hostages;

(3) the term "material support or resources" has the meaning given that term in section 2339A of title 18;

(4) the term "armed forces" has the meaning given that term in section 101 of title 10;

(5) the term "national of the United States" has the meaning given that term in section 101(a)(22) of the Immigration and Nationality Act (8 U.S.C. 1101(a)(22));

(6) the term "state sponsor of terrorism" means a country the government of which the Secretary of State has determined, for purposes of section 6(j) of the Export Administration Act of 1979 (50 U.S.C. App. 2405(j)), section 620A of the Foreign Assistance Act of 1961 (22 U.S.C. 2371), section 40 of the Arms Export Control Act (22 U.S.C. 2780), or any other provision of law, is a government that has repeatedly provided support for acts of international terrorism; and

(7) the terms "torture" and "extrajudicial killing" have the meaning given those terms in section 3 of the Torture Victim Protection Act of 1991 (28 U.S.C. 1350 note).

Sec. 1606. Extent of liability

As to any claim for relief with respect to which a foreign state is not entitled to immunity under section 1605 or 1607 of this chapter, the foreign state shall be liable in the same manner and to the same extent as a private individual under like circumstances; but a foreign state except for an agency or instrumentality thereof shall not be liable for punitive damages; if, however, in any case wherein death was caused, the law of the place where the action or omission occurred provides, or has been construed to provide, for damages only punitive in nature, the foreign state shall be liable for actual or compensatory damages measured by the pecuniary injuries resulting from such death which were incurred by the persons for whose benefit the action was brought.

Sec. 1607. Counterclaims

In any action brought by a foreign state, or in which a foreign state intervenes, in a court of the United States or of a State, the foreign state shall not be accorded immunity with respect to any counterclaim--

(a) for which a foreign state would not be entitled to immunity under section 1605 or 1605A of this chapter had such claim been brought in a separate action against the foreign state; or

(b) arising out of the transaction or occurrence that is the subject matter of the claim of the foreign state; or

(c) to the extent that the counterclaim does not seek relief exceeding in amount or differing in kind from that sought by the foreign state.

Sec. 1608. Service; time to answer; default

(a) Service in the courts of the United States and of the States shall be made upon a foreign state or political subdivision of a foreign state:

(1) by delivery of a copy of the summons and complaint in accordance with any special arrangement for service between the plaintiff and the foreign state or political subdivision; or

(2) if no special arrangement exists, by delivery of a copy of the summons and complaint in accordance with an applicable international convention on service of judicial documents; or

(3) if service cannot be made under paragraphs (1) or (2), by sending a copy of the summons and complaint and a notice of suit, together with a translation of each into the official language of the foreign state, by any form of mail requiring a signed receipt, to be addressed and dispatched by the clerk of the court to the head of the ministry of foreign affairs of the foreign state concerned, or

(4) if service cannot be made within 30 days under paragraph (3), by sending two copies of the summons and complaint and a notice of suit, together with a translation of each into the official language of the foreign state, by any form of mail requiring a signed receipt, to be addressed and dispatched by the clerk of the court to the Secretary of State in Washington, District of Columbia, to the attention of the Director of Special Consular Services--and the Secretary shall transmit one copy of the papers through diplomatic channels to the foreign state and shall send to the clerk of the court a certified copy of the diplomatic note indicating when the papers were transmitted.

As used in this subsection, a "notice of suit" shall mean a notice addressed to a foreign state and in a form prescribed by the Secretary of State by regulation.

(b) Service in the courts of the United States and of the States shall be made upon an agency or instrumentality of a foreign state:

(1) by delivery of a copy of the summons and complaint in accordance with any special arrangement for service between the plaintiff and the agency or instrumentality; or

(2) if no special arrangement exists, by delivery of a copy of the summons and complaint either to an officer, a managing or general agent, or to any other agent authorized by appointment or by law to receive service of process in the United States; or in accordance with an applicable international convention on service of judicial documents; or

(3) if service cannot be made under paragraphs (1) or (2), and if reasonably calculated to give actual notice, by delivery of a copy of the summons and complaint, together with a translation of each into the official language of the foreign state--

(A) as directed by an authority of the foreign state or political subdivision in response to a letter rogatory or request or

(B) by any form of mail requiring a signed receipt, to be addressed and dispatched by the clerk of the court to the agency or instrumentality to be served, or

(C) as directed by order of the court consistent with the law of the place where service is to be made.

(c) Service shall be deemed to have been made--

(1) in the case of service under subsection (a)(4), as of the date of transmittal indicated in the certified copy of the diplomatic note; and

(2) in any other case under this section, as of the date of receipt indicated in the certification, signed and returned postal receipt, or other proof of service applicable to the method of service employed.

(d) In any action brought in a court of the United States or of a State, a foreign state, a political subdivision thereof, or an agency or instrumentality of a foreign state shall serve an answer or other responsive pleading to the complaint within sixty days after service has been made under this section.

(e) No judgment by default shall be entered by a court of the United States or of a State against a foreign state, a political subdivision thereof, or an agency or instrumentality of a foreign state, unless the claimant establishes his claim or right to relief by evidence satisfactory to the court. A copy of any such default judgment shall be sent to the foreign state or political subdivision in the manner prescribed for service in this section.

Sec. 1609. Immunity from attachment and execution of property of a foreign state

Subject to existing international agreements to which the United States is a party at the time of enactment of this Act the property in the United States of a foreign state shall be immune from attachment arrest and execution except as provided in sections 1610 and 1611 of this chapter.

Sec. 1610. Exceptions to the immunity from attachment or execution

(a) The property in the United States of a foreign state, as defined in section 1603(a) of this chapter, used for a commercial activity in the United States, shall not be immune from attachment in aid of execution, or from execution, upon a judgment entered by a court of the United States or of a State after the effective date of this Act, if--

(1) the foreign state has waived its immunity from attachment in aid of execution or from execution either explicitly or by implication, notwithstanding any withdrawal of the waiver the foreign state may purport to effect except in accordance with the terms of the waiver, or

(2) the property is or was used for the commercial activity upon which the claim is based, or

(3) the execution relates to a judgment establishing rights in property which has been taken in violation of international law or which has been exchanged for property taken in violation of international law, or

(4) the execution relates to a judgment establishing rights in property--

(A) which is acquired by succession or gift, or

(B) which is immovable and situated in the United States: Provided, That such property is not used for purposes of maintaining a diplomatic or consular mission or the residence of the Chief of such mission, or

(5) the property consists of any contractual obligation or any proceeds from such a contractual obligation to indemnify or hold harmless the foreign state or its employees under a policy of automobile or other liability or casualty insurance covering the claim which merged into the judgment, or

(6) the judgment is based on an order confirming an arbitral award rendered against the foreign state, provided that attachment in aid of execution, or execution, would not be inconsistent with any provision in the arbitral agreement, or

(7) the judgment relates to a claim for which the foreign state is not immune under section 1605A, regardless of whether the property is or was involved with the act upon which the claim is based.

(b) In addition to subsection (a), any property in the United States of an agency or instrumentality of a foreign state engaged in commercial activity in the United States shall not be immune from attachment in aid of execution, or from execution, upon a judgment entered by a court of the United States or of a State after the effective date of this Act, if--

(1) the agency or instrumentality has waived its immunity from attachment in aid of execution or from execution either explicitly or implicitly, notwithstanding any withdrawal of the waiver the agency or instrumentality may purport to effect except in accordance with the terms of the waiver, or

(2) the judgment relates to a claim for which the agency or instrumentality is not immune by virtue of section 1605(a) (2), (3), or (5), 1605(b), or 1605A of this chapter, regardless of whether the property is or was involved in the act upon which the claim is based.

(c) No attachment or execution referred to in subsections (a) and (b) of this section shall be permitted until the court has ordered such attachment and execution after having determined that a reasonable period of time has elapsed following the entry of judgment and the giving of any notice required under section 1608(e) of this chapter.

(d) The property of a foreign state, as defined in section 1603(a) of this chapter, used for a commercial activity in the United States, shall not be immune from attachment prior to the entry of judgment in any action brought in a court of the United States or of a State, or prior to the elapse of the period of time provided in subsection (c) of this section, if--

(1) the foreign state has explicitly waived its immunity from attachment prior to judgment, notwithstanding any withdrawal of the waiver the foreign state may purport to effect except in accordance with the terms of the waiver, and

(2) the purpose of the attachment is to secure satisfaction of a judgment that has been or may ultimately be entered against the foreign state, and not to obtain jurisdiction.

(e) The vessels of a foreign state shall not be immune from arrest in rem, interlocutory sale, and execution in actions brought to foreclose a preferred mortgage as provided in section 1605(d).

(f)   (1)   (A) Notwithstanding any other provision of law, including but not limited to section 208(f) of the Foreign Missions Act (22 U.S.C. 4308(f)), and except as provided in subparagraph (B), any property with respect to which financial transactions are prohibited or regulated pursuant to section 5(b) of the Trading with the Enemy Act (50 U.S.C. App. 5(b)), section 620(a) of the Foreign Assistance Act of 1961 (22 U.S.C. 2370(a)), sections 202 and 203 of the International Emergency Economic Powers Act (50 U.S.C. 1701-1702), or any other proclamation, order, regulation, or license issued pursuant thereto, shall be subject to execution or attachment in aid of execution of any judgment relating to a claim for which a foreign state (including any agency or instrumentality or such state)

471

claiming such property is not immune under section 1605(a)(7) (as in effect before the enactment of section 1605A) or section 1605A.

(B) Subparagraph (A) shall not apply if, at the time the property is expropriated or seized by the foreign state, the property has been held in title by a natural person or, if held in trust, has been held for the benefit of a natural person or persons.

(2)(A) At the request of any party in whose favor a judgment has been issued with respect to a claim for which the foreign state is not immune under section 1605(a)(7) (as in effect before the enactment of section 1605A) or section 1605A, the Secretary of the Treasury and the Secretary of State should make every effort to fully, promptly, and effectively assist any judgment creditor or any court that has issued any such judgment in identifying, locating, and executing against the property of that foreign state or any agency or instrumentality of such state.

(B) In providing such assistance, the Secretaries--

(i) may provide such information to the court under seal; and

(ii) should make every effort to provide the information in a manner sufficient to allow the court to direct the United States Marshall's office to promptly and effectively execute against that property.

(3) Waiver.--The President may waive any provision of paragraph (1) in the interest of national security.

(g) Property in certain actions.--

(1) In general.--Subject to paragraph (3), the property of a foreign state against which a judgment is entered under section 1605A, and the property of an agency or instrumentality of such a state, including property that is a separate juridical entity or is an interest held directly or indirectly in a separate juridical entity, is subject to attachment in aid of execution, and execution, upon that judgment as provided in this section, regardless of--

(A) the level of economic control over the property by the government of the foreign state;

(B) whether the profits of the property go to that government;

(C) the degree to which officials of that government manage the property or otherwise control its daily affairs;

(D) whether that government is the sole beneficiary in interest of the property; or

(E) whether establishing the property as a separate entity would entitle the foreign state to benefits in United States courts while avoiding its obligations.

(2) United States sovereign immunity inapplicable.--Any property of a foreign state, or agency or instrumentality of a foreign state, to which paragraph (1) applies shall not be immune from attachment in aid of execution, or execution, upon a judgment entered under section 1605A because the property is regulated by the United States Government by reason of action taken against that foreign state under the Trading With the Enemy Act or the International Emergency Economic Powers Act.

(3) Third-party joint property holders.--Nothing in this subsection shall be construed to supersede the authority of a court to prevent appropriately the impairment of an interest held by a person who is not liable in the action giving rise to a judgment in property subject to attachment in aid of execution, or execution, upon such judgment.

Sec. 1611. Certain types of property immune from execution

(a) Notwithstanding the provisions of section 1610 of this chapter, the property of those organizations designated by the President as being entitled to enjoy the privileges, exemptions, and immunities provided by the International Organizations Immunities Act shall not be subject to attachment or any other judicial process impeding the disbursement of funds to, or on the order of, a foreign state as the result of an action brought in the courts of the United States or of the States.

(b) Notwithstanding the provisions of section 1610 of this chapter, the property of a foreign state shall be immune from attachment and from execution, if--

(1) the property is that of a foreign central bank or monetary authority held for its own account, unless such bank or authority, or its parent foreign government, has explicitly waived its immunity from attachment in aid of execution, or from execution, notwithstanding any withdrawal

of the waiver which the bank, authority or government may purport to effect except in accordance with the terms of the waiver; or

> (2) the property is, or is intended to be, used in connection with a military activity and
>> (A) is of a military character, or
>> (B) is under the control of a military authority or defense agency.

(c) Notwithstanding the provisions of section 1610 of this chapter, the property of a foreign state shall be immune from attachment and from execution in an action brought under section 302 of the Cuban Liberty and Democratic Solidarity (LIBERTAD) Act of 1996 to the extent that the property is a facility or installation used by an accredited diplomatic mission for official purposes.

CIVIL ACTION FOR DEPRIVATION OF RIGHTS
42 U.S.C. § 1983 (2006)

TITLE 42--THE PUBLIC HEALTH AND WELFARE
CHAPTER 21--CIVIL RIGHTS
SUBCHAPTER I--GENERALLY

Sec. 1983. Civil action for deprivation of rights

Every person who, under color of any statute, ordinance, regulation, custom, or usage, of any State or Territory or the District of Columbia, subjects, or causes to be subjected, any citizen of the United States or other person within the jurisdiction thereof to the deprivation of any rights, privileges, or immunities secured by the Constitution and laws, shall be liable to the party injured in an action at law, suit in equity, or other proper proceeding for redress, except that in any action brought against a judicial officer for an act or omission taken in such officer's judicial capacity, injunctive relief shall not be granted unless a declaratory decree was violated or declaratory relief was unavailable. For the purposes of this section, any Act of Congress applicable exclusively to the District of Columbia shall be considered to be a statute of the District of Columbia.

THE WESTFALL ACT
The Westfall Act, 28 U.S.C. § 2679 (2006)

TITLE 28--JUDICIARY AND JUDICIAL PROCEDURE
PART VI--PARTICULAR PROCEEDINGS
CHAPTER 171--TORT CLAIMS PROCEDURE

Sec. 2679. Exclusiveness of remedy

(a) The authority of any federal agency to sue and be sued in its own name shall not be construed to authorize suits against such federal agency on claims which are cognizable under section 1346(b) of this title, and the remedies provided by this title in such cases shall be exclusive.

> (b) (1) The remedy against the United States provided by sections 1346(b) and 2672 of this title for injury or loss of property, or personal injury or death arising or resulting from the negligent or wrongful act or omission of any employee of the Government while acting within the scope of his office or employment is exclusive of any other civil action or proceeding for money damages by reason of the same subject matter against the employee whose act or omission gave rise to the claim or against the estate of such employee. Any other civil action or proceeding for money damages arising out of or relating to the same subject matter against the employee or the employee's estate is precluded without regard to when the act or omission occurred.

> (2) Paragraph (1) does not extend or apply to a civil action against an employee of the Government—

    (A) which is brought for a violation of the Constitution of the United States, or

    (B) which is brought for a violation of a statute of the United States under which such action against an individual is otherwise authorized.

  (c) The Attorney General shall defend any civil action or proceeding brought in any court against any employee of the Government or his estate for any such damage or injury. The employee against whom such civil action or proceeding is brought shall deliver within such time after date of service or knowledge of service as determined by the Attorney General, all process served upon him or an attested true copy thereof to his immediate superior or to whomever was designated by the head of his department to receive such papers and such person shall promptly furnish copies of the pleadings and process therein to the United States attorney for the district embracing the place wherein the proceeding is brought, to the Attorney General, and to the head of his employing Federal agency.

  (d) (1) Upon certification by the Attorney General that the defendant employee was acting within the scope of his office or employment at the time of the incident out of which the claim arose, any civil action or proceeding commenced upon such claim in a United States district court shall be deemed an action against the United States under the provisions of this title and all references thereto, and the United States shall be substituted as the party defendant.

    (2) Upon certification by the Attorney General that the defendant employee was acting within the scope of his office or employment at the time of the incident out of which the claim arose, any civil action or proceeding commenced upon such claim in a State court shall be removed without bond at any time before trial by the Attorney General to the district court of the United States for the district and division embracing the place in which the action or proceeding is pending. Such action or proceeding shall be deemed to be an action or proceeding brought against the United States under the provisions of this title and all references thereto, and the United States shall be substituted as the party defendant. This certification of the Attorney General shall conclusively establish scope of office or employment for purposes of removal.

    (3) In the event that the Attorney General has refused to certify scope of office or employment under this section, the employee may at any time before trial petition the court to find and certify that the employee was acting within the scope of his office or employment. Upon such certification by the court, such action or proceeding shall be deemed to be an action or proceeding brought against the United States under the provisions of this title and all references thereto, and the United States shall be substituted as the party defendant. A copy of the petition shall be served upon the United States in accordance with the provisions of Rule 4(d)(4) of the Federal Rules of Civil Procedure. In the event the petition is filed in a civil action or proceeding pending in a State court, the action or proceeding may be removed without bond by the Attorney General to the district court of the United States for the district and division embracing the place in which it is pending. If, in considering the petition, the district court determines that the employee was not acting within the scope of his office or employment, the action or proceeding shall be remanded to the State court.

    (4) Upon certification, any action or proceeding subject to paragraph (1), (2), or (3) shall proceed in the same manner as any action against the United States filed pursuant to section 1346(b) of this title and shall be subject to the limitations and exceptions applicable to those actions.

    (5) Whenever an action or proceeding in which the United States is substituted as the party defendant under this subsection is dismissed for failure first to present a claim pursuant to section 2675(a) of this title, such a claim shall be deemed to be timely presented under section 2401(b) of this title if—

    (A) the claim would have been timely had it been filed on the date the underlying civil action was commenced, and

    (B) the claim is presented to the appropriate Federal agency within 60 days after dismissal of the civil action.

  (e) The Attorney General may compromise or settle any claim asserted in such civil action or proceeding in the manner provided in section 2677, and with the same effect.

COMPREHENSIVE ANTI-APARTHEID ACT OF 1986

Comprehensive Anti-Apartheid Act of 1986, Pub. L. No. 99-440, 100 Stat. 1087 (codified as amended in scattered sections of 22 U.S.C, repealed 1993)

An Act to prohibit loans to, other investments in, and certain other activities with respect to, South Africa, and for other purposes

Be it enacted by the Senate and House of Representatives of the United States of America in Congress assembled,

SHORT TITLE

SECTION 1. This Act may be cited as the "Comprehensive Anti-Apartheid Act of 1986" "22 USC 5001 note." * * *

DEFINITIONS

SEC. 3. "22 USC 5001." As used in this Act --

(1) the term "Code of Conduct" refers to the principles set forth in section 208(a);

(2) the term "controlled South African entity" means --

> (A) a corporation, partnership, or other business association or entity organized in South Africa and owned or controlled, directly or indirectly, by a national of the United States; or
>
> (B) a branch, office, agency, or sole proprietorship in South Africa of a national of the United States;

(3) the term "loan" --

> (A) means any transfer or extension of funds or credit on the basis of an obligation to repay or any assumption or guarantee of the obligation of another to repay an extension of funds or credit, including --
>
>> (i) overdrafts,
>>
>> (ii) currency swaps,
>>
>> (iii) the purchase of debt or equity securities issued by the Government of South Africa or a South African entity on or after the date of enactment of this Act,
>>
>> (iv) the purchase of a loan made by another person,
>>
>> (v) the sale of financial assets subject to an agreement to repurchase, and
>>
>> (vi) a renewal or refinancing whereby funds or credits are transferred or extended to the Government of South Africa or a South African entity, and
>
> (B) does not include --
>
>> (i) normal short-term trade financing, as by letters of credit or similar trade credits;
>>
>> (ii) sales on open account in cases where such sales are normal business practice; or
>>
>> (iii) rescheduling of existing loans, if no new funds or credits are thereby extended to a South African entity or the Government of South Africa;

(4) the term "new investment" --

> (A) means --
>
>> (i) a commitment or contribution of funds or other assets, and
>>
>> (ii) a loan or other extension of credit, and
>
> (B) does not include --
>
>> (i) the reinvestment of profits generated by a controlled South African entity into that same controlled South African entity or the investment of such profits in a South African entity;
>>
>> (ii) contributions of money or other assets where such contributions are necessary to enable a controlled South African entity to operate in an economically sound manner, without expanding its operations; or
>>
>> (iii) the ownership or control of a share or interest in a South African entity or a controlled South African entity or a debt or equity security issued by the Government of South Africa or a South African entity before the date of enactment of this Act, or the transfer or acquisition of such a share, interest, or debt or equity security, if any such transfer or acquisition does not result in a payment, contribution of funds or assets, or

475

credit to a South African entity, a controlled South African entity, or the Government of South Africa;

(5) the term "national of the United States" means --

    (A) a natural person who is a citizen of the United States or who owes permanent allegiance to the United States or is an alien lawfully admitted for permanent residence in the United States, as defined by section 101(a)(20) of the Immigration and Nationality Act (8 U.S.C. 1101(a)(20)); or

    (B) a corporation, partnership, or other business association which is organized under the laws of the United States, any State or territory thereof, or the District of Columbia;

(6) the term "South Africa" includes --

    (A) the Republic of South Africa;

    (B) any territory under the Administration, legal or illegal, of South Africa; and

    (C) the "bantustans" or "homelands", to which South African blacks are assigned on the basis of ethnic origin, including the Transkei, Bophuthatswana Ciskei, and Venda; and

(7) the term "South African entity" means --

    (A) a corporation, partnership, or other business association or entity organized in South Africa; or

    (B) a branch, office, agency, or sole proprietorship in South Africa of a person that resides or is organized outside South Africa; and

(8) the term "United States" includes the States of the United States, the District of Columbia, the Commonwealth of Puerto Rico, and any territory or possession of the United States.

PURPOSE

SEC. 4. "22 USC 5002." The purpose of this Act is to set forth a comprehensive and complete framework to guide the efforts of the United States in helping to bring an end to apartheid in South Africa and lead to the establishment of a nonracial, democratic form of government. This Act sets out United States policy toward the Government of South Africa, the victims of apartheid, and the other states in southern Africa. It also provides the President with additional authority to work with the other industrial democracies to help end apartheid and establish democracy in South Africa.

TITLE I -- POLICY OF THE UNITED STATES WITH RESPECT TO ENDING APARTHEID

POLICY TOWARD THE GOVERNMENT OF SOUTH AFRICA

SEC. 101. "22 USC 5011." (a) United States policy toward the Government of South Africa shall be designed to bring about reforms in that system of government that will lead to the establishment of a nonracial democracy.

(b) The United States will work toward this goal by encouraging the Government of South Africa to --

    (1) repeal the present state of emergency and respect the principle of equal justice under law for citizens of all races;

    (2) release Nelson Mandela, Govan Mbeki, Walter Sisulu, black trade union leaders, and all political prisoners;

    (3) permit the free exercise by South Africans of all races of the right to form political parties, express political opinions, and otherwise participate in the political process;

    (4) establish a timetable for the elimination of apartheid laws;

    (5) negotiate with representatives of all racial groups in South Africa the future political system in South Africa; and

    (6) end military and paramilitary activities aimed at neighboring states.

(c) The United States will encourage the actions set forth in subsection (b) through economic, political, and diplomatic measures as set forth in this Act. The United States will adjust its actions toward the Government of South Africa to reflect the progress or lack of progress made by the Government of South Africa in meeting the goal set forth in subsection (a).

POLICY TOWARD THE AFRICAN NATIONAL CONGRESS, ETC.

SEC. 102. "22 USC 5012." (a) United States policy toward the African National Congress, the Pan African Congress, and their affiliates shall be designed to bring about a suspension of violence that will lead to the start of negotiations designed to bring about a nonracial and genuine democracy in South Africa.

(b) The United States shall work toward this goal by encouraging the African National Congress and the Pan African Congress, and their affiliates, to --

476

(1) suspend terrorist activities so that negotiations with the Government of South Africa and other groups representing black South Africans will be possible;

(2) make known their commitment to a free and democratic post-apartheid South Africa;

(3) agree to enter into negotiations with the South African Government and other groups representing black South Africans for the peaceful solution of the problems of South Africa;

(4) reexamine their ties to the South African Communist Party.

(c) The United States will encourage the actions set forth in subsection (b) through political and diplomatic measures. The United States will adjust its actions toward the Government of South Africa not only to reflect progress or lack of progress made by the Government of South Africa in meeting the goal set forth in subsection 101(a) but also to reflect progress or lack of progress made by the ANC and other organizations in meeting the goal set forth in subsection (a) of this section.

POLICY TOWARD THE VICTIMS OF APARTHEID

SEC. 103. "22 USC 5013" (a) The United States policy toward the victims of apartheid is to use economic, political, diplomatic, and other effective means to achieve the removal of the root cause of their victimization, which is the apartheid system. In anticipation of the removal of the system of apartheid and as a further means of challenging that system, it is the policy of the United States to assist these victims of apartheid as individuals and through organizations to overcome the handicaps imposed on them by the system of apartheid and to help prepare them for their rightful roles as full participants in the political, social, economic, and intellectual life of their country in the post-apartheid South Africa envisioned by this Act.

(b) The United States will work toward the purposes of subsection (a) by --

(1) providing assistance to South African victims of apartheid without discrimination by race, color, sex, religious belief, or political orientation, to take advantage of educational opportunities in South Africa and in the United States to prepare for leadership positions in a post-apartheid South Africa;

(2) assisting victims of apartheid;

(3) aiding individuals or groups in South Africa whose goals are to aid victims of apartheid or foster nonviolent legal or political challenges to the apartheid laws;

(4) furnishing direct financial assistance to those whose nonviolent activities had led to their arrest or detention by the South African authorities and (B) to the families of those killed by terrorist acts such as "necklacings";

(5) intervening at the highest political levels in South Africa to express the strong desire of the United States to see the development in South Africa of a nonracial democratic society;

(6) supporting the rights of the victims of apartheid through political, economic, or other sanctions in the event the Government of South Africa fails to make progress toward the removal of the apartheid laws and the establishment of such democracy; and

(7) supporting the rights of all Africans to be free of terrorist attacks by setting a time limit after which the United States will pursue diplomatic and political measures against those promoting terrorism and against those countries harboring such groups so as to achieve the objectives of this Act.

POLICY TOWARD OTHER COUNTRIES IN SOUTHERN AFRICA

SEC. 104. "22 USC 5014" (a) The United States policy toward the other countries in the Southern African region shall be designed to encourage democratic forms of government, full respect for human rights, an end to cross-border terrorism, political independence, and economic development.

(b) The United States will work toward the purposes of subsection (a) by --

(1) helping to secure the independence of Namibia and the establishment of Namibia as a nonracial democracy in accordance with appropriate United Nations Security Council resolutions;

(2) supporting the removal of all foreign military forces from the region;

(3) encouraging the nations of the region to settle differences through peaceful means;

(4) promoting economic development through bilateral and multilateral economic assistance targeted at increasing opportunities in the productive sectors of national economies, with a particular emphasis on increasing opportunities for non-governmental economic activities;

(5) encouraging, and when necessary, strongly demanding, that all countries of the region respect the human rights of their citizens and noncitizens residing in the country, and especially the release of persons persecuted for their political beliefs or detained without trial;

(6) encouraging, and when necessary, strongly demanding that all countries of the region take effective action to end cross-border terrorism; and

(7) providing appropriate assistance, within the limitations of American responsibilities at home and in other regions, to assist regional economic cooperation and the development of interregional transportation and other capital facilities necessary for economic growth.

POLICY TOWARD "FRONTLINE" STATES

SEC. 105. "22 USC 5015" It is the sense of the Congress that the President should discuss with the governments of the African "frontline" states the effects on them of disruptions in transportation or other economic links through South Africa and of means of reducing those effects.

POLICY TOWARD A NEGOTIATED SETTLEMENT

SEC. 106. "22 USC 5016" (a)

(1) United States policy will seek to promote negotiations among representatives of all citizens of South Africa to determine a future political system that would permit all citizens to be full participants in the governance of their country. The United States recognizes that important and legitimate political parties in South Africa include several organizations that have been banned and will work for the unbanning of such organizations in order to permit legitimate political viewpoints to be represented at such negotiations. The United States also recognizes that some of the organizations fighting apartheid have become infiltrated by Communists and that Communists serve on the governing boards of such organizations.

(2) To this end, it is the sense of the Congress that the President, the Secretary of State, or other appropriate high-level United States officials should meet with the leaders of opposition organizations of South Africa, particularly but not limited to those organizations representing the black majority. Furthermore, the President, in concert with the major allies of the United States and other interested parties, should seek to bring together opposition political leaders with leaders of the Government of South Africa for the purpose of negotiations to achieve a transition to the post-apartheid democracy envisioned in this Act.

(b) The United States will encourage the Government of South Africa and all participants to the negotiations to respect the right of all South Africans to form political parties, express political opinions, and otherwise participate in the political process without fear of retribution by either governmental or nongovernmental organizations. It is the sense of the Congress that a suspension of violence is an essential precondition for the holding of negotiations. The United States calls upon all parties to the conflict to agree to a suspension of violence.

(c) The United States will work toward the achievement of agreement to suspend violence and begin negotiations through coordinated actions with the major Western allies and with the governments of the countries in the region.

(d) It is the sense of the Congress that the achievement of an agreement for negotiations could be promoted if the United States and its major allies, such as Great Britain, Canada, France, Italy, Japan, and West Germany, would hold a meeting to develop a four-point plan to discuss with the Government of South Africa a proposal for stages of multilateral assistance to South Africa in return for the Government of South Africa implementing --

(1) an end to the state of emergency and the release of the political prisoners, including Nelson Mandela;

(2) the unbanning of the African National Congress, the Pan African Congress, the Black Consciousness Movement, and all other groups willing to suspend terrorism and to participate in negotiations and a democratic process;

(3) a revocation of the Group Areas Act and the Population Registration Act and the granting of universal citizenship to all South Africans, including homeland residents; and

(4) the use of the international offices of a third party as an intermediary to bring about negotiations with the object of the establishment of power- sharing with the black majority.

POLICY TOWARD INTERNATIONAL COOPERATION ON MEASURES TO END APARTHEID

SEC. 107. "22 USC 5017" (a) The Congress finds that --
  (1) international cooperation is a prerequisite to an effective anti-apartheid policy and to the suspension of terrorism in South Africa; and
  (2) the situation in South Africa constitutes an emergency in international relations and that action is necessary for the protection of the essential security interests of the United States.
(b) Accordingly, the Congress urges the President to seek such cooperation among all individuals, groups, and nations.

POLICY TOWARD NECKLACING
SEC. 108. "22 USC 5018" It is the sense of the Congress that the African National Congress should strongly condemn and take effective actions against the execution by fire, commonly known as "necklacing", of any person in any country.

UNITED STATES AMBASSADOR TO MEET WITH NELSON MANDELA
SEC. 109. "22 USC 5019" It is the sense of the Senate that the United States Ambassador should promptly make a formal request to the South African Government for the United States Ambassador to meet with Nelson Mandela.

POLICY TOWARD the RECRUITMENT and TRAINING OF BLACK SOUTH AFRICANS BY UNITED STATES EMPLOYERS
SEC. 110. "22 USC 5020" (a) The Congress finds that --
  (1) the policy of apartheid is abhorrent and morally repugnant;
  (2) the United States believes strongly in the principles of democracy and individual freedoms;
  (3) the United States endorses the policy of political participation of all citizens;
  (4) a free, open, and vital economy is a primary means for achieving social equality and economic advancement for all citizens; and
  (5) the United States is committed to a policy of securing and enhancing human rights and individual dignity throughout the world.
(b) It is the sense of the Congress that United States employers operating in South Africa are obliged both generally to actively oppose the policy and practices of apartheid and specifically to engage in recruitment and training of black and colored South Africans for management responsibilities.

TITLE II -- MEASURES TO ASSIST VICTIMS OF APARTHEID SCHOLARSHIPS FOR THE VICTIMS OF APARTHEID
SEC. 201. "22 USC 2151c" (a) Section 105(b) of the Foreign Assistance Act of 1961 is amended --
  (1) by inserting "(1)" after "(b)"; and
  (2) by adding at the end thereof the following new paragraph:
    "(2)(A)(i) Of the amounts authorized to be appropriated to carry out this section for the fiscal years 1987, 1988, and 1989, not less than $4,000,000 shall be used in each such fiscal year to finance education, training, and scholarships for the victims of apartheid, including teachers and other educational professionals, who are attending universities and colleges in South Africa. Amounts available to carry out this subparagraph shall be provided in accordance with the provisions of section 802(c) of the International Security and Development Cooperation Act of 1985. "99 Stat. 260."
    "(ii) Funds made available for each such fiscal year for purposes of chapter 4 of part II of this Act "22 USC 2346" may be used to finance such education, training, and scholarships in lieu of an equal amount made available under this subparagraph.
    "(B)(i) In addition to amounts used for purposes of subparagraph (A), the agency primarily responsible for administering this part, in collaboration with other appropriate departments or agencies of the United States, shall use assistance provided under this section or chapter 4 of part II of this Act to finance scholarships for students pursuing secondary school education in South Africa. The selection of scholarship recipients shall be by a nationwide panel or by regional panels appointed by the United States chief of diplomatic mission to South Africa.

"(ii) Of the amounts authorized to be appropriated to carry out this section and chapter 4 of part II of this Act for the fiscal years 1987, 1988, and 1989, up to an aggregate of $1,000,000 may be used in each such fiscal year for purposes of this subparagraph.

"(C)(i) In addition to the assistance authorized in subparagraph (A), the agency primarily responsible for administering this part shall provide assistance for inservice teacher training programs in South Africa through such nongovernmental organizations as TOPS or teachers' unions.

"(ii) Of the amounts authorized to be appropriated to carry out this section and chapter 4 of part II of this Act, up to an aggregate of $500,000 for the fiscal year 1987 and up to an aggregate of $1,000,000 for the fiscal year 1988 may be used for purposes of this subparagraph, subject to standard procedures for project review and approval.".

(b) The Foreign Assistance Act of 1961 is amended by inserting after section 116 "22 USC 2151 note 22 USC 2151o" the following new section:

"SEC. 117. ASSISTANCE FOR DISADVANTAGED SOUTH AFRICANS. -- In providing assistance under this chapter or under chapter 4 of part II of this Act for disadvantaged South Africans, priority shall be given to working with and through South African nongovernmental organizations whose leadership and staff are selected on a nonracial basis, and which have the support of the disadvantaged communities being served. The measure of this community support shall be the willingness of a substantial number of disadvantaged persons to participate in activities sponsored by these organizations. Such organizations to which such assistance may be provided include the Educational Opportunities Council, the South African Institute of Race Relations, READ, professional teachers' unions, the Outreach Program of the University of the Western Cape, the Funda Center in Soweto, SACHED, UPP Trust, TOPS, the Wilgespruit Fellowship Center (WFC), and civic and other organizations working at the community level which do not receive funds from the Government of South Africa.".

HUMAN RIGHTS FUND

SEC. 202. (a) Section 116(e)(2)(A) of the Foreign Assistance Act "22 USC 2151n" of 1961 is amended --

(1) by striking out "1984 and" and inserting in lieu thereof "1984,"; and

(2) by inserting after "1985" a comma and the following: "and $1,500,000 for the fiscal year 1986 and for each fiscal year thereafter".

(b) Section 116 of such Act is amended by adding at the end thereof the following new subsection:

"(f)(1) Of the funds made available to carry out subsection (e)(2)(A) for each fiscal year, not less than $500,000 shall be used for direct legal and other assistance to political detainees and prisoners and their families, including the investigation of the killing of protesters and prisoners, and for support for actions of black-led community organizations to resist, through nonviolent means, the enforcement of apartheid policies such as --

"(A) removal of black populations from certain geographic areas on account of race or ethnic origin,

"(B) denationalization of blacks, including any distinctions between the South African citizenships of blacks and whites,

"(C) residence restrictions based on race or ethnic origin,

"(D) restrictions on the rights of blacks to seek employment in South Africa and to live wherever they find employment in South Africa, and

"(E) restrictions which make it impossible for black employees and their families to be housed in family accommodations near their place of employment.

"(2)(A) No grant under this subsection may exceed $100,000.

"(B) The average of all grants under this paragraph made in any fiscal year shall not exceed $70,000.

"(g) Of the funds made available to carry out subsection (e)(2)(A) for each fiscal year, $175,000 shall be used for direct assistance to families of victims of violence such as 'necklacing' and other such inhumane acts. An additional $175,000 shall be made available to black groups in South Africa which are actively working toward a multi-racial solution to the sharing of political power in that country through nonviolent, constructive means.".

EXPANDING PARTICIPATION IN THE SOUTH AFRICAN ECONOMY

SEC. 203. "22 USC 5031" (a) The Congress declares that --

    (1) the denial under the apartheid laws of South Africa of the rights of South African blacks and other nonwhites to have the opportunity to participate equitably in the South African economy as managers or owners of, or professionals in, business enterprises, and

    (2) the policy of confining South African blacks and other nonwhites to the status of employees in minority-dominated businesses, is an affront to the values of a free society.

(b) The Congress hereby --

    (1) applauds the commitment of nationals of the United States adhering to the Code of Conduct to assure that South African blacks and other nonwhites are given assistance in gaining their rightful place in the South African economy; and

    (2) urges the United States Government to assist in all appropriate ways the realization by South African blacks and other nonwhites of their rightful place in the South African economy.

(c) Notwithstanding any other provision of law, the Secretary of State and any other head of a department or agency of the United States carrying out activities in South Africa shall, to the maximum extent practicable, in procuring goods or services, make affirmative efforts to assist business enterprises having more than 50 percent beneficial ownership by South African blacks or other nonwhite South Africans.

EXPORT-IMPORT BANK OF THE UNITED STATES

SEC. 204. "12 USC 635" Section 2(b)(9) of the Export-Import Bank Act of 1945 is amended --

(1) by striking out "(9) In" and inserting in lieu thereof "(9)(A) Except as provided in subparagraph (B), in"; and

(2) by adding at the end thereof the following:

    "(B) The Bank shall take active steps to encourage the use of its facilities to guarantee, insure, extend credit, or participate in the extension of credit to business enterprises in South Africa that are majority owned by South African blacks or other nonwhite South Africans. The certification requirement contained in clause (c) of subparagraph (A) shall not apply to exports to or purchases from business enterprises which are majority owned by South African blacks or other nonwhite South Africans.".

LABOR PRACTICES OF THE UNITED STATES GOVERNMENT IN SOUTH AFRICA

SEC. 205. "22 USC 5032" (a) It is the sense of the Congress that the labor practices used by the United States Government --

    (1) for the direct hire of South Africans,

    (2) for the reimbursement out of official residence funds of South Africans and employees of South African organizations for their long-term employment services on behalf of the United States Government, and

    (3) for the employment services of South Africans arranged by contract, should represent the best of labor practices in the United States and should serve as a model for the labor practices of nationals of the United States in South Africa.

(b) The Secretary of State and any other head of a department or agency of the United States carrying out activities in South Africa shall promptly take, without regard to any provision of law, the necessary steps to ensure that the labor practices applied to the employment services described in paragraphs (1) through (3) of subsection (a) are governed by the Code of Conduct. Nothing in this section shall be construed to grant any employee of the United States the right to strike.

WELFARE AND PROTECTION OF VICTIMS OF APARTHEID BY THE UNITED STATES

SEC. 206. "22 USC 5033" (a) The Secretary of State shall acquire, through lease or purchase, residential properties in the Republic of South Africa that shall be made available, at rents that are equitable, to assist victims of apartheid who are employees of the United States Government in obtaining adequate housing. Such properties shall be acquired only in neighborhoods which would be open to occupancy by other employees of the United States Government in South Africa.

(b) There are authorized to be appropriated $10,000,000 for the fiscal year 1987 to carry out the purposes of this section.

EMPLOYMENT PRACTICES OF UNITED STATES NATIONALS IN SOUTH AFRICA

SEC. 207. "22 USC 5034" (a) Any national of the United States that employees more than 25 persons in South Africa shall take the necessary steps to insure that the Code of Conduct is implemented.
(b) No department or agency of the United States may intercede with any foreign government or foreign national regarding the export marketing activities in any country of any national of the United States employing more than 25 persons in South Africa that is not implementing the Code of Conduct.

CODE OF CONDUCT
SEC. 208. "22 USC 5035" (a) The Code of Conduct referred to in sections 203, 205, 207, and 603 of this Act is as follows:
> (1) desegregating the races in each employment facility;
> (2) providing equal employment opportunity for all employees without regard to race or ethnic origin;
> (3) assuring that the pay system is applied to all employees without regard to race or ethnic origin;
> (4) establishing a minimum wage and salary structure based on the appropriate local minimum economic level which takes into account the needs of employees and their families;
> (5) increasing by appropriate means the number of persons in managerial, supervisory, administrative, clerical, and technical jobs who are disadvantaged by the apartheid system for the purpose of significantly increasing their representation in such jobs;
> (6) taking reasonable steps to improve the quality of employees' lives outside the work environment with respect to housing, transportation, schooling, recreation, and health; and
> (7) implementing fair labor practices by recognizing the right of all employees, regardless of racial or other distinctions, to self-organization and to form, join, or assist labor organizations, freely and without penalty or reprisal, and recognizing the right to refrain from any such activity.

(b) It is the sense of the Congress that in addition to the principles enumerated in subsection (a), nationals of the United States subject to section 207 should seek to comply with the following principle: taking reasonable measures to extend the scope of influence on activities outside the workplace, including --
> (1) supporting the unrestricted rights of black businesses to locate in urban areas;
> (2) influencing other companies in South Africa to follow the standards of equal rights principles;
> (3) supporting the freedom of mobility of black workers to seek employment opportunities wherever they exist, and make provision for adequate housing for families of employees within the proximity of workers' employment; and
> (4) supporting the rescission of all apartheid laws.

(c) The President may issue additional guidelines and criteria to assist persons who are or may be subject to section 207 in complying with the principles set forth in subsection (a) of this section. The President may, upon request, give an advisory opinion to any person who is or may be subject to this section or would be considered to be in compliance with the principles set forth in subsection (a).
(d) The President may require all nationals of the United States referred to in section 207 to register with the United States Government.
(e) Notwithstanding any other provision of law, the President may enter into contracts with one or more private organizations or individuals to assist in implementing this section.

PROHIBITION ON ASSISTANCE
SEC. 209. "22 USC 5036" No assistance may be provided under this Act to any group which maintains within its ranks any individual who has been found to engage in gross violations of internationally recognized human rights (as defined in section 502B(d)(1) of the Foreign Assistance Act of 1961) "22 USC 2304."

USE OF THE AFRICAN EMERGENCY RESERVE
SEC. 210. "22 USC 5037" Whenever the President determines that such action is necessary or appropriate to meet food shortages in southern Africa, the President is authorized to utilize the existing, authorized, and funded reserve entitled the "Emergency Reserve for African Famine Relief" to provide food assistance and transportation for that assistance.

PROHIBITION ON ASSISTANCE TO ANY PERSON OR GROUP ENGAGING IN "NECKLACING"
SEC. 211. "22 USC 5038" No assistance may be provided under this Act, the Foreign Assistance Act of 1961 "22 USC 2151 note" or any other provision of law to any individual, group, organization, or member

thereof, or entity that directly or indirectly engages in, advocates, supports, or approves the practice of execution by fire, commonly know as "necklacing".

PARTICIPATION OF SOUTH AFRICA IN AGRICULTURAL EXPORT CREDIT AND PROMOTION PROGRAMS

SEC. 212. "22 USC 5039" Notwithstanding any other provision of this Act or any other provision of law, the Secretary of Agriculture may permit South Africa to participate in agricultural export credit and promotion programs conducted by the Secretary at similar levels, and under similar terms and conditions, as other countries that have traditionally purchased United States agricultural commodities and the products thereof.

TITLE III -- MEASURES BY THE UNITED STATES TO UNDERMINE APARTHEID
PROHIBITION ON THE IMPORTATION OF KRUGERRANDS

SEC. 301. "22 USC 5051" No person, including a bank, may import into the United States any South African krugerrand or any other gold coin minted in South Africa or offered for sale by the Government of South Africa.

PROHIBITION ON THE IMPORTATION OF MILITARY ARTICLES

SEC. 302. "22 USC 5052" No arms, ammunition, or military vehicles produced in South Africa or any manufacturing data for such articles may be imported into the United States.

PROHIBITION ON THE IMPORTATION OF PRODUCTS FROM PARASTATAL ORGANIZATIONS

SEC. 303. "22 USC 5053" (a) Notwithstanding any other provision of law, no article which is grown, produced, manufactured by, marketed, or otherwise exported by a parastatal organization of South Africa may be imported into the United States, (1) except for agricultural products during the 12-month period from the date of enactment; and (2) except for those strategic minerals for which the President has certified to the Congress that the quantities essential for the economy or defense of the United States are unavailable from reliable and secure suppliers and except for any article to be imported pursuant to a contract entered into before August 15, 1986 1986: Provided, that no shipments may be received by a national of the United States under such contract after April 1, 1987.

(b) For purposes of this section, the term "parastatal organization" means a corporation or partnership owned or controlled or subsidized by the Government of South Africa, but does not mean a corporation or partnership which previously received start-up assistance from the South African Industrial Development Corporation but which is now privately owned.

PROHIBITION ON COMPUTER EXPORTS TO SOUTH AFRICA

SEC. 304. "22 USC 5054" (a) No computers, computer software, or goods or technology intended to manufacture or service computers may be exported to or for use by any of the following entities of the Government of South Africa:

 (1) The military.
 (2) The police.
 (3) The prison system.
 (4) The national security agencies.
 (5) ARMSCOR and its subsidiaries or the weapons research activities of the Council for Scientific and Industrial Research.
 (6) The administering authorities for controlling the movements of the victims of apartheid.
 (7) Any apartheid enforcing agency.
 (8) Any local, regional, or homelands government entity which performs any function of any entity described in paragraphs (1) through (7).

(b) (1) Computers, computer software, and goods or technology intended to service computers may be exported, directly or indirectly, to or for use by an entity of the Government of South Africa other than those set forth in subsection (a) only if a system of end use verification is in effect to ensure that the computers involved will not be used for any function of any entity set forth in subsection (a).

 (2) The Secretary of Commerce may prescribe such rules and regulations as may be necessary to carry out this section.

PROHIBITION ON LOANS TO THE GOVERNMENT OF SOUTH AFRICA

SEC. 305. "22 USC 5055" (a) No national of the United States may make or approve any loan or other extension of credit, directly or indirectly, to the Government of South Africa or to any corporation, partnership or other organization which is owned or controlled by the Government of South Africa.

(b) The prohibiton contained in subsection (a) shall not apply to --

    (1) a loan or extension of credit for any education, housing, or humanitarian benefit which --

        (A) is available to all persons on a nondiscriminatory basis; or

        (B) is available in a geographic area accessible to all population groups without any legal or administrative restriction; or

    (2) a loan or extension of credit for which an agreement is entered into before the date of enactment of this Act.

PROHIBITION ON AIR TRANSPORTATION WITH SOUTH AFRICA

SEC. 306. "22 USC 5056" (a)

    (1) The President shall immediately notify the Government of South Africa of his intention to suspend the rights of any air carrier designated by the Government of South Africa under the Agreement Between the Government of the United States of America and the Government of the Union of South Africa Relating to Air Services Between Their Respective Territories, signed May 23, 1947, to service the routes provided in the Agreement. "61 Stat. 3057."

    (2) Ten days after the date of enactment of this Act, the President shall direct the Secretary of Transportation to revoke the right of any air carrier designated by the Government of South Africa under the Agreement to provide service pursuant to the Agreement.

    (3) Ten days after the date of enactment of this Act, the President shall direct the Secretary of Transportation not to permit or otherwise designate any United States air carrier to provide service between the United States and South Africa pursuant to the Agreement.

(b)   (1) The Secretary of State shall terminate the Agreement Between the Government of the United States of America and the Government of the Union of South Africa Relating to Air Services Between Their Respective Territories, signed May 23, 1947, in accordance with the provisions of that agreement.

    (2) Upon termination of such agreement, the Secretary of Transportation shall prohibit any aircraft of a foreign air carrier owned, directly or indirectly, by the Government of South Africa or by South African nationals from engaging in air transportation with respect to the United States.

    (3) The Secretary of Transportation shall prohibit the takeoff and landing in South Africa of any aircraft by an air carrier owned, directly or indirectly, or controlled by a national of the United States or by any corporation or other entity organized under the laws of the United States or of any State.

(c) The Secretary of Transportation may provide for such exceptions from the prohibition contained in subsection (a) or (b) as the Secretary considers necessary to provide for emergencies in which the safety of an aircraft or its crew or passengers is threatened.

(d) For purposes of this section, the terms "aircraft", "air transportation", and "foreign air carrier" have the meanings given those terms in section 101 of the Federal Aviation Act of 1958 (49 U.S. C. 1301). "49 USC app. 1301."

PROHIBITIONS ON NUCLEAR TRADE WITH SOUTH AFRICA

SEC. 307. "22 USC 5057 42 USC 2139" (a) Notwithstanding any other provision of law -

    (1) the Nuclear Regulatory Commission shall not issue any license for the export to South Africa of production or utilization facilities, any source or special nuclear material or sensitive nuclear technology, or any component parts, items, or substances which the Commission has determined, pursuant to section 109b. of the Atomic Energy Act, to be especially relevant from the standpoint of export control because of their significance for nuclear explosive purposes;

    (2) the Secretary of Commerce shall not issue any license for the export to South Africa of any goods or technology which have been determined, pursuant to section 309(c) "42 USC 2139a" of the Nuclear Non-Proliferation Act of 1978, to be of significance for nuclear explosive purposes for use in, or judged by the President to be likely to be diverted to, a South African production or utilization facility;

(3) the Secretary of Energy shall not, under section 57b.(2) of the Atomic Energy Act, "42 USC 2077" authorize any person to engage, directly or indirectly, in the production of special nuclear material in South Africa; and

(4) no goods, technology, source or special nuclear material, facilities, components, items, or substances referred to in clauses (1) through (3) shall be approved by the Nuclear Regulatory Commission or an executive branch agency for retransfer to South Africa,

unless the Secretary of State determines and certifies to the Speaker of the House of Representatives and the chairman of the Committee on Foreign Relations of the Senate that the Government of South Africa is a party to the Treaty on the Non-Proliferation of Nuclear Weapons, done at Washington, London, and Moscow on July 1, 1968, "21 UST 483" or otherwise maintains International Atomic Energy Agency safeguards on all its peaceful nuclear activities, as defined in the Nuclear Non-Proliferation Act of 1978. "22 USC 3201 note."

(b) Nothing in this section shall preclude --

(1) any export, retransfer, or activity generally licensed or generally authorized by the Nuclear Regulatory Commission or the Department of Commerce or the Department of Energy; or

(2) assistance for the purpose of developing or applying International Atomic Energy Agency or United States bilateral safeguards, for International Atomic Energy Agency programs generally available to its member states, for reducing the use of highly enriched uranium in research or test reactors, or for other technical programs for the purpose of reducing proliferation risks, such as programs to extend the life of reactor fuel and activities envisaged by section 223 of the Nuclear Waste Policy Act of 1982 "42 USC 10203" or which are necessary for humanitarian reasons to protect the public health and safety.

(c) The prohibitions contained in subsection (a) shall not apply with respect to a particular export, retransfer, or activity, or a group of exports, retransfers, or activities, if the President determines that to apply the prohibitions would be seriously prejudicial to the achievement of United States nonproliferation objectives or would otherwise jeopardize the common defense and security of the United States and, if at least 60 days before the initial export, retransfer, or activity is carried out, the President submits to the Speaker of the House of Representatives and the chairman of the Committee on Foreign Relations of the Senate a report setting forth that determination, together with his reasons therefor.

GOVERNMENT OF SOUTH AFRICA BANK ACCOUNTS

SEC. 308. "22 USC 5058" (a) A United States depository institution may not accept, receive, or hold a deposit account from the Government of South Africa or from any agency or entity owned or controlled by the Government of South Africa except for such accounts which may be authorized by the President for diplomatic or consular purposes. For purposes of the preceding sentence, the term "depository institution" has the same meaning as in section 19(b)(1) of the Federal Reserve Act. "12 USC 461."

(b) The prohibition contained in subsection (a) shall take effect 45 days after the date of enactment of this Act.

PROHIBITION ON IMPORTATION OF URANIUM AND COAL FROM SOUTH AFRICA

SEC. 309. "22 USC 5059" (a) Notwithstanding any other provision of law, no -- (1) uranium ore, (2) uranium oxide, (3) coal, or (4) textiles, that is produced or manufactured in South Africa may be imported into the United States.

(b) This section shall take effect 90 days after the date of enactment of this Act.

PROHIBITION ON NEW INVESTMENT IN SOUTH AFRICA

SEC. 310. "22 USC 5060" (a) No national of the United States may, directly or through another person, make any new investment in South Africa.

(b) The prohibition contained in subsection (a) shall take effect 45 days after the date of enactment of this Act.

(c) The prohibition contained in this section shall not apply to a firm owned by black South Africans.

TERMINATION OF CERTAIN PROVISIONS

SEC. 311. "22 USC 5061" (a) This title and sections 501(c) and 504(b) shall terminate if the Government of South Africa --

(1) releases all persons persecuted for their political beliefs or detained unduly without trial and Nelson Mandela from prison;

(2) repeals the state of emergency in effect on the date of enactment of this Act and releases all detainees held under such state of emergency;

(3) unbans democratic political parties and permits the free exercise by South Africans of all races of the right to form political parties, express political opinions, and otherwise participate in the political process;

(4) repeals the Group Areas Act and the Population Registration Act and institutes no other measures with the same purposes; and

(5) agrees to enter into good faith negotiations with truly representative members of the black majority without preconditions.

(b) The President may suspend or modify any of the measures required by this title or section 501(c) or section 504(b) thirty days after he determines, and so reports to the Speaker of the House of Representatives and the chairman of the Committee on Foreign Relations of the Senate, that the Government of South Africa has --

(1) taken the action described in paragraph (1) of subsection (a),

(2) taken three of the four actions listed in paragraphs (2) through (5) of subsection (a), and

(3) made substantial progress toward dismantling the system of apartheid and establishing a nonracial democracy,

unless the Congress enacts within such 30-day period, in accordance with section 602 of this Act, a joint resolution disapproving the determination of the President under this subsection.

(c) It is the policy of the United States to support the negotiations with the representatives of all communities as envisioned in this Act. If the South African Government agrees to enter into negotiations without preconditions, abandons unprovoked violence against its opponents, commits itself to a free and democratic post-apartheid South Africa under a code of law; and if nonetheless the African National Congress, the Pan African Congress, or their affiliates, or other oranizations, refuse to participate; or if the African National Congress, the Pan African Congress or other organizations --

(1) refuse to abandon unprovoked violence during such negotiations; and

(2) refuse to commit themselves to a free and democratice post-apartheid South Africa under a code of law,

then the United States will support negotiations which do not include these organizations.

POLICY TOWARD VIOLENCE OR TERRORISM

SEC. 312. "22 USC 5062" (a) United States policy toward violence in South Africa shall be designed to bring about an immediate end to such violence and to promote negotiations concluding with a removal of the system of apartheid and the establishment of a non-racial democracy in South Africa.

(b) The United States shall work toward this goal by diplomatic and other measures designed to isolate those who promote terrorist attacks on unarmed civilians or those who provide assistance to individuals or groups promoting such activities.

(c) The Congress declares that the abhorrent practice of "necklacing" and other equally inhumane acts which have been practices in South Africa by blacks against fellow blacks are an affront to all throughout the world who value the rights of individuals to live in an atmosphere free from fear of violent reprisals.

TERMINATION OF TAX TREATY AND PROTOCOL

SEC. 313. "22 USC 5063" The Secretary of State shall terminate immediately the following convention and protocol, in accordance with its terms, the Convention Between the Government of the United States of America and the Government of the Union of South Africa for the Avoidance of Double Taxation and for Establishing Rules of Reciprocal Administrative Assistance With Respect to Taxes on Income, done at Pretoria on December 13, 1946, and the protocol relating thereto.

PROHIBITION ON UNITED STATES GOVERNMENT PROCUREMENT FROM SOUTH AFRICA

SEC. 314. On or after the date of enactment of this Act, "22 USC 5064" no department, agency or any other entity of the United States Government may enter into a contract for the procurement of goods or services from parastatal organizations except for items necessary for diplomatic and consular purposes.

PROHIBITION ON THE PROMOTION OF UNITED STATES TOURISM IN SOUTH AFRICA

SEC. 315. "22 USC 5065" None of the funds appropriated or otherwise made available by any provision of law may be available to promote United States tourism in South Africa.

PROHIBITION ON UNITED STATES GOVERNMENT ASSISTANCE TO, INVESTMENT IN, OR SUBSIDY FOR TRADE WITH, SOUTH AFRICA

SEC. 316. "22 USC 5066" None of the funds appropriated or otherwise made available by any provision of law may be available for any assistance to investment in, or any subsidy for trade with, South Africa, including but not limited to funding for trade missions in South Africa and for participation in exhibitions and trade fairs in South Africa.

PROHIBITION ON SALE OR EXPORT OF ITEMS ON MUNITIONS LIST

SEC. 317. "22 USC 5067" (a) Except as provided in subsection (b), no item contained on the United States Munition List which is subject to the jurisdiction of the United States may be exported to South Africa.
(b) Subsection (a) does not apply to any item which is not covered by the United Nations Security Council Resolution 418 of November 4, 1977, and which the President determines is exported solely for commercial purposes and not exported for use by the armed forces, police, or other security forces of South Africa or for other military use.
(c) The President shall prepare and submit to Congress every six months a report describing any license issued pursuant to subsection (b).

MUNITIONS LIST SALES, NOTIFICATION

SEC. 318. (a) Notwithstanding any other provision of this Act, "22 USC 5068" the President shall:
    (i) notify the Congress of his intent to allow the export to South Africa any item which is on the United States Munition List and which is not covered by the United Nations Security Council Resolution 418 of November 4, 1977, and
    (ii) certify that such item shall be used solely for commercial purposes and not exported for use by the armed forces, police, or other security forces of South Africa or for other military use.
(b) The Congress shall have 30 calendar days of continuous session (compute as provided in section 906(b) of title 5, United States Code) to disapprove by joint resolution of any such sale.

PROHIBITION ON IMPORTATION OF SOUTH AFRICAN AGRICULTURAL PRODUCTS AND FOOD

SEC. 319. "22 USC 5069" Notwithstanding any other provision of law, no:
(1) agricultural commodity, product, byproduct of derivitive thereof,
(2) article that is suitable for human consumption, that is a product of South Africa may be imported into the customs territory of the United States after the date of enactment of this Act.

PROHIBITION ON IMPORTATION OF IRON AND STEEL

SEC. 320. "22 USC 5070" Notwithstanding any other provision of law, no iron or steel produced in South Africa may be imported into the United States.

PROHIBITION ON EXPORTS OF CRUDE OIL AND PETROLEUM PRODUCTS

SEC. 321. "22 USC 5071" (a) No crude oil or refined petroleum product which is subject to the jurisdiction of the United States or which is exported by a person subject to the jurisdiction of the United States may be exported to South Africa.
(b) Subsection (a) does not apply to any export pursuant to a contract entered into before the date of enactment of this Act.

PROHIBITION ON COOPERATION WITH THE ARMED FORCES OF SOUTH AFRICA

SEC. 322. "22 USC 5072" No agency or entity of the United States may engage in any form of cooperation, direct or indirect, with the armed forces of the Government of South Africa, except activities which are reasonably designed to facilitate the collection of necessary intelligence. Each such activity shall be considered a significant anticipated intelligence activity for purposes of section 501 of the National Security Act of 1947. "50 USC 413."

PROHIBITIONS ON SUGAR IMPORTS

SEC. 323. "22 USC 5073" (a)

    (1) Notwithstanding any other provision of law, no sugars,, sirups, or molasses that are products of the Republic of South Africa may be imported into the United States after the date of enactment of this Act.

    (2) The aggregate quantity of sugars, sirups, and molasses that --

        (A) are products of the Philippines, and

        (B) may be imported into the United States (determined without regard to this paragraph) under any limitation imposed by law on the quantity of all sugars, sirups, and molasses that may be imported into the United States during any period of time imported into the United States during any period of time occurring after the date of enactment of this Act, shall be increased by the aggregate quantity of sugars, sirups, and mollasses that are products of the Republic of South Africa which may have been imported into the United States under such limitation during such period if this section did not apply to such period.

(b)   (1) Paragraph (c)(i) of headnote 3 of subpart A of part 10 of schedule 1 of the Tariff Schedules of the United States is amended –

        (A) by striking out "13.5" in the item relating to the Philippines in the table and inserting in lieu thereof "15.8", and

        (B) by striking out the item relating to the Republic of South Africa in the table.

    (2) Paragraph (c) of headnote 3 of subpart A of part 10 of schedule 1 of the Tariff Schedules of the United States is amended by adding at the end thereof the following new subparagraph:

        "(iii) Notwithstanding any authority given to the United States Trade Representative under paragraphs (e) and (g) of this headnote --

        "(A) the percentage allocation made to the Philippines under this paragraph may not be reduced, and

        "(B) no allocation may be made to the Republic of South Africa, in allocating any limitation imposed under any paragraph of this headnote on the quantity of sugars, sirups, and molasses described in items 155.20 and 155.30 which may be entered."

TITLE IV -- MULTILATERAL MEASURES TO UNDERMINE APARTHEID NEGOTIATING AUTHORITY

SEC. 401. "22 USC 5081" (a) It is the policy of the United States to seek international cooperative agreements with the other industrialized democracies to bring about the complete dismantling of apartheid. Sanctions imposed under such agreements should be both direct and official executive or legislative acts of governments. The net economic effect of such cooperative should be measurably greater than the net economic effect of the measures imposed by this Act.

(b)   (1) Negotiations to reach international cooperative arrangements with the other industrialized democracies and other trading partners of South Africa on measures to bring about the complete dismantling of apartheid should begin promptly and should be concluded not later than 180 days from the enactment of this Act. During this period, the President or, at his direction, the Secretary of State should convene an international conference of the other industrialized democracies in order to reach cooperative agreements to impose sanctions against South Africa to bring about the complete dismantling of apartheid.

    (2) The President shall, not less than 180 days after the date of enactment of this Act, submit to the Congress a report containing

        (A) a description of United States efforts to negotiate multilateral measures to bring about the complete dismantling of apartheid; and

        (B) a detailed description of economic and other measures adopted by the other industrialized countries to bring about the complete dismantling of apartheid, including an assessment of the stringency with which such measures are enforced by those countries.

(c) If the President successfully concludes an international agreement described in subsection (b)(1), he may, after such agreement enters into force with respect to the United States, adjust, modify, or otherwise amend the measures imposed under any provision of sections 301 through 310 to conform with such agreement.

(d) Each agreement submitted to the Congress under this subsection shall enter into force with respect to the United States if (and only if) --

    (1) the President, not less than 30 days before the day on which he enters into such agreement, notifies the House of Representatives and the Senate of his intention to enter into such an agreement, and promptly thereafter publishes notice of such intention in the Federal Register;

    (2) after entering into the agreement, the President transmits to the House of Representatives and to the Senate a document containing a copy of the final legal text of such agreement, together with --

        (A) a description of any administrative action proposed to implement such agreement and an explanation as to how the proposed administrative action would change or affect existing law, and

        (B) a statement of his reasons as to how the agreement serves the interest of United States foreign policy and as to why the proposed administrative action is required or appropriate to carry out the agreement; and

    (3) a joint resolution approving such agreement has been enacted within 30 days of transmittal of such document to the Congress.

(e) It is the sense of the Congress that the President should instruct the Permanent Representative of the United States to the United Nations to propose that the United Nations Security Council, pursuant to Article 41 of the United Nations Charter, impose measures against South Africa of the same type as are imposed by this Act.

LIMITATION ON IMPORTS FROM OTHER COUNTRIES

SEC. 402. "22 USC 5082" The President is authorized to limit the importation into the United States of any product or service of a foreign country to the extent to which such foreign country benefits from, or otherwise takes commercial advantage of, any sanction or prohibition against any national of the United States imposed by or under this Act.

PRIVATE RIGHT OF ACTION

SEC. 403. (a) Any national of the United States who is required by this Act "22 USC 5083" to terminate or curtail business activities in South Africa may bring a civil action for damages against any person, partnership, or corporation that takes commercial advantage or otherwise benefits from such termination or curtailment.

(b) The action described in subsection (a) may only be brought, without respect to the amount in controversy, in the United States district court for the District of Columbia or the Court of International Trade. Damages which may be recovered include lost profits and the cost of bringing the action, including a reasonable attorney's fee.

(c) The injured party must show by a preponderance of the evidence that the damages have been the direct result of defendant's action taken with the deliberate intent to injure the party.

TITLE V -- FUTURE POLICY TOWARD SOUTH AFRICA
ADDITIONAL MEASURES

SEC. 501. "22 USC 5091" (a) It shall be the policy of the United States to impose additional measures against the Government of South Africa if substantial progress has not been made within twelve months of the date of enactment of this Act in ending the system of apartheid and establishing a nonracial democracy.

(b) The President shall prepare and transmit to the Speaker of the House of Representatives and the chairman of the Committee on Foreign Relations of the Senate within twelve months of the date of enactment of this Act, and every twelve months thereafter, a report on the extent to which significant progress has been made toward ending the system of apartheid, including --

    (1) an assessment of the extent to which the Government of South Africa has taken the steps set forth in section 101(b) of this Act;

    (2) an analysis of any other actions taken by the Government of South Africa in ending the system of apartheid and moving toward a nonracial democracy; and

    (3) the progress, or lack of progress, made in reaching a negotiated settlement to the conflict in South Africa.

(c) If the President determines that significant progress has not been made by the Government of South Africa in ending the system of apartheid and establishing a nonracial democracy, the President shall include in the report required by subsection (b) a recommendation on which of the following additional measures should be imposed:

(1) a prohibition on the importation of steel from South Africa;

(2) a prohibition on military assistance to those countries that the report required by section 508 identifies as continuing to circumvent the international embargo on arms and military technology to South Africa;

(3) a prohibition on the importation of food, agricultural products, diamonds, and textiles from South Africa;

(4) a prohibition on United States banks accepting, receiving, or holding deposit accounts from South African nationals; and

(5) a prohibition on the importation into the United States of strategic minerals from South Africa.

(d) A joint resolution which would enact part or all of the measures recommended by the President pursuant to subsection (c) shall be considered in accordance with the provisions of section 602 of this Act.

LIFTING OF PROHIBITIONS

SEC. 502. (a) Notwithstanding any other provision of this Act, the President may lift any prohibition contained in this Act imposed against South Africa if the President determines, after six months from the date of the imposition of such prohibition, and so reports to Congress, that such prohibition would increase United States dependence upon any member country or observer country of the Council for Mutual Economic Assistance (C.M.E.A.) for the importation of coal or any strategic and critical material by an amount which exceeds by weight the average amounts of such imports from such country during the period 1981 through 1985.

(b) (1) Not later than 30 days after the date of enactment of this Act, the Secretary of Commerce shall prepare and transmit to the Congress a report setting forth for each country described in subsection (a) --

(A) The average amount of such imports from such country during the period of 1981 through 1985; and

(B) the current amount of such imports from such country entering the United States.

(2) Thirty days after transmittal of the report required by paragraph (1) and every thirty days thereafter, the President shall prepare and transmit the information described in paragraph (1)(B).

STUDY OF HEALTH CONDITIONS IN THE "HOMELANDS" AREAS OF SOUTH AFRICA

SEC. 503. "22 USC 5093" The Secretary of State shall conduct a study to examine the state of health conditions and to determine the extent of starvation and malnutrition now prevalent in the "homelands" areas of South Africa and shall, not later than December 1, 1986, prepare and transmit to the Speaker of the House of Representatives and the chairman of the Committee on Foreign Relations of the Senate a report setting forth the results of such study.

REPORT ON SOUTH AFRICAN IMPORTS

SEC. 504. (a) Not later than 90 days after the date of enactment of this Act, "22 USC 5094" the President shall submit to the Speaker of the House of Representatives and the chairman of the Committee on Foreign Relations of the Senate a report on the extent to which the United States is dependent on the importation from South Africa of -- (1) chromium, (2) cobalt, (3) manganese, (4) platinum group metals, (5) ferroalloys, and (6) other strategic and critical materials (within the meaning of the Strategic and Critical Materials Stock Piling Act). "50 USC 98 et seq."

(b) The President shall develop a program which reduces the dependence, if any, of the United States on the importation from South Africa of the materials identified in the report submitted under subsection (a).

STUDY AND REPORT ON THE ECONOMY OF SOUTHERN AFRICA

SEC. 505. "22 USC 5095" (a) The President shall conduct a study on the role of American assistance in southern Africa to determine what needs to be done, and what can be done to expand the trade, private investment, and transport prospects of southern Africa's landlocked nations.

(b) Not later than 180 days after the date of enactment of this Act, the President shall prepare and transmit to the chairman of the Committee on Foreign Affairs of the House of Representatives and the chairman of the Committee on Foreign Relations of the Senate a report setting forth the findings of the study conducted under subsection (a).

REPORT ON RELATIONS BETWEEN OTHER INDUSTRIALIZED DEMOCRACIES AND SOUTH AFRICA

SEC. 506. "22 USC 5096" (a) Not later than 180 days after the date of enactment of this Act, the President shall prepare and transmit to the Speaker of the House of Representatives and the chairman of the Committee on Foreign Relations of the Senate a report containing a detailed assessment of the economic and other relationships of other industrialized democracies with South Africa. Such report shall be transmitted without regard to whether or not the President successfully concluded an international agreement under section 401.

(b) For purposes of this section, the phrase "economic and other relationships" includes the same types of matters as are described in sections 201, 202, 204, 205, 206, 207, sections 301 through 307, and sections 309 and 310 of this Act.

STUDY AND REPORT ON DEPOSIT ACCOUNTS OF SOUTH AFRICAN NATIONALS IN UNITED STATES BANKS

SEC. 507. "22 USC 5097"

(a)

(1) The Secretary of the Treasury shall conduct a study on the feasibility of prohibiting each depository institution from accepting, receiving, or holding a deposit account from any South African national.

(2) For purposes of paragraph (1), the term "depository institution" has the same meaning as in section 19(b)(1) of the Federal Reserve Act. "12 USC 461."

(b) Not later than 180 days after the date of enactment of this Act, the Secretary of the Treasury shall submit to the Speaker of the House of Representatives and the chairman of the Committee on Foreign Relations of the Senate a report detailing the findings of the study required by subsection (a).

STUDY AND REPORT ON THE VIOLATION OF THE INTERNATIONAL EMBARGO ON SALE AND EXPORT OF MILITARY ARTICLES TO SOUTH AFRICA

SEC. 508. "22 USC 5098" (a) The President shall conduct a study on the extent to which the international embargo on the sale and exports of arms and military technology to South Africa is being violated.

(b) Not later than 179 days after the date of enactment of this Act, the President shall submit to the Speaker of the House of Representatives and the chairman of the Committee on Foreign relations of the Senate a report setting forth the findings of the study required by subsection (a), including an identification of those countries engaged in such sale or export, with a view to terminating United States military assistance to those countries.

REPORT ON COMMUNIST ACTIVITIES IN SOUTH AFRICA

SEC. 509. (a) Not later than 90 days after the date of enactment of this Act, "22 USC 5099" the President shall prepare and transmit to the Speaker of the House of Representatives and the chairman of the Committee on Foreign Affairs of the House of Representatives and the chairman of the Committee on Foreign Relations of the Senate an unclassified version of a report, prepared with the assistance of the Director of the Central Intelligence Agency, the Director of the Defense Intelligence Agency, the National Security Advisor, and other relevant United States Government officials in the intelligence community, which shall set forth the activities of the Communist Party in South Africa, the extent to which Communists have infiltrated the many black and nonwhite South African organizations engaged in the fight against the apartheid system, and the extent to which any such Communist infiltration or influence sets the policies and goals of the organizations with which they are involved.

(b) At the same time the unclassified report in subsection (a) is transmitted as set forth in that subsection, a classified version of the same report shall be transmitted to the chairmen of the Select Committee on Intelligence of the Senate and of the Permanent Select Committee on Intelligence of the House of Representatives.

PROHIBITION ON THE IMPORTATION OF SOVIET GOLD COINS

SEC. 510. "22 USC 5100" (a) No person, including a bank, may import into the United States any gold coin minted in the Union of Soviet Socialist Republics or offered for sale by the Government of the Soviet Socialist Republics.

(b) For purposes of this section, the term "United States" includes the States of the United States, the District of Columbia, the Commonwealth of Puerto Rico, and any territory or possession of the United States.

(c) Any individual who violates this section or any regulations issued to carry out this section shall be fined not more than five times the value of the rubles involved.

ECONOMIC SUPPORT FOR DISADVANTAGED SOUTH AFRICANS

SEC. 511 (a) Chapter 4 of part II of the Foreign Assistance Act of 1961 is amended by adding at the end thereof the following new section:

"SEC. 535. "22 USC 2346d" ECONOMIC SUPPORT FOR DISADVANTAGED SOUTH AFRICANS. -- (a)(1) Up to $40,000,000 of the funds authorized to be appropriated to carry out this chapter for the fiscal year 1987 and each fiscal year thereafter shall be available for assistance for disadvantaged South Africans. Assistance under this section shall be provided for activities that are consistent with the objective of a majority of South Africans for an end to the apartheid system and the establishment of a society based on non-racial principles. Such activities may include scholarships, assistance to promote the participation of disadvantaged South Africans in trade unions and private enterprise, alternative education and community development programs. "(2) Up to $3,000,000 of the amounts provided in each fiscal year pursuant to subsection (a) shall be available for training programs for South Africa's trade unionists.

"(b) Assistance provided pursuant to the section shall be made available notwithstanding any other provision of law and shall not be used to provide support to organizations or groups which are financed or controlled by the Government of South Africa. Nothing in this subsection may be construed to prohibit programs which are consistent with subsection (a) and which award scholarships to students who choose to attend South African-supported institutions.".

(b) Not later than 90 days after the date of enactment of this Act, "22 USC 2346d note" the Secretary of State shall prepare and transmit to the Congress a report describing the strategy of the President during the five-year period beginning on such date regarding the assistance of black Africans pursuant to section 535 of the Foreign Assistance Act of 1961 and describing the programs and projects to be funded under such section.

REPORT ON THE AFRICAN NATIONAL CONGRESS

SEC. 512. "22 USC 5101" (a) Not later than 180 days after the date of enactment of this Act, the Attorney General shall prepare and transmit to the Congress a report on actual and alleged violations of the Foreign Agents Registration Act of 1938, "22 USC 611" and the status of any investigation pertaining thereto, by representatives of governments or opposition movements in Subsaharan Africa, including, but not limited to, members or representatives of the African National Congress.

(b) For purposes of conducting any investigations necessary in order to provide a full and complete report, the Attorney General shall have full authority to utilize civil investigative demand procedures, including but not limited to the issuance of civil subpenas.

TITLE VI -- ENFORCEMENT AND ADMINISTRATIVE PROVISIONS
REGULATORY AUTHORITY

SEC. 601. The President shall issue such rules, regulations, licenses, and orders as are necessary to carry out the provisions of this Act, "22 USC 5111" including taking such steps as may be necessary to continue in effect the measures imposed by Executive Order 12532 "50 USC 1701 note" of September 9, 1985, and Executive Order 12535 of October 1, 1985, and by any rule, regulation, license, or order issued thereunder (to the extent such measures are not inconsistent with this Act).

CONGRESSIONAL PRIORITY PROCEDURES

SEC. 602. "22 USC 5112" (a)

(1) The provisions of this subsection apply to the consideration in the House of Representatives of a joint resolution under sections 311(b), 401(d), and 501(d).

(2) a joint resolution shall, upon introduction, be referred to the Committee on Foreign Affairs of the House of Representatives.

(3)   (A) At any time after the joint resolution placed on the appropriate calendar has been on that calendar for a period of 5 legislative days, it is in order for any Member of the House

(after consultation with the Speaker as to the most appropriate time for the consideration of that joint resolution) to move that the House resolve itself into the Committee of the Whole House on the State of the Union for the consideration of that joint resolution. The motion is highly privileged and is in order even though a previous motion to the same effect has been disagreed to. All points of order against the joint resolution under clauses 2 and 6 of Rule XXI of the Rules of the House are waived. If the motion is agreed to, the resolution shall remain the unfinished business of the House until disposed of. A motion to reconsider the vote by which the motion is disagree to shall not be in order.

(B) Debate on the joint resolution shall not exceed ten hours, which shall be divided equally between a Member favoring and a Member opposing the joint resolution. A motion to limit debate is in order at any time in the House or in the Committee of the Whole and is not debatable.

(C) An amendment to the joint resolution is not in order.

(D) At the conclusion of the debate on the joint resolution, the Committee of the Whole shall rise and report the joint resolution back to the House, and the previous question shall be considered as ordered on the joint resolution to final passage without intervening motion.

(b)   (1) The provisions of this subsection apply to the consideration in the Senate of a joint resolution under section 311(b), 401(d), or 501(d).

(2) A joint resolution shall, upon introduction, be referred to the Committee on Foreign Relations of the Senate.

(3) a joint resolution described in this section shall be considered in the Senate in accordance with procedures contained in paragraphs (3) through (7) of section 8066(c) of the Department of Defense Appropriations Act, 1985 (as contained in Public Law 98-473), "98 Stat. 1935" except that --

(A) references in such paragraphs to the Committee on Appropriations of the Senate shall be deemed to be references to the Committee on Foreign Relations of the Senate; and

(B) amendments to the joint resolution are in order.

(c) For purposes of this subsection, the term "joint resolution" means only --

(A) in the case of section 311(b), a joint resolution which is introduced in a House of Congress within 3 legislative days after the Congress receives the report described in section 311(b) and for which the matter after the resolving clause reads as follows: "That the Congress, having received on . . . the report of the President containing the determination required by section 311(b) of the Comprehensive Anti-Apartheid Act of 1986, disapproves of such determination.", with the date of the receipt of the report inserted in the blank;

(B) in the case of section 401(d)(3), a joint resolution which is introduced in a House of Congress within 3 legislative days after the Congress receives the document described in section 401(d)(2) and for which the matter after the resolving clause reads as follows: "That the Congress, having received on the test of the international agreement described in section 401(d)(3) of the Comprehensive Anti-Apartheid Act of 1986, approves of such agreement.", with the date of the receipt of the text of the agreement inserted in the blank; and

(C) in the case of section 501(d), a joint resolution which is introduced in a House of Congress within 3 legislative days after the Congress receives the determination of the President pursuant to section 501(c) and for which the matter after the resolving clause reads as follows: "That the Congress, having received on . . . a determination of the President under section 501(c) of the Comprehensive Anti-Apartheid Act of 1986, approves the President's determination.", with the date of the receipt of the determination inserted in the blank.

(d) As used in this section, the term "legislative day" means a day on which the House of Representatives or the Senate is in session, as the case may be.

(e) This section is enacted --

(1) as an exercise of the rulemaking powers of the House of Representatives and the Senate, and as such it is deemed a part of the Rules of the House and the Rules of the Senate, respectively, but applicable only with respect to the procedure to be followed in the House and the Senate in the case of joint resolutions under this section, and it supersedes other rules only to the extent that it is inconsistent with such rules, and

(2) with full recognition of the constitutional right of the House and the Senate to change their rules at any time, in the same manner, and to the same extent as in the case of any other rule of the House or Senate, and of the right of the Committee on Rules of the House of Representatives to report a resolution for the consideration of any measure.

ENFORCEMENT AND PENALTIES

SEC. 603. "22 USC 5113" (a)

(1) The President with respect to his authorities under section 601 shall take the necessary steps to ensure compliance with the provisions of this Act and any regulations, licenses, and orders issued to carry out this Act, including establishing mechanisms to monitor compliance with this Act and such regulations, licenses, and orders.

(2) In ensuring such compliance, the President may --

(A) require any person to keep a full record of, and to furnish under oath, in the form of reports or otherwise, complete information relative to any act or transaction described in this Act either before, during, or after the completion thereof, or relative to any interest in foreign property, or relative to any property in which a foreign country or any national thereof has or has had any interest, or as may be otherwise necessary to enforce the provisions of this Act; and

(B) conduct investigations, hold hearings, administer oaths, examine witnesses, receive evidence, take depositions, and require by subpena the attendance and testimony of witnesses and the production of all books, papers, and documents relating to any matter under investigation.

(b) Except as provided in subsection (d) --

(1) any person that violates the provisions of this Act, or any regulation, license, or order issued to carry out this Act shall be subject to a civil penalty of $50,000;

(2) any person, other than an individual, that willfully violates the provisions of this Act, or any regulation, license, or order issued to carry out this Act shall be fined not more than $1,000,000;

(3) any individual who willfully violates the provisions of this Act or any regulation, license, or order issued to carry out this Act shall be fined not more than $50,000, or imprisoned not more than 10 years, or both; and

(4) any individual who violates section 301(a) or any regulations issued to carry out that section shall, instead of the penalty set forth in paragraph (2), be fined not more than 5 times the value of the krugerrands or gold coins involved.

(c)   (1) Whenever a person commits a violation under subsection (b) --

(A) any officer, director, or employee of such person, or any natural person in control of such person who knowingly and willfully ordered, authorized, acquiesced in, or carried out the act or practice constituting the violation, and

(B) any agent of such person who knowingly and willfully carried out such act or practice, shall be fined not more than $10,000, or imprisoned not more than 5 years, or both.

(2) Paragraph (1) shall not apply in the case of a violation by an individual of section 301(a) of this Act or of any regulation issued to carry out that section.

(3) A fine imposed under paragraph (1) on an individual for an act or practice constituting a violation may not be paid, directly or indirectly, by the person committing the violation itself.

(d)   (1) Any person who violates any regulation issued under section 208(d) or who, in a registration statement or report required by the Secretary of State, makes any untrue statement of a material fact or omits to state a material fact required to be stated therein or necessary to make the statements therein not misleading, shall be subject to a civil penalty of not more than $10,000 imposed by the Secretary of State. The provisions of subsections (d), (e), and (f) of section 11 of the Export Administration Act of 1979 "50 USC app. 2410" shall apply with respect to any such civil penalty.

(2) Any person who commits a willful violation under paragraph (1) shall upon conviction be fined not more than $1,000,000 or imprisoned not more than 2 years, or both.

(e) Nothing in this section may be construed to authorize the imposition of any penalty for failure to implement the Code of Conduct.

APPLICABILITY TO EVASIONS OF ACT

SEC. 604. This Act and the regulations issued to carry out this Act "22 USC 5114" shall apply to any person who undertakes or causes to be undertaken any transaction or activity with the intent to evade this Act or such regulations.

CONSTRUCTION OF ACT

SEC. 605. Nothing in this Act "22 USC 5115" shall be construed as constituting any recognition by the United States of the homelands referred to in this Act.

STATE OR LOCAL ANTI-APARTHEID LAWS, ENFORCE

SEC. 606. Notwithstanding section 210 of Public Law 99-349 "22 USC 5116" or any other provision of law --

(1) no reduction in the amount of funds for which a State or local government is eligible or entitled under any Federal law may be made, and

(2) no other penalty may be imposed by the Federal Government, by reason of the application of any State or local law concerning apartheid to any contract entered into by a State or local government for 90 days after the date of enactment of this Act.

TRAFFICKING VICTIMS PROTECTION ACT OF 2000

Trafficking Victims Protection Act of 2000, 22 U.S.C. §§ 7101-7112 (2006)

TITLE 22--FOREIGN RELATIONS AND INTERCOURSE
CHAPTER 78--TRAFFICKING VICTIMS PROTECTION

Sec. 7101. Purposes and findings

(a) Purposes

The purposes of this chapter are to combat trafficking in persons, a contemporary manifestation of slavery whose victims are predominantly women and children, to ensure just and effective punishment of traffickers, and to protect their victims.

(b) Findings

Congress finds that:

(1) As the 21st century begins, the degrading institution of slavery continues throughout the world. Trafficking in persons is a modern form of slavery, and it is the largest manifestation of slavery today. At least 700,000 persons annually, primarily women and children, are trafficked within or across international borders. Approximately 50,000 women and children are trafficked into the United States each year.

(2) Many of these persons are trafficked into the international sex trade, often by force, fraud, or coercion. The sex industry has rapidly expanded over the past several decades. It involves sexual exploitation of persons, predominantly women and girls, involving activities related to prostitution, pornography, sex tourism, and other commercial sexual services . The low status of women in many parts of the world has contributed to a burgeoning of the trafficking industry.

(3) Trafficking in persons is not limited to the sex industry. This growing transnational crime also includes forced labor and involves significant violations of labor, public health, and human rights standards worldwide.

(4) Traffickers primarily target women and girls, who are disproportionately affected by poverty, the lack of access to education, chronic unemployment, discrimination, and the lack of economic opportunities in countries of origin. Traffickers lure women and girls into their networks through false promises of decent working conditions at relatively good pay as nannies, maids, dancers, factory workers, restaurant workers, sales clerks, or models. Traffickers also buy children from poor families and sell them into prostitution or into various types of forced or bonded labor.

(5) Traffickers often transport victims from their home communities to unfamiliar destinations, including foreign countries away from family and friends, religious institutions, and other sources of protection and support, leaving the victims defenseless and vulnerable.

(6) Victims are often forced through physical violence to engage in sex acts or perform slavery-like labor. Such force includes rape and other forms of sexual abuse, torture, starvation, imprisonment, threats, psychological abuse, and coercion.

(7) Traffickers often make representations to their victims that physical harm may occur to them or others should the victim escape or attempt to escape. Such representations can have the same coercive effects on victims as direct threats to inflict such harm.

(8) Trafficking in persons is increasingly perpetrated by organized, sophisticated criminal enterprises. Such trafficking is the fastest growing source of profits for organized criminal enterprises worldwide. Profits from the trafficking industry contribute to the expansion of organized crime in the United States and worldwide. Trafficking in persons is often aided by official corruption in countries of origin, transit, and destination, thereby threatening the rule of law.

(9) Trafficking includes all the elements of the crime of forcible rape when it involves the involuntary participation of another person in sex acts by means of fraud, force, or coercion.

(10) Trafficking also involves violations of other laws, including labor and immigration codes and laws against kidnapping, slavery, false imprisonment, assault, battery, pandering, fraud, and extortion.

(11) Trafficking exposes victims to serious health risks. Women and children trafficked in the sex industry are exposed to deadly diseases, including HIV and AIDS. Trafficking victims are sometimes worked or physically brutalized to death.

(12) Trafficking in persons substantially affects interstate and foreign commerce. Trafficking for such purposes as involuntary servitude, peonage, and other forms of forced labor has an impact on the nationwide employment network and labor market. Within the context of slavery, servitude, and labor or services which are obtained or maintained through coercive conduct that amounts to a condition of servitude, victims are subjected to a range of violations.

(13) Involuntary servitude statutes are intended to reach cases in which persons are held in a condition of servitude through nonviolent coercion. In United States v. Kozminski, 487 U.S. 931 (1988), the Supreme Court found that section 1584 of Title 18, should be narrowly interpreted, absent a definition of involuntary servitude by Congress. As a result, that section was interpreted to criminalize only servitude that is brought about through use or threatened use of physical or legal coercion, and to exclude other conduct that can have the same purpose and effect.

(14) Existing legislation and law enforcement in the United States and other countries are inadequate to deter trafficking and bring traffickers to justice, failing to reflect the gravity of the offenses involved. No comprehensive law exists in the United States that penalizes the range of offenses involved in the trafficking scheme. Instead, even the most brutal instances of trafficking in the sex industry are often punished under laws that also apply to lesser offenses, so that traffickers typically escape deserved punishment.

(15) In the United States, the seriousness of this crime and its components is not reflected in current sentencing guidelines, resulting in weak penalties for convicted traffickers.

(16) In some countries, enforcement against traffickers is also hindered by official indifference, by corruption, and sometimes even by official participation in trafficking.

(17) Existing laws often fail to protect victims of trafficking, and because victims are often illegal immigrants in the destination country, they are repeatedly punished more harshly than the traffickers themselves.

(18) Additionally, adequate services and facilities do not exist to meet victims' needs regarding health care, housing, education, and legal assistance, which safely reintegrate trafficking victims into their home countries.

(19) Victims of severe forms of trafficking should not be inappropriately incarcerated, fined, or otherwise penalized solely for unlawful acts committed as a direct result of being trafficked, such as using false documents, entering the country without documentation, or working without documentation.

(20) Because victims of trafficking are frequently unfamiliar with the laws, cultures, and languages of the countries into which they have been trafficked, because they are often subjected

to coercion and intimidation including physical detention and debt bondage, and because they often fear retribution and forcible removal to countries in which they will face retribution or other hardship, these victims often find it difficult or impossible to report the crimes committed against them or to assist in the investigation and prosecution of such crimes.

(21) Trafficking of persons is an evil requiring concerted and vigorous action by countries of origin, transit or destination,and by international organizations.

(22) One of the founding documents of the United States, the Declaration of Independence, recognizes the inherent dignity and worth of all people. It states that all men are created equal and that they are endowed by their Creator with certain unalienable rights. The right to be free from slavery and involuntary servitude is among those unalienable rights. Acknowledging this fact, the United States outlawed slavery and involuntary servitude in 1865, recognizing them as evil institutions that must be abolished. Current practices of sexual slavery and trafficking of women and children are similarly abhorrent to the principles upon which the United States was founded.

(23) The United States and the international community agree that trafficking in persons involves grave violations of human rights and is a matter of pressing international concern. The international community has repeatedly condemned slavery and involuntary servitude, violence against women, and other elements of trafficking, through declarations, treaties, and United Nations resolutions and reports, including the Universal Declaration of Human Rights; the 1956 Supplementary Convention on the Abolition of Slavery, the Slave Trade, and Institutions and Practices Similar to Slavery; the 1948 American Declaration on the Rights and Duties of Man; the 1957 Abolition of Forced Labor Convention; the International Covenant on Civil and Political Rights; the Convention Against Torture and Other Cruel, Inhuman or Degrading Treatment or Punishment; United Nations General Assembly Resolutions 50/167, 51/66, and 52/98; the Final Report of the World Congress against Sexual Exploitation of Children (Stockholm, 1996); the Fourth World Conference on Women (Beijing, 1995); and the 1991 Moscow Document of the Organization for Security and Cooperation in Europe.

(24) Trafficking in persons is a transnational crime with national implications. To deter international trafficking and bring its perpetrators to justice, nations including the United States must recognize that trafficking is a serious offense. This is done by prescribing appropriate punishment, giving priority to the prosecution of trafficking offenses, and protecting rather than punishing the victims of such offenses. The United States must work bilaterally and multilaterally to abolish the trafficking industry by taking steps to promote cooperation among countries linked together by international trafficking routes. The United States must also urge the international community to take strong action in multilateral for a to engage recalcitrant countries in serious and sustained efforts to eliminate trafficking and protect trafficking victims.

Sec. 7102. Definitions

In this chapter:

(1) Appropriate Congressional committees

The term "appropriate congressional committees" means the Committee on Foreign Relations and the Committee on the Judiciary of the Senate and the Committee on International Relations and the Committee on the Judiciary of the House of Representatives.

(2) Coercion

The term "coercion" means--

(A) threats of serious harm to or physical restraint against any person;

(B) any scheme, plan, or pattern intended to cause a person to believe that failure to perform an act would result in serious harm to or physical restraint against any person; or

(C) the abuse or threatened abuse of the legal process.

(3) Commercial sex act

The term "commercial sex act" means any sex act on account of which anything of value is given to or received by any person.

(4) Debt bondage

The term "debt bondage" means the status or condition of a debtor arising from a pledge by the debtor of his or her personal services or of those of a person under his or her control as a security for debt, if the value of those services as reasonably assessed is not applied toward the liquidation of the debt or the length and nature of those services are not respectively limited and defined.

(5) Involuntary servitude

The term "involuntary servitude" includes a condition of servitude induced by means of--

(A) any scheme, plan, or pattern intended to cause a person to believe that, if the person did not enter into or continue in such condition, that person or another person would suffer serious harm or physical restraint; or

(B) the abuse or threatened abuse of the legal process.

(6) Minimum standards for the elimination of trafficking

The term "minimum standards for the elimination of trafficking" means the standards set forth in section 7106 of this title.

(7) Nonhumanitarian, nontrade-related foreign assistance

The term "nonhumanitarian, nontrade-related foreign assistance" means--

(A) any assistance under the Foreign Assistance Act of 1961 [22 U.S.C.A. § 2151 et seq.], other than--

(i) assistance under chapter 4 of part II of that Act [22 U.S.C.A. § 2346 et seq.] in support of programs of nongovernmental organizations that is made available for any program, project, or activity eligible for assistance under chapter 1 of part I of that Act [22 U.S.C.A. § 2151 et seq.];

(ii) assistance under chapter 8 of part I of that Act [22 U.S.C.A. § 2291 et seq.];

(iii) any other narcotics-related assistance under part I of that Act [22 U.S.C.A. § 2151 et seq.] or under chapter 4 or 5[4] part II of that Act [22 U.S.C.A. §§ 2346 et seq., 2347 et seq.], but any such assistance provided under this clause shall be subject to the prior notification procedures applicable to reprogrammings pursuant to section 634A of that Act [22 U.S.C.A. § 2394-1];

(iv) disaster relief assistance, including any assistance under chapter 9 of part I of that Act [22 U.S.C.A. § 2292 et seq.];

(v) antiterrorism assistance under chapter 8 of part II of that Act [22 U.S.C.A. § 1349aa et seq.];

(vi) assistance for refugees;

(vii) humanitarian and other development assistance in support of programs of nongovernmental organizations under chapters 1 and 10 of that Act;

(viii) programs under title IV of chapter 2 of part I of that Act [22 U.S.C.A. § 2191 et seq.], relating to the Overseas Private Investment Corporation; and

(ix) other programs involving trade-related or humanitarian assistance; and

(B) sales, or financing on any terms, under the Arms Export Control Act [22 U.S.C.A. § 2751 et seq.], other than sales or financing provided for narcotics-related purposes following notification in accordance with the prior notification procedures applicable to reprogrammings pursuant to section 634A of the Foreign Assistance Act of 1961 [22 U.S.C.A. § 2394-1].

(8) Severe forms of trafficking in persons

The term "severe forms of trafficking in persons" means--

(A) sex trafficking in which a commercial sex act is induced by force, fraud, or coercion, or in which the person induced to perform such act has not attained 18 years of age; or

(B) the recruitment, harboring, transportation, provision, or obtaining of a person for labor or services, through the use of force, fraud, or coercion for the purpose of subjection to involuntary servitude, peonage, debt bondage, or slavery.

(9) Sex trafficking

The term "sex trafficking" means the recruitment, harboring, transportation, provision, or obtaining of a person for the purpose of a commercial sex act.

(10) State

The term "State" means each of the several States of the United States, the District of Columbia, the Commonwealth of Puerto Rico, the United States Virgin Islands, Guam, American Samoa, the Commonwealth of the Northern Mariana Islands, and territories and possessions of the United States.

(11) Task Force

498

The term "Task Force" means the Interagency Task Force to Monitor and Combat Trafficking established under section 7103 of this title.

(12) United States

The term "United States" means the fifty States of the United States, the District of Columbia, the Commonwealth of Puerto Rico, the Virgin Islands, American Samoa, Guam, the Commonwealth of the Northern Mariana Islands, and the territories and possessions of the United States.

(13) Victim of a severe form of trafficking

The term "victim of a severe form of trafficking" means a person subject to an act or practice described in paragraph (8).

(14) Victim of trafficking

The term "victim of trafficking" means a person subjected to an act or practice described in paragraph (8) or (9).

Sec. 7103. Interagency Task Force to Monitor and Combat Trafficking

(a) Establishment

The President shall establish an Interagency Task Force to Monitor and Combat Trafficking.

(b) Appointment

The President shall appoint the members of the Task Force, which shall include the Secretary of State, the Administrator of the United States Agency for International Development, the Attorney General, the Secretary of Labor, the Secretary of Health and Human Services, the Director of National Intelligence, the Secretary of Defense, the Secretary of Homeland Security, and such other officials as may be designated by the President.

(c) Chairman

The Task Force shall be chaired by the Secretary of State.

(d) Activities of the Task Force

The Task Force shall carry out the following activities:

(1) Coordinate the implementation of this chapter.

(2) Measure and evaluate progress of the United States and other countries in the areas of trafficking prevention, protection, and assistance to victims of trafficking, and prosecution and enforcement against traffickers, including the role of public corruption in facilitating trafficking. The Task Force shall have primary responsibility for assisting the Secretary of State in the preparation of the reports described in section 7107 of this title.

(3) Expand interagency procedures to collect and organize data, including significant research and resource information on domestic and international trafficking. Any data collection procedures established under this subsection shall respect the confidentiality of victims of trafficking.

(4) Engage in efforts to facilitate cooperation among countries of origin, transit, and destination. Such efforts shall aim to strengthen local and regional capacities to prevent trafficking, prosecute traffickers and assist trafficking victims, and shall include initiatives to enhance cooperative efforts between destination countries and countries of origin and assist in the appropriate reintegration of stateless victims of trafficking.

(5) Examine the role of the international "sex tourism" industry in the trafficking of persons and in the sexual exploitation of women and children around the world.

(6) Engage in consultation and advocacy with governmental and nongovernmental organizations, among other entities, to advance the purposes of this chapter.

(7) Not later than May 1, 2004, and annually thereafter, the Attorney General shall submit to the Committee on Ways and Means, the Committee on International Relations, and the Committee on the Judiciary of the House of Representatives and the Committee on Finance, the Committee on Foreign Relations, and the Committee on the Judiciary of the Senate, a report on Federal agencies that are implementing any provision of this chapter, or any amendment made by this chapter, which shall include, at a minimum, information on--

(A) the number of persons who received benefits or other services under section 7105(b) of this title in connection with programs or activities funded or administered by the Secretary of Health and Human Services, the Secretary of Labor, the Board of Directors of the Legal Services Corporation, and other appropriate Federal agencies during the preceding fiscal year;

(B) the number of persons who have been granted continued presence in the United States under section 7105(c)(3) of this title during the preceding fiscal year;

(C) the number of persons who have applied for, been granted, or been denied a visa or otherwise provided status under section 1101(a)(15)(T)(i) of Title 8 during the preceding fiscal year;

(D) the number of persons who have been charged or convicted under one or more of sections 1581, 1583, 1584, 1589, 1590, 1591, 1592, or 1594 of Title 18, during the preceding fiscal year and the sentences imposed against each such person;

(E) the amount, recipient, and purpose of each grant issued by any Federal agency to carry out the purposes of sections 7104 and 7105 of this title, or section 2152d of this title, during the preceding fiscal year;

(F) the nature of training conducted pursuant to section 7105(c)(4) of this title during the preceding fiscal year;

(G) the amount, recipient, and purpose of each grant under sections 14044a and 14044c of Title 42; and

(H) the activities undertaken by the Senior Policy Operating Group to carry out its responsibilities under subsection (f) of this section.

(e) Support for the Task Force

The Secretary of State is authorized to establish within the Department of State an Office to Monitor and Combat Trafficking, which shall provide assistance to the Task Force. Any such Office shall be headed by a Director, who shall be appointed by the President, by and with the advice and consent of the Senate, with the rank of Ambassador-at-Large. The Director shall have the primary responsibility for assisting the Secretary of State in carrying out the purposes of this chapter and may have additional responsibilities as determined by the Secretary. The Director shall consult with nongovernmental organizations and multilateral organizations, and with trafficking victims or other affected persons. The Director shall have the authority to take evidence in public hearings or by other means. The agencies represented on the Task Force are authorized to provide staff to the Office on a nonreimbursable basis.

(f) Senior Policy Operating Group

(1) Establishment

There shall be established within the executive branch a Senior Policy Operating Group.

(2) Membership; related matters

(A) In general

The Operating Group shall consist of the senior officials designated as representatives of the appointed members of the Task Force (pursuant to Executive Order No. 13257 of February 13, 2002).

(B) Chairperson

The Operating Group shall be chaired by the Director of the Office to Monitor and Combat Trafficking of the Department of State.

(C) Meetings

The Operating Group shall meet on a regular basis at the call of the Chairperson.

(3) Duties

The Operating Group shall coordinate activities of Federal departments and agencies regarding policies (including grants and grant policies) involving the international trafficking in persons and the implementation of this chapter.

(4) Availability of information

Each Federal department or agency represented on the Operating Group shall fully share all information with such Group regarding the department or agency's plans, before and after final agency decisions are made, on all matters relating to grants, grant policies, and other significant actions regarding the international trafficking in persons and the implementation of this division.

(5) Regulations

Not later than 90 days after December 19, 2003, the President shall promulgate regulations to implement this section, including regulations to carry out paragraph (4).

Sec. 7104. Prevention of trafficking

(a) Economic alternatives to prevent and deter trafficking

The President shall establish and carry out international initiatives to enhance economic opportunity for potential victims of trafficking as a method to deter trafficking. Such initiatives may include--

(1) microcredit lending programs, training in business development, skills training, and job counseling;

(2) programs to promote women's participation in economic decisionmaking;

(3) programs to keep children, especially girls, in elementary and secondary schools, and to educate persons who have been victims of trafficking;

(4) development of educational curricula regarding the dangers of trafficking; and

(5) grants to nongovernmental organizations to accelerate and advance the political, economic, social, and educational roles and capacities of women in their countries.

(b) Public awareness and information

The President, acting through the Secretary of Labor, the Secretary of Health and Human Services, the Attorney General, and the Secretary of State, shall establish and carry out programs to increase public awareness, particularly among potential victims of trafficking, of the dangers of trafficking and the protections that are available for victims of trafficking.

(c) Border interdiction

The President shall establish and carry out programs of border interdiction outside the United States. Such programs shall include providing grants to foreign nongovernmental organizations that provide for transit shelters operating at key border crossings and that help train survivors of trafficking in persons to educate and train border guards and officials, and other local law enforcement officials, to identify traffickers and victims of severe forms of trafficking, and the appropriate manner in which to treat such victims. Such programs shall also include, to the extent appropriate, monitoring by such survivors of trafficking in persons of the implementation of border interdiction programs, including helping in the identification of such victims to stop the cross-border transit of victims. The President shall ensure that any program established under this subsection provides the opportunity for any trafficking victim who is freed to return to his or her previous residence if the victim so chooses.

(d) International media

The President shall establish and carry out programs that support the production of television and radio programs, including documentaries, to inform vulnerable populations overseas of the dangers of trafficking, and to increase awareness of the public in countries of destination regarding the slave-like practices and other human rights abuses involved in trafficking, including fostering linkages between individuals working in the media in different countries to determine the best methods for informing such populations through such media.

(e) Combating international sex tourism

(1) Development and dissemination of materials

The President, pursuant to such regulations as may be prescribed, shall ensure that materials are developed and disseminated to alert travelers that sex tourism (as described in subsections (b) through (f) of section 2423 of Title 18) is illegal, will be prosecuted, and presents dangers to those involved. Such materials shall be disseminated to individuals traveling to foreign destinations where the President determines that sex tourism is significant.

(2) Monitoring of compliance

The President shall monitor compliance with the requirements of paragraph (1).

(3) Feasibility report

Not later than 180 days after December 19, 2003, the President shall transmit to the Committee on International Relations of the House of Representatives and the Committee on Foreign Affairs of the Senate a report that describes the feasibility of such United States Government materials being disseminated through public-private partnerships to individuals traveling to foreign destinations.

(f) Consultation requirement

The President shall consult with appropriate nongovernmental organizations with respect to the establishment and conduct of initiatives and programs described in subsections (a) through (e) of this section.

(g) Termination of certain grants, contracts and cooperative agreements

The President shall ensure that any grant, contract, or cooperative agreement provided or entered into by a Federal department or agency under which funds are to be provided to a private entity, in whole or in part, shall include a condition that authorizes the department or agency to terminate the grant, contract, or cooperative agreement, without penalty, if the grantee or any subgrantee, or the contractor or any subcontractor (i) engages in severe forms of trafficking in persons or has procured a commercial sex act during the period of time that the grant, contract, or cooperative agreement is in effect, or (ii) uses forced labor in the performance of the grant, contract, or cooperative agreement.

(h) Prevention of trafficking in conjunction with post-conflict and humanitarian emergency assistance

The United States Agency for International Development, the Department of State, and the Department of Defense shall incorporate anti-trafficking and protection measures for vulnerable populations, particularly women and children, into their post-conflict and humanitarian emergency assistance and program activities.

Sec. 7105. Protection and assistance for victims of trafficking

(a) Assistance for victims in other countries

(1) In general

The Secretary of State and the Administrator of the United States Agency for International Development, in consultation with appropriate nongovernmental organizations, shall establish and carry out programs and initiatives in foreign countries to assist in the safe integration, reintegration, or resettlement, as appropriate, of victims of trafficking. Such programs and initiatives shall be designed to meet the appropriate assistance needs of such persons and their children, as identified by the Task Force. In addition, such programs and initiatives shall, to the maximum extent practicable, include the following:

(A) Support for local in-country nongovernmental organization-operated hotlines, culturally and linguistically appropriate protective shelters, and regional and international nongovernmental organization networks and databases on trafficking, including support to assist nongovernmental organizations in establishing service centers and systems that are mobile and extend beyond large cities.

(B) Support for nongovernmental organizations and advocates to provide legal, social, and other services and assistance to trafficked individuals, particularly those individuals in detention, and by facilitating contact between relevant foreign government agencies and such nongovernmental organizations to facilitate cooperation between the foreign governments and such organizations.

(C) Education and training for trafficked women and girls.

(D) The safe integration or reintegration of trafficked individuals into an appropriate community or family, with full respect for the wishes, dignity, and safety of the trafficked individual.

(E) Support for developing or increasing programs to assist families of victims in locating, repatriating, and treating their trafficked family members, in assisting the voluntary repatriation of these family members or their integration or resettlement into appropriate communities, and in providing them with treatment.

(2) Additional requirement

In establishing and conducting programs and initiatives described in paragraph (1), the Secretary of State and the Administrator of the United States Agency for International Development shall take all appropriate steps to enhance cooperative efforts among foreign countries, including countries of origin of victims of trafficking, to assist in the integration, reintegration, or resettlement, as appropriate, of victims of trafficking, including stateless victims.

(b) Victims in the United States

(1) Assistance

(A) Eligibility for benefits and services

Notwithstanding title IV of the Personal Responsibility and Work Opportunity Reconciliation Act of 1996, an alien who is a victim of a severe form of trafficking in persons, or an alien classified as a nonimmigrant under section 1101 (a)(15)(T)(ii) of Title 8, shall be eligible for benefits and services under any Federal or State program or activity funded or administered by any official or agency described in subparagraph (B) to the same extent as an alien who is admitted to the United States as a refugee under section 1157 of Title 8.

(B) Requirement to expand benefits and services

Subject to subparagraph (C) and, in the case of nonentitlement programs, to the availability of appropriations, the Secretary of Health and Human Services, the Secretary of Labor, the Board of Directors of the Legal Services Corporation, and the heads of other Federal agencies shall expand benefits and services to victims of severe forms of trafficking in persons in the United States, and aliens classified as a nonimmigrant under section 1101(a)(15)(T)(ii) of Title 8, without regard to the immigration status of such victims. In the case of nonentitlement programs funded by the Secretary of Health and Human Services, such benefits and services may include services to assist potential victims of trafficking in achieving certification and to assist minor dependent children of victims of severe forms of trafficking in persons or potential victims of trafficking.

(C) Definition of victim of a severe form of trafficking in persons

For the purposes of this paragraph, the term "victim of a severe form of trafficking in persons" means only a person--

(i) who has been subjected to an act or practice described in section 7102(8) of this title as in effect on October 28, 2000; and

(ii)   (I) who has not attained 18 years of age; or

(II) who is the subject of a certification under subparagraph (E).

(D) Repealed. Pub.L. 108-193, § 6(a)(2), Dec. 19, 2003, 117 Stat. 2880.

(E) Certification

(i) In general

Subject to clause (ii), the certification referred to in subparagraph (C) is a certification by the Secretary of Health and Human Services, after consultation with the Attorney General and the Secretary of Homeland Security, that the person referred to in subparagraph (C)(ii)(II)--

(I) is willing to assist in every reasonable way in the investigation and prosecution of severe forms of trafficking in persons; and

(II)   (aa) has made a bona fide application for a visa under section 1101(a)(15)(T) of Title 8, as added by subsection (e) of this section, that has not been denied; or

(bb) is a person whose continued presence in the United States the Attorney General and the Secretary of Homeland Security is ensuring in order to effectuate prosecution of traffickers in persons.

(ii) Period of effectiveness

A certification referred to in subparagraph (C), with respect to a person described in clause (i)(II)(bb), shall be effective only for so long as the Attorney General Secretary of Homeland Security determines that the continued presence of such person is necessary to effectuate prosecution of traffickers in persons.

(iii) Investigation and prosecution defined

For the purpose of a certification under this subparagraph, the term "investigation and prosecution" includes--

(I) identification of a person or persons who have committed severe forms of trafficking in persons;

(II) location and apprehension of such persons;

(III) testimony at proceedings against such persons; or

(IV) responding to and cooperating with requests for evidence and information.

(iv) Assistance to investigations

In making the certification described in this subparagraph with respect to the assistance to investigation or prosecution described in clause (i)(I), the Secretary of Health and Human Services shall consider statements from State and local law enforcement officials that the person referred to in subparagraph (C)(ii)(II) has been willing to assist in every reasonable way with respect to the investigation and prosecution of State and local crimes such as kidnapping, rape, slavery, or other forced labor offenses, where severe forms of trafficking appear to have been involved.

(2) Grants

(A) In general

Subject to the availability of appropriations, the Attorney General may make grants to States, Indian tribes, units of local government, and nonprofit, nongovernmental victims' service organizations to develop, expand, or strengthen victim service programs for victims of trafficking.

(B) Allocation of grant funds

Of amounts made available for grants under this paragraph, there shall be set aside--

(i) three percent for research, evaluation, and statistics;

(ii) two percent for training and technical assistance; and

(iii) one percent for management and administration.

(C) Limitation on Federal share

The Federal share of a grant made under this paragraph may not exceed 75 percent of the total costs of the projects described in the application submitted.

(c) Trafficking victim regulations

Not later than 180 days after October 28, 2000, the Attorney General, the Secretary of Homeland Security and the Secretary of State shall promulgate regulations for law enforcement personnel, immigration officials, and Department of State officials to implement the following:

(1) Protections while in custody

Victims of severe forms of trafficking, while in the custody of the Federal Government and to the extent practicable, shall--

(A) not be detained in facilities inappropriate to their status as crime victims;

(B) receive necessary medical care and other assistance; and

(C) be provided protection if a victim's safety is at risk or if there is danger of additional harm by recapture of the victim by a trafficker, including--

(i) taking measures to protect trafficked persons and their family members from intimidation and threats of reprisals and reprisals from traffickers and their associates; and

(ii) ensuring that the names and identifying information of trafficked persons and their family members are not disclosed to the public.

(2) Access to information

Victims of severe forms of trafficking shall have access to information about their rights and translation services. To the extent practicable, victims of severe forms of trafficking shall have access to information about federally funded or administered anti-trafficking programs that provide services to victims of severe forms of trafficking.

(3) Authority to permit continued presence in the United States

Federal law enforcement officials may permit an alien individual's continued presence in the United States, if after an assessment, it is determined that such individual is a victim of a severe form of trafficking and a potential witness to such trafficking, in order to effectuate prosecution of those responsible, and such officials in investigating and prosecuting traffickers shall protect the safety of trafficking victims, including taking measures to protect trafficked persons and their family members from intimidation, threats of reprisals, and reprisals from traffickers and their associates.

(4) Training of Government personnel

Appropriate personnel of the Department of State and the Department of Justice shall be trained in identifying victims of severe forms of trafficking and providing for the protection of such victims.

(d) Construction

Nothing in subsection (c) of this section shall be construed as creating any private cause of action against the United States or its officers or employees.

(e) Protection from removal for certain crime victims

(1) to (4) Omitted

(5) Statutory construction

Nothing in this section, or in the amendments made by this section, shall be construed as prohibiting the Secretary of Homeland Security from instituting removal proceedings under section 1229a of Title 8 against an alien admitted as a nonimmigrant under section

1101(a)(15)(T)(i) of Title 8, as added by subsection (e) of this section, for conduct committed after the alien's admission into the United States, or for conduct or a condition that was not disclosed to the Secretary of Homeland Security prior to the alien's admission as a nonimmigrant under such section 1101(a)(15)(T)(i) of Title.

(f) Omitted

(g) Annual reports

On or before October 31 of each year, the Attorney General or the Secretary of Homeland Security shall submit a report to the appropriate congressional committees setting forth, with respect to the preceding fiscal year, the number, if any, of otherwise eligible applicants who did not receive visas under section 1101(a)(15)(T) of Title 8, as added by subsection (e) of this section, or who were unable to adjust their status under section 1255(l) of Title 8, solely on account of the unavailability of visas due to a limitation imposed by section 1184(o)(2) or 1255(l)(4)(A) of Title 8.

Sec. 7106. Minimum standards for the elimination of trafficking

(a) Minimum standards

For purposes of this chapter, the minimum standards for the elimination of trafficking applicable to the government of a country of origin, transit, or destination for a significant number of victims of severe forms of trafficking are the following:

(1) The government of the country should prohibit severe forms of trafficking in persons and punish acts of such trafficking.

(2) For the knowing commission of any act of sex trafficking involving force, fraud, coercion, or in which the victim of sex trafficking is a child incapable of giving meaningful consent, or of trafficking which includes rape or kidnapping or which causes a death, the government of the country should prescribe punishment commensurate with that for grave crimes, such as forcible sexual assault.

(3) For the knowing commission of any act of a severe form of trafficking in persons, the government of the country should prescribe punishment that is sufficiently stringent to deter and that adequately reflects the heinous nature of the offense.

(4) The government of the country should make serious and sustained efforts to eliminate severe forms of trafficking in persons.

(b) Criteria

In determinations under subsection (a)(4) of this section, the following factors should be considered as indicia of serious and sustained efforts to eliminate severe forms of trafficking in persons:

(1) Whether the government of the country vigorously investigates and prosecutes acts of severe forms of trafficking in persons, and convicts and sentences persons responsible for such acts, that take place wholly or partly within the territory of the country. After reasonable requests from the Department of State for data regarding investigations, prosecutions, convictions, and sentences, a government which does not provide such data, consistent with the capacity of such government to obtain such data, shall be presumed not to have vigorously investigated, prosecuted, convicted or sentenced such acts. During the periods prior to the annual report submitted on June 1, 2004, and on June 1, 2005, and the periods afterwards until September 30 of each such year, the Secretary of State may disregard the presumption contained in the preceding sentence if the government has provided some data to the Department of State regarding such acts and the Secretary has determined that the government is making a good faith effort to collect such data.

(2) Whether the government of the country protects victims of severe forms of trafficking in persons and encourages their assistance in the investigation and prosecution of such trafficking, including provisions for legal alternatives to their removal to countries in which they would face retribution or hardship, and ensures that victims are not inappropriately incarcerated, fined, or otherwise penalized solely for unlawful acts as a direct result of being trafficked.

(3) Whether the government of the country has adopted measures to prevent severe forms of trafficking in persons, such as measures to inform and educate the public, including potential victims, about the causes and consequences of severe forms of trafficking in persons, measures to reduce the demand for commercial sex acts and for participation in international sex tourism by nationals of the country, measures to ensure that its nationals who are deployed abroad as part of a peacekeeping or other similar mission do not engage in or facilitate severe forms of trafficking in persons or exploit victims of such trafficking, and measures to prevent the use of forced labor or child labor in violation of international standards.

(4) Whether the government of the country cooperates with other governments in the investigation and prosecution of severe forms of trafficking in persons.

(5) Whether the government of the country extradites persons charged with acts of severe forms of trafficking in persons on substantially the same terms and to substantially the same extent as persons charged with other serious crimes (or, to the extent such extradition would be inconsistent with the laws of such country or with international agreements to which the country is a party, whether the government is taking all appropriate measures to modify or replace such laws and treaties so as to permit such extradition).

(6) Whether the government of the country monitors immigration and emigration patterns for evidence of severe forms of trafficking in persons and whether law enforcement agencies of the country respond to any such evidence in a manner that is consistent with the vigorous investigation and prosecution of acts of such trafficking, as well as with the protection of human rights of victims and the internationally recognized human right to leave any country, including one's own, and to return to one's own country.

(7) Whether the government of the country vigorously investigates, prosecutes, convicts, and sentences public officials who participate in or facilitate severe forms of trafficking in persons, including nationals of the country who are deployed abroad as part of a peacekeeping or other similar mission who engage in or facilitate severe forms of trafficking in persons or exploit victims of such trafficking, and takes all appropriate measures against officials who condone such trafficking. After reasonable requests from the Department of State for data regarding such investigations, prosecutions, convictions, and sentences, a government which does not provide such data consistent with its resources shall be presumed not to have vigorously investigated, prosecuted, convicted, or sentenced such acts. During the periods prior to the annual report submitted on June 1, 2004, and on June 1, 2005, and the periods afterwards until September 30 of each such year, the Secretary of State may disregard the presumption contained in the preceding sentence if the government has provided some data to the Department of State regarding such acts and the Secretary has determined that the government is making a good faith effort to collect such data.

(8) Whether the percentage of victims of severe forms of trafficking in the country that are non-citizens of such countries is insignificant.

(9) Whether the government of the country, consistent with the capacity of such government, systematically monitors its efforts to satisfy the criteria described in paragraphs (1) through (8) and makes available publicly a periodic assessment of such efforts.

(10) Whether the government of the country achieves appreciable progress in eliminating severe forms of trafficking when compared to the assessment in the previous year.

Sec. 7107. Actions against governments failing to meet minimum standards
(a) Statement of policy

It is the policy of the United States not to provide nonhumanitarian, nontrade-related foreign assistance to any government that--

(1) does not comply with minimum standards for the elimination of trafficking; and

(2) is not making significant efforts to bring itself into compliance with such standards.

(b) Reports to Congress

(1) Annual report

Not later than June 1 of each year, the Secretary of State shall submit to the appropriate congressional committees a report with respect to the status of severe forms of trafficking in persons that shall include--

(A) a list of those countries, if any, to which the minimum standards for the elimination of trafficking are applicable and whose governments fully comply with such standards;

(B) a list of those countries, if any, to which the minimum standards for the elimination of trafficking are applicable and whose governments do not yet fully comply with such standards but are making significant efforts to bring themselves into compliance;

(C) a list of those countries, if any, to which the minimum standards for the elimination of trafficking are applicable and whose governments do not fully comply with such standards and are not making significant efforts to bring themselves into compliance; and

(D) information on the measures taken by the United Nations, the Organization for Security and Cooperation in Europe, the North Atlantic Treaty Organization and, as appropriate, other multilateral organizations in which the United States participates, to prevent the involvement of the organization's employees, contractor personnel, and peacekeeping forces in trafficking in persons or the exploitation of victims of trafficking.

(2) Interim reports

In addition to the annual report under paragraph (1), the Secretary of State may submit to the appropriate congressional committees at any time one or more interim reports with respect to the status of severe forms of trafficking in persons, including information about countries whose governments--

(A) have come into or out of compliance with the minimum standards for the elimination of trafficking; or

(B) have begun or ceased to make significant efforts to bring themselves into compliance, since the transmission of the last annual report.

(3) Special watch list

(A) Submission of list

Not later than the date on which the determinations described in subsections (c) and (d) of this section are submitted to the appropriate congressional committees in accordance with such subsections, the Secretary of State shall submit to the appropriate congressional committees a list of countries that the Secretary determines requires special scrutiny during the following year. The list shall be composed of the following countries:

(i) Countries that have been listed pursuant to paragraph (1)(A) in the current annual report and were listed pursuant to paragraph (1)(B) in the previous annual report.

(ii) Countries that have been listed pursuant to paragraph (1)(B) pursuant to the current annual report and were listed pursuant to paragraph (1)(C) in the previous annual report.

(iii) Countries that have been listed pursuant to paragraph (1)(B) pursuant to the current annual report, where--

(I) the absolute number of victims of severe forms of trafficking is very significant or is significantly increasing;

(II) there is a failure to provide evidence of increasing efforts to combat severe forms of trafficking in persons from the previous year, including increased investigations, prosecutions and convictions of trafficking crimes, increased assistance to victims, and decreasing evidence of complicity in severe forms of trafficking by government officials; or

(III) the determination that a country is making significant efforts to bring themselves into compliance with minimum standards was based on commitments by the country to take additional future steps over the next year.

(B) Interim assessment

Not later than February 1st of each year, the Secretary of State shall provide to the appropriate congressional committees an assessment of the progress that each country on the special watch list described in subparagraph (A) has made since the last annual report.

(C) Relation of special watch list to annual trafficking in persons report

A determination that a country shall not be placed on the special watch list described in subparagraph (A) shall not affect in any way the determination to be made in the following year as to whether a country is complying with the minimum standards for the elimination of trafficking or whether a country is making significant efforts to bring itself into compliance with such standards.

(4) Significant efforts

In determinations under paragraph (1) or (2) as to whether the government of a country is making significant efforts to bring itself into compliance with the minimum standards for the elimination of trafficking, the Secretary of State shall consider--

(A) the extent to which the country is a country of origin, transit, or destination for severe forms of trafficking;

(B) the extent of noncompliance with the minimum standards by the government and, particularly, the extent to which officials or employees of the government have participated in, facilitated, condoned, or are otherwise complicit in severe forms of trafficking; and

(C) what measures are reasonable to bring the government into compliance with the minimum standards in light of the resources and capabilities of the government.

(c) Notification

Not less than 45 days or more than 90 days after the submission, on or after January 1, 2003, of an annual report under subsection (b)(1) of this section, or an interim report under subsection (b)(2) of this section, the President shall submit to the appropriate congressional committees a notification of one of the determinations listed in subsection (d) of this section with respect to each foreign country whose government, according to such report--

(A) does not comply with the minimum standards for the elimination of trafficking; and

(B) is not making significant efforts to bring itself into compliance, as described in subsection (b)(1)(C) of this section.

(d) Presidential determinations

The determinations referred to in subsection (c) of this section are the following:

(1) Withholding of nonhumanitarian, nontrade-related assistance

The President has determined that--

(A)   (i) the United States will not provide nonhumanitarian, nontrade- related foreign assistance to the government of the country for the subsequent fiscal year until such government complies with the minimum standards or makes significant efforts to bring itself into compliance; or

(ii) in the case of a country whose government received no nonhumanitarian, nontrade-related foreign assistance from the United States during the previous fiscal year, the United States will not provide funding for participation by officials or employees of such governments in educational and cultural exchange programs for the subsequent fiscal year until such government complies with the minimum standards or makes significant efforts to bring itself into compliance; and

(B) the President will instruct the United States Executive Director of each multilateral development bank and of the International Monetary Fund to vote against, and to use the Executive Director's best efforts to deny, any loan or other utilization of the funds of the respective institution to that country (other than for humanitarian assistance, for trade-related assistance, or for development assistance which directly addresses basic human needs, is not administered by the government of the sanctioned country, and confers no benefit to that government) for the subsequent fiscal year until such government complies with the minimum standards or makes significant efforts to bring itself into compliance.

(2) Ongoing, multiple, broad-based restrictions on assistance in response to human rights violations

The President has determined that such country is already subject to multiple, broad-based restrictions on assistance imposed in significant part in response to human rights abuses and such restrictions are ongoing and are comparable to the restrictions provided in paragraph (1). Such determination shall be accompanied by a description of the specific restriction or restrictions that were the basis for making such determination.

(3) Subsequent compliance

The Secretary of State has determined that the government of the country has come into compliance with the minimum standards or is making significant efforts to bring itself into compliance.

(4) Continuation of assistance in the National interest

Notwithstanding the failure of the government of the country to comply with minimum standards for the elimination of trafficking and to make significant efforts to bring itself into compliance, the President has determined that the provision to the country of nonhumanitarian, nontrade-related foreign assistance or funding for participation in educational and cultural exchange programs, or the multilateral assistance described in paragraph (1)(B), or both, would promote the purposes of this chapter or is otherwise in the national interest of the United States.

(5) Exercise of waiver authority

(A) In general

The President may exercise the authority under paragraph (4) with respect to--

(i) all nonhumanitarian, nontrade-related foreign assistance or funding for participation in educational and cultural exchange programs to a country;

   (ii) all multilateral assistance described in paragraph (1)(B) to a country; or

   (iii) one or more programs, projects, or activities of such assistance.

  (B) Avoidance of significant adverse effects

   The President shall exercise the authority under paragraph (4) when necessary to avoid significant adverse effects on vulnerable populations, including women and children.

 (6) Definition of multilateral development bank

   In this subsection, the term "multilateral development bank" refers to any of the following institutions: the International Bank for Reconstruction and Development, the International Development Association, the International Finance Corporation, the Inter-American Development Bank, the Asian Development Bank, the Inter-American Investment Corporation, the African Development Bank, the African Development Fund, the European Bank for Reconstruction and Development, and the Multilateral Investment Guaranty Agency.

(e) Certification

   Together with any notification under subsection (c) of this section, the President shall provide a certification by the Secretary of State that, with respect to any assistance described in clause (ii), (iii), or (v) of section 7102(7)(A) of this title, or with respect to any assistance described in section 7102(7)(B) of this title, no assistance is intended to be received or used by any agency or official who has participated in, facilitated, or condoned a severe form of trafficking in persons.

(f) After the President has made a determination described in subsection (d)(1) of this section with respect to the government of a country, the President may at any time make a determination described in paragraphs (4) and (5) of subsection (d) of this section to waive, in whole or in part, the measures imposed against the country by the previous determination under subsection (d)(1) of this section.

Sec. 7108. Actions against significant traffickers in persons

(a) Authority to sanction significant traffickers in persons

 (1) In general

   The President may exercise the authorities set forth in section 1702 of Title 50 without regard to section 1701 of Title 50 in the case of any of the following persons:

  (A) Any foreign person that plays a significant role in a severe form of trafficking in persons, directly or indirectly in the United States.

  (B) Foreign persons that materially assist in, or provide financial or technological support for or to, or provide goods or services in support of, activities of a significant foreign trafficker in persons identified pursuant to subparagraph (A).

  (C) Foreign persons that are owned, controlled, or directed by, or acting for or on behalf of, a significant foreign trafficker identified pursuant to subparagraph (A).

 (2) Penalties

   The penalties set forth in section 1705 of Title 50 apply to violations of any license, order, or regulation issued under this section.

(b) Report to Congress on identification and sanctioning of significant traffickers in persons

 (1) In general

   Upon exercising the authority of subsection (a) of this section, the President shall report to the appropriate congressional committees--

  (A) identifying publicly the foreign persons that the President determines are appropriate for sanctions pursuant to this section and the basis for such determination; and

  (B) detailing publicly the sanctions imposed pursuant to this section.

 (2) Removal of sanctions

   Upon suspending or terminating any action imposed under the authority of subsection (a) of this section, the President shall report to the committees described in paragraph (1) on such suspension or termination.

 (3) Submission of classified information

   Reports submitted under this subsection may include an annex with classified information regarding the basis for the determination made by the President under paragraph (1)(A).

(c) Law enforcement and intelligence activities not affected

Nothing in this section prohibits or otherwise limits the authorized law enforcement or intelligence activities of the United States, or the law enforcement activities of any State or subdivision thereof.

(d) Omitted

(e) Implementation

(1) Delegation of authority

The President may delegate any authority granted by this section, including the authority to designate foreign persons under paragraphs (1)(B) and (1)(C) of subsection (a) of this section.

(2) Promulgation of rules and regulations

The head of any agency, including the Secretary of Treasury, is authorized to take such actions as may be necessary to carry out any authority delegated by the President pursuant to paragraph (1), including promulgating rules and regulations.

(3) Opportunity for review

Such rules and regulations shall include procedures affording an opportunity for a person to be heard in an expeditious manner, either in person or through a representative, for the purpose of seeking changes to or termination of any determination, order, designation or other action associated with the exercise of the authority in subsection (a) of this section.

(f) "Foreign persons" defined

In this section, the term " foreign person" means any citizen or national of a foreign state or any entity not organized under the laws of the United States, including a foreign government official, but does not include a foreign state.

(g) Construction

Nothing in this section shall be construed as precluding judicial review of the exercise of the authority described in subsection (a) of this section.

Sec. 7109. Strengthening prosecution and punishment of traffickers

(a) Omitted

(b) Amendment to the sentencing guidelines

(1) Pursuant to its authority under section 994 of Title 28 and in accordance with this section, the United States Sentencing Commission shall review and, if appropriate, amend the sentencing guidelines and policy statements applicable to persons convicted of offenses involving the trafficking of persons including component or related crimes of peonage, involuntary servitude, slave trade offenses, and possession, transfer or sale of false immigration documents in furtherance of trafficking, and the Fair Labor Standards Act [29 U.S.C.A. § 201 et seq.] and the Migrant and Seasonal Agricultural Worker Protection Act [29 U.S.C.A. § 1801 et seq.].

(2) In carrying out this subsection, the Sentencing Commission shall--

(A) take all appropriate measures to ensure that these sentencing guidelines and policy statements applicable to the offenses described in paragraph (1) of this subsection are sufficiently stringent to deter and adequately reflect the heinous nature of such offenses;

(B) consider conforming the sentencing guidelines applicable to offenses involving trafficking in persons to the guidelines applicable to peonage, involuntary servitude, and slave trade offenses; and

(C) consider providing sentencing enhancements for those convicted of the offenses described in paragraph (1) of this subsection that--

(i) involve a large number of victims;

(ii) involve a pattern of continued and flagrant violations;

(iii) involve the use or threatened use of a dangerous weapon; or

(iv) result in the death or bodily injury of any person.

(3) The Commission may promulgate the guidelines or amendments under this subsection in accordance with the procedures set forth in section 21(a) of the Sentencing Act of 1987, as though the authority under that Act had not expired.

Sec. 7109a. Research on domestic and international trafficking in persons

(a) In general

The President, acting through the Council of Economic Advisors, the National Research Council of the National Academies, the Secretary of Labor, the Secretary of Health and Human Services, the Attorney General, the Secretary of State, the Administrator of the United States Agency for International

Development, and the the Director of National Intelligence, shall carry out research, including by providing grants to nongovernmental organizations, as well as relevant United States Government agencies and international organizations, which furthers the purposes of this chapter and provides data to address the problems identified in the findings of this chapter. Such research initiatives shall, to the maximum extent practicable, include, but not be limited to, the following:

(1) The economic causes and consequences of trafficking in persons.

(2) The effectiveness of programs and initiatives funded or administered by Federal agencies to prevent trafficking in persons and to protect and assist victims of trafficking.

(3) The interrelationship between trafficking in persons and global health risks, particularly HIV/AIDS.

(4) Subject to subsection (b) of this section, the interrelationship between trafficking in persons and terrorism, including the use of profits from trafficking in persons to finance terrorism.

(5) An effective mechanism for quantifying the number of victims of trafficking on a national, regional, and international basis.

(6) The abduction and enslavement of children for use as soldiers, including steps taken to eliminate the abduction and enslavement of children for use as soldiers and recommendations for such further steps as may be necessary to rapidly end the abduction and enslavement of children for use as soldiers.

(b) Role of Human Smuggling and Trafficking Center

The research initiatives described in subsection (a)(4) of this section shall be carried out by the Human Smuggling and Trafficking Center (established pursuant to section 1777 of Title 8).

(c) Definitions

In this section:

(1) AIDS: The term "AIDS" means the acquired immune deficiency syndrome.

(2) HIV: The term "HIV" means the human immunodeficiency virus, the pathogen that causes AIDS.

(3) HIV/AIDS: The term "HIV/AIDS" means, with respect to an individual, an individual who is infected with HIV or living with AIDS.

Sec. 7110. Authorizations of appropriations

(a) Authorization of appropriations in support of the Task Force

To carry out the purposes of section 104, and sections 7103(e), 7103(f) and 7107 of this title, there are authorized to be appropriated to the Secretary of State $1,500,000 for fiscal year 2001, $3,000,000 for each of the fiscal years 2002 and 2003, $5,000,000 for each of the fiscal years 2004 and 2005, and $5,500,000 for each of the fiscal years 2006 and 2007. In addition, there are authorized to be appropriated to the Office to Monitor and Combat Trafficking for official reception and representation expenses $3,000 for each of the fiscal years 2006 and 2007.

(b) Authorization of appropriations to the Secretary of Health and Human Services

To carry out the purposes of section 7105(b) of this title, there are authorized to be appropriated to the Secretary of Health and Human Services $5,000,000 for fiscal year 2001 and $10,000,000 for fiscal year 2002 and $15,000,000 for each of the fiscal years 2004, 2005, 2006, and 2007.

(c) Authorization of appropriations to the Secretary of State

(1) Bilateral assistance to combat trafficking

(A) Prevention

To carry out the purposes of section 7104 of this title, there are authorized to be appropriated to the Secretary of State $10,000,000 for each of the fiscal years 2004, 2005, 2006, and 2007.

(B) Protection

To carry out the purposes of section 7105(a) of this title, there are authorized to be appropriated to the Secretary of State $15,000,000 for fiscal year 2003 and $10,000,000 for each of the fiscal years 2004, 2005, 2006, and 2007.

(C) Prosecution and meeting minimum standards

To carry out the purposes of section 2152d of this title, there are authorized to be appropriated $10,000,000 for each of the fiscal years 2004, 2005, 2006, and 2007 to assist in promoting prosecution of traffickers and otherwise to assist countries in meeting the minimum standards described in section 7106 of this title, including $250,000 for each such fiscal year to carry out training activities for law enforcement officers, prosecutors, and members of the judiciary with respect to trafficking in persons at the International Law Enforcement Academies.

(2) Voluntary contributions to OSCE

To carry out the purposes of section 2152d of this title, there is authorized to be appropriated to the Secretary of State for each of the fiscal years 2001 through 2005 $300,000 for voluntary contributions to advance projects aimed at preventing trafficking, promoting respect for human rights of trafficking victims, and assisting the Organization for Security and Cooperation in Europe participating states in related legal reform for such fiscal year.

(3) Preparation of annual country reports on human rights

To carry out the purposes of section 104, there are authorized to be appropriated to the Secretary of State such sums as may be necessary to include the additional information required by that section in the annual Country Reports on Human Rights Practices, including the preparation and publication of the list described in subsection (a)(1) of that section.

(d) Authorization of appropriations to Attorney General

To carry out the purposes of section 7105(b) of this title, there are authorized to be appropriated to the Attorney General $5,000,000 for fiscal year 2001 and $10, 000,000 for fiscal year 2002 and $15,000, 000 for each of the fiscal years 2004, 2005, 2006, and 2007. To carry out the purposes of section 2152d of this title, there are authorized to be appropriated to the President, acting through the Attorney General and the Secretary of State, $250,000 for each of fiscal years 2004, 2005, 2006, and 2007 to carry out training activities for law enforcement officers, prosecutors, and members of the judiciary with respect to trafficking in persons at the International Law Enforcement Academies.

(e) Authorization of appropriations to President

(1) Foreign victim assistance

To carry out the purposes of section 7104 of this title, there are authorized to be appropriated to the President $5,000,000 for fiscal year 2001, $10,000,000 for fiscal year 2002, and $15,000,000 for each of the fiscal years 2003 through 2007.

(2) Assistance to foreign countries to meet minimum standards

To carry out the purposes of section 2152d of this title, there are authorized to be appropriated to the President $5,000,000 for fiscal year 2001, $10,000,000 for fiscal year 2002, and $15,000,000 for each of the fiscal years 2003 through 2007.

(3) Research

To carry out the purposes of section 7109a of this title, there are authorized to be appropriated to the President $300,000 for each of the fiscal years 2004 through 2007.

(f) Authorization of appropriations to the Secretary of Labor

To carry out the purposes of section 7105(b) of this title, there are authorized to be appropriated to the Secretary of Labor $5,000,000 for fiscal year 2001 and $10,000,000 for fiscal year 2002 and $10,000,000 for each of the fiscal years 2004, 2005, 2006, and 2007.

(g) Limitation on use of funds

(1) Restriction on programs

No funds made available to carry out this chapter, or any amendment made by this chapter, may be used to promote, support, or advocate the legalization or practice of prostitution. Nothing in the preceding sentence shall be construed to preclude assistance designed to promote the purposes of this Act by ameliorating the suffering of, or health risks to, victims while they are being trafficked or after they are out of the situation that resulted from such victims being trafficked.

(2) Restriction on organizations

No funds made available to carry out this chapter, or any amendment made by this division, may be used to implement any program that targets victims of severe forms of trafficking in persons described in section 7102(8)(A) of this title through any organization that has not stated in either a grant application, a grant agreement, or both, that it does not promote, support, or advocate the legalization or practice of prostitution. The preceding sentence shall not apply to organizations that provide services to individuals solely after they are no longer engaged in activities that resulted from such victims being trafficked.

(h) Authorization of appropriations to Director of the FBI

There are authorized to be appropriated to the Director of the Federal Bureau of Investigation $15,000,000 for fiscal year 2006, to remain available until expended, to investigate severe forms of trafficking in persons.

(i) Authorization of appropriations to the Secretary of Homeland Security

There are authorized to be appropriated to the Secretary of Homeland Security, $18,000,000 for each of the fiscal years 2006 and 2007, to remain available until expended, for investigations by the Bureau of Immigration and Customs Enforcement of severe forms of trafficking in persons.

Sec. 7111. Report by Secretary of State

At least 15 days prior to voting for a new or reauthorized peacekeeping mission under the auspices of the United Nations, the North Atlantic Treaty Organization, or any other multilateral organization in which the United States participates (or in an emergency, as far in advance as is practicable), the Secretary of State shall submit to the Committee on International Relations of the House of Representatives, the Committee on Foreign Relations of the Senate, and any other appropriate congressional committee a report that contains--

(A) a description of measures taken by the organization to prevent the organization's employees, contractor personnel, and peacekeeping forces serving in the peacekeeping mission from trafficking in persons, exploiting victims of trafficking, or committing acts of sexual exploitation or abuse, and the measures in place to hold accountable any such individuals who engage in any such acts while participating in the peacekeeping mission; and

(B) an analysis of the effectiveness of each of the measures referred to in subparagraph (A).

Sec. 7112. Additional activities to monitor and combat forced labor and child labor

(a) Activities of the Department of State

(1) Finding

Congress finds that in the report submitted to Congress by the Secretary of State in June 2005 pursuant to section 7107(b) of this title, the list of countries whose governments do not comply with the minimum standards for the elimination of trafficking and are not making significant efforts to bring themselves into compliance was composed of a large number of countries in which the trafficking involved forced labor, including the trafficking of women into domestic servitude.

(2) Sense of Congress

It is the sense of Congress that the Director of the Office to Monitor and Combat Trafficking of the Department of State should intensify the focus of the Office on forced labor in the countries described in paragraph (1) and other countries in which forced labor continues to be a serious human rights concern.

(b) Activities of the Department of Labor

(1) In general

The Secretary of Labor, acting through the head of the Bureau of International Labor Affairs of the Department of Labor, shall carry out additional activities to monitor and combat forced labor and child labor in foreign countries as described in paragraph (2).

(2) Additional activities described

The additional activities referred to in paragraph (1) are--

(A) to monitor the use of forced labor and child labor in violation of international standards;

(B) to provide information regarding trafficking in persons for the purpose of forced labor to the Office to Monitor and Combat Trafficking of the Department of State for inclusion in trafficking in persons report required by section 7107(b) of this title;

(C) to develop and make available to the public a list of goods from countries that the Bureau of International Labor Affairs has reason to believe are produced by forced labor or child labor in violation of international standards;

(D) to work with persons who are involved in the production of goods on the list described in subparagraph (C) to create a standard set of practices that will reduce the likelihood that such persons will produce goods using the labor described in such subparagraph; and

(E) to consult with other departments and agencies of the United States Government to reduce forced and child labor internationally and ensure that products made by forced labor and child labor in violation of international standards are not imported into the United States.

FOREIGN ASSISTANCE ACT OF 1961, § 116

Foreign Assistance Act of 1961, § 116, 22 U.S.C. § 2151n (2006)

TITLE 22--FOREIGN RELATIONS AND INTERCOURSE
CHAPTER 32--FOREIGN ASSISTANCE
SUBCHAPTER I--INTERNATIONAL DEVELOPMENT
Part I--Declaration of Policy; Development Assistance Authorizations

Sec. 2151n. Human rights and development assistance

(a) Violations barring assistance; assistance for needy people

No assistance may be provided under subchapter I of this chapter to the government of any country which engages in a consistent pattern of gross violations of internationally recognized human rights, including torture or cruel, inhuman, or degrading treatment or punishment, prolonged detention without charges, causing the disappearance of persons by the abduction and clandestine detention of those persons, or other flagrant denial of the right to life, liberty, and the security of person, unless such assistance will directly benefit the needy people in such country.

(b) Information to Congressional committees for realization of assistance for needy people; concurrent resolution terminating assistance

In determining whether this standard is being met with regard to funds allocated under subchapter I of this chapter, the Committee on Foreign Relations of the Senate or the Committee on Foreign Affairs of the House of Representatives may require the Administrator primarily responsible for administering subchapter I of this chapter to submit in writing information demonstrating that such assistance will directly benefit the needy people in such country, together with a detailed explanation of the assistance to be provided (including the dollar amounts of such assistance) and an explanation of how such assistance will directly benefit the needy people in such country. If either committee or either House of Congress disagrees with the Administrator's justification it may initiate action to terminate assistance to any country by a concurrent resolution under section 2367 of this title.

(b) [*sic*] Protection of children from exploitation

No assistance may be provided to any government failing to take appropriate and adequate measures, within their means, to protect children from exploitation, abuse or forced conscription into military or paramilitary services.

(c) Factors considered

In determining whether or not a government falls within the provisions of subsection (a) of this section and in formulating development assistance programs under subchapter I of this chapter, the Administrator shall consider, in consultation with the Assistant Secretary of State for Democracy, Human Rights, and Labor and in consultation with the Ambassador at Large for International Religious Freedom--

(1) the extent of cooperation of such government in permitting an unimpeded investigation of alleged violations of internationally recognized human rights by appropriate international organizations, including the International Committee of the Red Cross, or groups or persons acting under the authority of the United Nations or of the Organization of American States;

(2) specific actions which have been taken by the President or the Congress relating to multilateral or security assistance to a less developed country because of the human rights practices or policies of such country; and

(3) whether the government--

(A) has engaged in or tolerated particularly severe violations of religious freedom, as defined in section 6402 of this title; or

(B) has failed to undertake serious and sustained efforts to combat particularly severe violations of religious freedom (as defined in section 6402 of this title), when such efforts could have been reasonably undertaken.

514

(d) Report to Speaker of House and Committee on Foreign Relations of the Senate

The Secretary of State shall transmit to the Speaker of the House of Representatives and the Committee on Foreign Relations of the Senate, by February 25 of each year, a full and complete report regarding—

(1) the status of internationally recognized human rights, within the meaning of subsection (a) of this section—

(A) in countries that receive assistance under subchapter I of this chapter, and

(B) in all other foreign countries which are members of the United Nations and which are not otherwise the subject of a human rights report under this chapter;

(2) wherever applicable, practices regarding coercion in population control, including coerced abortion and involuntary sterilization;

(3) the status of child labor practices in each country, including--

(A) whether such country has adopted policies to protect children from exploitation in the workplace, including a prohibition of forced and bonded labor and policies regarding acceptable working conditions; and

(B) the extent to which each country enforces such policies, including the adequacy of the resources and oversight dedicated to such policies;

(4) the votes of each member of the United Nations Commission on Human Rights on all country-specific and thematic resolutions voted on at the Commission's annual session during the period covered during the preceding year;

(5) the extent to which each country has extended protection to refugees, including the provision of first asylum and resettlement;

(6) the steps the Administrator has taken to alter United States programs under subchapter I of this chapter in any country because of human rights considerations;

(7) wherever applicable, violations of religious freedom, including particularly severe violations of religious freedom (as defined in section 6402 of this title);

(8) wherever applicable, a description of the nature and extent of acts of anti-Semitism and anti-Semitic incitement that occur during the preceding year, including descriptions of—

(A) acts of physical violence against, or harassment of[5] Jewish people, and acts of violence against, or vandalism of Jewish community institutions, including schools, synagogues, and cemeteries;

(B) instances of propaganda in government and nongovernment media that attempt to justify or promote racial hatred or incite acts of violence against Jewish people;

(C) the actions, if any, taken by the government of the country to respond to such violence and attacks or to eliminate such propaganda or incitement;

(D) the actions taken by such government to enact and enforce laws relating to the protection of the right to religious freedom of Jewish people; and

(E) the efforts of such government to promote anti-bias and tolerance education;

(9) wherever applicable, consolidated information regarding the commission of war crimes, crimes against humanity, and evidence of acts that may constitute genocide (as defined in article 2 of the Convention on the Prevention and Punishment of the Crime of Genocide and modified by the United States instrument of ratification to that convention and section 2(a) of the Genocide Convention Implementation Act of 1987);

(10) for each country with respect to which the report indicates that extrajudicial killings, torture, or other serious violations of human rights have occurred in the country, the extent to which the United States has taken or will take action to encourage an end to such practices in the country; and

(11)   (A) wherever applicable, a description of the nature and extent--

(i) of the compulsory recruitment and conscription of individuals under the age of 18 by armed forces of the government of the country, government-supported paramilitaries, or other armed groups, and the participation of such individuals in such groups; and

(ii) that such individuals take a direct part in hostilities;

(B) what steps, if any, taken by the government of the country to eliminate such practices; and

(C) such other information related to the use by such government of individuals under the age of 18 as soldiers, as determined to be appropriate by the Secretary.

(e) Promotion of civil and political rights

The President is authorized and encouraged to use not less than 3,000,000 of the funds made available under this part, part X of this subchapter, and part IV of subchapter II of this chapter for each fiscal year for studies to identify, and for openly carrying out programs and activities which will encourage or promote increased adherence to civil and political rights, including the right to free religious belief and practice, as set forth in the Universal Declaration of Human Rights, in countries eligible for assistance under this part or under part X of this subchapter, except that funds made available under part X of this subchapter may only be used under this subsection with respect to countries in sub-Saharan Africa. None of these funds may be used, directly or indirectly, to influence the outcome of any election in any country.

(f) Annual country reports on human rights practices

(1) The report required by subsection (d) of this section shall include the following:

(A) A description of the nature and extent of severe forms of trafficking in persons, as defined in section 7102 of this title, in each foreign country.

(B) With respect to each country that is a country of origin, transit, or destination for victims of severe forms of trafficking in persons, an assessment of the efforts by the government of that country to combat such trafficking. The assessment shall address the following:

(i) Whether government authorities in that country participate in, facilitate, or condone such trafficking.

(ii) Which government authorities in that country are involved in activities to combat such trafficking.

(iii) What steps the government of that country has taken to prohibit government officials from participating in, facilitating, or condoning such trafficking, including the investigation, prosecution, and conviction of such officials.

(iv) What steps the government of that country has taken to prohibit other individuals from participating in such trafficking, including the investigation, prosecution, and conviction of individuals involved in severe forms of trafficking in persons, the criminal and civil penalties for such trafficking, and the efficacy of those penalties in eliminating or reducing such trafficking.

(v) What steps the government of that country has taken to assist victims of such trafficking, including efforts to prevent victims from being further victimized by traffickers, government officials, or others, grants of relief from deportation, and provision of humanitarian relief, including provision of mental and physical health care and shelter.

(vi) Whether the government of that country is cooperating with governments of other countries to extradite traffickers when requested, or, to the extent that such cooperation would be inconsistent with the laws of such country or with extradition treaties to which such country is a party, whether the government of that country is taking all appropriate measures to modify or replace such laws and treaties so as to permit such cooperation.

(vii) Whether the government of that country is assisting in international investigations of transnational trafficking networks and in other cooperative efforts to combat severe forms of trafficking in persons.

(viii) Whether the government of that country refrains from prosecuting victims of severe forms of trafficking in persons due to such victims having been trafficked, and refrains from other discriminatory treatment of such victims.

(ix) Whether the government of that country recognizes the rights of victims of severe forms of trafficking in persons and ensures their access to justice.

(C) Such other information relating to trafficking in persons as the Secretary of State considers appropriate.

(2) In compiling data and making assessments for the purposes of paragraph (1), United States diplomatic mission personnel shall consult with human rights organizations and other appropriate nongovernmental organizations.

FOREIGN ASSISTANCE ACT OF 1961, § 502B

Foreign Assistance Act of 1961, § 502B, 22 U.S.C. § 2304 (2006)

TITLE 22--FOREIGN RELATIONS AND INTERCOURSE
CHAPTER 32--FOREIGN ASSISTANCE
SUBCHAPTER II--MILITARY ASSISTANCE AND SALES
Part I--Declaration of Policy

Sec. 2304. Human rights and security assistance

(a) Observance of human rights as principal goal of foreign policy; implementation requirements

(1) The United States shall, in accordance with its international obligations as set forth in the Charter of the United Nations and in keeping with the constitutional heritage and traditions of the United States, promote and encourage increased respect for human rights and fundamental freedoms throughout the world without distinction as to race, sex, language, or religion. Accordingly, a principal goal of the foreign policy of the United States shall be to promote the increased observance of internationally recognized human rights by all countries.

(2) Except under circumstances specified in this section, no security assistance may be provided to any country the government of which engages in a consistent pattern of gross violations of internationally recognized human rights. Security assistance may not be provided to the police, domestic intelligence, or similar law enforcement forces of a country, and licenses may not be issued under the Export Administration Act of 1979 [50 App. U.S.C. 2401 et seq.] for the export of crime control and detection instruments and equipment to a country, the government of which engages in a consistent pattern of gross violations of internationally recognized human rights unless the President certifies in writing to the Speaker of the House of Representatives and the chairman of the Committee on Foreign Relations of the Senate and the chairman of the Committee on Banking, Housing, and Urban Affairs of the Senate (when licenses are to be issued pursuant to the Export Administration Act of 1979) that extraordinary circumstances exist warranting provision of such assistance and issuance of such licenses. Assistance may not be provided under part V of this subchapter to a country the government of which engages in a consistent pattern of gross violations of internationally recognized human rights unless the President certifies in writing to the Speaker of the House of Representatives and the chairman of the Committee on Foreign Relations of the Senate that extraordinary circumstances exist warranting provision of such assistance.

(3) In furtherance of paragraphs (1) and (2), the President is directed to formulate and conduct international security assistance programs of the United States in a manner which will promote and advance human rights and avoid identification of the United States, through such programs, with governments which deny to their people internationally recognized human rights and fundamental freedoms, in violation of international law or in contravention of the policy of the United States as expressed in this section or otherwise.

(4) In determining whether the government of a country engages in a consistent pattern of gross violations of internationally recognized human rights, the President shall give particular consideration to whether the government--

(A) has engaged in or tolerated particularly severe violations of religious freedom, as defined in section 6402 of this title; or

(B) has failed to undertake serious and sustained efforts to combat particularly severe violations of religious freedom when such efforts could have been reasonably undertaken.

(b) Report by Secretary of State on practices of proposed recipient countries; considerations

The Secretary of State shall transmit to the Congress, as part of the presentation materials for security assistance programs proposed for each fiscal year, a full and complete report, prepared with the assistance of the Assistant Secretary of State for Democracy, Human Rights, and Labor and with the assistance of the Ambassador at Large for International Religious Freedom, with respect to practices regarding the observance of and respect for internationally recognized human rights in each country proposed as a recipient of security assistance. Wherever applicable, such report shall include consolidated information regarding the commission of war crimes, crimes against humanity, and evidence of acts that may constitute genocide (as defined in article 2 of the Convention on the Prevention and Punishment of the Crime of Genocide and modified by the United States instrument of ratification to that convention and

517

section 2(a) of the Genocide Convention Implementation Act of 1987). Wherever applicable, such report shall include information on practices regarding coercion in population control, including coerced abortion and involuntary sterilization. Such report shall also include, wherever applicable, information on violations of religious freedom, including particularly severe violations of religious freedom (as defined in section 6402 of this title). Wherever applicable, a description of the nature and extent of acts of anti-Semitism and anti-Semitic incitement that occur, including the descriptions of such acts required under section 2151n(d)(8) of this title. Such report shall also include, for each country with respect to which the report indicates that extrajudicial killings, torture, or other serious violations of human rights have occurred in the country, the extent to which the United States has taken or will take action to encourage an end to such practices in the country. Each report under this section shall list the votes of each member of the United Nations Commission on Human Rights on all country-specific and thematic resolutions voted on at the Commission's annual session during the period covered during the preceding year. Each report under this section shall also include (i) wherever applicable, a description of the nature and extent of the compulsory recruitment and conscription of individuals under the age of 18 by armed forces of the government of the country, government-supported paramilitaries, or other armed groups, the participation of such individuals in such groups, and the nature and extent that such individuals take a direct part in hostilities, (ii) what steps, if any, taken by the government of the country to eliminate such practices, and (iii) such other information related to the use by such government of individuals under the age of 18 as soldiers, as determined to be appropriate by the Secretary of State. Each report under this section shall describe the extent to which each country has extended protection to refugees, including the provision of first asylum and resettlement. In determining whether a government falls within the provisions of subsection (a)(3) of this section and in the preparation of any report or statement required under this section, consideration shall be given to--

(1) the relevant findings of appropriate international organizations, including nongovernmental organizations, such as the International Committee of the Red Cross; and

(2) the extent of cooperation by such government in permitting an unimpeded investigation by any such organization of alleged violations of internationally recognized human rights.

(c) Congressional request for information; information required; 30-day period; failure to supply information; termination or restriction of assistance

(1) Upon the request of the Senate or the House of Representatives by resolution of either such House, or upon the request of the Committee on Foreign Relations of the Senate or the Committee on Foreign Affairs of the House of Representatives, the Secretary of State shall, within thirty days after receipt of such request, transmit to both such committees a statement, prepared with the assistance of the Assistant Secretary of State for Democracy, Human Rights, and Labor, with respect to the country designated in such request, setting forth—

(A) all the available information about observance of and respect for human rights and fundamental freedom in that country, and a detailed description of practices by the recipient government with respect thereto;

(B) the steps the United States has taken to—

(i) promote respect for and observance of human rights in that country and discourage any practices which are inimical to internationally recognized human rights, and

(ii) publicly or privately call attention to, and disassociate the United States and any security assistance provided for such country from, such practices;

(C) whether, in the opinion of the Secretary of State, notwithstanding any such practices—

(i) extraordinary circumstances exist which necessitate a continuation of security assistance for such country, and, if so, a description of such circumstances and the extent to which such assistance should be continued (subject to such conditions as Congress may impose under this section), and

(ii) on all the facts it is in the national interest of the United States to provide such assistance; and

(D) such other information as such committee or such House may request.

(2)   (A) A resolution of request under paragraph (1) of this subsection shall be considered in the Senate in accordance with the provisions of section 601(b) of the International Security Assistance and Arms Export Control Act of 1976.

(B) The term ``certification'', as used in section 601 of such Act, means, for the purposes of this subsection, a resolution of request of the Senate under paragraph (1) of this subsection.

(3) In the event a statement with respect to a country is requested pursuant to paragraph (1) of this subsection but is not transmitted in accordance therewith within thirty days after receipt of such request, no security assistance shall be delivered to such country except as may thereafter be specifically authorized by law from such country unless and until such statement is transmitted.

(4) (A) In the event a statement with respect to a country is transmitted under paragraph (1) of this subsection, the Congress may at any time thereafter adopt a joint resolution terminating, restricting, or continuing security assistance for such country. In the event such a joint resolution is adopted, such assistance shall be so terminated, so restricted, or so continued, as the case may be.

(B) Any such resolution shall be considered in the Senate in accordance with the provisions of section 601(b) of the International Security Assistance and Arms Export Control Act of 1976.

(C) The term ``certification'', as used in section 601 of such Act, means, for the purposes of this paragraph, a statement transmitted under paragraph (1) of this subsection.

(d) Definitions

For the purposes of this section—

(1) the term "gross violations of internationally recognized human rights" includes torture or cruel, inhuman, or degrading treatment or punishment, prolonged detention without charges and trial, causing the disappearance of persons by the abduction and clandestine detention of those persons, and other flagrant denial of the right to life, liberty, or the security of person; and

(2) the term "security assistance" means—

(A) assistance under part II (military assistance) or part IV (economic support fund) or part V (military education and training) or part VI (peacekeeping operations) or part VIII (antiterrorism assistance) of this subchapter.

(B) sales of defense articles or services, extensions of credits (including participations in credits, and guaranties of loans under the Arms Export Control Act [22 U.S.C. 2751 et seq.]); or

(C) any license in effect with respect to the export of defense articles or defense services to or for the armed forces, police, intelligence, or other internal security forces of a foreign country under section 38 of the Arms Export Control Act [22 U.S.C. 2778].

(e) Removal of prohibition on assistance

Notwithstanding any other provision of law, funds authorized to be appropriated under subchapter I of this chapter may be made available for the furnishing of assistance to any country with respect to which the President finds that such a significant improvement in its human rights record has occurred as to warrant lifting the prohibition on furnishing such assistance in the national interest of the United States.

(f) Allocations concerned with performance record of recipient countries without contravention of other provisions

In allocating the funds authorized to be appropriated by this chapter and the Arms Export Control Act [22 U.S.C. 2751 et seq.], the President shall take into account significant improvements in the human rights records of recipient countries, except that such allocations may not contravene any other provision of law.

(g) Report to Congress on use of certain authorities relating to human rights conditions

Whenever the provisions of subsection (e) or (f) of this section are applied, the President shall report to the Congress before making any funds available pursuant to those subsections. The report shall specify the country involved, the amount and kinds of assistance to be provided, and the justification for providing the assistance, including a description of the significant improvements which have occurred in the country's human rights record.

(h) Report on practices of recipient countries relating to trafficking in persons

(1) The report required by subsection (b) of this section shall include the following:

(A) A description of the nature and extent of severe forms of trafficking in persons, as defined in section 7102 of this title, in each foreign country.

(B) With respect to each country that is a country of origin, transit, or destination for victims of severe forms of trafficking in persons, an assessment of the efforts by the government of that country to combat such trafficking. The assessment shall address the following:

(i) Whether government authorities in that country participate in, facilitate, or condone such trafficking.

(ii) Which government authorities in that country are involved in activities to combat such trafficking.

(iii) What steps the government of that country has taken to prohibit government officials from participating in, facilitating, or condoning such trafficking, including the investigation, prosecution, and conviction of such officials.

(iv) What steps the government of that country has taken to prohibit other individuals from participating in such trafficking, including the investigation, prosecution, and conviction of individuals involved in severe forms of trafficking in persons, the criminal and civil penalties for such trafficking, and the efficacy of those penalties in eliminating or reducing such trafficking.

(v) What steps the government of that country has taken to assist victims of such trafficking, including efforts to prevent victims from being further victimized by traffickers, government officials, or others, grants of relief from deportation, and provision of humanitarian relief, including provision of mental and physical health care and shelter.

(vi) Whether the government of that country is cooperating with governments of other countries to extradite traffickers when requested, or, to the extent that such cooperation would be inconsistent with the laws of such country or with extradition treaties to which such country is a party, whether the government of that country is taking all appropriate measures to modify or replace such laws and treaties so as to permit such cooperation.

(vii) Whether the government of that country is assisting in international investigations of transnational trafficking networks and in other cooperative efforts to combat severe forms of trafficking in persons.

(viii) Whether the government of that country refrains from prosecuting victims of severe forms of trafficking in persons due to such victims having been trafficked, and refrains from other discriminatory treatment of such victims.

(ix) Whether the government of that country recognizes the rights of victims of severe forms of trafficking in persons and ensures their access to justice.

(C) Such other information relating to trafficking in persons as the Secretary of State considers appropriate.

(2) In compiling data and making assessments for the purposes of paragraph (1), United States diplomatic mission personnel shall consult with human rights organizations and other appropriate nongovernmental organizations.

UNITED STATES EXECUTIVE/LEGISLATIVE MATERIALS

SENATE RESOLUTION OF RATIFICATION OF THE U.N. CONVENTION AGAINST TORTURE AND OTHER CRUEL, INHUMAN OR DEGRADING TREATMENT OR PUNISHMENT
S. Exec. Rep. No. 101-30 (1990), 136 Cong. Rec. S17491 (1990) (ratified)

Resolved (two-thirds of the Senators present concurring therein), That the Senate advise and consent to the ratification of the Convention Against Torture and Other Cruel, Inhuman or Degrading Treatment or Punishment, adopted by unanimous agreement of the United Nations General Assembly on December 10, 1984, and signed by the United States on April 18, 1988: Provided, That:

I. The Senate's advice and consent is subject to the following reservations:

(1) That the United States considers itself bound by the obligation under Article 16 to prevent `cruel, inhuman or degrading treatment or punishment,' only insofar as the term `cruel, inhuman or degrading treatment or punishment' means the cruel, unusual and inhumane treatment or punishment prohibited by the Fifth, Eighth, and/or Fourteenth Amendments to the Constitution of the United States.

(2) That pursuant to Article 30(2) the United States declares that it does not consider itself bound by Article 30(1), but reserves the right specifically to agree to follow this or any other procedure for arbitration in a particular case.

II. The Senate's advice and consent is subject to the following understandings, which shall apply to the obligations of the United States under this Convention:

(1)   (a) That with reference to Article 1, the United States understands that, in order to constitute torture, an act must be specifically intended to inflict severe physical or mental pain or suffering and that mental pain or suffering refers to prolonged mental harm caused by or resulting from: (1) the intentional infliction or threatened infliction of severe physical pain or suffering; (2) the administration or application, or threatened administration or application, of mind altering substances or other procedures calculated to disrupt profoundly the senses or the personality; (3) the threat of imminent death; or (4) the threat that another person will imminently be subjected to death, severe physical pain or suffering, or the administration or application of mind altering substances or other procedures calculated to disrupt profoundly the senese or personality.

(b) That the United States understands that the definition of torture in Article 1 is intended to apply only to acts directed against persons in the offender's custody or physical control.

(c) That with reference to Article 1 of the Convention , the United States understands that `sanctions' includes judicially imposed sanctions and other enforcement actions authorized by United States law or by judicial interpretation of such law. Nonetheless, the United States understands that a State Party could not through its domestic sanctions defeat the object and purpose of the Convention to prohibit torture .

(d) That with reference to Article 1 of the Convention , the United States understands that the term `acquiescence' requires that the public official, prior to the activity constituting torture , have awareness of such activity and thereafter breach his legal responsibility to intervene to prevent such activity.

(e) That with reference to Article 1 of the Convention , the United States understands that noncompliance with applicable legal procedural standards does not per se constitute torture .

(2) That the United States understands the phrase, `where there are substantial grounds for believing that he would be in danger of being subjected to torture ,' as used in Article 3 of the Convention , to mean `if it is more likely than not that he would be tortured.'

(3) That it is the understanding of the United States that Article 14 requires a State Party to provide a private right of action for damages only for acts of torture committed in territory under the jurisdiction of that State Party.

(4) That the United States understands that international law does not prohibit the death penalty, and does not consider this Convention to restrict or prohibit the United States from applying the death penalty consistent with the Fifth, Eighth and/or Fourteenth Amendments to the Constitution of the United States, including any constitutional period of confinement prior to the imposition of the death penalty.

(5) That the United States understands that this Convention shall be implemented by the United States Government to the extent that it exercises legislative and judicial jurisdiction over the matters covered by the Convention and otherwise by the state and local governments. Accordingly, in implementing Articles 10-14 and 16, the United States Government shall take measures appropriate to the Federal system to the end that the competent authorities of the constituent units of the United States of America may take appropriate measures for the fulfillment of the Convention .

III. The Senate's advice and consent is subject to the following declarations:

(1) That the United States declares that the provisions of Articles 1 through 16 of the Convention are not self-executing.

(2) That the United States declares, pursuant to Article 21, paragraph 1, of the Convention , that it recognizes the competence of the Committee against Torture to receive and consider communications to the effect that a State Party claims that another State Party is not fulfilling its obligations under the

Convention . It is the understanding of the United States that, pursuant to the above mentioned article, such communications shall be accepted and processed only if they come from a State Party which has made a similar declaration.

IV. The Senate's advice and consent is subject to the following proviso, which shall not be included in the instrument of ratification to be deposited by the President:
The President of the United States shall not deposit the instrument of ratification until such time as he has notified all present and prospective ratifying parties to this Convention that nothing in this Convention requires or authorizes legislation, or other action, by the United States of America prohibited by the Constitution of the United States as interpreted by the United States.

SENATE RESOLUTION OF RATIFICATION OF THE INTERNATIONAL COVENANT ON CIVIL AND POLITICAL RIGHTS
S. Exec. Rep. No. 102-23 (1992), 138 Cong. Rec. S4783 (1992) (ratified)

Resolved (two-thirds of the Senators present concurring therein), That the Senate advise and consent to the ratification of the International Covenant on Civil and Political Rights, adopted by the United Nations General Assembly on December 16, 1966, and signed on behalf of the United States on October 5, 1977 (Executive E, 95-2), subject to the following Reservations, Understandings, Declarations and Proviso:

I. The Senate's advice and consent is subject to the following reservations:
(1) That Article 20 does not authorize or require legislation or other action by the United States that would restrict the right of free speech and association protected by the Constitution and laws of the United States.
(2) That the United States reserves the right, subject to its Constitutional constraints, to impose capital punishment on any person (other than a pregnant woman) duly convicted under existing or future laws permitting the imposition of capital punishment, including such punishment for crimes committed by persons below eighteen years of age.
(3) That the United States considers itself bound by Article 7 to the extent that `cruel, inhuman or degrading treatment or punishment' means the cruel and unusual treatment or punishment prohibited by the Fifth, Eighth and /or Fourteenth Amendments to the Constitution of the United States.
(4) That because U.S. law generally applies to an offender the penalty in force at the time the offense was committed, the United States does not adhere to the third clause of paragraph 1 of Article 15.
(5) That the policy and practice of the United States are generally in compliance with and supportive of the Covenant's provisions regarding treatment of juveniles in the criminal justice system. Nevertheless, the United States reserves the right, in exceptional circumstances, to treat juveniles as adults, notwithstanding paragraphs 2(b) and 3 Article 10 and paragraph 4 of Article 14. The United States further reserves to these provisions with respect to individuals who volunteer for military service prior to age 18.

II. The Senate's advice and consent is subject to the following understandings, which shall apply to the obligations of the United States under this Covenant :
(1) That the Constitution and laws of the United States guarantee all persons equal protection of the law and provide extensive protections against discrimination. The United States understands distinctions based upon race, colour, sex, language, religion, political or other opinion, national or social origin, property, birth or any other status--as those terms are used in Article 2, paragraph 1 and Article 26--to be permitted when such distinctions are, at minimum, rationally related to a legitimate governmental objective. The United States further understands the prohibition in paragraph 1 of Article 4 upon discrimination, in time of public emergency, based `solely' on the status of race, color, sex, language, religion or social origin not to bar distinctions that may have a disproportionate effect upon persons of a particular status.
(2) That the United States understands the right to compensation referred to in Articles 9(5) and 14(6) to require the provision of effective and enforceable mechanisms by which a victim of an unlawful arrest or detention or a miscarriage of justice may seek and , where justified, obtain compensation from either the

responsible individual or the appropriate governmental entity. Entitlement to compensation may be subject to the reasonable requirements of domestic law.

(3) That the United States understands the reference to 'exceptional circumstances' in paragraph 2(a) of Article 10 to permit the imprisonment of an accused person with convicted persons where appropriate in light of an individual's overall dangerousness, and to permit accused persons to waive their right to segregation from convicted persons. The United States further understands that paragraph 3 of Article 10 does not diminish the goals of punishment, deterrence, and incapacitation as additional legitimate purposes for a penitentiary system.

(4) That the United States understands that subparagraphs 3(b) and (d) of Article 14 do not require the provision of a criminal defendant's counsel of choice when the defendant is provided with court-appointed counsel on grounds of indigence, when the defendant is financially able to retain alternative counsel, or when imprisonment is not imposed. The United States further understands that paragraph 3(e) does not prohibit a requirement that the defendant make a showing that any witness whose attendance he seeks to compel is necessary for his defense. The United States understands the prohibition upon double jeopardy in paragraph 7 to apply only when the judgment of acquittal has been rendered by a court of the same governmental unit, whether the Federal Government or a constituent unit, as is seeking a new trial for the same cause.

(5) That the United States understands that this Covenant shall be implemented by the Federal Government to the extent that it exercises legislative and judicial jurisdiction over the matters covered therein, and otherwise by the state and local governments; to the extent that state and local governments exercise jurisdiction over such matters, the Federal Government shall take measures appropriate to the Federal system to the end that the competent authorities of the state or local governments may take appropriate measures for the fulfillment of the Covenant .

III. The Senate's advice and consent is subject to the following declarations:

(1) That the United States declares that the provisions of Articles 1 through 27 of the Covenant are not self-executing.

(2) That it is the view of the United States that States Party to the Covenant should wherever possible refrain from imposing any restrictions or limitations on the exercise of the rights recognized and protected by the Covenant , even when such restrictions and limitations are permissible under the terms of the Covenant . For the United States, Article 5, paragraph 2, which provides that fundamental human rights existing in any State Party may not be diminished on the pretext that the Covenant recognizes them to a lesser extent, has particular relevance to Article 19, paragraph 3, which would permit certain restrictions on the freedom of expression. The United States declares that it will continue to adhere to the requirements and constraints of its Constitution in respect to all such restrictions and limitations.

(3) That the United States declares that it accepts the competence of the Human Rights Committee to receive and consider communications under Article 41 in which a State Party claims that another State Party is not fulfilling its obligations under the Covenant

(4) That the United States declares that the right referred to in Article 47 may be exercised only in accordance with international law.

IV. The Senate's advice and consent is subject to the following proviso, which shall not be included in the instrument of ratification to be deposited by the President:

Nothing in this Covenant requires or authorizes legislation, or other action, by the United States of America prohibited by the Constitution of the United States as interpreted by the United States.

EXECUTIVE ORDER 13107 OF DECEMBER 10, 1998
IMPLEMENTATION OF HUMAN RIGHTS TREATIES
Exec. Order No. 13,107, 3 C.F.R. 234-36 (1999).

By the authority vested in me as President by the Constitution and the laws of the United States of America, and bearing in mind the obligations of the United States pursuant to the International Covenant on Civil and Political Rights (ICCPR), the Convention Against Torture and Other Cruel, Inhuman or

Degrading Treatment or Punishment (CAT), the Convention on the Elimination of All Forms of Racial Discrimination (CERD), and other relevant treaties concerned with the protection and promotion of human rights to which the United States is now or may become a party in the future, it is hereby ordered as follows:

Section 1. *Implementation of Human Rights Obligations.* (a) It shall be the policy and practice of the Government of the United States, being committed to the protection and promotion of human rights and fundamental freedoms, fully to respect and implement its obligations under the international human rights treaties to which it is a party, including the ICCPR, the CAT, and the CERD.

(b) It shall also be the policy and practice of the Government of the United States to promote respect for international human rights, both in our relationships with all other countries and by working with and strengthening the various international mechanisms for the promotion of human rights, including, inter alia, those of the United Nations, the International Labor Organization, and the Organization of American States.

Sec. 2. *Responsibility of Executive Departments and Agencies.* (a) All executive departments and agencies (as defined in 5 U.S.C. 101-105, including boards and commissions, and hereinafter referred to collectively as "agency" or "agencies") shall maintain a current awareness of United States international human rights obligations that are relevant to their functions and shall perform such functions so as to respect and implement those obligations fully. The head of each agency shall designate a single contact officer who will be responsible for overall coordination of the implementation of this order. Under this order, all such agencies shall retain their established institutional roles in the implementation, interpretation, and enforcement of Federal law and policy.

(b) The heads of agencies shall have lead responsibility, in coordination with other appropriate agencies, for questions concerning implementation of human rights obligations that fall within their respective operating and program responsibilities and authorities or, to the extent that matters do not fall within the operating and program responsibilities and authorities of any agency, that most closely relate to their general areas of concern.

Sec. 3. *Human Rights Inquiries and Complaints.* Each agency shall take lead responsibility, in coordination with other appropriate agencies, for responding to inquiries, requests for information, and complaints about violations of human rights obligations that fall within its areas of responsibility or, if the matter does not fall within its areas of responsibility, referring it to the appropriate agency for response.

Sec. 4. *Interagency Working Group on Human Rights Treaties.* (a) There is hereby established an Interagency Working Group on Human Rights Treaties for the purpose of providing guidance, oversight, and coordination with respect to questions concerning the adherence to and implementation of human rights obligations and related matters.

(b) The designee of the Assistant to the President for National Security Affairs shall chair the Interagency Working Group, which shall consist of appropriate policy and legal representatives at the Assistant Secretary level from the Department of State, the Department of Justice, the Department of Labor, the Department of Defense, the Joint Chiefs of Staff, and other agencies as the chair deems appropriate. The principal members may designate alternates to attend meetings in their stead.

(c) The principal functions of the Interagency Working Group shall include:

(i) coordinating the interagency review of any significant issues concerning the implementation of this order and analysis and recommendations in connection with pursuing the ratification of human rights treaties, as such questions may from time to time arise;

(ii) coordinating the preparation of reports that are to be submitted by the United States in fulfillment of treaty obligations;

(iii) coordinating the responses of the United States Government to complaints against it concerning alleged human rights violations submitted to the United Nations, the Organization of American States, and other international organizations;

(iv) developing effective mechanisms to ensure that legislation proposed by the Administration is reviewed for conformity with international human rights obligations and that these obligations are taken into account in reviewing legislation under consideration by the Congress as well;

(v) developing recommended proposals and mechanisms for improving the monitoring of the actions by the various States, Commonwealths, and territories of the United States and, where appropriate, of Native Americans and Federally recognized Indian tribes, including the review of State, Commonwealth, and territorial laws for their conformity with relevant treaties, the provision of relevant information for reports and other monitoring purposes, and the promotion of effective remedial mechanisms;

(vi) developing plans for public outreach and education concerning the provisions of the ICCPR, CAT, CERD, and other relevant treaties, and human rights-related provisions of domestic law;

(vii) coordinating and directing an annual review of United States reservations, declarations, and understandings to human rights treaties, and matters as to which there have been nontrivial complaints or allegations of inconsistency with or breach of international human rights obligations, in order to determine whether there should be consideration of any modification of relevant reservations, declarations, and understandings to human rights treaties, or United States practices or laws. The results and recommendations of this review shall be reviewed by the head of each participating agency;

(viii) making such other recommendations as it shall deem appropriate to the President, through the Assistant to the President for National Security Affairs, concerning United States adherence to or implementation of human rights treaties and related matters; and

(ix) coordinating such other significant tasks in connection with human rights treaties or international human rights institutions, including the Inter-American Commission on Human Rights and the Special Rapporteurs and complaints procedures established by the United Nations Human Rights Commission.

(d) The work of the Interagency Working Group shall not supplant the work of other interagency entities, including the President's Committee on the International Labor Organization, that address international human rights issues.

Sec. 5. *Cooperation Among Executive Departments and Agencies.* All agencies shall cooperate in carrying out the provisions of this order. The Interagency Working Group shall facilitate such cooperative measures.

Sec. 6. *Judicial Review, Scope, and Administration.* (a) Nothing in this order shall create any right or benefit, substantive or procedural, enforceable by any party against the United States, its agencies or instrumentalities, its officers or employees, or any other person.

(b) This order does not supersede Federal statutes and does not impose any justiciable obligations on the executive branch.

(c) The term "treaty obligations" shall mean treaty obligations as approved by the Senate pursuant to Article II, section 2, clause 2 of the United States Constitution.

(d) To the maximum extent practicable and subject to the availability of appropriations, agencies shall carry out the provisions of this order.

WILLIAM J. CLINTON

THE WHITE HOUSE,
December 10, 1998

DECLARATION OF SAMUEL M. WITTEN

Respondent's Opp'n to Petition for Habeas Corpus, Attach. 1, Decl. of Samuel M. Witten, *Corejo-Barreto v. Seifert*, No. 01-cv-662-AHS (C.D. Cal. Oct. 9, 2001), *available at* http://www.state.gov/documents/organization/16513.pdf

I, Samuel M. Witten, pursuant to 28 U.S.C. § 1746, hereby declare and say as follows:

1. I am the Assistant Legal Adviser for Law Enforcement and Intelligence ("L/LEI") in the Office of the Legal Adviser of the U.S. Department of State ("Department"), Washington, D.C. L/LEI, which I supervise, is responsible for providing legal advice to the Department on all law enforcement matters of significance to the Department and managing the Department's responsibilities in cases of international

extradition. I am a career member of the U.S. Government's Senior Executive Service and have supervised the management of the Department's international extradition responsibilities since December 17, 1996. The following statements provide a general overview of the process of extraditing a fugitive from the United States to a foreign country. They are not intended to be an exhaustive description of all of the steps that might be undertaken in particular cases. I make these statements based upon my personal knowledge and upon information made available to me in the performance of my official duties.

2. Extradition requests made to the United States begin when a formal extradition request is presented to the State Department by a diplomatic note from the requesting State's embassy in Washington, or through a similar diplomatic communication. Upon receiving the request with properly certified supporting documents, an attorney within L/LEI reviews the materials to determine: (a) whether an extradition treaty is in effect between the requesting State and the United States; (b) whether the request appears to come within the scope of the treaty; and (c) whether, on the face of the supporting documents, there is no clearly-evident defense to extradition under the treaty (for example, that the offense is a political offense). If the attorney is satisfied that the extradition request facially satisfies these requirements, L/LEI transmits the request and documents to the Department of Justice for further review and, if appropriate, the commencement of extradition proceedings before a United States magistrate judge or a United States district judge.

3. The extradition judge conducts a hearing to examine whether extradition would be lawful under the terms of the treaty and the relevant provisions of United States law, 18 U.S.C. §§ 3181 - 3196. If he or she finds that a fugitive is extraditable on any or all of the charges for which extradition is sought, the extradition judge will certify the fugitive's extraditability to the Secretary of State, who is the U.S. official responsible for determining ultimately whether to surrender the fugitive to the requesting State. See 18 U.S.C. §§ 3184, 3186. In U.S. practice, the extradition judge's decision whether to certify extraditability is not dependent on consideration of any humanitarian claims, such as the age or health of the fugitive, in determining the legality of extradition. Similarly, under the long-established "rule of noninquiry," consideration of the likely treatment of the fugitive if he were to be returned to the country requesting extradition should not be a part of the decision to certify extraditability. Instead, such issues are considered by the Secretary of State in making the final extradition decision.

4. After the Secretary of State receives a certification of extraditability from a magistrate judge or district judge as set forth above, the second phase of the extradition process begins, wherein the Secretary must decide whether a fugitive who has been found extraditable by a court should actually be extradited to a requesting State. In determining whether a fugitive should be extradited, the Secretary may consider de novo any and all issues properly raised before the extradition court (or a court to which the fugitive has submitted a petition for a writ of habeas corpus for review of the extradition court's decision), as well as any other considerations for or against surrender. Among these other considerations are humanitarian issues and matters historically arising under the rule of non-inquiry, including whether the extradition request was politically motivated, whether the fugitive is likely to be persecuted or denied a fair trial or humane treatment upon his return, and, since the entry into force for the United States of the Convention Against Torture and other Cruel, Inhuman or Degrading Treatment or Punishment ("Torture Convention") in 1994, specifically whether it is more likely than not that the fugitive would face torture in the requesting State.

5. The United States has undertaken the obligation under Article 3 of the Torture Convention not to extradite a person to a country where "there are substantial grounds for believing that he would be in danger of being subjected to torture." An Understanding included in the United States' instrument of ratification of the treaty establishes that the United States interprets this phrase to mean "if it is more likely than not that he would be tortured." As the U.S. official with ultimate responsibility for determining whether a fugitive will be extradited, the Secretary carries out the obligation of the United States under the Torture Convention.

6. The Department's regulations at 22 C.F.R. Part 95, which the Department promulgated pursuant to section 2242 of the Foreign Affairs Reform and Restructuring Act of 1998, P.L. 105-277, outline the procedures for considering the question of torture when the Secretary determines whether a fugitive will be extradited. Whenever allegations relating to torture are brought to the Department's attention by the fugitive or other interested parties, appropriate policy and legal offices within the Department with regional or substantive expertise review and analyze information relevant to the particular case in preparing a recommendation to the Secretary. The Department's Bureau of Democracy, Human Rights, and Labor, which drafts the U.S. Government's annual Human Rights Reports (discussed below in paragraph 7), is a key participant in this process. The views of the relevant regional bureau, country desk, or U.S. Embassy

also play an important role in the Department's evaluation of torture claims, because our regional bureaus, country desks, and Embassies are knowledgeable about matters such as human rights, prison conditions, and prisoners' access to counsel, in general and as they may apply to a particular case in a requesting State.

7. The Department will consider information concerning judicial and penal conditions and practices of the requesting State, including the Department's annual Human Rights Reports, and the relevance of that information to the individual whose surrender is at issue. * * * The Department will examine materials submitted by the fugitive, persons acting on his behalf, or other interested parties, and will examine other relevant materials that may come to its attention.

8. In determining whether a fugitive will be extradited, the Secretary must determine whether it is more likely than not that the particular fugitive will be tortured in the country requesting extradition. Based on the analysis of relevant information, the Secretary may decide to surrender the fugitive to the requesting State or to deny surrender of the fugitive. Or, in some cases, the Secretary might condition the extradition on the requesting State's provision of assurances related to torture or aspects of the requesting State's criminal justice system that protect against mistreatment, such as that the fugitive will have regular access to counsel and the full protections afforded under that State's constitution or laws. Whether such assurances are sought is decided on a case-by-case basis. In several cases in recent years, the Secretary signed a warrant only after the Department engaged in a diplomatic dialogue and received adequate assurances of humane treatment from the requesting State.

9. When evaluating assurances or other information provided by the requesting State, Department officials, including the Secretary, consider the identity, position, or other information concerning the official relaying the assurances, and political or legal developments in the requesting State that would provide context for the assurances provided. Department officials, including the Secretary, may also consider U.S. diplomatic relations with the requesting State when evaluating assurances. For instance, Department officials may make a judgment regarding the requesting State's incentives and capacities to fulfill its assurances to the United States, including the importance to the requesting State of maintaining an effective extradition relationship.

10. In some cases, the Department has asked governmental or non-governmental human rights groups in the requesting State to monitor the condition of a fugitive extradited from the United States. As with the issue of assurances, the decision whether to seek a monitoring arrangement is made on a case-by-case basis, based on the circumstances of a particular case, which could include the identity of the requesting State, the nationality of the fugitive, the groups or persons that might be available to monitor the fugitive's condition, the ability of such groups or persons to provide effective monitoring, and similar considerations.

11. The Department's ability to seek and obtain assurances from a requesting State depends in part on the Department's ability to treat dealings with the foreign government with discretion. Consistent with the diplomatic sensitivities that surround the Department's communications with requesting States concerning allegations relating to torture, the Department does not make public its decisions to seek assurances in extradition cases in order to avoid the chilling effects of making such discussions public and the possible damage to our ability to conduct foreign relations. Seeking assurances may be seen as raising questions about the requesting State's institutions or commitment to the rule of law, even in cases where the assurances are sought to highlight the issue for the requesting State and satisfy ourselves that the requesting State is aware of the concerns that have been raised and is in a position to undertake a commitment of humane treatment of a particular fugitive. There also may be circumstances where it may be important to protect sources of information (such as sources within a foreign government) about torture allegations, who want to keep their identity or the specific information they provide confidential.

12. If the Department is required to make public its communications with a requesting State concerning allegations of torture, that State, as well as other States, would likely be reluctant to communicate frankly with the United States concerning such issues. I know from experience that the delicate diplomatic exchange that is often required in these contexts cannot occur effectively except in a confidential setting. Later review in a public forum of the Department's dealings with a requesting State regarding extradition matters would thus seriously undermine our ability to investigate torture allegations and to reach acceptable accommodations with requesting States.

13. A judicial decision overturning a determination made by the Secretary after extensive discussions and negotiations with a requesting State could seriously undermine our foreign relations. Moreover, judicial review of the Secretary's determination to surrender a fugitive to a requesting State inevitably would add delays to extradition in what is already frequently a lengthy process. A new round of

judicial review and appeal could undermine the requesting State's ability to prosecute and also harm our efforts to press other countries to act more expeditiously in surrendering fugitives for trial in the United States.

I declare under the penalty of perjury that the foregoing is true and correct.

TREATY COMMITTEE DOCUMENTS

COMMITTEE ON THE ELIMINATION OF DISCRIMINATION AGAINST WOMEN GENERAL RECOMMENDATION 19
Violence against women

Comm. on the Elimination of Discrimination Against Women, *General Recommendation 19: Violence Against Women* (11th Sess., 1992), U.N. Doc. A/47/38(SUPP), at 1-8 (1993), *available in English at* http://www.un.org/womenwatch/daw/cedaw/recommendations/recomm.htm#recom19

Background

1. Gender-based violence is a form of discrimination that seriously inhibits women's ability to enjoy rights and freedoms on a basis of equality with men.

2. In 1989, the Committee recommended that States should include in their reports information on violence and on measures introduced to deal with it (General recommendation 12, eighth session).

3. At its tenth session in 1991, it was decided to allocate part of the eleventh session to a discussion and study on article 6 and other articles of the Convention relating to violence towards women and the sexual harassment and exploitation of women. That subject was chosen in anticipation of the 1993 World Conference on Human Rights, convened by the General Assembly by its resolution 45/155 of 18 December 1990.

4. The Committee concluded that not all the reports of States parties adequately reflected the close connection between discrimination against women, gender-based violence, and violations of human rights and fundamental freedoms. The full implementation of the Convention required States to take positive measures to eliminate all forms of violence against women.

5. The Committee suggested to States parties that in reviewing their laws and policies, and in reporting under the Convention, they should have regard to the following comments of the Committee concerning gender-based violence.

General comments

6. The Convention in article 1 defines discrimination against women. The definition of discrimination includes gender-based violence, that is, violence that is directed against a woman because she is a woman or that affects women disproportionately. It includes acts that inflict physical, mental or sexual harm or suffering, threats of such acts, coercion and other deprivations of liberty. Gender-based violence may breach specific provisions of the Convention, regardless of whether those provisions expressly mention violence.

7. Gender-based violence, which impairs or nullifies the enjoyment by women of human rights and fundamental freedoms under general international law or under human rights conventions, is discrimination within the meaning of article 1 of the Convention. These rights and freedoms include:

    (a) The right to life;

    (b) The right not to be subject to torture or to cruel, inhuman or degrading treatment or punishment;

    (c) The right to equal protection according to humanitarian norms in time of international or internal armed conflict;

    (d) The right to liberty and security of person;

    (e) The right to equal protection under the law;

(f) The right to equality in the family;

(g) The right to the highest standard attainable of physical and mental health;

(h) The right to just and favourable conditions of work.

8. The Convention applies to violence perpetrated by public authorities. Such acts of violence may breach that State's obligations under general international human rights law and under other conventions, in addition to breaching this Convention.

9. It is emphasized, however, that discrimination under the Convention is not restricted to action by or on behalf of Governments (see articles 2(e), 2(f) and 5). For example, under article 2(e) the Convention calls on States parties to take all appropriate measures to eliminate discrimination against women by any person, organization or enterprise. Under general international law and specific human rights covenants, States may also be responsible for private acts if they fail to act with due diligence to prevent violations of rights or to investigate and punish acts of violence, and for providing compensation.

Comments on specific articles of the Convention

Articles 2 and 3

10. Articles 2 and 3 establish a comprehensive obligation to eliminate discrimination in all its forms in addition to the specific obligations under articles 5-16.

Articles 2(f), 5 and 10(c)

11. Traditional attitudes by which women are regarded as subordinate to men or as having stereotyped roles perpetuate widespread practices involving violence or coercion, such as family violence and abuse, forced marriage, dowry deaths, acid attacks and female circumcision. Such prejudices and practices may justify gender-based violence as a form of protection or control of women. The effect of such violence on the physical and mental integrity of women is to deprive them the equal enjoyment, exercise and knowledge of human rights and fundamental freedoms. While this comment addresses mainly actual or threatened violence the underlying consequences of these forms of gender-based violence help to maintain women in subordinate roles and contribute to the low level of political participation and to their lower level of education, skills and work opportunities.

12. These attitudes also contribute to the propagation of pornography and the depiction and other commercial exploitation of women as sexual objects, rather than as individuals. This in turn contributes to gender-based violence.

Article 6

13. States parties are required by article 6 to take measures to suppress all forms of traffic in women and exploitation of the prostitution of women.

14. Poverty and unemployment increase opportunities for trafficking in women. In addition to established forms of trafficking there are new forms of sexual exploitation, such as sex tourism, the recruitment of domestic labour from developing countries to work in developed countries and organized marriages between women from developing countries and foreign nationals. These practices are incompatible with the equal enjoyment of rights by women and with respect for their rights and dignity. They put women at special risk of violence and abuse.

15. Poverty and unemployment force many women, including young girls, into prostitution. Prostitutes are especially vulnerable to violence because their status, which may be unlawful, tends to marginalize them. They need the equal protection of laws against rape and other forms of violence.

16. Wars, armed conflicts and the occupation of territories often lead to increased prostitution, trafficking in women and sexual assault of women, which require specific protective and punitive measures.

Article 11

17. Equality in employment can be seriously impaired when women are subjected to gender-specific violence, such as sexual harassment in the workplace.

18. Sexual harassment includes such unwelcome sexually determined behaviour as physical contact and advances, sexually coloured remarks, showing pornography and sexual demand, whether by words or actions. Such conduct can be humiliating and may constitute a health and safety problem; it is discriminatory when the woman has reasonable grounds to believe that her objection would disadvantage

her in connection with her employment, including recruitment or promotion, or when it creates a hostile working environment.

Article 12
19. States parties are required by article 12 to take measures to ensure equal access to health care. Violence against women puts their health and lives at risk.
20. In some States there are traditional practices perpetuated by culture and tradition that are harmful to the health of women and children. These practices include dietary restrictions for pregnant women, preference for male children and female circumcision or genital mutilation.

Article 14
21. Rural women are at risk of gender-based violence because traditional attitudes regarding the subordinate role of women that persist in many rural communities. Girls from rural communities are at special risk of violence and sexual exploitation when they leave the rural community to seek employment in towns.

Article 16 (and article 5)
22. Compulsory sterilization or abortion adversely affects women's physical and mental health, and infringes the right of women to decide on the number and spacing of their children.
23. Family violence is one of the most insidious forms of violence against women. It is prevalent in all societies. Within family relationships women of all ages are subjected to violence of all kinds, including battering, rape, other forms of sexual assault, mental and other forms of violence, which are perpetuated by traditional attitudes. Lack of economic independence forces many women to stay in violent relationships. The abrogation of their family responsibilities by men can be a form of violence, and coercion. These forms of violence put women's health at risk and impair their ability to participate in family life and public life on a basis of equality.

Specific recommendation
24. In light of these comments, the Committee on the Elimination of Discrimination against Women recommends that:

(a) States parties should take appropriate and effective measures to overcome all forms of gender-based violence, whether by public or private act;

(b) States parties should ensure that laws against family violence and abuse, rape, sexual assault and other gender-based violence give adequate protection to all women, and respect their integrity and dignity. Appropriate protective and support services should be provided for victims. Gender-sensitive training of judicial and law enforcement officers and other public officials is essential for the effective implementation of the Convention;

(c) States parties should encourage the compilation of statistics and research on the extent, causes and effects of violence, and on the effectiveness of measures to prevent and deal with violence;

(d) Effective measures should be taken to ensure that the media respect and promote respect for women;

(e) States parties in their reports should identify the nature and extent of attitudes, customs and practices that perpetuate violence against women and the kinds of violence that result. They should report on the measures that they have undertaken to overcome violence and the effect of those measures;

(f) Effective measures should be taken to overcome these attitudes and practices. States should introduce education and public information programmes to help eliminate prejudices that hinder women's equality (recommendation No. 3, 1987);

(g) Specific preventive and punitive measures are necessary to overcome trafficking and sexual exploitation;

(h) States parties in their reports should describe the extent of all these problems and the measures, including penal provisions, preventive and rehabilitation measures that have been taken to protect women engaged in prostitution or subject to trafficking and other forms of sexual exploitation. The effectiveness of these measures should also be described;

(i) Effective complaints procedures and remedies, including compensation, should be provided;

(j) States parties should include in their reports information on sexual harassment, and on measures to protect women from sexual harassment and other forms of violence of coercion in the workplace;

(k) States parties should establish or support services for victims of family violence, rape, sexual assault and other forms of gender-based violence, including refuges, specially trained health workers, rehabilitation and counselling;

(l) States parties should take measures to overcome such practices and should take account of the Committee's recommendation on female circumcision (recommendation No. 14) in reporting on health issues;

(m) States parties should ensure that measures are taken to prevent coercion in regard to fertility and reproduction, and to ensure that women are not forced to seek unsafe medical procedures such as illegal abortion because of lack of appropriate services in regard to fertility control;

(n) States parties in their reports should state the extent of these problems and should indicate the measures that have been taken and their effect;

(o) States parties should ensure that services for victims of violence are accessible to rural women and that where necessary special services are provided to isolated communities;

(p) Measures to protect them from violence should include training and employment opportunities and the monitoring of the employment conditions of domestic workers;

(q) States parties should report on the risks to rural women, the extent and nature of violence and abuse to which they are subject, their need for and access to support and other services and the effectiveness of measures to overcome violence;

(r) Measures that are necessary to overcome family violence should include:

    (i) Criminal penalties where necessary and civil remedies in cases of domestic violence;

    (ii) Legislation to remove the defence of honour in regard to the assault or murder of a female family member;

    (iii) Services to ensure the safety and security of victims of family violence, including refuges, counselling and rehabilitation programmes;

    (iv) Rehabilitation programmes for perpetrators of domestic violence;

    (v) Support services for families where incest or sexual abuse has occurred;

(s) States parties should report on the extent of domestic violence and sexual abuse, and on the preventive, punitive and remedial measures that have been taken;

(t) States parties should take all legal and other measures that are necessary to provide effective protection of women against gender-based violence, including, inter alia:

    (i) Effective legal measures, including penal sanctions, civil remedies and compensatory provisions to protect women against all kinds of violence, including inter alia violence and abuse in the family, sexual assault and sexual harassment in the workplace;

    (ii) Preventive measures, including public information and education programmes to change attitudes concerning the roles and status of men and women;

    (iii) Protective measures, including refuges, counselling, rehabilitation and support services for women who are the victims of violence or who are at risk of violence;

(u) States parties should report on all forms of gender-based violence, and such reports should include all available data on the incidence of each form of violence and on the effects of such violence on the women who are victims;

(v) The reports of States parties should include information on the legal, preventive and protective measures that have been taken to overcome violence against women, and on the effectiveness of such measures.

HUMAN RIGHTS COMMITTEE GENERAL COMMENT 24
General comment on issues relating to reservations made upon ratification or accession to the Covenant or the Optional Protocols thereto, or in relation to declarations under article 41 of the Covenant

Human Rights Comm., *General Comment 24: General Comment on Issues Relating to Reservations Made upon Ratification or Accession to the Covenant or the Optional Protocols Thereto, or in Relation to Declarations under Article 41 of the Covenant*, U.N. Doc. CCPR/C/21/Rev.1/Add.6 (52d Sess., 1994) (footnotes omitted)

1. As of 1 November 1994, 46 of the 127 States parties to the International Covenant on Civil and Political Rights had, between them, entered 150 reservations of varying significance to their acceptance of the obligations of the Covenant. Some of these reservations exclude the duty to provide and guarantee particular rights in the Covenant. Others are couched in more general terms, often directed to ensuring the continued paramountcy of certain domestic legal provisions. Still others are directed at the competence of the Committee. The number of reservations, their content and their scope may undermine the effective implementation of the Covenant and tend to weaken respect for the obligations of States parties. It is important for States parties to know exactly what obligations they, and other States parties, have in fact undertaken. And the Committee, in the performance of its duties under either article 40 of the Covenant or under the Optional Protocols, must know whether a State is bound by a particular obligation or to what extent. This will require a determination as to whether a unilateral statement is a reservation or an interpretative declaration and a determination of its acceptability and effects.

2. For these reasons the Committee has deemed it useful to address in a General Comment the issues of international law and human rights policy that arise. The General Comment identifies the principles of international law that apply to the making of reservations and by reference to which their acceptability is to be tested and their purport to be interpreted. It addresses the role of States parties in relation to the reservations of others. It further addresses the role of the Committee itself in relation to reservations. And it makes certain recommendations to present States parties for a reviewing of reservations and to those States that are not yet parties about legal and human rights policy considerations to be borne in mind should they consider ratifying or acceding with particular reservations.

3. It is not always easy to distinguish a reservation from a declaration as to a State's understanding of the interpretation of a provision, or from a statement of policy. Regard will be had to the intention of the State, rather than the form of the instrument. If a statement, irrespective of its name or title, purports to exclude or modify the legal effect of a treaty in its application to the State, it constitutes a reservation. Conversely, if a so-called reservation merely offers a State's understanding of a provision but does not exclude or modify that provision in its application to that State, it is, in reality, not a reservation.

4. The possibility of entering reservations may encourage States which consider that they have difficulties in guaranteeing all the rights in the Covenant none the less to accept the generality of obligations in that instrument. Reservations may serve a useful function to enable States to adapt specific elements in their laws to the inherent rights of each person as articulated in the Covenant. However, it is desirable in principle that States accept the full range of obligations, because the human rights norms are the legal expression of the essential rights that every person is entitled to as a human being.

5. The Covenant neither prohibits reservations nor mentions any type of permitted reservation. The same is true of the first Optional Protocol. The Second Optional Protocol provides, in article 2, paragraph 1, that "No reservation is admissible to the present Protocol, except for a reservation made at the time of ratification or accession that provides for the application of the death penalty in time of war pursuant to a conviction for a most serious crime of a military nature committed during wartime". Paragraphs 2 and 3 provide for certain procedural obligations.

6. The absence of a prohibition on reservations does not mean that any reservation is permitted. The matter of reservations under the Covenant and the first Optional Protocol is governed by international law. Article 19 (3) of the Vienna Convention on the Law of Treaties provides relevant guidance. It stipulates that where a reservation is not prohibited by the treaty or falls within the specified permitted categories, a State may make a reservation provided it is not incompatible with the object and purpose of the treaty. Even though, unlike some other human rights treaties, the Covenant does not incorporate a specific reference to the object and purpose test, that test governs the matter of interpretation and acceptability of reservations.

7. In an instrument which articulates very many civil and political rights, each of the many articles, and indeed their interplay, secures the objectives of the Covenant. The object and purpose of the Covenant is to create legally binding standards for human rights by defining certain civil and political rights and placing them in a framework of obligations which are legally binding for those States which ratify; and to provide an efficacious supervisory machinery for the obligations undertaken.

8. Reservations that offend peremptory norms would not be compatible with the object and purpose of the Covenant. Although treaties that are mere exchanges of obligations between States allow them to reserve *inter se* application of rules of general international law, it is otherwise in human rights treaties, which are for the benefit of persons within their jurisdiction. Accordingly, provisions in the Covenant that represent customary international law (and *a fortiori* when they have the character of peremptory norms) may not be the subject of reservations. Accordingly, a State may not reserve the right to engage in slavery, to torture, to subject persons to cruel, inhuman or degrading treatment or punishment, to arbitrarily deprive persons of their lives, to arbitrarily arrest and detain persons, to deny freedom of thought, conscience and religion, to presume a person guilty unless he proves his innocence, to execute pregnant women or children, to permit the advocacy of national, racial or religious hatred, to deny to persons of marriageable age the right to marry, or to deny to minorities the right to enjoy their own culture, profess their own religion, or use their own language. And while reservations to particular clauses of article 14 may be acceptable, a general reservation to the right to a fair trial would not be.

9. Applying more generally the object and purpose test to the Covenant, the Committee notes that, for example, reservation to article 1 denying peoples the right to determine their own political status and to pursue their economic, social and cultural development, would be incompatible with the object and purpose of the Covenant. Equally, a reservation to the obligation to respect and ensure the rights, and to do so on a non-discriminatory basis (article 2 (1)) would not be acceptable. Nor may a State reserve an entitlement not to take the necessary steps at the domestic level to give effect to the rights of the Covenant (article 2 (2)).

10. The Committee has further examined whether categories of reservations may offend the "object and purpose" test. In particular, it falls for consideration as to whether reservations to the non-derogable provisions of the Covenant are compatible with its object and purpose. While there is no hierarchy of importance of rights under the Covenant, the operation of certain rights may not be suspended, even in times of national emergency. This underlines the great importance of non-derogable rights. But not all rights of profound importance, such as articles 9 and 27 of the Covenant, have in fact been made non-derogable. One reason for certain rights being made non-derogable is because their suspension is irrelevant to the legitimate control of the state of national emergency (for example, no imprisonment for debt, in article 11). Another reason is that derogation may indeed be impossible (as, for example, freedom of conscience). At the same time, some provisions are non-derogable exactly because without them there would be no rule of law. A reservation to the provisions of article 4 itself, which precisely stipulates the balance to be struck between the interests of the State and the rights of the individual in times of emergency, would fall in this category. And some non-derogable rights, which in any event cannot be reserved because of their status as peremptory norms, are also of this character - the prohibition of torture and arbitrary deprivation of life are examples. While there is no automatic correlation between reservations to non-derogable provisions, and reservations which offend against the object and purpose of the Covenant, a State has a heavy onus to justify such a reservation.

11. The Covenant consists not just of the specified rights, but of important supportive guarantees. These guarantees provide the necessary framework for securing the rights in the Covenant and are thus essential to its object and purpose. Some operate at the national level and some at the international level. Reservations designed to remove these guarantees are thus not acceptable. Thus, a State could not make a reservation to article 2, paragraph 3, of the Covenant, indicating that it intends to provide no remedies for human rights violations. Guarantees such as these are an integral part of the structure of the Covenant and underpin its efficacy. The Covenant also envisages, for the better attainment of its stated objectives, a monitoring role for the Committee. Reservations that purport to evade that essential element in the design of the Covenant, which is also directed to securing the enjoyment of the rights, are also incompatible with its object and purpose. A State may not reserve the right not to present a report and have it considered by the Committee. The Committee's role under the Covenant, whether under article 40 or under the Optional Protocols, necessarily entails interpreting the provisions of the Covenant and the development of a jurisprudence. Accordingly, a reservation that rejects the Committee's competence to interpret the requirements of any provisions of the Covenant would also be contrary to the object and purpose of that treaty.

12. The intention of the Covenant is that the rights contained therein should be ensured to all those under a State party's jurisdiction. To this end certain attendant requirements are likely to be necessary. Domestic laws may need to be altered properly to reflect the requirements of the Covenant; and mechanisms at the domestic level will be needed to allow the Covenant rights to be enforceable at the local level.

Reservations often reveal a tendency of States not to want to change a particular law. And sometimes that tendency is elevated to a general policy. Of particular concern are widely formulated reservations which essentially render ineffective all Covenant rights which would require any change in national law to ensure compliance with Covenant obligations. No real international rights or obligations have thus been accepted. And when there is an absence of provisions to ensure that Covenant rights may be sued on in domestic courts, and, further, a failure to allow individual complaints to be brought to the Committee under the first Optional Protocol, all the essential elements of the Covenant guarantees have been removed.

13. The issue arises as to whether reservations are permissible under the first Optional Protocol and, if so, whether any such reservation might be contrary to the object and purpose of the Covenant or of the first Optional Protocol itself. It is clear that the first Optional Protocol is itself an international treaty, distinct from the Covenant but closely related to it. Its object and purpose is to recognize the competence of the Committee to receive and consider communications from individuals who claim to be victims of a violation by a State party of any of the rights in the Covenant. States accept the substantive rights of individuals by reference to the Covenant, and not the first Optional Protocol. The function of the first Optional Protocol is to allow claims in respect of those rights to be tested before the Committee. Accordingly, a reservation to an obligation of a State to respect and ensure a right contained in the Covenant, made under the first Optional Protocol when it has not previously been made in respect of the same rights under the Covenant, does not affect the State's duty to comply with its substantive obligation. A reservation cannot be made to the Covenant through the vehicle of the Optional Protocol but such a reservation would operate to ensure that the State's compliance with that obligation may not be tested by the Committee under the first Optional Protocol. And because the object and purpose of the first Optional Protocol is to allow the rights obligatory for a State under the Covenant to be tested before the Committee, a reservation that seeks to preclude this would be contrary to the object and purpose of the first Optional Protocol, even if not of the Covenant. A reservation to a substantive obligation made for the first time under the first Optional Protocol would seem to reflect an intention by the State concerned to prevent the Committee from expressing its views relating to a particular article of the Covenant in an individual case.

14. The Committee considers that reservations relating to the required procedures under the first Optional Protocol would not be compatible with its object and purpose. The Committee must control its own procedures as specified by the Optional Protocol and its rules of procedure. Reservations have, however, purported to limit the competence of the Committee to acts and events occurring after entry into force for the State concerned of the first Optional Protocol. In the view of the Committee this is not a reservation but, most usually, a statement consistent with its normal competence ratione temporis. At the same time, the Committee has insisted upon its competence, even in the face of such statements or observations, when events or acts occurring before the date of entry into force of the first Optional Protocol have continued to have an effect on the rights of a victim subsequent to that date. Reservations have been entered which effectively add an additional ground of inadmissibility under article 5, paragraph 2, by precluding examination of a communication when the same matter has already been examined by another comparable procedure. In so far as the most basic obligation has been to secure independent third party review of the human rights of individuals, the Committee has, where the legal right and the subject-matter are identical under the Covenant and under another international instrument, viewed such a reservation as not violating the object and purpose of the first Optional Protocol.

15. The primary purpose of the Second Optional Protocol is to extend the scope of the substantive obligations undertaken under the Covenant, as they relate to the right to life, by prohibiting execution and abolishing the death penalty. It has its own provision concerning reservations, which is determinative of what is permitted. Article 2, paragraph 1, provides that only one category of reservation is permitted, namely one that reserves the right to apply the death penalty in time of war pursuant to a conviction for a most serious crime of a military nature committed during wartime. Two procedural obligations are incumbent upon States parties wishing to avail themselves of such a reservation. Article 2, paragraph 1, obliges such a State to inform the Secretary-General, at the time of ratification or accession, of the relevant provisions of its national legislation during warfare. This is clearly directed towards the objectives of specificity and transparency and in the view of the Committee a purported reservation unaccompanied by such information is without legal effect. Article 2, paragraph 3, requires a State making such a reservation to notify the Secretary-General of the beginning or ending of a state of war applicable to its territory. In the view of the Committee, no State may seek to avail itself of its reservation (that is, have execution in time of war regarded as lawful) unless it has complied with the procedural requirement of article 2, paragraph 3.

16. The Committee finds it important to address which body has the legal authority to make determinations as to whether specific reservations are compatible with the object and purpose of the Covenant. As for international treaties in general, the International Court of Justice has indicated in the *Reservations to the Genocide Convention Case* (1951) that a State which objected to a reservation on the grounds of incompatibility with the object and purpose of a treaty could, through objecting, regard the treaty as not in effect as between itself and the reserving State. Article 20, paragraph 4, of the Vienna Convention on the Law of Treaties 1969 contains provisions most relevant to the present case on acceptance of and objection to reservations. This provides for the possibility of a State to object to a reservation made by another State. Article 21 deals with the legal effects of objections by States to reservations made by other States. Essentially, a reservation precludes the operation, as between the reserving and other States, of the provision reserved; and an objection thereto leads to the reservation being in operation as between the reserving and objecting State only to the extent that it has not been objected to.

17. As indicated above, it is the Vienna Convention on the Law of Treaties that provides the definition of reservations and also the application of the object and purpose test in the absence of other specific provisions. But the Committee believes that its provisions on the role of State objections in relation to reservations are inappropriate to address the problem of reservations to human rights treaties. Such treaties, and the Covenant specifically, are not a web of inter-State exchanges of mutual obligations. They concern the endowment of individuals with rights. The principle of inter-State reciprocity has no place, save perhaps in the limited context of reservations to declarations on the Committee's competence under article 41. And because the operation of the classic rules on reservations is so inadequate for the Covenant, States have often not seen any legal interest in or need to object to reservations. The absence of protest by States cannot imply that a reservation is either compatible or incompatible with the object and purpose of the Covenant. Objections have been occasional, made by some States but not others, and on grounds not always specified; when an objection is made, it often does not specify a legal consequence, or sometimes even indicates that the objecting party none the less does not regard the Covenant as not in effect as between the parties concerned. In short, the pattern is so unclear that it is not safe to assume that a non-objecting State thinks that a particular reservation is acceptable. In the view of the Committee, because of the special characteristics of the Covenant as a human rights treaty, it is open to question what effect objections have between States inter se. However, an objection to a reservation made by States may provide some guidance to the Committee in its interpretation as to its compatibility with the object and purpose of the Covenant.

18. It necessarily falls to the Committee to determine whether a specific reservation is compatible with the object and purpose of the Covenant. This is in part because, as indicated above, it is an inappropriate task for States parties in relation to human rights treaties, and in part because it is a task that the Committee cannot avoid in the performance of its functions. In order to know the scope of its duty to examine a State's compliance under article 40 or a communication under the first Optional Protocol, the Committee has necessarily to take a view on the compatibility of a reservation with the object and purpose of the Covenant and with general international law. Because of the special character of a human rights treaty, the compatibility of a reservation with the object and purpose of the Covenant must be established objectively, by reference to legal principles, and the Committee is particularly well placed to perform this task. The normal consequence of an unacceptable reservation is not that the Covenant will not be in effect at all for a reserving party. Rather, such a reservation will generally be severable, in the sense that the Covenant will be operative for the reserving party without benefit of the reservation.

19. Reservations must be specific and transparent, so that the Committee, those under the jurisdiction of the reserving State and other States parties may be clear as to what obligations of human rights compliance have or have not been undertaken. Reservations may thus not be general, but must refer to a particular provision of the Covenant and indicate in precise terms its scope in relation thereto. When considering the compatibility of possible reservations with the object and purpose of the Covenant, States should also take into consideration the overall effect of a group of reservations, as well as the effect of each reservation on the integrity of the Covenant, which remains an essential consideration. States should not enter so many reservations that they are in effect accepting a limited number of human rights obligations, and not the Covenant as such. So that reservations do not lead to a perpetual non-attainment of international human rights standards, reservations should not systematically reduce the obligations undertaken only to those presently existing in less demanding standards of domestic law. Nor should interpretative declarations or reservations seek to remove an autonomous meaning to Covenant obligations, by pronouncing them to be identical, or to be accepted only in so far as they are identical, with existing provisions of domestic law.

States should not seek through reservations or interpretative declarations to determine that the meaning of a provision of the Covenant is the same as that given by an organ of any other international treaty body.
20. States should institute procedures to ensure that each and every proposed reservation is compatible with the object and purpose of the Covenant. It is desirable for a State entering a reservation to indicate in precise terms the domestic legislation or practices which it believes to be incompatible with the Covenant obligation reserved; and to explain the time period it requires to render its own laws and practices compatible with the Covenant, or why it is unable to render its own laws and practices compatible with the Covenant. States should also ensure that the necessity for maintaining reservations is periodically reviewed, taking into account any observations and recommendations made by the Committee during examination of their reports. Reservations should be withdrawn at the earliest possible moment. Reports to the Committee should contain information on what action has been taken to review, reconsider or withdraw reservations.

COMMITTEE ON ECONOMIC, SOCIAL, AND CULTURAL RIGHTS GENERAL COMMENT 12
The Right to Adequate Food (Article 11)

Comm. on Econ., Soc., and Cultural Rights, *Substantive Issues Arising in the Implementation of the International Covenant on Economic, Social, and Cultural Rights, General Comment 12: The Right to Adequate Food (Art. 11)*, U.N. Doc. E/C.12/1999/5 (20th Sess., 1999)
(fotnotes omitted)

Introduction and basic premises
1. The human right to adequate food is recognized in several instruments under international law. The International Covenant on Economic, Social and Cultural Rights deals more comprehensively than any other instrument with this right. Pursuant to article 11.1 of the Covenant, States parties recognize "the right of everyone to an adequate standard of living for himself and his family, including adequate food, clothing and housing, and to the continuous improvement of living conditions", while pursuant to article 11.2 they recognize that more immediate and urgent steps may be needed to ensure "the fundamental right to freedom from hunger and malnutrition". The human right to adequate food is of crucial importance for the enjoyment of all rights. It applies to everyone; thus the reference in Article 11.1 to "himself and his family" does not imply any limitation upon the applicability of this right to individuals or to female-headed households.
2. The Committee has accumulated significant information pertaining to the right to adequate food through examination of State parties' reports over the years since 1979. The Committee has noted that while reporting guidelines are available relating to the right to adequate food, only few States parties have provided information sufficient and precise enough to enable the Committee to determine the prevailing situation in the countries concerned with respect to this right and to identify the obstacles to its realization. This General Comment aims to identify some of the principal issues which the Committee considers to be important in relation to the right to adequate food. Its preparation was triggered by the request of Member States during the 1996 World Food Summit, for a better definition of the rights relating to food in article 11 of the Covenant, and by a special request to the Committee to give particular attention to the Summit Plan of Action in monitoring the implementation of the specific measures provided for in article 11 of the Covenant.
3. In response to these requests, the Committee reviewed the relevant reports and documentation of the Commission on Human Rights and of the Sub-Commission on Prevention of Discrimination and Protection of Minorities on the right to adequate food as a human right; devoted a day of general discussion to this issue at its seventeenth session in 1997, taking into consideration the draft international code of conduct on the human right to adequate food prepared by international non-governmental organizations; participated in two expert consultations on the right to adequate food as a human right organized by the Office of the United Nations High Commissioner for Human Rights (OHCHR), in Geneva in December 1997, and in Rome in November 1998 co-hosted by the Food and Agriculture Organization of the United Nations (FAO), and noted their final reports. In April 1999 the Committee participated in a symposium on "The substance and politics of a human rights approach to food and nutrition policies and programmes",

organized by the Administrative Committee on Co-ordination/Sub-Committee on Nutrition of the United Nations at its twenty-sixth session in Geneva and hosted by OHCHR.

4. The Committee affirms that the right to adequate food is indivisibly linked to the inherent dignity of the human person and is indispensable for the fulfilment of other human rights enshrined in the International Bill of Human Rights. It is also inseparable from social justice, requiring the adoption of appropriate economic, environmental and social policies, at both the national and international levels, oriented to the eradication of poverty and the fulfilment of all human rights for all.

5. Despite the fact that the international community has frequently reaffirmed the importance of full respect for the right to adequate food, a disturbing gap still exists between the standards set in article 11 of the Covenant and the situation prevailing in many parts of the world. More than 840 million people throughout the world, most of them in developing countries, are chronically hungry; millions of people are suffering from famine as the result of natural disasters, the increasing incidence of civil strife and wars in some regions and the use of food as a political weapon. The Committee observes that while the problems of hunger and malnutrition are often particularly acute in developing countries, malnutrition, under-nutrition and other problems which relate to the right to adequate food and the right to freedom from hunger, also exist in some of the most economically developed countries. Fundamentally, the roots of the problem of hunger and malnutrition are not lack of food but lack of *access to* available food, <u>inter alia</u> because of poverty, by large segments of the world's population

Normative content of article 11, paragraphs 1 and 2

6. The right to adequate food is realized when every man, woman and child, alone or in community with others, has physical and economic access at all times to adequate food or means for its procurement. The *right to adequate food* shall therefore not be interpreted in a narrow or restrictive sense which equates it with a minimum package of calories, proteins and other specific nutrients. The *right to adequate food* will have to be realized progressively. However, States have a core obligation to take the necessary action to mitigate and alleviate hunger as provided for in paragraph 2 of article 11, even in times of natural or other disasters.

Adequacy and sustainability of food availability and access

7. The concept of *adequacy* is particularly significant in relation to the right to food since it serves to underline a number of factors which must be taken into account in determining whether particular foods or diets that are accessible can be considered the most appropriate under given circumstances for the purposes of article 11 of the Covenant. The notion of *sustainability* is intrinsically linked to the notion of adequate food or food *security*, implying food being accessible for both present and future generations. The precise meaning of "adequacy" is to a large extent determined by prevailing social, economic, cultural, climatic, ecological and other conditions, while "sustainability" incorporates the notion of long-term availability and accessibility.

8. The Committee considers that the core content of the right to adequate food implies: The availability of food in a quantity and quality sufficient to satisfy the dietary needs of individuals, free from adverse substances, and acceptable within a given culture; The accessibility of such food in ways that are sustainable and that do not interfere with the enjoyment of other human rights.

9. *Dietary needs* implies that the diet as a whole contains a mix of nutrients for physical and mental growth, development and maintenance, and physical activity that are in compliance with human physiological needs at all stages throughout the life cycle and according to gender and occupation. Measures may therefore need to be taken to maintain, adapt or strengthen dietary diversity and appropriate consumption and feeding patterns, including breast-feeding, while ensuring that changes in availability and access to food supply as a minimum do not negatively affect dietary composition and intake.

10. *Free from adverse substances* sets requirements for food safety and for a range of protective measures by both public and private means to prevent contamination of foodstuffs through adulteration and/or through bad environmental hygiene or inappropriate handling at different stages throughout the food chain; care must also be taken to identify and avoid or destroy naturally occurring toxins.

11. *Cultural or consumer acceptability* implies the need also to take into account, as far as possible, perceived non nutrient-based values attached to food and food consumption and informed consumer concerns regarding the nature of accessible food supplies.

12. *Availability* refers to the possibilities either for feeding oneself directly from productive land or other natural resources, or for well functioning distribution, processing and market systems that can move food from the site of production to where it is needed in accordance with demand.

13. *Accessibility* encompasses both economic and physical accessibility:
Economic accessibility implies that personal or household financial costs associated with the acquisition of food for an adequate diet should be at a level such that the attainment and satisfaction of other basic needs are not threatened or compromised. Economic accessibility applies to any acquisition pattern or entitlement through which people procure their food and is a measure of the extent to which it is satisfactory for the enjoyment of the right to adequate food. Socially vulnerable groups such as landless persons and other particularly impoverished segments of the population may need attention through special programmes. Physical accessibility implies that adequate food must be accessible to everyone, including physically vulnerable individuals, such as infants and young children, elderly people, the physically disabled, the terminally ill and persons with persistent medical problems, including the mentally ill. Victims of natural disasters, people living in disaster-prone areas and other specially disadvantaged groups may need special attention and sometimes priority consideration with respect to accessibility of food. A particular vulnerability is that of many indigenous population groups whose access to their ancestral lands may be threatened.

Obligations and violations
14. The nature of the legal obligations of States parties are set out in article 2 of the Covenant and has been dealt with in the Committee's General Comment No. 3 (1990). The principal obligation is to take steps to achieve *progressively* the full realization of the right to adequate food. This imposes an obligation to move as expeditiously as possible towards that goal. Every State is obliged to ensure for everyone under its jurisdiction access to the minimum essential food which is sufficient, nutritionally adequate and safe, to ensure their freedom from hunger.
15. The right to adequate food, like any other human right, imposes three types or levels of obligations on States parties: the obligations to *respect*, to *protect* and to *fulfil*. In turn, the obligation to *fulfil* incorporates both an obligation to *facilitate* and an obligation to *provide*. The obligation to *respect* existing access to adequate food requires States parties not to take any measures that result in preventing such access. The obligation to *protect* requires measures by the State to ensure that enterprises or individuals do not deprive individuals of their access to adequate food. The obligation to *fulfil (facilitate)* means the State must pro-actively engage in activities intended to strengthen people's access to and utilization of resources and means to ensure their livelihood, including food security. Finally, whenever an individual or group is unable, for reasons beyond their control, to enjoy the right to adequate food by the means at their disposal, States have the obligation to *fulfil (provide)* that right directly. This obligation also applies for persons who are victims of natural or other disasters.
16. Some measures at these different levels of obligations of States parties are of a more immediate nature, while other measures are more of a long-term character, to achieve progressively the full realization of the right to food.
17. Violations of the Covenant occur when a State fails to ensure the satisfaction of, at the very least, the minimum essential level required to be free from hunger. In determining which actions or omissions amount to a violation of the right to food, it is important to distinguish the inability from the unwillingness of a State party to comply. Should a State party argue that resource constraints make it impossible to provide access to food for those who are unable by themselves to secure such access, the State has to demonstrate that every effort has been made to use all the resources at its disposal in an effort to satisfy, as a matter of priority, those minimum obligations. This follows from Article 2.1 of the Covenant, which obliges a State party to take the necessary steps to the maximum of its available resources, as previously pointed out by the Committee in its General Comment No. 3, paragraph 10. A State claiming that it is unable to carry out its obligation for reasons beyond its control therefore has the burden of proving that this is the case and that it has unsuccessfully sought to obtain international support to ensure the availability and accessibility of the necessary food.
18. Furthermore, any discrimination in access to food, as well as to means and entitlements for its procurement, on the grounds of race, colour, sex, language, age, religion, political or other opinion, national or social origin, property, birth or other status with the purpose or effect of nullifying or impairing the equal enjoyment or exercise of economic, social and cultural rights constitutes a violation of the Covenant.
19. Violations of the right to food can occur through the direct action of States or other entities insufficiently regulated by States. These include: the formal repeal or suspension of legislation necessary for the continued enjoyment of the right to food; denial of access to food to particular individuals or groups, whether the discrimination is based on legislation or is pro-active; the prevention of access to humanitarian

food aid in internal conflicts or other emergency situations; adoption of legislation or policies which are manifestly incompatible with pre-existing legal obligations relating to the right to food; and failure to regulate activities of individuals or groups so as to prevent them from violating the right to food of others, or the failure of a State to take into account its international legal obligations regarding the right to food when entering into agreements with other States or with international organizations.

20. While only States are parties to the Covenant and are thus ultimately accountable for compliance with it, all members of society - individuals, families, local communities, non-governmental organizations, civil society organizations, as well as the private business sector - have responsibilities in the realization of the right to adequate food. The State should provide an environment that facilitates implementation of these responsibilities. The private business sector – national and transnational - should pursue its activities within the framework of a code of conduct conducive to respect of the right to adequate food, agreed upon jointly with the Government and civil society.

Implementation at the national level

21. The most appropriate ways and means of implementing the right to adequate food will inevitably vary significantly from one State party to another. Every State will have a margin of discretion in choosing its own approaches, but the Covenant clearly requires that each State party take whatever steps are necessary to ensure that everyone is free from hunger and as soon as possible can enjoy the right to adequate food. This will require the adoption of a national strategy to ensure food and nutrition security for all, based on human rights principles that define the objectives, and the formulation of policies and corresponding benchmarks. It should also identify the resources available to meet the objectives and the most cost-effective way of using them.

22. The strategy should be based on a systematic identification of policy measures and activities relevant to the situation and context, as derived from the normative content of the right to adequate food and spelled out in relation to the levels and nature of State parties' obligations referred to in paragraph 15 of the present general comment. This will facilitate coordination between ministries and regional and local authorities and ensure that related policies and administrative decisions are in compliance with the obligations under article 11 of the Covenant.

23. The formulation and implementation of national strategies for the right to food requires full compliance with the principles of accountability, transparency, people's participation, decentralization, legislative capacity and the independence of the judiciary. Good governance is essential to the realization of all human rights, including the elimination of poverty and ensuring a satisfactory livelihood for all.

24. Appropriate institutional mechanisms should be devised to secure a representative process towards the formulation of a strategy, drawing on all available domestic expertise relevant to food and nutrition. The strategy should set out the responsibilities and time-frame for the implementation of the necessary measures.

25. The strategy should address critical issues and measures in regard to *all* aspects of the food system, including the production, processing, distribution, marketing and consumption of safe food, as well as parallel measures in the fields of health, education, employment and social security. Care should be taken to ensure the most sustainable management and use of natural and other resources for food at the national, regional, local and household levels.

26. The strategy should give particular attention to the need to prevent discrimination in access to food or resources for food. This should include: guarantees of full and equal access to economic resources, particularly for women, including the right to inheritance and the ownership of land and other property, credit, natural resources and appropriate technology; measures to respect and protect self-employment and work which provides a remuneration ensuring a decent living for wage earners and their families (as stipulated in article 7 (a) (ii) of the Covenant); maintaining registries on rights in land (including forests).

27. As part of their obligations to protect people's resource base for food, States parties should take appropriate steps to ensure that activities of the private business sector and civil society are in conformity with the right to food.

28. Even where a State faces severe resource constraints, whether caused by a process of economic adjustment, economic recession, climatic conditions or other factors, measures should be undertaken to ensure that the right to adequate food is especially fulfilled for vulnerable population groups and individuals.

Benchmarks and framework legislation

29. In implementing the country-specific strategies referred to above, States should set verifiable benchmarks for subsequent national and international monitoring. In this connection, States should consider the adoption of a *framework law* as a major instrument in the implementation of the national strategy concerning the right to food. The framework law should include provisions on its purpose; the targets or goals to be achieved and the time-frame to be set for the achievement of those targets; the means by which the purpose could be achieved described in broad terms, in particular the intended collaboration with civil society and the private sector and with international organizations; institutional responsibility for the process; and the national mechanisms for its monitoring, as well as possible recourse procedures. In developing the benchmarks and framework legislation, States parties should actively involve civil society organizations.

30. Appropriate United Nations programmes and agencies should assist, upon request, in drafting the framework legislation and in reviewing the sectoral legislation. FAO, for example, has considerable expertise and accumulated knowledge concerning legislation in the field of food and agriculture. The United Nations Children's Fund (UNICEF) has equivalent expertise concerning legislation with regard to the right to adequate food for infants and young children through maternal and child protection including legislation to enable breast-feeding, and with regard to the regulation of marketing of breast milk substitutes.

Monitoring

31. States parties shall develop and maintain mechanisms to monitor progress towards the realization of the right to adequate food for all, to identify the factors and difficulties affecting the degree of implementation of their obligations, and to facilitate the adoption of corrective legislation and administrative measures, including measures to implement their obligations under articles 2.1 and 23 of the Covenant.

Remedies and accountability

32. Any person or group who is a victim of a violation of the right to adequate food should have access to effective judicial or other appropriate remedies at both national and international levels. All victims of such violations are entitled to adequate reparation, which may take the form of restitution, compensation, satisfaction or guarantees of non-repetition. National Ombudsmen and human rights commissions should address violations of the right to food.

33. The incorporation in the domestic legal order of international instruments recognizing the right to food, or recognition of their applicability, can significantly enhance the scope and effectiveness of remedial measures and should be encouraged in all cases. Courts would then be empowered to adjudicate violations of the core content of the right to food by direct reference to obligations under the Covenant.

34. Judges and other members of the legal profession are invited to pay greater attention to violations of the right to food in the exercise of their functions.

35. States parties should respect and protect the work of human rights advocates and other members of civil society who assist vulnerable groups in the realization of their right to adequate food.

International obligations

States parties

36. In the spirit of article 56 of the Charter of the United Nations, the specific provisions contained in articles 11, 2.1, and 23 of the Covenant and the Rome Declaration of the World Food Summit, States parties should recognize the essential role of international cooperation and comply with their commitment to take joint and separate action to achieve the full realization of the right to adequate food. In implementing this commitment, States parties should take steps to respect the enjoyment of the right to food in other countries, to protect that right, to facilitate access to food and to provide the necessary aid when required. States parties should, in international agreements whenever relevant, ensure that the right to adequate food is given due attention and consider the development of further international legal instruments to that end.

37. States parties should refrain at all times from food embargoes or similar measures which endanger conditions for food production and access to food in other countries. Food should never be used as an instrument of political and economic pressure. In this regard, the Committee recalls its position, stated in its General Comment No. 8, on the relationship between economic sanctions and respect for economic, social and cultural rights.

States and international organizations

38. States have a joint and individual responsibility, in accordance with the Charter of the United Nations, to cooperate in providing disaster relief and humanitarian assistance in times of emergency, including

assistance to refugees and internally displaced persons. Each State should contribute to this task in accordance with its ability. The role of the World Food Programme (WFP) and the Office of the United Nations High Commissioner for Refugees (UNHCR), and increasingly that of UNICEF and FAO is of particular importance in this respect and should be strengthened. Priority in food aid should be given to the most vulnerable populations.

39. Food aid should, as far as possible, be provided in ways which do not adversely affect local producers and local markets, and should be organized in ways that facilitate the return to food self-reliance of the beneficiaries. Such aid should be based on the needs of the intended beneficiaries. Products included in international food trade or aid programmes must be safe and culturally acceptable to the recipient population.

The United Nations and other international organizations

40. The role of the United Nations agencies, including through the United Nations Development Assistance Framework (UNDAF) at the country level, in promoting the realization of the right to food is of special importance. Coordinated efforts for the realization of the right to food should be maintained to enhance coherence and interaction among all the actors concerned, including the various components of civil society. The food organizations, FAO, WFP and the International Fund for Agricultural Development (IFAD) in conjunction with the United Nations Development Programme (UNDP), UNICEF, the World Bank and the regional development banks, should cooperate more effectively, building on their respective expertise, on the implementation of the right to food at the national level, with due respect to their individual mandates.

41. The international financial institutions, notably the International Monetary Fund (IMF) and the World Bank, should pay greater attention to the protection of the right to food in their lending policies and credit agreements and in international measures to deal with the debt crisis. Care should be taken, in line with the Committee's General Comment No. 2, paragraph 9, in any structural adjustment programme to ensure that the right to food is protected.

INTERNATIONAL CRIMINAL TRIBUNAL DOCUMENTS

CHARTER OF THE INTERNATIONAL MILITARY TRIBUNAL
Agreement for the Prosecution and Punishment of the Major War Criminals of the European Axis, *adopted* Aug. 8, 1945, 58 Stat. 1544, 82 U.N.T.S. 279

Whereas the United Nations have from time to time made declarations of their intention that war criminals shall be brought to justice;

And *whereas* the Moscow Declaration of 30 October 1943, on German atrocities in Occupied Europe stated that those German officers and men and members of the Nazi Party who have been responsible for or have taken a consenting part in atrocities and crimes will be sent back to the countries in which their abominable deeds were done in order that they may be judged and punished according to the laws of these liberated countries and of the free Governments that will be created therein;

And *whereas* this Declaration was stated to be without prejudice to the case of major criminals whose offences have no particular geographical location and who will be punished by the joint decision of the Governments of the Allies;

Now therefore the Government of the United Kingdom of Great Britain and Northern Ireland, the Government of the United States of America, the Provisional Government of the French Republic and the Government of the Union of Soviet Socialist Republics (hereinafter called "the Signatories") acting in the interests of all the United Nations and by their representatives duly authorized thereto have concluded this Agreement.

Article 1

There shall be established after consultation with the Control Council for Germany an International Military Tribunal for the trial of war criminals whose offences have no particular geographical location whether they be accused individually or in their capacity as members of organizations or groups or in both capacities.

Article 2

The constitution, jurisdiction and functions of the International Military Tribunal shall be those set out in the Charter annexed to this Agreement, which Charter shall form an integral part of this Agreement.

Article 3

Each of the Signatories shall take the necessary steps to make available for the investigation of the charges and trial the major war criminals detained by them who are to be tried by the International Military Tribunal. The Signatories shall also use their best endeavours to make available for investigation of the charges against and the trial before the International Military Tribunal such of the major war criminals as are not in the territories of any of the Signatories.

Article 4

Nothing in this Agreement shall prejudice the provisions established by the Moscow Declaration concerning the return of war criminals to the countries where they committed their crimes.

Article 5

Any Government of the United Nations may adhere to this Agreement by notice given through the diplomatic channel to the Government of the United Kingdom, who shall inform the other signatory and adhering Governments of each such adherence.

Article 6

Nothing in this Agreement shall prejudice the jurisdiction or the powers of any national or occupation court established or to be established in any Allied territory or in Germany for the trial of war criminals.

Article 7

This Agreement shall come into force on the day of signature and shall remain in force for the period of one year and shall continue thereafter, subject to the right of any Signatory to give, through the diplomatic channel, one month's notice of intention to terminate it. Such termination shall not prejudice any proceedings already taken or any findings already made in pursuance of this Agreement.

In witness whereof the undersigned have signed the present Agreement. Done in quadruplicate in London this eighth day of August 1945, each in English, French and Russian, and each text to have equal authenticity.

CHARTER OF THE INTERNATIONAL MILITARY TRIBUNAL

I. CONSTITUTION OF THE INTERNATIONAL MILITARY TRIBUNAL

Article 1

In pursuance of the Agreement signed on the 8th day of August 1945 by the Government of the United States of America, the Provisional Government of the French Republic, the Government of the United Kingdom of Great Britain and Northern Ireland and the Government of the Union of Soviet Socialist Republics, there shall be established an International Military Tribunal (hereinafter called "the Tribunal") for the just and prompt trial and punishment of the major war criminals of the European Axis.

Article 2

The Tribunal shall consist of four members, each with an alternate. One member and one alternate shall be appointed by each of the Signatories. The alternates shall, so far as they are able, be present at all sessions of the Tribunal. In case of illness of any member of the Tribunal or his incapacity for some other reason to fulfill his functions, his alternate shall take his place.

Article 3

Neither the Tribunal, its members nor their alternates can be challenged by the prosecution, or by the Defendants or their Counsel. Each Signatory may replace its members of the Tribunal or his alternate for reasons of health or for other good reasons, except that no replacement may take place during a Trial, other than by an alternate.

Article 4

(a) The presence of all four members of the Tribunal or the alternate for any absent member shall be necessary to constitute the quorum.

(b) The members of the Tribunal shall, before any trial begins, agree among themselves upon the selection from their number of a President, and the President shall hold office during the trial, or as may otherwise be agreed by a vote of not less than three members. The principle of rotation of presidency for successive trials is agreed. If, however, a session of the Tribunal takes place on the territory of one of the four Signatories, the representative of that Signatory on the Tribunal shall preside.

(c) Save as aforesaid the Tribunal shall take decisions by a majority vote and in case the votes are evenly divided, the vote of the President shall be decisive: provided always that convictions and sentences shall only be imposed by affirmative votes of at least three members of the Tribunal.

Article 5

In case of need and depending on the number of the matters to be tried, other Tribunals may be set up; and the establishment, functions, and procedure of each Tribunal shall be identical, and shall be governed by this Charter.

II. JURISDICTION AND GENERAL PRINCIPLES

Article 6

The Tribunal established by the Agreement referred to m Article 1 hereof for the trial and punishment of the major war criminals of the European Axis countries shall have the power to try and punish persons who, acting in the interests of the European Axis countries, whether as individuals or as members of organizations, committed any of the following crimes.

The following acts, or any of them, are crimes coming within the jurisdiction of the Tribunal for which there shall be individual responsibility:

(a) CRIMES AGAINST PEACE: namely, planning, preparation, initiation or waging of a war of aggression, or a war in violation of international treaties, agreements or assurances, or participation in a common plan or conspiracy for the accomplishment of any of the foregoing;

(b) WAR CRIMES: namely, violations of the laws or customs of war. Such violations shall include, but not be limited to, murder, ill-treatment or deportation to slave labor or for any other purpose of civilian population of or in occupied territory, murder or ill-treatment of prisoners of war or persons on the seas, killing of hostages, plunder of public or private property, wanton destruction of cities, towns or villages, or devastation not justified by military necessity;

(c)CRIMES AGAINST HUMANITY: namely, murder, extermination, enslavement, deportation, and other inhumane acts committed against any civilian population, before or during the war; or persecutions on political, racial or religious grounds in execution of or in connection with any crime within the jurisdiction of the Tribunal, whether or not in violation of the domestic law of the country where perpetrated.

Leaders, organizers, instigators and accomplices participating in the formulation or execution of a common plan or conspiracy to commit any of the foregoing crimes are responsible for all acts performed by any persons in execution of such plan.

Article 7

The official position of defendants, whether as Heads of State or responsible officials in Government Departments, shall not be considered as freeing them from responsibility or mitigating punishment.

Article 8

The fact that the Defendant acted pursuant to order of his Government or of a superior shall not free him from responsibility, but may be considered in mitigation of punishment if the Tribunal determines that justice so requires.

Article 9

At the trial of any individual member of any group or organization the Tribunal may declare (in connection with any act of which the individual may be convicted) that the group or organization of which the individual was a member was a criminal organization.

After the receipt of the Indictment the Tribunal shall give such notice as it thinks fit that the prosecution intends to ask the Tribunal to make such declaration and any member of the organization will be entitled to apply to the Tribunal for leave to be heard by the Tribunal upon the question of the criminal character of the organization. The Tribunal shall have power to allow or reject the application. If the application is allowed, the Tribunal may direct in what manner the applicants shall be represented and heard.

Article 10

In cases where a group or organization is declared criminal by the Tribunal, the competent national authority of any Signatory shall have the right to bring individual to trial for membership therein before national, military or occupation courts. In any such case the criminal nature of the group or organization is considered proved and shall not be questioned.

Article 11

Any person convicted by the Tribunal may be charged before a national, military or occupation court, referred to in Article 10 of this Charter, with a crime other than of membership in a criminal group or organization and such court may, after convicting him, impose upon him punishment independent of and additional to the punishment imposed by the Tribunal for participation in the criminal activities of such group or organization.

Article 12

The Tribunal shall have the right to take proceedings against a person charged with crimes set out in Article 6 of this Charter in his absence, if he has not been found or if the Tribunal, for any reason, finds it necessary, in the interests of justice, to conduct the hearing in his absence.

Article 13

The Tribunal shall draw up rules for its procedure. These rules shall not be inconsistent with the provisions of this Charter.

III. COMMITTEE FOR THE INVESTIGATION AND PROSECUTION OF MAJOR WAR CRIMINALS

Article 14

Each Signatory shall appoint a Chief Prosecutor for the investigation of the charges against and the prosecution of major war criminals. the Chief Prosecutors shall act as a committee for the following purposes:

(a) to agree upon a plan of the individual work of each of the Chief Prosecutors and his staff,
(b) to settle the final designation of major war criminals to be tried by the Tribunal,
(c) to approve the Indictment and the documents to be submitted therewith,
(d) to lodge the Indictment and the accompany documents with the Tribunal,
(e) to draw up and recommend to the Tribunal for its approval draft rules of procedure, contemplated by Article 13 of this Charter. The Tribunal shall have the power to accept, with or without amendments, or to reject, the rules so recommended.

The Committee shall act in all the above matters by a majority vote and shall appoint a Chairman as may be convenient and in accordance with the principle of rotation: provided that if there is an equal division of · vote concerning the designation of a Defendant to be tried by the Tribunal, or the crimes with which he shall be charged, that proposal will be adopted which was made by the party which proposed that the particular Defendant be tried, or the particular charges be preferred against him.

Article 15

The Chief Prosecutors shall individually, and acting in collaboration with one another, also undertake the following duties:

(a) investigation, collection and production before or at the Trial of all necessary evidence,

(b) the preparation of the Indictment for approval by the Committee in accordance with paragraph (c) of Article 14 hereof,

(c) the preliminary examination of all necessary witnesses and of all Defendants,

(d) to act as prosecutor at the Trial,

(e) to appoint representatives to carry out such duties as may be assigned them,

(f) to undertake such other matters as may appear necessary to them for the purposes of the preparation for and conduct of the Trial.

It is understood that no witness or Defendant detained by the Signatory shall be taken out of the possession of that Signatory without its assent.

IV. FAIR TRIAL FOR DEFENDANTS

Article 16

In order to ensure fair trial for the Defendants, the following procedure shall be followed:

(a) The Indictment shall include full particulars specifying in detail the charges against the Defendants. A copy of the Indictment and of all the documents lodged with the Indictment, translated into a language which he understands, shall be furnished to the Defendant at reasonable time before the Trial.

(b) During any preliminary examination or trial of a Defendant he will have the right to give any explanation relevant to the charges made against him.

(c) A preliminary examination of a Defendant and his Trial shall be conducted in, or translated into, a language which the Defendant understands.

(d) A Defendant shall have the right to conduct his own defense before the Tribunal or to have the assistance of Counsel.

(e) A Defendant shall have the right through himself or through his Counsel to present evidence at the Trial in support of his defense, and to cross-examine any witness called by the Prosecution.

V. POWERS OF THE TRIBUNAL AND CONDUCT OF THE TRIAL

Article 17

The Tribunal shall have the power

(a) to summon witnesses to the Trial and to require their attendance and testimony and to put questions to them

(b) to interrogate any Defendant,

(c) to require the production of documents and other evidentiary material,

(d) to administer oaths to witnesses,

(e) to appoint officers for the carrying out of any task designated by the Tribunal including the power to have evidence taken on commission.

Article 18

The Tribunal shall

(a) confine the Trial strictly to an expeditious hearing of the cases raised by the charges,

(b) take strict measures to prevent any action which will cause reasonable delay, and rule out irrelevant issues and statements of any kind whatsoever,

(c) deal summarily with any contumacy, imposing appropriate punishment, including exclusion of any Defendant or his Counsel from some or all further proceedings, but without prejudice to the determination of the charges.

Article 19

The Tribunal shall not be bound by technical rules of evidence. It shall adopt and apply to the greatest possible extent expeditious and nontechnical procedure, and shall admit any evidence which it deems to be of probative value.

Article 20

The Tribunal may require to be informed of the nature of any evidence before it is entered so that it may rule upon the relevance thereof.

Article 21

The Tribunal shall not require proof of facts of common knowledge but shall take judicial notice thereof. It shall also take judicial notice of official governmental documents and reports of the United Nations, including the acts and documents of the committees set up in the various allied countries for the investigation of war crimes, and of records and findings of military or other Tribunals of any of the United Nations.

Article 22

The permanent seat of the Tribunal shall be in Berlin. The first meetings of the members of the Tribunal and of the Chief Prosecutors shall be held at Berlin in a place to be designated by the Control Council for Germany. The first trial shall be held at Nuremberg, and any subsequent trials shall be held at such places as the Tribunal may decide.

Article 23

One or more of the Chief Prosecutors may take part in the prosecution at each Trial. The function of any Chief Prosecutor may be discharged by him personally, or by any person or persons authorized by him. The function of Counsel for a Defendant may be discharged at the Defendant's request by any Counsel professionally qualified to conduct cases before the Courts of his own country, or by any other person who may be specially authorized thereto by the Tribunal.

Article 24

The proceedings at the Trial shall take the following course:
    (a) The Indictment shall be read in court.
    (b) The Tribunal shall ask each Defendant whether he pleads "guilty" or "not guilty."
    (c) The prosecution shall make an opening statement.
    (d) The Tribunal shall ask the prosecution and the defense what evidence (if any) they wish to submit to the Tribunal, and the Tribunal shall rule upon the admissibility of any such evidence.
    (e) The witnesses for the Prosecution shall be examined and after that the witnesses for the Defense. Thereafter such rebutting evidence as may be held by the Tribunal to be admissible shall be called by either the Prosecution or the Defense.
    (f) The Tribunal may put any question to any witness and to any defendant, at any time.
    (g) The Prosecution and the Defense shall interrogate and may crossexamine any witnesses and any Defendant who gives testimony.
    (h) The Defense shall address the court.
    (i) The Prosecution shall address the court.
    (j) Each Defendant may make a statement to the Tribunal.
    (k) The Tribunal shall deliver judgment and pronounce sentence.

Article 25

All official documents shall be produced, and all court proceedings conducted, in English, French and Russian, and in the language of the Defendant. So much of the record and of the proceedings may also be translated into the language of any country in which the Tribunal is sitting, as the Tribunal is sitting, as the Tribunal considers desirable in the interests of the justice and public opinion.

VI. JUDGMENT AND SENTENCE

Article 26

The judgment of the Tribunal as to the guilt or the innocence of any Defendant shall give the reasons on which it is based, and shall be final and not subject to review.

Article 27
The Tribunal shall have the right to impose upon a Defendant, on conviction, death or such other punishment as shall be determined by it to be just.

Article 28
In addition to any punishment imposed by it, the Tribunal shall have the right to deprive the convicted person of any stolen property and order its delivery to the Control Council for Germany.

Article 29
In case of guilt, sentences shall be carried out in accordance with the orders of the Control Council for Germany, which may at any time reduce or otherwise alter the sentences, but may not increase the severity thereof. If the Control Council for Germany, after any Defendant has been convicted and sentenced, discovers fresh evidence which, in its opinion, would found a fresh charge against him, the Council shall report accordingly to the Committee established under Article 14 hereof, for such action as they may consider proper, having regard to the interests of justice.

VII. EXPENSES

Article 30
The expenses of the Tribunal and of the Trials, shall be charged by the Signatories against the funds allotted for maintenance of the Control Council of Germany.

CONTROL COUNCIL LAW NO. 10
Punishment of Persons Guilty of War Crimes, Crimes Against Peace and Against Humanity

Allied Control Council Law No 10: Punishment of Persons Guilty of War Crimes, Crimes against Peace and against Humanity, enacted 20 December 1945, art II(a)(b), 3 Official Gazette Control Council for Germany (1946) at 50-55, (1946)

In order to give effect to the terms of the Moscow Declaration of 30 October 1943 and the London Agreement of 8 August 1945, and the Charter issued pursuant thereto and in order to establish a uniform legal basis in Glermany for the prosecution of war criminals and other similar offenders, other than those dealt with by the International Military Tribunal, the Control Council enacts as follows:

Article I
The Moscow Declaration of 30 October 1943 "Concerning Responsibility of Hitlerites for Committed Atrocities" and the London Agreement of 8 August 1945 "Concerning Prosecution and Punishment of Major War Criminals of European Axis" are made integral parts of this Law. Adherence to the provisions of the London Agreement by any of the United Nations, as provided for in Article V of that Agreement, shall not entitle such Nation to participate or interfere in the operation of this Law within the Control Council area of authority in Germany.

Article II
1. Each of the following acts is recognized as a crime:
> (a) *Crimes against Peace*. Initiation of invasions of other countries and wars of aggression in violation of international laws and treaties, including but not limited to planning, preparation, initiation or waging a war of aggression, or a war of violation of international treaties, agreements

547

or assurances, or participation in a common plan or conspiracy for the accomplishment of any of the foregoing.

(b) *War Crimes*. Atrocities or offenses against persons or property constituting violations of the laws or customs of war, including but not limited to, murder, ill treatment or deportation to slave labour or for any other purpose, of civilian population from occupied territory, murder or ill treatment of prisoners of war or persons on the seas, killing of hostages, plunder of public or private property, wanton destruction of cities, towns or villages, or devastation not justified by military necessity.

(c) *Crimes against Humanity*. Atrocities and offenses, including but not limited to murder, extermination, enslavement, deportation, imprisonment, torture, rape, or other inhumane acts committed against any civilian population, or persecutions on political, racial or religious grounds whether or not in violation of the domestic laws of the country where perpetrated.

(d) Membership in categories of a criminal group or organization declared criminal by the International Military Tribunal.

2. Any person without regard to nationality or the capacity in which he acted, is deemed to have committed a crime as defined in paragraph 1 of this Article, if he was (a) a principal or (b) was an accessory to the commission of any such crime or ordered or abetted the same or (c) took a consenting part therein or (d) was connected with plans or enterprises involving its commission or (e) was a member of any organization or group connected with the commission of any such crime or (f) with reference to paragraph 1 (a) if he held a high political, civil or military (including General Staff) position in Germany or in one of its Allies, co-belligerents or satellites or held high position in the financial, industrial or economic life of any such country.

3. Any persons found guilty of any of the crimes above mentioned may upon conviction be punished as shall be determined by the tribunal to be just. Such punishment may consist of one or more of the following:

    (a) Death.

    (b) Imprisonment for life or a term of years, with or without hard labor.

    (c) Fine, and imprisonment with or without hard labour, in lieu thereof.

    (d) Forfeiture of property.

    (e) Restitution of property wrongfully acquired.

    (f) Deprivation of some or all civil rights.

Any property declared to be forfeited or the restitution of which is ordered by the Tribunal shall be delivered to the Control Council for Germany, which shall decide on its disposal.

4.   (a) The official position of any person, whether as Head of State or as a responsible official in a Government Department, does not free him from responsibility for a crime or entitle him to mitigation of punishment.

    (b) The fact that any person acted pursuant to the order of his Government or of a superior does not free him from responsibility for a crime, but may be considered in mitigation.

5. In any trial or prosecution for a crime herein referred to, the accused shall not be entitled to the benefits of any statute of limitation in respect to the period from 30 January 1933 to 1 July 1945, nor shall any immunity, pardon or amnesty granted under the Nazi regime be admitted as a bar to trial or punishment.

Article III

1. Each occupying authority, within its Zone of Occupation,

    (a) shall have the right to cause persons within such Zone suspected of having committed a crime, including those charged with crime by one of the United Nations, to be arrested and shall take under control the property, real and personal, owned or controlled by the said persons, pending decisions as to its eventual disposition.

    (b) shall report to the Legal Directorate the name of all suspected criminals, the reasons for and the places of their detention, if they are detained, and the names and location of witnesses.

    (c) shall take appropriate measures to see that witnesses and evidence will be available when required.

    (d) shall have the right to cause all persons so arrested and charged, and not delivered to another authority as herein provided, or released, to be brought to trial before an appropriate tribunal. Such tribunal may, in the case of crimes committed by persons of German citizenship or nationality against other persons of German citizenship or nationality, or stateless persons, be a German Court, if authorized by the occupying authorities.

2. The tribunal by which persons charged with offenses hereunder shall be tried and the rujles and procedure thereof shall be determined or designated by each Zone Conimander for his respective Zone. Nothing herein is intended to, or shall impair or limit the Jurisdiction or power of any court or tribunal now or hereafter established in any Zone by the Commander thereof, or of the International Military Tribunal established by the London Agreement of 8 August 1945.

3. Persons wanted for trial by an International Military Tribunal will not be tried without the consent of the Committee of Chief Prosecutors. Each Zone Commander will deliver such persons who are within his Zone to that committee upon request and will make witnesses and evidence available to it.

4. Persons known to be wanted for trial in another Zone or outside Germany will not be tried prior to decision under Article IV unless the fact of their apprehension has been reported in accordance with Section 1 (b) of this Article, three months have elapsed thereafter, and no request for delivery of the type contemplated by Article IV has been received by the Zone Commander concerned.

5. The execution of death sentences may be deferred by not to exceed one month after the sentence has become final when the Zone Commander concerned has reason to believe that the testimony of those under sentence would be of value in the investigation and trial of crimes within or without his zone.

6. Each Zone Commander will cause such effect to be given to the judgments Of courts of competent jurisdiction, with respect to the property taken under his control pursuant thereto, as he may deem proper in the interest of Justice.

Article IV

1. When any person in a Zone in Germany is alleged to have committed a crime, as defined in Article II, in a country other than Germany or in another Zone, the government of that nation or the Commander of the latter Zone, as the case may be, may request the Commander of the Zone which the person is located for his arrest and delivery for trial to the country or Zone in which the crime was committed. Such request for delivery shall be granted by the Commander receiving it unless he believes such person is wanted for trial or as a witness by an International Military Tribunal, or in Germany, or in a nation other than the one making the request, or the Commander is not satisfied that delivery should be made, in any of which cases he shall have the right to forward the said request to the Legal Directorate of the Allied Control Authority. A similar procedure shall apply to witnesses, material exhibits and other forms of evidence.

2. The Legal Directorate shall consider all requests referred to it, and shall determine the same in accordance with the following principles, its determination to be communicated to the Zone Commander.

   (a) A person wanted for trial or as a witness by an International Military Tribunal shall not be delivered for trial or required to give evidence outside Germany, as the case may be, except upon approval by the Committee of Chief Prosecutors acting under the London Agreement of 8 August 1945.

   (b) A person wanted for trial by several authorities (other than an International Military Tribunal) shall be disposed of in accordance with the following priorities:

   (1) If wanted for trial in the Zone in which he is, he should not be delivered unless arrangements are made for his return after trial elsewhere;

   (2) If wanted for trial in a Zone other than that in which he is, he should be delivered to that Zone in preference to delivery outside Germany unless arrangements are made for his return to that Zone after trial elsewhere;

   (3) If wanted for trial outside Germany by two or more of the United Nations, of one of which he is a citizen, that one should have priority;

   (4) If wanted for trial outside Germany by several countries, not all of which are United Nations, United Nations should have priority;

   (5) If wanted for trial outside Germany by two or more of the United Nations, then, subject to Article IV 2 (b) (3) above, that which has the most serious charges against him, which are moreover supported by evidence, should have priority.

Article V

The delivery, under Article IV of this law, of persons for trial shall be mades on demands of the Governments or Zone Commanders in such a manner that the delivery of criminals to one jurisdiction will not become the means of defeating or unnecessarily delaying the carrying out of justice in another place. If within six months the delivered person has not been convicted by the Court of the Zone or country to which he has been delivered, then such person shall be returned upon demand of the Commander of the Zone where the person was located prior to delivery

Done at Berlin, 20 December 1945.

STATUTE OF THE INTERNATIONAL CRIMINAL TRIBUNAL FOR THE FORMER YUGOSLAVIA

Statute of the International Criminal Tribunal for the Former Yugoslavia, *adopted by* S.C. Res. 827, U.N. Doc. S/RES/827 (May 25, 1993), *as amended by* S.C. Res. 1166, U.N. Doc. S/RES/1166 (May 13, 1998); S.C. Res. 1329, U.N. Doc. S/RES/1329 (Nov. 30, 2000); S.C. Res. 1411, U.N. Doc. S/RES/1411 (May 17, 2002); S.C. Res. 1431, U.N. Doc. S/RES/1431 (Aug. 14, 2002); S.C. Res. 1481, U.N. Doc. S/RES/1481 (May 19, 2003); S.C. Res. 1597, U.N. Doc. S/RES/1597 (Apr. 20, 2005); S.C. Res. 1660, U.N. Doc. S/RES/1660 (Feb. 28, 2006), *available at* http://www.un.org/icty/legaldoc-e/basic/statut/statute-feb08-e.pdf

Having been established by the Security Council acting under Chapter VII of the Charter of the United Nations, the International Tribunal for the Prosecution of Persons Responsible for Serious Violations of International Humanitarian Law Committed in the Territory of the Former Yugoslavia since 1991 (hereinafter referred to as "the International Tribunal") shall function in accordance with the provisions of the present Statute.

Article 1
Competence of the International Tribunal

The International Tribunal shall have the power to prosecute persons responsible for serious violations of international humanitarian law committed in the territory of the former Yugoslavia since 1991 in accordance with the provisions of the present Statute.

Article 2
Grave breaches of the Geneva Conventions of 1949

The International Tribunal shall have the power to prosecute persons committing or ordering to be committed grave breaches of the Geneva Conventions of 12 August 1949, namely the following acts against persons or property protected under the provisions of the relevant Geneva Convention:

(a) wilful killing;
(b) torture or inhuman treatment, including biological experiments;
(c) wilfully causing great suffering or serious injury to body or health;
(d) extensive destruction and appropriation of property, not justified by military necessity and carried out unlawfully and wantonly;
(e) compelling a prisoner of war or a civilian to serve in the forces of a hostile power;
(f) wilfully depriving a prisoner of war or a civilian of the rights of fair and regular trial;
(g) unlawful deportation or transfer or unlawful confinement of a civilian;
(h) taking civilians as hostages.

Article 3
Violations of the laws or customs of war

The International Tribunal shall have the power to prosecute persons violating the laws or customs of war. Such violations shall include, but not be limited to:

(a) employment of poisonous weapons or other weapons calculated to cause unnecessary suffering;
(b) wanton destruction of cities, towns or villages, or devastation not justified by military necessity;
(c) attack, or bombardment, by whatever means, of undefended towns, villages, dwellings, or buildings;

(d) seizure of, destruction or wilful damage done to institutions dedicated to religion, charity and education, the arts and sciences, historic monuments and works of art and science;
(e) plunder of public or private property.

Article 4
Genocide

1. The International Tribunal shall have the power to prosecute persons committing genocide as defined in paragraph 2 of this article or of committing any of the other acts enumerated in paragraph 3 of this article.
2. Genocide means any of the following acts committed with intent to destroy, in whole or in part, a national, ethnical, racial or religious group, as such:
(a) killing members of the group;
(b) causing serious bodily or mental harm to members of the group;
(c) deliberately inflicting on the group conditions of life calculated to bring about its physical destruction in whole or in part;
(d) imposing measures intended to prevent births within the group;
(e) forcibly transferring children of the group to another group.
3. The following acts shall be punishable:
(a) genocide;
(b) conspiracy to commit genocide;
(c) direct and public incitement to commit genocide;
(d) attempt to commit genocide;
(e) complicity in genocide.

Article 5
Crimes against humanity

The International Tribunal shall have the power to prosecute persons responsible for the following crimes when committed in armed conflict, whether international or internal in character, and directed against any civilian population:
(a) murder;
(b) extermination;
(c) enslavement;
(d) deportation;
(e) imprisonment;
(f) torture;
(g) rape;
(h) persecutions on political, racial and religious grounds;
(i) other inhumane acts.

Article 6
Personal jurisdiction

The International Tribunal shall have jurisdiction over natural persons pursuant to the provisions of the present Statute.

Article 7
Individual criminal responsibility

1. A person who planned, instigated, ordered, committed or otherwise aided and abetted in the planning, preparation or execution of a crime referred to in articles 2 to 5 of the present Statute, shall be individually responsible for the crime.
2. The official position of any accused person, whether as Head of State or Government or as a responsible Government official, shall not relieve such person of criminal responsibility nor mitigate punishment.
3. The fact that any of the acts referred to in articles 2 to 5 of the present Statute was committed by a subordinate does not relieve his superior of criminal responsibility if he knew or had reason to know that the subordinate was about to commit such acts or had done so and the superior failed to take the necessary and reasonable measures to prevent such acts or to punish the perpetrators thereof.

551

4. The fact that an accused person acted pursuant to an order of a Government or of a superior shall not relieve him of criminal responsibility, but may be considered in mitigation of punishment if the International Tribunal determines that justice so requires.

Article 8
Territorial and temporal jurisdiction

The territorial jurisdiction of the International Tribunal shall extend to the territory of the former Socialist Federal Republic of Yugoslavia, including its land surface, airspace and territorial waters. The temporal jurisdiction of the International Tribunal shall extend to a period beginning on 1 January 1991.

Article 9
Concurrent jurisdiction

1. The International Tribunal and national courts shall have concurrent jurisdiction to prosecute persons for serious violations of international humanitarian law committed in the territory of the former Yugoslavia since 1 January 1991.

2. The International Tribunal shall have primacy over national courts. At any stage of the procedure, the International Tribunal may formally request national courts to defer to the competence of the International Tribunal in accordance with the present Statute and the Rules of Procedure and Evidence of the International Tribunal.

Article 10
Non-bis-in-idem

1. No person shall be tried before a national court for acts constituting serious violations of international humanitarian law under the present Statute, for which he or she has already been tried by the International Tribunal.

2. A person who has been tried by a national court for acts constituting serious violations of international humanitarian law may be subsequently tried by the International Tribunal only if:

(a) the act for which he or she was tried was characterized as an ordinary crime; or

(b) the national court proceedings were not impartial or independent, were designed to shield the accused from international criminal responsibility, or the case was not diligently prosecuted.

3. In considering the penalty to be imposed on a person convicted of a crime under the present Statute, the International Tribunal shall take into account the extent to which any penalty imposed by a national court on the same person for the same act has already been served.

Article 11
Organization of the International Tribunal

The International Tribunal shall consist of the following organs:

(a) the Chambers, comprising three Trial Chambers and an Appeals Chamber;

(b) the Prosecutor; and

(c) a Registry, servicing both the Chambers and the Prosecutor.

Article 12
Composition of the Chambers

1. The Chambers shall be composed of sixteen permanent independent judges, no two of whom may be nationals of the same State, and a maximum at any one time of twelve *ad litem* independent judges appointed in accordance with article 13 *ter*, paragraph 2, of the Statute, no two of whom may be nationals of the same State.

2. Three permanent judges and a maximum at any one time of nine *ad litem* judges shall be members of each Trial Chamber. Each Trial Chamber to which *ad litem* judges are assigned may be divided into sections of three judges each, composed of both permanent and *ad litem* judges, except in the circumstances specified in paragraph 5 below. A section of a Trial Chamber shall have the same powers and responsibilities as a Trial Chamber under the Statute and shall render judgement in accordance with the same rules.

3. Seven of the permanent judges shall be members of the Appeals Chamber. The Appeals Chamber shall, for each appeal, be composed of five of its members.

4. A person who for the purposes of membership of the Chambers of the International Tribunal could be regarded as a national of more than one State shall be deemed to be a national of the State in which that person ordinarily exercises civil and political rights.

5. The Secretary-General may, at the request of the President of the International Tribunal appoint, from among the *ad litem* judges elected in accordance with Article 13 *ter*, reserve judges to be present at each stage of a trial to which they have been appointed and to replace a judge if that judge is unable to continue sitting.

6. Without prejudice to paragraph 2 above, in the event that exceptional circumstances require for a permanent judge in a section of a Trial Chamber to be replaced resulting in a section solely comprised of *ad litem* judges, that section may continue to hear the case, notwithstanding that its composition no longer includes a permanent judge.

Article 13
Qualifications of judges

The permanent and *ad litem* judges shall be persons of high moral character, impartiality and integrity who possess the qualifications required in their respective countries for appointment to the highest judicial offices. In the overall composition of the Chambers and sections of the Trial Chambers, due account shall be taken of the experience of the judges in criminal law, international law, including international humanitarian law and human rights law.

Article 13 *bis*
Election of permanent judges

1. Fourteen of the permanent judges of the International Tribunal shall be elected by the General Assembly from a list submitted by the Security Council, in the following manner:

(a) The Secretary-General shall invite nominations for judges of the International Tribunal from States Members of the United Nations and non-member States maintaining permanent observer missions at United Nations Headquarters;

(b) Within sixty days of the date of the invitation of the Secretary-General, each State may nominate up to two candidates meeting the qualifications set out in article 13 of the Statute, no two of whom shall be of the same nationality and neither of whom shall be of the same nationality as any judge who is a member of the Appeals Chamber and who was elected or appointed a permanent judge of the International Criminal Tribunal for the Prosecution of Persons Responsible for Genocide and Other Serious Violations of International Humanitarian Law Committed in the Territory of Rwanda and Rwandan Citizens Responsible for Genocide and Other Such Violations Committed in the Territory of Neighbouring States, between 1 January 1994 and 31 December 1994 (hereinafter referred to as "The International Tribunal for Rwanda") in accordance with article 12 *bis* of the Statute of that Tribunal;

(c) The Secretary-General shall forward the nominations received to the Security Council. From the nominations received the Security Council shall establish a list of not less than twenty-eight and not more than forty-two candidates, taking due account of the adequate representation of the principal legal systems of the world;

(d) The President of the Security Council shall transmit the list of candidates to the President of the General Assembly. From that list the General Assembly shall elect fourteen permanent judges of the International Tribunal. The candidates who receive an absolute majority of the votes of the States Members of the United Nations and of the non-member States maintaining permanent observer missions at United Nations Headquarters, shall be declared elected. Should two candidates of the same nationality obtain the required majority vote, the one who received the higher number of votes shall be considered elected.

2. In the event of a vacancy in the Chambers amongst the permanent judges elected or appointed in accordance with this article, after consultation with the Presidents of the Security Council and of the General Assembly, the Secretary-General shall appoint a person meeting the qualifications of article 13 of the Statute, for the remainder of the term of office concerned.

3. The permanent judges elected in accordance with this article shall be elected for a term of four years. The terms and conditions of service shall be those of the judges of the International Court of Justice. They shall be eligible for re-election.

Article 13 *ter*
Election and appointment of *ad litem* judges

1. The *ad litem* judges of the International Tribunal shall be elected by the General Assembly from a list submitted by the Security Council, in the following manner:

(a) The Secretary-General shall invite nominations for *ad litem* judges of the International Tribunal from States Members of the United Nations and non-member States maintaining permanent observer missions at United Nations Headquarters.

(b) Within sixty days of the date of the invitation of the Secretary-General, each State may nominate up to four candidates meeting the qualifications set out in article 13 of the Statute, taking into account the importance of a fair representation of female and male candidates.

(c) The Secretary-General shall forward the nominations received to the Security Council. From the nominations received the Security Council shall establish a list of not less than fifty-four candidates, taking due account of the adequate representation of the principal legal systems of the world and bearing in mind the importance of equitable geographical distribution.

(d) The President of the Security Council shall transmit the list of candidates to the President of the General Assembly. From that list the General Assembly shall elect the twenty-seven *ad litem* judges of the International Tribunal. The candidates who receive an absolute majority of the votes of the States Members of the United Nations and of the non-member States maintaining permanent observer missions at United Nations Headquarters shall be declared elected.

(e) The *ad litem* judges shall be elected for a term of four years. They shall be eligible for re election.

2. During any term, *ad litem* judges will be appointed by the Secretary-General, upon request of the President of the International Tribunal, to serve in the Trial Chambers for one or more trials, for a cumulative period of up to, but not including, three years. When requesting the appointment of any particular *ad litem* judge, the President of the International Tribunal shall bear in mind the criteria set out in article 13 of the Statute regarding the composition of the Chambers and sections of the Trial Chambers, the considerations set out in paragraphs 1 (b) and (c) above and the number of votes the *ad litem* judge received in the General Assembly.

Article 13 *quater*
Status of *ad litem* judges

1. During the period in which they are appointed to serve in the International Tribunal, *ad litem* judges shall:

(a) Benefit from the same terms and conditions of service mutatis mutandis as the permanent judges of the International Tribunal;

(b) Enjoy, subject to paragraph 2 below, the same powers as the permanent judges of the International Tribunal;

(c) Enjoy the privileges and immunities, exemptions and facilities of a judge of the International Tribunal;

(d) Enjoy the power to adjudicate in pre-trial proceedings in cases other than those that they have been appointed to try.

2. During the period in which they are appointed to serve in the International Tribunal, *ad litem* judges shall not:

(a) Be eligible for election as, or to vote in the election of, the President of the Tribunal or the Presiding Judge of a Trial Chamber pursuant to article 14 of the Statute;

(b) Have power:

(i) To adopt rules of procedure and evidence pursuant to article 15 of the Statute. They shall, however, be consulted before the adoption of those rules;

(ii) To review an indictment pursuant to article 19 of the Statute;

(iii) To consult with the President in relation to the assignment of judges pursuant to article 14 of the Statute or in relation to a pardon or commutation of sentence pursuant to article 28 of the Statute.

3. Notwithstanding, paragraphs 1 and 2 above, an *ad litem* judge who is serving as a reserve judge shall, during such time as he or she so serves:

(a) Benefit from the same terms and conditions of service mutatis mutandis as the permanent judges of the International Tribunal;

(b) Enjoy the privileges and immunities, exemptions and facilities of a judge of the International Tribunal;

(c) Enjoy the power to adjudicate in pre-trial proceedings in cases other than those that they have been appointed to and for that purpose to enjoy subject to paragraph 2 above, the same powers as permanent judges.

4. In the event that a reserve judge replaces a judge who is unable to continue sitting, he or she will, as of that time, benefit from the provisions of paragraph 1 above.

Article 14
Officers and members of the Chambers

1. The permanent judges of the International Tribunal shall elect a President from amongst their number.

2. The President of the International Tribunal shall be a member of the Appeals Chamber and shall preside over its proceedings.

3. After consultation with the permanent judges of the International Tribunal, the President shall assign four of the permanent judges elected or appointed in accordance with Article 13 *bis* of the Statute to the Appeals Chamber and nine to the Trial Chambers.

4. Two of the permanent judges of the International Tribunal for Rwanda elected or appointed in accordance with article 12 *bis* of the Statute of that Tribunal shall be assigned by the President of that Tribunal, in consultation with the President of the International Tribunal, to be members of the Appeals Chamber and permanent judges of the International Tribunal.

5. After consultation with the permanent judges of the International Tribunal, the President shall assign such *ad litem* judges as may from time to time be appointed to serve in the International Tribunal to the Trial Chambers.

6. A judge shall serve only in the Chamber to which he or she was assigned.

7. The permanent judges of each Trial Chamber shall elect a Presiding Judge from amongst their number, who shall oversee the work of the Trial Chamber as a whole.

Article 15
Rules of procedure and evidence

The judges of the International Tribunal shall adopt rules of procedure and evidence for the conduct of the pre-trial phase of the proceedings, trials and appeals, the admission of evidence, the protection of victims and witnesses and other appropriate matters.

Article 16
The Prosecutor

1. The Prosecutor shall be responsible for the investigation and prosecution of persons responsible for serious violations of international humanitarian law committed in the territory of the former Yugoslavia since 1 January 1991.

2. The Prosecutor shall act independently as a separate organ of the International Tribunal. He or she shall not seek or receive instructions from any Government or from any other source.

3. The Office of the Prosecutor shall be composed of a Prosecutor and such other qualified staff as may be required.

4. The Prosecutor shall be appointed by the Security Council on nomination by the Secretary-General. He or she shall be of high moral character and possess the highest level of competence and experience in the conduct of investigations and prosecutions of criminal cases. The Prosecutor shall serve for a four-year term and be eligible for reappointment. The terms and conditions of service of the Prosecutor shall be those of an Under-Secretary-General of the United Nations.

5. The staff of the Office of the Prosecutor shall be appointed by the Secretary-General on the recommendation of the Prosecutor.

Article 17
The Registry

1. The Registry shall be responsible for the administration and servicing of the International Tribunal.

2. The Registry shall consist of a Registrar and such other staff as may be required.

3. The Registrar shall be appointed by the Secretary-General after consultation with the President of the International Tribunal. He or she shall serve for a four-year term and be eligible for reappointment. The terms and conditions of service of the Registrar shall be those of an Assistant Secretary-General of the United Nations.

4. The staff of the Registry shall be appointed by the Secretary-General on the recommendation of the Registrar.

Article 18
Investigation and preparation of indictment

1. The Prosecutor shall initiate investigations *ex-officio* or on the basis of information obtained from any source, particularly from Governments, United Nations organs, intergovernmental and nongovernmental organisations. The Prosecutor shall assess the information received or obtained and decide whether there is sufficient basis to proceed.

2. The Prosecutor shall have the power to question suspects, victims and witnesses, to collect evidence and to conduct on-site investigations. In carrying out these tasks, the Prosecutor may, as appropriate, seek the assistance of the State authorities concerned.

3. If questioned, the suspect shall be entitled to be assisted by counsel of his own choice, including the right to have legal assistance assigned to him without payment by him in any such case if he does not have sufficient means to pay for it, as well as to necessary translation into and from a language he speaks and understands.

4. Upon a determination that a *prima facie* case exists, the Prosecutor shall prepare an indictment containing a concise statement of the facts and the crime or crimes with which the accused is charged under the Statute. The indictment shall be transmitted to a judge of the Trial Chamber.

Article 19
Review of the indictment

1. The judge of the Trial Chamber to whom the indictment has been transmitted shall review it. If satisfied that a *prima facie* case has been established by the Prosecutor, he shall confirm the indictment. If not so satisfied, the indictment shall be dismissed.

2. Upon confirmation of an indictment, the judge may, at the request of the Prosecutor, issue such orders and warrants for the arrest, detention, surrender or transfer of persons, and any other orders as may be required for the conduct of the trial.

Article 20
Commencement and conduct of trial proceedings

1. The Trial Chambers shall ensure that a trial is fair and expeditious and that proceedings are conducted in accordance with the rules of procedure and evidence, with full respect for the rights of the accused and due regard for the protection of victims and witnesses.

2. A person against whom an indictment has been confirmed shall, pursuant to an order or an arrest warrant of the International Tribunal, be taken into custody, immediately informed of the charges against him and transferred to the International Tribunal.

3. The Trial Chamber shall read the indictment, satisfy itself that the rights of the accused are respected, confirm that the accused understands the indictment, and instruct the accused to enter a plea. The Trial Chamber shall then set the date for trial.

4. The hearings shall be public unless the Trial Chamber decides to close the proceedings in accordance with its rules of procedure and evidence.

Article 21
Rights of the accused

1. All persons shall be equal before the International Tribunal.

2. In the determination of charges against him, the accused shall be entitled to a fair and public hearing, subject to article 22 of the Statute.

3. The accused shall be presumed innocent until proved guilty according to the provisions of the present Statute.

4. In the determination of any charge against the accused pursuant to the present Statute, the accused shall be entitled to the following minimum guarantees, in full equality:

(a) to be informed promptly and in detail in a language which he understands of the nature and cause of the charge against him;

(b) to have adequate time and facilities for the preparation of his defence and to communicate with counsel of his own choosing;

(c) to be tried without undue delay;

(d) to be tried in his presence, and to defend himself in person or through legal assistance of his own choosing; to be informed, if he does not have legal assistance, of this right; and to have legal assistance assigned to him, in any case where the interests of justice so require, and without payment by him in any such case if he does not have sufficient means to pay for it;

(e) to examine, or have examined, the witnesses against him and to obtain the attendance and examination of witnesses on his behalf under the same conditions as witnesses against him;

(f) to have the free assistance of an interpreter if he cannot understand or speak the language used in the International Tribunal;

(g) not to be compelled to testify against himself or to confess guilt.

Article 22
Protection of victims and witnesses

The International Tribunal shall provide in its rules of procedure and evidence for the protection of victims and witnesses. Such protection measures shall include, but shall not be limited to, the conduct of in camera proceedings and the protection of the victim's identity.

Article 23
Judgement

1. The Trial Chambers shall pronounce judgements and impose sentences and penalties on persons convicted of serious violations of international humanitarian law.

2. The judgement shall be rendered by a majority of the judges of the Trial Chamber, and shall be delivered by the Trial Chamber in public. It shall be accompanied by a reasoned opinion in writing, to which separate or dissenting opinions may be appended.

Article 24
Penalties

1. The penalty imposed by the Trial Chamber shall be limited to imprisonment. In determining the terms of imprisonment, the Trial Chambers shall have recourse to the general practice regarding prison sentences in the courts of the former Yugoslavia.

2. In imposing the sentences, the Trial Chambers should take into account such factors as the gravity of the offence and the individual circumstances of the convicted person.

3. In addition to imprisonment, the Trial Chambers may order the return of any property and proceeds acquired by criminal conduct, including by means of duress, to their rightful owners.

Article 25
Appellate proceedings

1. The Appeals Chamber shall hear appeals from persons convicted by the Trial Chambers or from the Prosecutor on the following grounds:

(a) an error on a question of law invalidating the decision; or

(b) an error of fact which has occasioned a miscarriage of justice.

2. The Appeals Chamber may affirm, reverse or revise the decisions taken by the Trial Chambers.

Article 26
Review proceedings

Where a new fact has been discovered which was not known at the time of the proceedings before the Trial Chambers or the Appeals Chamber and which could have been a decisive factor in reaching the decision, the convicted person or the Prosecutor may submit to the International Tribunal an application for review of the judgement.

Article 27
Enforcement of sentences

Imprisonment shall be served in a State designated by the International Tribunal from a list of States which have indicated to the Security Council their willingness to accept convicted persons. Such imprisonment shall be in accordance with the applicable law of the State concerned, subject to the supervision of the International Tribunal.

Article 28
Pardon or commutation of sentences

If, pursuant to the applicable law of the State in which the convicted person is imprisoned, he or she is eligible for pardon or commutation of sentence, the State concerned shall notify the International Tribunal accordingly. The President of the International Tribunal, in consultation with the judges, shall decide the matter on the basis of the interests of justice and the general principles of law.

Article 29
Co-operation and judicial assistance

1. States shall co-operate with the International Tribunal in the investigation and prosecution of persons accused of committing serious violations of international humanitarian law.
2. States shall comply without undue delay with any request for assistance or an order issued by a Trial Chamber, including, but not limited to:
    (a) the identification and location of persons;
    (b) the taking of testimony and the production of evidence;
    (c) the service of documents;
    (d) the arrest or detention of persons;
    (e) the surrender or the transfer of the accused to the International Tribunal.

Article 30
The status, privileges and immunities of the International Tribunal

1. The Convention on the Privileges and Immunities of the United Nations of 13 February 1946 shall apply to the International Tribunal, the judges, the Prosecutor and his staff, and the Registrar and his staff.
2. The judges, the Prosecutor and the Registrar shall enjoy the privileges and immunities, exemptions and facilities accorded to diplomatic envoys, in accordance with international law.
3. The staff of the Prosecutor and of the Registrar shall enjoy the privileges and immunities accorded to officials of the United Nations under articles V and VII of the Convention referred to in paragraph 1 of this article.
4. Other persons, including the accused, required at the seat of the International Tribunal shall be accorded such treatment as is necessary for the proper functioning of the International Tribunal.

Article 31
Seat of the International Tribunal

The International Tribunal shall have its seat at The Hague.

Article 32
Expenses of the International Tribunal

The expenses of the International Tribunal shall be borne by the regular budget of the United Nations in accordance with Article 17 of the Charter of the United Nations.

Article 33
Working languages

The working languages of the International Tribunal shall be English and French.

Article 34
Annual report

The President of the International Tribunal shall submit an annual report of the International Tribunal to the Security Council and to the General Assembly.

STATUTE OF THE INTERNATIONAL TRIBUNAL FOR RWANDA

Statute of the International Tribunal for Rwanda, *adopted by* S.C. Res. 955, U.N. Doc. S/RES/955 (Nov. 8, 1994), *as amended by* S.C. Res. 1165, U.N. Doc. S/RES/1165 (Nov. 30, 2000); S.C. Res. 1411, U.N. Doc. S/RES/1411 (May 17, 2002); S.C. Res. 1431, U.N. Doc. S/RES/1431 (Aug. 14, 2002), *available at* http://www2.ohchr.org/english/law/itr.htm

As amended by the Security Council acting under Chapter VII of the Charter of the United Nations, the International Criminal Tribunal for the Prosecution of Persons Responsible for Genocide and Other Serious Violations of International Humanitarian Law Committed in the Territory of Rwanda and Rwandan Citizens responsible for genocide and other such violations committed in the territory of neighbouring States, between 1 January 1994 and 31 December 1994 (hereinafter referred to as "The International Tribunal for Rwanda") shall function in accordance with the provisions of the present Statute.

Article 1: Competence of the International Tribunal for Rwanda

The International Tribunal for Rwanda shall have the power to prosecute persons responsible for serious violations of international humanitarian law committed in the territory of Rwanda and Rwandan citizens responsible for such violations committed in the territory of neighbouring States between 1 January 1994 and 31 December 1994, in accordance with the provisions of the present Statute.

Article 2: Genocide

1. The International Tribunal for Rwanda shall have the power to prosecute persons committing genocide as defined in paragraph 2 of this Article or of committing any of the other acts enumerated in paragraph 3 of this Article.
2. Genocide means any of the following acts committed with intent to destroy, in whole or in part, a national, ethnical, racial or religious group, as such:
> (a) Killing members of the group;
> (b) Causing serious bodily or mental harm to members of the group;
> (c) Deliberately inflicting on the group conditions of life calculated to bring about its physical destruction in whole or in part;
> (d) Imposing measures intended to prevent births within the group;
> (e) Forcibly transferring children of the group to another group.
3. The following acts shall be punishable:
> (a) Genocide;
> (b) Conspiracy to commit genocide;
> (c) Direct and public incitement to commit genocide;
> (d) Attempt to commit genocide;
> (e) Complicity in genocide.

Article 3: Crimes against Humanity

The International Tribunal for Rwanda shall have the power to prosecute persons responsible for the following crimes when committed as part of a widespread or systematic attack against any civilian population on national, political, ethnic, racial or religious grounds:
> (a) Murder;
> (b) Extermination;
> (c) Enslavement;
> (d) Deportation;
> (e) Imprisonment;
> (f) Torture;

(g) Rape;

(h) Persecutions on political, racial and religious grounds;

(i) Other inhumane acts.

Article 4: Violations of Article 3 Common to the Geneva Conventions and of Additional Protocol II

The International Tribunal for Rwanda shall have the power to prosecute persons
committing or ordering to be committed serious violations of Article 3 common to the Geneva Conventions of 12 August 1949 for the Protection of War Victims, and of Additional Protocol II thereto of 8 June 1977. These violations shall include, but shall not be limited to:

(a) Violence to life, health and physical or mental well-being of persons, in particular murder as well as cruel treatment such as torture, mutilation or any form of corporal punishment;

(b) Collective punishments;

(c) Taking of hostages;

(d) Acts of terrorism;

(e) Outrages upon personal dignity, in particular humiliating and degrading treatment, rape, enforced prostitution and any form of indecent assault;

(f) Pillage;

(g) The passing of sentences and the carrying out of executions without previous judgement pronounced by a regularly constituted court, affording all the judicial guarantees which are recognized as indispensable by civilised peoples;

(h) Threats to commit any of the foregoing acts.

Article 5: Personal Jurisdiction

The International Tribunal for Rwanda shall have jurisdiction over natural persons pursuant to the provisions of the present Statute.

Article 6: Individual Criminal Responsibility

1. A person who planned, instigated, ordered, committed or otherwise aided and abetted in the planning, preparation or execution of a crime referred to in Articles 2 to 4 of the present Statute, shall be individually responsible for the crime.

2. The official position of any accused person, whether as Head of state or government or as a responsible government official, shall not relieve such person of criminal responsibility nor mitigate punishment.

3. The fact that any of the acts referred to in Articles 2 to 4 of the present Statute was committed by a subordinate does not relieve his or her superior of criminal responsibility if he or she knew or had reason to k now that the subordinate was about to commit such acts or had done so and the superior failed to take the necessary and reasonable measures to prevent such acts or to punish the perpetrators thereof.

4. The fact that an accused person acted pursuant to an order of a government or of a superior shall not relieve him or her of criminal responsibility, but may be considered in mitigation of punishment if the International Tribunal for Rwanda determines that justice so requires.

Article 7: Territorial and Temporal Jurisdiction

The territorial jurisdiction of the International Tribunal for Rwanda shall extend to the territory of Rwanda including its land surface and airspace as well as to the territory of neighbouring States in respect of serious violations of international humanitarian law committed by Rwandan citizens. The temporal jurisdiction of the International Tribunal for Rwanda shall extend to a period beginning on 1 January 1994 and ending on 31 December 1994.

Article 8: Concurrent Jurisdiction

1. The International Tribunal for Rwanda and national courts shall have concurrent jurisdiction to prosecute persons for serious violations of international humanitarian law committed in the territory of Rwanda and Rwandan citizens for such violations committed in the territory of the neighbouring States, between 1 January 1994 and 31 December 1994.

2. The International Tribunal for Rwanda shall have the primacy over the national courts of all States. At any stage of the procedure, the International Tribunal for Rwanda may formally request national courts to

defer to its competence in accordance with the present Statute and the Rules of Procedure and Evidence of the International Tribunal for Rwanda.

Article 9: *Non Bis in Idem*

1. No person shall be tried before a national court for acts constituting serious violations of international humanitarian law under the present Statute, for which he or she has already been tried by the Internationa l Tribunal for Rwanda.

2. A person who has been tried before a national court for acts constituting serious violations of international humanitarian law may be subsequently tried by the International Tribunal for Rwanda only if:

(a) The act for which he or she was tried was characterised as an ordinary crime; or

(b) The national court proceedings were not impartial or independent, were designed to shield the accused from international criminal responsibility, or the case was not diligently prosecuted.

3. In considering the penalty to be imposed on a person convicted of a crime under the present Statute, the International Tribunal for Rwanda shall take into account the extent to which any penalty imposed by a national court on the same person for the same act has already been served.

Article 10: Organisation of the International Tribunal for Rwanda

The International Tribunal for Rwanda shall consist of the following organs:

(a) The Chambers, comprising three Trial Chambers and an Appeals Chamber;

(b) The Prosecutor;

(c) A Registry.

Article 11: Composition of the Chambers

1. The Chambers shall be composed of sixteen permanent independent judges, no two of whom may be nationals of the same State, and a maximum at any one time of nine *ad litem* independent judges appointed in accordance with article 12 *ter*, paragraph 2, of the present Statute, no two of whom may be nationals of the same State.

2. Three permanent judges and a maximum at any one time of six *ad litem* judges shall be members of each Trial Chamber. Each Trial Chamber to which *ad litem* judges are assigned may be divided into sections of three judges each, composed of both permanent and *ad litem* judges. A section of a Trial Chamber shall have the same powers and responsibilities as a Trial Chamber under the present Statute and shall render judgement in accordance with the same rules.

3. Seven of the permanent judges shall be members of the Appeals Chamber. The Appeals Chamber shall, for each appeal, be composed of five of its members.

4. A person who for the purposes of membership of the Chambers of the International Tribunal for Rwanda could be regarded as a national of more than one State shall be deemed to be a national of the State in which that person ordinarily exercises civil and political rights.

Article 12: Qualification and Election of Judges

The permanent and *ad litem* judges shall be persons of high moral character, impartiality and integrity who possess the qualifications required in their respective countries for appointment to the highest judicia l offices. In the overall composition of the Chambers and sections of the Trial Chambers, due account shall be taken of the experience of the judges in criminal law, international law, including international humanitarian law and human rights law.

Article 12 *bis*: Election of Permanent Judges

1. Eleven of the permanent judges of the International Tribunal for Rwanda shall be elected by the General Assembly from a list submitted by the Security Council, in the following manner:

(a) The Secretary-General shall invite nominations for permanent judges of the International Tribunal for Rwanda from States Members of the United Nations and non-member States maintaining permanent observer missions at United Nations Headquarters;

(b) Within sixty days of the date of the invitation of the Secretary-General, each State may nominate up to two candidates meeting the qualifications set out in article 12 of the present Statute, no two of whom shall be of the same nationality and neither of whom shall be of the same nationality as any judge who is a member of the Appeals Chamber and who was elected or appointed a permanent judge of the International Tribunal for the Prosecution of Persons

Responsible for Serious Violations of International Humanitarian Law Committed in the Territory of the Former Yugoslavia since 1991 (hereinafter referred to as 'the International Tribunal for the Former Yugoslavia') in accordance with article 13 *bis* of the Statute of that Tribunal;

(c) The Secretary-General shall forward the nominatio ns received to the Security Council. From the nominations received the Security Council shall establish a list of not less than twenty-two and not more than thirty-three candidates, taking due account of the adequate representation on the International Tribunal for Rwanda of the principal legal systems of the world;

(d) The President of the Security Council shall transmit the list of candidates to thePresident of the General Assembly. From that list the General Assembly shall elect eleven permanent judges of the International Tribunal for Rwanda. The candidates who receive an absolute majority of the votes of the States Members of the United Nations and of the non-member States maintaining permanent observer missions at United Nations Headquarters, shall be declared elected. Should two candidates of the same nationality obtain the required majority vote, the one who received the higher number of votes shall be considered elected.

2. In the event of a vacancy in the Chambers amongst the permanent judges elected or appointed in accordance with this article, after consultation with the Presidents of the Security Council and of the General Assembly, the Secretary-General shall appoint a person meeting the qualifications of article 12 of the present Statute, for the remainder of the term of office concerned.

3. The permanent judges elected in accordance with this article shall be elected for a term of four years. The terms and conditions of service shall be those of the permanent judges of the International Tribunal for the Former Yugoslavia. They shall be eligible for re-election.

Article 12 *ter*: Election and Appointment of *Ad litem* Judges

1. The *ad litem* judges of the International Tribunal for Rwanda shall be elected by the General Assembly from a list submitted by the Security Council, in the following manner:

(a) The Secretary-General shall invite nominations for *ad litem* judges of the International Tribunal for Rwanda from States Members of the United Nations and non-member States maintaining permanent observer missions at United Nations Headquarters;

(b) Within sixty days of the date of the invitation of the Secretary-General, each State may nominate up to four candidates meeting the qualifications set out in article 12 of the present Statute, taking into account the importance of a fair representation of female and male candidates;

(c) The Secretary-General shall forward the nominations received to the Security Council. From the nominations received the Security Council shall establish a list of not less than thirty-six candidates, taking due account of the adequate representation of the principal legal systems of the world and bearing in mind the importance of equitable geographical distribution;

(d) The President of the Security Council shall transmit the list of candidates to the President of the General Assembly. From that list the General Assembly shall elect the eighteen *ad litem* judges of the International Tribunal for Rwanda. The candidates who receive an absolute majority of the votes of the States Members of the United Nations and of the non-member States maintaining permanent observer missions at United Nations Headquarters shall be declared elected;

(e) The *ad litem* judges shall be elected for a term of four years. They shall not be eligible for re election.

2. During their term, *ad litem* judges will be appointed by the Secretary-General, upon request of the President of the International Tribunal for Rwanda, to serve in the Trial Chambers for one or more trials, for a cumulative period of up to, but not including, three years. When requesting the appointment of any particular *ad litem* judge, the President of the International Tribunal for Rwanda shall bear in mind the criteria set out in article 12 of the present Statute regarding the composition of the Chambers and sections of the Trial Chambers, the considerations set out in paragraphs 1 (b) and (c) above and the number of votes the *ad litem* judge received in the General Assembly.

Article 12 *quater*: Status of *Ad litem* Judges

1. During the period in which they are appointed to serve in the International Tribunal for Rwanda, *ad litem* judges shall:

(a) Benefit from the same terms and conditions of service *mutatis mutandis* as the permanent judges of the International Tribunal for Rwanda;

(b) Enjoy, subject to paragraph 2 below, the same powers as the permanent judges of the International Tribunal for Rwanda;

(c) Enjoy the privileges and immunities, exemptions and facilities of a judge of the International Tribunal for Rwanda;

(d) Enjoy the power to adjudicate in pre-trial proceedings in cases other than those that they have been appointed to try.

2. During the period in which they are appointed to serve in the International Tribunal for Rwanda, *ad litem* judges shall not:

(a) Be eligible for election as, or to vote in the election of, the President of the International Tribunal for Rwanda or the Presiding Judge of a Trial Chamber pursuant to article 13 of the present Statute;

(b) Have power:

(i) To adopt rules of procedure and evidence pursuant to article 14 of the present Statute. They shall, however, be consulted before the adoption of those rules;

(ii) To review an indictment pursuant to article 18 of the present Statute;

(iii) To consult with the President of the International Tribunal for Rwanda in relation to the assignment of judges pursuant to article 13 of the present Statute or in relation to a pardon or commutation of sentence pursuant to article 27 of the present Statute.

Article 13: Officers and Members of the Chambers

1. The permanent judges of the International Tribunal for Rwanda shall elect a President from amongst their number.

2. The President of the International Tribunal for Rwanda shall be a member of one of its Trial Chambers.

3. After consultation with the permanent judges of the International Tribunal for Rwanda, the President shall assign two of the permanent judges elected or appointed in accordance with article 12 *bis* of the present Statute to be members of the Appeals Chamber of the International Tribunal for the Former Yugoslavia and eight to the Trial Chambers o f the International Tribunal for Rwanda.

4. The members of the Appeals Chamber of the International Tribunal for the Former Yugoslavia shall also serve as the members of the Appeals Chamber of the International Tribunal for Rwanda.

5. After consultation with the permanent judges of the International Tribunal for Rwanda, the President shall assign such *ad litem* judges as may from time to time be appointed to serve in the International Tribunal for Rwanda to the Trial Chambers.

6. A judge shall serve only in the Chamber to which he or she was assigned.

7. The permanent judges of each Trial Chamber shall elect a Presiding Judge from amongst their number, who shall oversee the work of that Trial Chamber as a whole.

Article 14: Rules of Procedure and Evidence

The Judges of the International Tribunal for Rwanda shall adopt, for the purpose of proceedings before the International Tribunal for Rwanda, the Rules of Procedure and Evidence for the conduct of the pre-trial phase of the proceedings, trials and appeals, the admission of evidence, the protection of victims and witnesses and other appropriate matters of the International Tribunal for the former Yugoslavia with such changes as they deem necessary.

Article 15: The Prosecutor

1. The Prosecutor shall be responsible for the investigation and prosecution of persons responsible for serious violations of international humanitarian law committed in the territory of Rwanda and Rwandan citizens responsible for such violations committed in the territory of neighbouring States, between 1 January 1994 and 31 December 1994.

2. The Prosecutor shall act independently as a separate organ of the International Tribunal for Rwanda. He or she shall not seek or receive instructions from any government or from any other source.

3. The Office of the Prosecutor shall be composed of a Prosecutor and such other qualified staff as may be required.

4. The Prosecutor shall be appointed by the Security Council on nomination by the Secretary-General. He or she shall be of high moral character and possess the highest level of competence and experience in the conduct of investigations and prosecutions of criminal cases. The Prosecutor shall serve for a four-year

term and be eligible for reappointment. The terms and conditions of service of the Prosecutor shall be those of an Under-Secretary-General of the United Nations.

5. The staff of the Office of the Prosecutor shall be appointed by the Secretary-General on the recommendation of the Prosecutor.

Article 16: The Registry

1. The Registry shall be responsible for the administration and servicing of the International Tribunal for Rwanda.

2. The Registry shall consist of a Registrar and such other staff as may be required.

3. The Registrar shall be appointed by the Secretary-General after consultation with the President of the International Tribunal for Rwanda. He or she shall serve for a four-year term and be eligible for re-appointment. The terms and conditions of service of the Registrar shall be those of an Assistant Secretary-General of the United Nations.

4. The Staff of the Registry shall be appointed by the Secretary-General on the recommendation of the Registrar.

Article 17: Investigation and Preparation of Indictment

1. The Prosecutor shall initiate investigations ex-officio or on the basis of information obtained from any source, particularly from governments, United Nations organs, intergovernmental and non-governmental organizations. The Prosecutor shall assess the information received or obtained and decide whether there is sufficient basis to proceed.

2. The Prosecutor shall have the power to question suspects, victims and witnesses, to collect evidence and to conduct on-site investigations. In carrying out these tasks, the Prosecutor may, as appropriate, seek the assistance of the State authorities concerned.

3. If questioned, the suspect shall be entitled to be assisted by Counsel of his or her own choice, including the right to have legal assistance assigned to the suspect without payment by him or her in any such case if he or she does not have sufficient means to pay for it, as well as necessary translation into and from a language he or she speaks and understands.

4. Upon a determination that a *prima facie* case exists, the Prosecutor shall prepare an indictment containing a concise statement of the facts and the crime or crimes with which the accused is charged under the Statute. The indictment shall be transmitted to a judge of the Trial Chamber.

Article 18: Review of the Indictment

1. The judge of the Trial Chamber to whom the indictment has been transmitted shall review it. If satisfied that a *prima facie* case has been established by the Prosecutor, he or she shall confirm the indictment. If not so satisfied, the indictment shall be dismissed.

2. Upon confirmation of an indictment, the judge may, at the request of the Prosecutor, issue such orders and warrants for the arrest, detention, surrender or transfer of persons, and any other orders as may be required for the conduct of the trial.

Article 19: Commencement and Conduct of Trial Proceedings

1. The Trial Chambers shall ensure that a trial is fair and expeditious and that proceedings are conducted in accordance with the Rules of Procedure and Evidence, with full respect for the rights of the accused and due regard for the protection of victims and witnesses.

2. A person against whom an indictment has been confirmed shall, pursuant to an order or an arrest warrant of the International Tribunal for Rwanda, be taken into custody, immediately informed of the charges against him or her and transferred to the International Tribunal for Rwanda.

3. The Trial Chamber shall read the indictment, satisfy itself that the rights of the accused are respected, confirm that the accused understands the indictment, and instruct the accused to enter a plea. The Trial Chamber shall then set the date for trial.

4. The hearings shall be public unless the Trial Chamber decides to close the proceedings in accordance with its Rules of Procedure and Evidence.

Article 20: Rights of the Accused

1. All persons shall be equal before the International Tribunal for Rwanda.

2. In the determination of charges against him or her, the accused shall be entitled to a fair and public hearing, subject to Article 21 of the Statute.

3. The accused shall be presumed innocent until proven guilty according to the provisions of the present Statute.

4. In the determination of any charge against the accused pursuant to the present Statute, the accused shall be entitled to the following minimum guarantees, in full equality:

> (a) To be informed promptly and in detail in a language which he or she understands of the nature and cause of the charge against him or her;
>
> (b) To have adequate time and facilities fo r the preparation of his or her defence and to communicate with counsel of his or her own choosing;
>
> (c) To be tried without undue delay;
>
> (d) To be tried in his or her presence, and to defend himself or herself in person or through legal assistance of his or her own choosing; to be informed, if he or she does not have legal assistance, of this right; and to have legal assistance assigned to him or her, in any case where the interest of justice so require, and without payment by him or her in any such case if he or she does not have sufficient means to pay for it;
>
> (e) To examine, or have examined, the witnesses against him or her and to obtain the attendance and examination of witnesses on his or her behalf under the same conditions as witnesses against him or her;
>
> (f) To have the free assistance of an interpreter if he or she cannot understand or speak the language used in the International Tribunal for Rwanda;
>
> (g) Not to be compelled to testify against himself or herself or to confess guilt.

Article 21: Protection of Victims and Witnesses

The International Tribunal for Rwanda shall provide in its Rules of Procedure and Evidence for the protection of victims and witnesses. Such protection measures shall include, but shall not be limited to, the conduct of in camera proceedings and the protection of the victim's identity.

Article 22: Judgement

1. The Trial Chambers shall pronounce judgements and impose sentences and penalties on persons convicted of serious violations of international humanitarian law.

2. The judgement shall be rendered by a majority of the judges of the Trial Chamber, and shall be delivered by the Trial Chamber in public. It shall be accompanied by a reasoned opinion in writing, to which separate or dissenting opinions may be appended.

Article 23: Penalties

1. The penalty imposed by the Trial Chamber shall be limited to imprisonment. In determining the terms of imprisonment, the Trial Chambers shall have recourse to the general practice regarding prison sentences in the courts of Rwanda.

2. In imposing the sentences, the Trial Chambers should take into account such factors as the gravity of the offence and the individual circumstances of the convicted person.

3. In addition to imprisonment, the Trial Chambers may order the return of any property and proceeds acquired by criminal conduct, including by means of duress, to their rightful owners.

Article 24: Appellate Proceedings

1. The Appeals Chamber shall hear appeals from persons convicted by the Trial Chambers or from the Prosecutor on the following grounds:

> (a) An error on a question of law invalidating the decision; or
>
> (b) An error of fact which has occasioned a miscarriage of justice.

2. The Appeals Chamber may affirm, reverse or revise the decisions taken by the Trial Chambers.

Article 25: Review Proceedings

Where a new fact has been discovered which was not known at the time of the proceedings before the Trial Chambers or the Appeals Chamber and which could have been a decisive factor in reaching the decision, the convicted person or the Prosecutor may submit to the International Tribunal for Rwanda an application for review of the judgement.

Article 26: Enforcement of Sentences

Imprisonment shall be served in Rwanda or any of the States on a list of States which have indicated to the Security Council their willingness to accept convicted persons, as designated by the International Tribunal for Rwanda. Such imprisonment shall be in accordance with the applicable law of the State concerned, subject to the supervision of the International Tribunal for Rwanda.

Article 27: Pardon or Commutation of Sentences

If, pursuant to the applicable law of the State in which the convicted person is imprisoned, he or she is eligible for pardon or commutation of sentence, the State concerned shall notify the International Tribunal for Rwanda accordingly. There shall only be pardon or commutation of sentence if the President of the International Tribunal for Rwanda, in consultation with the judges, so decides on the basis of the interests of justice and the general principles of law.

Article 28: Cooperation and Judicial Assistance

1. States shall cooperate with the International Tribunal for Rwanda in the investigation and prosecution of persons accused of committing serious violations of international humanitarian law.
2. States shall comply without undue delay with any request for assistance or an order issued by a Trial Chamber, including but not limited to:
> (a) The identification and location of persons;
> (b) The taking of testimony and the production of evidence;
> (c) The service of documents;
> (d) The arrest or detention of persons;
> (e) The surrender or the transfer of the accused to the International Tribunal for Rwanda.

Article 29: The Status, Privileges and Immunities of the International Tribunal for Rwanda

1. The Convention on the Privileges and Immunities of the United Nations of 13 February 1946 shall apply to the International Tribunal for Rwanda, the judges, the Prosecutor and his or her staff, and the Registrar and his or her staff.
2. The judges, the Prosecutor and the Registrar shall enjoy the privileges and immunities, exemptions and facilities accorded to diplomatic envoys, in accordance with international law.
3. The staff of the Prosecutor and of the Registrar shall enjoy the privileges and immunities accorded to officials of the United Nations under Articles V and VII of the Convention referred to in paragraph 1 of this article.
4. Other persons, including the accused, required at the seat or meeting place of the International Tribunal for Rwanda shall be accorded such treatment as is necessary for the proper functioning of the International Tribunal for Rwanda.

Article 30: Expenses of the International Tribunal for Rwanda

The expenses of the International Tribunal for Rwanda shall be expenses of the Organisation in accordance with Article 17 of the Charter of the United Nations.

Article 31: Working Languages

The working languages of the International Tribunal for Rwanda shall be English and French.

Article 32: Annual Report

The President of t he International Tribunal for Rwanda shall submit an annual report of the International Tribunal for Rwanda to the Security Council and to the General Assembly.

ROME STATUTE OF THE INTERNATIONAL CRIMINAL COURT

Rome Statute of the International Criminal Court, *adopted* July 17, 1998, 2187 U.N.T.S. 90

PREAMBLE

The States Parties to this Statute,

Conscious that all peoples are united by common bonds, their cultures pieced together in a shared heritage, and concerned that this delicate mosaic may be shattered at any time,

Mindful that during this century millions of children, women and men have been victims of unimaginable atrocities that deeply shock the conscience of humanity,

Recognizing that such grave crimes threaten the peace, security and well being of the world,

Affirming that the most serious crimes of concern to the international community as a whole must not go unpunished and that their effective prosecution must be ensured by taking measures at the national level and by enhancing international cooperation,

Determined to put an end to impunity for the perpetrators of these crimes and thus to contribute to the prevention of such crimes,

Recalling that it is the duty of every State to exercise its criminal jurisdiction over those responsible for international crimes,

Reaffirming the Purposes and Principles of the Charter of the United Nations, and in particular that all States shall refrain from the threat or use of force against the territorial integrity or political independence of any State, or in any other manner inconsistent with the Purposes of the United Nations,

Emphasizing in this connection that nothing in this Statute shall be taken as authorizing any State Party to intervene in an armed conflict in the internal affairs of any State,

Determined to these ends and for the sake of present and future generations, to establish an independent permanent International Criminal Court in relationship with the United Nations system, with jurisdiction over the most serious crimes of concern to the international community as a whole,

Emphasizing that the International Criminal Court established under this Statute shall be complementary to national criminal jurisdictions,

Resolved to guarantee lasting respect for the enforcement of international justice,

Have agreed as follows:

PART 1. ESTABLISHMENT OF THE COURT

Article 1
The Court

An International Criminal Court ("the Court") is hereby established. It shall be a permanent institution and shall have the power to exercise its jurisdiction over persons for the most serious crimes of international concern, as referred to in this Statute, and shall be complementary to national criminal jurisdictions. The jurisdiction and functioning of the Court shall be governed by the provisions of this Statute.

Article 2
Relationship of the Court with the United Nations

The Court shall be brought into relationship with the United Nations through an agreement to be approved by the Assembly of States Parties to this Statute and thereafter concluded by the President of the Court on its behalf.

Article 3
Seat of the Court

1. The seat of the Court shall be established at The Hague in the Netherlands ("the host State").
2. The Court shall enter into a headquarters agreement with the host State, to be approved by the Assembly of States Parties and thereafter concluded by the President of the Court on its behalf.
3. The Court may sit elsewhere, whenever it considers it desirable, as provided in this Statute.

Article 4
Legal status and powers of the Court

1. The Court shall have international legal personality. It shall also have such legal capacity as may be necessary for the exercise of its functions and the fulfilment of its purposes.
2. The Court may exercise its functions and powers, as provided in this Statute, on the territory of any State Party and, by special agreement, on the territory of any other State.

PART 2. JURISDICTION, ADMISSIBILITY AND APPLICABLE LAW

Article 5
Crimes within the jurisdiction of the Court

1. The jurisdiction of the Court shall be limited to the most serious crimes of concern to the international community as a whole. The Court has jurisdiction in accordance with this Statute with respect to the following crimes:
> (a) The crime of genocide;
> (b) Crimes against humanity;
> (c) War crimes;
> (d) The crime of aggression.

2. The Court shall exercise jurisdiction over the crime of aggression once a provision is adopted in accordance with articles 121 and 123 defining the crime and setting out the conditions under which the Court shall exercise jurisdiction with respect to this crime. Such a provision shall be consistent with the relevant provisions of the Charter of the United Nations.

Article 6
Genocide

For the purpose of this Statute, "genocide" means any of the following acts committed with intent to destroy, in whole or in part, a national, ethnical, racial or religious group, as such:
> (a) Killing members of the group;
> (b) Causing serious bodily or mental harm to members of the group;
> (c) Deliberately inflicting on the group conditions of life calculated to bring about its physical destruction in whole or in part;
> (d) Imposing measures intended to prevent births within the group;
> (e) Forcibly transferring children of the group to another group.

Article 7
Crimes against humanity

1. For the purpose of this Statute, "crime against humanity" means any of the following acts when committed as part of a widespread or systematic attack directed against any civilian population, with knowledge of the attack:
> (a) Murder;
> (b) Extermination;
> (c) Enslavement;
> (d) Deportation or forcible transfer of population;
> (e) Imprisonment or other severe deprivation of physical liberty in violation of fundamental rules of international law;
> (f) Torture;
> (g) Rape, sexual slavery, enforced prostitution, forced pregnancy, enforced sterilization, or any other form of sexual violence of comparable gravity;

(h) Persecution against any identifiable group or collectivity on political, racial, national, ethnic, cultural, religious, gender as defined in paragraph 3, or other grounds that are universally recognized as impermissible under international law, in connection with any act referred to in this paragraph or any crime within the jurisdiction of the Court;

(i) Enforced disappearance of persons;

(j) The crime of apartheid;

(k) Other inhumane acts of a similar character intentionally causing great suffering, or serious injury to body or to mental or physical health.

2. For the purpose of paragraph 1:

(a) "Attack directed against any civilian population" means a course of conduct involving the multiple commission of acts referred to in paragraph 1 against any civilian population, pursuant to or in furtherance of a State or organizational policy to commit such attack;

(b) "Extermination" includes the intentional infliction of conditions of life, inter alia the deprivation of access to food and medicine, calculated to bring about the destruction of part of a population;

(c) "Enslavement" means the exercise of any or all of the powers attaching to the right of ownership over a person and includes the exercise of such power in the course of trafficking in persons, in particular women and children;

(d) "Deportation or forcible transfer of population" means forced displacement of the persons concerned by expulsion or other coercive acts from the area in which they are lawfully present, without grounds permitted under international law;

(e) "Torture" means the intentional infliction of severe pain or suffering, whether physical or mental, upon a person in the custody or under the control of the accused; except that torture shall not include pain or suffering arising only from, inherent in or incidental to, lawful sanctions;

(f) "Forced pregnancy" means the unlawful confinement of a woman forcibly made pregnant, with the intent of affecting the ethnic composition of any population or carrying out other grave violations of international law. This definition shall not in any way be interpreted as affecting national laws relating to pregnancy;

(g) "Persecution" means the intentional and severe deprivation of fundamental rights contrary to international law by reason of the identity of the group or collectivity;

(h) "The crime of apartheid" means inhumane acts of a character similar to those referred to in paragraph 1, committed in the context of an institutionalized regime of systematic oppression and domination by one racial group over any other racial group or groups and committed with the intention of maintaining that regime;

(i) "Enforced disappearance of persons" means the arrest, detention or abduction of persons by, or with the authorization, support or acquiescence of, a State or a political organization, followed by a refusal to acknowledge that deprivation of freedom or to give information on the fate or whereabouts of those persons, with the intention of removing them from the protection of the law for a prolonged period of time.

3. For the purpose of this Statute, it is understood that the term "gender" refers to the two sexes, male and female, within the context of society. The term "gender" does not indicate any meaning different from the above.

Article 8
War crimes

1. The Court shall have jurisdiction in respect of war crimes in particular when committed as part of a plan or policy or as part of a large-scale commission of such crimes.

2.   For the purpose of this Statute, "war crimes" means:

(a) Grave breaches of the Geneva Conventions of 12 August 1949, namely, any of the following acts against persons or property protected under the provisions of the relevant Geneva Convention:

(i) Wilful killing;

(ii) Torture or inhuman treatment, including biological experiments;

(iii) Wilfully causing great suffering, or serious injury to body or health;

(iv) Extensive destruction and appropriation of property, not justified by military necessity and carried out unlawfully and wantonly;

(v) Compelling a prisoner of war or other protected person to serve in the forces of a hostile Power;

(vi) Wilfully depriving a prisoner of war or other protected person of the rights of fair and regular trial;

(vii) Unlawful deportation or transfer or unlawful confinement;

(viii) Taking of hostages.

(b) Other serious violations of the laws and customs applicable in international armed conflict, within the established framework of international law, namely, any of the following acts:

(i) Intentionally directing attacks against the civilian population as such or against individual civilians not taking direct part in hostilities;

(ii) Intentionally directing attacks against civilian objects, that is, objects which are not military objectives;

(iii) Intentionally directing attacks against personnel, installations, material, units or vehicles involved in a humanitarian assistance or peacekeeping mission in accordance with the Charter of the United Nations, as long as they are entitled to the protection given to civilians or civilian objects under the international law of armed conflict;

(iv) Intentionally launching an attack in the knowledge that such attack will cause incidental loss of life or injury to civilians or damage to civilian objects or widespread, long-term and severe damage to the natural environment which would be clearly excessive in relation to the concrete and direct overall military advantage anticipated;

(v) Attacking or bombarding, by whatever means, towns, villages, dwellings or buildings which are undefended and which are not military objectives;

(vi) Killing or wounding a combatant who, having laid down his arms or having no longer means of defence, has surrendered at discretion;

(vii) Making improper use of a flag of truce, of the flag or of the military insignia and uniform of the enemy or of the United Nations, as well as of the distinctive emblems of the Geneva Conventions, resulting in death or serious personal injury;

(viii) The transfer, directly or indirectly, by the Occupying Power of parts of its own civilian population into the territory it occupies, or the deportation or transfer of all or parts of the population of the occupied territory within or outside this territory;

(ix) Intentionally directing attacks against buildings dedicated to religion, education, art, science or charitable purposes, historic monuments, hospitals and places where the sick and wounded are collected, provided they are not military objectives;

(x) Subjecting persons who are in the power of an adverse party to physical mutilation or to medical or scientific experiments of any kind which are neither justified by the medical, dental or hospital treatment of the person concerned nor carried out in his or her interest, and which cause death to or seriously endanger the health of such person or persons;

(xi) Killing or wounding treacherously individuals belonging to the hostile nation or army;

(xii) Declaring that no quarter will be given;

(xiii) Destroying or seizing the enemy's property unless such destruction or seizure be imperatively demanded by the necessities of war;

(xiv) Declaring abolished, suspended or inadmissible in a court of law the rights and actions of the nationals of the hostile party;

(xv) Compelling the nationals of the hostile party to take part in the operations of war directed against their own country, even if they were in the belligerent's service before the commencement of the war;

(xvi) Pillaging a town or place, even when taken by assault;

(xvii) Employing poison or poisoned weapons;

(xviii) Employing asphyxiating, poisonous or other gases, and all analogous liquids, materials or devices;

(xix) Employing bullets which expand or flatten easily in the human body, such as bullets with a hard envelope which does not entirely cover the core or is pierced with incisions;

(xx) Employing weapons, projectiles and material and methods of warfare which are of a nature to cause superfluous injury or unnecessary suffering or which are inherently indiscriminate in violation of the international law of armed conflict, provided that such weapons, projectiles and material and methods of warfare are the subject of a comprehensive prohibition and are included in an annex to this Statute, by an amendment in accordance with the relevant provisions set forth in articles 121 and 123;

(xxi) Committing outrages upon personal dignity, in particular humiliating and degrading treatment;

(xxii) Committing rape, sexual slavery, enforced prostitution, forced pregnancy, as defined in article 7, paragraph 2 (f), enforced sterilization, or any other form of sexual violence also constituting a grave breach of the Geneva Conventions;

(xxiii) Utilizing the presence of a civilian or other protected person to render certain points, areas or military forces immune from military operations;

(xxiv) Intentionally directing attacks against buildings, material, medical units and transport, and personnel using the distinctive emblems of the Geneva Conventions in conformity with international law;

(xxv) Intentionally using starvation of civilians as a method of warfare by depriving them of objects indispensable to their survival, including wilfully impeding relief supplies as provided for under the Geneva Conventions;

(xxvi) Conscripting or enlisting children under the age of fifteen years into the national armed forces or using them to participate actively in hostilities.

(c) In the case of an armed conflict not of an international character, serious violations of article 3 common to the four Geneva Conventions of 12 August 1949, namely, any of the following acts committed against persons taking no active part in the hostilities, including members of armed forces who have laid down their arms and those placed hors de combat by sickness, wounds, detention or any other cause:

(i) Violence to life and person, in particular murder of all kinds, mutilation, cruel treatment and torture;

(ii) Committing outrages upon personal dignity, in particular humiliating and degrading treatment;

(iii) Taking of hostages;

(iv) The passing of sentences and the carrying out of executions without previous judgement pronounced by a regularly constituted court, affording all judicial guarantees which are generally recognized as indispensable.

(d) Paragraph 2 (c) applies to armed conflicts not of an international character and thus does not apply to situations of internal disturbances and tensions, such as riots, isolated and sporadic acts of violence or other acts of a similar nature.

(e) Other serious violations of the laws and customs applicable in armed conflicts not of an international character, within the established framework of international law, namely, any of the following acts:

(i) Intentionally directing attacks against the civilian population as such or against individual civilians not taking direct part in hostilities;

(ii) Intentionally directing attacks against buildings, material, medical units and transport, and personnel using the distinctive emblems of the Geneva Conventions in conformity with international law;

(iii) Intentionally directing attacks against personnel, installations, material, units or vehicles involved in a humanitarian assistance or peacekeeping mission in accordance with the Charter of the United Nations, as long as they are entitled to the protection given to civilians or civilian objects under the international law of armed conflict;

(iv) Intentionally directing attacks against buildings dedicated to religion, education, art, science or charitable purposes, historic monuments, hospitals and places where the sick and wounded are collected, provided they are not military objectives;

(v) Pillaging a town or place, even when taken by assault;

(vi) Committing rape, sexual slavery, enforced prostitution, forced pregnancy, as defined in article 7, paragraph 2 (f), enforced sterilization, and any other form of sexual violence also constituting a serious violation of article 3 common to the four Geneva Conventions;

(vii) Conscripting or enlisting children under the age of fifteen years into armed forces or groups or using them to participate actively in hostilities;

(viii) Ordering the displacement of the civilian population for reasons related to the conflict, unless the security of the civilians involved or imperative military reasons so demand;

(ix) Killing or wounding treacherously a combatant adversary;

(x) Declaring that no quarter will be given;

(xi) Subjecting persons who are in the power of another party to the conflict to physical mutilation or to medical or scientific experiments of any kind which are neither justified by the medical, dental or hospital treatment of the person concerned nor carried out in his or her interest, and which cause death to or seriously endanger the health of such person or persons;

(xii) Destroying or seizing the property of an adversary unless such destruction or seizure be imperatively demanded by the necessities of the conflict;

(f) Paragraph 2 (e) applies to armed conflicts not of an international character and thus does not apply to situations of internal disturbances and tensions, such as riots, isolated and sporadic acts of violence or other acts of a similar nature. It applies to armed conflicts that take place in the territory of a State when there is protracted armed conflict between governmental authorities and organized armed groups or between such groups.

3. Nothing in paragraph 2 (c) and (e) shall affect the responsibility of a Government to maintain or re-establish law and order in the State or to defend the unity and territorial integrity of the State, by all legitimate means.

Article 9
Elements of Crimes

1.Elements of Crimes shall assist the Court in the interpretation and application of articles 6, 7 and 8. They shall be adopted by a two-thirds majority of the members of the Assembly of States Parties.

2. Amendments to the Elements of Crimes may be proposed by:

(a) Any State Party;

(b) The judges acting by an absolute majority;

(c) The Prosecutor.

Such amendments shall be adopted by a two-thirds majority of the members of the Assembly of States Parties.

3. The Elements of Crimes and amendments thereto shall be consistent with this Statute.

Article 10

Nothing in this Part shall be interpreted as limiting or prejudicing in any way existing or developing rules of international law for purposes other than this Statute.

Article 11
Jurisdiction *ratione temporis*

1. The Court has jurisdiction only with respect to crimes committed after the entry into force of this Statute.

2. If a State becomes a Party to this Statute after its entry into force, the Court may exercise its jurisdiction only with respect to crimes committed after the entry into force of this Statute for that State, unless that State has made a declaration under article 12, paragraph 3.

Article 12
Preconditions to the exercise of jurisdiction

1. A State which becomes a Party to this Statute thereby accepts the jurisdiction of the Court with respect to the crimes referred to in article 5.

2. In the case of article 13, paragraph (a) or (c), the Court may exercise its jurisdiction if one or more of the following States are Parties to this Statute or have accepted the jurisdiction of the Court in accordance with paragraph 3:

(a) The State on the territory of which the conduct in question occurred or, if the crime was committed on board a vessel or aircraft, the State of registration of that vessel or aircraft;

(b) The State of which the person accused of the crime is a national.

3. If the acceptance of a State which is not a Party to this Statute is required under paragraph 2, that State may, by declaration lodged with the Registrar, accept the exercise of jurisdiction by the Court with respect to the crime in question. The accepting State shall cooperate with the Court without any delay or exception in accordance with Part 9.

Article 13
Exercise of jurisdiction

The Court may exercise its jurisdiction with respect to a crime referred to in article 5 in accordance with the provisions of this Statute if:

(a) A situation in which one or more of such crimes appears to have been committed is referred to the Prosecutor by a State Party in accordance with article 14;

(b) A situation in which one or more of such crimes appears to have been committed is referred to the Prosecutor by the Security Council acting under Chapter VII of the Charter of the United Nations; or

(c) The Prosecutor has initiated an investigation in respect of such a crime in accordance with article 15.

Article 14
Referral of a situation by a State Party

1. A State Party may refer to the Prosecutor a situation in which one or more crimes within the jurisdiction of the Court appear to have been committed requesting the Prosecutor to investigate the situation for the purpose of determining whether one or more specific persons should be charged with the commission of such crimes.

2. As far as possible, a referral shall specify the relevant circumstances and be accompanied by such supporting documentation as is available to the State referring the situation.

Article 15
Prosecutor

1. The Prosecutor may initiate investigations *proprio motu* on the basis of information on crimes within the jurisdiction of the Court.

2. The Prosecutor shall analyse the seriousness of the information received. For this purpose, he or she may seek additional information from States, organs of the United Nations, intergovernmental or non-governmental organizations, or other reliable sources that he or she deems appropriate, and may receive written or oral testimony at the seat of the Court.

3. If the Prosecutor concludes that there is a reasonable basis to proceed with an investigation, he or she shall submit to the Pre-Trial Chamber a request for authorization of an investigation, together with any supporting material collected. Victims may make representations to the Pre-Trial Chamber, in accordance with the Rules of Procedure and Evidence.

4. If the Pre-Trial Chamber, upon examination of the request and the supporting material, considers that there is a reasonable basis to proceed with an investigation, and that the case appears to fall within the jurisdiction of the Court, it shall authorize the commencement of the investigation, without prejudice to subsequent determinations by the Court with regard to the jurisdiction and admissibility of a case.

5. The refusal of the Pre-Trial Chamber to authorize the investigation shall not preclude the presentation of a subsequent request by the Prosecutor based on new facts or evidence regarding the same situation.

6. If, after the preliminary examination referred to in paragraphs 1 and 2, the Prosecutor concludes that the information provided does not constitute a reasonable basis for an investigation, he or she shall inform those who provided the information. This shall not preclude the Prosecutor from considering further information submitted to him or her regarding the same situation in the light of new facts or evidence.

Article 16
Deferral of investigation or prosecution

No investigation or prosecution may be commenced or proceeded with under this Statute for a period of 12 months after the Security Council, in a resolution adopted under Chapter VII of the Charter of the United Nations, has requested the Court to that effect; that request may be renewed by the Council under the same conditions.

Article 17
Issues of admissibility

1. Having regard to paragraph 10 of the Preamble and article 1, the Court shall determine that a case is inadmissible where:

(a) The case is being investigated or prosecuted by a State which has jurisdiction over it, unless the State is unwilling or unable genuinely to carry out the investigation or prosecution;

(b) The case has been investigated by a State which has jurisdiction over it and the State has decided not to prosecute the person concerned, unless the decision resulted from the unwillingness or inability of the State genuinely to prosecute;

(c) The person concerned has already been tried for conduct which is the subject of the complaint, and a trial by the Court is not permitted under article 20, paragraph 3;

(d) The case is not of sufficient gravity to justify further action by the Court.

2. In order to determine unwillingness in a particular case, the Court shall consider, having regard to the principles of due process recognized by international law, whether one or more of the following exist, as applicable:

(a) The proceedings were or are being undertaken or the national decision was made for the purpose of shielding the person concerned from criminal responsibility for crimes within the jurisdiction of the Court referred to in article 5;

(b) There has been an unjustified delay in the proceedings which in the circumstances is inconsistent with an intent to bring the person concerned to justice;

(c) The proceedings were not or are not being conducted independently or impartially, and they were or are being conducted in a manner which, in the circumstances, is inconsistent with an intent to bring the person concerned to justice.

3. In order to determine inability in a particular case, the Court shall consider whether, due to a total or substantial collapse or unavailability of its national judicial system, the State is unable to obtain the accused or the necessary evidence and testimony or otherwise unable to carry out its proceedings.

Article 18
Preliminary rulings regarding admissibility

1. When a situation has been referred to the Court pursuant to article 13 (a) and the Prosecutor has determined that there would be a reasonable basis to commence an investigation, or the Prosecutor initiates an investigation pursuant to articles 13 (c) and 15, the Prosecutor shall notify all States Parties and those States which, taking into account the information available, would normally exercise jurisdiction over the crimes concerned. The Prosecutor may notify such States on a confidential basis and, where the Prosecutor believes it necessary to protect persons, prevent destruction of evidence or prevent the absconding of persons, may limit the scope of the information provided to States.

2. Within one month of receipt of that notification, a State may inform the Court that it is investigating or has investigated its nationals or others within its jurisdiction with respect to criminal acts which may constitute crimes referred to in article 5 and which relate to the information provided in the notification to States. At the request of that State, the Prosecutor shall defer to the State's investigation of those persons unless the Pre-Trial Chamber, on the application of the Prosecutor, decides to authorize the investigation.

3. The Prosecutor's deferral to a State's investigation shall be open to review by the Prosecutor six months after the date of deferral or at any time when there has been a significant change of circumstances based on the State's unwillingness or inability genuinely to carry out the investigation.

4. The State concerned or the Prosecutor may appeal to the Appeals Chamber against a ruling of the Pre-Trial Chamber, in accordance with article 82. The appeal may be heard on an expedited basis.

5. When the Prosecutor has deferred an investigation in accordance with paragraph 2, the Prosecutor may request that the State concerned periodically inform the Prosecutor of the progress of its investigations and any subsequent prosecutions. States Parties shall respond to such requests without undue delay.

6. Pending a ruling by the Pre-Trial Chamber, or at any time when the Prosecutor has deferred an investigation under this article, the Prosecutor may, on an exceptional basis, seek authority from the Pre-Trial Chamber to pursue necessary investigative steps for the purpose of preserving evidence where there is a unique opportunity to obtain important evidence or there is a significant risk that such evidence may not

be subsequently available.

7. A State which has challenged a ruling of the Pre-Trial Chamber under this article may challenge the admissibility of a case under article 19 on the grounds of additional significant facts or significant change of circumstances.

Article 19
Challenges to the jurisdiction of the Court or the admissibility of a case

1. The Court shall satisfy itself that it has jurisdiction in any case brought before it. The Court may, on its own motion, determine the admissibility of a case in accordance with article 17.

2. Challenges to the admissibility of a case on the grounds referred to in article 17 or challenges to the jurisdiction of the Court may be made by:

> (a) An accused or a person for whom a warrant of arrest or a summons to appear has been issued under article 58;
>
> (b) A State which has jurisdiction over a case, on the ground that it is investigating or prosecuting the case or has investigated or prosecuted; or
>
> (c) A State from which acceptance of jurisdiction is required under article 12.

3. The Prosecutor may seek a ruling from the Court regarding a question of jurisdiction or admissibility. In proceedings with respect to jurisdiction or admissibility, those who have referred the situation under article 13, as well as victims, may also submit observations to the Court.

4. The admissibility of a case or the jurisdiction of the Court may be challenged only once by any person or State referred to in paragraph 2. The challenge shall take place prior to or at the commencement of the trial. In exceptional circumstances, the Court may grant leave for a challenge to be brought more than once or at a time later than the commencement of the trial. Challenges to the admissibility of a case, at the commencement of a trial, or subsequently with the leave of the Court, may be based only on article 17, paragraph 1 (c).

5. A State referred to in paragraph 2 (b) and (c) shall make a challenge at the earliest opportunity.

6. Prior to the confirmation of the charges, challenges to the admissibility of a case or challenges to the jurisdiction of the Court shall be referred to the Pre-Trial Chamber. After confirmation of the charges, they shall be referred to the Trial Chamber. Decisions with respect to jurisdiction or admissibility may be appealed to the Appeals Chamber in accordance with article 82.

7. If a challenge is made by a State referred to in paragraph 2 (b) or (c), the Prosecutor shall suspend the investigation until such time as the Court makes a determination in accordance with article 17.

8. Pending a ruling by the Court, the Prosecutor may seek authority from the Court:

> (a) To pursue necessary investigative steps of the kind referred to in article 18, paragraph 6;
>
> (b) To take a statement or testimony from a witness or complete the collection and examination of evidence which had begun prior to the making of the challenge; and
>
> (c) In cooperation with the relevant States, to prevent the absconding of persons in respect of whom the Prosecutor has already requested a warrant of arrest under article 58.

9. The making of a challenge shall not affect the validity of any act performed by the Prosecutor or any order or warrant issued by the Court prior to the making of the challenge.

10. If the Court has decided that a case is inadmissible under article 17, the Prosecutor may submit a request for a review of the decision when he or she is fully satisfied that new facts have arisen which negate the basis on which the case had previously been found inadmissible under article 17.

11. If the Prosecutor, having regard to the matters referred to in article 17, defers an investigation, the Prosecutor may request that the relevant State make available to the Prosecutor information on the proceedings. That information shall, at the request of the State concerned, be confidential. If the Prosecutor thereafter decides to proceed with an investigation, he or she shall notify the State to which deferral of the proceedings has taken place.

Article 20
Ne bis in idem

1. Except as provided in this Statute, no person shall be tried before the Court with respect to conduct which formed the basis of crimes for which the person has been convicted or acquitted by the Court.

2. No person shall be tried by another court for a crime referred to in article 5 for which that person has already been convicted or acquitted by the Court.

3. No person who has been tried by another court for conduct also proscribed under article 6, 7 or 8 shall be tried by the Court with respect to the same conduct unless the proceedings in the other court:

  (a) Were for the purpose of shielding the person concerned from criminal responsibility for crimes within the jurisdiction of the Court; or

  (b) Otherwise were not conducted independently or impartially in accordance with the norms of due process recognized by international law and were conducted in a manner which, in the circumstances, was inconsistent with an intent to bring the person concerned to justice.

Article 21
Applicable law

1. The Court shall apply:

  (a) In the first place, this Statute, Elements of Crimes and its Rules of Procedure and Evidence;

  (b) In the second place, where appropriate, applicable treaties and the principles and rules of international law, including the established principles of the international law of armed conflict;

  (c) Failing that, general principles of law derived by the Court from national laws of legal systems of the world including, as appropriate, the national laws of States that would normally exercise jurisdiction over the crime, provided that those principles are not inconsistent with this Statute and with international law and internationally recognized norms and standards.

2. The Court may apply principles and rules of law as interpreted in its previous decisions.

3. The application and interpretation of law pursuant to this article must be consistent with internationally recognized human rights, and be without any adverse distinction founded on grounds such as gender as defined in article 7, paragraph 3, age, race, colour, language, religion or belief, political or other opinion, national, ethnic or social origin, wealth, birth or other status.

PART 3. GENERAL PRINCIPLES OF CRIMINAL LAW

Article 22
Nullum crimen sine lege

1. A person shall not be criminally responsible under this Statute unless the conduct in question constitutes, at the time it takes place, a crime within the jurisdiction of the Court.

2. The definition of a crime shall be strictly construed and shall not be extended by analogy. In case of ambiguity, the definition shall be interpreted in favour of the person being investigated, prosecuted or convicted.

3. This article shall not affect the characterization of any conduct as criminal under international law independently of this Statute.

Article 23
Nulla poena sine lege

A person convicted by the Court may be punished only in accordance with this Statute.

Article 24
Non-retroactivity *ratione personae*

1. No person shall be criminally responsible under this Statute for conduct prior to the entry into force of the Statute.

2. In the event of a change in the law applicable to a given case prior to a final judgement, the law more favourable to the person being investigated, prosecuted or convicted shall apply.

Article 25
Individual criminal responsibility

1. The Court shall have jurisdiction over natural persons pursuant to this Statute.

2. A person who commits a crime within the jurisdiction of the Court shall be individually responsible and liable for punishment in accordance with this Statute.

3. In accordance with this Statute, a person shall be criminally responsible and liable for punishment for a crime within the jurisdiction of the Court if that person:

  (a) Commits such a crime, whether as an individual, jointly with another or through another person, regardless of whether that other person is criminally responsible;

(b) Orders, solicits or induces the commission of such a crime which in fact occurs or is attempted;

(c) For the purpose of facilitating the commission of such a crime, aids, abets or otherwise assists in its commission or its attempted commission, including providing the means for its commission;

(d) In any other way contributes to the commission or attempted commission of such a crime by a group of persons acting with a common purpose. Such contribution shall be intentional and shall either:

> (i) Be made with the aim of furthering the criminal activity or criminal purpose of the group, where such activity or purpose involves the commission of a crime within the jurisdiction of the Court; or

> (ii) Be made in the knowledge of the intention of the group to commit the crime;

(e) In respect of the crime of genocide, directly and publicly incites others to commit genocide;

(f) Attempts to commit such a crime by taking action that commences its execution by means of a substantial step, but the crime does not occur because of circumstances independent of the person's intentions. However, a person who abandons the effort to commit the crime or otherwise prevents the completion of the crime shall not be liable for punishment under this Statute for the attempt to commit that crime if that person completely and voluntarily gave up the criminal purpose.

4. No provision in this Statute relating to individual criminal responsibility shall affect the responsibility of States under international law.

Article 26
Exclusion of jurisdiction over persons under eighteen

The Court shall have no jurisdiction over any person who was under the age of 18 at the time of the alleged commission of a crime.

Article 27
Irrelevance of official capacity

1. This Statute shall apply equally to all persons without any distinction based on official capacity. In particular, official capacity as a Head of State or Government, a member of a Government or parliament, an elected representative or a government official shall in no case exempt a person from criminal responsibility under this Statute, nor shall it, in and of itself, constitute a ground for reduction of sentence.

2. Immunities or special procedural rules which may attach to the official capacity of a person, whether under national or international law, shall not bar the Court from exercising its jurisdiction over such a person.

Article 28
Responsibility of commanders and other superiors

In addition to other grounds of criminal responsibility under this Statute for crimes within the jurisdiction of the Court:

(a) A military commander or person effectively acting as a military commander shall be criminally responsible for crimes within the jurisdiction of the Court committed by forces under his or her effective command and control, or effective authority and control as the case may be, as a result of his or her failure to exercise control properly over such forces, where:

> (i) That military commander or person either knew or, owing to the circumstances at the time, should have known that the forces were committing or about to commit such crimes; and

> (ii) That military commander or person failed to take all necessary and reasonable measures within his or her power to prevent or repress their commission or to submit the matter to the competent authorities for investigation and prosecution.

(b) With respect to superior and subordinate relationships not described in paragraph (a), a superior shall be criminally responsible for crimes within the jurisdiction of the Court committed by subordinates under his or her effective authority and control, as a result of his or her failure to exercise control properly over such subordinates, where:

> (i) The superior either knew, or consciously disregarded information which clearly indicated, that the subordinates were committing or about to commit such crimes;

(ii) The crimes concerned activities that were within the effective responsibility and control of the superior; and

(iii) The superior failed to take all necessary and reasonable measures within his or her power to prevent or repress their commission or to submit the matter to the competent authorities for investigation and prosecution.

Article 29
Non-applicability of statute of limitations

The crimes within the jurisdiction of the Court shall not be subject to any statute of limitations.

Article 30
Mental element

1. Unless otherwise provided, a person shall be criminally responsible and liable for punishment for a crime within the jurisdiction of the Court only if the material elements are committed with intent and knowledge.

2. For the purposes of this article, a person has intent where:

(a) In relation to conduct, that person means to engage in the conduct;

(b) In relation to a consequence, that person means to cause that consequence or is aware that it will occur in the ordinary course of events.

3. For the purposes of this article, "knowledge" means awareness that a circumstance exists or a consequence will occur in the ordinary course of events. "Know" and "knowingly" shall be construed accordingly.

Article 31
Grounds for excluding criminal responsibility

1. In addition to other grounds for excluding criminal responsibility provided for in this Statute, a person shall not be criminally responsible if, at the time of that person's conduct:

(a) The person suffers from a mental disease or defect that destroys that person's capacity to appreciate the unlawfulness or nature of his or her conduct, or capacity to control his or her conduct to conform to the requirements of law;

(b) The person is in a state of intoxication that destroys that person's capacity to appreciate the unlawfulness or nature of his or her conduct, or capacity to control his or her conduct to conform to the requirements of law, unless the person has become voluntarily intoxicated under such circumstances that the person knew, or disregarded the risk, that, as a result of the intoxication, he or she was likely to engage in conduct constituting a crime within the jurisdiction of the Court;

(c) The person acts reasonably to defend himself or herself or another person or, in the case of war crimes, property which is essential for the survival of the person or another person or property which is essential for accomplishing a military mission, against an imminent and unlawful use of force in a manner proportionate to the degree of danger to the person or the other person or property protected. The fact that the person was involved in a defensive operation conducted by forces shall not in itself constitute a ground for excluding criminal responsibility under this subparagraph;

(d) The conduct which is alleged to constitute a crime within the jurisdiction of the Court has been caused by duress resulting from a threat of imminent death or of continuing or imminent serious bodily harm against that person or another person, and the person acts necessarily and reasonably to avoid this threat, provided that the person does not intend to cause a greater harm than the one sought to be avoided. Such a threat may either be:

(i) Made by other persons; or

(ii) Constituted by other circumstances beyond that person's control.

2. The Court shall determine the applicability of the grounds for excluding criminal responsibility provided for in this Statute to the case before it.

3. At trial, the Court may consider a ground for excluding criminal responsibility other than those referred to in paragraph 1 where such a ground is derived from applicable law as set forth in article 21. The procedures relating to the consideration of such a ground shall be provided for in the Rules of Procedure and Evidence.

Article 32

578

Mistake of fact or mistake of law

1. A mistake of fact shall be a ground for excluding criminal responsibility only if it negates the mental element required by the crime.

2. A mistake of law as to whether a particular type of conduct is a crime within the jurisdiction of the Court shall not be a ground for excluding criminal responsibility. A mistake of law may, however, be a ground for excluding criminal responsibility if it negates the mental element required by such a crime, or as provided for in article 33.

Article 33
Superior orders and prescription of law

1. The fact that a crime within the jurisdiction of the Court has been committed by a person pursuant to an order of a Government or of a superior, whether military or civilian, shall not relieve that person of criminal responsibility unless:

    (a) The person was under a legal obligation to obey orders of the Government or the superior in question;

    (b) The person did not know that the order was unlawful; and

    (c) The order was not manifestly unlawful.

2. For the purposes of this article, orders to commit genocide or crimes against humanity are manifestly unlawful.

PART 4. COMPOSITION AND ADMINISTRATION OF THE COURT

Article 34
Organs of the Court

The Court shall be composed of the following organs:

    (a) The Presidency;

    (b) An Appeals Division, a Trial Division and a Pre-Trial Division;

    (c) The Office of the Prosecutor;

    (d) The Registry.

Article 35
Service of judges

1. All judges shall be elected as full-time members of the Court and shall be available to serve on that basis from the commencement of their terms of office.

2. The judges composing the Presidency shall serve on a full-time basis as soon as they are elected.

3. The Presidency may, on the basis of the workload of the Court and in consultation with its members, decide from time to time to what extent the remaining judges shall be required to serve on a full-time basis. Any such arrangement shall be without prejudice to the provisions of article 40.

4. The financial arrangements for judges not required to serve on a full-time basis shall be made in accordance with article 49.

Article 36
Qualifications, nomination and election of judges

1. Subject to the provisions of paragraph 2, there shall be 18 judges of the Court.

2. (a) The Presidency, acting on behalf of the Court, may propose an increase in the number of judges specified in paragraph 1, indicating the reasons why this is considered necessary and appropriate. The Registrar shall promptly circulate any such proposal to all States Parties.

(b) Any such proposal shall then be considered at a meeting of the Assembly of States Parties to be convened in accordance with article 112. The proposal shall be considered adopted if approved at the meeting by a vote of two thirds of the members of the Assembly of States Parties and shall enter into force at such time as decided by the Assembly of States Parties.

(c) (i) Once a proposal for an increase in the number of judges has been adopted under subparagraph (b), the election of the additional judges shall take place at the next session of the Assembly of States Parties in accordance with paragraphs 3 to 8, and article 37, paragraph 2;

(ii) Once a proposal for an increase in the number of judges has been adopted and brought into effect under subparagraphs (b) and (c) (i), it shall be open to the Presidency at any time thereafter, if the workload of the Court justifies it, to propose a reduction in the number of judges, provided that the number of judges shall not be reduced below that specified in paragraph 1. The proposal shall be dealt with in accordance with theprocedure laid down in subparagraphs (a) and (b). In the event that the proposal is adopted, the number ofjudges shall be progressively decreased as the terms of office of serving judges expire, until the necessary number has been reached.

3. (a) The judges shall be chosen from among persons of high moral character, impartiality and integrity who possess the qualifications required in their respective States for appointment to the highest judicial offices.

(b) Every candidate for election to the Court shall:

(i) Have established competence in criminal law and procedure, and the necessary relevant experience,

whether as judge, prosecutor, advocate or in other similar capacity, in criminal proceedings; or

(ii) Have established competence in relevant areas of international law such as international humanitarian

law and the law of human rights, and extensive experience in a professional legal capacity which is of

relevance to the judicial work of the Court;

(c) Every candidate for election to the Court shall have an excellent knowledge of and be fluent in at least one of the working languages of the Court.

4. (a) Nominations of candidates for election to the Court may be made by any State Party to this Statute, and shall be made either:

(i) By the procedure for the nomination of candidates for appointment to the highest judicial offices in the State in question; or

(ii) By the procedure provided for the nomination of candidates for the International Court of Justice in the Statute of that Court.

Nominations shall be accompanied by a statement in the necessary detail specifying how the candidate fulfils the requirements of paragraph 3.

(b) Each State Party may put forward one candidate for any given election who need not necessarily be a national of that State Party but shall in any case be a national of a State Party.

(c) The Assembly of States Parties may decide to establish, if appropriate, an Advisory Committee on nominations. In that event, the Committee's composition and mandate shall be established by the Assembly of States Parties.

5. For the purposes of the election, there shall be two lists of candidates:

List A containing the names of candidates with the qualifications specified in paragraph 3 (b) (i); and

List B containing the names of candidates with the qualifications specified in paragraph 3 (b) (ii).

A candidate with sufficient qualifications for both lists may choose on which list to appear. At the first election to the Court, at least nine judges shall be elected from list A and at least five judges from list B. Subsequent elections shall be so organized as to maintain the equivalent proportion on the Court of judges qualified on the two lists.

6. (a) The judges shall be elected by secret ballot at a meeting of the Assembly of States Parties convened for that purpose under article 112. Subject to paragraph 7, the persons elected to the Court shall be the 18 candidates who obtain the highest number of votes and a two-thirds majority of the States Parties present and voting.

(b) In the event that a sufficient number of judges is not elected on the first ballot, successive ballots shall be held in accordance with the procedures laid down in subparagraph (a) until the remaining places have been filled.

7. No two judges may be nationals of the same State. A person who, for the purposes of membership of the Court, could be regarded as a national of more than one State shall be deemed to be a national of the State in which that person ordinarily exercises civil and political rights.

8. (a) The States Parties shall, in the selection of judges, take into account the need, within the membership of the Court, for:

(i) The representation of the principal legal systems of the world;

   (ii) Equitable geographical representation; and

   (iii) A fair representation of female and male judges.

  (b) States Parties shall also take into account the need to include judges with legal expertise on specific issues, including, but not limited to, violence against women or children.

9. (a) Subject to subparagraph (b), judges shall hold office for a term of nine years and, subject to subparagraph (c) and to article 37, paragraph 2, shall not be eligible for re-election.

  (b) At the first election, one third of the judges elected shall be selected by lot to serve for a term of three years; one third of the judges elected shall be selected by lot to serve for a term of six years; and the remainder shall serve for a term of nine years.

  (c) A judge who is selected to serve for a term of three years under subparagraph (b) shall be eligible for re-election for a full term.

10. Notwithstanding paragraph 9, a judge assigned to a Trial or Appeals Chamber in accordance with article 39 shall continue in office to complete any trial or appeal the hearing of which has already commenced before that Chamber. * * *

Article 39
Chambers

1. As soon as possible after the election of the judges, the Court shall organize itself into the divisions specified in article 34, paragraph (b). The Appeals Division shall be composed of the President and four other judges, the Trial Division of not less than six judges and the Pre-Trial Division of not less than six judges. The assignment of judges to divisions shall be based on the nature of the functions to be performed by each division and the qualifications and experience of the judges elected to the Court, in such a way that each division shall contain an appropriate combination of expertise in criminal law and procedure and in international law. The Trial and Pre-Trial Divisions shall be composed predominantly of judges with criminal trial experience.

2. (a) The judicial functions of the Court shall be carried out in each division by Chambers.

  (b) (i) The Appeals Chamber shall be composed of all the judges of the Appeals Division;

   (ii) The functions of the Trial Chamber shall be carried out by three judges of the Trial Division;

   (iii) The functions of the Pre-Trial Chamber shall be carried out either by three judges of the Pre-Trial Division or by a single judge of that division in accordance with this Statute and the Rules of Procedure and Evidence;

  (c) Nothing in this paragraph shall preclude the simultaneous constitution of more than one Trial Chamber or Pre-Trial Chamber when the efficient management of the Court's workload so requires.

3. (a) Judges assigned to the Trial and Pre-Trial Divisions shall serve in those divisions for a period of three years, and thereafter until the completion of any case the hearing of which has already commenced in the division concerned.

  (b) Judges assigned to the Appeals Division shall serve in that division for their entire term of office.

4. Judges assigned to the Appeals Division shall serve only in that division. Nothing in this article shall, however, preclude the temporary attachment of judges from the Trial Division to the Pre-Trial Division or vice versa, if the Presidency considers that the efficient management of the Court's workload so requires, provided that under no circumstances shall a judge who has participated in the pre-trial phase of a case be eligible to sit on the Trial Chamber hearing that case.

Article 40
Independence of the judges

1. The judges shall be independent in the performance of their functions.

2. Judges shall not engage in any activity which is likely to interfere with their judicial functions or to affect confidence in their independence.

3. Judges required to serve on a full-time basis at the seat of the Court shall not engage in any other occupation of a professional nature.

4. Any question regarding the application of paragraphs 2 and 3 shall be decided by an absolute majority of the judges. Where any such question concerns an individual judge, that judge shall not take part in the

decision.

Article 41
Excusing and disqualification of judges

1. The Presidency may, at the request of a judge, excuse that judge from the exercise of a function under this Statute, in accordance with the Rules of Procedure and Evidence.

2.   (a)   A judge shall not participate in any case in which his or her impartiality might reasonably be doubted on any ground. A judge shall be disqualified from a case in accordance with this paragraph if, *inter alia*, that judge has previously been involved in any capacity in that case before the Court or in a related criminal case at the national level involving the person being investigated or prosecuted. A judge shall also be disqualified on such other grounds as may be provided for in the Rules of Procedure and Evidence.

        (b)   The Prosecutor or the person being investigated or prosecuted may request the disqualification of a judge under this paragraph.

        (c)   Any question as to the disqualification of a judge shall be decided by an absolute majority of the judges. The challenged judge shall be entitled to present his or her comments on the matter, but shall not take part in the decision.

Article 42
The Office of the Prosecutor

1. The Office of the Prosecutor shall act independently as a separate organ of the Court. It shall be responsible for receiving referrals and any substantiated information on crimes within the jurisdiction of the Court, for examining them and for conducting investigations and prosecutions before the Court. A member of the Office shall not seek or act on instructions from any external source.

2. The Office shall be headed by the Prosecutor. The Prosecutor shall have full authority over the management and administration of the Office, including the staff, facilities and other resources thereof. The Prosecutor shall be assisted by one or more Deputy Prosecutors, who shall be entitled to carry out any of the acts required of the Prosecutor under this Statute. The Prosecutor and the Deputy Prosecutors shall be of different nationalities. They shall serve on a full-time basis.

3. The Prosecutor and the Deputy Prosecutors shall be persons of high moral character, be highly competent in and have extensive practical experience in the prosecution or trial of criminal cases. They shall have an excellent knowledge of and be fluent in at least one of the working languages of the Court.

4. The Prosecutor shall be elected by secret ballot by an absolute majority of the members of the Assembly of States Parties. The Deputy Prosecutors shall be elected in the same way from a list of candidates provided by the Prosecutor. The Prosecutor shall nominate three candidates for each position of Deputy Prosecutor to be filled. Unless a shorter term is decided upon at the time of their election, the Prosecutor and the Deputy Prosecutors shall hold office for a term of nine years and shall not be eligible for re-election.

5. Neither the Prosecutor nor a Deputy Prosecutor shall engage in any activity which is likely to interfere with his or her prosecutorial functions or to affect confidence in his or her independence. They shall not engage in any other occupation of a professional nature.

6. The Presidency may excuse the Prosecutor or a Deputy Prosecutor, at his or her request, from acting in a particular case.

7. Neither the Prosecutor nor a Deputy Prosecutor shall participate in any matter in which their impartiality might reasonably be doubted on any ground. They shall be disqualified from a case in accordance with this paragraph if, *inter alia*, they have previously been involved in any capacity in that case before the Court or in a related criminal case at the national level involving the person being investigated or prosecuted.

8. Any question as to the disqualification of the Prosecutor or a Deputy Prosecutor shall be decided by the Appeals Chamber.

        (a) The person being investigated or prosecuted may at any time request the disqualification of the Prosecutor or a Deputy Prosecutor on the grounds set out in this article;

        (b) The Prosecutor or the Deputy Prosecutor, as appropriate, shall be entitled to present his or her comments on the matter;

9. The Prosecutor shall appoint advisers with legal expertise on specific issues, including, but not limited to, sexual and gender violence and violence against children.

Article 43
The Registry

1. The Registry shall be responsible for the non-judicial aspects of the administration and servicing of the Court, without prejudice to the functions and powers of the Prosecutor in accordance with article 42.

2. The Registry shall be headed by the Registrar, who shall be the principal administrative officer of the Court. The Registrar shall exercise his or her functions under the authority of the President of the Court.

3. The Registrar and the Deputy Registrar shall be persons of high moral character, be highly competent and have an excellent knowledge of and be fluent in at least one of the working languages of the Court.

4. The judges shall elect the Registrar by an absolute majority by secret ballot, taking into account any recommendation by the Assembly of States Parties. If the need arises and upon the recommendation of the Registrar, the judges shall elect, in the same manner, a Deputy Registrar.

5. The Registrar shall hold office for a term of five years, shall be eligible for re-election once and shall serve on a full-time basis. The Deputy Registrar shall hold office for a term of five years or such shorter term as may be decided upon by an absolute majority of the judges, and may be elected on the basis that the Deputy Registrar shall be called upon to serve as required.

6. The Registrar shall set up a Victims and Witnesses Unit within the Registry. This Unit shall provide, in consultation with the Office of the Prosecutor, protective measures and security arrangements, counselling and other appropriate assistance for witnesses, victims who appear before the Court, and others who are at risk on account of testimony given by such witnesses. The Unit shall include staff with expertise in trauma, including trauma related to crimes of sexual violence.

Article 44
Staff

1. The Prosecutor and the Registrar shall appoint such qualified staff as may be required to their respective offices. In the case of the Prosecutor, this shall include the appointment of investigators.

2. In the employment of staff, the Prosecutor and the Registrar shall ensure the highest standards of efficiency, competency and integrity, and shall have regard, mutatis mutandis, to the criteria set forth in article 36, paragraph 8.

3. The Registrar, with the agreement of the Presidency and the Prosecutor, shall propose Staff Regulations which include the terms and conditions upon which the staff of the Court shall be appointed, remunerated and dismissed. The Staff Regulations shall be approved by the Assembly of States Parties.

4. The Court may, in exceptional circumstances, employ the expertise of gratis personnel offered by States Parties, intergovernmental organizations or non-governmental organizations to assist with the work of any of the organs of the Court. The Prosecutor may accept any such offer on behalf of the Office of the Prosecutor. Such gratis personnel shall be employed in accordance with guidelines to be established by the Assembly of States Parties. * * *

Article 46
Removal from office

1. A judge, the Prosecutor, a Deputy Prosecutor, the Registrar or the Deputy Registrar shall be removed from office if a decision to this effect is made in accordance with paragraph 2, in cases where that person:

    (a)   Is found to have committed serious misconduct or a serious breach of his or her duties under this Statute, as provided for in the Rules of Procedure and Evidence; or

    (b)   Is unable to exercise the functions required by this Statute.

2. A decision as to the removal from office of a judge, the Prosecutor or a Deputy Prosecutor under paragraph 1 shall be made by the Assembly of States Parties, by secret ballot:

    (a)   In the case of a judge, by a two-thirds majority of the States Parties upon a recommendation adopted by a two-thirds majority of the other judges;

    (b)   In the case of the Prosecutor, by an absolute majority of the States Parties;

    (c)   In the case of a Deputy Prosecutor, by an absolute majority of the States Parties upon the recommendation of the Prosecutor.

3. A decision as to the removal from office of the Registrar or Deputy Registrar shall be made by an absolute majority of the judges.

4. A judge, Prosecutor, Deputy Prosecutor, Registrar or Deputy Registrar whose conduct or ability to exercise the functions of the office as required by this Statute is challenged under this article shall have full opportunity to present and receive evidence and to make submissions in accordance with the Rules of

Procedure and Evidence. The person in question shall not otherwise participate in the consideration of the matter.

Article 47
Disciplinary measures

A judge, Prosecutor, Deputy Prosecutor, Registrar or Deputy Registrar who has committed misconduct of a less serious nature than that set out in article 46, paragraph 1, shall be subject to disciplinary measures, in accordance with the Rules of Procedure and Evidence.

Article 48
Privileges and immunities

1. The Court shall enjoy in the territory of each State Party such privileges and immunities as are necessary for the fulfilment of its purposes.

2. The judges, the Prosecutor, the Deputy Prosecutors and the Registrar shall, when engaged on or with respect to the business of the Court, enjoy the same privileges and immunities as are accorded to heads of diplomatic missions and shall, after the expiry of their terms of office, continue to be accorded immunity from legal process of every kind in respect of words spoken or written and acts performed by them in their official capacity.

3. The Deputy Registrar, the staff of the Office of the Prosecutor and the staff of the Registry shall enjoy the privileges and immunities and facilities necessary for the performance of their functions, in accordance with the agreement on the privileges and immunities of the Court.

4. Counsel, experts, witnesses or any other person required to be present at the seat of the Court shall be accorded such treatment as is necessary for the proper functioning of the Court, in accordance with the agreement on the privileges and immunities of the Court.

5. The privileges and immunities of:

    (a)   A judge or the Prosecutor may be waived by an absolute majority of the judges;

    (b)   The Registrar may be waived by the Presidency;

    (c)   The Deputy Prosecutors and staff of the Office of the Prosecutor may be waived by the Prosecutor;

    (d)   The Deputy Registrar and staff of the Registry may be waived by the Registrar.

Article 49
Salaries, allowances and expenses

The judges, the Prosecutor, the Deputy Prosecutors, the Registrar and the Deputy Registrar shall receive such salaries, allowances and expenses as may be decided upon by the Assembly of States Parties. These salaries and allowances shall not be reduced during their terms of office.

Article 50
Official and working languages

1. The official languages of the Court shall be Arabic, Chinese, English, French, Russian and Spanish. The judgements of the Court, as well as other decisions resolving fundamental issues before the Court, shall be published in the official languages. The Presidency shall, in accordance with the criteria established by the Rules of Procedure and Evidence, determine which decisions may be considered as resolving fundamental issues for the purposes of this paragraph.

2. The working languages of the Court shall be English and French. The Rules of Procedure and Evidence shall determine the cases in which other official languages may be used as working languages.

3. At the request of any party to a proceeding or a State allowed to intervene in a proceeding, the Court shall authorize a language other than English or French to be used by such a party or State, provided that the Court considers such authorization to be adequately justified.

Article 51
Rules of Procedure and Evidence

1. The Rules of Procedure and Evidence shall enter into force upon adoption by a two-thirds majority of the members of the Assembly of States Parties.

2. Amendments to the Rules of Procedure and Evidence may be proposed by:

    (a)   Any State Party;

    (b)   The judges acting by an absolute majority; or

    (c)   The Prosecutor.

Such amendments shall enter into force upon adoption by a two-thirds majority of the members of the Assembly of States Parties.

3. After the adoption of the Rules of Procedure and Evidence, in urgent cases where the Rules do not provide for a specific situation before the Court, the judges may, by a two-thirds majority, draw up provisional Rules to be applied until adopted, amended or rejected at the next ordinary or special session of the Assembly of States Parties.

4. The Rules of Procedure and Evidence, amendments thereto and any provisional Rule shall be consistent with this Statute. Amendments to the Rules of Procedure and Evidence as well as provisional Rules shall not be applied retroactively to the detriment of the person who is being investigated or prosecuted or who has been convicted.

5. In the event of conflict between the Statute and the Rules of Procedure and Evidence, the Statute shall prevail.

Article 52
Regulations of the Court

1. The judges shall, in accordance with this Statute and the Rules of Procedure and Evidence, adopt, by an absolute majority, the Regulations of the Court necessary for its routine functioning.

2. The Prosecutor and the Registrar shall be consulted in the elaboration of the Regulations and any amendments thereto.

3. The Regulations and any amendments thereto shall take effect upon adoption unless otherwise decided by the judges. Immediately upon adoption, they shall be circulated to States Parties for comments. If within six months there are no objections from a majority of States Parties, they shall remain in force.

PART 5. INVESTIGATION AND PROSECUTION

Article 53
Initiation of an investigation

1. The Prosecutor shall, having evaluated the information made available to him or her, initiate an investigation unless he or she determines that there is no reasonable basis to proceed under this Statute. In deciding whether to initiate an investigation, the Prosecutor shall consider whether:

    (a)   The information available to the Prosecutor provides a reasonable basis to believe that a crime within the jurisdiction of the Court has been or is being committed;

    (b)   The case is or would be admissible under article 17; and

    (c)   Taking into account the gravity of the crime and the interests of victims, there are nonetheless substantial reasons to believe that an investigation would not serve the interests of justice.

If the Prosecutor determines that there is no reasonable basis to proceed and his or her determination is based solely on subparagraph (c) above, he or she shall inform the Pre-Trial Chamber.

2. If, upon investigation, the Prosecutor concludes that there is not a sufficient basis for a prosecution because:

    (a)   There is not a sufficient legal or factual basis to seek a warrant or summons under article 58;

    (b)   The case is inadmissible under article 17; or

    (c)   A prosecution is not in the interests of justice, taking into account all the circumstances, including the gravity of the crime, the interests of victims and the age or infirmity of the alleged perpetrator, and his or her role in the alleged crime;

the Prosecutor shall inform the Pre-Trial Chamber and the State making a referral under article 14 or the Security Council in a case under article 13, paragraph (b), of his or her conclusion and the reasons for the conclusion.

3.(a) At the request of the State making a referral under article 14 or the Security Council under article 13, paragraph (b), the Pre-Trial Chamber may review a decision of the Prosecutor under paragraph 1 or 2 not to proceed and may request the Prosecutor to reconsider that decision.

(b) In addition, the Pre-Trial Chamber may, on its own initiative, review a decision of the Prosecutor not to proceed if it is based solely on paragraph 1 (c) or 2 (c). In such a case, the decision of the Prosecutor shall be effective only if confirmed by the Pre-Trial Chamber.

4. The Prosecutor may, at any time, reconsider a decision whether to initiate an investigation or prosecution based on new facts or information.

Article 54
Duties and powers of the Prosecutor with respect to investigations

1. The Prosecutor shall:

>   (a)   In order to establish the truth, extend the investigation to cover all facts and evidence relevant to an assessment of whether there is criminal responsibility under this Statute, and, in doing so, investigate incriminating and exonerating circumstances equally;

>   (b)   Take appropriate measures to ensure the effective investigation and prosecution of crimes within the jurisdiction of the Court, and in doing so, respect the interests and personal circumstances of victims and witnesses, including age, gender as defined in article 7, paragraph 3, and health, and take into account the nature of the crime, in particular where it involves sexual violence, gender violence or violence against children; and

>   (c)   Fully respect the rights of persons arising under this Statute.

2. The Prosecutor may conduct investigations on the territory of a State:

>   (a)   In accordance with the provisions of Part 9; or

>   (b)   As authorized by the Pre-Trial Chamber under article 57, paragraph 3 (d).

3. The Prosecutor may:

>   (a)   Collect and examine evidence;

>   (b)   Request the presence of and question persons being investigated, victims and witnesses;

>   (c)   Seek the cooperation of any State or intergovernmental organization or arrangement in accordance with its respective competence and/or mandate;

>   (d)   Enter into such arrangements or agreements, not inconsistent with this Statute, as may be necessary to facilitate the cooperation of a State, intergovernmental organization or person;

>   (e)   Agree not to disclose, at any stage of the proceedings, documents or information that the Prosecutor obtains on the condition of confidentiality and solely for the purpose of generating new evidence, unless the provider of the information consents; and

>   (f)   Take necessary measures, or request that necessary measures be taken, to ensure the confidentiality of information, the protection of any person or the preservation of evidence.

Article 55
Rights of persons during an investigation

1. In respect of an investigation under this Statute, a person:

>   (a)   Shall not be compelled to incriminate himself or herself or to confess guilt;

>   (b)   Shall not be subjected to any form of coercion, duress or threat, to torture or to any other form of cruel, inhuman or degrading treatment or punishment;

>   (c)   Shall, if questioned in a language other than a language the person fully understands and speaks, have, free of any cost, the assistance of a competent interpreter and such translations as are necessary to meet the requirements of fairness; and

>   (d)   Shall not be subjected to arbitrary arrest or detention, and shall not be deprived of his or her liberty except on such grounds and in accordance with such procedures as are established in this Statute.

2. Where there are grounds to believe that a person has committed a crime within the jurisdiction of the Court and that person is about to be questioned either by the Prosecutor, or by national authorities pursuant to a request made under Part 9, that person shall also have the following rights of which he or she shall be informed prior to being questioned:

(a)   To be informed, prior to being questioned, that there are grounds to believe that he or she has committed a crime within the jurisdiction of the Court;

(b)   To remain silent, without such silence being a consideration in the determination of guilt or innocence;

(c)   To have legal assistance of the person's choosing, or, if the person does not have legal assistance, to have legal assistance assigned to him or her, in any case where the interests of justice so require, and without payment by the person in any such case if the person does not have sufficient means to pay for it; and

(d)   To be questioned in the presence of counsel unless the person has voluntarily waived his or her right to counsel.

Article 56
Role of the Pre-Trial Chamber in relation
to a unique investigative opportunity

1.   (a)   Where the Prosecutor considers an investigation to present a unique opportunity to take testimony or a statement from a witness or to examine, collect or test evidence, which may not be available subsequently for the purposes of a trial, the Prosecutor shall so inform the Pre-Trial Chamber.

(b)   In that case, the Pre-Trial Chamber may, upon request of the Prosecutor, take such measures as may be necessary to ensure the efficiency and integrity of the proceedings and, in particular, to protect the rights of the defence.

(c)   Unless the Pre-Trial Chamber orders otherwise, the Prosecutor shall provide the relevant information to the person who has been arrested or appeared in response to a summons in connection with the investigation referred to in subparagraph (a), in order that he or she may be heard on the matter.

2. The measures referred to in paragraph 1 (b) may include:

(a)   Making recommendations or orders regarding procedures to be followed;

(b)   Directing that a record be made of the proceedings;

(c)   Appointing an expert to assist;

(d)   Authorizing counsel for a person who has been arrested, or appeared before the Court in response to a summons, to participate, or where there has not yet been such an arrest or appearance or counsel has not been designated, appointing another counsel to attend and represent the interests of the defence;

(e)   Naming one of its members or, if necessary, another available judge of the Pre-Trial or Trial Division to observe and make recommendations or orders regarding the collection and preservation of evidence and the questioning of persons;

(f)   Taking such other action as may be necessary to collect or preserve evidence.

3.   (a)   Where the Prosecutor has not sought measures pursuant to this article but the Pre-Trial Chamber considers that such measures are required to preserve evidence that it deems would be essential for the defence at trial, it shall consult with the Prosecutor as to whether there is good reason for the Prosecutor's failure to request the measures. If upon consultation, the Pre-Trial Chamber concludes that the Prosecutor's failure to request such measures is unjustified, the Pre-Trial Chamber may take such measures on its own initiative.

(b)   A decision of the Pre-Trial Chamber to act on its own initiative under this paragraph may be appealed by the Prosecutor. The appeal shall be heard on an expedited basis.

4. The admissibility of evidence preserved or collected for trial pursuant to this article, or the record thereof, shall be governed at trial by article 69, and given such weight as determined by the Trial Chamber.

Article 57
Functions and powers of the Pre-Trial Chamber

1. Unless otherwise provided in this Statute, the Pre-Trial Chamber shall exercise its functions in accordance with the provisions of this article.

2.   (a)   Orders or rulings of the Pre-Trial Chamber issued under articles 15, 18, 19, 54, paragraph 2, 61, paragraph 7, and 72 must be concurred in by a majority of its judges.

(b)   In all other cases, a single judge of the Pre-Trial Chamber may exercise the functions provided for in this Statute, unless otherwise provided for in the Rules of Procedure and Evidence or by a majority of the Pre-Trial Chamber.

3. In addition to its other functions under this Statute, the Pre-Trial Chamber may:

(a)   At the request of the Prosecutor, issue such orders and warrants as may be required for the purposes of an investigation;

(b)   Upon the request of a person who has been arrested or has appeared pursuant to a summons under article 58, issue such orders, including measures such as those described in article 56, or seek such cooperation pursuant to Part 9 as may be necessary to assist the person in the preparation of his or her defence;

(c)   Where necessary, provide for the protection and privacy of victims and witnesses, the preservation of evidence, the protection of persons who have been arrested or appeared in response to a summons, and the protection of national security information;

(d)   Authorize the Prosecutor to take specific investigative steps within the territory of a State Party without having secured the cooperation of that State under Part 9 if, whenever possible having regard to the views of the State concerned, the Pre-Trial Chamber has determined in that case that the State is clearly unable to execute a request for cooperation due to the unavailability of any authority or any component of its judicial system competent to execute the request for cooperation under Part 9.

(e)   Where a warrant of arrest or a summons has been issued under article 58, and having due regard to the strength of the evidence and the rights of the parties concerned, as provided for in this Statute and the Rules of Procedure and Evidence, seek the cooperation of States pursuant to article 93, paragraph 1 (k), to take protective measures for the purpose of forfeiture, in particular for the ultimate benefit of victims.

Article 58
Issuance by the Pre-Trial Chamber of a warrant of arrest or a summons to appear

1. At any time after the initiation of an investigation, the Pre-Trial Chamber shall, on the application of the Prosecutor, issue a warrant of arrest of a person if, having examined the application and the evidence or other information submitted by the Prosecutor, it is satisfied that:

(a)   There are reasonable grounds to believe that the person has committed a crime within the jurisdiction of the Court; and

(b)   The arrest of the person appears necessary:

(i)   To ensure the person's appearance at trial,

(ii)   To ensure that the person does not obstruct or endanger the investigation or the court proceedings, or

(iii)   Where applicable, to prevent the person from continuing with the commission of that crime or a related crime which is within the jurisdiction of the Court and which arises out of the same circumstances.

2. The application of the Prosecutor shall contain:

(a)   The name of the person and any other relevant identifying information;

(b)   A specific reference to the crimes within the jurisdiction of the Court which the person is alleged to have committed;

(c)   A concise statement of the facts which are alleged to constitute those crimes;

(d)   A summary of the evidence and any other information which establish reasonable grounds to believe that the person committed those crimes; and

(e)   The reason why the Prosecutor believes that the arrest of the person is necessary.

3. The warrant of arrest shall contain:

(a)   The name of the person and any other relevant identifying information;

(b)   A specific reference to the crimes within the jurisdiction of the Court for which the person's arrest is sought; and

(c)   A concise statement of the facts which are alleged to constitute those crimes.

4. The warrant of arrest shall remain in effect until otherwise ordered by the Court.

5. On the basis of the warrant of arrest, the Court may request the provisional arrest or the arrest and surrender of the person under Part 9.

6. The Prosecutor may request the Pre-Trial Chamber to amend the warrant of arrest by modifying or

adding to the crimes specified therein. The Pre-Trial Chamber shall so amend the warrant if it is satisfied that there are reasonable grounds to believe that the person committed the modified or additional crimes.

7. As an alternative to seeking a warrant of arrest, the Prosecutor may submit an application requesting that the Pre-Trial Chamber issue a summons for the person to appear. If the Pre-Trial Chamber is satisfied that there are reasonable grounds to believe that the person committed the crime alleged and that a summons is sufficient to ensure the person's appearance, it shall issue the summons, with or without conditions restricting liberty (other than detention) if provided for by national law, for the person to appear.
The summons shall contain:

(a)   The name of the person and any other relevant identifying information;

(b)   The specified date on which the person is to appear;

(c)   A specific reference to the crimes within the jurisdiction of the Court which the person is alleged to have committed; and

(d)   A concise statement of the facts which are alleged to constitute the crime.
The summons shall be served on the person.

Article 59
Arrest proceedings in the custodial State

1. A State Party which has received a request for provisional arrest or for arrest and surrender shall immediately take steps to arrest the person in question in accordance with its laws and the provisions of Part 9.

2. A person arrested shall be brought promptly before the competent judicial authority in the custodial State which shall determine, in accordance with the law of that State, that:

(a)   The warrant applies to that person;

(b)   The person has been arrested in accordance with the proper process; and

(c)   The person's rights have been respected.

3. The person arrested shall have the right to apply to the competent authority in the custodial State for interim release pending surrender.

4. In reaching a decision on any such application, the competent authority in the custodial State shall consider whether, given the gravity of the alleged crimes, there are urgent and exceptional circumstances to justify interim release and whether necessary safeguards exist to ensure that the custodial State can fulfil its duty to surrender the person to the Court. It shall not be open to the competent authority of the custodial State to consider whether the warrant of arrest was properly issued in accordance with article 58, paragraph 1 (a) and (b).

5. The Pre-Trial Chamber shall be notified of any request for interim release and shall make recommendations to the competent authority in the custodial State. The competent authority in the custodial State shall give full consideration to such recommendations, including any recommendations on measures to prevent the escape of the person, before rendering its decision.

6. If the person is granted interim release, the Pre-Trial Chamber may request periodic reports on the status of the interim release.

7. Once ordered to be surrendered by the custodial State, the person shall be delivered to the Court as soon as possible.

Article 60
Initial proceedings before the Court

1. Upon the surrender of the person to the Court, or the person's appearance before the Court voluntarily or pursuant to a summons, the Pre-Trial Chamber shall satisfy itself that the person has been informed of the crimes which he or she is alleged to have committed, and of his or her rights under this Statute, including the right to apply for interim release pending trial.

2. A person subject to a warrant of arrest may apply for interim release pending trial. If the Pre-Trial Chamber is satisfied that the conditions set forth in article 58, paragraph 1, are met, the person shall continue to be detained. If it is not so satisfied, the Pre-Trial Chamber shall release the person, with or without conditions.

3. The Pre-Trial Chamber shall periodically review its ruling on the release or detention of the person, and may do so at any time on the request of the Prosecutor or the person. Upon such review, it may modify its ruling as to detention, release or conditions of release, if it is satisfied that changed circumstances so require.

4. The Pre-Trial Chamber shall ensure that a person is not detained for an unreasonable period prior to trial due to inexcusable delay by the Prosecutor. If such delay occurs, the Court shall consider releasing the person, with or without conditions.

5. If necessary, the Pre-Trial Chamber may issue a warrant of arrest to secure the presence of a person who has been released.

Article 61
Confirmation of the charges before trial

1. Subject to the provisions of paragraph 2, within a reasonable time after the person's surrender or voluntary appearance before the Court, the Pre-Trial Chamber shall hold a hearing to confirm the charges on which the Prosecutor intends to seek trial. The hearing shall be held in the presence of the Prosecutor and the person charged, as well as his or her counsel.

2. The Pre-Trial Chamber may, upon request of the Prosecutor or on its own motion, hold a hearing in the absence of the person charged to confirm the charges on which the Prosecutor intends to seek trial when the person has:

    (a)   Waived his or her right to be present; or

    (b)   Fled or cannot be found and all reasonable steps have been taken to secure his or her appearance before the Court and to inform the person of the charges and that a hearing to confirm those charges will be held.

    In that case, the person shall be represented by counsel where the Pre-Trial Chamber determines that it is in the interests of justice.

3. Within a reasonable time before the hearing, the person shall:

    (a)   Be provided with a copy of the document containing the charges on which the Prosecutor intends to bring the person to trial; and

    (b)   Be informed of the evidence on which the Prosecutor intends to rely at the hearing.

    The Pre-Trial Chamber may issue orders regarding the disclosure of information for the purposes of the hearing.

4. Before the hearing, the Prosecutor may continue the investigation and may amend or withdraw any charges. The person shall be given reasonable notice before the hearing of any amendment to or withdrawal of charges. In case of a withdrawal of charges, the Prosecutor shall notify the Pre-Trial Chamber of the reasons for the withdrawal.

5. At the hearing, the Prosecutor shall support each charge with sufficient evidence to establish substantial grounds to believe that the person committed the crime charged. The Prosecutor may rely on documentary or summary evidence and need not call the witnesses expected to testify at the trial.

6. At the hearing, the person may:

    (a)   Object to the charges;

    (b)   Challenge the evidence presented by the Prosecutor; and

    (c)   Present evidence.

7. The Pre-Trial Chamber shall, on the basis of the hearing, determine whether there is sufficient evidence to establish substantial grounds to believe that the person committed each of the crimes charged. Based on its determination, the Pre-Trial Chamber shall:

    (a)   Confirm those charges in relation to which it has determined that there is sufficient evidence, and commit the person to a Trial Chamber for trial on the charges as confirmed;

    (b)   Decline to confirm those charges in relation to which it has determined that there is insufficient evidence;

    (c)   Adjourn the hearing and request the Prosecutor to consider:

        (i) Providing further evidence or conducting further investigation with respect to a particular charge; or

        (ii) Amending a charge because the evidence submitted appears to establish a different crime within the jurisdiction of the Court.

8. Where the Pre-Trial Chamber declines to confirm a charge, the Prosecutor shall not be precluded from subsequently requesting its confirmation if the request is supported by additional evidence.

9. After the charges are confirmed and before the trial has begun, the Prosecutor may, with the permission of the Pre-Trial Chamber and after notice to the accused, amend the charges. If the Prosecutor seeks to add additional charges or to substitute more serious charges, a hearing under this article to confirm those

charges must be held. After commencement of the trial, the Prosecutor may, with the permission of the Trial Chamber, withdraw the charges.

10. Any warrant previously issued shall cease to have effect with respect to any charges which have not been confirmed by the Pre-Trial Chamber or which have been withdrawn by the Prosecutor.

11. Once the charges have been confirmed in accordance with this article, the Presidency shall constitute a Trial Chamber which, subject to paragraph 9 and to article 64, paragraph 4, shall be responsible for the conduct of subsequent proceedings and may exercise any function of the Pre-Trial Chamber that is relevant and capable of application in those proceedings.

PART 6. THE TRIAL

Article 62
Place of trial

Unless otherwise decided, the place of the trial shall be the seat of the Court.

Article 63
Trial in the presence of the accused

1. The accused shall be present during the trial.

2. If the accused, being present before the Court, continues to disrupt the trial, the Trial Chamber may remove the accused and shall make provision for him or her to observe the trial and instruct counsel from outside the courtroom, through the use of communications technology, if required. Such measures shall be taken only in exceptional circumstances after other reasonable alternatives have proved inadequate, and only for such duration as is strictly required.

Article 64
Functions and powers of the Trial Chamber

1. The functions and powers of the Trial Chamber set out in this article shall be exercised in accordance with this Statute and the Rules of Procedure and Evidence.

2. The Trial Chamber shall ensure that a trial is fair and expeditious and is conducted with full respect for the rights of the accused and due regard for the protection of victims and witnesses.

3. Upon assignment of a case for trial in accordance with this Statute, the Trial Chamber assigned to deal with the case shall:

    (a)   Confer with the parties and adopt such procedures as are necessary to facilitate the fair and expeditious conduct of the proceedings;

    (b)   Determine the language or languages to be used at trial; and

    (c)   Subject to any other relevant provisions of this Statute, provide for disclosure of documents or information not previously disclosed, sufficiently in advance of the commencement of the trial to enable adequate preparation for trial.

4. The Trial Chamber may, if necessary for its effective and fair functioning, refer preliminary issues to the Pre-Trial Chamber or, if necessary, to another available judge of the Pre-Trial Division.

5. Upon notice to the parties, the Trial Chamber may, as appropriate, direct that there be joinder or severance in respect of charges against more than one accused.

6. In performing its functions prior to trial or during the course of a trial, the Trial Chamber may, as necessary:

    (a)   Exercise any functions of the Pre-Trial Chamber referred to in article 61, paragraph 11;

    (b)   Require the attendance and testimony of witnesses and production of documents and other evidence by obtaining, if necessary, the assistance of States as provided in this Statute;

    (c)   Provide for the protection of confidential information;

    (d)   Order the production of evidence in addition to that already collected prior to the trial or presented during the trial by the parties;

    (e)   Provide for the protection of the accused, witnesses and victims; and

    (f)   Rule on any other relevant matters.

7. The trial shall be held in public. The Trial Chamber may, however, determine that special circumstances require that certain proceedings be in closed session for the purposes set forth in article 68, or to protect confidential or sensitive information to be given in evidence.

8.	(a)	At the commencement of the trial, the Trial Chamber shall have read to the accused the charges previously confirmed by the Pre-Trial Chamber. The Trial Chamber shall satisfy itself that the accused understands the nature of the charges. It shall afford him or her the opportunity to make an admission of guilt in accordance with article 65 or to plead not guilty.

(b)	At the trial, the presiding judge may give directions for the conduct of proceedings, including to ensure that they are conducted in a fair and impartial manner. Subject to any directions of the presiding judge, the parties may submit evidence in accordance with the provisions of this Statute.

9. The Trial Chamber shall have, inter alia, the power on application of a party or on its own motion to:

(a)	Rule on the admissibility or relevance of evidence; and

(b)	Take all necessary steps to maintain order in the course of a hearing.

10. The Trial Chamber shall ensure that a complete record of the trial, which accurately reflects the proceedings, is made and that it is maintained and preserved by the Registrar.

Article 65
Proceedings on an admission of guilt

1. Where the accused makes an admission of guilt pursuant to article 64, paragraph 8(a), the Trial Chamber shall determine whether:

(a)	The accused understands the nature and consequences of the admission of guilt;

(b)	The admission is voluntarily made by the accused after sufficient consultation with defence counsel; and

(c)	The admission of guilt is supported by the facts of the case that are contained in:

(i)	The charges brought by the Prosecutor and admitted by the accused;

(ii)	Any materials presented by the Prosecutor which supplement the charges and which the accused accepts; and

(iii)	Any other evidence, such as the testimony of witnesses, presented by the Prosecutor or the accused.

2. Where the Trial Chamber is satisfied that the matters referred to in paragraph 1 are established, it shall consider the admission of guilt, together with any additional evidence presented, as establishing all the essential facts that are required to prove the crime to which the admission of guilt relates, and may convict the accused of that crime.

3. Where the Trial Chamber is not satisfied that the matters referred to in paragraph 1 are established, it shall consider the admission of guilt as not having been made, in which case it shall order that the trial be continued under the ordinary trial procedures provided by this Statute and may remit the case to another Trial Chamber.

4. Where the Trial Chamber is of the opinion that a more complete presentation of the facts of the case is required in the interests of justice, in particular the interests of the victims, the Trial Chamber may:

(a)	Request the Prosecutor to present additional evidence, including the testimony of witnesses; or

(b)	Order that the trial be continued under the ordinary trial procedures provided by this Statute, in which case it shall consider the admission of guilt as not having been made and may remit the case to another Trial Chamber.

5. Any discussions between the Prosecutor and the defence regarding modification of the charges, the admission of guilt or the penalty to be imposed shall not be binding on the Court.

Article 66
Presumption of innocence

1. Everyone shall be presumed innocent until proved guilty before the Court in accordance with the applicable law.

2. The onus is on the Prosecutor to prove the guilt of the accused.

3. In order to convict the accused, the Court must be convinced of the guilt of the accused beyond reasonable doubt.

Article 67
Rights of the accused

1. In the determination of any charge, the accused shall be entitled to a public hearing, having regard to the provisions of this Statute, to a fair hearing conducted impartially, and to the following minimum guarantees, in full equality:

(a)　To be informed promptly and in detail of the nature, cause and content of the charge, in a language which the accused fully understands and speaks;

(b)　To have adequate time and facilities for the preparation of the defence and to communicate freely with counsel of the accused's choosing in confidence;

(c)　To be tried without undue delay;

(d)　Subject to article 63, paragraph 2, to be present at the trial, to conduct the defence in person or through legal assistance of the accused's choosing, to be informed, if the accused does not have legal assistance, of this right and to have legal assistance assigned by the Court in any case where the interests of justice so require, and without payment if the accused lacks sufficient means to pay for it;

(e)　To examine, or have examined, the witnesses against him or her and to obtain the attendance and examination of witnesses on his or her behalf under the same conditions as witnesses against him or her. The accused shall also be entitled to raise defences and to present other evidence admissible under this Statute;

(f)　To have, free of any cost, the assistance of a competent interpreter and such translations as are necessary to meet the requirements of fairness, if any of the proceedings of or documents presented to the Court are not in a language which the accused fully understands and speaks;

(g)　Not to be compelled to testify or to confess guilt and to remain silent, without such silence being a consideration in the determination of guilt or innocence;

(h)　To make an unsworn oral or written statement in his or her defence; and

(i)　Not to have imposed on him or her any reversal of the burden of proof or any onus of rebuttal.

2. In addition to any other disclosure provided for in this Statute, the Prosecutor shall, as soon as practicable, disclose to the defence evidence in the Prosecutor's possession or control which he or she believes shows or tends to show the innocence of the accused, or to mitigate the guilt of the accused, or which may affect the credibility of prosecution evidence. In case of doubt as to the application of this paragraph, the Court shall decide.

Article 68
Protection of the victims and witnesses and their participation in the proceedings

1. The Court shall take appropriate measures to protect the safety, physical and psychological well-being, dignity and privacy of victims and witnesses. In so doing, the Court shall have regard to all relevant factors, including age, gender as defined in article 7, paragraph 3, and health, and the nature of the crime, in particular, but not limited to, where the crime involves sexual or gender violence or violence against children. The Prosecutor shall take such measures particularly during the investigation and prosecution of such crimes. These measures shall not be prejudicial to or inconsistent with the rights of the accused and a fair and impartial trial.

2. As an exception to the principle of public hearings provided for in article 67, the Chambers of the Court may, to protect victims and witnesses or an accused, conduct any part of the proceedings in camera or allow the presentation of evidence by electronic or other special means. In particular, such measures shall be implemented in the case of a victim of sexual violence or a child who is a victim or a witness, unless otherwise ordered by the Court, having regard to all the circumstances, particularly the views of the victim or witness.

3. Where the personal interests of the victims are affected, the Court shall permit their views and concerns to be presented and considered at stages of the proceedings determined to be appropriate by the Court and in a manner which is not prejudicial to or inconsistent with the rights of the accused and a fair and impartial trial. Such views and concerns may be presented by the legal representatives of the victims where the Court considers it appropriate, in accordance with the Rules of Procedure and Evidence.

4. The Victims and Witnesses Unit may advise the Prosecutor and the Court on appropriate protective measures, security arrangements, counselling and assistance as referred to in article 43, paragraph 6.

5. Where the disclosure of evidence or information pursuant to this Statute may lead to the grave endangerment of the security of a witness or his or her family, the Prosecutor may, for the purposes of any proceedings conducted prior to the commencement of the trial, withhold such evidence or information and

instead submit a summary thereof. Such measures shall be exercised in a manner which is not prejudicial to or inconsistent with the rights of the accused and a fair and impartial trial.

6. A State may make an application for necessary measures to be taken in respect of the protection of its servants or agents and the protection of confidential or sensitive information.

Article 69
Evidence

1. Before testifying, each witness shall, in accordance with the Rules of Procedure and Evidence, give an undertaking as to the truthfulness of the evidence to be given by that witness.

2. The testimony of a witness at trial shall be given in person, except to the extent provided by the measures set forth in article 68 or in the Rules of Procedure and Evidence. The Court may also permit the giving of *viva voce* (oral) or recorded testimony of a witness by means of video or audio technology, as well as the introduction of documents or written transcripts, subject to this Statute and in accordance with the Rules of Procedure and Evidence. These measures shall not be prejudicial to or inconsistent with the rights of the accused.

3. The parties may submit evidence relevant to the case, in accordance with article 64. The Court shall have the authority to request the submission of all evidence that it considers necessary for the determination of the truth.

4. The Court may rule on the relevance or admissibility of any evidence, taking into account, inter alia, the probative value of the evidence and any prejudice that such evidence may cause to a fair trial or to a fair evaluation of the testimony of a witness, in accordance with the Rules of Procedure and Evidence.

5. The Court shall respect and observe privileges on confidentiality as provided for in the Rules of Procedure and Evidence.

6. The Court shall not require proof of facts of common knowledge but may take judicial notice of them.

7. Evidence obtained by means of a violation of this Statute or internationally recognized human rights shall not be admissible if:

    (a)   The violation casts substantial doubt on the reliability of the evidence; or

    (b)   The admission of the evidence would be antithetical to and would seriously damage the integrity of the proceedings.

8. When deciding on the relevance or admissibility of evidence collected by a State, the Court shall not rule on the application of the State's national law.

Article 70
Offences against the administration of justice

1. The Court shall have jurisdiction over the following offences against its administration of justice when committed intentionally:

    (a)   Giving false testimony when under an obligation pursuant to article 69, paragraph 1, to tell the truth;

    (b)   Presenting evidence that the party knows is false or forged;

    (c)   Corruptly influencing a witness, obstructing or interfering with the attendance or testimony of a witness, retaliating against a witness for giving testimony or destroying, tampering with or interfering with the collection of evidence;

    (d)   Impeding, intimidating or corruptly influencing an official of the Court for the purpose of forcing or persuading the official not to perform, or to perform improperly, his or her duties;

    (e)   Retaliating against an official of the Court on account of duties performed by that or another official;

    (f)   Soliciting or accepting a bribe as an official of the Court in connection with his or her official duties.

2. The principles and procedures governing the Court's exercise of jurisdiction over offences under this article shall be those provided for in the Rules of Procedure and Evidence. The conditions for providing international cooperation to the Court with respect to its proceedings under this article shall be governed by the domestic laws of the requested State.

3. In the event of conviction, the Court may impose a term of imprisonment not exceeding five years, or a fine in accordance with the Rules of Procedure and Evidence, or both.

4.   (a)   Each State Party shall extend its criminal laws penalizing offences against the integrity of its own investigative or judicial process to offences against the administration of justice referred to in this article, committed on its territory, or by one of its nationals;

(b)   Upon request by the Court, whenever it deems it proper, the State Party shall submit the case to its competent authorities for the purpose of prosecution. Those authorities shall treat such cases with diligence and devote sufficient resources to enable them to be conducted effectively.

Article 71
Sanctions for misconduct before the Court

1. The Court may sanction persons present before it who commit misconduct, including disruption of its proceedings or deliberate refusal to comply with its directions, by administrative measures other than imprisonment, such as temporary or permanent removal from the courtroom, a fine or other similar measures provided for in the Rules of Procedure and Evidence.

2. The procedures governing the imposition of the measures set forth in paragraph 1 shall be those provided for in the Rules of Procedure and Evidence.

Article 72
Protection of national security information

1. This article applies in any case where the disclosure of the information or documents of a State would, in the opinion of that State, prejudice its national security interests. Such cases include those falling within the scope of article 56, paragraphs 2 and 3, article 61, paragraph 3, article 64, paragraph 3, article 67, paragraph 2, article 68, paragraph 6, article 87, paragraph 6 and article 93, as well as cases arising at any other stage of the proceedings where such disclosure may be at issue.

2. This article shall also apply when a person who has been requested to give information or evidence has refused to do so or has referred the matter to the State on the ground that disclosure would prejudice the national security interests of a State and the State concerned confirms that it is of the opinion that disclosure would prejudice its national security interests.

3. Nothing in this article shall prejudice the requirements of confidentiality applicable under article 54, paragraph 3 (e) and (f), or the application of article 73.

4. If a State learns that information or documents of the State are being, or are likely to be, disclosed at any stage of the proceedings, and it is of the opinion that disclosure would prejudice its national security interests, that State shall have the right to intervene in order to obtain resolution of the issue in accordance with this article.

5. If, in the opinion of a State, disclosure of information would prejudice its national security interests, all reasonable steps will be taken by the State, acting in conjunction with the Prosecutor, the defence or the Pre-Trial Chamber or Trial Chamber, as the case may be, to seek to resolve the matter by cooperative means. Such steps may include:

(a)   Modification or clarification of the request;

(b)   A determination by the Court regarding the relevance of the information or evidence sought, or a determination as to whether the evidence, though relevant, could be or has been obtained from a source other than the requested State;

(c)   Obtaining the information or evidence from a different source or in a different form; or

(d)   Agreement on conditions under which the assistance could be provided including, among other things, providing summaries or redactions, limitations on disclosure, use of *in camera* or *ex parte* proceedings, or other protective measures permissible under the Statute and the Rules of Procedure and Evidence.

6. Once all reasonable steps have been taken to resolve the matter through cooperative means, and if the State considers that there are no means or conditions under which the information or documents could be provided or disclosed without prejudice to its national security interests, it shall so notify the Prosecutor or the Court of the specific reasons for its decision, unless a specific description of the reasons would itself necessarily result in such prejudice to the State's national security interests.

7. Thereafter, if the Court determines that the evidence is relevant and necessary for the establishment of the guilt or innocence of the accused, the Court may undertake the following actions:

(a)   Where disclosure of the information or document is sought pursuant to a request for cooperation under Part 9 or the circumstances described in paragraph 2, and the State has invoked the ground for refusal referred to in article 93, paragraph 4:

(i)   The Court may, before making any conclusion referred to in subparagraph 7 (a) (ii), request further consultations for the purpose of considering the State's representations, which may include, as appropriate, hearings in camera and ex parte;

(ii)   If the Court concludes that, by invoking the ground for refusal under article 93, paragraph 4, in the circumstances of the case, the requested State is not acting in accordance with its obligations under this Statute, the Court may refer the matter in accordance with article 87, paragraph 7, specifying the reasons for its conclusion; and

(iii)   The Court may make such inference in the trial of the accused as to the existence or non-existence of a fact, as may be appropriate in the circumstances; or

(b)   In all other circumstances:

(i)   Order disclosure; or

(ii)   To the extent it does not order disclosure, make such inference in the trial of the accused as to the existence or non-existence of a fact, as may be appropriate in the circumstances.

Article 73
Third-party information or documents

If a State Party is requested by the Court to provide a document or information in its custody, possession or control, which was disclosed to it in confidence by a State, intergovernmental organization or international organization, it shall seek the consent of the originator to disclose that document or information. If the originator is a State Party, it shall either consent to disclosure of the information or document or undertake to resolve the issue of disclosure with the Court, subject to the provisions of article 72. If the originator is not a State Party and refuses to consent to disclosure, the requested State shall inform the Court that it is unable to provide the document or information because of a pre-existing obligation of confidentiality to the originator.

Article 74
Requirements for the decision

1. All the judges of the Trial Chamber shall be present at each stage of the trial and throughout their deliberations. The Presidency may, on a case-by-case basis, designate, as available, one or more alternate judges to be present at each stage of the trial and to replace a member of the Trial Chamber if that member is unable to continue attending.

2. The Trial Chamber's decision shall be based on its evaluation of the evidence and the entire proceedings. The decision shall not exceed the facts and circumstances described in the charges and any amendments to the charges. The Court may base its decision only on evidence submitted and discussed before it at the trial.

3. The judges shall attempt to achieve unanimity in their decision, failing which the decision shall be taken by a majority of the judges.

4. The deliberations of the Trial Chamber shall remain secret.

5. The decision shall be in writing and shall contain a full and reasoned statement of the Trial Chamber's findings on the evidence and conclusions. The Trial Chamber shall issue one decision. When there is no unanimity, the Trial Chamber's decision shall contain the views of the majority and the minority. The decision or a summary thereof shall be delivered in open court.

Article 75
Reparations to victims

1. The Court shall establish principles relating to reparations to, or in respect of, victims, including restitution, compensation and rehabilitation. On this basis, in its decision the Court may, either upon request or on its own motion in exceptional circumstances, determine the scope and extent of any damage, loss and injury to, or in respect of, victims and will state the principles on which it is acting.

2. The Court may make an order directly against a convicted person specifying appropriate reparations to, or in respect of, victims, including restitution, compensation and rehabilitation.

Where appropriate, the Court may order that the award for reparations be made through the Trust Fund provided for in article 79.

3. Before making an order under this article, the Court may invite and shall take account of representations from or on behalf of the convicted person, victims, other interested persons or interested States.

4. In exercising its power under this article, the Court may, after a person is convicted of a crime within the jurisdiction of the Court, determine whether, in order to give effect to an order which it may make under this article, it is necessary to seek measures under article 93, paragraph 1.

5. A State Party shall give effect to a decision under this article as if the provisions of article 109 were applicable to this article.

6. Nothing in this article shall be interpreted as prejudicing the rights of victims under national or international law.

Article 76
Sentencing

1. In the event of a conviction, the Trial Chamber shall consider the appropriate sentence to be imposed and shall take into account the evidence presented and submissions made during the trial that are relevant to the sentence.

2. Except where article 65 applies and before the completion of the trial, the Trial Chamber may on its own motion and shall, at the request of the Prosecutor or the accused, hold a further hearing to hear any additional evidence or submissions relevant to the sentence, in accordance with the Rules of Procedure and Evidence.

3. Where paragraph 2 applies, any representations under article 75 shall be heard during the further hearing referred to in paragraph 2 and, if necessary, during any additional hearing.

4. The sentence shall be pronounced in public and, wherever possible, in the presence of the accused.

PART 7. PENALTIES

Article 77
Applicable penalties

1. Subject to article 110, the Court may impose one of the following penalties on a person convicted of a crime referred to in article 5 of this Statute:

    (a)   Imprisonment for a specified number of years, which may not exceed a maximum of 30 years; or

    (b)   A term of life imprisonment when justified by the extreme gravity of the crime and the individual circumstances of the convicted person.

2. In addition to imprisonment, the Court may order:

    (a)   A fine under the criteria provided for in the Rules of Procedure and Evidence;

    (b)   A forfeiture of proceeds, property and assets derived directly or indirectly from that crime, without prejudice to the rights of bona fide third parties.

Article 78
Determination of the sentence

1. In determining the sentence, the Court shall, in accordance with the Rules of Procedure and Evidence, take into account such factors as the gravity of the crime and the individual circumstances of the convicted person.

2. In imposing a sentence of imprisonment, the Court shall deduct the time, if any, previously spent in detention in accordance with an order of the Court. The Court may deduct any time otherwise spent in detention in connection with conduct underlying the crime.

3. When a person has been convicted of more than one crime, the Court shall pronounce a sentence for each crime and a joint sentence specifying the total period of imprisonment. This period shall be no less than the highest individual sentence pronounced and shall not exceed 30 years imprisonment or a sentence of life imprisonment in conformity with article 77, paragraph 1 (b).

Article 79
Trust Fund

1. A Trust Fund shall be established by decision of the Assembly of States Parties for the benefit of victims of crimes within the jurisdiction of the Court, and of the families of such victims.

2. The Court may order money and other property collected through fines or forfeiture to be transferred, by order of the Court, to the Trust Fund.

3. The Trust Fund shall be managed according to criteria to be determined by the Assembly of States Parties.

Article 80
Non-prejudice to national application of penalties and national laws

Nothing in this Part affects the application by States of penalties prescribed by their national law, nor the law of States which do not provide for penalties prescribed in this Part.

PART 8. APPEAL AND REVISION

Article 81
Appeal against decision of acquittal or conviction or against sentence

1. A decision under article 74 may be appealed in accordance with the Rules of Procedure and Evidence as follows:

    (a)   The Prosecutor may make an appeal on any of the following grounds:

        (i) Procedural error,

        (ii) Error of fact, or

        (iii) Error of law;

    (b)   The convicted person, or the Prosecutor on that person's behalf, may make an appeal on any of the following grounds:

        (i) Procedural error,

        (ii) Error of fact,

        (iii) Error of law, or

        (iv) Any other ground that affects the fairness or reliability of the proceedings or decision.

2.   (a)   A sentence may be appealed, in accordance with the Rules of Procedure and Evidence, by the Prosecutor or the convicted person on the ground of disproportion between the crime and the sentence;

    (b)   If on an appeal against sentence the Court considers that there are grounds on which the conviction might be set aside, wholly or in part, it may invite the Prosecutor and the convicted person to submit grounds under article 81, paragraph 1 (a) or (b), and may render a decision on conviction in accordance with article 83;

    (c)   The same procedure applies when the Court, on an appeal against conviction only, considers that there are grounds to reduce the sentence under paragraph 2 (a).

3.   (a)   Unless the Trial Chamber orders otherwise, a convicted person shall remain in custody pending an appeal;

    (b)   When a convicted person's time in custody exceeds the sentence of imprisonment imposed, that person shall be released, except that if the Prosecutor is also appealing, the release may be subject to the conditions under subparagraph (c) below;

    (c)   In case of an acquittal, the accused shall be released immediately, subject to the following:

        (i)   Under exceptional circumstances, and having regard, _inter alia_, to the concrete risk of flight, the seriousness of the offence charged and the probability of success on appeal, the Trial Chamber, at the request of the Prosecutor, may maintain the detention of the person pending appeal;

        (ii)   A decision by the Trial Chamber under subparagraph (c) (i) may be appealed in accordance with the Rules of Procedure and Evidence.

4. Subject to the provisions of paragraph 3 (a) and (b), execution of the decision or sentence shall be suspended during the period allowed for appeal and for the duration of the appeal proceedings.

Article 82
Appeal against other decisions

1. Either party may appeal any of the following decisions in accordance with the Rules of Procedure and Evidence:

    (a)   A decision with respect to jurisdiction or admissibility;

(b)   A decision granting or denying release of the person being investigated or prosecuted;
(c)   A decision of the Pre-Trial Chamber to act on its own initiative under article 56, paragraph 3;
(d)   A decision that involves an issue that would significantly affect the fair and expeditious conduct of the proceedings or the outcome of the trial, and for which, in the opinion of the Pre-Trial or Trial Chamber, an immediate resolution by the Appeals Chamber may materially advance the proceedings.
2. A decision of the Pre-Trial Chamber under article 57, paragraph 3 (d), may be appealed against by the State concerned or by the Prosecutor, with the leave of the Pre-Trial Chamber. The appeal shall be heard on an expedited basis.
3. An appeal shall not of itself have suspensive effect unless the Appeals Chamber so orders, upon request, in accordance with the Rules of Procedure and Evidence.
4. A legal representative of the victims, the convicted person or a bona fide owner of property adversely affected by an order under article 75 may appeal against the order for reparations, as provided in the Rules of Procedure and Evidence.

Article 83
Proceedings on appeal
1. For the purposes of proceedings under article 81 and this article, the Appeals Chamber shall have all the powers of the Trial Chamber.
2. If the Appeals Chamber finds that the proceedings appealed from were unfair in a way that affected the reliability of the decision or sentence, or that the decision or sentence appealed from was materially affected by error of fact or law or procedural error, it may:
(a)   Reverse or amend the decision or sentence; or
(b)   Order a new trial before a different Trial Chamber.
For these purposes, the Appeals Chamber may remand a factual issue to the original Trial Chamber for it to determine the issue and to report back accordingly, or may itself call evidence to determine the issue. When the decision or sentence has been appealed only by the person convicted, or the Prosecutor on that person's behalf, it cannot be amended to his or her detriment.
3. If in an appeal against sentence the Appeals Chamber finds that the sentence is disproportionate to the crime, it may vary the sentence in accordance with Part 7.
4. The judgement of the Appeals Chamber shall be taken by a majority of the judges and shall be delivered in open court. The judgement shall state the reasons on which it is based. When there is no unanimity, the judgement of the Appeals Chamber shall contain the views of the majority and the minority, but a judge may deliver a separate or dissenting opinion on a question of law.
5. The Appeals Chamber may deliver its judgement in the absence of the person acquitted or convicted.

Article 84
Revision of conviction or sentence
1. The convicted person or, after death, spouses, children, parents or one person alive at the time of the accused's death who has been given express written instructions from the accused to bring such a claim, or the Prosecutor on the person's behalf, may apply to the Appeals Chamber to revise the final judgement of conviction or sentence on the grounds that:
(a)   New evidence has been discovered that:
(i)   Was not available at the time of trial, and such unavailability was not wholly or partially attributable to the party making application; and
(ii)   Is sufficiently important that had it been proved at trial it would have been likely to have resulted in a different verdict;
(b)   It has been newly discovered that decisive evidence, taken into account at trial and upon which the conviction depends, was false, forged or falsified;
(c)   One or more of the judges who participated in conviction or confirmation of the charges has committed, in that case, an act of serious misconduct or serious breach of duty of sufficient gravity to justify the removal of that judge or those judges from office under article 46.
2. The Appeals Chamber shall reject the application if it considers it to be unfounded. If it determines that the application is meritorious, it may, as appropriate:
(a)   Reconvene the original Trial Chamber;

(b)   Constitute a new Trial Chamber; or

(c)   Retain jurisdiction over the matter,

with a view to, after hearing the parties in the manner set forth in the Rules of Procedure and Evidence, arriving at a determination on whether the judgement should be revised.

Article 85
Compensation to an arrested or convicted person

1. Anyone who has been the victim of unlawful arrest or detention shall have an enforceable right to compensation.

2. When a person has by a final decision been convicted of a criminal offence, and when subsequently his or her conviction has been reversed on the ground that a new or newly discovered fact shows conclusively that there has been a miscarriage of justice, the person who has suffered punishment as a result of such conviction shall be compensated according to law, unless it is proved that the non-disclosure of the unknown fact in time is wholly or partly attributable to him or her.

3. In exceptional circumstances, where the Court finds conclusive facts showing that there has been a grave and manifest miscarriage of justice, it may in its discretion award compensation, according to the criteria provided in the Rules of Procedure and Evidence, to a person who has been released from detention following a final decision of acquittal or a termination of the proceedings for that reason.

PART 9. INTERNATIONAL COOPERATION AND JUDICIAL ASSISTANCE

Article 86
General obligation to cooperate

States Parties shall, in accordance with the provisions of this Statute, cooperate fully with the Court in its investigation and prosecution of crimes within the jurisdiction of the Court.

Article 87
Requests for cooperation: general provisions

1.   (a)   The Court shall have the authority to make requests to States Parties for cooperation. The requests shall be transmitted through the diplomatic channel or any other appropriate channel as may be designated by each State Party upon ratification, acceptance, approval or accession. Subsequent changes to the designation shall be made by each State Party in accordance with the Rules of Procedure and Evidence.

(b)   When appropriate, without prejudice to the provisions of subparagraph (a), requests may also be transmitted through the International Criminal Police Organization or any appropriate regional organization.

2. Requests for cooperation and any documents supporting the request shall either be in or be accompanied by a translation into an official language of the requested State or one of the working languages of the Court, in accordance with the choice made by that State upon ratification, acceptance, approval or accession.

Subsequent changes to this choice shall be made in accordance with the Rules of Procedure and Evidence.

3. The requested State shall keep confidential a request for cooperation and any documents supporting the request, except to the extent that the disclosure is necessary for execution of the request.

4. In relation to any request for assistance presented under this Part, the Court may take such measures, including measures related to the protection of information, as may be necessary to ensure the safety or physical or psychological well-being of any victims, potential witnesses and their families. The Court may request that any information that is made available under this Part shall be provided and handled in a manner that protects the safety and physical or psychological well-being of any victims, potential witnesses and their families.

5.   (a)   The Court may invite any State not party to this Statute to provide assistance under this Part on the basis of an ad hoc arrangement, an agreement with such State or any other appropriate basis.

(b)   Where a State not party to this Statute, which has entered into an ad hoc arrangement or an agreement with the Court, fails to cooperate with requests pursuant to any such arrangement or agreement, the Court may so inform the Assembly of States Parties or, where the Security Council referred the matter to the Court, the Security Council.

6. The Court may ask any intergovernmental organization to provide information or documents. The Court may also ask for other forms of cooperation and assistance which may be agreed upon with such an organization and which are in accordance with its competence or mandate.

7. Where a State Party fails to comply with a request to cooperate by the Court contrary to the provisions of this Statute, thereby preventing the Court from exercising its functions and powers under this Statute, the Court may make a finding to that effect and refer the matter to the Assembly of States Parties or, where the Security Council referred the matter to the Court, to the Security Council.

Article 88
Availability of procedures under national law

States Parties shall ensure that there are procedures available under their national law for all of the forms of cooperation which are specified under this Part.

Article 89
Surrender of persons to the Court

1. The Court may transmit a request for the arrest and surrender of a person, together with the material supporting the request outlined in article 91, to any State on the territory of which that person may be found and shall request the cooperation of that State in the arrest and surrender of such a person. States Parties shall, in accordance with the provisions of this Part and the procedure under their national law, comply with requests for arrest and surrender.

2. Where the person sought for surrender brings a challenge before a national court on the basis of the principle of *ne bis in idem* as provided in article 20, the requested State shall immediately consult with the Court to determine if there has been a relevant ruling on admissibility. If the case is admissible, the requested State shall proceed with the execution of the request. If an admissibility ruling is pending, the requested State may postpone the execution of the request for surrender of the person until the Court makes a determination on admissibility.

3.   (a)   A State Party shall authorize, in accordance with its national procedural law, transportation through its territory of a person being surrendered to the Court by another State, except where transit through that State would impede or delay the surrender.

      (b)   A request by the Court for transit shall be transmitted in accordance with article 87. The request for transit shall contain:

           (i)   A description of the person being transported;

           (ii)   A brief statement of the facts of the case and their legal characterization; and

           (iii)   The warrant for arrest and surrender;

      (c)   A person being transported shall be detained in custody during the period of transit;

      (d)   No authorization is required if the person is transported by air and no landing is scheduled on the territory of the transit State;

      (e)   If an unscheduled landing occurs on the territory of the transit State, that State may require a request for transit from the Court as provided for in subparagraph (b). The transit State shall detain the person being transported until the request for transit is received and the transit is effected, provided that detention for purposes of this subparagraph may not be extended beyond 96 hours from the unscheduled landing unless the request is received within that time.

4. If the person sought is being proceeded against or is serving a sentence in the requested State for a crime different from that for which surrender to the Court is sought, the requested State, after making its decision to grant the request, shall consult with the Court.

Article 90
Competing requests

1. A State Party which receives a request from the Court for the surrender of a person under article 89 shall, if it also receives a request from any other State for the extradition of the same person for the same conduct which forms the basis of the crime for which the Court seeks the person's surrender, notify the Court and the requesting State of that fact.

2. Where the requesting State is a State Party, the requested State shall give priority to the request from the Court if:

(a) The Court has, pursuant to article 18 or 19, made a determination that the case in respect of which surrender is sought is admissible and that determination takes into account the investigation or prosecution conducted by the requesting State in respect of its request for extradition; or

(b) The Court makes the determination described in subparagraph (a) pursuant to the requested State's notification under paragraph 1.

3. Where a determination under paragraph 2 (a) has not been made, the requested State may, at its discretion, pending the determination of the Court under paragraph 2 (b), proceed to deal with the request for extradition from the requesting State but shall not extradite the person until the Court has determined that the case is inadmissible. The Court's determination shall be made on an expedited basis.

4. If the requesting State is a State not Party to this Statute the requested State, if it is not under an international obligation to extradite the person to the requesting State, shall give priority to the request for surrender from the Court, if the Court has determined that the case is admissible.

5. Where a case under paragraph 4 has not been determined to be admissible by the Court, the requested State may, at its discretion, proceed to deal with the request for extradition from the requesting State.

6. In cases where paragraph 4 applies except that the requested State is under an existing international obligation to extradite the person to the requesting State not Party to this Statute, the requested State shall determine whether to surrender the person to the Court or extradite the person to the requesting State. In making its decision, the requested State shall consider all the relevant factors, including but not limited to:

(a) The respective dates of the requests;

(b) The interests of the requesting State including, where relevant, whether the crime was committed in its territory and the nationality of the victims and of the person sought; and

(c) The possibility of subsequent surrender between the Court and the requesting State.

7. Where a State Party which receives a request from the Court for the surrender of a person also receives a request from any State for the extradition of the same person for conduct other than that which constitutes the crime for which the Court seeks the person's surrender:

(a) The requested State shall, if it is not under an existing international obligation to extradite the person to the requesting State, give priority to the request from the Court;

(b) The requested State shall, if it is under an existing international obligation to extradite the person to the requesting State, determine whether to surrender the person to the Court or to extradite the person to the requesting State. In making its decision, the requested State shall consider all the relevant factors, including but not limited to those set out in paragraph 6, but shall give special consideration to the relative nature and gravity of the conduct in question.

8. Where pursuant to a notification under this article, the Court has determined a case to be inadmissible, and subsequently extradition to the requesting State is refused, the requested State shall notify the Court of this decision.

Article 91
Contents of request for arrest and surrender

1. A request for arrest and surrender shall be made in writing. In urgent cases, a request may be made by any medium capable of delivering a written record, provided that the request shall be confirmed through the channel provided for in article 87, paragraph 1 (a).

2. In the case of a request for the arrest and surrender of a person for whom a warrant of arrest has been issued by the Pre-Trial Chamber under article 58, the request shall contain or be supported by:

(a) Information describing the person sought, sufficient to identify the person, and information as to that person's probable location;

(b) A copy of the warrant of arrest; and

(c) Such documents, statements or information as may be necessary to meet the requirements for the surrender process in the requested State, except that those requirements should not be more burdensome than those applicable to requests for extradition pursuant to treaties or arrangements between the requested State and other States and should, if possible, be less burdensome, taking into account the distinct nature of the Court.

3. In the case of a request for the arrest and surrender of a person already convicted, the request shall contain or be supported by:

(a)   A copy of any warrant of arrest for that person;

(b)   A copy of the judgement of conviction;

(c)   Information to demonstrate that the person sought is the one referred to in the judgement of conviction; and

(d)   If the person sought has been sentenced, a copy of the sentence imposed and, in the case of a sentence for imprisonment, a statement of any time already served and the time remaining to be served.

4. Upon the request of the Court, a State Party shall consult with the Court, either generally or with respect to a specific matter, regarding any requirements under its national law that may apply under paragraph 2 (c). During the consultations, the State Party shall advise the Court of the specific requirements of its national law.

Article 92
Provisional arrest

1. In urgent cases, the Court may request the provisional arrest of the person sought, pending presentation of the request for surrender and the documents supporting the request as specified in article 91.

2. The request for provisional arrest shall be made by any medium capable of delivering a written record and shall contain:

(a)   Information describing the person sought, sufficient to identify the person, and information as to that person's probable location;

(b)   A concise statement of the crimes for which the person's arrest is sought and of the facts which are alleged to constitute those crimes, including, where possible, the date and location of the crime;

(c)   A statement of the existence of a warrant of arrest or a judgement of conviction against the person sought; and

(d)   A statement that a request for surrender of the person sought will follow.

3. A person who is provisionally arrested may be released from custody if the requested State has not received the request for surrender and the documents supporting the request as specified in article 91 within the time limits specified in the Rules of Procedure and Evidence. However, the person may consent to surrender before the expiration of this period if permitted by the law of the requested State. In such a case, the requested State shall proceed to surrender the person to the Court as soon as possible.

4. The fact that the person sought has been released from custody pursuant to paragraph 3 shall not prejudice the subsequent arrest and surrender of that person if the request for surrender and the documents supporting the request are delivered at a later date.

Article 93
Other forms of cooperation

1. States Parties shall, in accordance with the provisions of this Part and under procedures of national law, comply with requests by the Court to provide the following assistance in relation to investigations or prosecutions:

(a)   The identification and whereabouts of persons or the location of items;

(b)   The taking of evidence, including testimony under oath, and the production of evidence, including expert opinions and reports necessary to the Court;

(c)   The questioning of any person being investigated or prosecuted;

(d)   The service of documents, including judicial documents;

(e)   Facilitating the voluntary appearance of persons as witnesses or experts before the Court;

(f)   The temporary transfer of persons as provided in paragraph 7;

(g)   The examination of places or sites, including the exhumation and examination of grave sites;

(h)   The execution of searches and seizures;

(i)   The provision of records and documents, including official records and documents;

(j)   The protection of victims and witnesses and the preservation of evidence;

(k)   The identification, tracing and freezing or seizure of proceeds, property and assets and instrumentalities of crimes for the purpose of eventual forfeiture, without prejudice to the rights of bona fide third parties; and

(l)   Any other type of assistance which is not prohibited by the law of the requested State, with a view to facilitating the investigation and prosecution of crimes within the jurisdiction of the Court.

2. The Court shall have the authority to provide an assurance to a witness or an expert appearing before the Court that he or she will not be prosecuted, detained or subjected to any restriction of personal freedom by the Court in respect of any act or omission that preceded the departure of that person from the requested State.

3. Where execution of a particular measure of assistance detailed in a request presented under paragraph 1, is prohibited in the requested State on the basis of an existing fundamental legal principle of general application, the requested State shall promptly consult with the Court to try to resolve the matter. In the consultations, consideration should be given to whether the assistance can be rendered in another manner or subject to conditions. If after consultations the matter cannot be resolved, the Court shall modify the request as necessary.

4. In accordance with article 72, a State Party may deny a request for assistance, in whole or in part, only if the request concerns the production of any documents or disclosure of evidence which relates to its national security.

5. Before denying a request for assistance under paragraph 1 (l), the requested State shall consider whether the assistance can be provided subject to specified conditions, or whether the assistance can be provided at a later date or in an alternative manner, provided that if the Court or the Prosecutor accepts the assistance subject to conditions, the Court or the Prosecutor shall abide by them.

6. If a request for assistance is denied, the requested State Party shall promptly inform the Court or the Prosecutor of the reasons for such denial.

7.   (a)   The Court may request the temporary transfer of a person in custody for purposes of identification or for obtaining testimony or other assistance. The person may be transferred if the following conditions are fulfilled:

(i)   The person freely gives his or her informed consent to the transfer; and

(ii)   The requested State agrees to the transfer, subject to such conditions as that State and the Court may agree.

(b)   The person being transferred shall remain in custody. When the purposes of the transfer have been fulfilled, the Court shall return the person without delay to the requested State.

8.   (a)   The Court shall ensure the confidentiality of documents and information, except as required for the investigation and proceedings described in the request.

(b)   The requested State may, when necessary, transmit documents or information to the Prosecutor on a confidential basis. The Prosecutor may then use them solely for the purpose of generating new evidence.

(c)   The requested State may, on its own motion or at the request of the Prosecutor, subsequently consent to the disclosure of such documents or information. They may then be used as evidence pursuant to the provisions of Parts 5 and 6 and in accordance with the Rules of Procedure and Evidence.

9.   (a)   (i)   In the event that a State Party receives competing requests, other than for surrender or extradition, from the Court and from another State pursuant to an international obligation, the State Party shall endeavour, in consultation with the Court and the other State, to meet both requests, if necessary by postponing or attaching conditions to one or the other request.

(ii)   Failing that, competing requests shall be resolved in accordance with the principles established in article 90.

(b)   Where, however, the request from the Court concerns information, property or persons which are subject to the control of a third State or an international organization by virtue of an international agreement, the requested States shall so inform the Court and the Court shall direct its request to the third State or international organization.

10.   (a)   The Court may, upon request, cooperate with and provide assistance to a State Party conducting an investigation into or trial in respect of conduct which constitutes a crime within the jurisdiction of the Court or which constitutes a serious crime under the national law of the requesting State.

(b)   (i)   The assistance provided under subparagraph (a) shall include, inter alia:

a.   The transmission of statements, documents or other types of evidence obtained in the course of an investigation or a trial conducted by the Court; and
b.   The questioning of any person detained by order of the Court;

(ii)   In the case of assistance under subparagraph (b) (i) a:

a.   If the documents or other types of evidence have been obtained with the assistance of a State, such transmission shall require the consent of that State;
b.   If the statements, documents or other types of evidence have been provided by a witness or expert, such transmission shall be subject to the provisions of article 68.

(c)   The Court may, under the conditions set out in this paragraph, grant a request for assistance under this paragraph from a State which is not a Party to this Statute.

Article 94
Postponement of execution of a request in respect of ongoing investigation or prosecution

1. If the immediate execution of a request would interfere with an ongoing investigation or prosecution of a case different from that to which the request relates, the requested State may postpone the execution of the request for a period of time agreed upon with the Court. However, the postponement shall be no longer than is necessary to complete the relevant investigation or prosecution in the requested State. Before making a decision to postpone, the requested State should consider whether the assistance may be immediately provided subject to certain conditions.

2. If a decision to postpone is taken pursuant to paragraph 1, the Prosecutor may, however, seek measures to preserve evidence, pursuant to article 93, paragraph 1 (j).

Article 95
Postponement of execution of a request in respect of an admissibility challenge

Where there is an admissibility challenge under consideration by the Court pursuant to article 18 or 19, the requested State may postpone the execution of a request under this Part pending a determination by the Court, unless the Court has specifically ordered that the Prosecutor may pursue the collection of such evidence pursuant to article 18 or 19.

Article 96
Contents of request for other forms of assistance under article 93

1. A request for other forms of assistance referred to in article 93 shall be made in writing. In urgent cases, a request may be made by any medium capable of delivering a written record, provided that the request shall be confirmed through the channel provided for in article 87, paragraph 1 (a).

2. The request shall, as applicable, contain or be supported by the following:

(a)   A concise statement of the purpose of the request and the assistance sought, including the legal basis and the grounds for the request;
(b)   As much detailed information as possible about the location or identification of any person or place that must be found or identified in order for the assistance sought to be provided;
(c)   A concise statement of the essential facts underlying the request;
(d)   The reasons for and details of any procedure or requirement to be followed;
(e)   Such information as may be required under the law of the requested State in order to execute the request; and
(f)   Any other information relevant in order for the assistance sought to be provided.

3. Upon the request of the Court, a State Party shall consult with the Court, either generally or with respect to a specific matter, regarding any requirements under its national law that may apply under paragraph 2 (e). During the consultations, the State Party shall advise the Court of the specific requirements of its national law.

4. The provisions of this article shall, where applicable, also apply in respect of a request for assistance made to the Court.

Article 97
Consultations

Where a State Party receives a request under this Part in relation to which it identifies problems which may impede or prevent the execution of the request, that State shall consult with the Court without delay in order to resolve the matter. Such problems may include, <u>inter alia</u>:

    (a)   Insufficient information to execute the request;

    (b)   In the case of a request for surrender, the fact that despite best efforts, the person sought cannot be located or that the investigation conducted has determined that the person in the requested State is clearly not the person named in the warrant; or

    (c)   The fact that execution of the request in its current form would require the requested State to breach a pre-existing treaty obligation undertaken with respect to another State.

Article 98
Cooperation with respect to waiver of immunity and consent to surrender

1. The Court may not proceed with a request for surrender or assistance which would require the requested State to act inconsistently with its obligations under international law with respect to the State or diplomatic immunity of a person or property of a third State, unless the Court can first obtain the cooperation of that third State for the waiver of the immunity.

2. The Court may not proceed with a request for surrender which would require the requested State to act inconsistently with its obligations under international agreements pursuant to which the consent of a sending State is required to surrender a person of that State to the Court, unless the Court can first obtain the cooperation of the sending State for the giving of consent for the surrender.

Article 99
Execution of requests under articles 93 and 96

1. Requests for assistance shall be executed in accordance with the relevant procedure under the law of the requested State and, unless prohibited by such law, in the manner specified in the request, including following any procedure outlined therein or permitting persons specified in the request to be present at and assist in the execution process.

2. In the case of an urgent request, the documents or evidence produced in response shall, at the request of the Court, be sent urgently.

3. Replies from the requested State shall be transmitted in their original language and form.

4. Without prejudice to other articles in this Part, where it is necessary for the successful execution of a request which can be executed without any compulsory measures, including specifically the interview of or taking evidence from a person on a voluntary basis, including doing so without the presence of the authorities of the requested State Party if it is essential for the request to be executed, and the examination without modification of a public site or other public place, the Prosecutor may execute such request directly on the territory of a State as follows:

    (a)   When the State Party requested is a State on the territory of which the crime is alleged to have been committed, and there has been a determination of admissibility pursuant to article 18 or 19, the Prosecutor may directly execute such request following all possible consultations with the requested State Party;

    (b)   In other cases, the Prosecutor may execute such request following consultations with the requested State Party and subject to any reasonable conditions or concerns raised by that State Party. Where the requested State Party identifies problems with the execution of a request pursuant to this subparagraph it shall, without delay, consult with the Court to resolve the matter.

5. Provisions allowing a person heard or examined by the Court under article 72 to invoke restrictions designed to prevent disclosure of confidential information connected with national security shall also apply to the execution of requests for assistance under this article.

Article 100
Costs

1. The ordinary costs for execution of requests in the territory of the requested State shall be borne by that State, except for the following, which shall be borne by the Court:

    (a)   Costs associated with the travel and security of witnesses and experts or the transfer under article 93 of persons in custody;

    (b)   Costs of translation, interpretation and transcription;

(c)   Travel and subsistence costs of the judges, the Prosecutor, the Deputy Prosecutors, the Registrar, the Deputy Registrar and staff of any organ of the Court;

(d)   Costs of any expert opinion or report requested by the Court;

(e)   Costs associated with the transport of a person being surrendered to the Court by a custodial State; and

(f)   Following consultations, any extraordinary costs that may result from the execution of a request.

2. The provisions of paragraph 1 shall, as appropriate, apply to requests from States Parties to the Court. In that case, the Court shall bear the ordinary costs of execution.

Article 101
Rule of speciality

1. A person surrendered to the Court under this Statute shall not be proceeded against, punished or detained for any conduct committed prior to surrender, other than the conduct or course of conduct which forms the basis of the crimes for which that person has been surrendered.

2. The Court may request a waiver of the requirements of paragraph 1 from the State which surrendered the person to the Court and, if necessary, the Court shall provide additional information in accordance with article 91. States Parties shall have the authority to provide a waiver to the Court and should endeavour to do so.

Article 102
Use of terms

For the purposes of this Statute:

(a)   "surrender" means the delivering up of a person by a State to the Court, pursuant to this Statute.

(b)   "extradition" means the delivering up of a person by one State to another as provided by treaty, convention or national legislation.

PART 10. ENFORCEMENT

Article 103
Role of States in enforcement of sentences of imprisonment

1.   (a)   A sentence of imprisonment shall be served in a State designated by the Court from a list of States which have indicated to the Court their willingness to accept sentenced persons.

(b)   At the time of declaring its willingness to accept sentenced persons, a State may attach conditions to its acceptance as agreed by the Court and in accordance with this Part.

(c)   A State designated in a particular case shall promptly inform the Court whether it accepts the Court's designation.

2.   (a)   The State of enforcement shall notify the Court of any circumstances, including the exercise of any conditions agreed under paragraph 1, which could materially affect the terms or extent of the imprisonment. The Court shall be given at least 45 days' notice of any such known or foreseeable circumstances. During this period, the State of enforcement shall take no action that might prejudice its obligations under article 110.

(b)   Where the Court cannot agree to the circumstances referred to in subparagraph (a), it shall notify the State of enforcement and proceed in accordance with article 104, paragraph 1.

3. In exercising its discretion to make a designation under paragraph 1, the Court shall take into account the following:

(a)   The principle that States Parties should share the responsibility for enforcing sentences of imprisonment, in accordance with principles of equitable distribution, as provided in the Rules of Procedure and Evidence;

(b)   The application of widely accepted international treaty standards governing the treatment of prisoners;

(c)   The views of the sentenced person;

(d)   The nationality of the sentenced person;

(e)   Such other factors regarding the circumstances of the crime or the person sentenced, or the effective enforcement of the sentence, as may be appropriate in designating the State of enforcement.

4. If no State is designated under paragraph 1, the sentence of imprisonment shall be served in a prison facility made available by the host State, in accordance with the conditions set out in the headquarters agreement referred to in article 3, paragraph 2. In such a case, the costs arising out of the enforcement of a sentence of imprisonment shall be borne by the Court.

Article 104
Change in designation of State of enforcement

1. The Court may, at any time, decide to transfer a sentenced person to a prison of another State.
2. A sentenced person may, at any time, apply to the Court to be transferred from the State of enforcement.

Article 105
Enforcement of the sentence

1. Subject to conditions which a State may have specified in accordance with article 103, paragraph 1 (b), the sentence of imprisonment shall be binding on the States Parties, which shall in no case modify it.
2. The Court alone shall have the right to decide any application for appeal and revision. The State of enforcement shall not impede the making of any such application by a sentenced person.

Article 106
Supervision of enforcement of sentences and conditions of imprisonment

1. The enforcement of a sentence of imprisonment shall be subject to the supervision of the Court and shall be consistent with widely accepted international treaty standards governing treatment of prisoners.
2. The conditions of imprisonment shall be governed by the law of the State of enforcement and shall be consistent with widely accepted international treaty standards governing treatment of prisoners; in no case shall such conditions be more or less favourable than those available to prisoners convicted of similar offences in the State of enforcement.
3. Communications between a sentenced person and the Court shall be unimpeded and confidential.

Article 107
Transfer of the person upon completion of sentence

1. Following completion of the sentence, a person who is not a national of the State of enforcement may, in accordance with the law of the State of enforcement, be transferred to a State which is obliged to receive him or her, or to another State which agrees to receive him or her, taking into account any wishes of the person to be transferred to that State, unless the State of enforcement authorizes the person to remain in its territory.
2. If no State bears the costs arising out of transferring the person to another State pursuant to paragraph 1, such costs shall be borne by the Court.
3. Subject to the provisions of article 108, the State of enforcement may also, in accordance with its national law, extradite or otherwise surrender the person to a State which has requested the extradition or surrender of the person for purposes of trial or enforcement of a sentence.

Article 108
Limitation on the prosecution or punishment of other offences

1. A sentenced person in the custody of the State of enforcement shall not be subject to prosecution or punishment or to extradition to a third State for any conduct engaged in prior to that person's delivery to the State of enforcement, unless such prosecution, punishment or extradition has been approved by the Court at the request of the State of enforcement.
2. The Court shall decide the matter after having heard the views of the sentenced person.
3. Paragraph 1 shall cease to apply if the sentenced person remains voluntarily for more than 30 days in the territory of the State of enforcement after having served the full sentence imposed by the Court, or returns to the territory of that State after having left it.

Article 109
Enforcement of fines and forfeiture measures

1. States Parties shall give effect to fines or forfeitures ordered by the Court under Part 7, without prejudice to the rights of bona fide third parties, and in accordance with the procedure of their national law.

2. If a State Party is unable to give effect to an order for forfeiture, it shall take measures to recover the value of the proceeds, property or assets ordered by the Court to be forfeited, without prejudice to the rights of bona fide third parties.

3. Property, or the proceeds of the sale of real property or, where appropriate, the sale of other property, which is obtained by a State Party as a result of its enforcement of a judgement of the Court shall be transferred to the Court.

Article 110
Review by the Court concerning reduction of sentence

1. The State of enforcement shall not release the person before expiry of the sentence pronounced by the Court.

2. The Court alone shall have the right to decide any reduction of sentence, and shall rule on the matter after having heard the person.

3. When the person has served two thirds of the sentence, or 25 years in the case of life imprisonment, the Court shall review the sentence to determine whether it should be reduced. Such a review shall not be conducted before that time.

4. In its review under paragraph 3, the Court may reduce the sentence if it finds that one or more of the following factors are present:

   (a)   The early and continuing willingness of the person to cooperate with the Court in its investigations and prosecutions;

   (b)   The voluntary assistance of the person in enabling the enforcement of the judgements and orders of the Court in other cases, and in particular providing assistance in locating assets subject to orders of fine, forfeiture or reparation which may be used for the benefit of victims; or

   (c)   Other factors establishing a clear and significant change of circumstances sufficient to justify the reduction of sentence, as provided in the Rules of Procedure and Evidence.

5. If the Court determines in its initial review under paragraph 3 that it is not appropriate to reduce the sentence, it shall thereafter review the question of reduction of sentence at such intervals and applying such criteria as provided for in the Rules of Procedure and Evidence.

Article 111
Escape

If a convicted person escapes from custody and flees the State of enforcement, that State may, after consultation with the Court, request the person's surrender from the State in which the person is located pursuant to existing bilateral or multilateral arrangements, or may request that the Court seek the person's surrender, in accordance with Part 9. It may direct that the person be delivered to the State in which he or she was serving the sentence or to another State designated by the Court.

PART 11. ASSEMBLY OF STATES PARTIES

Article 112
Assembly of States Parties

1. An Assembly of States Parties to this Statute is hereby established. Each State Party shall have one representative in the Assembly who may be accompanied by alternates and advisers. Other States which have signed this Statute or the Final Act may be observers in the Assembly.

2. The Assembly shall:

   (a)   Consider and adopt, as appropriate, recommendations of the Preparatory Commission;

   (b)   Provide management oversight to the Presidency, the Prosecutor and the Registrar regarding the administration of the Court;

   (c)   Consider the reports and activities of the Bureau established under paragraph 3 and take appropriate action in regard thereto;

   (d)   Consider and decide the budget for the Court;

   (e)   Decide whether to alter, in accordance with article 36, the number of judges;

   (f)   Consider pursuant to article 87, paragraphs 5 and 7, any question relating to non-cooperation;

(g)   Perform any other function consistent with this Statute or the Rules of Procedure and Evidence.

3.   (a)   The Assembly shall have a Bureau consisting of a President, two Vice-Presidents and 18 members elected by the Assembly for three-year terms.

(b)   The Bureau shall have a representative character, taking into account, in particular, equitable geographical distribution and the adequate representation of the principal legal systems of the world.

(c)   The Bureau shall meet as often as necessary, but at least once a year. It shall assist the Assembly in the discharge of its responsibilities.

4. The Assembly may establish such subsidiary bodies as may be necessary, including an independent oversight mechanism for inspection, evaluation and investigation of the Court, in order to enhance its efficiency and economy.

5. The President of the Court, the Prosecutor and the Registrar or their representatives may participate, as appropriate, in meetings of the Assembly and of the Bureau.

6. The Assembly shall meet at the seat of the Court or at the Headquarters of the United Nations once a year and, when circumstances so require, hold special sessions. Except as otherwise specified in this Statute, special sessions shall be convened by the Bureau on its own initiative or at the request of one third of the States Parties.

7. Each State Party shall have one vote. Every effort shall be made to reach decisions by consensus in the Assembly and in the Bureau. If consensus cannot be reached, except as otherwise provided in the Statute:

(a)   Decisions on matters of substance must be approved by a two-thirds majority of those present and voting provided that an absolute majority of States Parties constitutes the quorum for voting;

(b)   Decisions on matters of procedure shall be taken by a simple majority of States Parties present and voting.

8. A State Party which is in arrears in the payment of its financial contributions towards the costs of the Court shall have no vote in the Assembly and in the Bureau if the amount of its arrears equals or exceeds the amount of the contributions due from it for the preceding two full years. The Assembly may, nevertheless, permit such a State Party to vote in the Assembly and in the Bureau if it is satisfied that the failure to pay is due to conditions beyond the control of the State Party.

9. The Assembly shall adopt its own rules of procedure.

10. The official and working languages of the Assembly shall be those of the General Assembly of the United Nations.

PART 12. FINANCING

Article 113
Financial Regulations

Except as otherwise specifically provided, all financial matters related to the Court and the meetings of the Assembly of States Parties, including its Bureau and subsidiary bodies, shall be governed by this Statute and the Financial Regulations and Rules adopted by the Assembly of States Parties.

Article 114
Payment of expenses

Expenses of the Court and the Assembly of States Parties, including its Bureau and subsidiary bodies, shall be paid from the funds of the Court.

Article 115
Funds of the Court and of the Assembly of States Parties

The expenses of the Court and the Assembly of States Parties, including its Bureau and subsidiary bodies, as provided for in the budget decided by the Assembly of States Parties, shall be provided by the following sources:

(a)   Assessed contributions made by States Parties;

(b)   Funds provided by the United Nations, subject to the approval of the General Assembly, in particular in relation to the expenses incurred due to referrals by the Security Council.

Article 116
Voluntary contributions

Without prejudice to article 115, the Court may receive and utilize, as additional funds, voluntary contributions from Governments, international organizations, individuals, corporations and other entities, in accordance with relevant criteria adopted by the Assembly of States Parties.

Article 117
Assessment of contributions

The contributions of States Parties shall be assessed in accordance with an agreed scale of assessment, based on the scale adopted by the United Nations for its regular budget and adjusted in accordance with the principles on which that scale is based.

Article 118
Annual audit

The records, books and accounts of the Court, including its annual financial statements, shall be audited annually by an independent auditor.

PART 13. FINAL CLAUSES

Article 119
Settlement of disputes

1. Any dispute concerning the judicial functions of the Court shall be settled by the decision of the Court.
2. Any other dispute between two or more States Parties relating to the interpretation or application of this Statute which is not settled through negotiations within three months of their commencement shall be referred to the Assembly of States Parties. The Assembly may itself seek to settle the dispute or may make recommendations on further means of settlement of the dispute, including referral to the International Court of Justice in conformity with the Statute of that Court.

Article 120
Reservations

No reservations may be made to this Statute.

Article 121
Amendments

1. After the expiry of seven years from the entry into force of this Statute, any State Party may propose amendments thereto. The text of any proposed amendment shall be submitted to the Secretary-General of the United Nations, who shall promptly circulate it to all States Parties.
2. No sooner than three months from the date of notification, the Assembly of States Parties, at its next meeting, shall, by a majority of those present and voting, decide whether to take up the proposal. The Assembly may deal with the proposal directly or convene a Review Conference if the issue involved so warrants.
3. The adoption of an amendment at a meeting of the Assembly of States Parties or at a Review Conference on which consensus cannot be reached shall require a two-thirds majority of States Parties.
4. Except as provided in paragraph 5, an amendment shall enter into force for all States Parties one year after instruments of ratification or acceptance have been deposited with the Secretary-General of the United Nations by seven-eighths of them.
5. Any amendment to articles 5, 6, 7 and 8 of this Statute shall enter into force for those States Parties which have accepted the amendment one year after the deposit of their instruments of ratification or acceptance. In respect of a State Party which has not accepted the amendment, the Court shall not exercise its jurisdiction regarding a crime covered by the amendment when committed by that State Party's nationals or on its territory.
6. If an amendment has been accepted by seven-eighths of States Parties in accordance with paragraph 4, any State Party which has not accepted the amendment may withdraw from this Statute with immediate effect, notwithstanding article 127, paragraph 1, but subject to article 127, paragraph 2, by giving notice no later than one year after the entry into force of such amendment.

7. The Secretary-General of the United Nations shall circulate to all States Parties any amendment adopted at a meeting of the Assembly of States Parties or at a Review Conference.

Article 122
Amendments to provisions of an institutional nature

1. Amendments to provisions of this Statute which are of an exclusively institutional nature, namely, article 35, article 36, paragraphs 8 and 9, article 37, article 38, article 39, paragraphs 1 (first two sentences), 2 and 4, article 42, paragraphs 4 to 9, article 43, paragraphs 2 and 3, and articles 44, 46, 47 and 49, may be proposed at any time, notwithstanding article 121, paragraph 1, by any State Party. The text of any proposed amendment shall be submitted to the Secretary-General of the United Nations or such other person designated by the Assembly of States Parties who shall promptly circulate it to all States Parties and to others participating in the Assembly.
2. Amendments under this article on which consensus cannot be reached shall be adopted by the Assembly of States Parties or by a Review Conference, by a two-thirds majority of States Parties. Such amendments shall enter into force for all States Parties six months after their adoption by the Assembly or, as the case may be, by the Conference.

Article 123
Review of the Statute

1. Seven years after the entry into force of this Statute the Secretary-General of the United Nations shall convene a Review Conference to consider any amendments to this Statute. Such review may include, but is not limited to, the list of crimes contained in article 5. The Conference shall be open to those participating in the Assembly of States Parties and on the same conditions.
2. At any time thereafter, at the request of a State Party and for the purposes set out in paragraph 1, the Secretary-General of the United Nations shall, upon approval by a majority of States Parties, convene a Review Conference.
3. The provisions of article 121, paragraphs 3 to 7, shall apply to the adoption and entry into force of any amendment to the Statute considered at a Review Conference.

Article 124
Transitional Provision

Notwithstanding article 12, paragraphs 1 and 2, a State, on becoming a party to this Statute, may declare that, for a period of seven years after the entry into force of this Statute for the State concerned, it does not accept the jurisdiction of the Court with respect to the category of crimes referred to in article 8 when a crime is alleged to have been committed by its nationals or on its territory. A declaration under this article may be withdrawn at any time. The provisions of this article shall be reviewed at the Review Conference convened in accordance with article 123, paragraph 1.

Article 125
Signature, ratification, acceptance, approval or accession

1. This Statute shall be open for signature by all States in Rome, at the headquarters of the Food and Agriculture Organization of the United Nations, on 17 July 1998. Thereafter, it shall remain open for signature in Rome at the Ministry of Foreign Affairs of Italy until 17 October 1998. After that date, the Statute shall remain open for signature in New York, at United Nations Headquarters, until 31 December 2000.
2. This Statute is subject to ratification, acceptance or approval by signatory States. Instruments of ratification, acceptance or approval shall be deposited with the Secretary-General of the United Nations.
3. This Statute shall be open to accession by all States. Instruments of accession shall be deposited with the Secretary-General of the United Nations.

Article 126
Entry into force

1. This Statute shall enter into force on the first day of the month after the 60th day following the date of the deposit of the 60th instrument of ratification, acceptance, approval or accession with the Secretary-General of the United Nations.

2. For each State ratifying, accepting, approving or acceding to this Statute after the deposit of the 60th instrument of ratification, acceptance, approval or accession, the Statute shall enter into force on the first day of the month after the 60th day following the deposit by such State of its instrument of ratification, acceptance, approval or accession.

Article 127
Withdrawal

1. A State Party may, by written notification addressed to the Secretary-General of the United Nations, withdraw from this Statute. The withdrawal shall take effect one year after the date of receipt of the notification, unless the notification specifies a later date.

2. A State shall not be discharged, by reason of its withdrawal, from the obligations arising from this Statute while it was a Party to the Statute, including any financial obligations which may have accrued. Its withdrawal shall not affect any cooperation with the Court in connection with criminal investigations and proceedings in relation to which the withdrawing State had a duty to cooperate and which were commenced prior to the date on which the withdrawal became effective, nor shall it prejudice in any way the continued consideration of any matter which was already under consideration by the Court prior to the date on which the withdrawal became effective.

Article 128
Authentic texts

The original of this Statute, of which the Arabic, Chinese, English, French, Russian and Spanish texts are equally authentic, shall be deposited with the Secretary-General of the United Nations, who shall send certified copies thereof to all States.

LAW OF THE SUPREME IRAQI CRIMINAL TRIBUNAL

Al-Waqa'i Al-Iraqiya [Official Gazette of the Republic of Iraq], No. 4006, Law No. 10 of 2005: Law of the Supreme Iraqi Criminal Tribunal, Oct. 18, 2005, *translated by* the International Center for Transitional Justice, *available at* http://www.ictj.org/static/MENA/Iraq/iraq.statute.engtrans.pdf

SECTION ONE
Establishment and Organization of the Tribunal

PART ONE
Establishment
Article 1

First: A Tribunal is hereby established and shall be known as The Supreme Iraqi Criminal Tribunal (the "Tribunal"). The Tribunal shall enjoy complete independence.

Second: The Tribunal shall have jurisdiction over every natural person, whether Iraqi or non-Iraqi resident of Iraq, accused of committing any of the crimes listed in Articles 11, 12, 13 and 14 of this law, committed during the period from 17 July 1968 to 1 May 2003, in the Republic of Iraq or elsewhere, including the following crimes:

    A. Genocide;

    B. Crimes against humanity;

    C. War crimes; and

    D. Violations of Iraqi laws listed in Article 14 of this law.

Article 2

The Tribunal shall have its seat in the city of Baghdad. It may hold its sessions in any governorate, pursuant to a decree by the Council of Ministers upon the recommendation of the President of the Tribunal.

PART TWO
Organizational Structure of the Tribunal

Article 3

The Tribunal shall consist of:

First:

    A. An Appeals Chamber with the power to review the rulings and decisions of the Trial Chambers or Investigative Judges

    B. One or more Trial Chambers.

    C. Investigative judges.

Second: Prosecutions Department

Third: An administration providing administrative and financial services to the Tribunal and the Public Prosecution.

Fourth:

    A. The Appeals Chamber shall consist of nine judges who shall elect one of its members as a President. The President of the Appeals Chamber shall be the senior President of the Tribunal and shall supervise its administrative and financial affairs.

    B. The Trial Chamber shall consist of five judges, who shall elect one of them as a President to supervise their work.

Fifth: The Council of Ministers may, if necessary, and on the basis of a proposal by the President of the Tribunal, appoint non-Iraqi judges who have experience in the crimes stipulated in this Law, and who shall be persons of high moral character, honesty and integrity, in the event that one of the parties is a State. These judges shall be appointed with the assistance of the international community, including the United Nations.

PART THREE
Selection of Judges and Prosecutors and Termination of Service

Article 4

First: Judges and prosecutors shall be persons of high moral character, honesty and integrity, and shall have experience in the field of criminal law and meet conditions for appointment stipulated in the Judicial Organization Law 160 of 1979 and the Public Prosecution Law 159 of 1979

Second: As an exception to the provisions of paragraph First of this Article, candidates for the positions of judges at the Appeals Chamber and the Trial Chambers, and for investigative judges and prosecutors shall be serving judges and prosecutors. Retired judges and prosecutors can be nominated regardless of age, as can Iraqi lawyers who possess a high level of, efficiency and experience, and absolute competence in accordance with the Legal Profession Law. 173 of 1965, and service of a judicial or legal nature or in the field of legal practice of no less than 15 years.

Third:

    A. The Supreme Judicial council shall nominate all judges and prosecutors to the Tribunal. Following approval by the Council of Ministers, a decision for their appointment shall be issued by the Presidency Council. The appointments shall be of the first category, as an exception to the provisions of the Judicial Organization Lawand the Public Prosecution Law. Their salaries and remunerations shall be specified through instructions issued by the Council of Ministers.

B. The judges, prosecutors and employees appointed in accordance with the law prior to this legislation shall be deemed legally approved as of the date of their appointment according to the provisions of Article (4)(Third)(A) taking into account the provisions of Article (33) of this law.

Fourth: The Presidency Council, upon a recommendation from the Council of Ministers, may transfer judges and prosecutors from the Tribunal to the Supreme Judicial Council for any reason.

Fifth: The services of a judge or prosecutor covered by the provisions of this law shall be terminated for one of the following reasons:

1. If he is convicted of a non-political felony.
2. If he presents false information.
3. If he fails to fulfill his duties without good reason.

Article 6

First: A committee comprised of five members elected from among the Tribunal's judges and prosecutors shall be established under the supervision of the Tribunal's Appeals Chamber, and they shall select a president of the committee, which shall be called "Judges and Public Prosecutors Affairs Committee". The committee shall operate for one year and shall have the powers stipulated in the Judicial Organization Law and the Public Prosecution Law. It shall review matters relating to disciplinary measures and conditions of service pertaining to judges and prosecutors. Its decisions can be appealed before the full chamber of the Federal Appeal Court where they involve the termination of the services of a judge or prosecutor.

Second: The Committee shall, if the appeal before the full chamber of the Federal Appeal Court is rejected, submit a recommendation to the Council of Ministers for the issuance of an order by the Presidency Council to terminate the services of the judge or prosecutor, including the President of the Tribunal if any of the conditions in Article 6 of this Article (sic) is met.

Third: Upon completion of the work of the Tribunal, the judges and prosecutors shall be transferred to the Supreme Judiciary Council to work in the federal courts. Those who have reached retirement age shall be pensioned off in accordance with the provisions of the law.

PART FOUR
The Presidency of the Tribunal

Article 7

First: The president of the Tribunal shall:

A. Preside over the hearings of the Appeals Chamber.

B. Assign permanent and reserve judges to the Trial Chambers.

C. Assign a judge to a Trial Chamber in case of absence.

D. Ensure the completion of the administrative work of the Tribunal.

E. Appoint the Tribunal's Administrative Director, Security Director, Public Relations Director and Archives and Documentation Director and terminate their services in accordance with the law.

F. Name an official spokesperson for the Tribunal from among the judges or prosecutors.

Second: The President of the Tribunal may appoint non-Iraqi experts to work in the Trial Chambers and the Appeals Chamber to provide assistance in the field of international law and similar areas, whether international or otherwise. The appointment of these experts shall be undertaken with the assistance of the international community, including the United Nations.

Third: Non-Iraqi experts provided for in paragraph Second of this Article shall be persons of high moral character, honesty and integrity. The non-Iraqi expert shall preferably be a person who has previously worked in the judiciary or public prosecution in his country or in international war crimes tribunals.

PART FIVE
Investigative Judges

Article 8

First: A Sufficient number of Investigative Judges shall be appointed.

Second: The Tribunal's Investigative Judges shall be responsible for investigating those accused of committing crimes stipulated in Article 1(Second) of this law.

Third: The Investigative Judges shall elect a Chief Investigative Judge and a Deputy from amongst them.

Fourth: The Chief Investigative Judge shall assign cases under investigation to individual Investigative Judges.

Fifth: Each of the Investigative Judges' Offices shall be composed of an Investigative Judge and such other qualified staff necessary as may be required for the work of the Investigative Judge.

Sixth: An Investigative Judge may gather prosecution evidence from whatever source he deems appropriate and to communicate directly with all relevant parties.

Seventh: The Investigative Judge shall act with complete independence as a separate organ of the Tribunal. He shall not be subject to or respond to requests or instructions from any governmental body or any other party.

Eight: The decisions of the Investigative Judge can be challenged by appeal to the Appeals Chamber within fifteen days of the notification or deemed notification of the decision in accordance with the law.

Ninth: The Investigative Judge, after consultation with the President of the Tribunal, may appoint non-Iraqi experts to provide judicial assistance to the Investigative Judges in the investigation of cases provided for in this Law, whether international or otherwise. The Chief Investigative Judge may appoint these experts with the assistance of the international community, including the United Nations.

Tenth: The non-Iraqi experts and observers referred to in paragraph Ninth of this Article shall be persons of high moral character, honesty and integrity. The non-Iraqi expert or observer shall preferably be a person who has worked in the judiciary or public prosecution in his country or at international war crimes tribunals.

PART SIX
The Public Prosecution

Article 9

First: A sufficient number of Prosecutors shall be appointed.

Second: The Prosecution Department shall be composed of a number of Prosecutors who shall be responsible for the prosecution of persons accused of crimes that fall within the jurisdiction of the Tribunal.

Third: Prosecutors shall elect a Chief Prosecutor and a Deputy from among them.

Fourth: Each Prosecution Office shall be composed of a Prosecutor and such other qualified staff as may be required for the Prosecutor's work.

Fifth: Each prosecutor shall act with complete independence since he is considered as a separate entity from the Court. He shall not fall under, nor receive instructions from, any government department or from any other party. Each Prosecutor shall act with complete independence as a separate organ of the Tribunal. He shall not be subject to or respond to requests or instructions from the government or any other party.

Sixth: The Chief Prosecutor shall assign to Prosecutors cases requiring investigation and prosecution in court [Literally, presenting the case at the stage of trial] in accordance with the powers granted to the Prosecutors by law.

Seventh: The Chief Prosecutor, in consultation with the President of the Tribunal, may appoint non-Iraqi experts to provide assistance to the Prosecutors with regard to the investigation and prosecution of cases provided for in this Law, whether international or otherwise. The Chief Prosecutor may appoint these experts with the assistance of the international community, including the United Nations.

Eighth: The non-Iraqi experts referred to in paragraph Seventh of this Article shall be persons of high moral character, honesty and integrity. The non-Iraqi expert shall preferably be a person who has acted in a prosecutorial capacity in his country or at international war crimes tribunals.

PART SEVEN
The Administration Department

Article 10

First: The Administration Department shall be managed by an officer with the title of Department Director who holds a bachelor degree in law and has judicial and administrative experience. He shall be assisted by a number of employees in managing the affairs of the department.

Second: The Administration Department shall be responsible for the administrative, financial and servicing affairs of the Tribunal and the Prosecutions Department.

SECTION TWO
Court Jurisdiction

PART ONE
The Crime of Genocide

Article 11
First: For the purposes of this Law and in accordance with the Convention on the Prevention and Punishment of the Crime of Genocide, dated 9 December 1948, as ratified by Iraq on 20 January 1959, "genocide" means any of the following acts committed with intent to destroy, in whole or in part, a national, ethnic, racial or religious group as such:

A. Killing members of the group;

B. Causing serious bodily or mental harm to members of the group;

C. Deliberately inflicting on the group living conditions calculated to bring about its physical destruction in whole or in part;

D. Imposing measures intended to prevent births within the group.

E. Forcibly transferring children of the group to another group.

Second: The following acts shall be punishable

A. Genocide.

B. Conspiracy to commit genocide.

C. Direct and public incitement to commit genocide.

D. Attempt to commit genocide.

E. Complicity in genocide.

PART TWO
Crimes AgainstHumanity

Article 12
First: For the purposes of this Law, "crimes against humanity" means any of the following acts when committed as part of a widespread or systematic attack directed against any civilian population, with knowledge of the attack:

A.Willful killing;

B. Extermination;

C. Enslavement;

D. Deportation or forcible transfer of population;

E. Imprisonment or other severe deprivation of physical liberty in violation of fundamental norms of international law;

F. Torture;

G. Rape, sexual slavery, enforced prostitution, forced pregnancy, or any other form of sexual violence of comparable gravity;

H. Persecution against any specific party or population on political, racial, national, ethnic, cultural, religious, gender or other grounds that are impermissible under international law, in connection with any act referred to as a form of sexual violence of comparable gravity;

I. Enforced disappearance of persons; and

J. Other inhumane acts of a similar character intentionally causing great suffering, or serious injury to the body or to the mental or physical health.

Second: For the purposes of implementing the provisions of paragraph First of this Article:

A. "Attack directed against any civilian population" means a course of conduct involving the multiple panel of acts referred to in paragraph First of this Article against any civilian population, pursuant to or in furtherance of a state or organizational policy to commit such attack;

B. "Extermination" means the intentional infliction of living conditions, such as the deprivation of access to food and medicine, with the intent to bring about the destruction of part of the population;

C. "Enslavement" means the exercise of any or all of the powers entailed by the right of ownership over a person and includes the exercise of such power in the course of trafficking in persons, particularly women and children;

617

D. "Deportation or forcible transfer of population" means forced displacement of the persons concerned by expulsion or other coercive acts from the area in which they are lawfully present, without grounds permitted under international law;

E. "Torture" means the intentional infliction of severe pain or suffering, whether physical or mental, upon a person in the custody or under the control of the accused; except that torture shall not include pain or suffering arising from, or related to legal punishments;

F. "Persecution" means the intentional and severe deprivation of fundamental rights contrary to international law by reason of the identity of the group or population; and

G. "Enforced disappearance of persons" means the arrest, detention or abduction of persons by, or with the authorization, support or acquiescence of, the State or a political organization, followed by a refusal to acknowledge that deprivation of freedom or to give information on the fate or whereabouts of those persons, with the intention of removing them from the protection of the law for a prolonged period of time.

PART THREE
War Crimes

Article 13

For the purposes of this Law, "war crimes" shall mean the following:

First: Grave breaches of the Geneva Conventions of 12 August 1949, namely any of the following acts against persons or property protected under the provisions of the relevant Geneva Convention:

    A. Willful killing;

    B. Torture or inhuman treatment, including biological experiments;

    C. Willfully causing great suffering, or serious injury to body or health;

    D. Extensive destruction and appropriation of property not justified by military necessity and carried out unlawfully and wantonly;

    E. Compelling a prisoner of war or other protected person to serve in the forces of a hostile power;

    F. Willfully denying the right of a fair regular trial to a prisoner of war or other protected person;

    G. Unlawful confinement;

    H. Unlawful deportation or transfer; and

    I. Taking of hostages.

Second: Other serious violations of the laws and customs applicable in international armed conflicts, within the established framework of international law, namely any of the following acts:

    A. Intentionally directing attacks against the civilian population as such or against individual civilians not taking direct part in hostilities;

    B. Intentionally directing attacks against civilian objects, including objects which do not constitute military objectives;

    C. Intentionally directing attacks against personnel, installations, material, units or vehicles used in humanitarian assistance or peacekeeping missions in accordance with the Charter of the United Nations, as long as such missions are entitled to the protection given to civilians or civilian objects under the international law of armed conflicts;

    D. Intentionally launching an attack in the knowledge that such attack will cause incidental loss of life or injury to civilians or civilian damage which would be clearly excessive in relation to the concrete and direct overall military advantages anticipated;

    E. Intentionally launching an attack in the knowledge that such attack will cause widespread, long-term and severe damage to the natural environment, which would be clearly excessive in relation to the concrete and direct overall military advantage anticipated;

    F. Attacking or bombarding, by whatever means, towns, villages, dwellings or buildings which are undefended and which are not military objectives;

    G. Killing or wounding a combatant who, having laid down his arms or having no longer means of defense, has clearly surrendered;

    H. Making improper use of a flag of truce, or the flag, or the military insignia and uniform of the enemy or of the United Nations, as well as of the distinctive emblems of the Geneva Conventions, resulting in death or serious personal injury;

I. The transfer, directly or indirectly, by the Government of Iraq or any of its agencies (including, for clarification, any of the agencies of the Arab Ba'ath Socialist Party), of parts of its own civilian population into any territory it occupies, or the deportation or transfer of all or parts of the population of the occupied territory within or outside this territory;

J. Intentionally directing attacks against buildings which do not constitute military objectives, and are dedicated to religious, educational, artistic, scientific or charitable purposes, or against historic monuments, hospitals and places where the sick and wounded are collected;

K. Subjecting persons of another nation to physical mutilation or to medical or scientific experiments of any kind that are neither justified by the medical, dental or hospital treatment of the person concerned nor carried out in his or her interest, and which cause death to or seriously endanger the health of such person or persons;

L. Killing or wounding treacherously individuals belonging to a hostile nation or army;

M. Declaring that no person is still alive [*i.e.* declaring that no quarter will be given];

N. Destroying or seizing the civilian property of an adverse party unless such destruction or seizure be imperatively required by the necessities of war;

O. Declaring the abolition, suspension or prohibition of access to a court of law, with the intention of depriving the nationals of the hostile party from seeking their rights;

P. Compelling the nationals of the hostile party to take part inmilitary operations directed against their own country, even if they were in the belligerent's service before the commencement of the war;

Q. Pillaging a town or place, even when taken by force;

R. Using poisons or poisoned weapons;

S. Using asphyxiating, poisonous or any other gases, as well as any other similar liquids, materials or devices;

T. Using bullets, which expand or flatten easily in the human body, such as bullets with a hard envelope, which does not entirely cover the core or is pierced

U. Committing outrages upon personal dignity, in particular humiliating and degrading treatment;

V. Committing rape, sexual slavery, enforced prostitution, forced pregnancy, or any other form of sexual violence of comparable gravity;

W. Utilizing the presence of civilians or other protected persons to render certain points, areas or military forces immune from military operations;

X. Intentionally directing attacks against buildings, material and medical units, means of transport, and personnel using the distinctive emblems of the Geneva Conventions in conformity with international law;

Y. Intentionally using starvation of civilians as a method of warfare by depriving them ofmaterial indispensable to their survival, including willfully impeding relief supplies as provided for under international law; and

Z. Conscripting or enlisting children under the age of fifteen years into the national armed forces or using them to participate actively in hostilities.

Third: In the case of an armed conflict, any of the following acts committed against
persons taking no active part in the hostilities, including members of armed forces who have laid down their arms and those placed *hors de combat* by sickness, injury, detention or any other cause:

A. Use of violence against life and persons, in particular killing of all kinds, mutilation, cruel treatment and torture;

B. Committing outrages upon personal dignity, in particular humiliating and degrading treatment;

C. Taking of hostages; and

D. The passing of sentences and the carrying out of executions without previous judgment pronounced by a regularly constituted court, affording all recognized and indispensable judicial guarantees.

Fourth: Other serious violations of the laws and customs of war applicable in armed conflict not of an international character. [*sic*] within the established framework of international law, specifically any of the following acts:

A. Intentionally directing attacks against the civilian population as such or against civilian individuals not taking direct part in hostilities;

B. Intentionally directing attacks against buildings, materials, medical transportation units and means, and personnel using the distinctive emblems of the Geneva Conventions in conformity with international law;

C. Intentionally directing attacks against personnel, installations, materials, units, or vehicles used in humanitarian assistance or peacekeeping missions in accordance with the Charter of the United Nations, as long as they are entitled to the protection given to civilians or civilian targets under the international law of armed conflict;

D. Intentionally directing attacks against buildings dedicated to religious, educational, artistic, scientific or charitable purposes, or against historic monuments, hospitals and places where the sick and wounded are collected, provided they are not military objectives;

E. Pillaging any town or place, even when taken over by force;

F. Committing rape, sexual slavery, enforced prostitution, forced pregnancy, or any other form of sexual violence of comparable gravity;

G. Conscripting or listing children under the age of fifteen years into armed forces or groups or using them to participate actively in hostilities;

H. Ordering the displacement of the civilian population for reasons related to the conflict, unless the security of the civilians involved or imperative military reasons so demand;

I. Killing or wounding treacherously a combatant adversary;

J. Declaring that no person is still alive;

K. Subjecting persons who are under the power of the other party in the conflict to physical mutilation or to medical or scientific experiments of any kind that are neither justified by the medical, dental or hospital treatment of the person concerned nor carried out in his or her interest, causing death to such person or persons, or seriously endangering their health; and

L. Destroying or seizing the property of an adversary, unless such destruction or seizure is imperatively demanded by the necessities of the conflict.

PART FOUR
Violations of Iraqi Laws

Article 14

The Tribunal shall have the power to prosecute persons who have committed the following crimes:

First: Interference in the affairs of the judiciary or attempting to influence its functioning.

Second: The wastage and squandering of national resources, pursuant to Article 2(g) of the Punishment of Conspirators against Public Safety and Corrupters of the System of Governance Law 7 of 1958.

Third: The abuse of position and the pursuit of policies that have almost led [*i.e.,* may lead to] to the threat of war or the use of the Iraqi armed forces against an Arab country, in accordance with Article 1 of Law 7 of 1958.

Fourth: If the Tribunal finds that the special element of any of the crimes stipulated in Articles 11, 12 and 13 of this Law is missing, and establishes that the act involved constitutes a crime punishable under the Penal Code or any other penal law at the time of its commission, the Tribunal shall be competent to hear the case.

SECTION THREE
Individual Criminal Responsibility

Article 15

First: A person who commits a crime within the jurisdiction of this Tribunal shall be individually responsible and liable for punishment in accordance with this Law.

Second: In accordance with this Law, and the provisions of the Penal Code, a person shall be criminally responsible if he [or she]:

A. Commits such a crime, whether as an individual, jointly with another or through another person, regardless of whether that [other] person is criminally responsible;

B. Orders, solicits or induces the commission of such a crime, which has occurred or has been attempted;

C. For the purpose of facilitating the commission of such a crime, aids, abets or by any other means assists in its commission or its attempted commission, including providing the means for its commission;

D. Contributing by any other means, together with a group of persons with a common criminal intent, to the commission or attempted commission of such a crime provided such contribution is intentional and is either:

    1. Made with the aim of furthering the criminal activity or criminal purpose of the group, where such activity or purpose involves the commission of a crime within the jurisdiction of the Tribunal;

    2. Made with the knowledge of the intention of the group to commit the crime;

E. In respect of the crime of genocide, directly and publicly incites others to commit this crime;

F. Attempts to commit such a crime by taking action with the intention of committing it, but the crime does not occur because of circumstances independent of the person's intentions. However, a person who takes an action that precludes the commission or completion of the crime shall not be liable for punishment, nor will he be liable for punishment under this Law if he completely and voluntarily abandons his criminal purpose.

Third: The official position of any accused person, whether as president of the State, chairman or member of the Revolution Command Council, prime minister or member of the cabinet, or a member of the leadership of the Ba'ath Party, shall not relieve such person of criminal responsibility nor mitigate punishment. No person is entitled to any immunity with respect to any of the crimes stipulated in Articles 11, 12, 13 and 14 of this Law.

Fourth: A superior is not relieved of the criminal responsibility for crimes committed by his subordinates, if he knew or had reason to know that the subordinate had committed, or was about to commit such acts, and the superior failed to take the necessary and reasonable measures to prevent such acts or to refer the matter to the competent authorities for investigation and prosecution.

Fifth: The fact that an accused person acted pursuant to an order of the Government or of his superior shall not relieve him of criminal responsibility, but may be considered in mitigation of punishment if the Tribunal determines that justice so requires.

Sixth: Amnesty decrees issued prior to this Law coming into force do not apply to persons accused of committing any of the crimes stipulated in it.

SECTION FOUR
Rules of Procedure and Evidence

Article 16

The Tribunal shall follow the rules of procedure provided for in the Criminal Procedure Law 23 of 1971 and the Rules of Procedures and Evidence appended to this Law, of which it shall be considered an integral part.

SECTION FIVE
General Principles of Criminal Law

Article 17

First: In the absence of provisions in this Law and the rules made thereunder, the general principles of criminal law contained in the following laws shall be applicable in connection with the prosecution and trial of any accused persons:

    A- For the period 17/7/1968 to 14/12/1969, the Baghdadi Penal Code of 1919

    B- For the period 15/12/1969 to 1/5/2003, the Penal Code No. 111 of 1969, which was in force in 1985 (Third Edition),

    C- The Military Penal Code No.13 of 1940, and the Code of Military Procedure No. 44 of 1941.

Second: In interpreting Articles 11, 12 and 13 of this Law, the Trial Chamber and Appeals Chamber may resort to the [relevant] decisions of international criminal tribunals.

Third: Grounds for exclusion of criminal responsibility under the Penal Code shall be implemented in a manner consistent with this Law and with international legal obligations concerning crimes within the jurisdiction of the Tribunal.

Fourth: The crimes stipulated in Articles 11, 12, 13, and 14 of this Law shall not be subject to any statute of limitations.

SECTION SIX
Investigations and Indictment

Article 18

First: The Tribunal Investigative Judge shall initiate investigations on the basis of information obtained from any source, particularly from the police or any governmental or non-governmental source. The Investigative Judge shall assess the information received and decide whether there is sufficient basis to proceed.

Second: The Investigative Judge shall have the power to question suspects, victims or their relatives, and witnesses, to collect evidence and to conduct on-site investigations. In carrying out his tasks, the Investigative Judge may, as appropriate, request the assistance of the relevant governmental authorities, who shall be required to provide full cooperation with the request.

Third: Upon a determination that a *prima facie* case exists, the Investigative Judge shall prepare an indictment containing a concise statement of the facts and the crime with which the accused is charged under the Law, and shall refer the case to the Trial Chamber.

PART ONE
Rights of the Accused

Article 19

First: All persons shall be equal before the Tribunal.

Second: The accused shall be presumed innocent until proven guilty before the Tribunal in accordance with this law.

Third Every accused shall be entitled to a public hearing, in accordance with the provisions of this law and the rules of procedure made hereunder.

Fourth: When bringing charges against the accused pursuant to this Law, the accused shall be entitled to a fair impartial trial in accordance with the following minimum guarantees:

> A. To be informed promptly and in detail of the content, nature and cause of the charge against him;
>
> B. To have adequate time and facilities for the preparation of his defense and to communicate freely with counsel of his own choosing and to meet with him in private. The accused is entitled to have non-Iraqi legal representation so long as the principal lawyer of such accused is Iraqi;
>
> C. To be tried without undue delay;
>
> D. To be tried in his presence, and to be assisted by counsel of his own choosing, or to be informed of his right to request legal assistance if he cannot afford it; and to have the right to seek such assistance that will allow him to appoint a lawyer without paying the fees;
>
> E. To have the right to call and examine defence and prosecution witnesses, and to present any evidence in his defense in accordance with the law.
>
> F. Not to be compelled to confess guilt, and to have the right to remain silent and not to testify without such silence being interpreted as evidence of guilt or innocence

SECTION SEVEN
Trial Proceedings

Article 20

First: A person against whom an indictment has been issued shall be taken into custody, pursuant to an arrest order or warrant issued by the Tribunal Investigative Judge, and shall be immediately informed of the charges against him and transferred to the Tribunal.

Second: The Trial Chamber shall ensure a fair and expeditious trial conducted in accordance with this Law and the Rules of Procedure and Evidence annexed it, with full respect for the rights of the accused and due regard for the protection of victims or their relatives, and witnesses.

Third: The Trial Chamber shall read the indictment, satisfy itself that the rights of the accused are respected and guaranteed, ensure that the accused understands the charge or charges against him, and instruct the accused to enter a plea.

Fourth: The hearings shall be public unless the Trial Chamber decides to close the proceedings in accordance with the Rules of Procedure and Evidence annexed to this Law. The decision to close the proceedings shall be exercised on a very limited basis.

Article 21

The Trial Chamber shall provide for the protection of victims or their relatives, and witnesses, in accordance with the Rules of Procedure and Evidence annexed to this Law, including the protection of the identity of the victims or their relatives, and witnesses.

Article 22

Relatives of victims and harmed persons who are Iraqi nationals may bring civil suits against the accused for damages resulting from acts which constitute crimes under this Law. The Tribunal shall have the power to adjudicate such claims in accordance with the Code of Criminal Procedure No 23 of 1971 and other relevant laws.

Article 23

First: The Trial Chamber shall pronounce judgments and impose sentences and penalties on persons convicted of crimes within the jurisdiction of the Court.

Second: The judgment shall be rendered by a majority of the judges of the Trial Chamber, and shall be delivered by the Trial Chamber in public. The judgment shall not be issued except on the basis of a decision to convict, to which the opinions of dissenting judges may be appended.

Article 24

First: The penalties imposed by the Tribunal shall be those prescribed by the Penal Code No. 111 of 1969, except for a sentence of life imprisonment that means the remaining natural life of the convicted person, taking into account the provisions stipulated in Article 17 of this Law.

Second: The penalties for the crimes under Article 14 of this Statute shall be those prescribed under Iraqi Penal Code and other penal laws.

Third: Taking into account paragraphs Fourth and Fifth of this article, the Trial Chambers shall determine the penalties for the crimes under Articles 11, 12 and 13 of this Law

Fourth: A person convicted of crimes stipulated in the Penal Code shall be punished if committed:

    A. Murder or rape as defined under the Penal Code.

    B. Complicity in the commission of murder or rape.

Fifth: The penalty for any crimes under Articles 11, 12, 13 which do not have a counterpart under Iraqi law shall be determined by the Trial Chambers taking into account such factors as the gravity of the crime, the individual circumstances of the convicted person, guided by judicial precedents and relevant sentences issued by the international criminal tribunals.

Sixth: The Trial Chambers may order the forfeiture of assets, property or proceeds derived directly or indirectly from a crime, without prejudice to the rights of the *bona fide* third parties.

Seventh: In accordance with Article 307 of the Code of Criminal Procedure, the Trial Chambers shall have the authority to confiscate any material or goods prohibited by law regardless of whether the case has been discharged for any lawful reason.

SECTION EIGHT
Appeals Proceedings

PART ONE
Cassation

Article 25

First: The convicted person or the Prosecutor may contest the verdicts and decisions by appealing in cassation to the Appeals Chamber on the following grounds:

    A. If the verdict is in contradiction with the law or there is an error in interpreting it.

B. An error of procedure.

C. An error of material fact which has occasioned a miscarriage of justice.

Second: The Appeals Chamber may affirm, reverse or revise the decisions taken by the Trial Chambers or the Investigative Judge.

Third: Where the Appeals Chamber reverses a verdict of acquittal or release issued by the Trial Chamber or the Investigative Judge, the case shall be referred back to the Trial Chamber for retrial or to the Investigative Judge for implementation of its decision.

Fourth: The period allowed for the lodging of appeals shall be in accordance with the provisions of the Code of Criminal Procedure No. 23 of 1971, unless otherwise provided for.

PART TWO
Retrial

Article 26

First: Where new findings or facts have been discovered which were not known at the time of the proceedings before the Trial Chamber or the Appeals Chamber and which could have been a decisive factor in reaching the verdict, the convicted person or the Prosecutor may submit to the Tribunal an application for a retrial

Second: The Tribunal shall reject the application if it considers it to be unfounded. If the Tribunal determines that the application has merit, it may, after hearing the parties, and with a view to amending the judgment:

A. Send the case back to the original Trial Chamber to review it; or

B. Send the case to another Trial Chamber; or

C. The Appeals Chamber reviews the case.

SECTION NINE
Enforcement of Sentences

Article 27

First: Sentences shall be carried out in accordance with the law.

Second: No authority, including the President of the Republic, may grant a pardon or reduce the penalties issued by this Tribunal. Penalties shall be enforceable within thirty days of the sentence or decision reaching finality.

SECTION TEN
General and Final Provisions

Article 28

Investigative judges, Trial Chamber judges, members of the Prosecutions Department, Director of the Administration Department and Tribunal personnel shall be Iraqi nationals, taking into account Article 4 (Third) of this Law.

Article 29

First: The Tribunal and the national courts shall have concurrent jurisdiction to prosecute persons accused of the crimes prescribed in Article 14 of this Statute

Second: The Tribunal shall have primacy over all other Iraqi courts with respect to its jurisdiction over the crimes prescribed in Articles 11, 12 and 13 of this Law.

Third: At any stage of the proceedings, the Tribunal may demand of any other court to transfer any case being tried by it involving any crimes prescribed inArticles 11, 12, 13 and 14 of this Law, and such court shall be required to transfer such case on demand.

Fourth: At any stage of the proceedings, the Tribunal may demand of any other court
to transfer any case being tried by it involving any crimes prescribed in Articles 13,
14, 15 and 16 of this Law, and such court shall be required to transfer such case upon demand.

Article 30

First: No person shall be tried before any other Iraqi court for crimes for which he has already been tried by the Tribunal, in accordance with Articles 300 and 301 of the Code of Criminal Procedure.

Second: A person who has been tried by any Iraqi court for a crime or crimes within the jurisdiction of the Tribunal may not be subsequently tried by the Tribunal unless the Tribunal determines that the previous court proceedings were not impartial or independent, or were designed to shield the accused from criminal responsibility. When taking a decision to order a retrial, one of the conditions contained in Article 196 of the Code of Civil Procedure and the requirements of Article 303 of the Code of Criminal Procedure must be met.

Third: In determining the penalty to be imposed on a person convicted of a crime under this Law, the Tribunal shall take into account the time served of any penalty imposed by an Iraqi court on the same person for the same crime.

Article 31

First: The President of the Tribunal, the Judges, the Investigation Judges, the Prosecutors, the Director of the Administration Department and the Tribunal staff shall have immunity from civil suits with respect to their official duties.

Second: Other persons, including the accused, shall be accorded such treatment as is necessary for the proper functioning of the Tribunal.

Article 32

Arabic shall be the official language of the Tribunal.

Article 33

No person belonging to the Ba'ath Party may be appointed as a Judge, Investigative Judge, Prosecutor, employee or any of the Tribunal's staff.

Article 34

The expenses of the Tribunal shall be borne by the regular budget of the State

Article 35

The President of the Tribunal shall prepare an annual report on the Tribunal's work for submission to the Council of Ministers.

Article 36

The provisions of the Civil Service Law No. 24 of 1960, Personnel Law No. 25 of 1960, State And Socialist Sector Employees Disciplinary Law No 14 of 1991 and Civil Service Retirement Law No.33 of 1966 shall apply to the Tribunal's employees other than the judges and members of Public Prosecution.

Article 37

The Statute of the Iraqi Special Tribunal for Crimes Against Humanity, Law No. 1 of 2003, and the Rules of Procedure issued under Article 16 thereof shall be abolished with effect from the date of the coming into force of this Law.

Article 38

All decisions and rules of procedure issued under Law No. 1 of 2003 are considered correct and in accordance with the law.

Article 39

In coordination with the President of the Tribunal, the Council of Ministers shall issue instructions to facilitate the implementation of this Law.

Article 40

This Law shall come into force on the date of its publication in the Official Gazette.

INTERNATIONAL FINANCIAL INSTITUTIONS

IBRD ARTICLES OF AGREEMENT

International Bank for Reconstruction and Development Articles of Agreement, 60 Stat. 1440, 2 U.N.T.S. 134 (as amended 1965 and 1989), *available at* http://siteresources.worldbank.org/EXTABOUTUS/Resources/ibrd-articlesofagreement.pdf

ARTICLE I
Purposes

The purposes of the Bank are:

(i) To assist in the reconstruction and development of territories of members by facilitating the investment of capital for productive purposes, including the restoration of economies destroyed or disrupted by war, the reconversion of productive facilities to peacetime needs and the encouragement of the development of productive facilities and resources in less developed countries.

(ii) To promote private foreign investment by means of guarantees or participations in loans and other investments made by private investors; and when private capital is not available on reasonable terms, to supplement private investment by providing, on suitable conditions, finance for productive purposes out of its own capital, funds raised by it and its other resources.

(iii) To promote the long-range balanced growth of international trade and the maintenance of equilibrium in balances of payments by encouraging international investment for the development of the productive resources of members, thereby assisting in raising productivity, the standard of living and conditions of labor in their territories.

(iv) To arrange the loans made or guaranteed by it in relation to international loans through other channels so that the more useful and urgent projects, large and small alike, will be dealt with first.

(v) To conduct its operations with due regard to the effect of international investment on business conditions in the territories of members and, in the immediate postwar years, to assist in bringing about a smooth transition from a wartime to a peacetime economy.

The Bank shall be guided in all its decisions by the purposes set forth above

ARTICLE II
Membership in and Capital of the Bank

SECTION 1. Membership

(a) The original members of the Bank shall be those members of the International Monetary Fund which accept membership in the Bank before the date specified in Article XI, Section 2 (e).

(b) Membership shall be open to other members of the Fund, at such times and in accordance with such terms as may be prescribed by the Bank. * * *

ARTICLE III
General Provisions Relating to Loans and Guarantees

SECTION 1. Use of Resources

(a) The resources and the facilities of the Bank shall be used exclusively for the benefit of members with equitable consideration to projects for development and projects for reconstruction alike.

(b) For the purpose of facilitating the restoration and reconstruction of the economy of members whose metropolitan territories have suffered great devastation from enemy occupation or hostilities, the Bank, in determining the conditions and terms of loans made to such members, shall pay special regard to lightening the financial burden and expediting the completion of such restoration and reconstruction. * * *

SECTION 4. Conditions on which the Bank may Guarantee or Make Loans

The Bank may guarantee, participate in, or make loans to any member or any political sub-division thereof and any business, industrial, and agricultural enterprise in the territories of a member, subject to the following conditions:

(i) When the member in whose territories the project is located is not itself the borrower, the member or the central bank or some comparable agency of the member which is acceptable to the Bank, fully guarantees the repayment of the principal and the payment of interest and other charges on the loan.

(ii) The Bank is satisfied that in the prevailing market conditions the borrower would be unable otherwise to obtain the loan under conditions which in the opinion of the Bank are reasonable for the borrower.

(iii) A competent committee, as provided for in Article V, Section 7, has submitted a written report recommending the project after a careful study of the merits of the proposal.

(iv) In the opinion of the Bank the rate of interest and other charges are reasonable and such rate, charges and the schedule for repayment of principal are appropriate to the project.

(v) In making or guaranteeing a loan, the Bank shall pay due regard to the prospects that the borrower, and, if the borrower is not a member, that the guarantor, will be in position to meet its obligations under the loan; and the Bank shall act prudently in the interests both of the particular member in whose territories the project is located and of the members as a whole.

(vi) In guaranteeing a loan made by other investors, the Bank receives suitable compensation for its risk.

(vii) Loans made or guaranteed by the Bank shall, except in special circumstances, be for the purpose of specific projects of reconstruction or development.

SECTION 5. Use of Loans Guaranteed, Participated in or Made by the Bank

(a) The Bank shall impose no conditions that the proceeds of a loan shall be spent in the territories of any particular member or members.

(b) The Bank shall make arrangements to ensure that the proceeds of any loan are used only for the purposes for which the loan was granted, with due attention to considerations of economy and efficiency and without regard to political or other non-economic influences or considerations.

(c) In the case of loans made by the Bank, it shall open an account in the name of the borrower and the amount of the loan shall be credited to this account in the currency or currencies in which the loan is made. The borrower shall be permitted by the Bank to draw on this account only to meet expenses in connection with the project as they are actually incurred. * * *

ARTICLE IV
Operations
SECTION 1. Methods of Making or Facilitating Loans

(a) The Bank may make or facilitate loans which satisfy the general conditions of Article III in any of the following ways:

> (i) By making or participating in direct loans out of its own funds corresponding to its unimpaired paid-up capital and surplus and, subject to Section 6 of this Article, to its reserves.
>
> (ii) By making or participating in direct loans out of funds raised in the market of a member, or otherwise borrowed by the Bank.
>
> (iii) By guaranteeing in whole or in part loans made by private investors through the usual investment channels.

(b) The Bank may borrow funds under (a) (ii) above or guarantee loans under (a) (iii) above only with the approval of the member in whose markets the funds are raised and the member in whose currency the loan is denominated, and only if those members agree that the proceeds may be exchanged for the currency of any other member without restriction. * * *

SECTION 4. Payment Provisions for Direct Loans

Loan contracts under Section 1 (a) (i) or (ii) of this Article shall be made in accordance with the following payment provisions:

(a) The terms and conditions of interest and amortization payments, maturity and dates of payment of each loan shall be determined by the Bank. The Bank shall also determine the rate and any other terms and conditions of commission to be charged in connection with such loan. In the case of loans made under Section 1 (a) (ii) of this Article during the first ten years of the Bank's operations, this rate of commission shall be not less than one percent per annum and not greater than one and one-half percent per annum, and shall be charged on the outstanding portion of any such loan. At the end of this period of ten years, the rate of commission may be reduced by the Bank with respect both to the outstanding portions of loans already made and to future loans, if the reserves accumulated by the Bank under Section 6 of this Article and out of other earnings are considered by it sufficient to justify a reduction. In the case of future loans the Bank shall also have discretion to increase the rate of commission beyond the above limit, if experience indicates that an increase is advisable.

(b) All loan contracts shall stipulate the currency or currencies in which payments under the contract shall be made to the Bank. At the option of the borrowers however, such payments may be made in gold, or subject to the agreement of the Bank, in the currency of a member other than that prescribed in the contract.

(i) In the case of loans made under Section 1 (a) (i) of this Article, the loan contracts shall provide that payments to the Bank of interest, other charges and amortization shall be made in the currency loaned, unless the member whose currency is loaned agrees that such payments shall be made in some other specified currency or currencies. These payments, subject to the provisions of Article II, Section 9 (c), shall be equivalent to the value of such contractual payments at the time the loans were made, in terms of a currency specified for the purpose by the Bank by a three-fourths majority of the total voting power.

(ii) In the case of loans made under Section 1 (a) (ii) of this Article, the total amount outstanding and payable to the Bank in any one currency shall at no time exceed the total amount of the outstanding borrowings made by the Bank under Section 1 (a) (ii) and payable in the same currency.

(c) If a member suffers from an acute exchange stringency, so that the service of any loan contracted by that member or guaranteed by it or by one of its agencies cannot be provided in the stipulated manner, the member concerned may apply to the Bank for a relaxation of the conditions of payment. if the Bank is satisfied that some relaxation is in the interests of the particular member and of the operations of the Bank and of its members as a whole, it may take action under either, or both, of the following paragraphs with respect to the whole, or part, of the annual service:

(i) The Bank may, in its discretion, make arrangements with the member concerned to accept service payments on the loan in the member's currency for periods not to exceed three years upon appropriate terms regarding the use of such currency and the maintenance of its foreign exchange value; and for the repurchase of such currency on appropriate terms.

(ii) The Bank may modify the terms of amortization or extend the life of the loan, or both. * * *

SECTION 8. Miscellaneous Operations

In addition to the operations specified elsewhere in this Agreement, the Bank shall have the power:

(i) To buy and sell securities it has issued and to buy and sell securities which it has guaranteed or in which it has invested, provided that the Bank shall obtain the approval of the member in whose territories the securities are to be bought or sold.

(ii) To guarantee securities in which it has invested for the purpose of facilitating their sale.

(iii) To borrow the currency of any member with the approval of that member.

(iv) To buy and sell such other securities as the Directors by a three-fourths majority of the total voting power may deem proper for the investment-of all or part of the special reserve under Section 6 of this Article.

In exercising the powers conferred by this Section, the Bank may deal with any person, partnership, association, corporation or other legal entity in the territories of any member. * * *

SECTION 10. Political Activity Prohibited

The Bank and its officers shall not interfere in the political affairs of any member; nor shall they be influenced in their decisions by the political character of the member or members concerned. Only economic considerations shall be relevant to their decisions, and these considerations shall be weighed impartially in order to achieve the purposes stated in Article I.

ARTICLE V
Organization and Management

SECTION 1. Structure of the Bank

The Bank shall have a Board of Governors, Executive Directors, a President and such other officers and staff to perform such duties as the Bank may determine.

SECTION 2. Board of Governors

(a) All the powers of the Bank shall be vested in the Board of Governors consisting of one governor and one alternate appointed by each member in such manner as it may determine. Each governor and each alternate shall serve for five years, subject to the pleasure of the member appointing him, and may be reappointed. No alternate may vote except in the absence of his principal. The Board shall select one of the Governors as chairman.

(b) The Board of Governors may delegate to the Executive Directors authority to exercise any powers of the Board, except the power to:

(i) Admit new members and determine the conditions of their admission;

(ii) Increase or decrease the capital stock;

(iii) Suspend a member;

(iv) Decide appeals from interpretations of this agreement given by the Executive Directors;

(v) Make arrangements to cooperate with other international organizations (other than informal arrangements of a temporary and administrative character);

(vi) Decide to suspend permanently the operations of the Bank and to distribute its assets;

(vii) Determine the distribution of the net income of the Bank.

(c) The Board of Governors shall hold an annual meeting and such other meetings as may be provided for by the Board or called by the Executive Directors. Meetings of the Board shall be called by the Directors whenever requested by five members or by members having one quarter of the total voting power.

(d) A quorum for any meeting of the Board of Governors shall be a majority of the Governors, exercising not less than two-thirds of the total voting power.

(e) The Board of Governors may by regulation establish a procedure whereby the Executive Directors, when they deem such action to be in the best interests of the Bank, may obtain a vote of the Governors on a specific question without calling a meeting of the Board.

(f) The Board of Governors, and the Executive Directors to the extent authorized, may adopt such rules and regulations as may be necessary or appropriate to conduct the business of the Bank

(g) Governors and alternates shall serve as such without compensation from the Bank, but the Bank shall pay them reasonable expenses incurred in attending meetings.

(h) The Board of Governors shall determine the remuneration to be paid to the Executive Directors and the salary and terms of the contract of service of the President. * * *

SECTION 4. Executive Directors

(a) The Executive Directors shall be responsible for the conduct of the general operations of the Bank, and for this purpose, shall exercise all the powers delegated to them by the Board of Governors.

(b) There shall be twelve Executive Directors, who need not be governors, and of whom:

(i) five shall be appointed, one by each of the five members having the largest number of shares;

(ii) seven shall be elected according to Schedule B by all the Governors other than those appointed by the five members referred to in (i) above.

For the purpose of this paragraph, "members" means governments of countries whose names are set forth in Schedule A, whether they are original members or become members in accordance with Article 11, Section I (b). When governments of other countries become members, the Board of Governors may, by a four-fifths majority of the total voting power, increase the total number of directors by increasing the number of directors to be elected. Executive Directors shall be appointed or elected every two years. (c) Each executive director shall appoint an alternate with full power to act for him when he is not present. When the executive directors appointing them are present, alternates may participate in meetings but shall not vote.

(d) Directors shall continue in office until their successors are appointed or elected. If the office of an elected director becomes vacant more than ninety days before the end of his term, another director shall be elected for the remainder of the term by the governors who elected the former director. A majority of the votes cast shall be required for election. While the office remains vacant, the alternate of the former director shall exercise his powers, except that of appointing an alternate.

(e) The Executive Directors shall function in continuous session at the principal office of the Bank and shall meet as often as the business of the Bank may require.

(f) A quorum for any meeting of the Executive Directors shall be a majority of the Directors, exercising not less than one-half of the total voting power.

(g) Each appointed director shall be entitled to cast the number of votes allotted under Section 3 of this Article to the member appointing him. Each elected director shall be entitled to cast the number of votes which counted toward his election. All the votes which a director is entitled to cast shall be cast as a unit.

(h) The Board of Governors shall adopt regulations under which a member not entitled to appoint a director under (b) above may send a representative to attend any meeting of the Executive Directors when a request made by, or a matter particularly affecting, that member is under consideration.

(i) The Executive Directors may appoint such committees as they deem advisable. Membership of such committees need not be limited to governors or directors or their alternates.

SECTION 5. President and Staff

(a) The Executive Directors shall select a President who shall not be a governor or an executive director or an alternate for either. The President shall be Chairman of the Executive Directors, but shall have no vote except a deciding vote in case of an equal division. He may participate in meetings of the Board of Governors, but shall not vote at such meetings. The President shall cease to hold office when the Executive Directors so decide.

(b) The President shall be chief of the operating staff of the Bank and shall conduct, under the direction of the Executive Directors, the ordinary business of the Bank. Subject to the general control of the Executive Directors, he shall be responsible for the organization, appointment and dismissal of the officers and staff.

(c) The President, officers and staff of the Bank, in the discharge of their offices, owe their duty entirely to the Bank and to no other authority. Each member of the Bank shall respect the international character of this duty and shall refrain from all attempts to influence any of them in the discharge of their duties.

(d) In appointing the officers and staff the President shall, subject to the paramount importance of securing the highest standards of efficiency and of technical competence, pay due regard to the importance of recruiting personnel on as wide a geographical basis as possible.

SECTION 6. Advisory Council

(a) There shall be an Advisory Council of not less than seven persons selected by the Board of Governors including representatives of banking, commercial, industrial, labor, and agricultural interests, and with as wide a national representation as possible. In those fields where specialized international organizations exist, the members of the Council representative of those fields shall be selected in agreement with such organizations. The Council shall advise the Bank on matters of general policy. The Council shall meet annually and on such other occasions as the Bank may request.

(b) Councillors shall serve for two years and may be reappointed. They shall be paid their reasonable expenses incurred on behalf of the Bank.

SECTION 7. Loan Committees

The committees required to report on loans under Article III, Section 4, shall be appointed by the Bank. Each such committee shall include an expert selected by the governor representing the member in whose territories the project is located and one or more members of the technical staff of the Bank.

SECTION 8. Relationship to Other International Organizations

(a) The Bank, within the terms of this Agreement, shall cooperate with any general international organization and with public international organizations having specialized responsibilities in related fields. Any arrangements for such cooperation which would involve a modification of any provision of this Agreement may be effected only after amendment to this Agreement under Article VIII.

(b) In making decisions on applications for loans or guarantees relating to matters directly within the competence of any international organization of the types specified in the preceding paragraph and participated in primarily by members of the Bank, the Bank shall give consideration to the views and recommendations of such organization. * * *

ARTICLE VII
Status, Immunities and Privileges

SECTION 1. Purposes of the Article

To enable the Bank to fulfill the functions with which it is entrusted, the status, immunities and privileges set forth in this Article shall be accorded to the Bank in the territories of each member.

SECTION 2. Status of the Bank

The Bank shall possess full juridical personality, and, in particular, the capacity:

      (i) to contract;

(ii) to acquire and dispose of immovable and movable property;

(iii) to institute legal proceedings.

SECTION 3. Position of the Bank with Regard to judicial Process
Actions may be brought against the Bank only in a court of competent jurisdiction in the territories of a member in which the Bank has an office, has appointed an agent for the purpose of accepting service or notice of process, or has issued or guaranteed securities. No actions shall, however, be brought by members or persons acting for or deriving claims from members. The property and assets of the Bank shall, wheresoever located and by whomsoever held, be immune from all forms of seizure, attachment or execution before the delivery of final judgment against the Bank.

SECTION 4. Immunity of Assets from Seizure
Property and assets of the Bank, wherever located and by whomsoever held, shall be immune from search, requisition, confiscation, expropriation or any other form of seizure by executive or legislative action.

SECTION 5. Immunity of Archives
The archives of the Bank shall be inviolable.

SECTION 6. Freedom of Assets from Restrictions
To the extent necessary to carry out the operations provided for in this Agreement and subject to the provisions of this Agreement, all property and assets of the Bank shall be free from restrictions, regulations, controls and moratoria of any nature.

SECTION 7. Privilege for Communications
The official communications of the Bank shall be accorded by each member the same treatment that it accords to the official communications of other members.

SECTION 8. Immunities and Privileges of Officers and Employees
All governors, executive directors, alternates, officers and employees of the Bank

(i) shall be immune from legal process with respect to acts performed by them in their official capacity except when the Bank waives this immunity;

(ii) not being local nationals, shall be accorded the same immunities from immigration restrictions, alien registration requirements and national service obligations and the same facilities as regards exchange restrictions as are accorded by members to the representatives, officials, and employees of comparable rank of other members;

(iii) shall be granted the same treatment in respect of travelling facilities as is accorded by members to representatives, officials and employees of comparable rank of other members.

SECTION 9. Immunities from Taxation
(a) The Bank, its assets, property, income and its operations and transactions authorized by this Agreement, shall be immune from all taxation and from all customs duties. The Bank shall also be immune from liability for the collection or payment of any tax or duty.

(b) No tax shall be levied on or in respect of salaries and emoluments paid by the Bank to executive directors, alternates, officials or employees of the Bank who are not local citizens, local subjects, or other local nationals.

(c) No taxation of any kind shall be levied on any obligation or security issued by the Bank (including any dividend or interest thereon) by whomsoever held:

> (i) which discriminates against such obligation or security solely because it is issued by the Bank; or

> (ii) if the sole jurisdictional basis for such taxation is the place or currency in which it is issued, made payable or paid, or the location of any office or place of business maintained by the Bank.

(d) No taxation of any kind shall be levied on any obligation or security guaranteed by the Bank (including any dividend or interest thereon) by whomsoever held:

> (i) which discriminates against such obligation or security solely because it is guaranteed by the Bank; or

(ii) if the sole jurisdictional basis for such taxation is the location of any office or place of business maintained by the Bank.

SECTION 10. Application of Article

Each member shall take such action as is necessary in its own territories for the purpose of making effective in terms of its own law the principles set forth in this Article and shall inform the Bank of the detailed action which it has taken. * * *

ARTICLE IX
Interpretation

(a) Any question of interpretation of the provisions of this Agreement arising between any member and the Bank or between any members of the Bank shall be submitted to the Executive Directors for their decision. If the question particularly affects any member not entitled to appoint an Executive Director, it shall be entitled to representation in accordance with Article V, Section 4 (h).

(b) In any case where the Executive Directors have given a decision under (a) above, any member may require that the question be referred to the Board of Governors, whose decision shall be final. Pending the result of the reference to the Board, the Bank may, so far as it deems necessary, act on the basis of the decision of the Executive Directors.

(c) Whenever a disagreement arises between the Bank and a country which has ceased to be a member, or between the Bank and any member during the permanent suspension of the Bank, such disagreement shall be submitted to arbitration by a tribunal of three arbitrators, one appointed by the Bank, another by the country involved and an umpire who, unless the parties otherwise agree, shall be appointed by the President of the Permanent Court of International justice or such other authority as may have been prescribed by regulation adopted by the Bank. The umpire shall have full power to settle an questions of procedure in any case where the parties are in disagreement with respect thereto. * * *

WORLD BANK INSPECTION PANEL OPERATING PROCEDURE

World Bank Inspection Panel, *Operating Procedure, adopted* August 19, 1994, *reprinted in* Ibrahim F. Shihata, *The World Bank Inspection Panel*, Annex III, 373, published for the World Bank by Oxford University Press (1994), *available at* www.worldbank.org

INTRODUCTION

The Inspection Panel (the "Panel") is an independent forum established by the Executive Directors of the International Bank for Reconstruction and Development ("IBRD") and the International Development Assocation ("IDA") by IBRD Resolution No. 93-10 and the identical IDA Resolution No. 93-6 both adopted by the Executive Directors of the respective institutions on September 22, 1993 (collectively the "Resolution"). The text of the Resolution is in Annex 1. References in these procedures to the "Bank" includes the IBRD and IDA.

The Panel's authority is dictated by the Resolution: within that framework, these Operating Procedures are adopted by the Panel to provide detail to the operational provisions. The text is based on the Resolution and takes into account suggestions from outside sources.

In view of the unprecedented nature of the new inspection function the current procedures are provisional: the Panel will review them within 12 months, and in light of experience and comments received, will revise thme if necessary and will recommend to the Bank's Executive Directors ("Executive Directors") amendments to the Resolution that would allow a more effective role for the Panel.

Compostion

The Panel consists of three Inspectors. At the outset one Inspector, the Chairperson, will work on a full-time basis: the other two will work part-time. This arrangement is provisional. The Panel's workload will be dicatated by the number and nature of requests received. If necessary, the Panel will recommend alternative arrangements to the Executive Directors.

Purpose

The Panel has established for the purpose of providing people directly and adversely affected by a Bank-financed project with an independent forum through which they can request the Bank to act in accordance with its own policies and procedures. It follows that this forum is available when adversely affected people believe the Bank itself has failed, or has failed to require others, to comply with its policies and procedures, and only after efforts have been made to ask Bank Managment ("Management") itself to deal with the problem.

Functions

The role of the Panel is to carry out independent investigations. Its function, which will be triggered when it receives a request for inspection, is to inquire and recommend: it will make a preliminary review of a request for inspection and the response of Management, independently assess the information and then recommend to the Board of Executive Directors whether or not the matters complained of should be investigated. If the Board decides that a request shall be investigated, the Panel will collect information and provide its findings, independent assessment and conclusions to the Board. On the basis of the Panel's findings and Management's recommendations, the Executive Directors will consider the actions, if any, to be taken by the Bank.

Participants

During the preliminary review period—up to the time the Panel makes a recommendation to the Board on whether or not the matter should be investigated—the Panel will accept statements or evidence from (a) the Requester, i.e. either the affected people and/or their duly appointed representative, or an Executive Director; (b) Management; and (c) any other individual or entity invited by the Panel to present information or comments.

During an investigation, any person who is either a party to the investigation or who is either a party to the investigation or who provides the designated Inspector(s) with satisfactory evidence that he/she has an interest, apart from any interest in common with the public, will be entitled to submit information or evidence relevant to the investigation.

Administration

The Panel has approved separate Administrative Procedures which are available from the Office of the Inspection Panel.

*Please note that all headings are for ease of reference only. They do not form part of these procedures and do not constitute an interpretation thereof.

I. SUBJECT MATTER OF REQUESTS

Scope

1. The Panel is authorized to accept requests for inspection ("Request(s)") which claim that an actual or threatened material adverse effect on the affected party's rights or interests arises directly out of an action or omission of the Bank to follow its own operational policies and procedures during the design, appraisal and/or implementation of a Bank-financed project. Before submitting a Request steps must have already been taken (or efforts made) to bring the matter to the attention of Management with a result unsatisfactory to the Requester.

Limitations

2. The Panel is not authorized to deal with the following:

> (a) complaints with respect to actions which are the responsibility of other parties, such as the borrower, or potential borrower, and which do not involve any action or omission on the part of the Bank;
>
> (b) complaints against procurement decisions by Bank borrowers from suppliers of goods and services financed by the Bank under a loan/credit agreement, or from losing tenderers for the supply of any such goods and services, which will continue to be addressed by Bank staff under existing procedures;
>
> (c) Requests filed after the Closing Date of the loan/credit financing the project with respect to which the Request is filed or when 95% or more of the loan/credits proceeds have been disbursed; or

(d) Requests related to a particular matter or matters over which the Panel has already made its recommendation after having received a prior Request, unless justified by new evidence or circumstances not known at the time of the prior Request.

II. PREPARATION OF A REQUEST

3. The Panel's operational proceeding begin when a Request is received. This section of the procedures is primarily designed to give further guidance to potential Requesters on what facts and explanations they should provide.

A. Who Can File A Request
4. The Panel has authority to receive Requests which complain of a violation of the Bank's policies and procedures from the following people or entities:
> (a) any group of two or more people in the country where the Bank-financed project is located who believe that as a result of the Bank's violation their rights or interests have been, or are likely to be adversely affected in a direct and material way. They may be an organization, association, society or other grouping of individuals; or
> (b) a duly appointed local representative acting on explicit instructions as the agent of adversely affected people; or
> (c) in the exceptional case referred to in paragraph 11 below, a foreign representative acting as agent of adversely affected people; or
> (d) an Executive Director of the Bank in special cases of serious alleged violations of the Bank's policies and procedures.

B. Contents of a Request
5. In accordance with the Resolution, Requests should contain the following information:
> (a) a description of the project, stating all the relevant facts including the harm suffered by or threatened to the affected party;
> (b) an explanation of how Bank policies, procedures or contractual documents were seriously violated;
> (c) a description of how the act or omission on the part of the Bank has led or may lead to a violation of the specific provision;
> (d) a description of how the party was, or is likely to be, materially and adversely affected by the Bank's act or omission and what rights or interests of the claimant were directly affected;
> (e) a description of the steps taken by the affected party to resolve the violations with Bank staff, and explanation of why the Bank's response was inadequate;
> (f) in Requests relating to matters previously submitted to the Panel, a statement specifying what new evidence or changed circumstances justify the Panel revisiting the issue; and
> (g) if some of the information cannot be provided, an explanation should be included.

C. Form of Request
Written
6. All Request must be submitted in writing, dated and signed by the Requester and contain his/her name and contact address.

Format
7. No specific form is necessary: a letter will suffice. A Requester may wish to refer to the guidance and use the model form specifying required information. (Attached as Annex 2)
Language
8. The working language of the Panel is English. Requests submitted directly by affected people themselves may be in their local language if they are unable to obtain a translation. If requests are not in English, the time needed to translate and ensure an accurate and agreed translation may delay acceptance and consideration by the Panel.
Representatives

9. If the Requester is a directly affected person or entity representing affected people, written signed proof that the representative has authority to act on their behalf must be attached.

10. If the Request is submitted by a non-affected representative, he/she must provide evidence of representational authority and the names and contact address of the party must be provided. Proof of the original signed copy of the affected party's explicit instructions, must be attached.

11. In addition, in cases of non-local representation, the Panel will require clear evidence that there is no adequate or appropriate representation in the country where the project is located.

Documents

12. The following documents should be attached:

> (a) all correspondence with Bank staff;
> (b) notes of meetings with Bank staff;
> (c) a map or diagram, if relevant, showing the location of the affected party or area affected by the project; and
> (d) any other evidence supporting the complaint.

13. If all the information listed cannot be provided an explanation should be included.

D. Delivery of Request

14. Requests must be sent by registered or certified mail or delivered by hand in a sealed envelope against receipt to the Office of the Inspection Panel at 1818 H Street, N.W., Washington, D.C. 20433, U.S.A. or to the Bank's resident representative in the country where the project is located. In the latter case, the resident representative shall, after issuing a receipt to the Requester, forward the Request to the Panel through the next pouch.

E. Advice on Preparation

15. People or entities seeking advice on how to prepare and submit a Request may contact the Office of the Inspection Panel, which will provide information or may meet and discuss the requirements with potential requesters.

III. PROCEDURES ON RECEIPT OF A REQUEST

16. When the Panel receives a Request the Chairperson, on the basis of the information contained in the Request, shall either promptly register the Request, or ask for additional information, or find the Request outside the Panel's mandate.

A. Register

17. If the Request, appears to contains sufficient required information the Chairperson shall register the Request in the Panel Register; promptly notify the Requester, the Executive Directors and the Bank President ("President") of the registration; and transmit to the President a copy of the Request with the accompanying documentation, if any.

A. Contents of Notice

18. The notice of registration shall:

> (a) record that the Request is registered and indicate the date of the registration and dispatch of that notice;
> (b) the notice will include the name of the project, the country where the project is located, the name of the Requester unless anonymity is requested, and a brief description of the Request;
> (c) notify the Requestor that all communications in connection with the Request will be sent to the address stated in the Request, unless another address is indicated to the Panel Secretariat; and
> (d) request Management to provide the Panel, within 21 days after receipt of the notice and Request, with written evidence that it has complied, or intends to comply with the Bank's relevant policies and procedures. The notice shall specify the due date of the response.

B. Request Additional Information

19. If the Chairperson finds the contents of the Request or documentation on representation insufficient, he/she may ask the Requester to supply further information.

20. Upon a receipt of a Request, the Chairperson shall send a written acknowledgement to the Requester, and will specify what additional information is required.

21. The Chairperson may refuse to register a Request until all necessary information and documentation is filed.

C. Outside Scope

22. If the Chairperson finds that the matter is without doubt manifestly outside the Panel's mandate, he/she will notify the Requesters of his/her refusal to register the Request and of the reasons therefor; this will include but not limited to the following types of communications:

(a) Requests which are clearly outside the Panel's mandate including those listed above at paragraph 2;

(b) Requests which do not show the steps taken or effort made to resolve the matter with Management;

(c) Requests from an individual or from a non-authorized representative of an affected party;

(d) any correspondence, including but not limited to letters, memoranda, opinions, submissions or requests on any matter within the Panel's mandate which are not requests for an inspection; and

(e) Requests that are manifestly frivolous, absurd or anonymous.

Records

23. The number of such Requests and communications received shall be noted in the Register on a quarterly basis and the yearly total included in the Annual Report.

D. Need for Review

24. In cases where additional information is required, or where it is not clear whether a Request is manifestly outside the Panel's mandate, the Chairperson shall designate a Panel member to review the Request.

E. Revised Request

25. If the Requester receives significant new evidence or information at any time after the initial Request was submitted, he/she may consider whether or not it is serious enough to justify the submission of a revised Request.

26. If a revised Request is submitted, the time periods for Management's response and the Panel recommendation will begin again from the time such Request is registered.

IV. MANAGEMENT'S RESPONSE

27. Within 21 days after being notified of a Request, Management shall provide the Panel with evidence that it has complied, or intends to comply with the Bank's relevant policies and procedures. After the Panel receives Management's response, it shall promptly enter the date of receipt in the Panel Register.

28. If there is no response from Management within 21 days, the Panel shall notify the President and the Executive Directors and send a copy to the Requester.

Clarification

29. In order to make an informed recommendation, the Panel may request clarification from Management; in the light of Management's response, request more information from the Requester; and provide relevant portions of Management's response for comment. A time limit for receipt of the information requested shall be specified; and

(a) whether or not such clarification or information is received within the time limit, make its recommendation to the Executive Driectors within 21 days after receipt of Management's response; or

(b) in the event it is not possible for the Requester to provide the information quickly, the Panel may advise the Requester to submit an amended Request; the Executive Directors and Bank Management will be notified that the process will begin again when the amended Request is received.

V. PANEL RECOMMENDATION

30. Within 21 days after receiving Management's response, the Panel shall make a recommendation to the Executive Directors as to whether the matter should be investigated.

A. Basis
31. The Panel shall prepare its recommendation on the basis of the information contained in:
>   (a) the Request;
>   (b) Management's response;
>   (c) any further information the Panel may have requested and received from the Requester and/or Management and/or third parties; and
>   (d) any findings of the Panel during this stage.

B. Required Criteria
32. If, on the basis of the information contained in the Request, it has not already been established that the Request meets the following three conditions required by the Resolution, the Chairperson, in consultation with the other Panel members may, if necessary, designates a Panel member to conduct a preliminary review to determine whether the Request:
>   (a) was filed by an eligible party;
>   (b) is not time-barred; and
>   (c) relates to a matter falling within the Panel's mandate.

Criteria for Satisfactory Response
33. The Panel may proceed to recommend that there should not be an investigation, if, on the basis of the information contained in the Request and Management's response, the Panel is satisfied that Management has done the following:
>   (a) dealt appropriately with the subject matter of the Request; and
>   (b) demonstrated clearly that it has followed the required policies and procedures; or
>   (c) admitted that it has failed to follow the required policies and procedures but has provided a statement of specific remedial actions and a time-table for implementing them, which will, in the judgement of the Panel, adequately correct the failure and any adverse effects such failure has already caused.

Preliminary Review
34. If, on the basis of the information contained in Management's response and any clarifications provided, the Panel is satisfied that Management has failed to demonstrate that it has followed, or is taking adequate steps to follow the Bank's policies and procedures, the Panel will conduct a preliminary review in order to determine whether conditions required by provisions of the Resolution exist.

35. Although it may not investigate Management's actions in depth at this stage, it will determine whether Management's failure to comply with Bank policies and procedures meets the following three conditions:
>   (a) whether such failure has had, or threatens to have, a material adverse effect;
>   (b) whether, the alleged violation of the Bank's policies and procedures are, in the judgement of the Panel, of a serious character; and
>   (c) whether remedial actions proposed by Management do not appear to adequate to meet the concerns of the Requester as to the application of the Bank's policies and procedures.

Initial Study
36. If the Chairperson considers, after the preliminary review and consultation with the other Panel members, that more factual data not already provided by the Requester, Management or any other source is required to make an informed recommendation to the Executive Directors, he/she may designate a Panel member to undertake a preliminary study. The study may include, but need not be limited to, a desk study and/or a visit to the project site.

C. Contents
37. On the basis of the review, the Panel shall make its recommendation to the Board as to whether the matter should be investigated. Every recommendation shall include a clear explanation setting forth reasons for the recommendation and be accompanied by:
>   (a) the text of the Request and, where applicable, any other relevant information provided by the Requester;
>   (b) the text of Management's response and, where applicable, any clarifications provided;
>   (c) the text of any advice received from the Bank's Legal Department;
>   (d) any other relevant documents or information received; and

(e) statements of the majority and minority views in the absence of a consensus by the Panel.

D. Submission
38. The recommendation shall be circulated by the Executive Secretary of the Panel to the Executive Directors for decision. The Panel will notify the Requester that a recommendation has been sent to the Executive Directors.

VI. BOARD DECISION AND PUBLIC RELEASE

39. The Board decides whether or not to accept or reject the Panel's recommendation; and, if the Requester is a non-local representative, whether exceptional circumstances exist and suitable local representation is not available.
Notification
40. The Panel shall promptly inform the Requester of the Board's decision on whether or not to investigate the Request and shall send the Requester a copy of the Panel's recommendation.
Public Information
41. After the Executive Directors have considered a Request the Bank shall make such a Request publicly available together with the Panel's recommendation on whether to proceed with the inspection and the decision of the Executive Directors in this respect.

VII. AN INVESTIGATION

A. Initial Procedures
42. When a decision to investigate a Request is made by the Board, or the Board itself requests an investigation, the Chairperson shall promptly:
>   (a) designate one or more of the Panel's members (Inspector(s)) to take primary responsibility for the investigation;
>   (b) arrange for all Panel members to consult, taking into account the nature of the particular Request, on:
>>   (i) the methods of investigation that at the outset appear the most appropriate;
>>   (ii) an initial schedule for the conduct of the investigation;
>>   (iii) when the Inspector(s) shall report his/her (their) findings to the Panel, including any interim findings; and
>>   (iv) any additional procedures for the conduct of the investigation.
43. The designated Inspector(s) shall, as needed, arrange for a meeting with the Requester and schedule discussions with directly affected people.
44. The name of the Inspector(s) and in initial work plan shall be made public as soon as possible.

B. Methods of Investigation
45. The Panel may, taking into account the nature of the particular Request, use a variety of investigatory methods, including but not limited to:
>   (a) meetings with the Requester, affected people, Bank staff, government officials and project authorities of the country where the project is located, and representatives of local and international non-governmental organizations;
>   (b) holding public hearings in the project area;
>   (c) visiting project sites;
>   (d) requesting written or oral submissions on specific issues from the Requester, affected people, independent experts, government or project officials, Bank staff, or local or international non-governmental organizations;
>   (e) hiring independent consultants to research specific issues relating to the Request;
>   (f) researching Bank files; and
>   (g) any other reasonable methods the Inspector(s) consider appropriate to the specific investigation.
Consent Required
46. In accordance with the Resolution, physical inspection in the country where the project is located will be carried out with prior consent. The Chairperson shall request the Executive Director representing such

country to provide written consent.

C. Participation of Requester
47. During the course of the investigation, in addition to any information requested by the Inspector(s), the Requester (and affected people if the Requester is a non-affected Representative or an Executive Director) or Bank staff may provide the Inspector(s) either directly or through the Executive Secretary with supplemental information that they believe is relevant to evaluating the Request.
48. The Inspector(s) may notify the Requester of any new material facts provided by Bank staff or by the Executive Director for, or authorities in, the country where the project is located.
49. To facilitate understanding of specific points, the Panel may discuss its preliminary findings of fact with the Requester.

D. Participation of Third Parties
50. During the course of the investigation, in addition to any information requested by the Inspector(s), any member of the public may provide the Inspector(s), either directly or through the Executive Secretary, with supplemental information that they believe is relevant to evaluating the Request.
51. Information should not exceed ten pages and include a one-page summary. Supporting documentation may be listed and attached. The Inspector(s) may request more details if necessary.

VIII. PANEL REPORT

Contents
52. The report of the Panel (the "Report") shall include the following:
> (a) a summary discussion of the relevant facts and of steps taken to conduct the investigation;
> (b) a conclusion showing the Panel's findings on whether the Bank has complied with relevant Bank policies and procedures;
> (c) a list of supporting documents which will be available on request from the Office of The Inspection Panel; and
> (d) statements of the majority and minority views in the absence of a consensus by the Panel.

Submission
53. Upon its completion, the Panel shall submit the Report to:
> (a) the Executive Directors: accompanied by notification that the Report is being submitted to the President on the same date; and
> (b) the President: accompanied by a notice against receipt that within 6 weeks of receipt of the Report, Management must submit to the Executive Directors for their consideration a report indicating Management's recommendations in response to the Panel's findings.

IX. MANAGEMENT'S RECOMMENDATIONS

54. Within 6 weeks after receiving the Panel's findings, Management will submit to the Executive Directors for their consideration a report indicating its recommendations in response to the Panel's findings. Upon receipt of a copy of the report, the Panel will notify the Requester.

X. BOARD DECISION AND PUBLIC RELEASE

55. Within 2 weeks after the Executive Directors consider the Panel's Report and the Management's response, the Bank shall inform the Requester of the results of the investigation and the action decided by the Executive Directors, if any.
56. After the Bank has informed the Requester, the Bank shall make publicly available:
> (a) the Panel's Report;
> (b) Management's recommendations; and
> (c) the Board's decision.

These documents will also be available at the Office of The Inspection Panel.
57. The Panel will seek to enhance public awareness of the results of investigations through all available information sources.

XI. GENERAL

Business Days
58. "Days" under these procedures means days on which the Bank is open for business in Washington, D.C.

Copies
59. Consideration of Requests and other documents submitted throughout the process will be expedited if an original and two copies are filed. When any document contains extensive supporting documentation the Panel may ask for additional copies.

Consultations
60. The borrower and the Executive Director representing the borrowing (or guaranteeing) country shall be consulted on the subject matter before the Panel's recommendation and during an investigation.

Access to Bank Staff and Information
61. Pursuant to the Resolution and in discharge of their functions, the members of the Panel shall have access to all Bank staff who may contribute information and to all pertinent Bank records and shall consult as needed with the Director General, Operations Evaluation Department and the Internal Auditor.

Legal Advice
62. The Panel shall seek, through the Vice President and General Counsel of the Bank, the written advice of the Bank's Legal Department on matters related to the Bank's rights and obligations with respect to the Request under consideration. Any such advice will be included as an attachment to the Panel's recommendation and/or Report to the Executive Directors.

Confidentiality
63. Documents, or portions of documents of a confidential nature will not be released by the Panel without the express written consent of the party concerned.

Information to Requester and Public
64. The Executive Secretary shall record in the Register all actions taken in connection with the processing of the Request, the dates thereof, and the dates on which any document or notification under these procedures is received in or sent from the Office of The Inspection Panel. The Requester shall be informed promptly. The Register will be publicly available.

65. A notice that a Request has been registered and all other notices or documents issued by the Panel will be available to the public through the Bank's PIC in Washington, D.C.; at the Bank's Resident Mission in the country where the project is located or at the relevant regional office; at the Bank's Paris, London and Tokyo offices; or on request from the Executive Secretary of the Panel.

ANNEX 1

September 22, 1993
INTERNATIONAL BANK FOR RECONSTRUCTION AND DEVELOPMENT INTERNATIONAL DEVELOPMENT ASSOCIATION

Resolution No. 93-10
Resolution No. IDA 93-6
"The World Bank Inspection Panel"

The Executive Directors:
Hereby resolve:

1. There is established an independent Inspection Panel (hereinafter called the Panel), which shall have the powers and shall function as stated in this resolution.

Composition of the Panel
2. The Panel shall consist of three members of different nationalities from Bank member countries. The President, after consultation with the Executive Directors, shall nominate the members of the Panel to be appointed by the Executive Directors.
3. The first members of the Panel shall be appointed as follows: one for three years, one for four years and

one for five years, provided that no member may serve for more than one term. The term of apointment of each member shall be subject to the continuity of the inspection function established by this Resolution.

4. Members of the Panel shall be selected on the basis of their ability to deal thoroughly and fairly with the requests brought to them, their integrity and their independence from the Bank's Management, and their exposure to developmental issues and to living conditions in developing countries. Knowledge and experience of the Bank's operations will also be desirable.

5. Executive Directors, Alternates, Advisors and staff members of the Bank Group may not serve on the Panel until two years have elapsed since the end of their service in the Bank Group. For purposes of this Resolution, the term "staff" shall mean all persons holding Bank Group appointments as defined in Staff Rule 4.01 including persons holding consultant and local consultant appointments.

6. A Panel member shall be disqualified from participation in the hearing and investigation of any request related to a matter in which he/she has a personal interest or had significant involvement in any capacity.

7. The Panel member initially appointed for five years shall be the first Chairperson of the Panel, and shall hold such office for one year. Thereafter, the members of the Panel shall elect a Chairperson for a period of one year.

8. Members of the Panel may be removed from office only by decision of the Executive Directors, for cause.

9. With the exception of the Chairperson who shall work on a full-time basis at Bank headquarters, members of the Panel shall be expected to work on a full-time basis only when their workload justifies such an arrangement, as will be decided by the Executive Directors on the recommendation of the Panel.

10. In the performance of their functions, members of the Panel shall be officials of the Bank enjoying the privileges and immunities accorded to Bank officials, and shall be subject to the requirements of the Bank's Articles of Agreement concerning their exclusive loyalty to the Bank and to the obligations of subparagraphs (c) and (d) of paragraph 3.1 and paragraph 3.2 of the Principles of Staff Employment concerning their conduct as officials of the Bank. Once they begin to work on a full-time basis, they shall receive remuneration at a level to be determined by the Executive Directors upon a recommendation of the President, plus normal benefits available to Bank fixed-term staff. Prior to that time, they shall be remunerated on a per diem basis and shall be reimbursed for their expenses on the same basis as the members of the Bank's Administrative Tribunal. Members of the Panel may not be employed by the Bank Group, following the end of their service on the Panel.

11. The President, after consultation with the Executive Directors, shall assign a staff member to the Panel as Executive Secretary, who need not act on a full-time basis until the workload so justifies. The Panel shall be given such budgetary resources as shall be sufficient to carry out its activities.

Powers of the Panel

12. The Panel shall receive requests for inspection presented to it by an affected party in the territory of the borrower which is not a single individual (i.e., a community of persons such as an organization, association, society or other grouping of individuals), or by the local representative of such party or by another representative in the exceptional cases where the party submitting the request contends that appropriate representation is not locally available and the Executive Directors so agree at the time they consider the request for inspection. Any such representative shall present to the Panel written evidence that he is acting as agent of the party on behalf of which the request is made. The affected party must demonstrate that its rights or interests have been or are likely to be directly affected by an action of omission of the Bank as a result of a failure of the Bank to follow its operational policies and procedures with respect to the design, appraisal and/or implementation of a project financed by the Bank (including situations where the Bank is alleged to have failed in its follow-up on the borrower's obligations under loan agreements with respect to such policies and procedures) provided in all cases that such failure has had, or threatens to have, a material adverse effect. In view of the institutional responsibilities of Executive Directors in the observance by the Bank of its operational policies and procedures, an Executive Directors in the observance by the Bank of its operational policies and procedures, and Executive Director may in special cases of serious alleged violations of such policies and procedures ask the Panel for an investigation, subject to the requirements of paragraphs 13 and 14 below. The Executive Directors, acting as a Board, may at any time instruct the Panel to conduct an investigation. For purposes of this Resolution, "operational policies and procedures" consist of the Bank's Procedures and Operational Directives, and similar documents issued before these series were started, and does not include Guidelines and Best Practices and similar documents or statements.

13. The Panel shall satisfy itself before a request for inspection is heard that the subject matter of the

request has been dealt with by the Management of the Bank and Management has failed to demonstrate that it has followed, or is taking adequate steps to follow the Bank's policies and procedures is of a serious character.

14. In considering requests under paragraph 12 above, the following requests shall not be heard by the Panel:

     (a) Complaints with respect to action which are the responsibility of other parties, such as a borrower, or potential borrower, and which do not involve any action or omission on the part of the Bank.

     (b) Complaints against procurement decisions by Bank borrowers from suppliers of goods and services financed or expected to be financed by the Bank under a loan agreement, or from losing tenderers for the supply of any such goods and services, which will continue to be addressed by staff under existing procedures.

     (c) Requests filed after the Closing Date of the loan financing the project with respect to which the request is filed or after the loan financing the project has been substantially disbursed. * * *

     (d) Requests related to a particular matter or matters over which the Panel has already made its recommendation upon having received a prior request, unless justified by new evidence or circumstances not known at the time of the prior request.

15. The Panel shall seek advice of the Bank's Legal Department on matters related to the Bank's rights and obligations with respect to the request under consideration.

Procedures

16. Requests for inspection shall be in writing and shall state all relevant facts, including, in the case of a request by an affected party, the harm suffered by or threatened to such party or parties by the alleged action or omission of the Bank. All requests shall explain the steps already taken to deal with the issue, as well as the nature of the alleged actions or omissions and shall specify the actions taken to bring the issue to the attention of the Management, and Management's response to such action.

17. The Chairperson of the Panel shall inform the Executive Directors and the President of the Bank promptly upon receiving a request for inspection.

18. Within 21 days of being notified of a request for inspection, the Management of the Bank shall provide the Panel with evidence that it has complied, or intends to comply with the Bank's relevant policies and procedures.

19. Within 21 days of receiving the response of the Management as provided in the preceding paragraph, the Panel shall determine whether the request meets the eligibility criteria set out in paragraphs 12 to 14 above and shall make a recommendation to the Executive Directors as to whether the matter should be investigated. The recommendation of the Panel shall be circulated to the Executive Directors for decision within the normal distribution period. In case the request was initiated by an affected party, such party shall be informed of the decision of the Executive Directors within two weeks of the date of such decision.

20. If a decision is made by the Executive Directors to investigate the request, the Chairperson of the Panel shall designate one or more of the Panel's members (Inspectors) who shall have primary responsibility for conducting the inspection. The Inspector(s) shall report his/her (their) findings to the Panel within a period to be determined by the Panel taking into account the nature of each request.

21. In the discharge of their functions, the members of the Panel shall have access to all staff who may contribute information and to all pertinent Bank records and shall consult as needed with the Director General, Operations Evaluation Department and the Internal Auditor. The borrower and the Executive Director representing the borrowing (or guaranteeing) country shall be consulted on the subject matter both before the Panel's recommendation on whether to proceed with the investigation and during the investigation. Inspection in the territory of such country shall be carried out with its prior consent.

22. The Panel shall submit its report to the Executive Directors and the President. The report of the Panel shall consider all relevant facts, and shall conclude with the Panel's findings on whether the Bank has complied with all relevant Bank policies and procedures.

23. Within six weeks from receiving the Panel's findings, Management will submit to the Executive Directors for their consideration a report indicating its recommendations in response to such findings. The findings of the Panel and the actions completed during project preparation also will be discussed in the Staff Appraisal Report when the project is submitted to the Executive Directors for financing. In all cases of a request made by an affected party, the Bank shall, within two weeks of the Executive Directors' consideration of the matter, inform such party of the results of the investigation and the action taken in its

respect, if any.

Decisions of the Panel

24. All decisions of the Panel on procedural matters, its recommendations to the Executive Directors on whether to proceed with the investigation of a request, and its reports pursuant to paragraph 22, shall be reached by consensus and, in the absence of a consensus, the majority and minority views shall be stated.

Reports

25. After the Executive Directors have considered a request for an inspection as set out in paragraph 19, the Bank shall make such request publicly available together with the recommendation of the Panel on whether to proceed with the inspection and the decision of the Executive Directors in this respect. The Bank shall make publicly available the report submitted by the Panel pursuant to paragraph 22 and the Bank's response thereon within two weeks after consideration by the Executive Directors of the report.
26. In addition to the material referred to in paragraph 25, the Panel shall furnish an annual report to the President and the Executive Directors concerning its activities. The annual report shall be published by the Bank.

Review

27. The Executive Directors shall review the experience of the inspection function established by this Resolution after two years from the date of the appointment of the first members of the Panel.

Application to IDA projects

28. In this resolution, references to the Bank and to loans include references to the Association and to development credits.

ANNEX 2

GUIDANCE ON HOW TO PREPARE A REQUEST FOR INSPECTION

The Inspection Panel needs some basic information in order to process a Request for Inspection:

1. Name, contact address and telephone number of the group or people making the request.
2. Name and description of the Bank project.
3. Adverse effects of the Bank project.
4. If you are a representative of affected people attach explicit written instructions from them authorizing you to act on their behalf.

These key questions must be answered:

1. Can you elaborate on the nature and importance of the damage caused by the project to you or those you represent?
2. Do you know that the Bank is responsible for the aspects of the project that has or may affect you adversely? How did you determine this?
3. Are you familiar with Bank policies and procedures that apply to this type of project? How do you believe the Bank may have violated them?
4. Have you contacted or attempted to contact Bank staff about the project? Please provide information about all contacts, and the responses, if any, you received from the Bank. You must have done this before you can file a request.
5. Have you tried to resolve your problem through any other means?
6. If you know that the Panel has dealt with this matter before, do you have new facts or evidence to submit?

Please provide a summary of the information in no more than a few pages. Attach as much other information as you think necessary as separate documents. Please note and identify attachments in your summary. * * *

INTERNATIONAL CODES OF CONDUCT

INTERNATIONAL BAR ASSOCIATION
CODE OF ETHICS

International Bar Association, *International Code of Ethics* (1988), *available at* http://www.ibanet.org/images/downloads/International_Ethics.pdf

1. A lawyer who undertakes professional work in a jurisdiction where he is not a full member of the local profession shall adhere to the standards of professional ethics in the jurisdiction in which he has been admitted. He shall also observe all ethical standards which apply to lawyers of the country where he is working.

2. Lawyers shall at all times maintain the honour and dignity of their profession. They shall, in practice as well as in private life, abstain from any behaviour which may tend to discredit the profession of which they are members.

3. Lawyers shall preserve independence in the discharge of their professional duty. Lawyers practising on their own account or in partnership where permissible, shall not engage in any other business or occupation if by doing so they may cease to be independent.

4. Lawyers shall treat their professional colleagues with the utmost courtesy and fairness. Lawyers who undertake to render assistance to a foreign colleague shall always keep in mind that the foreign colleague has to depend on them to a much larger extent than in the case of another lawyer of the same country. Therefore their responsibility is much greater, both when giving advice and when handling a case. For this reason it is improper for lawyers to accept a case unless they can handle it promptly and with due competence, without undue interference by the pressure of other work. To the fees in these cases Rule 19 applies.

5. Except where the law or custom of the country concerned otherwise requires, any oral or written communication between lawyers shall in principle be accorded a confidential character as far as the Court is concerned, unless certain promises or acknowledgements are made therein on behalf of a client.

6. Lawyers shall always maintain due respect towards the Court. Lawyers shall without fear defend the interests of their clients and without regard to any unpleasant consequences to themselves or to any other person. Lawyers shall never knowingly give to the Court incorrect information or advice which is to their knowledge contrary to the law.

7. It shall be considered improper for lawyers to communicate about a particular case directly with any person whom they know to be represented in that case by another lawyer without the latter's consent.

8. A lawyer should not advertise or solicit business except to the extent and in the manner permitted by the rules of the jurisdiction to which that lawyer is subject. A lawyer should not advertise or solicit business in any country in which such advertising or soliciting is prohibited.

9. A lawyer should never consent to handle a case unless: (a) the client gives direct instructions, or, (b) the case is assigned by a competent body or forwarded by another lawyer, or (c) instructions are given in any other manner permissible under the relevant local rules or regulations.

10. Lawyers shall at all times give clients a candid opinion on any case. They shall render assistance with scrupulous care and diligence. This applies also if they are assigned as counsel for an indigent person. Lawyers shall at any time be free to refuse to handle a case, unless it is assigned by a competent body. Lawyers should only withdraw from a case during its course for good cause, and if possible in such a manner that the client's interests are not adversely affected. The loyal defence of a client's case may never cause advocates to be other than perfectly candid, subject to any right or privilege to the contrary which clients choose them to exercise, or knowingly to go against the law.

11   Lawyers shall, when in the client's interest, endeavour to reach a solution by settlement out of court rather than start legal proceedings. Lawyers should never stir up litigation.

12   Lawyers should not acquire a financial interest in the subject matter of a case which they are conducting. Neither should they, directly or indirectly, acquire property about which litigation is pending before the Court in which they practice.

13   Lawyers should never represent conflicting interests in litigation. In non-litigation matters, lawyers should do so only after having disclosed all conflicts or possible conflicts of interest to all parties concerned and only with their consent. This Rule also applies to all lawyers in a firm.

14   Lawyers should never disclose, unless lawfully ordered to do so by the Court or as required by Statute, what has been communicated to them in their capacity as lawyers even after they have ceased to be the client's counsel. This duty extends to their partners, to junior lawyers assisting them and to their employees.

15   In pecuniary matters lawyers shall be most punctual and diligent. They should never mingle funds of others with their own and they should at all times be able to refund money they hold for others. They shall not retain money they receive for their clients for longer than is absolutely necessary.

16   Lawyers may require that a deposit is made to cover their expenses, but the deposit should be in accordance with the estimated amount of their charges and the probable expenses and labour required.

17   Lawyers shall never forget that they should put first not their right to compensation for their services, but the interests of their clients and the exigencies of the administration of justice. The Lawyer's right to ask for a deposit or to demand payment of out of-pocket expenses and commitments, failing payment of which they may withdraw from the case or refuse to handle it, should never be exercised at a moment at which the client may be unable to find other assistance in time to prevent irreparable damage being done. Lawyers' fees should, in the absence or non-applicability of official scales, be fixed on a consideration of the amount involved in the controversy and the interest of it to the client, the time and labour involved and all other personal and factual circumstances of the case.

18   A contract for a contingent fee, where sanctioned by the law or by professional rules and practice, should be reasonable under all circumstances of the case, including the risk and uncertainty or the compensation and subject to supervision of a court as to its reasonableness.

19   Lawyers who engage a foreign colleague to advise on a case or to cooperate in handling it, are responsible for the payment of the latter's charges except where there has been express agreement to the contrary. When lawyers direct a client to a foreign colleague they are not responsible for the payment of the latter's charges, but neither are they entitled to a share of the fee of this foreign colleague.

20   Lawyers should not permit their professional services or their names to be used in any way which would make it possible for persons to practice law who are not legally authorised to do so. Lawyers shall not delegate to a legally unqualified person not in their employ and control any functions which are by the law or custom of the country in which they practice only to be performed by a qualified lawyer.

21   It is not unethical for lawyers to limit or exclude professional liability subject to the rules of their local Bar Association and to there being no statutory or constitutional prohibitions.

CODE OF CONDUCT FOR EUROPEAN LAWYERS

Council of Bars and Law Societies of Europe, *Code of Conduct for European Lawyers* (2006) *available at* http://www.ccbe.org/fileadmin/user_upload/NTCdocument/2006_code_enpdf1_1182240432.pdf

1. PREAMBLE

1.1. The Function of the Lawyer in Society
In a society founded on respect for the rule of law the lawyer fulfils a special role. The lawyer's duties do not begin and end with the faithful performance of what he or she is instructed to do so far as the law permits. A lawyer must serve the interests of justice

as well as those whose rights and liberties he or she is trusted to assert and defend and it is the lawyer's duty not only to plead the client's cause but to be the client's adviser. Respect for the lawyer's professional function is an essential condition for the rule of law and democracy in society.

A lawyer's function therefore lays on him or her a variety of legal and moral obligations (sometimes appearing to be in conflict with each other) towards:

- the client;
- the courts and other authorities before whom the lawyer pleads the client's cause or acts on the client's behalf;
- the legal profession in general and each fellow member of it in particular;
- the public for whom the existence of a free and independent profession, bound together by respect for rules made by the profession itself, is an essential means of safeguarding human rights in face of the power of the state and other interests in society.

1.2. The Nature of Rules of Professional Conduct

1.2.1. Rules of professional conduct are designed through their willing acceptance by those to whom they apply to ensure the proper performance by the lawyer of a function which is recognised as essential in all civilised societies. The failure of the lawyer to
observe these rules may result in disciplinary sanctions.

1.2.2. The particular rules of each Bar or Law Society arise from its own traditions. They are adapted to the organisation and sphere of activity of the profession in the Member State concerned and to its judicial and administrative procedures and to its national legislation. It is neither possible nor desirable that they should be taken out of their context nor that an attempt should be made to give general application to rules which are inherently incapable of such application.

The particular rules of each Bar and Law Society nevertheless are based on the same values and in most cases demonstrate a common foundation.

1.3. The Purpose of the Code

1.3.1. The continued integration of the European Union and European Economic Area and the increasing frequency of the cross-border activities of lawyers within the European Economic Area have made necessary in the public interest the statement of common rules which apply to all lawyers from the European Economic Area whatever Bar or Law Society they belong to in relation to their cross-border practice. A particular purpose of the statement of those rules is to mitigate the difficulties which result from the application of "double deontology", notably as set out in Articles 4 and 7.2 of Directive 77/249/EEC and Articles 6 and 7 of Directive 98/5/EC.

1.3.2. The organisations representing the legal profession through the CCBE propose that the rules codified in the following articles:

- be recognised at the present time as the expression of a consensus of all the Bars and Law Societies of the European Union and European Economic Area;
- be adopted as enforceable rules as soon as possible in accordance with national or EEA procedures in relation to the crossborder activities of the lawyer in the European Union and European Economic Area;
- be taken into account in all revisions of national rules of deontology or professional practice with a view to their progressive harmonisation.

They further express the wish that the national rules of deontology or professional practice be interpreted and applied whenever possible in a way consistent with the rules in this Code.

After the rules in this Code have been adopted as enforceable rules in relation to a lawyer's cross-border activities the lawyer will remain bound to observe the rules of the Bar or Law Society to which he or she belongs to the extent that they are consistent with
the rules in this Code.

1.4. Field of Application *Ratione Personae*

This Code shall apply to lawyers as they are defined by Directive 77/249/EEC and by Directive 98/5/EC and to lawyers of the Observer Members of the CCBE.

1.5. Field of Application *Ratione Materiae*

Without prejudice to the pursuit of a progressive harmonisation of rules of deontology or professional practice which apply only internally within a Member State, the following rules shall apply to the cross-border activities of the lawyer within the European Union
and the European Economic Area. Cross-border activities shall mean:

(a) all professional contacts with lawyers of Member States other than the lawyer's own;

(b) the professional activities of the lawyer in a Member State other than his or her own, whether or not the lawyer is physically present in that Member State.

1.6. Definitions

In this Code:

"Member State" means a member state of the European Union or any other state whose legal profession is included in Article 1.4.

"Home Member State" means the Member State where the lawyer acquired the right to bear his or her professional title.

"Host Member State" means any other Member State where the lawyer carries on cross-border activities.

"Competent Authority" means the professional organisation(s) or authority(ies) of the Member State concerned responsible for the laying down of rules of professional conduct and the administration of discipline of lawyers.

"Directive 77/249/EEC" means Council Directive 77/249/EEC of 22 March 1977 to facilitate the effective exercise by lawyers of freedom to provide services.

"Directive 98/5/EC" means Directive 98/5/EC of the European Parliament and of the Council of 16 February 1998 to facilitate practice of the profession of lawyer on a permanent basis in a Member State other than that in which the qualification was obtained.

2. GENERAL PRINCIPLES

2.1. Independence

2.1.1. The many duties to which a lawyer is subject require the lawyer's absolute independence, free from all other influence, especially such as may arise from his or her personal interests or external pressure. Such independence is as necessary to trust in the
process of justice as the impartiality of the judge. A lawyer must therefore avoid any impairment of his or her independence and be careful not to compromise his or her professional standards in order to please the client, the court or third parties.

2.1.2. This independence is necessary in non-contentious matters as well as in litigation. Advice given by a lawyer to the client has no value if the lawyer gives it only to ingratiate him- or herself, to serve his or her personal interests or in response to outside pressure.

2.2. Trust and Personal Integrity

Relationships of trust can only exist if a lawyer's personal honour, honesty and integrity are beyond doubt. For the lawyer these traditional virtues are professional obligations.

2.3. Confidentiality

2.3.1. It is of the essence of a lawyer's function that the lawyer should be told by his or her client things which the client would not tell to others, and that the lawyer should be the recipient of other information on a basis of confidence. Without the certainty of confidentiality there cannot be trust. Confidentiality is therefore a primary and fundamental right and duty of the lawyer.
The lawyer's obligation of confidentiality serves the interest of the administration of justice as well as the interest of the client. It is therefore entitled to special protection by the State.

2.3.2. A lawyer shall respect the confidentiality of all information that becomes known to the lawyer in the course of his or her professional activity.

2.3.3. The obligation of confidentiality is not limited in time.

2.3.4. A lawyer shall require his or her associates and staff and anyone engaged by him or her in the course of providing professional services to observe the same obligation of confidentiality.

2.4. Respect for the Rules of Other Bars and Law Societies

When practising cross-border, a lawyer from another Member State may be bound to comply with the professional rules of the Host Member State. Lawyers have a duty to inform themselves as to the rules which will affect them in the performance of any particular activity.
Member organisations of the CCBE are obliged to deposit their codes of conduct at the Secretariat of the CCBE so that any lawyer can get hold of the copy of the current code from the Secretariat.

2.5. Incompatible Occupations

2.5.1. In order to perform his or her functions with due independence and in a manner which is consistent with his or her duty to participate in the administration of justice a lawyer may be prohibited from undertaking certain occupations.

2.5.2. A lawyer who acts in the representation or the defence of a client in legal proceedings or before any public authorities in a Host Member State shall there observe the rules regarding incompatible occupations as they are applied to lawyers of the Host
Member State.
2.5.3. A lawyer established in a Host Member State in which he or she wishes to participate directly in commercial or other activities not connected with the practice of the law shall respect the rules regarding forbidden or incompatible occupations as they are applied to lawyers of that Member State.

2.6. Personal Publicity
2.6.1. A lawyer is entitled to inform the public about his or her services provided that the information is accurate and not misleading, and respectful of the obligation of confidentiality and other core values of the profession.
2.6.2. Personal publicity by a lawyer in any form of media such as by press, radio, television, by electronic commercial communications or otherwise is permitted to the extent it complies with the requirements of 2.6.1.

2.7. The Client's Interest
Subject to due observance of all rules of law and professional conduct, a lawyer must always act in the best interests of the client and must put those interests before the lawyer's own interests or those of fellow members of the legal profession.

2.8. Limitation of Lawyer's Liability towards the Client
To the extent permitted by the law of the Home Member State and the Host Member State, the lawyer may limit his or her liabilities towards the client in accordance with the professional rules to which the lawyer is subject.

3. RELATIONS WITH CLIENTS

3.1. Acceptance and Termination of Instructions
3.1.1. A lawyer shall not handle a case for a party except on that party's instructions. The lawyer may, however, act in a case in which he or she has been instructed by another lawyer acting for the party or where the case has been assigned to him or her by a competent body.
The lawyer should make reasonable efforts to ascertain the identity, competence and authority of the person or body who instructs him or her when the specific circumstances show that the identity, competence and authority are uncertain.
3.1.2. A lawyer shall advise and represent the client promptly, conscientiously and diligently. The lawyer shall undertake personal responsibility for the discharge of the client's instructions and shall keep the client informed as to the progress of the matter with which the lawyer has been entrusted.
3.1.3. A lawyer shall not handle a matter which the lawyer knows or ought to know he or she is not competent to handle, without cooperating with a lawyer who is competent to handle it.
A lawyer shall not accept instructions unless he or she can discharge
those instructions promptly having regard to the pressure of other work.
3.1.4. A lawyer shall not be entitled to exercise his or her right to withdraw from a case in such a way or in such circumstances that the client may be unable to find other legal assistance in time to prevent prejudice being suffered by the client.

3.2. Conflict of Interest
3.2.1. A lawyer may not advise, represent or act on behalf of two or more clients in the same matter if there is a conflict, or a significant risk of a conflict, between the interests of those clients.
3.2.2. A lawyer must cease to act for both or all of the clients concerned when a conflict of interests arises between those clients and also whenever there is a risk of a breach of confidence or where the lawyer's independence may be impaired.
3.2.3. A lawyer must also refrain from acting for a new client if there is a risk of breach of a confidence entrusted to the lawyer by a former client or if the knowledge which the lawyer possesses of the affairs of the former client would give an undue advantage to the new client.
3.2.4. Where lawyers are practising in association, paragraphs 3.2.1 to 3.2.3 above shall apply to the association and all its members.

3.3. *Pactum de Quota Litis*

3.3.1. A lawyer shall not be entitled to make a *pactum de quota litis*.

3.3.2. By "*pactum de quota litis*" is meant an agreement between a lawyer and the client entered into prior to final conclusion of a matter to which the client is a party, by virtue of which the client undertakes to pay the lawyer a share of the result regardless of

whether this is represented by a sum of money or by any other benefit achieved by the client upon the conclusion of the matter.

3.3.3. "*Pactum de quota litis*" does not include an agreement that fees be charged in proportion to the value of a matter handled by the lawyer if this is in accordance with an officially approved fee scale or under the control of the Competent Authority having

jurisdiction over the lawyer.

3.4. Regulation of Fees

A fee charged by a lawyer shall be fully disclosed to the client, shall be fair and reasonable, and shall comply with the law and professional rules to which the lawyer is subject.

3.5. Payment on Account

If a lawyer requires a payment on account of his or her fees and/or disbursements such payment should not exceed a reasonable estimate of the fees and probable disbursements involved. Failing such payment, a lawyer may withdraw from the case or refuse to handle it, but subject always to paragraph 3.1.4 above.

3.6. Fee Sharing with Non-Lawyers

3.6.1. A lawyer may not share his or her fees with a person who is not a lawyer except where an association between the lawyer and the other person is permitted by the laws and the professional rules to which the lawyer is subject.

3.6.2. The provisions of 3.6.1 above shall not preclude a lawyer from paying a fee, commission or other compensation to a deceased lawyer's heirs or to a retired lawyer in respect of taking over the deceased or retired lawyer's practice.

3.7. Cost of Litigation and Availibility of Legal Aid

3.7.1. The lawyer should at all times strive to achieve the most cost effective resolution of the client's dispute and should advise the client at appropriate stages as to the desirability of attempting a settlement and/or a reference to alternative dispute resolution.

3.7.2. A lawyer shall inform the client of the availability of legal aid where applicable.

3.8. Client Funds

3.8.1. Lawyers who come into possession of funds on behalf of their clients or third parties (hereinafter called "client funds") have to deposit such money into an account of a bank or similar institution subject to supervision by a public authority (hereinafter called a "client account"). A client account shall be separate from any other account of the lawyer. All client funds received by a lawyer should be deposited into such an account unless the owner of such funds agrees that the funds should be dealt with otherwise.

3.8.2. The lawyer shall maintain full and accurate records showing all the lawyer's dealings with client funds and distinguishing client funds from other funds held by the lawyer. Records may have to be kept for a certain period of time according to national rules.

3.8.3. A client account cannot be in debit except in exceptional circumstances as expressly permitted in national rules or due to bank charges, which cannot be influenced by the lawyer. Such an account cannot be given as a guarantee or be used as a security for any reason. There shall not be any set-off or merger between a client account and any other bank account, nor shall the client funds in a client account be available to defray money owed by the lawyer to the bank.

3.8.4. Client funds shall be transferred to the owners of such funds in the shortest period of time or under such conditions as are authorized by them.

3.8.5. The lawyer cannot transfer funds from a client account into the lawyer's own account for payment of fees without informing the client in writing.

3.8.6. The Competent Authorities in Member States shall have the power to verify and examine any document regarding client funds, whilst respecting the confidentiality or legal professional privilege to which it may be subject.

3.9. Professional Indemnity Insurance

3.9.1. Lawyers shall be insured against civil legal liability arising out of their legal practice to an extent which is reasonable having regard to the nature and extent of the risks incurred by their professional activities.

3.9.2. Should this prove impossible, the lawyer must inform the client of this situation and its consequences.

4. RELATIONS WITH THE COURTS

4.1. Rules of Conduct in Court
A lawyer who appears, or takes part in a case, before a court or tribunal must comply with the rules of conduct applied before that court or tribunal.

4.2. Fair Conduct of Proceedings
A lawyer must always have due regard for the fair conduct of proceedings.

4.3. Demeanour in Court
A lawyer shall while maintaining due respect and courtesy towards the court defend the interests of the client honourably and fearlessly without regard to the lawyer's own interests or to any consequences to him- or herself or to any other person.

4.4. False or Misleading Information
A lawyer shall never knowingly give false or misleading information to the court.

4.5. Extension to Arbitrators etc.
The rules governing a lawyer's relations with the courts apply also to the lawyer's relations with arbitrators and any other persons exercising judicial or quasi-judicial functions, even on an occasional basis.

5. RELATIONS BETWEEN LAWYERS

5.1. Corporate Spirit of the Profession
5.1.1. The corporate spirit of the profession requires a relationship of trust and co-operation between lawyers for the benefit of their clients and in order to avoid unnecessary litigation and other behaviour harmful to the reputation of the profession. It can, however, never justify setting the interests of the profession against those of the
client.

5.1.2. A lawyer should recognise all other lawyers of Member States as professional colleagues and act fairly and courteously towards them.

5.2. Co-operation among Lawyers of Different Member States
5.2.1. It is the duty of a lawyer who is approached by a colleague from another Member State not to accept instructions in a matter which the lawyer is not competent to undertake. The lawyer should in such case be prepared to help that colleague to obtain
the information necessary to enable him or her to instruct a lawyer who is capable of providing the service asked for.

5.2.2. Where a lawyer of a Member State co-operates with a lawyer from another Member State, both have a general duty to take into account the differences which may exist between their respective legal systems and the professional organisations, competences and obligations of lawyers in the Member States concerned.

5.3. Correspondence between Lawyers
5.3.1. If a lawyer intends to send communications to a lawyer in another Member State, which the sender wishes to remain confidential or without prejudice he or she should clearly express this intention prior to communicating the documents.

5.3.2. If the prospective recipient of the communications is unable to ensure their status as confidential or without prejudice he or she should inform the sender accordingly without delay.

5.4. Referral Fees
5.4.1. A lawyer may not demand or accept from another lawyer or any other person a fee, commission or any other compensation for referring or recommending the lawyer to a client.

5.4.2. A lawyer may not pay anyone a fee, commission or any other compensation as a consideration for referring a client to him- or herself.

5.5. Communication with Opposing Parties
A lawyer shall not communicate about a particular case or matter directly with any person whom he or she knows to be represented or advised in the case or matter by another lawyer, without the consent of that other lawyer (and shall keep the other
lawyer informed of any such communications).

5.6. (Deleted by decision of the Plenary Session in Dublin on 6 December 2002)

5.7. Responsibility for Fees

In professional relations between members of Bars of different Member States, where a lawyer does not confine him- or herself to recommending another lawyer or introducing that other lawyer to the client but instead him- or herself entrusts a correspondent with a particular matter or seeks the correspondent's advice, the instructing lawyer is personally bound, even if the client is insolvent, to pay the fees, costs and outlays which are due to the foreign correspondent. The lawyers concerned may, however, at the outset of the relationship between them make special arrangements on this matter. Further, the instructing lawyer may at any time limit his or her personal responsibility to the amount of the fees, costs and outlays incurred before intimation to the foreign lawyer of the instructing lawyer's disclaimer of responsibility for the future.

5.8. Continuing Professional Development

Lawyers should maintain and develop their professional knowledge and skills taking proper account of the European dimension of their profession.

5.9. Disputes amongst Lawyers in Different Member States

5.9.1. If a lawyer considers that a colleague in another Member State has acted in breach of a rule of professional conduct the lawyer shall draw the matter to the attention of that colleague.

5.9.2. If any personal dispute of a professional nature arises amongst lawyers in different Member States they should if possible first try to settle it in a friendly way.

5.9.3. A lawyer shall not commence any form of proceedings against a colleague in another Member State on matters referred to in 5.9.1 or 5.9.2 above without first informing the Bars or Law Societies to which they both belong for the purpose of allowing both Bars or Law Societies concerned an opportunity to assist in reaching a settlement.

CODE OF PROFESSIONAL CONDUCT FOR COUNSEL APPEARING BEFORE THE INTERNATIONAL TRIBUNAL

International Criminal Tribunal for the former Yugoslavia, *Code of Professional Conduct for Counsel Appearing Before the International Tribunal*, U.N. Doc. IT/125 REV. 2 (2006), *available at* http://www.un.org/icty/legaldoc-e/basic/counsel/IT125-Rev2e.pdf.

PREAMBLE

The Registrar of the Tribunal,

Considering the Statute of the Tribunal adopted by Security Council under Resolution 827 of 25 May 1993, as subsequently amended, and in particular Article 21 thereof;

Considering the Rules of Procedure and Evidence ("Rules") adopted by the Tribunal on 11 February 1994, as subsequently amended, and in particular Rules 44 to 46, 77 and 91 thereof;

Considering the Directive on Assignment of Defence Counsel (IT/73) adopted on 1 August 1994, as subsequently amended;

Considering that counsel shall adhere to a Code of Professional Conduct in the performance of their duties;

Considering that counsel appearing before the Tribunal come from various jurisdictions, and that the interests of justice require all counsel to adhere to the same Code of Professional Conduct;

Considering that this first revision of the Code of Professional Conduct for Defence Counsel Appearing Before the International Tribunal is adopted in accordance with Article 6 of the Code;

Pursuant to Rules 44 to 46 of the Rules;

ISSUES REVISION 1 OF THE CODE OF PROFESSIONAL CONDUCT FOR COUNSEL APPEARING BEFORE THE INTERNATIONAL TRIBUNAL AS FOLLOWS:

PART ONE
GENERAL PROVISIONS

Article 1
Definitions

(A) In this Code, unless the context otherwise requires, the following terms shall mean:

Code:	The Code of Professional Conduct for Counsel Appearing Before the International Tribunal in force;
Directive:	The Directive on Assignment of Defence Counsel (IT/73) adopted on 1 August 1994, as subsequently amended;
Rules:	The Rules of Procedure and Evidence of the Tribunal adopted on 11 February 1994, as subsequently amended;
Statute:	The Statute of the Tribunal adopted by Security Council resolution 827 of 25 May 1993, as subsequently amended;
Tribunal:	The International Tribunal for the Prosecution of Persons Responsible for Serious Violations of International Humanitarian Law Committed in the Territory of the Former Yugoslavia since 1991, established by Security Council resolution 827 of 25 May 1993.

* * *

Advisory Panel:	Body established to assist the President and the Registrar in all matters relating to defence counsel under Rule 44 (D) of the Rules;
Association of Counsel:	An association recognised by the Registrar in accordance with Rule 44 of the Rules;
Client:	An accused, suspect, detainee, witness or other person who has engaged counsel or has been assigned counsel by the Registry;
Counsel:	Any person who is or has been engaged by a client and has filed a power of attorney with the Registrar; who is or has been assigned by the Registrar to represent a client; or who is in communication with a prospective client;
Firm:	Persons belonging to a private firm, a legal department of an organisation or a legal services organisation;
Parties:	The Prosecution and the Defence;
Team:	Counsel, co-counsel, legal and non-legal associates and other persons who perform services for counsel for the purpose of representing a client before the Tribunal.

(B) Any term not defined in this Code has the same meaning given to it by the Statute or by the Rules.
(C) General provisions of this Code should not be read or applied in a restrictive way by reason of any particular or illustrative provisions.
(D) In this Code, the masculine shall include the feminine and the singular the plural, and vice versa.

Article 2
Entry into Force

This Code shall enter into force on 12 June 1997.

Article 3
Basic Principles

This Code is based, in particular, on the fundamental principles that:

i. clients have the right to legal assistance of their own choosing;
ii. as legal practitioners, counsel shall maintain high standards of professional conduct;
iii. the role of counsel as advocates in the administration of justice requires them to act honestly, independently, fairly, skilfully, diligently, efficiently and courageously;
iv. counsel have a duty of loyalty to their clients consistent with their duty to the Tribunal to act with independence in the administration of justice;

v.vcounsel shall take all necessary steps to ensure that their actions do not bring proceedings before the Tribunal into disrepute; and

vi. counsel may be subject to disciplinary proceedings and should be informed of the circumstances under which such proceedings may take place and his rights and obligations in those proceedings.

Article 4
Conflicts

If there is any inconsistency between this Code and any other codes of practice and ethics governing counsel, the terms of this Code prevail in respect of counsel's conduct before the Tribunal.

Article 5
Authentic Texts

The English and French texts of this Code shall be equally authentic. In case of discrepancy, the version that is more consonant with the spirit of the Statute, the Rules, the Directive and this Code shall prevail.

Article 6
Amendment

A. Under the supervision of the President, amendments shall be promulgated by the Registrar after consultation with the permanent Judges, the Association of Counsel and the Advisory Panel.

B. An amendment shall enter into force seven days after the date of issue of an official Tribunal document containing the amendment, but shall not operate to prejudice the rights of counsel or clients in any pending case.

PART TWO
OBLIGATIONS OF COUNSEL

Article 7
Purpose

The purpose of this Part is to provide for standards of conduct for counsel in the interests of the fair and proper administration of justice.

Section 1: Obligations of Counsel to Clients

Article 8
Scope of Representation

A. Counsel shall advise and represent a client until counsel's representation is terminated by the client or withdrawn by the Registrar.

B. When representing a client, counsel shall:

i. abide by the client's decisions concerning the objectives of representation;

ii. consult with the client about the means by which those objectives are to be pursued, but is not bound by the client's decision; and

iii. seek or accept only those instructions which emanate from the client and which are not given as the result of an inducement from any person, organisation or State.

C. Counsel shall not advise or assist a client to engage in conduct which counsel knows is criminal or fraudulent, in breach of the Statute, the Rules, this Code or any other applicable law and, where counsel has been assigned to the client, the Directive. However, counsel may discuss the legal consequences of any proposed course of conduct with a client and may advise or assist a client in good faith to determine the validity, scope or meaning of the applicable law.

Article 9
Declining, Terminating or Withdrawing Representation

A. Counsel shall not represent a client if:

i. representation will result in conduct which is criminal, fraudulent or a violation of the Statute, the Rules, this Code or any other applicable law;

653

ii. counsel's physical or mental condition materially impairs counsel's ability to represent the client; or

iii. counsel's representation is terminated by the client or withdrawn by the Registrar.

B. Counsel may terminate or request, if applicable subject to the provisions of the Directive, withdrawal of his representation of a client if such termination or withdrawal can be accomplished without material adverse effect on the interests of the client, or if:

i. the client has used counsel's services to perpetrate a crime or fraud, or persists in a course of action involving counsel's services that counsel reasonably believes is criminal or fraudulent;

ii. the client insists upon pursuing an objective that counsel considers repugnant or imprudent;

iii. the client fails to substantially fulfil an obligation to counsel regarding counsel's services and has been given reasonable warning that counsel will terminate or request withdrawal of his representation unless the obligation is fulfilled; or

iv. other good cause for termination or withdrawal exists.

C. Subject to leave from the Chamber, if representation by counsel is to be terminated or withdrawn, counsel shall not do so until a replacement counsel is engaged by the client or assigned by the Registrar, or the client has notified the Registrar in writing of his intention to conduct his own defence.

D. Upon termination or withdrawal of representation, counsel shall take steps to the extent reasonably practicable to protect the client's interests, such as giving sufficient notice to the client, surrendering papers and property to which the client or the Tribunal is entitled and refunding any advance payment of fee that has not been earned.

Article 10
Competence, Integrity and Independence

In the course of providing representation to a client, counsel shall:

i. act with competence, skill, care, honesty and loyalty;

ii. exercise independent professional judgement and render open and honest advice;

iii. never be influenced in the matter of his representation;

iv. preserve their own integrity and that of the legal profession as a whole;

v. never permit their independence, integrity and standards to be compromised by external pressures.

Article 11
Diligence

Counsel shall represent a client diligently and promptly in order to protect the client's best interests. Unless the representation is terminated or withdrawn, counsel shall carry through to conclusion all matters undertaken for a client within the scope of his legal representation.

Article 12
Communication

Counsel shall keep a client informed about the status of a matter before the Tribunal in which the client is an interested party and must promptly comply with all reasonable requests for information.

Article 13
Confidentiality

A. Whether or not counsel continues to represent a client, counsel shall preserve the confidentiality of the client's affairs and shall not reveal to any other person, other than to members of his team who need such information for the performance of their duties, information which has been entrusted to him in confidence or use such information to the client's detriment or to his own or another client's advantage.

B. Notwithstanding paragraph (A), counsel may reveal information which has been entrusted to him in confidence under the following circumstances:

i. when the client has been fully consulted and knowingly consents; or

ii. when the client has voluntarily disclosed the content of the communication to a third party, and that third party then gives evidence of that disclosure; or

iii. when essential to establish a claim or defence on behalf of counsel in a controversy between counsel and the client, to establish a defence to a criminal or disciplinary charge or other claim

formally instituted against counsel based upon conduct in which the client was involved, or to respond to allegations in any proceeding concerning counsel's representation of the client; or
iv. for counsel assigned by the Registrar pursuant to the Directive, when necessary to comply with that counsel's obligations under Article 17 of the Directive; or
C. to prevent an act which counsel reasonably believes:
i. is, or may be, criminal within the territory in which it may occur or under the Statute or the Rules; and
ii. may result in death or substantial bodily harm to any person unless the information is disclosed.

Article 14
Conflict of Interest

A. Counsel owes a duty of loyalty to a client. Counsel also has a duty to the Tribunal to act with independence in the interests of justice and shall put those interests before his own interests or those of any other person, organisation or State.
B. Counsel shall exercise all care to ensure that no conflict of interest arises.
C. Counsel shall not represent a client in connection with a matter in which counsel participated personally and substantially as an official or staff member of the Tribunal or in any other capacity, unless the Registrar determines, after consultation with the parties and taking account the views of the Chamber, that there is no real possibility shown that a conflict between the former and present assignment exists.
D. Counsel or his firm shall not represent a client with respect to a matter if:
i. such representation will be, or may reasonably be expected to be, adversely affected by representation of another client;
ii. representation of another client will be, or may reasonably be expected to be, adversely affected by such representation;
ii. the matter is the same or substantially related to another matter in which counsel or his firm had formerly represented another client ("former client"), and the interests of the client are materially adverse to the interests of the former client; or
iv. counsel's professional judgement on behalf of the client will be, or may reasonably be expected to be, adversely affected by:
1. counsel's responsibilities to, or interests in, a third party; or
2. to counsel's own financial, business, property or personal interests.
E. Where a conflict of interest does arise, counsel shall:
i. promptly and fully inform each potentially affected present and former client of the nature and extent of the conflict; and
ii. either:
1. take all steps necessary to remove the conflict; or
2. obtain the full and informed consent of all potentially affected present and former clients to continue the representation unless such consent is likely to irreversibly prejudice the administration of justice.

Article 15
Sexual Relations with Clients

Counsel shall not:
i. require or demand sexual relations with a client as a condition of professional representation;
ii. employ coercion, intimidation or undue influence in sexual relations with a client; or
ii. represent or continue to represent a client with whom counsel has or had sexual relations if such sexual relations may reasonably be expected to result in violations of this Code.

Article 16
Client under a Disability

When a client's ability to make adequately considered decisions in connection with his representation is affected because of a mental disability, his status as a minor or any other reason, counsel shall:

i. inform the Judge or Chamber hearing the matter, if any, of the client's mental disability or status as a minor; and

ii. take such steps as are necessary to ensure the adequate legal representation of that client.

Article 17
Consultations with Clients on Provisional Release or at Liberty

A. Counsel shall not consult with a client on provisional release or at liberty at the client's place of residence.

B. Notwithstanding paragraph (A), counsel may exceptionally consult with a client at his residence if illness, physical disability or other constraints restrict the client's mobility and preferably in the presence of an independent person.

Article 18
Fee-splitting

A. Fee-splitting arrangements, including but not limited to financial arrangements, between assigned counsel and their clients, relatives and/or agents of their clients are prohibited by the Tribunal.

B. Where assigned counsel are being requested, induced or encouraged by their clients to enter into fee-splitting arrangements, they shall advise their clients on the prohibition of such practice and shall report the incident to the Registrar forthwith.

C. Counsel shall inform the Registrar of any alleged fee-splitting arrangement by any member of his or any other defence team.

D. Following receipt of information regarding possible fee-splitting arrangements between assigned counsel and their clients, the Registrar shall investigate such information in order to determine whether it is substantiated.

E. Where assigned counsel is found to have engaged in a practice of fee-splitting or to have entered into a fee-splitting arrangement with his client, the Registrar shall consider taking action in accordance with the Directive.

F. Where the Registrar has granted leave, counsel may provide their clients with equipment and materials necessary for the preparation of their defence.

Article 19
Fees and Compensation

A. Counsel, other than counsel assigned by the Registrar, shall provide to a client, in writing and before counsel is engaged to represent a client, a statement of costs of representation, including:

i. the basis for calculating the costs;

ii. the billing arrangements; and

iii. the client's right to receive a bill of costs.

B. Counsel, other than counsel assigned by the Registrar, shall not accept compensation for representing a client from a source other than that client unless:

i. that client consents in writing after being fully informed by counsel of the source and any other information relevant to the interests of the client; and

ii. there is no interference with counsel's independence of professional judgement nor with the client-counsel relationship.

C. Counsel, if assigned by the Registrar, shall not accept compensation for representing a client except as provided for under the Directive.

Section 2: Conduct before the Tribunal

Article 20
Rules of the Tribunal

Counsel shall at all times comply with the Statute, the Rules, this Code or any other applicable law including such rulings as to conduct and procedure as may be issued by the Tribunal in its proceedings. Counsel shall at all times have due regard to the fair conduct of proceedings.

Article 21
Discriminatory Conduct

Counsel shall not engage directly or indirectly in discriminatory conduct in relation to any other person because of race, colour, ethnic or national origin, nationality, citizenship, sex, sexual orientation, marital status, disability, religion or political persuasion.

Article 22
Communications with the Chambers

Unless permitted by the Rules, this Code or the Judge or Chamber hearing the matter, counsel shall not:
> i. make contact with a Judge or Chamber in relation to the merits of a particular case, except within the proper context of the proceedings in the case; or
> ii. submit exhibits, notes or documents to a Judge or Chamber without transmitting them through the Registry, except in an emergency or when at the same time transmitted to the Registry.

Article 23
Candour Toward the Tribunal

A. Counsel shall be personally responsible toward the Tribunal for the conduct and presentation of a client's case.

B. Counsel shall not knowingly:
> i. make an incorrect statement of material fact or law to the Tribunal; or
> ii. offer evidence which counsel knows to be incorrect.

C. Notwithstanding paragraph (B)(i), counsel will not have made an incorrect statement of material fact or law to another party to the proceedings or to the Tribunal simply by failing to correct an error on any matter stated to counsel or to the Tribunal during proceedings.

D. Counsel shall take all necessary steps to correct an incorrect statement of material fact or law by counsel in proceedings before the Tribunal as soon as possible after counsel becomes aware that the statement was incorrect.

E. Counsel may refuse to offer evidence if counsel makes a reasoned determination that the material in question is irrelevant or lacks probative value.

Article 24
Integrity of Evidence

Counsel shall at all times maintain the integrity of evidence, whether in written, oral or any other form, which is or may be submitted to the Tribunal.

Article 25
Meritorious Proceedings and Claims

Counsel shall not bring or defend a proceeding or action unless there is a basis for doing so that is not frivolous. It shall not be considered frivolous for counsel to defend a proceeding so as to require that every element of the case be established.

Article 26
Counsel as Witness

Counsel shall not act as an advocate in a proceeding in which counsel is likely to be a necessary witness except where:
> i. the testimony relates to an uncontested issue;
> ii. the testimony relates to the nature and value of legal services rendered in the case; or
> iii. substantial hardship would be caused to the client if that counsel does not so act.

Section 3: Obligations of Counsel to Others

Article 27
Persons Facilitating or Participating in the Proceedings

A. Counsel shall demonstrate respect, integrity and courtesy for officials and staff members of the Tribunal and for all persons who facilitate and participate in the proceedings.

B. Counsel shall not seek to influence or communicate with a Judge, official, or staff member of the Tribunal by means prohibited by the Statute, the Rules, this Code or any other applicable law.

C. Counsel shall recognise the representatives of the parties as professional colleagues and shall act fairly, honestly and courteously towards them.

D. Counsel shall not communicate with the client of another counsel without the authorisation of that client's counsel unless permitted under the Rules, this Code or any other applicable law.

Article 28
Victims and Witnesses

A. Counsel shall not use any means that have no substantial purpose other than to embarrass, delay or burden victims and witnesses, or use coercive or other methods of obtaining evidence that violate the Statute, the Rules or this Code.

B. Counsel shall not make any payments in monies or assets to witnesses or potential witnesses for the purpose of unduly influencing or inducing such witnesses or potential witnesses.

Article 29
Unrepresented Persons

A. Counsel communicating, on behalf of a client, with a person who is not represented by counsel ("unrepresented person"), shall not:

    i. knowingly mislead the unrepresented person, to the prejudice of that person, concerning the identity and interests of counsel's client;

    ii. coerce, harass or threaten the unrepresented person or his relatives;

    iii. state or imply that counsel is disinterested;

    iv. make other statements prohibited by applicable law;

    v. fail to disclose information required by applicable law; or

    vi. give advice to the unrepresented person, except to retain counsel and in relation to matters specified under paragraph (B), if the interests of that person are or may reasonably be expected to be in conflict with the interests of his client.

B. Whether or not a conflict exists or may exist with the interests of counsel's client, counsel shall inform the unrepresented person of:

    i. the role counsel plays in the matter;

    ii. the person's right to counsel under the Rules; and

    iii. the nature of legal representation in general.

Article 30
Prospective Clients

Counsel shall not:

    i. contact a prospective client, his relatives or acquaintances directly or indirectly;

    ii. solicit work from a prospective client, if:

        1. the prospective client, his relatives or acquaintances have made known to counsel a desire not to be solicited by counsel; or

        2. the solicitation involves behaviour such as fraud, undue influence, coercion, duress or harassment; or

    ii. make false, misleading or deceptive communications to a prospective client, his relatives or acquaintances about the counsel or another counsel's services.

Article 31
Referral Fees

A. Counsel shall not demand or accept from another counsel or any other person a fee, commission or any other compensation for referring or recommending the counsel to a client.

B. Counsel shall not pay any person a fee, commission or any other compensation as a consideration for referring a client to the counsel.

Section 4: Supervisory and Subordinate Conduct

Article 32
Responsibilities of Supervisory Counsel

658

A. Counsel having direct supervisory authority over another counsel in his team shall make reasonable efforts to ensure that the other counsel adheres to this Code.

B. Counsel shall be responsible for another counsel's violation of this Code if:

> i. counsel orders, or with knowledge of the specific conduct, approves the conduct involved; or
>
> ii. counsel has direct supervisory authority over the other counsel, and knew or had reason to know of the conduct at a time when its consequences can be avoided or mitigated but fails to take reasonable remedial action.

Article 33
Responsibilities of Subordinate Counsel

A. Counsel is bound by this Code notwithstanding that counsel acted at the direction of another counsel.

B. Counsel reasonably acting in accordance with a supervisory counsel's reasonable resolution of an arguable question of professional duty shall not be considered to have violated this Article.

Article 34
Responsibility for other Team Members

A. Counsel having direct supervisory authority over other members of his team shall make reasonable efforts to ensure that such members' conduct is compatible with the professional obligations of counsel.

B. Counsel shall be responsible for the conduct of other members of his team who provide services for counsel that would be a violation of this Code if engaged by counsel if:

> i. counsel orders or, with knowledge of the specific conduct, approves the conduct involved; or
>
> ii. counsel has direct supervisory authority over the team member, and knows of the conduct at a time when its consequences can be avoided or mitigated but fails to take reasonable remedial action.

Section 5: Maintenance of the Integrity of the Profession

Article 35
Misconduct

It shall be professional misconduct for counsel, inter alia, to:

> i. violate or attempt to violate the Statute, the Rules, this Code or any other applicable law, or to knowingly assist or induce another person to do so, or to do so through the acts of another person;
>
> ii. commit a criminal act which reflects adversely on counsel's honesty, trustworthiness or fitness as counsel;
>
> iii. engage in conduct involving dishonesty, fraud, deceit or misrepresentation;
>
> iv. engage in conduct which is prejudicial to the proper administration of justice before the Tribunal; or
>
> v. provide inaccurate information or fail to disclose information regarding counsel's qualifications to practice before the Tribunal as set out in the Rules and, where counsel has been assigned to a client, the Directive.

Article 36
Reporting Misconduct

In accordance with the disciplinary regime set out in Part Three of this Code, counsel shall inform the Disciplinary Panel if counsel knows that another counsel has breached this Code or has otherwise engaged in professional misconduct.

PART THREE
DISCIPLINARY REGIME

Article 37
Purpose

The purposes of this Part are:

      a. to protect clients and other individuals, and particularly witnesses from counsel who have not discharged, will not discharge or are unlikely to discharge their professional responsibilities and to provide every person the right to submit a complaint about the conduct of counsel;

      b. to ensure compliance by individual counsel with the necessary standards of professionalism, competence, diligence and honesty and to maintain at a significantly high level the ethics and practice of the legal system operated by the Tribunal; and

      c. to guarantee that procedural fairness is applied to any disciplinary proceedings taken against counsel.

Article 38
Inherent Powers of the Tribunal

This Part shall not affect the inherent powers of the Tribunal to deal with conduct which interferes with the administration of justice under the Statute, the Rules or any other applicable law.

Article 39
Filings, Decisions and Orders

Unless otherwise provided in this disciplinary regime, all filings, decisions and orders in relation to the disciplinary regime shall be submitted in confidence to, or transmitted by, the Registry in a working language of the Tribunal. The Registry shall maintain all records for the purposes of this disciplinary regime.

Article 40
Disciplinary Panel

A. A Disciplinary Panel shall deal with all matters relating to counsel ethics. The Panel shall consist of:

      i. a member of the Association of Counsel to be appointed in accordance with the Association's statute;

      ii. a member of the Advisory Panel having practised at the Tribunal to be appointed by the President of the Advisory Panel;

      iii. the Registrar of the Tribunal, or a senior Registry legal official designated by him.

B. The members of the Panel shall select at its first meeting a counsel chairperson from amongst its members. The chairperson shall be appointed for a term of two years.

C. Except as otherwise provided by this Code, the Panel may determine its own procedure for the filing of briefs and presentation of argument.

D. Complaints concerning the conduct of a counsel or a member of his team relating to matters before the Tribunal and specified in Article 35 shall be submitted to the Chairperson of the Panel in accordance with Article 39. Where the Panel itself has reasonable grounds to suspect that counsel or a member of his team has engaged in such conduct, it may commence, proprio motu, an investigation into the matter.

Article 41
Submission of Complaints

1. Complaints may be submitted by a client, a party to proceedings before the Tribunal, or any other person, organisation or State whose rights or interests could be substantially affected by an alleged misconduct.

2. The complaint, which shall be in writing and submitted in accordance with Article 39, shall identify the complainant and the counsel against whom the complaint is made, and describe in sufficient detail the alleged misconduct of the counsel.

3. The complaint shall be submitted within twelve months after the alleged misconduct is brought to the attention of the complainant or within twelve months after the complainant should have reasonably known about the existence or occurrence of the alleged misconduct. The Disciplinary Panel may pursue complaints after these deadlines if the matter is of general importance for the Tribunal or in the interests of justice in a pending case.

Article 42
Summary Dismissal of Complaints

In consultation with the Duty Judge of the Tribunal, the Disciplinary Panel may dismiss a complaint if it is vexatious, misconceived, frivolous, lacking in substance or out of time.

Article 43
Withdrawal of Complaints

A. By notice in writing served on the Chairperson of the Disciplinary Panel, a complaint may be withdrawn by the complainant in writing. The withdrawal of a complaint does not impact upon the Panel's competencies under Article 40 (D) to investigate the matter raised in the complaint.

B. The withdrawal of the complaint does not prevent a further complaint being made under this Part by the same or any other complainant, with respect to the subject matter of the withdrawn complaint; or action being taken on any other complaint made with respect to that matter.

Article 44
Investigation of Alleged Misconduct

A. The Disciplinary Panel shall conduct, as soon as possible, an investigation into the alleged misconduct specified in Article 35, provided that a complaint is not summarily dismissed.

B. In the investigation of the conduct, the Panel:

   i. shall send particulars of the conduct to the respective counsel or team member ("respondent") in a language he understands, and invite him to submit a written explanation in response to the complaint;

   ii. may order, by notice served in writing, the respondent to:

   1. produce, at any time and place specified in the notice, any books, documents, papers, accounts or records that are in his possession or under his control and that relate to the subject-matter of the complaint; or

   2. otherwise assist in, or co-operate with, the investigation of the complaint in a specified manner.

C. The Disciplinary Panel may inspect any book, document, paper, account or record produced in accordance with paragraph (B)(ii)(1) and may retain it for such period as it deems necessary for the purposes of the investigation. For the purpose of investigating an alleged misconduct of counsel involving allegations of fee-sharing, the Panel may request the Registrar to provide information on his related inquiries into the financial status of an accused, if any.

D. Any respondent who, without reasonable justification or excuse, refuses or fails to comply with any order or requirement of the Disciplinary Panel under this Article may be fined by the Disciplinary Panel with a penalty of up to 10.000 €.

Article 45
Interim Suspension from Practice

A. At any time after a complaint against a respondent has been filed or the Disciplinary Panel has commenced an investigation propriu motu, if there are reasonable grounds to conclude that the alleged misconduct is likely to cause immediate and irreparable harm to the interests of justice, a party to the proceedings, a witness, the respondent's client or any other prospective client, the Panel may, without prior notice to the respondent, issue a reasoned order that the respondent be suspended from practising before the Tribunal until the charge has been heard and disposed of.

B. If counsel is representing a suspect or accused while the Disciplinary Panel considers an order for suspension, the Panel must obtain approval from the Presiding Judge of the Chamber in front of which counsel appears before issuing an order.

C. The respondent, or his client, may at any time apply to the President of the Tribunal for the revocation of the order. The President of the Tribunal shall review such application within seven days after it has been received and may grant or refuse the application as he deems fit.

Article 46
Charges against Counsel and Institution of Proceedings and Hearings

A. The Disciplinary Panel shall inquire into each particularised allegation, and if there are reasonable grounds that the counsel has committed misconduct, formulate charges against counsel.

B. The Disciplinary Panel may order, if it is in the interests of justice, the joinder of:

   i. more than one charge against the same respondent; or

ii. a charge against one or more respondents if all the charges are founded on the same, or closely related, acts or omissions.

C. During the course of the inquiry, the respondent shall be provided the opportunity to file a reply to the allegation in the charge in accordance with the rules of the Disciplinary Panel.

D. If there are any material issues of fact raised in the pleadings or if the respondent requests the opportunity to be heard in mitigation, the Disciplinary Panel shall hold a hearing in public at the seat of the Tribunal unless it decides, proprio motu or upon application by the respondent, to exclude the public.

E. During the hearing the respondent shall have the right to be represented by counsel, to examine evidence submitted by the complainant or gathered by the Disciplinary Panel, cross-examine witnesses and to present evidence. The complainant, if any, shall be permitted to address the Disciplinary Panel concerning the respondent's alleged misconduct and its effect on him.

F. The Disciplinary Panel may admit any evidence which is relevant or which has probative value, whether oral or written, whether direct or hearsay and whether or not the same would be admissible in a court of law.

G. Every witness appearing before the Disciplinary Panel shall, before giving evidence, make the solemn declaration as set out in the Rules. The provisions of the Rules relating to false testimony under solemn declaration shall apply, mutatis mutandis, to witnesses appearing before the Disciplinary Panel.

Article 47
Findings and Sanctions

A. The findings of the Disciplinary Panel on each charge shall be rendered, in consultation with the Duty Judge of the Tribunal, by the majority of its members and shall be accompanied by a reasoned opinion in writing, to which separate or dissenting opinions may be appended.

B. The Disciplinary Panel may conclude its proceedings without a finding of misconduct, or dismiss any charge. The Panel may suspend or dismiss a complaint, before, during or after the investigation of the complaint, if it is in the interests of justice to do so or it fails to find reasonable grounds to conclude that the respondent committed the alleged misconduct.

C. A respondent against whom a charge of professional misconduct has been found proved beyond a reasonable doubt may be sentenced by the Disciplinary Panel to be, either alternatively or cumulatively:

    i. admonished by the Disciplinary Panel;

    ii. given advice by the Disciplinary Panel as to his future conduct;

    iii. publicly reprimanded by the Disciplinary Panel;

    iv. ordered to pay a fine of up to 50,000 € to the Tribunal;

    v. suspended from practising before the Tribunal for an appropriate fixed period of time not exceeding two years;

    vi. banned from practising before the Tribunal.

D. In determining the sentence imposed, the Disciplinary Panel must take into account any mitigating factors it considers relevant, including, inter alia, the fact that the respondent was acting pursuant to a provision of another code of practice and ethics which governs his conduct and that provision is inconsistent with this Code. A sentence must be proportionate in view of the misconduct.

E. The decision of the Disciplinary Panel shall be notified in writing to the complainant, if any, and to the respondent in a language the respondent understands.

F. A copy of the decision shall be communicated to the Association of Counsel as well as the professional body regulating the conduct of the respondent in his State of admission, or to the governing body of the university where counsel is a law professor.

G. The Registry shall take such action as may be required to enforce the sentence.

Article 48
Appeal to the Disciplinary Board

A. In cases where one or more charges of professional misconduct have been proved, the respondent may file an appeal with a Disciplinary Board within fourteen days of notification of the decision of the Disciplinary Panel.

B. In cases where the Disciplinary Panel has decided that a charge has not been proved, the Registrar may file an appeal with the Disciplinary Board within fourteen days of notification of the decision to the respondent.

C. The Disciplinary Board shall consist of:

i. three Judges to be appointed by the President of the Tribunal;

ii. two members of the Association of Counsel, to be appointed for a two year period, and in accordance with the Association's statute. No member of the Disciplinary Panel shall be a member of the Disciplinary Board at the same time.

D. No Judge who sat as a member of the Chamber before which the respondent appeared shall be eligible to sit as a member of the Disciplinary Board on the hearing or determination of any charge against the respondent for professional misconduct.

E. The members of the Disciplinary Board shall, at its first meeting, select a chairperson from amongst their number.

F. Except as otherwise provided by this Code, the Disciplinary Board may determine its own procedure for the filing of briefs and presentation of argument. During its review, however, the Disciplinary Board shall not receive or consider any evidence that was not presented to the Disciplinary Panel, unless it considers that the interests of justice so require.

G. Any respondent who, without reasonable justification or excuse, refuses or fails to comply with any order or requirement of the Disciplinary Board under this Article may be fined by the Board with a penalty of up to 10.000 €.

H. The Disciplinary Board may confirm, reverse or modify the decision on appeal.

I. In any case in which the respondent has given notice of appeal to the Disciplinary Board, the actions set out in Article 47 paragraph (G) shall be deferred until the appeal has been disposed of by the Disciplinary Board with or without a hearing. The Board may at any time after it was seized order a measure in accordance with Article 45 (A). Article 45 (B) does not apply.

J. The decision of the Disciplinary Board is final, and shall in particular not be subject to any remedy before the President or a Chamber of the Tribunal.

Article 49
Costs

A. If a respondent is sentenced by the Disciplinary Panel, and an appeal is not filed, or by the Disciplinary Board, the respondent shall bear the costs of the procedure. These costs consist of necessary and reasonable travel costs of the Panel or Board members in accordance with the Tribunal's practice for travel of defence counsel, if any, and an office expenses lump sum of up to 1000 € to be determined by the Disciplinary Panel or Board.

B. If a proceeding or complaint is dismissed by the Disciplinary Panel, and an appeal is not filed, or by the Disciplinary Board, the Tribunal bears the costs of the proceedings, unless the Panel or Board decides, on the basis of reasonable cause, that the respondent should bear up to fifty percent of the costs. * * *

Article 50
Non Bis In Idem

Once a proceeding or complaint has been finally adjudicated by the Disciplinary Board and an appeal has not been filed to the Disciplinary Board within fourteen days of notification, or by the Disciplinary Panel, no further action shall be taken by the Disciplinary Panel or Disciplinary Board against the respondent with respect to the subject matter of the proceeding or complaint.

INTERNATIONAL CRIMINAL TRIBUNAL FOR RWANDA (ICTR) CODE OF PROFESSIONAL CONDUCT FOR DEFENCE COUNSEL

International Criminal Tribunal for Rwanda, *Code of Professional Conduct for Defence Counsel* (2008), *available at*
http://69.94.11.53/ENGLISH/basicdocs/080314/04Code%20of%20Conduct%20for%20Defence%20Counsel.pdf

INTRODUCTION

This Code is made in the belief that:

1. As legal practitioners, Counsel must maintain high standards of professional conduct;

2. The role of Counsel as specialist advocates in the administration of justice requires them to act honestly, fairly, skillfully, diligently and courageously;

3. Counsel have an overriding duty to defend their client's interests, to the extent that they can do so without acting dishonestly or by improperly prejudicing the administration of justice;

4. Counsel may be subject to disciplinary proceedings under Rule 46 of the Rules of Procedure and Evidence of the Tribunal. It is therefore necessary that Counsel be aware of their rights and obligations toward the Tribunal;

To these ends, this Code and its Articles of conduct have been formulated.

Part I: Preliminary

Article 1
Definitions

(1) In this Code, unless a different interpretation is required by the provisions of the Code or the context in which they appear, the following terms shall mean:

Client: An accused, suspect, detainee, witness or other person who has engaged Counsel for the purposes of his legal representation before the Tribunal;

Counsel: Any person who has satisfied the Registrar that he is admitted to the practice of law in a State, or is a University professor of law, and

(a) Has filed his or her power of attorney with the Registrar; or

(b) Has been assigned under the Rules to a suspect, accused, detainee, witness or other person.

Any reference to Counsel includes a reference to any Co-counsel jointly and to each of them severally.

Directive: The directive entitled "Directive on Assignment of Defence Counsel", as amended (No. 1/96 (ICTR/2/L.2);

Rules: The Rules of Procedure and Evidence of the Tribunal adopted on 5 July 1995, as amended;

Statute: The Statute of the Tribunal adopted by Security Council Resolution 955 of 8 November 1994;

Tribunal: The International Criminal Tribunal for the Prosecution of Persons Responsible for Genocide and Other Serious Violations of International Humanitarian Law Committed in the Territory of Rwanda and Rwandan Citizens Responsible for Genocide and other such violations committed in the territory of neighbouring States, between 1 January 1994 and 31 December 1994, established by Security Council Resolution 955 of 8 November 1994.

(2) In the event of any inconsistency between this Code and the Directive, the terms and provisions of the Directive prevail.

(3) Any term not defined in this Code has the same meaning given to it by the Statute or by the Rules.

(4) While Counsel is bound by this Code, it is not, and should not be read as if it were a complete or detailed Code of Conduct for Counsel. Other standards and requirements ay be imposed on the conduct of Counsel by virtue of the Tribunal's inherent jurisdiction and the code of conduct of any national body to which Counsel belongs.

(5) This Code must be read and applied so as to most effectively attain the objects and uphold the values expressed in the Preamble.

(6) General provisions of this Code should not be read or applied in a restrictive way by reason of any particular or illustrative provisions.

(7) The singular includes the plural and vice versa.

Article 2
Entry into Force

This Code enters into force on 4 June 1998.

Article 3
General Purpose and Application

(1) The general purpose of this Code is to provide for standards of conduct on the part of Counsel which are appropriate in the interests of the fair and proper administration of justice.

(2) This Code applies to Counsel as defined in Article 1(1) of this Code.

Part II: General Obligations of Counsel to Clients

Article 4
Scope and Termination of Representation

(1) Counsel must advise and represent their client until the client duly terminates Counsel's position, or Counsel is otherwise withdrawn with the consent of the Tribunal.

(2) When representing a client, Counsel must:

(a) Abide by a client's decisions concerning the objectives of representation if not inconsistent with Counsels ethical duties; and

(b) Consult with the client about the means by which those objectives are to be pursued.

(3) Counsel must not advise or assist a client to engage in conduct which Counsel knows is in breach of the Statute, the Rules or this Code and, where Counsel has been assigned to the client, the Directive.

Article 5
Competence and Independence

In providing representation to a client, Counsel must:

(a) Act with competence, dignity, skill, care, honesty and loyalty;

(b) Exercise independent professional judgement and render open and honest advice;

(c) Never be influenced by improper or patently dishonest behaviour on the part of a client;

(d) Preserve their own integrity and that of the legal profession as a whole;

(e) Never permit their independence, integrity and standards to be compromised by external pressures.

Article 5 *bis*
Fee Splitting

(1) Fee-splitting arrangements, including but not limited to financial arrangements, between Counsel and their clients, relatives and/or agent of their clients are not permitted by the Tribunal.

(2) Where Counsel are being requested, induced or encouraged by their clients to enter into fee splitting arrangements, they shall advise their clients on the unlawfulness of such practice and shall report the incident to the Registrar forthwith.

(3) Counsel shall inform the Registrar of any alleged fee splitting arrangement by any member of his Defence team.

(4) Following receipt of information regarding possible fee splitting arrangements between Counsel and their clients, the Registrar shall investigate such information in order to determine whether it is substantiated.

(5) Where Counsel is found to have engaged in a practice of fee splitting or to have entered into a fee splitting arrangement with his client, the Registrar shall take action in accordance with Article 19 (A) (iii) of the Directive on assignment of Defence Counsel.

(6) In exceptional circumstances, and only where the Registrar has granted leave, Counsel may provide their clients with equipment and materials necessary for the preparation of their defence.

Article 6
Diligence

Counsel must represent a client diligently in order to protect the client's best interests. Unless the representation is terminated, Counsel must carry through to conclusion all matters undertaken for a client within the scope of his legal representation.

Article 7
Communication

Counsel must keep a client informed about the status of a matter before the Tribunal in which the client is an interested party and must promptly comply with all reasonable requests for information.

Article 8
Confidentiality

(1) Whether or not the relation of Counsel and client continues, Counsel must preserve the confidentiality of his client's affairs and, subject to sub-article (2), must not reveal to any other person, other than to any assistants who need to know it for the performance of their duties, information which has been entrusted to him in confidence or use such information to his client's detriment or to his own or another client's advantage.

(2) Notwithstanding sub-article (1), and subject to Article 19 ("Conflicts"), Counsel may reveal information which has been entrusted to him in confidence in any one of the following circumstances:

(a) When the client has been fully consulted and knowingly consents; or

(b) When the client has voluntarily disclosed the content of the communication to a third party, and that third party then gives evidence of that disclosure; or

(c) When essential to establish a defence to a criminal or disciplinary charge or civil claim formally instituted against Counsel; or

(d) To prevent an act which Counsel reasonably believes:

(i) Is, or may be, criminal within the territory in which it may occur or under the Statute or the Rules; and

(ii) May result in death or substantial bodily harm to any person unless the information is disclosed.

(3) For the purposes of this Article, Counsel includes employees or associates of Counsel and all others whose services are used by Counsel.

Article 9
Conflict of Interest

(1) Counsel owes a duty of loyalty to his or her client. Counsel must at all times act in the best interests of the client and must put those interests before their own interests or those of any other person.

(2) In the course of representing a client, Counsel must exercise all care to ensure that no conflict of interest arises.

(3) Without limiting the generality of sub-articles (1) and (2), Counsel must not represent a client with respect to a matter if:

(a) Such representation will be or is likely to be adversely affected by representation of another client;

(b) Representation of another client will be or is likely to be adversely affected by such representation;

(c) The Counsels professional judgement on behalf of the client will be, or may reasonably be expected to be, adversely affected by:

(i) The Counsels responsibilities to, or interests in, a third party; or

(ii) The Counsels own financial, business, property or personal interests; or

(iii) The matter is the same or substantially related to another matter in which Counsel had formerly represented another client (the former client); and the interests of the client are materially adverse to the interests of the former client, unless the former client consents after consultation.

(4) Counsel must not accept compensation for representing a client from a source other than that client or, if assigned by the Tribunal, from a source other than the Tribunal, unless:

(a) That client consents after consultation; and

(b) There is no interference thereby with the Counsels independence of professional judgement nor with the client-Counsel relationship.

(5) Where a conflict of interest does arise, Counsel must:

(a) Promptly and fully inform each potentially affected client of the nature and extent of the conflict; and

(b) Either:

(i) Take all steps necessary to remove the conflict; or

(ii) Obtain the full and informed consent of all potentially affected clients to continue the representation, so long as Counsel is able to fulfil all other obligations under this Code.

Article 10

Client under a Disability
When a client's ability to make adequately considered decisions in connection with their representation is impaired because of minority, mental disability or any other reason, Counsel must:

(a) Inform the Judge or Chamber of the Tribunal hearing the matter, if any, of the disability;

(b) Take such steps as are necessary to ensure the adequate legal representation of that client; and

(c) As far as reasonably possible maintain a normal Counsel-client relationship with the client.

Article 11
Accounting for Time
Counsel should account in good faith for the time spent working on a case and maintain and preserve detailed records of time spent. Counsel is under a duty to set his bills and fees with moderation.

Part III: Conduct before the Tribunal

Article 12
Rules of the Tribunal
(1) Counsel must at all times comply with the Rules and such rulings as to conduct and procedure as may be applied by the Tribunal in its proceedings. Counsel must at all times have due regard to the fair conduct of proceedings.

(2) Counsel must not, unless permitted by the Rules or this Code or the Judge or Chamber hearing the matter:

(a) Make contact with a Judge or Chamber of the Tribunal without first or concurrently informing Counsel acting for any other party to the proceedings;

(b) Submit exhibits, notes or documents to the Judge without communicating them first or concurrently to Counsel acting for any other party to the proceedings.

Article 13
Candour Toward the Tribunal
(1) Counsel is personally responsible for the conduct and presentation of their Client's case, and must exercise personal judgement upon the substance and purpose of statements made and questions asked.

(2) Counsel must not knowingly:

(a) Make an incorrect statement of material fact to the Tribunal; or

(b) Offer evidence which the Counsel knows to be incorrect.

(3) Despite sub-article (2) (a), Counsel will not have made an incorrect statement to another party to the proceedings or to the Tribunal simply by failing to correct an error on any matter stated to Counsel or to the Tribunal during proceedings.

(4) Counsel must take all necessary steps to correct an incorrect statement made by Counsel in proceedings before the Tribunal as soon as possible after Counsel becomes aware that the statement was incorrect.

Article 14
Integrity of Evidence
(1) Counsel must at all times maintain the integrity of evidence, whether in written, oral or any other form, which is or may be submitted to the Tribunal.

(2) If Counsel's representation of a client terminates for any reason, Counsel shall return evidence and other materials, which have come into his possession as a result of the said representation, to his former client, to the latter's Counsel, or under seal to the Registrar for onward transmission to the said client or Counsel, as appropriate.

Article 15
Impartiality of the Tribunal
(1) Counsel must take all necessary steps to ensure that their actions do not bring proceedings before the Tribunal into disrepute.

(2) Counsel must not seek to influence a Judge or other official of the Tribunal by means prohibited by the Statute, the Rules or this Code.

Article 16
Counsel as Witness

Counsel must not act as advocate in a trial in which the Counsel is likely to be a necessary witness except where the testimony relates to an uncontested issue or where substantial hardship would be caused to the client if that Counsel does not so act.

Part IV: Duty of Counsel to Others

Article 17
Fairness and Courtesy

(1) Counsel must act fairly, honestly and courteously towards all persons with whom they have professional contact, namely other Counsel, their clients, Judges, members of the Office of the Prosecutor and Registry staff. Counsel shall recognize all other Counsel appearing or acting in relation to proceedings before the Tribunal as professional colleagues.

(2) Counsel must not communicate with the client of another Counsel except through or with the permission of that client's Counsel.

Article 18
Dealing with Unrepresented Persons

(1) If, on behalf of a client, Counsel is dealing with a person who is not represented by Counsel, Counsel:
>   (a) Must not give advice to this unrepresented person if the interests of the person are, or have a reasonable possibility of being, in conflict with the interests of the Counsel's client; but
>   (b) May advise the unrepresented person to secure legal representation.

(2) Counsel must inform the unrepresented person of the role Counsel plays in the matter, the persons right to Counsel under the Rules, and the nature of legal representation in general.

This information must be given whether or not a conflict exists or may exist with the interests of Counsel's client.

Part V: Maintenance of the Integrity of the Profession

Article 19
Conflicts

If there is any inconsistency between this Code and any other code which Counsel is bound to honour, the terms of this Code prevail in respect of Counsel's conduct before the Tribunal.

Article 20
Misconduct

It is professional misconduct for Counsel, *inter alia,* to:
>   (a) Violate or attempt to violate this Code or to knowingly assist or induce another person to do so, or to do so through the acts of another person;
>   (b) Commit a reprehensible act which reflects adversely on Counsel's honesty, trustworthiness or fitness as Counsel;
>   (c) Engage in conduct involving dishonesty, fraud, deceit or misrepresentation;
>   (d) Engage in conduct which is prejudicial to the proper administration of justice before the Tribunal; or
>   (e) Attempt to influence an officer of the Tribunal in an improper manner.

Article 21
Reporting Misconduct

(1) If:
>   (a) Counsel knows that another Counsel has breached this Code or has otherwise engaged in professional misconduct; and

(b) That violation or conduct raises a substantial question as to the other Counsel's honesty, trustworthiness or fitness as Counsel.

Counsel shall inform the Judge or Chamber of the Tribunal before which Counsel is appearing.
(2) The Registrar may also communicate any misconduct of Counsel to the professional body regulating the conduct of Counsel in his State of admission or, if a Professor and not otherwise admitted to the profession, to the governing body of his University.

Article 22
Enforcement

Counsel must abide by and voluntarily submit to any enforcement and disciplinary procedures as may be established by the Tribunal in accordance with the Rules.

Article 23
Amendment

This Code may be amended by the Registrar, after consultation with the Judges.

INTERNATIONAL CRIMINAL COURT
CODE OF PROFESSIONAL CONDUCT FOR COUNSEL

International Criminal Court, *Code of Professional Conduct for Counsel*, U.N. Doc. ICC-ASP/4/32 (2005), *available at* http://www.icc-cpi.int/library/about/officialjournal/ICC-ASP-4-32-Res.1_English.pdf

Chapter 1
General provisions

Article 1
Scope

This Code shall apply to defence counsel, counsel acting for States, *amici curiae* and counsel or legal representatives for victims and witnesses practising at the International Criminal Court, hereinafter referred to as "counsel".

Article 2
Use of terms

1. Unless otherwise defined in this Code, all terms are used as defined in the Statute, the Rules of Procedure and Evidence and the Regulations of the Court.
2. In this Code:
   - "Court" refers to the International Criminal Court;
   - "associate" refers to lawyers who practise in the same law firm as counsel;
   - "national authority" refers to the bar association of which counsel is a member or any other organ competent to regulate and control the activity of lawyers, judges, prosecutors or professors of law, or other qualified counsel according to rule 22, paragraph 1, of the Rules of Procedure and Evidence;
   - "client" refers to all those assisted or represented by counsel;
   - "defence team" refers to counsel and all persons working under his or her oversight; and
   - "agreement" refers to the oral or written legal relationship which binds counsel to his or her client before the Court.

Article 3
Amendment procedure

1. States Parties, judges, the Registrar, counsel and independent organizations representing lawyers' associations and counsel may submit proposals for amendments to this Code. Any proposal for amendments to this Code shall be submitted to the Registrar, together with explanatory material, in one or both working languages of the Court.

2. The Registrar shall transmit the proposals to the Presidency, together with a reasoned report prepared after consultation with the Prosecutor and, as appropriate, with any independent organization representing lawyers' associations and counsel.

3. Any proposal to amend this Code, submitted by one or more States Parties, shall be transmitted by the Presidency to the Assembly of States Parties together with any comments the Presidency may have, taking into account the report of the Registrar.

4. Any proposal to amend this Code, other than one submitted by one or more States Parties, shall be transmitted by the Presidency to the Assembly of States Parties together with any comments the Presidency may have, taking into account the report of the Registrar. In such circumstances, the Presidency shall provide the Assembly of States Parties with the Presidency's reasoned recommendations as to whether or not any such proposal should be adopted. If the Presidency recommends adoption, it shall submit a draft amendment in relation to that proposal to the Assembly of States Parties for the purpose of adoption.

5. Amendments to this Code shall be adopted by the Assembly of States Parties in accordance with article 112, paragraph 7, of the Statute.

Article 4
Primacy of the Code of Professional Conduct for counsel

Where there is any inconsistency between this Code and any other code of ethics or professional responsibility which counsel are bound to honour, the terms of this Code shall prevail in respect of the practice and professional ethics of counsel when practising before the Court.

Article 5
Solemn undertaking by counsel

Before taking office, counsel shall give the following solemn undertaking before the Court: "I solemnly declare that I will perform my duties and exercise my mission before the International Criminal Court with integrity and diligence, honourably, freely, independently, expeditiously and conscientiously, and that I will scrupulously respect professional secrecy and the other duties imposed by the Code of Professional Conduct for Counsel before the International Criminal Court".

Article 6
Independence of counsel

1. Counsel shall act honourably, independently and freely.
2. Counsel shall not:
    (a) Permit his or her independence, integrity or freedom to be compromised by external pressure; or
    (b) Do anything which may lead to any reasonable inference that his or her independence has been compromised.

Article 7
Professional conduct of counsel

1. Counsel shall be respectful and courteous in his or her relations with the Chamber, the Prosecutor and the members of the Office of the Prosecutor, the Registrar and the members of the Registry, the client, opposing counsel, accused persons, victims, witnesses and any other person involved in the proceedings.
2. Counsel shall maintain a high level of competence in the law applicable before the Court. He or she shall participate in training initiatives required to maintain such competence.
3. Counsel shall comply at all times with the Statute, the Rules of Procedure and Evidence, the Regulations of the Court and such rulings as to conduct and procedure as may be made by the Court, including the enforcement of this Code.
4. Counsel shall supervise the work of his or her assistants and other staff, including investigators, clerks and researchers, to ensure that they comply with this Code.

Article 8
Respect for professional secrecy and confidentiality

1. Counsel shall respect and actively exercise all care to ensure respect for professional secrecy and the confidentiality of information in accordance with the Statute, the Rules of Procedure and Evidence and the Regulations of the Court.

2. The relevant provisions referred to in paragraph 1 of this article include, inter alia, article 64, paragraph 6 (c), article 64, paragraph 7, article 67, paragraph 1 (b), article 68, and article 72 of the Statute, rules 72, 73, and 81 of the Rules of Procedure and Evidence and regulation 97 of the Regulations of the Court. Counsel shall also comply with the relevant provisions of this Code and any order of the Court.

3. Counsel may only reveal the information protected under paragraphs 1 and 2 of this article to co-counsel, assistants and other staff working on the particular case to which the information relates and solely to enable the exercise of his or her functions in relation to that case.

4. Subject to paragraph 3 of this article, counsel may only disclose the information protected under paragraphs 1 and 2 of this article, where such disclosure is provided for by a particular provision of the Statute, the Rules of Procedure and Evidence, the Regulations of the Court or this Code or where such disclosure is ordered by the Court. In particular, Counsel shall not reveal the identity of protected victims and witnesses, or any confidential information that may reveal their identity and whereabouts, unless he or she has been authorized to do so by an order of the Court.

Article 9
Counsel-client relationship

1. Counsel shall not engage in any discriminatory conduct in relation to any other person, in particular his or her client, on grounds of race, colour, ethnic or national origin, nationality, citizenship, political opinions, religious convictions, gender, sexual orientation, disability, marital status or any other personal or economic status.

2. In his or her relations with the client, counsel shall take into account the client's personal circumstances and specific needs, in particular where counsel is representing victims of torture or of physical, psychological or sexual violence, or children, the elderly or the disabled.

3. Where a client's ability to make decisions concerning representation is impaired because of mental disability or for any other reason, counsel shall inform the Registrar and the relevant Chamber. Counsel shall also take the steps necessary to ensure proper legal representation of the client according to the Statute and the Rules of Procedure and Evidence.

4. Counsel shall not engage in any improper conduct, such as demanding sexual relations, coercion, intimidation, or exercise any other undue influence in his or her relations with a client.

Article 10
Advertising

Counsel may advertise provided the information is:
> (a) Accurate; and
> (b) Respectful of counsel's obligations regarding confidentiality and privilege.

Chapter 2
Representation by counsel

Article 11
Establishment of the representation agreement

The agreement is established when counsel accepts a request from a client seeking representation or from the Chamber.

Article 12
Impediments to representation

1. Counsel shall not represent a client in a case:
> (a) If the case is the same as or substantially related to another case in which counsel or his or her associates represents or formerly represented another client and the interests of the client are incompatible with the interests of the former client, unless the client and the former client consent after consultation; or
> (b) In which counsel was involved or was privy to confidential information as a staff member of the Court relating to the case in which counsel seeks to appear. The lifting of this impediment may, however, at counsel's request, be ordered by the Court if deemed justified in the interests of justice. Counsel shall still be bound by the duties of confidentiality stemming from his or her former position as a staff member of the Court.

2. In the case of paragraph 1 (a) of this article, where consent has been obtained after consultation, counsel shall inform the Chamber of the Court seized with the situation or case of the conflict and the consent obtained. Such notice shall be provided in a manner consistent with counsel's duties of confidentiality pursuant to article 8 of this Code and rule 73, sub-rule 1 of the Rules of Procedure and Evidence.

3. Counsel shall not act in proceedings in which there is a substantial probability that counsel or an associate of counsel will be called to appear as a witness unless:

    (a) The testimony relates to an uncontested issue; or

    (b) The testimony relates to the nature and value of legal services rendered in the case.

4. This article is without prejudice to article 16 of this Code.

Article 13
Refusal by counsel of a representation agreement

1. Counsel has the right to refuse an agreement without stating reasons.

2. Counsel has a duty to refuse an agreement where:

    (a) There is a conflict of interest under article 16 of this Code;

    (b) Counsel is incapable of dealing with the matter diligently; or

    (c) Counsel does not consider that he or she has the requisite expertise.

Article 14
Performance in good faith of a representation agreement

1. The relationship of client and counsel is one of candid exchange and trust, binding counsel to act in good faith when dealing with the client. In discharging that duty, counsel shall act at all times with fairness, integrity and candour towards the client.

2. When representing a client, counsel shall:

    (a) Abide by the client's decisions concerning the objectives of his or her representation as long as they are not inconsistent with counsel's duties under the Statute, the Rules of Procedure and Evidence, and this Code; and

    (b) Consult the client on the means by which the objectives of his or her representation are to be pursued.

Article 15
Communication between counsel and the client

1. Counsel shall provide the client with all explanations reasonably needed to make informed decisions regarding his or her representation.

2. When counsel is discharged from or terminates the agreement, he or she shall convey as promptly as possible to the former client or replacement counsel any communication that counsel received relating to the representation, without prejudice to the duties which subsist after the end of the representation.

3. When communicating with the client, counsel shall ensure the confidentiality of such communication.

Article 16
Conflict of interest

1. Counsel shall exercise all care to ensure that no conflict of interest arises. Counsel shall put the client's interests before counsel's own interests or those of any other person, organization or State, having due regard to the provisions of the Statute, the Rules of Procedure and Evidence, and this Code.

2. Where counsel has been retained or appointed as a common legal representative for victims or particular groups of victims, he or she shall advise his or her clients at the outset of the nature of the representation and the potential conflicting interests within the group. Counsel shall exercise all care to ensure a fair representation of the different yet consistent positions of his or her clients.

3. Where a conflict of interest arises, counsel shall at once inform all potentially affected clients of the existence of the conflict and either:

    (a) Withdraw from the representation of one or more clients with the prior consent of the Chamber; or

(b) Seek the full and informed consent in writing of all potentially affected clients to continue representation.

Article 17
Duration of the representation agreement

1. Counsel shall advise and represent a client until:
    (a) The case before the Court has been finally determined, including all appeals;
    (b) Counsel has withdrawn from the agreement in accordance with article 16 or 18 of this Code; or
    (c) A counsel assigned by the Court has been withdrawn.
2. The duties of counsel towards the client continue until the representation has ended, except for those duties which subsist under this Code.

Article 18
Termination of the representation

1. With the prior consent of the Chamber, counsel may withdraw from the agreement in accordance with the Regulations of the Court if:
    (a) The client insists on pursuing an objective that counsel considers repugnant; or
    (b) The client fails to fulfil an obligation to counsel regarding counsel's services and has been given reasonable warning that counsel will withdraw unless the obligation is fulfilled.
2. Where counsel withdraws from the agreement, he or she remains subject to article 8 of this Code, as well as any provisions of the Statute and the Rules of Procedure and Evidence relating to confidentiality.
3. Where counsel is discharged by the client, counsel may be discharged in accordance with the Regulations of the Court.
4. Where counsel's physical or mental condition materially impairs his or her ability to represent the client, counsel may be withdrawn by the Chamber at his or her request or at the request of the client or the Registrar.
5. In addition to complying with the duties imposed by article 15, paragraph 2, of this Code, counsel shall convey to replacement counsel the entire case file, including any material or document relating to it.

Article 19
Conservation of files

Following the termination of the representation, counsel shall keep files containing documents and records of work carried out in fulfilment of the agreement for five years. Counsel shall allow the former client to inspect the file unless he or she has substantial grounds for refusing to do so. After this time counsel shall seek instructions from the former client, his or her heirs or the Registrar on the disposal of the files, with due regard to confidentiality.

Article 20
Counsel's fees

Prior to establishing an agreement, counsel shall inform the client in writing of the rate of fees to be charged and the criteria for setting them, the basis for calculating the costs, the billing arrangements and the client's right to receive a bill of costs.

Article 21
Prohibitions

1. Notwithstanding article 22, counsel shall not accept remuneration, in cash or in kind, from a source other than the client unless the client consents thereto in writing after consultation and counsel's independence and relationship with the client are not thereby affected.
2. Counsel shall never make his or her fees contingent on the outcome of a case in which he or she is involved.
3. Counsel shall not mix funds of a client with his or her own funds, or with funds of counsel's employer or associates. Counsel shall not retain money received on behalf of a client.
4. Counsel shall not borrow monies or assets from the client.

Article 22
Remuneration of counsel in the framework of legal assistance

1. The fees of counsel where his or her client benefits from legal assistance shall be paid exclusively by the Registry of the Court. Counsel shall not accept remuneration in cash or in kind from any other source.

2. Counsel shall neither transfer nor lend all or part of the fees received for representation of a client or any other assets or monies to a client, his or her relatives, acquaintances, or any other third person or organization in relation to which the client has a personal interest.

3. Counsel shall sign an undertaking to respect the obligations under this article when accepting the appointment to provide legal assistance. The signed undertaking shall be sent to the Registry.

4. Where counsel is requested, induced or encouraged to violate the obligations under this article, counsel shall advise the client of the prohibition of such conduct.

5. Breach of any obligations under this article by Counsel shall amount to misconduct and shall be subject to a disciplinary procedure pursuant to this Code. This may lead to a permanent ban on practising before the Court and being struck off the list of counsel, with transmission to the respective national authority.

Chapter 3
Relations with the Court and others

Article 23
Communications with the Chambers and judges

Unless the judge or the Chamber dealing with a case permits counsel to do so in exceptional circumstances, counsel shall not:

    (a) Make contact with a judge or Chamber relative to the merits of a particular case other than within the proper context of the proceedings; or

    (b) Transmit evidence, notes or documents to a judge or Chamber except through the Registry.

Article 24
Duties towards the Court

1. Counsel shall take all necessary steps to ensure that his or her actions or those of counsel's asSistants or staff are not prejudicial to the ongoing proceedings and do not bring the Court into disrepute.

2. Counsel is personally responsible for the conduct and presentation of the client's case and shall exercise personal judgement on the substance and purpose of statements made and questions asked.

3. Counsel shall not deceive or knowingly mislead the Court. He or she shall take all steps necessary to correct an erroneous statement made by him or her or by assistants or staff as soon as possible after becoming aware that the statement was erroneous.

4. Counsel shall not submit any request or document with the sole aim of harming one or more of the participants in the proceedings.

5. Counsel shall represent the client expeditiously with the purpose of avoiding unnecessary expense or delay in the conduct of the proceedings.

Article 25
Evidence

1. Counsel shall at all times maintain the integrity of evidence, whether in written, oral or any other form, which is submitted to the Court. He or she shall not introduce evidence which he or she knows to be incorrect.

2. If counsel, while collecting evidence, reasonably believes that the evidence found may be destroyed or tampered with, counsel shall request the Chamber to issue an order to collect the evidence pursuant to rule 116 of the Rules of Procedure and Evidence.

Article 26
Relations with unrepresented persons

1. When required in the course of representation, counsel may communicate with and meet an unrepresented person in the client's interest.

2. When counsel communicates with unrepresented persons he or she shall:

    (a) Inform them of their right to assistance from counsel and, if applicable, to their right to legal assistance; and

    (b) Without infringing upon the confidentiality of counsel-client privilege, inform them of the interest that counsel represents and the purpose of the communication.

3. If counsel becomes aware of a potential conflict of interest in the course of a communication or meeting with an unrepresented person, he or she shall, notwithstanding paragraph 1 of this article, refrain immediately from engaging in any further contact or communication with the person.

Article 27
Relations with other counsel

1. In dealing with other counsel and their clients, counsel shall act fairly, in good faith and courteously.
2. All correspondence between counsel representing clients with a common interest in a litigated or non-litigated matter and who agree on exchanging information concerning the matter, shall be presumed confidential and privileged by counsel.
3. When counsel does not expect particular correspondence between counsel to be confidential, he or she shall state clearly at the outset that such correspondence is not confidential.

Article 28
Relations with persons already represented by counsel

Counsel shall not address directly the client of another counsel except through or with the permission of that counsel.

Article 29
Relations with witnesses and victims

1. Counsel shall refrain from intimidating, harassing or humiliating witnesses or victims or from subjecting them to disproportionate or unnecessary pressure within or outside the courtroom.
2. Counsel shall have particular consideration for victims of torture or of physical, psychological or sexual violence, or children, the elderly or the disabled.

Chapter 4
Disciplinary regime

Article 30
Conflict with other disciplinary regimes

Subject to article 38 of this Code, the present chapter is without prejudice to the disciplinary powers of any other disciplinary authority that may apply to counsel subject to this Code.

Article 31
Misconduct

Counsel commits misconduct when he or she:

(a) Violates or attempts to violate any provisions of this Code, the Statute, the Rules of Procedure and Evidence and the Regulations of the Court or of the Registry in force imposing a substantial ethical or professional duty on him or her;

(b) Knowingly assists or induces another person to commit any misconduct, referred to in paragraph (a) of this article, or does so through the acts of another person; or

(c) Fails to comply with a disciplinary decision rendered pursuant to this chapter.

Article 32
Liability for conduct of assistants or other staff

1. Counsel shall be liable for misconduct under article 31 of this Code by his or her assistants or staff when he or she:

(a) Orders or approves the conduct involved; or

(b) Knows or has information suggesting that violations may be committed and takes no reasonable remedial action.

2. Counsel shall instruct his or her assistants or staff in the standards set by this Code.

Article 33
The Commissioner

1. A Commissioner responsible for investigating complaints of misconduct in accordance with this chapter shall be appointed for four years by the Presidency. The Commissioner shall be chosen from amongst persons with established competence in professional ethics and legal matters.

2. The Commissioner shall not be eligible for re-appointment. A Commissioner who is involved in an investigation when his or her mandate expires shall continue to conduct such an investigation until it is concluded.

Article 34
Filing a complaint of misconduct

1. Complaints against counsel regarding misconduct as referred to in articles 31 and 32 of this Code may be submitted to the Registry by:

    (a) The Chamber dealing with the case;

    (b) The Prosecutor; or

    (c) Any person or group of persons whose rights or interests may have been affected by the alleged misconduct.

2. The complaint shall be made in writing or, if the complainant is unable to do so, orally before a staff member of the Registry. It shall identify the complainant and the counsel against whom the complaint is made and shall describe in sufficient detail the alleged misconduct.

3. The Registrar shall transmit the complaint to the Commissioner.

4. The Registrar may, on his or her own initiative, make complaints to the Commissioner regarding the misconduct referred to in articles 31 and 32 of this Code.

5. All complaints shall be kept confidential by the Registry.

Article 35
Limitation period

The right to file a complaint against counsel for misconduct shall lapse five years after the termination of the representation agreement.

Article 36
Composition and management of the Disciplinary Board

1. The Disciplinary Board shall comprise three members, two of whom shall be permanent and one *ad hoc*.

2. The members of the Disciplinary Board shall perform their functions under this Code in an independent and impartial manner.

3. The Registry shall make appropriate arrangements for the elections, provided for in paragraph 4 of this article, in consultation with counsel and, as appropriate, national authorities.

4. The two permanent members, as well as one alternate member who may serve as a replacement in accordance with paragraph 10 of this article, shall be elected for four years by all counsel entitled to practise before the Court. They shall be chosen from amongst persons with established competence in professional ethics and legal matters.

5. The *ad hoc* member shall be a person appointed by the national authority competent to regulate and control the activities of counsel subject to the disciplinary procedure.

6. The permanent members shall not be eligible for re-election.

7. Notwithstanding paragraph 4 of this article, at the first election one of the permanent members shall be selected by lot to serve for a term of six years.

8. After each election and in advance of the first meeting of the newly-elected Disciplinary Board, the permanent and alternate members shall elect one of the permanent members as a chairperson.

9. All members of the Disciplinary Board shall have the same rights and votes. The Disciplinary Board shall decide by majority vote. An alternate member serving on a case pursuant to paragraph 10 of this article shall have the same rights and votes as permanent and *ad hoc* members serving on the same case.

10. If one of the permanent members is unavailable to deal with the case or serve on the Disciplinary Board, the chairperson or, where the chairperson is the permanent member concerned, the other permanent member, shall request the alternate member to serve as a replacement on the Disciplinary Board.

11. Permanent members or the alternate member whose mandates have expired shall continue to deal with the cases they already have under consideration until such cases are finally determined including all appeals.

12. The Registrar shall appoint a staff member of the Registry who will render secretariat services to the Disciplinary Board. Once appointed, the relevant staff member of the Registry shall act at arm's length from the Registry and, subject to article 44, paragraph 12 of this Code, solely as the secretariat of the Disciplinary Board.

Article 37
Preliminary procedures

1. If the complaint filed meets the requirements in article 34 of this Code, the Commissioner shall forward it to counsel subject to the disciplinary procedure, who shall submit a response within sixty days from the date the complaint is forwarded.
2. The response shall indicate whether the alleged misconduct has been or is the subject of a disciplinary procedure before the national authority. If so, it shall include:
   (a) The identity of the national authority deciding on the alleged misconduct; and
   (b) A certified communication by the national authority stating the alleged facts that are the basis of the disciplinary procedure before it.

Article 38
Complementarity of disciplinary measures

1. The disciplinary procedure in this Code shall be applied by the Disciplinary Board.
2. The *ad hoc* member of the Disciplinary Board shall serve as the contact point with the relevant national authority for all communication and consultation regarding the procedure.
3. Counsel subject to the disciplinary procedure shall request the national authority dealing with the matter to inform the Disciplinary Board of the progress of any national disciplinary procedure concerning the alleged misconduct and of its final decision, and shall take all measures necessary to facilitate such communication.
4. When the alleged misconduct is the basis of a disciplinary procedure which has already been initiated before the relevant national authority, the procedure before the Disciplinary Board shall be suspended until a final decision is reached regarding the former procedure, unless:
   (a) the national authority does not respond to communications and consultations in accordance with paragraph 2 of this article within a reasonable time;
   (b) the Disciplinary Board considers that the information received is not satisfactory; or
   (c) the Disciplinary Board considers that, in the light of the information received, the national authority is unable or unwilling to conclude the disciplinary procedure.
5. As soon as it receives the decision of the national authority, the Disciplinary Board shall:
   (a) declare the procedure closed, unless the decision adopted does not adequately address a complaint of misconduct under this Code; or
   (b) declare that the decision of the national authority does not cover or only partially covers the misconduct brought before the Disciplinary Board and that therefore the procedure is to be continued.
6. In the case of paragraphs 3 and paragraph 4 (b) of this article, the Disciplinary Board may ask counsel subject to the disciplinary procedure to provide detailed information about the procedure, including any minute or evidence which might have been submitted.
7. A decision by the Disciplinary Board based on this article may be appealed before the Disciplinary Appeals Board.

Article 39
Disciplinary procedure

1. The Commissioner conducting the investigation may dismiss a complaint without any further investigation if he or she considers on the basis of the information at his or her disposal that the allegation of misconduct is unfounded in fact or in law. He or she shall notify the complainant accordingly.
2. Should the Commissioner consider otherwise, he or she shall promptly investigate the counsel's alleged misconduct and decide either to submit a report to the Disciplinary Board or to bring the procedure to an end.
3. The Commissioner shall take into consideration all evidence, whether oral, written or any other form, which is relevant and has probative value. He or she shall keep all information concerning the disciplinary procedure confidential.

4. The Commissioner may try to find an amicable settlement if he or she deems it appropriate. The Commissioner shall report the outcome of any such efforts to reach an amicable settlement to the Disciplinary Board, which may take it into consideration. Any amicable settlement shall be without prejudice to the competence or powers of the Disciplinary Board under this Code.

5. The report of the Commissioner shall be submitted to the Disciplinary Board.

6. The Disciplinary Board hearing shall be public. However, the Disciplinary Board may decide to hold a hearing or parts of it in closed session, in particular to safeguard the confidentiality of information in the report of the Commissioner or to protect victims and witnesses.

7. The Commissioner and the counsel subject to the disciplinary procedure shall be called and heard. The Disciplinary Board may also call and hear any other person deemed useful for the establishment of the truth.

8. In exceptional cases, where the alleged misconduct is of such a nature as to seriously prejudice the interests of justice, the Commissioner may lodge an urgent motion with the Chamber before which the counsel who is the subject of the complaint is appearing, so that it may, as appropriate, declare a temporary suspension of such counsel.

Article 40
Rights of counsel subject to the disciplinary procedure

1. Counsel subject to the disciplinary procedure shall be entitled to assistance from other counsel.

2. Counsel shall have the right to remain silent before the Disciplinary Board, which may draw any inferences it deems appropriate and reasonable from such silence in the light of all the information submitted to it.

3. Counsel shall have the right to full disclosure of the information and evidence gathered by the Commissioner as well as the Commissioner's report.

4. Counsel shall be given the time required to prepare his or her defence.

5. Counsel shall have the right to question, personally or through his or her counsel, any person called by the Disciplinary Board to testify before it.

Article 41
Decisions by the Disciplinary Board

1. The Disciplinary Board may conclude the procedure finding no misconduct on the basis of the evidence submitted to it or finding that counsel subject to disciplinary procedure committed the alleged misconduct.

2. The decision shall be made public. It shall be reasoned and issued in writing.

3. The decision shall be notified to counsel subject to the disciplinary procedure and to the Registrar.

4. When the decision is final, it shall be published in the Official Journal of the Court and transmitted to the national authority.

Article 42
Sanctions

1. When misconduct has been established, the Disciplinary Board may impose one or more of the following sanctions:

    (a) Admonishment;

    (b) Public reprimand with an entry in counsel's personal file;

    (c) Payment of a fine of up to €30,000;

    (d) Suspension of the right to practise before the Court for a period not exceeding two years; and

    (e) Permanent ban on practising before the Court and striking off the list of counsel.

2. The admonishment may include recommendations by the Disciplinary Board.

3. The costs of the disciplinary procedure shall be within the discretion of the Disciplinary Board.

Article 43
Appeals

1. Sanctioned counsel and the Commissioner shall have the right to appeal the decision of the Disciplinary Board on factual or legal grounds.

2. The appeal shall be notified to the secretariat of the Disciplinary Board within thirty days from the day on which the decision has been delivered.

3. The secretariat of the Disciplinary Board shall transmit the notification of the appeal to the secretariat of the Disciplinary Appeals Board.

4. The Disciplinary Appeals Board shall decide on the appeal according to the procedure followed before the Disciplinary Board.

Article 44
Composition and management of the Disciplinary Appeals Board

1. The Disciplinary Appeals Board shall decide on appeals against decisions of the Disciplinary Board.

2. The members of the Disciplinary Appeals Board shall perform their functions under this Code in an independent and impartial manner.

3. The Registry shall make appropriate arrangements for the elections provided for in paragraph 5 of this article, in consultation with counsel and, as appropriate, national authorities.

4. The Disciplinary Appeals Board shall comprise five members:

    (a) The three judges of the Court who take precedence under regulation 10 of the Regulations of the Court, not including:

        (i) the judges dealing with the case from which the complaint subject to the disciplinary procedure arose; or

        (ii) any members or former members of the Presidency who appointed the Commissioner.

    (b) Two persons elected in accordance with paragraph 5 of this article.

5. The two members of the Disciplinary Appeals Board referred to in paragraph 4 (b) of this article, as well as an alternate member who may serve as a replacement in accordance with paragraph 6 of this article, shall be elected for four years by all counsel entitled to practise before the Court. They shall be chosen from amongst persons with established competence in professional ethics and legal matters.

6. If one of the elected members is unavailable to deal with the case or serve on the Disciplinary Appeal Board, the chairperson shall request the alternate member to serve as a replacement on the Disciplinary Appeals Board.

7. The functions of members of the Disciplinary Appeals Board are incompatible with those of members of the Disciplinary Board.

8. The elected members shall not be eligible for re-election.

9. The judge who takes precedence among the three judges referred to in paragraph 4 (a) of this article shall be the chairperson of the Disciplinary Appeals Board.

10. All members of the Disciplinary Appeals Board shall have the same rights and votes. The Disciplinary Appeals Board shall decide by majority vote. An alternate member serving on a case pursuant to paragraph 6 of this article shall have the same rights and votes as other members serving on the same case.

11. Members whose mandates have expired shall continue to deal with the cases they already have under consideration until such cases are finally determined.

12. The staff member of the Registry appointed by the Registrar pursuant to article 36, paragraph 12, of this Code to provide secretariat services to the Disciplinary Board shall also act as the secretariat of the Disciplinary Appeals Board. Once appointed, the relevant staff member of the Registry shall act at arm's length from the Registry.

Chapter 5
Final provisions

Article 45
Entry into force

This Code and any amendments to it shall enter into force 30 days after their adoption by the Assembly of States Parties in accordance with article 112, paragraph 2, of the Rome Statute.

Article 46
Publication

The Code adopted by the Assembly of States Parties shall be published in the Official Journal of the Court.

NGO DOCUMENTS

AMNESTY INTERNATIONAL
14 PRINCIPLES ON THE EFFECTIVE EXERCISE OF UNIVERSAL
JURISDICTION

Amnesty International, *14 Principles on the Effective Exercise of Universal Jurisdiction*, AI Index No. IOR
53/001/1999 (May 1, 1999)

INTRODUCTION

In 1945, the courts of the victorious Allies began exercising universal jurisdiction under Allied Control
Council Law No. 10 on behalf of the international community over crimes against humanity and war
crimes committed during the Second World War outside their own territories and against victims who were
not citizens or residents. However, for half a century afterwards, only a limited number of states provided
for universal jurisdiction under their national law for such crimes. No more than a handful of these states
had ever exercised such jurisdiction during those 50 years, including Australia, Canada, Israel and the
United Kingdom, and then only for crimes committed during the Second World War. Sadly, states failed to
exercise universal jurisdiction over grave crimes under international law committed since that war ended,
even though almost every single state is a party to at least four treaties giving states parties universal
jurisdiction over grave crimes under international law.

The power and duty under international law to exercise universal jurisdiction. Traditionally, courts of
one state would only exercise jurisdiction over persons who had committed a crime in their own territory
(territorial jurisdiction). Gradually, international law has recognized that courts could exercise other forms
of extraterritorial jurisdiction, such as jurisdiction over crimes committed outside the territory by the state's
own nationals (active personality jurisdiction), over crimes committed against the state's essential security
interests (protective principle jurisdiction) and, although this form of jurisdiction is contested by some
states, over crimes committed against a state's own nationals (passive personality jurisdiction). In addition,
beginning with piracy committed on the high seas, international law began to recognize that courts of a
state could exercise jurisdiction on behalf of the entire international community over certain grave crimes
under international law which were matters of international concern. Since such crimes threatened the
entire international framework of law, any state where persons suspected of such crimes were found could
bring them to justice. International law and standards now permit, and, in some cases, require states to
exercise jurisdiction over persons suspected of certain grave crimes under international law, no matter
where these crimes occurred, even if they took place in the territory of another state, involved suspects or
victims who are not nationals of their state or posed no direct threat to the state's own particular security
interests (universal jurisdiction).

Grave breaches of the Geneva Conventions. The four Geneva Conventions for the Protection of War
Victims of 1949, which have been ratified by almost every single state in the world, require each state party
to search for persons suspected of committing or ordering to be committed grave breaches of these
Conventions, to bring them to justice in their own courts, to extradite them to states which have made out a
prima facie case against them or to surrender them to an international criminal court. Grave breaches of
those Conventions include any of the following acts committed during an international armed conflict
against persons protected by the Conventions (such as shipwrecked sailors, wounded sailors or soldiers,
prisoners of war and civilians): wilful killing, torture or inhuman treatment, including biological
experiments, wilfully causing great suffering or serious injury to body or health, extensive destruction and
appropriation of property not justified by military necessity and carried out unlawfully and wantonly,
compelling a prisoner of war or an inhabitant of an occupied territory to serve in the forces of the hostile
power, wilfully depriving a prisoner of war or an inhabitant of an occupied territory of the rights of fair and
regular trial, taking of hostages and unlawfully deporting or transferring or unlawfully confining an
inhabitant of an occupied territory.

Genocide, crimes against humanity, extrajudicial executions, enforced disappearances and torture. It is also now widely recognized that under international customary law and general principles of law states may exercise universal jurisdiction over persons suspected of genocide, crimes against humanity, war crimes in international armed conflict other than grave breaches of the Geneva Conventions and war crimes in non-international armed conflict, extrajudicial executions, enforced disappearances and torture. Crimes against humanity are now defined in the Rome Statute of the International Criminal Court to include the following conduct when committed on a widespread or systematic basis: murder, extermination, enslavement, deportation or forcible transfer of population, imprisonment or other severe deprivation of physical liberty in violation of fundamental rules of international law, torture, rape and other sexual violence, persecution, enforced disappearance, apartheid and other inhumane acts.

It is also increasingly recognized that states not only have the power to exercise universal jurisdiction over these crimes, but also that they have the duty to do so or to extradite suspects to states willing to exercise jurisdiction. For example, the Convention against Torture and Other Cruel, Inhuman or Degrading Treatment or Punishment (Convention against Torture) adopted in 1984 requires states parties when persons suspected of torture are found in their territories to bring them to justice in their own courts or to extradite them to a state able and willing to do so.

Exercise by national courts of universal jurisdiction over post-war crimes. For many years, most states failed to give their courts such jurisdiction under national law. A number of states, most notably in Latin America, enacted legislation providing for universal jurisdiction over certain crimes under international law committed since the Second World War, including Austria, Belgium, Bolivia, Brazil, Canada, Chile, Colombia, Costa Rica, Denmark, Ecuador, El Salvador, France, Germany, Guatemala, Honduras, Mexico, Nicaragua, Norway, Panama, Peru, Spain, Switzerland, Uruguay and Venezuela. Few of these ever exercised it.

However, in the past few years, beginning with the establishment of the International Criminal Tribunals for the former Yugoslavia and Rwanda (Yugoslavia and Rwanda Tribunals) in 1993 and 1994, states have finally begun to fulfil their responsibilities under international law to enact legislation permitting their courts to exercise universal jurisdiction over grave crimes under international law and to exercise such jurisdiction. Courts in Austria, Denmark, Germany, the Netherlands, Sweden and Switzerland have exercised universal jurisdiction over grave crimes under international law committed in the former Yugoslavia. Courts in Belgium, France and Switzerland have opened criminal investigations or begun prosecutions related to genocide, crimes against humanity or war crimes committed in 1994 in Rwanda in response to Security Council Resolution 978 urging "States to arrest and detain, in accordance with their national law and relevant standards of international law, pending prosecution by the International Tribunal for Rwanda or by the appropriate national authorities, persons found within their territory against whom there is sufficient evidence that they were responsible for acts within the jurisdiction of the International Tribunal for Rwanda".

Italy and Switzerland have opened criminal investigations of torture, extrajudicial executions and enforced disappearances in Argentina in the 1970s and 1980s. Spain, as well as Belgium, France and Switzerland, have sought the extradition from the United Kingdom of the former head of state of Chile, Augusto Pinochet, who has been indicted for such crimes. On 24 March 1999, the United Kingdom's House of Lords held that he was not immune from criminal prosecution on charges that he was responsible for torture or conspiracy to torture and the Home Secretary has permitted the courts to consider the request by Spain for his extradition on these charges.

The need for states to fill the gap in the Rome Statute by exercising universal jurisdiction. An overwhelming majority of states at the Diplomatic Conference in Rome in June and July 1998 favoured giving the International Criminal Court the same universal jurisdiction over genocide, crimes against humanity and war crimes which they themselves have. However, as a result of a last-minute compromise in an attempt to persuade certain states not to oppose the Court, the Rome Statute omits such jurisdiction when the Prosecutor acts based on information from sources other than the Security Council. Article 12 limits the Court's jurisdiction to crimes committed within the territory of a state party or on its ships and aircraft and to crimes committed by the nationals of a state party, unless a non-state party makes a special declaration under that article recognizing the Court's jurisdiction over crimes within its territory, on its ships or aircraft or by its nationals. However, the Security Council, acting pursuant to Chapter VII of the United Nations (UN) Charter to maintain or restore international peace and security or in a case of aggression, may refer a situation to the Court involving crimes committed in the territory of a non-state party.

The international community must ensure that this gap in international protection is filled. National legislatures in states which have signed and ratified the Rome Statute will need to enact implementing legislation permitting the surrender of accused persons to the Court and requiring their authorities to cooperate with the Court. When enacting such legislation, they should ensure that national courts can be an effective complement to the International Criminal Court, not only by defining the crimes within the Court's jurisdiction as crimes under national law consistently with definitions in the Rome Statute, but also by providing their courts with universal jurisdiction over grave crimes under international law, including genocide, crimes against humanity, war crimes, extrajudicial executions, enforced disappearances and torture. Such steps - by reinforcing an integrated system of investigation and prosecution of crimes under international law - will help reduce and, eventually, eliminate safe havens for those responsible for the worst crimes in the world.

14 PRINCIPLES ON THE EFFECTIVE EXERCISE OF UNIVERSAL JURISDICTION

1. *Crimes of universal jurisdiction.* **States should ensure that their national courts can exercise universal and other forms of extraterritorial jurisdiction over grave human rights violations and abuses and violations of international humanitarian law.**

States should ensure that their national courts exercise universal jurisdiction on behalf of the international community over grave crimes under international law when a person suspected of such crimes is found in their territories or jurisdiction. If they do not do so, they should extradite the suspect to a state able and willing to do so or surrender the suspect to an international court with jurisdiction. When a state fails to fulfil this responsibility, other states should request the suspect's extradition and exercise universal jurisdiction.

Among the human rights violations and abuses over which national courts may exercise universal jurisdiction under international law are genocide, crimes against humanity, war crimes (whether committed in international or in non-international armed conflict), other deliberate and arbitrary killings and hostage-taking, whether these crimes were committed by state or by non-state actors, such as members of armed political groups, as well as extrajudicial executions, "disappearances" and torture.

In defining grave crimes under international law as extraterritorial crimes under their national criminal law, national legislatures should ensure that the crimes are defined in ways consistent with international law and standards, as reflected in international instruments such as the Hague Convention (IV) Respecting the Laws and Customs of War on Land and the annexed Hague Regulations Respecting the Laws and Customs of War on Land (1907), the Nuremberg and Tokyo Charters (1945 and 1946), Allied Control Council Law No. 10 (1945), the Convention on the Prevention and Punishment of the Crime of Genocide (1948), the four Geneva Conventions for the Protection of Victims of War (1949) and their two Additional Protocols (1977), the Convention Against Torture and Other Cruel, Inhuman or Degrading Treatment or Punishment (Convention against Torture) (1984), the UN Principles on the Effective Prevention and Investigation of Extra-legal, Arbitrary and Summary Executions (1989), the UN Declaration on the Protection of All Persons from Enforced Disappearance (1992), the Draft Code of Crimes against the Peace and Security of Mankind (1996) and the Rome Statute of the International Criminal Court (1998). In defining these crimes national legislatures should also take into account the Statutes and jurisprudence of the Yugoslavia and Rwanda Tribunals.

National legislatures should ensure that under their criminal law persons will also be liable to prosecution for extraterritorial inchoate and ancillary crimes, such as conspiracy to commit genocide and attempt to commit grave crimes under international law, direct and public incitement to commit them or complicity in such crimes. National laws should also fully incorporate the rules of criminal responsibility of military commanders and civilian superiors for the conduct of their subordinates.

2. *No immunity for persons in official capacity.* National legislatures should ensure that their national courts can exercise jurisdiction over anyone suspected or accused of grave crimes under international law, whatever the official capacity of the suspect or accused at the time of the alleged crime or any time thereafter.

Any national law authorizing the prosecution of grave crimes under international law should apply equally to all persons irrespective of any official or former official capacity, be it head of state, head or member of government, member of parliament or other elected or governmental capacity. The Charters of the Nuremberg and Tokyo Tribunals, the Statutes of the Yugoslavia and Rwanda Tribunals and the Rome Statute of the International Criminal Court have clearly confirmed that courts may exercise jurisdiction over persons suspected or accused of grave crimes under international law regardless of the official position or capacity at the time of the crime or later. The Nuremberg Charter provided that the official position of a person found guilty of crimes against humanity or war crimes could not be considered as a ground for mitigating the penalty.

The UN General Assembly unanimously affirmed in Resolution 95 (I) on 11 December 1946 "the principles of international law recognized in the Charter of the Nuremberg Tribunal and the judgment of the Tribunal". These principles have been applied by national, as well as international, courts, most recently in the decision by the United Kingdom's House of Lords that the former head of state of Chile, Augusto Pinochet, could be held criminally responsible by a national court for the crime under international law of torture.

3. *No immunity for past crimes.* National legislatures should ensure that their courts can exercise jurisdiction over grave crimes under international law no matter when they occurred.

The internationally recognized principle of nullum crimen sine lege (no crime without a prior law), also known as the principle of legality, is an important principle of substantive criminal law. However, genocide, crimes against humanity, war crimes and torture were considered as crimes under general principles of law recognized by the international community before they were codified. Therefore, national legislatures should ensure that by law courts have extraterritorial criminal jurisdiction over grave crimes under international law no matter when committed. As Article 15 (2) of the International Covenant on Civil and Political Rights (ICCPR) makes clear, such legislation is fully consistent with the nullum crimen sine lege principle. That provision states that nothing in the article prohibiting retrospective punishment "shall prejudice the trial and punishment of any person for any act or omission which, at the time when it was committed, was criminal according to the general principles of law recognized by the community of nations". Thus, the failure of a state where the crime under international law took place to have provided at the time the conduct occurred that it was a crime under national law does not preclude that state - or any other state exercising universal jurisdiction on behalf of the international community - from prosecuting a person accused of the crime.

4. *No statutes of limitation.* National legislatures should ensure that there is no time limit on the liability to prosecution of a person responsible for grave crimes under international law.

It is now generally recognized that time limits found in many national criminal justice systems for the prosecution of ordinary crimes under national law do not apply to grave crimes under international law. Most recently, 120 states voted on 17 July 1998 to adopt the Rome Statute of the International Criminal Court, which provides in Article 29 that genocide, crimes against humanity and war crimes "shall not be subject to any statutes of limitations". Similarly, the UN Convention on the Non-Applicability of Statutory Limitations to War Crimes and Crimes Against Humanity (1968) states that these crimes are not subject to any statutes of limitation regardless when they were committed. Neither the UN Principles on the Effective Prevention and Punishment of Extra-legal, Arbitrary and Summary Executions nor the Convention against Torture contain provisions exempting states from the duty to bring to justice those responsible for such crimes through statutes of limitations.

683

The international community now considers that when enforced disappearances are committed on a widespread or systematic basis, they are not subject to statutes of limitations. Article 29 of the Rome Statute of the International Criminal Court provides that crimes within the Court's jurisdiction, including enforced disappearances when committed on a widespread or systematic basis, are not subject to statutes of limitation, and Article 17 of the Statute permits the Court to exercise its concurrent jurisdiction when states parties are unable or unwilling genuinely to investigate or prosecute such crimes. Thus, the majority of states have rejected as out of date that part of Article 17 (3) in the UN Declaration on the Protection of All Persons from Enforced Disappearances which appears to permit statutes of limitation for enforced disappearances. However, even to the limited extent that this provision still has any force, it requires that where statutes of limitations exist they shall be "commensurate with the extreme seriousness of the offence", and Article 17 (2) states that when there are no effective remedies available, statutes of limitations "be suspended until these remedies are re- established". Moreover, the Declaration also clearly establishes that "[a]cts constituting enforced disappearances shall be considered a continuing offence [emphasis added] as long as the perpetrators continue to conceal the fate and the whereabouts of persons who have disappeared and these facts remain unclarified" (Article 17(1)).

5. *Superior orders, duress and necessity should not be permissible defences.* National legislatures should ensure that persons on trial in national courts for the commission of grave crimes under international law are only allowed to assert defences that are consistent with international law. Superior orders, duress and necessity should not be permissible defences.

Superior orders should not be allowed as a defence. The Nuremberg and Tokyo Charters and the Statutes of the Yugoslavia and Rwanda Tribunals all exclude superior orders as a defence. Article 33 (2) of the Rome Statute of the International Criminal Court provides that "orders to prohibit genocide or crimes against humanity are manifestly unlawful", and, therefore, superior orders are prohibited as a defence with respect to these crimes. Article 33 (1) provides that a superior order does not relieve a person of criminal responsibility unless three exceptional circumstances are present: "(a) The person was under a legal obligation to obey orders of the Government or superior in question; (b) The person did not know the order was unlawful; and (c) The order was not manifestly unlawful." Since subordinates are only required to obey lawful orders, most military subordinates receive training in humanitarian law and the conduct within the Court's jurisdiction is all manifestly unlawful, the number of situations where superior orders could be a defence in the Court to war crimes are likely to be extremely rare. In any event, this defence is limited to cases before the Court and does not affect current international law prohibiting superior orders as a defence to war crimes in national courts or other international courts.

Principle 19 of the UN Principles on the Effective Prevention and Investigation of Extra-legal, Arbitrary and Summary Executions states that "an order from a superior officer or a public authority may not be invoked as a justification for extra-legal, arbitrary or summary executions". Article 6 of the UN Principles on the Protection of All Persons from Enforced Disappearances provides: "No order or instruction of any public authority, civilian, military or other, may be invoked to justify an enforced disappearance. Any person receiving such an order or instruction shall have the right and duty not to obey it." Similarly, Article 2 (3) of the Convention against Torture states: "An order from a superior officer or a public authority may not be invoked as a justification of torture."

Duress or coercion (by another person) should also be excluded as a permissible defence. In many cases, and certainly in war crimes cases, allowing duress or coercion as a defence would enable defendants to assert the superior orders defence in disguise. In many national systems of criminal law duress or coercion is a permissible defence to ordinary crimes, if the harm supposedly inflicted by the defendant is less than the serious bodily harm he or she had to fear, had he or she withstood the duress or coercion. In cases such as genocide, crimes against humanity, extrajudicial executions, enforced disappearance and torture it is hard to conceive how committing such crimes could result in the lesser harm. However, duress or coercion can, in some cases, be considered as a mitigating circumstance when determining the appropriate sentence for such grave crimes.

No circumstances such as state of war, state of siege or any other state of public emergency should exempt persons who have committed grave crimes under international law from criminal responsibility on the ground of necessity. This principle is recognized in provisions of a number of instruments, including Article 2 (2) of the Convention against Torture, Article 7 of the UN Declaration on the Effective Protection of All Persons from Enforced Disappearances and Article 19 of the UN Principles on the Effective Prevention and Punishment of Extra-legal, Arbitrary and Summary Executions.

6. *National laws and decisions designed to shield persons from prosecution cannot bind courts in other countries.* **National legislatures should ensure that national courts are allowed to exercise jurisdiction over grave crimes under international law in cases where the suspects or accused were shielded from justice in any other national jurisdiction.**

The international community as a whole has a legitimate interest in the prosecution of grave crimes under international law in order to deter the commission of such crimes in the future, to punish the commission of these crimes in the past and in order to contribute to the redress for victims. Indeed, each state has a duty to do so on behalf of the entire international community. Therefore, when one state fails to fulfil its duty to bring those responsible for such crimes to justice, other states have a responsibility to act. Just as international courts are under no obligation to respect decisions of the judicial, executive or legislative branch of government in a national jurisdiction aimed at shielding perpetrators of these crimes from justice by amnesties, sham criminal procedures or any other schemes or decisions, no national court exercising extraterritorial jurisdiction over such crimes is under an obligation to respect such steps in other jurisdictions to frustrate international justice.

Bringing perpetrators to justice who were shielded from justice in another national jurisdiction is fully consistent with the ne bis in idem principle (the prohibition of double jeopardy) that no one should be brought to trial or should be punished for the same crime twice in the same jurisdiction. As the Human Rights Committee, a body of experts established under the ICCPR to monitor implementation of that treaty has explained, Article 14 (7) of the ICCPR "does not guarantee non bis in idem with regard to the national jurisdictions of two or more States. The Committee observes that this provision prohibits double jeopardy only with regard to an offence adjudicated in a given State." (A.P. v. Italy, NO. 204/1986, 2 November 1987, 2 Selected Decisions of the Human Rights Committee under the Optional Protocol 67, U.N. Doc. CCPR/C/OP/2, U.N. Sales No. E.89.XIV.1). The International Law Commission, a body of experts established by the UN General Assembly to codify and progressively develop international law, has declared that "international law [does] not make it an obligation for States to recognize a criminal judgement handed down in a foreign State" and that where a national judicial system has not functioned independently or impartially or where the proceedings were designed to shield the accused from international criminal responsibility, "the international community should not be required to recognize a decision that is the result of such a serious transgression of the criminal justice process" (Report of the International Law Commission's 48th session - 6 May to 26 July 1996, U.N. Doc. A/51/10, 1996, p. 67).

Provisions in the Statutes of the Yugoslavia and Rwanda tribunals and the Rome Statute of the International Criminal Court which permit international courts to try persons who have been acquitted by national courts in sham proceedings or where other national decisions have shielded suspects or the accused from international justice for grave crimes under international law are, therefore, fully consistent with international law guaranteeing the right to fair trial.

7. *No political interference.* **Decisions to start or stop an investigation or prosecution of grave crimes under international law should be made only by the prosecutor, subject to appropriate judicial scrutiny which does not impair the prosecutor's independence, based solely on legal considerations, without any outside interference.**

Decisions to start, continue or stop investigations or prosecutions should be made on the basis of independence and impartiality. As Guideline 14 of the UN Guidelines on the Role of Prosecutors makes clear, "Prosecutors shall not initiate or continue prosecution, or shall make every effort to stay proceedings, when an impartial investigation shows the charge to be unfounded." Moreover, Guidelines 13 (a) and (b) provide that decisions to initiate or continue prosecutions should be free from political, social, religious, racial, cultural, sexual or any other kind of discrimination and should be guided by international obligations of the state to bring, and to help bring, perpetrators of serious violations of human rights and international humanitarian law to justice, the interests of the international community as a whole and the interests of the victims of the alleged crimes.

8. *Grave crimes under international law must be investigated and prosecuted without waiting for complaints of victims or others with a sufficient interest.* National legislatures should ensure that national law requires national authorities exercising universal jurisdiction to investigate grave crimes under international law and, where there is sufficient admissible evidence, to prosecute, without waiting for a complaint by a victim or any other person with a sufficient interest in the case.

The duty to bring to justice on behalf of the international community those responsible for grave crimes under international law requires that states not place unnecessary obstacles in the way of a prosecution. For example, there should be no unnecessary thresholds such as a requirement that an investigation or prosecution can only start after a complaint by a victim or someone else with a sufficient interest in the case. If there is sufficient evidence to start an investigation or sufficient admissible evidence to commence a prosecution, then the investigation or prosecution should proceed. Only in an exceptional case would it ever be in the interest of justice, which includes the interests of victims, not to proceed in such circumstances.

9. *Internationally recognized guarantees for fair trials.* National legislatures should ensure that criminal procedure codes guarantee persons suspected or accused of grave crimes under international law all rights necessary to ensure that their trials will be fair and prompt in strict accordance with international law and standards for fair trials. All branches of government, including the police, prosecutor and judges, must ensure that these rights are fully respected.

Suspects and accused must be accorded all rights to a fair and prompt trial recognized in international law and standards. These rights are recognized in provisions of a broad range of international instruments, including Articles 9, 10 and 11 of the Universal Declaration of Human Rights, Articles 9, 14 and 15 of the ICCPR, the UN Standard Minimum Rules for the Treatment of Prisoners, the UN Body of Principles for the Protection of All Persons under Any Form of Detention or Imprisonment (1988), Articles 7 and 15 of the Convention against Torture, the UN Basic Principles on the Independence of the Judiciary, the UN Guidelines on the Role of the Prosecutors and the UN Basic Principles on the Role of Lawyers. These rights are also recognized in the Rome Statute of the International Criminal Court and the Statutes and Rules of Procedure and Evidence of the Yugoslavia and Rwanda Tribunals, as well as in the Geneva Conventions and their Protocols.

When a suspect or an accused is facing trial in a foreign jurisdiction it is essential that he or she receive translation and interpretation in a language he or she fully understands and speaks in every stage of the proceedings, during questioning as a suspect and from the moment he or she is detained. The right to translation and interpretation is part of the right to prepare a defence.

Suspects and accused have the right to legal assistance of their own choice at all stages of the criminal proceedings, from the moment they are questioned as a suspect or detained. When a suspect is detained in a jurisdiction outside his or her own country, the suspect must be notified of his or her right to consular assistance, in accordance with the Vienna Convention on Consular Relations and Principle 16 (2) of the Body of Principles for the Protection of All Persons under Any Form of Detention or Imprisonment. The latter provision states that if the person is a refugee or is otherwise under the protection of an international organization, he or she must be notified of the right to communicate with the competent international organization.

To ensure that the right to be tried in one's presence, recognized in Article 14 (3) (d) of the ICCPR, is fully respected and the judgments of courts are implemented, national legislatures should ensure that legislation does not permit trials in absentia in cases of grave crimes under international law. Neither the Rome Statute of the International Criminal Court nor the Statutes of the Yugoslavia and Rwanda Tribunals provide for trials in absentia.

10. *Public trials in the presence of international monitors.* **To ensure that justice is not only done but also seen to be done, intergovernmental and non-governmental organizations should be permitted by the competent national authorities to attend and monitor the trials of persons accused of grave crimes under international law.**

The presence and the public reports by international monitors of the trials of persons accused of grave crimes under international law will clearly demonstrate that the fair prosecution of these crimes is of interest to the international community as a whole. The presence and reports of these monitors will also help to ensure that the prosecution of these crimes will not go unnoticed by victims, witnesses and others in the country where the crimes were committed. The presence and reports of international monitors at a public trial serves the fundamental principle of criminal law that justice must not only be done, but be seen to be done, by helping to ensure that the international community trusts and respects the integrity and fairness of the proceedings, verdicts and sentences. When trials are fair and prompt, then the presence of international monitors can assist international criminal courts in determining that there will be no need to exercise their concurrent jurisdiction over such crimes. Therefore, courts should invite intergovernmental and non-governmental organizations to observe such trials.

11. *The interests of victims, witnesses and their families must be taken into account.* **National courts must protect victims, witnesses and their families. Investigation of crimes must take into account the special interests of vulnerable victims and witnesses, including women and children. Courts must award appropriate redress to victims and their families.**

States must take effective security measures to protect victims, witnesses and their families from reprisals. These measures should encompass protection before, during and after the trial until that security threat ends. Since investigation and prosecution of grave crimes under international law is a responsibility of the entire international community, all states should assist each other in protecting victims and witnesses, including through relocation programs. Protection measures must not, however, prejudice the rights of suspects and accused to a fair trial, including the right to cross-examine witnesses.

Special measures are needed to deal with the particular demands of investigating, prosecuting and judging crimes involving violence against women, including rape and other forms of sexual violence. Women who have suffered such violence may be reluctant to come forward to testify. Prosecutors must ensure that investigators have expertise in a sensitive manner. Investigations must be conducted in a manner which does not cause unnecessary trauma to the victims and their families. Investigation and prosecution of crimes against children and members of other vulnerable groups also will require a special sensitivity and expertise.

Courts must award victims and their families with adequate redress. Such redress should include restitution, compensation, rehabilitation, satisfaction and guarantees of non- repetition.

12. *No death penalty or other cruel, inhuman or degrading punishment.* **National legislatures should ensure that grave crimes under international law are not punishable by the death penalty or any other cruel, inhuman or degrading punishment.**

Amnesty International believes that the death penalty violates the right to life guaranteed by Article 3 of the Universal Declaration of Human Rights and is the ultimate form of cruel, inhuman and degrading punishment prohibited by Article 5 of that Declaration. It should never be imposed for any crime, no matter how serious. Indeed, the Rome Statute of the International Criminal Court and the Statutes of the Yugoslavia and Rwanda Tribunals exclude this penalty for the worst crimes in the world: genocide, crimes against humanity and war crimes. National legislatures should also ensure that prison sentences are served in facilities and under conditions that meet the international standards for the protection of persons in detention such as the UN Standard Minimum Rules for the Treatment of Prisoners and the UN Body of Principles for the Protection of All Persons under Any Form of Detention or Imprisonment. To ensure that the treatment in prison of those convicted for grave crimes under international law is in accordance with international standards on the treatment of prisoners, international monitors, as well as the consul of the convicted person's state, should be allowed regular, unrestricted and confidential access to the convicted person.

13. *International cooperation in investigation and prosecution.* **States must fully cooperate with investigations and prosecutions by the competent authorities of other states exercising universal jurisdiction over grave crimes under international law.**

The UN General Assembly has declared that all states must assist each other in bringing to justice those responsible for grave crimes under international law. In Resolution 3074 (XXVIII) of 3 December 1973 it adopted the Principles of International Co-operation in the Detection, Arrest, Extradition and Punishment of Persons Guilty of War Crimes and Crimes against Humanity which define the scope of these responsibilities in detail. In addition, states parties under the Convention on the Prevention and Punishment of the Crime of Genocide, the Geneva Conventions for the Protection of Victims of War and their First Additional Protocol, the UN Convention against Torture are required to assist each other in bringing those responsible for genocide, war crimes and torture to justice. The UN Principles on the Effective Prevention and Investigation of Extra-legal, Arbitrary and Summary Executions and the UN Declaration on the Protection of All Persons from Enforced Disappearance require states to cooperate with other states by extraditing persons accused of extrajudicial executions or enforced disappearances if they do not bring them to justice in their own courts.

National legislatures should ensure that the competent authorities are required under national law to assist the authorities of other states in investigations and prosecutions of grave crimes under international law, provided that such proceedings are in accordance with international law and standards and exclude the death penalty and other cruel, inhuman or degrading punishment. Such assistance should include the identification and location of persons, the taking of testimony and the production of evidence, the service of documents, the arrest or detention of persons and the extradition of accused persons.

14. *Effective training of judges, prosecutors, investigators and defence lawyers.* **National legislatures should ensure that judges, prosecutors and investigators receive effective training in human rights law, international humanitarian law and international criminal law.**

They should be trained concerning the practical implementation of relevant international instruments, state obligations deriving from these instruments and customary law, as well as the relevant jurisprudence of tribunals and courts in other national and international jurisdictions.

Judges, prosecutors, investigators and defence lawyers should also receive proper training in culturally sensitive methods of investigation and in methods of investigating and prosecuting grave crimes under international law against women, children and other persons from vulnerable groups.

Princeton University Program in Law and Public Affairs
The Princeton Principles on Universal Jurisdiction 28 (2001)
Available at http://www1.umn.edu/humanrts/instree/princeton.html

The participants in the Princeton Project on Universal Jurisdiction propose the following principles for the purposes of advancing the continued evolution of international law and the application of international law in national legal systems:

Principle 1 -- Fundamentals of Universal Jurisdiction

1. For purposes of these Principles, universal jurisdiction is criminal jurisdiction based solely on the nature of the crime, without regard to where the crime was committed, the nationality of the alleged or convicted perpetrator, the nationality of the victim, or any other connection to the state exercising such jurisdiction.

2. Universal jurisdiction may be exercised by a competent and ordinary judicial body of any state in order to try a person duly accused of committing serious crimes under international law as specified in Principle 2(1), provided the person is present before such judicial body.

3. A state may rely on universal jurisdiction as a basis for seeking the extradition of a person accused or convicted of committing a serious crime under international law as specified in Principle 2(1) provided that it has established a prima facie case of the person's guilt and that the person sought to be extradited will be tried or the punishment carried out in accordance with international norms and standards on the protection of human rights in the context of criminal proceedings.

4. In exercising universal jurisdiction or in relying upon universal jurisdiction as a basis for seeking extradition, a state and its judicial organs shall observe international due process norms including but not limited to those involving the rights of the accused and victims, the fairness of the proceedings, and the independence and impartiality of the judiciary (hereinafter referred to as "international due process norms").

5. A state shall exercise universal jurisdiction in good faith and in accordance with its rights and obligations under international law.

Principle 2 -- Serious Crimes Under International Law

1. For purposes of these Principles, serious crimes under international law include: (1) piracy; (2) slavery; (3) war crimes; (4) crimes against peace; (5) crimes against humanity; (6) genocide; and (7) torture.

2. The application of universal jurisdiction to the crimes listed in paragraph 1 is without prejudice to the application of universal jurisdiction to other crimes under international law.

Principle 3 -- Reliance on Universal Jurisdiction in the Absence of National Legislation

With respect to serious crimes under international law as specified in Principle 2(1), national judicial organs may rely on universal jurisdiction even if their national legislation does not specifically provide for it.

Principle 4 -- Obligation to Support Accountability

1. A state shall comply with all international obligations that are applicable to: prosecuting or extraditing persons accused or convicted of crimes under international law in accordance with a legal process that complies with international due process norms, providing other states investigating or prosecuting such crimes with all available means of administrative and judicial assistance, and under-taking such other necessary and appropriate measures as are consistent with international norms and standards.

2. A state, in the exercise of universal jurisdiction, may, for purposes of prosecution, seek judicial assistance to obtain evidence from another state, provided that the requesting state has a good faith basis and that the evidence sought will be used in accordance with international due process norms.

Principle 5 -- Immunities

With respect to serious crimes under international law as specified in Principle 2(1), the official position of any accused person, whether as head of state or government or as a responsible government official, shall not relieve such person of criminal responsibility nor mitigate punishment.

Principle 6 -- Statutes of Limitations

Statutes of limitations or other forms of prescription shall not apply to aerious crimes under international law as specified in Principle 2(1).

Principle 7 -- Amnesties

1. Amnesties are generally inconsistent with the obligation of states to provide accountability for serious crimes under international law as specified in Principle in 2(1).

2. The exercise of universal jurisdiction with respect to serious crimes under international law as specified in Principle 2(1) shall not be precluded by amnesties which are incompatible with the international legal obligations of the granting state.

Principle 8 -- Resolution of Competing National Jurisdictions

Where more than one state has or may assert jurisdiction over a person and where the state that has custody of the person has no basis for jurisdiction other than the principle of universality, that state or its judicial organs shall, in deciding whether to prosecute or extradite, base their decision on an aggregate balance of the following criteria:

(a) multilateral or bilateral treaty obligations;

(b) the place of commission of the crime;

(c) the nationality connection of the alleged perpetrator to the requesting state;

(d) the nationality connection of the victim to the requesting state;

(e) any other connection between the requesting state and the alleged perpetrator, the crime, or the victim;

(f) the likelihood, good faith, and effectiveness of the prosecution in the requesting state;

(g) the fairness and impartiality of the proceedings in the requesting state;

(h) convenience to the parties and witnesses, as well as the availability of evidence in the requesting state; and

(i) the interests of justice.

Principle 9 -- *Non Bis In Idem*/ Double Jeopardy

1. In the exercise of universal jurisdiction, a state or its judicial organs shall ensure that a person who is subject to criminal proceedings shall not be exposed to multiple prosecutions or punishment for the same criminal conduct where the prior criminal proceedings or other accountability proceedings have been conducted in good faith and in accordance with international norms and standards. Sham prosecutions or derisory punishment resulting from a conviction or other accountability proceedings shall not be recognized as falling within the scope of this Principle.

2. A state shall recognize the validity of a proper exercise of universal jurisdiction by another state and shall recognize the final judgment of a competent and ordinary national judicial body or a competent international judicial body exercising such jurisdiction in accordance with international due process norms.

3. Any person tried or convicted by a state exercising universal jurisdiction for serious crimes under international law as specified in Principle 2(1) shall have the right and legal standing to raise before any national or international judicial body the claim of *non bis in idem* in opposition to any further criminal proceedings.

Principle 10 -- Grounds for Refusal of Extradition

1. A state or its judicial organs shall refuse to entertain a request for extradition based on universal jurisdiction if the person sought is likely to face a death penalty sentence or to be subjected to torture or any other cruel, degrading, or inhuman punishment or treatment, or if it is likely that the person sought will be subjected to sham proceedings in which international due process norms will be violated and no satisfactory assurances to the contrary are provided.

2. A state which refuses to extradite on the basis of this Principle shall, when permitted by international law, prosecute the individual accused of a serious crime under international law as specified in Principle 2(1) or extradite such person to another state where this can be done without exposing him or her to the risks referred to in paragraph 1.

Principle 11 -- Adoption of National Legislation

A state shall, where necessary, enact national legislation to enable the exercise of universal jurisdiction and the enforcement of these Principles.

Principle 12 -- Inclusion of Universal Jurisdiction in Future Treaties

In all future treaties, and in protocols to existing treaties, concerned with serious crimes under international law as specified in Principle 2(1), states shall include provisions for universal jurisdiction.

Principle 13 -- Strengthening Accountability and Universal Jurisdiction

1. National judicial organs shall construe national law in a manner that is consistent with these Principles.

2. Nothing in these Principles shall be construed to limit the rights and obligations of a state to prevent or punish, by lawful means recognized under international law, the commission of crimes under international law.

3. These Principles shall not be construed as limiting the continued development of universal jurisdiction in international law.

Principle 14 -- Settlement of Disputes

1. Consistent with international law and the Charter of the United Nations, states should settle their disputes arising out of the exercise of universal jurisdiction by all available means of peaceful settlement of disputes and in particular by submitting the dispute to the International Court of Justice.

2. Pending the determination of the issue in dispute, a state seeking to exercise universal jurisdiction shall not detain the accused person nor seek to have that person detained by another state unless there is a reasonable risk of flight and no other reasonable means can be found to ensure that person's eventual appearance before the judicial organs of the state seeking to exercise its jurisdiction.

STATUTE OF AMNESTY INTERNATIONAL

Amnesty International, *Statute of Amnesty International* (2007), http://www.amnesty.org/en/who-we-are/accountability/statute-of-amnesty-international

VISION AND MISSION

1. Amnesty International's vision is of a world in which every person enjoys all of the human rights enshrined in the Universal Declaration of Human Rights and other international human rights instruments. In pursuit of this vision, Amnesty International's mission is to undertake research and action focused on preventing and ending grave abuses of these rights.

CORE VALUES

2. AMNESTY INTERNATIONAL forms a global community of human rights defenders with the principles of international solidarity, effective action for the individual victim, global coverage, the universality and indivisibility of human rights, impartiality and independence, and democracy and mutual respect.

METHODS

3. AMNESTY INTERNATIONAL addresses governments, intergovernmental organizations, armed political groups, companies and other non-state actors.

AMNESTY INTERNATIONAL seeks to disclose human rights abuses accurately, quickly and persistently. It systematically and impartially researches the facts of individual cases and patterns of human rights abuses. These findings are publicized, and members, supporters and staff mobilize public pressure on governments and others to stop the abuses.

In addition to its work on specific abuses of human rights, AMNESTY INTERNATIONAL urges all governments to observe the rule of law, and to ratify and implement human rights standards; it carries out a wide range of human rights educational activities; and it encourages intergovernmental organizations, individuals, and all organs of society to support and respect human rights.

INTEGRATED STRATEGIC PLAN

4. There will be at all times for AMNESTY INTERNATIONAL an Integrated Strategic Plan covering a period of six years.

ORGANIZATION

5. AMNESTY INTERNATIONAL is an organization based on worldwide voluntary membership and it shall consist of sections, structures, international networks, affiliated groups and international members.

6. Ultimate authority for the conduct of the affairs of AMNESTY INTERNATIONAL is vested in the International Council. The primary functions of the International Council are:

    i. to focus on strategy;

ii. to set AMNESTY INTERNATIONAL's vision, mission and core values;

iii. to determine AMNESTY INTERNATIONAL's Integrated Strategic Plan including its financial strategy;

iv. to establish systems and bodies of governance and delegation for the movement, to elect members to those bodies, and to hold those bodies and their members accountable;

v. to evaluate the movement's performance against its agreed strategies and plans;

vi. to hold sections, structures and other bodies accountable.

7. There is an International Executive Committee. The primary role of the International Executive Committee is to provide leadership and stewardship for the whole of AMNESTY INTERNATIONAL worldwide. The functions of the International Executive Committee are:

i. to take international decisions on behalf of AMNESTY INTERNATIONAL;

ii. to ensure that there is a sound financial policy for AMNESTY INTERNATIONAL and that the financial policy is consistently implemented across the international organization;

iii. to ensure implementation of the Integrated Strategic Plan;

iv. to make any necessary adjustments to the Integrated Strategic Plan and other decisions of the International Council;

v. to ensure compliance with the Statute;

vi. to ensure human resources development;

vii. to hold sections, structures and other bodies of AMNESTY INTERNATIONAL accountable for their functioning by presenting reports to the International Council;

viii. to perform the other functions conferred on it by the Statute.

8. The day-to-day affairs of AMNESTY INTERNATIONAL shall be conducted by the International Secretariat headed by a Secretary General under the direction of the International Executive Committee.

9. The office of the International Secretariat shall be in London or such other place as the International Executive Committee shall decide and which is ratified by at least one half of the sections.

10. Responsibility for AMNESTY INTERNATIONAL work on abuses of human rights in any country or territory, including the collection and evaluation of information, and the sending of delegations, lies with the international governing bodies of the organization, and not with the section, structure, groups or members in the country or territory concerned.

SECTIONS

11. A section of AMNESTY INTERNATIONAL may be established in any country, state, territory or region with the consent of the International Executive Committee. In order to be recognized as such, a section shall:

i. prior to its recognition have demonstrated its ability to organize and maintain basic AMNESTY INTERNATIONAL activities;

ii. submit its Statute to the International Executive Committee for approval;

iii. pay such annual fee as may be determined by the International Council;

iv. be registered as such with the International Secretariat on the decision of the International Executive Committee.

Sections shall take no action on matters that do not fall within the stated vision and mission of AMNESTY INTERNATIONAL. The International Secretariat shall maintain a register of sections. Sections shall act in accordance with the core values and methods of AMNESTY INTERNATIONAL, as well as any Integrated Strategic Plans, working rules and guidelines that are adopted from time to time by the International Council.

STRUCTURES

12. An AMNESTY INTERNATIONAL structure is an AMNESTY INTERNATIONAL national or regional body established by the International Executive Committee, to promote and implement the movement's vision and mission. The purpose of a structure is to coordinate a sustained programme of human rights activities and consolidate its national or regional organization. A structure must consist of at least a board and active volunteers, unless otherwise determined by the International Executive Committee, and must meet any other criteria determined by the International Executive Committee.

INTERNATIONAL NETWORKS

13. An AMNESTY INTERNATIONAL "International Network" exists to promote and implement the movement's vision and mission, primarily on the basis of a specific theme or identity.
An International Network must meet the following requirements:

  i. have AMNESTY INTERNATIONAL members from at least five different sections and/or structures;

  ii. have AMNESTY INTERNATIONAL members from at least two International Secretariat programme regions;

  iii. be theme or identity based;

  iv. have terms of reference that meet the Statute and core values of AMNESTY INTERNATIONAL;

  v. have terms of reference approved by the International Executive Committee;

  vi. be formally recognized by, and registered with, the International Executive Committee.

AFFILIATED GROUPS

14. Groups of not less than five members may, on payment of an annual fee determined by the International Council, become affiliated to AMNESTY INTERNATIONAL or a section thereof. Any dispute as to whether a group should be or remain affiliated shall be decided by the International Executive Committee. An affiliated adoption group shall accept for adoption such prisoners as may from time to time be allotted to it by the International Secretariat, and shall adopt no others as long as it remains affiliated to AMNESTY INTERNATIONAL. No group shall be allotted a prisoner of conscience detained in its own country. Each section shall maintain and make available to the International Secretariat a register of affiliated AMNESTY INTERNATIONAL groups. Groups in a country, state, territory or region without a section shall be registered with the International Secretariat. Groups shall take no action on matters that do not fall within the stated vision and mission of AMNESTY INTERNATIONAL. Groups shall act in accordance with the core values and methods of AMNESTY INTERNATIONAL, as well as any Integrated Strategic Plans, working rules and guidelines that are adopted from time to time by the International Council.

INDIVIDUAL MEMBERSHIP

15. An individual member of AMNESTY INTERNATIONAL is any person who contributes to the advancement of the mission of AMNESTY INTERNATIONAL, who acts in accordance with the core values and policies of AMNESTY INTERNATIONAL, and who has been recognized and registered as a member by an AMNESTY INTERNATIONAL section, structure or affiliated group by virtue of payment of annual dues or having been granted a dues waiver.

Individuals residing in countries, states, territories, or regions where there is no section or structure and who are not members of an affiliated group, may, on payment to the International Secretariat of an annual subscription fee determined by the International Executive Committee, become international members of AMNESTY INTERNATIONAL. In countries where a section or structure exists, individuals may become international members of AMNESTY INTERNATIONAL with the consent of the section or structure and of the International Executive Committee. The International Secretariat shall maintain a register of such international members.

INTERNATIONAL COUNCIL

16. The International Council shall consist of the members of the International Executive Committee and of representatives of sections and structures and shall meet at intervals of not more than two years on a date fixed by the International Executive Committee. Only representatives of sections and structures shall have the right to vote at the International Council.

17. All sections and structures shall have the right to appoint one representative to the International Council. In addition, a section may appoint:

  more than 250 members 1 representative

  more than 2,500 members 2 representatives

  more than 15,000 members 3 representatives

  more than 40,000 members 4 representatives

  more than 80,000 members 5 representatives

or, if a section so chooses:

  10 – 49 groups 1 representative

  50 – 99 groups 2 representatives

100 – 199 groups 3 representatives
200 – 399 groups 4 representatives
400 groups and over 5 representatives

Only sections having paid in full their annual fee as assessed by the International Council for the two previous financial years shall vote at the International Council. This requirement may be waived in whole or in part by the International Council. If a section has not provided its standardized financial report to the International Secretariat within three months of the final date for submission on each of the last two occasions such a report was required, the section is not entitled to vote at the International Council. This requirement may be waived in whole or in part by the International Council.

18. The International Executive Committee may invite to the International Council delegates from international networks and other individuals as non-voting participants.

19. A section or structure unable to participate at an International Council may appoint a proxy or proxies to vote on its behalf and a section represented by a lesser number of persons than its entitlement under Article 17 hereof may authorize its representative or representatives to cast votes up to its maximum entitlement under Article 17 hereof.

20. Notice of the number of representatives proposing to attend an International Council, and of the appointment of proxies, shall be given to the International Secretariat not later than one month before the meeting of the International Council. This requirement may be waived by the International Executive Committee.

21. A quorum shall consist of the representatives or proxies of not less than one quarter of the sections and structures entitled to be represented.

22. The Chairperson of the International Council and an alternate shall be elected by the preceding International Council. The Chairperson or, in his or her absence, the alternate, shall preside at the International Council. In the absence of the Chairperson and the alternate, the Chairperson of the International Executive Committee or such other person as the International Executive Committee may appoint shall open the proceedings of the International Council which shall elect a Chairperson. Thereafter the elected Chairperson, or such other person as the Chairperson may appoint, shall preside at the International Council.

23. Except as otherwise provided in the Statute, the International Council shall make its decisions by a simple majority of the votes cast. In case of an equality of votes the Chairperson of the International Council shall have a casting vote.

24. The International Council shall be convened by the International Secretariat by notice to all sections and structures not later than 90 days before the date thereof.

25. The Chairperson of the International Executive Committee shall at the request of the Committee or of not less than one third of the sections and structures call an extraordinary meeting of the International Council by giving not less than 21 days' notice in writing to all sections and structures.

26. The International Council shall elect a Treasurer, who shall be a member of the International Executive Committee.

27. The agenda for the meetings of the International Council shall be prepared by the International Secretariat under the direction of the Chairperson of the International Executive Committee.

INTERNATIONAL EXECUTIVE COMMITTEE

28. The International Executive Committee shall consist of the Treasurer and eight regular members, who shall be individual or international members of AMNESTY INTERNATIONAL. The regular members and Treasurer shall be elected by the International Council. Not more than one member in any section, structure or affiliated group, or international member of AMNESTY INTERNATIONAL voluntarily resident in a country, state or territory in which there is no section or structure, may be elected as a regular member of the Committee, and once such a member has received sufficient votes to be elected, any votes cast for other members in that section, structure or affiliated group, or for international members resident in that country, state or territory, shall be disregarded.

29. The International Executive Committee shall meet not less than twice a year at a place to be decided by itself.

30. Members of the International Executive Committee shall hold office for a period of two years and shall be eligible for re-election for a maximum tenure of three consecutive terms.

31. The Committee may co-opt not more than two additional members who shall hold office until the close of the next meeting of the International Council; they shall be eligible to be reco-opted once. Co-opted members shall not have the right to vote.

32. In the event of a vacancy occurring on the Committee, it may co-opt a further member to fill the vacancy until the next meeting of the International Council, which shall elect such members as are necessary to replace retiring members and to fill the vacancy.

33. If a member of the Committee is unable to attend a meeting, such member may appoint an alternate.

34. The Committee shall each year appoint one of its members to act as Chairperson.

35. The Chairperson may, and at the request of the majority of the Committee shall, summon meetings of the Committee.

36. A quorum shall consist of not fewer than five members of the Committee or their alternates.

37. The agenda for meetings of the Committee shall be prepared by the International Secretariat under the direction of the Chairperson.

38. The Committee may make regulations for the conduct of the affairs of AMNESTY INTERNATIONAL and for the procedure to be followed at the International Council, and may take such steps as it sees fit to establish and maintain a system of effective committees, including standing committees, intermediate structures, or other forums, in support of its functions.

INTERNATIONAL SECRETARIAT

39. The International Executive Committee may appoint a Secretary General who shall be responsible under its direction for the conduct of the affairs of AMNESTY INTERNATIONAL and for the implementation of the decisions of the International Council.

40. The Secretary General may appoint senior executive staff in close cooperation with the International Executive Committee, and may appoint all other staff as are necessary for the proper conduct of the affairs of AMNESTY INTERNATIONAL.

41. In the case of the absence or illness of the Secretary General, or of a vacancy in the post of Secretary General, the Chairperson of the International Executive Committee shall, after consultation with the members of that Committee, appoint an Acting Secretary General to act until the next meeting of the Committee.

42. The Secretary General or Acting Secretary General and such members of the International Secretariat as may appear to the Chairperson of the International Executive Committee to be necessary shall attend meetings of the International Council and of the International Executive Committee and may speak thereat but shall not be entitled to vote.

TERMINATION OF MEMBERSHIP

43. Membership of or affiliation to AMNESTY INTERNATIONAL may be terminated at any time by resignation in writing.

44. The International Executive Committee may impose sanctions (which may consist of a warning, intervention, temporary suspension or permanent exclusion or closure) on any section, structure, international network, affiliated group, or international member if in its opinion that section, structure, international network, affiliated group, or international member does not act within the spirit of the vision, mission, core values and methods set out in Articles 1, 2 and 3 or does not organize and maintain basic AMNESTY INTERNATIONAL activities, or does not observe any of the provisions of this Statute, and constitutes an immediate threat to the reputation, integrity or operation of AMNESTY INTERNATIONAL. None of these sanctions shall be imposed until the concerned section, structure, international network, affiliated group, or international member is informed in writing of the grounds of the sanctions. When closure of a section is the sanction under consideration, all other sections shall also be informed in the same manner before such an action is taken.

In the case of closure or permanent exclusion, the concerned section, structure, international network, affiliated group, or international member shall be provided with an opportunity to make its or such international member's case to the International Executive Committee within six months before the sanction of closure or permanent exclusion is imposed. Once the International Executive Committee has decided to impose any sanction in respect of a section, structure, international network, affiliated group, or international member, the party concerned may appeal to the Membership Appeals Committee. This committee shall consist of five members and two alternate members who shall be elected by the

International Council in the same manner and subject to the same conditions as provided for in Article 28 for the International Executive Committee.

During any period of temporary suspension, or once closure or permanent exclusion has been agreed, a section, structure, international network, affiliated group, or international member may no longer represent or use the name of AMNESTY INTERNATIONAL.

FINANCE

45. An auditor appointed by the International Council shall annually audit the accounts of AMNESTY INTERNATIONAL, which shall be prepared by the International Secretariat and presented to the International Executive Committee and the International Council.

46. No part of the income or property of AMNESTY INTERNATIONAL shall directly or indirectly be paid or transferred otherwise than for valuable and sufficient consideration to any of its members by way of dividend, gift, division, bonus or otherwise howsoever by way of profit.

AMENDMENTS OF STATUTE

47. The Statute may be amended by the International Council by a majority of not less than two thirds of the votes cast. Amendments may be submitted by the International Executive Committee or by a section or structure. Proposed amendments shall be submitted to the International Secretariat not less than seven months before the International Council meets, and presentation to the International Council shall be supported in writing by at least five sections or structures. Proposed amendments shall be communicated by the International Secretariat to all sections and structures and to members of the International Executive Committee.

MISCELLANEOUS MATERIALS

PROMOTION OF NATIONAL UNITY AND RECONCILIATION ACT (SOUTH AFRICA)

Promotion of National Unity and Reconciliation Act 34 of 1995 (S. Afr.), *available at* http://www.doj.gov.za/trc/trc_frameset.htm.

It is hereby notified that the President has assented to the following Act which is hereby published for general information:-

ACT

To provide for the investigation and the establishment of as complete a picture aspossible of the nature, causes and extent of gross violations of human rights committed during the period from 1 March 1960 to the cut-off date contemplated in the Constitution, within or outside the Republic, emanating from the conflicts of the past, and the fate or whereabouts of the victims of such violations; the granting of amnesty to persons who make full disclosure of all the relevant facts relating to acts associated with a political objective committed in the course of the conflicts of the past during the said period; affording victims an opportunity to relate the violations they suffered; the taking of measures aimed at the granting of reparation to, and the rehabilitation and the restoration of the human and civil dignity of, victims of violations of human rights; reporting to the Nation about such violations and victims; the making of recommendations aimed at the prevention of the commission of gross violations of human rights; and for the said purposes to provide for the establishment of a Truth and Reconciliation Commission, a Committee on Human Rights Violations, a Committee on Amnesty and a Committee on Reparation and Rehabilitation; and to confer certain powers on, assign certain functions to and impose certain duties upon that Commission and those Committees; and to provide for matters connected therewith.

SINCE the Constitution of the Republic of South Africa, 1993 (Act No. 200 of 1993), provides a historic bridge between the past of a deeply divided society characterized by strife, conflict, untold suffering and injustice, and a future founded on the recognition of human rights, democracy and peaceful co-existence for all South Africans, irrespective of colour, race, class, belief or sex;

AND SINCE it is deemed necessary to establish the truth in relation to past events as well as the motives for and circumstances in which gross violations of human rights have occurred, and to make the findings known in order to prevent a repetition of such acts in future;

AND SINCE the Constitution states that the pursuit of national unity, the well-being of all South African citizens and peace require reconciliation between the people of South Africa and the reconstruction of society;

AND SINCE the Constitution states that there is a need for understanding but not for vengeance, a need for reparation but not for retaliation, a need for ubuntu but not for victimization;

AND SINCE the Constitution states that in order to advance such reconciliation and reconstruction amnesty shall be granted in respect of acts, omissions and offences associated with political objectives committed in the course of the conflicts of the past;

AND SINCE the Constitution provides that Parliament shall under the Constitution adopt a law which determines a firm cut-off date, which shall be a date after 8 October 1990 and before the cut-off date envisaged in the Constitution, and providing for the mechanisms, criteria and procedures, including tribunals, if any, through which such amnesty shall be dealt with;

(English text signed by the President.) (Assented to 19 July 1995.)

BE IT THEREFORE ENACTED by the Parliament of the Republic of South Africa, as follows:-

CHAPTER 1
Interpretation and application

Definitions

1. (1) In this Act, unless the context otherwise indicates-
    (i) "act associated with a political objective" has the meaning ascribed thereto in section 20(2) and (3); (ii)

    (ii) "article" includes any evidence, book, document, file, object, writing, recording or transcribed computer printout produced by any mechanical or electronic device or any device by means of which information is recorded, stored or transcribed; (xix)

    (iii) "Commission" means the Truth and Reconciliation Commission established by section 2; (ix)

    (iv) "commissioner" means a member of the Commission appointed in terms of section 7(2)(a); (viii)

    (v) "committee" means the Committee on Human Rights Violations, the Committee on Amnesty or the Committee on Reparation and Rehabilitation, as the case may be; (vii)

    (vi) "Constitution" means the Constitution of the Republic of South Africa, 1993 (Act No. 200 of 1993); (iv)

    (vii) "cut-off date" means the latest date allowed as the cut-off date in terms of the Constitution as set out under the heading "National Unity and Reconciliation"; (i)

    (viii) "former state" means any state or territory which was established by an Act of Parliament or by proclamation in terms of such an Act prior to the commencement of the Constitution and the territory of which now forms part of the Republic; (xvii)

    (ix) "gross violation of human rights" means the violation of human rights through-
        (a) the killing, abduction, torture or severe ill-treatment of any person; or
        (b) any attempt, conspiracy, incitement, instigation, command or procurement to commit an act referred to in paragraph (a), which emanated from conflicts of the past and which was committed during the period 1 March 1960 to the cut-off date within or outside the Republic, and the commission of which was advised, planned, directed, commanded or ordered, by any person acting with a political motive; (v)

(x) "joint committee" means a joint committee of the Houses of Parliament appointed in accordance with the Standing Orders of Parliament for the purpose of considering matters referred to it in terms of this Act; (iii)

(xi) "Minister" means the Minister of Justice; (x)

(xii) "prescribe" means prescribe by regulation made under section 40; (xviii)

(xiii) "President" means the President of the Republic; (xi)

(xiv) "reparation" includes any form of compensation, ex gratia payment, restitution, rehabilitation or recognition; (vi)

(xv) "Republic" means the Republic of South Africa referred to in section 1(2) of the Constitution; (xvi)

(xvi) "security forces" includes any full-time or part-time-

      (a) member or agent of the South African Defence Force, the South African Police, the National Intelligence Service, the Bureau of State Security, the Department of Correctional Services, or any of their organs;

      (b) member or agent of a defence force, police force, intelligence agency or prison service of any former state, or any of their organs; (xvi)

(xvii) "State" means the State of the Republic; (xiv)

(xviii) "subcommittee" means any subcommittee established by the Commission in terms of section 5(c);* * *

(xix) "victims" includes-

      (a) persons who, individually or together with one or more persons, suffered harm in the form of physical or mental injury, emotional suffering, pecuniary loss or a substantial impairment of human rights-

            (i) as a result of a gross violation of human rights; or

            (ii) as a result of an act associated with a political objective for which amnesty has been granted;

      (b) persons who, individually or together with one or more persons, suffered harm in the form of physical or mental injury, emotional suffering, pecuniary loss or a substantial impairment of human rights, as a result of such person intervening to assist persons contemplated in paragraph (a) who were in distress or to prevent victimization of such persons; and

      (c) such relatives or dependants of victims as may be prescribed. (xiii)

(2) For the purposes of sections 10(1), (2) and (3) and II and Chapters 6 and 7 "Commission" shall be construed as including a reference to "committee" or subcommittee", as the case may be, and "Chairperson", "Vice-Chairperson" or commissioner" shall be construed as including a reference to the chairperson, vice-chairperson or a member of a committee or subcommittee, as the case may be.

CHAPTER 2
Truth and Reconciliation Commission

Establishment and seat of Truth and Reconciliation Commission

2. (1) There is hereby established a juristic person to be known as the Truth and Reconciliation Commission.

(2) The seat of the Commission shall be determined by the President.

Objectives of Commission

3. (1) The objectives of the Commission shall be to promote national unity and reconciliation in a spirit of understanding which transcends the conflicts and divisions of the past by-

      (a) establishing as complete a picture as possible of the causes, nature and extent of the gross violations of human rights which were committed during the period from I March 1960 to the cut-off date, including the antecedents, circumstances, factors and context of such violations, as well as the perspectives of the victims and the motives and perspectives of the persons responsible for the commission of the violations, by conducting investigations and holding hearings;

      (b) facilitating the granting of amnesty to persons who make full disclosure of all the relevant facts relating to acts associated with a political objective and comply with the requirements of this Act;

      (c) establishing and making known the fate or whereabouts of victims and by restoring the human and civil dignity of such victims by granting them an opportunity to relate their own accounts of the violations of which they are the victims, and by recommending reparation measures in respect of them;

(d) compiling a report providing as comprehensive an account as possible of the activities and findings of the Commission contemplated in paragraphs (a), (b) and (c), and which contains recommendations of measures to prevent the future violations of human rights.

(2) The provisions of subsection (1) shall not be interpreted as limiting the power of the Commission to investigate or make recommendations concerning any matter with a view to promoting or achieving national unity and reconciliation within the context of this Act.

(3) In order to achieve the objectives of the Commission-

(a) the Committee on Human Rights Violations, as contemplated in Chapter 3, shall deal, among other things, with matters pertaining to investigations of gross violations of human rights;

(b) the Committee on Amnesty, as contemplated in Chapter 4, shall deal with matters relating to amnesty;

(c) the Committee on Reparation and Rehabilitation, as contemplated in Chapter 5, shall deal with matters referred to it relating to reparations;

(d) the investigating unit referred to in section 5(d) shall perform the investigations contemplated in section 28(4)(a); and

(e) the subcommittees shall exercise, perform and carry out the powers, functions and duties conferred upon, assigned to or imposed upon them by the Commission.

Functions of Commission

4. The functions of the Commission shall be to achieve its objectives, and to that end the Commission shall-

(a) facilitate, and where necessary initiate or coordinate, inquiries into-

(i) gross violations of human rights, including violations which were part of a systematic pattern of abuse;

(ii) the nature, causes and extent of gross violations of human rights, including the antecedents, circumstances, factors, context, motives and perspectives which led to such violations;

(iii) the identity of all persons, authorities, institutions and organisations involved in such violations;

(iv) the question whether such violations were the result of deliberate planning on the part of the State or a former state or any of their organs, or of any political organisation, liberation movement or other group or individual; and

(v) accountability, political or otherwise, for any such violation;

(b) facilitate, and initiate or coordinate, the gathering of information and the receiving of evidence from any person, including persons claiming to be victims of such violations or the representatives of such victims, which establish the identity of victims of such violations, their fate or present whereabouts and the nature and extent of the harm suffered by such victims;

(c) facilitate and promote the granting of amnesty in respect of acts associated with political objectives, by receiving from persons desiring to make a full disclosure of all the relevant facts relating to such acts, applications for the granting of amnesty in respect of such acts, and transmitting such applications to the Committee on Amnesty for its decision, and by publishing decisions granting amnesty, in the Gazette;

(d) determine what articles have been destroyed by any person in order to conceal violations of human rights or acts associated with a political objective;

(e) prepare a comprehensive report which sets out its activities and findings, based on factual and objective information and evidence collected or received by it or placed at its disposal;

(f) make recommendations to the President with regard to-

(i) the policy which should be followed or measures which should be taken with regard to the granting of reparation to victims or the taking of other measures aimed at rehabilitating and restoring the human and civil dignity of victims;

(ii) measures which should be taken to grant urgent interim reparation to victims;

(g) make recommendations to the Minister with regard to the development of a limited witness protection programme for the purposes of this Act;

(h) make recommendations to the President with regard to the creation of institutions conducive to a stable and fair society and the institutional, administrative and legislative measures which should be taken or introduced in order to prevent the commission of violations of human rights.

Powers of Commission

5. In order to achieve its objectives and to perform its functions the Commission shall have the power to-

(a) determine the seat, if any, of every committee;

(b) establish such offices as it may deem necessary for the performance of its functions;

(c) establish subcommittees to exercise, carry out or perform any of the powers, duties and functions assigned to them by the Commission;

(d) conduct any investigation or hold any hearing it may deem necessary and establish the investigating unit referred to in section 28;

(e) refer specific or general matters to, give guidance and instructions to, orreview the decisions of, any committee or subcommittee or the investigating unit with regard to the exercise of its powers, the performance of its functions and the carrying out of its duties, the working procedures which should be followed and the divisions which should be set up by any committee in order to deal effectively with the work of the committee: Provided that no decision, or the process of arriving at such a decision, of the Committee on Amnesty regarding any application for amnesty shall be reviewed by the Commission; direct any committee or subcommittee to make information which it has in its possession available to any other committee or subcommittee;

(g) direct the submission of and receive reports or interim reports from any committee or subcommittee;

(h) have the administrative and incidental work connected with the exercise of its powers, the execution of its duties or the performance of its functions carried out by persons-

(i) employed or appointed by it;

(ii) seconded to its service by any department of State at the request of the Commission and after consultation with the Public Service Commission;

(iii) appointed by it for the performance of specified tasks;

(i) in consultation with the Minister and through diplomatic channels, obtain permission from the relevant authority of a foreign country to receive evidence or gather information in that country;

(j) enter into an agreement with any person, including any department of State, in terms of which the Commission will be authorized to make use of any of the facilities, equipment or personnel belonging to or under the control or in the employment of such person or department;

(k) recommend to the President that steps be taken to obtain an order declaring a person to be dead;

(l) hold meetings at any place within or outside the Republic;

(m) on its own initiative or at the request of any interested person inquire or investigate into any matter, including the disappearance of any person or group of persons.

Certain powers shall be exercised in consultation with Minister

6. Subject to the provisions of section 45, any power referred to in section 5(a), (b) and (c), and, if it is to be exercised outside the Republic, any power referred to in sections 5(d) and (1), 10(1) and 29(1), shall be exercised in consultation with the Minister.

Constitution of Commission

7. (1) The Commission shall consist of not fewer than 11 and not more than 17 commissioners, as may be determined by the President in consultation with the Cabinet.

(2)   (a) The President shall appoint the commissioners in consultation with the Cabinet.

(b) The commissioners shall be fit and proper persons who are impartial and who do not have a high political profile: Provided that not more than two persons who are not South African citizens may be appointed as commissioners.

(3) The President shall make the appointment of the commissioners known by proclamation in the Gazette.

(4) The President shall designate one of the commissioners as the Chairperson, and another as the Vice-Chairperson, of the Commission.

(5) A commissioner appointed in terms of subsection (2)(a) shall, subject to the provisions of subsections (6) and (7), hold office for the duration of the Commission.

(6) A commissioner may at any time resign as commissioner by tendering his or her resignation in writing to the President.

(7) The President may remove a commissioner from office on the grounds of misbehaviour, incapacity or incompetence, as determined by the joint committee and upon receipt of an address from the National Assembly and an address from the Senate.

(8) If any commissioner tenders his or her resignation under subsection (6), or is removed from office under subsection (7), or dies, the President in consultation with the Cabinet, may fill the vacancy by appointing a person for the unexpired portion of the term of office of his or her predecessor or may allow the seat vacated as a result of a resignation, removal from office or death to remain vacant.

Acting Chairperson of Commission
8. If both the Chairperson and Vice-Chairperson are absent or unable to perform their duties, the other commissioners shall from among their number nominate an Acting Chairperson for the duration of such absence or incapacity.

Conditions of service, remuneration, allowances and other benefits of staff of Commission
9. (1) The persons appointed or employed by the Commission who are not officials of the State, shall receive such remuneration, allowances and other employment benefits and shall be appointed or employed on such terms and conditions and for such periods as the Commission with the approval of the Minister, granted in concurrence with the Minister of Finance, may determine.

(2)　　(a) A document setting out the remuneration, allowances and other conditions of employment determined by the Commission in terms of subsection (1), shall be tabled in Parliament within 14 days after each such determination.
　　　　(b) If Parliament disapproves of any determination, such determination shall cease to be of force to the extent to which it is so disapproved.
　　　　(c) If a determination ceases to be of force as contemplated in paragraph (b)-
　　　　　　(i) anything done in terms of such determination up to the date on which such determination ceases to be of force shall be deemed to have been validly done; and
　　　　　　(ii) any right, privilege, obligation or liability acquired, accrued or incurred up to the said date under and by virtue of such determination, shall lapse upon the said date.

Meetings, procedure at and quorum for meetings of Commission and recording of proceedings
10. (1) A meeting of the Commission shall be held at a time and place determined by the Chairperson of the Commission or, in the absence or inability of such Chairperson, by the Vice-Chairperson of the Commission or, in the absence or inability of both such Chairperson and Vice-Chairperson, by the Acting Chairperson of the Commission.

(2) Subject to section 40, the Commission shall have the power to determine the procedure for its meetings, including the manner in which decisions shall be taken.

(3) The Commission shall cause a record to be kept of its proceedings.

(4) The quorum for the first meeting of the Commission shall be two less than the total number of the Commission.

Principles to govern actions of Commission when dealing with victims
11. When dealing with victims the actions of the Commission shall be guided by the following principles:
　　(a) Victims shall be treated with compassion and respect for their dignity;
　　(b) victims shall be treated equally and without discrimination of any kind, including race, colour, gender, sex, sexual orientation, age, language, religion, nationality, political or other opinion, cultural beliefs or practices, property, birth or family status, ethnic or social origin or disability;
　　(c) procedures for dealing with applications by victims shall be expeditious, fair, inexpensive and accessible;
　　(d) victims shall be informed through the press and any other medium of their rights in seeking redress through the Commission, including information of-
　　　　(i) the role of the Commission and the scope of its activities;
　　　　(ii) the right of victims to have their views and submissions presented and considered at appropriate stages of the inquiry;

(e) appropriate measures shall be taken in order to minimize inconvenience to victims and, when necessary, to protect their privacy, to ensure their safety as well as that of their families and of witnesses testifying on their behalf, and to protect them from intimidation;

(f) appropriate measures shall be taken to allow victims to communicate in the language of their choice;

(g) informal mechanisms for the resolution of disputes, including mediation, arbitration and any procedure provided for by customary law and practice shall be applied, where appropriate, to facilitate reconciliation and redress for victims.

CHAPTER 3
Investigation of Human Rights Violations

Committee on Human Rights Violations

12. There is hereby established a committee to be known as the Committee on Human Rights Violations, which shall in this Chapter be referred to as the Committee.

Constitution of Committee

13. (1) The Committee shall consist of-

    (a)   (i) a Chairperson; and

            (ii) two Vice-Chairpersons, who shall be commissioners designated by the Commission;

    (b) such other commissioners as may be appointed by the Commission; and

    (c) not more than three other members.

(2) The Commission shall appoint, as the members referred to in subsection (1)(c), South African citizens who are fit and proper persons and broadly representative of the South African community and shall, when making such appointments, give preference to persons possessing knowledge of the content and application of human rights or of investigative or fact-finding procedures.

Powers, duties and functions of Committee

14. (1) In addition to the powers, duties and functions conferred on, imposed upon and assigned to it in this Act, and for the purpose of achieving the objectives of the Commission, referred to in section 3(1)(a), (c) and (d)-

    (a) the Committee shall-

            (i) institute the inquiries referred to in section 4(a);

            (ii) gather the information and receive the evidence referred to in section 4(b);

            (iii) determine the facts contemplated in section 4(d);

            (iv) take into account the gross violations of human rights for which indemnity has been granted during the period between 1 March 1960 and the date of commencement of this Act or for which prisoners were released or had their sentences remitted for the sake of reconciliation and for the finding of peaceful solutions during that period;

            (v) record allegations and complaints of gross violations of human rights;

    (b) the Committee may-

            (i) collect or receive from any organisation, commission or person, articles relating to gross violations of human rights;

            (ii) make recommendations to the Commission with regard to the matters referred to in section 4(f), (g) or (h);

            (iii) make information which is in its possession available to a committee referred to in Chapter 4 or 5, a subcommittee or the investigating unit;

            (iv) submit to the Commission interim reports indicating the progress made by the Committee with its activities or with regard to any other particular matter;

            (v) exercise the powers referred to in Chapters 6 and 7.

(2) The Committee shall at the conclusion of its functions submit to the Commission a comprehensive report of all its activities and findings in connection with the performance of its functions and the carrying out of its duties in terms of this Act.

Referrals to Committee on Reparation and Rehabilitation

15. (1) When the Committee finds that a gross violation of human rights has been committed and if the Committee is of the opinion that a person is a victim of such violation, it shall refer the matter to the Committee on Reparation and Rehabilitation for its consideration in terms of section 26.

(2) After a referral to the Committee on Reparation and Rehabilitation has been made by the Committee in terms of subsection (1), it shall, at the request of the Committee on Reparation and Rehabilitation, furnish that Committee with all the evidence and other information relating to the victim concerned or conduct such further investigation or hearing as the said Committee may require.

CHAPTER 4
Amnesty mechanisms and procedures

Committee on Amnesty

16. There is hereby established a committee to be known as the Committee on Amnesty, which shall in this Chapter be referred to as the Committee.

Constitution of Committee

17. (1) The Committee shall consist of a Chairperson, a Vice-Chairperson and three other members who are fit and proper persons, appropriately qualified, South African citizens and broadly representative of the South African community.

(2) The President shall appoint the Chairperson, the Vice-Chairperson, one other person and, after consultation with the Commission, two commissioners as members of the Committee.

(3) The Chairperson of the Committee shall be-
      (a) a judge as defined in section 1(1) of the Judges' Remuneration and Conditions of Employment Act, 1989 (Act No. 88 of 1989); or
      (b) a judge who has been discharged from active service in terms of section 3 of the said Act.

(4) Any vacancies in the Committee shall be filled in accordance with this section.

Applications for granting of amnesty

18. (1) Any person who wishes to apply for amnesty in respect of any act, omission or offence on the grounds that it is an act associated with a political objective, shall within 12 months from the date of the proclamation referred to in section 7(3), or such extended period as may be prescribed, submit such an application to the Commission in the prescribed form.

(2) The Committee shall give priority to applications of persons in custody and shall prescribe measures in respect of such applications after consultation with the Minister and the Minister of Correctional Services.

Committee shall consider applications for amnesty

19. (1) Upon receipt of any application for amnesty, the Committee may return the application to the applicant and give such directions in respect of the completion and submission of the application as may be necessary or request the applicant to provide such further particulars as it may deem necessary.

(2) The Committee shall investigate the application and make such enquiries as it may deem necessary: Provided that the provisions of section 30(2) shall, with the necessary changes, apply in respect of such investigation.

(3) After such investigation, the Committee may-
      (a)   (i) inform the applicant that the application, judged on the particulars or further particulars contained in the application or provided by the applicant or revealed as a result of enquiries made by the Committee, if any, does not relate to an act associated with a political objective;
            (ii) afford the applicant the opportunity to make a further submission; and
            (iii) decide whether the application, judged on the particulars referred to in subparagraph (i), and in such further submission, relates to such an act associated with a political objective, and if it is satisfied that the application does not relate to such an act, in the absence of the applicant and without holding a hearing refuse the application and inform the applicant accordingly; or
     (b) if it is satisfied that-
            (i) the requirements mentioned in section 20(i) have been complied with;
            (ii) there is no need for a hearing; and

(iii) the act, omission or offence to which the application relates, does not constitute a gross violation of human rights, in the absence of the applicant and without holding a hearing, grant amnesty and inform the applicant accordingly.

(4) If an application has not been dealt with in terms of subsection (3), the Committee shall conduct a hearing as contemplated in Chapter 6 and shall, subject to the provisions of section 33-

(a) in the prescibed manner, notify the applicant and any victim or person implicated, or having an interest in the application, of the place where and the time when the application will be heard and considered;

(b) inform the persons referred to in paragraph (a) of their right to be present at the hearing and to testify, adduce evidence and submit any article to be taken into consideration;

(c) deal with the application in terms of section 20 or 21 by granting or refusing amnesty.

(5)   (a) The Committee shall, for the purpose of considering and deciding upon an application referred to in subsection (1), have the same powers as those conferred upon the Commission in section 5(l) and (m) and Chapters 6 and 7.

(b) Notwithstanding the provisions of section 18(1), the Committee may consider jointly the individual applications in respect of any particular act, omission or offence to which such applications relate.

(6) If the act or omission which is the subject of an application under section 18 constitutes the ground of any claim in civil proceedings instituted against the person who submitted that application, the court hearing that claim may at the request of such person, if it is satisfied that the other parties to such proceedings have been informed of the request and afforded the opportunity to address the court or to make further submissions in this regard, suspend those proceedings pending the consideration and disposal of the application.

(7) If the person who submitted an application under section 18 is charged with any offence constituted by the act or omission to which the application relates, or is standing trial upon a charge of having committed such an offence, the Committee may request the appropriate authority to postpone the proceedings pending the consideration and disposal of the application for amnesty.

(8)   (a) Subject to the provisions of section 33, the applications, documentation in connection therewith, further information and evidence obtained before and during an investigation by the Commission, the deliberations conducted in order to come to a decision or to conduct a hearing contemplated in section 33, shall be confidential.

(b) Subject to the provisions of section 33, the confidentiality referred to in paragraph (a) shall lapse when the Commission decides to release such information or when the hearing commences.

Granting of amnesty and effect thereof

20. (1) If the Committee, after considering an application for amnesty, is satisfied that-

(a) the application complies with the requirements of this Act;

(b) the act, omission or offence to which the application relates is an act associated with a political objective committed in the course of the conflicts of the past in accordance with the provisions of subsections (2) and (3); and

(c) the applicant has made a full disclosure of all relevant facts, it shall grant amnesty in respect of that act, omission or offence.

(2) In this Act, unless the context otherwise indicates, "act associated with a political objective" means any act or omission which constitutes an offence or delict which, according to the criteria in subsection (3), is associated with a political objective, and which was advised, planned, directed, commanded, ordered or committed within or outside the Republic during the period I March 1960 to the cut-off date, by-

(a) any member or supporter of a publicly known political organisation or liberation movement on behalf of or in support of such organization or movement, bona fide in furtherance of a political struggle waged by such organisation or movement against the State or any former state or another publicly known political organisation or liberation movement;

(b) any employee of the State or any former state or any member of the security forces of the State or any former state in the course and scope of his or her duties and within the scope of his or her express or implied authority directed against a publicly known political organisation or liberation movement engaged in a political struggle against the State or a former state or against any members or supporters of such organisation or movement, and which was committed bona fide with the object of countering or otherwise resisting the said struggle;

(c) any employee of the State or any former state or any member of the security forces of the State or any former state in the course and scope of his or her duties and within the scope of his or her express or implied authority directed-

     (i) in the case of the State, against any former state; or

     (ii) in the case of a former state, against the State or any other former state, whilst engaged in a political struggle against each other or against any employee of the State or such former state, as the case may be, and which was committed bona fide with the object of countering or otherwise resisting the said struggle;

(d) any employee or member of a publicly known political organisation or liberation movement in the course and scope of his or her duties and within the scope of his or her express or implied authority directed against the State or any former state or any publicly known political organisation or liberation movement engaged in a political struggle against that political organisation or liberation movement or against members of the security forces of the State or any former state or members or supporters of such publicly known political organisation or liberation movement, and which was committed bona fide in furtherance of the said struggle;

(e) any person in the performance of a coup d' etat to take over the government of any former state, or in any attempt thereto;

(f) any person referred to in paragraphs (a), (b), (c) and (d), who on reasonable grounds believed that he or she was acting in the course and scope of his or her duties and within the scope of his or her express or implied authority;

(g) any person who associated himself or herself with any act or omission committed for the purposes referred to in paragraphs (a), (b), (c), (d), (e) and (f).

(3) Whether a particular act, omission or offence contemplated in subsection (2) is an act associated with a political objective, shall be decided with reference to the following criteria:

(a) The motive of the person who committed the act, omission or offence;

(b) the context in which the act, omission or offence took place, and in particular whether the act, omission or offence was committed in the course of or as part of a political uprising, disturbance or event, or in reaction thereto;

(c) the legal and factual nature of the act, omission or offence, including the gravity of the act, omission or offence;

(d) the object or objective of the act, omission or offence, and in particular whether the act, omission or offence was primarily directed at a political opponent or State property or personnel or against private property or individuals;

(e) whether the act, omission or offence was committed in the execution of an order of, or on behalf of, or with the approval of, the organisation, institution, liberation movement or body of which the person who committed the act was a member, an agent or a supporter; and

(f) the relationship between the act, omission or offence and the political objective pursued, and in particular the directness and proximity of the relationship and the proportionality of the act, omission or offence to the objective pursued, but does not include any act, omission or offence committed by any person referred to in subsection (2) who acted-

     (i) for personal gain: Provided that an act, omission or offence by any person who acted and received money or anything of value as an informer of the State or a former state, political organisation or liberation movement, shall not be excluded only on the grounds of that person having received money or anything of value for his or her information; or

     (ii) out of personal malice, ill-will or spite, directed against the victim of the acts committed.

(4) In applying the criteria contemplated in subsection (3), the Committee shall take into account the criteria applied in the Acts repealed by section 48.

(5) The Commission shall inform the person concerned and, if possible, any victim, of the decision of the Committee to grant amnesty to such person in respect of a specified act, omission or offence and the Committee shall submit to the Commission a record of the proceedings, which may, subject to the provisions of this Act, be used by the Commission.

(6) The Committee shall forthwith by proclamation in the Gazette make known the full names of any person to whom amnesty has been granted, together with sufficient information to identify the act, omission or offence in respect of which amnesty has been granted.

(7)   (a) No person who has been granted amnesty in respect of an act, ommission or offence shall be criminally or civilly liable in respect of such act, omission or offence and no body or organisation or the State shall be liable, and no person shall be vicariously liable, for any such act, omission or offence.

(b) Where amnesty is granted to any person in respect of any act, omission or offence, such amnesty shall have no influence upon the criminal liability of any other person contingent upon the liability of the first-mentioned person.

(c) No person, organisation or state shall be civilly or vicariously liable for an act, omission or offence committed between 1 March 1960 and the cut-off date by a person who is deceased, unless amnesty could not have been granted in terms of this Act in respect of such an act, omission or offence.

(8) If any person-

(a) has been charged with and is standing trial in respect of an offence constituted by the act or omission in respect of which amnesty is granted in terms of this section; or

(b) has been convicted of, and is awaiting the passing of sentence in respect of, or is in custody for the purpose of serving a sentence imposed in respect of, an offence constituted by the act or omission in respect of which amnesty is so granted, the criminal proceedings shall forthwith upon publication of the proclamation referred to in subsection (6) become void or the sentence so imposed shall upon such publication lapse and the person so in custody shall forthwith be released.

(9) If any person has been granted amnesty in respect of any act or omission which formed the ground of a civil judgment which was delivered at any time before the granting of the amnesty, the publication of the proclamation in terms of subsection (6) shall not affect the operation of the judgment in so far as it applies to that person.

(10) Where any person has been convicted of any offence constituted by an act or omission associated with a political objective in respect of which amnesty has been granted in terms of this Act, any entry or record of the conviction shall be deemed to be expunged from all official documents or records and the conviction shall for all purposes, including the application of any Act of Parliament or any other law, be deemed not to have taken place: Provided that the Committee may recommend to the authority concerned the taking of such measures as it may deem necessary for the protection of the safety of the public.

Refusal of amnesty and effect thereof

21. (1) If the Committee has refused any application for amnesty, it shall as soon as practicable notify-

(a) the person who applied for amnesty;

(b) any person who is in relation to the act, omission or offence concerned, a victim; and

(c) the Commission, in writing of its decision and the reasons for its refusal.

(2)   (a) If any criminal or civil proceedings were suspended pending a decision on an application for amnesty, and such application is refused, the court concerned shall be notified accordingly.

(b) No adverse inference shall be drawn by the court concerned from the fact that the proceedings which were suspended pending a decision on an application for amnesty, are subsequently resumed.

Referrals to Committee on Reparation and Rehabilitation

22. (1) Where amnesty is granted to any person in respect of any act, omission or offence and the Committee is of the opinion that a person is a victim in relation to that act, omission or offence, it shall refer the matter to the Committee on Reparation and Rehabilitation for its consideration in terms of section 26.

(2) Where amnesty is refused by the Committee and if it is of the opinion that-

(a) the act, omission or offence concerned constitutes a gross violation of human rights; and

(b) a person is a victim in the matter, it shall refer the matter to the Committee on Reparation and Rehabilitation for consideration in terms of section 26.

CHAPTER 5

Reparation and rehabilitation of victims

Committee on Reparation and Rehabilitation
23. There is hereby established a committee to be known as the Committee on Reparation and Rehabilitation, which shall in this Chapter be referred to as the Committee.

Constitution of Committee
24. (1) The Committee shall consist of-
    (a) a Chairperson;
    (b) a Vice-Chairperson;
    (c) not more than five other members; and
    (d) in addition to the commissioners referred to in subsection (2), such other commissioners as may be appointed to the Committee by the Commission.
(2) Commissioners designated by the Commission shall be the Chairperson and Vice-Chairperson of the Committee.
(3) The Commission shall for the purpose of subsection (1)(c) appoint as members of the Committee fit and proper persons who are suitably qualified, South African citizens and broadly representative of the South African community.

Powers, duties and functions of Committee
25. (1) In addition to the powers, duties and functions in this Act and for the purpose of achieving the Commission's objectives referred to in section 3(1)(c) and (d)-
    (a) the Committee shall-
        (i) consider matters referred to it by-
            (aa) the Commission in terms of section 5(e);
            (bb) the Committee on Human Rights Violations in terms of section 15(1); and
            (cc) the Committee on Amnesty in terms of section 22(1);
        (ii) gather the evidence referred to in section 4(b);
    (b) the Committee may-
        (i) make recommendations which may include urgent interim measures as contemplated in section 4(f)(ii), as to appropriate measures of reparation to victims;
        (ii) make recommendations referred to in section 4(h);
        (iii) prepare and submit to the Commission interim reports in connection with its activities;
        (iv) may exercise the powers referred to in section 5(l) and (m) and Chapters 6 and 7.
(2) The Committee shall submit to the Commission a final comprehensive report on its activities, findings and recommendations.

Applications for reparation
26. (1) Any person who is of the opinion that he or she has suffered harm as a result of a gross violation of human rights may apply to the Committee for reparation in the prescribed form.
(2)   (a) The Committee shall consider an application contemplated in subsection (1) and may exercise any of the powers conferred upon it by section 25.
          (b) In any matter referred to the Committee, and in respect of which a finding as to whether an act, omission or offence constitutes a gross violation of human rights is required, the Committee shall refer the matter to the Committee on Human Rights Violations to deal with the matter in terms of section 14.
(3) If upon consideration of any matter or application submitted to it under subsection (1) and any evidence received or obtained by it concerning such matter or application, the Committee is of the opinion that the applicant is a victim, it shall, having regard to criteria as prescribed, make recommendations as contemplated in section 25(1)(b)(i) in an endeavour to restore the human and civil dignity of such victim.

Parliament to consider recommendations with regard to reparation of victims
27. (1) The recommendations referred to in section 4(f)(i) shall be considered by the President with a view to making recommendations to Parliament and making regulations.

(2) The recommendations referred to in subsection (1) shall be considered by the joint committee and the decisions of the said joint committee shall, when approved by Parliament, be implemented by the President by making regulations.

(3) The regulations referred to in subsection (2)-

    (a) shall-

        (i) determine the basis and conditions upon which reparation shall be granted;

        (ii) deter-mine the authority responsible for the application of the regulations; and

    (b) may-

        (i) provide for the revision and, in appropriate cases, the discontinuance or reduction of any reparation;

        (ii) prohibit the cession, assignment or attachment of any reparation in terms of the regulations, or the right to any such reparation;

        (iii) determine that any reparation received in terms of the regulations shall not form part of the estate of the recipient should such estate be sequestrated; and

        (iv) provide for any other matter which the President may deem fit to prescribe in order to ensure an efficient application of the regulations.

(4) The joint committee may also advise the President in respect of measures that should be taken to grant urgent interim reparation to victims.

CHAPTER 6
Investigations and hearings by Commission

Commission may establish investigating unit

28. (1) The Commission may establish an investigating unit which shall consist of such persons, including one or more commissioners, as may be determined by the Commission.

(2) The period of appointment of such members shall be determined by the Commission at the time of appointment, but such period may be extended or curtailed by the Commission.

(3) The Commission shall appoint a commissioner as the head of the investigating unit.

(4)   (a) The investigating unit shall investigate any matter failing within the scope of the Commission's powers, functions and duties, subject to the directions of the Commission, and shall at the request of a committee investigate any matter failing within the scope of the powers, functions and duties of that committee, subject to the directions of the committee.

    (b) The investigating unit shall in the performance of its functions follow such procedure as may be determined by the Commission or the committee concerned, as the case may be.

(5) Subject to section 33, no article or information obtained by the investigating unit shall be made public, and no person except a member of the investigating unit, the Commission, the committee concerned or a member of the staff of the Commission shall have access to such article or information until such time as the Commission or the committee determines that it may be made public or until the commencement of any hearing in terms of this Act which is not held behind closed doors.

Powers of Commission with regard to investigations and hearings

29. (1) The Commission may for the purposes of or in connection with the conduct of an investigation or the holding of a hearing, as the case may be-

    (a) at any time before the commencement or in the course of such investigation or hearing conduct an inspection in loco;

    (b) by notice in writing call upon any person who is in possession of or has the custody of or control over any article or other thing which in the opinion of the Commission is relevant to the subject matter of the investigation or hearing to produce such article or thing to the Commission, and the Commission may inspect and, subject to subsection (3), retain any article or other thing so produced for a reasonable time;

    (c) by notice in writing call upon any person to appear before the Commission and to give evidence or to answer questions relevant to the subject matter of the hearing;

    (d) in accordance with section 32 seize any article or thing referred to in paragraph (b) which is relevant to the subject matter of the investigation or hearing.

(2) A notice referred to in subsection (1) shall specify the time when and the place where the person to whom it is directed shall appear, shall be signed by a commissioner, shall be served by a member of the

staff of the Commission or by a sheriff, by delivering a copy thereof to the person concerned or by leaving it at such person's last known place of residence or business, and shall specify the reason why the article is to be produced or the evidence is to be given.

(3) If the Commission is of the opinion that the production of any article in the possesion or custody or under the control of the State, any department of State, the Auditor-General or any Attorney-General may adversely affect any intended or pending judicial proceedings or the conduct of any investigation carried out with a view to the institution of judicial proceedings, the Commission shall take steps aimed at the prevention of any undue delay in or the disruption of such investigation or proceedings.

(4) The Commission may require any person who in compliance with a requirement in terms of this section appears before it, to take the oath or to make an affirmation and may through the Chairperson or any member of the staff of the Commission administer the oath to or accept an affirmation from such person.

(5) No person other than a member of the staff of the Commission or any person required to produce any article or to give evidence shall be entitled or be permitted to attend any investigation conducted in terms of this section, and the Commission may, having due regard to the principles of openness and transparency, declare that any article produced or information submitted at such investigation shall not be made public until the Commission determines otherwise or, in the absence of such a determination, until the article is produced at a hearing in terms of this Act, or at any proceedings in any court of law.

Procedure to be followed at investigations and hearings of Commission, committees and subcommittees

30. (1) The Commission and any committee or subcommittee shall in any investigation or hearing follow the prescribed procedure or, if no procedure has been prescribed, the procedure determined by the Commission, or, in the absence of such a determination, in the case of a committee or subcommittee the procedure determined by the committee or subcommittee, as the case may be.

(2) If during any investigation by or any hearing before the Commission-

(a) any person is implicated in a manner which may be to his detriment;

(b) the Commission contemplates making a decision which may be to the detriment of a person who has been so implicated;

(c) it appears that any person may have suffered harm as a result of a gross violation of human rights, the Commission shall, if such person is available, afford him or her an opportunity to submit representations to the Commission within a specified time with regard to the matter under consideration or to give evidence at a hearing of the Commission.

Compellability of witnesses and inadmissibility of incriminating evidence given before Commission

31. (1) Any person who is questioned by the Commission in the exercise of its powers in terms of this Act, or who has been subpoenaed to give evidence or to produce any article at a hearing of the Commission shall, subject to the provisions of subsections (2), (3) and (5), be compelled to produce any article or to answer any question put to him or her with regard to the subject-matter of the hearing notwithstanding the fact that the article or his or her answer may incriminate him or her.

(2) A person referred to in subsection (1) shall only be compelled to answer a question or to produce an article which may incriminate him or her if the Commission has issued an order to that effect, after the Commission-

(a) has consulted with the attorney-general who has jurisdiction;

(b) has satisfied itself that to require such information from such a person is reasonable, necessary and justifiable in an open and democratic society based on freedom and equality; and

(c) has satisfied itself that such a person has refused or is likely to refuse to answer a question or produce an article on the grounds that such an answer or article might incriminate him or her.

(3) Any incriminating answer or information obtained or incriminating evidence directly or indirectly derived from a questioning in terms of subsection (1) shall not be admissible as evidence against the person concerned in criminal proceedings in a court of law or before any body or institution established by or under any law: Provided that incriminating evidence arising from such questioning shall be admissible in criminal proceedings where the person is arraigned on a charge of perjury or a charge contemplated in section 39(d)(ii) of this Act or in section 319(3) of the Criminal Procedure Act, 1955 (Act No. 56 of 1955).

(4) Subject to the provisions of this section, the law regarding privilege as applicable to a witness summoned to give evidence in a criminal case in a court of law shall apply in relation to the questioning of a person in terms of subsection (1).

(5) Any person appearing before the Commission by virtue of the provisions of subsection (1) shall be entitled to peruse any article referred to in that subsection, which was produced by him or her, as may be reasonably necessary to refresh his or her memory.

Entry upon premises, search for and seizure and removal of certain articles or other things
32. (1) Any commissioner, member of the staff of the Commission or police officer authorized thereto by a commissioner may on the authority of an entry warrant, issued in terms of subsection (2), enter upon any premises in or upon which any article or thing-

(a) which is concerned with or is upon reasonable grounds suspected to be concerned with any matter which is the subject of any investigation in terms of this Act;

(b) which contains, or is upon reasonable grounds suspected to contain, information with regard to any such matter, is or is upon reasonable grounds suspected to be, and may on the authority of a search warrant, issued in terms of subsection (2)-

(i) inspect and search such premises and there make such inquiries as he or she may deem necessary;

(ii) examine any article or thing found in or upon such premises;

(iii) request from the person who is in control of such premises or in whose possession or under whose control any article or thing is when it is found, or who is upon reasonable grounds believed to have information with regard to any article or thing, an explanation or information;

(iv) make copies of or extracts from any such article found upon or in such premises;

(v) seize any article or thing found upon or in such premises which he or she upon reasonable grounds suspects to be an article or thing mentioned in paragraph (a) or (b);

(vi) after having issued a receipt in respect thereof remove any article or thing found on such premises and suspected upon reasonable grounds to be an article or thing mentioned in paragraph (a) or (b), and retain such article or thing for a reasonable period for the purpose of further examination or, in the case of such article, the making of copies thereof or extracts therefrom: Provided that any article or thing that has been so removed, shall be returned as soon as possible after the purpose of such removal has been accomplished.

(2) An entry or search warrant referred to in subsection (1) shall be issued by a judge of the Supreme Court or by a magistrate who has jurisdiction in the area where the premises in question are situated, and shall only be issued if it appears to the judge or magistrate from information on oath that there are reasonable grounds for believing that an article or thing mentioned in paragraph (a) or (b) of subsection (I) is upon or in such premises, and shall specify which of the acts mentioned in paragraph (b)(i) to (vi) of that subsection may be performed thereunder by the person to whom it is issued.

(3) A warrant issued in terms this section shall be executed by day unless the person who issues the warrant authorizes the execution thereof by night at times which shall be reasonable, and any entry upon or search of any premises order, including-

(a) a person's right to, respect for and the protection of his or her dignity;

(b) the right of a person to freedom and security; and

(c) the right of a person to his or her personal privacy.

(4) Any person executing a warrant in terms of this section shall immediately before commencing with the execution-

(a) identify himself or herself to the person in control of the premises, if such person is present, and hand to such person a copy of the warrant or, if such person is not present, affix such copy to a prominent place on the premises;

(b) supply such person at his or her request with particulars regarding his or her authority to execute such a warrant.

(5) (a) Any commissioner, or any member of the staff of the Commission or police officer at the request of a commissioner, may without a warrant enter upon any premises, other than a private dwelling, and search for, seize and remove any article or thing referred to in subsection (1)-

(i) if the person who is competent to do so consents to such entry, search, seizure and removal; or

(ii) if he or she upon reasonable grounds believes that-

(aa) the required warrant will be issued to him or her in terms of subsection (2) if he or she were to apply for such warrant; and

(bb) the delay caused by the obtaining of any such warrant would defeat the object of the entry, search, seizure and removal.

(b) Any entry and search in terms of paragraph (a) shall be executed by day, unless the execution thereof by night is justifiable and necessary.

(6)   (a) Any person who may on the authority of a warrant issued in terms of subsection (2), or under the provisions of subsection (5), enter upon and search any premises, may use such force as may be reasonably necessary to overcome resistance to such entry or search.

(b) No person may enter upon or search any premises unless he or she has audibly demanded admission to the premises and has notified the purpose of his or her entry, unless such person is upon reasonable grounds of the opinion that any article or thing may be destroyed if such admission is first demanded and such purpose is first notified.

(7) If during the execution of a warrant or the conducting of a search in terms of this section, a person claims that an article found on or in the premises concerned contains privileged information and refuses the inspection or removal of such article, the person executing the warrant or conducting the search shall, if he or she is of the opinion that the article contains information which is relevant to the investigation and that such information is necessary for the investigation or hearing, request the registrar of the Supreme Court which has jurisdiction or his or her delegate, to seize and remove that article for safe custody until a court of law has made a ruling on the question whether the information concerned is privileged or not.

(8) A warrant issued in terms of this section may be issued on any day and shall be of force until-

(a) it is executed; or

(b) it is cancelled by the person who issued it or, if such person is not available, by any person with like authority; or

(c) the expiry of one month from the day of its issue; or

(d) the purpose for the issuing of the warrant has lapsed, whichever may occur first.

Hearings of Commission to be open to public

33. (1)   (a) Subject to the provisions of this section, the hearings of the Commission shall be open to the public.

(b) If the Commission, in any proceedings before it, is satisfied that-

(i) it would be in the interest of justice; or

(ii) there is a likelihood that harm may ensue to any person as a result of the proceedings being open, it may direct that such proceedings be held behind closed doors and that the public or any category thereof shall not be present at such proceedings or any part thereof: Provided that the Commission shall permit any victim who has an interest in the proceedings concerned, to be present.

(c) An application for proceedings to be held behind closed doors may be brought by a person referred to in paragraph (b) and such application shall be heard behind closed doors.

(d) The Commission may at any time review its decision with regard to the question whether or not the proceedings shall be held behind closed doors.

(2) Where the Commission under subsection (1)(b) on any grounds referred to in that subsection directs that the public or any category thereof shall not be present at any proceedings or part thereof, the Commission may, subject to the provisions of section 20(6)-

(a) direct that no information relating to the proceedings, or any part thereof held behind closed doors, shall be made public in any manner;

(b) direct that no person may, in any manner, make public any information which may reveal the identity of any witness in the proceedings;

(c) give such directions in respect of the record of proceedings as may be necessary to protect the identity of any witness:

Provided that the Commission may authorize the publication of so much information as it considers would be just and equitable.

Legal representation

34. (1) Any person questioned by an investigation unit and any person who has been subpoenaed or called upon to appear before the Commission is entitled to appoint a legal representative.

(2) The Commission may, in order to expedite proceedings, place reasonable limitations with regard to the time allowed in respect of the cross-examination of witnesses or any address to the Commission.

(3) The Commission may appoint a legal representative to appear on behalf of the person concerned if it is satisfied that the person is not financially capable of appointing a legal representative himself or herself, and if it is of the opinion that it is in the interests of justice that the person be represented by a legal representative.

(4) A person referred to in subsection (1) shall be informed timeously of his or her right to be represented by a legal representative.

Limited witness protection programme

35. (1) The Minister shall, in consultation with the Commission, promote the establishment of a witness protection programme in order to provide for the protection and safety of witnesses in any manner when necessary.

(2) The witness protection programme contemplated in subsection (1) shall be prescribed by the President as soon as possible after the date referred to in section 7(3).

(3) The regulations providing for a witness protection programme shall-

    (a) provide for, among others, the appointment of a private person or the secondment of an official or employee of any department of State in terms of the Public Service Act, 1994 (Proclamation No. 103 of 1994), to act as the witness protector; and

    (b) be Tabled in Parliament for approval.

(4)   (a) Until such time as the witness protection programme has been established the President may, in consultation with the Minister and the Commission, prescribe interim measures to be followed in order to provide for the protection and the safety of a witness:

Provided that the provisions of section 185A of the Criminal Procedure Act, 1977 (Act No. 51 of 1977), shall, with the necessary changes, apply in the absence of such interim measures.

    (b) The interim measures contemplated in paragraph (a) shall be Tabled in Parliament for approval.

(5) In this section "witness" means a person who wishes to give evidence, gives evidence or gave evidence for the purposes of this Act and includes any member of his or her family or household whose safety is being threatened by any person or group of persons, whether known to him or her or not, as a result thereof.

CHAPTER 7
General provisions

Independence of Commission

36. (1) The Commission, its commissioners and every member of its staff shall function without political or other bias or interference and shall, unless this Act expressly otherwise provides, be independent and separate from any party, government, administration, or any other functionary or body directly or indirectly representing the interests of any such entity.

(2) To the extent that any of the personnel of the entities referred to in subsection (1) may be involved in the activities of the Commission, such personnel will be accountable solely to the Commission.

(3)   (a) If at any stage during the course of proceedings at any meeting of the Commission it appears that a commissioner has or may have a financial or personal interest which may cause a substantial conflict of interests in the performance of his or her functions as such a commissioner, such a commissioner shall forthwith and fully disclose the nature of his or her interest and absent himself or herself from that meeting so as to enable the remaining commissioners to decide whether the commissioner should be precluded from participating in the meeting by reason of that interest.

    (b) Such a disclosure and the decision taken by the remaining commissioners shall be entered on the record of the proceedings.

(4) If a commissioner fails to disclose any conflict of interest as required by subsection (3) and is present at a meeting of the Commission or in any manner participates in the proceedings, such proceedings in relation to the relevant matter shall, as soon as such non-disclosure is discovered, be reviewed and be varied or set aside by the Commission without the participation of the commissioner concerned.

(5) Every commissioner and member of a committee shall-

(a) notwithstanding any personal opinion, preference or party affiliation, serve impartially and independently and perform his or her duties in good faith and without fear, favour, bias or prejudice;

(b) serve in a full-time capacity to the exclusion of any other duty or obligation arising out of any other employment or occupation or the holding of another office: Provided that the Commission may exempt a commissioner from the provisions of this paragraph.

(6) No commissioner or member of a committee shall-

(a) by his or her membership of the Commission, association, statement, conduct or in any other manner jeopardize his or her independence or in any other manner harm the credibility, impartiality or integrity of the Commission;

(b) make private use of or profit from any confidential information gained as a result of his or her membership of the Commission or a committee; or

(c) divulge any such information to any other person except in the course of the performance of his or her functions as such a commissioner or member of a committee.

Commission to decide on disclosure of identity of applicants and witnesses

37. Subject to the provisions of sections 20(6), 33 and 35 the Commission shall, with due regard to the purposes of this Act and the objectives and functions of the Commission, decide to what extent, if at all, the identity of any person who made an application under this Act or gave evidence at the hearing of such application or at any other inquiry or investigation under this Act may be disclosed in any report of the Commission.

Confidentiality of matters and information

38. (1) Every commissioner and every member of the staff of the Commission shall, with regard to any matter dealt with by him or her, or information which comes to his or her knowledge in the exercise, performance or carrying out of his or her powers, functions or duties as such a commissioner or member, preserve and assist in the preservation of those matters which are confidential in terms of the provisions of this Act or which have been declared confidential by the Commission.

(2)   (a) Every commissioner and every member of the staff of the Commission shall, upon taking office, take an oath or make an affirmation in the form specified in subsection (6).

(b) A commissioner shall take the oath or make the affirmation referred to in paragraph (a) before the Chairperson of the Commission or, in the case of the Chairperson, before the Vice-Chairperson.

(c) A member of the staff of the Commission shall take the oath or make the affirmation referred to in paragraph (a) before a commissioner.

(3) No commissioner shall, except for the purpose of the exercise of his or her powers, the performance of his or her functions or the carrying out of his or her duties or when required by a court of law to do so, or under any law, disclose to any person any information acquired by him or her as such a commissioner or while attending any meeting of the Commission.

(4) Subject to the provisions of subsection (3) and sections 20(6) and 33, no person shall disclose or make known any information which is confidential by virtue of any provision of this Act.

(5) No person who is not authorized thereto by the Commission shall have access to any information which is confidential by virtue of any provision of this Act.

(6) For the purposes of this section the oath or affirmation shall be in the following form:

" I, A B, hereby declare under oath/solemnly affirm that I understand and shall honour the obligation of confidentiality imposed upon me by any provision of the Promotion of National Unity and Reconciliation Act, 1995, and shall not act in contravention thereof.".

Offences and penalties

39. Any person who-

(a) anticipates any finding of the Commission regarding an investigation in a manner calculated to influence its proceedings or such findings;

(b) does anything calculated improperly to influence the Commission in respect of any matter being or to be considered by the Commission in connection with an investigation;

(c) does anything in relation to the Commission which, if done in relation to a court of law, would constitute contempt of court;

(d)   (i) hinders the Commission, any commissioner or member of the staff of the Commission in the exercise, performance or carrying out of its, his or her powers, functions or duties under this Act;

            (ii) wilfully furnishes the Commission, any such commissioner or member with any information which is false or misleading;

(e)   (i) having been subpoenaed in terms of this Act, without sufficient cause fails to attend at the time and place specified in the subpoena, or fails to remain in attendance until the conclusion of the meeting in question or until excused from further attendance by the person presiding at that meeting, or fails to produce any article in his or her possession or custody or under his or her control;

            (ii) having been subpoenaed in terms of this Act, without sufficient cause refuses to be sworn or to make affirmation as a witness or fails or refuses to answer fully and satisfactorily to the best of his or her knowledge and belief any question lawfully put to him or her; fails to perform any act as required in terms of sections 36(6) and 38;

(g) discloses any confidential information in contravention of any provision of this Act;

(h) destroys any article relating to or in anticipation of any investigation or proceedings in terms of this Act, shall be guilty of an offence and liable on conviction to a fine, or to imprisonment for a period not exceeding two years or to both such fine and such imprisonment.

Regulations

40. (1) The President may make regulations-

    (a) prescribing anything required to be prescribed for the proper application of this Act;

    (b) prescribing the remuneration and allowances and other benefits, if any, of commissioners: Provided that such remuneration shall not be less than that of a judge of the Supreme Court of South Africa;

    (c) determining the persons who shall for the purposes of this Act be regarded as the dependants or relatives of victims;

    (d) providing, in the case of interim measures for urgent reparation payable over a period of time, for the revision, and, in appropriate cases, for the discontinuance or reduction of any reparation so paid;

    (e) prohibiting the cession, attachment or assignment of any such reparation so granted; determining that any such reparation received in terms of a recommendation shall not form part of the estate of the recipient, should such estate be sequestrated;

    (g) providing for the payment or reimbursement of expenses incurred in respect of travel and accommodation by persons attending any hearing of the Commission in compliance with a subpoena issued in terms of this Act;

    (h) with regard to any matter relating to the affairs of the Fund, established in terms of section 42;

    (i) with regard to any matter which the President deems necessary or expedient to prescribe in order to achieve the objects of this Act.

(2) Any regulation made in terms of subsection (1) which may result in the expenditure of State money shall be made in consultation with the Minister and the Minister of Finance.

Liability of Commission, commissioners and members of staff

41. (1) Subject to the provisions of subsection (2), the State Liability Act, 1957 (Act No. 20 of 1957), shall apply, with the necessary changes, in respect of the Commission, a member of its staff and a commissioner, and in such application a reference in that Act to "the State" shall be construed as a reference to "the Commission", and a reference to "the Minister of the department concerned" shall be construed as a reference to the Chairperson of the Commission.

(2) No-

    (a) commissioner;

    (b) member of the staff of the Commission; or

    (c) person who performs any task on behalf of the Commission, shall be liable in respect of anything reflected in any report, finding, point of view or recommendation made or expressed in good faith and submitted or made known in terms of this Act.

President's Fund

42. (1) The President may, in such manner as he or she may deem fit, in consultation with the Minister and the Minister of Finance, establish a Fund into which shall be paid-

(a) all money appropriated by Parliament for the purposes of the Fund; and

(b) all money donated or contributed to the Fund or accruing to the Fund from any source.

(2) There shall be paid from the Fund all amounts payable to victims by way of reparation in terms of regulations made by the President.

(3) Any money of the Fund which is not required for immediate use may be invested with a financial institution approved by the Minister of Finance and may be withdrawn when required.

(4) Any unexpended balance of the money of the Fund at the end of a financial year, shall be carried forward as a credit to the Fund for the next financial year.

(5) The administrative work, including the receipt of money appropriated by Parliament for, or donated for the purposes of, the Fund or accruing to the Fund from any source, and the making of payments from the Fund in compliance with a recommendation in terms of this Act, shall be performed by officers in the Public Service designated by the Minister.

(6) The Minister shall appoint an officer designated under subsection (5) as accounting officer in respect of the Fund.

(7) The Auditor-General shall audit the Fund and all financial statements relating thereto, and the provisions of section 6 of the Auditor-General Act, 1989 (Act No. 52 of 1989), shall apply in respect of any such audit. Completion of report by Commission and dissolution of Commission

43. (1) Subject to the provisions of subsection (2), the Commission shall within a period of 18 months from its constitution or the further period, not exceeding six months, as the President may determine, complete its work.

(2) The Commission shall within three months, from the date contemplated in subsection (1), complete its final report.

(3) The Commission shall be dissolved on a date determined by the President by proclamation in the Gazette.

Publication of final report of Commission

44. The President shall, in such manner as he or she may deem fit, bring the final report of the Commission to the notice of the Nation, among others, by laying such report, within two months after having received it, upon the Table in Parliament.

Approach to and review by joint committee of, and reports to, Parliament

45. (1)　(a) The Commission may, at any time, approach the joint committee with regard to any matter pertaining to the functions and powers of the Commission.

(b) The Minister may at any time approach the joint committee with regard to any matter pertaining to functions and powers which may be performed or exercised by him or her in terms of this Act.

(c) The joint committee may at any time review any regulation made under section 40 and request the President to amend certain regulations or to make further regulations in terms of that section.

(2) The Commission shall submit to Parliament half-yearly financial reports:

Provided that the Commission may, at any time, submit a financial report to Parliament on specific or general matters if-

(a) it deems it necessary;

(b) it deems it in the public interest;

(c) it requires the urgent attention of, or an intervention by, Parliament;

(d) it is requested to do so by the Speaker of the National Assembly or the President of the Senate.

Chief executive officer, secretaries, expenditure and estimates of Commission

46. (1) The Commission shall appoint in its service a person as the chief executive officer of the Commission and four other persons as secretaries to the Commission, the Committee on Human Rights Violations, the Committee on Amnesty and the Committee on Reparation and Rehabilitation, respectively.

(2) The chief executive officer-

(a) shall for the purposes of section 15 of the Exchequer Act, 1975 (Act No.66 of 1975), be the accounting officer in respect of all State moneys received in respect of and paid out of the account of the Commission referred to in subsection (4), and shall keep proper accounting records of all financial transactions of the Commission;

(b) shall carry out such duties and perform such functions as the Commission may from time to time impose upon or assign to him or her in order to achieve the objectives of the Commission.

(3) The expenses in connection with the exercise of the powers, the performance of the functions and the carrying out of the duties of the Commission shall be defrayed out of money appropriated by Parliament for that purpose.

(4) The Commission shall, in consultation with the Minister of Finance, open an account with a banking institution, into which shall be deposited all moneys appropriated as mentioned in subsection (3) and from which all money required to pay for the expenses so mentioned shall be paid.

(5)   (a) The Commission shall within three months from the date referred to in section 7(3), for the first financial year, and thereafter in each financial year for the following financial year, in a format determined by the Audit Commission established by section 2 of the Audit Arrangements Act, 1992 (Act No. 122 of 1992), prepare the necessary estimate of revenue and expenditure of the Commission, which shall, after consultation with the said Audit Commission, be submitted to the Minister for his or her approval, granted in concurrence with the Minister of Finance, for furtherance in terms of subsection (3).

(b) The Commission shall not incur any expenditure which exceeds the total amount approved in terms of paragraph (a).

(6) As from the date on which the Commission is dissolved in terms of section 43(3) and after all the expenses referred to in subsection (3) have been paid, the account opened in terms of subsection (4) shall be closed and the balance of the moneys deposited into that account, if any, shall be transferred to the fiscus.

Consequences of dissolution

47. (1) As from the date on which the Commission is dissolved in terms of section 43(3), all the funds and property which vested in the President's Fund immediately prior to that date shall be transferred to the Disaster Relief Fund referred to in Chapter 11 of the Fund-raising Act, 1978 (Act No. 107 of 1978), and shall vest in the Disaster Relief Fund.

(2) After the date referred to in subsection (1), all the funds and property which would have accrued to the President's Fund, if the Commission had not been dissolved, shall vest in the Disaster Relief Fund.

(3) Any funds or property which, by trust, donation or bequest were vested in, orwould have accrued to, the President's Fund, and which vest in the Disaster Relief Fund in terms of subsection (1), shall be dealt with by the board of the Disaster Relief Fund in accordance with the conditions of such trust, donation or bequest.

(4) As from the date referred to in subsection (1) the liabilities incurred by the Commission or the President's Fund in terms of this Act, shall pass to the Disaster Relief Fund: Provided that such a liability shall be defrayed only from funds or property which vest in the Disaster Relief Fund in terms of this section.

(5) No transfer duty, stamp duty or registration fees shall be payable in respect of the acquisition of any funds or property in terms of this section.

Acts repealed

48. (1) The Indemnity Act, 1990 (Act No. 35 of 1990), the Indemnity Amendment Act, 1992 (Act No. 124 of 1992), and the Further Indemnity Act, 1992 (Act No. 151 of 1992), are hereby repealed.

(2) Any indemnity granted under the provisions of the Indemnity Act, 1990, the Indemnity Amendment Act, 1992, or the Further Indemnity Act, 1992, shall remain in force notwithstanding the repeal of those Acts.

(3) Any temporary immunity or indemnity granted under an Act repealed in terms of subsection (1) shall remain in force for a period of 12 months after the date referred to in section 7(3) notwithstanding the repeal of that Act.

Short title and commencement

49. This Act shall be called the Promotion of National Unity and Reconciliation Act, 1995, and shall come into operation on a date fixed by the President by proclamation in the Gazette.

RESTATEMENT (THIRD) OF FOREIGN RELATIONS LAW §§ 404, 702 (1987)

Part IV. Jurisdiction And Judgments
Chapter 1. Jurisdiction To Prescribe
Subchapter A. Principles Of Jurisdiction To Prescribe

§ 404. Universal Jurisdiction To Define And Punish Certain Offenses

A state has jurisdiction to define and prescribe punishment for certain offenses recognized by the community of nations as of universal concern, such as piracy, slave trade, attacks on or hijacking of aircraft, genocide, war crimes, and perhaps certain acts of terrorism, even where none of the bases of jurisdiction indicated in § 402 is present.

Part VII. Protection Of Persons (Natural And Juridical)
Chapter 1. International Law Of Human Rights

§ 702. Customary International Law Of Human Rights

A state violates international law if, as a matter of state policy, it practices, encourages, or condones

(a) genocide,
(b) slavery or slave trade,
(c) the murder or causing the disappearance of individuals,
(d) torture or other cruel, inhuman, or degrading treatment or punishment,
(e) prolonged arbitrary detention,
(f) systematic racial discrimination, or
(g) a consistent pattern of gross violations of internationally recognized human rights.
